Concepts of Chemical Dependency

EIGHTH EDITION

HAROLD E. DOWEIKO

Gundersen-Lutheran Medical Center
La Crosse, WI

BROOKS/COLE
CENGAGE Learning™

Australia • Brazil • Japan • Korea • Mexico • Singapore • Spain • United Kingdom • United States

**Concepts of Chemical Dependency,
Eighth Edition, International Edition**
Harold E. Doweiko

Publisher: Linda Schreiber-Ganster

Executive Editor: Jon-David Hague

Senior Editor: Jaime Perkins

Acquisitions Editor: Seth Dobrin

Assistant Editor: Nicolas Albert

Editorial Assistant: Rachel McDonald

Marketing Manager: Trent Whatcott

Marketing Assistant/Associate: Gurpreet Saran

Marketing Communications Manager: Tami Strang

Content Project Management: PreMediaGlobal

Art Director: Caryl Gorska

Print Buyer: Mary Beth Hennebury

Rights Acquisition Director: Bob Kauser

Rights Acquisition Specialist, Text/Image: Roberta Broyer

Production Service/Compositor: PreMediaGlobal

Cover Designer: Denise Davidson

Cover Image: Jorg Greue/Getty Images

Library of Congress Control Number: 2010933371

International Edition:

ISBN-13: 978-0-8400-3391-8

ISBN-10: 0-8400-3391-5

Cengage Learning International Offices

Asia
www.cengageasia.com
tel: (65) 6410 1200

Australia/New Zealand
www.cengage.com.au
tel: (61) 3 9685 4111

Brazil
www.cengage.com.br
tel: (55) 11 3665 9900

India
www.cengage.co.in
tel: (91) 11 4364 1111

Latin America
www.cengage.com.mx
tel: (52) 55 1500 6000

UK/Europe/Middle East/Africa
www.cengage.co.uk
tel: (44) 0 1264 332 424

Represented in Canada by Nelson Education, Ltd.
tel: (416) 752 9100 / (800) 668 0671
www.nelson.com

Cengage Learning is a leading provider of customized learning solutions with office locations around the globe, including Singapore, the United Kingdom, Australia, Mexico, Brazil and Japan. Locate your local office at **www.cengage.com/global**.

For product information: **www.cengage.com/international**
Visit your local office: **www.cengage.com/global**
Visit our corporate website: **www.cengage.com**

Printed in the United States of America
2 3 4 5 6 7 14 13 12 11

To Jan,
who lit the spark of love within.

Contents

Preface to the Eighth Edition

The world of the neurosciences is constantly changing. New discoveries about the process of neurotransmission and how certain chemicals damage neurons or aid in their recovery from trauma all impact the world of substance abuse and the treatment of these disorders. Many long-cherished theories have been discarded, whereas new information leads to the formation of new theories or suggests new directions for theoretical inquiry. An excellent example is Koob's (2009) assertion that scientists are only now starting to explore the glial[1] cells, which comprise 90% of the brain's mass, play roles in the process of neurogenesis, provide metabolic support of the neurons, and are involved in the process of neurotransmission itself. The adherence to the "Neuron Doctrine" (Kolb, 2009, p. 1) is drawing to an end, and scientists are starting to study these long-overlooked components of the brain. The effects of the various drugs of abuse on the neural networks of the brain are not even fully understood, and there has been virtually no research into how the various drugs of abuse affect the glial cells, which by far make up the majority of the brain's mass.

Over the years, there have been a number of changes made to this text, and this process has continued with the current edition. New research is cited, and the process of publishing journal articles online before the publication of the printed version has resulted in the citation of numerous journal articles that were "published online prior to print." Further, because research suggests that substance use patterns between young adults who go on to attend college and those who do not might differ, a new chapter that focuses just on substance use issues in the college student population has been added to the text.

Over the years, several instructors have contacted the author to inquire as to why there was a discussion of the drugs of abuse and their effects. The answer to this question is quite complex: First, many readers will be unaware of the effects of the chemicals of abuse, or at least have only a vague awareness of their effects. Second, many people, including health care professionals, are unaware of the dosage levels of these compounds being used by people with a substance use disorder. At one seminar in which the author of this text was a speaker, a physician stood up and said, "But using those chemicals at that dosage level is dangerous!" Which is exactly the point: These compounds are not used in the same manner that they might be used by a physician (this assumes that the compound under discussion is a pharmaceutical). On more than one occasion, students or seminar participants have expressed surprise at some of the contaminants or adulterants found in illicit drugs. For these reasons, the author of this text has adopted the philosophy that in order to understand and treat the substance use disorders, you need to first understand the chemicals being abused and their effects.

Acknowledgments

It is not possible to thank all of those people who have provided so much support during the preparation of this edition. I would like to especially thank the staff of the Health Services Library of Gundersen Lutheran Medical Center in La Crosse, Wisconsin, for their assistance in tracking down various journal articles over the years. I would also like to thank Dr. David Metzler for his willingness to part company with copies of many journals over the years. This allowed me access to many of the references cited in this text, and his kindness is appreciated.

---

[1]See Glossary

CHAPTER 1

Why Worry About Substance Abuse?

Introduction

Historical evidence would suggest that substance abuse has been a problem for society for thousands of years (Kilts, 2004). At the end of the first decade of the 21st century, substance use disorders collectively remain the most prevalent mental health issue facing society (Vuchinich, 2002). As will be discussed in Chapter 37, the response of the United States and many other nations has been to declare "war" on substance use disorders, a war that has demonstrated remarkably little success. In spite of this minor detail, society continues along the same path, trying to punish those who seek to alter their sense of consciousness through the use of chemicals deemed unacceptable to those in power.

Substance use disorders (SUDs) might take any number of forms, including the subset of SUDs known as alcohol use disorders (AUDs) and nicotine use disorders (NUDs). Another subform of the SUDs is composed of those who abuse prescription drugs. The most prominent form of SUDs is the abuse of illegal drugs such as hallucinogens, cocaine, narcotics, and marijuana.[1] Finally, there are those who abuse compounds not normally intended for human use such as inhalants or anabolic steroids.[2]

The face of SUDs changes over time as one compound or another gains widespread acceptance among those who wish to engage in its use, and then is replaced by the next popular drug of abuse. Alcohol and nicotine again hold a unique position in this process, in that the use of each substance has remained fairly stable within society in spite of widespread acknowledgment of the physical, social, and financial toll that each causes to society. There have been initiatives to ban the use of these compounds over the years; however, they have continued to be used in spite of legal efforts at control. In contrast to the relative stability of the abuse of legal substances, the illicit drugs follow a curious

---

[1]This is because most people are loath to classify alcohol abuse or addiction as a *substance* use disorder. After all, it is only alcohol, right?

[2]Although many of the steroid compounds being abused were indeed intended for human use, they are used at dosage levels far in excess of what is deemed medically acceptable, and thus could be said not to be intended for human use. Furthermore, many of the steroid compounds being abused were not intended for humans, but rather were designed for use with animals, and were diverted to the illicit market.

cycle: First one compound becomes a popular drug of abuse, and then it is slowly replaced by another, "better" drug of abuse. After the physical and emotional dangers of that form of substance abuse are discovered, drug abusers switch to another, purportedly "better" and "safer" drug of abuse. In this chapter we will begin to examine the impact of SUDs on society.

The SUDs as Unsuspected Influences on Society

In spite of the best efforts of those who have attempted to interdict illicit drugs or punish those who engage in their use, at the end of the first decade of the 21st century recreational substance use remains a deeply ingrained aspect of life in the United States that is intertwined with other social problems that face this nation. When all the direct and indirect costs of substance abuse and addiction are added up, it has been found that *over 15% of the average state's budget is devoted* to the costs of substance use disorders[3] (National Center on Addiction and Substance Abuse at Columbia University, 2009a). The U.S. share of the global illicit-drug trade is an estimated $264 billion a year, whereas the indirect costs of the "war on drugs" are estimated to be another $200 billion a year. These indirect costs of include (Cafferty, 2009): (a) salaries of the police officers and sheriff's deputies working to enforce the existing laws against illicit-drug use, (b) staff to transport suspects from the jails to the courts, (c) prosecutors and district attorney staff members who must prosecute those charged with drug-related offenses, (d) the collective expenditure in time of the judges, bailiffs, courthouse security officers and stenographers during the trials of those accused of breaking the laws against drug abuse, (e) the cost of prisons to house those convicted of drug-related offenses, (f) the salaries of the prison guards, (g) the cost of feeding and housing those convicted of drug-related crimes, and (h) the salaries of the probation and parole officers to supervise those released from prison after serving their sentence for drug-related offenses.

Further indirect costs of the "war on drugs" include the financial expenditure of providing financial and health care support for the families of those convicted of drug-related crimes, as well as the cost of substance-related health care expenses and lost productivity by those who abuse these substances (Dobbs, 2007). Yet

the "war on drugs" continues, and politicians hide the full cost of this "war" by sliding part of the expense from one budgetary column to the next (National Center on Addiction and Substance Abuse at Columbia University, 2009a). For example, the cost of incarcerating those who are convicted of drug-related offenses is part of the Department of Corrections budget, whereas the cost of providing health care for families of those convicted of drug-related offenses is part of the Human Services budget, and so forth.

Politicians speak at length about the rising cost of health care, but ignore the impact of substance use disorders, as evidenced by the fact that:

- *Approximately 25% of patients seen by primary care physicians have a substance use disorder (E. M. Jones, Knutson, & Haines, 2004).*
- *Excessive alcohol use was a factor in 50% of all deaths from acute traumatic injuries (D. Baron, Garbely, & Boyd, 2009).*
- *Approximately 40% of hospital admissions can be tied either directly or indirectly to alcohol use/abuse (D. Baron, Garbely, & Boyd, 2009; Greenfield, 2007; Greenfield & Hennessy, 2008a).*
- *Approximately 25% of those individuals on Medicaid have a substance use disorder. As this group ages, their medical costs increase at a higher rate than for age-matched individuals without an SUD ("Substance abuse adds millions to Medicaid's total health care costs," 2008).*

The SUDs are also intertwined with other forms of psychiatric problems as evidenced by the fact that:

- *SUDs are a factor in 50–75% of all psychiatric hospital admissions (N. S. Miller, 2004).*
- *Alcohol dependence is the second most common psychiatric diagnosis made in the United States (Mariani & Levin, 2004).*
- *Approximately 10% of those people with an SUD will eventually commit suicide (Getzfeld, 2006).*
- *Between 40 and 60% of individuals who commit suicide were intoxicated at the time of their deaths,*

---

[3]This figure includes the contribution made to the problem by alcohol and tobacco use disorders.

and 10% had evidence of other drugs of abuse in their bodies at the time of their death as well (D. Karch, Cosby, & Simon, 2006; Scott & Marcotte, 2010).

- *Traumatic brain injury (TBI) accounts for almost one-third of trauma-related deaths in the United States each year, with most of those individuals who die from a severe TBI not living long enough to reach the hospital. Between 29 and 52% of patients who do live long enough to be admitted to the hospital following a TBI have alcohol in their bodies at the time of admission (N. S. Miller & Adams, 2006).*

- *In the year 2008[4] an estimated 10 million people 12 years of age or older reported having driven a motor vehicle while under the influence of an illicit drug (Substance Abuse and Mental Health Services Administration, 2009). This is in addition to those who drove a motor vehicle while under the influence of alcohol in the past year.*

Substance Use Disorders and Interpersonal Violence

There is a well-documented relationship between SUDs and violent behavior that has remained relatively constant over the years. In the United States, fully 56% of all cases of criminal assault each year involve alcohol (Dyehouse & Sommers, 1998). It has also been found that adults with an SUD were 2.7 times as likely to have been physically abused a child, and 4.2 times as likely to have neglected a child, than were their non-substance-abusing peers (Ireland, 2001). In both the United States and Europe, half of all perpetrators of a violent crime had been drinking before the commission of that crime (Coghlan, 2008; Parrott & Giancola, 2006). It has been found that alcohol is a factor in 40–86% of all homicides committed in the United States (Parrott & Giancola, 2006)[5], as well as in 40% of homicide cases in Europe (Coghlan, 2008). And according to Parrott and Giancola, illicit-drug use increases the woman's chance of being murdered by her significant other by as much as 28-fold, even if she was not abusing chemicals herself at the time of her murder.

The Scope of the Problem of SUDs

It should be clear by now that each year the various substance use disorders extract a terrible toll on the individual, the family unit, and the society in which that individual lives. At least half of the world's population has used at least one psychoactive substance (Leamon, Wright, & Myrick, 2008); however, only about 200 million people, or about 5% of the entire population of the world, has *abused* an illicit substance at least once (United Nations, 2008). This distinction is important because the majority of those who use a psychoactive substance do so without abusing the privilege, and thus rarely present a problem to society because of substance abuse. For a minority of people however, substance abuse becomes desirable, and a thriving "black market"[6] has evolved to meet the world's demand for these chemicals. The worldwide illicit-drug trade is estimated to be an $800 billion per year industry, making it larger than the annual gross domestic product of 90% of the world's countries ("Vital Signs," 2007; United Nations, 2008).

In a sense, illicit-drug use might be said to be an "American way of life," as reflected in the fact that this single country, with just under 5% of the world's total population, consumed 60% of the illicit drugs produced on this planet ("Drug War Success Claims Challenged," 2006). In the United States, 20.1 million individuals 12 years of age and older used an illicit drug in the 30 days prior to being surveyed (Substance Abuse and Mental Health Services Administration, 2009). This figure is approximately 8% of the population of the country above the age of 12 years, and has remained relatively stable since 2002 (Substance Abuse and Mental Health Services Administration, 2009). During 2008, 2.1 million people above the age of 12 abused an illicit drug for the first time, with an average age at the time of such drug use being 18.8 years (Substance Abuse and Mental Health Services Administration, 2009).

Alcohol is the most commonly abused substance in the United States, although illicit-drug use is still popular there. Each day in the United States alone, approximately 8000 people will try an illicit drug for the first time (Lemonick & Park, 2007; Substance Abuse and Mental Health Services Administration, 2009). The most commonly abused illicit substance is marijuana, with 75.7% of illicit-drug users abusing marijuana, and 57.3% of

---

[4]The last year for which data is available at this time.

[5]These different estimates reflect the different methodologies utilized by different research studies.

---

[6]See Glossary.

illict-drug abusers using only marijuana (Substance Abuse and Mental Health Services Administration, 2009). This figure still means that 8.6 million people over the age of 12 abused an illicit compound other than marijuana in the month preceding the survey (Substance Abuse and Mental Health Services Administration, 2009). Such illicit-drug use has been detected through the use of a unique research methodology utilized by Banta-Greene et al. (2009). The authors examined the waste water from rural and urban areas for signs of illicit drug use in the population served by that system. They found that although cocaine metabolites were found in both urban and rural water samples, they were higher in urban areas.

Methamphetamine metabolites were ubiquitous across both urban- and rural-area water samples examined. However, the Substance Abuse and Mental Health Services Administration (2009) suggested that methamphetamine is becoming less and less popular as a drug of abuse, as evidenced by the drop in past-month methamphetamine abusers by about 50% to 314,000 people and the increase in past-month cocaine abusers to 1.9 million people. Many of these individuals will experiment with the use of illicit drugs for only 12 months or less, suggesting that for the most part illicit-drug use might reflect experimentation or curiosity (Center for Substance Abuse Research, 2008). However, it is important to keep in mind that even those who are merely curious about the effects of an illicit drug run the risk of becoming addicted. In the next section, we will closely examine the scope of the problem of SUDs in this country.

Alcohol Use, Abuse, and Addiction

Alcohol is a popular recreational beverage, with an estimated 119 million people in this country ingesting it at least once a year (Office of National Drug Control Policy, 2006). For most of these people, alcohol will not become a problem in any sphere of their lives. However, there are an estimated 8–16 million people in the United States who become physically dependent on alcohol, whereas another 5.6 million are believed to abuse it on a regular basis (Bankole & Ait-Daoud, 2005). This may underestimate the total number of people with an alcohol use disorder, since many high-functioning people with an AUD are able to successfully hide this fact from friends, family, and coworkers, possibly for decades (Benton, 2009).

It should not be surprising to learn that a minority of those who drink consume a disproportionate amount of the alcohol produced. Ten percent of drinkers consume

60% of the alcohol consumed in the United States; however, the top 30% of drinkers consume 90% of the U.S.-consumed alcohol (Killbourne, 2002). Those whose drinking has resulted in their suffering social, physical, emotional, or vocational consequences[7] are said to have an alcohol use disorder (AUD). The majority of those in the United States who do develop an AUD are male by a ratio of approximately two to three men to every woman (Kranzler & Ciraulo, 2005a). These figures underscore the danger of alcohol use and abuse in spite of its legal status as a socially acceptable recreational compound for adults.

Estimates of the Problem of Opiate Abuse and Addiction[8]

When many people hear the term *narcotics,* they immediately think of heroin, a drug that does indeed account for 71% of the opiate use disorders around the world (United Nations, 2007). Globally, it has been estimated that 15.6 million people either abuse or are addicted to heroin (United Nations, 2008). It has been estimated that approximately 3 million people have abused heroin at one point in their lives, and that there are between 810,000 and 1 million people in the United States who are currently dependent on this compound (Jaffe & Strain, 2005). The states with the largest numbers of opioid abusers are thought to be California, New York, Massachusetts, and New Jersey, although this problem is found in every state of the union (Jaffe & Strain, 2005), with a male-to-female ratio of 4 to 1.

Unfortunately, heroin is only one of a wide range of opioids that might be obtained and abused.[9] Heroin continues to be a significant part of the problem of the opioid use disorders in the United States, but there has been a growing awareness of medication diversion in this country. Many of those addicted to narcotic analgesics in the United States have never used heroin but support their addiction through prescribed narcotic analgesics or prescription medications diverted to the illicit market. The growing trend of opioid addicts relying on prescribed medications could very well result in the estimate of 800,000 to 1 million heroin addicts

---

[7]The topic of determining whether a person has an AUD will be discussed later in this book.

[8]For the purpose of this text, the terms *opioid, opiate,* and *narcotic* will be used interchangeably; although, as will be discussed in Chapter 14, there are technical differences between these terms.

[9]The topic of opioid abuse and addiction is discussed in Chapter 14.

being an *underestimate* of the scope of the U.S. opiate addiction problem.

Estimates of the Problem of Stimulant Abuse and Addiction[10]

Globally, the problem of central nervous system (CNS) stimulant abuse[11] has apparently reached a plateau, approximately 25 million people around the world still abuse a CNS stimulant (United Nations, 2008). In North America, the demand for the most potent of the CNS stimulants, the amphetamines (especially methamphetamine), has been stable, with about 3.8 million people[12] abusing these compounds at least once each year (United Nations, 2008). Although the media in the United States often focus on local CNS stimulant use disorders, in reality only 15% of CNS stimulant abusers live in North America (United Nations, 2008).

Estimates of the Problem of Cocaine Abuse and Addiction

The number of cocaine abusers/addicts has remained relatively stable around the globe over the past decade (United Nations, 2008). Globally, approximately 14 million people are cocaine abusers or addicts, the vast majority of whom are thought to live in North America[13] (United Nations, 2008). The true scope of cocaine abuse/addiction in the United States is confused by the fact that in spite of its reputation, researchers during the last wave of U.S. cocaine abuse concluded that only 3–20% of those who abused cocaine would go on to become addicted to it[14] (Musto, 1991).

Estimates of the Problem of Marijuana Use, Abuse and Addiction

Globally, it is estimated that at least 160 million people have used marijuana in the past 12 months (United Nations, 2008). Just under 30 million people are thought to be current users of marijuana in North America[15] (United Nations, 2008). Approximately 25% of the entire U.S. population is thought to have abused marijuana at least once, and 3 million people are thought to be addicted to it (Grinfeld, 2001).[16]

Estimates of the Problem of Hallucinogen Abuse[17]

Many researchers question whether it is possible to become *addicted* to hallucinogens. But it is thought that perhaps 10% of the U.S. population has abused a hallucinogen at least once in their lives (Sadock & Sadock, 2007). The Substance Abuse and Mental Health Services Administration (2009) estimated that 1.1 million people in the United States have abused a hallucinogenic compound in the past month.

Estimates of the Problem of Tobacco Abuse and Addiction

Tobacco is a special product. It might be legally purchased by adults, yet it is acknowledged to be destructive and addictive. Unfortunately, tobacco products are easily available to adolescents, and in some cases to children. Researchers estimate that approximately 25% of the entire U.S. population are current cigarette smokers, 25% are former smokers, and 50% have never smoked (Sadock & Sadock, 2007).

The Cost of Chemical Abuse/Addiction

Globally, drug use disorders are the sixth leading cause of disease in adults (Leamon et al., 2008). This translates into a financial impact of $880 billion per year, with alcohol use disorders costing the world economy another $880 billion per year ("Vital Signs," 2007). In the United States, alcohol and drug use disorders are thought to drain at least $375 billion per year from the economy (Falco, 2005). The annual toll from the

---

[10]This topic is discussed in more detail in Chapter 11.

[11]Which includes the abuse of methylphenidate and the various amphetamines.

[12]Which, as noted earlier in this chapter, includes both Canada and the United States.

[13]The United Nations defines "North America" as including both Canada and the United States.

[14]The danger, as will be discussed again in Chapter 12, is that it is impossible to predict at this time *which* individual will go on to become addicted to cocaine, and thus the use of this compound is discouraged, if only for this reason. Other dangers associated with cocaine use/abuse/addiction will be discussed in Chapter 12.

---

[15]Remember, again, that this includes *both* the United States and Canada.

[16]Although most people do not think of marijuana as a potentially addictive substance, as will be discussed in Chapter 13, some abusers do indeed become addicted to it.

[17]This is a difficult subject to discuss in depth since some researchers classify MDMA (commonly known as "Ecstasy") as a hallucinogen, others classify it as an amphetamine, and still others call it a hallucinogenic amphetamine compound. For the sake of this text it will be classified as a hallucinogen. See Chapter 17 for more details on this issue.

various diseases associated with illicit drug use in the United States, combined with the number of drug-related infant deaths, suicides, homicides, and motor vehicle accidents, is estimated to be approximately 12,000–17,000 people a year (Donovan, 2005; N. S. Miller & Brady, 2004; Mokdad, Marks, Stroup, & Gerberding, 2004).

All of the estimates cited in the last paragraph are in addition to the 440,000 people who are thought to die each year from smoking-related illness brought on by their own tobacco use, and the additional 35,000 to 56,000 people each year in the United States who are thought to lose their lives to illness brought on by exposure to "secondhand" or "environmental" tobacco smoke (R. T. Benson & Sacco, 2000; Bialous & Sarna, 2004; Mokdad et al., 2004). Furthermore, approximately 100,000 people die each year in the United States as a direct result of their alcohol use (Naimi et al., 2003; Small, 2002). Notice that the last sentence stated "as a *direct* result" of the individual's alcohol use. Alcohol use disorders contribute to or exacerbate 60 different medical disorders (B. Room, Babor, & Rehm, 2005). A person might die from one of the disease states exacerbated by their drinking, but the disease state, not the alcohol abuse, will be identified on the death certificate as the primary cause of death. If one were to include these "indirect" alcohol-related deaths, it becomes clear that alcohol either directly or indirectly causes as many deaths each year in the United States as do tobacco products (B. Room et al., 2005).

The Cost of Alcohol Use/Abuse/Addiction

Globally, alcohol use is thought to be a direct factor in 10–11% of all deaths each year (Stevenson & Sommers, 2005). The annual economic impact of alcohol use/abuse/addiction in the United States is thought to be at least $185 billion per year, of which $26 billion is for direct health care costs, and $37 billion is a result of lost productivity brought on by alcohol-related premature death (Belenko, Patapis, & French, 2005; Gilpin & Kolb, 2008; Petrakis, Gonzalez, Rosenheck, & Krystal, 2002; Smothers, Yahr, & Ruhl, 2004). It has been estimated that the complications brought on by alcohol use account for 15–25% of the annual total expenditure for health care each year in the United States (Anton, 2005; R. M. Swift, 2005). Clearly, although only 5–10% of the population in this country appears to have an alcohol use disorder, they consume a disproportionate amount of the yearly health care expenditure in the United States. For example, between 15 and 30% of

those individuals in nursing homes are thought to be there as either a direct or indirect result of their alcohol use disorders (Schuckit, 2006a & b). On a more personal level, it has been estimated that AUDs cost every man, woman, and child in the United States $638 per year whether they use alcohol or not (B. F. Grant et al., 2006).

Alcohol use is a factor in numerous motor vehicle accidents, with an estimated economic loss from such accidents being estimated at $24.7 billion per year (Craig, 2004). Alcohol is thought to be involved in approximately 40% of all motor vehicle accidents and 40–60% of all traumatic injury cases involve patients with an SUD (Craig, 2004; Savage, Kirsh, & Passik, 2008).

The Cost of Tobacco Use Disorders

Although it is legally produced, purchased, and used by adults without restriction, tobacco use extracts a terrible toll around the globe. Globally more than 3 million people per year die around the world as a direct result of their use of tobacco products, of whom about 435,000 live in the United States (Mokdad et al., 2004). In the United States, tobacco-related illness consumes 60% or more of the annual expenditure for health care, with one in every five deaths being directly traced to smoking-related illness (Sadock & Sadock, 2007). And this figure does not include those people who die as a result to exposure to "secondhand" or "environmental" tobacco smoke each year in this country.

The Cost of Substance Use Disorders

The cost of illicit-substance use, which includes the cost of premature death and illness, lost wages, financial losses by victims of substance-related crime, combined with the cost of law enforcement activities directly aimed at the problem of SUDs, has been calculated as at least $900 for every person 18 years or older in the United States each year (Heyman, 2009). When the cost of disability, accidental injuries, health care, and absenteeism from work are added together, the total annual economic impact of SUDs on the U.S. economy is estimated to be $428 billion (Gonzalez, Vasisileva, & Scott, 2009).

The health care problem has received much publicity in recent years. The team of Santora and Hutton (2008) concluded that hospitalized alcohol abusers had average hospital care expenses that were 120% higher than for a nonabuser, and that opioid abusers who are hospitalized require health care expenditures that are 482% than for nonabusers. Yet, as will be discussed in the next section of this chapter, the response to this ongoing problem has been haphazard, ineffective, and, in many cases, become a part of the problem.

Who Treats People with an SUD?

Having established that substance use disorders are a legitimate problem thus far, we are left with the question: Who treats those people with such disorders? It is not society in general: Only four cents of every dollar spent by state governments is devoted to the prevention and treatment of people with a substance use disorder (Grinfeld, 2001). Nor do physicians typically treat substance abusers, who comprise between 15 and 30% of patients seen by a primary care physician. Less than one-fifth of the physicians surveyed reported that they thought they were trained to treat patients with AUDs, whereas less than 17% thought that their training was sufficient to enable them to work with patients with other forms of SUDs (Clay, Allen, & Parran, 2008; National Center on Addiction and Substance Abuse at Columbia University, 2000). Furthermore, most physicians emerge from graduate training with a negative attitude toward individuals with an SUD (Renner, 2004a).

Possibly as a result of this deficit in their training, fewer than one-third of physicians carefully screen for substance use disorders among their patients (Greenfield & Hennessy, 2008a). Less than 50% of patients who go to see a physician about alcohol-related problems are even *asked* about their alcohol use (J. Pagano, Graham, Frost-Pineda, & Gold, 2005). This failure to inquire about a patient's substance use habits might be a major reason why SUDs are both underdiagnosed and undertreated (Clay et al., 2008; Greenfield & Hennessy, 2008a). This conclusion is supported by the observation that less than 1% of internal medicine and family practice consultations and only 5.1% of psychiatric consultations result in an accurate diagnosis of an SUD when it is present (Banta & Montgomery, 2007).

Although it has been repeatedly demonstrated in the professional journals that the addictions are chronic, treatable disorders, physicians "more often than not [will] view the addicted patient as challenging at best and not worthy of customary compassion" (R. Brown, 2006, p. 5). Physician postgraduate educational programs have attempted to address this problem, but the average length of such training programs is only about eight hours (Renner, 2004a). Nor is this professional blindness limited to physicians. Although nursing professionals frequently have more contact with patients than do physicians, "the majority of nursing schools … required only 1 to 5 clock hours of instruction on alcohol and drug abuse content during their entire undergraduate curricula" (Stevenson & Sommers, 2005, p. 15). Thus those health professionals who will have the most contact with the patient, the nursing staff, are ill-prepared to work with patients with SUDs.

Marriage and family therapists frequently encounter situations that are either caused or exacerbated by a substance-abusing family member. However, such problems are rarely identified, vital clues to the nature of the disorder within the family are missed, and therapy might be rendered ineffective. *If* these disorders are identified, they are usually addressed by a referral to another therapist of another discipline by the marriage or family therapist. This interrupts the continuity of care, and even if therapy is at all effective, it proceeds in a haphazard manner. Furthermore, if there is a dual-diagnosis situation (substance abuse with co-occurring mental illness), there is a definite need for family therapy, although this is rarely initiated (Minkoff, 2008).

In spite of the obvious relationship between SUDs and various forms of psychopathology, "most clinical psychologists are not well prepared to deal with issues involving substance use or abuse" (Sobell & Sobell, 2007, p. 2). Fully 74% of the psychologists surveyed admitted that they had no formal training in the identification or treatment of the addictions, and rated their graduate school training in this area as being inadequate (Aanavi, Taube, Ja, & Duran, 2000). Thus like their counterparts in other areas of the health care industry, psychologists are often ill-prepared to work with patients with SUDs. Only professional substance abuse counselors are required to have a high level of professional training in the recognition and treatment of SUDs, with national standards for individuals working in this field having recently been established. Because such counselors make up only a minority of those in the health care industry, the most common response to the question of who treats those individuals who are addicted to alcohol or drugs is, all too often, "nobody."

Society's Response

For the last half of the 20th century through the first decade of the 21st century, the response to substance use disorders has been a "war on drugs." Yet this has been a most curious "war," in the sense that the most destructive substances (alcohol and tobacco products) are exempt from attack. Furthermore, the deliberate use of false information, or *disinformation,* has become an almost unspoken official policy. As Szalavitz (2005) observed, "entire government bureaucracies—from the US Drug Enforcement Administration and the drug tsar to state police and prosecutors—have invested a great deal of time, effort and money to convince us that 'exposure to corrupting substances inevitably causes addiction and death'" (p. 19). As was noted earlier, about half of those who begin to use an illicit substance discontinue it in the first year, a finding that suggests that although addiction and death during this period of experimental use are possible (Center for Substance Abuse Research, 2008).

Unfortunately, society's response to the problem of substance use disorders has been much like its response to adolescent sexuality: Because of political/social/religious agendas of one group or another, the truth is either ignored or manipulated, or abstinence-based programs are assumed to be sufficient. Based on the number of adolescent pregnancies each year in the United States, it should be clear that abstinence-based sex education programs do not work. Why should this be different in the field of the substance use disorders? It is the purpose of this text to provide factual information about the mechanism(s) by which the various drugs of abuse work and the dangers associated with their use. And though it is not the purpose of this text to encourage the use of any compound, I hope that the information herein will allow individuals to make an informed decision about substance use based on the most current available information.

CHAPTER **2**

The Nature of the Beast

(Being an Examination of the Problem of SUDs)

Introduction

Substance use disorders (SUDs) and their impact on society in the United States can be examined from a number of different, often contradictory perspectives. For example, it has been suggested by some biologists that at least some mammals appear to have an inborn predisposition to seek out compounds such as fermented apples or mushrooms, which can alter that creature's perceptions of the world. Cat owners have long known this: They give their cat "catnip," which alters the cat's perception of the world in a way that they seem to enjoy.[1] Animal biologists have long recorded incidents where birds or other animals have apparently gone out of their way to find fermented apples or berries to ingest, apparently seeking the effects of the alcohol obtained in this manner. It would appear that we share this characteristic with our mammal cousins.

Why do People Choose to Use Drugs or Alcohol?

On the simplest of levels, this question might be answered with the observation that they want to do so. Virtually every known society encourages, if not actively supports, the use of some chemicals to alter the individual's perception of reality[2] (Glennon, 2008). Behavioral scientists now believe that recreational chemical use might serve several functions within a given culture. It might facilitate social bonding, serve as a means of religious communion with the gods, or provide a means of rebellion by a subgroup within the larger community.

Individuals might use chemicals to express a previously forbidden impulse, cope with emotional or physical pain, or explore alternative realities perceived to be either within themselves or in the world around them. Some individuals seek to substitute a substance-induced feeling of euphoria for the less mundane reality in which they live. People who have been marginalized by society might choose to use chemicals as a way to escape from the pain of their social status (Rasmussen, 2008). Unfortunately, in this process some users become ensnared by the ability of many compounds to trigger a reward cascade within their brain that is many times more powerful than that induced by regular reinforcers like food, water, or sex.

Our hedonistic society would seem to encourage the at least occasional use of chemicals, and they have become so pervasive in our culture that every one of us

---

[1] The cats, not their owners, although on occasion owners have also been known to sample the product out of curiosity. It is not known whether they stop to lick themselves or cough up fur balls after doing so.

[2] Before you begin to argue against this statement, consider the case of caffeine: How many of us would like to begin the day without that first cup of coffee or two (or three ...) in our system? Remember: Caffeine is a chemical, too!

must make a conscious choice every day to use or not use a recreational chemical(s).[3] Admittedly, for most of us this decision is so automatic that it does not even require conscious thought. If the individual should elect to use a drug(s) whose use is not approved of by society, or even use a socially accepted drug in a manner that is not acceptable to society,[4] the legal system can step in to punish this socially unacceptable act. Indeed, the legal system functions on the premise that substance use/abuse/addiction is the result of a choice, and that the individual can thus be held accountable for his/her actions.[5]

The Continuum of Chemical Use

It is surprising how often people confuse the terms substance *use*, *abuse*, and *addiction*. Indeed, these terms are often used synonymously, even in clinical research studies (Minkoff, 1997). In reality, substance use "is considered a normal learned behavior that falls on a continuum ranging from patterns of little use and few problems to excessive use and dependence" (Budney, Sigmon, & Higgons, 2003, p. 249).

The end points of this continuum are total abstinence on one end through to the pathological or repetitive pattern of use that is the hallmark of addiction. For this text, we will use the continuum in Figure 2-1 to examine substance use.

Admittedly, this continuum, as is true for any such tool, is an artificial construct. There are few clear

demarcations between one stage and the next, and it should not be assumed that a substance user will automatically move from one stage to the next (Brust, 2004; Washton & Zweben, 2006). This is perhaps seen most clearly in the observation that there is no clear consensus as to what constitutes normal use as opposed to abuse of even our oldest recreational chemical: alcohol (Cooney, Kadden, & Steinberg, 2005). Still, for the sake of this classification system, the various stages are defined as follows:

Level 0: *Total abstinence* from all recreational chemicals.

Level 1: *Rare to social use* of recreational chemicals, which might include the limited experimental use of a drug that is, technically, illegal.

Level 2: *Heavy social use/early problem use:* Individuals' use of a compound(s) is clearly above the norm for that society, and they might experience some legal, social, vocational, or medical consequences caused by their substance use.[6]

Level 3: *Late problem use/early addiction:* Individuals in this category may be physically dependent on a compound(s) and, if they should abruptly stop using their drug(s) of choice,[7] they may also experience the classic withdrawal syndrome for the compound(s) being abused.

Level 4: *Middle- to Late-Stage Addiction:* Individuals whose substance use would fall in this category demonstrate all of the classic signs of addiction: physical, medical, legal, occupational, and/or personal problems, as well as a possible physical dependency on alcohol/drugs.

Clearly, this classification system is imperfect. The criteria used to define whether an individual falls into one category or another are arbitrary and subject to debate. Furthermore, there are no clear points of demarcation between one stage and the next (Jaffe & Anthony, 2005). A further complicating factor is that the issue of whether the substance abuse is a current ongoing problem or has been resolved is often overlooked (Heyman, 2009). Many people with a history of a substance use disorder will either discontinue or at least significantly reduce their alcohol or drug use as a result of the

---

[3]In response to those of you who wish to argue this point, consider the following: Where is the nearest liquor store, or bar? If you wanted to do so, would you know where to buy some marijuana? If you did not know, would you know the name of a person to ask who would know? Are there certain people that you know of (coworkers, friends, etc.) whose company you avoid because you do not approve of their substance use? You see, we are not so removed from the problem of recreational drug use as we would like to believe, are we?

[4]Even in this category, there are contradictions. For example, the recreational use of a narcotic is illegal and a matter for the courts to handle. However, if individuals have a prescription from a physician, they now become a "patient" for whom the use of the same compound is sanctioned.

[5]It is frequently argued that because by definition the addiction requires that a person continue to use a compound(s) to avoid withdrawal symptoms, that she should not be punished for the substance use. The courts disagree, holding that the individual is responsible for decisions made to start to use recreational chemicals, even if the initial decision to use that compound was made sometime in the past. Furthermore, the courts hold that the individual is responsible for how she chooses to support that addiction.

---

[6]This does not automatically mean that the individual is *addicted* to that compound, although the term *abuser* would not be inappropriate here.

[7]The claim that "I can stop any time that I want to!" might be a motto for individuals whose substance use falls in this category.

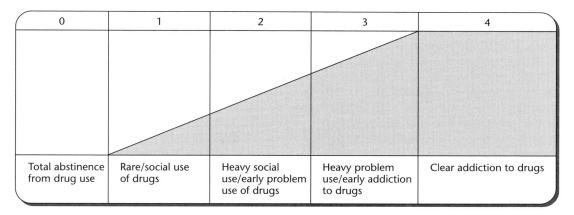

0	1	2	3	4
Total abstinence from drug use	Rare/social use of drugs	Heavy social use/early problem use of drugs	Heavy problem use/early addiction to drugs	Clear addiction to drugs

FIGURE 2-1 The Continuum of Recreational Chemical Use

maturation process (Heyman, 2009). A college student who might meet the established diagnostic criteria for alcohol abuse at the age of 20 might not, for example, meet the diagnostic for any form of an alcohol use disorder at the age of 30.

If They Are So Destructive, Why Do People Abuse Chemicals?

On the simplest of levels, the answer is: "because they make the user feel good." In reality, there are a number of factors that influence the individual's decision to use/abuse a certain chemical(s). They are as follows.

Blindness to the Compound's Effects

Unfortunately, one side effect of alcohol, the drugs of abuse, and some prescription medications is that users will report that they *feel* better, when an objective observer would say that they are actually decompensating in terms of their interpersonal behaviors, ability to handle finances, ability to maintain cognitive function, and ability to attend to the activities of daily living that make it so nice to be around other people (Breggin, 2008).

Pharmacological Reward Potential of That Compound

Another factor that contributes to the individual's choice to abuse a chemical is the reward potential. The drugs of abuse *are* drugs of abuse because they are able to induce pleasurable effects (Budney et al., 2003; O'Brien, 2006). The reward potential of a compound depends in large part upon its chemical structure and the route of administration. Those compounds that

have a rapid onset of action and that induce a sense of pleasure have the highest reward potential for abuse (O'Brien, 2006). Not surprisingly, this is a common characteristic of the drugs of abuse. When a chemical-electrical brain such as ours encounters a compound(s) that triggers the reward cascade (G. Marcus, 2008), that compound becomes a potential drug of abuse.

The basic laws of behavioral psychology hold that if something (a) increases the individual's sense of pleasure or (b) decreases his discomfort, then he is likely to repeat the behavior (in this case using alcohol or a drug). In contrast, if a compound were to (c) decrease the individual's sense of discomfort or (d) reduce the individual's sense of pleasure, he would be unlikely to repeat that behavior. Finally, the *immediacy of effect* is another factor that must be considered in a drug's potential for abuse[8] (Kalivas, 2003). It must be remembered, however, that the reward potential of a given compound, though it might be a powerful incentive for repeated use, is not sufficient in itself to cause addiction to that compound (Kalivas, 2003).

The Social Learning Component

An individual does not start life expecting to abuse a chemical(s). Rather, the individual must learn (a) that the use of a given compound is socially acceptable, (b) to recognize the effects of that compound, and (c) how to interpret them as desirable. All these tasks are accomplished through the process of social learning, which takes place through peer groups, mass media,

---

[8]Compare the abuse potential of a hypothetical compound that will induce a sense of pleasure in 4–5 minutes, as compared with that of a second hypothetical compound that will induce a sense of pleasure in 4–6 weeks, and you will understand this point.

familial feedback, and so on (Cape, 2003; Mueser, Noordsy, Drake, & Fox, 2003). For instance, the mass media's emphasis on how a celebrity has developed an SUD might be interpreted as a form of acceptance of substance use at the same time that celebrity is serving as a role model for others (A. Brown, 2007).

Alcohol provides an excellent example of the social learning component of SUDs. First-time drinkers are complimented by their drinking companions for their alcohol use, and reminded that this was "fun" even while the new drinker conducts a close inspection of the interior of a toilet bowl. Another example is provided by marijuana abusers, who must be taught by their drug-abusing peers (a) how to obtain it, (b) how to use it, (c) how to recognize the effects, and (d) why intoxication is so desirable (Monti, Kadden, Rohsenow, Cooney, & Abrams, 2002). Popular media portrayals of substance use also provide a conduit for social learning, although many people do not think of the media in this light.

Individual Expectations

Individual expectations often serve as an arena in which the individual will interpret the effect(s) of a chemical(s). These expectations begin to manifest in childhood or early adolescence, and evolve over time as a result of such influences as peer groups, childhood exposure to advertising, parental substance use behaviors, and the individual's past experience with the use of that compound(s) (Monti et al., 2002; Sher, Wood, Richardson, & Jackson, 2005). Individuals' expectations for a substance are also strongly influenced by the context in which they uses that chemical and by the cultural traditions that surround the use of a substance such as alcohol (Lindman, Sjoholm, & Lang, 2000; Sher et al., 2005).

Not surprisingly, individuals' expectations about the effects of a compound(s) play a very powerful role in their substance use pattern (A. W. Blume, 2005). For example, it has been found that many of those people who are likely to abuse MDMA ("Ecstasy")[9] are those who anticipate gaining self-knowledge (Engels & ter Bogt, 2004). As will be discussed in more detail in Chapter 15, those individuals who have a negative expectation set for LSD are more likely to experience a "bad trip" than those who anticipate more positive experiences. Finally, many older pharmaceuticals that were marketed as central nervous system stimulants[10]

are now classified as "cognitive enhancers," a label that belies the fact that there is only minimal, if any, improvement in cognitive performance with the use of these compounds (Stix, 2009). However, if people *expect* these compounds to improve cognitive abilities, they might very well achieve that result through the placebo effect.

An individual's expectations for any aspect of life are not static and unchanging but rather, as a result of personal experience and interpersonal feedback, are subject to modification. For example, a person who was raised in a home where there was a violent, abusive, alcohol-dependent parent might swear never to engage in the use of alcohol. However, under the influence of peer pressure at a party this same person might conclude that *moderate* alcohol use is acceptable.

Cultural/Social Influences

Each individual lives in a cultural environment in which behavioral norms are transmitted through modeling and tradition. People's substance use decisions are made in this cultural context as well as the context of the social group(s) to which they belong (Monti et al., 2002; D. L. Rosenbloom, 2000, 2005). This cultural influence might express itself in one or more of five different ways (Pihl, 1999): (a) the general cultural environment, (b) the specific community in which the individual lives, (c) subcultures within the parent community, (d) family/peer influences, and (e) the context in which the compound (such as alcohol) is used. At each level, the *availability* of a given chemical (s) of abuse also influences substance use behavior, although this is often overlooked by researchers.

It is important to remember that within each culture there are various subgroups that may, perhaps only to a limited degree, adopt the standards of the parent culture. The relationship between different social groups within a parent culture might be viewed in the manner shown in Figure 2-2.

Unfortunately, cultural guidelines might require generations, or even centuries, to evolve (Westermeyer, 1995). The discrepancy between the availability of substances and the stage of cultural sanctions against them might clearly be seen in the unfolding drama in which younger Jewish generations, wishing to explore new behaviors that they observe in their non-Jewish peers, are starting to experiment with the use of recreational chemicals that are "unclean" by their traditional standards. Their cultural and educational heritage has failed to warn them about the addictive potential of these compounds, leaving them vulnerable to physical

---

[9]Discussed in Chapter 15.

[10]Compounds such as methylphenidate, or the amphetamine compounds.

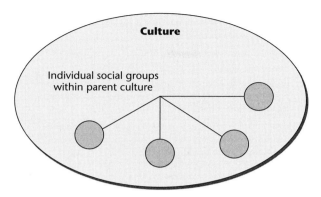

FIGURE 2-2 The Relationship Between Different Subgroups and the Parent Culture

Individual Life Goals

Individual life goals help to shape whether people begin to use, or continue to use, a chemical(s). At each point in the process of substance abuse, they must determine whether the use of that substance is consistent with their long-term life goals. This is rarely a problem with socially approved compounds such as alcohol and tobacco. But consider a low-level business executive who is being considered for a major promotion and who discovers that the new department is in a branch of the company that has a strict no-smoking policy. People in this circumstance have a choice of either changing their smoking habits, allowing them to either accept the promotion, or reject the promotion because of the no-smoking policy. A flowchart of the decision-making process that the individual goes through might look like the one in Figure 2-3.

It should be noted that the forces that help to shape a given individual's decision to *initiate* substance use have been found to be different from those that help to *maintain* it (Washton & Zweben, 2006). For example, avowed nondrinkers who agree to "try some beer" on a date might discover that they like the effects,

dependence on them (K. R. Roane, 2000). Thus while cultural traditions might have a potential to protect individuals from potential substance use disorders, there is a very real danger that they will find that their culture fails to provide such behavioral guidelines.

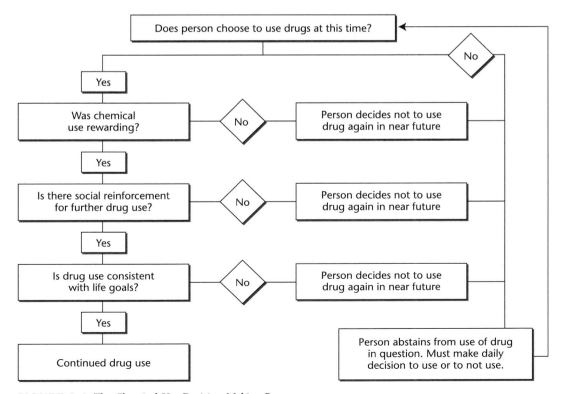

FIGURE 2-3 The Chemical Use Decision-Making Process

continue to use it, and now find it to be an essential component to a social event. If they should become physically dependent on alcohol, the fear of withdrawal then helps to shape continued use of that substance. In this hypothetical example, the force that helped to initiate the alcohol use (social approval) was far different from the force that maintained it (physical addiction). This is a common phenomenon in the world of substance use, and is frequently overlooked by those who are attempting to assess[11] the individual's use of a substance to determine if it is problematic (Washton & Zweben, 2006).

What Do We Mean When We Say that Somebody Is "Addicted" to a Chemical?

In the hypothetical example used in the last paragraph, the individual could be said to be physically dependent on alcohol by the end of the paragraph. Physical dependence on a substance is one of the traditionally accepted signs of addiction. Surprisingly, there is no universally accepted definition of the term *addiction* (Brust, 2004). Indeed, it is often quite surprising for students to learn that terms such as *substance abuse* or *addiction* are quite arbitrary (O'Brien, 2006).

Medical professionals use a list of standardized diagnostic criteria, such as those outlined in the American Psychiatric Association's (2000)[12] *Diagnostic and Statistical Manual of Mental Disorders*, 4th edition, text revision (or *DSM-IV-TR*) to assist them in making the determination whether a given individual does or does not have an SUD. Some of the criteria outlined in the *DSM-IV-TR* are listed in the following table:[13]

DSM-IV-TR DIAGNOSTIC CRITERIA

1. Users are *preoccupied* with substance use during periods of abstinence.
2. They will *use more than planned.*
3. Users *develops tolerance* to the substance(s) being abused.
4. Users will experience a *characteristic withdrawal syndrome* if they should discontinue to use that (or similar) substances.
5. Users *begins to use more of a substance to avoid the withdrawal syndrome* noted in item 4.

6. Users *make repeated attempts to cut back or discontinue* the use of that substance without success.
7. Users are *under the influence of the chemical at inappropriate times* (such as in class or while at work).
8. Continued substance use *interferes with normal daily functioning* (for example, the individual is unable to go to work/class because of a hangover).
9. Users *reduce non-substance-centered activities* in favor of activities that allow for further substance use (for example: not going to a family reunion where substance use is discouraged in favor of a fishing trip with substance-abusing friends).
10. Users *continue to abuse chemicals in spite of physical, emotional, social, or vocational* problems.

NOTE: This table is intended for illustrative purposes only. It is not intended to be nor should it be used as, a guide to patient diagnosis.

Individuals who meet four or more of the *DSM-IV-TR* criteria are said to be addicted to a substance. Although the *DSM-IV-TR* is the most widely used diagnostic system in the United States, there are other systems in use.[14] For instance, Shaffer (2001) suggested the criteria listed in the following table as signs of an addiction to alcohol or drugs:

DIAGNOSTIC CRITERIA SUGGESTED BY SHAFFER (2001)

1. *Craving/compulsion* to use the chemical, or another chemical that serves as a substitute. Individuals' thoughts are centered on the possibility of substance use, obtaining the substance, or memories of the last time that they used that (or other) chemicals.
2. *Loss of control*, exhibited by using significantly more of a compound than was planned, being unable to cut back on the amount used, or being unable to stop the use of the chemical at all.
3. *Continued use in spite of consequences* brought on by the abuse of that compound(s). Such consequences might involve the physical, psychosocial, vocational, or financial spheres of the individual's life.

NOTE: This list is intended for illustrative purposes only, and is not intended to be, nor should it be used as, a guide to patient diagnosis.

Both lists, and other definitions of SUDs not discussed in this text, share certain common elements, including: (1) substance use is a primary disease; (2) it has multiple manifestations in the user's life, including the social, psychological, spiritual, vocational, interpersonal, and economic spheres of their lives; (3) it is often progressive; (4) it is potentially fatal; (5) it is marked by users' inability to control (or, at least to control consistently) their substance use; (6) it is

[11]The process of assessment is discussed in Chapter 28.

[12]The *Diagnostic and Statistical Manual of Mental Disorders* (5th edition) is tentatively scheduled for publication in 2012.

[13]The reader is advised to consult the *DSM-IV-TR* for a full list of diagnostic criteria.

[14]The *ICD-10* is one example.

marked by preoccupation with drug use; (7) users develop a distorted way of looking at the world so that it supports their continued use of that compound(s); (8) users become *tolerant* to the effects of that compound(s), and they either must go through "drug holidays" in which they lose some of that tolerance, or must use larger and larger amounts in a manner designed to overcome their tolerance; and (9) users will experience a characteristic *withdrawal syndrome* if they should discontinue using that compound(s).

Definitions of Terms Used in This Text

At this point it is necessary to establish a common language so that we are "all on the same page." Therefore in this text, the following definitions will be utilized:

Social use: A point of confusion is that use of a substance is equated with a substance use disorder, especially when the person is abusing illicit drugs. However, "being a substance user does not mean invariably that one has a substance use disorder" (Gonzalez et al., 2009, p. 456). An individual's culture defines the frequency with which the individual might use these substances and under what conditions. Currently, alcohol and tobacco are the only products that can legally be used in a social setting, although marijuana use is arguably also a "social" compound given its frequency of abuse.

Substance abuse: This term is used when an individual uses a compound when there is no legitimate medical need to do so, or when that compound is used in excess of social standards (Schuckit, 2006a & b). There is no physical dependence on the chemical(s) in question at this time. Individuals might best be viewed as making a *poor choice* concerning the use of that compound(s) (Minkoff, 1997). But they are not dependent on that compound, and it does not automatically progress to physical addiction of that compound (Swift, 2005).

Dependence: This is said to exist when the individual meets the *DSM-IV-TR* criteria for alcohol or drug dependence.

Drug of choice: Clinicians once spoke about the individual's *drug of choice* as an important component of the disease of addiction. Indeed, this was why Narcotics Anonymous (NA) was founded. The early members of NA did not feel that Alcoholics Anonymous (AA)[15] was able to meet their needs. In many cases, drug addicts who attempted to join AA in the 1950s and 1960s were actually told that they could talk only about their alcohol use disorder at meetings, as AA not intended for drug addiction. As a larger and larger percentage of younger members joined AA with poly-drug dependency issues, the concept of *drug of choice* has fallen into some degree of disfavor, and clinicians place little emphasis on this concept in the first decade of the 21st century.

Loss of Control: This is a poorly defined term. In essence, individuals who continue to abuse alcohol/drugs in spite of legal, psychosocial, or medical consequences of their substance use are said to have lost control over the use of that compound.

Addiction/dependence: These are poorly defined terms. Most clinicians now prefer the term *dependence* to a chemical, although a large percentage still use the older term *addiction* (Shaffer, 2001). Dependence is marked by the development of a characteristic *withdrawal syndrome* for the compound(s) being abused, each of which will be discussed in the chapter devoted to that drug(s) of abuse.

Tolerance: This is said to develop when the individual must use more of the drug(s) of abuse in order to achieve the desired effects because the initial dose is no longer as effective. For the sake of this text, we will limit our discussion to just two subforms of tolerance: *metabolic tolerance* and *pharmacodynamic tolerance*. In metabolic tolerance, the body becomes more effective in breaking down or eliminating the compound(s) in question, so it does not remain in the body for as long a period of time as it initially did, and thus has a diminished effect. The liver is the organ in the body that breaks down most drugs of abuse, and this is carried out in a process known as *biotransformation*[16]

Pharmacodynamic tolerance is the term applied to the body's ability to develop some degree of insensitivity to the drug's effects, so that the cells in the body might continue to function normally in spite of the continued presence of the chemical. When either form of tolerance has developed, the individual usually can overcome it by (a) going on a drug-free "holiday" so that the body reverses its tolerance to that compound, (b) using increasing amounts of the chemical to overcome the body's growing tolerance, or (c) using

---

[15]Both Alcoholics Anonymous and Narcotics Anonymous are discussed later in this text.

[16]In older pharmacology textbooks this was called *metabolism*, but this choice of word caused endless confusion between the body's natural metabolic processes and the breakdown of alcohol and drugs. Professionals now use the term *biotransformation* if the compound was prescribed, and *metabolism* if it is a drug of abuse.

more potent delivery methods so that a greater amount of the drug(s) in question is introduced into the body more quickly.

Withdrawal syndrome: This is a phenomenon experienced when individuals either stop or significantly reduces their intake of a specific compound(s). The withdrawal syndrome is usually the opposite of the compound's effects on the user's body. Thus, for example, alcohol acts like a chemical "brake" on the neurons of the brain. The neurons struggle to compensate, increasing the number of neurotransmitter receptor sites for excitatory neurotransmitters to overcome the inhibitory effects of the persistent alcohol use. When the alcohol-dependent individual stops drinking, this "brake" is removed, and neurons in the brain might become overactive. This is experienced by the heavy drinker as anxiety, withdrawal tremors, and in extreme cases the delirium tremens (DTs), all of which are discussed in more detail in Chapter 6.

The world of the addictions is replete with a range of other terms, which serve as a form of professional shorthand for individuals who work in the field, but those just discussed should serve as a solid foundation on which the reader can begin to build an understanding of the world of substance use disorders.

The Growth of New "Addictions"

One of the more frustrating aspects of the subfield of the behavioral sciences that addresses the SUDs is that the term *addiction* is applied to a range of other conditions. For example, there are sex, food, men, women, play, shopping, shoplifting, carbohydrates, unhappy relationships, french fries, lip balm, and credit cards are all said to be an "addiction" by one group or another (Barber, 2008; Jaffe & Anthony, 2005). Barber argued convincingly that physicians are now catering to the "worried well" rather than those who are physically sick, and there is an ever-growing number of antidepressants, stimulants, or anxiolytics[17] that might be dispensed for the cash-carrying worried well. Fortunately, there is little physical evidence at this time that non-drug-centered behaviors can result in a physical addiction such as can result from the physical dependence on alcohol or the other compounds commonly called the "drugs of abuse," which are the focus of this text.

---

[17]See Glossary.

What Do We *Really* Know about Substance Use Disorders?

If you were a devotee of the television talk shows, or read a small sample of the self-help books that line the bookstore shelves, you would easily be left with the impression that researchers have discovered the cause(s) of and the treatment(s) for alcoholism and addiction to the other drugs of abuse. Unfortunately, *nothing could be further from the truth!* Much of what is "known" about SUDs is based on mistaken assumptions, distorted data, clinical myth, theory, or, in many cases, incomplete data. An excellent example of how incomplete or distorted data might influence the evolution of treatment theory can be seen in the manner in which clinical research is carried out. There is a difference between *lifetime prevalence*, which is whether a person has abused a given chemical at any point in their lives, and *period prevalence*, which is whether the individual has abused a given chemical in a specified period of time (usually one year) (Brook, Pahl, & Rubenstone, 2008).

Another example of how clinical theory is based on distorted data is the fact that much of the research conducted to date involves people in either inpatient or outpatient substance abuse rehabilitation, although it is not clear whether these individuals are typical of *all* substance abusers, or a subset of substance abusers who are unable to quit the abuse of a chemical(s) without professional intervention (Heyman, 2009). Virtually nothing is known about the natural history of SUDs, or the percentage of those substance abusers who discontinue their chemical abuse without professional assistance (Heyman, 2009).

Many of those who abuse a compound do so simply out of curiosity about the effects of that substance, and after a period stop abusing it. A percentage of these people go on to become regular abusers of that compound, and an even smaller percentage become addicted to it. A seldom studied subpopulation of abusers are those people who use chemicals on a social basis, with possibly weeks or months between isolated episodes of use, but who apparently never go on to become addicted. These people are known as "chippers." Finally, there has been little research on the similarities and/or differences between men and women with SUDs.

There are, therefore, serious questions that face researchers in the field of the addictions:

1. Are those individuals who seek treatment the same as those who do not?
2. Are those individuals who are "chippers" different in some poorly understood way from those individuals who go on to become physically dependent on a drug or alcohol?
3. Is research carried out on those individuals who seek treatment through the Veterans Administration Hospital system applicable to the general population?
4. How do men and women who have SUDs differ? Do the same treatment techniques work on each subgroup?
5. Are those substance abusers who hold full-time employment the same as or different from those substance abusers who hold part-time jobs, and are individuals in either group the same as or different from those who are unemployed?
6. Are those people addicted to only alcohol the same as those people who are poly-drug abusers or addicts?

It is difficult to answer these questions, in part because much of the clinical literature addresses only the AUDs. There are probable differences between a person with an AUD and one with, as an example, an opioid dependence, but there is a dearth of clinical research into such differences. The assumption that the forces that shape SUDs in men automatically are the same as those that apply to women has also been challenged.[18] As will be discussed in Chapter 23, the problem of child and adolescent substance abuse/addiction has virtually been ignored until recently, and much of what was thought to be "known" about this problem reflected assumptions based on adult populations.

Thus what much of what we think we know about substance use disorders is not based on scientific research, but on assumptions, guesses, and limited data. However, it is on this foundation that an entire rehabilitation "industry" has been based. It is not the purpose of this text to deny that SUDs cause a terrible cost in individual suffering and to society, but hopefully the reader has started to understand how little is really known about SUDs.

The State of the Art: Unanswered Questions, Uncertain Answers

As the reader may have concluded by now, there is much to be learned about SUDs and how they manifest in the life of the individual. For example, 30–45% of all adults will demonstrate at least one sign of an alcohol use disorder (alcohol-related "blackout," legal problem, etc.). This does not mean that 30–45% of the adult population of this country is or will become alcohol-dependent! Most people either use alcohol socially or abstain from it entirely, and neither clinical researchers nor substance abuse rehabilitation professionals know how to identify the individual who will go on to develop an alcohol use disorder[19] from the one who will experience a transient substance use problem, and then either go on to abstain from further chemical use or at least simply be a "social" user from that point on. As will be discussed later in Chapters 4 and 5, there is still much to be discovered about even the use, abuse, and addiction to humanity's oldest compound of abuse: alcohol.

Chapter Summary

In this chapter, many of the basic concepts used by researchers and clinicians who work in the field of substance abuse rehabilitation were introduced. Also discussed was the fact that substance use can be classified along a continuum. Information about the extent of the problem of substance use/abuse in the United States and around the world was discussed. The scope of the toll that the drug(s) of abuse extract on the individual was briefly touched on. Unanswered questions about chemical use, abuse, and addiction were raised and briefly discussed, as was the fact that there is still a great deal to learn about SUDs.

---

[18]See Chapter 18.

[19]The alcohol use disorders (AUDs) are a subset of substance use disorders. When the discussion is limited only to alcohol, the terms *alcohol use disorders* or *AUDs* will be used. When the topic is limited to cocaine abuse or addiction, the term *cocaine use disorders* will be used, and so on.

CHAPTER 3

A Brief Introduction to the Science of Pharmacology[1]

Introduction

It is virtually impossible to discuss the effects of the various drugs of abuse without touching on a number of basic pharmacological concepts. Although a complete understanding of the science of pharmacology can take years to attain, in this chapter we will discuss the impact that the different drugs of abuse might have on the user's body, and the pharmacological principles by which these effects take place.

A Basic Misconception

It is surprising how often people discuss the drugs of abuse as if they were somehow a special class of chemicals that are unique. In reality most of the drugs of abuse were pharmaceutical agents in the past, and of those that were not actual pharmaceuticals, many were investigated as possible medications at one point in time. Thus, they work in the same manner that the other pharmaceuticals do: by changing the biological function of target cells through chemical actions (Katzung, 1995). As is true for most of the pharmaceuticals in use today, the drugs of abuse strengthen/weaken a potential that exists within the cells of the body. In the case of the drugs of abuse, the target cells are usually in the central nervous system.

The Prime Effect and Side Effects of Chemicals

It is often surprising for students to learn that it is virtually impossible to develop a mind-altering drug without unwanted side effects. This is "because the brain is so highly integrated, it is not possible to circumscribe mental functions without impairing a variety of other functions, typically causing generalized dysfunction of the brain and mind" (Breggin, 2008, p. 2).

Thus in order to achieve the *prime effect*[2] of a compound, the user must endure the *side effects*[3] of that compound as well. Some of the side effects will be relatively minor, whereas others might be life threatening. This rule is true both for pharmaceutical agents prescribed by a physician for a patient, and for drug abusers.

For example, a person might ingest a dose of aspirin to help them cope with the pain of a minor injury. Aspirin does this by inhibiting the production of a family of chemicals known as the *prostaglandins,* a subtype of which is produced at the site of the injury. This is the primary effect of the aspirin dose. However, aspirin also blocks the production of another subtype of prostaglandin used to regulate kidney and stomach function, possibly placing the user's life at risk from the unwanted inhibition of prostaglandin production in these organs.

---

[1]This chapter is designed to provide the reader with a brief overview of some of the more important principles of pharmacology. It is not intended to serve as, nor should it be used for, a guide to patient care.

[2]See Glossary.

[3]See Glossary.

Another example of the difference between the primary and side effects of a medication is seen in the patient who has developed a bacterial infection in the middle ear (a condition known as *otitis media*) who is prescribed an antibiotic such as amoxicillin. The desired effect is the elimination of the offending bacteria in the middle ear, but an unwanted side effect might also be the death of bacteria in the gastrointestinal tract, where they perform a useful function in the process of digestion. The point to keep in mind is that there are the desired *primary effects* and unwanted *side effects,* or what are also known as *secondary effects,* of every compound. The side effects can range in intensity from making the patient mildly uncomfortable to being life threatening.

The Method by Which a Compound is Administered

One factor that influences the intensity of the drug's primary and side effects is the manner in which it is administered. The specific *form* in which a compound is administered will have a major impact on (a) the speed with which that compound begins to have an effect on the body, (b) the way that the compound is distributed throughout the body, (c) the intensity of its effects, and (d) the speed with which the individual will begin to experience any side effects from the compound. Kamienski and Keogy (2006) identified 13 different ways that a compound could be introduced into the body. Fortunately, most of the drugs of abuse are administered either by the *enteral* or the *parenteral* route.

Enteral Forms of Drug Administration

Compounds administered by the enteral route enter the body by the gastrointestinal (GI) tract (T. N. M. Brody, 1994). Such compounds are usually administered in oral, sublingual, or rectal forms (A. J. Jenkins, 2007; B. R. Williams & Baer, 1994). The most common method of enteral drug administration is through the use of a tablet, which is essentially a selected dose of a compound mixed with a binding agent that acts to give it shape and hold its form until it enters the GI tract. In most cases the tablet is designed to be ingested whole, although in some cases it might be broken up to allow the patient to ingest a small dose, if desired. A number of compounds are administered in enteral form, including many pharmaceuticals, over-the-counter medications,[4] and some illicit drugs.

Once in the GI tract the compound begins to break down and separate from the binding agent and is absorbed into the body.

Another common method of administration of an oral medication is the capsule. This is a modified form of tablet, with the medication being suspended in a solution and surrounded by a gelatin capsule. The capsule is designed to be swallowed whole, and once it reaches the GI tract it breaks down and the medication (and the solution in which it is suspended) is released, allowing the absorption of the desired compound. Some compounds are simply administered as liquids, such as children's medication(s). This allows for the titration of the dose according to a child's weight. An excellent example of a drug of abuse that is administered in liquid form is alcohol.

A number of compounds might be absorbed through the blood-rich tissues found under the tongue. A chemical that is administered in this manner is said to be administered *sublingually,* which is a variation of the oral form of drug administration. Some of the compounds administered sublingually include nitroglycerin and fentanyl. The sublingual method of drug administration avoids the danger of the "first pass metabolism" effect (discussed later in this chapter) (A. J. Jenkins, 2007). But in spite of this advantage, the sublingual form of drug administration is only rarely used.

While many compounds are rapidly absorbed rectally, this method of drug administration is uncommon in medical practice, and virtually unheard of by drug abusers (A. J. Jenkins, 2007). Thus methods of rectal drug administration will not be discussed further in this text.

Parenteral Forms of Drug Administration

The parenteral method of drug administration essentially involves the injection of a compound directly into the body. There are several advantages to parental forms of drug administration, including the fact that the drug(s) are not exposed to gastric juices, delays caused by the stomach-emptying process, or the danger of being mixed with food in the GI tract rather than being absorbed by the body. But the parenteral method of drug administration also presents dangers to the user, which will be discussed later.

Depending on the substance being discussed, parenteral administration might be the preferred method of administration, especially when a rapid onset of effects is desired. The *subcutaneous* method of drug administration involves the injection of a given amount of a compound (and the agent in which it is suspended)

---

[4]See Glossary.

just under the skin. While this avoids the dangers of exposing the drug(s) to the digestive juices of the GI tract, compounds administered subcutaneously are only slowly absorbed. This is often a method by which illicit narcotics are first injected and is referred to as "skin popping" by injection drug addicts. While the onset of the drug's effects is slower than other forms of parental drug administration, subcutaneous drug administration methods allow for a reservoir of the drug to be established just under the skin.

A second method of parenteral drug administration involves the injection of a compound(s) into muscle tissue (IM injection). Muscle tissues have a good supply of blood, and many compounds injected into muscle tissue will be absorbed into the general circulation more rapidly than compounds injected just under the skin. This method of drug administration is used both for the administration of some pharmaceuticals in medical practice and sometimes by illicit drug abusers. Anabolic steroid abusers will often inject the drug(s) being abused into muscle tissue, for example; however, there are many compounds, such as the benzodiazepine chlordiazepoxide, that are poorly absorbed by muscle tissue and are thus rarely, if ever, administered by this route (DeVane, 2004).

A third method of parenteral drug administration is the *intravenous* (or IV) injection. In this process the compound(s) of choice are injected directly into a vein, thus being deposited directly into the general circulation (DeVane, 2004). This is a common method by which legitimate pharmaceuticals, and many drugs of abuse, are administered. One serious disadvantage of the intravenous method of drug administration is that it does not allow the body very much time to adapt to the foreign chemical, and thus the individual is at risk for a serious adverse reaction to that compound within seconds of when it was administered.

Although a compound might be administered via a parenteral method, that drug(s) will not have an instantaneous effect. The speed at which any drug will begin to have an effect depends on a number of factors, which will be discussed in the section titled Distribution, later in this chapter.

Other Forms of Drug Administration

There are a number of additional forms of drug administration, which will be discussed only briefly in this text. The *transdermal* method of drug administration involves a compound being slowly absorbed through the skin. This has the advantage of allowing a low,

but relatively steady blood level of the compound(s) in question being established in the user's body. But this method of drug administration does not allow one to rapidly establish any significant blood level of a compound in the user's body. This can be seen in the fact that transdermal nicotine patches might require up to 24 hours before a sufficient level of nicotine is established in the user's blood to block nicotine withdrawal symptoms.

Another method of drug administration, one that is used more frequently by drug abusers than in medical practice, is the *intranasal* method. In this method of drug administration, the compound is "snorted," depositing it on to the blood-rich tissues in the sinuses. Both cocaine and heroin powder are occasionally abused in this manner. This allows for a relatively rapid absorption of the drug(s) in question, but the rate of absorption is slower than the intravenous route of administration, and absorption is rather erratic.

The process of "snorting" is similar to the process of *inhalation,* which is used both in medical practice and with certain compounds by drug abusers. The process of inhalation takes advantage of the fact that the circulatory system is separated from direct exposure to the air only by a layer of tissue less than 1/100,000ths of an inch (0.64 micron) thick (Garrett, 1994). Many drug molecules are small enough to pass across this barrier relatively easily, entering the individual's circulation quickly. An example of this would be surgical anesthetic gasses. When smoked, many of the drugs of abuse become able to cross over this barrier as well, gaining access to the circulation. Some of these compounds include heroin and cocaine. Finally, in the case of some compounds, the process of inhalation is able to introduce small particles into the deep tissues of the lungs, where they are deposited. In a brief period of time, these particles are then broken down into small units until they are small enough to pass though the tissue barrier of the lungs into the circulation. This is the process that takes place when tobacco cigarettes are smoked, for example.

Each subform of inhalation takes advantage of the fact that the lungs offer a blood-rich, extremely large surface area, allowing for the rapid absorption of many compounds (A. J. Jenkins, 2007). But the amount of a given compound that actually is absorbed into the general circulation is highly variable for two reasons:

1. The individual must inhale the compound(s) at exactly the right point in the respiratory cycle to allow the drug molecules to reach the desired point in the lungs.

2. Some chemicals are able to pass through the tissues of the lung into the circulation only very slowly.

Marijuana is a good example of this problem, as the compounds in marijuana smoke are able to cross into the general circulation only slowly. The individual must hold his breath for as long as possible to allow as large a percentage of the compounds inhaled to cross into the circulation as might be accomplished before the person must exhale.

Bioavailability

To have an effect, a compound must enter the body in sufficient strength to achieve the desired effect. This is referred to as the *bioavailability* of a compound. Essentially the bioavailability of a compound is the *concentration of unchanged chemical at the site of action* (Bennett & Brown, 2003). The bioavailability of a compound, in turn, is affected by the factors of absorption, distribution, biotransformation, and elimination (A. J. Jenkins, 2007; Bennett & Brown, 2003). Each of these processes will be discussed in more detail in the following sections.

Absorption

Except for topical agents such as an antifungal cream, which are deposited directly on the site of action, most compounds must be absorbed into the body in order to have any effect (A. J. Jenkins, 2007). This involves the drug molecules moving from the site of entry, through various cell boundaries, to the circulatory system, where it is transported to the site of action. Compounds that are weakly acidic are usually absorbed through the stomach lining, whereas compounds that are a weak base[5] are absorbed in the small intestine (A. J. Jenkins, 2007; DeVane, 2004).

The human body is composed of layers of specialized cells, organized into specific patterns in order to carry out designated functions. The cells of the circulatory system are organized to form tubes (blood vessels) that contain the cells and fluids found in blood. Each layer of tissue that a compound must pass through in order to reach the circulatory system will slow absorption that much more. For example, as noted earlier the circulation is separated from the air in the lungs by a single layer of tissue (the cell wall of the individual alveoli). Compounds that are able to cross this one

cell layer are able to reach the general circulation in just a matter of seconds. In contrast to this, a compound that is ingested orally must pass through the layers of cells lining the GI tract and the blood vessels the surround it, before it reaches the circulation. Thus the oral method of drug administration is recognized as being much slower than inhalation, for example.

There are a number of specialized *cellular transport mechanisms* that the body uses to move necessary substances into/away from the circulatory system that drug molecules can take advantage of in order to move from the site of administration to the site of action. Without going into too much detail, it is possible to classify these cellular transport mechanisms as being either *active* or *passive* means of transport (A. J. Jenkins, 2007). The most common method by which drug molecules move across cell membranes, diffusion, is also a passive method of molecular transport. Active methods involve the drug molecule taking advantage of one of several natural molecular transport mechanisms that move essential molecules into or out of cells. Collectively, these different molecular transport mechanisms provide a system of active transport across the cell boundaries and into the interior of the body.

The process of drug absorption is variable, depending on a number of factors, the most important of which is the *method of administration,* as discussed earlier in this chapter. Another major variable is the *rate of blood flow* at the site of entry. For example, an intramuscular injection into the deltoid muscle of a person suffering from hypothermia will result in poor absorption, because the blood has been routed to the interior of the body to conserve body heat. Under these conditions, the muscle tissue will receive relatively little blood flow, and this will reduce the speed at which the drug molecules injected into muscle tissue(s) might be absorbed into the general circulation.

Yet another variable is the *molecular characteristics of the compound itself*. Some drug molecules are more easily absorbed than others. Also, if the compound is administered orally, a factor that affects absorption of that drug is whether or not it is ingested on an empty stomach (DeVane, 2004). Most compounds are better absorbed when ingested on an empty stomach, although some are better absorbed if ingested right after a meal (DeVane, 2004). Furthermore, one compound might best be absorbed if it does not have to compete with other drug molecules for admission into the body. All of these factors limit the absorption of the compound into the circulation. The next section addresses the second factor that influences the manner in which a

[5]See Glossary.

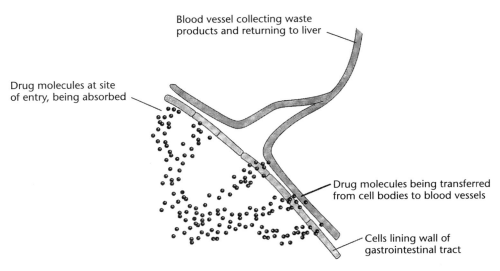

Blood vessel collecting waste
products and returning to liver

Drug molecules at site
of entry, being absorbed

Drug molecules being transferred
from cell bodies to blood vessels

Cells lining wall of
gastrointestinal tract

FIGURE 3-1 The Process of Drug Absorption

given compound in the body, its *distribution*. The process of drug absorption is shown in Figure 3-1.

Distribution

The process of *distribution* refers to how the chemical molecules are transported within the body. This includes both the process of drug transport and the pattern of drug accumulation within the body. As a general rule, very little is known about drug distribution patterns in overdose situations (A. J. Jenkins, 2007). Although the process of distribution would seem relatively straightforward, in reality it is affected by factors such as the individual's age, sex, muscle/adipose tissue ratio, state of hydration, genetic heritage, and health. Because of such factors, there are significant interindividual differences in the distribution pattern of the same compound when the same dose is ingested (DeVane, 2004; A. J. Jenkins & Cone, 1998).

Transport

Once the drug molecules reach the general circulation, they can then be transported to the *site of action*. This would give the impression that the circulatory system exists just to provide a distribution system for drug molecules. In reality a drug molecule is a foreign substance that takes advantage of the body's own natural chemical distribution system to move from the site of entry to the site of action. There are several different methods by which this might be accomplished, depending on the chemical characteristics of the specific compound(s) in question.

Some chemicals are able to mix freely with the blood plasma, and as such are often referred to as *water-soluble*

compounds. Such compounds, of which alcohol is a fine example, then are intermixed with the blood plasma and pumped through the body by the circulatory system. Because much of the human body is water, this provides a fine medium in which a compound might be suspended and pumped around the body. Again, depending on the chemical properties of the drug molecules, it might be possible for them to bind to one of the fat molecules that circulate through the body. Such compounds are called *lipid-soluble* compounds. The body uses lipids for a variety of purposes, including maintenance of cell walls, and any drug molecule that has attached itself to the lipid molecule will then be dragged along by that lipid as it circulates. Body tissues are constantly absorbing lipid molecules from the circulatory system as part of the cellular maintenance process. Compounds attached to the lipid molecules will then gain rapid access to body tissues because the human body organs ranges from 6 to 20% lipid molecules.

It is important to keep in mind some characteristics of molecular binding. First, as will be discussed in more detail later, drug molecular "binding" is usually not permanent. While the drug molecule is "bound" to the lipid molecule it is safe from elimination from the body, but it is also unable to achieve its desired effects. To become active again, it must detach from the lipid molecule. A compound that is 98% lipid soluble means that 98% of the drug molecules absorbed into the circulation are bound to blood lipids, leaving just 2% of the drug molecules to actually be biologically active. There are advantages and disadvantages to this characteristic of lipid binding. The process of lipid binding provides a drug reservoir within the body, as drug molecules detach from the lipid molecule over time. This allows new drug molecules to become active to replace those that have been biotransformed and eliminated from the body. But the lipid-bound drug molecules are unable to have an effect until they detach from the blood lipids.

In contrast to the rest of the body organs, which are 6–20% lipid molecules, 50% of the brain is actually lipid molecules (J. R. Cooper, Bloom, & Roth, 2002). So a compound that is lipid soluble will be concentrated in the brain tissues fairly rapidly. The ultra-short-acting and short-acting barbiturates[6] are excellent examples of this process. Some forms of the parent barbiturate molecule are able to form bonds with blood lipids very rapidly, thus allowing them to have a rapid effect. This is what makes them so useful as a surgical anesthetic agent. In contrast to the lipid binding compounds, some drug molecules might bind to one of the protein molecules that circulates throughout the body in the circulation.[7] Different drug molecules differ in their ability to "bind" with protein or lipid molecules. The antidepressant amitriptyline is 95% protein bound, for example, whereas nicotine is only 5% protein bound (A. J. Jenkins, 2007). The antianxiety agent diazepam is 99% protein bound, and so its effects are actually caused by the 1% of the drug molecules that are unbound.

As with the process of lipid binding, some drug molecules form stronger bonds with the protein molecule than do others, and this is one factor that determines how long a given drug will remain in the body. Also, as is true for lipid-bound molecules, protein-bound drug molecules are unable to have any biological effect. So, it is the percentage of the drug molecules that are unattached from a blood protein/lipid that causes that compound's biological activity. The "bound" fraction provides a reservoir of drug molecules that will replace those molecules that are removed from the body by its natural defense mechanisms. It is important to keep in mind that drug molecules are foreign substances, and their presence in the body is tolerated by the body only until its natural elimination/defense mechanisms are able to latch onto and remove it. Thus there is a constant process of drug molecule replacement during the period of active dosing, as some molecules are eliminated from the body, and others break their bonds with the protein/lipid molecules and replace them.

Another point to keep in mind is that protein molecules can "bind" only to a limited number of drug molecules. Thus if an individual were to take an unusually large dose of a drug, or if the molecules of more than one compound were competing for the binding sites on the protein molecule, then those binding sites might become saturated, leaving a larger than normal percentage of the drug molecules free in the blood to have a biological effect. This is one of the mechanisms through which drugs might have a *synergistic*[8] effect. This brings us to the process of Biotransformation.

Biotransformation

The biotransformation mechanisms in the human body evolved over millions of years to help the organism cope with potentially dangerous compounds found in food sources (Wynn, Oesterheld, Cozza, & Armstrong, 2009). These defensive detoxification systems are nonselective, eliminating poisons found in food with the same enthusiasm that they eliminate prescribed medications, because drug molecules are foreign to the body. In some cases, the body is able to simply filter the drug from the blood. Penicillin is an excellent example of such a compound. The penicillin molecules are filtered from the blood by the kidneys almost immediately without being altered. There are other compounds that are removed from the body unchanged. However, in the majority of cases the chemical structure of the drug(s) must be modified before they can be eliminated from the body.

This is accomplished through a process that was once referred to as *detoxification* or *drug metabolism*. However, because of the confusion over whether physicians were discussing the metabolic processes in the body or the process of breaking down a foreign chemical, the term *biotransformation* has gradually been gaining favor as the proper term when a pharmaceutical agent is being discussed, whereas the older term *detoxification* is applied to the drugs of abuse. Biotransformation is usually carried out in the liver, although on occasion other tissue(s) might also be

---

[6]Discussed in Chapter 9.

[7]The most common of which is *albumin*. Sometimes, compounds are referred to as albumin bound, rather than protein bound. Technically, drug molecules that are more acidic tend to bind to albumin, whereas those that are more basic tend to bind to the alpha1-acid glycoprotein molecules in the blood.

[8]See Glossary.

involved. The *microsomal endoplasmic reticulum* of the liver produces a number of enzymes[9] that transform toxic molecules into a form that might be eliminated from the body. This is accomplished through one or more of the following mechanisms: oxidation, reduction, hydrolysis, and conjugation (Ciraulo, Shader, Greenblatt, & Creelman, 2006; Wynn et al. 2009). There are essentially two forms of biotransformation: (a) the *zero-order biotransformation* process and (b) the *first-order Biotransformation* process. In the zero-order biotransformation process, the biotransformation mechanism(s) quickly become saturated, and only a set amount of a compound can thus be biotransformed each hour (Bennett & Brown, 2003). Alcohol is an example of a compound that is biotransformed through a zero-order biotransformation process.[10] In the zero-order biotransformation process, the speed at which biotransformation progresses is relatively independent of the concentration of the drug molecules in the user's body.

In the first-order biotransformation process, a set percentage of the compound(s) in question is biotransformed each hour. Certain antibiotics are eliminated from the body in this manner, with a certain percentage being biotransformed each hour. The specifics of each subform of the process of biotransformation are quite complex and are best reserved for those readers who wish to pick up a pharmacology textbook to review the biochemistry involved in each phase of this process. It is enough for the reader to remember that there are four different subforms and two different pathways of biotransformation.

In both forms of biotransformation, the drug molecules are chemically altered only as rapidly as the enzymes involved in each step can do so. This takes place one atom at a time, at the rate at which the enzymes necessary for the biotransformation of that molecule can carry out their effect. In some cases, depending on the chemical characteristics of the drug(s) ingested, this process might involve several steps. For example, compounds that are highly lipid soluble require extensive biotransformation before they become less lipid soluble and are more easily eliminated from the body (A. J. Jenkins, 2007).

Technically, the compound that emerges at each step of the biotransformation process is referred to as a *metabolite* of the original compound. The original compound is referred to as the *parent compound*. Metabolites may have their own psychoactive effect on the user, a factor that must be considered by physicians when prescribing a pharmaceutical for a patent. If the parent compound had no or minimal biological effect, and its major impact is achieved by the metabolites of that compound, then the parent compound is referred to as a *prodrug*. Most compounds in use today are biologically active, and there are few that are used as prodrugs, but this is not always the case.

To add an element of confusion, normal variations in the individual's biological heritage, drug interactions, or various diseases can alter the speed at which some individuals can biotransform a compound. Sometimes the enzymes necessary for the biotransformation of one compound will increase the speed of the biotransformation of a second compound, reducing its effectiveness, for example. Furthermore, as a result of genetic variations some individuals are able to biotransform a given compound more rapidly than are others, making them *rapid metabolizers* of that compound. Also, by chance other people have a body that makes them slower at breaking down a given compound than is normal, making them a *slow metabolizer* of that compound. To date, there is no way to identify these individuals other than clinical experience obtained by giving the patient a drug and observing their reaction. Disease states, such as alcohol-induced liver damage,[11] can also alter the liver's ability to biotransform many compounds, a situation that the attending physician must also consider when prescribing a pharmaceutical to treat an ill patient.

The First-Pass Metabolism Effect

The human digestive tract is designed not to let any chemical that is absorbed pass directly into the circulation, but to filter it first through the liver. This is called the first-pass metabolism effect (DeVane, 2004). By taking chemicals absorbed from the GI tract and passing them through the liver, any toxin in that food or drug might be identified and the biotransformation process started, hopefully before that compound can do any damage to the body itself. One consequence of the first-pass metabolism process is that the effectiveness of many orally administered compounds is limited. For example, much of an orally administered

---

[9]The most common of which is the P-450 metabolic process, or the microsomal P-450 pathway.

[10]Although, technically, alcohol's biotransformation at extremely high doses does not follow the zero-order biotransformation cycle exactly. But alcohol's deviation(s) from the zero-order biotransformation cycle is best reserved for toxicology texts.

[11]Discussed in Chapter 8.

dose of morphine is biotransformed by the first-pass metabolism effect before it reaches the site of action, limiting its effectiveness as an analgesic unless injected into the body.

Collectively, the first-pass metabolism process, and the various subforms of biotransformation, work to prepare foreign chemicals for the last stage of pharmacokinetics,[12] that of *elimination*.

Elimination

So closely intertwined are the processes of biotransformation and elimination that some pharmacologists consider them to be a single topic. The process of biotransformation changes the chemical structure of a compound so that the metabolites are more water soluble, so they can then be removed from the circulation by the organs involved in filtering the blood. This usually is carried out by the kidneys, although the lungs, sweat glands, and biliary tract might also be involved in the process of drug elimination (B. A. Wilson, Shannon, Shields, & Stang, 2007). For example, a small percentage of alcohol ingested will be eliminated through the sweat and breath when the person exhales, giving the intoxicated person a characteristic smell.

The process of drug elimination does not happen instantly. Rather, depending on the speed at which the process of biotransformation is carried out, it might take a period of time before the drug molecule(s) are transformed into a water-soluble metabolite that can be eliminated from the body. This bring us to another necessary concept to consider: the drug *half-life*.

The Drug Half-Life

The concept of a drug half-life provides a useful yardstick by which to make a *rough* estimate of a compound's effectiveness, duration of effect, and the length of time that it will remain in the body. But there are several different forms of drug half-life, depending on different aspects of the compound's actions in the body. We will discuss some of the more important of these half-life forms in this section.

The *distribution half-life* is the time that it takes a compound to work its way into the general circulation, once it is administered (Reiman, 1997). This information is important to physicians in overdose situations, where it is necessary to anticipate the long-term effects of compounds administered but that might not have

reached the general circulation. It is also of importance in planning pharmacological interventions: If a patient is in acute pain, you would want to administer a compound that was able to reach the circulation as rapidly as possible, rather than a compound that is slowly absorbed. Patients in chronic pain might benefit more from a compound that is more slowly absorbed, providing more steady analgesia for their chronic discomfort.

Therapeutic half-life is a rough measure of the compound's duration of effect. The therapeutic half-life is the time necessary for the body to inactivate 50% of a compound. This may be complicated by compounds where the metabolites also have a biological action on the body. The therapeutic half-life usually is a reference to a single dose of a compound, and regular dosing of that compound can alter the therapeutic half-life by prolonging it.

Finally, there is the *elimination half-life* of a compound. This is the time that the body requires to eliminate 50% of a compound. Again, the elimination half-life is usually a reference to the time that it takes for 50% of a single dose of a compound to be eliminated from the body. In medical practice it is usually assumed that after the fifth dose, the individual will have achieved a *steady state* of a compound in her blood, although this is only a rough estimate and there are multiple factors that affect when a steady state is achieved. Furthermore, the concept of an elimination half-life is based on the assumption that the user has normal liver and kidney function. Patients with impaired liver or kidney function might require smaller than normal doses to achieve the same desired effect as a normal person, because the body will require more time to eliminate the compound.

The various half-lives of a compound are not the same. A compound might have a therapeutic half-life of minutes, for example, but an elimination half-life of hours. Several of the ultra-short-acting barbiturates[13] are excellent examples of how a compound might have a short duration of effect, but a prolonged elimination period. Furthermore, all half-life estimates are based on the assumption that the patient has used only one compound. If the patient is using multiple compounds, it becomes more difficult to estimate the drug half-lives, because multiple drugs would then compete for the processes of absorption, distribution, biotransformation, and elimination. For example, proteins found in the blood offer only a limited number of molecular binding locations, and if the patient is receiving multiple medications, the binding sites on the

---

[12]See Glossary.

[13]Discussed in Chapter 9.

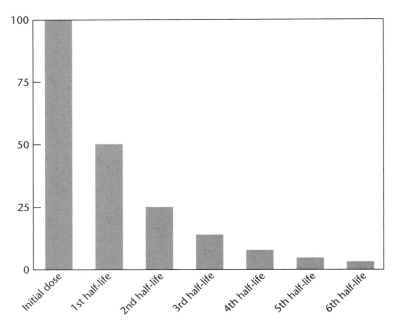

FIGURE 3-2 Drug Elimination in Half-Life Stages

protein molecules might become saturated. This would force higher-than-normal levels of the drug to remain unbound and thus biologically active. This is one reason why drug overdoses involving different agents might be lethal at doses that, independently, might not cause the user's death.

One popular misconception is that it takes only two elimination half-life periods to remove a compound from the body. In reality, fully 25% of the initial dose remains after the end of the second half-life period, and 12% is still in the body after three half-life periods. As a general rule, pharmacologists estimate that it will take five half-life periods before all of a single dose of a chemical is eliminated from the user's body, as illustrated in Figure 3-2.

Generally, compounds with longer half-life periods tend to remain biologically active for longer periods of time, whereas the reverse also is generally true. This is where the process of protein or lipid binding comes into play: Compounds with longer half-lives are more likely to become protein bound, with only a small percentage of the drug molecules actually being biologically active at any time. Those drug molecules that are still protein bound provide a reservoir of that drug, allowing new molecules to gradually be released back into the general circulation as the chemical bonds between the drug and the protein molecule become weaker and weaker until

that molecule becomes "unbound" and it enters the circulation where it becomes biologically active.

Drug Interactions

In cases where a patient is receiving multiple medications, there is a very real danger of these compounds interacting in ways not anticipated by the user. Wynn et al. (2009) estimated that 5% of all hospitalizations in the United States were the result of adverse drug–drug interactions, and numerous less severe interactions result in consequences for the patient who does not require hospitalization. Serious drug–drug interactions result in an estimated 7000 deaths in this country alone. This is only an estimate, however, and many fatal drug–drug interactions probably are not reported, or the deaths are attributed to other conditions, according to the authors.

The Effective Dose

The concept of the *effective dose* (ED) is based on dose-response calculations in which scientists have calculated the approximate dose at which a given percentage of the population will respond to a given dose of a compound. For example, the dose at which 10% of the general population is expected to have the desired response would be identified as the ED_{10}, whereas the dose at which 50% of the general population is expected to have the desired response would be identified as the ED_{50}. Obviously, if you were a biochemist developing a new compound, you would want to find a dosage where as large a percentage of the general population as possible would achieve the desired response. However, as you increase the dose, you are more and more likely to (a) encounter the *ceiling dose effect,* and (b) develop toxic reactions.

The *ceiling dose effect* is just that: a dose above which additional drug molecules will not have any additional effect. Acetaminophen and ibuprofen, for example, are compounds with ceiling doses, and if the patient were to ingest a dose larger than this he would only be more likely to experience a toxic reaction.

The Lethal Dose and Therapeutic Index

This brings us to another useful concept: the *lethal dose.* Drugs are, by definition, foreign to the body, and although they might disrupt a body function(s) in a specific manner, they also present the risk of altering that body function so much that the user dies. For example, a hypothetical compound that suppressed respiration at a certain dose might be a useful pharmaceutical for certain forms of surgery. However, too large a dose would run the risk of the individual's respiration being suppressed permanently, hardly a desired response!

Drawing on the calculations as to how much radiation a person might be exposed to without becoming terminally ill, scientists have developed dose-response curves that estimate what percentage of the population would die as a result of being exposed to a certain dose of a chemical or toxin. This figure is then expressed in terms of the *lethal dose* (LD) ratio. A dose of a drug that would cause 1% of the population to die would be abbreviated as the LD01 and the dose that in theory would kill 25% of the population would be abbreviated as the LD25, etc. For example, as will be discussed in the next chapter, 1% of patients with a blood alcohol concentration of 0.350 mg/mL would be expected to die without medical help. Thus for alcohol, the LD01 would be 0.350 mg/mL of blood.

By comparing the effective dose and lethal dose ratios, it is possible to obtain a raw estimate of the *therapeutic window* or the *therapeutic index* of a compound. If you had a hypothetical chemotherapy compound used to treat cancer that had an ED_{99} of 100 mg and an LD_{001} (meaning only one death per thousand patients receiving this dose), that compound would be said to have a wide therapeutic window. In contrast,

another hypothetical compound that caused 10% of the patients receiving it to die at a dose of 100 mg without medical intervention would be said to have a smaller therapeutic window. As should be obvious by now, you would want to use compounds with as large a therapeutic window as possible to reduce the risk to the user's life. Unfortunately, as will be discussed in the next few chapters, many of the drugs of abuse have very narrow "therapeutic" windows, with the result being that it is very easy to overdose on these compounds.

Therapeutic Threshold and Peak Effects

As the drug absorption process progresses following a single dose of a compound, the amount of a compound in the user's circulation will increase until it reaches the minimal level at which that compound might be effective. This is the *therapeutic threshold* for that compound. As the blood levels rise over time, the effects will continue to become stronger and stronger until the drug reaches its *peak effect dose.* Then, as the process of biotransformation proceeds, the effects of that compound will diminish until the blood levels of that compound fall below the therapeutic threshold. Scientists have learned to calculate dose-response curves for many compounds in order to estimate the potential for that compound to have an effect on the user after a single dose. For example, the period of peak effects varies from one compound to another. The peak effects of one of the ultrashort-acting barbiturates, for instance, might be achieved in a matter of seconds after the compound is injected into a vein, whereas a long-term barbiturate might take hours to achieve its peak effects. Further variables that affect absorption, distribution, biotransformation, and elimination will also impact on when a given compound reaches its peak effects.

The Site of Action

Essentially, the site of action is where the compound(s) introduced into the body carry out their main effects. For most of the psychoactive pharmaceuticals, and the various drugs of abuse, various neurons in the central nervous system (CNS)[14] will be the site of action. The

---

[14]Although the CNS is by itself worthy of a lifetime of study, for the purposes of this text the beauty and complexities of the CNS must be compressed into a few short paragraphs. Those who wish to learn more about the CNS are advised to seek a good neuroanatomy, neuropsychology, or neurology textbook.

CNS is, without question, the most complex organ system found in the human body. At its most fundamental level, the CNS is comprised of an estimated 100 billion neurons, each of which receives input from tens, hundreds, or perhaps thousands of other neurons. This is accomplished through the use of molecular neurotransmitters that are released by one neuron[15] with the goal of activating a receptor site on the next neuron in that neural chain.[16] It has been estimated that one mature human brain has more synaptic junctions than there are individual grains of sand on all of the beaches of the planet Earth (Stahl, 2008).

Although most of the CNS is squeezed into the confines of the skull, the individual neurons usually do not actually touch. Rather, they are separated by a microscopic space called the *synapse*. To communicate across the synaptic void, or synaptic gap, one neuron will release a cloud of chemical molecules that function as *neurotransmitters*. To date more than 150 compounds have been identified that function as a neurotransmitter within the brain, but the greater percentage of these neurotransmitters will remain outside of the scope of this text.[17]

The Process of Neurotransmission[18]

When a sufficient number of receptor sites in a given neuron are occupied by the right chemical messenger, a profound change is triggered in the postsynaptic neuron. There are two classes of neural responses to the reception of a neurotransmitter: the *fast* or *inotropic* responses. These usually involve the downstream neuron opening or closing a gated ion channel, which will alter the speed with which the downstream neuron can "fire." Another inotropic response might be for the downstream neuron to release a cloud of neurotransmitter molecules at select synaptic junctions in turn, passing the electrochemical message on to the next neuron in the chain. Longer-term responses, known as *metabotropic responses,* involve long-term alterations in the downstream neuron as it constantly adapts to the ever-changing input from upstream neurons. This includes the processes of: making or destroying synaptic junctions, reinforcing neural networks, urging axions to sprout, and the synthesis of various proteins, enzymes, and neurotransmitter receptors that regulate the function of the target neuron (Stahl, 2008).

To prevent premature or unnecessary neural activity, there is a "fail-safe" system built into the process of neurotransmission. A large percentage of the receptor sites must be occupied by neurotransmitter molecules at the same instant before the electrochemical potential of the downstream neuron is altered. For the sake of illustration, let us say that 70% of the receptor sites must be occupied by neurotransmitter molecules at the same instant before neurotransmission occurs.[19] If a lower number of receptor sites are occupied, say by stray neurotransmitter molecules that have "leaked" into the synaptic junction from other sites, then the receptor site is not activated.

Cotransmission

When neurotransmitters were first discovered, scientists believed that each neuron utilized just one neurotransmitter type. But in the last years of the 20th century, scientists began to uncover evidence that neurons both transmit and receive *secondary* neurotransmitter molecules, which often have far different characteristics from those of the primary neurotransmitter. The process of releasing both types of neurotransmitter is called *cotransmission,* and this helps to explain why many drugs that affect the CNS have such wide-reaching, secondary or side effects. For example, some neurons that utilize serotonin as the primary neurotransmitter might also release small amounts of norepinephrine during the process of neurotransmission.

The Receptor Site

This is usually a large protein molecule(s) in the cell wall (Bennett & Brown, 2003; Olson, 2006). To understand how a receptor site works, imagine the analogy of slipping a key into a lock. The structure of the neurotransmitter molecule fits into the receptor site much as a key does into a lock, although on a molecular scale. But by coincidence, some natural and artificial chemicals closely mimic the shape of the molecular "key," or neurotransmitter molecule, that activates the "lock"

---

[15]Called the "upstream" neuron.

[16]Called the "downstream" or "postsynaptic" neuron.

[17]I bet you thought that I was going to name them all, didn't you?

[18]Admittedly, this is a very simplified summary of the neurotransmission cascade, but it should be sufficient for the purposes of this text. There are a number of very good books on neuroanatomy that provide a detailed description of this process, if you should wish to pursue this area for further study.

---

[19]The number of receptor sites that must be occupied before the neurotransmission cascade is initiated is called the *affinity* of the compound to the receptor sites.

(receptor site). The closer that the drug molecule matches the natural neurotransmitter molecule, the stronger that compound's effects will be on the neuron.[20] The drugs of abuse fall into one of two groups: (a) those that cause the target neuron(s) to increase the rate at which they fire, or (b) those that cause the target neuron(s) to decrease the rate at which they fire. By achieving either effect, the drug(s) of abuse alter the normal function of the CNS.

Neurotransmitter Reuptake/Destruction

Once a neurotransmitter has been released, there is a danger that it will "leak" from the synaptic junction, float into other synaptic junctions, and activate other receptor sites than the one it was intended to reach. To prevent this, many neurons utilize what are known as molecular *reuptake pumps* that absorb as many of the just-released neurotransmitter molecules as possible for reuse. In the case of those neurons that utilize serotonin mentioned earlier, the norepinephrine molecules that are also released seem to activate the reuptake pumps on both the upstream and downstream neurons, allowing for those molecules to be recycled to the greatest degree possible. But many neurotransmitters are also broken down after release by one of a number of specific enzymes designed for this purpose. Thus if the neurotransmitter should escape the reuptake process, the enzymes will hopefully destroy them before they cause false signals in the neural net.

Up-Regulation/Down-Regulation

The individual neurons of the CNS are not passive participants in the process of information transfer, but are constantly rewiring themselves to allow for greater/reduced sensitivity to the neurotransmitters being thrown at them. If a receptor site is constantly exposed to high levels of a given neurotransmitter, it might decrease the number of receptor sites available to those molecules (*down-regulate*) (Bennett & Brown, 2003). This is accomplished by the neuron absorbing, or inactivating, some of the receptor sites, making that neuron less sensitive to that neurotransmitter. The analogy of somebody turning down the sound on a car radio would not be entirely out of place here.

But if the neuron is not being stimulated enough by the neurotransmitter molecules at the synapse, then that neuron might build new receptor sites, to give the limited number of neurotransmitter molecules the largest possible number of "targets" to hit (bind at). This is the process known as *up-regulation* (Bennett & Brown, 2003). The analogy of somebody using a directional microphone as opposed to a regular microphone might be useful in explaining this concept.

Tolerance/Cross-Tolerance

Tolerance to a compound is defined as "a shortened duration and decreased intensity of drug effects after repeated administration" (Ghoneim, 2004b, p. 1279). Technically, this process is also known as *neuroadaptation*, especially when the compound has been prescribed by a physician, but many people still use the older term *tolerance* for both prescribed and illicit use of a compound.[21]

Because the molecules of the drugs of abuse alter the normal function of the brain, it attempts to chemically alter the influence of that compound at a neural level (Breggin, 2008; Cruz, Bajo, Schweitzer, & Roberto, 2008). One mechanism of neuroadaptation is the alteration of the number of receptor sites in the neural wall through either up-regulation[22] or down-regulation[23] of the number of receptor sites. This process helps to explain both the phenomena of tolerance/neuroadaptation to a compound, as well as that of "cross-tolerance" to related compounds. As the neurons adapt to the continued use of the compound(s) in question, the subjective experience will be one of a reduced reaction to the effects of a given dose of a compound. To overcome neuroadaptation (or tolerance), the user must often increase the dosage, possibly to dangerous levels.

However, multiple compounds might effect the body through similar mechanisms, and thus the adaptive changes made for one chemical might also help the brain adjust to the effects of other, similar chemicals. This is referred to as cross-tolerance. Alcohol provides a good example: The person who drinks frequently might find that benzodiaze pines do not provide the same degree of sedation as for the nondrinker, because they are cross-tolerant to the effects of the latter compounds.

Another process that is often seen with frequent, heavy use of a compound is the process of *metabolic tolerance*. Through this process, the body becomes

---

[20]Technically, this is called the *sensitivity* of the compound for the receptor site.

[21]In this text the term *tolerance* will be used when illicit drugs are being discussed, and the term *neuroadaptation* will be used when discussing prescription substances.

[22]See Glossary.

[23]See Glossary.

more proficient in the process of biotransformation, at least for a limited period. This is commonly seen in the early stages of alcohol dependence, for example, where drinkers will report that they must use more alcohol to achieve the same level of intoxication once achieved with a lower level of alcohol intake (T. Nelson, 2000). Unfortunately, the liver can maintain this extra effort at alcohol biotransformation for only a limited period before it starts to break down, resulting in the phenomenon of lower tolerance to alcohol often found later in the drinker's life.

Behavioral tolerance reflects the behavioral outcome of the brain's efforts to maintain normal function in spite of the presence of foreign molecules. Individuals' behavior appears almost normal in spite of the presence of a compound in their body. Again, using alcohol as an example, even law enforcement or health care professionals are shocked to discover that the individual who appeared to be mildly intoxicated was in reality significantly over the legal blood alcohol level.

Drug Agonists/Antagonists

Essentially, a drug *agonist* is a compound that activates a receptor site by being able to mimic the actions of a natural neurotransmitter or enhancing its the actions (B. A. Wilson et al. 2007). The more closely a chemical molecule resembles that of natural chemical the more normally will that receptor site be activated.[24] For the drugs of abuse, the receptor sites are the individual neurons of the brain, and the more closely the molecule resembles that of a naturally occurring neurotransmitter, the stronger the drug's effect will be on the neuron. The analogy of a "skeleton" key for a lock would not be out of place here: The narcotic analgesic family of compounds use binding sites normally utilized by the brain for pain perception. However, the narcotics are not perfect matches for the receptor site.

Some compounds are able to fit into the receptor site *without activating it*. Such compounds are called *antagonists* (or, antagonists). The drug Narcan (used to treat narcotic overdoses) functions as an opioid antagonist, blocking the opioid receptor sites without activating them and thus preventing the narcotic molecules from reaching the receptor sites in the brain. The analogy of a key that was broken off just beyond the handle might not be out of place here. There are also compounds that are *partial agonists*. This means that the drug molecules are able to activate the receptor site very weakly if at all, while preventing other drug

molecules the opportunity to bind at that receptor site. Again, using the lock-and-key analogy, imagine the night watchman with a ring full of keys, who is forced to go through key after key to find the right one for a specific lock. Some of the keys might match some of the tumblers in the lock, but only one will match the specific combination necessary to open that lock.

Potency

Essentially, a neuropharmaceutical's potency is the ratio between the size of a dose and the behavioral response (Ghoneim, 2004b). Imagine that you had two hypothetical compounds with the same side-effect profiles, which impacted at the same receptor site and had the same mechanism of action to accomplish the same effect. One compound requires that you take an oral dose of 1000 mg to achieve a certain effect, whereas the second compound will achieve the same goal with an oral dose of just 100 mg. The latter compound would be said to be more *potent* than the former and is often the preferred compound. For example, as will be discussed in the chapter on narcotic analgesics, a standard conversion formula is that it takes 10 mg of morphine to achieve the same degree of analgesia that 4 mg of heroin can induce. Thus heroin is said to be more potent than morphine, although the pharmacology of both compounds will be discussed in Chapter 14.

The Blood–Brain Barrier

The human brain is an energy-intensive organ, and 20% of the blood pumped with each heartbeat is sent to the brain to supply it with needed nutrients and oxygen. But the capillaries involved in cerebral blood flow differ from those found elsewhere in the body in that the endothelial cells are tightly joined together around the capillaries. This forms part of the *blood–brain barrier* (or BBB), which is composed of the tightly knit endothelial cells and a thin layer of tissue contributed by the astrocytes[25] of the brain, which separate the brain from direct contact with the circulatory system.

Although it is referred to as a "barrier," the BBB is better thought of as a selective screen. Specialized cellular transport mechanisms, each one adapted to allow one type of water-soluble molecule such as glucose, iron, and certain vitamins, to pass through the BBB into the neurons beyond. Lipids are also able to pass through the endothelial cells by first binding with, and

---

[24]Which is referred to as the *ligand* in professional literature.

[25]See Glossary.

slowly passing through the cell walls of the endothelial cells to reach the brain. In the process, compounds that are lipid soluble are also admitted into the brain in spite of the BBB.

But all of this is a reflection of normal conditions. If the BBB were to be damaged as a result of trauma or infection, then it would lose its ability to filter out many unwanted compounds, and the individual might experience an atypical response to some compounds. The BBB is thus an important element of the individual's health.

Chapter Summary

Although the field of pharmacology, and the subspecialty of neuropharmacology, are each worthy of a lifetime of study by themselves, it is not possible to do justice to either topic in this text. However, some of the basic concepts necessary to better understand how the drugs of abuse might exert their effects, including how such compounds are administered, absorbed, distributed, and biotransformed/eliminated from the body, were discussed. Also discussed were concepts such as the drug agonist, the antiagonist (or antagonist), and the mixed agonist/antagonist were introduced. A brief overview of the blood–brain barrier, and its function, was provided, and the concepts of tolerance and cross-tolerance to a compound(s) were reviewed. These basic concepts should provide a foundation on which the student might begin to build an understanding of the drugs of abuse, and the mechanism(s) by which they work.

CHAPTER 4

An Introduction to Alcohol: Man's Oldest Recreational Chemical

Introduction

Ethyl alcohol[1] does occur in the natural world, especially in various forms of fruit that ripen in the wild. There is thus an emerging body of scientific data, and supposition supported by biological data and cross-species observations suggesting that alcohol derived from fermenting fruits plays an important role in the lives of many insect and animal species, including our hominid ancestors. Humans have used alcohol at least since the beginning of civilization, and it would be unreasonable to assume that "civilized"[2] man suddenly discovered alcohol's intoxicating effects. As should be apparent from this information, alcohol plays an intriguing role in the animal kingdom, including that of the hominid line, from which homo sapiens evolved, that is, prehistoric humans, and it continues to play an important role in society today. Indeed, the use of alcohol might predate civilization by 1–2 million years, if not more. It is thus important for the reader to have a working understanding of alcohol, how it is obtained, and the effects of social alcohol use.

Why Do People Consume Alcohol?

Theoretically, alcohol is but one of a rather extensive range of compounds ingested by humans for their psychoactive effects (McGovern, 2009). Prior to the emergence of modern chemistry, which allowed for the development of a range of artificial psychoactive chemicals, various species of mushroom or naturally occurring toxins were also used for their psychoactive effects. However, alcohol is the easiest to obtain and is safer, and so it assumed a role of central importance in the emergence of civilization. Beverages containing alcohol were less likely to contain dangerous bacteria in an era when bacterial contamination was the rule rather than the exception (S. Johnson, 2006). The beverage also supplied at least some of the fluids necessary for the individual's survival each day, and as noted earlier was a valuable source of energy derived from the glucose that resulted from alcohol biotransformation (McGovern, 2009). These facts underscore anthropological evidence suggesting that early civilization emerged

---

[1]The designation *ethyl alcohol* is important to chemists, as there are at least 45 other compounds that might be classified as a form of alcohol. Many of these are very toxic, if not potentially lethal, to humans. *Ethyl alcohol* is the one most commonly consumed by humans, and these other forms of alcohol will not be discussed further in this chapter.

[2]An arguable point.

in response to the perceived need for a stable home base from which to brew alcoholic beverages. Scientists exploring the ruins of various cities in what was once the ancient Sumerian empire have found numerous clay tablets devoted to the process of brewing beer, especially a form of beer made from fermented honey known as mead (Cahill, 1998).

Ethyl alcohol plays a number of roles in modern society. Although the consumer was unlikely to have been aware of the fact, beer, wine, and liquors have mild antibacterial properties that made them safer to ingest than the local water (S. Johnson, 2006). For example, there was a cholera epidemic that broke out in London in the year 1854 that modern science knows was caused by well water contaminated with fecal matter (S. Johnson, 2006). Although alcohol still presented the user with risks inherent in the use of alcohol-containing beverages, from a reproductive perspective it is still more advantageous for individuals to die of cirrhosis of the liver sometime in their 40s than of a water-borne disease such as cholera as a child or adolescent (S. Johnson, 2006).

Alcohol induces a sense of well-being or in some cases euphoria in the drinker, feelings that added to the allure of alcohol-containing beverages throughout history. Alcohol also facilitates social interactions. It is used in certain religious rituals, and on very rare occasions by physicians for medicinal purposes. Individuals may consume alcohol for a variety of reasons: In limited quantities it has some health benefits, and some people use it as a hypnotic.[3] Folk medicine holds that a teaspoon of brandy helps to break up mucus in the lungs, allowing the patient to breathe more easily. Although this theory is attractive, it is for its ability to induce a sense of well-being and euphoria that most people consume alcohol, even if it is done under the pretense of being "my cough medicine."

Daily consumption of one glass of wine a day appeared to lower the individual's risk of developing cancer of the esophagus by approximately 56% (Kubo et al., 2009). However, as will be discussed in the next chapter, heavy alcohol use is a risk factor for the development of cancer of the esophagus, and this effect was found only for wine drinkers (Kubo et al., 2009).

A Brief History of Alcohol

There is strong evidence that some insects and animals are attuned to the smell of fruit and are drawn to it, a trait that early naturalists capitalized on to capture specimens (McGovern, 2009). Since the seed pods, which are the fruit that we consume, are also usually quite visually striking, animal species that use visual cues to obtain food will also be drawn to these fruit pods. Some plants capitalize on the insects' attraction to them as a means of pollination, whereas animals that ingest the seed pods play a role in the distribution of that species by spreading seeds across their respective territories (thoughtfully complete with a little packet of fertilizer).

However, from time to time the outer skin of the fruit will crack or break open, allowing microorganisms[4] entry to the lush interior of the fruit pod. Some will begin the process of fermentation. Ethyl alcohol is not the goal of fermentation but is only a by-product of this process. In spite of its status as waste from the process of fermentation, it is a concentrated source of energy and as such insects and animals are drawn to it. The intoxicating effects of alcohol apparently are an additional incentive for many animal species to seek out and consume it, an observation that is supported by evidence that bird species seem to consume alcohol simply for its intoxicating effects. Some birds have even been known to die from an acute alcohol overdose (McGovern, 2009). Researchers have observed tree shrews, distant biological cousins of human beings, selectively sipping nectar from certain palm flower clusters in which the process of fermentation takes place. The liquid found in these palm flower clusters after fermentation has an alcohol content of 3.8%, approximately the same as modern beer. Based on this evidence, it is not unreasonable to assume that ancient hominids shared this preference for alcohol when it could be obtained.[5] Thus there is strong evidence suggesting that insects and many animal species might have a "taste" for alcohol, possibly acquired through the evolutionary process ("A Tree Shrew's Favorite Tipple," 2008; McGovern, 2009).

Historical evidence suggests that humans have long been aware of ethyl alcohol's intoxicating effects (McGovern, 2009). *Mead*, a form of beer made from fermented honey, appears to have been in widespread

---

[3]See Glossary.

[4]Discussed in the section How Alcohol Is Produced, later in this chapter.

[5]This is only a theory as there is little evidence of intoxicated hominids in the geological strata in which these fossils are found. A *Homo habilis* skeleton from an intoxicated member of that species, when found by anthropologists, would look the same as any member of the *H. habilis* genera, although one might argue that their intoxication might have contributed to their opportunity to become fossilized if it made them ignore predators in the area.

use during the latter part of the Paleolithic era,[6] whereas beer made from other ingredients might date back to 9000 BCE.[7] (Gallagher, 2005). These early forms of beer were quite thick and nutritious, and by comparison modern forms of beer are rather thin and almost anemic, contributing little to the drinker's dietary needs. The widespread use of beer and wine as social beverages and as dietary agents is reflected in the fact that both are mentioned in Homer's epic stories, *The Iliad* and *The Odyssey*.

The earliest written record of wine making is found in an Egyptian tomb that dates back to 3000 BCE., although there is evidence that the Sumerians might have used wine made from fermented grapes around 5400 BCE. ("A Very Venerable Vintage," 1996). By the time of the Green and Roman empires, wine was a central part of civilized life (Walton, 2002). This is reflected in the fact that ancient Greek prayers for warriors suggested that they would enjoy a state of continuous intoxication in the afterlife, whereas in pre-Christian Rome intoxication was seen as a religious experience[8] (McGovern, 2009; Walton, 2002). The Holy Bible referred to alcohol as nothing less than a gift from God, and during the Dark Ages monks in various abbeys experimented with methods of wine production and discovered how to produce champagne (J. T. Woods, 2005).

Beer and wine consumption continued through the Renaissance in Europe, the Age of Exploration, and into the early Colonial period when the first colonies in the New World were established. However, alcohol use was not always viewed as a positive aspect of life, as reflected by the fact that the Puritan ethic that emerged in England in the 14th and 15th centuries placed restrictions on the use of alcoholic beverages. By the start of the 19th century, public intoxication in European culture was viewed not as a sign of religious ecstasy but as a public disgrace. This debate has continued into the early 20th century, where the use of alcohol has been both defended and attacked. In the post–World War I era, the United States embarked on a social experiment known as Prohibition[9] in which alcohol use was prohibited. It was repealed after approximately 13 years, and was openly flaunted even when the law was still in effect.

When scientists developed the means to explore the chemical properties of ethyl alcohol, they discovered that it was an extraordinary source of energy for the drinker. The body is able to obtain as much energy from alcohol as it can from fat, and far more energy than from carbohydrates and proteins (Lieber, 1998). The alcohol also curbed, if not eliminated, bacterial growth in the fluid, allowing it to be consumed safely. Although ancient cultures probably did not understand these facts, they obviously did understand that alcoholic beverages were an essential part of the diet. This belief has continued until the present era.[10]

Alcohol in the Modern World

In the time since the process of distillation was developed, various fermented beverages made with a wide variety of flavors and in different concentrations of alcohol have evolved.[11] Alcohol remains very popular in spite of the perception in some quarters that it holds great potential for harm, and it has been estimated that the vast majority of adults in the United States will consume alcohol at least once in their lives. Most certainly it is a common intoxicant, and at any given moment 0.7% of the population of the world is intoxicated (Raw Data, 2009b).

Since the beginning of the 21st century, beer sold in the United States usually has had an alcohol content of 3.5 and 5%, although some specialty beers have an alcohol content of less than 3% or greater than 9% (Devour, 1999). Wine made in the United States is usually made by fermenting grapes or other fruits. In other countries, other substances than grapes are used for the process of fermentation, such as the famous "rice wine" of Japan known as *sake*. In the United States, wine usually has an alcohol content of between 8 and 17%, although light wines might have as little as 7% alcohol and wine "coolers" only 5–7% by weight (Devour, 1999). Sometimes, a distilled spirit is added back to wine, to form a wine with a higher content than is normally possible. These are the "fortified" wines, which may have an alcohol content as high as 20–24%

---

[6]During what is commonly called the late "stone age."

[7]Which stands for "before the Common Era."

[8]For example, a Roman proverb suggested that "bathing, wine, and Venus exhaust the body; that is what life is about."

[9]Prohibition started in 1920 and ended in 1933.

[10]When the Puritans set sail for the New World, for example, they stocked their ship with 14 tons of water, 10,000 gallons of wine, and 42 tons of beer (McPherson, Yudko, Murray-Bridges, Rodriguez, & Lindo-Moulds, 2009). Historians have suggested that the main reason why they elected to settle in Plymouth was because they had exhausted their supply of beer on the voyage across the Atlantic and needed to grow crops with which to produce more beer (McAnalley, 1996).

[11]A standard "yardstick" by which alcoholic beverages are measured is that the beverage must contain 12 grams of ethanol. This is the amount of alcohol found in one standard 12-ounce can of beer, 1.5 ounces of an 80-proof liquor, or 4 ounces of regular wine.

(Devour, 1999). "Hard" liquors usually contain 30–50% alcohol content, although in some cases the alcohol content might be as high as 80% or more (Devour, 1999). Although high levels of alcohol ingestion can result in a sense of intoxication, scientists are attempting to identify ways in which this might be avoided, or ways in which the individual might recover from this intoxication more rapidly (Motluk, 2006).

How Alcohol Is Produced

Alcohol is produced when microscopic yeast spores of two species known as *Saccharomyces cerevisiae* and *Saccharomyces bayanus* settle on sugar-rich environments, such as those found in fruit pods, and begin ingesting the organic material found within. A waste product, ethyl alcohol, is produced during this process. Although it is a waste product, alcohol is also a biochemical defense against competing microorganisms in that it can deter competing microorganisms. However, animals, and later prehistoric humans, discovered the intoxicating effects of alcohol and began to seek it out for its intoxicating effects.

Initially this happened only in the wild when the fruit pods split open, but at some unknown point in prehistory it was discovered that if you crush certain forms of fruit, then let it sit in a container and allow it to stand, sometimes the same process would take place, producing the same fluid found in the wild fruit pods. It is known that the yeast cells break down the carbon, hydrogen, and oxygen atoms that they find in the crushed fruit, producing ethyl alcohol and carbon dioxide as waste products. This is the process known as *fermentation*. Waste products are often toxic to the organism that produces them, and so it is with ethyl alcohol: When the concentration of alcohol in the container reaches about 15%, it becomes toxic to the yeast cells, and the fermentation process will cease. Thus the highest concentration of alcohol that can be achieved by natural means is about 15%.

Although Plato wrote about how a "strange water" would form when one boiled wine (Walton, 2002), it was not until around the year 800 BCE that an Arabian chemist experimented by boiling wine and collecting the steam that was produced by this process. Because alcohol boils at about 172°F whereas the open-air boiling point for water is 212°F, it is possible to boil a container of wine and collect the steam, which will contain a higher concentration of alcohol than the original wine. This is the process of *distillation*, which historical evidence suggests was developed in the Middle East, and

which had reached Europe by around 1100 BCE (el-Guebaly, 2008; Walton, 2002). Over time, it was discovered that one could place a cap over the container in which the wine was heated to catch the vapors. A metal coil attached to the cap would collect the vapors and allow them to cool, forming a liquid again. This liquid could be collected and then consumed. This is the famous *still* of lore and legend (Walton, 2002).

Around the year 1100 BCE wine growers in Italy started using distillation to obtain concentrated "spirits." Over the years, they learned to mix these spirits with various herbs and spices to produce different flavored beverages, which were then sold. Physicians were quick to seize on the new beverages as a possible medicine in an era when little was known about disease or its treatment. Consumers were quick to recognize that the resulting beverage allowed the drinker to more quickly achieve a state of intoxication than would be possible with wine and that distilled spirits did not spoil as rapidly as did wine (if at all); for these reasons the alcohol-containing beverages soon gained popularity for both medicinal and recreational use.[12]

Unfortunately, during the process of distillation many of the amino acids and vitamins found in the original wine are lost. Thus although they are a rapid source of intoxication, the concentrated alcohol that results from the process of distillation is nutritionally empty. This nutritionally neutral alcoholic beverage can, if consumed to excess, contribute to the condition known as *avitaminosis*, which will be discussed in the next chapter. However, alcohol is prized for its ability to produce a state of relaxation and a state of altered consciousness, which at its extreme is called *intoxication*. In a very real sense we have come full circle, producing at will the same fluid so prized by insects and animals in the wild so that we might share the joys of intoxication with them.

A Working Definition of Rare or Social Drinking

For the purpose of this chapter, people are defined as suffering from alcohol abuse or addiction if they (a) require the daily use of alcohol to function, (b) make attempts to limit their heavy alcohol use to a specific time (weekends, for example), with periods of abstinence in between the episodes of heavy alcohol

---

[12]A little known fact is that, after leaving the White House after his second term in office ended, Washington went into the distillation business and was able to produce up to 11,000 gallons of whiskey per year on his plantation, much of which was sold for profit (Zax, 2008).

use, (c) engage in continuous "binges"[13] that last for days, weeks, or months, interspaced with periods of abstinence, or (d) engage in the daily use of alcohol in excess of what is prudent for health or for social norms. People with an alcohol use disorder will experience any of a wide range of medical, social, legal, or vocational consequences associated with heavy alcohol use. They would possibly have engaged in multiple attempts to cut back or control their alcohol use, and may have continued to use alcohol in spite of an awareness that its use caused or exacerbated a medical condition in their bodies. The rare or social drinker does not meet any of these criteria.

Scope of Alcohol Use in the United States Today

It has been estimated that 90% of the adults in the United States have consumed alcohol at least once, that 70% have done so in the past year, and that 51% of the population 12 years of age or older consume alcohol at least once per month (O'Brien, 2006; Kranzler & Ciraulo, 2005a; Sadock & Sadock, 2007; Substance Abuse and Mental Health Services Administration, 2009). These figures mean that there are 129 million active drinkers in the United States 12 years of age or older (Substance Abuse and Mental Health Services Administration, 2009). An estimated 12,000 people join this number each day as they take their first drink of an alcohol-containing beverage (Lemonick & Park, 2007).

Over the decades, there has been a marked fluctuation in the per capita amount of alcohol consumed in the United States. In the 1790s, it was estimated that the average American consumed 5.8 gallons of pure ethyl alcohol, which by the 1830s had increased to 7.1 gallons of ethanol per person annually (Brust, 2004). In 1920, alcohol consumption was outlawed in the United States and remained illegal until 1933. This forced a reduction in the amount of alcohol consumed, although this is only a guess because so many people were making their own alcohol-containing beverages or buying them illegally. After the repeal of Prohibition, there was a gradual decline in the amount of alcohol consumed by each person in the United States annually, until the year 1996, when this trend was reversed (Naimi et al., 2003). At the present time it is thought

that the per capita consumption of alcohol is 8.29 liters (or 2.189 gallons) of pure alcohol, as compared to 12.34 liters per year for residents of Greenland, 9.44 liters per year for the average adult in Finland, and 16.01 liters per year for the average adult living in the Republic of Ireland (Schmid et al., 2003).

These figures are *averages,* as there is a significant variation in the level of individual alcohol consumption. It has been estimated that just 10% of those who consume alcohol will drink 60% of all of the alcohol consumed in the United States each year, whereas the top 30% of drinkers consume 90% of all of the alcohol ingested (Kilbourne, 2002). At the present time, beer is the most popular alcohol-containing beverage in the United States (Naimi et al., 2003). Unfortunately, as the amount and/or frequency of alcohol use increases, individuals become increasingly vulnerable to the potential for physical harm and addiction to alcohol. It is surprising how little alcohol it takes before individuals are at risk for physical harm from their alcohol use (Motluk, 2004). In addition to the risk for physical harm, it is thought that 8% of those who consume alcohol will become addicted to it at some point in their lives (Sterling et al., 2006). The impact of the AUDs will be discussed in the next chapter. In this chapter we will focus on social alcohol use by those people who do not have an alcohol use disorder.

The Pharmacology of Ethyl Alcohol

The alcohol molecule is quite small and is soluble in both lipids and water, although it shows a preference for the latter (A. W. Jones, 1996). It might be introduced into the body intravenously or as a vapor,[14] but the most common form of alcohol administration is as a liquid. Following absorption, the alcohol molecules are rapidly distributed throughout the body, especially to blood-rich organs such as the brain, where the concentration soon surpasses that found in the blood (Kranzler & Ciraulo 2005a). This is because alcohol is able to bind to lipids and to water, both of which are found in abundance in the brain. The alcohol molecule does diffuse into adipose[15] and muscle tissues, but it does so with more difficulty than it does into the tissues of the CNS. Still, this characteristic of alcohol

---

[13]A "binge" is defined as when a man consumes five or more standard drinks, glasses of wine or cans of beer in a 24-hour period, or when a woman consumes four or more standard drinks, glasses of wine, or cans of beer in a 24-hour period.

[14]Although devices have been introduced to take advantage of this characteristic of ethyl alcohol, many states have banned their use, and others are expected to do so, soon.

[15]See Glossary.

distribution means that a heavier person will have a slightly lower blood alcohol level than a smaller person after both consume the same amount of alcohol.

Ten to 20% of the alcohol ingested is absorbed through the stomach wall if consumed on an empty stomach, with the first alcohol molecules being detectable in the blood in as little as 1 minute (J. D. Levin, 2002; I. M. Rose, 1988; Sadock & Sadock, 2007; R. M. Swift, 2005; Zakhari, 2006). The main site of alcohol absorption, however, is the small intestine, and following the ingestion of a single drink, peak blood alcohol levels are achieved in 30 minutes (Knapp, Ciraulo, & Kranzler, 2008) to 60 minutes (Sadock & Sadock, 2007). There are a number of factors that will influence the speed at which alcohol is absorbed. It has been suggested that alcohol mixed with carbonated beverages might result in more rapid absorption, although this theory remains unproven (Sadock & Sadock, 2007; Schuckit, 2008a). When mixed with food, especially high-fat foods, the absorption of alcohol is slowed down to the point where peak alcohol levels might not be achieved until 1–6 hours after it was consumed (Baselt, 1996; Sher et al., 2005). Thus by mixing alcohol with food, its absorption will be slower; however, eventually all the alcohol will be absorbed into the body.

The mechanism through which alcohol is able to induce a state of intoxication remains poorly understood. Different theories have been advanced to account for alcohol's intoxicating effects (Motluk, 2006). In the early 20th century, it was suggested that alcohol might be able to affect the molecular structure and function of lipids in the neural walls (Brust, 2004; Tabakoff & Hoffman, 2004). This was known as the *membrane fluidization theory* or the *membrane hypothesis*. According to this theory, alcohol's ability to bind to lipids allowed it to bind to the lipids in the neural walls, making it more difficult for that neuron to maintain normal function. Though appealing, this theory has fallen into disfavor and there are few proponents of it at this time.

Scientists now believe that alcohol is a "dirty" compound. It does not seem to show a preference for specific receptor sites, but alters the action of various neurotransmitters as well as interferes with the action of messenger molecules within the neuron itself (Knapp et al., 2008; Lovinger, 2008).[16] Some of the

neurotransmitter systems altered by the ingestion of alcohol include: GABAa, glutamate, nicotinic, endogenous cannabinoids and voltage gated calcium ion channels, to name but a few (Cruz et al., 2008; Knapp et al., 2008).

Alcohol enhances the effects of gamma-amino-butyric acid (GABA),[17] the main inhibitory neurotransmitter in the brain, by binding at receptor sites utilized by GABA. When alcohol molecules bind at the GABAa-1 receptor, it enhances the influx of chloride atoms into the neuron, slowing the rate at which that neuron can "fire" (Tabakoff & Hoffman, 2004). When the alcohol molecules bind at the GABAa2s receptor site, it induces a subjective sense of relaxation for the individual. When alcohol binds to the GABAa5s receptor site in sufficient quantities, it can induce memory loss and psychomotor impairment, and indirectly contributes to the experience of alcohol-induced euphoria (Motluk, 2006).

Alcohol ingestion also alters the *N-methyl-D-aspartate* (NMDA) receptor sites in the CNS, receptor sites utilized by the neurotransmitter glutamate (Schuckit, 2008a). Glutamate is the main excitatory neurotransmitter found in the brain, increasing the firing rate of downstream neurons when it reaches the NMDA receptors (Pinel, 2003;). Thus alcohol blocks the action of glutamate at the receptor site and as such might be said to be a glutamate antagonist.

The subjective effect of alcohol is usually a feeling of gentle euphoria, reflecting alcohol's action on the endogenous opioid receptor system. When the drinker drinks enough alcohol to achieve moderate to high blood levels, the alcohol molecules are known to promote the binding process at the mu opioid receptor site[18] (Cruz et al., 2008; Modesto-Lowe & Fritz, 2005; Stahl, 2008). The mu opioid receptor site appears to be associated with the experience of alcohol-induced euphoria, an observation supported by experimental research that suggests that the administration of opioid antagonists like Naltrexone reduce alcohol consumption by chronic alcohol users. In contrast to this, the activation of the sigma opioid receptor site by high doses of alcohol appears associated with the aversive effects of alcohol (vomiting and the like).

A competing theory suggests that alcohol-induced euphoria is caused by its ability to force neurons to empty their stores of dopamine back into the synaptic junction (Heinz et al., 1998). High levels of dopamine release in the nucleus accumbens region of the brain appears to be involved in the reward cascade. The

---

[16]To illustrate how little is known about alcohol and its effects, it was recently discovered that alcohol molecules alter the norepinephrine receptor sites in the brain, although the consequences of this process are yet to be identified.

[17]See Glossary.

[18]Discussed in Chapter 14.

disinhibitory actions of alcohol appear to reflect its ability to enhance the effects of the neurotransmitter *serotonin* at the 5HT3 receptor site (Tabakoff & Hoffman, 2004). This serotonin receptor subtype is involved in the process of inhibition of behavioral inhibition. Technically, alcohol intoxication is an acute confusional state reflecting cortical dysfunction (Filley, 2004; Schuckit, 2006a). When consumed in sufficient quantities, alcohol is capable of interfering with the formation of memories in the drinker's brain. This condition is called *anteriorgrade amnesia* (Ghoneim, 2004a, 2004b). At mild to moderate intensities, this cortical dysfunction can result in neuromuscular dysfunction, cognitive dysfunction, and speech problems. At its extreme, it can be fatal through cardiopulmonary arrest. However, there is little evidence to suggest that social drinking is associated with the long-term neurocognitive changes found in persistent heavy drinkers (Rourke, & Grant, 2009).

The Biotransformation of Alcohol

The liver is the primary organ that biotransforms alcohol, and the primary method of biotransformation is oxidation (Sadock & Sadock, 2003; Zakhari, 2006). But about 10% of the alcohol ingested is either unchanged or is broken down in other sites in the body (Edenberg, 2007). At extremely high blood levels, the percentage of alcohol that is excreted unchanged through the lungs, urine, and skin is increased, giving the intoxicated person the characteristic smell of intoxication (Sadock & Sadock, 2007; Schuckit, 2006a).

For the rare social drinker, alcohol biotransformation begins in the stomach, which produces small amounts of an enzyme known as *alcohol dehydrogenase* (ADH) ("Alcohol Metabolism: An Update," 2007; Sadock & Sadock, 2007). However, the stomach's ability to produce this enzyme is impaired by the concurrent use of aspirin. Surprisingly, the regular or chronic use of alcohol blocks the stomach's ability to produce alcohol dehydrogenase. Alcohol dehydrogenase production is dependent on the level of testosterone in the user's blood. Because women produce less testosterone than do men, they produce less alcohol dehydrogenase, contributing to the tendency for women to become more intoxicated on a given amount of alcohol than men (Sadock & Sadock, 2007; R. M. Swift, 2005). Women also usually have a lower muscle-to-body mass ratio, and about 10% less water volume then men (Zealberg & Brady, 1999), factors that also contribute to the tendency for women to become more intoxicated on a given amount of alcohol than do men.

The liver is where the majority of alcohol is biotransformed. First, the liver produces large amounts of ADH, breaking alcohol down into a metabolite called *acetaldehyde*. It has been suggested that in prehistoric times the liver's ability to produce ADH evolved so that mammals could biotransform natural alcohol when fermented fruits were ingested or to help the body deal with the small amount of alcohol produced endogenously[19] (A. W. Jones, 1996). This metabolite, acetaldehyde, has been found to be extremely toxic to the human body (Melton, 2007). Normally, this is not a problem, because the body produces a family of enzymes[20] that are collectively known as *aldehyde dehydrogenase*. These enzymes, especially the form known as *aldehyde dehydrogenase # 2,*[21] rapidly breaks acetaldehyde down into acetic acid, which can be burned by the muscles as fuel (Melton, 2007). Ultimately, alcohol is biotransformed into carbon dioxide, water, and fatty acids (carbohydrates).

The Speed of Alcohol Biotransformation

There is some interindividual variability in the speed at which alcohol is biotransformed and eliminated (Edenberg, 2007; Zakhari, 2006). However, the average person might biotransform one standard mixed drink of 80-proof alcohol, 4 ounces of wine, or one 12-ounce can of beer, every 60–90 minutes (M. Fleming, Mihic, & Harris, 2006; Nace, 2005a, 2005b; Renner, 2004a). Alcohol is biotransformed through a zero-order biotransformation process, and the rate of alcohol biotransformation is relatively independent of the alcohol blood level. Thus if the person should consume alcohol at a rate faster than the speed of biotransformation, the blood alcohol level will increase. The outcome of this process will be discussed in the section titled the Subjective Effects of Alcohol.

The Alcohol Flush Reaction

After drinking even a small amount of alcohol, between 3 and 29% of people of European descent and 47–85% of people of Asian descent experience the *alcohol flush reaction* (R. L. Collins & McNair, 2002; Sher & Wood, 2005). The alcohol flush reaction is the result of a genetic

---

[19]Occasionally, people arrested for driving while under the influence of alcohol will try to argue that it is because of this naturally occurring alcohol that they were intoxicated, and not because they had ingested alcohol-containing beverages. Unfortunately, the bacteria in the gastrointestinal tract produce about 1–2 teaspoons of ethyl alcohol in a 24-hour period, which is hardly sufficient to induce intoxication.

[20]Sometimes referred to as the *ALDHs*.

[21]Referred to in some of the literature as $ALDH_2$.

mutation that prevents the liver from being able to produce sufficient amounts of aldehyde dehydrogenase, thus allowing high levels of acetaldehyde to accumulate in the drinker's blood. The individual will experience symptoms such as facial flushing, heart palpitations, dizziness, and nausea, as acetaldehyde levels climb to perhaps 20 times those seen in the normal person who has consumed a similar amount of alcohol. Because the alcohol flush reaction is so uncomfortable, this is thought to be one reason why alcohol use disorders are less common in people of Asian descent.

The Blood Alcohol Level

Because it is not possible to measure the alcohol level in the drinker's brain, physicians have to settle for a measurement of the alcohol concentration in the drinker's blood, known as the *blood alcohol level* (BAL)[22]. The BAL is reported in terms of milligrams of alcohol per 100 milliliters of blood (mg/mL). A BAL of 0.10 would be one-tenth of a milligram of alcohol per 100 milliliters of blood. The BAL provides a *rough approximation* of the individual's level of intoxication and the behavioral effects of alcohol that should be expected from an

individual with the measured BAL (Knapp et al., 2008). The same individual might have different behaviors at different times with exactly the same BAL in response to different mood states and environmental factors (Stein & Rogers, 2009). Furthermore, the drinker's subjective sense of intoxication appears to be stronger while the BAL is still rising, a phenomenon known as the *Mellanby effect* (Drummer & Odell, 2001; Sher et al., 2005). The Mellanby effect might reflect the individual's body starting to become tolerant to the effects of alcohol after even just one drink, although this theory has not been proven.

As noted earlier, the BAL that will be achieved by two people who consume the same amount of alcohol will vary as a result of a number of factors, including whether they had recently had a meal and their body size. A person who weighs 100 lbs and who consumed two regular drinks in an hour's time would have a BAL of 0.09 (just above the amount needed to be legally intoxicated). A second person who also had consumed two regular drinks in an hour's time who weighed 200 lbs would have a BAL of only 0.04 mg/mL, however, as the alcohol would be distributed in a larger body volume in the latter case. Figure 4-1 provides a rough estimate of the BAL that might result if various people of different weights were to consume different amounts of alcohol.[23]

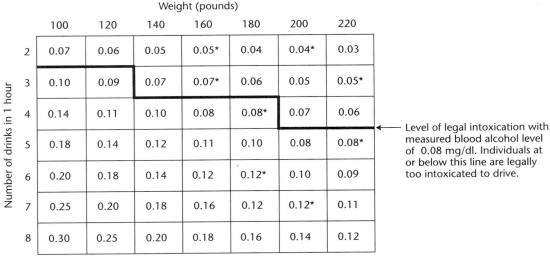

Weight (pounds)

Number of drinks in 1 hour	100	120	140	160	180	200	220
2	0.07	0.06	0.05	0.05*	0.04	0.04*	0.03
3	0.10	0.09	0.07	0.07*	0.06	0.05	0.05*
4	0.14	0.11	0.10	0.08	0.08*	0.07	0.06
5	0.18	0.14	0.12	0.11	0.10	0.08	0.08*
6	0.20	0.18	0.14	0.12	0.12*	0.10	0.09
7	0.25	0.20	0.18	0.16	0.12	0.12*	0.11
8	0.30	0.25	0.20	0.18	0.16	0.14	0.12

← Level of legal intoxication with measured blood alcohol level of 0.08 mg/dl. Individuals at or below this line are legally too intoxicated to drive.

*Rounded off.

FIGURE 4-1 Approximate Blood Alcohol Levels
Note: The chart is provided only as an illustration and is not sufficiently accurate to be used as legal evidence or as a guide to "safe" drinking. Individual blood alcohol levels from the same dose of alcohol vary widely, and these figures provide an average blood alcohol level for an individual of a given body weight.

---

[22]Occasionally the term *blood alcohol concentration* (BAC) is used.

[23]This table is provided only to illustrate the process of intoxication at different levels of alcohol consumption, and is *not* intended to function as an aid to diagnosis or as a guide to safe drinking.

Subjective Effects of Alcohol on the Individual at Normal Doses in the Social Drinker

Alcohol is both a neurotoxin and a psychoactive compound. It also has very mild analgesic effect. To achieve the same degree of analgesia accomplished by 10 mg of morphine, a person would have to ingest 15,000–20,000 mg of alcohol (A. W. Jones, 1996). However, most drinkers do not consume alcohol for the analgesic effect of this compound, but rather for its psychoactive properties. However, alcohol's effects are not automatic for the drinker. At low to moderate BALs, individuals' *expectations* play a major role in how they interpret the effects of alcohol, and in their drinking behavior (Sher et al., 2005). Alcohol use expectations begin to form early in life, perhaps as early as 3 years of age, and become more entrenched between the ages of 3–7 years (R. T. Jones & McMahon, 1998). It has been found, for example, that alcohol users tend to have more positive expectations for the outcome of their alcohol use than do nondrinkers.

One effect that the individual does encounter after just one to two drinks is the *disinhibition effect*. It is believed that this is caused when alcohol interferes with the normal function of the cortex region responsible for inhibitions, as well as for abstract thinking and speech. As the BAL increases, individuals begin to "forget" social inhibitions (Julien, 2005) and might end up doing something they might later regret. The effects of alcohol for the social or rare drinker are summarized in the following Table 4-1.

Medical Complications of Alcohol Use for the Social Drinker

The Hangover

The hangover has been known to be an aftereffect to drinking for thousands of years. Physical manifestations of the hangover include fatigue, malaise, sensitivity to light, thirst, tremor, nausea, dizziness, depression, and anxiety (Sher et al., 2005; Schuckit, 2006a). In spite of the individual's subjective discomfort, alcohol-induced hangovers usually resolve in 8–24 hours and will require only conservative medical treatments such as antacids, bed rest, and over-the-counter analgesics, along with adequate fluids.

The exact mechanism by which alcohol use is able to induce a hangover is still not known (R. Swift & Davidson, 1998). Researchers are still divided over the question of whether the hangover is caused by: (a) the direct effects of alcohol on the drinker's brain, (b) the effects of a metabolite of alcohol biotransformation (such as acetaldehyde), (c) some of the flavoring agents mixed with liquors (called *congeners*), (d) an alcohol-induced state of dehydration, which affects brain function, (e) reflects an early alcohol-withdrawal syndrome, or (f) the effects of an alcohol-induced reduction in brain ß-endorphin levels (Mosier, 1999; R. Swift & Davidson, 1998). Some of the congeners contained in alcohol-containing beverages include acetone, acetaldehyde, fusel oil, tannins, and furfural, although the proportion of these compounds varies as a result of the form of alcohol-containing beverage

TABLE 4-1 EFFECTS OF ALCOHOL ON THE INFREQUENT DRINKER

BLOOD ALCOHOL LEVEL (BAL)	BEHAVIORAL AND PHYSICAL EFFECTS
0.02	Feeling of warmth, relaxation.
0.05–0.09	Skin becomes flushed. Drinker is more talkative, feels euphoria. At this level, psychomotor skills are slightly to moderately impaired, and ataxia develops. Loss of inhibitions, increased reaction time, and visual field disturbances.
0.10–0.19	Slurred speech, severe ataxia, mood instability, drowsiness, nausea and vomiting, staggering gait, confusion.
0.20–0.29	Lethargy, combativeness, stupor, severe ataxia, incoherent speech, amnesia, unconsciousness.
0.30–0.39	Coma, respiratory depression, anesthesia, respiratory failure.
Above 0.40	Death.

SOURCES: Based on Baselt (1996), T. M. Brown and Stoudemire (1998), Brust (2004).

(Roshsenow et al., 2009). Bourbon, for example, contains 37 times the concentration of congeners as does vodka (Roshsenow et al., 2009).

Approximately 75% of drinkers will experience a hangover at some point in their lives, although most people do not experience a hangover every time they consume alcoholic beverages. There is evidence to suggest that some individuals are more prone to this alcohol withdrawal effect than others, possibly as a result of genetic variability (R. Swift & Davidson, 1998). Once the hangover develops, there is little that can be done to speed its resolution in spite of the wide variety of folk remedies purported to do this (Erickson, 2007).

The Effects of Alcohol on the Gastrointestinal Tract

At high blood alcohol levels, the stomach begins to excrete more mucus than normal and will close the pyloric valve between the stomach and the small intestine in an attempt to slow further alcohol absorption. The drinker will experience a sense of nausea and might possibly vomit as the body attempts to rid itself of the poison, alcohol. Alcohol also interferes with the normal vomiting reflex, with one result being that the drinker's body might even attempt regurgitation while the person is unconscious. This will expose the unconscious drinker to the danger of possible aspiration of the material being regurgitated, which can contribute to a condition known as *aspirative pneumonia*.[24] If the airway should become blocked, the unconscious drinker might very possibly die during this process.

The Effects of Alcohol on Sleep for the Social Drinker

Although alcohol, like other CNS depressants, might induce a form of sleep, it does not allow the drinker to follow a normal sleep cycle. Alcohol-induced sleep problems, though strongest in the chronic drinker,[25] can occur even in the social drinker especially after a binge-drinking episode (Roshsenow et al., 2009). For example, even a modest amount of alcohol consumed within 2 hours of when the individual goes to bed can contribute to both more frequent and longer episodes of sleep apnea.[26] Alcohol use prior to sleep has been shown to weaken pharyngeal muscle tone, increasing the tendency for the drinker to snore while asleep and to experience sleep breathing problems (Qureshi & Lee-Chiong, 2004). Thus even rare social drinkers with known sleep respiratory problems should consult a physician before using alcohol.

Social Drinking and Stroke

There is mixed evidence suggesting that rare or social drinking increases the individual's risk for a stroke. D. Smith (1997) suggested that even light drinking, defined as ingesting 1–4 ounces of pure ethanol per month, more than doubled the individual's chances of a hemorrhagic stroke. Yet Jackson, Sesso, Buring, and Gaziano (2003) concluded that moderate alcohol use (defined as no more than one standard drink in 24 hours) reduced the individual's risk of both ischemic and hemorrhagic stokes in a sample of male physicians who had already suffered one stroke. The reasons for these apparently contradictory conclusions are not known at this time; however until a definitive answer is found, it must be suspected that even casual or social alcohol use will raise the individual's risk for a stroke. There was no observed relationship between level of alcohol use and functional outcome after the individual suffered a stroke, however, indicating that level of alcohol use was not a factor in poststroke recovery (Rist et al., 2010).

Alcohol Use and Neurocognitive Effects

There is a growing body of evidence that alcohol can start to induce brain damage even in social drinkers. The team of Biller, Bartsch, Homola, and Bendszus (2009) administered either three beers or two glasses of wine to a sample of 15 healthy volunteers. The authors then examined the brains of their volunteers through a process known as magnetic resonance spectroscopy and found that creatine, a chemical that helps to protect neurons, decreases as the individual's blood alcohol level increases. The brain's ability to recover from the exposure to alcohol decreased as the blood alcohol level increased, the authors found, and they postulated that this might be one of the mechanisms through which heavy drinking might cause brain damage. Acute intoxication has been identified as a factor in the disruption of the process of neurogenesis in the individual's brain (Crews, 2008). Even social drinking can induce some degree of depression in the drinker, possibly levels of depression that will contribute to self-abusive behavior(s), as evidenced by the fact that as many as two-thirds of those individuals who commit

---

[24]See Glossary.

[25]Discussed in the next chapter.

[26]See Glossary.

self-injurious acts used alcohol prior to the commission of that act (McClosky & Berman, 2003).

The observed neurocognitive deficits appear to persist for hours after the individual's body has finished the process of biotransformation and elimination of the alcohol that was consumed (Roshsenowet al., 2009). The authors found that binge drinkers in their study suffered reduced reaction times in spite of the participants' subjective belief that they were capable of driving safely, suggesting that binge drinkers present a higher risk for motor vehicle accidents than do abstainers or those who choose not to drive the next day.

Other Consequences of Rare/Social Drinking

The most significant consequence of rare/social alcohol use is quite simply the death of the drinker. Alcohol is responsible for more deaths from chemical overdose than any other drug of abuse (Schuckit, 2006b). The amount of alcohol that must be ingested to induce intoxication is already a significant fraction of the lethal dose, and the higher that the individual's blood alcohol level becomes, the closer she will be to death from an alcohol overdose.

Alcohol also interferes with the body's ability to excrete uric acid from the body. This is a matter of some concern for individuals who suffer from high uric acid levels (such as those found in gout). The team of Zhang et al. (2006) concluded that even occasional alcohol use would increase individuals' risk of an acute attack of gout if they were predisposed to this condition, with such attacks usually taking place within 24 hours of the individual's alcohol use. Another relatively common consequence of social alcohol use is the dreaded "beer goggle" effect (Aldhous, 2008). In brief, alcohol consumption appears to make the drinker less selective in the choice of potential partner(s), resulting in a possible shock next day when the drinker awakens. Alcohol use by young adults has been found to alter the drinker's perception of the sexual attractiveness both of the drinker and of potential sexual partners (Aldhous, 2008). Furthermore, as noted earlier, the disinhibition effect of alcohol encourages individuals to engage in behavior(s) that they would normally avoid.

Although many binge drinkers believe that they are immune to the dangers of alcohol use, it has been determined that even binge drinking can speed up the formation of plaque in the coronary arteries of the drinker (Redmond, Morrow, Kunkiml, Miller-Graziano, & Cullen, 2008). The causal mechanism appears to be that acetaldehyde, an intermediate step in the biotransformation of alcohol, can induce the binding of body cells known as monocytes to artery walls, thus inducing the formation of plaque in the drinker's body (Redmond et al., 2008).

Drug Interactions Involving Social Alcohol Use[27]

There has been little research into the effects of social drinking (defined as one to two standard drinks a day) on the action of various pharmaceutical agents (Weathermon & Crabb, 1999). It is known that because alcohol is a CNS depressant, it might potentiate the effects of other CNS depressants such as over-the-counter/prescribed antihistamines, benzodiazepines,[28] barbiturates,[29] opiates,[30] and various anesthetic agents used in medical practice (Weathermon & Crabb, 1999; Zernig & Battista, 2000), to name but a few of the CNS depressants that interact with alcohol.

Patients who take nitroglycerine, used to treat certain heart conditions, should not use alcohol under any circumstances, as the combination of these compounds can cause a significant, potentially serious, drop in blood pressure (Zernig & Battista, 2000). Patients taking the anticoagulant medication warfarin should not drink, as alcohol's anticoagulant effects will cause abnormal biotransformation patterns of the warfarin being used, with potentially dangerous results for the drinker.

Although there is evidence that the antidepressant amitriptyline might enhance the euphoric effects of alcohol, the concurrent use of both medications might cause rapid, potentially dangerous, blood pressure changes for the drinker (Weathermon & Crabb, 1999). While the selective serotonin reuptake inhibitors (SSRIs) are antidepressants with fewer side effects or risks than the older antidepressant medications, the use of alcohol with the SSRIs increases the individual's risk for the development of the *serotonin syndrome*[31] (T. M. Brown & Stoudemire, 1998).

---

[27]The list of medications that might interact with alcohol is quite extensive. This is only a partial list of medications that might interact with alcohol. The reader is advised to consult a pharmacist and/or physician before mixing ethyl alcohol with *any* form of over-the-counter or prescription medication.

[28]Discussed in Chapter 10.

[29]Discussed in Chapter 9.

[30]Discussed in Chapter 14.

[31]See Glossary.

Alcohol itself has an anticoagulant effect, as does aspirin, and the danger of unwanted bleeding is increased when these compounds are used concurrently. Although acetaminophen, a common alternative to aspirin, does not have an anticoagulant effect, the use of acetaminophen and alcohol increases the risk of acetaminophen toxicity even if used at regular dosage levels (Ciraulo et al., 2006; Zernig & Battista, 2000). Thus the use of alcohol with over-the-counter analgesics should be avoided.

Diabetic patients taking oral medications for their diabetes should not drink, as the alcohol ingested can interfere with the body's ability to biotransform alcohol and can result in acute alcohol poisoning at even moderate BALs. Furthermore, the antidiabetic medication prevents the body from being able to break the alcohol down, extending the period of alcohol intoxication. Patients on monoamine oxidase inhibitors (MAO inhibitors or MAOIs) should not consume alcohol under *any* circumstances to avoid the risk of intermixing their medication with the amino acid tyramine. This amino acid is produced during fermentation, and when mixed with an MAOI may cause dangerously high, perhaps fatal, blood pressure levels (T. M. Brown & Stoudemire, 1998).

Researchers have found that verapamil hydrochloride[32] inhibits the process of alcohol biotransformation, increasing the duration of intoxication (T. M. Brown & Stoudemire, 1998). Although early research suggested a negative interaction between alcohol and the medications ranitidine and cimtidine (now sold as over-the-counter agents for control of stomach acid), later research failed to support this hypothesis. However, the mixture of these compounds should be avoided whenever possible. This is clearly seen in cases where the patient is taking an antibiotic compound such as chloramphenicol, furazolidone, or metronidazole, or the antimalarial medication quinacrine. When mixed with these medications, alcohol produces a flush reaction type of response that can be both uncomfortable, and potentially dangerous. Although the antibiotic erythromycine does not cause an alcohol flush reaction response, it does speed gastric emptying, causing abnormally high BALs (Zernig & Battista, 2000). Patients who are on the antibiotic compound doxycycline and who drink will find that the alcohol decreases the antibiotic blood levels, possibly to the point where it will no longer be effective (T. M. Brown & Stoudemire,

1998). Finally, the antitubercular medication isoniazid (or INH) can induce hepatitis when mixed with alcohol, and its effectiveness will be reduced while the patient is drinking.

Alcohol use can interfere with the effects of many of the drugs of abuse. As will be discussed in Chapter 12, the concurrent use of alcohol and cocaine interferes with the pharmacokinetics of both compounds. Although there has been limited research into possible interactions between alcohol and marijuana, preliminary evidence suggests that alcohol's depressant effects might exacerbate the CNS depressant effects of marijuana (Garriott, 1996). As this list would suggest, alcohol is a very potent compound that has the potential to interact with a wide range of chemicals, and it should not be consumed by patients taking any over-the-counter or prescription medication.

Alcohol Ingestion and Injury

Pennock (2007) argues persuasively that following World War II what might collectively be called the "alcohol industry" had adopted several advertising strategies, all of which were designed to project an image of alcohol consumption as a mark of sophistication, a way to share a pleasant time, and a way to entertain guests. Missing from such advertisements were admissions that alcohol consumption also played a role in accidental injury, interpersonal violence, and death. Even drinkers have a BAL of only between 0.05 and 0.079, levels below that used to define legal intoxication, their odds of being in a motor vehicle accident increase by 546% if they were to drive, whereas a BAL of 0.08 increases the odds of those individuals being in a motor vehicle accident by 1,500% (Movig et al., 2004).

In addition to its role in motor vehicle accidents, alcohol use has been found to be a factor in 51% of all boating facilities (G. S. Smith et al., 2001). Ethyl alcohol use has also been found to be a factor in 17–53% of all falls and 40–67% of all fire-related fatalities (D. C. Lewis, 1997). Although bicycling is not usually thought of as a high-risk activity, 32% of the adults who die in a bicycle accident were found to have alcohol in their systems at the time of their accident (Li, Baker, Smialek, & Soderstrom, 2001). This is consistent with the observation that 52% of patients treated at one major trauma center were found to have alcohol in their blood at the time of admission (Cornwell et al., 1998), because bike accidents are one potential form of major trauma. This list, although incomplete, does demonstrate that even casual alcohol use carries with it a significant risk of accidental injury or death.

---

[32]A "calcium channel blocker" used for control of hypertension, and sold under the a variety of brand names.

There is a known association between alcohol use and interpersonal violence. It has been suggested that the alcohol-related disinhibition effect might explain, in part, the relationship between alcohol use and aggressive behavior. Alcohol was found to be involved in 38% of loud arguments, 57% of disputes that involve a threat being made, and 68% of incidents in which there is physical aggression of some kind (Giancola et al., 2009). In approximately 86% of homicides, 60% of sex offenses, 37% of physical assault, and 30% of child abuse, the perpetrator was under the influence of alcohol at the time of the offense (Greenfield, 2007; Parrott & Giancola, 2006). Furthermore, an unknown percentage of victims in each category of crime just identified were also using alcohol. The association between alcohol use and injury is so strong that any patient who has been injured while under the influence of alcohol be assessed for a full alcohol use disorder (discussed in the next chapter).

As this information suggests, although alcohol is man's most popular recreational beverage, its use is not without significant danger. Alcohol is not as innocuous as many both in and outside of what might loosely be called the "liquor industry" would have us believe; it interacts with numerous pharmaceuticals, and its habitual use is responsible for death from various forms of organ failure as well as from accidents.

Chapter Summary

Although people consume ethyl alcohol as a recreational substance, research has shown that its use carries with it a significant potential for harm. It may be the first recreational chemical produced by humans, and over the years its production has become more sophisticated as its production moved through the use of fermented honey, to fermented fruits, on to distilled spirits. Distillation allowed manufacturers to increase the alcohol content in the beverage being produced above the 15% limit imposed by nature itself, allowing more concentrated beverages with higher alcohol contents to be developed. Alcohol's effects on the rare social drinker were reviewed, and some of the more significant interactions between alcohol and pharmaceutical agents were discussed. In the next chapter, the effects of chronic and heavy alcohol use will be explored.

CHAPTER 5

The Effects of Alcohol Abuse and Addiction

Introduction

The focus of the last chapter was on the effects of ethyl alcohol on the social drinker. Even limited alcohol use is associated with an increased risk of accidental death, as was discussed. But there are those who come to enjoy the effects of alcohol so much that they do not limit themselves to the rare or social use of this compound. There are many reasons why they come to make this decision: They might do so because they enjoy the euphoric effects of alcohol, or they might do so because they believe that they need alcohol in order to cope with the pain of living. Many have abused alcohol for so long that they have now become physically addicted to it. About the only characteristic that these groups share is that they all use alcohol more frequently, and consume more alcohol, than the rare/social drinker.

In that common characteristic we find the root of the problem. Where rare or social drinking carried with it some degree of risk, the risks are multiplied for the heavy or chronic alcohol use.

A Working Definition of the Alcohol Use Disorders

In the last chapter, individuals with an alcohol use disorder were said to be those who will: (a) require the daily use of alcohol to function, (b) make attempts to limit their heavy alcohol use to a specific time (weekends, for example), with periods of abstinence in between the episodes of heavy alcohol use, (c) engages in binge-type[1] drinking for days, weeks, or months, interspersed with periods of abstinence, or (d) engage in the daily use of alcohol in excess of what is prudent for health or for social norms.

This definition includes a wide range of drinking behaviors. Some people will be weekend drinkers, abstaining from alcohol during the workweek to avoid problems at the job site. Others will abstain from alcohol during work hours, but will start to consume alcohol after the end of the workday, and possibly throughout the weekend. Yet other drinkers will intermix periods of alcohol heavy use with periods of lower use, or possibly even abstinence. Some drinkers will "hide" their drinking behavior(s) from significant others, whereas still others will openly consume alcohol abusively, demanding that family/friends accept their drinking as a price for their presence. The common element to all of these different drinking styles is the abusive use of alcohol, possibly to the point where the drinker becomes physically dependent on it.

---

[1]"Binge" drinking was defined in Chapter 4.

It is generally accepted by health care professionals that the consumption of 16 ounces of an 80- to 100-proof liquor, or 11–15 twelve-ounce cans of beer, each day for 2–3 weeks will produce a physical dependency on alcohol (Perry et al., 2007). The body will have attempted to compensate for the constant use of alcohol during this period, and upon cessation or significant reduction of alcohol intake, the compensatory mechanisms will then cause a characteristic alcohol withdrawal syndrome (AWS). The person with an AUD typically will experience any of a wide range of medical, social, legal, or vocational consequences associated with heavy alcohol use. People with an AUD would possibly have engaged in multiple attempts to cut back or control their alcohol use. Such individuals might have continued to use alcohol in spite of an awareness that its use caused or exacerbated a medical condition in their bodies. A formal diagnosis of alcohol abuse, or dependence, using the diagnostic criteria identified in the *Diagnostic and Statistical Manual of Mental Disorders* (4th ed., text revision) (American Psychiatric Association, 2000) also would identify a person with an AUD.

Scope of the Problem

During the first decade of the 21st century, Europeans had the dubious distinction of being the heaviest drinkers in the world, with 5% of men and 1% of women meeting the diagnostic criteria for alcohol dependence ("Europeans Heaviest Drinkers in the World," 2006). Globally, 2.4 million people lose their lives to alcohol-related illness or injuries each year, a death toll that is approximately half of that wrought by tobacco-related illness ("First Shots in the War on Alcohol," 2009). This amounts to 3.8% of all deaths and 4.6% of all cases of disability around the world each year.

In the United States, it is thought that 90% of all adults will consume alcohol at some point in their lives and that 65% of adults are current alcohol users (Nace, 2005b; Schuckit, 2009). Furthermore, it is estimated that more than 60% of adults in the United States drank to the point of intoxication in the past year. Although these statistics would suggest that AUDs are widespread, in reality only a minority of these individuals have an alcohol use disorder. Depending on the criteria used, perhaps 10–20% of the adults who consume alcohol[2] will meet the diagnostic criteria for an

AUD at some point in their lives,[3] although the team of Hasin, Stinson, Ogburn, and Grant (2007) suggested that the percentage of adults who will meet the diagnostic criteria for an AUD at some point in their lives might be as high as 30%! This figure should be considered a high-end estimate, and most clinicians estimate that the range of AUDs is more in the range of 10–20% of drinkers. However, it must be remembered that of this percentage a smaller subgroup will currently be drinking abusively, whereas others begin to abuse alcohol at a later point in their lives.

To complicate matters, people's alcohol use patterns do not remain stable over the course of their lifetime. Rather, there are several different pathways that a person's alcohol use pattern might follow. Some abusive drinkers remain abusive drinkers, whereas others alternate between periods of abusive drinking and periods of abstinence or controlled drinking (Hasin et al., 2007). Some heavy drinkers "mature out" of their abusive drinking,[4] learning either to be social drinkers or to abstain from further alcohol use. Some drinkers who once met the diagnostic criteria for alcohol dependence based on their past drinking patterns might currently be abstinent from alcohol use. Some heavy drinkers might be abstinent due to situational stressors, such as being under court supervision or at risk for losing their job, but without any desire to stop drinking once the external motivation for abstinence is removed.

A popular misconception of the heavy drinker is that of a person who is unemployed and who spends much of the day sitting on the curb drinking cheap whiskey from a bottle wrapped in a brown paper bag. In reality the majority of people with an AUD live lives that appear on the surface to be successful and productive (Aldhous, 2010). This is why so few heavy drinkers are easily identified to either the general public or health care professionals. Still, an estimated 10.7 million people, or 7.7% of the population, are thought to have an active AUD at any given point in time (Lemonick & Park, 2007). Drawing on the National Epidemiologic Survey on Alcohol and Related Drug Conditions, the team of B. F. Grant et al. (2006) concluded that 4.65% of the adults in the United States had abused alcohol in the proceeding 12 months, but only 3.81% of the adult

---

[2]Remember that because 90% of the adults are thought to drink at some point in their lives, in reality this is about 9–18% of the adults in this country.

[3]This figure includes those who *abuse* alcohol, and the smaller percentage of those who go on to become alcohol dependent at some point in their lives.

[4]As will be discussed in Chapters 23 and 24, this pattern is often seen in young adults and in college students who abuse alcohol for a period of time, then set it aside when they assume the duties and responsibilities of adulthood.

population was actively addicted to and abusing alcohol during that period. Alcohol-dependent people are thought to lose about 15 years of potential life as a result of their AUD (Schuckit, 2006a). The estimated economic impact of the alcohol use disorders in the United States alone was $234 billion, with 13% of this amount being just for health care costs for people injured or ill as a result of their alcohol abuse or addiction (Rehm et al., 2009). In addition, AUDs are also associated with problems in the interpersonal, educational, vocational, educational, and legal spheres of functioning. Alcohol abusers are predominately male by a factor of 3:1 or 4:1 (Anton, 2005; Schuckit, 2005).

Who is the Typical Person With an Alcohol Use Disorder?

This is a difficult question to answer, in part because alcohol use disorders take so many different forms. Table 5-1 provides an overview of the subtypes of people with an alcohol use disorder identified thus far.

Daily drinking is often seen in people with an alcohol use disorder. However, other people with an AUD present with a pattern of binge drinking, which was the topic of a study by Naimi et al. (2003). This was defined by the authors as a person who was (a) not a daily drinker who (b) consumed five or more cans of beer or standard mixed drinks in a single episode of alcohol consumption. Using this definition, the authors concluded that 15% of the adults in the United States had engaged in at least one period of binge drinking

in the proceeding 30 days, and that 15% reported having done so on 12 or more days in the preceding year. An estimated 1.5 *billion* episodes of binge drinking take place each year in just the United States alone (Freiberg & Samet, 2005). Not surprisingly, heavy drinkers were more likely to engage in binge drinking, and to consume more alcohol during a binge, than were light to moderate drinkers.

The typical alcohol-dependent person in the United States will experience their first psychosocial or medical problem as a result of their drinking in their 20s or 30s, and they will probably enter treatment for the first time when they are in their 40s (Schuckit, 2006a). Although this data would suggest that it is easy to identify adults with an AUD, they are "masters of denial" (Knapp, 1996, p. 19). When confronted, many people with an AUD are able to offer a thousand and one reasons why they cannot possibly have an alcohol use disorder. Such excuses may include the fact that they are nothing like the "skid row" daily drinker, that they hold a regular job, that they always go to work, that they can tell you the names of 10 people who drink 10 times as much as they do, that they never go to the bars, and so on. In reality, only about 5% of heavy drinkers fit the role of the "skid row" derelict (Brust, 2004). Many of those who drink heavily are high-functioning drinkers, with jobs, families, and a public image to protect (Aldhous, 2010; Benton, 2009). Such people include many health care professionals, business executives, political figures, and so forth. These individuals will often go to great lengths to hide their growing dependence on alcohol

TABLE 5-1 SUBTYPES OF ALCOHOLISM

SUBTYPE OF ALCOHOLISM	PERCENTAGE OF SAMPLE	AVERAGE AGE OF DEPENDENCE ONSET	SELECT CHARACTERISTICS
Young Adult	31.5%	*20 years*	*Low rates of other drug abuse, low rates of mental illness, and about one-third still in higher education.*
Young Antisocial	21.1%	*21.1 years*	*Some familial history of AUDs, high rates of mental health problems and drug abuse.*
Functional	19.4%	*37 years*	*Well educated, usually with stable jobs and families. Limited history of alcohol use disorders in family of origin. Moderate rates of depression.*
Intermediate familial	18.8%	*32 years*	*Familial history of alcohol use disorders in many cases. High levels of depression and/or bipolar affective disorders. Drug use disorders often present.*
Chronic Severe	9.2%	*29 years*	*Frequent history of familial AUDs. High rates of mental health issues and other SUDs.*

Note: Based on Aldhous (2010) and Moss, Chen, and Yi (2007).

from others, while their personality defenses protect them from being aware of it themselves. It is only in moments of quiet introspection that the drinker might wonder why they do not drink like a "normal person."[5] As the disease progresses, these moments of introspection become increasingly infrequent. As these studies suggest, there is no "typical" person with an AUD.

Alcohol Dependence, Tolerance, and "Craving": Signposts of Alcohol Use Disorders

There are many symptoms that, when present, suggest that drinkers have moved past simple social drinking, or even heavy alcohol use, to the point where they have developed a serious alcohol use disorder. Perhaps the most important of these is the development of *tolerance*. As drinkers continue to consume alcohol over periods of time, the body begins to adapt to the continuous presence of alcohol, which is said to demonstrate *tolerance* to alcohol. This process reflects the individual's (a) drinking history and (b) genetic inheritance (R. M. Swift, 2005). A person who consumed alcohol two times a week would be less likely to develop the same degree of tolerance to alcohol's effects than would a drinker who consumed alcohol daily, for example.

It is not unusual for physicians or drug counselors to have a client report that they needed to drink more to achieve a given level of intoxication than they required

in the past, which is a reflection of the process of metabolic tolerance (T. Nelson, 2000). Research has shown that after 1–2 weeks of habitual daily drinking there is a 30% increase in the speed of alcohol biotransformation, allowing the drinker to consume more alcohol (Schuckit, 2006b). Over time however, chronic drinkers might discover that they do not require as much alcohol to achieve a given level of intoxication as they did when they were younger. At this point, the individual's tolerance to alcohol is said to be decreasing, as a result of aging and the accumulated damage to the liver caused by the constant presence of alcohol. The phenomenon of tolerance to alcohol is seen by comparing the effects of alcohol on the chronic drinker in Table 5-2 to those in Table 4-1 (Chapter 4).

Tolerance is rather energy-intensive, and if the individual is continuously exposed to a given compound, eventually the different organs will prove to be unequal to the task of maintaining the high level of tolerance that has developed. At this point, drinkers will find that they will achieve a certain level of intoxication after consuming much less alcohol, and their tolerance would "be on the downswing."

Individuals with an AUD often come to depend on alcohol for psychological support as well as to avoid physical withdrawal symptoms. In such cases, individuals are said to be *psychologically dependent* on alcohol. They would believe that they need alcohol in order to relax, engage in intimate relations, sleep, cope with stress, and so on. In contrast to this, the phenomenon of *physical dependence* manifests when the individual suddenly stops drinking and experiences

TABLE 5-2 EFFECTS OF ALCOHOL ON THE CHRONIC DRINKER	
BLOOD ALCOHOLLEVEL (BAL)	**BEHAVIORAL AND PHYSICAL EFFECTS**
0.05–0.09	None to minimal effect observed.
0.10–0.19	Mild ataxia, euphoria.
0.20–0.29	Mild emotional changes.
	Ataxia is more severe.
0.30–0.39	Drowsiness, lethargy, stupor.
0.40–0.49	Coma. Death is possible.
0.50–0.60	Respiratory paralysis that may result in drinker's death.[a]

[a]Brust (2004) discussed how, on rare occasions, a patient with a measured BAL of up to 0.80 might be alert or conscious, although such exceptions are rare, and usually a BAL of 0.50 is fatal.
Sources: Based on information in Baselt (1996); Lehman, Pilich, & Andrews (1994); Morrison, Rogers, & Thomas (1995); Renner (2004a).

[5]Often referred to at 12-step meetings as "Normies."

the characteristic *alcohol withdrawal syndrome* (AWS) (discussed later in this chapter).

The TIQ Hypothesis

It was once thought that alcohol use significantly reduced the brain's production of natural opioid-like molecules known as *enkephalins* and the *dynorphins*. Furthermore, during the process of alcohol biotransformation, an alcohol metabolite and naturally occurring neurotransmitters combined to form the toxic compound *tetrahydroisoquinoline* (TIQ) (K. Blum, 1988). TIQ was thought to bind to the opioid receptor sites within the brain's reward system, causing euphoria and a sense of well-being (K. Blum & Payne, 1991; Trachenberg & Blum, 1988). However, TIQ's effects are short lived, a characteristic that would force the individual to continue to drink in order to maintain the initial feeling of well-being achieved through alcohol use according to the authors.

Over time, heavy habitual alcohol use was thought to cause the brain to reduce its productions of natural opioid-like molecules as the ever-present TIQ was substituted for these natural neurotransmitters (K. Blum & Payne, 1991; Trachtenberg & Blum, 1988). The individual's cessation of drinking would result in a lack of stimulation in the reward system, which the individual would experience as "craving" for further alcohol use. Although the TIQ theory had many proponents in the latter part of the 20th century and still is occasionally suggested as accounting for alcohol-induced feelings of euphoria and well-being experienced by drinkers, a number of research studies have failed to find evidence supporting the TIQ hypothesis and there are few advocates of this theory now.

Complications of Chronic Alcohol Use

Globally, alcohol is thought to be a factor in 2.5 million deaths each year. In the United States, alcohol is thought to cause or be a factor in 85,000 to 90,000 deaths each year[6] (Danaei et al., 2009; Myrick & Wright, 2008). Although used as an intoxicant, alcohol is a mild toxin that, after extended exposure, may result in damage to one or more organs. This is clearly seen in the fact that habitual heavy drinkers are thought to lose up to 25 years of potential life compared with nondrinkers (Sullivan, 2007). There is a dose-dependent relationship between the amount of alcohol ingested by an individual, in both the frequency and the length of stay in hospitals, placing an additional strain on a struggling health care system (C. L. Hart & Smith, 2009). Surprisingly, it has been found that episodic or binge alcohol abuse can result in many of the same effects on the body seen in habitual alcohol abusers or those who are addicted to this compound.

The question of alcohol-related organ damage has been proven beyond question. However, a variable that has rarely been considered is the effect of *age* on the drinker's body. The aging process will itself extract a toll on the individual's body. Unfortunately, it is impossible to determine the percentage of the damage observed in a given individual due to the aging process as opposed to the habitual use of alcohol. It is known, however, that habitual drinkers demonstrate a greater number of health problems, and more serious health problems, than do nondrinkers of the same age.

The amount of physical damage that alcohol causes to the drinker's body is mitigated or enhanced by his genetic inheritance. We do not understand the relationship between specific genes and alcohol-induced organ damage, but there are strong reasons to suspect that variations in genetic heritage results in higher or lower levels of vulnerability for alcohol induced organ damage. For example, the individual's risk for developing Wernicke-Korsakoff's disorder[7] is mediated by genetically determined variations in the production of the enzyme transketolase (Rourke & Grant, 2009). This should not be interpreted to mean that individuals who lack predisposing genetic histories are free from the risk of alcohol-induced organ damage. We do not know enough about genetics to make such a statement. Rather, it should be assumed that as with other aspects of life, individuals' genetic heritage is one factor that contributes to or detracts from their ability to resist alcohol-induced organ damage.

The Effects of Chronic Alcohol Use on the Digestive System

Alcohol has a profound impact on the digestive system. The body of the heavy drinker loses some of its ability to absorb needed nutrients from food that is ingested. First, there is the method by which modern distilled spirits are obtained. As was discussed in the last

---

[6]These figures include not only those deaths directly caused by alcohol, but also indirect alcohol-related deaths such as injuries, violence, cancer, and so forth.

[7]Discussed later in this chapter.

chapter, during the process of distillation many of the vitamins, minerals, and amino acids found in the original wine are lost. Where the original wine might have contributed something to the individual's daily nutritional requirements, even this modest contribution is lost through the distillation process.

Also, the end product of alcohol biotransformation results in the formation of carbohydrates, which often make the drinker not feel the need to eat. These are called "empty calories" by nutritional experts, because they contribute nothing to the individual's dietary requirements of protein, amino acids, and so on. In severe cases, daily drinkers may obtain up to 50% of their daily caloric requirement with alcohol-derived calories rather than with calories from more traditional foods (Griffith & Schenker, 2006). Although drinkers might not feel hungry, their body may be starving for necessary nutrients. However, even if chronic drinkers should consume food, their ability to absorb needed nutrients is often blocked by alcohol's ability to interfere with the absorption of nutrients from the digestive system (M. Fleming, Mihic, & Harris, 2006; Sadock & Sadock, 2007). One mechanism that causes this is alcohol-induced diarrhea. The condition will interfere with the body's ability to absorb necessary nutrients from the food (Brunton et al., 2008). Collectively, alcohol-induced diarrhea, anorexia, and the empty calories that result from alcohol biotransformation contribute to the development of malnutrition for the drinker. Drinkers' bodies that become vitamin-deficient, a common outcome of habitual heavy alcohol use, are said to have developed *avitaminosis*.[8]

Another possible gastrointestinal problem seen in heavy drinkers is the development of an inflammation of the pancreas, a condition known as *pancreatitis*. This condition can develop after a single episode of heavy drinking, but prolonged heavy drinking is the more common cause of alcohol-induced pancreatitis (Brunton et al., 2008). The causal mechanism for alcohol-induced pancreatitis seems to be the exposure of pancreatic cells to alcohol, which is a toxic compound. Although there are other reasons why a given patient might develop pancreatitis, the AUDs are the most common cause of this condition in the United States, and about 10% of heavy drinkers eventually develop this disorder (Brunton et al., 2008; Schuckit, 2008a).

Daily alcohol use has been found to increase the individual's risk for developing cancer of the pancreas (Genkinger et al., 2009), as well as an increased risk of cancer in various other parts of the body, causing an estimated 389,000 new cases of cancer in the United States (Druesne-Peccolo et al., 2009). The authors suggested, based on their review of the clinical literature, that alcohol can induce the development of cancer in the oral cavity, pharynx, liver, stomach, colon, rectum, breast, and esophagus (Brunton et al., 2008; Druesne-Peccolo et al., 2009). The observed relationship between alcohol ingestion and esophageal cancer is especially important because the long-term survival rate for patients with this form of cancer is quite low (Khushalani, 2008). The combination of cigarette smoking and heavy alcohol use is especially dangerous. Chronic drinkers experience almost a sixfold increase in the risk of developing cancer of the mouth or pharynx (Pagano et al., 2005). Whereas cigarette smoking is associated with a sevenfold increase in such cancers, chronic drinkers who also smoke cigarettes have a *38-fold higher risk* of cancer of the mouth or pharynx than do nonsmokers/nondrinkers (Pagano et al., 2005). On a positive note, the individual's risk of developing cancer of the mouth or throat is reduced after 5 years of abstinence, and at the end of 20 years of abstinence is virtually the same as that of a person who never had an AUD (Rehm, Patra, & Popova, 2007).

The Effects of Chronic Alcohol Use on the Liver

The liver is a unique organ, which is sometimes classified as a part of the digestive system and sometimes as an organ apart from the digestive tract. Because of its role in protecting us from the effects of many environmental toxins, it is classified as a separate organ in this text, in spite of the fact that it is most heavily involved in the process of alcohol biotransformation/elimination. This may be why the liver is the organ most heavily damaged by chronic alcohol use (Sadock & Sadock, 2007). The chronic use of alcohol is the most common cause of liver disease in the United States (D. B. Hill & Kugelmas, 1998). One possible mechanism for alcohol-induced liver damage is by its ability to interfere with the production of the enzyme glutathione. The liver produces this enzyme to protect itself from various toxins. It also is involved with the inflammatory response when tissues are damaged. Heavy drinkers demonstrate an 80% lower glutathione level when compared with nondrinkers, suggesting that this is one mechanism by which alcohol (a toxin) is able to damage the liver (Kershaw & Guidot, 2008).

---

[8]There are a number of causes for this condition, but the chronic use of alcohol is one of the most significant.

Between 80 and 90% of heavy drinkers will develop an early manifestation of alcohol-related liver disease known as a "fatty liver."[9] Individuals who have this condition have a liver that is enlarged and does not function normally (Bankole & Ait-Daoud, 2005). The fatty liver can develop after just a few days of heavy drinking (Khan, Morrow, & McCarron, 2009). Although there are few physical manifestations of this disorder that the patient might detect, blood tests would reveal abnormalities in the drinker's liver enzymes that would suggest liver damage (Schuckit, 2006a). Fortunately, in its early stages this condition will usually reverse itself with abstinence from alcohol (Khan et al., 2009). However, patients with active liver steatosis are at risk for premature death.

Persistent heavy drinkers who manifest liver steatosis and who continue to drink can experience a more severe form of liver damage: *alcoholic hepatitis*. This is a condition that can manifest as abdominal pain, the buildup of various toxins in the blood, and blood chemistry changes (Schuckit, 2006a; D. B. Hill & Kugelmas, 1998). Between 20 and 65% of patients who develop alcohol-induced hepatitis suffer a premature death (Bondesson & Sapperston, 1996). The usual patient with alcohol-induced hepatitis will develop this condition after about 15–20 years of heavy drinking, although there are cases on record where alcohol-related hepatitis has developed more rapidly in some drinkers. Such patients are poor surgical risks because of their hepatitis, increasing the odds that they will not survive surgery if the surgeon was unaware of the individual's drinking history.

Of those individuals who develop alcohol-induced hepatitis, 10–35%[10] go on to develop a condition known as *cirrhosis* of the liver (Bankole & Ait-Daoud, 2005; Karsan, Rojter, & Saab, 2004; Nace, 2005a, 2005b). In cirrhosis, individual liver cells die and are replaced by scar tissue. Although structurally important for helping the liver maintain its shape, scar tissue is nonfunctional. If the level of liver damage is great enough, the body becomes unable to cleanse itself and will eventually die. A physical examination of a patient with hepatitis will reveal a hard, nodular liver, an enlarged spleen, surface blood vessel changes producing "spider" angiomas, tremor, confusion, blood chemistry changes, and in males possible testicular atrophy (Nace, 2005a, 2005b).

Although it would seem at first glance that alcoholic hepatitis would predate the development of cirrhosis, some heavy drinkers appear to manifest cirrhosis without previous signs of hepatitis ("Alcohol and the Liver," 1993). Alcohol-induced cirrhosis has been documented in people who have consumed as little as two to four standard drinks a day for just 10 years (Karsan et al., 2004), which would seem to be somewhat counterintuitive in that one would expect that it would take a longer period of heavy drinking to cause this level of damage to the liver.

It has been suggested that the formation of what are known as *free radicals*[11] generated during the process of alcohol biotransformation might contribute to the death of individual liver cells, initiating the development of liver cirrhosis (Brust, 2004; K. Walsh & Alexander, 2000). The liver produces an enzyme, glutathione, to protect itself from free radicals. However, it is thought that heavy drinkers do not produce sufficient glutathione to protect their livers, leading to eventual liver damage. Surprisingly, there is evidence that coffee consumption might reduce the individual's risk for developing alcohol-related cirrhosis (Klatsky, Morton, Udaltsova, & Friedman, 2006). The authors suggested that the individual's risk of developing cirrhosis was reduced by 22% for each cup of coffee consumed in a day, although the exact mechanism for this effect is still not clear at this time.

At one point, it was thought that malnutrition was a factor in the development of alcohol-induced liver disease. However, subsequent research has failed to support that hypothesis. Scientists have discovered, however, that alcohol-dependent people are at increased risk of contracting the hepatitis C virus.[12] This, in turn, increases the drinker's risk for the eventual development of cirrhosis and exacerbates the level of damage to the liver. Why alcohol-dependent people would be at increased risk for hepatitis C infection remains a mystery. There is a strong relationship between alcohol-induced cirrhosis and the development of liver cancer (Bagnardi, Blangiardo, La Vecchia, & Corrao, 2001; Schuckit, 2006a). However, hepatitis C is also associated with an increased risk of liver cancer, and it is currently not clear whether or not this accounts

---

[9]Also known as liver *steatosis,* which is a condition in which more than 5% of the liver is made up of fat cells (Griffith & Schenker, 2006).

[10]Khan et al. (2009) reported that up to 70% of patients who develop alcohol-related hepatitis go on to develop cirrhosis of the liver. It is not known why these different authors provided such disparate estimates.

---

[11]See Glossary.

[12]Discussed in Chapter 36.

for the association between heavy drinking and the development of liver cancer.

Another problem associated with alcohol-induced cirrhosis is sodium and water retention, a problem that indirectly affects cardiac function (Nace, 2005b; Schuckit, 2006a). Furthermore, as the liver becomes enlarged in response to inflammation and cellular damage, it compresses the blood vessels that pass through it. This causes the blood and plasma to build up pressure. In turn, this places additional stress on the drinker's heart and veins returning to the heart from the body, a condition known as *portal hypertension.* The higher pressure levels can cause blood vessels in the esophagus to swell and become weak, forming *esophageal varicies,*[13] which may rupture with little warning. Ruptured esophageal varicies are a medical emergency, with a 20–30% death rate even with the best of medical care (Hegab & Luketic, 2001). Between 50 and 60% of those who survive the initial episode of a bleeding esophageal varix will develop a second episode, which will carry with it an additional 20–30% death rate with the result being that ultimately 60% of patients with esophageal varicies will die from this condition (Giacchino & Houdek, 1998).

Scientists once thought that chronic alcohol use could reduce stomach's mucosal barrier, exposing it to its own digestive juices (Fleming et al., 2006). This was originally attributed to habitual alcohol abuse, but questions have recently been raised as to the possible role of the *Helicobacter pylori* strain of bacteria, known to cause stomach ulcers in nondrinkers. It is not clear at this time whether the condition known as alcohol-induced *gastritis* is indeed caused by high levels of alcohol ingestion, as originally thought, infection of the stomach lining by the *H. pylori* strain of bacteria, or some combination of these two factors. It is known that the ingestion of alcohol-containing beverages that have a 40% or higher concentration of alcohol[14] have a direct toxic effect on the gastric mucosa and can interfere with the normal recovery process from *H. pylori* bacterial infection (Brunton et al., 2008).

If the ulcers should form over a major blood vessel, it may rupture, causing bleeding into the stomach. This is a "bleeding" ulcer, which in extreme cases will require the surgical resection of the stomach. Even consuming just three or more standard drinks per day increases the individual's chance of a gastrointestinal "bleed" by 300%.

Habitual drinking also contributes to the development of vitamin malabsorption syndromes, leaving the drinker at risk for the development of such infections as tuberculosis (TB).[15] In reality, the term *vitamin malabsorption syndrome* is something of a misnomer, because habitual drinkers are known to have trouble absorbing not only vitamins such as vitamin A, vitamin D, and the B family of vitamins, but also minerals such as calcium, sodium, phosphorus, and magnesium. During the process of biotransformation, alcohol produces "empty" calories from the glucose that is one of the end products of the alcohol biotransformation process. The infusion of glucose into the drinker's circulation will prevent her from feeling hungry, but it will not provide her with the necessary nutrients necessary for healthy living. Some heavy drinkers obtain up to 50% of their daily caloric requirements from the biotransformation of ingested alcohol rather than from more appropriate foods, contributing to a state of malnutrition. This, in turn, can contribute to a reduction in the effectiveness of the body's immune system. The effects of the alcohol-induced malnutrition might be seen in the fact that there is a 300–700% increase in risk of death from pneumonia for heavy drinkers as compared to nondrinkers (Schirmer, Wiedermann, & Konwalinka, 2000).

The heavy use of alcohol has been observed to alter the normal pattern of bacterial growth in the mouth, contributing to the condition known as *glossitis*[16] and to a possible stricture of the esophagus known as Barrett's esophagus (Fleming et al., 2006). This latter condition develops after the esophageal tissues have repeatedly been exposed to digestive juices during gastric reflux, as well as a possible traumatic rupture of the esophagus (Brunton et al., 2008). These conditions further contribute to the drinker's failure to ingest an adequate diet, adding to possible alcohol-related dietary deficiencies. Finally, the chronic use of alcohol has also been identified as a contributing factor for a number of metabolic disorders, including the development of type 2 diabetes[17] (Wannamethee, Camargo, Manson, Willett, & Rimm, 2003). A significant percentage of drinkers with liver disease are either glucose intolerant or diabetic, conditions that reflect alcohol-related interference with the body's normal glucose control mechanisms. Schuckit (2006b, 2008a) suggested

---

[13]The singular is an esophageal *varix.*

[14]Which is to say 80 proof or higher.

[15]Discussed in Chapter 36.

[16]See Glossary.

[17]Once referred to as "adult-onset" or "non-insulin-dependent" diabetes.

that the diagnosis of true diabetes, as opposed to an alcohol-related metabolic dysfunction, would require 2–4 weeks of abstinence on the part of the drinker.

Effects of Chronic Alcohol Use on the Cardiopulmonary System

Clinical researchers have long been aware of what has come to be called the "French Paradox," which is a phenomenon in which the French, in spite of a diet rich in foods that are assumed to contribute to cardiovascular disease, actually have a lower incidence of such disorders (I. J. Goldberg, 2003). The *moderate* use of alcohol, defined as the consumption of no more than two standard drinks per day for a man and half that for a woman, has been found to bring about a 10–40% reduction in the drinker's risk of developing coronary heart disease (CHD) (Fleming et al., 2006; Klatsky, 2003).

This cardioprotective effect appears to be moderated by the individual's genetic heritage, lifestyle, and current health status with some drinkers obtaining more of a protective effect than others (Britton, Marmot & Shipley, 2008; L. M. Hines et al., 2001).[18] This cardioprotective effect is mainly seen in healthy people who engage in a healthy lifestyle (Britton et al., 2008; Karlamangla et al., 2009). Furthermore, this cardioprotective effect is achieved at a price, as there is a dose-dependent relationship between alcohol consumption and loss of brain volume that is seen even with just one to two drinks a day (Paula et al., 2008). This effect is stronger in women than in men, but does affect both women and men, according to the authors.

It has been suggested that the moderate use of alcohol is cardioprotective because of its ability to function as an anticoagulant and reduce fibrinogen levels (Klatsky, 2003). By inhibiting the ability of the blood to form clots, it is estimated that moderate alcohol use may lower an individual's risk of a heart attack by 30–40% (Stoschitzky, 2000). The moderate use of alcohol also appears to increase HDL levels of cholesterol (the "good" cholesterol) in the blood, making it more difficult for atherosclerotic plaque to build up on the walls of the drinker's arteries (A. D. O'Connor, Rusyniak, & Bruno, 2005). In spite of these apparent benefits from moderate drinking, physicians still hesitate to recommend that nondrinkers turn to alcohol as a way of reducing

their cardiovascular risk. Furthermore, the cardiovascular benefits may very well be offset by increased risk of damage to the central nervous system, especially if the drinker should engage in heavy, as opposed to moderate, alcohol use.

Heavy alcohol use will increase the individual's risk of CHD by as much as 600% (Schuckit, 2006a). Heavy alcohol use can cause anemia and acts as an anticoagulant (Brust, 2004). It can also exacerbate hypertension and induces an increased risk of stroke (C. M. Chen, Smith, Harbord, & Lewis, 2008; A. D. O'Connor et al., 2005). However, the risk of stroke is not equal for both sexes. Ikehara et al. (2008) examined the health histories of 34,776 men and 48,906 women in Japan and found that heavy alcohol use was associated with an increased risk of death from strokes for men, but not for women, with heavy drinkers of either sex sharing an increased risk for coronary artery heart disease. This might reflect alcohol's ability to increase the blood levels of angiotensin II, a compound that, among other things, causes the blood vessels to constrict. This forces the heart to expend extra energy in an effort to pump the blood through the constricted blood vessels, contributing to the individual's possible hypertension (Kershaw & Guidot, 2008). Thus where light to moderate drinkers have a 200% higher risk of stroke, heavy drinkers are thought to have a 300% chance of a stroke (Ordorica & Nace, 1998). These statistics suggest that an individuals' increased risk of a stroke might outweigh any benefit they might gain from using alcohol to reduce cardiovascular risk.

It has been proven that alcohol is *cardiotoxic*. It inhibits the synthesis of proteins in the muscles, especially the myobibrillar protein necessary for normal cardiac muscle function (Ponnappa & Rubin, 2000). So toxic is chronic alcohol use on the drinker's body that up to a quarter of chronic drinkers will develop early-onset cardiovascular disease (Schuckit, 2006a). Clinical *cardiomyopathy* is thought to be present in 25–40% of chronic drinkers, although it is thought that virtually all chronic drinkers will demonstrate some degree of alcohol-induced muscle damage on special tests (Figueredo, 1997; Lee & Regan, 2002). The ingestion of six cans of beer per day, or a pint of whiskey per day may induce permanent damage to the heart muscle tissue, causing a general weakening of the heart muscle (A. D. O'Connor et al., 2005; Schuckit, 2005, 2006a). Statistically, 40–50% of all cases of cardiomyopathy in the United States are alcohol related (Wadland & Ferenchick, 2004; Zakhari, 1997). Between 40 and 80% of those individuals with alcohol-induced

---

[18]Although alcohol use advocates point to this fact as a reason why people should drink alcohol in moderation, they overlook the fact that the French, as a whole, have a higher incidence of alcohol-related liver disease (Walton, 2002).

cardiomyopathy will die within 4 years of being diagnosed with this disorder if they continue to drink (Brust, 2004; Figueredo, 1997; Stoschitzky, 2000).

Although many drinkers take comfort in the fact that they drink to excess only on occasion, even binge drinking is not without its dangers. Alcohol binges have been implicated as a cause of a condition known as the *holiday heart syndrome* (Bankole & Ait-Daoud, 2005; Klatsky, 2003; Raghaven, Decker, & Meloy, 2005). The sudden influx of a large amount of alcohol interferes with the normal flow of electrical impulses within the heart, causing an arrhythmia known as atrial fibrillation, which is potentially fatal. It has been suggested that 15–30% of all new cases of atrial fibrillation have developed this condition as a result of their alcohol binge (A. D. O'Connor et al., 2005). It has also been discovered that binge drinking more than triples the drinker's risk of a fatal hemorrhagic stroke (Sull, Sang-Wook, Nam, & Ohrr, 2009). Thus even limited periods of alcohol abuse can be potentially harmful to the drinker.

The Effects of Chronic Alcohol Use on the Central Nervous System (CNS)

Although it is often assumed that the liver would be the first organ to be damaged by the chronic use of alcohol, this is not always true. The exact mechanism(s) by which heavy alcohol abuse causes damage to the CNS is not known at this time but may reflect such factors as the amount of alcohol consumed over the life span, the individual's pattern of alcohol ingestion, the frequency and intensity of alcohol withdrawal episodes, and the individual's genetic heritage (M. J. Rosenbloom & Pefferbaum, 2008).

Even heavy, acute alcohol use can induce neurological dysfunction. Research has demonstrated evidence of alcohol-induced memory deficits after as little as one drink. Fortunately, the drinker normally needs to consume more than five standard drinks in an hour's time before alcohol is able to significantly impair the process of memory formation, leaving gaps in the drinker's memory known as *blackouts*. The alcohol-induced blackout develops only after a blood alcohol level of 0.14 to 0.20 is achieved. In an alcohol-induced blackout, the individual may appear conscious to bystanders, answer questions, and possibly carry on a coherent conversation and carry out many complex tasks, but later is unable to recall part or all of the period of intoxication. The alcohol-induced blackout is a form of anterograde amnesia induced by alcohol's ability to

disrupt the action of the neurotransmitters gamma-amiobutyric acid (GABA) and *N*-methyl-d-aspartate (NMDA) (E. C. Nelson et al., 2004). Approximately two-thirds of alcohol-dependent people will report having experienced at least one alcohol-induced blackout, which can last for hours or even days (Schuckit, 2008a). This might reflect the fact that the alcoholics' vulnerability to alcohol-related blackouts is influenced by their genetic heritage, with the result being that some individuals are more vulnerable to developing this condition than others (E. C. Nelson et al., 2004).

As a group, long-term alcohol abusers have been found to demonstrate evidence of impaired neurological testing up to 4 weeks after their last drink, and in 10% of the cases the level of neuropsychological impairment is found to be severe (Rourke & Grant, 2009). This impairment in neuropsychological test function appears to reflect the physical damage to the brain found during autopsies or through noninvasive imaging studies such as a computerized tomography (CT) scan or magnetic resonance imaging (MRI) studies. Researchers have found, for example, that up to 50–70% of habitual drinkers demonstrate enlarged ventricles (Gilpin & Kolb, 2008; M. J. Rosenbloom & Pefferbaum, 2008; Schuckit, 2006a, 2006b). With abstinence many heavy drinkers show evidence of subsequent neural growth on later neuroimaging studies, suggesting that some degree of recovery from alcohol-related neurological damage is possible with long-term abstinence (Schuckit, 2005, 2006). However, it is not clear whether the former drinker can return to normal neurological functioning or not at this time.

Habitual drinkers demonstrate evidence of damage to the prefrontal cortex[19] region of the brain, which is involved in the process of working memory (Brunton et al., 2008; Rourke & Grant, 2009). Neuropsychological testing confirms the presence of prefrontal cortex damage in between one-half and two-thirds of chronic drinkers (Zahr & Sullivan, 2008). Another region of the brain that seems vulnerable to alcohol-induced damage is the *cerebellum*,[20] and about 1% of chronic drinkers develop a condition known as *cerebellar atrophy*,[21] which is seen in approximately 50% of heavy drinkers (Schuckit, 2008a; Tomb, 2008). Symptoms of this condition include a characteristic psychomotor dysfunction, gait disturbance, and problems coordinating muscle movements (T. Berger, 2000; Oehmichen,

---

[19]See Glossary.

[20]See Glossary.

[21]See Glossary.

Auer, & Konig, 2005; Schuckit, 2009). Another CNS complication seen in the persistent alcohol abuser is known as *vitamin deficiency amblyopia*. Symptoms of this condition include blurred vision, a loss of visual perception in the center of the visual field,[22] and in extreme cases, atrophy of the optic nerve, all of which may become permanent in spite of the most aggressive medical care (Brust, 2004).

These findings suggest that alcohol is quite neurotoxic. This neurological damage has been compared with that seen in other forms of neurodegenerative disease, and is clearly seen in MRI studies of heavy drinkers. Such neurodegeneration is observed in both chronic and heavy binge drinkers (Crews, 2008). Unfortunately, although suggestive, these studies cannot determine the exact relationship between habitual alcohol use and neurological damage, because researchers lack predrinking neuropsychological test data or radiographic imaging studies from large numbers of habitual drinkers in order to compare pre- and postdrinking test results (Crews, 2008).

Alcoholism is also a known cause of a form of dementia,[23] although researchers disagree as to the causal mechanism for this condition. One theory holds that alcohol-induced dementia is the direct result of alcohol's toxic effects on the brain. A second theory is that alcohol-induced vitamin deficiencies are the direct causal mechanism (Berent & Albert, 2005; Filley, 2004). A third theory is that alcohol-induced liver damage results in the brain being chronically exposed to toxins normally filtered from the blood, resulting in neuronal loss. Pfefferbaum, Rosenbloom, Serventi, and Sullivan (2004) suggested that all three of these factors contributed to alcohol-induced neurological damage.

A limited degree of cognitive function recovery is possible for *some* habitual drinkers who stop drinking, however maximum recovery might take months (Filley, 2004; Gilpin & Kolb, 2008) to years (Rourke & Grant, 2009) of abstinence. However, the degree to which a given individual might recover from such neurological trauma is not known at this time, and many heavy drinkers demonstrate only a modest level of cognitive improvement after prolonged periods of abstinence and aggressive nutritional therapy (Mancall, 2008; Schuckit, 2006a). In many cases, the drinker does not recover from the long-term effects of their drinking and must be institutionalized. It has been estimated that 15–30% of all nursing home patients are there

because of permanent alcohol-induced brain damage, which places a further strain on the health care system (Schuckit, 2006a). Still, it is possible for some persistent drinkers to recover at least some of the cognitive functions lost to heavy alcohol use. After just 2 months of abstinence, scientists have measured a 1.85% increase in brain volume[24] and a 20% improvement in communications efficiency in some heavy drinkers (Bartsch et al., 2007). Unfortunately if the drinker should return to the use of alcohol, this recovery in brain function will be lost and the progression of alcohol-induced brain damage will continue.

Wernicke-Korsakoff's Disease[25]

In 1881, the physician Carl Wernicke first described a neurological disorder seen in chronic drinkers that has since been called *Wernicke's encephalopathy* (Day, Bentham, Callagham, Kuruvilla, & George, 2004). According to Mattingley and Groon (2008), patients with Wernicke's encephalopathy demonstrated a distinctive triad of symptoms: (a) ataxia, (b) mental-status changes, and (c) nystagmus or ocular changes (Day et al., 2004; Schuckit, 2006a). Now it is known that only 10% of patients with Wernicke's disease demonstrate all three of these symptoms, and that 19% of patients do not demonstrate *any* of these traditionally accepted symptoms, possibly contributing to the underdiagnosis of this disorder while the drinker is still alive (Kinsella & Riley, 2007; Mattingley & Groon, 2008). In some patients with Wernicke's disease, the only symptoms are irritability and fatigue, or hyperthermia, chronic dyskinesias, and decreased muscle tone in the later stages of this disorder (Mancall, 2008; Mattingley & Groon, 2008; Tse & Koller, 2004).

It must be noted that there are causes of Wernicke's disorder other than chronic alcoholism. Those who suffer from Crohn's disease, anorexia nervosa, and AIDS, as well as cancer chemotherapy patients and patients who had gastric bypass surgery are also at risk for this disorder (Kinsella & Riley, 2007; Mattingley & Groon, 2008). However, a common cause is persistent heavy alcohol abuse. The causal mechanism for alcohol-induced Wernicke's disease is thought to be the thiamine[26] depletion from the body. The body's thiamine reserves are limited and must constantly be replaced

---

[22]A condition known as *central scotomata*.

[23]Sometimes called *encephalopathy*.

[24]It is not known whether this increase in brain volume reflects neurogenesis, the development of new dendritic connections between existing neurons, or a combination of these two factors.

[25]Called *alcohol-induced persisting amnestic disorder* in some texts.

[26]See Glossary.

through the individual's dietary intake (Kinsella & Riley, 2007). Poor diet, vitamin malabsorption syndrome, and tendency to rely on alcohol-based calories rather than to ingest a normal diet all interfere with the individual's ability to maintain adequate thiamine levels. The drinker's genetic heritage has also been suggested as a factor that might influence the development of thiamine depletion (Mancall, 2008). Vitamin depletion is quite rapid and can be detected after just 7–8 weeks of daily heavy alcohol use, although between 30 and 80% of these individuals will not demonstrate signs of Wernicke's disease (Harper & Matsumoto, 2005; Ropper & Brown, 2005).[27]

The signs of Wernicke's encephalopathy begin to express themselves in the first few hours or days after the heavy drinker discontinues the use of alcohol (Fernandez, Eisenschenk, & Okun, 2010; Rourke & Grant, 2009). It is estimated that 20% of patients with untreated or inadequately treated Wernicke's encephalopathy will die, usually of cardiovascular collapse (Mattingley & Groon, 2008). It is thus imperative that the body's thiamine stores be built up as rapidly as possible. So important is the process of thiamine replacement that Ropper and Brown (2005) recommended *automatic* intramuscular injections of thiamine, even if the physician only *suspects* the possibility that the patient has Wernicke's encephalopathy. To limit the amount of neurological damage induced by thiamine depletion, the standard treatment protocol calls for intramuscular injections of 100 mg of thiamine for 3 days, followed by oral supplements of thiamine. However, Mattingley and Groon (2008) suggested that the standard protocol was too conservative and recommended injected doses of 500 mg of thiamine three times daily, for a minimum of 3 days, with concurrent blood tests to determine the drinker's magnesium level once daily.

In the early 1900s, before aggressive thiamine replacement therapies were instituted, up to 80% of those patients who developed Wernicke's encephalopathy developed *Korsakoff's syndrome* (Day et al., 2003; Rourke & Grant, 2009). These conditions were originally viewed as separate disorders, although it is now recognized that Wernicke's disease reflects the acute stage whereas Korsakoff's syndrome is the end stage of thiamine depletion–induced brain damage. These disorders are often referred to as Wernicke-Korsakoff's disease or Wernicke-Korsakoff's syndrome. Even with the most aggressive of thiamine replacement therapies

available, 1 in 500 heavy drinkers develops Wernicke-Korsakoff's disease (Schuckit, 2008a).

It was long thought that one of the characteristic symptoms of Korsakoff's syndrome was the inability of the individual to acquire new information, or anterograde amnesia. Some degree of retrograde amnesia is also present in many cases, although long-term memory is relatively resistant to alcohol-induced memory loss (Lezak, Hannay, & Fischer, 2004; Mancall, 2008). Individuals will be able to recall events from their distant past, although with some degree of confusion, but will be unable to retain new information (Mancall, 2008). Many alcohol-dependent patients with alcohol-induced memory loss and organic brain damage show a marked indifference to their plight. When faced with evidence of a memory loss, they have been known to provide the assessor with "memories" of a past that never took place, a process known as *confabulation*[28] (Mancall, 2008; Ropper & Brown, 2005). In the past, confabulation was viewed as one of the diagnostic criteria for patients with Korsakoff's disorder. Mankcall (2008) suggested that confabulation reflects *suggestibility* by the patient: When the medical staff ask patients a question(s) in a manner that they interpret as requiring an answer, they manufacture one to please the inquirer. Although dramatic, it should be noted that not every patient with Wernicke-Korsakoff's will confabulate (Brust, 2004; Ropper & Samuels, 2009), and when present it is usually seen in the earlier stages of Wernicke-Korsakoff's disease (Rourke & Grant, 2009).

In extreme cases of Wernicke-Korsakoff's, the patient will appear to be almost "frozen" in time. The neurologist Oliver Sacks (1970) offered the example of a man who was unable to recall anything that had transpired after the late 1940s. If asked, the patient would answer the question as if he were still living in the late 1940s, and he was unable to assimilate information from after that point. The author of this text has encountered several such patients. When interviewed in the 1980s, they expressed surprise upon being told that astronauts have visited the moon, that President John F. Kennedy was assassinated, and so on. These are extreme examples of this process, and most patients with alcohol-induced amnesia will be able to remember some of the past while being unable to recall other events from their past.

There is an emerging body of research data suggesting that the chronic use of alcohol does not directly destroy neurons so much as induce a *disconnection*

---

[27]Another name for Wernicke's encephalopathy that is often used in clinical literature.

[28]See Glossary.

syndrome in which the neural connections between neurons are destroyed (Harper & Matsumoto, 2005). Because neurons require regular stimulation, it is thought that the isolated neurons begin to wither and eventually die, accounting for the neural loss observed in the brains of chronic alcohol use. However, these theories remain unproven. It is known that at least 10% of those individuals who develop Wernicke-Korsakoff's will be left with a permanent memory impairment in spite of the most aggressive of vitamin replacement therapies, although with abstinence some degree of recovery of lost cognitive function is possible with long-term abstinence from alcohol use (Fernandez et al., 2010; Rourke & Grant, 2009).

The persistent heavy use of alcohol has also been identified as a risk factor for the development of a movement disorder known as *tardive dyskinesia* (TD) (Lopez & Jeste, 1997). TD is a common complication seen in patients who were treated with neuroleptic drugs for the control of psychotic disorders for extended periods of time, but is occasionally found in chronic drinkers who have never been exposed to neuroleptic agents (Lopez & Jeste, 1997). The causal mechanism for this neurological condition as a result of chronic drinking is not known at this time, but when it does develop in a chronic drinker, it is usually only after 10–20 years of heavy alcohol consumption (Lopez & Jeste, 1997).

Alcohol's Effects on the Sleep Cycle

There is still a great deal to be discovered about how alcohol impacts on the normal sleep cycle, but it is known that the chronic use of alcohol interferes with the normal sleep cycle (Conroy, Arnedt, & Brower, 2008; Karam-Hage, 2004). Chronic drinkers report that they require more time to fall asleep and that their sleep is both less sound and less restful than that of nondrinkers the same age (Karam-Hage, 2004). Approximately 60% of chronic drinkers report symptoms of insomnia (Brower, Aldrich, Robinson, Zucker, & Greden, 2001; Conroy et al., 2008). This may reflect alcohol's ability, when used on a chronic basis, to suppress the production of melatonin in the brain, which has the potential result of interfering with the normal sleep/wake cycle (Karem-Hage, 2004). However, a second hypothesis was offered by Milne (2007), who suggested that chronic drinkers tend to overestimate the amount of time necessary for them to fall asleep.[29]

Unfortunately, physicians will often treat patients who complain about sleep problems but do not reveal to their doctor that they have an AUD. There is a double danger in this: First, extended periods of insomnia can serve as a relapse trigger for the person in the early stages of abstinence (Brower et al., 2001). Second, most of the current pharmaceutical agents used to treat insomnia have a high abuse potential (Conroy et al., 2008). Karam-Hage (2004) suggested that gabapentin (sold under the brand name Neurontin) is quite useful as a hypnotic agent in alcohol-dependent people, and it lacks the abuse potential found in other more traditional hypnotics.

Alcohol use suppresses rapid eye movement (REM) sleep, and this effect is most pronounced in the chronic drinker (Hobson, 2005; Schuckit, 2008a). It has been demonstrated that we need to sleep and to dream, although scientists are still not sure why this is necessary. About 85% of our dream experiences take place during REM sleep. By suppressing the individuals' REM sleep cycles, the chronic use of alcohol will interfere with their cognitive function during their waking hours. Furthermore, if REM sleep is suppressed by extended periods of alcohol abuse, individuals will spend more time in the REM sleep stage when they finally do stop drinking. This phenomenon is known as *REM rebound.* During REM rebound, the individual will experience longer, more intense REM dreams, which are often difficult for the newly abstinent drinker to separate from reality (Ropper & Brown, 2005). Some of these dreams might be so intense and so frightening for the dreamer that they can serve as a relapse trigger for the former drinker, who may be tempted to return to the use of alcohol to "get a good night's sleep again." REM rebound has been found to last for up to 6 months after the individual's last drink (Brower et al., 2001; Schuckit & Tapert, 2004). Furthermore, scientists have documented sleep disturbances for up to 1–2 *years* after the individual's last alcohol use (Brower et al., 2001; Karam-Hage, 2004).

Although alcohol is a known neurotoxin, there is evidence that at some doses it might suppress some of the involuntary movements of Huntington's disease (Lopez & Jeste, 1997). Although this is not to suggest that alcohol is an accepted treatment for this disorder, it might account for the finding that patients with Huntington's disease tend to abuse alcohol more often than close relatives who do not have this condition (Lopez & Jeste, 1997).

There is also evidence suggesting that chronic alcohol use can contribute to long-term psychomotor

---

[29]See "Sleep latency" in Glossary.

coordination problems (DeWilde, Dom, Hulstjn, & Sabbe, 2007). The authors found that recently detoxified alcohol-dependent people required longer to complete psychomotor tasks than what would normally be expected. There was some degree of improvement in the speed of psychomotor responses as the individual abstained from alcohol for longer and longer periods of time, but even people who had been abstinent from alcohol for extended periods of time still required longer periods of time to complete assigned tasks than were required by their nondrinking peers.

The Effects of Habitual Alcohol Use on the Peripheral Nervous System

The human nervous system is usually viewed as two interconnected systems: the central nervous system (CNS) and the peripheral nervous system (PNS). Unfortunately, alcohol-induced avitaminosis involves both subunits of the nervous system. One of the most common manifestations of alcohol-induced effects on the nervous system is known as *peripheral neuropathy*. This condition develops in 15% of chronic drinkers (Schuckit, 2005, 2008a; Tomb, 2008). Symptoms of peripheral neuropathy include feelings of weakness, pain, and a burning sensation in the affected region of the body at the time of onset, followed by a loss of sensation in the peripheral regions of the body (Ropper & Brown, 2005).

The causal mechanism for alcohol-induced peripheral neuropathies are not known as this time. The individual's genetic predisposition appears to be one factor that influences the development of peripheral neuropathies. Other possible factors that appear to influence the development of alcohol-related peripheral neuropathies include the effects of chronic alcohol exposure and possibly alcohol-related dietary deficiencies. Currently, it is thought that alcohol's ability to deplete the body of the B family of vitamins is a major factor in the development of alcohol-induced peripheral neuropathies (J. D. Levin, 2002; Tomb, 2008).

The Effects of Alcohol Use Disorders on the Drinker's Emotions

Chronic drinkers are subject to a wide range of psychiatric problems including depression, which is seen in approximately 40% of alcoholics (Schuckit, 2008a). Another problem often encountered in chronic drinkers is anxiety, which is seen in 10–30% of alcoholics (Schuckit, 2008a). This anxiety might take the form of a generalized anxiety disorder or panic attacks

(Schuckit, 2005, 2006). Some of these symptoms are secondary to the process of alcohol withdrawal, as evidenced by the fact that up to 80% of patients going through alcohol withdrawal report symptoms of anxiety (Schuckit, 2005, 2006). However, alcohol-induced anxiety is also common, and some drinkers turn to either further alcohol use or anxiolytic[30] medications to help control what is perceived as a subjective sense of anxiety. Newly abstinent patients who report anxiety symptoms may require as long as 2 weeks for complete sobriety before their need for antianxiety medications can be adequately assessed.

It has been discovered that 10–20% of patients with an anxiety disorder will also admit to an AUD (Cox & Taylor, 1999). Conversely, 10–40% of patients in treatment for an AUD will report having an anxiety disorder of some kind (Schuckit, 2008b). The diagnostic dilemma for the clinician is complicated by the fact that withdrawal-related symptoms are virtually the same as those experienced by patients having anxiety attacks or generalized anxiety disorder (GAD) (Schuckit, 2005). This determination is further complicated by the fact that chronic alcohol users might experience feelings of anxiety for months after their last drink (Schuckit, 2005, 2006, 2008a). Only a careful diagnostic history will reveal whether patients' anxiety symptoms predated, or followed, the development of their AUD.

As will be discussed later in this chapter, one of the subjective experiences of the alcohol withdrawal process is a sense of anxiety or dread. Unfortunately, it is not uncommon for alcohol-dependent people to discuss their "anxiety" symptoms with a general physician without revealing their AUD. Physicians, believing they are treating the patient's apparent anxiety, will often prescribe a benzodiazepine[31] for anxiety control. As will be discussed in Chapter 10, the benzodiazepine molecule binds at the same chloride channel in the neuron as does alcohol, both enhancing the effects of alcohol and providing a pharmaceutical replacement for alcohol. So similar are the two compounds that benzodiazepines have been called alcohol in pill form (Longo, 2005), or "freeze dried alcohol" (McGuinness & Fogger, 2006, p. 25).

There is a strong relationship between alcoholism and the development of depression. The AUD appears to precede the development of a major depression in most cases, it would appear, strongly suggesting that in most

---

[30]See Glossary.

[31]Discussed in Chapter 10.

cases the individual's alcohol abuse induced the depression through an unknown mechanism (Fergusson, Boden, & Horwood, 2009). These findings are consistent with those of Hasin and Grant (2002), who examined the histories of 6,050 recovering heavy drinkers, and found that former drinkers had a fourfold increased incidence of depression as compared to nondrinkers the same age.

Depression has a negative impact on the individual's ability to benefit from alcohol rehabilitation programs and might contribute to higher dropout rates for those who do enter treatment (Charney, 2004). Unfortunately, the differentiation between alcohol-induced depression and a primary depressive disorder can be quite difficult, although alcohol-induced depression will usually moderate after 2–5 weeks of abstinence. Although there is some controversy over whether antidepressant medications should be used because of this fact, Charney (2004) recommended that every case of depression be aggressively treated as soon as it is identified.

Unfortunately, there is a strong relationship between suicide and AUDs. At least one-third of those people who end their lives are thought to have an alcohol use disorder (Connor et al., 2006). Because chronic drinkers are at risk for the development of depression, and depression is associated with an increased risk for suicide, it is logical to assume that as a group chronic drinkers are also at high risk for suicide. Indeed, research has suggested that suicide is 58–85 times as likely to take place in alcohol-dependent people as in those who are not alcohol dependent (Frierson, Melikian, & Wadman, 2002). Suicide is quite rare in the general population, but it has been estimated that the lifetime risk of suicide for chronic drinkers is as high as 5% (Preuss et al., 2003) to 7% (Connor, Li, Meldrum, Duberstein & Conwell, 2003) to possibly as high as 18% (Bongar, 1997; Preuss & Wong, 2000). Such alcohol-related suicides are more likely to occur in late middle adulthood, when the effects of the drinker's extended alcohol abuse begin to manifest as physical organ damage (Nisbet, 2000).

The team of Preuss et al. (2003) followed a cohort of 1237 alcohol-dependent people for 5 years and discovered that during this period of time that subjects were more than twice as likely to end their lives in suicide as were nonalcoholic individuals. The team of Dumais et al. (2005) concluded that alcohol's disinhibiting effect, combined with the impulsiveness demonstrated by many of those with a personality disorder, combined with the presence of a major depression, were all significant risk factors for suicide in male heavy drinkers. The topic of suicide, suicide prediction and

intervention, are far too complicated to discuss in detail in this text, as entire books have been devoted to this subject.

One causal mechanism through which chronic alcohol use might contribute to the increased risk of depression in chronic drinkers (with the concurrent risk of suicide in those who are depressed, because this is the most common psychiatric diagnosis in completed suicides) is alcohol's ability to affect dopamine turnover in the brain. The constant alcohol-induced release of dopamine might cause a reduction in dopamine binding sites as the brain attempts to adapt to the constant presence of high levels of this compound (Heinz, 2006).

Chronic Alcohol Use and Medication Abuse

Individuals with an alcohol use disorder are at higher risk for the abuse of prescription medications. The teams of McCabe, Cranford, and Boyd, (2006) and McCabe, Cranford, Morales, and Young (2006) concluded that people with an alcohol use disorder are 18 times more likely to abuse prescription drugs than those individuals who do not have an AUD. The younger the individual was at the initiation of alcohol use, and the more alcohol consumed per episode of alcohol use, were found to be positively correlated with the concurrent abuse of prescription medications, with young adults being at highest risk for this problem, according to the authors.

Between 25 and 50% of alcohol-dependent people also have a benzodiazepine addiction (Sattar & Bhatia, 2003). So similar are the effects of alcohol and the benzodiazepines that the benzodiazepines can be substituted for alcohol in situations where it would be unwise to use alcohol. Alcohol-dependent people can then avoid withdrawal symptoms and be around people without the smell of alcohol on their body. However, the combination of two CNS depressants such as alcohol and a benzodiazepine also increases the individual's risk for an accidental, possibly fatal, overdose. Thu, the use of these medications by people with an AUD is not without very real dangers. It was once thought that either alcohol alone or the combination of alcohol with a benzodiazepine might lower cortical inhibitions to the point where the individual would experience a *paradoxical rage reaction*.[32] However, the

---

[32]The rage reaction being paradoxical because it develops after the patient has ingested a CNS depressant, not a stimulant.

existence of this possible disorder has been challenged by some health care professionals, and it remains a only hypothetical construct at this time.

The Effects of Habitual Alcohol Use on the Respiratory System

The chronic use of alcohol has been found to both cause and exacerbate sleep apnea[33] both during the periods of active alcohol use and for a number of weeks after the individual's last drink (Brust, 2004; Schuckit, 2008a). Sleep apnea itself has been identified as a cause of such problems as poor sleep hygiene, hypertension, depression, reduced concentration, daytime fatigue, and possibly falling asleep while driving.

The association between heavy drinking and pneumonia has been recognized for centuries. Chronic alcohol abusers are at increased risk for aspiration pneumonia[34] and various forms of respiratory failure (Kershaw & Guidot, 2008). It has been demonstrated that the chronic use of alcohol alters the body's natural defense mechanisms from the mouth down to the alveolar spaces in the lungs, in part by reducing the effectiveness of the macrophages[35] in the lungs. But as was noted earlier, the heavy use of alcohol alters the normal pattern of bacterial growth in the mouth, also increasing the chronic drinker's risk for pneumonia (Schuckit, 2006a).

The Effects of Chronic Alcohol Use on Other Body Systems

The social image of alcohol is that it enhances sexual performance. In reality, heavy, regular drinkers have been known to suffer from a variety of sexual dysfunctions including decreased libido and, in women, menstrual irregularities (Brunton et al., 2008; Schuckit, 2006a). Male drinkers might experience decreased sperm production and motility, decreased ejaculate volume, reduced sperm count, and possible impotence[36] (Schuckit, 2006a). As will be discussed in Chapter 20, alcohol use by a woman in pregnancy can have profound, devastating effects for the developing fetus.

There is also evidence that suggests that heavy, regular alcohol abuse will result in calcium loss for both men and women, which then weakens the drinker's

bones (Jerslid, 2001). This will, in turn, increase the drinker's chances for injury and death when the individual falls or is involved in an automobile accident. Traumatic brain injuries (TBIs) are two to four times more common in drinkers as opposed to nondrinkers (Rourke & Grant, 2009). Between 29 and 56% of TBI patients who live long enough to reach the hospital[37] will test positive for alcohol at the time of admission (Kraus & Chu, 2005; N. S. Miller & Adams, 2006).[38] The individual's postinjury use of alcohol can both mediate and complicate the patient's recovery from the TBI (N. S. Miller & Adams, 2006). Although it is widely believed that the patient is using alcohol to self-medicate the pain and frustration of the aftereffects of the TBI, research data suggests that in most cases the AUD preceded the TBI (N. S. Miller & Adams, 2006).

AUDs have also been identified as a causal factor in 40–50% of all motor vehicle deaths and up to 67% of home injuries (N. S. Miller, 1999). Statistically, the typical drinker is 10 times as likely to develop cancer as the nondrinker (Ordorica & Nace, 1998). It has been estimated that possibly as many as 4% of cancer deaths in men and 1% of all cancer-related deaths in women are alcohol related. The role of the alcohol metabolite acetaldehyde is thought to play at least a limited role in the development of some of these forms of cancer (Melton, 2007). Habitual alcohol use appears to facilitate the spread of certain forms of cancer of the breast and colon (Forsyth et al., 2009). Chronic use of alcohol is also implicated as a causal agent in certain forms of gum disease (Schuckit, 2005, 2006). Furthermore, the consumption of four to eight standard drinks per day has been found to interfere with normal immune system function, further increasing the drinker's risk for various infectious diseases such as pneumonia and TB (Jaffe & Anthony, 2005).

The Alcohol Withdrawal Syndrome

The alcohol withdrawal syndrome (AWS) is interpreted by health care professionals as proof that the individual has become physically dependent on alcohol. The intensity of the withdrawal syndrome depends in part on the duration and severity of the individual's alcohol use (Perry et al., 2007). In severe cases, it can be

---

[33]See Glossary.

[34]Discussed in Chapter 34.

[35]See Glossary.

[36]Possibly as a manifestation of alcohol-induced peripheral neuropathy, discussed elsewhere in this chapter.

[37]A significant percentage of patients who receive a TBI die before reaching the hospital.

[38]Although rare/social drinkers might also suffer TBI, it is less likely to be as a result of their alcohol use, and thus this topic was reserved for this chapter.

life threatening[39] (Fadem, 2009). The causal mechanism is the sudden reduction or cessation of alcohol intake after the body has become alcohol tolerant. Because alcohol is a CNS depressant, the drinker's brain becomes relatively insensitive to the effects of the inhibitory neurotransmitter GABA over time, while significantly increasing the number of NMDA (an excitatory neurotransmitter) receptor sites. When the alcohol level is markedly reduced, the neurons begin to work erratically because the delicate balance between excitatory and inhibitory neurotransmission processes in these neurons has been disrupted.

Clinically, the AWS is an acute brain syndrome that presents in such a manner that it might be mistaken for such conditions as a subdural hematoma, pneumonia, meningitis, or infection involving the central nervous system unless the attending physician is aware of the individual's drinking history (Saitz, 1998).[40] Once it has been identified as AWS, the severity of the alcohol withdrawal is often assessed with the Clinical Institute Withdrawal Assessment for Alcohol Scale, Revised (CIWA-Ar) (Baron et al., 2009; A. McKay, Koranda, & Axen, 2004; V. A. Kelly & Saucier, 2004). This noncopyrighted instrument measures 15 symptoms of alcohol withdrawal, with each symptom rated in severity, for a maximum score of 67 points. A score of 0–4 is interpreted as minimal discomfort from the AWS; 5–12 points is interpreted as evidence of mild alcohol withdrawal. Patents whose score on the CIWA-Ar is between 13 and 19 points are thought to be in moderately severe withdrawal, whereas scores of 20+ points are interpreted as evidence of severe alcohol withdrawal. One advantage of the CIWA-Ar is that it might be administered repeatedly over time, providing a baseline measure of the patient's status over time and a measure of the client's improvement.

Mild alcohol withdrawal is marked by symptoms such as agitation, anxiety, tremor, diarrhea, abdominal discomfort, exaggerated reflexes, insomnia, vivid dreams or nightmares, nausea, vomiting, tachycardia, headache, memory impairment, problems in concentration, and possible withdrawal seizures (Kelly & Saucier, 2004; Messing, 2008; Perry et al., 2007). The first alcohol withdrawal symptoms are usually seen

8–12 hours after the individual's last drink, although if the patient has suffered significant levels of liver damage this time period might be extended for up to 10 days after the individual's last drink (Baron et al., 2009; A. McKay et al., 2004; Saitz, 1998). Tremor is often one of the first withdrawal signs noted, and it is not uncommon for many heavy alcohol users to keep a drink, or in some cases even a bottle, next to their bed, so that they can have a drink even before getting up for the day. This is often done on the pretense of "helping steady my nerves" or needing an "eye opener," although in reality the drinker will awaken to the early signs of AWS and self-medicate it with their first drink of the day. Although the withdrawal tremor usually resolves in a few hours or days, on rare occasions it can persist for weeks after the individual's last drink (Kinsella & Riley, 2007).

On occasion even mild-intensity AWS will also include hallucinations. This condition is known as *alcoholic hallucinosis,* which is seen in about 10% of the cases of AWS. This condition usually starts 1–2 days after the individual's last drink. These hallucinations might involve visual, tactile, or auditory hallucinations (Kelly & Saucier, 2004; Olmedo & Hoffman, 2000; Ropper & Brown, 2005). They usually resolve within a few days of the individual's last alcohol use, although in rare cases they can continue for months (Tekin & Cummings, 2003; Tse & Koller, 2004). In about 10–20% of the cases, the individual develops an ongoing psychosis (Soyka, 2000).[41] Alcohol withdrawal hallucinations are often quite frightening for the individual, who might not recognize the nature of the hallucinations (Tse & Koller, 2004). On occasion, the individual has been known to respond to the hallucinations as if they were actual experiences (Ropper & Brown, 2005), possibly attempting suicide or become violent in an attempt to escape from their hallucinations (Soyka, 2000; Tekin & Cummings, 2003). This condition is not usually life threatening,[42] and the exact mechanism for alcohol withdrawal hallucinations is not known at the present time.

Mild alcohol withdrawal symptoms peak at about 24 hours and usually subside within 48–72 hours after

---

[39]All real or suspected cases of alcohol withdrawal should be assessed by and treatment should be carried out under the supervision of a physician.

[40]This is not to say that these or any range of other life-threatening conditions might not also be present, complicating the task of the attending physician(s) working with a patient experiencing AWS.

[41]Which raises an interesting question: Was the individual (a) already psychotic and using alcohol to self-medicate his psychiatric problems, (b) a latent person with a latent psychosis that was activated by the AWS, or (c) a person whose alcohol use disorder induced a psychotic state through an unknown mechanism?

[42]Although a physician should be consulted if this complication to alcohol withdrawal should develop while alcohol withdrawal is being attempted.

the individual's last drink (Perry et al., 2007). Although not usually associated with mild alcohol withdrawal syndromes, it is still possible for the individual to experience withdrawal seizures. Such seizures usually occur 72–96 hours after the individual's last drink. It has been estimated that between 10-16% of heavy drinkers will experience seizures during the AWS (T. Berger, 2000; Perry et al., 2007). Withdrawal-induced seizures do not usually reflect a preexisting seizure disorder, and anticonvulsant medication is rarely needed in such cases (Sadock & Sadock, 2007). It was once thought that the individual would experience only one or two alcohol withdrawal seizures, but research has demonstrated that in about 60% of the cases the patient will have multiple withdrawal seizures (Aminoff, Greenbergh, & Simon, 2005; D'Onofrio, Rathlev, Ulrich, Fish, & Greedland, 1999). The benzodiazepines are thought to be the most effective intervention for such patients (Perry et al., 2007; Sadock & Sadock, 2007; Traub, 2009).

Although it is generally assumed that seizures that develop during AWS are a result of the withdrawal process, in 2–4% of the cases the patient had a preexisting seizure disorder. The seizure disorder may have been exacerbated by the alcohol withdrawal process, but it should be remembered that medication compliance is often poor in heavy drinkers (Tse & Koller, 2004). In cases where the patient has a known seizure disorder, the attending physician might wish to check the patient's blood levels of anticonvulsant medications to ensure that adequate blood levels of prescribed medications are in their blood to minimize potential seizures (Parent & Aminoff, 2008; Perry et al., 2007).

Individuals who experience withdrawal seizures are at increased risk for another complication of alcohol withdrawal: *delirium tremens* (DTs)[43]. The DTs reflect a severe organic brain syndrome that is the result of extended periods of heavy drinking, often as little as 5 years (Fadem, 2009). Before the development of effective treatments for this withdrawal syndrome, 10–40% of patients experiencing the DTs would die, usually of cardiovascular collapse (Kinsella & Riley, 2007; Perry et al., 2007). Even today, with the best of medical care, the DTs carry a 1–2% risk of death[44] (Filley, 2004; Perry et al., 2007). Once the DTs develop they are very difficult to control. Some of the symptoms of DTs include profound delirium, hallucinations, delusional beliefs, fever,

hypotension, hyperthermia, peripheral vascular collapse, and tachycardia (Perry et al., 2007; Traub, 2009).

Current medical practice is carried out on the assumption that it is best to block the development of the DTs with appropriate doses of benzodiazepines during withdrawal than to wait for their development and then attempt to control this condition. Drawing on the clinical history of 334 patients in Stockholm, Sweden, Palmstierna (2001) identified five markers that seemed to identify the patient at risk for the development of the DTs: (a) existence of concurrent infections such as pneumonia during the withdrawal process, (b) tachycardia, (c) signs of autonomic nervous system overactivity in spite of an alcohol concentration at or above 1 gram per liter of body fluid, (d) history of previous epilepsy, and (e) a history of having previously experienced the DTs. The author advocated the aggressive use of benzodiazepines to minimize the risk that the patient will experience another episode of the DTs during the current hospital admission. Patients in severe alcohol withdrawal run the risk of sepsis, cardiac and/ or circulatory system collapse, arrhythmia, hyperthermia, and, possibly, suicide (Brunton et al., 2008).

Alcohol also inhibits the release of what has been called the *antidiuretic hormone*[45] (ADH), altering the fluid balance in the drinker's body (Brunton et al., 2008). This results in the typical heavy drinker being in a state of fluid depletion while intoxicated, and with the onset of abstinence the drinker's body will often begin to retain fluids as the compensatory mechanism for the constant presence of ADH breakdown. This will further increase the drinker's risk for cardiovascular and neurological damage. Such fluid retention, and cardiac arrhythmias, will require pharmacological intervention to increase the patient's chances of survival. The pharmacological treatment of the AWS will be discussed in Chapter 33. Patients going through the DTs are also at high risk for alcohol-related muscle damage and the development of *rhabdomyolysis*[46] (Richards, 2000; Sauret, Marinides, & Wang, 2002). It is possible that there are other symptoms of the alcohol withdrawal process, but the information reviewed in this section provides a fairly comprehensive overview of the dangers of the acute AWS.

Extended Alcohol Withdrawal

The acute withdrawal process typically begins about 8 hours after the individual's last drink, peaks in intensity about the 4th or 5th day, and then becomes less

---

[43]Once called the "rum fits" (Ropper & Brown, 2005).

[44]Baron et al. (2009) gave a figure of 5–15% mortality rate from the DTs.

[45]Technically, vasopressin.

[46]See Glossary.

intense over a period of a few days. Some symptoms of the AWS, such as anxiety, sleep problems, and neuropathies, might persist for months after the individual's last drink (Schuckit, 2005, 2006). During this period the individual will be exquisitely sensitive to alcohol use "cues" that might trigger a return to active drinking. Many of these cues will be found in the individual's environment, making it difficult for her to abstain from alcohol during those first critical days (Gilpin & Kolb, 2008).

Part of this vulnerability to relapse is mediated by a subjective sense of craving for alcohol that continues long after individuals stopped drinking. This is often referred to as being "thirsty." During such times individuals find themselves preoccupied with drinking as a result of exposure to drinking-related cues. Such cues include events, times, and other stimuli associated with alcohol use. Surprisingly, the smell of cigarettes often serves as a relapse "cue," because there is often a great deal of smoking in bars where many people drink. There is also evidence that repeated periods of alcohol use interspersed with alcohol withdrawal may enhance the negative effects of alcohol withdrawal, adding to the individual's motivation to continue drinking.

The Benefits of Moderate Drinking

Ever since the 1980s, physicians have been aware of the fact that there appear to be certain health benefits to the use of *limited amounts* of alcohol on a daily basis.[47] This finding has proven to be a point of contention even among physicians, for there has been little systematic research into this possible medical benefit of moderate alcohol use. Physicians often hesitate to recommend even limited alcohol use for nondrinkers and most certainly will not recommend even limited alcohol use to people with a history of an AUD. However, many heavy drinkers justify their alcohol use on the basis of evidence that suggests that moderate drinking might have some health benefits, although they overlook the fact that in their enthusiasm for drinking they pass through "moderate" alcohol use to the point of "excessive" alcohol use.

But moderate alcohol use does appear to have some health benefits. The team of Kallberg et al. (2008) found that moderate daily alcohol consumption[48] appeared to attenuate some of the risk factors of rheumatoid arthritis for the subjects in their research study. The exact mechanism by which this was accomplished is not known at this time. However, the authors also pointed out that there is a known relationship between rheumatoid arthritis and cigarette smoking, which exacerbates the symptoms of arthritis. Thus cigarette smokers might negate any health benefits of moderate alcohol use by their cigarette use. There is a need for further research into this area to replicate this study.

Chapter Summary

Ethyl alcohol, though a popular social beverage, carries with it some risk for the rare drinker. These risks are magnified in persons with an AUD, as alcohol is a toxin that affects virtually every organ system when consumed to excess. Unfortunately, the short-term reinforcement potential of alcohol entices a small percentage of those who consume it to drink to excess, placing their lives (and often the lives of those around them) at risk. Individuals with an alcohol use disorder risk damage to the central nervous system, cardiovascular system, pulmonary system, and digestive system, through a variety of mechanisms. In spite of these dangers, some individuals persist in drinking to the point where they become physically dependent on alcohol and must go through the "detoxification" process to help their bodies return to normal functioning.

---

[47]Defined as no more than two standard drinks per day for a man or one for a woman.

[48]The authors of this study defined "heavy" alcohol use as 3.8 standard drinks *per week,* or less than 1 standard drink per day.

CHAPTER 6

Abuse of and Addiction to Barbiturates and Barbiturate-Like Compounds

Introduction

The charge has been made that the anxiety disorders have become society's most fashionable neurotic complaint, a position they have held since the 1950s (Rasmussen, 2008). This might explain why the anxiety disorders are the most common form of mental illness in the United States, affecting approximately 14% of the general population (Getzfelt, 2006). Furthermore, each year approximately one-third of the population will experience at least a period of transitory insomnia (Ghoneim, 2004b). For thousands of years, alcohol was the only agent that could reduce anxiety or help the individual fall asleep. However, as discussed in the last chapter, alcohol's effectiveness as an antianxiety agent or a hypnotic both is limited and carries with it some danger.

At the start of the chemical revolution in the 19th century, chemists began to identify compounds that were able to reduce the individual's sense of dread and induce a form of sleep that was, if not normal, at least as close to a normal state of sleep that could be chemically induced at the time. These compounds were found to be rather dangerous, but in some cases also became popular drugs of abuse in the period from 1950 to 1980. In this chapter, we will discuss the various medications used to control anxiety or promote sleep prior to the introduction of the benzodiazepines in the 1960s, and the benzodiazepines will be discussed in the next chapter.

Early Medical Treatment of Anxiety and Insomnia

Many of the early anxiolytic/hypnotic agents introduced in the late 18th and early 19th centuries produced a dose-dependent effect on the user. Depending on the dose used, the effects could range from sedation, to sleep, to a profound loss of consciousness, to a state of surgical anesthesia, and, ultimately, to death

(Charney et al., 2006). The first of these compounds was *chloral hydrate,* which was originally introduced as a hypnotic agent in 1870. This medication was administered orally, and it had been found that a dose of 1–2 grams would cause the patient to fall asleep in less than an hour. The effects lasted for 8–11 hours, making it appear to be ideal as a hypnotic agent.

Unfortunately, physicians soon discovered that chloral hydrate had several side effects that made its use

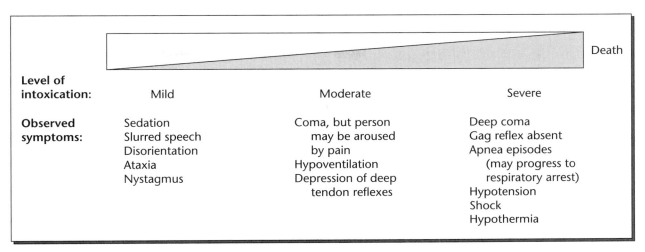

FIGURE 6-1 Spectrum of CNS Depressant Intoxication

problematic. It was discovered that chloral hydrate was quite irritating to the stomach lining, and that repeated administration of this compound could cause significant levels of damage to the stomach lining. Furthermore, it was found that chloral hydrate is quite addictive, and it has a narrow therapeutic window[1] of between 1:2 and 1:3 (Ciraulo & Sarid-Segal, 2005; T. M. Brown & Stoudemire, 1998). Finally, after it had been in use for a period of time, physicians discovered that withdrawal from chloral hydrate could result in life-threatening seizures (T. M. Brown & Stoudemire, 1998).

Technically, chloral hydrate is a prodrug, which is rapidly biotransformed into *trichloroethanal* after oral administration. This is the active agent of chloral hydrate that actually causes it to function as a hypnotic. This medication is still occasionally used in helping elderly patients sleep, although its use is increasingly rare in the practice of medicine.

Paraldehyde was first isolated in 1829 and first used as a hypnotic in 1882. It proved to be an effective hypnotic, producing little cardiac or respiratory depression. But it tends to produce a very noxious taste in the user's mouth, and users develop a strong, unpleasant odor on their breath after ingestion. Because paraldehyde is irritating to the mucous membranes of the mouth and throat, it is usually diluted in another liquid before use. Its therapeutic half-life ranges from 3.4 to 9.8 hours. Between 70 and 80% of a single dose leaves the body unchanged, usually through exhalation, which accounts for the unpleasant odor on the user's breath.

Paraldehyde has an abuse potential similar to that of alcohol, and paraldehyde intoxication resembles that of alcohol intoxication in many ways. After the barbiturates were introduced, paraldehyde gradually fell into disfavor, and at the start of the 21st century it has virtually disappeared (Doble, Martin, & Nutt, 2004).

The *bromide salts* were introduced in the mid-1800s, and as was typical for medications of the era, were available without prescription. These compounds were originally introduced as a treatment for epilepsy, and later as a sedative and hypnotic (Bisaga, 2008). Soon after their introduction it was discovered that even after a few days' continuous use, a reservoir of these compounds built up in the user's body, causing a drug-induced depression. The bromide salts also had a very narrow therapeutic window, and withdrawal from the bromide salts after periods of extended use can include such symptoms as seizures, psychosis, and delirium (Bisaga, 2008). The bromide salts have been totally replaced by newer compounds and are no longer available in the United States.

Diphenhydramine is an antihistamine with a strong sedative side effect. Because of this, it is often used as an over-the-counter sleep aid either by itself or in combination with other compounds. Although it has some degree of success in this application, the risk of anticholinergic-induced delirium is significant, especially when abused at higher than normal doses, in the elderly or chronic users (Perry et al., 2007).

Despite superficial differences in their chemical structures, all of these compounds are CNS depressants. The relative potency of these barbiturate-like compounds are reviewed in Figure 6-1.

---

[1]Discussed in Chapter 3.

Surprisingly, in spite of their different chemical structures, these compounds have many characteristics in common. They all *potentiate* the effects of other CNS depressants, for example, and all have significant abuse potentials. Still, these compounds were the treatment(s) of choice for insomnia until the barbiturates were introduced in the early 20th century.

History and Current Medical Uses of Barbiturates

In 1864 the German chemist Aldolph von Baeyer discovered barbituric acid, the parent compound from which all of the barbiturates are derived (Nemeroff & Putnam, 2005). Barbituric acid is itself inactive, but derivatives of this parent compound yielded a large family of chemicals that could be used as sedatives or (at higher doses) hypnotic agents. The first of these compounds, barbital, was introduced in 1903. In a short period of time a flood of barbiturates were introduced, so dominating the market that for the first half of the 20th century that no nonbarbiturate sedative hypnotic compounds were introduced (T. Nelson, 2000; Nemeroff & Putnam, 2005). Another measure of their impact is found in the fact that, at the height of their popularity, more than *1 million pounds* of barbiturate compounds were manufactured each year just in the United States (Brust, 2004).

More than 2500 different barbiturate compounds were developed, although most were never marketed and remained only laboratory curiosities. Only about 50 of these compounds were ever introduced into clinical use, of which perhaps 20 are still used by physicians (Nishino, Mishima, Mignot, & Dement, 2004). The relative potency of the most commonly used barbiturates are reviewed in Table 6-1, below.

Originally thought to be nonaddictive, clinical experience with these compounds soon revealed the truth

(Ivanov, Schulz, Palmero, & Newcorn, 2006). Legally, barbiturates are classified as Category II controlled compounds[2] and are available only by prescription. After the introduction of the benzodiazepines[3] in the 1960's, the barbiturates slowly fell into disfavor with physicians, although their abuse does continue (Brust, 2004).

Furthermore, in spite of the pharmacological revolution that began in the latter half of the 20th century, there are still some areas of medicine where barbiturates remain the pharmaceutical of choice (Ciraulo, Ciraulo, Sands, Knapp, & Sarid-Segal, 2005). These include certain surgical procedures, possible control of swelling of the brain after traumatic injury, treatment of some forms of migraine headache, and seizure control on both an emergency and long-term basis (Charney et al., 2006; Nemeroff & Putnam, 2005; Ropper & Brown, 2005).

As they enter their second century of use, controversy still swirls around the appropriate use of many of these compounds. Physicians have long thought that barbiturates were helpful in controlling the swelling of the brain following trauma, although this belief has been challenged (Brain Trauma Foundation, 2000; Nemeroff & Putnam, 2005). Questions have been raised about their use in inducing a coma in a terminally ill patient in extreme pain, as well. Perhaps the most controversial application of the barbiturates at this time is their role in the process of "lethal injection" of criminals sentenced to the death penalty.

The Abuse Potential of Barbiturates

Barbiturates have a significant abuse potential and are quite dangerous to use. In light of all that has been discovered about their abuse potential, it is surprising to learn they have enjoyed a minor resurgence in popularity. Older generations, especially those above the age of 60, became addicted to these compounds decades ago and often continue to abuse these compounds. Also, a small number of physicians have attempted to avoid the extra paperwork imposed by some state regulatory agencies on benzodiazepine prescriptions by prescribing barbiturates to their patients. Finally, this group of compounds has enjoyed an ongoing popularity with some illicit-drug users (Ropper & Brown, 2005).

TABLE 6-1 DOSAGE EQUIVALENCY FOR BARBITURATE-LIKE DRUGS	
GENERIC NAME OF DRUG	**DOSE EQUIVALENT TO 30 MG OF PHENOBARBITAL**
Chloral hydrate	500 mg
Ethchlorvynol	350 mg
Meprobamate	400 mg
Methyprylon	300 mg
Glutethimide	250 mg

---

[2]See Appendix 4.

[3]Discussed in the next chapter.

TABLE 6-2 CLINICAL APPLICATIONS OF BARBITURATES

DURATION OF EFFECT	APPLICATION
Ultra-short-acting barbiturates	When injected, effects begin in seconds, and last for <30 minutes. Very lipid soluble. Useful in dental surgical procedures.
Short-acting barbiturates	Usually administered orally. Effects begin in 10–20 minutes and last for 3–4 hours. Elimination half-life may be longer than duration of effect. Lipid solubility falls between that of ultra-short-acting and intermediate-duration barbiturates.
Intermediate-duration barbiturates	Usually administered orally. Effects begin in approximately 1 hour. Effects of a single dose last for 6–8 hours. Elimination half-life may be longer than duration of effect. Moderately lipid soluble.
Long-acting barbiturates	Usually administered orally. Effects of a single dose begin in about an hour and last for 6–12 hours. Elimination half-life may be longer than duration of effect. Lipid solubility less than that of Intermediate-duration barbiturates.

NOTE: Based on Schuckit (2006), J. S. Meyer and Quenzer (2005), Brunton et al. (2008), and Zevin and Benowitz (1998).

Pharmacology of the Barbiturates

As stated earlier, there are minor differences in the chemical structure between various members of the barbiturate family of compounds, differences that translate into variations in absorption, distribution, biotransformation, and elimination between various barbiturates. However, they all have their main effects in the central nervous system, which is "exquisitely sensitive" (Brunton et al., 2008, p. 270) to the effects of these drugs.

Different barbiturate compounds have different degrees of lipid solubility. The barbiturates that have greater degrees of lipid solubility tend to be more potent and have a more rapid onset of action, although they also have a shorter duration of effect than barbiturates with less lipid solubility (J. D. Levin, 2002; Ropper & Brown 2005). This is clearly seen in the difference between the effects of pentobarbital as compared with phenobarbital. A single dose of pentobarbital, which is very lipid soluble, will begin to have an effect in 10–15 minutes, whereas a single dose of phenobarbital, which is poorly lipid soluble, might require an hour or more to begin to have an effect.

In spite of the differences in lipid solubility, the barbiturates share the same mechanism of action (Nemeroff & Putnam, 2005). At the level of the neuron, the barbiturate molecule inhibits the closing of the GABAa channel to close, slowing the rate at which that neuron can establish the electrical differential necessary for it to "fire" (Ciraulo & Sarid-Segal, 2005; Doble et al.,

2004; Nemeroff & Putnam, 2005; Nishino et al., 2004). Unlike the benzodiazepines, which replaced them as the preferred CNS depressant starting in the 1960s, the barbiturates can cause this effect even in the absence of the GABA molecule itself (Doble et al., 2004; Parrott, Morinan, Moss, & Scholey, 2004). However, the pattern of GABAa channel activation achieved by benzodiazepines is different from that of GABA itself, as barbiturate-facilitated activation forces the chloride channels to remain open longer as opposed to open more rapidly, than normal (Brunton et al., 2008).

Clinically, barbiturates are classified on the basis of their *duration of action,*[4] as reviewed in Table 6-2.

One point that must be made here is that the duration of effect of the various barbiturates is often different from the elimination half-life of the same compound. As was discussed in Chapter 3, the therapeutic half-life of a compound provides a *rough* estimate of the time that that chemical will remain in the body. A very good example of this is provided by the short-acting barbiturate Nembutal, which begins to take effect on the user in 10–15 minutes after a single dose, lasts for 3–4 hours, and yet, because of the manner in which the compound is redistributed around the body following absorption, might require 10–50 hours before all of a single dose is eliminated (J. D. Levin, 2002; Nemeroff & Putnam, 2005). The speed of this redistribution process varies from one

---

[4]A number of different classification systems for barbiturates have been suggested over the years. This text will follow the system suggested by Zevin and Benowitz (1998).

barbiturate to another, depending on its ability to form chemical bonds with protein and lipid molecules in the blood.

Following absorption, significant amounts of some of the shorter-acting barbiturates are stored in different body tissues and then released back into the general circulation. This means that many of the barbiturates have a "hangover" effect on the user, reducing psychomotor function for a significant period of time after the desired effects have ended. Generally shorter-term barbiturates require biotransformation by the liver before elimination, whereas long-term barbiturates are eliminated from the body virtually unchanged. Thus the barbiturate methohexital, with a half-life of 3–6 hours, is extensively biotransformed by the liver before elimination, whereas 25–50% of a single dose of phenobarbital, which has a half-life of 2–6 days, will be excreted from the body unchanged (American Society of Health System Pharmacists, 2008). Another difference between the various barbiturates is the degree to which the drug molecules become protein bound, with longer-duration barbiturates having greater degrees of protein binding.

Barbiturates are usually administered orally, although many of the ultra-short-duration barbiturates are used intravenously to rapidly induce anesthesia for surgical procedures. On rare occasions, barbiturates may be administered through suppositories. Orally administered barbiturates are rapidly absorbed through the small intestine (J. D. Levin, 2002; Nemeroff & Putnam, 2005). Once in the general circulation, the barbiturate molecules are distributed throughout the body, with the highest concentrations being found in the liver and the brain (American Society of Health System Pharmacists, 2008).

Behaviorally, the effects of barbiturates are very similar to those of alcohol (Ciraulo & Sarid-Segal, 2005; Nishino et al., 2004). The barbiturates will depress the level of neural activity, as is seen with alcohol ingestion, but they also have a minor impact on the heart, muscle tissues, and the respiration process (Ciraulo et al., 2005). In the brain, the barbiturate molecules tend to have their greatest impact on the cortex, the reticular activating system, and the medulla oblongata.[5] Not surprisingly, these are the neurons with the highest number of GABA receptor sites, which is where the barbiturate molecules are therapeutically active. By reducing the level of neural activity in the neurons in the cortex, at low doses the barbiturates are able to induce a sense of

relaxation, and at slightly higher doses induce a form of sleep. However, because of their effects on the respiratory center of the brain, it is suggested that patients with a respiratory disorder not use a barbiturate except under a physician's supervision (Nishino et al., 2004). At high dosage levels or when mixed with other CNS depressants, the barbiturates are capable of causing death from respiratory depression.

Barbiturate-induced death can occur either as a result of a deliberate act or as a result of a miscalculation, because many barbiturates have a therapeutic window of only 1:3 to 1:10 (Brunton et al., 2008; Ciraulo et al., 2005; J. S. Meyer & Quenzer, 2005). Before the introduction of the benzodiazepines, which have a larger therapeutic window and thus are safer to prescribe, an annual death rate of 118 per each 100,000 barbiturate prescriptions was not uncommon (Drummer & Odell, 2001). The use of these compounds is now discouraged because of their narrow therapeutic window and high lethality in overdose situations (Perry et al., 2007).

Subjective Effects of Barbiturates at Normal Dosage Levels

At low doses, barbiturates cause the user to experience a sense of relaxation or even a sense of euphoria (Ciraulo et al., 2005). Some users also report a sense of sedation or fatigue, possibly to the point of drowsiness, ataxia, and an increase in reaction time similar to that seen in alcohol intoxication (Nishino et al., 2004; Filley, 2004). Because both the barbiturates and alcohol affect the same gated chloride ion channel in the neural wall, the pharmacological mechanism by which they achieve their effects is very similar, and thus the subjective experience is about the same. Indeed, to rule out this possibility, patients who appear intoxicated but who have no sign of alcohol in their bodies should be tested for barbiturate ingestion.

Complications of Barbiturate Use at Normal Dosage Levels

Like alcohol, barbiturates interfere with the normal function of the neurons of the cortex, possibly causing a *paradoxical rage reaction* (Ciraulo et al., 2005). Other side effects of barbiturates when used at normal dosage levels include feelings of nausea, dizziness, and mental slowness. But anxious patients report that their sense of

---

[5]See Glossary.

anxiety is reduced, if not eliminated, and patients with insomnia report that they can slip into a state of drug-induced sleep. Unfortunately, tolerance to the hypnotic effects of barbiturates will develop after a few days of continuous use (Drummer & Odell, 2001). This is a very real problem, because patients might go to see a physician with a complaint of insomnia, without revealing their barbiturate use to the practitioner. If physicians should prescribe another CNS depressant in an attempt to help patients sleep, there is a danger that the patients will experience an unexpected, possibly lethal, overdose. Furthermore, the users' growing tolerance to the hypnotic effects of barbiturates does not alter the lethal threshold for these drugs. Thus, if they should increase their dose, or intermix barbiturates with other CNS depressants in an effort to regain the original anxiolytic or hypnotic effect, it is very possible for them to die from an overdose.

Furthermore, the sleep induced by barbiturates is not a normal form of sleep. Barbiturates interfere with the normal progression of sleep stages and suppress the duration of the REM sleep stage (Nemeroff & Putnam, 2005; Nishino et al., 2004). Following the nightly use of barbiturates for as little as 2 weeks, REM sleep time has been reduced by as much as 50% (Brunton et al., 2008). Although reduced REM sleep time for one or two nights is not thought to be dangerous, long-term REM sleep impairment is thought to have long-term emotional and physical effects on the individual. When the barbiturates are discontinued after an extended period of use, they will induce the phenomenon of REM *rebound*[6] with dream intensity bordering on nightmares for the individual. These REM rebound dreams may serve as an incentive for the person to return to the use of barbiturates, or similar compounds, to "get a good night's sleep."

Barbiturates are able to cause the user to experience a drug-induced "hangover" the day after using one of these drugs (B. A. Wilson et al., 2007). The subjective experience for the user is of "just not being able to get going," if not of continued intoxication by barbiturates. This drug-induced hangover effect is the result of the distribution and elimination characteristics of the barbiturate being used. As was discussed in Chapter 3, physicians estimate that it takes five elimination half-life periods to eliminate a single chemical from the body. But the extended elimination half-lives of many barbiturates means that significant amounts of the drug might remain in the user's body for days after a single

dose of that compound. For example, although the therapeutic effects of a single dose of secobarbital might last for 6–8 hours, the hangover effect might cause impaired motor coordination abilities for 10–20 hours after that same dose (Charney et al., 2006). If the person adds to the reservoir of nonmetabolized drug by ingesting an additional dose(s) of the barbiturate, there is a greater chance that the individual will experience a drug hangover. Individuals with impaired liver function, such as the elderly or people with advanced liver disease, are especially prone to barbiturate hangover effects.

One application of the barbiturate phenobarbital is seizure control in patients who are prone to this problem. Individuals who have taken phenobarbital for seizure control on a long-term basis have been found to suffer an 8-point drop in IQ, although it is not clear whether this is an artifact, a drug-induced effect, or the cumulative impact of the seizure disorder (Breggin, 1999). It also is not known whether this measured loss of IQ is reversible or if this effect is limited to phenobarbital.

Other known complications of barbiturates when used at therapeutic doses include sexual-performance problems and a loss of libido for both men and women (Finger, Lund, & Slagel, 1997). Hypersensitivity reactions have been reported in patients receiving a barbiturate, especially patients who suffer from asthma. Other known complications include nausea, vomiting, diarrhea, skin rashes, and in some cases constipation. Finally, some patients develop an extreme sensitivity to sunlight known as *photosensitivity,* placing them at risk for sunburn after even short exposures to sunlight.

Patients who suffer from attention deficit hyperactivity disorder (ADHD) who also receive a barbiturate experience a resurgence or intensification of the ADHD symptoms. This effect would appear to reflect the ability of barbiturates to suppress the action of the reticular activating system (RAS) in the brain. It is thought that ADHD is caused by an underactive RAS, so any medication that reduces the level of RAS activity will probably intensify the symptoms of ADHD.

Drug Interactions Involving Barbiturates

When used at therapeutic doses, barbiturates are able to potentiate the effects of other CNS depressants, including those of alcohol, narcotic analgesics, phenothiazines, benzodiazepines, and antihistamines. The interaction between the barbiturates and antihistamines is especially problematic because the latter class of chemicals is often contained in over-the-counter

---

[6]See Glossary.

cold or allergy remedies, resulting in unintended over-dose effects. Patients using monoamine oxidase inhibitor (MAO) medications should not take a barbiturate except under a physician's supervision, because MAO inhibitors can block the biotransformation of barbiturates, placing the patient at an unintended risk for a barbiturate overdose (Ciraulo et al., 2006; Tatro, 2009). Barbiturates also reduce the effectiveness of the antibiotic doxycycline and speed up the biotransformation of the class of antidepressant medications known as "tricyclic" antidepressants (Ciraulo et al., 2006). They also speed up the biotransformation of oral contraceptives, corticosteroids, the anticoagulant medication warfarin, and the antibiotic metronidazole. Barbiturates are biotransformed by the same region of the liver that biotransforms the antiasthma medication theophylline, which may interfere with asthma control. Finally, patients using barbiturates and the over-the-counter analgesic acetaminophen are at increased risk for liver damage (Tatro, 2009). As this list would suggest, barbiturates are exceptionally potent compounds, which should not be intermixed with other medications except under the supervision of a physician.

Effects of Barbiturates at Above-Normal Dosage Levels

Individuals who ingest higher-than-normal levels of barbiturates demonstrate behaviors similar to those seen in alcohol intoxication, including slurred speech and ataxia. The use of these medications may be confirmed through the use of appropriate urine toxicology tests. When they discontinue the intake of barbiturates, long-term users may experience a *delirium tremens* (DT)-like reaction (Ciraulo & Sarid-Segal, 2005). Barbiturates interfere with the normal cough reflex, placing the abuser at risk for conditions such as pneumonia and bronchitis.

The barbiturates cause a dose-dependent reduction in respiration, which at its extreme can result in respiratory arrest as the barbiturates cause the respiratory centers in the medulla oblongata to become less sensitive to the rising blood carbon dioxide levels. Hypothermia is also seen when the barbiturates are used at above-normal dosage levels (Ciraulo et.al., 2005; Pagliaro & Pagliaro, 1998). Other symptoms seen when barbiturates are ingested at above-normal doses include a progressive loss of reflex activity, tachycardia, hypotension, coma, and possible death (Nemeroff & Putnam, 2005).

Although physicians have had access to a range of safer medications, even in the early 21st century intentional or unintentional barbiturate overdoses are not unheard of. Fortunately, barbiturates do not cause direct damage to the CNS. If overdose victims reach support before they develop shock or hypoxia, there is a good chance they may fully recover from the overdose (Nishino et al., 2005). If only for this reason *any suspected barbiturate overdose should immediately be assessed and treated by a physician.*

Neuroadaptation, Tolerance, and Physical Dependence on Barbiturates

With periods of continuous use, the individual's body will begin a process of neuroadaptation,[7] with the result being that over a surprisingly short period of time the individual becomes tolerant to many of the effects of the barbiturate. The process of barbiturate-induced neuroadaptation is not uniform, however. For example, when a barbiturate such as phenobarbital is used to control seizures, neuroadaptation does not appear to be a major problem, and after patients adapt to the sedative effects of the medication, they might be maintained on the same dose for extended periods of time without becoming tolerant to the anticonvulsant effects of this medication. But if patients were to take a barbiturate for its hypnotic effects, they might become tolerant to this effect after just a couple of weeks of continuous use (Nemeroff & Putnam, 2005).

Both patients and drug abusers have been known to try and overcome their increasing tolerance to a given barbiturate by increasing their dose. Unfortunately, whereas people might become tolerant to the sedating effects of a barbiturate, they do not appear to develop any significant tolerance to the respiratory depressant effect of barbiturates, resulting in many unintentional or intentional overdoses. In spite of the process of neuroadaptation, the lethal dose to a barbiturate remains relatively unchanged (Charney et al., 2006; J. S. Meyer & Quenzer, 2005). Thus by increasing the dose, the user runs the risk of a barbiturate overdose, with possibly lethal consequences.

Barbiturate abusers also develop tolerance to the euphoric effects of these drugs, which again might prompt many abusers to increase the dosage level or

---

[7]Or, if the drug is being abused, the same process is called "tolerance."

intermix barbiturates with other CNS depressants. As stated earlier, the outcome of either process might be a fatal suppression of the respiratory reflex. Furthermore, barbiturates have been documented to induce *cross-tolerance.*[8] Cross tolerance between alcohol and barbiturates is common, as is cross-tolerance between barbiturates and narcotic analgesics, and between barbiturates and the hallucinogenic PCP, among others. Chronic barbiturate use is able to induce a state of physical dependence on barbiturates, with a characteristic withdrawal syndrome if people were to discontinue or drastically reduce their barbiturate use. *Barbiturate withdrawal is potentially life threatening and should be attempted only under the supervision of a physician* (Erickson, 2007; J. S. Meyer & Quenzer, 2005).

As a general rule longer-acting barbiturates will tend to have longer withdrawal periods. The barbiturate withdrawal syndrome is similar to that of the alcohol withdrawal syndrome and might bring about symptoms including confusion, seizures, muscle weakness, anorexia, muscle twitches, rebound anxiety and trembling, agitation, a DT-like state, brain damage, and possible death. Barbiturate withdrawal seizures may begin on the 2nd or 3rd day of abstinence and are rare after the 12th day of abstinence. The acute withdrawal syndrome normally lasts 3–14 days, and physicians may use any of a wide range of pharmaceuticals to help control the severity of the withdrawal process. However, patients should be warned that there is no symptom-free withdrawal.

The Barbiturate-Like Drugs

Because physicians quickly became aware of the many adverse side effects of barbiturates, pharmaceutical companies began to look for substitutes that might be both effective, yet safe to use. This resulted in a number of compounds that were introduced in the 1950s to replace the barbiturates, including *meprobamate, methaqualone, glutethimide, ethchlorvynol,* and *methyprylon.*

Although each of these compounds was originally thought to be "nonaddicting," subsequent clinical experience demonstrated that each had an abuse potential very similar to that of the barbiturates. This is not surprising, because the chemical structure of some of these compounds (such as gutethimide and methyprylon) is very similar to that of the barbiturates (Julien, 2005). Furthermore, like the barbiturates, glutethimide and methyprylon are mainly biotransformed in the liver.

TABLE 6-3 NORMAL DOSAGE LEVELS OF COMMONLY USED BARBITURATES		
BARBITURATE	**SEDATIVE DOSE***	**HYPNOTIC DOSE****
Amobarbital	50–150 mg/day	65–200 mg
Aprobarbital	120 mg/day	40–60 mg
Butabarbital	45–120 mg/day	50–100 mg
Mephobarbital	96–400 mg/day	Not used as hypnotic
Pentobarbital	60–80 mg/day	100 mg
Phenobarbital	30–120 mg/day	100–320 mg
Secobarbital	90–200 mg/day	50–200 mg
Talbutal	30–120 mg/day	120 mg

SOURCE: Based on information provided in Uhde & Trancer (1995).
*Administered in divided doses.
**Administered as a single dose at bedtime.

Gluethimide was widely used after its introduction, but subsequent use of this compound revealed that there were wide variations in its absorption both between patients and within the same patient over time. Furthermore, users were found to rapidly develop tolerance to its effects, and the discontinuance syndrome was found to be rather severe (Kranzler & Ciraulo, 2005b). Abusers reported that when ingested with codeine it caused a sense of euphoria, although this has not been independently confirmed. The symptoms of a glutethimide overdose can take up to 120 hours to resolve (Kranzler & Ciraulo, 2005b). Glutethimide withdrawal symptoms can include seizures, tremulousness, nausea, tachycardia, fever, as well as catatonia-like symptoms (Kranzler & Ciraulo, 2005b).

The therapeutic dose of glutethimide is just a little below the toxic dosage range, placing the user at high risk for an overdose. Detoxification with controlled doses of a long-term barbiturate such as phenobarbital was recommended at the rate of 60 mg of phenobarbital for each 500 mg of glutethimide ingested daily for stabilization, followed by a gradual reduction in each day's dose of phenobarbital until the patient was drug free (Kranzler & Ciraulo, 2005b). Because of the complications associated with its use, neither ethchlorvynol or glutethimide is used by physicians except under special circumstances (Schuckit, 2006a). The prolonged use of ethchlorvynol can induce a loss of vision known as *amblyopia,* which will slowly clear after the drug is discontinued.

Meprobamate was first introduced in 1955 as a "nonbarbiturate" compound that could be used in the

---

[8]See Glossary.

daytime to treat anxiety and at higher dosage levels as a hypnotic agent at night. Shortly after it was introduced, it was discovered that it could also induce a sense of euphoria when abused at high dosage levels (Bisaga, 2008). This compound's chemical structure is very similar to that of the barbiturate, but is just different enough so that the claim that it is not a barbiturate is justified. However, in the mid-1950s the use of these "minor" tranquilizers was an accepted part of life for middle-class America,[9] at least until the introduction of the safer benzodiazepines, which are discussed in the next chapter. By current standards it is considered obsolete and is very rarely prescribed today. Surprisingly, an over-the-counter prodrug, *carisoprodol,* is biotransformed in part into meprobamate after ingestion, and there have been reports of physical dependence on carisoprodol (Bisaga, 2008; Gitlow, 2007).

Peak blood levels of meprobamate are seen in 1–3 hours after a single dose, and the half-life is between 6 and 17 hours, although when used on an extended basis the half-life might be extended to between 24 and 48 hours (Cole & Yonkers, 1995). The LD50 of meprobamate is estimated to be about 28,000 mg, however some patients have expired after ingesting only 12,000 mg (Cole & Yonkers, 1995). When combined with other CNS depressants, the therapeutic window for meprobamate is reduced and fatal overdoses were not uncommon. Physical dependence on meprobamate is common when patients require 3, 200 mg per day to achieve the desired effects (Cole & Yonkers, 1995).

Methaqualone was introduced as a safe, nonaddicting barbiturate substitute in 1965, and it quickly gained a following among illicit drug abusers in the late 1960s and early 1970s (Neubauer, 2005). Illicit-drug users discovered that, if you resisted the hypnotic effects of this compound, you were able to induce a feeling of euphoria. Following oral administration methaqualone is rapidly absorbed from the gastrointestinal tract, and the effects begin in 15–20 minutes. Anxiolytic doses were usually about 75 mg, whereas hypnotic doses were between 150 and 300 mg. Tolerance to the sedative and hypnotic effects of methaqualone develop rapidly. Unfortunately, after the development of tolerance many abusers would increase their dosage levels in an attempt to maintain the initial effect, ignoring the fact that methaqualone has a narrow therapeutic window and that the lethal dose remains the same in spite of possible tolerance to the drug's effects. This made the user vulnerable to accidental overdoses, especially when this compound was mixed with other CNS depressants such as alcohol. In the United States, methaqualone is a Schedule I[10] compound and was withdrawn from the market. It is, however, still manufactured in other countries, or manufactured in illicit markets, and so the alcohol and drug counselor should have at least a working knowledge of its effects.

Chapter Summary

The twin problems of anxiety and insomnia have plagued humans for thousands of years. For much of that time, alcohol was the only compound that was even marginally effective in relieving either disorder, although tolerance to the anxiolytic and hypnotic effects of alcohol develops rapidly when it is used on a continuous basis. Then the chemical revolution that began in the 1800s resulted in the development of a number of compounds with a hypnotic effect, although each also had serious side effects that limited its use. Then, in the early 1900s the first of a new family of compounds, the barbiturates, were introduced. These chemicals were in use for decades before it was discovered that they had a mechanism of action very similar to that of alcohol. It was, however, quickly discovered that cross-tolerance between alcohol and the barbiturates was possible and that they had a high abuse potential.

Following World War II, a number of new compounds were introduced as safe, nonaddicting replacements for the barbiturates. However, it was soon discovered that each of these compounds also had an abuse potential similar to that of the barbiturates. Since the introduction of the benzodiazepines (discussed in the next chapter), most of these compounds have fallen into disfavor. However, a small number of the barbiturates have a limited role in medicine even today, and the health care professional will occasionally encounter a patient who abuses these compounds.

---

[9]A popular comedian, Milton Berle, once introduced himself at the start of an episode of his television program as "Miltown®" (a brand name of this compound) Berle. This joke resulted in uproarious laughter, which is perhaps a reflection of popularity of this compound in middle-class America.

[10]See Appendix 4.

CHAPTER 7

Abuse of and Addiction to the Benzodiazepines and Similar Agents

Introduction

In 1960, the first of a new class of antianxiety compounds, chlordiazepoxide, was introduced in the United States. The benzodiazepines (BZs) were identified as a result of the search for safe replacements for the barbiturates, and more than 3000 different variations of benzodiazepines have been identified. Approximately 50 BZs have been introduced around the world, and several are used as pharmaceuticals in the United States. Since the time of their introduction, the BZs have been found to be useful either as the primary or as an adjunct to the treatment of a wide range of disorders, including anxiety states, insomnia, muscle strains, and the emergency control of seizures (Bisaga, 2008). Each year, between 10 and 15% of the adults in the Western world will use a benzodiazepine, a Schedule II[1] class of drugs, at least once (Dubovsky, 2005; A. J. Jenkins, 2007). Collective benzodiazepines, which are the main focus of this chapter, have become the most frequently prescribed class of psychotropic medications in the world (Gitlow, 2007).

Medical Uses of the Benzodiazepines

Although the BZs were developed as a result of the ongoing search for safe and effective alternatives to the barbiturates, they are no longer viewed as the "frontline" anxiolytic medications (Shear, 2003). Physicians now view the selective serotonin reuptake inhibitors (SSRIs) as the drugs of choice for long-term anxiety control, although the BZs are still used to control *acute* anxiety (anxiety attacks, or short-term

anxiety from a specific time-limited stressor), and they continue to have a role in the treatment of such conditions as generalized anxiety disorder (GAD) (Stevens & Pollack, 2005).

One of the reasons the benzodiazepines became so popular is that they offer the advantage of a mechanism of action that is more selective than that of the barbiturates. This, plus their relatively large therapeutic windows, made physicians feel more comfortable prescribing them for patients. Some of the more frequently prescribed benzodiazepines are reviewed in the next section of this chapter.

Some benzodiazepines currently in the United States, such as diazepam, have been found to be of

---

[1]See Appendix 4.

value in such problems as seizure control and helping muscles recover from strains. The benzodiazepine clonazepam has been found to be very effective in long-term control of anxiety and increasingly is being used in this capacity (Raj & Sheehan, 2004). In addition, the benzodiazepines were often used as hypnotic agents. Researchers estimate that between 25 and 35% of the adults in this country suffer from occasional insomnia, whereas 10–15% suffer from chronic insomnia (Neubauer, 2005). During the latter part of the 20th century, the benzodiazepines flurazepam, quazepam, triazolam, and tamazepam were introduced as hypnotic agents for use in the control of insomnia in this country. However, since the introduction of a new class of medications known as *benzodiazepine receptor agonists* (or BRAs), the benzodiazepines are rarely used as hypnotics. The BRAs are more selective than the BZs and are thought to have a lower abuse potential than the BZs ("Insomnia in Later Life," 2006). These medications will be discussed later in this chapter.

Patients being treated for depression will often receive a benzodiazepine as an adjunct to their antidepressant medication. Alprazolam has been shown to have a minor antidepressant action and is a good short-term anxiolytic (Dubovsky, 2005). The benzodiazepine adinazolam was introduced as having a direct antidepressant effect, but for the most part has been eclipsed by the SSRIs as antidepressants and is rarely used as an anxiolytic or antidepressant at this time.

Benzodiazepines and Suicide Attempts

An ever-present danger when treating depressed patients is that one will attempt to commit suicide. Because of their high therapeutic index,[2] the BZs have traditionally been viewed as being far safer to use with depressed patients than were the barbiturates. Research using animals as test subjects suggests that the LD50 for diazepam is around 720 mg per kilogram of body weight for mice, and 1240 mg per kilogram of weight for rats (Thompson PDR, 2007), for example. Although the LD50 in humans is not known, these figures do suggest that diazepam has a far larger margin of safety than the barbiturates. However, other BZs have different therapeutic indexes than does diazepam, and if the patient should ingest another CNS depressant (such as alcohol, narcotic analgesics, and the like) the margin of safety is significantly reduced. Thus *any suspected drug overdose should immediately be assessed and treated by medical professionals.*

Although pharmacists have developed a benzodiazepine antagonist called flumazenil, which will bind at and block the receptor sites where the BZ molecules normally bind, it is effective for only 20–45 minutes and is specific to benzodiazepines (Brust, 1998, 2007b). A greater problem is that the sudden blockade of the receptor sites normally occupied by benzodiazepine molecules can initiate sudden withdrawal if the individual were a long-term benzodiazepine abuser. As discussed elsewhere in this chapter, benzodiazepine withdrawal can induce seizures and is potentially life threatening (Traub, 2009). Thus flumazenil is of value only in acute overdose situations with patients who have limited histories of benzodiazepine abuse or addiction, and a continuous infusion of flumazenil, or repeated doses of this medication, must be administered in a benzodiazepine overdose situation.

When initially used as an anxiolytic at normal dosage levels, patients report a reduction in anxiety and a sense of gentle relaxation. Very few patients report a sense of euphoria at therapeutic dosage levels. When used as a hypnotic, the BZs initially reduce sleep latency,[3] and upon awakening the user reports having experienced a deep, restful period of sleep. However, when used in the control of anxiety, and when used as a hypnotic, patients may experience some degree of ataxia, as well as a clouding of consciousness that has been described as a sense of floating, or detachment, from external reality.[4] These effects are compounded if the patient should be using other CNS depressants, including over-the-counter medications such as antihistamines or alcohol.

The Pharmacology of the Benzodiazepines

In terms of their main effects, the benzodiazepines and the minor variations in chemical structure between different benzodiazepines mainly affect their duration of action (Dubovsky, 2005). The relative potency and biological half-lives of some of the benzodiazepines currently in use in the United States are reviewed in Table 7-1.

---

[2]Discussed in Chapter 6.

[3]See Glossary

[4]Individuals who have been exposed to a traumatic stressor and thus are at risk for the development of posttraumatic stress disorder (PTSD) have been found not to benefit from benzodiazepine intervention. This is possibly because the dissociative effect of this class of medications contributes to feelings of not being in control, which is one of the factors that contributes to the development of PTSD (Shalev, 2009).

TABLE 7-1 COMMONLY PRESCRIBED BENZODIAZEPINES AND THEIR PHARMACOKINETICS

GENERIC NAME	EQUIPOTENT DOSE	ESTIMATED HALF-LIFE
Alprazolam	0.5 mg	6–20 hours
Chlordiazepoxide	25 mg	30–100 hours
Clonazepam	0.20 mg	20–40 hours
Clorazepate	7.5 mg	30–100 hours
Diazepam	5 mg	50–100 hours
Flurazepam	30 mg	50–100 hours
Halzepam	20 mg	30–100 hours
Lorazepam	1 mg	10–20 hours
Oxazepam	15 mg	5–21 hours
Prazepam	10 mg	30–100 hours
Temazepam	30 mg	9.5–12.4 hours
Triazolam	0.25 mg	1.7–3.0 hours

NOTE: Based on Brunton et al. (2008), and Schuckit (2006a).

Like many pharmaceuticals, it is possible to classify the BZs on the basis of their pharmacological characteristics (such as degree of lipid or protein binding). Those BZs that are most lipid soluble will pass from the gastrointestinal tract into the circulation more rapidly than those that are not as lipid soluble after a BZ is ingested (Ciraulo et al., 2005; Raj & Sheehan, 2004). Another way to classify the BZs is on the basis of their therapeutic half-lives:[5] (a) ultra-short-acting (<4 hours), (b) short-acting (<6 hours), (c) intermediate duration (6–24 hours), and (d) long-lasting (24+ hours) (Charney et al., 2006).

Once in the circulation, the benzodiazepine molecules bind to protein molecules in the blood. Between 70 and 99% of the benzodiazepine molecules become protein bound, although the degree of protein binding varies from one benzodiazepine to the next. Diazepam is more than 99% protein bound, whereas only 80% of the benzodiazepine alprazolam molecules become protein bound, for example (Thompson PDR, 2007). Protein binding and distribution pattern of that specific BZ are factors that influence the therapeutic effects of that compound on the body (Raj & Sheehan, 2004). Some of the BZs are sequestered in body tissues such as body fat and are then slowly released back into the

general circulation over extended periods of time, allowing that compound to have an extended half-life. This is often an advantage when a physician is trying to decide on a BZ to offer the patient for use as an anxiolytic or hypnotic.

Lipid solubility determines how rapidly the unbound molecules of a specific benzodiazepine might pass through the blood–brain barrier into the brain, where the primary site of action is the GABAa receptor site in various regions of the brain (Bisaga, 2008; Raj & Sheehan, 2004). However, researchers have identified more than 20 subtypes of the GABA receptor site, and the role of each in human behavior is still being explored. Thus it is not clear whether the BZs must bind to GABAA receptors in only one part of the brain to induce their anxiolytic effect or if there are multiple sites of action within the brain. The chemical structure of many benzodiazepines makes the absorption of those compounds very erratic when they are injected into muscle tissue, and thus they are not usually used in intramuscular injections but are usually administered orally. One exception to this rule is when the patient is experiencing a seizure. In such cases intravenous injections of diazepam, or a similar benzodiazepine, can aid in seizure control. Another exception to this rule is midazolam, which is sold under the brand name of Versed®, which is used as a presurgical anesthetic or for procedures that require "conscious sedation."

Many benzodiazepines require biotransformation before these compounds can be eliminated from the body. In the process of biotransformation, some benzodiazepines produce metabolites that are themselves biologically active for a period of time. Thus, the *duration of effect* for many BZs might be different from the elimination half-life of that same compound (Dubovsky, 2005). An excellent example of this is the benzodiazepine flurazepam, which will produce five different metabolites during the process of biotransformation. Each of these metabolites has its own biological effect on the user. Because of normal variation in the speed at which a given individual's body can biotransform and eliminate flurazepam and its metabolites, a single dose might continue to have an effect on the user for *280 hours after a single dose.*[6] Fortunately, there are benzodiazepines such as lorazepam and oxazepam that are eliminated unchanged from the body or they produce metabolites that have minimal biological effect, making them ideal for some patients.

---

[5]Remember: There is the *therapeutic* half-life, the *distribution* half-life, and the *elimination* half-life. This table is based on the therapeutic half-life of the BZs being considered.

[6]To put this into perspective, there are only 168 hours in a 7-day week.

Although the benzodiazepines are often compared with the barbiturates, the mechanism of action of the BZs is more specific than that of the barbiturates, which is one factor that contributes to their large therapeutic index. The benzodiazepine molecules bind at the same gated chloride channel activated by GABA, but require that GABA molecules be present before they have an effect on the neuron. In contrast the barbiturates activate this ion channel even in the absence of GABA (Bisaga, 2008; Brunton et al., 2008; Charney et al., 2006). Thus the benzodiazepines enhance the effects of GABA, forcing the chloride channel to remain open far longer than normal and reducing the "firing" rate of that neuron (Brust, 2004; Raj & Sheehan, 2004; Ramadan, Werder, & Preskorn, 2006).

Surprisingly, although the BZs have been used for more than a half century as anxiolytic medications, there is strong disagreement as to their long-term effectiveness in anxiety control. Some researchers believe that the BZs are effective anxiolytics for only 1–2 months, after which they become less effective (Ayd, Janicak, Davis, & Preskor, 1996; Berry & Mugford, 2007; Fricchione, 2004). It is for this reason that the current theory is that benzodiazepines should be used concurrently with SSRIs for long-term anxiolytic purposes, with the former class of drugs slowly being discontinued after 6–8 weeks (Fricchione, 2004; Raj & Sheehan, 2004). This treatment protocol avoids the danger of BZ-withdrawal "rebound" anxiety, or the "plateau effect" seen when the prescribed BZ becomes less effective as an anxiolytic over time.

It has been suggested that the duration of effects for alprazolam, marketed as an anxiolytic, is too short to provide optimal control of anxiety. Because of the short duration of effect there is a danger that the patient will begin to experience "rebound" anxiety, which is misinterpreted as evidence that he or she needs to continue taking the medication. Many physicians recommend that alprazolam be used for only short periods of time. These observations are not universally accepted, and some physicians view the BZs as being effective for the control of anxiety even over extended periods of time. There is little evidence to suggest that patients become tolerant to the antianxiety effects of the BZs, although they do seem to reach a plateau after which the patient will often report that it "just doesn't work like it used to" (Ciraulo et al., 2005; Raj & Sheehan, 2004). In this case, a dosage adjustment might be called for, although Raj and Sheehan warn that the patient might be seeking that initial sense of relaxation achieved when the medication was first started. Thus even within the medical community there is disagreement as to the optimal use of the benzodiazepines, and as we will discuss later in this chapter, their potential for abuse.

Side Effects of the Benzodiazepines When Used at Normal Dosage Levels

The benzodiazepines are usually prescribed as antianxiety agents. But between 4 and 9% of patients will report a moderate to severe level of sedation when they first start a benzodiazepine. That effect will pass in a few days as the user's body becomes tolerant to the effects of these medications (Stevens & Pollack, 2005). In cases of excess sedation, the physician must consider whether the prescribed dose was too high, the possibility of medication interactions, medication abuse, and the effects of age on the user's ability to biotransform and eliminate the benzodiazepines administered. If a benzodiazepine is required for an older patient, the physician will often prescribe a compound with a shorter half-life, such as lorazepam or oxazepam, compounds that do not require extensive biotransformation prior to elimination.

Some benzodiazepines require extensive biotransformation before elimination might proceed. If patients were to ingest a second, or third dose of the medication before the first dose was entirely biotransformed, they might begin to accumulate a reservoir of nonmetabolized medication in their body that will slowly return to the circulatory system and cause an extended effect on the user's body. Originally developed as a treatment for insomnia, flurazepam was found to produce a metabolite that itself remained biologically active for between 40 and 280 hours[7] after just a single dose (Doghramji, 2003). If patients were to ingest a second dose the following night, they might develop significant levels of drug metabolites, causing extended periods of sedation for the patient. A single dose of the benzodiazepine diazepam might interfere with individuals' ability to drive for up to 7 hours after the dose was ingested, and therapeutic doses of this compound have been shown to prolong users' reaction time, increasing their risk of a motor vehicle accident by 500% (Gitlow, 2007).

There are rare reports of benzodiazepine-induced suicidal thinking in patients who did not demonstrate

---

[7]This is a period of 12 *days*.

such thoughts prior to starting these medications (Breggin, 2008). These medications have also been implicated in the development of a sense of emotional dulling, in which the user finds it difficult to express normal emotions such as grief following the death of a loved one (Breggin, 2008).

Neuroadaptation to, Abuse of, and Addiction to, the Benzodiazepines

Within a few years of their introduction as pharmaceuticals, reports of benzodiazepine abuse and addiction began to surface. Such reports immediately became a source of significant controversy and confusion for a number of reasons. First, even when used as prescribed for just a few months, patients were reported to experience a *discontinuation syndrome*. This process was confused with the development of tolerance seen in drug abusers, and many health care professionals have mistakenly interpreted this as a sign of benzodiazepine abuse or addiction.

The brain is constantly adapting to environmental demands, a process known as *neuroadaptation*[8] (O'Brien, 2005, 2006). This process is natural, and reflects the ongoing process of adaptation in the brain as it develops new neural pathways and changes in receptor site responsiveness to the neurotransmitters that it receives from other neurons. If used on a continual basis, even if used as prescribed, the brain will adapt to the continual presence of the benzodiazepine molecules by making changes in the GABA receptor site responsiveness. If the patient should abruptly discontinue the benzodiazepine (or any other mood-altering compound), the brain must now adapt to the sudden absence of the BZ molecules, causing a "rebound" or "discontinuance" syndrome that can cause significant distress for the user (O'Brien, 2005). Because of this process, the Royal College of Psychiatrists in Great Britain recommend that benzodiazepines not be used on a continual basis for more than 4 weeks (Gitlow, 2007).

One point of confusion is that the discontinuance syndrome is just a milder version of the withdrawal syndrome seen when a person abuses a sedative-hypnotic for extended periods of time. Patients experiencing the discontinuation syndrome often object when being told that they are experiencing "withdrawal" because they are

TABLE 7-2 BENZODIAZEPINE WITHDRAWAL SYMPTOMS FOLLOWING EXTENDED PERIODS OF USE AT HIGH DOSAGE LEVELS
Abdominal cramps
Agitation (possibly to the point of mania)
Anxiety (often "rebound" anxiety)
Anorexia
Ataxia
Confusion
Delirium
Depersonalization/derealization
Depression
Dizziness/hypotension
Fatigue or muscle weakness
Formication
Irritability
Insomnia
Nausea/vomiting
Nightmares
Postural hypotension
Seizures (possibly leading to death)
Sweating
Withdrawal psychosis

NOTE: Based on Bisaga (2008), Ciraulo et al. (2005), N. S. Miller and Adams (2006), and G. E. Smith and Wesson (2004).

certainly *not* drug addicts! So the term *discontinuance syndrome* is applied to the adjustment process when the patient was taking a sedative-hypnotic as prescribed, and the term *withdrawal* is used when the patient has been abusing the BZs. Some of the more common symptoms of the benzodiazepine withdrawal syndrome are identified in Table 7-2.

The discontinuance or withdrawal syndrome in long-term BZ users might prove to be rather severe, and appears similar to that seen in the barbiturate withdrawal syndrome. Thus in extreme cases the benzodiazepine withdrawal syndrome has the potential to be life threatening[9] (Perry et al., 2007). In such cases, a gradual "taper" may be instituted over a period of 6–12 months to minimize the withdrawal discomfort

---

[8]See Glossary.

[9]It is for this reason that benzodiazepine withdrawal should be attempted *only* under the supervision of a physician.

(Bisaga, 2008). The symptoms of the discontinuance syndrome will vary as a result of (a) the duration the patient received a BZ, (b) the dose prescribed, (c) the half-life of the medication used, and (d) the individual's expectations. Approximately 44% of patients who took a low dose of a prescribed benzodiazepine reported withdrawal symptoms, some of which were quite distressing to the user (Perry et al., 2007).

To minimize the patient's distress during the discontinuation of benzodiazepine use, the patient is often placed on a slow "taper" from these medications. When the individual's daily dosage level reaches 10–25% of their former dose, they may experience "rebound" anxiety, which might actually be more intense than the original episode of anxiety for a few weeks (Wesson & Smith, 2005). The use of mood stabilizers, or Seroquel® (quetiapine fumarate), has been suggested as an anxiolytic if patients should request help with their anxiety during the taper (Wesson & Smith, 2005). Further anticipatory guidance might prove of value for patients going through the discontinuance syndrome, so that they might understand the symptoms and their cause, and that this is a transitory phase.

It is of interest to learn that, unlike the other drugs of abuse, the benzodiazepines actually *lower* rather than the dopamine levels in the mesolimbic system of the brain (Bisaga, 2008). This might be the reason why the abuse potential of the benzodiazepines is quite low and only a subset of people intentionally abuse these compounds (Bisaga, 2008). Research has found that 80% of those who abuse benzodiazepines also have other substance use disorders, and in such cases the BZs are usually not the primary drug of abuse (Longo, Parran, Johnson, & Kinsey, 2000; Sattar & Bhatia, 2003).

Benzodiazepine abusers (a) use these compounds to enhance the effects of the primary drug of abuse, (b) control some of the unwanted side effects of the primary drug of abuse, or (c) help control the effects of the withdrawal process from their primary drug of abuse (Longo et al., 2000). For example, the BZ diazepam might be substituted for heroin when it is unavailable, or intermixed with low-quality heroin to enhance its effects. It will also be abused by patients on methadone maintenance programs to obtain a sense of euphoria when these compounds are intermixed. The exact mechanism for this is not known but may reflect the suppression of cortical inhibitions (Ciraulo et al., 2005), or indirect activation of the Mu opioid receptor site (Bisaga, 2008). Benzodiazepine intoxication is very similar to alcohol intoxication, with the exception of

the fact that it does not cause slurred speech. Thus although the BZs are not popular drugs of abuse as such, they do have some abuse potential.

Patients who are recovering from *any* SUD are "at risk" for a reactivation of their addiction if they should receive a prescription for a BZ. For example, approximately 25% of recovering alcoholics relapse after receiving a prescription for a benzodiazepine (Fricchione, 2004; Gitlow, 2007; Sattar & Bhatia, 2003). At best, there is only limited evidence that the BZs can be used safely with patients who have an SUD (Drake, 2007; Sattar & Bhatia, 2003). This is most clearly seen in the results of the study conducted by the team of R. E. Clark, Xie, and Brunette (2004), who found that whereas the BZs are often used as an adjunct to the treatment of various forms of mental illness, their use did not improve clinical outcomes and that people with an SUD were likely to try and abuse their BZs. It is for this reason that it is recommended that benzodiazepines be used *only* after alternative treatments have failed in people with a substance use disorder (Ciraulo & Nace, 2000; Seppala, 2004; Sommer, 2005). Further, *if* benzodiazepine treatment is necessary, the prescribing physician should put special restrictions in place to limit the patient's access to large amounts of the medication, and that a BZ such as clonazepam should be prescribed (Seppala, 2004) to minimize the danger of misuse of the benzodiazepines.

Complications of Benzodiazepine Use When Used as Prescribed

In spite of their popularity as prescribed medications, the benzodiazepine family of compounds has many side effects, especially in older users. Some side effects seen when these medications are used at normal dosage levels include irritability, hostility, rage, or aggression (Drummer & Odell, 2001; Breggin, 2008; Brust, 2004). The aggression/rage response appears to reflect the benzodiazepine-induced cortical disinhibition effect. Because both alcohol and the benzodiazepines affect the same calcium channel in the neural wall through the action of each chemical on the GABA molecule, cross-tolerance between alcohol and the BZs is common (O'Brien, 2006). The mixture of a BZ with another CNS depressant, such as alcohol, over-the-counter or prescribed antihistamine, narcotic analgesics, or other compounds, might have a synergistic[10] effect, increasing the

---

[10]See Glossary.

CNS depressant-induced sedation possibly to the point where death can occur (Ciraulo et al., 2006).

Benzodiazepines have been found to interfere with normal sexual function in both men and women (Finger et al., 1997). Also, although many BZs were marketed as hypnotic agents, they have been found to interfere with normal sleep patterns even when used at normal dosage levels (Qureshi & Lee-Chiong, 2004). Further, when discontinued the BZs have been found to sometimes cause a phenomenon called *rebound insomnia,* in which the original problem returns until the body adapts to the absence of the drug molecules (Doghramji, 2003; Qureshi & Lee-Chiong, 2004). This may result in patients again starting to take the BZ to help them sleep again (Gitlow, 2007).

Even when used at normal dosage levels, the BZs can interfere with normal memory function, a condition called *anterograde amnesia.* This condition, most commonly seen in older patients, still is so common that 10% of patients assessed for a memory problem are thought to experience benzodiazepine-induced memory impairment (Curran et al., 2003). The mechanism for the BZ-induced memory impairment appears to be similar to that of the alcohol-related "blackout," and it will last for the duration of the BZ's effects on the user (Drummer & Odell, 2001). The mechanism has been compared with that of Korsakoff's syndrome in that the same regions of the brain are involved in each condition (Ghoneim, 2004a).

Although marketed as anxiolytic agents, the benzodiazepines reduce the level of neural function in virtually every region of the brain to some degree (Breggin, 2008). This is consistent with the findings of Gonzalez et al. (2009), who suggested that there was "compelling evidence" that long-term benzodiazepine use even at therapeutic levels can induce "significant and widespread neuropsychological impairments that persist even after many months abstinence" (p. 436). Currently, it is not known whether these cognitive impairments will resolve over time or the time line required for such resolution.

Benzodiazepine-related psychomotor impairment is common. For example, the risk of a motor vehicle accident was found to be 50% higher for a person who had ingested *just a single dose* of the benzodiazepine diazepam (Drummer & Odell, 2001). Further, even at recommended dosage levels, there have been rare reports of benzodiazepine-induced respiratory depression, especially in patients with preexisting breathing problems, such as sleep apnea or chronic lung disease (Charney et al., 2006). In such patients, BZ-related respiratory depression might be serious or even fatal (Charney et al., 2006; Drummer & Odell, 2001). Also, patients who suffer from Alzheimer's disease should not use a benzodiazepine except under a physician's supervision to avoid BZ-related confusion (Drummer & Odell, 2001).

Although often used as an adjunct to the treatment of depression, on rare occasions benzodiazepines can induce, or exacerbate, a depressive reaction in the patient (Breggin, 2008; Drummer & Odell, 2001; N. S. Miller & Adams, 2006). Further, benzodiazepine-related thoughts of suicide have been identified as a potential side effect of these medications (Drummer & Odell, 2001). Although it is not possible to identify every potential side effect of these medications, this list should illustrate the fact that in spite of their relative safety, the benzodiazepines present risks to the user even when used at normal dosage levels.

Drug Interactions Between Pharmaceuticals and the Benzodiazepines

The most popular method of BZ administration is orally, a process that can be significantly slowed if the patient should also take a dose of an over-the-counter antacid (Raj & Sheehan, 2004). The concurrent use of cimetidine (Tagamet®) can result in increased benzodiazepine blood levels (Tatro, 2009), and thus these medications should be used only under a physician's supervision. There have been a "few anecdotal case reports" (Ciraulo et al., 2006, p. 267) of patients who had an adverse reaction while taking BZs and lithium. The authors reviewed a single case report of a patient who developed profound hypothermia that was attributed to this combination of medications. Further, the authors suggested that the combination of lithium and the benzodiazepines diazepam and oxazepam may cause higher levels of depression in patients who intermix these medications.

Patients who are taking disulfiram (Antabuse®) should use benzodiazepines with caution, because the combination of these medications can reduce the speed at which the liver can biotransform benzodiazepines such as diazepam and chlordiazepoxide (DeVane & Nemeroff, 2002; Tatro, 2009). Surprisingly, grapefruit juice has been found to slow the P-450 metabolic pathway in the liver, slowing the rate at which the benzodiazepines might be biotransformed (Charney et al., 2001). Further, benzodiazepine use can alter the blood levels of many antipsychotic medications such as haloperidol and fluphenazine by competing with the BZ molecules for access to the liver's biotransformation enzymes (Ciraulo et al., 2006).

There is limited evidence to suggest that benzodiazepines may enhance the respiratory depressant effect of buprenorphine, possibly to lethal levels if these medications are used concurrently (Ciraulo et al., 2006). Benzodiazepine use has been shown to alter the blood levels of digoxin, and patients receiving both medications should have frequent blood level tests to avoid the danger of drug-induced digoxin toxicity. Patients receiving prescription medications such as phenytoin, mephenytoin, ethotoin, fluoxetine, propranolol, and metoprolol should be aware of the danger that these medications might interfere with the biotransformation of benzodiazepines such as diazepam (DeVane & Nemeroff, 2002). Patients who are taking the anxiolytic medication alprazolam who also take St. John's wort might experience *more* anxiety than usual, as the latter compound induces a more rapid biotransformation of alprazolam thus limiting its anxiolytic effects (DeVane & Nemeroff, 2002).

Because of the potential for a synergistic effect between the two medications, patients taking *any* form of CNS depressant medication should not take a BZ except under the supervision of their physician. The effects of two or more CNS depressants might result in higher than anticipated levels of sedation to perhaps life-threatening levels of respiratory depression. Patients who use the herbal medicine Kava should not use a benzodiazepine, as the former compound will enhance the sedative effects of the benzodiazepine to potentially dangerous levels. There have been case reports indicating that the benzodiazepine blood levels in women using hormone-based birth control medications might be lower than normal because the birth control medication increased the speed of the benzodiazepine biotransformation (Tatro, 2009). In contrast to this, patients using propoxyphene might experience higher than normal blood levels of benzodiazepines because the former medication inhibits the biotransformation of the BZs (Tatro, 2009).

It is important to note that patients taking valproic acid and lorazepam might become comatose because of the interaction between these two compounds (Wynn et al., 2009). Although this list does not include every potential interaction between benzodiazepines and other compounds, it should alert the reader to the need for the patient to check with a pharmacist or physician before mixing benzodiazepines with other prescribed, over-the-counter, or herbal compounds.

Long-Term Consequences of Chronic Benzodiazepine Use

The benzodiazepines were originally introduced in the 1960s as safe and nonaddicting substitutes for the barbiturates, to be used both as anxiolytic and hypnotic agents. Surprisingly, the benzodiazepines have been found to be neither safe nor nonaddicting. Health care professionals have learned that they must weigh the potential benefits of the use of benzodiazepines against their potential dangers. Further, although frequently prescribed as anxiolytic agents, their use in the long-term treatment of anxiety has not been studied in detail (P. T. White, 2009).

Benzodiazepines have an abuse potential, especially those BZs with shorter half-lives such as diazepam, lorazepam, alprazolam, and triazolam (Ciraulo & Sarid-Segal, 2005). There is also emerging evidence that the benzodiazepine clonazepam is gaining favor with some drug abusers (Longo & Johnson, 2000). Benzodiazepine abusers might be viewed as falling into one of two groups (O'Brien, 2005, 2006): (a) those individuals who abuse these compounds to achieve a sense of euphoria, and (b) those individuals who begin to abuse a prescribed BZ by taking more of it, or for longer periods, than was prescribed. The first subgroup is rather small, as the majority of those who take a benzodiazepine do not report experiencing any significant sense of euphoria. However, there are those who do experience some degree of euphoria from benzodiazepines, and *intravenous* BZ abusers report a greater sense of euphoria than do oral abusers (Bisaga, 2008; Brust, 2004). Abusers who wish to achieve a sense of euphoria are usually polydrug abusers, a fact that reinforces the injunction that these medications should rarely, if ever, be used to treat patients with SUDs (E. M. Jones et al., 2003; O'Brien, 2006). Polydrug abusers will usually take a benzodiazepine(s) to supplement the effects of their drug(s) of choice, to minimize the effects of drug withdrawal, and only rarely as a source of euphoria.

The second subgroup might overlap with the first group of BZ abusers to a small degree, but for the most part were prescribed benzodiazepines by a physician and became tolerant to the anxiolytic effects of these medications over time. In their attempt to overcome their growing tolerance to the anxiolytic effect of the benzodiazepines, these patients might slowly increase their daily dose of a benzodiazepine to dangerous levels.[11] For example, although 5–10 mg of diazepam two or three times a day might initially cause sedation and relief from anxiety, there have been reports of abusers building their intake level to 1000 mg/day as their tolerance to this compound develops over time, a dosage level that might prove fatal to the drug-naive user (O'Brien, 2006). Unfortunately, individuals who abuse BZs in this manner rarely are motivated to discontinue using benzodiazepines, in spite of their protests to the contrary (Work Group on Substance Use Disorders, 2007).

Even when just taken as prescribed over extended periods of time, patients may come to rely on the benzodiazepine and anticipate their next dose to help them deal with what they view as insurmountable anxiety. This is a form of "psychological" dependency that is independent of the process of neuroadaptation. Such patients may engage in "clock watching" as the time nears for their next anticipated dose, and then eagerly take the dose to help them cope with what might actually be "rebound" anxiety induced when the previous dose begins to wear off (Raj & Sheehan, 2004). For example, it is possible to start to experience withdrawal symptoms between doses of alprazolam (Breggin, 2008). To minimize this danger, BZs with longer half-lives have been suggested, which is one reason why clonazepam is gaining popularity as an anxiolytic. The longer half-life of this compound means that the blood levels will drop more slowly between doses, controlling "rebound" anxiety.

Following periods of extended use, the BZs are able to induce a characteristic withdrawal syndrome similar to that of the alcohol withdrawal syndrome, as was discussed earlier. All CNS depressants, including the benzodiazepines, are capable of producing a *toxic psychosis* or *organic brain syndrome,* especially when the medications are taken in exceptionally high doses. Some of the symptoms of this drug-induced disruption of normal brain function include visual and auditory hallucinations, paranoid delusions, hyperthermia, delirium, seizures, and possible death (Ciraulo & Sarid-Segal, 2005). Because of the potential for death, *medical supervision during the withdrawal process is imperative.* The attending physician will have a wide range of pharmaceutical support agents to call on to help minimize the withdrawal discomfort and to treat complications.

Although once widely used as a hypnotic, evidence suggests that the process of neuroadaptation to the hypnotic effects of the benzodiazepines causes them to lose effectiveness after perhaps a week or two of nightly use (Carvey, 1998). It is for this reason that the BZs are recommended for only the *short-term* treatment of insomnia, and only after other potential causes of insomnia are ruled out (Conroy et al. 2008; S. Taylor, McCracken, Wilson, & Copeland, 1998). Surprisingly, patients report having used a BZ as a hypnotic for weeks, months, or even years, suggesting that the process of taking these medications has become part of the psychological ritual that the individual follows to ensure proper sleep more than a pharmacological effect of the BZs (Carvey, 1998).

As discussed earlier, the BZs also interfere with the normal sleep cycle and suppress rapid eye movement (REM) sleep. If used for an extended period of time, the REM suppression might cause the sleeper to experience REM "rebound," a phenomenon in which the dreamer spends more time than usual in REM sleep, apparently in an attempt to "catch up" on lost dream time. Dreams during REM rebound periods can be rather intense and frightening, and the patient should be warned that this is a possible reaction to the discontinuance of the benzodiazepine. It has been suggested that therapeutic doses of melatonin[12] might also prove useful in promoting normal sleep in the former benzodiazepine user (Garfinkel, Zisapel, Wainstein, & Laundon, 1999; Peles et al., 2007; Pettit, 2000).

There is a small, controversial body of evidence that suggests that chronic BZ use might cause transient changes in cognition, which may or may not resolve with abstinence (Stewart, 2005). Thus medical and mental health professionals should be aware of this potential consequence of chronic benzodiazepine use/abuse.

Benzodiazepines as a Substitute for Other Drugs of Abuse

Individuals who abuse the BZs usually do so more in order to help them compensate for the use of other compounds than because they desire its effects; although as noted earlier in this chapter, on rare occasions BZ abusers are found who desire the effects of these compounds in their own right (Bisaga, 2008).

---

[11]Usually by obtaining prescriptions from multiple doctors, different pharmacies, or illicit suppliers, or by buying drugs from "Internet 'pharmacies.'"

[12]See Glossary.

Because of their ability to mitigate alcohol withdrawal distress, the BZs are often abused by alcohol-dependent people who wish to avoid the smell of alcohol on their breath during the day. The author of this text has been told by several patients who engage in this practice that 10 mg of diazepam has the same physical effect on them as three to four "stiff" drinks, which would certainly abort the alcohol withdrawal syndrome in most alcohol-dependent people! So, patients go to the doctor with a complaint of "anxiety" (which is to say a misdiagnosed early alcohol withdrawal syndrome, with patients conveniently not mentioning their alcohol use to the prescribing physician) and emerge with a prescription for a benzodiazepine. This will allow them to work throughout the day, without the smell of alcohol on their breath.

It has been found that between 40 and 50 percent of patients in methadone maintenance programs also use benzodiazepines (Bisaga, 2008). It is not known how many of these individuals *need* a benzodiazepine as opposed to *want* them because of the potential for an intentional interactive effect between these two medications. The usual practice is for the patient to ingest a massive dose of a benzodiazepine (the equivalent of 100–300 mg of diazepam) between 30 and 120 minutes after ingesting the methadone, in order to "boost" the effects of the methadone (Drummer & Odell, 2001; O'Brien, 2005, 2006). People who are heroin dependent who are going through unsupervised heroin withdrawal may use large doses of a benzodiazepine to eliminate or mitigate their withdrawal distress, and people who abuse a central nervous stimulant such as cocaine or the amphetamines may use benzodiazepines to control the unwanted side effects of their primary drug of choice.

Section Summary

As should be evident by this point, the benzodiazepines offer the user a double-edged sword. Although they have a number of potent applications, they also have many side effects that make their use problematic at best, if not life threatening. These compounds may be abused in a number of ways, and drug abusers may seek them out for their primary effects. More commonly, the benzodiazepines are abused to control/mitigate the effects of the individual's primary drug(s) of choice, to control the symptoms of withdrawal from other compounds, or as a substitute for other compounds that may not be available to the

drug abuser at that time. Because of these drawbacks, pharmaceutical companies have continued the search for compounds that may offer a safer alternative to the benzodiazepines, many of which will be discussed in the next section of this chapter.

Buspirone

In 1986, a new medication marketed under the name of BuSpar (buspirone) was introduced as an antianxiety agent. Buspirone is a member of a new class of compounds known as the *azapirones*,[13] which are chemically different from the benzodiazepines. Buspirone was initially discovered as a result of a search for an antipsychotic compound that lacked the harsh side effects of the existing agents. Although the antipsychotic effects of buspirone were limited, researchers were impressed by its ability to reduce the individual's anxiety level and initially thought that it was as effective as the benzodiazepines as an anxiolytic (Drummer & Odell, 2001). Further, unlike the BZs buspirone did not appear to potentiate the effects of alcohol.

These safety advantages are outweighed by the fact that the patient must take the medication for up to 2–6 weeks before it becomes effective (Doble et al., 2004; Perry et al., 2007). This is a major disadvantage in patients who desire immediate relief from their anxiety symptoms. Some of the more major side effects of buspirone include gastrointestinal problems, drowsiness, decreased concentration, dizziness, agitation, headache, lightheadedness, nervousness, diarrhea, excitement, sweating/clamminess, nausea, depression, nasal congestion, and rare feelings of fatigue (Hudziak & Waterman, 2005; Perry et al., 2007). Patients who have Parkinson's disease who receive buspirone might experience an exacerbation of their Parkinson's disease symptoms, although this does not occur in every patient (Perry et al., 2007).

Unlike benzodiazepines, buspirone has no significant anticonvulsant action, and it is most effective in controlling generalized anxiety disorder (GAD) but does not seem to mitigate the discomfort of panic attacks (Hudziak & Waterman, 2005). It does seem to help augment the effects of the SSRI class of antidepressants, and at high doses may even function as an antidepressant in its own right. It is not of value in treating the alcohol or benzodiazepine withdrawal

---

[13]The team of Perry wet al. (2007) suggested that it was a member of the *azaspriodecanedione* family of chemicals.

syndromes (Hudziak & Waterman, 2005). There is also limited evidence that it might assist patients who wish to discontinue the use of cigarettes who experience a degree of anxiety in this process (Covey et al., 2000).

The Pharmacology of Buspirone

Buspirone's mechanism of action is not well understood at this time. There is little evidence that buspirone interacts with GABA receptors, as is true for the benzodiazepines, but rather that it has a dual action. Presynaptically, it functions as a full agonist at the serotonin[14] 5-HT1A receptor site of the dorsal midbrain raphe, inhibiting the synthesis of serotonin in this region of the brain (Perry et al., 2007). It also appears to function as a partial agonist of the 5-HT1A receptor sites in the limbic region and cortex (Perry et al., 2007; Ramadan et al., 2006). The combined effects of these mechanisms of action appear to balance serotonin levels, stimulating the production if it is low and reducing it if it is high.

Depending on the individual's biochemistry, the peak blood levels of buspirone are achieved in 60–90 minutes following a single dose, although the absorption might be doubled if it is taken with food (Perry et al., 2007). It is extensively biotransformed during the "first-pass metabolism" process (Hudziak & Waterman, 2005). During biotransformation at least seven major and five minor metabolites are produced, only one of which is biologically active to any degree.[15] This may be the metabolite that causes some of buspirone's adverse effects. In the body 99% becomes protein bound, and its elimination half-life is approximately 2.5 hours. This requires the patient to take a dose three to four times a day, as opposed to just once or twice a day for the benzodiazepines with long half-lives like clonazepam or diazepam. However, there is no cross-tolerance between buspirone and alcohol or the benzodiazepines, which is an advantage in some situations. However, patients taking these compounds may have to be "tapered" off of the original compound before being started on buspirone (Perry et al., 2007). The abuse potential of buspirone is limited (G. E. Smith & Wesson, 2004). There is no evidence of a discontinuation process similar to that seen in benzodiazepines, and no evidence of buspirone-related memory impairment or tolerance to its effects.

Adverse Effects of Buspirone Use

The most serious adverse effect of buspirone use is the development of the *serotonin syndrome*.[16] This is more common when buspirone is used concurrently with the antidepressant medications bloxetine or fluvoxamine but can develop under other conditions (Sternbach, 2003). Deaths from overdoses *involving buspirone alone* have not been reported as of this time (Perry et al., 2007).

Some of the reported side effects associated with buspirone use include headaches, dizziness, drowsiness, nervousness, a sense of disquiet, dysphoria, and a degree of psychomotor impairment that is still less than that seen with benzodiazepine use (Perry et al., 2007).

Drug Interactions Involving Buspirone

Buspirone is known to interact with the antidepressant medications known as monoamine oxidase inhibitors (MAO inhibitors or MAOIs), and it is recommended that patients taking these antidepressant medications discontinue them 2 weeks or more before starting buspirone to avoid drug-induced hypertensive episodes (Ramadan, Werder, & Preskorn, 2006). Patients taking the medications diltiazem, verapamil, erythromycin, intraconazole, or clarithromycline should not take buspirone, as they block its biotransformation and cause buspirone blood levels to rise beyond the recommended level (Ramadan et al., 2006; Venkatakrishnan, Shader, & Greenblatt, 2006). Patients taking this medication should avoid large amounts of grapefruit juice (*Monthly Prescribing Reference*, 2008). Although this list is not all inclusive, it does demonstrate the need for the patient to consult a psychiatrist before taking buspirone concurrently with any other medication.

Although initially advertised as a different anxiolytic that was safer than benzodiazepines, buspirone has failed to live up to its initial promise except in certain special applications.

Zolpidem

Zolpidem is a member of the *benzodiazepine receptor agonist* (BRA) class of medications, introduced in 1993 and sold under the brand name of Ambien®. The BRAs have come to dominate the market for hypnotics, although on occasion one will still find a patient who is taking a benzodiazepine for this purpose. Buspirone is

[14]See Glossary.

[15]Which, if you must know, is 1-pryrimidinylpiperazine.

[16]See Glossary.

designed for oral use in the short-term treatment (<4 weeks) of insomnia, and is available only by prescription. This compound belongs to the *imidazopryidine* family of compounds, and is more selective than the benzodiazepines in that it binds at just a subset of the benzodiazepine receptors in the brain. This allows zolpidem to have only a minor anticonvulsant effect, and that is usually seen above the hypnotic dose (Doble, Martin, & Nutt, 2004).

Zolpidem is administered orally, and after a single dose peak blood levels are achieved in 2–3 hours (Dubovsky, 2005; Schuckit, 2006a). The elimination half-life is between 2 and 3 hours in the normal adult and slightly longer in the geriatric adult (Charney et al., 2006; Doble et al., 2004; Dubovsky, 2005). The majority of a single dose of zolpidem is biotransformed in the liver into inactive metabolites, which are then excreted by the kidneys. When used as directed, there is little evidence of neuroadaptation to zolpidem's hypnotic effects even after as long as 1 year of regular use (Folks & Burke, 1998; Holm & Goa, 2000). However, Schuckit (2006a) disagreed with this assessment, noting that a limited degree of neuoradaptation can develop after zolpidem has been used each night for as little as 2 weeks. There have also been rare reports of patients becoming tolerant to its hypnotic effects after using it at very high dosage levels for a number of years (Holm & Goa, 2000).

Unlike the benzodiazepines, zolpidem causes only a minor reduction in REM sleep when used at normal dosage levels, and it does not interfere with the normal progression through the stages of sleep, allowing for a more restful night's sleep (Doble et al., 2004; Schuckit, 2006a).

Adverse Effects of Zolpidem at Normal Dosage Levels

The adverse effects of zolpidem are dose-related, although patients taking this medication at prescribed dosage levels have also experienced one or more of the following side effects: nightmares, headache, gastrointestinal upset, agitation, residual drowsiness, and in rare cases hallucinations or psychosis (Breggin, 2008; Schuckit, 2006a). Some users have reported "sleepwalking" like behaviors including driving motor vehicles, eating meals, or other complex tasks, without any subsequent recall of these events (Breggin, 2008).

Zolpidem is contraindicated in persons with sleep apnea as it increases both the frequency and duration of apnea episodes (Holm & Goa, 2000). There have also

been reports of users experiencing suicidal thoughts when taking zolpidem as prescribed.

Effects of Zolpidem at Above-Normal Dosage Levels

At dosage levels above 20 mg/day zolpidem has been found to reduce REM sleep time, and there are reports of patients experiencing REM "rebound" when they discontinue the medication (Ciraulo et al., 2005). Volunteers who ingested 50 mg doses reported such symptoms as visual perceptual disturbances, ataxis, dizziness, nausea, and/or vomiting. Patients who ingested up to 40 times the maximum recommended dosage have recovered without ill effects. *There will be a synergistic effect between zolpidem and other CNS depressants possibly ingested in an overdose, and some such overdoses have proven fatal.*[17]

The Abuse Potential of Zolpidem

Since the time of its introduction, evidence has emerged suggesting that its abuse potential might be far higher than was originally thought. Ciraulo and Sarid-Segal (2005) presented a case summary of an individual who increased his daily dose from 5 to 10 mg/day to over 800 mg/day over a period of time, for example. On a positive note, the abuse potential of zolpidem appears to be highest in people with a prior history of an SUD (Gitlow, 2007; Holm & Goa, 2000). Its abuse potential appears to be about the same as that of the benzodiazepines (Charney et al., 2001), and like the BZs its use may trigger thoughts of returning to active drug use (E. M. Jones et al., 2003).

In the late 1960s and early 1970s, there were reports of drug abusers who would ingest the medication methaqualone and then resist its effects to achieve a sense of euphoria. Surprisingly, there are rare reports of patients who will do the same with zolpidem, which means that after 50 years of dedicated research, we are right back to where we were in the middle of the 20th century.

Zaleplon

The compound zaleplon is sold in the United States under the brand name *Sonata®*, is a member of the *pryazolpyrimidine* class of pharmaceuticals, and also functions as a BRA ("Insomnia in Later Life," 2006). Animal research suggests that zaleplon has some

---

[17]Any known or suspected overdose should immediately be assessed and treated by a physician.

sedative and anticonvulsant effects, but it is approved for use in the United States only as a hypnotic (Danjou et al., 1999). Zaleplon is administered orally, in capsules containing 5 mg, 10 mg, or 20 mg of the drug. In most cases the 10-mg dose is thought to be the most effective, although in people with low body weight the 5 mg dose might be more appropriate (Danjou et al., 1999).

The strongest effects are observed in the first 4 hours after ingestion, and although it seems to improve sleep latency, there is little evidence that it affects total sleep time at therapeutic doses (Perry et al., 2007). This is consistent with the observed half-life of 1 hour (Doble et al., 2006).[18] The liver is the site of zaleplon biotransformation, with about 30% of the dose becoming biotransformed through the first-pass metabolism process, and less than 1% of the dose is eliminated from the body unchanged. The majority of a dose is biotransformed by the liver into less active metabolites, which are eliminated in the feces and urine (Charney et al., 2006).

It is thought that the zaleplon molecule binds at the same benzodiazepine subtype receptor site utilized by zolpidem (Charney et al., 2006; J. K. Walsh, Pollak, Scharf, Schweitzer, & Vogel, 2000). There is little evidence of a drug "hangover" effect, but the patient is still advised not to attempt to operate machinery for 4 hours after taking the last dose (Danjou et al., 1999; Doble et al., 2003; J. K. Walsh et al., 2000). Some of the side effects observed at therapeutic doses include headache, rhinitis, nausea, myalgia, anterograde amnesia, dizziness, depersonalization, drug-induced hangover effects, constipation, dry mouth, gout, bronchitis, asthma attacks, nervousness, depression, ataxia, and paradoxical insomnia.

Tolerance to the hypnotic effects of zaleplon develops rapidly, and for this reason this compound is intended only for the *short-term* treatment of insomnia. Patients have reported rebound insomnia after discontinuation, although this is more common when the patient was using higher dosage levels (Dubovsky, 2005). The abuse potential is similar to that of the benzodiazepines, especially triazolam (G. E. Smith & Wesson, 2004). When used even at therapeutic doses for more than 2 weeks, it has been implicated as the cause of problems such as muscle cramps, tremor, vomiting, and on rare occasions withdrawal seizures. Because of its potential to trigger addictive thinking, the team of E. M. Jones (2003) does not recommend that it be used in patients with a SUD.

Ramelteon

Ramelteon is sold in the United States under the brand name of Rozerem, and is a novel hypnotic agent that binds at the melatonin receptor (Conroy et al., 2008; Winkelman, 2006). It is thought that by enhancing the effects of melatonin, ramelteon is able to facilitate the sleep cycle, an advantage for patients with alcohol use disorders because their melatonin levels are usually depleted when they stop drinking and enter the early stages of abstinence.

Ramelteon is administered orally, is rapidly absorbed through the gastrointestinal tract, and peak blood levels following a single dose are found approximately 45 minutes after the medication was ingested (Neubauer, 2005; Winkelman, 2006). But the drug is extensively biotransformed in the first-pass metabolism process, with less than 2% of the dose ingested actually reacting the brain (Neubauer, 2005; Winkelman, 2006). About 85% of the metabolites are found in the urine (Neubauer, 2005). There is no apparent potentiation effect between ramelteon and the benzodiazepines, and the compound has an elimination half-life of between 1.0 and 2.6 hours (Neubauer, 2005). It does not seem to exacerbate sleep breathing problems or chronic obstructive pulmonary disease (COPD), but there is a minor potentiation effect between ramelteon and alcohol (Neubauer, 2006). Although it would appear to be safe to use in patients with an SUD, the possibility that it will trigger a relapse has not been ruled out as of this time.

Rohypnol

Flunitrazepam, which is sold in other countries under the brand name of Rohypnol, is a benzodiazepine that is not legally sold in the United States. It is thus a Schedule IV compound under the Controlled Substances Act of 1970.[19] Possession of or trafficking in flunitrazepam might be punished by up to 20 years in prison at this time.

Flunitrazepam is used by physicians in other countries as a presurgical medication, a muscle relaxant, and a hypnotic (Gahlinger, 2004; Gwinnell & Adamec, 2006; Palmer & Edmunds, 2003). Its abuse was first

---

[18]Remember: It is generally accepted that it takes five half-life periods to eliminate almost all of a compound from the body, so after 5 hours, virtually all of the drug would have been eliminated from the patient's body, allowing the patient to awaken naturally.

[19]See Appendix 4.

identified in the United States during the mid-1990s, when it gained a reputation as a "date rape" drug (Gahlinger, 2004). Its pharmacological characteristics, especially when mixed with alcohol, could induce a state of anterograde amnesia that would last for 8–24 hours, a characteristic that many men are reputed to have taken advantage of to facilitate a date rape. To combat this, the manufacturer added a harmless compound that would turn the drink a dark blue if it were to be added to alcohol, thus alerting the drinker that it had been tampered with (Klein & Kramer, 2004).

Flunitrazepam is estimated to be 10 times as potent as diazepam, and this makes it hard to be detected with standard urine toxicology tests. The manufacturer has provided a program of free urine drug testing to law enforcement officials who suspect that the drinker was the victim of a "date rape" (Palmer & Edmunds, 2003). Illicit-drug abusers will often mix flunitrazepam with other compounds (such as marijuana and alcohol) to enhance their effects. The combination of marijuana and flunitrazepam is said to produce a "floating" sensation. Adolescents have been reported to use flunitrazepam to remain intoxicated in class, while avoiding detection with standard drug urine toxicology test kits (Greydanus & Patel, 2003; Wesson & Smith, 2005).

Chemically, flunitrazepam is a derivative of chlordiazepoxide, and is reportedly 10 times as potent as diazepam (Gahlinger, 2004; Klein & Kramer, 2004). Physicians usually prescribe 0.5–2 mg of flunitrazepam. Peak blood levels are achieved in between 30 and 120 minutes following a single oral dose (Saum & Inciardi, 1997). Flurintrazepam has an elimination half-life that is significantly longer than its duration of effect, because it is rapidly sequestered in body tissues following absorption. The elimination half-life can last from 15 to 66 hours (J. H. Woods & Winger, 1997), whereas the effects last only 8–10 hours (Klein & Kramer, 2004) because of this distribution pattern. Less than 1% of a dose of flunitrazepam is excreted unchanged.

Drug abusers usually take double the recommended dose, which begins to produce sedation in 20–30 minutes and which will cause an effect for 8–12 hours. Because it is a member of the benzodiazepine family of drugs, the effects are similar to those seen with other BZs in use in this country (Klein & Kramer, 2004). It is capable of causing a pharmacological state of dependence, and when discontinued will cause the characteristic benzodiazepine withdrawal syndrome. Withdrawal after extended periods of use is potentially dangerous, and like the other BZs flunitrazepam can induce withdrawal seizures. For this reason, *flunitrazepam withdrawal should be carried out only under the supervision of a physician*. Although it is a potent compound, evidence would suggest that the legitimate medical applications for which flunitrazepam is used around the globe can be met through the use of other benzodiazepine compounds here in the United States, and it is unlikely to ever be legalized in this country.

Chapter Summary

In the middle of the 20th century, pharmaceutical companies began to search for compounds that might be used as anxiolytics and hypnotics, but with a larger therapeutic index than was possible with the barbiturates. In the 1960s, a class of compounds known as the *benzodiazepines* was introduced, and rapidly became the treatment of choice for anxiety control and to help the individual fall asleep. Unfortunately, although they were introduced as "nonaddicting" and "safe" compounds that might be substituted for barbiturates, there is now evidence that they have an abuse potential similar to that of the barbiturates, and they have become a part of the drug abuse problem in the United States.

Pharmaceutical companies have continued the search for safe, nonaddicting compounds that might be used to control anxiety and induce sleep. The first of these nonbenzodiazepine compounds was buspirone, introduced in the United States as an anxiolytic, and zolpidem, introduced as a hypnotic compound. The former compound has found only limited applications in the medical field, whereas the latter has been found to have an abuse potential similar to that of the benzodiazepines. The search continues for a new family of compounds that might help treat anxiety and induce sleep controls.

CHAPTER 8

Abuse of and Addiction to Central Nervous System Stimulants

Introduction

Although the average person thinks of central nervous system (CNS) abuse as a modern problem, historical evidence suggests that the use and abuse of CNS stimulants dates back thousands of years. Chinese physicians would prescribe the ephedra plant for patients with a respiratory disorder, for example (G. R. King & Ellinwood, 2005). When a plant was discovered to have a stimulant effect, people would use the stimulatory effects of those plants to enable them to work, or fight, longer.

Later, as chemists began to isolate the active agent(s) in these plants, those compounds were also used to enable the user to work longer, fight longer, or control the manifestations of certain diseases. Ephedrine is a classic example of this process. Chemists isolated the active agent in the ephedra plant in 1887, which was subsequently named ephedrine after the plant from which it was derived (Rasmussen, 2008). The effects of this compound were found to be similar to that of adrenaline, and it shared adrenaline's ability to treat the manifestations of asthma. However, unlike adrenaline, ephedrine could be taken by mouth, and it was found to reverse the symptoms of asthma and also relieve sinus congestion, as well as have a mild stimulant effect on the CNS. In the years since ephedrine was introduced, chemists have developed a wide range of compounds that function as CNS stimulants. Besides ephedrine, other CNS stimulants include cocaine, the amphetamines, amphetamine-like compounds such as methylphenidate, and the hallucinogen MDMA.[1] In spite of the chemical differences, the behavioral effects of these compounds are very similar. A recent entry into the field of CNS stimulants is modafinil, which is sold under the brand name of Provigil®. However, these compounds are rather controversial and are the source of much confusion both in the medical

---

[1]Classified by some neuropharmacologists as an amphetamine compound, whereas other neuropharmacologists classify it as a hallucinogenic compound. Still other psychopharmacologists take a middle-of-the-road approach and classify MDMA as a hallucinogenic amphetamine-like compound.

community and among the lay public. For this reason, this chapter will be divided into two parts: In the first part the medical uses of the CNS stimulants including their effects, side effects, and complications from their use will be discussed. In the second part, the complications of CNS stimulant abuse are discussed.

I. CNS Stimulants as Used in Medical Practice

The Amphetamine-Like Drugs

Ephedrine

Scientists have found ephedra plants at Neanderthal burial sites in Europe that are thought to be 60,000 years old (S. B. Karch, 2009). It is not known whether the plants were used for medical purposes or were placed in the grave sites for decorative or religious purposes, but the fact that they were placed in the grave site is suggestive of the possibility that Neanderthal man was aware of the plant's CNS stimulatory effects. It is known that Chinese physicians were using the ephedra plant for medicinal purposes 5000 years ago (G. R. King & Ellinwood, 2005). The main active agent in the ephedra plant, called ephedrine, was first isolated by chemists in 1897, but remained nothing more than a laboratory curiosity until 1930 when a report in a medical report appeared suggesting that ephedrine might be of value in treating asthma (S. B. Karch, 2009). Soon there was a large demand for ephedrine, and fears began to develop that the demand might exhaust the available supply. This spurred efforts to find a substitute compound(s) that might be as effective as ephedra, but without the danger of demand exceeding supplies of this compound (discussed later in the section History of the Amphetamines).

Medical Uses of Ephedrine In the past, the medical uses of ephedrine included the treatment of asthma and respiratory problems associated with bronchitis, emphysema, and chronic obstructive pulmonary disease (COPD) (Westfall & Westfall, 2006). Although once considered as a treatment for nasal congestion, it is no longer used for this purpose. In hospitals, ephedrine is used to treat symptoms of shock and, because it is such a potent vasoconstrictor, in some surgical procedures where low blood pressure is a problem (S. B. Karch, 2009; Westfall & Westfall, 2006). Ephedrine is still used for some forms of nasal surgery, because it is a vasoconstrictor and thus will limit blood loss when

these delicate tissues are injured. It was once used to treat some cardiac conditions, but the advent of newer, more effective medications has made its use in this arena rare (Westfall & Westfall, 2006). However, ephedrine is still used as an adjunct to the treatment of myasthenia gravis (B. A. Wilson et al., 2007).

Pharmacology of Ephedrine In the human body, ephedrine's primary effects are in the peripheral regions of the body rather than the CNS, with an effect very similar to that of adrenaline (G. R. King & Ellinwood, 2005; Westfall & Westfall, 2006). The ephedrine molecule binds at the acetylcholine receptor sites[2] responsible for modulating the constriction or dilation of peripheral blood vessels (Rothman et al., 2003). When the capillaries constrict, the heart compensates by increasing the force with which it pumps, increasing blood pressure. This makes clinical sense because ephedrine blocks the reuptake of norepinephrine[3] (NE) as the receptor sites used by NE in the regulation of the individual's state of arousal, cardiac response, and so on. At the same time, ephedrine is able to cause the smooth muscles surrounding the bronchial passages to relax, improving air flow into and out of the lungs (Westfall & Westfall, 2008).

Depending on the patient's condition, ephedrine might be administered orally or injected. Intramuscular or subcutaneous doses are completely absorbed, as are orally administered doses (S. B. Karch, 2009; Westfall & Westfall, 2006). Peak blood levels after a single dose are achieved in about 1 hour (Drummer & Odell, 2001). In light of the fact that it has been in use for almost a century now, surprisingly little is known about the distribution pattern of ephedrine in the body. The half-life is estimated at between 2.7 and 3.6 hours (Samenuk et al., 2002). Virtually all of a single dose is eliminated unchanged, and the amount that is eliminated unchanged

---

[2]Technically, the alpha-2 receptor sites, which control the degree of constriction in the muscles that surround these blood vessels.

[3]A stimulatory neurotransmitter. See Glossary.

depends on the level of acidity in the urine (Westfall & Westfall, 2006).

Tolerance to the bronchodilation effect of ephedrine develops rapidly, and because of this fact physicians recommend that the use of ephedrine to treat asthma be limited to short periods of time. Further, the chronic use of ephedrine use can cause or exacerbate cardiac or respiratory problems for the patient, again limiting its use to short periods of time. Though marketed as an over-the-counter diet aid, in reality ephedrine appears to have only a modest anorexic effect. The team of Shekelle et al. (2003) found in their meta-analysis of the medical literature that ephedrine can help the patient lose 0.9 kilograms over a short period of time, but there is no data on its long-term effectiveness nor is there evidence that it will enhance athletic ability as is commonly believed (Shekelle et al., 2003).

Side Effects of Ephedrine at Normal Dosage Levels   Because the therapeutic index of ephedrine is rather small, it is possible to have toxic effects from even low dosage levels. Even at therapeutic doses, ephedrine users are 200–300% more likely than nonusers to experience autonomic nervous system problems, upper gastrointestinal tract problems, and heart palpitations (Shekelle et al., 2003). Although some patients have reported experiencing a sense of euphoria when ephedrine is used at normal dosage levels, patients have also reported problems such as urinary retention, anxiety or feelings of apprehension, insomnia, headache, hallucinations, tremor, and seizures (American Society of Health System Pharmacists, 2008; Samenuk et al., 2002; Zevin & Benowitz, 2007). It was once thought that ephedrine could induce potentially fatal cardiac arrhythmias when used at normal dosage levels, but there is little evidence to support this belief (Hallas, Bjerrum, Støvring, & Andersen, 2008).

Medication Interactions Involving Ephedrine   It is recommended that patients taking one of the "tricyclic" antidepressants avoid the use of ephedrine, as these medications will enhance the stimulant effect of ephedrine, possibly to uncomfortable levels (Devane & Nemeroff, 2002).[4]

Methylphenidate

Methylphenidate has become a rather controversial compound. It was originally introduced as an antidepressant compound in the late 1950s, but research quickly found that it was not very effective in this capacity (Rasmussen, 2008). Currently, it is frequently used to control the symptoms of attention deficit hyperactivity disorder (ADHD) (Breggin, 2008). An astounding 80% of the world's total production of methylphenidate is consumed in the United States each year, a fact that raises questions about whether ADHD is being overdiagnosed and methylphenidate overprescribed (Breggin, 2008; Diller, quoted in Marsa, 2005). Further, the challenge has been made that parents "medicate our kids more, and for more trivial reasons, than any other culture. We'd rather give them a pill than discipline them" (Diller, quoted in Marsa, 2005, p. 164). Such children are being turned into chemical "zombies" through prescribed methylphenidate or similar agents in the name of behavioral control (Aldhous, 2006; Breggin, 2008).

Methylphenidate does not seem to be the most effective treatment for attention deficit disorder, as evidenced by the fact that about half of the prescriptions for this medication are never renewed (Breggin, 1999). There have been strident arguments both for and against the use of methylphenidate in the treatment of ADHD, and it is certain to remain a most controversial compound for many years to come.

Pharmacology of Methylphenidate   This compound functions as a CNS stimulant, originally developed as a possible nonaddicting substitute for the amphetamines (discussed later) (Diller, 1998). The habit-forming potential of the amphetamines had been identified by then, and so it was hoped that methylphenidate could serve as a safer substitute. Chemically, it is a close cousin to the amphetamine family of compounds, and some neuropharmacologists classify it as a member of the amphetamine family of drugs. In this text it will be classified as an amphetamine-like compound.

When used in the treatment of ADHD, patients are prescribed daily doses of between 15 and 90 mg. Orally administered doses are rapidly absorbed through the gastrointestinal tract (Greenhill, 2006). Peak blood levels are usually achieved around 2 hours following a single dose, although with extended-release forms of methylphenidate this might not occur until 4–7 hours after the medication was ingested (B. A. Wilson , 2007). The estimated therapeutic window of methylphenidate is 1:100, which is to say that the effective dose is approximately 1/100th the estimated lethal dose (Greenhill, 2006). The half-life is between 1 and 3 hours, with the effects lasting 3–6 hours following a single oral dose. These figures are extended in situations where the patient has ingested an extended release form of methylphenidate, and might last for up to 8 hours. About 80% of a single dose is

---

[4]Always consult a physician or pharmacist before using ephedrine with another drug.

biotransformed into ritanic acid in the intestinal tract, which is then excreted by the kidneys (S. B. Karch, 2009).

Within the brain, methylphenidate blocks the molecular dopamine reuptake pump[5] in the neural wall, allowing the dopamine molecules to remain in the synaptic junction longer, enhancing their effect (Volkow et al., 1998; Volkow & Swanson, 2003). One region of the brain that benefits from this effect is the reticular activating system (RAS), a region of the brain involved in the process of focusing attention. The RAS neurons are very sensitive to dopamine, and thus there is a dose-related response to methylphenidate with higher doses having a stronger effect on the neural reuptake pumps. At normal therapeutic doses, methylphenidate is able to block 50% of the dopamine reuptake pumps within 60–90 minutes of the time that the medication was ingested, thus allowing children to focus their attention on a given task more effectively (Jaffe, Rawson, & Ling, 2005).

Medical Uses of Methylphenidate Methylphenidate functions as a CNS stimulant and is of value in the treatment of ADHD and of a rare neurological condition known as *narcolepsy*. It also is occasionally used as an adjunct in the treatment of depression. There are few, if any, other medical applications of methylphenidate at this time.

Side Effects of Methylphenidate Methylphenidate's long-term effects have not been studied, because most follow-up studies involving methylphenidate are discontinued after a few weeks. Even studies involving the administration of methylphenidate to animals are usually discontinued after a few weeks to months, in part because of the cost of maintaining the animals over extended periods of time. Although it is reportedly safe at prescribed doses, there is emerging evidence that casts some doubt on this claim (Higgins, 2009). This is a matter of some concern because there is a growing trend for patients to be told that they must continue taking methylphenidate through childhood into adulthood (Higgins, 2009).

Methylphenidate has been implicated as the cause of cardiac problems in a limited number of cases, and it is now recommended that children receiving methylphenidate or one of the amphetamine compounds have a preliminary cardiovascular assessment and a baseline electrocardiogram (EKG) to minimize the danger of unexpected death from previously undiagnosed heart disease (Vetter et al., 2008). Further, up to 5% of the children who receive therapeutic doses of methylphenidate will experience visual hallucinations (Aldhous, 2006). Children prescribed methylphenidate have been noted to demonstrate behaviors suggestive of the obsessive-compulsive disorder, symptoms that were not present prior to the initiation of this medication (Breggin, 2008). Other identified side effects of therapeutic doses of methylphenidate include anorexia, insomnia, weight loss or failure to gain weight, dry mouth, heart palpitations, angina, anxiety, liver dysfunctions, skin rashes, dizziness, headache, hypertension, exacerbation of Tourette's syndrome, blurred vision, leukopenia, anemia, perseveration, and possible cerebral hemorrhage (Breggin, 2008; Higgins, 2009; S. B. Karch, 2009; Newcorn & Ivanov, 2007). Further, there is evidence that some patients on methylphenidate might experience a drug-induced psychosis at therapeutic doses (Higgins, 2009).

Methylphenidate can interfere with normal physical growth. It has a mild anorexic side effect that appears to be one mechanism by which this compound interferes with weight gain or physical growth (G. R. King & Ellinwood, 2005). However, research involving animals has revealed that the CNS stimulants (including methylphenidate) can, by increasing the dopamine levels in the brain, interfere with the pituitary's[6] normal function, contributing to growth retardation for the child (Higgins, 2009). Patients with a known seizure disorder should not be placed on methylphenidate, as this compound can exacerbate such disorders (Breggin, 1998). These seizures may be due to drug-induced changes in cerebral blood flow patterns, although this has not been proven.

Children who take prescribed doses of methylphenidate frequently report that the drug made them feel like a "zombie" and makes them resistant to taking it (Breggin. 1998). This appears to be a common effect of methylphenidate (Diller, 1998). However, such reports are disputed. For example, Pliszka (1998) denied that this was a drug-induced effect. Further, a small number of studies have suggested that there is a relationship between methylphenidate use in childhood and possible affective disorders in adulthood (Higgins, 2009). On rare occasions therapeutic methylphenidate use can also induce a state of depression that may reach suicidal proportions (Breggin, 1998). There is early research data suggesting a *possible* connection between the use of prescribed doses of methylphenidate and the development of Parkinson's disease later in life (Rothenberger & Banaschewski, 2004). This obviously

---

[5]See Glossary.

[6]See Glossary.

is a matter of some concern, and further research into possible mechanisms, treatment options, and alternatives is needed in this area. These studies suggest a need for further research into the benefits and long-term consequences of methylphenidate use even at therapeutic doses.

Medication Interactions Involving Methylphenidate Patients who are using any of the "tricyclic" antidepressants should not use methylphenidate, as the interaction of these compounds can cause potentially toxic levels of the antidepressant medication to build up in the patient's blood (DeVane & Nemeroff, 2002). Patients using any of the MAO inhibitors should not use methylphenidate because of a potential toxic reaction between these compounds. Further, the use of methylphenidate with the SSRI family of antidepressants reportedly can lower the seizure threshold, causing seizures (DeVane & Nemeroff, 2002). Finally, patients taking antihypertensive medications might find that their blood pressure control is inadequate, as methylphenidate interferes with the effectiveness of blood pressure medications (DeVane & Nemeroff, 2002). Although it is not possible to identify every potential drug interaction involving methylphenidate, this list should highlight the need for the patient to check with a physician or pharmacist before taking methylphenidate with any other medication.

The Amphetamine Compounds

Although methamphetamine has been in the headlines for much of the last decade, it is only one of a family of related compounds collectively known as the *amphetamines*. Like methylphenidate, their use in medicine remains controversial and are the matter of much debate. In this section we will discuss the medical uses of the amphetamines.

History of the Amphetamines The history of the amphetamine compounds is filled with twists and turns worthy of a movie plot. Although the first amphetamine compound was discovered in 1887, these compounds remained little more than laboratory curiosities until 1927 because they were *analogs*[7] of ephedrine, which was already being used to treat asthma. However, with growing demand for ephedrine, there was serious concern that the demand for ephedrine might exceed the supply.

The answer to this dilemma was the amphetamine compound Benzedrine®, which was found to share many of the medical applications of ephedrine. As a treatment for asthma, Benzedrine® was contained in a small glass vial with a cap on one end, surrounded by several layers of cloth. In the 1930s this vial contained approximately 325 mg of Benzedrine®. When needed, the patient would twist the ampule, breaking the glass and releasing the amphetamine compound into the surrounding layers of cloth. Then the patient would inhale the fumes, counteracting the effects of the asthma attack. It was not long, however, before the first reports of habituation among patients taking an amphetamine compound at prescribed doses and of amphetamine abuse began to surface (S. B. Karch, 2009; G. R. King & Ellinwood, 2007; Rasmussen, 2008). Drug abusers quickly discovered that one could carefully unwrap the cloth, take out the ampule of concentrated Benzedrine®, carefully unscrew the cap or break it open at one end, and obtain the concentrated amphetamine contained within. Some abusers would inject it directly into a vein. By the 1940s the amount of Benzedrine® in each ampule had been reduced to 250 mg, which still was the equivalent of 50 of the 5 mg tablets prescribed for oral use (Rasmussen, 2008). At these dosage levels the effects were found to be very similar to those of cocaine, which at the time was known to be dangerous when abused, but were longer lasting and thought to be a safe substitute for cocaine, a belief that fueled its abuse.

In World War II, both sides exploited the CNS stimulatory effects of the amphetamines to counteract the effects of fatigue and allow military personnel to work or fight longer. This was done in spite of the limited evidence that it was effective for these purposes, that it was about as effective as caffeine, and that extended periods of use resulted in visual hallucinations (Rasmussen, 2008). Historical evidence strongly suggests that Adolf Hitler himself was addicted to amphetamines as part of a cocktail of compounds injected into him on a daily basis by his personal physician. Whether this addiction contributed to his ultimate breakdown and the defeat of Germany is open to debate.

Medical historians now believe that it was the arrival of large amounts of amphetamine compounds, especially methamphetamine, that contributed to the outbreak of drug-related violence that ended the "Summer of Love" in 1967 (D. Smith, 1997, 2001). By that time amphetamine abusers had discovered that high doses of amphetamines could cause agitation and death from cardiovascular collapse. It has also been discovered that following periods of intense amphetamine abuse, users would enter a depressive state that might last for days or weeks after their last use that might reach suicidal

---

[7]See Glossary.

proportions. Although it was originally believed that CNS stimulants lacked the dangers associated with cocaine use, by the mid-1970s abusers had coined the phrase "speed kills" as a warning about the dangers of amphetamine abuse (D. Smith, 1997, 2001). Because of their identified abuse potential, and the discovery that the amphetamines were not as effective in the treatment of depression or obesity as originally thought, they were classified as Schedule II[8] compounds in the Controlled Substances Act of 1970.

Current Medical Uses of the Amphetamines As was discussed earlier in this chapter, the amphetamines have been classified as compounds in search for a disease that they might be used to treat (Rasmussen, 2008). It is known that the amphetamines improve the action of smooth muscles in the body, leading some to believe that they can improve athletic performance. In reality, the amphetamines have an unpredictable effect on muscle performance, possibly inducing a *decrease* in athletic performance rather than the desired improvement. Because of their reputed use as athletic performance enhancement agents however, they were abused for this reputed enhancement effect and now sports regulatory agencies routinely test for amphetamine compounds, making their use by athletes rather rare.

The amphetamines in medical use have an *anorexic*[9] side effect, and were extensively prescribed by physicians in the 1960s and 1970s for patients who wanted to lose weight. However, research soon demonstrated that tolerance to the anorexic effects of the amphetamines develops rapidly and that it is not uncommon for patients to then regain the weight that they had initially lost. It was also discovered that simple dieting and exercise would result in the same degree of weight loss.

The amphetamines were once thought to have an antidepressant effect, although research has demonstrated that the antidepressant effects of the amphetamines currently in use are short-lived at best. They are still occasionally used as an *adjunct* to the treatment of depression, as they augment the effects of many antidepressant medications. Physicians will occasionally exploit the euphoric effect of the amphetamines to counteract depression in the terminally ill or to counteract the respiratory depression induced by other compounds (Brunton et al., 2007; Fadem, 2009). Although the Food and Drug Administration (FDA) approves of the use of amphetamine compounds only in the treatment of narcolepsy, "off-label" uses of these compounds include the treatment of some of the effects of AIDS,[10] dysthymia, chronic fatigue syndrome, and lethargy (Sadock & Sadock, 2007).

Narcolepsy, one of the few diseases amphetamine compounds are approved to treat, is thought to be the result of a deficit in dopamine levels in certain regions of the brain. Because the amphetamines force neurons to release stores of dopamine, it would appear to be an ideal treatment for narcolepsy and certain forms of depression. In 1938 it was discovered that the amphetamines had a paradoxical calming effect on patients with ADHD. Subsequent research has revealed that the amphetamines are about as effective in controlling the symptoms of ADHD as is methylphenidate, calming about 50% of the patients with this disorder, and that an additional 25% will experience some degree of improvement when they take prescribed amphetamine compounds (T. Spencer et al., 2001). This effect is thought to reflect the amphetamine's ability to enhance the function of the neurons in the RAS.[11] However, as is true with methylphenidate, the use of the amphetamines to treat ADHD is controversial, and there is little research into the long-term benefits or consequences of amphetamine use for this purpose. There are those who believe that these compounds may do more harm than good for patients who take them for the control of ADHD (T. J. Spencer et al., 2001; Breggin, 2008).

Pharmacology of the Amphetamines The amphetamines have been in clinical use for almost a century and yet the pharmacokinetics of these compounds have not been studied in detail (Payer & London, 2009). The most common forms of amphetamine are dextroamphetamine (*d*-ampheta-mine sulfate), methamphetamine, and a combination of dextroamphetamine and pure amphetamine salts (Sadock & Sadock, 2007). Because of its longer half-life, and its ability to rapidly cross the blood–brain barrier, drug abusers seem to prefer methamphetamine over dextroamphetamine, however both compounds are abused (Albertson, Derlet, & Van Hoozen, 1999). The various amphetamines in use have only minor variations in chemical structure, which affect only the potency and pharmacological characteristics of that compound. The chemical structure of the basic amphetamine molecule is similar to that of the norepinephrine and dopamine

---

[8]See Appendix 4.

[9]See Glossary.

[10]Discussed in Chapter 34.

[11]See Glossary.

molecules, and technically the amphetamines might be classified as an agonist of these compounds (G. R. King & Ellinwood, 2007).

When ingested orally, the amphetamine molecule is easily absorbed through the lining of the small intestine, and the usual route of administration in medical practice is orally administered tablets or capsules. On rare occasions it is administered through intramuscular or intravenous injection in medical practice. In the brain the effects of any amphetamine are region specific, causing an increase in neurotransmitter activity in one region while inducing a simultaneous decrease in the release of other neurotransmitters in other regions of the brain (Hanson & Fleckenstein, 2009).

The main effects of the amphetamines on the central nervous system when administered in therapeutic doses appear to be their ability to alter the dopamine neurotransmission system (Fadem, 2009; G. R. King and Ellinwood, 2007). The amphetamine molecule causes the release of catecholamine molecules from the upstream neurotransmitters, especially dopamine, into the synaptic junction (Fadem, 2009; G. R. King & Ellinwood, 2007; Sadock & Sadock, 2007). Then the amphetamine blocks the reuptake pumps, allowing the dopamine to remain in the synaptic junction for an extended period of time and enhancing its effects on the downstream neurons. However, they also induce the release and block the reuptake of glutamate, and the effects of the amphetamines on the acetylcholine neurotransmission system have not been studied in detail (Hanson & Fleckenstein, 2009).

The effects of a single oral dose of an amphetamine begin in about 20–30 minutes, and peak blood levels are achieved in 1–3 hours (Drummer & Odell, 2001). The biological half-life of dextroamphetamine is between 10 and 34 hours, but there is some controversy as to the elimination half-life of methamphetamine. B. A. Wilson et al. (2007) suggested that this was only 4–5 hours after a single dose in the normal, healthy patient, whereas S. B. Karch (2002) suggested that the half-life might be as long as 12.2 hours. These discrepant estimates of the half-life reflect the lack of firm data of the pharmacokinetics of these compounds.

The various forms of amphetamine in clinical use are lipid soluble; however, because of the limited research into the pharmacokinetics of the amphetamines, it is not known whether one form of amphetamine is more lipid soluble than any other form of amphetamine. The peripheral effects of the amphetamine compounds are the result of their ability to stimulate the release of norepinephrine, whereas the CNS effects appear to reflect their ability to stimulate the release of dopamine molecules while blocking the dopamine reuptake pumps at thy synaptic junction (Hanley, 2004). This effect is especially in the mesolimbic region of the brain, which has a large number of dopamine-based neurons and is also thought to be part of the brain's pleasure center. This, plus the effects of the amphetamines on the medulla, where the respiratory centers of the brain are located, and their effects on the cortex, make the patient breathe more deeply and feel less fatigued (Sadock & Sadock, 2003).

There is significant interindividual variability to the effects of the amphetamines. Under normal conditions 45–70% of a single dose of an amphetamine compound will be excreted unchanged in the urine within 24 hours (S. B. Karch, 2009). The exact percentage of the dose that is excreted unchanged depends in large part on the acidity level of the user's blood. The more acidic the individual's blood, the greater the percentage of a given dose that will be excreted unchanged. But if the blood is more alkaline, then the kidneys tend to reabsorb the amphetamine molecules and return them to the circulatory system. The remaining amphetamine molecules are biotransformed by the liver. Depending on the specific amphetamine ingested, the number of metabolites produced during the biotransformation process will vary. For example, during the process of methamphetamine biotransformation seven different metabolites are formed before the drug molecules are finally eliminated.

At one point it was thought that making the patient's urine acidic would speed up the elimination of amphetamine molecules from the circulation, especially if the patient had ingested an overdose (G. R. King & Ellinwood, 2005). However, some clinicians believe that this process also increases the patient's chance(s) of developing a cardiac arrhythmia and/or seizures, placing the patient's life at risk (Venkatakrishnan et al., 2006). Thus it is not clear which course of action the attending physician should follow if the patient should take an overdose of an amphetamine.

There is also a great deal of interindividual variability in toxic reactions to the amphetamines. The estimated lethal dose of an amphetamine compound will vary depending on the (a) specific compound being abused, (b) individuals' substance use history, (c) the route of administration, (d) the individuals' state of health, (e) whether they had developed any degree of tolerance to amphetamine compounds, and (f) their genetic heritage. Some patients have tolerated exceptionally large doses of amphetamines, such as in overdose attempts, without apparent ill effect. Other patients have been unable to tolerate even low therapeutic doses without experiencing a range of potentially fatal side effects (discussed later).

Although classified as central nervous system stimulants, almost 6% of patients taking an amphetamine compound in a clinical trial reported that they felt drowsy and less alert while taking one of these substances. Just under 4% reported feeling confused, and 8.7% reported feeling that they were depressed. Over 17% reported feeling irritable, agitated, and restless, adverse effects that the mainstream media often ignore (Breggin, 2008). These findings illustrate the fact that these compounds neither are perfect nor is their use without risk.

Neuroadaptation to Amphetamine Compounds The steady use of an amphetamine at therapeutic dosage levels will result in an incomplete state of neuroadaptation. Shortly after the time of their introduction, the first clinical reports of amphetamine addiction began to appear in the clinical literature, and the pharmaceuticals industry quickly settled on the term *habit forming* to avoid the charge that these compounds were addictive (Rasmussen, 2008).

When used to treat narcolepsy, the patient might remain on the same dose of the amphetamine for years, without any loss of efficacy (Jaffe, Ling, & Rawson, 2005). In contrast to this, patients soon develop tolerance to the anorexic effect of amphetamines after only a few weeks, and the drug-induced sense of euphoria does not last beyond the first few doses when amphetamines are used at therapeutic dosage levels.

Medication Interactions Involving the Amphetamine Compounds Patients who are taking any medication, even if it is an over-the-counter medication, should consult with a physician or pharmacist before starting to take an amphetamine, to avoid the danger of potentially dangerous drug interactions. For example, there is limited evidence that individuals taking any of the monoamine oxidase inhibitors[12] (MAO inhibitors or MAO-Is) should not take an amphetamine compound for several days after they discontinue the MAO-I in order to avoid potentially lethal hypertensive episodes (Ciraulo et al., 2006). Although the potential for these compounds to cause such a hypertensive episode remains unproven, the danger has not been ruled out, and to avoid this possibility patients

should not take these compounds until they have completed an MAO-I "wash out" period of 72 hours or longer.

There is evidence to suggest that amphetamine compounds may interact with at least some of the antipsychotic medications currently in use in the United States at (Ciraulo et al., 2006). Although this list is hardly exhaustive, it does illustrate that the amphetamines have the potential to interact with other pharmaceuticals in use. A physician or pharmacist should always be consulted about the possible interaction between two different medications if used concurrently.

Subjective Experience of Amphetamine Use in Medical Practice

The subjective effects of an amphetamine administered under a physician's supervision will depend on a number of factors, including the individual's mental state, the manner in which the drug is administered, the relative potency of the dose administered, and the individual's substance use history. For example, a hypothetical soldier who has gone without sleep for 48 hours who ingests a 5 mg tablet of an amphetamine will have a different reaction than that same soldier would if well rested. The reaction of the hypothetical soldier mentioned in the last sentence would be far different still if she or he were to have a 5 mg dose of the amphetamine injected into a vein rather than orally.

Amphetamine compounds do have a very small, virtually insignificant analgesic property of their own, although they may multiply the analgesic effect of a given dose of a narcotic analgesic (G. R. King & Ellinwood, 2005). However, amphetamine compounds are rarely if ever used for their analgesic effects, and this property of amphetamine compounds will not be discussed further in this chapter. When used in medical practice, the amphetamines are usually administered orally, in doses of between 5 and 60 mg/day (A. G. Jenkins, 2007). At such dosage levels, the user will experience enhanced mood, less mental fatigue, an improved ability to concentrate, and perhaps a mild euphoria especially when the medication is first started (Sadock & Sadock, 2003). Users may also notice that they are not hungry as often and may not feel the need to eat as much as before. As noted earlier, the amphetamines do have an anorexic effect, especially before the development of neuroadaptation to these compounds (G. R. King & Ellinwood, 2005).

About 10% of patients started on an amphetamine compound will experience drug-induced tachycardia (Breggin, 2008; Fuller & Sajatovic, 1999). It is for this

---

[12]See Glossary.

reason that the physician should conduct tests to rule out preexisting cardiac problems in the patient before starting the medication. Rarely, patients taking an amphetamine compound at therapeutic doses will develop a drug-induced psychosis (Ciraulo et al., 2006). More commonly encountered are stereotypical, repetitive behaviors, which are especially common when these medications are used at high dosage levels.

Patients with *Tourette's disorder*[13] often find that amphetamine use exacerbates the symptoms of their Tourette's. Some patients begin to engage in the characteristic vocalizations and movements of Tourette's disorder when they begin to take a prescribed amphetamine. Further, although the amphetamines are CNS stimulants, about 40% of patients taking them at therapeutic doses experience a drug-induced feeling of depression, which might become so profound as to reach suicidal proportions (Breggin, 1998). When the patient discontinues a prescribed amphetamine, they also are prone to experience a depressive reaction, as well as fatigue and lethargy, lasting a few hours or days. These compounds have also been known to interfere with normal growth in children. As this information suggests, the amphetamines are quite potent compounds, which even at therapeutic doses have the potential to harm the user.

Modafinil (Provigil®)

A recent entry into the field of CNS stimulants is modafinil, which is sold under the brand name of Provigil® (Baker, 2009). Provigil® was introduced in 1998 as a "wake-promoting agent" (Price, 2009, p. 3), a term that the author suggested was a carefully selected term to avoid the suspect term *stimulant*.[14] This compound is recommended as a treatment of ADHD and narcolepsy (Thompson PDR, 2007). One off-label[15] use of modafinil is to enhance cognitive endurance for people suffering from fatigue (Baker, 2009). Like the other CNS stimulants, modafinil stimulates the release of dopamine within the brain, and as such has a mild abuse potential (Price, 2009; Volkow et al., 2009). For example, it is often abused by those who wish to improve concentration although they do not have ADHD. In this capacity it is often abused by college students who wish to enhance concentration during all-night study sessions.

Pharmacology of Modafinil The pharmacokinetics of modafinil are not well understood at this time. At clinical doses it appears to block the dopamine transporter system in various regions of the brain, thus enhancing the effects of dopamine in the receptor site. This includes the dopamine receptors in the nucleus accumbens region of the brain, increasing its abuse potential in a manner similar to that seen with the amphetamines (Volkow et al., 2009). It does not appear to bind at the norepinephrine, serotonin, GABA, adenosine, histamine, melatonin, or benzodiazepine receptor sites in the brain (Thompson PDR, 2007). Following the administration of two to four doses (one per day) to establish steady-state plasma levels, the elimination half-life is approximately 15 hours (Thompson PDR, 2007).

Following oral ingestion, the peak blood plasma levels of modafinil are seen in 2–4 hours when ingested on an empty stomach. Although it may be ingested with food, absorption of modafinil will be delayed by approximately 1 hour. Approximately 60% of the drug molecules bind to protein molecules in the blood (mainly albumin). It is biotransformed in the liver, with only 10% of the modafinil being excreted unchanged by the kidneys (Thompson PDR, 2007). This medication is not to be used by patients with a known allergic reaction to this compound (Thompson PDR, 2007).

Side Effects of Modafinil Use This medication can induce shortness of breath, heart palpitations, chest pain, and transient changes in the electrocardiogram (Thompson PDR, 2007). Its use in patients who have suffered a recent myocardial infarction (heart attack) has not been studied in detail and should be used in such patients only under a physician's supervision. One patient did develop symptoms of a drug-induced psychosis after taking exceptionally large doses of modafinil, but these symptoms resolved after the medication was discontinued (Thompson PDR, 2007). Modafinil does not appear to induce the sense of CNS overstimulation seen when a patient receives methylphenidate or an amphetamine compound (Baker, 2009). It does, however, appear to have an addiction potential (Wakefulness Drug: New Safety Concerns, 2009).

Medication Interactions Involving Modafinil This medication is known to reduce the effectiveness of oral contraceptives. Possible interactions with alcohol have not been studied. It is recommended that the patient consult with a pharmacist before taking another medication (including over-the-counter compounds) with modafinil.

Strattera® (Atomoxetine Hydrochloride)

Technically, atomoxetine hydrochloride is not classified as a CNS stimulant by the manufacturer but has been

---

[13]See Glossary.

[14]A term associated in the minds of many with drugs of abuse such as cocaine and the like.

[15]See Glossary.

classified as such by the *Physician's Desk Reference* (Thompson PDR, 2007). It will be classified as such in this text because, like the other compounds reviewed in this chapter, it is recommended for the treatment of ADHD.

Pharmacokinetics Atomoxetine hydrochloride is administered orally, and following absorption approximately 98% becomes protein bound (Thompson PDR, 2007). The exact mechanism of action remains unclear, but it is assumed to be a result of the drug's ability to alter norepinephrine release patterns in the neurons. The half-life of this compound is estimated to be approximately 5 hours in the typical patient.

Side Effects Identified side effects include a mild increase in heart rate (approximately six beats a minute). Breggin (2008) noted that other reported side effects include irritability, mood swings, and aggressive behaviors by the child receiving this medication. Other reported side effects include grandiosity, hyperactivity, and insomnia, and in overdose situations it can induce seizures. The FDA has also required the manufacturer to include a "black box" warning about this compound apparently causing suicidal thinking or suicidal acts in children receiving it (Breggin, 2008).

Medication Interactions Numerous medication interactions are identified in the 2007 edition of the *Physician's Desk Reference,* and a pharmacist should be consulted before intermixing atomoxetine hydrochloride with other compounds.

Challenges to the Use of CNS Stimulants to Treat Identified Disorders

It has been observed that the amphetamines are "orphan" drugs in search of a disease to treat. Touted first as a treatment for asthma in the 1930s and 1940s, they were then sold as reputed antidepressants in the 1950s, and eventually as an anorexic that could be used to assist in weight loss programs in the 1960s (Breggin, 2008; Rasmussen, 2008). Currently, they are recommended as a pharmacological treatment for the attention deficit disorders and narcolepsy. Admittedly, new applications for existing pharmaceuticals are discovered after their introduction. At the peak of their popularity as pharmaceutical agents in the mid-1960s, 5% of the adults in the United States were taking a prescribed amphetamine compound. About half of these patients were abusing amphetamines for their euphoric effects, which underscores the abuse potential of this class of drugs (G. R. King & Ellinwood, 2005; Rasmussen, 2008).

Surprisingly, in spite of their use as agents to treat ADHD for more than a generation, there is little evidence of the long-term effectiveness of such compounds for treating such disorders, and a mounting body of evidence suggests that psychosocial interventions are far more superior (Breggin, 2008; McDonagh & Peterson, 2006). Obviously, because psychosocial interventions cannot be patented by a pharmaceutical company, they are not mentioned in advertisements for CNS stimulants. Unfortunately, as noted earlier in this chapter, the amphetamine-like drugs have also been identified as possibly causing neural damage even when used as prescribed (Breggin, 2008), raising questions whether the cure might be worse than the disease states that they are supposed to control.

II. CNS Stimulant Abuse
Scope of the Problem
The Amphetamines
Discussion of the problem of amphetamine abuse is complicated by the fact that different researchers define the term *amphetamine* in different ways: Some researchers limit the term to only the compound methamphetamine, whereas others differentiate between the abuse of methamphetamine and other amphetamine compounds (Rutkowski & Maxwell, 2009, p. 6). Some researchers apply the term *amphetamine* only to diverted pharmaceuticals, whereas others include both diverted and amphetamine compounds produced in illicit "labs" under the rubric of "amphetamine" (Rutkowski & Maxwell, 2009). Finally, some researchers include the hallucinogen MDMA ("Ecstasy") as an "amphetamine," whereas others classify it as a hallucinogenic[16] compound.

In the United States the amphetamines, especially methamphetamine, are the second most popular class of illicit drugs of abuse, exceeded in popularity only by marijuana. Twenty-five percent of the students at some colleges have used the amphetamine sold under the brand name of Adderall® to help them study for examinations or stay up all night to finish assigned projects (Owen, 2008). The abuse of prescribed amphetamine compounds is widespread, and it has been argued that at the end of the first decade of the 21st century the "pusher"[17] for the current generation of young adults is not the seedy man on the

---

[16]The practice that is followed in this book is to classify MDMA, or "Ecstasy," as a hallucinogenic, not an amphetamine compound.

[17]One who sells illicit drugs.

street selling little white packets of drugs, but the health care professional in a white lab coat and armed with a prescription pad who authorizes the use of these compounds (Owen, 2008; Rasmussen, 2008).

Globally, the abuse of the amphetamines or amphetamine-like compounds is thought to be a $65 billion per year industry (United Nations, 2008). The total number of people who abuse methamphetamine around the globe is estimated to outnumber the number of heroin and cocaine abusers *combined* (BBC News, 2006). The mass media in the United States have often spoken about a "meth crisis" in this country, although in reality three-quarters of methamphetamine abusers live in Asia or Southeast Asia (Ling, Rawson, & Shoptaw, 2006). To put the problem of methamphetamine abuse in the United States into perspective, consider the following facts: Just under 73 million people have used a cigarette, 125 million people have used alcohol, 2.4 million people have abused cocaine, and 7 million people were thought to have abused prescription narcotic analgesics in the past year (Fadem, 2009). In contrast only about 583,000 people are thought to be regular methamphetamine abusers in the United States, and 257,000 people are estimated to be addicted to it (Acosta, Haller, & Schnoll, 2005; M. C. Miller, 2005; Owen, 2007). Although this is not to downplay the dangers associated with methamphetamine abuse or addiction, it does underscore how the media help to shape our perception of substance use disorders on a day-to-day basis.

Young adults, or those who are about to become young adults, represent a special risk group for methamphetamine abuse. In a recent survey, 11.4% of high school seniors admitted to having used an amphetamine compound, and 3.0% admitted to the use of methamphetamine at least once (L. D. Johnston, O'Malley, Backman, & Schulenberg, 2008a). As these figures demonstrate, the abuse of amphetamine compounds in the United States is both common and widespread. However, there is still much to be discovered about the epidemiology of amphetamine abuse both in the United States and around the world.

Ephedrine   Because it was once sold over the counter as a diet aid and treatment for asthma, the true scope of ephedrine abuse is simply not known (S. B. Karch, 2009). It is often sold under the guise of other, more potent compounds. The side effects of ephedrine abuse include all of those noted earlier in this chapter, plus coronary artery vasoconstriction, myocardial infarction, cardiac arrhythmias, stroke, and death (Brust, 2004; Neergaard, 2004; Samenuk

et al., 2002). Ephedrine is also a precursor of the amphetamines, especially methamphetamine, and so restrictions were placed on its access in the United States in 2004. Such restrictions have been found to have minimal effect on methamphetamine production, and the ban was overturned by the courts a year later ("Utah Judge Strikes Down FAD Ban on Ephedra," 2005). The legal status of ephedrine thus remains to be settled in this country.

Methylphenidate   There simply is no way to estimate the percentage of methylphenidate pills that are diverted to the illicit drug market, although it is known that they are popular drugs of abuse and that a significant percentage of those tablets prescribed to patients are diverted. A conversion formula suggests that 15 mg of methylphenidate is about as potent as 5 mg of dextroamphetamine, a popular drug of abuse in the 1970s (Rasmussen, 2008).

Modafinil   The abuse potential of modafinil remains poorly defined, although it is acknowledged that a small percentage of users take the medication to help them remain cognitively alert for longer than normal. It is also increasingly being diverted into the hands of those for whom the drug was not prescribed (Price, 2009). Given the report that it was pharmacologically different from the amphetamine compounds when it was introduced, health care professionals have become complacent about the potential risks associated with modafinil abuse, which is rather frightening in light of its growing popularity as a drug of abuse.

Atomoxetine Hydrochloride   No identified pattern of abuse for this medication has been reported as of this time.

Methods of CNS Stimulant Abuse and Their Effects

Ephedrine

Effects of Ephedrine When Abused   The effects of ephedrine abuse are essentially an exaggeration of the adverse effects of ephedrine when used at normal doses.[18] This makes sense, because even when used as recommended higher doses of ephedrine increase the user's chances of suffering an adverse effect. Unfortunately, because ephedrine can induce a feeling of euphoria when used in very high doses, there is an incentive for some people to abuse it. This sense of euphoria is less intense than that seen in amphetamine

---

[18]This assumes that the abuser is taking *only* ephedrine.

abusers, but it sill is experienced when abusers ingest high levels of ephedrine (Erickson, 2007).

Methods of Ephedrine Abuse   The most common method of ephedrine abuse is for the individual to ingest over-the-counter ephedrine tablets. On rare occasions, the pills might be crushed and the resulting power "snorted." On even more rare occasions, the pills are crushed, mixed with water, and then injected into a vein.

Complications of Ephedrine Abuse   The therapeutic window for ephedrine is quite small, and as indicated earlier it can induce toxic effects even at therapeutic doses. Ephedrine abuse can result in impaired judgment, agitation, necrosis[19] of the lining of the gastrointestinal tract, nausea, vomiting, stroke, irritation of cardiac tissues (especially in abusers who have damaged their hearts), potentially fatal heart arrhythmias, and heart attacks. The causal mechanism for ephedrine-induced heart attacks appears to be a drug-induced increase of the cardiac muscle, increasing the oxygen demand by those tissues. This is potentially dangerous if the person should have some form of coronary artery disease that independently limits the blood flow to the heart muscle.

Ephedrine abuse can also result in the formation of ephedrine-based kidney stones, which is seen in people who use exceptionally large doses of ephedrine on a chronic basis. These kidney stones are found to be almost entirely ephedrine when they are examined by physicians, and are quite painful when they move down the urinary tract of the abuser to the bladder.

Methylphenidate

Effects of Methylphenidate When Abused   There are multiple causes for methylphenidate abuse: Some abusers want to engage in tasks such as driving delivery trucks or studying for exams for extended periods of time (Vedantam, 2006). Other abusers wish to stay awake at parties longer or counteract the sedating effects of alcohol so that they can drink longer, whereas others seek a drug-induced feeling of euphoria (Aldhous, 2006; Arria & Wish, 2006). Such abuse is stimulated by the mistaken belief that this medication is not addicting.

Although a favorite stimulate for students who wish to "cram" before an examination, on occasion methylphenidate abusers whose motivation is a bit different from that of college students will also use pills (Vedantam, 2006). Serious methylphenidate abusers will crush the pills into a fine powder, then either inhale the powder or inject it into a vein (S. B. Karch,

2009; Stahl, 2008; Volkow & Swanson, 2003). The strongest effects are achieved when the compound is injected into a vein. When injected, methylphenidate can induce a 50% blockade of the dopamine transport system within seconds, inducing a feeling of euphoria for the user (Volkow et al., 1998; Volkow & Swanson, 2003). For many abusers, this drug-induced sense of euphoria becomes desirable and serves as a source of motivation for further methylphenidate abuse.

Consequences of Methylphenidate Abuse   One unanticipated consequence of methylphenidate abuse is physical addiction to the compound. The team of Y. Kim et al. (2009) administered methylphenidate to mice and found at the end of their trial period that the mice that received the methylphenidate had developed a greater number of spiny neurons in the nucleus accumbens than did the control mice. This is a region of the brain known to be associated with addiction to chemicals. However, the impact of this compound on the brain varies with the individual's motivation to use it: Patients who receive this medication for the control of ADHD usually do not develop signs of addiction to methylphenidate, whereas recreational abusers are prone to do so. This might reflect the timing or dosage of methylphenidate used by abusers as opposed to patients on this compound, or it might reflect another, as yet unidentified, process.

The physical consequences of methylphenidate abuse are essentially an extension of those seen when this compound is used medically. Even when used under a doctor's supervision, at recommended dosage levels, methylphenidate can occasionally trigger a toxic psychosis, with symptoms similar to those seen in paranoid schizophrenia (Aldhous, 2006; S. B. Karch, 2009). Most certainly large doses, such as those seen when this compound is abused, can trigger a toxic psychosis as well (M. Weiss, 2007). A small percentage of abusers will experience a methylphenidate-induced stroke or cardiac problems (S. B. Karch, 2009).

When methylphenidate abusers crush a tablet to use intravenously, they will inject not only the active agent of the compound but also various "fillers"[20] designed to give the tablet shape and form (Volkow et al., 1998). The fillers may then form a thrombosis, causing damage to body tissues that depend on the now-blocked artery for oxygenated blood and food. Sometimes, such damage occurs to the retina, causing visual field disturbance and possible blindness (S. B. Karch, 2009).

---

[19]See Glossary.

[20]See Glossary.

As this information would suggest, methylphenidate is not a safe compound, and abusers take on a very real risk of potential harm and addiction when they abuse this compound.

The Amphetamine Compounds

Effects of Amphetamine Abuse The amphetamine compounds, especially methamphetamine, might be ingested orally, used intranasally (that is, "snorted"), smoked, or injected intravenously. Depending on the individuals' tolerance to the effects of the amphetamines, they might experience a state of heightened alertness, confidence, and euphoria. The effects depend on several factors: (a) dose, (b) method of administration, (c) possible concurrent use of other compounds, (d) the individual's state of health, and (e) the individual's past substance use history.

Orally administered amphetamine compounds will begin to take effect in 20 minutes, whereas a "snorted" (intranasal) dose will begin to take effect in about 5 minutes. When injected or smoked, an amphetamine compound will begin to have an effect on the abuser in a matter of seconds (Gwinnell & Adamec, 2006; Rawson & Ling, 2008). The amphetamines and related compounds are popular drugs of abuse on the college campus, especially as students prepare for examinations (Azar, 2008). Surprisingly, there is no evidence to suggest that these compounds actually improve the individual's performance on the examination(s). Students still abuse them around exam time in the hope that they will give them an edge as they study. Then, having discovered that these compounds allow them to remain awake for longer periods of time than is normal, they often begin to abuse them so that they might party longer (Azar, 2008).

During the 1970s much of the methamphetamine abused in the United States came from small "laboratories" that would produce relatively small amounts of methamphetamine for local consumption[21] using various easily obtained compounds. These "kitchen labs" proliferated in the 1990s when methamphetamine again became a popular drug of abuse. However, the process is dangerous, and even legitimate pharmaceutical companies will suffer the occasional explosion in the facility devoted to the production of an amphetamine compound. Illicit laboratories are much more likely to experience an explosion during the manufacturing process. So common were the explosions of "labs" that local police departments would wait for the explosion to help them identify a methamphetamine production site.

Methods for methamphetamine production are available on the Internet. "Nazi meth" is one such preparation of illicit methamphetamine. The name is obtained from the Nazi symbols that decorated the paper on which the formula was originally written ("Nazi Meth on the Rise," 2003). Unlike some of the other formulas for methamphetamine manufacture, this method does not rely on the use of red phosphorus,[22] but rather uses lithium (obtained from batteries) and ammonia ("Nazi Meth on the Rise," 2003). The use of these compounds for the production of illicit methamphetamine exposes the abuser to contaminants (a matter of little concern to the abuser or, for that matter, the manufacturer) (Graber, 2007). To combat the production of illicit methamphetamine, precursor compounds such as ephedrine and pseudo-ephedrine were subjected to strict control, with people being able to purchase only a small amount each month for self-medication of colds or allergies. The impact of this restriction has been minimal, at best (J. K. Cunningham, Liu, & Callaghan, 2009), and illicit methamphetamine remains rampant.

There is a financial incentive for producing methamphetamine. An investment of $200 in the chemicals used for illicit production of methamphetamine might produce enough to sell for $2,500 on the illegal market. This financial incentive attracted the attention of organized-crime cartels, which set up large-scale production facilities (known as "super labs") in Mexico, and then the methamphetamine is smuggled across the border (Graber, 2007). These "super labs" have essentially replaced the smaller production facilities once commonly found in the United States, although on occasion they are still discovered by police.

Adverse Effects of Amphetamine Abuse Generally, the higher the blood level of the amphetamine compound being abused, the more likely it will be toxic to the abuser (Julien, 2005). Unfortunately, there is a significant interindividual variability for the development of amphetamine toxicity, with some individuals demonstrating evidence of toxic reactions at therapeutic dosage levels (Breggin, 2008). Some of the symptoms of a toxic reaction to an amphetamine include agitation, confusion, hallucinations, delirium, panic and assaultiveness, tremor, convulsions, coma, sweating, flushing, headache, cardiac arrhythmias, nausea, vomiting, cramps,

---

[21]It has been estimated that for every pound of methamphetamine produced, *5–7 pounds* of toxic waste are also produced, which then becomes an expensive hazardous-waste problem for the community where the "lab" was located (Rollo et al., 2007).

---

[22]Usually obtained from matches.

increased respiration, and circulatory collapse (Breggin, 2008).

There is also evidence suggesting that the clinical pharmacokinetics of methamphetamine, the most popular amphetamine being abused, at low doses is not the same as when it is used at high doses (Hanson & Fleckenstein, 2009). Finally, illicit amphetamine compounds are often adulterated by impurities during the production process. These adulterants also produce adverse effects and prevent health care providers from developing a formula by which they might calculate the toxic dosage level for an amphetamine for a given individual or what adverse reactions one might expect for that person. The more serious consequences of amphetamine abuse or addiction will be discussed in the section Consequences of Amphetamine Abuse.

Methods of Amphetamine Abuse There are multiple methods of amphetamine abuse. The amphetamine molecule is easily absorbed through the gastrointestinal tract, and thus oral administration is one common method by which the amphetamines are abused. The amphetamines are also well absorbed from intramuscular injections, the nasal mucosa, through the lungs if it is smoked, and from the general circulation if it is injected into a vein. When smoked, the amphetamine molecule is able to cross into the circulation easily, where it is then transported to the brain in just a matter of seconds. When injected into a vein, the amphetamine molecule is also able to reach the brain in just a matter of a few seconds. Amphetamine smoking and intravenous injection are the most common methods of amphetamine abuse in the United States (Rollo et al., 2007). The amphetamine molecules are also easily absorbed through the tissues of the nasopharynx, allowing them to be "snorted" (Rollo et al., 2007). Although it might be absorbed through the tissues of the rectum, this is not a popular method of amphetamine administration among abusers.

Subjective Effects of Amphetamines When Abused The subjective effects of amphetamine abuse depend on such factors as (a) possible concurrent use of other drugs, (b), whether individuals have developed any degree of tolerance to the effects of these drugs, (c) the method by which they abuse the compound, (d) the purity of the compound being abused, (e) the method of administration, (f) the dose administered, (g) the duration of the amphetamine abuse, and (h) the users' state of health. All of these factors interact with the individuals' expectations for the drug to produce the subjective drug experience. For example, whereas intravenous drug abusers might report a period of intense,

almost orgasmic feeling at first, followed by a gentle state of euphoria following the drug administration, those who take amphetamines orally or who "snort" it reported just the sense of gentle euphoria, which may last for a number of hours. In the case of methamphetamine, this "high" might last for 8–24 hours, a feature of this compound that makes it more addictive than cocaine[23] (Castro, Barrington, Walton, & Rawson, 2000; Rawson, Sodano, & Hillhouse, 2005). Abusers also report feeling less need for sleep and a reduced appetite. These are the effects that make amphetamine abuse desirable to the individual. The consequences of amphetamine abuse will be discussed later in the next section.

Amphetamine abusers quickly become tolerant to the euphoric effects of these compounds (Hanley, 2004). In an attempt to recapture the initial sense of euphoria, many amphetamine abusers will engage only in episodic amphetamine abuse. Other amphetamine abusers "graduate" from the oral use of these compounds to intranasal use, amphetamine smoking, or even injection. When amphetamine injectors become tolerant to the effects of the amphetamine being abused, they might embark on a "speed run," injecting more amphetamine every few minutes. In many cases, the cumulative dose injected within a 24-hour span of time might be enough to kill a drug-naive person, and is well within the range of neurotoxicity found in animal studies (Haney, 2008). Such "speed runs" might last for a number of hours, or even days, after which time the abuser will usually fall into a state of deep sleep and/or depression that might reach suicidal proportions.

Consequences of Amphetamine Abuse

Because the amphetamines have a reputation for enhancing normal body functions (increased alertness, concentration, and so on), they are mistakenly viewed by some abusers as being less dangerous than other illicit compounds (United Nations, 2008). The amphetamines, especially methamphetamine, have the potential to induce significant physical damage to the body if not be fatal to the abuser. We will look at the toxic effects of amphetamine abuse on the major body organs in the sections that follow.

Brain Damage Researchers have found that the abuse of any amphetamine can cause damage to the brain on both a regional and a cellular level, although it is not clear whether some of the amphetamine compounds are more likely to cause this effect than others (Yudko, Hall, & McPherson, 2009). At the neural level,

---

[23]Discussed in the next chapter.

methamphetamine, and similar compounds[24] have been found to damage or destroy up to 50% of the dopamine-producing neurons even at low dosage levels (Rawson et al., 2005). The danger of neurotoxicity from methamphetamine appears to be strongest at higher doses of the compound (Hanson & Fleckenstein, 2009). At high doses the amphetamine compounds, especially methamphetamine, also appear to be highly toxic to both the dopaminergic and the serotonergic neural networks (Yudko et al., 2009). Animal research has found that dopamine and norepinephrine neurotransmitter levels might not return to normal for at least 6 months of abstinence (G. R. King & Ellinwood, 2005).

The causal mechanism(s) for this neurotoxicity is not clear, and there are at least two competing theories to account for this observed effect. First, it is thought that at high dosage levels methamphetamine and similar compounds will induce the release of peroxide and hydroxyquinone family of compounds, both of which function as "free radicals" at the synaptic junction (Ling et al., 2006). In theory, these toxins might then poison the neurons (especially those in the serotonergic neurotransmission system), inducing neural death (Jaffe, Ling, & Rawson, 2005; G. R. King & Ellinwood, 2005). A competing theory is that high doses of an amphetamine compound force the release of large amounts of glutamate, which in large amounts is also known to be neurotoxic. However, the mechanism by which the amphetamines, especially methamphetamine, induces neural death when abused remains unknown at this time.

Methamphetamine addicts have been found to have a significant reduction in the "gray" matter in the brains[25] on high-resolution magnetic resonance imaging (MRI) tests when compared with age-matched control subjects (P. M. Thompson et al., 2004). The causal mechanism is not clear at this time, but might be a result of the observed amphetamine-induced temporary and permanent changes in cerebral blood flow patterns (Buffenstein, Heaster, & Ko, 1999; Payer & London, 2009). The amphetamine compounds have a profound impact on the cerebral circulatory system. Other complications of methamphetamine abuse include cerebral vasculitis and cerebral vasospasm. Available evidence also suggests that high doses of methamphetamine might break down the blood–brain barrier,[26] increasing the risk of neurotoxicity and

possible cerebral infections. Further, there is evidence of specific alterations in brain function, with some regions of the brain actually increasing in size during periods of active amphetamine abuse. This is thought to reflect localized trauma to regions of the brain such as the parietal cortex and caudate nucleus induced by long-term amphetamine abuse (Jernigan et al., 2005).

Other identified neurological consequences of methamphetamine abuse include agitation, delirium, and seizures (Graber, 2007). Following methamphetamine cessation, many former abusers report having trouble concentrating, and although there is a measurable cognitive decline that is attributed to methamphetamine abuse, research has demonstrated at least some degree of recovery in cognitive function after the abuser has abstained from alcohol and drug abuse for at least a year (Salo et al., 2009).

There are rare reports of amphetamine-induced episodes of the serotonin syndrome.[27] It is not known at this time whether these observed effects are found in people who abuse other amphetamine compounds besides methamphetamine or just to abusers of the latter compound. However, the fact that MDMA can also induce the serotonin syndrome suggests that at least one other member of the amphetamine family of compounds besides methamphetamine can cause this life-threatening problem. Further, long-term amphetamine abuse can induce sleep disturbances that can persist for a number of months after the last use of such drugs, and there is evidence of abnormal EEG tracings (a measure of electrical activity in the brain) that might persist for as long as 3 months after the last drug use (Schuckit, 2006a).

Effects of Amphetamine Abuse on the Emotions Amphetamine abusers will often experience periods of deep depression between periods of active amphetamine use (Rawson et al., 2005). These depressive episodes can reach suicidal proportions. Further, the abuse of amphetamines can cause the user to experience significant levels of anxiety and possibly panic attacks (Ballas, Evans, & Dinges, 2004; Breggin, 1998). Amphetamine-induced anxiety episodes may persist for weeks or even years after the individual's last use of an amphetamine, possibly because of drug-induced sensitization of those regions of the brain involved in the anxiety response (London et al., 2004). Often, the amphetamine abuser will attempt to control drug-induced anxiety through anxiolytics, marijuana, or alcohol.

During periods of active amphetamine use, the abuser might experience periods of drug-induced confusion,

---

[24]Some researchers, for example, classify MDMA as an amphetamine compound.

[25]See Glossary.

[26]See Glossary.

[27]See Glossary.

irritability, fear, suspicion, hallucinations, or delusional thinking (Julien, 2005; G. R. King & Ellinwood, 2005; M. C. Miller, 2005). Other consequences of amphetamine abuse include agitation, assaultiveness, tremor, headache, irritability, weakness, and suicidal and homicidal tendencies (Albertson et al., 1999; Ballas et al., 2004; Rawson et al., 2005). The amphetamines as a group have the potential to induce a psychotic state, although methamphetamine appears to be the most likely to do so (Ballas et al., 2004; Batki, 2001; Kosten & Sofuoglu, 2004). It was once thought that intravenous diazepam and haloperidol were the most effective in treating the toxic reaction to an amphetamine (Brust, 2004). However, recent evidence suggests that haloperidol might be neurotoxic to the cells of the substantia nigra region of the brain when used to treat amphetamine-induced psychotic states (Hatzipetros, Raudensky, Soghomonian, & Wamamoto, 2007). Thus the optimal treatment of amphetamine-induced psychosis remains to be identified.

Using the process of positron emission tomography (PET) scans, the team of Sekine et al. (2001) were able to document long-lasting reductions in the number of dopamine transporter molecules in the brains of methamphetamine abusers. The authors suggested that this might be one mechanism through which methamphetamine abuse is able to induce a psychotic state in the abuser. In its early stages this drug-induced psychosis is often indistinguishable from paranoid schizophrenia, and might include symptoms such as confusion, suspiciousness, paranoia, auditory and/or visual hallucinations, delusional thinking, anxiety, and possibly aggressive behavior (Haney, 2008; G. R. King & Ellinwood, 2005; United Nations, 2008). Less common symptoms of an amphetamine-related psychosis include psychomotor retardation, incoherent speech, inappropriate or flattened affect, and depression (Srisurapanont, Marsden, Sunga, Wada, & Monterio, 2003).

It was once thought that amphetamine-induced psychotic symptoms were rare. But researchers have found that two-thirds of people with a methamphetamine use disorder (MUD) will report at least some symptoms of a psychotic reaction upon detailed inquiry (Rawson et al., 2005). Again, it is not known whether or not other members of the amphetamine family of compounds share this characteristic. There is also evidence that the methamphetamine-related aggression may appear both during periods of acute intoxication, especially during the toxic psychosis and during the withdrawal stage (Sekine et al., 2001et al., 2006). Further research is needed to determine whether this is a characteristic specific to methamphetamine or is shared by the other forms of amphetamine.

It was once thought that the amphetamine psychosis was more common in people predisposed to schizophrenia and that this condition was simply uncovered by the amphetamine abuse. This theory is supported by the findings of C. K. Chen et al. (2003), who discovered that individuals who developed an amphetamine-related psychosis in Taipei (Taiwan) were younger at the time of their first amphetamine use, had used larger doses, and had premorbid personalities with schizoid or schizotypal personalities as compared with those who did not develop an amphetamine-induced psychosis.

There is a known relationship between amphetamine abuse and violent behaviors. Amphetamine-related aggression is thought to reflect amphetamine-related reductions in the serotonin transporter system in the brain, and such changes in the serotonin transporter system seem to continue for at least a year after the individual's last amphetamine (Sekine et al., 2006). This is consistent with clinical observations that reveal that an amphetamine-induced psychosis usually clears within a few days to a few weeks, although Rawson and Ling (2008) suggested that in 28% of the cases this condition might last longer than 6 months, if not become permanent (Haney, 2004; Rawson et al., 2005). Researchers in Japan noted in the years after World War II, when there was an epidemic of amphetamine abuse and subsequent amphetamine-induced psychosis, that in 15% of the cases it took up to 5 years for the condition to clear (Flaum & Schultz, 1996). Chronic amphetamine abuse can also result in the development of a condition known as *formication*[28] (Fadem, 2009; Tekin & Cummings, 2003). Individuals with this condition have the subjective sensation of having bugs crawling on or just under their skin and have been known to scratch or burn their skin in an attempt to rid themselves of these unseen creatures. The experience of formication appears to reflect the overstimulation of the nervous system, and it clears with abstinence.

Effects of Amphetamine Abuse on the Digestive System The amphetamines have a long history of being prescribed as anorexic agents to aid in weight loss programs, but their abuse can also result in such problems as diarrhea, constipation, nausea, vomiting, and ischemic colitis (Rawson et al., 2005; Sadock & Sadock, 2003). Further, because of their anorexic side effect, individuals who abuse these compounds tend to

---

[28]See Glossary.

neglect their daily dietary requirements, developing various dietary deficiencies as the body's stores of protein and various vitamins and amino acids are depleted (Mooney, Glasner-Edwards, Rawson, & Ling, 2009).

Methamphetamine abuse is associated with acute abdominal pain and gastroduodenal ulcers that sometimes can reach impressive size (Mooney et al., 2009). A poorly understood consequence of long-term methamphetamine abuse is a condition known as "meth mouth" (Davey, 2005; Rawsom et al., 2005). Individuals who suffer from this condition rapidly develop so much tooth decay or damage that extensive dental repairs/extractions are often necessary. There are several competing theories about the cause of "meth mouth." First, methamphetamine abuse reduces saliva production to about one-fourth its normal level.[29] This interferes with saliva's role as a defense against dental decay. A second theory is that because methamphetamine abusers substitute sugar-sweetened soda/candy for food, their risk for dental decay is increased (Rawson et al., 2005). A third possibility is that the compounds used to manufacture illicit methamphetamine cause or exacerbate dental decay, sometimes to the point where it becomes necessary to remove the individual's teeth and insert dental prosthetics (Davey, 2005; Rollo et al., 2007). This might reflect the fact that the first dental care the methamphetamine abusers receive for many years is when they are first incarcerated.

Effects of Amphetamine Abuse on the Cardiovascular System   There is strong evidence that amphetamine abusers are at higher risk for a myocardial infarction[30] than are nonabusers. The team of Westover, Nakonezny, and Haley (2008) examined the records of 3 million adults, aged 18–44 years from the state of Texas and concluded that amphetamine abusers were 61% more likely to suffer a myocardial infarction as nonusers the same age. One possible causal mechanism is the ability of compounds like methamphetamine to join sugar molecules to protein molecules (Treweek, Wee, Koob, Dickerson, & Janda, 2007). This then alters the function of those protein molecules, possibly causing them to become toxic to the muscle cells of the heart.

Long-term amphetamine abuse, but especially the abuse of methamphetamine, has been implicated in the acceleration of plaque development in the coronary arteries of the user, contributing to coronary artery disease for the abuser (S. B. Karch, 2009). Amphetamine abuse can also result in hypertensive episodes, tachycardia, arrhythmias, and sudden cardiac death, when abused at high doses (Ballas et al., 2004; Brust, 2004; Fadem, 2009; Gitlow, 2007; S. B. Karch, 2009; Rawson et al., 2005). Other suspected cardiac complications from amphetamine abuse include cardiac ischemia, myocardial ischemia, angina, and possible congestive heart failure (Acosta et al., 2005; Diercks et al., 2008; Oehmichen et al., 2005; Wadland & Ferenchick, 2004). Methamphetamine abusers have been found to have a 350% higher incidence of cardiomyopathy[31] than nonabusers of the same age, a finding that underscores the cardiotoxic effects of this compound (Yeo et al., 2007). Although this remains only a theory, the ability of high-dose chronic amphetamine abuse to induce myocardial infarctions is thought to be through the same mechanism as is observed in cocaine abusers[32].

Amphetamine-induced hypertensive episodes are associated with an increased risk of stroke for the user. The amphetamine-related hypertension places stress on the walls of cerebral blood vessels, and if they are weakened by a birth defect, there is a danger of a hemorrhagic stroke as the weakened artery wall ruptures (S. C. Johnston & Elkins, 2008). Methamphetamine-related strokes are predominantly (but not exclusively) found in the abuser's frontal lobes of the brain of the abuser (Mooney et al., 2009). Rare cases of methamphetamine-related cortical blindness have also been identified, as well as rare reports of subarachnoid hemorrhages (Mooney et al., 2009).

Effects of Amphetamine Abuse on the Pulmonary System   Amphetamine abuse has been identified as the cause of such respiratory problems as sinusitis, pulmonary infiltrates, pulmonary edema, exacerbation of asthma in patients with this condition, pulmonary hypertension, and possible pulmonary hemorrhage or infarct (Acosta et al., 2005; Rawson et al., 2005). Methamphetamine smoking has been identified as the cause of shortness of breath, some forms of pneumonia, and emphysema, possibly as a consequence of crushing tablets for smoking, thus admitting talc and other foreign agents into the lungs (Mooney et al., 2009).

Other Consequences of Amphetamine Abuse   The abuse of the amphetamines has been identified as a possible cause of rhabdomyolysis in some individuals, although the causal mechanism remains unclear at this time (Mooney et al., 2009). Amphetamine abuse has also been implicated as the cause of sexual

---

[29]A condition known as *xerostomia.*

[30]Commonly called a "heart attack."

[31]See Glossary.

[32]Discussed in the next chapter.

performance problems for both men and women (Albertson et al., 1999; Finger et al., 1997; Sadock & Sadock, 2007). The chronic use of high doses of amphetamine compounds can cause an inhibition of orgasm for both sexes and an inhibition of ejaculation in men. Individuals who abuse the amphetamines at high doses are at high risk for episodes of potentially fatal body hyperthermia (Ballas et al., 2004; G. R. King & Ellinwood, 2005; Rawson & Ling, 2008; Winslow, Voorhees, & Pehl, 2007).

There is evidence suggesting that methamphetamine abuse is the cause of liver damage (S. B. Karch, 2009; Rawson & Ling, 2008). Researchers have found that a "fatty liver" was present in 15.4% of methamphetamine abusers examined; and 9% of methamphetamine abusers demonstrated cirrhosis of the liver (S. B. Karch, 2009). However, most methamphetamine abusers are polydrug abusers, and thus it is hard to determine whether methamphetamine itself is the cause of the observed liver damage or just one of a range of compounds that induces the observed liver damage. Other identified consequences of amphetamine abuse include agitation, muscle twitching (Graber, 2007), and rarely hemorrhagic pancreatitis (Mooney et al., 2009).

The Addiction Potential of Amphetamines There is no test by which people might assess their potential to become addicted to these compounds, and if only for this reason even the experimental use of amphetamines is not recommended. There is evidence, however, that the amphetamines might induce an addiction in less time than cocaine (Payer & London, 2009). When abused, these compounds stimulate the brain's reward system (Haney, 2004), which is one of the reasons why they are such popular drugs of abuse. This effect, plus the brain's natural tendency to form strong memories of things that triggered the reward system, help to sensitize the abuser to drug use "cues." Brust (2004) suggested that some individuals progress from their initial amphetamine abuse on through to full amphetamine addiction in just a few months, underscoring the addictive potential of these compounds.

Amphetamine Abstinence Syndrome Following extended periods of amphetamine abuse at high doses, abusers or those who are addicted to amphetamines will experience a withdrawal syndrome including anhedonia,[33] irritability, depression (which might reach the level of suicidal proportions), fatigue, increased need for sleep, sleep disturbance, REM "rebound," and poor concentration (Brust, 2004; M. C. Miller, 2005). Post-amphetamine abuse anhedonia might last for a period

of months after the individual's last amphetamine use (M. C. Miller, 2005; Schuckit, 2006a). Other symptoms noted in the first few days following extended periods of amphetamine abuse include musculoskeletal pain, anorexia, "craving" for amphetamines, and impaired social function. These symptoms wax and wane in intensity over the first few weeks of abstinence (Brust, 2004). The amphetamine abstinence syndrome is noted for all cases where the individual was abusing an amphetamine at high doses for extended periods of time, although it is strongest in those individuals who abuse or are addicted to methamphetamine.

"Ice"

Essentially, "ice" is a form of methamphetamine prepared for smoking. The chemical properties of methamphetamine allow for it to be concentrated in a crystal that resembles a chip of ice (thus the name) or a piece of clear rock candy. The chip of concentrated methamphetamine is smoked, allowing the fumes to gain rapid access to the lungs and thus the general circulation, where it is transported to the brain in a matter of seconds. The practice of smoking Ice apparently began in Japan following World War II, and knowledge of the practice was carried back to Hawaii by Army troops involved in the postwar occupation of Japan. The practice became popular in Hawaii and eventually spread to the continental United States, where it has become popular in some parts of the country (S. B. Karch, 2009).

In the United States, the wave of Ice abuse went through three different phases: (1) In the earliest stages it was manufactured in Mexico and California, then shipped to various parts of the country (Rutkowski & Maxwell, 2009). As the demand increased, (2) local "meth labs" developed to meet local demand. These "labs" were most commonly found in the South and Midwest of the United States, because cocaine was still a popular stimulant in the northeastern United States. In response to this the government placed restrictions on precursor chemicals used in the production of methamphetamine, causing huge price increases (up to 185%) (Rutkowski & Maxwell, 2009). Although there are still local illicit labs that produce small quantities of methamphetamine for the illicit market, the major sources of methamphetamine have moved to Mexico, and the drug is then smuggled into the United States for consumption. A concurrent phenomenon is that methamphetamine abuse is now becoming popular in different ethnic groups besides white, middle-class young adults (Rutkowski & Maxwell, 2009).

---

[33]See Glossary.

How Ice Is Abused   Ice is a colorless, odorless, concentrated form of crystal methamphetamine. It is usually smoked, allowing abusers to titer effects to suit their perceived needs. Ice is usually less expensive than cocaine on a dose-per-dose basis because it will last longer than cocaine when smoked (Rawson et al., 2005). Because of its duration of effect, in many cases it is *perceived* by the abuser to be more potent than crack cocaine. It does not require the elaborate equipment necessary for cocaine smoking and does not produce a smell to alert others that it is being abused. Finally, if the individual should decide to stop smoking that "chip," it will reform as a crystal as it cools, allowing for the remainder to be used at another time. As will be discussed in the next chapter, when smoked, cocaine will burn off almost immediately, forcing the abuser to use it all at once.

Thus the preferred method of methamphetamine abuse is smoking, although it may also be injected. On occasion the chip of methamphetamine is melted down into a liquid and injected by intravenous methamphetamine abusers. This is usually seen if other forms of methamphetamine are not available to the user.

Subjective Effects of Ice   In contrast to cocaine-induced euphoria, which will last only 20 minutes, the euphoria induced by methamphetamine smoking is reported to last for hours. This is consistent with the pharmacological differences between cocaine and the amphetamines, in that the stimulant effect of cocaine lasts for a short period of time, whereas that of an amphetamine compound might last for a period of hours.

The complications of methamphetamine smoking are essentially extensions of those seen with other forms of amphetamine abuse, because ice is simply a form of methamphetamine and as such it shares the same side-effect and overdose profiles as other forms of amphetamine. Some abusers have reported experiencing a myocardial infarction up to 36 hours after their last use of ice, although the causal mechanism is not clear at this time (Tominaga, Garcia, Dzierba, & Wong, 2004). Thus ice shares the potential for incredible physical, social, and emotional damage seen with the abuse or addiction to other forms of the amphetamines.

Khat

In the 1990s it was feared that methcathinone ("Kat", "Quat," or "Khat," also known as "miraa" in some areas) might become the next popular drug of abuse in the United States. However, by the start of the 21st century methcathinone has virtually disappeared from the illicit-drug market in the United States and is rarely abused except by some immigrants from sub-Saharan Africa who continue the practice of chewing the leaves for their psychoactive effect ("Khat Calls," 2004; S. B. Karch, 2009). On the other hand, it is of growing concern in England, where the basic molecule has been modified by illicit-drug dealers so that it then becomes a "legal" drug ("Concern at New 'Legal High' Drugs," 2008). These drugs are then sold as a "safe" alternative to Ecstasy[34] to illicit-drug abusers. These variations on the methcathinone molecule were declared illegal in 2009 ("Concern at New 'Legal High' Drugs, 2008).

Where Khat Is Obtained   Khat is naturally found in several parts of the world, including east Africa and southern Arabia (Community Anti-Drug Coalitions of America, 1997; Haroz & Greenberg, 2005). In the natural world the plant grows to between 10 and 20 feet in height, and the leaves produce the alkaloids cathinone and cathine. Illicit-drug manufacturers began to produce an analog of cathinone known as methcathinone, which has a chemical structure very similar to that of compounds such as the amphetamines and ephedrine (S. B. Karch, 2009). It was then made available to drug abusers in the United States.

The Legal Status of Khat   Khat was classified as a Schedule I compound in 1992, and its manufacture or possession in the United States is illegal. However, it is easily manufactured in illicit laboratories using such products as drain cleaner, epsom salts, battery acid, acetone, toulene, and various dyes, to transform the basic ephedrine molecule by adding an oxygen atom to it. The end product is a compound with the chemical structure 2-methylamino-1-pheylpropan-l-1, which is then sold to illicit-drug users. By the year 2008, illicit laboratories had been found in at least 10 different states in the United States ("Parkinson-Like Symptoms Linked to Illicit Kat Use," 2008).

Methods of Khat Administration   Abusers typically smoke Khat, although it can be injected. On rare occasions the leaves are also chewed.

The Effects of Khat   The effects of Khat are very similar to those of the amphetamines. This is understandable because the Khat plant contains norephedrine and cathinone, which is biotransformed into norephedrine in the body following ingestion. Like the amphetamines, Khat can induce dopamine release and a sense of euphoria that is longer lasting and more intense than that induced by cocaine (Community Anti-Drug Coalitions of America, 1997). Indeed, the effects of Khat are thought to last for 24 hours or longer (Community Anti-Drug Coalitions of America, 1997). However, methamphetamine

---

[34]Discussed in Chapter 15.

is easier to manufacture, and so Khat never became a popular drug of abuse in the United States.

Adverse Effects of Khat   There has been little research into the actions of Khat on the body. What little is known is drawn from clinical data from physicians who have treated patient(s) who have abused this compound. Known adverse effects of Khat include vasoconstriction, hyperthermia, hypertension, insomnia, anorexia, constipation, a drug-induced psychosis, hallucinations, paranoia, aggressive episodes, anxiety, cardiac arrhythmias, mood swings, and depression (Haroz & Greenberg, 2005). Following extended periods of abuse, it is not uncommon for the abuser to fall into an extended period of sleep that might last days.

There is preliminary evidence suggesting that Khat is capable of inducing a Parkinson's disease-like syndrome ("Parkinson-Like Symptoms Linked to Illicit Kat Use," 2008). In one of the few studies to be published in this area, A. Stephens et al. (2008) drew on clinical evidence from 23 adult intravenous Khat addicts from Latvia, where Khat abuse is common. The research subjects had an average period of injected Khat use of 6.7 years and their average age was 37.5 years. It was noted that a gait disturbance predated the development of other symptoms, and there were no psychiatric problems noted in the research sample. Unfortunately, it was discovered that even if patients discontinued the use of Khat, there was no improvement in their neuropsychiatric status, suggesting that the damage to the brain is permanent (A. Stephens et al., 2008)

Chapter Summary

There are a number of compounds that function as central nervous system stimulants, including the natural substance ephedrine, which was isolated from the ephedra plant. This was found to be useful in the treatment of asthma, but fears developed that the demand for ephedrine might outstrip supply. Chemists examined compounds that had similar chemical structures in the hope of finding substitutes. The analogs of ephedrine known as the amphetamines were isolated in the 1880s, but it was not until the early 1930s that they were introduced for the treatment of asthma. Later these compounds were also found to have a paradoxical calming effect on some children who had what was then known as *hyperactivity*.

Drug abusers also found that the effects of the amphetamines were similar to those of cocaine, which was known to be quite dangerous to abuse. The ampules of amphetamine-containing liquid could be carefully unwrapped, broken open, and the contents injected, providing a "high" similar to that seen with cocaine but that lasted for a longer period of time. At the same time, physicians were prescribing amphetamines for their anorexic side effect and as an aid to the treatment of depression. However, as physicians have come to better understand the abuse potential of amphetamines, they have come under increasingly strict controls.

Unfortunately, the amphetamines might also be easily manufactured in illicit laboratories, so when drug addicts were unable to gain access to pharmaceutical quality amphetamines, they switched to illicit sources of these compounds, and there is a thriving manufacture/distribution system for the amphetamines. The most commonly abused amphetamine is methamphetamine, although the other members of the amphetamine family may also be abused from time to time. In the process, the current generation of drug abusers has come to relearn the lesson that amphetamine abusers of the 1960s had discovered through grim experience: "Speed kills."

CHAPTER 9

Cocaine Abuse and Dependence

Introduction

Future historians will note that there have been at least two cocaine use "epidemics" in the United States, during which time the generation of current cocaine abusers go through a process in which (a) the warnings of earlier generations of cocaine abusers are ignored, (b) cocaine becomes a rare drug of abuse, (c) its abuse becomes widespread, (d) the warnings of earlier generations are confirmed, (e) cocaine abuse is again deemed to be both dangerous and not a panacea, and (f) its abuse becomes less and less common.

This cycle was clearly seen in the United States in the last century. Cocaine abuse was common in the first decade(s) of the 20th century, and its dangers were well known to both drug abusers and physicians. In part because of the dangers associated with cocaine abuse, in the 1930s the recently introduced amphetamine compounds became the stimulant of choice. Then as the dangers associated with amphetamine abuse became known, there was a resurgence of cocaine abuse in the early- to mid-1980s. This wave of cocaine abuse peaked around the year 1986 and then gradually declined as drug abusers again returned to the abuse of the amphetamine compounds. However, the problem of cocaine abuse has never entirely disappeared, and there is evidence that cocaine abuse is again growing in popularity in some social groups (Acosta et al., 2005; Haney, 2008). Thus the cycle appears to be starting again. In this chapter, we will discuss the use and abuse of cocaine.

A Brief History of Cocaine

Biologists believe that at some distant point in the past a member of the plant species Erythroxylon coca began to produce a toxin in its leaves to protect itself from predation by insects or animals (Breiter, 1999). This neurotoxin, which we know as cocaine, was quite effective in this role, allowing the plant to thrive in the relatively thin atmosphere of the high Andes mountain region of South America. Then, at least 5000 years ago, it was discovered by early settlers of the region that by chewing the leaves of the coca plant, it was possible to ease feelings of fatigue, thirst, and hunger, allowing them to work for longer periods of time in the thin mountain air (Levis & Garmel, 2005).

By the time that the first European explorers arrived, they discovered that a thriving empire, the Incas, had developed in that region of what they called the "New World," and that the coca plant was used extensively by these people, who believed it to be a gift from the sun god (Brust, 2004). Prior to the arrival of the European explorers, the use of cocaine was generally reserved for the upper classes of the Inca society (Brust, 2004). However, the Inca empire did not survive its encounter with European civilization and was conquered. The European conquerors soon discovered that by giving native workers coca leaves to chew on, they would become more productive. The coca plant became associated with exploitation of South Americans by Europeans, who encouraged its widespread use. Even today, the practice of chewing coca leaves, or drinking a form of "tea" brewed from coca leaves, is commonplace.

In South America, the native workers will chew coca leaves mixed with lime obtained from sea shells, a practice that helps to negate the bitter taste of the coca leaf itself. The cocaine that is released by the practice of chewing is then absorbed into the chewer's system, providing a stimulatory effect that negates the fatigue normally felt when working at the high altitudes of the Andes mountains. This practice may also allow the chewer to gain some small measure of nutritional benefit, although this has not been scientifically studied. European scientists of the 19th century took a passing interest in the coca plant and attempted to isolate the compound(s) that made it so effective in warding off hunger and fatigue. In 1855[1] a chemist by the name of Albert Neiman isolated a compound that was later named cocaine. This accomplishment allowed scientists of the era to obtain large amounts of relatively pure cocaine, for research purposes. One experiment was the injection of concentrated cocaine into the bloodstream through the use of another recent invention: the hypodermic needle. The world has not been the same since.

Chemists of the era soon discovered that even orally administered doses of concentrated cocaine made the user feel good. Extracts from the coca leaf were used to make a wide range of drinks and elixirs, one of which even won an endorsement from the Pope himself (Martensen, 1996). Physicians and chemists of the era, lacking many effective pharmaceuticals to treat human suffering, began to experiment with concentrated cocaine as a possible way to ease human suffering. No less a figure than Sigmund Freud experimented with cocaine as a possible treatment for depression, and at first he endorsed its use for this disorder or as a possible treatment for narcotic withdrawal symptoms. When Freud later tried to warn others of his mistaken perception that cocaine was an effective treatment for these disorders, and of its previously unknown dangers, he was ignored by scientists of the era (Gold & Jacobs, 2005). Cocaine had entered European society, and even today it remains stubbornly entrenched in society as a drug of abuse.

Through all of this time, the natives of the high Andes mountains have continued to chew cocaine leaves to help them work in the rarified mountain air. Some researchers think that the fact that these natives are able to discontinue cocaine use when they descend to lower altitudes is evidence that it is not as addictive as law enforcement officials claim. However, this argument is undermined by the fact that chewing the coca leaf is not an effective method of administration. Much of the cocaine that is released during cocaine chewing is destroyed by digestive juices and the "first-pass" metabolism process.[2] Still, the blood levels of cocaine obtained when cocaine leaves are chewed are in the lower end of the blood levels achieved when a cocaine abuser "snorts" cocaine powder, and although the amount of cocaine that reaches the brain is barely enough to have a psychoactive effect because of this, cocaine chewers are still thought to become addicted to it by some scientists (S. B. Karch, 2009). Thus the question of whether coca chewing results in cocaine addiction has not been resolved.

Cocaine in U.S. History

The history of cocaine use in the United States is, surprisingly, intertwined with attempts to control alcohol use by the town fathers of Atlanta, Georgia. In response to the prohibition against alcohol use on Sundays, John Stith-Pemberton developed a "temperance drink" (Martensen, 1996, p. 1615) that, although alcohol-free, did up until 1903 contain 60 mg of cocaine per 8-ounce serving (M. S. Gold & W. S. Jacobs, 2005). In time, the world would come to know Stith-Pemberton's product by the name of "Coke-Cola," and it has become one of the more popular soft drinks sold.

The fact that Coke-Cola once contained cocaine is surprising to modern readers. But it is important to keep in mind that at the turn of the 20th century consumer protection laws were virtually nonexistent, and compounds such as cocaine and morphine were available without a prescription. Such compounds were also widely

---

[1]Schuckit (2006) reported that cocaine was first isolated in 1857, not 1855.

[2]Discussed in Chapter 3.

used in a range of "patent" medicines and other products, often as hidden ingredients. This practice contributed to a wave of cocaine abuse in Europe between the years 1886 and 1991, and in the United States between 1894 and 1899, and again between 1921 and 1929. These waves of cocaine abuse or addiction were fueled by the common practice of using cocaine as a "hidden" ingredient in so many products. Fears that cocaine was corrupting southern blacks prompted both the passage of the Pure Food and Drug Act of 1906 and the classification of cocaine as a "narcotic" in 1914 (Martensen, 1996). The Pure Food and Drug Act of 1906 did not prohibit the use of cocaine in products, but it did require that the ingredients be identified on the label, allowing consumers to avoid products that contained compounds such as cocaine. This prompted many manufacturers to remove it from their products. When the Harrison Narcotics Act of 1914 was passed, the nonmedical use of cocaine in the United States became illegal.

These regulations, combined with the geographical isolation of the United States in World War I prior to the entry of this country into the conflict, and the introduction of the amphetamines in the 1930s virtually eliminated cocaine abuse in the United States. It did not resurface as a major drug of abuse until the late 1960s, when it reappeared with the reputation as being the "Champagne of drugs" (P. T. White, 1989, p. 34). It became increasingly popular as a drug of abuse in the 1970s and 1980s, as a new generation of drug abusers discovered its euphoric effects. Reports of the physical damage induced by cocaine abuse at the turn of the 20th century were dismissed as exaggerations or, given the primitive state of medicine in the era, as being a misdiagnosis of another condition (Walton, 2002).

Also, there was a growing disillusionment with the amphetamines as drugs of abuse that started in the mid-1960s. The amphetamines had gained the reputation as dangerous, potentially fatal, drugs of abuse. Drug users would warn each other that "speed kills," a reference to the dangers associated with the use of "speed" (the slang term for amphetamines). Cocaine had gained the reputation as being able to bring about the same sense of euphoria as amphetamines, without their dangers. This, plus the emerging restrictions on amphetamine production and use, and its reputation as a "glamorous" drug, all helped to focus the attention of illicit-drug abusers on cocaine in the late 1960s.

By the middle of the 1980s, the cocaine distribution and sales network in the United States had become the seventh largest industry of its time, generating an estimated $21 billion per year in profits. This in turn attracted the attention of what has come to loosely be called "organized crime." Cocaine distributors were looking for ways to increase sales and open new markets for their "product" in the United States. The primary method of cocaine abuse during this era was intranasal inhalation of cocaine powder, although some abusers did smoke it after going through a long, dangerous process of transforming the powder into a smokable form of cocaine. After a period of experimentation, "crack" cocaine was developed. Essentially crack is cocaine prepared for smoking before sale to the abuser, and its abuse now accounts for approximately 50% of the illicit cocaine market in the United States (Greydanus & Patel, 2005).

The wave of cocaine abuse that swept across the United States in the 1980s and early 1990s is a topic worthy of a book in its own right and will be mentioned only in passing in this text. Just as the recently introduced amphetamines were adopted as a replacement for the known dangers of cocaine by drug abusers in the 1930s, cocaine came to be viewed as a safe alternative to amphetamine abuse in the 1970s and 1980s. The wave of cocaine abuse peaked in the mid-1980s, and the numbers of cocaine abusers in this country have slowly declined in the years since then. However, it has not disappeared entirely, and there is evidence that it might again be growing in popularity in some parts of the country (Acosta et al., 2005; Gold & Jacobs, 2005).

Current Medical Uses of Cocaine

Cocaine was once a respected pharmaceutical compound, used in the treatment of a variety of conditions. It was found to function as a local anesthetic by its ability to block the movement of sodium ions into the neuron, thus reducing or eliminating the ability of the neuron to transmit pain messages to the brain (Drummer & Odell, 2001). In this capacity it was used by physicians in surgical procedures in the ear, nose, throat, rectum, and vagina. As a topical anesthetic its effects would begin in about 1 minute, and would last for up to 2 hours (B. A. Wilson et al., 2007). No less a figure than Sigmund Freud exploited this characteristic of cocaine toward the end of his life, when he struggled with cancer of the tongue (Stahl, 2008). Cocaine is still frequently used by otolaryngologists,[3] especially because of its vasoconstrict and analgesic effects, but for the most part it has been supplanted by newer, safer compounds.

---

[3]Ear, nose, and throat specialists.

Scope of the Problem of the Cocaine Use Disorders

An estimated 994 metric tons of cocaine was produced in 2008 to meet the global demand for cocaine (United Nations, 2008). The vast majority is intended for the illicit-drug market. Of the 994 metric tons produced, an estimated 46% (or 450 metric tons) was shipped to North America,[4] 25% (or 250 metric tons) was shipped to Europe, and about 17% (or 17 metric tons) was used in South America. Authorities were able to interdict 42% of the total amount of cocaine produced, leaving 568 metric tons available to cocaine abusers around the globe for use. For the first time in over a decade, law enforcement officials in the United States were able to interdict sufficient amounts of cocaine to cause the price of cocaine at the retail level to increase, while the purity of cocaine sold to illicit users fell (United Nations, 2008).

In the United States it has been estimated that 2000 people use cocaine for the first time each day (McCord et al., 2008). Nationally 5–10% of the population, or about 30 million people, have abused cocaine at least once (Hahn & Hoffman, 2001; A. D. O'Connor et al., 2005). Many of those who have abused cocaine have done so out of curiosity, and the number of regular cocaine abusers in this country is estimated to be only between 1.7 and 2 million people (Acosta et al., 2005; C. M. Carroll & Ball, 2005). But cocaine abusers in the United States alone are thought to spend an estimated $35 billion per year to obtain this substance (Levis & Garmel, 2005).

In spite of mass media campaigns to the contrary, cocaine is not automatically addictive. Perhaps 15% of those who begin to use cocaine will ultimately become addicted to it (Budney, Forrman, Stephens, & Walker, 2007), whereas 28% become regular users[5] (Leamon et al., 2008). There are wide variations in the popularity of cocaine abuse around the United States. It has been estimated that the per capita cocaine abuse in New York City alone is 172 grams per person, whereas Washington, DC, takes second place with 73 grams per person per year and San Francisco earns the third-place prize with an estimated per capita consumption of 40 grams per year ("New York Remains Cocaine Capital of the World," 2007).

Pharmacology of Cocaine

Cocaine is best absorbed into the body when it is administered as cocaine hydrochloride, which is a water-soluble compound. After entering the circulation, it is quickly transported to the brain and other blood-rich organs of the body. The level of cocaine in the brain is usually higher than the blood plasma levels, especially in the first 2 hours following the drug administration ("Cocaine and the Brain," 1994; S. B. Karch, 2009). Cocaine's effects on the user appear to be stronger when the levels are rising, with the same blood concentration that causes euphoria when the blood levels are rising causing dysphoria[6] when the blood levels are falling (S. B. Karch, 2009; O'Brien, 2006).

The pharmacological effects of cocaine are quite short-lived. The effects of "snorted" cocaine begin in 3–5 minutes, peak in about 10–20 minutes, and last about an hour (Mendelson, Mello, Schuckit, & Segal, 2006). Cocaine smoking and injected cocaine results in an almost instantaneous "rush" experience as the drug begins to work, and the half-life of injected or "snorted" cocaine is estimated to be between 30 and 90 minutes (Jaffe, Rawson, & Ling, 2005; Leamon et al., 2008). Mendelson and Mello (2008) offered a more conservative estimate of cocaine's half-life as between 40 and 60 minutes. The difference between these two estimates might reflect the significant inter-individual variability in the speed with which the body is able to biotransform and eliminate cocaine.

During the process of cocaine biotransformation, the liver will produce about a dozen metabolites of cocaine (S. B. Karch, 2009). About 80% of a single dose of intravenously administered cocaine is biotransformed into *benzoylecgonine* (BEG) and *ecogonine methyl ester* (Levis & Garmel, 2005). Between 5 and 10% of a single dose is eliminated from the body unchanged, and about 10% is biotransformed into other compounds that are of minor importance and will not be mentioned again. Neither of the primary metabolites of cocaine has any known psychoactive effect. BEG has a half-life of about 7.5 hours and might be detected in urine samples for 48–72 hours, or about two to three times as long as cocaine itself might be detected. Thus urine toxicology tests usually attempt to isolate this cocaine metabolite rather than cocaine itself as evidence of cocaine use.

At the neural level, cocaine forces the release of dopamine stores from the presynaptic[7] neurons involved in the reward network of the brain, establishing strong

---

[4]Which the United Nations classified as including the United States, Canada, and Mexico.

[5]Regular cocaine use is a stepping-stone to addiction. Some of these regular abusers will become addicted, and others will step back from the brink of addiction. Thus about half of those who become regular users will become addicted to it.

[6]See Glossary.

[7]See Glossary.

drug-centered memories (Brust, 2004). This makes clinical sense as in the natural world it would be advantageous for sources of positive reinforcers such as food, water, or sex to produce a strong memory trace in people's brains so they can find that positive reinforcer again when they wanted to. Unfortunately, cocaine abuse "short-circuits" this reward system, causing a reward cascade stronger than that produced by natural reinforcers (Hanley, 2004). On the basis of their research on mice, Maze et al. (2010) found that cocaine suppressed the action of gene 9A, which in turn controls the production of an enzyme that either activates or suppresses the action of other genes, in effect locking the "pleasure center" of the brain into the "on" position. This in turn results in an increased craving for more of the drug. It is not known whether this same mechanism is found in humans, but their findings are suggestive of one mechanism through which cocaine is able to induce craving for additional cocaine use in abusers.

Cocaine's reinforcing effects appear to involve those neurons that use dopamine as their primary neurotransmitter. There are at least five subtypes of dopamine receptors in the brain, and cocaine's reinforcing effects appear to involve the dopamine D1 receptor subtype (Romach et al., 1999). The authors administered an experimental dopamine D1-blocking compound to cocaine-abusing volunteers and discovered that they failed to experience any major euphoria when they received cocaine. Not surprisingly, the dopamine D1 receptor sites are located in the limbic system of the brain, where the brain's reward system is thought to be located.

Research evidence suggests that cocaine activates the opioid mu and kappa receptor sites, possibly as an indirect result of its ability to activate the dopamine D1 receptor site. Habitual cocaine abuse can also cause long-term changes in the activity of compounds such as the ΔFosB[8] (Nestler, 2005). These findings appear to account, at least in part, for the intensity of the subjective experience of "craving" reported by cocaine-dependent people when they are abstaining from the compound. Cocaine abuse also impacts on the serotonin and norepinephrine neurotransmitter systems, although the significance of this effect is not known at this time (Acosta et al., 2005; Reynolds & Bada, 2003).

Cocaine also alters the function of a protein known as *Postsynaptic density-95* (Sanna & Koob, 2004). Long-term changes in this protein, which is involved in the process of helping the synaptic junction between neurons adjust to changes in neurotransmitter density, are

also thought to be involved in the process of learning and memory formation. This is thought to be one reason why cocaine abusers form such intense memories of their cocaine use and why the relapse rate among newly abstinent cocaine abusers is so high (Acosta et al., 2005; Sanna & Koob, 2004).

After periods of prolonged abuse, the neurons in the abuser's brain will have exhausted virtually all of their dopamine stores and there will be a loss of the initial euphoria. To overcome this effect, many habitual cocaine abusers will inject new cocaine two to three times an hour in an attempt to regain the euphoria initially achieved when the drug was first injected (Mendelson et al., 2006). However, eventually the neurons have exhausted the available stores of dopamine because cocaine blocks the reuptake of cocaine from the synaptic junction. This pharmacological effect of cocaine might explain the phenomenon in which cocaine abusers are known to become depressed after periods of cocaine abuse, a depressive state that might reach suicidal proportions in some abusers.

Although abused for its euphoric effects, tolerance to cocaine-induced euphoria develops very rapidly (Schuckit, 2006a). To counteract the tolerance, the abuser may increase the amount of cocaine abused to the point where it may be lethal to the drug-naive abuser. Also, the ever-increasing dosage level of cocaine interferes with the normal function of the region of the brain known as the diencephalon, which helps to regulate body temperature. At the same time, the cocaine will cause the surface blood vessels to constrict, making it harder for the body to cool itself. This cocaine-induced hyperthermia[9] may become life threatening as the abuser's body attempts to retain body heat at the very time that it will need to release excess heat (Gold & Jacobs, 2005; Jaffe, Rawson, & Ling, 2005; Mendelson & Mello, 2008).

Drug Interactions Involving Cocaine

Although cocaine is a common drug of abuse, there has been remarkably little research into cocaine-pharmaceutical interactions (S. B. Karch, 2009). There is a significant problem with cross-addiction, with cocaine abusers turning to other chemicals as a way to control the unwanted side effects of their cocaine use (Mendelson & Mello, 2008). For example, more than 62–90 percent of cocaine abusers have a concurrent alcohol use disorder (Gold & Jacobs, 2005).

The use of cocaine during alcohol intoxication can alter the pharmacokinetics of both compounds.

---

[8]See Glossary.

[9]See Glossary.

Scientists have observed a 30% increase in the blood plasma levels of cocaine in persons who abuse both alcohol and cocaine simultaneously, as the alcohol interferes with the ability of the liver to biotransform the cocaine. Further, a small amount (<10%) of the cocaine in the abuser's body will be transformed into *cocaethylene* (S. B. Karch, 2009; Repetto & Gold, 2005). Cocaethylene is a toxic compound that is thought to be 25–30 times as likely to induce death as the cocaine in the abuser's body (Karan, Haller, & Schnoll, 1998). Cocaethylene is thought to function as a calcium channel-blocking agent in the heart and has a biological half-life that is five times longer than that of cocaine alone, factors that are thought to increase the user's risk of sudden cardiac death 18-fold over that of cocaine abuse alone (Acosta et al., 2005; Hahn & Hoffman, 2001; Repetto & Gold, 2005). The concurrent use of alcohol and cocaine has also been identified as an element in the development of a potentially fatal pulmonary edema (Ciraulo et al., 2006). Unfortunately, cocaethylene may extend the period of cocaine-induced euphoria, possibly by blocking dopamine reuptake, which acts as an incentive for the individual to continue to coadminister these compounds in spite of these dangers.

It is not uncommon for cocaine abusers to use both cocaine and a narcotic analgesic[10] simultaneously. For reasons that are not well understood, cocaine appears to enhance the respiratory depressive effects of the narcotic analgesics, possibly contributing to potentially fatal respiratory arrest. Further, as will be discussed later in this chapter, cocaine can induce feelings of irritation or anxiety, feelings that the abuser often attempts to control through alcohol, sedating agents, and/or marijuana.

There is evidence that patients taking disulfiram as part of a treatment program for alcoholism achieve higher blood levels when they take cocaine, and this combination appears to cause a higher heart rate then when the person abuses just cocaine (S. B. Karch, 2009). There is also evidence that people taking antiviral medications may achieve higher blood concentrations of cocaine as the two compounds compete for biotransformation through the same metabolic pathway in the liver.

How Illicit Cocaine Is Produced

The production of illicit cocaine has changed little over the years. First, the cocaine leaves are harvested. In some parts of Bolivia, this might be done as often as once every 3–4 months, as the plant thrives in certain regions of that country. Then the collected leaves are dried in the open sunlight for a few hours to a few days. Although this is technically illegal, the local authorities are quite tolerant and do little to interfere with this process for the most part. Then the dried leaves are placed in a plastic-lined pit and mixed with water and sulfuric acid (P. T. White, 1989). The leaves are then crushed by workers who wade into the pit in their bare feet, stomping the mixture and from time to time draining off the liquids. Lime is mixed with the residue, which then forms a paste, which is called "cocaine base." It takes 500 kilograms of leaves to produce just 1 kilogram of cocaine base (P. T. White, 1989).

Next, compounds like water, gasoline, acid, potassium permanganate, and ammonia are added to the cocaine paste. This forms a reddish-grown liquid that is then mixed with a few drops of ammonia. This produces a milky solid that is dried and then dissolved in a solution of hydrochloric acid and acetone. It settles to the bottom of the tank, forming cocaine hydrochloride. This is filtered then dried under heating lights, where it forms a white, crystalline powder that is collected, packed, and shipped, usually in kilogram packages. As the cocaine moves through the distribution network, it is usually repeatedly adulterated, increasing its bulk and thus the profits for the dealer at each level of the distribution process.

Methods of Cocaine Abuse

Cocaine is abused in a number of ways. First, cocaine hydrochloride powder might be inhaled through the nose ("intranasal" use, or "snorting," technically known as "insufflation"). It may also be injected directly into a vein. Cocaine hydrochloride is a water-soluble compound and thus is well adapted to both intranasal and intravenous use. Cocaine "base" might be smoked, and the fumes then rapidly gain access to the circulation for transport to the brain. Finally, cocaine might be administered sublingually (under the tongue), where the blood-rich tissues under the tongue allow it to gain access to the circulation as it is absorbed. Each method of administration, though offering advantages to abusers, also exposes them to potentially toxic levels of cocaine in spite of the assertion of drug dealers that they are "safe" (Repetto & Gold, 2005).

Insufflation

Historical evidence suggests that the practice of "snorting" cocaine hydrochloride began in 1903, which is the year that the first case reports of septal perforation began to appear in medical journals (S. B. Karch, 2009). Currently,

---

[10]A practice known as "speedballing."

those who "snort" cocaine arrange the powder on a piece of glass (such as a mirror), usually in thin lines of 1/2 to 2 inches long and about 1/8 of an inch wide (Acosta et al., 2005). One gram of cocaine will usually yield around 30 such "lines" of cocaine (Acosta et al., 2005). The powder is diced up, usually with a razor blade, in order to make the particles as small as possible to enhance absorption. The powder is then inhaled through a tube such as a drinking straw or rolled-up paper, allowing it to be deposited on the blood-rich tissues of the sinus membranes.

About 60% of the cocaine deposited in the nasal passages is rapidly absorbed, with the first cocaine reaching the general circulation in 30–90 seconds after which it is then rapidly transported to the brain. The physical sensations reach peak intensity about 15–30 minutes after ingestion and begin to wear off in about 45–60 minutes following a single dose (Kosten & Sofuoglu, 2004). With repeated administrations, the peak effects might last twice as long as this (Hoffman & Hollander, 1997).

Researchers have suggested that 70–80% of the cocaine absorbed through the nasal passages is biotransformed by the liver *before* it is able to reach the brain, limiting the intensity of cocaine-induced euphoria experienced by the abuser. Further, because cocaine is a potent vasoconstrictor, it tends to limit its own absorption through the nasal mucosa, with the result being that only 60% of the cocaine deposited into the nasal passages is absorbed (Gold & Jacobs, 2005). These limiting factors make the inhalation of cocaine an ineffective means of cocaine abuse, and it is usually seen in casual or inexperienced abusers.

Intravenous Cocaine Administration

It is possible to mix cocaine hydrochloride power with water and then inject it directly into a vein. Intravenously administered cocaine will reach the brain in under 30 seconds (Kosten & Sofuoglu, 2004), with virtually all of the injected cocaine being absorbed into the user's body (Acosta et al., 2005). Although this allows for the rapid introduction of cocaine into the user's body, it does not allow the abuser to titrate the dose for optimal effects, and this may cause unwanted agitation to the cocaine abuser. However, it is an effective way to achieve the "rush" or "flash" experience so desired by intravenous cocaine abusers (discussed later in the Subjective Effects of Cocaine Abuse section). Following the "rush," cocaine abusers will experience a feeling of euphoria that lasts for about 10–15 minutes, during which time they might feel invulnerable. These feelings often contribute to abusers' reason(s) to deny that they have a cocaine use disorder (Gitlow, 2007).

Sublingual Cocaine Abuse

Cocaine hydrochloride powder is well adapted for absorption through the blood-rich tissues of the mouth, where it is rapidly absorbed and then transported to the brain in a manner similar to that seen with intranasal cocaine use. An unknown percentage of the cocaine that is absorbed will be subjected to the "first-pass metabolism" effect, and it is not known what percentage of the cocaine that is absorbed will actually reach the brain.

Rectal Cocaine Abuse

This practice is popular among certain groups, such as male homosexuals (S. B. Karch, 2009). Cocaine's local anesthetic properties provide some degree of relief from what would otherwise be painful forms of sexual activity. Unfortunately, the anesthetic properties of cocaine might also mask the pain signals that would warn the individual of physical trauma to the tissues of the rectal area, increasing the individual's risk for infection and possible death (S. B. Karch, 2009).

Cocaine Smoking

Historical evidence would suggest that the practice of burning, or smoking, different parts of the coca plant dates back to at least 3000 BCE when the Incas would burn leaves at religious festivals (Hahn & Hoffman, 2001). The practice of smoking cocaine resurfaced in the late 1800s, when coca cigarettes were used to treat hay fever and opiate addiction. By the year 1890, cocaine smoke was being used in the United States for the treatment of whooping cough, bronchitis, asthma, and a range of other conditions. But although the practice of cocaine smoking for medicinal reasons dates back for more than a century, recreational cocaine smoking did not become popular until the mid-1980s.

Although cocaine hydrochloride was a popular drug of abuse in the 1970s and 1980s, abusers discovered that it could not be easily smoked. It had to be transformed back into the cocaine base ("freebase" or "base") through a complex, labor-intensive process that involved the use of potentially explosive compounds. The obtained mixture was then passed through a filter in an attempt to remove the impurities, although many impurities remain in the cocaine "base." The cocaine "base" itself can be smoked. Abusers who smoked cocaine "base" discovered that the compound could induce an intense sense of pleasure. One of the reasons for this appears to be because 70–90% of the cocaine enters the circulation from the lungs when it is smoked, reaching the brain in as little as 7 seconds (Hahn & Hoffman, 2001; Mendelson & Mello, 2008).

However, the risk of fire and/or explosion inherent in this process limited the popularity of smoking cocaine "freebase" in the United States. To solve this problem, and expand their market by allowing more people to smoke cocaine, illicit distributors introduced a form of cocaine base that was already prepared for smoking. This form of cocaine is called "crack," because of the sound that it makes when smoked (Schuckit, 2006a). It is essentially a solid chunk of cocaine base designed to be smoked before sale at the local level. This was done in illicit "factories" or "laboratories" before distribution to individual dealers for sale in small, ready-to-use pellets that allow one or two inhalations. This form of cocaine for smoking has almost entirely replaced "freebase" cocaine in the United States (S. B. Karch, 2009). Although it would appear to be less expensive than cocaine prepared for intravenous injection, in reality crack is about as expensive on a gram-per-gram basis (S. B. Karch, 2009). Further, in spite of its reputation in some quarters as being safer than intravenously administered cocaine, it shares the same dangers as those found in cocaine injection. Since its introduction, crack has arguably become the most widely recognized method of cocaine abuse.

On rare occasions, intravenous cocaine abusers have been known to attempt to dissolve pellets of crack in alcohol, lemon juice, vinegar, or water, then inject the resulting mixture (Acosta et al., 2005). This is usually done by intravenous cocaine addicts who are unable to obtain cocaine hydrochloride for injection.

Gastrointestinal Absorption

It is possible to absorb cocaine through the gastrointestinal tract. If the person were to be a body packer[11] and one of the packets were to rupture, the individual would develop a massive cocaine overdose with probable death being the result (S. B. Karch, 2009). Coca-tea (commonly used in South America) will also allow the individual to absorb significant amounts of cocaine if too much is consumed. This can cause the abuser to test "positive" for cocaine and its metabolites on urine toxicology testing, and thus the use of such compounds should be avoided by those people subject to urine toxicology testing (S. B. Karch, 2009).

Subjective Effects of Abused Cocaine

There are several factors that influence people's subjective experience of cocaine abuse. First are their expectations for the compound's effects. Memories of past episodes of cocaine abuse both help to shape expectations for the drug's effects and trigger memories of past cocaine abuse that then contributes to the urge to engage in its abuse again (Gold & Jacobs, 2005). The actual dose being abused is also a factor, although this is often difficult to estimate because of differences in the purity of cocaine sold in different locations. Finally, the physiological effects of the chemical help to shape how it is abused. For example, cocaine smokers are able to stop smoking it when the side effects become uncomfortable.

Low blood levels of cocaine tend to cause an increase in the individual's libido, a feeling of increased energy, and a generalized feeling of arousal. At higher blood levels, such as those achieved through smoked or intravenously administered cocaine, a sense of intense euphoria known as the "flash" or the "rush" will be induced within seconds of the time that the drug was introduced into the body (Jaffe, Rawson, & Ling, 2005; Stahl, 2008). This experience has been compared to the sexual orgasm in intensity, and some male cocaine abusers have reported spontaneous ejaculation without direct genital stimulation as a result of cocaine injection or smoking. Within a few seconds the "rush" fades into a feeling of excitation or euphoria that lasts for 10–20 minutes. Tolerance to the euphoric effects of cocaine develops rapidly. To overcome this tolerance, abusers have been known to engage in several behaviors. Some abusers switch from methods of cocaine abuse that introduces small amounts of cocaine into their system to more efficient methods of cocaine dosing. Others attempt to overpower cocaine-induced tolerance by engaging in extended periods of continuous cocaine abuse known as the "coke run." Cocaine "runs" last between 12 hours and 7 days, during which time the abuser will inject additional cocaine perhaps as often as two to three times an hour until the cumulative dose reaches levels that would kill the cocaine-naive individual (Mendelson & Mello, 2008). At the end of the coke "run," the individual may fall into a prolonged, deep sleep that may last for hours, or even days, and experience a profound, possibly suicidal level of depression.

Complications of Cocaine Abuse/Addiction

Sometimes cocaine abuse can exacerbate medical conditions that were present, even if only in subclinical forms, before the individual began to abuse this compound (Mendelson & Mello, 2008). This may help to explain why cocaine abuse is a factor in between 40 and

---

[11]See Glossary.

50 percent of all deaths associated with illicit-drug use (S. B. Karch, 2009). In some cases, death occurs so rapidly that the abusers do not have a chance to reach a hospital, and the coroner is the only physician who will see them. Unfortunately, this will be after the abuser's death. But in addition to simply killing the abuser, cocaine abuse can induce a wide range of other complications, including the following.

Addiction

It was believed in the 1960s and 1970s that cocaine was not physically addictive, a misperception brought on by the fact that cocaine was so expensive and so difficult to find during that era that few abusers could afford to use it long enough to become addicted. With the availability of cheaper, more potent[12] cocaine, it has been discovered that cocaine addiction is not only possible, but that it also develops more rapidly than addiction to other compounds such as alcohol or marijuana. The addiction potential of cocaine might best be illustrated by the observation that a monkey would spend hours pushing a lever until it had pushed it 6000 times, just to get a shot of cocaine (Rasmussen, 2008).

Cocaine is often portrayed as a universally addictive substance, whereas in reality only about 6% of those who begin to abuse cocaine will be physically addicted to it within the first year (C. M. Carroll & Ball, 2005).[13] If the individual continues to abuse cocaine, the percentage who become physically addicted to it increases until eventually 15% of those who initiated the use of cocaine will end up being addicted to it (Jaffe, Rawson, & Ling, 2005; C. M. Carroll & Ball, 2005).

Respiratory System Problems

Cocaine smokers experience side effects such as chest pain, cough, and damage to the bronchioles of the lungs (Gold & Jacobs, 2005; J. H. Jones & Weir, 2005). Approximately one-third of habitual crack abusers develop wheezing sounds when they breathe, and many experience an asthma-like condition known as chronic bronchiolitis ("crack lung"). It has been suggested that this might be due, at least in part, to contaminants in the cocaine that is smoked (Mendelson & Mello, 2008). Other cocaine smokers risk the development of hemorrhage, pneumonia, and a chronic inflammation of the throat. On occasion the smoker will experience a situation where the alveoli of the lungs will rupture, allowing the escape of air (and bacteria) into the surrounding tissues, known as a "pneumothorax," establishing the potential for an infection to develop as well as compromising the ability of the smoker's lungs to function properly. There is evidence suggesting that cocaine-induced lung damage may be permanent.

Cocaine smoking appears to be associated with an observed increase in the number of fatal asthma cases ("Asthma Deaths Blamed on Cocaine Use," 1997). Although cocaine abuse is not the cause of all asthma-related deaths, it is known that the practice of smoking cocaine can cause/exacerbate asthma in cocaine smokers. Chronic cocaine "snorters" experience sore throats, inflamed sinuses, bleeding from the sinuses, hoarseness, and on occasion a breakdown in the cartilage in the nose, a condition that may develop after just a few weeks of intranasal cocaine use (S. B. Karch, 2009). It is also common for intranasal cocaine abusers to experience the development of ulcers in the nasal passages, as cocaine-induced vasoconstriction and the impurities in illicit cocaine contribute to bacterial infections in these tissues.

Cardiovascular System Damage

Cocaine abuse appears to be a major risk factor contributing to the buildup of plaque in the coronary arteries of abusers between the ages of 18 and 45 (S. B. Karch, 2009; Lai et al., 2005; Levis & Garmel, 2005; McCord et al., 2008). If the abuser is also infected with HIV-1 infection,[14] the process of plaque buildup is accelerated (Lai et al., 2005).

Repeated episodes of cocaine abuse seems to trigger the "complement cascade" normally seen when the body is invaded by foreign microorganisms. The complement cascade allows the buildup of protein molecules on the cell walls of invading organisms, thus alerting the body's macrophages[15] as to which cells to attack. This would explain the theory that atherosclerotic plaque is formed when the macrophage cells mistakenly attack cholesterol molecules circulating in the blood and then attach these cells to the endothelial cells of the coronary arteries. Over time, significant amounts of cholesterol accumulate, reducing the flow of blood through that vessel and contributing to the development of coronary artery disease.

Although this theory is attractive, it has been challenged by Pletcher et al. (2005). Drawing on the data

---

[12]As compared to what it cost in the 1960s and early 1970s.

[13]If only because it is not possible to predict who is in danger of becoming addicted to cocaine and who is not, the experimentation with cocaine is not recommended.

---

[14]Discussed in Chapter 34.

[15]See Glossary.

obtained from the CARDIA study, the authors found that one-third of the 5000 subjects had abused cocaine at some point in their lives. Yet after having factored in the effects of age and the participant's sex, ethnicity, familial medical history, and alcohol and tobacco use patterns, the authors were unable to find *any* impact from having a history of cocaine abuse on coronary artery health status. The factors that were the strongest predictors of coronary artery disease were being male and alcohol and cigarette abuse problems. Indeed, 50% of cocaine abusers who present at the hospital emergency room with heart pain have no evidence of atherosclerotic plaque buildup in their coronary arteries (Leamon et al., 2008). These contradictory findings suggest that there is much to learn about cocaine's relationship to coronary artery disease in abusers.

Cocaine abuse is associated with cardiovascular problems such as severe hypertension, sudden dissection of the coronary arteries, cardiac ischemia, tachycardia, micro-infarcts myocarditis, cardiomyopathy, and sudden cardiac death (Greenberg & Bernard, 2005; S. B. Karch, 2009; Jaffe, Rawson, & Ling, 2005; Mendelson & Mello, 2008; Stahl, 2008). However, the mechanism(s) by which cocaine abuse causes such problems is often not what clinicians have been taught. For example, clinical wisdom suggested that cocaine-induced coronary artery spasms might cause the heart attacks so often seen in cocaine abusers. Although such spasms do take place, they seem to play only a minor role in cocaine-induced heart attacks. Rather, cocaine abuse appears to first cause the buildup of plaque coronary artery where the endothelium has already been damaged and then cause the coronary artery to constrict at these points during subsequent periods of abuse.

This process is seen most often in cigarette smokers, although it does occasionally occur in nonsmokers as well (J. H. Jones & Weir, 2005). Patrizi et al. (2006) concluded that cocaine-induced coronary artery disease was the most common cause of myocardial infarctions in cocaine abusers. Further, the authors noted that cocaine abusers had significantly higher levels of atherosclerosis in the coronary arteries than nonabusers. So strong is the association between cocaine abuse and heart attacks that Tomb (2008) recommended that physicians assume that cocaine abuse was involved when a young adult experiences a heart attack until proven otherwise.

Cocaine abuse can cause a significant increase in the heart rate, and it is not uncommon for the abuser to state that their heart was beating so fast that they thought that they were about to die (S. B. Karch,

2009; Levis & Garmel, 2005). These are characteristics that contribute to the 24- to 27.5-fold *higher* risk of a heart attack in the first hour after the individual began to use cocaine (Wadland & Ferenchick, 2004; S. B. Karch, 2009; Khan et al., 2009). Further, it is thought that cocaine abuse can cause or exacerbate cardiac ischemia for up to 18 hours after the individual's last cocaine use, because of the time that it takes for the rupture of atherosclerotic plaque to manifest as coronary artery blockage (S. B. Karch, 2009). There is some evidence that suggests that women are at higher risk for cocaine-induced cardiac problems than their male counterparts, although these problems are seen in either sex (Lukas, 2006).

Cocaine has been found to be directly toxic to the muscle tissues of the heart and can disrupt the normal electrical flow pattern necessary for normal heartbeat (S. B. Karch, 2009). This might explain why cocaine abuse can induce cardiac arrhythmias such as atrial fibrillation, sinus tachycardia, and ventricular tachycardia, as well as the potentially fatal *torsade de pointes*[16] (Gold & Jacobs, 2005; Khan et al., 2009; O'Connor et al., 2005). Scientists continue to search for a compound(s) that might mitigate cocaine's cardiovascular effects, offering the promise that physicians might soon have new tools to protect the hearts of those foolish enough to abuse cocaine.

In the 1990s it was believed that cocaine abuse altered the normal action of the catecholamines[17] in the heart, causing the cocaine-induced cardiac problems (S. B. Karch, 2009). However, the team of Tuncel et al. (2002) challenged this theory, noting that in rare cocaine abusers, a normal physiological response known as the baroreflex would block the release of excess norepinephrine, reducing the stress on the heart. Thus the theory that cocaine abuse causes increased levels of norepinephrine in the blood, placing an increased workload on the heart, especially the left ventricle, and is therefore the suspected mechanism for cocaine-induced sudden cardiac death, remains unproven.

Some scientists believe that cocaine abuse causes "micro-infarcts"[18] in the cardiac muscle (Gold & Jacobs, 2005). These micro-infarcts each slightly reduce the heart's ability to carry out its role as the circulatory system pump, and cumulatively may cause the abuser's heart to fail. It is

---

[16]See Glossary.

[17]See Glossary.

[18]Microscopic areas where the blood supply to cardiac tissue was disrupted, resulting in damage to the tissue supplied by those blood vessels.

not known whether these micro-infarcts are the cause of the chest pain reported by some cocaine abusers, but it is known that cocaine abuse can induce areas of ischemia in body organs, especially the heart and brain.

There does not appear to be a specific pattern to cocaine-induced cardiac problems, and both first-time abusers and those with a long history of prior cocaine abuse may present with symptoms of a heart attack. Cocaine's contribution to heart disease in young adults is often underrecognized, and it has been estimated that 25% of heart attack patients between the ages of 18 and 45 suffered a cocaine-related heart attack (J. H. Jones & Weir, 2005). Cocaine abusers frequently have abnormal electrocardiograms (EKGs), even if they are not actively abusing cocaine at the time of the EKG. These abnormal EKG tracings may reflect subclinical drug-induced heart damage, which will be exacerbated if the individual should continue to abuse cocaine. Unfortunately, some illicit-drug dealers have been known to tell their clients that if the cocaine causes chest pain, it is a sign that the cocaine is very potent, not a sign of a possible cocaine-induced heart problem. If abusers should then fail to tell the physician that they were a cocaine abuser, the physician might attempt to treat the suspected heart attack with medications such as the beta-adrenergic antagonists (β-blockers), which can exacerbate the cocaine-induced vasoconstriction and possibly kill the patient (J. P. Thompson, 2004).

A rare, but potentially fatal complication seen with cocaine abuse is the *acute aortic dissection* (Gold & Jacobs, 2005; S. B. Karch, 2009; O'Brien, 2006; Repetto & Gold, 2005). In this condition, a weak spot develops in the wall of the aorta and eventually the inner lining of the aorta rips away from the outer parts. Each heartbeat causes this tear to move farther down the aorta, until it eventually results in death. Although not every case of acute aortic dissection is related to cocaine, it is a medical emergency that requires immediate surgery if the patient should have any chance to survive. As the preceding information demonstrates, cocaine abuse carries with it a significant cardiovascular risk.

Cocaine Abuse as a Cause of Digestive System Damage

There is evidence that some of the metabolites of cocaine, especially cocaethylene, are quite toxic to the liver (Brust, 2004). However, the theory that cocaine abuse can directly cause/contribute to liver disease remains controversial (S. B. Karch, 2009). Still, some individuals have a genetic defect that prevents their bodies from producing an enzyme that plays a crucial role in cocaine biotransformation. This condition is the pseudocholinesterase deficiency, and people with this condition are at risk for potentially fatal reactions to even small amounts of cocaine (Brust, 2004; Schuckit, 2006a).

Cocaine abuse has been identified as the cause of bruxism, decreased gastric motility, perforation of the bowel, gangrene of the bowel, and ischemia to different regions of the intestinal tract. These later complications of cocaine abuse might become so severe that surgical intervention is necessary to remove the damaged portions of the intestinal tract, with all of the risks associated with such surgery.

Cocaine Abuse as a Cause of Central Nervous System Damage

Researchers have found that like the amphetamines, cocaine abuse causes a reduction in cerebral blood flow in at least 50% of those who abuse it (Balamuthusamy & Desai, 2006; Brust, 2004). Neuroimaging studies have found evidence of cerebral atrophy and enlarged ventricles within the brain, both indicators of the death of neural tissue (Bolla & Cadet, 2007). The observed changes in both the vasculature and structure of the brain might contribute to or even cause the lower cognitive functions seen in cocaine abusers. Researchers have found deficits in the areas of verbal learning, memory, and attention of chronic cocaine abusers on neuropsychological test batteries (Kosten & Sofuoglu, 2004; Kosten, Sofuoglu, & Gardner, 2008). These neurocognitive deficits appear to continue for months after the individual's last cocaine use, and it is not known at this time whether they will resolve with extended abstinence or not (Gonzalez et al., 2009).

Cocaine abuse is associated with an increased risk for either obstructive or hemorrhagic strokes (Bolla & Cadet, 2007; Khan et al., 2009; Mendelson et al., 2006). These cocaine-induced strokes might be microscopic in size ("micro-strokes") or may involve major regions of the central nervous system. Kaufman et al. (1998) suggested that cocaine abusers were twice as likely as nonabusers of the same age to suffer a stroke, whereas B. A. Johnson, Devous, Ruiz, and Alt-Daoud (2001) suggested that the risk might be as much as 14 times higher. Such strokes have been identified in the brain, retina, and spinal cord of cocaine abusers (Jaffe, Rawson, & Ling, 2005). The risk of suffering a cocaine-related stroke is apparently cumulative, with long-term abusers being at higher risk than new abusers, although both groups are at risk for a cocaine-induced stroke.

The causal mechanism for cocaine-induced strokes is thought to be the cycle of drug-induced vasospasm during periods of active drug abuse and the reperfusion[19] that occurs in between these periods of cocaine use (Bolla & Cadet, 2007; B. A. Johnson et al., 2001; S. B. Karch, 2009). This can lead to damage to the blood vessel walls of the cerebral vasculature, facilitating the development of a stroke. Cocaine abusers are also at higher risk for *transient ischemic attacks* (TIAs) brought on as a result of their cocaine abuse, possibly because of the effects of cocaine-induced vasoconstriction on the brain (Kaufman et al., 1998).

Cocaine abuser are at higher than normal risk for the development of seizures, although the mechanism for this remains unknown (Fadem, 2009; Gold & Jacobs, 2005). These seizures may be the result of cocaine-induced interruptions in cerebral blood flow, although this is not proven. There is strong evidence that cocaine might initiate a neurological process known as *kindling*,[20] with the individual's cocaine abuse both causing and exacerbating seizure disorders in abusers (Gold & Jacobs, 2005; S. B. Karch, 2009). Even first-time abusers have been known to suffer a cocaine-induced seizure, and there is no evidence to suggest that these seizures are dose related (Gold & Jacobs, 2005). One region of the brain thought to be involved in the kindling process is the amygdala, although other regions of the brain might also be sensitive to cocaine use–related kindling.

Cocaine abuse is thought to interfere with the process of body temperature regulation, causing periods of *malignant hyperthermia* (S. B. Karch, 2009). The brain can operate only within a very narrow temperature range, and if the body temperature exceeds these limits, there is a very real danger of damage to the brain, if not even the death of the patient. There is also an emerging body of evidence that suggests that cocaine abusers are at high risk for alterations of the brain at the level of the individual neuron (Tannu, Mash, & Hemby, 2006). The authors compared samples of brain tissue from 10 cocaine overdose victims with those of people who had died from noncocaine-related causes. They found alterations in the expression of 50 different proteins involved in the process of forming and maintaining neural connections in neurons in the nucleus accumbens of abusers. As all of the preceding information demonstrates, cocaine abusers place themselves at high risk for neural damage, if not death.

Finally, there is also evidence suggesting that cocaine abuse may alter the blood–brain barrier,[21] facilitating the entry of the human immunodeficiency virus type 1 (HIV-1) into the brain. Further, because of the various bacterial, fungal, or viral contaminants in some samples of illicit cocaine, abusers are being exposed to a number of potentially fatal infectious agents through their cocaine abuse (Acosta et al., 2005). The intranasal use of cocaine induces a state of intense vasoconstriction in the tissues of the sinuses. This might cause tissue death in the affected areas, establishing focal colonization points for bacteria, and in turn can result in sinusitis, loss of a sense of smell, nose bleeds, or even a potentially fatal brain abscess if the bacteria are able to access the brain through the nasal cavity (Roldan & Patel, 2008).

Cocaine's Effects on the Abuser's Emotions and Perceptions

According to Oehmichen et al. (2005), statistically, cocaine abusers are at increased risk for premature death from both suicide and homicide. The authors found that suicide accounted for 10% of the deaths of the cocaine abusers who died, whereas homicide accounted for 20%[22] of the cocaine abusers who died. Further, cocaine abuse can exacerbate symptoms of conditions such as Tourette's syndrome and tardive dyskinesia (Lopez & Jeste, 1997). After extended periods of abuse, some cocaine abusers develop the sensation of having bugs crawling on or just under their skin. These hallucinations are known as formication,[23] and cocaine abusers have been known to scratch, burn, or cut themselves in an attempt to relieve themselves of the torment of these nonexistent insects (Gold & Jacobs, 2005).

Cocaine abusers frequently report experiencing some degree of anxiety as a side effect of their drug use. In one study conducted during the height of the wave of cocaine abuse in the United States that peaked in the 1990s, *one-quarter* of those patients being assessed for an anxiety disorder eventually admitted to the abuse of cocaine (Louie, 1990). Up to 64% of cocaine abusers surveyed had experienced some degree of anxiety as a result of their cocaine abuse, according to Louie. Cocaine abusers frequently attempt to control this anxiety by concurrently abusing sedating agents such as marijuana, benzodiazepines, alcohol, narcotic analgesics, and, on occasion, barbiturates.

---

[19]See Glossary.

[20]See Glossary.

[21]Discussed in Chapter 3.

[22]Cocaine-induced heart disease, infections (including HIV-1), strokes, and accidents accounted for the other 70% of those cocaine abusers who died.

[23]See Glossary.

Cocaine-related anxiety attacks might persist for months after the individual's last cocaine use (Gold & Jacobs, 2005; Schuckit, 2006a). Further, there is evidence that cocaine abuse might lower the threshold at which the individual will experience an anxiety attack (Gold & Jacobs, 2005).

Cocaine abuse has also been identified as the cause of a drug-induced psychosis (Schuckit, 2006a). A significant percentage of chronic cocaine abusers will exhibit symptoms of a psychosis that are very similar to those seen in paranoid schizophrenia. This condition, known as "coke paranoia" by abusers, usually clears within a few hours or days of the individual's last cocaine use (Hanley, 2004; S. B. Karch, 2009; Schuckit, 2006a; Stahl, 2008). The mechanism through which extended periods of cocaine abuse is able to cause a drug-induced psychosis is not known, and there is little research being conducted into this phenomenon.

Habitual cocaine abuse has been implicated in the death of neurons, possibly because of cocaine's ability to alter the normal function of the *synuclein* family of proteins in the brain. Under normal conditions these proteins help to regulate dopamine transport within the neuron. Recent evidence suggests that chronic cocaine abuse can alter the process of synuclein production within the neuron, ultimately causing or contributing to the death of these neurons (Mash et al., 2003).

Other Problems Associated with Cocaine Abuse

Men who abuse cocaine run the risk of developing erectile dysfunctions, including a painful, potentially dangerous condition known as priapism[24] (S. B. Karch, 2009). Further, as noted earlier in this chapter, the rectal use of cocaine may, although it reduces the individual's awareness of pain, contribute to tissue damage, development of infection, and possible death.

As discussed earlier, cocaine abuse/addiction can cause the individual's death as a direct result of the cocaine on the individual's body. But it can also indirectly contribute to the abuser's premature demise through a variety of mechanisms. One such indirect method of cocaine-induced death is that it can cause rhabdomyolsis,[25] which can cause or contribute to the individual's death (Khan et al., 2009; Schuckit, 2006a). Rhabdomyolsis is thought to be the result of cocaine-induced vasoconstriction, causing ischemia in the muscle tissue (S. B. Karch, 2009; Repetto & Gold, 2005; Richards, 2000).

[24]See Glossary.
[25]See Glossary.

Cocaine Withdrawal

A few hours after the individual last "snorted" cocaine, or within 15 minutes of the last intravenous or smoked dose, the individual will slide into a state of deep depression that may reach suicidal proportions (Gold & Jacobs, 2005). Roy (2001) found that one-fifth of all suicides of adults under the age of 60 in New York City were cocaine related. This depressive effect is thought to reflect the cocaine-induced depletion of the neurotransmitters dopamine and norepinephrine in the brain. After a period of abstinence, the neurotransmitter levels slowly return to normal. But there is a possibility that the individual's cocaine abuse masked a preexisting depressive disorder, which will become apparent only after the individual discontinues the abuse of cocaine. In such cases, compounds such as desipramine or buproprion might be the best choices for antidepressant medications (Rounsaville, 2004).

Other symptoms frequently seen during cocaine withdrawal include fatigue, vivid and intense dreams, sleep disorders (both insomnia and hypersomnia), anorexia, and psychomotor agitation or retardation (C. M. Carroll & Ball, 2005). Many cocaine abusers report experiencing cognitive problems upon cessation that may continue for 6 months or longer (P. T. Morgan et al., 2006). There is evidence to suggest that cocaine abusers are less likely than the abusers of other compounds to report insomnia when they discontinue the use of cocaine, and that there is a positive relationship between the abuser's postcessation insomnia and the possibility of relapse (P. T. Morgan et al., 2006).

Chapter Summary

It is often surprising for students to learn that cocaine is nothing more than a natural pesticide produced by the coca plant in an attempt to ward off insects or animals that might otherwise consume the leaves of the plant. By coincidence, this compound also has a strong impact on the central nervous system (CNS). Early settlers in the high Andes mountain regions found that by chewing the cocaine leaf, they could enhance their endurance while working at these high altitudes. It soon became a valued part of the culture prior to the arrival of European explorers.

With the development of the methods to chemically extract cocaine from the leaf and concentrate it, and the almost simultaneous development of the hypodermic needle, the world entered a new era of cocaine abuse. It was found that if concentrated cocaine were to be smoked or injected, it could induce a powerful sense of euphoria that is, at least in the opinion of some abusers, "better than sex." This soon made cocaine the stimulant of choice for many. Over time, it was discovered that although cocaine might indeed make the abuser feel good, it also contributed to a wide range of potentially lethal problems, and abusers drifted away from cocaine abuse to the supposedly safer pleasures of the amphetamines in the 1930s. By the 1960s or 1970s, they had

discovered that these compounds were dangerous, but the lessons so painfully learned by cocaine abusers at the turn of the 20th century had been forgotten. Cocaine again became a major drug of abuse, and the dangers associated with its use were rediscovered. It remains a significant component of the drug-abuse problem in the United States in spite of the known dangers associated with its use.

CHAPTER 10

Marijuana Abuse and Addiction

Introduction

The earliest written reference to marijuana possibly dates to 2727 BCE, although the exact age of this Chinese manuscript is disputed (Grinspoon, Bakalar, & Russo, 2005). The fact that the exact age of the manuscript is controversial is in a symbolic way quite appropriate, for even back then marijuana was controversial. It remains the subject of controversy, sparks fierce debate, and has been the source of many "urban myths." People discuss marijuana as if it were a chemical or a drug: In reality it is a plant, a member of the *Cannabis sativa* family, which has long been known and used by humans. Indeed, the very name *Cannabis sativa* is Latin for "cultivated hemp" (J. Green, 2002). Historical evidence suggests that some varieties of the cannabis plant have been cultivated for the hemp fiber that it produces for over 12,000 years (Welch, 2005). The hemp fibers are then used to manufacture a variety of products,[1] the range of which often surprises the student.

In the United States the topic of marijuana has reached such a point of hysteria that *any* member of the *Cannabis sativa* family of plants is automatically assumed to have a major abuse potential (T. Williams, 2000). This is hardly the truth, for some varieties produce hemp *fiber,* which has little or no abuse potential, whereas other strains are bred to produce large amounts of those compounds that give marijuana a psychoactive effect. To differentiate between these two plant varieties, T. Williams (2000) suggested that the term *hemp* be applied to those plants grown for their ability to produce fiber, whereas the term *marijuana* be reserved for just those members of the *Cannabis sativa* family grown for their ability to produce compounds with a psychoactive effect. This is the convention that we will follow in this text.

---

[1]For example: Clothing has been made from hemp for thousands of years. The King James translation of the Bible was printed on paper manufactured from hemp. Both Rembrandt and Van Gogh painted on "canvas" made from hemp (T. Williams, 2000). Although George Washington cultivated cannabis to obtain hemp, which was used to manufacture rope and other products during the era, there is no direct evidence that he smoked marijuana.

A History of Marijuana Use/Abuse

Almost 5000 years ago, physicians in China were using marijuana as a treatment for malaria and constipation, to ease the pain of childbirth, and, when mixed with wine, as a surgical anesthetic (Robson, 2001). There is historical evidence that suggests that the settlers in Jamestown, Virginia, began to harvest cannabis for its ability to produce hemp fibers in 1611, fibers that, among other uses, were used to produce rope for the expanding world of commerce (Grinspoon et al., 2005). Its intoxicating effects have been known at least since the 1800s, although there is evidence that in Central and South America people may have used marijuana for its intoxicating effects even before this time (Grinspoon et al., 2005). Physicians in Asia, Europe, and the New World viewed cannabis/marijuana as a treatment for a wide variety of disorders. In the United States, for example, physicians were trained to prescribe marijuana as a sedative, a hypnotic, a treatment for migraine headaches, and an anticonvulsant. By the turn of the 20th century, no less a company than Sears, Roebuck and Company sold marijuana as a cure for the then-prevalent morphine addiction (Brust, 2004).

By the 1930s law enforcement officials and physicians had come to view marijuana use with some degree of suspicion (Walton, 2002). This suspicion was fueled by Henry Anslinger, who was the U.S. Commissioner of Narcotics in the 1920s. The main focus of this agency was on the interdiction of alcohol during Prohibition, but with the end of this social experiment he searched for a new "problem" to justify the continued existence of his agency. Marijuana was the ideal candidate. Whereas in 1931 he testified before Congress that marijuana abuse was not a major problem in the Untied States, by 1935 he testified that it had become as much of a problem as heroin (McPherson et al., 2009). Lurid stories of marijuana-related axe murders and other criminal acts were used to justify the criminalization of marijuana (although there is evidence suggesting that these supposed criminal acts were entirely fictitious), and Anslinger suggested the now famous "gateway" theory that marijuana abuse leads to the abuse of hard drugs (McPherson et al., 2009). Its use was also associated with socially unpopular minority groups. At the same time, marijuana was found to be less effective than, or at best only as effective as, many of the new pharmaceuticals being introduced into clinical practice. By the late 1930s it had been removed from the physician's pharmacopoeia, and in 1937 the Marijuana Tax Act[2] was passed and marijuana was officially classified as an illegal substance.

However, by historical coincidence, the *recreational* use of marijuana was becoming increasingly popular during the pre-Prohibition years. The practice of recreational marijuana smoking for its psychoactive effects was introduced into the United States by immigrant and itinerant workers from Mexico who had come north to find work (J. Mann, 2000; Nicoll & Alger, 2004). Further, the start of Prohibition in 1920 left the common person in this country without a recreational substance to use, and many members of the working class turned to marijuana as a substitute, at least until the end of Prohibition when alcohol again could be legally obtained.

Even after the end of Prohibition a small minority of the population continued to smoke marijuana, a fact seized upon by some politicians to further their political careers as they railed against the marijuana abuse "problem." However, the "problem"[3] of illicit marijuana use never really went away, and by the 1960s it was a popular drug of abuse in spite of the best efforts of law enforcement authorities. Its abuse has waxed and waned since then until by the start of the 21st century it became the most commonly abused illicit drug in the United States.[4] A measure of its popularity might be seen in the fact that more than 50% of the population admits to having used it at least once (Gold, Frost-Pineda, & Jacobs, 2004; Gruber & Pope, 2002).

A Medico-Legal Conundrum

As a substance of abuse, marijuana is illegal. In spite of this technicality, physicians have offered anecdotal evidence for more than half a century suggesting that marijuana,

---

[2]In spite of popular opinion, the Marijuana Tax Act of 1937 did not make the *possession* of marijuana illegal. The Stamp Act imposed a small tax on marijuana, which the person could pay. Obviously, the act of buying the stamp would alert authorities to the fact that this person either had marijuana or was planning to buy it. So it was rather unusual for abusers to pay the tax and receive the stamp that signified that they had done so. However, the stamp did become a popular item for stamp collectors, many of whom did pay the necessary tax to receive the stamp. In 1992 the United States Supreme Court ruled the Act unconstitutional, although many states still have similar laws ("Stamp Out Drugs," 2003).

[3]Whether marijuana use is itself a problem is an issue that has been debated for many decades without clear resolution. Reader is left to draw their own conclusions.

[4]Remember, the operative word is *illicit* drug. Alcohol, though abused more often than is marijuana, is legally available to adults in the United States.

or at least a compound(s) in marijuana, is useful in treating one or more diseases that continue to plague humankind. Case reports surfaced in the 1970s that cancer chemotherapy patients reported having less nausea after smoking marijuana (Robson, 2001). These case reports resulted in the development of a synthetic drug Marinol® (dronabinol), which is concentrated Δ-9-tetrahydrocannabinol (THC).[5] This compound met with only limited success in controlling chemotherapy-related nausea, possibly because the antinausea effects were induced by another compound than THC (D. Smith, 1997).

Patients with multiple sclerosis (MS) also reported improved functioning after smoking marijuana.[6] Based on such reports, the compound Sativex® was introduced in Canada. This compound is made from cannabis and designed to be sprayed under the tongue, as an aid to the treatment of MS (Wilson, 2005). In the Netherlands, early research suggested that marijuana use could ease the symptoms of neurological disorders, ease pain, and help reverse the "wasting syndrome" so often seen in cancer and AIDS patients (Gorter, Butorac, Coblan, & Van der Sluis, 2005).

Other researchers found evidence that suggested that at least one of the compounds in marijuana smoke might be of possible value in treating Alzheimer's disease (Eubanks et al., 2006). There is also limited evidence suggesting that a compound in marijuana might have at least a short-term beneficial effect for patients with amyotrophic lateral sclerosis (ALS) (Amtmann, Weydt, Johnson, Jensen, & Carter, 2004). Further, several researchers have concluded that smoking marijuana might help control some forms of chronic-pain disorders (J. Green, 2002; Robson, 2001; Watson, Benson, & Joy, 2000; Welch, 2005). The team of Karst et al. (2003) explored the potential of a synthetic analog of THC known as CT-3[7] to treat neuropathic pain, and found that it was not only effective but that it also did not appear to induce any major adverse effects. The team of D. I. Abrams et al. (2007) concluded that one or more compounds in marijuana might prove to be of value in controlling neuropathic pain associated with HIV-1 infection.

Using animal research, other scientists found that a compound(s) in marijuana seemed to function as a potent antioxidant, and thus that it might prove of value in limiting the amount of damage caused by a stroke or neurological trauma (Hampson et al., 2002; Papathanasopoulous et al., 2008). Preliminary research suggested that smoking marijuana might help control certain forms of otherwise unmanageable glaucoma; however, follow-up studies failed to replicate the initial findings and this claim is now disputed (J. Green, 2002; Watson et al., 2000).

Physicians have reason to believe that a compound in marijuana might prove to be useful in treating asthma, Crohn's disease, anorexia, emphysema, epilepsy, and possibly hypertension (J. Green, 2002). There is also strong evidence that a compound in marijuana might inhibit tumor growth, including gliomas[8] (B. R. Martin, 2004; Salazar et al., 2009). Based on such reports, the Institute of Medicine concluded that there was enough evidence to warrant an in-depth study of possible medicinal uses for marijuana. However, in 2006 the Food and Drug Administration (FDA) dismissed this conclusion, using as a justification for the action their conclusion that because there are no well-designed scientific research studies documenting possible medical applications for any variety of the cannabis plant, there is no need to look for possible medical applications for any member of this plant family ("No Dope on Dope," 2006). This is done in the name of the people who pay the taxes that pay the salaries of those who draw such conclusions. Because of this line of reasoning, it is quite unlikely that legitimate medical research into possible medical applications of any compound found in marijuana will ever be conducted in this country. The federal government's monopoly on legal marijuana production for research allows it to refuse to provide marijuana for research studies that might reveal a medical application for marijuana (Doblin, quoted in Frood, 2008).

In response to citizen initiatives, a number of different states have legalized the medical use of marijuana, although the federal government continues to assert that federal law takes precedence over the desires of these citizens.[9] Thus it is safe to say that marijuana

---

[5]A compound thought to be the primary psychoactive agent in marijuana.

[6]However, Papathanasopoulous, Messinis, Epameinondas, Kastellakis, and Panagis (2008) questioned whether cannabinoids might also induce changes in brain function that would contribute to cognitive decline in patients with MS, a matter of some concern for patients with this condition.

[7]Which is chemical shorthand for: 1′,1′Dimethylheptyl-Δ8tetrahydro-cannabinol-11-oric acid.

---

[8]See Glossary.

[9]In the play *1776* there is a line in which the character of Stephen Hopkins, a delegate to the Continental Congress from Rhode Island, states that he had never heard, seen, or smelled an idea that was so dangerous that it could not be openly debated (Stone & Edwards, 1970). This is apparently a sentiment that is not shared by the federal government, which refuses to allow such investigations into possible medical applications of any compound found in marijuana.

will retain its status as a controversial substance for many years to come.

A Question of Potency

Ever since it became a popular compound of abuse in the 1960s, marijuana abusers have sought ways to enhance its effects either by intermixing the marijuana with other compounds or by obtaining strains with the highest possible concentration of those compounds thought to give marijuana its psychoactive effects (Δ-9-tetrahydro-cannabinol,[10] or THC, being the primary compound). There were also clandestine efforts to cross-breed high-potency marijuana to produce strains with even higher THC content (Coghlan, 2009). These efforts have been successful. In 1992 the average concentration of THC in marijuana seized by police was 3.08%, which had increased to 5.11% by the year 2002 (W. M. Compton, Grant, Colliver, Glantz, & Stinson, 2004) and averaged 9.6% by 2004 (Office of National Drug Control Policy, 2008). There is evidence that the THC content of some strains of marijuana being sold today is between 60 and 200 mg per cigarette (Hunnault et al., 2008; "Potent Pot," 2008). However, there is so much variation between samples of marijuana that only a properly trained chemist can assess the potency of any given sample.

Unfortunately, much of the research on marijuana and its potential uses, abuses, and dangers was carried out 25 years ago when less-potent strains were commonly abused, and thus there are questions as to its current applicability ("Potent Pot," 2008). Thus the conclusions of much of the early research into the safety of marijuana is no longer applicable.

A Technical Point

THC is found throughout the marijuana plant, but the highest concentrations are found in the small upper leaves and the flowering tops of the plant (W. Hall & Solowij, 1998). Historically, the term *marijuana* is applied to preparations of the plant used for smoking or eating. *Hashish* is used to identify the thick resin that is obtained from the flowers of the cannabis plant. This resin is dried, providing a brown or black substance that has a high concentration of THC. The resin is then either ingested orally (often mixed with a sweet substance to mask its flavor) or smoked. *Hash oil* is a liquid extract from the plant, usually containing 25–60%

THC, which is added to marijuana or hashish to enhance its effect. For the purpose of this chapter, the generic term *marijuana* will be used for any part of the plant that is to be smoked or ingested, except when the term *hashish* is specifically used.

Scope of the Problem

Marijuana is the most commonly abused illicit substance on this planet (Coghlan, 2009). Globally, an estimated 166 million people over the age of 15 use marijuana on a regular basis (Coghlan, 2009). Fully 31% of marijuana abusers (49 million people) live in Asia, whereas another 24% (38 million people) live in North America,[11] 19% (31 million people) live in Europe, and 24% (38 million people) live in Africa (United Nations, 2008).

In the United States, marijuana is the most commonly abused illicit substance, and in terms of retail value it is *the* biggest cash crop raised in the United States at this time ("Grass Is Greener," 2007). The number of past and current marijuana abusers in the United States has been estimated to be just under 43% of people over the age of 18 years, and each day approximately 6000 more people in the United States use marijuana for the first time ("Going to Pot," 2009; Sadock & Sadock, 2007). The average age at which individuals begin to smoke marijuana in the United States is around 18–19 years of age (Ellickson, Martino, & Collins, 2004). Although it has been known to happen, it is uncommon for the marijuana abuser to start abusing it after the age of 20 (Ellickson et al., 2004). Marijuana use peaks in the early adult years and is usually limited to the 20s and early 30s, although there are those who continue to smoke marijuana past this phase of life (Ellickson et al., 2004). As those who grew up with marijuana age, it is possible that they will continue to use it into middle and old age, although only time will tell whether this prediction is accurate.

There are parallels between marijuana abuse patterns and those of alcohol: 14% of those who smoke marijuana do so daily, consuming 95% of the marijuana sold on the illicit market in this country (United Nations, 2008). The other marijuana abusers engage in rare marijuana use, and only a small percentage of abusers use more than 10 grams a month (enough for about 25–35 cigarettes) (MacCoun & Reuter, 2001). In spite of its reputation as being nonaddictive, some abusers do develop a psychological dependency on it, and 10–20% of marijuana abusers will become physically addicted to it (Lynskey & Lukas, 2005; Sadock & Sadock, 2007).

---

[10]Discussed elsewhere in this chapter.

[11]Which the United Nations (2008) defined as Mexico, the United States, and Canada.

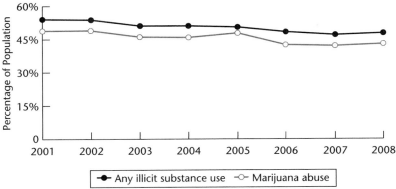

FIGURE 10-1 Exploring the Future data
Source: Johnston, L.D., O'Malley, P.M., Backman, J.G., & Schulenberg, J.E. (2010). Monitoring the Future: National Results on Adolescent Drug Use. Bethesda, MD: National Institute on Drug Abuse

Because of its popularity as a substance of abuse, the legal and social sanctions against marijuana use have repeatedly changed over the past half century, and are expected to continue to change in the years to come. In some states, possession of small amounts of marijuana for personal use is subject only to a fine, whereas in other states the possession of the same amount of marijuana would result in major legal sanctions. It has been decriminalized in some states, though recriminalized in some of those same states just a few years later. Currently, the legal status of marijuana varies from state to state, although it should be noted that the federal authorities continue to assert that federal law takes precedence over state law and that *any* marijuana abuse is illegal under federal law. It has also been asserted that the prohibition against marijuana is far worse than the damage that marijuana itself might do (Beckley Foundation, quoted in Coghlan, 2009, p. 6).

The Pharmacology of Marijuana

In spite of its long history as a popular substance of abuse, the pharmacokinetics of marijuana are still not completely understood (Grinspoon et al., 2005). It is known that the *Cannabis sativa* plant contains at least 400 different compounds, of which 61 or more are psychoactive (Gold et al., 2004; Mendelson & Mello, 2008; Sadock & Sadock, 2007). In the 1960s researchers discovered that the majority of marijuana's effects are caused by a compound known as Δ-9-tetrahydrocannabinol ("THC"); however some of the other psychoactive compounds in marijuana are also thought to contribute to its effects. For example, a compound

known as *cannabidiol* (CBD) is also inhaled when marijuana is smoked, and clinical research would suggest that although it does not bind at known THC receptor sites, it does appear to modify the effects of THC through an unknown mechanism[12] (Borgwardt et al., 2008).

There is no "standard" dose of marijuana, because the potency among samples varies significantly. Further, if it is smoked, intraindividual and interindividual variability in the smoking process can influence the amount of marijuana smoke reaching the lungs. Such factors as the number of "puffs," the time interval between puffs, the depth of inhalation, and the time that smokers hold their breath influence the amount of THC that reaches the circulation. Once it reaches the circulation, THC is rapidly distributed to blood-rich organs such as the heart, lungs, and brain. Then, over time it slowly works its way into less blood-rich tissues such as the body's fat reserves, where THC will be stored. Chronic daily abuse results in significant amounts of THC being stored in the body's fat cells, and upon cessation it slowly is released back into the blood, probably in amounts too small to have any psychoactive effect in cases of rare marijuana abuse (McDowell, 2005). In spite of strident claims to the contrary, rare marijuana abusers will usually have only marijuana metabolites in their urine for about

---

[12]There is also significant evidence suggesting that CBD might be useful in the treatment of seizure disorders, have an antiinflammatory effect, and might even be useful in the treatment of schizophrenia. But as discussed in Chapter 37, the Drug Enforcement Administration (DEA) will not allow research into possible medical applications for marijuana, or any compound found in the cannabis plant, for reasons discussed in Chapter 38.

72 hours after their last use of this substance.[13] About 65% of a single dose of marijuana is excreted in the feces and only 20% in the urine (Huestis, 2009). Chronic marijuana abusers might test "positive" for THC in their urine for up to 30 days, but this happens only with exceptionally heavy levels of marijuana abuse (R. S. Stephens & Roffman, 2005).

In the body, THC is biotransformed into a compound known as 11-hydroxy-Δ9-THC, and this metabolite is thought to cause marijuana's psychoactive effects (Sadock & Sadock, 2007). Between 97 and 99% of the THC that reaches the blood is protein bound, with the result being that its immediate psychoactive effects are caused by the 1–3% that remains unbound (Huestis, 2009; Jenkins, 2007). When it is smoked the peak blood levels are seen within 10 minutes, and THC blood levels drop to 10% of the peak level within 1 hour (Gonzalez et al., 2009; W. Hall & Degenhardt, 2005). The absorption, distribution, biotransformation, and elimination of marijuana is slower when it is ingested orally, but after absorption from the gastrointestinal tract the THC is still protein bound in the same pattern as noted previously.

THC mimics the action of two naturally occurring neurotransmitters in the brain collectively called *endocannabinoids*[14] (U. Kraft, 2006; Lovinger, 2008). Receptor sites for the endocannabinoids have been found throughout the brain, including in the hippocampus, cerebral cortex, basal ganglia, the cerebellum, and the dorsal horns of the spinal cord (Cruz et al., 2008; Gonzalez et al., 2009; B. R. Martin, 2004; Nicoll & Alger, 2004; Welch, 2005; Zajicek et al., 2003). There are virtually no known receptor sites for any of the endocannabinoids in the brain stem, which is consistent with the clinical observation that THC has no apparent effect on respiration (Sadock & Sadock, 2007).

The principal endocannabinoids that have been identified to date are the compounds *anandamide* and *sn-2 arachidonyglycerol* (or simply, 2-AG) (Cruz et al., 2008). Both of these compounds are synthesized in the body from lipid molecules, and are emerging from obscurity to be recognized as essential components not only of current neural function and future growth and development of the brain. Animal research, for example, suggests that anandamide helps to guide the

specification of what are known as pyramidal cells in the brain and the pattern of axon growth in new neurons[15] (Berghuis et al., 2007; G. Fields 2009; Lovinger, 2008; Mulder et al., 2008). It also appears to function as a toxin to immature neurons[16] (G. Fields, 2009). These discoveries might be the reason why marijuana use interferes with the abuser's ability to learn new material (which involves the development of new neural networks).

Following birth, anandamide appears to be involved in such activities as the regulation of mood, memory, cognition, perception, muscle coordination, the regulation of sleep, body temperature regulation, appetite, pain perception, and possibly regulation of the immune system (Gruber & Pope, 2002; B. R. Martin, 2004; Nowak, 2004; Parrott et al., 2004; Reynolds & Bada, 2003; Welch, 2005). The CB1 receptor site appears to be involved in the regulation of the body's immune system. Research evidence now suggests that this site is deactivated by colon cancer cells, allowing these cancer cells to replicate without being attacked by the body's defenses ("Cannabis Chemical Clue to Colon Cancer," 2008). It currently is not known whether a similar phenomenon occurs in other forms of human cancer, but this discovery does open up exciting avenues of research for the treatment of cancer. It would appear that CB1 is also involved in cellular necrosis, marking diseased cells for destruction and absorption by the body.

In the brain, THC mimics the actions of anandamide, although it is thought to be between 4 and 20 times as potent as this compound and thus has a far stronger effect on anandamide receptor sites (Lovinger, 2008; B. R. Martin, 2004). Anandamide functions as a *retrograde transmitter molecule*, which modulates the release of many neurotransmitters from one neuron to the next (Lovinger, 2008). This reduces the firing rate of those neurons, which subjectively is experienced as a calming effect. Normally, this neurotransmitter inhibition continues for as long as the endocannabinoid molecules are present at the synaptic junction. Experimental research suggests that by blocking the endocannabinoid receptors, it is possible to reduce drug-seeking behaviors not only for marijuana, but also for food, nicotine, and possibly other drugs of abuse. These findings suggest

---

[13]Some abusers will claim that their urine toxicology test was "positive" for THC because they had consumed a form of beer made from hemp. Although creative, this claim has not been supported by research evidence.

[14]A contraction of the term *endogenous cannabinoids*.

[15]A process known as corticogenesis, which is discussed in the Glossary.

[16]Although in the mature brain, it appears to have a neuroprotective effect (R. D. Fields, 2009). The reason for this contrast between its effects on the immature and the mature neuron is not known at the present time.

new avenues of possible treatment for individuals with SUDs and eating disorders (Kraft, 2006; Le Foll & Goldberg, 2005).

A rather mysterious endocannabinoid is Sn-2 archidonoyglycerol, thought to be manufactured in the hippocampus region of the brain (Parrott et al., 2004). This region of the brain is thought to be involved in the process of memory formation, and evidence suggests that the endocannabinoids play a role in elimination of aversive memories (Cruz et al., 2008; B. R. Martin, 2004; Marsicano et al., 2002; Robbe et al., 2006). The available evidence would suggest that under normal conditions, Sn-2 arachidonoyglycerol interferes with the firing sequence of subunits of the hippocampus involved in normal memory formation, a finding that is consistent with clinical experience with marijuana abusers, who report having some memory problems.

Marijuana has also been found to affect the synthesis of acetylcholine[17] in the limbic system and the cerebellum regions of the brain (Fortgang, 1999). This might be the mechanism by which marijuana causes the user to feel sedated and relaxed. Marijuana has also been found to have a mild analgesic effect and is known to potentiate the analgesic effects of narcotic analgesics (Anand et al., 2008; B. R. Martin, 2004; Welch, 2005). Because the cannabinoids are involved in peripheral pain perception, it may be possible to develop drugs that will target this pain perception system without the intoxicating effects of marijuana (Anand et al., 2008).

This effect appears to reflect marijuana-induced inhibition of the enzyme *adenylate cyclase,* which is involved in the process of transmission of pain messages in the CNS. Marijuana is also able to inhibit the production of cyclooxygenase,[18] which is possibly another mechanism through which it is able to inhibit pain perception, without the sedation seen when narcotic analgesics are used (Carvey, 1998; Whitten, 2008b). The analgesic effects of marijuana appear to peak about 5 hours after use (Welch, 2005). Although originally thought to be about as potent as codeine in terms of its analgesic potential, animal research suggests that it might possibly be more potent than this, and further research into its potential analgesic potential is clearly called for (Welch, 2005).

The mechanism through which marijuana is able to induce a sense of mild euphoria is not understood. Like other drugs of abuse, marijuana's euphoric effects appear to reflect its effects on the brain's endogenous opioid neurotransmitter system (Welch, 2005). The primary site of THC biotransformation is in the liver, and more than 100 metabolites are produced during this process (R. H. Hart, 1997). The half-life of THC appears to depend on whether metabolic tolerance to its effects has developed or not. Even under the best of conditions, the body is not able to biotransform THC quickly, and in chronic abusers the half-life might vary from 24 to 96 hours (Oehmichen et al., 2005). About 65% of THC metabolites are excreted in the feces, and the remainder is eliminated from the body in the urine (Hubbard, Franco, & Onaivi, 1999). Tolerance to the effects of THC develops rapidly (O'Brien, 2006; Welch, 2005). After the development of tolerance, abusers must either wait a few days before using marijuana again until the body begins to lose its tolerance to marijuana, or change the method by which they use marijuana. For example, oral abusers might switch to smoking marijuana, or marijuana smokers might switch to more potent varieties for smoking.

Interactions Between Marijuana and Other Chemicals

There has been relatively little research into potential interactions between marijuana and other compounds. Thus there is a significant possibility that there are undiscovered interactions between marijuana and various pharmaceuticals or drugs of abuse, and if only for this reason this list is not all-inclusive.

Clinical evidence would suggest that marijuana use by patients on lithium can cause the lithium levels in the blood to increase, possibly to toxic levels (Ciraulo et al., 2006). Given the fact that lithium has only a very narrow "therapeutic window" and if too high may be fatal, the possible interaction between these compounds is thus potentially life threatening. There is a single case report of a patient who abused marijuana while taking the antidepressant medication fluoxetine who developed a possible drug-induced psychotic reaction (Brust, 2004).

Cocaine abusers often will abuse marijuana in an attempt to counteract the agitation and excessive stimulation induced by high levels of cocaine abuse. It is known that marijuana abuse will cause an increase in the heart rate between 20 and 50%, and it is known that cocaine can cause a wide variety of cardiac problems (W. Hall & Degenhardt, 2005). Unfortunately, there has been no research into possible interactional effects as to the effects of concurrent cocaine and marijuana abuse either on previously healthy patients or on those with unsuspected or known cardiac disease.

---

[17]See Glossary.

[18]See Glossary.

Many alcohol abusers will also abuse marijuana while drinking, a practice that is potentially dangerous because marijuana inhibits nausea and vomiting. Because one of the body's natural defenses against poisons is to eject the poison from the body by vomiting, in theory individuals who have ingested too much alcohol are at increased risk of a potentially fatal alcohol overdose if they were also using marijuana (Craig, 2004). This is only a theory, and it has not been tested. However, as this rather short list demonstrates, there is a dire need for further research into potential interactional effects between marijuana and both pharmaceuticals as well as the drugs of abuse.

Methods of Marijuana Abuse

Although it is possible to inject THC into the body, this is a very difficult process. The preferred methods of marijuana abuse are oral ingestion or by smoking (Brust, 2004; Erickson, 2007). Oral abusers will usually bake marijuana into cookies or brownies, which are then ingested. Orally administered marijuana is slowly absorbed, with the results being that the abuser does not feel the first effects of THC until 30–120 minutes after ingesting it. Only about 4–12% of the available THC will reach the abuser's circulation when it is abused in this manner, as a large amount of the remainder is destroyed in the gastrointestinal tract by digestive juices before absorption (Drummer & Odell, 2001; Gold et al., 2004; Stimmel, 1997a).

The oral user must thus ingest approximately three times as much marijuana as a smoker to achieve the same effect (Sadock & Sadock, 2007). Peak THC levels are usually seen in 1–5 hours after the marijuana-laced cookie or brownie was ingested, and the effects last for 5 to possibly as long as 24 hours after ingestion (Brust, 2004; Drummer & Odell, 2001; Gruber & Pope, 2002). Another advantage of oral ingestion is that it avoids the tell-tale smell of marijuana smoke, which would alert employers, law enforcement, or school officials that the individual has been abusing marijuana.

The most popular method of marijuana abuse is by smoking it, a practice that can be traced back for at least 5000 years (Gruber & Pope, 2002; Walton, 2002). Neuropharmacologists disagree as to the amount of THC that reaches the circulation when marijuana is smoked. R. S. Stephens and Roffman (2005) suggested that 30–80% of the available THC was destroyed in the process of smoking, or lost in "sidestream" smoke. Only 5–24% of the remaining THC was actually absorbed into the smoker's body, according to the authors. In contrast to this, Gold et al. (2004) suggested that almost 60% of the available THC was absorbed into the body when it was smoked. These two estimates of the amount of THC that is absorbed into the smoker's body might reflect the fact that there is significant intraindividual variability in THC absorption rates when it is smoked. However, as these discrepant estimates suggest, there is much to be learned about the process of marijuana smoking and the absorption of THC when it is smoked.

Although it might be intermixed with other compounds, marijuana is usually smoked alone in cigarettes commonly called "joints." The typical marijuana cigarette is estimated to contain between 500 and 750 mg of marijuana, providing an effective dose of 2.5–20 mg of THC to the smoker, depending on the potency of the marijuana being smoked. The average marijuana joint contains about 0.02 ounces of marijuana (Raw Data, 2008). A variation on the marijuana cigarette is the "blunt," made by removing some of the outer leaves of a cigar, unrolling it, filling the core with high-potency marijuana mixed with chopped cigar tobacco, then rerolling the cigar (Gruber & Pope, 2002). When smoked in this manner, abusers often report some degree of stimulation, possibly from the nicotine in the tobacco in the cigar, in addition to marijuana's effects.

The process of smoking a joint is somewhat different from that used to smoke normal tobacco cigarettes. Users must inhale the smoke deeply into their lungs, then hold their breath for as long as possible (ideally 20–30 seconds) in an attempt to allow as much THC as possible to cross over from the lungs into the general circulation. Because THC passes across into the circulation very slowly, only about 25–50% of the THC in the smoke actually will be absorbed into the smoker's circulation (McDowell, 2005). But the effects of the THC that does enter the circulation are felt within seconds to perhaps a few minutes (Brust, 2004).

Subjective Effects of Marijuana Abuse

Marijuana smokers achieve the strongest effects, producing a mild sense of euphoria, relaxation, some sensory distortions, and altering the individual's perception of ordinary activities such as eating, watching television or movies, and having sex (W. Hall & Degenhardt, 2005). Some abusers report enhanced perception of sounds and colors as well (Earlywine, 2005; Zevin & Benowitz, 2007). Some abusers report a dysphoric experience (Tomb, 2008). In social settings, marijuana smokers are prone to infectious laughter, excessive talkativeness, and a feeling of relaxation.

THC is relatively potent, and the smoker must inhale 25–50 *micro*grams of THC for every kilogram of body weight, whereas the oral user must ingest 50–200 micrograms of THC, to achieve a marijuana "high" (J. Mann, 2000). If the blood levels are five times this amount, the abuser might experience a hallucinatory effect from the marijuana being abused (J. Mann, 2000). Marijuana abusers in other countries often have access to high-potency marijuana and are thus easily able to achieve doses high enough to induce hallucinations, but this is only rarely reported in the United States in spite of its official classification as a hallucinogenic compound.

When smoked, the effects of marijuana reach peak intensity in 20–30 minutes and begin to decline in about an hour (McDowell, 2005; Sadock & Sadock, 2007). The effects of marijuana progress through two phases, which are influenced, in part, by the abuser's expectations for them (Brust, 2004). In the first phase, which begins shortly after THC enters the circulation, the individual experiences some mild anxiety and decreased salivation. This phase is thought to last from 2 to 4 hours (Grinspoon et al., 2005; O'Brien, 2006; Sadock & Sadock, 2007; Zevin & Benowitz, 2007). The inexperienced user's reaction to these effects, combined with the selective activation of certain brain regions[19] by THC itself, combined with the unexpected increase in cardiac rate and marijuana-induced periods of depersonalization, may be reasons why inexperienced abusers experience some degree of anxiety.

However, experienced abusers report a positive experience from marijuana use, including mild euphoria, a sense of relaxation, and reduction in anxiety (Brust, 2004; Grinspoon et al., 2005; W. Hall & Degenhardt, 2005). These effects of marijuana appear to be caused by the THC isomer cannabidiol (CBD), which appears to selectively suppress function of those regions of the brain involved in the fear response[20] (Fusar-Poli et al., 2009). These effects blend into the second phase of marijuana intoxication, in which the abuser will experience residual psychomotor problems, mood swings, and possible depression. These feelings last for at least 5–12 hours after a single dose, suggesting that marijuana's effects on the abuser should be classified as falling into the period of either acute or extended effects (Freimuth, 2005; O'Brien, 2006; Sadock & Sadock, 2007; Tomb, 2008). Marijuana-related depression is usually short-lived and only rarely requires professional intervention (Grinspoon et al., 2005).

Individuals who smoke high-potency marijuana report a synesthesia[21]-like experience, in which the sensations of one sensory modality slip over into another (Earlywine, 2005). Over half of marijuana abusers report enhanced tactile sensations, and although the sense of taste is not improved, abusers speak of enjoying taste sensations more (Earlywine, 2005). Some abusers also report that marijuana's effects contribute to enhanced sexual pleasure (Earlywine, 2005). These claims have not been verified by scientific research.

Clinicians often hear depressed patients claim that they abuse marijuana because it helps their depression. Research has demonstrated that very low doses of marijuana does seem to stimulate the release of serotonin in the brain and thus might have an antidepressant effect in much the same manner that the selective serotonin reuptake inhibitors (SSRIs) do. However, there is only a very narrow dosing "window" for this effect, and if the abuser should use more marijuana than necessary it can actually contribute to feelings of depression (Bambico, Katz, Debonnel, & Govvi, 2007). Thus marijuana's antidepressant effects are too limited to be of clinical significance.

Marijuana abusers often report a sense of being on the threshold of a significant personal insight, but they are unable to put this insight into words. Such drug-induced insights are rarely recalled after the period of acute intoxication ends. Further, marijuana-related creative efforts are usually found somewhat less than inspirational when the individual recovers from the period of acute intoxication. In such cases, abusers' subjective sense of insight and creativity appears to reflect the drug's effects on the brain rather than actual new perception of the self or the world around them.

Adverse Effects of Marijuana Abuse

Dangers of Marijuana Abuse

An Ongoing Debate

Marijuana is viewed by many people as being relatively harmless, a perception that is supported by observations that the effective dose is estimated to be between 1/20,000th and 1/40,000th the lethal dose (Grinspoon et al., 2005). To express this safety margin in other

---

[19]Frontal lobes and parietal regions of the brain.

[20]In this case the amygdala and cingulate cortex regions of the brain.

[21]See Glossary.

terms, it has been estimated that a 160-pound person would have to smoke 900 marijuana cigarettes simultaneously to reach the lethal level (Cloud, 2002). An even higher estimate was offered by Schlosser (2003), who suggested that the average person would need to smoke *100 pounds* of marijuana every minute for 15 minutes to achieve a lethal overdose.[22] In contrast to the estimated 200,000 deaths caused by the other forms of illicit-drug use around the world each year, there are two documented cases of a lethal marijuana overdose, although Coghlan (2009) did not provide information as to how this was accomplished. Although this information would suggest that marijuana has an impressive safety margin, it is not totally without risk.

Known and Suspected Adverse Effects of Short-Term Abuse

In the last decades of the 20th century, scientists began to identify adverse effects of marijuana abuse (Aharonovich et al., 2005). However, with 400 known compounds in marijuana and more than 2000 known metabolites of these compounds being produced during the biotransformation process, there is much to be discovered about marijuana's short-term and long-term effects on the body. Some of these metabolites might remain in the individual's body for weeks after a single period of marijuana use. In spite of this fact, research into the physical effects of marijuana on the brain of the abuser has been "surprisingly scarce" (Aharonovich et al., 2005, p. 1057). Rare social users of marijuana do not appear to experience long-term cognitive impairment following the cessation of marijuana abuse (Filley, 2004; Gonzalez et al., 2009; Zevin & Benowitz, 2007). Long-term abusers might suffer cognitive impairment that could last up to 2 years after their last use of marijuana (Gonzalez et al., 2009; Khan et al., 2009).

There have been rare reports of anaphylactic reactions in marijuana abusers, although it is not clear whether these reactions were triggered by the marijuana itself or contaminants or adulterants found in illicit marijuana samples (Brust, 2004). It is not uncommon for illicit marijuana to be adulterated, and these compounds add to the flood of chemicals introduced into the body when an individual abuses marijuana. To further cloud the issue, illicit marijuana is often exposed to herbicides sprayed on it by law enforcement officials in an attempt to destroy the plants before they are harvested and sold.

If the plants are harvested and sold, those herbicides are still on the plants and will also be introduced into the body by the abuser.

A more common reaction for rare abusers is the development of "bloodshot" eyes (Mendelson et al., 2006). This effect is caused by marijuana-induced dilation of the blood vessels in the conjunctiva of the eyes. This effect itself is relatively harmless, although quite striking to see for the first time. However, 40–60% of abusers will report at least one other adverse effect beyond bloodshot eyes (Hubbard et al., 1999). Further, marijuana intoxication impairs the motor skills necessary to safely drive a motor vehicle on about the same level as does a blood alcohol level of between 0.07 and 0.1% (W. Hall & Degenhardt, 2005). Even occasional episodes of marijuana abuse increase the individual's risk of being in a motor vehicle accident by 300 to 700%, possibly because of marijuana-induced loss of depth perception (Brust, 2004; Lamon et al., 2005).

Marijuana can induce a splitting of consciousness or periods of depersonalization for the abuser (Earlywine, 2005; Johns, 2001). This might be one reason why 50–60% of marijuana abusers report experiencing at least one episode of marijuana-induced anxiety (O'Brien, 2006). Such episodes of anxiety are seen most often in novice abusers (Grinspoon et al., 2005; Gruber & Pope, 2002). Because marijuana smokers are able to titrate their dose more easily than those who ingest it orally, there is a tendency for oral abusers to experience anxiety more than marijuana smokers because the latter group can simply stop smoking it if they find its effects uncomfortable (Brust, 2004; Gold et al., 2004). Usually the only treatment that is necessary is a gentle reassurance that it will soon pass (Brust, 2004; Sadock & Sadock, 2007).

Marijuana use has been identified as a cause of increased heart rate and arrhythmias. In rare cases myocardial infarction and atrial fibrillation have been found in individuals who have just used marijuana, although the causal mechanism still remains to be identified (Khan et al., 2009). There are reports of abusers experiencing angina,[23] especially if they have coronary insufficiency, and patients with known or suspected cardiac problems are advised not to use marijuana (Mendelson et al., 2006).

There is one case report of a child suffering an episode of transient global amnesia after the child was accidentally exposed to it, which resolved after a period of several hours (Prem & Uzoma, 2004). Although often believed to be an aphrodisiac, even limited marijuana

---

[22]It should be noted that some abusers have made commendable efforts to reach this level of marijuana intoxication, although apparently with little success.

[23]See Glossary.

use is known to reduce sexual desire, and for male abusers may result in erectile dysfunction, reduced sperm count, and delayed ejaculation (Greydanus & Patel, 2005; W. Hall & Degenhardt, 2005).

"Secondhand" Marijuana Smoke

One topic that has rarely been explored until recently is the possibility that toxic compounds might be intermixed with the "sidestream" or secondhand smoke produced by marijuana smoking. The team of Moir et al. (2007) examined this very topic. The authors utilized two "smoking machines" to "smoke" marijuana blunts under controlled conditions and found that the sidestream marijuana smoke had 20 times as much ammonia as did cigarette smoke, whereas other toxic compounds such as hydrogen cyanide and nitric oxide were also found in the secondhand smoke at three to five times the concentration found in sidestream smoke from tobacco cigarettes. Further, the authors detected known carcinogenic compounds in sidestream smoke produced by the marijuana blunts, possibly as a result of the tobacco leaves that are also smoked in the process.

Consequences of Chronic Marijuana Abuse

Marijuana abusers are known to be at risk for the development of a *drug-induced* psychosis. The regions of the brain known as the striatum and the cingulate each have a high number of cannabinoid receptor sites (Bhattacharyya et al., 2009). These regions of the brain are also thought to be involved in the development of the symptoms of schizophrenia, which appears to explain why marijuana abusers have an increased risk for the development of a psychosis. An alternative theory is that marijuana can interfere with the normal function of the endocannabinoid 2-arachidonoyl-glycerol in the cortex and hippocampus of the brain. These competing theories suggest that there is still a great deal to be discovered about marijuana and its effects on the brain.

Most marijuana-induced psychotic reactions are short-lived and clear up in a few hours or days (Johns, 2001). There is debate over whether an ongoing psychosis reflected a predisposition toward a psychosis that was possibly unmasked by marijuana abuse (M. T. Compton et al., 2009; W. Hall & Degenhardt, 2005). Another theory is that the psychotic reaction was induced by the individual's marijuana abuse, a theory that is supported by the findings of McGrath et al. (2010), who found an increased risk of psychosis in young adulthood for individuals who engaged in marijuana use earlier in life as compared to nonabusing siblings. Thus marijuana-induced psychosis might be viewed as a form of a toxic psychosis that may become permanent. The age at which the individual begins to abuse marijuana is one apparent critical variable in the development of a later psychotic reaction, with research finding that individuals who had abused marijuana during adolescence, especially before the age of 15, have a higher incidence of schizophrenia later in life (Raby, 2009). Another variable affecting the possible development was the intensity of the individual's marijuana use. One study conducted in Sweden found, for example, that Army recruits who had abused marijuana more than 50 times had a 670% higher incidence of psychosis than nonabusers who were also Army recruits (Iverson, 2005).

An interesting hypothesis for the apparent relationship between marijuana use and the development of psychosis was offered by Feilding and Morrison (2010). The authors, drawing upon recent research into the role of the compound cannabidiol (CBD) in marijuana, noted that as strains of marijuana have been developed with higher levels of THC, CBD levels have dropped almost proportionally. Yet new evidence suggests that CBD has an antipsychotic effect, counteracting the potential for THC to induce a psychosis. In essence, by developing new strains of marijuana with higher levels of THC and low levels of CBD, the more potent strains of marijuana reduce the individual's exposure to a compound that might protect them from a possible psychosis.

Using new high-resolution structural magnetic resonance imaging (MRI) technology, Yucel et al. (2008) found that chronic marijuana smokers had an approximate 12% reduction in volume of the hippocampus and a 6% reduction in the size of the amygdala in the brain. These regions of the brain have a high density of cannabinoid receptors, and there was a clear relationship between duration of marijuana use and the degree of shrinkage in these regions of the brain, although it is not clear at this time whether this reduction in regional brain volume is permanent or not.

It has also been discovered that the habitual use of marijuana suppresses REM sleep, although it is not clear whether isolated episodes of marijuana abuse have any significant impact on REM sleep (McDowell, 2005). The consequences of REM sleep suppression on the individual's health has yet to be determined, although some research has suggested that long-term REM sleep suppression might have a negative effect on the individual's health. Researchers have also found precancerous changes in the cells of the respiratory tract in chronic marijuana smokers similar to those seen in tobacco smokers (Gold et al., 2004; Tashkin, 2005; Tetrault et al., 2007). Preliminary evidence would suggest that the chronic smoking of one marijuana joint a day might increase users' cancer risk as much as if they were to smoke a pack of cigarettes a day (Brambilla & Colonna, 2008). Brambilla and Colonna found that marijuana smokers who had smoked just one joint a day for 10 years had a 570% higher risk of lung cancer as nonsmokers in spite of whether they smoked tobacco cigarettes or not.

Marijuana smokers were also found to have an increased incidence of cough and wheezing in a manner similar to that seen in cigarette smokers (Khan et al., 2009; Tetrault et al., 2007). Researchers have found that marijuana smokers who also smoke cigarettes have an increased risk for chronic obstructive pulmonary disease (COPD) later in life (W. C. Tan et al., 2009). These effects might reflect the ability of marijuana to reduce the effectiveness of the respiratory system to resist infection (Gruber & Pope, 2002; W. Hall & Degenhardt, 2005). Marijuana smokers are exposed to virtually all the toxic compounds found in tobacco cigarettes except nicotine, unless they were to use a blunt. In this case, the marijuana smoker is exposed to *all* of the toxins found in tobacco in addition to those found in marijuana (Gruber & Pope, 2002). The typical marijuana cigarette has 10–20 times as much "tar" as tobacco cigarettes (T. Nelson, 2000). Marijuana smokers are also exposed to higher levels of carbon monoxide than tobacco smokers, and there is a dose-related reduction in pulmonary function. Unlike tobacco smoking, which produces microscopic particles that block the lung passages in the lowest levels of the lungs, marijuana smoking produces larger particles that block the larger air passages of the respiratory system (Aldington et al., 2007).

Marijuana smoke has been found to contain many of the same carcinogens found in tobacco cigarettes, often in higher amounts than those found in regular tobacco cigarettes, placing marijuana smokers at higher risk for cancer of the mouth, tongue, and throat (Gruber & Pope, 2002; W. Hall & Degenhardt, 2005). In terms of absolute numbers, marijuana smokers tend to smoke fewer joints than tobacco smokers do tobacco cigarettes, but they also smoke unfiltered joints, increasing their exposure to microscopic contaminants in marijuana. They also inhale more deeply than do cigarette smokers, all factors that increase the risk of the marijuana abuser to respiratory diseases such as COPD (Gruber & Pope, 2002).

Animal research also confirms that heavy marijuana abuse appears to suppress the immune system's effectiveness, although the relevance of these findings to humans is not clear at the present time (Abrams et al., 2003; Gold et al., 2004). However, this finding is of potential significance to those people who struggle with an HIV-1[24] viral infection, which has already weakened their immune system. Chronic marijuana abuse has been implicated as the cause of a number of reproductive system dysfunctions such as reduced sperm count, lower testosterone levels, and smaller testicular size in male abusers (Hubbard et al., 1999; Schuckit, 2006a). Habitual female marijuana abusers have been found to experience menstrual abnormalities, including possible failure to ovulate (Gold et al., 2004; Hubbard et al., 1999). These problems are so severe that women who wish to conceive are advised to abstain from marijuana use prior to attempting to become pregnant.

People who have abused a hallucinogenic such as LSD often experience marijuana-triggered "flashbacks" (W. Hall & Degenhardt, 2005). Such "flashbacks" are usually limited to the 6-month period following the individual's last use of marijuana and usually will stop on their own. However, it is not clear whether marijuana alone can trigger such "flashback" experiences by itself or not (Sadock & Sadock, 2007). This topic will be discussed in more detail in Chapter 12.

Further, there is growing evidence suggesting that marijuana use might be associated with an increased risk of cancer in the testicles (Daling et al., 2009). In a retrospective study involving patients already diagnosed with testicular cancer, Daling et al. found that individuals with testicular cancer were 30% more likely to report past abuse of marijuana and *70%* more likely to be current abusers. The authors theorized that adolescence is a "window of opportunity" for environmental factors such as marijuana abuse to influence stem cells to turn cancerous, although the exact causal mechanism for marijuana-related testicular cancer is not known at this time. This parallels the decision by the state of California to list marijuana as a carcinogen and to require medical marijuana dispensaries to label marijuana sold through such centers as a carcinogen (Dembosky, 2009).

Heavy marijuana abuse has been identified as a cause of cardiac arrhythmias, although with chronic use the abuser can develop some tolerance to this effect (Khan et al., 2009). Older marijuana smokers who suffer an acute myocardial infarction (heart attack) were less likely to survive than were nonsmokers who had also suffered an acute myocardial infarction (Mukamal, Maclure, Muller, & Mittleman, 2008). Mukamal et al.

---

[24]Discussed in Chapter 36.

also found that heart attack survivors who continued to use marijuana were at higher risk for death than were nonsmokers who survived. It was not clear whether these findings were a direct result of the individual's marijuana use, or whether there were other causes (cigarette smoking, for example) that explained the observed findings, according to the authors.

A small but growing body of evidence suggests that chronic marijuana abuse can cause brain cognitive dysfunctions (Vik, Cellucci, Jarchow, & Hedt, 2004). It is possible to detect evidence of cognitive deficits on psychological tests for up to 7–14 days after habitual marijuana abusers last used marijuana (H. G. Pope et al., 2001; Vik et al., 2004). These identified memory deficits appear to be progressive worse in heavy marijuana abusers (Gruber et al., 2003; Lundqvist, 2005; Solowij et al., 2002). In light of the discovery that heavy marijuana abuse has been identified as a causal agent in altered brain structure, it would not be unreasonable to state that these cognitive dysfunctions might reflect the neurological changes identified in the brains of habitual marijuana abusers.

Many chronic marijuana abusers have been found to have abnormal electroencephalographic (EEG) studies. It is possible that these EEG changes predate the individual's marijuana or other chemical abuse, although there is little evidence to support this hypothesis. The observed changes suggest that repeated, heavy episodes of marijuana use are associated with dose-dependent changes in the brain's internal electrical activity (Herning, Better, & Cadet, 2008). Herning et al. speculated that the observed EEG changes might reflect altered brain perfusion (blood flow in the brain). Sneider et al. (2006) suggested that these altered changes in regional blood flow patterns in the abuser's brain might persist for at least the first few weeks after the individual stopped abusing marijuana. In another study addressing regional blood flow patterns in habitual marijuana abusers, Herning, Better, Tate, and Cadet (2001) discovered that even after 4 weeks of abstinence the blood flow pattern in marijuana abusers was still comparable to that seen in normal 60-year-old adults. This would suggest that these regional blood flow changes might be long-lasting after extended periods of marijuana abuse.

Under normal conditions the occasional activation of the endogenous cannabinoid CB1 receptor might have a neuroprotective effect (Freedman, 2008). However, the persistent activation of this receptor site appears to make the CB1 receptor less responsive, thus negating this neuroprotective function. The affected neurons are no longer protected against the increased levels of excitation and neural death produced by such conditions as schizophrenia or continual marijuana abuse. This might account for the findings of the research team of Matochik, Eldreth, Cadet, and Bolla (2005), who found evidence of significant levels of neural tissue loss in the right parahippocampal gyrus and in the left parietal lobe in the brains of 11 marijuana abusers on neuroimaging studies. This loss of neural tissue was strongly correlated with the duration of marijuana use, according to the authors.

Paradoxically, Jacobus et al. (2009) found evidence that adolescent marijuana abusers appear to have less damage to the "white matter"[25] of the brain after episodes of binge drinking as compared with adolescents who engage in binge drinking but who do not smoke marijuana. The mechanism through which marijuana might provide a neuroprotective effect in such circumstances is not known at this time, and the findings of this study must be replicated in future research to confirm that this process does indeed take place.

There is also an emerging body of evidence that suggests that long-term marijuana abuse might contribute to periodontal disease (W. M. Thomson et al., 2008). Thomson et al. reported that after examinations of 903 young adults, they found evidence of periodontal disease in 32% of those who used marijuana at least once a week, in 12% who used marijuana less frequently than once a week, and in only 4% of nonusers in their research sample. This was independent of the individual's tobacco use, which itself increased the individual's risk for potential periodontal disease by a small margin, the authors suggested.

Although some clinicians believe that marijuana might contain a compound(s) of value in the treatment of MS, other researchers have suggested that at least one compound(s) in marijuana might speed up the cognitive decline seen in patients with MS through some unknown mechanism (Ghaffar & Feinstein, 2008). In contrast, Lakhan and Rowland (2009) concluded that a combination of THC and cannabidiol reduced patient distress induced by MS-associated spasticity, and there was mixed evidence of a physical reduction in spasticity. Thus the potential value of marijuana as an adjunct to the treatment of multiple sclerosis is not clear at this time. A more disturbing finding is that marijuana abuse seems to be associated with a more rapid progression of liver damage in patients infected with the hepatitis C virus[26] (Ishida et al., 2008). Ishida et al. speculated

---

[25]See Glossary.

[26]Discussed in Chapter 36.

that at least some of the abusers identified in their research sample had switched from alcohol to marijuana because of their fear that their alcohol use might accelerate the damage being done to their liver by the viral infection. However, it was pointed out that marijuana abuse might also be associated with an acceleration in liver damage in hepatitis C patients.

The "Amotivational Syndrome"

Scientists have found conflicting evidence that chronic marijuana abuse might cause the so-called "amotivational" syndrome. This hypothetical condition is marked by short attention span, decreased drive and ambition, easy distractibility, and a tendency not to make plans beyond the present day (W. Hall & Degenhardt, 2005). Indirect evidence that such a condition might exist was provided by Gruber et al. (2003). The authors compared the psychological and demographic measures of 108 individuals who had smoked marijuana more than 5000 times against 72 age-matched control subjects who reported having abused marijuana 50 times or less. The authors found that those individuals with the greatest level of marijuana use had significantly lower income levels and educational achievement levels than did the control group, in spite of the fact that these two groups were from similar families. Although suggestive, this study does not answer the question of whether these findings reflect the effects of marijuana, or if individuals prone to heavy marijuana abuse tend to have less drive and initiative prior to their marijuana abuse.

Indeed, the very existence of the amotivational syndrome is subject to question. It was pointed out that even chronic heavy marijuana abusers demonstrate "remarkable energy and enthusiasm in the pursuit of their goals" (C. J. Weiss & Millman, 1998, p. 211). It has been suggested that the amotivational syndrome reflects nothing more than the acute effects of marijuana intoxication on the abuser (Johns, 2001). Sadock & Sadock (2007) pointed out that the characteristics of the amotivational syndrome might reflect personality style rather than a drug-induced effect. Thus the question of whether there is a specific amotivational syndrome that might be attributed to marijuana abuse has not been determined as of this time (Brunton et al., 2008).

Marijuana Abuse as a Cause of Death

There is a significant body of evidence that suggests that chronic marijuana use is associated with, or at least contributes to, a number of potentially serious medical problems. Marijuana abuse, for example, is associated with a 30–50% increase in cardiac rate that might last for as long as 3 hours after the initiation of an episode of marijuana abuse (Craig, 2004; W. Hall & Degenhardt, 2005). This is potentially harmful for individuals who have a cardiac condition. Marijuana abuse is also associated with a reduction in the strength of cardiac muscle contractions and the amount of oxygen reaching cardiac tissues, which again are of importance to patients with cardiac disease. This also might be one mechanism by which marijuana abuse causes an increased risk of heart attacks in older abusers during the first few hours following the initiation of an episode of abuse ("Marijuana-Related Deaths?", 2002; Mittleman, Lewis, Maclure, Sherwood, & Muller, 2001; Mukamal et al., 2008; Schuckit, 2006a).

The Myth of Marijuana-Induced Violence

In the 1930s and 1940s, it was widely believed that marijuana abuse would trigger episodes of violence. This belief was reinforced by politicians who wished to further their political agenda by using it as a justification to outlaw marijuana. But researchers have never found evidence that supports this belief. Indeed, "only the unsophisticated continue to believe that cannabis [abuse] leads to violence and crime" (Grinspoon et al., 2005, p. 267). It is believed by clinicians that the sedating and euphoric effects of marijuana actually *reduce* the tendency toward violent behavior on the part of abusers (Grinspoon et al., 2005; Husak, 2004). However, the chronic abuser will be more tolerant to the sedating effects of marijuana and thus capable of reacting violently if they have such a predisposition (Walton, 2002).

Addiction to Marijuana

In spite of the belief of many abusers, marijuana is indeed addictive. There is some degree of controversy as to the danger of marijuana addiction. Zevin and Benowitz (2007) suggested that 8–20% of chronic marijuana abusers will become dependent on it (see also Lynskey & Lukas, 2005). A low estimate that 9% of those who try marijuana will ultimately become addicted to it was offered by Budney, Roffman, Stephens, and Walker (2007).[27] Although this percentage is lower than the percentage of cocaine or heroin abusers who become addicted to those substances according to Budney et al., it still indicates that marijuana presents a significant addiction potential for the abuser.

---

[27]Unfortunately, it is not possible to determine *who* will become addicted to marijuana, and so its use is not recommended, if only for this reason.

Marijuana does not induce the same dramatic withdrawal symptoms seen in alcohol- or narcotic-dependent people who discontinue the abuse of their desired drug(s). For this reason, people have long underestimated the addiction potential of marijuana. However, tolerance, one of the hallmarks of physical addiction to a substance, does rapidly develop to marijuana (R. S. Stephens & Roffman, 2005). Another diagnostic characteristic of the addiction to a substance is the development of a characteristic withdrawal syndrome. It has been found that upon cessation of marijuana use, marijuana abusers experience withdrawal symptoms such as irritability, aggression, anxiety, depression, insomnia, sweating nausea, tachycardia, anorexia, a "craving" for marijuana, and vomiting (Brunton et al., 2008; Budney et al., 2007; Leamon et al., 2008; Raby, 2009; R. S. Stephens & Roffman, 2005).

These withdrawal symptoms begin 1–3 days after the individual's last use of marijuana, peak between the 2nd and 10th day, and the total duration of the marijuana withdrawal syndrome has been estimated to last between 12 and 115 days depending on the duration and intensity with which the individual was abusing marijuana (Budney, Moore, Bandrey, & Hughes, 2003; Leamon et al., 2008; Sussman & Westreich, 2003).

Marijuana withdrawal syndrome has been classified as flu-like in intensity, although in some abusers it might approach the intensity of nicotine withdrawal (Budney et al., 2007; Vandry, Budney, & Ligouori, 2008). There is no specific treatment for marijuana withdrawal other than complete abstinence from this compound or other drugs of abuse. However, the marijuana withdrawal syndrome can serve as a "trigger" for further marijuana use, starting the abuser back down the road toward addictive marijuana use (Crowley, 2007). As this evidence suggests, marijuana meets the established criteria for an addictive compound.

Chapter Summary

Cannabis sativa has been cultivated for its fibers for thousands of years, and at one point no less a person than George Washington cultivated it as a commercial crop. Indeed, hemp fibers have been used for a variety of purposes over the course of history. But at some unknown point in time it was discovered that some varieties of cannabis produced a substance, later to be called THC, that produced a sense of euphoria if it should be smoked. Certain strains of *Cannabis sativa* were selectively bred to produce higher levels of THC, and these strains came to be viewed not as sources of hemp fiber, but as producing a compound(s) that could be used to induce euphoria at will. These plants have since come to be known as marijuana.

Public perception of marijuana was transformed during the 20th century. During the Prohibition era, a significant percentage of the population turned to marijuana as a recreational compound to replace the alcohol that was forbidden by law. Following the repeal of Prohibition, several politicians seized on its use by certain minority groups as justification to have it classified as a dangerous and illegal substance to further their own careers. In spite of the classification of marijuana as illegal, its abuse never did disappear, and during the 1960s it emerged as a popular drug of abuse in the United States. Over the last half of the 20th century, drug abusers sought strains of marijuana with ever-increasing levels of THC for its enhanced effects, and its use became a mark of rebellion against the established authorities in the eyes of some abusers. These forces interacted to make its use so common that by the start of the 21st century, more than 50% of the adults in the United States are thought to have used it at least once.

At the end of the first decade of the 21st century, the federal government continues to maintain that there is no medicinal value in any compound found in marijuana and that for this reason research into possible industrial/medical applications of any compound found in marijuana is not necessary. In spite of this circular reasoning, physicians began to find evidence that there were indeed possible benefits of marijuana use for some patients with certain conditions, but further research into these possible benefits is prohibited by federal mandate. Thus it is still classified as an illegal substance by the federal government.

Although proponents of the lifting of marijuana use restrictions point to its relative safety, there is an emerging body of evidence suggesting that the chronic use of marijuana for recreational purposes is not without certain dangers. Further, it has been found to be an addictive substance, capable of producing a characteristic withdrawal syndrome. This information is certain to become part of the controversy surrounding the use, and possible abuse, of marijuana in the 21st century.

CHAPTER 11
Opioid Use, Abuse, and Addiction

Introduction

Pain is the oldest problem known to medicine (Meldrum, 2003). The fact that each year in the United States more than 70% of adults will experience at least one episode of acute pain also is evidence that it is one of the most common complaints by patients (Meldrum, 2003; D. A. Williams, 2004). Throughout history the treatment of pain was virtually synonymous with the use of opioids such as morphine or codeine. With the advent of the chemical revolution that began in the late 19th century and continued through the 20th century, new semisynthetic and synthetic opioids have been introduced, providing options for the physician who wishes to treat the patient with acute pain.

The problem of both acute and chronic pain continues to baffle scientists in spite of the advances made in the past century. For example, there is no objective method by which to measure pain, and the physician must rely almost exclusively on the patient's self-report (Cheatle & Gallagher, 2006; D. A. Williams, 2004). Further, even after a century of study, scientists still do not fully understand the neurobiological process of pain sensation (C. R. Chapman & Okifuji, 2004). In light of the fact that scientists have only an imperfect understanding of the process of pain perception, it should not be surprising that narcotic analgesics, the compounds most commonly used to treat many forms of pain, are also a source of confusion for both physicians and the patient who relies on them. Because of their perceived potential for abuse, both physicians and the general public tend to view these medications with distrust (Vourakis, 1998). Over the years, myths about narcotic[1] analgesics have been repeated so often that they ultimately have been incorporated into professional journals and textbooks as clinical "fact," shaping patient care practice and further complicating pain control (Vourakis, 1998).

This is clearly seen in the fact that because of the widespread problem of opioid *addiction,* many physicians hesitate to prescribe large doses of narcotic analgesics because of their fear that they might cause a substance use disorder (SUD) (Antoin & Beasley, 2004). Thus, many physicians *underprescribe* narcotic analgesics to patients and then view their request for additional analgesics as

---

[1]Unfortunately, the legal definition of *narcotic* is different from the pharmacological definition. Legally, cocaine is classified as a "narcotic" but it is not an opiate or opioid. In this chapter, the term *narcotic* will be used for compounds that produce effects similar to those of morphine, as in the term *narcotic analgesic.*

evidence of drug-seeking behavior(s) (Carvey, 1998; Kuhl, 2002).[2] Because of this fear, as many as 73% of patients in moderate to severe levels of pain receive less than adequate doses of narcotic analgesics (Gunderson & Stimmel, 2004; Stimmel, 1997a). Given the fact that fully 3% of the general population receives a prescription for a narcotic analgesic for long-term pain control (Dunn et al., 2010), it is easy to see where it would be easy for some of these medications to be diverted to the illicit-drug market. Although introduced to control moderate to severe levels of pain, compounds such as OxyContin have now emerged as a significant part of the drug abuse problem in the United States (Meier, 2003).[3] The efforts of various governments around the world to control drug abuse have resulted in untold thousands of people having to live in pain during what might be the last months of their lives (Nowak, 2008). However, a counterargument might lie in the finding of A. J. Hall et al. (2008), who concluded that narcotic analgesics diverted from the intended patient accounted for just under two-thirds of the accidental drug overdose deaths in West Virginia in 2006 (the last year for which statistics were available to the researchers).

In order to try and avoid some of the confusion that surrounds the use and abuse of narcotic analgesics, this chapter will be split into two parts: In the first part, the use of narcotic analgesics within the medical setting will be discussed. In the second part, the opioid use disorders (OUDs) will be discussed.

A Short History of the Natural and Synthetic Opioids

At some unknown point in time, it was discovered that if you made an incision on the top of the *Papaver somniferum* plant during a brief period in its life cycle, the plant would extrude a thick resin that had medicinal value. Anthropologists now believe that opium has been in use as an analgesic for at least 3500 years, and there is evidence that the opium poppy was cultivated as a crop 10,000 years ago (Jaffe & Strain, 2005; Walton, 2002). Whether or not the poppy was cultivated to obtain opium 10,000 years ago is not known. However, during the chemical revolution that began in the 19th century, this resin was found to contain: "an elaborate cocktail containing sugars, proteins, ammonia, latex, gums, plant wax, tars, sulphuric acid and lactic acids, water, meconic acid, and a wide range of alkaloids" (Booth, 1996, p. 4).

Prehistoric humans did not need this information: They just understood that something in the resin helped control pain. Thousands of years later, chemists began to tease out the chemical secrets of the resin that would one day be called opium (A. J. Jenkins, 2007). The English word *opium* can be traced to the Greek word *opion*, which means "poppy juice" (Stimmel, 1997a). Opium was viewed in many cultures as a gift from the gods, because it could be used to control pain as well as severe diarrhea from conditions such as dysentery.[4] By the 18th century, physicians had discovered that opium also had a limited anxiolytic effect as well as a limited antipsychotic effect. These were all important discoveries in an era when physicians had few medications that really worked. Its use as a recreational substance had also been discovered, although little is known about opium abuse patterns prior to the 18th century.

Then, in 1806 a chemist by the name of Friedrich W. A. Serturner isolated a compound that would later

---

[2]As opposed to a patient who simply has not received an adequate dose for analgesia.

[3]It is of interest to note that the International Narcotics Control Board (2008), an agency funded by and a part of the United Nations, stated that "[the] diversion of narcotic drugs from the licit to the illicit market are [sic] virtually non-existent" (p. iii).

[4]See Glossary.

be determined to be the active ingredient of opium (Gutstein & Akil, 2006). Because it could make the user feel tired, this alkaloid base was named *morphine* after the Greek god of dreams, Morpheus. As scientists explored the properties of morphine, it was discovered that this compound was a waste product produced by the opium poppy. Morphine, which is about 10 times as potent as opium, is 1 of 20 distinct alkaloid compounds produced by that plant (Gutstein & Akil, 2006; Heyman, 2009). Another of these alkaloid compounds was codeine, which was first isolated in 1832 and which will be discussed in more detail later in this chapter (Gutstein & Akil, 2006; Jaffe & Strain, 2005).

The problems associated with the use of opium were first discussed in Europe in the early 18th century (Schuckit, 2006a). But in 1857, about a half century after morphine was isolated, Alexander Wood invented the hypodermic needle. This device made it possible to rapidly and relatively painlessly introduce compounds such as morphine directly into the body. Almost concurrently physicians had discovered that morphine was an effective analgesic, a discovery that, in retrospect, appears obvious. By the time of the Civil War in the United States, both the hypodermic needle and morphine were freely available for a modest price without prescriptions being necessary. Morphine was widely used for medicinal purposes both on the battlefields of the middle to late 19th century and by those in general society who suffered from any of a wide range of ailments.

Morphine was also a hidden ingredient in many "patent" medicines[5] sold without prescription in the United States during the 19th century. These compounds were often sold under brand names that, to the unsophisticated person at least, gave them an aura of authenticity as a medicinal compound (Rasmussen, 2008). Surprisingly, research has found that the vast majority of physicians actually recommended them to patients at least on occasion (Rasmussen, 2008). The unregulated use of morphine and other dangerous compounds as hidden ingredients in various elixirs, plus the extensive use of morphine in the battlefield and military hospitals, combined with the recently invented intravenous needle, plus the practice of opium smoking, which had been introduced into the United States on a large scale by Chinese immigrants who came to this country to work in the late 19th century, all contributed to the growing epidemic of narcotics addiction in the late 19th and early 20th centuries. By the year 1900 *more than 4%* of the entire population of the United States was addicted to opium or other narcotics (Brust, 2004).

Faced with this growing epidemic of unrestrained narcotic abuse, the U.S. Congress passed the Pure Food and Drug Act of 1906. This law required that manufacturers list the ingredients of their product on the label, although the exact amounts could be kept a secret. Suddenly many members of the general public could see that many of their most trusted home remedies contained a narcotic compound(s), a discovery that helped contribute to the demise of the "patent" medicine movement. Other laws, especially the Harrison Narcotics Act of 1914, ruled that only a licensed physician or dentist could prescribe a narcotic analgesic, ending the public's unrestricted access to these compounds. Historians attribute the reduction in recreational opioid abuse seen after the passage of this act to the Harrison Narcotics Act, although in reality the wave of opioid addiction had peaked approximately a decade earlier and the problem of illicit narcotics abuse was on the decline (Heyman, 2009).

Society's efforts to eliminate recreational opioid abuse has been less than successful, in spite of an ongoing "war" on illicit drug abuse.[6] A part of this program to eliminate opioid abuse has been an ongoing search by chemists for a compound that would allow physicians to control pain at least as effectively as they can with morphine, without the potential for opioid-induced side effects or addiction. This search has continued for more than a century now and has resulted in a range of natural, semisynthetic, and synthetic narcotic analgesics being developed over the years. However, to date this search has failed to yield a compound with morphine's potential for analgesia yet at the same time lacking its addictive potential, for reasons that will be discussed later in this chapter. Thus the opioids have become, and remain, an enigma: They are both popular illicit recreational compounds and effective analgesics.

I. The Medical Applications of Narcotic Analgesics
The Classification of Narcotic Analgesics

Since morphine was first isolated, chemists have developed a wide variety of compounds that have similar pharmacological effects as morphine. These compounds

---

[5]The phenomenon of "patent" medicines in the 19th century is a topic worthy of a book in its own right, but must be mentioned only in passing here.

[6]Discussed in Chapters 37 and 38.

are classified as falling into three groups: (a) natural opiates, which are obtained directly from the opium poppy (morphine and codeine are examples of this category), (b) semisynthetic opiates, which are chemically altered derivatives of natural opiates (dihydromorphine and heroin are examples of this category), and (c) synthetic opioids, which are synthesized in laboratories and not derived from natural opiates at all (methadone and propoxyphene are examples of this category of compounds). Although there are significant differences in the chemical structure of the different compounds in each category, for the sake of this text they will all be called *opioids, opiates,* or *narcotic analgesics* because they have very similar analgesic effects.

The Problem of Pain

We tend to view pain as something to avoid, if possible. The very word *pain* comes from the Latin word *poena*, meaning a punishment or penalty, which summarizes our perspective on pain (Cheatle & Gallagher, 2006; Stimmel, 1997a). However, the word *pain* is too simplistic. In reality there are several subforms of pain: (a) acute pain, (b) noncancer chronic (or persistent) pain, and (c) cancer-induced pain (Gunderson & Stimmel, 2004; Holleran, 2002). *Acute* pain is short and intense, and resolves when the cause (incision, broken bone, and so on) heals. *Persistent pain* is not associated with cancer and is the result of pathological conditions in the body (neuropathic pain, for example), whereas *cancer-related* pain is the result of a tumor's growth or expansion.

There are three different classes of compounds used to treat pain. The first are general anesthetic agents used to induce a loss of consciousness, so that the person (hopefully) is unable to feel pain. Local anesthetic agents, the second category of analgesics, are used to block the nerve transmission of pain from the source of an injury to the brain. Cocaine was once extensively used in this capacity, but it has since been replaced by other, safer compounds for the most part, although on occasion it is still used as a local anesthetic for special procedures. The third group of compounds used to control pain are those that reduce/block the individual's awareness of pain within the central nervous system (CNS) without causing a loss of consciousness. There are several subforms in this category: (a) narcotic analgesics, which are "unsurpassed analgesic agents" (C. P. Bailey & Connor, 2005, p. 60), (b) the peripheral mu opioid receptor antagonists, a new class of opioid analgesic that does not work in the CNS, and (c) the over-the-counter analgesics, which will be discussed in Chapter 15.

Where Opium Is Produced

As was noted earlier, the natural and semisynthetic opioids are derived from raw opium, which is obtained from the opium poppy. The world's need for medicinal opium can be met by the opium fields of India. However, there are vast fields of opium poppies being grown in other countries, usually producing opium for the illicit market. It has been estimated that Afghanistan alone is estimated to produce 82% of the opium produced on this planet, all for the illicit-narcotics trade (United Nations, 2008). Painfully, the total amount of land devoted to growing opium poppies for the illicit-drug trade increased by 17% in just 2007 alone (United Nations, 2008).

Current Medical Uses of Narcotic Analgesics

For thousands of years, opium was used to treat pain (Gutstein & Akil, 2006). With the isolation of morphine. the main agent for pain control gradually evolved from opium to morphine, and before aspirin was introduced, narcotic analgesics were used to treat even mild levels of pain such as that seen in a toothache. At the start of the 21st century, narcotic analgesics are most commonly used to control severe, acute pain (O'Brien, 2006) and some forms of chronic pain (D. A. Marcus, 2003).[7] During the Civil War in the United States, soldiers on both sides would use intravenous doses of morphine to control pain from wounds, the symptoms of diarrhea, and to reduce the cough reflex. In the time since then, a large number of opiate-based analgesics have been introduced, although they all work through the same general mechanism(s) and for the most part have only minor variations in potency, absorption characteristics, and duration of effect. The generic and brand names of some of the more commonly used narcotic analgesics are provided in Table 11-1.

Nationally, it has been estimated that approximately 5% of the adult population in the United States took an opioid in the past 12 months (J. P. Kelly et al., 2008). Nearly half of narcotic analgesic users had been using one or more of these medications for more than 2 years, and one-fifth had been doing so for at

---

[7]The use of narcotic analgesics to control chronic pain is controversial and has sparked fierce debate among health care professionals; to date, there is no resolution insight (Antoin & Beasley, 2004). The team of Martell et al. (2007) suggested after their review of the literature, for example, that the efficacy of narcotic analgesics for the control of chronic pain for periods longer than 16 weeks has not been demonstrated.

TABLE 11-1 SOME COMMON NARCOTIC ANALGESICS*

GENERIC NAME	BRAND NAME	APPROXIMATE EQUIANALGESIC PARENTERAL DOSE
Morphine	—	10 mg every 3–4 hours
Hydromorphone	Dilaudid	1.5 mg every 3–4 hours
Meperidine	Demerol	100 mg every 3 hours
Methadone	Dolophine	10 mg every 6–8 hours
Oxymorphone	Numorphan	1 mg every 3–4 hours
Fentanyl	Sublimaze	0.1 mg every 1–2 hours
Pentazocine	Talwin	60 mg every 3–4 hours
Buprenorphine	Buprenex	0.3–0.4 mg every 6–8 hours
Codeine	—	75–130 mg every 3–4 hours**
Oxycodone	Perdocet, Tylox	Not available in parenteral dosage forms

SOURCE: Based on information contained in Thomson PDR (2007) and Cherny & Foley (1996).

*This chart is for comparison purposes only. It is not intended to serve as, nor should it be used as, a guide to patient care.

**It is not recommended that doses of codeine above 65 mg be used because doses above this level do not produce significantly increased analgesia and may result in increased risk of unwanted side effects.

least 5 years, according to the authors. This study will spark lively debate about whether these medications are overprescribed. It also has been found that approximately one-third of regular opioid users utilized more than five other, nonopioid medications on a regular basis, whereas just one-tenth of patients not prescribed a narcotic analgesic used that many medications, according to Kelly et al. (2008).

Pharmacology of the Narcotic Analgesics

Collectively, the narcotic analgesics utilize several different mechanisms to inhibit pain awareness. These compounds will inhibit the transmission of pain from the spinal cord to the brain, while simultaneously activating pain-suppression systems in the brain and spinal cord to inhibit the action of pain receptors in peripheral tissues. Concurrently, opiate-induced stimulation of the limbic system will also alter the patient's perception and emotional response to the pain that is perceived (Savage et al., 2008). All known narcotic analgesics are able to achieve their effects by binding at the mu and kappa opioid receptor sites in the brain (Savage et al., 2008). In the sections that follow, we will look at the more frequently prescribed narcotic analgesics in more detail.

As the wonders of neurotransmission have been revealed, it has become apparent that narcotic analgesics mimic the action of endogenous opioid peptides known as the *enkephalins, endorphins,* and *dynorphins* (Gutstein & Akil, 2006). These natural opioid peptides function as neurotransmitters in the brain and spinal cord. Each of these families of opioid peptides tends to be found mainly in a specific region of the brain, although there is a degree of overlap (Jaffe & Strain).[8]

The endogenous opioids are also involved in such activities in the CNS as—moderation of the emotions, anxiety, sedation, appetite suppression, the reward cascade—they seem to have an anticonvulsant effect. In the body, endogenous opioids are involved in the process of smooth muscle motility and regulation of various body functions such as temperature, cardiac rate, respiration, and blood pressure. In the CNS, narcotic analgesics affect the activity of a wide range of primary and secondary neurotransmitters such as norepinephrine, serotonin, acetylcholine, adenosine, glutamate, the endogenous cannabinoid receptors, nitric oxide receptor sites, throtropin-releasing hormone (TRH), and histamine. As this list would suggest, the endogenous opioids are quite powerful compounds. For example, the endogenous opioid peptide beta endorphin (ß-endorphin) is, on a milligram-per-milligram basis, estimated to be 200 times as potent as morphine.

Researchers believe that narcotic analgesics function as opioid peptide agonists, occupying the receptor site (s)

---

[8]The specific pattern of neurotransmitter distribution in the brain, and those regions where these endogenous opioid receptor sites overlap, is beyond the scope of this text. Readers are referred to a good neuropharmacology text if they are interested in learning more about this phenomenon.

normally utilized by endogenous opioids, to simulate or enhance the effects of these naturally occurring compounds (Vanderah, 2006). A number of these receptor sites have been identified in the brain, and their distribution patterns have been mapped. Researchers have used the Greek letters *mu, kappa,* and *delta* to identify different endogenous opioid receptor sites. Each receptor site in turn has subtypes: There are two known *mu* receptor subtypes, three known *kappa* receptor subtypes, and two known subtypes of the *delta* receptor subtype (A. J. Jenkins, 2007). A fourth receptor, now called the *sigma* receptor,[9] has been identified, but its distribution pattern and role in the brain is still being explored. The primary function of these endogenous opioid receptor subtypes are reviewed Table 11-2.

There is much to be discovered about the impact of narcotic analgesics on normal brain function. There is strong evidence that when used at therapeutic doses, the narcotic analgesics alter the blood flow pattern within the brain, although the significance of this has yet to be determined. This process was visualized through the process of the single photon emission computed tomography (SPECT) scan, which identified changes in cerebral blood flow patterns following the administration of narcotic analgesics (Schlaepfer et al., 1998; Schuckit, 2006a).

The effects of drug-induced mu opioid receptor activation are dose related and include respiratory depression, cognitive blurring, meiosis, and urinary retention. At high doses they can result in the activation of the brain's reward system (Savage et al., 2008; Stahl, 2008). In contrast to this, activation of the kappa opioid receptor sites results in sedation, respiration depression, nausea, and analgesia. Activation of the kappa receptor site appears to induce less analgesia, and medications that bind to this receptor site thus are effective only for mild to moderate levels of pain (Savage et al., 2008). It should be noted that the kappa endogenous opioid system functions as an antagonist with the mu receptor system. Narcotic analgesics that are mu receptor agonists cannot be utilized with kappa receptor agonists, as activation of the kappa receptor site negates any analgesia achieved by activation of the mu receptor site (Savage et al., 2008).

Surprisingly, the subjective effects of a single dose of a narcotic analgesic are different for patients experiencing significant levels of pain, as opposed to those who are not. Volunteers who are not in pain and who have received therapeutic doses of narcotic analgesics usually report experiencing a feeling of *dysphoria*[10] and rarely report any degree of euphoria (Schuckit, 2006a). This would appear to reflect the activation of the sigma and kappa receptors when the pain recognition system is not active. If narcotic analgesics *do* induce a sense of euphoria, that is caused by the effects of these compounds on the ventral tegmental region in the brain (Schuckit, 2006a). This region of the brain is rich in dopamine receptor sites and is connected with the limbic system, which might be the mechanism through which these compounds cause euphoria. Narcotic analgesics bind to what are known as interneurons, which inhibit dopamine production in the central nervous system, especially the limbic reward system (Savage et al., 2008). Without GABA neuron inhibition, the limbic reward system produces large amounts of dopamine, triggering the reward system in the brain (Savage et al., 2008). Chronic administration of morphine causes the dopamine-utilizing neurons to shrink in volume by about 25% (Sklair-Tavron et al., 1996). One implication of this is that over time the euphoric effects of morphine might wear off as the brain's ventral tegmental region shrinks, while the subjective effect of morphine might become more ordinary and induce less euphoria.

The amygdalae (singular: amygdala[11]) region of the brain has large number of opioid receptor sites. Currently, it is thought that the amygdalae will release endogenous opioids in response to sensory data, thus influencing the formation of emotionally laden memories (Jaffe & Strain, 2005). The sense of joy and accomplishment that people feel when they finally solve a complex math problem, for example, is the result of the amygdala's release of endogenous opioid neuropeptide molecules, making it more likely that students will remember the solution to that problem if they should encounter it again. The amygdala is also involved in the initiation of the "fight or flight" response, and thus it is not surprising to learn that the endogenous opioids also play a role in dampening the fear response (Motluk, 2008).

The narcotic analgesic molecules tend to preferentially bind to the *mu* receptor sites in the brain, reducing the individual's pain awareness and possibly inducing a sense of well-being that will last for about 30–60 minutes after administration of a single dose (Giannini, 2000; Jaffe & Strain, 2005; Schuckit, 2006a). When opioid molecules bind to the *kappa* receptor site(s), the individual will feel somewhat sedated and will experience

---

[9]This receptor site is sometimes referred to as the *nonciceptin/orphanin FQ* (N/OFQ) site.

[10]See Glossary.

[11]See Glossary.

TABLE 11-2 OPIOID BRAIN RECEPTORS AND THEIR FUNCTION

RECEPTOR SUBTYPE	FUNCTION IN CENTRAL NERVOUS SYSTEM
mu (subtype 1)	analgesia
mu (subtype 2)	gastrointestinal motility, bradycardia, respiratory depression
delta	analgesia (at level of spinal cord) meiosis, sedation, minor changes in psychomotor function to limited degree
kappa	analgesia (at level of spinal cord), sedation, changes in respiration
sigma	dysphoria, hallucinations, decreased respiration, some increase in psychomotor activity levels
epsilon	function remains unknown at this time
lambda	function remains unknown at this time
orphan opioid-like receptor-1 (ORL-1)	function remains unknown at this time

NOTE: Based on information proved in M. Barnett (2001), Jaffe and Jaffe (2004), W. A. Katz (2000), C. M. Knapp, Ciraulo, and Jaffe (2005), and Stout (2009).

constriction of the pupils of the eyes (Schuckit, 2006a). Research evidence suggests that opioid molecules binding at the *kappa* receptor sites in the locus ceruleus region of the brain tend to be the mechanism through which dysphoria is induced. Further, when the *kappa* receptor sites in the medulla are occupied by opioid molecules, the individual's vomiting reflex is triggered.

In an animal research study involving genetically engineered mice that did not produce any of the neurotransmitter serotonin, Zhao et al. (2007) concluded that there was no apparent analgesic effect from the narcotic analgesics administered to the mice, suggesting that the serotonin neurotransmitter system is somehow involved in analgesia through an unknown mechanism. As the preceding information demonstrates, there is still a great deal to be learned about how the narcotic analgesics impact the normal function of the human brain. In the sections that follow, we will look at some of the pharmacological properties of the more commonly prescribed narcotic analgesics.

Carfentanil

This is a chemical cousin to fentanyl (discussed later). It is estimated that this compound is 10,000 times as potent as morphine. It is sold under the brand name of Wildnil® and used in veterinary practice used to immobilize large animals (S. B. Karch, 2009). It is not intended for human use, and there is no data about the pharmacokinetics of this compound in humans.

Codeine

Codeine is another alkaloid compound found in the milky sap from the papaver somniferum plant bulb, and was first isolated in 1832 (Gutstein & Akil, 2006). Like its chemical cousin morphine, codeine is able to suppress the cough reflex, and it has a mild analgesic potential (Dilts & Dilts, 2005). This is because about 10% of the codeine administered is biotransformed into morphine as an intermediate stage of the biotransformation process (Brunton et al., 2008; Gutstein & Akil, 2006). The analgesic potential of codeine is estimated as being about one-fifth that of morphine, and thus it is most commonly used to control mild to moderate levels of pain. Following a single dose of codeine, the peak blood levels are seen in 1–2 hours, and the half-life is thought to be between 2.4 and 3.6 hours (Gutstein & Akil, 2006; S. B. Karch, 2009; Stout, 2009). It has been found that the analgesic potential of codeine is enhanced when it is mixed with over-the-counter analgesics such as aspirin or acetaminophen, and it is commonly mixed with such compounds in tablet form (Gutstein & Akil, 2006).

One problem with the use of codeine for analgesia is that a genetic mutation found in 7–10% of Caucasians and 50% of Chinese patients have a genetic mutation that prevents their body from being able to biotransform codeine into morphine. This thus prevents these patients from obtaining analgesia from codeine and reduces the body's ability to biotransform and eliminate this compound (Brunton et al., 2008; D. Goldstein, 2005; Stout, 2009; Zevin & Benowitz, 2007). In such cases, patient complaints that they have not obtained the desired level of relief from the codeine might not reflect drug seeking on their part, but rather an honest report that for them the codeine simply is not effective.

Fentanyl

Fentanyl is a synthetic opioid, introduced into the United States in 1968. It offers several advantages over traditional narcotic analgesics and is especially popular during and immediately after surgery (B. A. Wilson , 2007). It is well absorbed from muscle tissue, allowing for intramuscular injection, and also is well absorbed following intravenous injection. Unlike morphine, it does not stimulate the release of large amounts of histamine, an important consideration in some cases (Brunton et al., 2008; Gutstein & Akil, 2006).

Fentanyl is quite lipid soluble, a characteristic that makes it possible to be absorbed into the body through the skin. One common method of fentanyl administration for chronic pain is through a transdermal patch. Unfortunately, therapeutic levels of fentanyl will not build up for 12 hours after a transdermal patch is applied, a characteristic that requires the use of more traditional narcotic analgesics in the first 12 hours following application of the transdermal patch.

Pharmacology and Subjective Effects of Fentanyl
Fentanyl is quite potent, although there remains some controversy as to the relative potency of this compound as compared with morphine. Various researchers have estimated that fentanyl is 10 times (Greydanus & Patel, 2005) to perhaps 50–100 times as potent as morphine (Gutstein & Akil; 2006; S. B. Karch, 2009; Zevin &

Benowitz, 2007). A typical intravenous dose is 1 microgram.[12] It is highly lipid soluble, with 80% binding to lipid molecules in the blood after intravenous administration, and it reaches the brain rapidly after intravenous administration, providing analgesia in a matter of minutes after intravenous administration.

The biological half-life of a single intravenous dose of fentanyl is 1–6 hours, depending on the individual's biochemistry.[13] Most physicians use the average figure of 3 hours when planning for the patient's analgesia. Fentanyl primary site of action is the mu receptor site in the brain (T. M. Brown & Stoudemire, 1998). Its analgesic effects when it is administered intravenously peak in 5 minutes and last for 30–120 minutes, both important consideration when planning the patient's postsurgical analgesia (Brunton et al., 2008). It is rapidly biotransformed in the liver and excreted by the body in the urine (S. B. Karch, 2009). Unfortunately, fentanyl suppresses respiration for longer than it induces analgesia, a characteristic of this compound that physicians must keep in mind when planning for postsurgical analgesia (B. A. Wilson et al., 2007).

Between 3 and 10% of patients who receive a therapeutic dose of fentanyl will experience some degree of somnolence and/or confusion, drug-induced anxiety, hallucinations, and/or feelings of depression (T. M. Brown & Stoudemire, 1998). Approximately 1% will experience some degree of paranoia, agitation, and/or drug-induced amnesia. Other identified side effects include blurred vision, euphoria, nausea, vomiting, dizziness, delirium, and constipation (B. A. Wilson et al., 2007). Fentanyl can cause a 20% drop in the patient's blood, and it can also induce up to a 25% reduction in cardiac rate of 25. Thus as with all compounds, the attending physician must weigh the potential benefits of fentanyl use against the possible dangers inherent in its use.

Hydrocodone/Hydromorphone

Hydrocodone is a semisynthetic narcotic derived from codeine, although it is more toxic than the parent compound. It is used to control coughs and mild to moderate levels of pain. Technically it is a prodrug,[14] and most of its analgesic effects are thought to reflect the action of a metabolite, hydromorphone. Orally administered doses of hydromorphone are thought to be

---

[12]Which is about 1/60,000th the weight of a postage stamp.

[13]Some individuals will be "fast" metabolizers, whereas others will be "slow" metabolizers. See Glossary.

[14]See Glossary.

five to seven times as potent as morphine, although in opioid abusers its potency might be reduced to approximately half of this figure (Stout, 2009). Intravenously administered doses of hydromorphone have a rapid onset of analgesia (5 minutes) and provide 3–4 hours of pain relief (Stout, 2009). Orally administered doses begin to provide analgesia in 60–180 minutes, and the elimination half-life of intravenously administered hydromorphone is estimated to be around 2–3 hours (Stout, 2009). The elimination half-life of orally administered hydrophone has been estimated to be approximately 4 hours, and oral doses are subject to the first-pass metabolism effect. Side effects can include dizziness, sedation, mental confusion, anxiety fear, nausea and/or vomiting, dysphoria, and respiratory depression. Patients receiving exceptionally large doses also experience allodynia and possible seizures (Stout, 2009). A controlled-release preparation of hydromorphone is available in Canada, but has not been approved for use in the United States as of this time.

Meperidine

Meperidine was once recommended for the treatment of persistent pain. Because many of the metabolites of this compound are toxic, its use is limited to 48 hours or less (Gutstein & Akil, 2006).

Methadone

Methadone is a synthetic opioid developed by German chemists in the 1930's and later used as a substitute for morphine by German physicians during World War II (Traub, 2009). Although it is a useful pharmacological agent, there is a great deal of confusion surrounding this compound. It is used as an analgesic, especially in cases where the patient has persistent pain that requires long-term pain control (Toombs & Kral, 2005). However, because of its utilization in *methadone maintenance programs*,[15] many patients object to its use because "I'm not an addict!" To ease some of patients' reservations about being placed on a compound that in their minds is associated with opioid addiction, the brand-name form of methadone known as Dolophine® is often prescribed (Lipman, 2008; Schuckit, 2006a).

The methadone molecule is structurally similar to the morphine molecule. It is well absorbed from the gastrointestinal tract, with about 80% of a single oral dose being absorbed into the patient's body (Lipman, 2008). It is also well absorbed from muscle tissue when administered in an intramuscular injection, can be

injected subcutaneously, and may be administered intravenously (Toombs & Kral, 2005). Because of its long therapeutic half-life, it can provide extended periods of analgesia and reduce "breakthrough" pain episodes, which can cause distress to the patient. In the opiate-naive patient, analgesia is usually achieved with small oral doses of methadone (5–20 mg two to four times a day).

Methadone is highly lipophilic, and once in the circulatory system is rapidly distributed to blood-rich organs such as the brain, liver, lungs, and kidneys. The analgesic effects of methadone begin within 30–60 minutes, peak about 2–4 hours after the dose was administered, and continue to be effective for 4–6 hours depending on the individual's biochemistry (Lipman, 2008). Repeated doses of methadone provide a reservoir of methadone buildup in the body, which is then slowly released back in the circulation over time, providing a relatively steady blood level in the patient's blood. However, methadone provides a prime example of how the therapeutic half-life might be shorter than the elimination half-life. In contrast to the therapeutic half-life, the elimination half-life of methadone is between 13 and 58 hours, and depending on the individual's biochemistry possibly as long as 128 hours at first (Schottenfeld, 2008).

Toxicity to methadone varies from individual to individual, with doses of 50 mg or less proving to be fatal to nontolerant adults in some cases, whereas doses of 180 mg/day are often used in methadone maintenance programs. The potential for a lethal overdose is higher for children who accidentally obtain this medication, with doses as low as 5–10 mg being fatal to children in some cases (Schottenfeld, 2008). The speed at which methadone is eliminated from the body is dependent upon the individual's biochemistry and the acidity level of the individual's urine (Drummer & Odell, 2001; S. B. Karch, 2009). If the individual's urine is very acidic, the elimination half-life of a single dose of methadone is reduced by 50% (Drummer & Odell, 2001). When administered over extended periods of time to treat persistent pain, the methadone biotransformation period becomes shorter, reducing the elimination half-life to around 48 hours (Schottenfeld, 2008).

As an analgesic, methadone is about as potent as morphine (Stout, 2009). The major route of biotransformation is through the liver, and nine different metabolites, none of which appear to have any analgesic potential of their own, have been identified (Lipman, 2008; Stout, 2009). The majority of these metabolites are then excreted in the bile (Lipman, 2008). Tolerance

---

[15]Which will be discussed in Chapter 33.

to the respiratory depression effects of methadone is incomplete, and whereas methadone induces its own biotransformation when used on a regular basis, the danger of respiratory depression is always present. The long elimination half-life of methadone can result in a significant reservoir of this medication in the body when used for extended periods of time, placing the patient at risk for respiratory depression (Baron et al., 2009). When used to treat noncancer pain, it is recommended that the patient be started at very low doses to avoid respiratory distress, and then the dose can be slowly increased every few days until the patient reaches a desired level of analgesia. Thus physicians use the rule of "start low and go slow" in the upward titration process, increasing the patient's dose only every 4–5 days to avoid inducing respiratory depression and possible death (Lipman, 2008). However, because of this it might take up to 12 days of dosage adjustments before the patient achieves a steady-state level of methadone and thus optimal levels of analgesia (Chou et al., 2009). As is true with its chemical cousin morphine, tolerance to the effects of methadone develops unevenly. The patient might quickly become tolerant to the euphoric effects of methadone, whereas tolerance to the gastrointestinal effects (constipation) might develop slowly if at all (Lipman, 2008). Tolerance to the respiratory depressant effect of methadone might be magnified by the concurrent use of other CNS depressants such as alcohol or other pharmaceuticals. Further, neuroadaptation to effects of methadone are rapidly reversed after abstinence, so that if patients should resume this medication, it will be necessary for them to again "start low and go slow" to avoid the danger of a methadone overdose (Lipman, 2008).

This compound does present some unique dangers, however. Methadone can induce cardiac arrhythmias both when used at therapeutic doses and when it is abused (Chou et al., 2009). It is thought that methadone can prolong the QT interval[16] of the normal heart rhythm and induce a potentially fatal arrhythmia known as *Torsade de Pointes* (Chugh et al., 2008; Schottenfeld, 2008). The causal mechanism appears to be methadone's ability to block the normal action of the potassium channels in the cardiac heart muscles, which are required for the rapid repolarization of the muscles for the next heartbeat (Malik & Stillman, 2009). Between 10 and 15% of those people on methadone who develop this arrhythmia are thought to have a

subclinical form of ventricular tachycardia,[17] which is then exacerbated by methadone.[18] The exact percentage of patients on methadone who go on to develop *Torsade de Pointes* is thought to be <1%, but physicians are advised to assess the patient for this possible drug-complication through the use of serial electrocardiogram (EKG) studies because the mortality rates of these cardiac problems is so high.

In recent years the media have focused attention on the "epidemic" of methadone-related deaths. Although this is not meant to ignore the dangers associated with methadone use, the concurrent use of other CNS depressants, and even over-the-counter compounds such as antihistamines, can increase the risk of an overdose (Lipman, 2008). Methadone overdoses can be treated by blocking agents such as Narcan®, but the extended half-life of methadone makes it imperative that the patient continue to repeatedly receive the appropriate dose of this antidote over extended periods of time. Methadone overdose deaths have been known to occur up to 24 hours after the individual's overdose was ingested or after the narcotic blocker was discontinued (Schottenfeld, 2008).

However, when used as prescribed, methadone has a very good safety profile. Even after years of prescribed use, there is no evidence of drug-induced damage to the lungs, kidneys, liver, brain, stomach, or spleen. Methadone will interact with *at least* 100 different pharmaceuticals currently in use in the United States (Schottenfeld, 2004; "Taming Drug Interactions," 2003). Depending on the exact nature of the drug(s) involved, the methadone-drug interaction might range from inconvenient to life threatening.[19] Some of the medications that might interact with methadone include (but are not limited to) carbamazepine, phenytoin, risperidone, Ritonavir, and the herbal medication St. John's wort, all of which may reduce the patient's blood methadone levels. Other medications such as fluoxetine, fluvoximine, sanquinavir, cimetidine, erythromycin, and ciprofloxcin may slow the rate of methadone biotransformation, causing higher than normal (possibly fatal) blood levels of the latter compound (Drummer & Odell, 2001; "Methadone-Cipro Interactions," 2002; Schottenfeld, 2004). Patients taking methadone should avoid the use of other CNS

---

[16]Technically the time required for the activation and then recovery from a single heartbeat on an electrocardiogram.

[17]See Glossary.

[18]It is important to keep in mind that ventricular tachycardia has a number of causes, not just the use of methadone.

[19]As always, patients on *any* prescribed medication should consult with a physician or pharmacist before taking either another prescribed medication or an over-the-counter product.

depressants such as alcohol or antihistamines to avoid a potentially fatal potentiation effect between the chemicals being abused. This is one reason why polydrug abusers are at increased risk for a potentially fatal overdose, especially in the early stages of methadone treatment. For example, there is one known case report of a fatal drug interaction effect for a patient taking both methadone and a benzodiazepine (Schottenfeld, 2008).

There is also evidence that methadone might interfere with the antithrombotic action of aspirin, thus allowing the blood to form clots more easily, possibly contributing to a heart attack, stroke, or other serious medical problem (Malinin, Callahan, & Serebruany, 2001). Although this list of potential drug interactions is far from being inclusive, it does illustrate the potential for potentially fatal drug interactions between methadone and a wide range of other compounds.

Morphine

The resin that is collected from *Papaver somniferum* as the poppy head is lanced at the proper time contains 10–17% morphine and at last 20 other compounds, many of which have analgesic properties of their own (Brust, 2004; A. J. Jenkins, 2007; A. J. Jenkins & Cone, 2008). Morphine was first isolated more than 150 years ago, but it still remains the gold standard against which other narcotic analgesics are measured (D'Arcy, 2005; Gutstein & Akil, 2006; Traub, 2009).

Although morphine can be administered orally and is rapidly absorbed through the gastrointestinal tract, between 60 and 80% of a dose of morphine will be biotransformed through the first-pass metabolism[20] effect before it reaches the brain (Stout, 2009). This fact makes orally administered morphine of limited value in the treatment of moderate to severe levels of pain. This, plus the fact that it is well absorbed from both intramuscular and intravenous injection sites, results in the usual routes of administration being intramuscular or intravenous injections. A standard conversion formula is that 10 mg of injected morphine induces the same level of analgesia as 60 mg of orally administered morphine (Cherny & Foley, 1996). A rare, but effective, route of administration is rectal suppositories. This takes advantage of the fact that morphine is easily absorbed through the mucous membranes of the body such as those found in the rectum. However, this method of morphine administration is so rare that it will not be discussed again in this text.

The peak blood levels of a single dose of morphine are achieved in about 60 minutes after an oral dose, and within 30–60 minutes following intravenous injection (B. A. Wilson et al., 2007). After absorption into the body, about one-third of the morphine will become plasma bound, providing a reservoir of morphine in the body for several hours. This is an advantage because the unbound morphine molecules will be rapidly distributed to every blood-rich organ, including the lungs, muscle tissues, kidneys, liver, spleen, and brain. The analgesic effects of a single dose of morphine last approximately 4 hours (Gutstein & Akil, 2006). The biotransformation half-life of a single dose of morphine ranges from 1 to 8 hours depending on the individual's biochemistry, with most textbooks offering an average figure of 2–3 hours (Drummer & Odell, 2001). Morphine crosses through the blood–brain barrier slowly, taking between 20 and 30 minutes to actually reach the neurons within the brain to reach the appropriate receptor sites. Thus the analgesic effects of morphine are not immediate and might require as long as a half hour to reach full effect.

The majority of the morphine is broken down into the metabolite *morphine-3-glucuronide* (M3G). A smaller amount will be biotransformed into *morphine-6-glucur-onide* (M6G), and the remainder is biotransformed into several additional metabolites (Brunton et al., 2008; S. B. Karch, 2009). Interestingly, M6G has a stronger analgesic effect than its parent compound (Wynn et al., 2009). When morphine is administered on a repeated basis, the analgesic effect of M6G has been estimated to be between 2 and 20 times that of morphine itself, possibly accounting for morphine's analgesic effects in such cases (Gutstein & Akil, 2005; Wynn et al., 2009). The elimination half-life of morphine is thought to be between 2 and 3 hours, but is slightly longer in men than in women (Lipman, 2008).

OxyContin

OxyContin was introduced in 1995 as a time-released form of oxycodone, itself a synthetic opioid. It was designed for use in cases where the patient was suffering long-term pain that could be controlled by oral medications, thus reducing the need for intravenously administered medications. A relatively stable blood level of OxyContin could be reached after two to three doses, providing better pain control than could be achieved using short-acting narcotic analgesics. Unfortunately OxyContin has become a major drug of abuse, which will be discussed later in this chapter.

---

[20]Discussed in Chapter 3 and in Glossary.

Heroin

Technically, heroin is just two morphine molecules joined together by an oxygen molecule, thus yielding its chemical name, diacetylmorphine (Brunton et al., 2008). As an analgesic, it is thought to be approximately twice as potent as morphine, and a standard conversion formula is that 10 mg of morphine has the same analgesic potential as 3 mg of diacetylmorphine (Brust, 2004). Its major first-stage metabolite[21] is 6-monoacetylmorphine (6-MAM), which is then broken down into morphine. The importance of this metabolite is that it crosses over the blood–brain barrier much more quickly than does morphine itself (Gutstein & Akil, 2005). In the United States, heroin has no recognized medical use and is classified as a Schedule I substance[22] under the Controlled Substances Act of 1970 (A. J. Jenkins, 2007). It remains a recognized pharmaceutical in some other countries, used by physicians to treat severe pain.[23] Further, there is an emerging body of evidence that suggests that heroin might have a cardioprotective potential during periods of cardiac ischemia, although the exact mechanism for this is not clear at the present time (Gutstein & Akil, 2006; Mamer, Penn, Wildmer, Levin, & Maslansky, 2003; Peart & Gross, 2004). This effect, if proven in future research, may make diacetylmorphine of value in treating heart attack patients; however, there is a need for further clinical research to identify the mechanism that causes this effect. Heroin as a drug of abuse in the United States will be discussed later in this chapter.

Propoxyphene

This is a synthetic narcotic analgesic that is almost as effective an analgesic as codeine (Graedon & Graedon, 1996). It is widely prescribed for mild to moderate levels of pain, often in combination with over-the-counter analgesics such as acetaminophen. In February of 2009 an advisory panel to the Food and Drug Administration (FDA) recommended that production of this compound be discontinued and that it be removed from the market. The FDA rejected this recommendation. However, in Great Britain this product was removed from the market in 2005.

Propoxyphene is a very mild mu receptor antagonist when taken at recommended doses, and for this reason was used for mild to moderate levels of pain. However, when taken concurrently with other CNS depressants such as alcohol, or in overdose situations, it can induce respiratory depression and possible death. This compound has a reputation as being popular for suicide gestures, attempts, and completed suicides ("Propoxyphene Pharmacokinetics," 2009).

Even when used at therapeutic doses, propoxyphene was not without its dangers. A metabolite produced during the biotransformation process, norpropoxyphene (NP), is able to induce 2.5 times the level of cardiac depression than the parent compound. Further, the elimination half-life of NP is approximately 36 hours, or three times that of propoxyphene itself. Thus, with repeated propoxyphene doses being administered for analgesia, significant levels of NP can accumulate in the user's body. Further, propoxyphene (or its metabolite NP) inhibits the ability of the liver to biotransform a wide range of other compounds, some of which are used to control seizures ("Propoxyphene Pharmacokinetics," 2009).

Tramadol

Tramadol is a distant chemical cousin to codeine (discussed earlier). It is used to treat mild to moderate levels of pain and is thought to be of value in controlling the pain of childbirth because it induces less neonatal respiratory depression following birth (Brunton et al., 2008). As an analgesic, it is thought to be about as potent as morphine (Brunton et al., 2008). Between 70 and 75% of a single oral dose reaches the circulation and 20% of this is protein-bound. Peak plasma levels are reached in about 2.3 hours, and the half-life is 5.5 hours following a single oral dose (Brunton, Lazo, & Parker, 2006).

Although tramadol has long been viewed as a safe narcotic analgesic for use in mild to moderate pain, the team of Daubin et al. (2008) described at length the clinical course of a patient who had ingested a drug overdose of various compounds, including tramadol. The authors concluded that the prescribing physician needed to be vigilant when prescribing this compound, which is possibly more toxic than originally thought.

---

[21]As with many compounds, heroin biotransformation goes through a number of stages.

[22]See Appendix 4.

[23]Obviously, the heroin used for medicinal purposes in medical centers overseas is produced by pharmaceutical companies under controlled conditions, producing a medication of known potency and purity. The only thing that this heroin has in common with illicit heroin is its name.

Sufentanil

This is a chemical cousin to fentanyl and is sold under the brand name of Sufenta®. It is a pharmaceutical commonly used in cardiac surgery and is estimated to be 1000 times as potent as morphine (Brunton et al., 2008; S. B. Karch, 2009). The pharmacokinetics of this compound are similar to that of fentanyl.

Buprenorphine

Buprenorphine is a synthetic opioid introduced into clinical use in the 1960s. As an analgesic, it is well absorbed through intramuscular and intravenous injections and is estimated to be 25–50 times as potent as morphine (Fudala & O'Brien, 2005; S. B. Karch, 2009). A standard conversion formula is that 0.3 mg of intravenously administered buprenorphine is approximately as powerful as 10 mg of morphine. However, the analgesic potential of this medication is limited, and it has a slow onset of action. These characteristics, plus its long elimination half-life (up to 37 hours), are all reasons why it is a rarely used pain medication (Baron et al., 2009; U.S. Department of Health and Human Services, 2004).

Approximately 95% of the buprenorphine in the blood is protein bound. It is biotransformed in the liver, with 79% being excreted in the feces and only 3.9% being excreted in the feces. Surprisingly, animal research suggests that the various buprenorphine metabolites are unable to cross the blood–brain barrier, suggesting that the analgesic effects of buprenorphine are induced by those buprenorphine molecules that cross over into the brain.

Once in the brain, buprenorphine binds to the same receptor sites that are used by morphine. It functions as a partial *mu* receptor agonist, but with some interesting properties. When the buprenorphine molecule binds at a *mu* receptor site, it initially activates that receptor. Rather than disconnecting from the receptor site after the initial activation however, the molecule remains at the receptor site, preventing other opioid molecules from reaching that same receptor site until the buprenorphine molecule finally disconnects from that receptor. At high dosage levels, buprenorphine acts as an opioid antagonist, limiting not only its own effects but that of other narcotic analgesics as well (U.S. Department of Health and Human Services, 2004). It also binds at the kappa receptor sites and will bind only weakly with the sigma receptor site, although the significance of these observations is not known at the present time (Fudala & O'Brien, 2005).

Between 40 and 70% of patients who receive buprenorphine will experience sedation, constipation, and urinary retention, and 5–40% will experience dizziness (Donaher & Welsh, 2006). In rare cases (<1%) patients will experience drug-induced anxiety, euphoria, hallucinations, and possibly depression (T. M. Brown & Stoudemire, 1998). It is a powerful narcotic analgesic that unfortunately is gaining popularity as a drug of abuse.

Nonopioid Analgesics

A new analgesic compound is ziconotide (Prialt®), a substance derived from the venom of the marine snail *Conus magus*. This compound blocks calcium channels in neurons responsible for pain transmission signals, reducing the sensitivity of neurons involved in the process of pain recognition. This compound is not effective as a primary analgesic for acute injuries, but is of value for persistent pain conditions. It is extremely potent and is administered through an in-dwelling pump. Ziconotide is capable of inducing neurological side effects including (but not limited to) blurred vision, nystagmus, sedation, drug-induced psychotic reactions, and depression that might reach suicidal proportions. Thus close clinical monitoring is necessary to identify these consequences and immediately discontinue the medication. However, for those patients who are able to benefit from this medication, it offers the hope of relief from persistent pain without the use of narcotic analgesics.

Peripheral Mu Opioid Receptor Antagonists

These are a new class of compounds, two of which, methylnaltrexone and alvimopan, have recently been introduced in the United States. These compounds have poor lipid solubility and possess an electrical charge that prevents them from crossing the blood–brain barrier. Therefore they do not reverse opioid-induced analgesia in the CNS, but do bind at mu opioid receptor sites in the intestines, blocking the opioid-induced constipation that so often limits the use of traditional opioids in pain control (Moss & Rosow, 2008). These compounds are also first in the class of a new family of compounds that may limit, or reverse, many of the adverse effects of opioids, allowing the latter drugs to be used more effectively as analgesics.

Neuroadaptation to Narcotic Analgesics

Analgesia is not a static process but is influenced by a host of factors such as (a) genetic heritage, (b) disease progression, (c) increase/decrease in level of physical activity, (d) medication compliance/noncompliance, and (e) medication interaction effects and the process of neuroadaptation to the narcotic analgesic(s) being administered to the patient. The first point, the individual's genetic heritage, is occasionally a source of some confusion in that a small percentage of the population possesses what is known as *innate tolerance* to a narcotic analgesic (G. Chang, Chen, & Mao, 2007). This is observed from the very first dose of a narcotic analgesic and reflects the fact that the individual's genetic heritage is such that the individual is less responsive to some narcotic analgesics than others.

In contrast to innate tolerance is acquired tolerance, which reflects adaptive changes within the neurons on the brain to the presence of narcotic molecules. The development of neuroadaptation to narcotic analgesics is rapid, incomplete, and proceeds at an uneven pace (Jaffe & Jaffe, 2004). Animal research has demonstrated changes in neuronal responsiveness to an opioid after just a single dose, suggesting that the process of neuroadaptation begins almost immediately (C. P. Bailey & Connor, 2005). There is wide variation between individuals as to the speed at which neuroadaptation develops, with some patients becoming tolerant to opioid-induced analgesia after just a few days of continuous use at a set dosage level (Ivanov, Schulz, Palmero, & Newcorn, 2006). The process of neuroadaptation is often incomplete, as evidenced by the fact that patients on narcotic analgesics might never fully adapt to narcotic-induced constriction of the pupils even after extended periods of narcotic use (Schuckit, 2006a).[24]

Unfortunately, neuroadaptation is occasionally misinterpreted as evidence of patient opiate addiction, making the physician reluctant to adequately treat the patient's pain. This condition is now termed *pseudoaddiction* as opposed to a real substance use disorder. The differentiation between these two conditions lies in the fact that once patients' pain is adequately controlled, they will not request additional narcotic analgesics.

As the process of neuroadaptation evolves over time, the individual's daily medication requirements might change. Physicians have discovered that the use of the anticough compound dextromethorphan, an NMDA receptor antagonist, will slow the development of neuroadaptation and improve analgesia without the need for a dosage increase (O'Brien, 2006). It has also been found that the concurrent use of over-the-counter analgesics potentiates the effects of prescribed narcotic analgesics through an unknown mechanism (Gutstein & Akil, 2006). Thus a dosage increase is not the only answer to the development of neuroadaptation to narcotic analgesics.

The Problem of Hyperalgesia

In rare cases, once the neural pain receptors have been repeatedly activated they might become sensitized, responding to noxious stimuli more strongly than before (Vanderah, 2006). This process is not a sign of tolerance to the effects of the narcotic analgesic being used, but rather a neurological overresponse to what would normally be a less painful stimuli. Surprisingly, in even less common cases the pain recognition system neurons might respond to normal stimuli as if they were a sign of injury, sending pain messages to the brain without trauma to the body. This condition is known as *allodynia* and is exceptionally rare.

Withdrawal from Narcotic Analgesics When Used in Medical Practice

Most patients who receive narcotic analgesics, even those who do so for an extended period of time, are able to discontinue the use of these medications when the time comes without significant distress. A small percentage of these patients will develop a *discontinuance syndrome*. The discontinuance syndrome might develop in patients who receive as little as 15 mg of morphine three times a day for 3 days (Ropper & Brown, 2005). This discontinuance syndrome is usually mild and does not require treatment, although in some cases the patient is advised to gradually "taper" from the medication rather than to just discontinue it.

Drug Interactions Involving Narcotic Analgesics[25]

Even a partial list of potential medication interactions involving narcotic analgesics clearly underscores the potential for these compounds to do harm if taken by a patient receiving certain other medications. Narcotic analgesics should not be used in patients who are taking, or have recently used, a monoamine oxidase inhibitor (MAOI or, more commonly, MAO inhibitor). Patients receiving or who have received an MAO inhibitor in the past 14 days may experience a potentially fatal reaction if they should intermix these compounds within the specified time period.

Patients on narcotic analgesics should not mix their medications with other central nervous system

---

[24]Unless, as the author pointed out, the patient has suffered some degree of brain damage, in which case the pupils might be dilated, not constricted.

[25]Always consult a physician or pharmacist before mixing two different medications.

depressants, which include (but is not limited to) alcohol, the benzodiazepines, and the over-the-counter antihistamines, without consulting a physician or pharmacist first. They also should avoid the concurrent use of the "tricyclic" antidepressants while on morphine (Ciraulo et al., 2006). The combination of different CNS depressants carries with it the danger of excessive sedation, respiratory depression, and possibly even death (Ciraulo et al., 2006).

Given the growing use of methadone in pain control for chronic pain disorders and methadone maintenance programs, it is important to be aware of the range of methadone-drug interactions that are possible.[26] Compounds that activate the liver's cytochrome P450 metabolic pathway might then either cause premature biotransformation of methadone (resulting in opioid withdrawal symptoms), or by competing with the methadone for biotransformation, cause higher than normal blood levels of both compounds. An example of this is how the use of the selective serotonin reuptake inhibitor fluvoxamine might, when taken with methadone, cause toxic, possibly fatal, levels of the latter compound to build up in the patient's blood.

It was found that 21 of 30 patients on a methadone maintenance program who took the antibiotic rifampin experienced the opioid withdrawal syndrome in spite of their continued use of methadone through an unknown interaction effect between these two chemicals (Ciraulo et al., 2006). Such withdrawal symptoms did not manifest until the 5th day of treatment, suggesting that the interaction effect between these two medications might require some time to develop.

This is only a partial list of the possible interactions between the narcotic analgesics and various other pharmaceuticals, but does underscore the potential for harm if a patient should intermix a narcotic analgesic(s) with the wrong medication(s). As always, consult a physician or pharmacist before taking two medications concurrently.

Subject Effects of Narcotic Analgesics When Used in Medical Practice

There are several factors that influence the effects that a narcotic analgesic will have on patients, including the (a) route of administration, (b) interval between doses, (c) the actual dose of the medication being used, (d) the half-life of the medication being used, (e) the individual's anxiety level, (f) their expectations for the medication,

(g) length of time that they have used a given narcotic analgesic, (h) their expectations for the medication's effects, and (i) their biochemistry. The latter point is illustrated by the earlier observation that a certain percentage of the population lacks the ability to manufacture an enzyme necessary to break down codeine and thus are unable to receive any benefit from this medication.

The primary application of narcotic analgesics is in pain control. Between 80 and 95% of patients in pain who receive a dose of morphine report that their fear, anxiety, and/or tension levels are lower when the medication begins to work (T. M. Brown & Stoudemire, 1998). Other descriptions include less intense pain, less discomfort, that they become sleepy, and possibly that their pain might have disappeared entirely (Knapp et al., 2005). When used to control cough, patients report that their cough is less frequent and that they are able to get more rest. In rare circumstances, narcotic analgesics are administered to control massive diarrhea, although with the introduction of newer medications this use of opioids is rather rare.

Complications Caused by Narcotic Analgesics When Used in Medical Practice

Constriction of the Pupils

When used at therapeutic doses, narcotic analgesics causes the pupils of the eyes to become constricted (meiosis). Some patients will experience this effect, even in total darkness (B. A. Wilson et al., 2007). Some physicians interpret this as a sign of opiate addiction, but actually it is a side effect of the narcotic analgesics and is rarely encountered in a patient who is not taking or abusing these medications.

Respiratory Depression

At therapeutic doses, narcotic analgesics make the brain stem less responsive to blood carbon dioxide levels and thus can cause some degree of respiratory depression (Brunton, et al., 2008; Brust, 2004). The level of respiratory depression is not significant in the healthy patient in good health who is in pain. But even a single dose of a narcotic analgesic might impact respiration for up to 24 hours (T. M. Brown & Stoudemire, 1998). Because of this effect, there is an ongoing debate concerning whether narcotic analgesics can safely be used by patients with breathing disorders. It would appear that if the attending physician were to increase the patient's dose in a timely and appropriate manner, there is little danger even for patients whose breathing

---

[26]This list is not complete, and a pharmacist should be consulted prior to the use of two or more medications simultaneously.

has been compromised by disease (Estfan et al., 2007). Indeed, the danger is not so much the narcotic analgesic as it is the skill and knowledge of the prescribing physician (George & Regnard, 2007). As always, the narcotic analgesics are the drugs of choice *if* the benefits outweigh the dangers associated with the use of such medications (McNichol et al., 2003).

Gastrointestinal Side Effects

When used even at therapeutic levels, narcotic analgesics can induce nausea and vomiting, especially during the first 48 hours of treatment or with a major dose increase (M. Barnett, 2001; Dilts & Dilts, 2005). At therapeutic doses, following the administration of their medication 10–40% of ambulatory patients will experience some degree of nausea and approximately 15% will actually vomit (Swegle & Logemann, 2006). This unwanted effect of narcotic analgesics appears to be most common in the ambulatory patient, and patients are advised to rest for a short period of time after receiving a dose of medication to minimize this effect. Further, people's vulnerability to this effect is mediated, in part, by their genetic heritage, with some individuals demonstrating opioid-induced nausea/vomiting even at very low dosage levels (Brunton et al., 2008). To combat this side effect, some clinicians advocate the use of *ultralow* doses of the narcotic blocker naloxone to block the opioid-induced nausea (Cepeda, Alvarez, Morales, & Carr, 2004).

At therapeutic dosage levels, narcotic analgesics have been found to alter the normal function of the gastrointestinal tract in a number of ways. All narcotic analgesics decrease the secretion of hydrochloric acid in the stomach, and slow the muscle contractions of peristalsis[27] (Dilts & Dilts, 2005; Gutstein & Akil, 2006). This side effect is of great value in controlling the diarrhea caused by dysentery or similar disorders, but is also a bothersome, occasionally life-threatening problem for patients receiving narcotic analgesics for pain control. The muscle contractions might slow to such a degree that patients develop constipation or possibly even an intestinal blockage (Jaffe & Jaffe, 2004; Swegle & Logemann, 2006). Tolerance to this effect does not appear to develop even after periods of extended use (Swegle & Logemann, 2006). Mild cases might be controlled by over-the-counter laxatives (M. Barnett, 2001), and experimental evidence suggests that the compound methylnaltrexone might be used to relieve extreme opioid-induced constipation (M. Barnett, 2001; Moon, 2008b).

Blood Pressure Effects

Narcotic analgesics should be used with great caution immediately following head trauma. Edema[28] in such cases is common, and if the narcotic analgesic administered to the patient should reduce respiration, the heart will pump even more blood to the brain to compensate for the increased carbon dioxide levels, exacerbating cerebral edema if present.

Other Side Effects

At therapeutic doses, narcotic analgesics stimulate the smooth muscles surrounding the bladder, while simultaneously reducing the voiding reflex, causing urinary retention (Brunton et al., 2008; Dilts & Dilts, 2005). Sedation, although a desired side effect in many settings, may interfere with the individual's ability to safely handle power tools or a motor vehicle, and contribute to an increase in accidental injuries (Blondell & Ashrafioun, 2008). The initial dose(s) of a narcotic analgesic can induce transitory changes in cognition and compound the effects of infection(s), dehydration, metabolic dysfunctions, or late-stage cancer (Swegle & Logemann, 2006). It has been demonstrated that between 4 and 35% of patients receiving a narcotic analgesic for the control of pain will experience some degree of drug-induced irritability and that 4–25% will experience some degree of drug-induced depression. The initial doses of a narcotic analgesic can reduce blood testosterone levels (Schuckit, 2008b). Nightmares, although well documented, have not been studied in detail. When used at high dosage levels, all narcotic analgesics can induce seizures, although this side effect is more commonly seen when these compounds are abused because abusers are more likely to utilize the higher dosage levels necessary to induce seizures (Gutstein & Akil, 2006).

Narcotic analgesics can cause the patient to become dizzy, lose their balance, and fall, possibly compounding the problem(s) for which they were taking these medications. Although advancing age is a risk factor for falls and injury, even young adults are not entirely safe from this side effect. Finally, narcotic analgesics can induce memory loss and/or an acute confusional state, which will usually resolve with abstinence (Filley, 2004).

The Danger of Physician-Induced Addiction

Many health care workers will admit to an ongoing fear that they will cause the patient to become addicted to narcotic analgesics.[29] In reality, unless the patient has a

---

[27]See Glossary.

[28]See Glossary.

[29]Which would, technically, be an *iatrogenic addiction.*

prior history of a substance use disorder, only 1 in every 14,000 patients who receives a narcotic analgesic for the short-term control of acute pain is thought to be at risk for the development of an iatrogenic addiction. This risk is higher with patients who have a prior history of a substance use disorder. Yet such patients are often injured or require surgery for one reason or other, sparking a treatment dilemma for the attending physician(s).

A New Approach to Pain

The team of Zylka et al. (2008) have uncovered a new approach to pain, one that does not use narcotic analgesics. Rather, on the basis of animal research, the authors suggested that a previously unknown protein molecule known as prostatic acid phosphatase (PAP) helps neurons generate adenosine, a molecule known for its ability to suppress pain at the neural level. This process appears to generate a level of analgesia eight times as powerful as that achieved by morphine and seems to be applicable to neurogenic pain as well as possibly acute pain, without the sedation seen with narcotic analgesics, for a longer period of time than is achieved by morphine alone. Further research into this novel approach to pain control is needed, but this does offer an exciting nonopioid approach that seems promising.

Part Summary

As is evident in the preceding information, the narcotic analgesics are powerful compounds that have the potential to bring great benefit to the patient, but only at significant risk. The narcotic analgesics, be they natural, semisynthetic, or synthetic compounds, have similar effects on the brain: They block patients' awareness of pain, bringing relief to them at a time when they are in distress. However, they are not perfect compounds, forcing patients to experience any of a wide variety of side effects such as constipation, alterations in consciousness, respiratory depression, and so on. Although scientists have searched for a compound that might produce analgesia without the side effects brought on by narcotic analgesics, thus far they have been unable to do so.

II. Opiates As Drugs of Abuse

The popular image of narcotics abusers is that of heroin addicts huddled in the corner of a building, with a belt around their arm injecting the heroin into their circulation. Such people make up only a small percentage of drug abusers according to the popular media, and students are often surprised to learn that this image is false. After marijuana, prescription narcotics are the most

commonly abused class of chemicals (A. W. Blume, 2005; Davis & Johnson, 2008). This is not to dismiss the problem of heroin addiction but to clarify the fact that the narcotic use disorders include not only the abuse of illicit compounds such as heroin, but also the abuse of prescribed narcotic analgesics that have been diverted to the illicit-drug market. Surprisingly, 97% of those people who abuse prescription narcotic analgesics obtained their drug not from illicit-drug dealers, but from a friend or relative who had a prescription for medications such as Vicodin® or OxyConti® ("Adult Use of Prescription Opioid Pain Medications—Utah, 2008," 2010). To clarify such misunderstandings about the abuse of narcotic analgesics in this part, the opiate use disorders will be examined.

Why Do People Abuse Opiates?

At first glance it would appear that the answer to this question is simple: They make the abuser feel good.[30] The exact mechanism by which opioids might induce a sense of pleasure remains unknown but appears to reflect a drug-induced release of dopamine in the reward system of the brain (Gutstein & Akil, 2006; Schuckit, 2008b). Depending on the specific compound being abused, the method by which it is administered, the individuals' drug use history, and their expectations for the drug(s) abused, the intensity of these feelings can vary from mild to such that it has been compared to the sexual orgasm in intensity (Jaffe & Strain, 2005; Sadock & Sadock, 2007).

Narcotics mimic the action of naturally occurring, opiate-like neurotransmitters, in the nucleus accumbens and the ventral tegmentum areas of the brain, regions that appear to be involved in the pleasure cascade reported by many opioid abusers when they use these compounds (Kosten & George, 2002).

However, the abuse of prescribed narcotics has become a greater problem than heroin abuse or addiction (Davis & Johnson, 2008). This aspect of prescribed narcotic analgesics will be discussed later in the section on opioid misuse and addiction.

The Mystique of Heroin

Heroin is the first drug that most people think about when they hear the words *narcotics addiction,* although there is widespread abuse of prescription opioids. Still, there is some foundation for this belief: Ever since

---

[30]Does anybody *ever* abuse a drug because it makes them feel bad?

the U.S.-led invasion of Afghanistan, it has become the predominant supplier of heroin for the illicit drug trade, producing *93%* of the total amount of heroin produced in 2007 (Reuter, 2009). Heroin abuse or addiction accounts for 71% of the opioid use problem around the world (United Nations, 2008). If, as the United Nations (2008) estimated, there are 16.5 million illicit opioid abusers around the world, then some 11.7 million people are either heroin abusers or addicts. Of this number of opioid abusers, it is estimated that 9.3 million live in Asia, 3.6 million in Europe, and 1.2 million in the United States (United Nations, 2008).

A Short History of Heroin

Like aspirin, heroin was first developed by chemists at the Bayer pharmaceutical company of Germany and was first introduced in 1898. The chemists who developed this compound tried it on themselves, found that it made them feel "heroic," and so it was given the brand name *Heroin* (C. C. Mann & Plummer, 1991, p. 26). Like its chemical cousin morphine, heroin is obtained from raw opium. One ton of raw opium will, after processing, yield 100 kilograms of heroin ("South American Drug Production Increases," 1997).

During the Civil War in the United States, and the various wars between nations in Europe during the latter quarter of the 19th century, large numbers of men became addicted to morphine, which was freely administered to treat battlefield wounds or illness. Heroin was found to stop morphine withdrawal at low doses, and because of this was thought at the time to be a treatment for morphine addiction (Walton, 2002). Further, both morphine and heroin were found to suppress the coughs associated with conditions such as pneumonia and tuberculosis, both leading causes of death at that time. Thus both compounds were freely administered to patients with either condition.

It was not until 12 years later that the addictive potential of heroin was generally recognized. However, by that time, heroin abuse and addiction had become a fixture in the United States. By the 1920s the term *junkie* was coined for heroin addicts who supported their drug habit by collecting scrap metal from industrial dumps for resale to junk-metal collectors (I. Scott, 1998). This money would then be used to pay for their daily heroin. Although the procedure(s) by which heroin addicts obtain their money has changed over the years, the process has not: Heroin addicts must still feed their "habit" every day.

The Pharmacology of Heroin

Essentially heroin is a prodrug[31] (A. J. Jenkins & Cone, 1998). The heroin molecule is essentially a pair of morphine molecules that have been joined chemically. The result of this process is an analgesic that is more potent than morphine, and a standard conversion formula is that 3 mg of heroin has the same analgesic potential as 10 mg of morphine (Brust, 2004). The half-life of heroin has been estimated as between 2 and 3 minutes (Drummer & Odell, 2001) to perhaps as long as 36 minutes (S. B. Karch, 2009). Eventually heroin is biotransformed into morphine, but an intermediate metabolite of heroin biotransformation has been found to be exceptionally lipid soluble, allowing the metabolite to cross the blood–brain barrier up to 100 times as rapidly as does morphine (Brunton et al., 2008). It would not be unreasonable to assume that this metabolite is biologically active and may have an analgesic potential in its own right. However, the current theory is that heroin's analgesic power is the result of its breakdown into morphine (Drummer & Odell, 2001; S. B. Karch, 2009). After it has been biotransformed into morphine, its distribution pattern and elimination pattern follow that of medicinal morphine, discussed in the first part of this chapter.

Subjective Effects of Heroin When Abused

There are a number of factors that influence the subjective effects of heroin, including the (a) individual's expectations for the drug, (b) dose utilized, and (c) method of heroin abuse. Intranasally administered heroin, for example, is poorly absorbed by the body, with only 25% of the available heroin reaching the general circulation. The absorption of intranasally administrated heroin is slower than that of intramuscular or intravenous injections as well. In contrast with this is the virtual 100% absorption rate achieved when heroin is administered intravenously.

Where intranasal abusers report achieving a gentle sense of euphoria after the compound reaches the brain, experienced intravenous drug abusers report a "rush" or "flash" experience that is very similar to the sexual orgasm and that lasts for about 1 minute (Stahl, 2008). Other sensations reported by heroin abusers include a feeling of warmth under the skin, dry mouth, nausea, and a feeling of heaviness in the extremities. There is some degree of nasal congestion that develops, as heroin stimulates the release of histamine in the body. Heroin abusers also report a sensation of floating

---

[31]See Glossary.

or light sleep ("nodding off"), which lasts for about 2 hours, accompanied by clouded mental function. In contrast to alcohol, heroin abusers do not experience slurred speech, ataxia, or emotional lability (Gutstein & Akil, 2006).

Other Opioids of Abuse

At the time of their admission to a methadone maintenance program, a significant proportion of abusers identify a physician as their main source for drugs at the time of their admission. We will discuss some of the more commonly abused narcotic analgesics in the sections that follow.

Codeine

Codeine has emerged as a drug of abuse, accounting for 10% of all drug-related deaths (S. B. Karch, 2009). There is little information available about codeine abuse, as this compound was long thought to be too weak to be of interest to drug abusers. It is possible that heroin abusers miscalculate the amount of codeine necessary to block opioid withdrawal symptoms, thus contributing to their deaths. However, this is only a theory.

OxyContin

OxyContin was released in 1995 and became a drug of abuse shortly afterward. A generic form was introduced in 2004. It has been estimated that 13.7 million people in the United States have used OxyContin for nonmedical purposes in the year 2003 (the last year for which data was available to the authors) (G. B. Collins & Leak, 2008). Abusers often crush the time-release spheres in the capsule and inject the material into a vein. Other abusers simply chew the tablets, defeating the time-release coating on the spheres, or take larger-than-prescribed doses for the euphoric effects.

OxyContin was heavily marketed as having a low abuse potential by the company that introduced it, and only later was it revealed that they were quite aware of its abuse potential but did not discuss this with prescribing physicians, instead placing emphasis on its supposedly low abuse potential (Meier, 2003). Further, the pharmaceutical company that introduced it overlooked the fact that:

> While prescription-drug abusers may differ in their pharmaceutical choices, the dynamic of abuse shares a common theme: whatever a manufacturer's claims about a drug's "abuse liability," both hard core addicts and recreational users will quickly find ways to make a drug their own. (Meier, 2003, p. 89)

It has been estimated that OxyContin alone is involved in approximately half of the estimated 4 million episodes of nonprescribed narcotic analgesic abuse that takes place each year in the United States (Office of National Drug Control Policy, 2006). Indeed, there is evidence that the pharmacokinetics of this medication makes it especially attractive to drug abusers, which clouds the issue of whether it is a valuable drug in treating pain or not.

Buprenorphine

Buprenorphine has emerged as a drug of abuse. When administered sublingually, it is a valuable alternative to methadone maintenance as a treatment for opioid addiction. But *intravenously* administered buprenorphine has a significant abuse potential. This practice is not common in the United States at this time (Ling, Wesson, & Smith, 2005). It has been reported that this compound is abused either alone or in combination with diazepam, cyclizine, or temazepax.

Hydromorphone

Hydromorphone was introduced under the brand name of Dilaudid, although it has since been introduced in a generic form. Hydromorphone was intended for oral use and (in medical settings) for intravenous use. When used orally, it is used in tablet form in dosage levels of 1–4 mg. Illicit-drug abusers often crush the tablets and inject them, although the manufacturers do attempt to block this method of abuse by adding compounds to make this process difficult or impossible to achieve. This is one of the reasons why oral hydromorphone is usually abused by oral ingestion.

Fentanyl

Fentanyl has long been a popular drug of abuse because of its high potency. It is a prescription-only medication, which is often diverted to the illicit-drug market. Abusers have been known to smoke it, use it intranasally, or take transdermal patches, heat them, and inhale the fumes (S. B. Karch, 2009). Some abusers also take transdermal patches, poke holes in them, and consume the medication reservoir for use in any of the methods noted previously. However, because of its high potency, it is easy to overdose on fentanyl, possibly with fatal results.

Propoxyphene

Propoxyphene is a compound that was sold under a number of brand names in the last quarter of the 20th century. This compound has little potential to induce euphoria by itself, but it is often used concurrently with methadone, providing a feeling of euphoria from the combined effects of these compounds.

While this list is not all inclusive, it does underscore the abuse potential inherent in the use of all prescription narcotic analgesics.

Methods of Opiate Abuse

When opiates are abused, the preferred method of abuse depends on individuals' experience with the compound. These compounds might be taken orally, injected under the skin ("skin popping"), administered intravenously, smoked, or used intranasally (technically "insufflation"). Historically, the practice of smoking opium has not been common in the United States in the past half century, although it does continue in some quarters. However, the practice of smoking opium wastes a great deal of potential opium, and if supplies are limited (as they are in the United States), it is not a popular method of opioid abuse.

Some abusers take large doses of the opioid of choice, whereas others have been known to chew time-release capsules such as OxyContin, thus defeating the manufacturer's attempts to provide an even level of this compound in the blood for analgesia. Then there is the problem of heroin, which is abused in a variety of methods. The practices of insufflation and smoking heroin powder have become popular in the United States, fueled in part by the popular myth that you cannot become addicted to narcotics unless you *inject* drugs such as heroin into your body (Drummer & Odell, 2001; Greydanus & Patel, 2005; Gwinnell & Adamec, 2006; D. Smith, 2001). When heroin is used intranasally, the method of administration is very similar to that of cocaine when used through insufflation. The abuser will place the powder on a glass, then use a razor blade or knife edge to "dice" up the power until it is a fine, talcum-like powder, arrange it in a line on the glass, and then inhale it through a straw. In contrast to injected heroin, where the effects are felt almost instantly, it takes 10–15 minutes before inhaled heroin powder begins to take effect. Injected heroin provides an intense rush, followed by a gentle sense of euphoria, which is the desired effect, and frequently a severe itching of the skin, nausea, and vomiting[32] (Gwinnell & Adamec, 2006).

Heroin is well absorbed through the lungs when it is smoked, although the onset of its effects is slower than when it is injected. The effects of heroin when it is smoked begin in 10–15 minutes, in contrast to the estimated 8 seconds before injected heroin begins to

work (Gwinnell & Adamec, 2006). Smoking heroin is an ineffective method of delivery, with up to 80% of the available heroin being destroyed by the heat produced by the smoking process (Drummer & Odell, 2001). The level of inefficiency seen with smoked heroin is seen in the fact that blood levels are only about 50% as high as those when heroin is injected (Drummer & Odell, 2001). The practice of "chasing the dragon" is a variation on the process of smoking heroin. In this procedure, the abuser heats some heroin powder on a piece of aluminum foil, using a cigarette lighter or match as the heat source. The resulting fumes are then inhaled, avoiding the exposure to intravenous needles that might be contaminated by earlier abusers (S. B. Karch, 2009). Another variation of the practice of smoking heroin is seen when abusers intermix heroin with "crack" cocaine pellets. This combination is said to enhance the "high" induced by these chemicals, although possibly at the cost of exacerbating the respiratory depression seen when narcotics are abused.

The most concentrated blood levels of heroin are achieved when the abuser injects the compound into a vein. Sometimes the heroin addict will mix:

> heroin in the spoon with water, or glucose and water, in order to dissolve it. Lemon juice, citric acid or vitamin C may be added to aid dissolving. This cocktail is headed until it boils, drawn into the syringe through a piece of cotton wool or cigarette filter to remove impurities, and injected whilst still warm. (Booth, 1996, p. 14)

This method of abuse allows for the rapid introduction of concentrated heroin into the body, inducing an intense reaction, as noted elsewhere in this chapter. Although veins in the arm are often used, some abusers or addicts will use arteries in the groin or the neck, on the theory that this will allow the heroin to more rapidly reach the brain.

Sources of Illicit Narcotics

Pharmaceuticals, which are prized by illicit-drug addicts because of their known purity and potency, are obtained in a variety of ways. Currently, the available evidence would suggest that prescribed narcotic analgesics are the most commonly abused prescribed medication in New York City and are more commonly abused in that city than is heroin (Davis & Johnson, 2008). Davis and Johnson found that the majority of the 586 drug abusers in their study obtained medications from physicians. The authors discovered that methadone was the most commonly diverted substance, although other narcotic

---

[32]Sometimes called "the good sick" by heroin addicts.

analgesics such as OxyContin, Vicodin, or Percocet were also diverted or misused by abusers.

Sometimes the individual will "make a doctor"[33] or dentist for a prescription, or will arrange for a patient who receives medication for legitimate medical reasons to "divert" the medication to the illicit-drug market. Some opioid abusers have been known to befriend a person with a terminal illness in order to steal narcotics from the patient for their own use. Others have burglarized pharmacies or brazenly held up the pharmacy to demand narcotic analgesics, while "Internet" pharmacies have become a source of "prescribed" medications that are used for illicit purposes.

But these sources cannot supply the drug abuser with heroin, which is illegal in the United States. An elaborate distribution network has evolved to smuggle heroin into the United States, distribute it across the country, and from there get it to the individual abuser. In order to avoid conflict over territory, upper-level distributors agreed that the heroin abused west of the Mississippi River would be smuggled through Mexico, whereas the heroin abused east of the Mississippi would be smuggled into the United States from other sources.

At each level of the distribution process, the heroin powder is intermixed with adulterants, increasing the bulk (at the price of potency) and thus increasing profits for the distributor at that level of the distribution network. Eventually, the heroin reaches the level of the individual dealer, who sells the drug in small plastic packets (the condom is often used for this purpose) containing one dose of heroin. It has been estimated that the purity of heroin at this level is around 47%, although occasionally one will find a sample that is up to 85% pure being sold on the street level (O'Brien, 2008). The individual abuser will take this powder, mix it with water, heat the mixture, and then pour it into a hypodermic needle for injection into the body.

Health care professionals have been known to divert pharmaceuticals for their own use, although the strict controls over access and the use of narcotic analgesics makes this increasingly difficult. But the health care professional is more likely to have access to sterile needles and to follow appropriate injection procedures to avoid infection(s)[34] often associated with illicit drug injection. Further, health care professionals will rarely reuse an intravenous needle, even if they are abusing an opioid, whereas illicit-drug abusers frequently not only reuse needles, but also share them. This process exposes each abuser to all of the viral infections in the blood of the previous abuser(s), unless special precautions are used to sterilize the needle, precautions that intravenous drug abusers rarely take time to perform.

As noted earlier, illicit-narcotics abusers will often attempt to inject a tablet or capsule originally intended for oral use. These oral-administration vehicles contain compounds known as "fillers"[35] intended to give the capsule or tablet bulk, making it easier for the patient to handle them. These compounds are not intended for intravenous injection and are either destroyed by gastric juices or pass harmlessly through the gastrointestinal tract. Either the fillers or adulterants often mixed into illicit heroin then go on to form an emboli, or damage the vessel lining and thus contribute to the formation of a blood clot at the site of injection. Repeated exposure to such compounds can cause extensive scarring at the site of injection, forming the famous "tracks" associated with illicit opioid abuse/addiction.[36]

The Development of Tolerance

The mechanism through which tolerance to a narcotic analgesic develops is poorly understood (Kreek, 2008). It is known that tolerance to a narcotic will develop rapidly, and with continuous use the illicit-opioid abuser will develop significant tolerance to the analgesic, respiratory, and sedating effects of opioids. They also become tolerant to the rush or flash effect that is initially experienced when they begin intravenously administered opioids (Jaffe & Strain, 2005). However, they still experience the narcotic-induced sense of gentle euphoria that is by itself an incentive for continued opioid use (Jaffe & Strain, 2005). In spite of their growing tolerance to opioids, illicit-narcotics abusers never fully become tolerant to the meiotic and constipating effects induced by narcotic analgesics (Jaffe & Jaffe, 2004; Jaffe & Strain, 2005). Indeed, the chronic abuse of opioids may result in significant constipation problems for abusers, possibly to the point where they will form an intestinal blockage and require emergency surgery.

In their attempt to reachieve the rush experience, some abusers will increase their dosage level, possibly as much as 100-fold over an extended period of time in an attempt to overcome their tolerance to the opioid-induced rush (O'Brien, 2006). Such doses would be fatal

---

[33]See Glossary.

[34]Discussed in Chapter 36.

[35]See Glossary.

[36]Which IV drug abusers might attempt to hide through the use of strategically placed tattoos (Greydanus & Patel, 2005).

to an opiate-naive person, and it is not uncommon for opioid abusers/addicts to miscalculate their level of tolerance and accidentally overdose on narcotics. Schuckit (2008b) reported that approximately 50% of opioid abusers will experience at least one drug overdose. Other abusers will go through cycles of drug use until their tolerance is such that they can no longer afford the necessary drugs to induce euphoria and so then go through a period of withdrawal (usually with support from other illicit drugs, such as illicit benzodiazepines). Upon completion of the withdrawal cycle, they will restart the abuse of opiates again. Eventually, they reach the point where they no longer use drugs to achieve a high, but "just to maintain" their intoxicated state.

Addiction

Physical dependence on opioids can develop in a very short time, possibly after just a few days of continuous use (Ivanov et al., 2006; Stahl, 2008). This is the same process as "neuroadaptation" seen in patients being treated with narcotic analgesics and reflects the same biological mechanisms at work in the brain.

Scope of the Problem of Narcotic Abuse and Addiction

Only a fraction of those who *briefly* abuse opiates, perhaps only 1:3 to 1:4 people, will go on to become addicted to narcotics (O'Brien, 2006; Sommer, 2005).[37] This is clearly seen in the subpopulation of opioid abusers known as "chippers," who abuse opioids in response to social cues but have no trouble abstaining from narcotics when they wish to do so. However, very little is known about opioid chippers. Some of those who once were classified as a chipper go on to become addicted, some discontinue the use of these compounds, and still others remain a chipper.

Males tend to predominate the opioid addiction problem by a ratio of about 3:1 (Sadock & Sadock, 2007). Given the estimate of 1 million people with a narcotic use disorder in the United States, this would mean that approximately 750,000 are male and 250,000 are female. It has been estimated that there are just under 16 million opioid abusers around the world, of whom an estimated 1.4–4 million live in North America[38] (Brust, 2004; United Nations, 2008). Another 3.8 million are thought to live in

Europe, 8.4 million in Asia, and approximately 1 million in Africa (United Nations, 2008).

Prescription narcotic analgesics have become a significant part of the narcotic use disorders. In the United States, the abuse of prescription narcotics appears to be more common than is heroin addiction (Davis & Johnson, 2008; Hasemyer, 2006). An estimated 2.4 million people over the age of 12 start to abuse prescribed narcotic analgesics each year in this country (National Survey on Drug Use and Health, 2006). Admittedly, not all of those who begin to abuse prescription narcotics will become dependent on them, as evidenced by the fact that whereas an estimated 31.8 million people over the age of 12 have abused a narcotic analgesic at some point in their lives (National Survey on Drug Use and Health, 2006), only a small percentage have become addicted to them.

When the term *opiate use disorders* is used, it is important to keep in mind that there are various subsets of narcotics abusers/addicts. Some abusers are simply curious about these compounds, use them for a limited time, and then abstain from further narcotics abuse. Some individuals with an opiate use disorder are medical patients who became addicted to narcotic analgesics after prolonged use of these compounds to treat an accident or the effects of illness.[39] These individuals may attempt to avoid being identified as being dependent on narcotics through the continued sanctioned use of a prescribed medication. It is often difficult to separate drug-seeking patients from those with a legitimate need for pain relief, especially in a patient who has a physical illness.

Finally, there are those individuals with an opioid use disorder who fit the stereotypical picture of a narcotics addict. But these individuals will intermix the abuse of illicit narcotics with prescribed medication (s). It is not uncommon for such patients to visit different physicians or hospital emergency rooms to obtain multiple prescriptions for a desired medication(s). Such abusers will often study medical textbooks to be able to simulate symptoms of a disorder virtually guaranteed to provide them with a prescription for a narcotic analgesic. It has even been known for some individuals to have a tattoo that simulates the scar of a surgical procedure, especially a back surgery, to justify a prescription for narcotic analgesics from a new physician. If stopped by the police, they are able to

---

[37]However, because it is not possible to identify *who* will become addicted, the abuse of the narcotic analgesics is not recommended.

[38]Which the United Nations defines as Canada, the United States, and Mexico.

[39]Known as an *iatrogenic* addiction. As noted in the section devoted to the medical uses of narcotic analgesics, this is rare. Still, it does happen.

produce a prescription bottle with their name on it, affirming that there is a legitimate need for them to use that medication.

These patients know the physician's schedule and know exactly when to come to the office or the emergency room with exaggerated signs of physical distress. They do so with the hope of obtaining a prescription from the overworked physician who is looking forward to the end of the shift/day. Such medical emergencies are often seen on Fridays, at 4 p.m., for example, and the narcotics addict hopes that the physician will just write out a prescription rather than spend time arguing with the patient. Both claims of physician abandonment, often intermixed with threats, and exaggerated complaints of physical illness are used to obtain desired prescriptions. These behaviors, plus reports that the patient is "allergic" to less powerful narcotic analgesics such as tramadol, or that these compounds do not work for the patient, should alert the physician to the possibility of drug-seeking behaviors. Still, because it is the end of the shift, there is a small mountain of paperwork waiting to be filled out, and the physician wants to go home, it is not uncommon for the physician to write out a prescription just to get the patient to leave.

The diversion of prescribed narcotic analgesics has become a major problem in recent years. The individual's motivation for abusing prescribed narcotic analgesics, especially methadone, ranges from a desire to obtain narcotic-induced euphoria to attempts to "taper" themselves from narcotic analgesics using illicit compounds (Davis & Johnson, 2008). Other people were using the opioids to self-medicate pain, according to the authors. Seventy-two percent of the subjects in their study used methadone, and 65% sold it. Indeed, the authors found that methadone abuse was more common than that of OxyContin, Vicodin, or Percocet. The findings of this study underscore the problem of diversion of prescribed narcotic analgesics.

All of these factors make it difficult to estimate the scope of the narcotics use disorders in the United States. Still, it has been suggested that there are approximately 800,000 to 1 million people in the United States who are physically dependent on narcotics at this time (Hasemyer, 2006; O'Brien; 2008; Tinsley, 2005). This figure should be accepted as a low estimate, in the opinion of the author of this text.

Scope of Illicit Heroin Abuse in the United States

There are those who *abuse* heroin, some of whom *go on to become addicted* to this compound, and those who are *currently addicted* to this compound. Heroin addiction does not develop instantly, but will usually require approximately 2 years between the initiation of heroin use and the time that the individual has become physically dependent on it. Each year in the United States approximately 146,000 people try heroin (Jaffe & Anthony, 2005). Approximately 3 million people in this country are thought to have used heroin at least once, and between 600,000 and 800,000 people in the United States are addicted to it (Jaffe & Strain, 2005).

In the late 1990s heroin use was viewed as a sign of rebellion, possibly reaching its pinnacle with the rise of the "heroin chic" culture during that era (Jonnes, 2002). This contributed to a change in heroin abuse patterns in that decade: In 1988 the average age of the individual's first heroin use was 27, but by the mid-1990s this had dropped to the age of 19 (Hopfer, Mikulich, & Crowley, 2000). Adolescents were found to make up just under 22% of those who admitted to heroin abuse, a trend fueled by the availability of low price, high-potency heroin and its status as a sign of rebellion (Hopfer et al., 2000).[40]

Each year in just the United States alone, heroin abusers are thought to consume between 13 and 18 metric *tons* of heroin (Office of National Drug Control Policy, 2006). Although this is a staggering figure, it is not the entirety of the heroin use problem in the United States. Heroin abusers do not just limit their opioid use to heroin. Rather, they intermix their abuse of heroin with the use of pharmaceuticals diverted to the illicit drug market, other opioids that were prescribed to them for what appeared to be legitimate medical reasons, and medications stolen from legitimate patients for their use, and the heroin that they can obtain from illicit sources. All of these different factors contribute to problems in estimating the scope of heroin abuse and addiction in the United States at this time.

Complications Induced by Opiate Abuse or Addiction

Collectively, the abuse of opioid analgesics is so widespread and so dangerous that in many states there are more fatal overdoses involving this class of medications than deaths from motor vehicle accidents ("Increase in Fatal Poisonings Involving," 2009). The complications of chronic opiate abuse fall into two categories: (a) those that

---

[40]In contrast to the typical heroin sample of the 1960s, which was perhaps 4% heroin and the rest fillers and adulterants, O'Brien (2008) noted that currently a heroin addict can expect to find illicit heroin to be around 45% heroin, and noted that some samples have been up to 85% pure heroin.

are exaggerations of the complications seen when these compounds are seen in medical practice and (b) those that are forced on the individual by the lifestyle of the opioid-dependent person.

Addiction to narcotics exposes the individual to a significant threat of premature death, the most common causes of which are accidental overdose and cardiopulmonary failure (Fiellin, 2008; Smyth, Hoffman, Fan, & Hser, 2007). This is illustrated by the findings of the team of Smyth et al., who reported the results of a longitudinal study of 581 heroin addicts who originally lived in California. Thirty-three years after the subjects were initially admitted to treatment, the authors found that 48.5% of the original sample pool had died. The leading causes of death in the sample were overdose (17%), chronic liver disease (15%), cardiovascular disorders (12%), cancer (11%), accidents (8%), and homicide (7%). The typical heroin addict lost approximately 18.3 years[41] of potential life either directly or indirectly as a result of their addiction (Smyth et al., 2007). Other potential causes of death for opiate abusers or addicts include cerebral infarction and the formation of a thrombosis that can result in a stroke (Ricaurte, Langston, & McCann, 2008).

Narcotic Withdrawal Syndrome

The narcotic withdrawal syndrome experienced by opiate abusers or addicts is simply the opioid discontinuance syndrome observed when patients use these medications under a physician's supervision. The narcotic withdrawal syndrome is on a possibly more intense scale than the discontinuance syndrome seen in normal medical practice because abusers or addicts use higher doses of opiates for longer periods of time than is the norm in medical practice. It should be noted, however, that in spite of common claims by those who abuse opioids, the narcotic withdrawal syndrome is only rarely a life-threatening condition[42] (Fadem, 2009). In reality, withdrawal distress has been compared to a severe case of influenza (Kosten & O'Connor, 2003; Tomb, 2008). There are two stages to the opioid withdrawal syndrome: (a) the stage of *acute* withdrawal and (b) the stage of *extended* withdrawal. Both of these stages are influenced by such factors as (a) the specific compound(s) being abused,[43] (b) the length of time that these compounds have been abused, (c) the speed at which the withdrawal processes progresses, and (c) the individual's cognitive "set" (Jaffe & Jaffe, 2004; Kosten & O'Connor, 2003). Health care professionals might use the Clinical Institute Narcotics Assessment (CINA) to obtain an objective assessment tool for the withdrawal process (Mee-Lee & Gastfriend, 2008).

Obviously, the specific compound being abused will influence the withdrawal process. Heroin withdrawal symptoms, for example, peak 36–72 hours after the individual's last dose and last for 7–10 days. In contrast to this, the withdrawal symptoms from methadone peak 4–6 days after the last dose and continue for 14–21 days (E. D. Collins & Kleber, 2004; Kosten & O'Connor, 2003; Kreek, 2008). The withdrawal patterns for other opioids are similar, although there might be some variation depending on the half-life of the compound(s) being abused and thus the duration of the acute phase of the withdrawal syndrome.

The speed of the opioid withdrawal process is another factor that influences the symptoms experienced and their duration. Opioid-dependent people who are placed on a methadone "taper" will experience the withdrawal symptoms over a prolonged period of time, as their medication is slowly reduced from day to day. However, these withdrawal symptoms will be less intense than if they just stopped abusing drugs ("cold turkey"). But the withdrawal distress would be of shorter duration in the latter case. Thus physicians must balance the individual's discomfort with the speed of the withdrawal process.

The individual's cognitive "set" also influences the withdrawal process and the individual's perception of it. This reflects such factors as their knowledge, attention, motivation, and degree of suggestibility. The influence of the individual's cognitive "set" might be seen in extreme cases, where the individual develops an almost phobic-like fear of withdrawal, contributing to the urge to continue to abuse opioids (E. D. Collins & Kleber, 2004; Kenny, Chen, Kitamura, Marku, & Koob, 2006). Another example is seen in the case of individuals forced to go through the opioid withdrawal process because of incarceration, for example. These individuals might have no personal investment in the success of the withdrawal process and thus are motivated to respond to every symptom as if it were major trauma being inflicted on them. In contrast to this,

---

[41]If you assume that average addicts would have lived 80 years if they were not addicted to heroin, this means that typical heroin addicts lose about 22% of their estimated lifetime because of their addiction to heroin.

[42]All cases of drug withdrawal should be assessed and treated by a physician to ensure proper medical care during this process.

---

[43]Including the half-life of each compound being abused.

the highly motivated client might be eased through the withdrawal process through the use of hypnotic suggestion (L. B. Erlich, 2001).

A complicating factor during the opiate withdrawal process is that the individual becomes more sensitive to pain as a result of increased muscle activity and the stimulation of the sympathetic nervous system (Gunderson & Stimmel, 2004; Kreek, 2008).[44] Further, the opioid withdrawal process induces a sense of "craving" for additional opioids as well as anxiety, both emotional states that lower people's pain threshold and increase their sensitivity to pain. In the section to follow, we will examine the acute withdrawal process more closely.

Acute Opioid Withdrawal for the Addicted Person

One of the more pronounced symptoms experienced by the individual going through the opioid withdrawal process is intense "craving" for more narcotics. Other symptoms include tearing of the eyes, runny nose, repeated yawning,[45] sweating, restless sleep, dilated pupils, anxiety, anorexia, irritability, insomnia, weakness, abdominal pain, nausea, vomiting, gastrointestinal upset, chills, diarrhea, muscle spasms, and in males possible ejaculation (Brust, 2004; E. D. Collins & Kleber, 2004; Gunderson Stimmel, 2004; Kreek, 2008). It has been suggested that 600–800 mg of ibuprofen every 4–6 hours can provide significant relief from the muscle pain experienced by many patients during this phase of withdrawal (E. D. Collins & Kleber, 2004). However, the etiology of the pain must first be identified to avoid the danger of not treating a real medical problem because it was assumed to be a withdrawal manifestation (Gunderson & Stimmel, 2004).

Whereas constipation is a problem for the person taking narcotics, during the withdrawal process the individual might experience diarrhea as the gastrointestinal tract returns to a normal self-regulating state. On very rare occasions, the opioid withdrawal process can cause seizures or exacerbate a preexisting seizure disorder (E. D. Collins & Kleber, 2004; Gutstein & Akil, 2006; Kreek, 2008). One exception to this rule is when the person abuses the narcotic meperidine, which is known to lower the patient's seizure threshold. Anxiety is common

during opioid withdrawal and might be so intense as to serve as a relapse trigger (E. D. Collins & Kleber, 2004). It has been recommended that rather than a benzodiazepine, the compound Seroquel® (quetiapine fumarate) be used to control withdrawal-induced anxiety (Winegarden, 2001).

A Cautionary Note   Many opiate-dependent people will emphasize their physical distress during the withdrawal process, in the hopes of obtaining drugs to limit their distress and possibly obtain a substitute for the unavailable opioid. Such displays are often quite dramatic, but are hardly realistic for the most part. Mild to moderate opioid withdrawal is, although uncomfortable, rarely a medical emergency in healthy adults[46] (Baron et al., 2009). The subjective experience has been compared to a bad case of influenza and will abate in the healthy individual even without medical intervention.

Extended Opioid Withdrawal Symptoms

During this phase, which might last for several months in some individuals, the individual might experience symptoms such as fatigue, heart palpitations, "urges" to return to opioid use, and a general feeling of restlessness (Jaffe & Strain, 2006). Some people also report concentration problems that might last 3–6 months after their last use of narcotics. These feelings become less intense over time, and the individual's level of function returns to normal over a period of weeks to months.

Organ Damage

Some patients who experience extreme pain, such as that seen in some forms of cancer, for example, receive massive doses of narcotic analgesics for extended periods of time but fail to demonstrate any sign of drug-induced organ damage (Ricaurte et al., 2008). For example the famed surgeon William Halsted was addicted to morphine for 50 years without suffering apparent physical harm (Brust, 2004). However, these are cases where the person is using pharmaceutical-quality narcotic analgesics and not the "street" drugs commonly abused by illicit-drug abusers. These compounds are of questionable purity as they are usually intermixed with compounds not intended for injection.

---

[44]A medical examination will reveal whether the reported withdrawal distress is caused or exacerbated by a concurrent medical condition that needs treatment (Gunderson & Stimmel, 2004).

[45]A process that, according to Newberg and Walkman (2009), reflects the brain's efforts to "reset" the cognitive pathways so that they can adjust to the change in the level of neurotransmitters within the opioid neurotransmitter system.

---

[46]Assuming they were abusing *only* narcotics and have not overdosed on an opioid or combination of drugs. The latter situation is a medical emergency that requires immediate intervention by a trained medical team (O'Brien, 2001; Sadock & Sadock, 2007; Work Group on Substance Use Disorders, 2007; Zevin & Benowitz, 2007).

There is little data on the health consequences of the abuse of other opioids beyond heroin.

Common health complications seen in heroin abusers include strokes, cerebral vasospasm, infectious endocarditis, botulism, tetanus, peptic ulcer disease, liver failure, disorders of the body's ability to form blood clots, malignant hypertension, nephropathy pulmonary edema, and uremia (Brust, 2004; Greydanus & Patel, 2005; S. B. Karch, 2009). Given the fact that heroin has been used as a pharmaceutical in many countries for more than a century without evidence of organ damage, it must be assumed that these complications of heroin abuse in the United States are caused either by adulterants mixed in with the heroin or by the conditions under which it is abused.

The chronic abuse of illicit narcotics has also been found to reduce the effectiveness of the immune system, although again the exact mechanism for this disorder is not understood at this time (S. B. Karch, 2009). Intravenous opioid addicts are at increased risk for rhabdomyolysis, but it is not clear whether this is because of the effects of the narcotics or one or more adulterants mixed in with illicit narcotics (Karch, 2009). For reasons that are not clear at this time, oxycodone abusers appear to be vulnerable to developing an autoimmune disorder that attacks the kidneys, causing significant damage to these vital organs (P. Hill, Dwyer, Kay, & Murphy, 2002).

The recreational abuse of opioids appears to induce the shrinkage of the brain's reward system. This appears to reflect an adaptive response by the brain to the constant presence of an opioid such as heroin and may reflect the biological basis for tolerance to the euphoric effects of such compounds. With extended abstinence, this effect appears to reverse itself. The practice of smoking heroin has been identified as causing a progressive spongiform leukoencephalophy[47] in rare cases (Zevin & Benowitz, 2007). It is not known whether this effect is induced by the heroin itself or by one of the adulterants mixed into the illicit heroin before sale (Ropper & Brown, 2005; Schuckit, 2008b). There was an outbreak of heroin-induced progressive spongiform leukoencephalophy in the Netherlands in the 1990s, a condition that is rarely encountered in the United States. Intravenous opioid abuse also has been seen to induce damage to peripheral nerves, because the individual rests for extended periods of time in the same position, cutting off the blood flow to the affected nerves. Also, nerves near the injection site might be damaged by the adulterants mixed with the illicit drug being injected (Ropper & Brown, 2005).

Cotton Fever

As noted earlier, heroin addicts will attempt to "purify" the heroin about to be injected by pouring it through wads of cotton or cigarette filters. During times of hardship, some abusers will attempt to use the residual heroin found in these "filters" and in the process will inject microscopic cotton particles as well as the impurities that had originally been filtered out. This will induce a condition known as pulmonary arteritis[48] (which is called "cotton fever" by addicts).

Overdose of Illicit Narcotics[49]

Ropper and Brown (2005) identified four mechanisms by which the abuser might overdose: (a) a suicide attempt, (b) the use of substitute or contaminated illicit drugs, (c) unusual sensitivity on the part of the individual to the drug(s) being abused, and (d) errors in calculating the proper dosage. It has been estimated that at least 50% of illicit-heroin users will overdose at least once, possibly with fatal results. Indeed, death may result so quickly that abusers are found with the needle still in their arm. It is thought that death is the result of respiratory depression (Gutstein & Akil, 2006). An unknown but significant number of people overdose on prescription narcotic analgesics diverted to the illicit-drug market as well (Dunn et al., 2010).

Some of the symptoms of an opioid overdose include reduced level of consciousness, pinpoint pupils, cerebral edema, and respiratory depression (Drummer & Odell, 2001; Schuckit, 2006a). Even if the individual should survive the overdose attempt, there might be residual effects such as partial paralysis or blindness, or peripheral neuropathies, induced by the overdose (Dilts & Dilts, 2005). The onset of specific overdose symptoms is dependent on the compound(s) ingested or injected. For example, if methadone were the compound ingested, the first symptoms might not manifest for up to 3.2 *hours* after the overdose, and respiratory depression might require up to 8 hours to begin to appear (Lovecchio et al., 2007). To further complicate matters, the practice of polydrug abuse and the effects of various adulterants in the drug(s) being abused often cloud the clinical presentation of an overdose. For example, there is evidence that the concurrent use of

---

[47]Similar to "mad cow" disease.

[48]See Glossary.

[49]*Any* real or suspected case of a drug overdose should be assessed and treated by a physician.

marijuana and heroin might increase the individual's risk of a narcotics overdose through an unknown mechanism (Drummer & Odell, 2001). The practice of using amphetamines or cocaine might hide the symptoms of the overdose until it is too late to seek medical attention, because the stimulants might mask the early symptoms of an opioid overdose.

Even in the best-equipped hospital, an opioid overdose can be fatal. The current treatment of choice for an opioid overdose is a combination of respiratory and cardiac support and the intravenous administration of *Narcan®* (naloxone hydrochloride) (Ropper & Brown, 2005). This compound binds at the opioid receptor sites, blocking the opioid molecules from reaching them. If administered in time, this will reverse the narcotics overdose. However, the therapeutic half-life of Narcan® is only 60–90 minutes, and several doses might be necessary before the patient fully recovers from the overdose. In the case of long-acting narcotic analgesics such as methadone, the individual might require Narcan® infusions for days to avoid long-term overdose effects. There is the additional danger of side effects of naloxone hydrochloride. These side effects will need to be assessed by the attending physician, and if severe enough to warrant intervention will need to be addressed by the attending health care professionals as well.

Chapter Summary

The opioids have been effectively used for thousands of years to treat pain. After alcohol, one could argue that opium is the second-oldest drug used by humans, with a known history going back thousand of years prior to the invention of writing. With the onset of the chemical revolution of the 18th and 19th centuries, chemists began to isolate the active compounds found in opium, producing a family of compounds that were found to be useful in controlling severe pain, severe cough, and severe diarrhea. But it was also discovered that the compounds isolated from opium and their chemical cousins presented the user with a significant abuse potential as well as the potential for addiction.

With the advent of semisynthetic and synthetic opioids, chemists attempted to find a compound that would retain the analgesic potential of morphine, which has emerged as the gold standard for analgesia, without the negative effects associated with the use of opioids. Unfortunately, this search has failed to yield such a compound, although it has provided a wide range of narcotic analgesics that have the potential to be abused and to induce addiction. These compounds have become the subject of great controversy both in the field of medicine and between members of the general public.

CHAPTER 12
Abuse of and Addiction to Hallucinogens

Introduction

To older people the term *hallucinogen* is associated with the "Summer of Love"[1] in San Francisco, when arguably the "psychedelic" era of the 1960s reached its pinnacle (Traub, 2009). In the time since then, these compounds have waxed and waned in popularity as drugs of abuse. Although they are perhaps less commonly abused now than they were in decades past, hallucinogenic compounds are still occasionally either intentionally or unintentionally ingested by illicit-drug users. Some of these compounds are used to bolster the apparent effect of low-quality marijuana, for example, to make users think they acquired high-potency cannabis. Some of the hallucinogens are also often sold under the guise of other compounds. As will be discussed in Chapter 37, in the world of illicit drugs it is a case of "let the buyer beware."

In the last century, scientists have concluded that there are thousands of different species of plants that contain compounds that might, if smoked or ingested, alter the user's state of consciousness. The tobacco plant, which is discussed in Chapter 16, is one such plant, although it is rarely thought of in this light. Some of the hallucinogenic compounds that were discovered by early humans have been used in religious ceremonies, healing rituals, and for predicting the future (Metzner, 2005; Sessa, 2005; Traub, 2009). One example is peyote, which anthropologists believe has been used for its hallucinogenic effects for at least 4000 years (Nichols, 2006; Traub, 2009). A range of natural and synthetic hallucinogenic compounds have been identified since then, and certain religious groups continue to use mushrooms that contain hallucinogenic psilocybin as part of their ceremony.

Currently, scientists are actively investigating whether at least some of the known hallucinogenic compounds might have some medicinal value (D. J. Brown, 2007; Horgan, 2005; S. B. Karch, 2009). The U.S. Army experimented with LSD (discussed later) as a possible chemical warfare agent, going so far as to administer doses of this compound to soldiers without their knowledge or consent (Talty, 2003). The Central Intelligence Agency (CIA) is known to have experimented with them as possible agents to aid interrogation.

---

[1] 1968 for those who are just a little too young to remember this year from personal experience.

During this same period, some individuals advocated their use as a way to explore alternative realities or gain self-knowledge, a trend that has continued until the present day (Metzner, 2002). As a result of this trend, they became drugs of abuse in the 1960s and have continued to be abused for their hallucinogenic effects since then. In this chapter, some of the most popular hallucinogenic compounds will be examined.

A Short History of Hallucinogens

Over the years chemists have isolated approximately 100 different hallucinogenic compounds that are found in various plants or mushrooms.[2] Some of these compounds have been isolated and studied by scientists. Psilocybin is an example of one such compound. Psilocybin is in certain mushrooms found in the southwestern United States and the northern regions of Mexico, and it has been extensively studied. However there are a large number of other natural hallucinogenic compounds that have never been isolated or studied, and much remains to be discovered about these chemicals and their effects on a user (Glennon, 2004). Experimental pharmacologists have also developed synthetic compounds with hallucinogenic effects, one of which, phencyclidine (PCP),[3] has been a part of the drug abuse problem in the United States since shortly after it was developed.

One family of compounds that has been subjected to intense scientific scrutiny are those chemicals produced by the ergot fungus, which grows on various forms of grain. Some compounds produced by the ergot fungus have been found to induce such severe vasoconstriction that the entire limb has been known to auto-amputate[4] or cause the individual to die of gangrene (Walton, 2002). Historians believe that ergot fungus induced a widespread illness in the Aquitaine province of France around the year 1000 CE,[5] causing the death of at least 40,000 people who consumed bread made from contaminated grain during the epidemic that took place in France at that time (Walton, 2002).

Because these compounds were so potent, scientists tried to isolate them to see whether they might have medicinal value. In 1943, during a clinical research project exploring the possible application of a compound obtained from the rye ergot fungus *Claviceps pirpurea,* a scientist named Albert Hoffman accidently ingested a small amount of the fungus. The intention was to isolate a compound that might be used to treat headaches, but Hoffman began to experience hallucinations and visual perceptual distortions, which he correctly attributed to a compound produced by the strain of *Claviceps pirpurea* that he had been working on. The next day, after recovering from the effects of the first unintentional exposure, he ingested a small amount of the fungus and again experienced the same effects. His experiences sparked research to isolate the compound responsible for these effects, eventually yielding lysergic acid diethylamide-25 (LSD-25, or simply, LSD) as the causal agent.

Following World War II, there was a great deal of scientific interest in the effects of various hallucinogenics, sparked in part by the similarities between those effects and the symptoms of various forms of mental illness. During the 1950s, scientists coined the term *psychedelics* or *hallucinogenics* to identify this class of compounds. They were the focus both of scientific investigation into the nature of schizophrenia and also of the military as possible weapons of war. This latter area of investigation is perhaps most clearly demonstrated by the Army's administration of LSD to unsuspecting service personnel in the 1960s to observe its effects on the soldiers (O'Meara, 2009). Such a potent compound also became the focus of informal experiments by drug abusers in the 1960s and early 1970s as a way toliberate the mind from the shackles of conventional thought. The most popular of these compounds, LSD and later PCP, were classified as Schedule I controlled substances by the

---

[2]Although at first glance this statement might seem at conflict with the statement in the introduction that "thousands" of plant species contain hallucinogenic compounds, it is important to keep in mind that the same compound might be found in a number of different plants.

[3]Discussed later in this chapter.

[4]See Glossary, under the term *auto-amputation.*

[5]Or *Common Era.* This term replaces the older term *AD.*

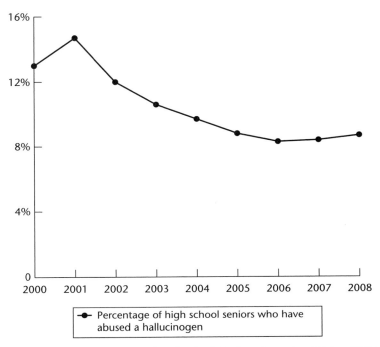

FIGURE 12-1 Percentage of High School Students Reporting Lifetime LSD USE: 1999–2007
Source: Johnston, L.D., O'Malley, P.M., Backman, J.G., & Schulenberg, J.E. (2010). Monitoring The Future: National Results on Adolescent Drug Use. Bethesda, MD: National Institute on Drug Abuse.

Drug Enforcement Administration.[6] However, this did not prevent these compounds from becoming popular drugs of abuse in the last four decades of the 20th century.

Abuse of hallucinogens appears to go through cycles. For example, the abuse of LSD reached a low point in the late 1970s, then gradually increased until it peaked in 1996 and started to decline in prevalence after that time (Markel, 2000). This pattern is reflected in the fact that 12% of high school seniors admitted to the use of LSD at least once in 2000, whereas only 8% admitted to using this compound in 2000 and just over 3% admitted to its use at least once in 2006 (L. D. Johnston et al., 2008). The reported levels of LSD abuse by high school seniors, those who are most likely to abuse this compound, is reviewed in Figure 12-1.

The compound PCP deserves special mention. It was originally developed as the first of a new class of anesthetic compounds that would cause the patient to dissociate during surgery (Mozayani, 2009). As is true with other therapeutic agents, PCP was also found to be a viable drug of abuse, although its popularity appears to have peaked in the middle 1990s and since then its

abuse has been declining. It is still occasionally abused in its own right, especially in the larger cities on the East and West coasts (Drummer & Odell, 2001). PCP is also a popular adulterant mixed in with (or sold as) other compounds. A recent trend has been for abusers to mix PCP with formaldehyde and methanol before smoking this mixture, often calling this combination of chemicals "dope dip" or "dip" (Mendyk & Fields, 2002).

Another compound, MDMA,[7] emerged as a major drug of abuse in the last quarter of the 20th century and has remained a popular drug of abuse ever since. Both MDMA and PCP will be discussed later in this chapter.

Scope of the Problem

In the United States, it was estimated that approximately 23 million people over the age of 12 years had ever used LSD, 6.6 million people in the same age bracket had ever used PCP, and 12 million people had ever used MDMA (National Survey on Drug Use and Health, 2008). However, of this number, fewer than 700,000 were thought to have used LSD in the year

[6]See Appendix 4.

[7]Which is short for N, alpha-dimethyl-1,3-benzodioxole-t-ethanamine.

preceding the study, fewer than 200,000 people were thought to have used PCP, and 2.1 million had used MDMA (National Survey on Drug Use and Health, 2008). However, most of these individuals were casual users, possibly using it only out of curiosity, and there are only an estimated 450,000 regular users of MDMA in the United States (Lawton, 2009).

These numbers suggest that for the most part the abuse of hallucinogens is declining in the United States. Still, it was estimated that 943,000 persons over the age of 12 abused a hallucinogenic compound for the first time in the year 2007 (National Survey on Drug Use and Health, 2008). An exception to the general decline in hallucinogen abuse is *Salvia divinorum,* a compound that has exploded onto the drug scene in the United States. It is thought that 1.8 million people over the age of 12 years had ever abused this substance, with 750,000 doing so in the year preceding the National Survey on Drug Use and Health (2008).

Pharmacology of the Hallucinogens

Surprisingly, the effects of these compounds have not been studied in depth (Glennon, 2008). As a class, the hallucinogens exert their effects on the serotonin neurotransmitter receptor system in the brain, especially the serotonin 2a receptor site. The effects of a given hallucinogen are dependent on dose, the specific compound used, and the route of administration (M. Weiss, 2007). The general effect of hallucinogens is to alter the delicate balance of neurotransmitters in the brain, thus producing their effects.[8]

Although compounds such as dopamine and serotonin are viewed as neurotransmitters, it has been suggested that they might also be viewed as *neuromodulators,* shifting the activity of neurons from one state to another. Subjectively, the experience of these neural activity shifts is reflected in such activities as concentration on a specific task, the euphoria experienced in a new love relationship, or the amnesia of sleep (Hobson, 2001). Disorders of this neurological balance would then cause various abnormal brain states, such as those induced by the hallucinogens (Hobson, 2001). By altering the balance of neurotransmitters in the brain, it is

possible to change the individual's subjective experience of consciousness.

The commonly abused hallucinogens are divided into two major groups (Glennon, 2008): (a) the phenylalkylamines (mescaline and MDMA fall into this class of compounds), and (b) the indolealkyamines (which includes psilocybin and DMT). LSD belongs to a subgroup of the indolealkyamines known as the *lstergamides* (Glennon, 2008). There are also atypical hallucinogens, which includes ibogaine. This latter group is of minor interest to drug abusers and will not be discussed further in this text. The mechanism through which these compounds alter the normal balance of neurotransmitters is still being explored. Research evidence, for example, would suggest that LSD, like most of the other hallucinogenic compounds, acts as an agonist to the 5-HT serotonin receptor site, and the effects of this compound are blocked by experimental 5-HT serotonin receptor site antagonists (Drummer & Odell, 2001; Glennon, 2004).

In spite of their classification as *hallucinogens,* these compounds do not produce frank hallucinations except at very high doses[9] (R. T. Jones, 2005). At the doses normally used by drug abusers in the United States, these compounds induce perceptual distortions (R. T. Jones, 2005; Tacke & Ebert, 2005). Further, abusers tend to adjust their intake of the compound being abused to produce just the effects that they desire, but at the usual dosage level being abused frank hallucinations are rare and the abuser will experience perceptual distortions more than hallucinations (Schuckit, 2006a).

It is common for hallucinogen abusers to believe they have achieved a new insight into reality as a result of their abuse of a given compound. These perceptions do not usually prove to be of value and are usually recognized by the abuser as being drug induced. Because LSD is the prototypical hallucinogen and has been best studied, this chapter will focus on LSD first and focus on other compounds only as needed.

Methods of Abuse

Hallucinogens might be ingested orally, smoked, or injected, although the latter method of abuse is rather rare and will not be discussed again in this chapter (Weaver & Schnoll, 2008). The exact method of abuse depends on the specific compound being abused. For example, LSD is usually ingested orally, whereas PCP

---

[8]The truth of this statement is easily proven by the experience of people who suffer from a high fever during illness, or diabetic patients whose blood sugar levels fall to dangerously low levels. Each group of patients reports distorted perceptions of reality and behave in abnormal ways.

---

[9]To avoid confusion, these compounds will continue to be referred to as *hallucinogens.*

(discussed later in this chapter) can be ingested orally, injected, or smoked.

The Pharmacology of LSD

Although LSD has been subjected to intense scientific scrutiny, there is still much to be discovered about how this compound affects the brain (Sadock & Sadock, 2007). LSD has been estimated to be between 100 and 1000 times as potent as natural hallucinogens such as psilocybin and peyote, and perhaps 3000 times as potent as mescaline (O'Brien, 2006). But it is also thought to be weaker than the synthetic hallucinogen DOM/STP (Schuckit, 2006a).

Abusers usually ingest LSD orally, although it can be administered intranasally, intravenously, or by inhalation (Klein & Kramer, 2004; Tacke & Ebert, 2005). Casual abusers might find that a dose of 50 micrograms will cause the desired effects, although the classic LSD "trip" usually requires at least twice that dose. Current illicit LSD samples are usually lower than those sold in the 1960s and 1970s, possibly to make the effects less frightening and more acceptable to the first-time abuser. Experienced users will thus use two or three typical doses in order to achieve the desired effects.

The LSD molecule is water soluble, making it possible for it to be both rapidly and completely absorbed from the gastrointestinal tract when it is ingested (Tacke & Ebert, 2005). Once in the circulation, LSD is distributed to all blood-rich organs in the body, with one result being that only a small percentage of the original dose is thought to reach the brain (Tacke & Ebert, 2005). The chemical structure is very similar to that of the neurotransmitter serotonin, and in the brain LSD appears to function as a serotonin agonist (A. J. Jenkins, 2007; Klein & Kramer, 2004). It is thought to bind most strongly at the 5-HT2a receptor site, although other binding sites might be discovered in the future (Glennon, 2004).

The highest brain LSD concentrations are found in the regions associated with vision, the limbic system, and the reticular activating system (RAS).[10] In retrospect this should not be surprising, because these regions of the brain are involved in the process of interpreting, and the emotional response to, external reality. Experimental evidence would suggest that LSD and similar agents alter the normal function of serotonin in the dorsal midbrain raphe region of the brain (Hobson, 2001; A. J. Jenkins, 2007). By binding at the

5-HT2a receptor sites in this region of the brain, LSD is able to induce the activation of acetylcholine-based neurons most active in the suppression of rapid eye movement (REM) sleep during the waking state. This allows those neurons to then become active during the waking state, allowing perceptional and emotional changes normally seen only during sleep to slip over into the waking state, inducing perceptual distortions and emotions characteristic of the LSD experience (Hobson, 2001; A. J. Jenkins, 2007).

Tolerance to LSD's effects develops rapidly, often after just 2–4 days of continuous use (Commission on Adolescent Substance and Alcohol Abuse, 2005; R. T. Jones, 2005). After tolerance develops, abusers must wait for 2–4 days for the tolerance to abate before they can achieve the same effects again (R. T. Jones, 2005). Because cross-tolerance between hallucinogens is common, the abuser must alternate between periods of active hallucinogen abuse and periods of abstinence to achieve the desired effects. There is no known withdrawal syndrome from LSD (Fadem, 2009).

Scientists have yet to determine the lethal dose of LSD, making it perhaps the safest compound known to modern medicine (Erickson, 2007; Pechnick & Ungerleider, 2004).[11] Death for LSD abusers is rare and usually involves accidental death possibly caused by the perceptual distortions induced by LSD (Drummer & Odell, 2001; Pechnick & Ungerleider, 2004). But this is not to imply that LSD is entirely safe. There are reports suggesting that LSD-induced seizures might occur up to 60 days after the individual's last use of this compound, although the causal mechanism for such seizures remains unknown (Klein & Kramer, 2004).

The biological half-life of LSD is estimated to be approximately 2.5–3 hours (A. J. Jenkins, 2007; Oehmichen et al., 2005). It is rapidly biotransformed in the liver, with only 1–3% of a single dose of LSD being excreted from the body unchanged. The rest is eliminated in the bile (Drummer & Odell, 2001; Tacke & Ebert, 2005). The biotransformation/elimination process is so rapid

---

[10]See Glossary.

[11]Boese (2007) discussed an incident from 1962 in which a trio of scientists decided to investigate the effects of LSD on an elephant for undisclosed reasons. They injected an elephant at the Denver zoo with a dose of LSD estimated to be 3000 times larger than the typical dose used by a human. The elephant died within 1 hour. This outcome raises questions about the elephant's death. Are these creatures especially sensitive to LSD's effects, was the elephant's death drug-induced, or did the elephant die of another, unrelated cause? The results of this study does suggest that it is possible to die from an LSD overdose. What made the scientists decide to inject the elephant with the LSD has never been revealed.

that the major metabolite of LSD, 2-oxy-LSD, remains in the abuser's urine for only 12–36 hours after it is ingested. Although illicit-drug abusers often claim that the LSD detected in their urine was a result of passive absorption through the skin, there is little evidence that this is possible.

The subjective effects of LSD last far longer than its biological half-life, and for the typical abuser the perceptual distortions usually last for 12–18 hours after the drug was first ingested (Drummer & Odell, 2001; M. Weiss, 2007). The discrepancy between the drug's duration of effects and its elimination half-life might reflect the fact that some abusers ingest large doses, thus allowing residual LSD to remain in their bodies to continue to cause perceptual distortions for extended periods of time. Another possibility is that the brain requires an extended period of time to reestablish the delicate balance of the neuromodulators normally found in the brain.

The Subjective Effects Of LSD

The subjective effects of LSD begin about 5–10 minutes after the dose was ingested. The negative effects include such symptoms as anxiety, gastric distress, tachycardia, increased blood pressure, increased body temperature, dilation of the pupils, nausea and muscle weakness, exaggerated muscle reflexes,[12] dizziness, and possible muscle tremor (Tacke & Ebert, 2005). These effects are usually easily tolerated by the experienced abuser. Inexperienced abusers may overreact to these negative drug-induced effects at the start of the LSD trip, as users refer to it, thus inducing a "bad trip." LSD-induced hallucinations or perceptual distortions begin 3–60 minutes after the drug was ingested, last at full intensity for 2–4 hours, and gradually wane over the next 8–12 hours (O'Brien, 2006; Pechnick & Ungerleider, 2004).[13] Individuals' subjective interpretation of LSD's effects are thought to reflect their (a) personality, (b) expectations, (c) the environment in which the drug was used, and (d) the dose ingested (Tacke & Ebert, 2005; Weaver & Schnoll, 2008).

As stated earlier, abusers often refer to the LSD experience as a trip, during which time the abuser might experience a sensation of not having psychological boundaries, enhanced insight, a heightened awareness of sensory perception(s), enhanced memory recall, a feeling of contentment, and a sense of being "at one" with the universe (Callaway & McKenna, 1998). The trip is made up of several distinct phases: The first phase, which begins within a few minutes, is experienced as a release of inner tension. During this phase, the LSD abuser might feel the need to laugh or cry, and experience a sense of euphoria (Tacke & Ebert, 2005). Stage two begins between 30 and 90 minutes after the drug was ingested, and will involve sensations such as perceptual distortions, synesthesia,[14] and visual illusions (Pechnick & Ungerleider, 2004; Sacks, 2008; Tacke & Ebert, 2005; Traub, 2009).

The third phase of the LSD experience begins 3–4 hours after the drug was ingested, and during this phase the individual experiences a distortion of the sense of time. Some individuals report a sense of ego disintegration, and anxiety/panic reactions are occasionally experienced during this phase (which are the bad-trip experiences from LSD, discussed in the next section). During this phase, individuals might express a belief that they have quasi-magical powers or that they are somehow in control of events around them (Tacke & Ebert, 2005). Such beliefs are potentially fatal, as LSD abusers have been known to jump from windows or operate motor vehicles during this phase. On rare occasions LSD abusers might experience suicidal thoughts or even attempt suicide during this phase (S. C. Shea, 2002; Tacke & Ebert, 2005). These reactions might reflect LSD's ability to induce feelings of depression on rare occasions (Weaver & Schnoll, 2008).

The effects of LSD normally start to wane 4–12 hours after ingestion (Pechnick & Ungerleider, 2004). As individuals begin to recover, they will experience periods of normal perception, interspaced with periods in which they continue to experience residual effects of LSD, until eventually they are again fully in touch with reality. Following the last phase of the LSD trip, the abuser might experience a residual sense of emotional numbness that might last for hours to days.

The "Bad Trip"

As noted earlier, LSD abusers are prone to panic reactions, which LSD abusers call a "bad trip." Although it was once thought that only inexperienced abusers were prone to such reactions, it is now known that even experienced LSD abusers are vulnerable to this experience. Several factors that seem to influence the probability and course of a bad trip are (a) the individual's

---

[12]Known as *hyperreflexia*.

[13]Weiss (2007) suggested that some abusers might simultaneously use cocaine or an amphetamine compound to prolong the effects of LSD.

[14]See Glossary.

expectations for LSD, (b) the setting in which LSD is used, and (c) the psychological health of the user (Strassman, 2005). Feedback from others also influences how the individual interprets the drug's effects.[15] If the abusers develop an LSD-related panic reaction, they will usually respond to calm, gentle reminders from others that the feelings are a reaction to the drug and that they will pass. This is known as "talking down" the LSD abuser.

Pharmacological intervention is necessary only in the most extreme cases,[16] and there is evidence that the "atypical" antipsychotic medications clozapine and risperidone bind to the same receptor sites utilized by LSD, aborting the drug trip within 30 minutes of the time that either compound was administered (Walton, 2002). Although some physicians advocate the use of diazepam as an anxiolytic for such reactions, diazepam might further distort the individual's perception of reality, contributing to even more anxiety for the LSD abuser. Normally, benzodiazepine-induced sensory distortion is so slight as to be unnoticed by the typical patient, but when combined with the effects of LSD might become quite substantial and contribute to the problem being treated.

Even without treatment, the LSD-related "bad trip" will last only 6–12 hours at most and will resolve as the drug's effects wear off (R. T. Jones, 2005). On rare occasions, however, LSD appears to be able to "activate" a latent psychosis within the abuser, compounding the problem of treatment for that person (Erickson, 2007; Tacke & Ebert, 2005). This does not appear to be a drug effect so much as the activation of a latent psychosis within the abuser, as studies have found that Native American tribes who use mescaline as part of their religious practices do not have higher rates of psychoses than the general population (Carvey, 1998). However, the ultimate answer to this question remains unclear, because "LSD experience is so exceptional that there is a tendency for abusers to attribute *any* later

psychiatric illness to the use of LSD" (L. A. Henderson, 1994, p. 65, italics added). As the Henderson points out, psychiatric disorders that manifest weeks, months, or even years after the individual's last use of LSD are often attributed to the drug abuse and not to other possible causes.

In spite of the claims of some drug dealers, it *is* possible to overdose on LSD, although this is quite rare. Symptoms seen in an LSD overdose include convulsions and hyperthermia[17] as well as an exaggeration of the normal effects of LSD. As is true for *any* suspected drug overdose, medical care is imperative to minimize the possibility of death for the patient and allow for timely intervention for cardiac problems and the like.

The LSD "Flashback"

A "flashback" is a period of perceptual distortion similar to those experienced during LSD use but during a period when the individual has not used a hallucinogen. The first clinical reports of hallucinogenic-related flashbacks are more than 100 years old (R. T. Jones, 2005). These cases involved persons who had used mescaline and who continued to experience sensitivity to light, shade, or sounds for extended periods after their last use of this compound.

The symptoms of the LSD-related flashback[18] fall into one of three categories: (a) perceptual, (b) somatic, or (c) emotional issues, as well as feelings of depersonalization. These latter flashbacks may involve the individual reexperiencing distressing emotions first experienced when the individual abused LSD (C. J. Weiss & Millman, 1998). Reported symptoms include visual field distortions, hallucinations, "flashes" of light or color, halos surrounding objects in the visual field, the perception that things are growing larger or smaller, and depersonalization (Pechnick & Ungerleider, 2004). Between 15 and 77% of LSD abusers will experience at least one flashback, which can be a source of anxiety for the inexperienced LSD abuser who first encounters this phenomenon. Experienced LSD abusers might not report flashbacks unless specifically questioned about these experiences, accepting them as a

---

[15]Individuals who provide such feedback are often called "ground control," and are usually not abusing LSD at the time they function in this role.

[16]On occasion, physicians will encounter a patient who took LSD mixed with belladonna or another anticholinergic compounds. If the physician were to attempt to treat the patient's anxiety and agitation with a phenothiazine (an older class of antipsychotic medications), the combination of these compounds might induce a coma, or even death from cardiorespiratory failure. This is one reason why attending physicians should be alerted about what compound(s) have possibly been ingested by patients and if possible be provided with a sample of the drug(s) ingested, so that they might avoid potentially dangerous chemical interactions.

---

[17]See Glossary.

[18]Although a common consequence of LSD abuse, similar experiences might occur in patients with cerebral lesions, infections, a form of epilepsy that causes visual field disturbances, or delirium. Thus a physician should be consulted in cases of suspected LSD flashbacks to determine whether the patient might have another cause of what appears to be an LSD-related flashback.

normal consequence of their LSD abuse (Batzer, Ditzer, & Brown, 1999).

The exact mechanism behind the LSD flashback experience remains unclear at this time, but it is recognized by the American Psychiatric Association (2000) as the *hallucinogen persisting perceptual disorder* (see also Drummer & Odell, 2001; Pechnick & Ungerleider, 2004). The possibility that LSD functions as a selective neurotoxin, destroying the neurons that inhibit excessive stimulation of the visual cortex, has been suggested (Gitlow, 2007).

Clinical evidence with past LSD abusers suggests that the LSD-related flashback experiences most commonly occur in the first 6 months following the individual's last use of LSD, although they have been reported to occur up to 5 years after the individual's last episode of drug abuse (R. T. Jones, 2005). In rare cases it remains a permanent aftereffect of the individual's LSD abuse (Gitlow, 2007). It was once thought that the flashback required repeated episodes of LSD use, but clinical experience has revealed that even first-time abusers have flashback experiences (Commission on Adolescent Substance and Alcohol Abuse, 2005; Pechnick & Ungerleider, 2004). Flashbacks might be triggered by such things as stress, fatigue, marijuana abuse, emerging from a dark room into the light, infections, and the use of CNS stimulants (R. T. Jones, 2005; Weaver & Schnoll, 2008). Armed with this knowledge, some people will intentionally try to experience a flashback to experience and enjoy the effects of this phenomenon. The use of sedating agents like alcohol can also trigger flashbacks for unknown reasons (Batzer et al., 1999).

Treatment for the LSD-related flashback is usually limited to simple reassurance that this experience will last for a short period of time (usually hours, but sometimes longer than this) and that it is a normal consequence of LSD abuse (Sadock & Sadock, 2007). In some cases, the use of anxiolytic[19] medications are useful for acute flashback-related anxiety, if reassurance is not sufficient.

Drug Interactions Involving LSD

Unfortunately, there has been little clinical research into the possible drug interactions between LSD and other compounds. There are case reports suggesting that the selective serotonin reuptake inhibitor (SSRIs) antidepressants might trigger/exacerbate LSD-related "flashbacks" (Ciraulo et al., 2007). There are reports

of LSD/SSRI-induced grand mal seizures, although it was not known whether this was a drug-induced seizure or a seizure caused by another factor. LSD can interact with the antiviral agent Ritonavir, used in the treatment of HIV infection,[20] resulting in higher blood concentrations of LSD with unknown consequences (Weiss, 2007). There are other potential interactions between LSD and other compounds, but there has been little research into this area.

Phencyclidine (PCP)

Phencyclidine (PCP) was first introduced in 1957 as an experimental surgical anesthetic and was designed for intravenous administration (Tacke & Ebert, 2005). The compound was found to have serious side effects that precluded its use in humans, including agitation and a drug-induced delirium and/or psychotic reaction that lasted up to 10 days, and its use in human patients was quickly discontinued (Javitt & Zukin, 2005; A. J. Jenkins, 2007; McDowell, 2004). It still was used as a veterinary anesthetic agent until 1978, when all legal production of PCP in the United States was discontinued. It has since been classified as a Schedule I compound.[21] It continues to be used as a veterinary anesthetic compound in other parts of the world and thus is still legally manufactured by pharmaceutical companies in other countries.

By the time that its use in humans was discontinued, illicit-drug abusers had discovered PCP, and the first reports of PCP abuse began to appear in the clinical literature around 1965 (Javitt & Zukin, 2005). Its abuse has waxed and waned in the United States over the years, and currently it is not a popular drug of abuse (Javitt & Zukin, 2005). However, it is still occasionally abused by some people and is a common adulterant added to other drugs of abuse. For these reasons, we will review the effects of PCP.

Scope of Phencyclidine Abuse

Currently, PCP is not a popular drug of abuse, even in the United States, and its use outside of this country is rare (Mozayani, 2009). Even in the United States, *intentional* PCP use is uncommon (Zukin, Sloboda, & Javitt, 2005). However, it is often found as an adulterant in other compounds or is sold as other drugs of abuse. Unintentional PCP exposure, which might cause

---

[19]See Glossary.

[20]Discussed in Chapter 36.

[21]See Appendix 4.

significant anxiety for the unsuspecting drug abuser, compounds the side effects noted later (Zukin et al., 2005). Currently, it is thought that less than 0.5% of the total population of the United States has ever abused PCP.

Methods of PCP Administration

PCP might be used intranasally, ingested orally, injected either into muscle tissue or intravenously, and when mixed with other substances, it might be smoked (S. B. Karch, 2009). This latter method of PCP abuse is the most popular, as it allows the individual to titrate their total PCP intake to a level suitable to their taste, after which time they can just discontinue further PCP smoking for a few minutes, hours, or days.

Subjective Experience of PCP

When abused, PCP's effects have been found to last for several days, an observation that is consistent with clinical experience with this compound when it was first used as an experimental anesthetic agent for surgery in human patients. During the time that abusers are under the influence of PCP, they will experience rapid fluctuations in their level of consciousness, a sense of dissociation in which reality appears to be distorted or distant, euphoria, decreased inhibitions, a feeling of immense power, analgesia, an altered sense of time, and a loss of sensation or the feeling that body parts are no longer attached to their body (Brust, 2004; Weaver, Jarvis, & Schnoll, 1999). These latter experiences can be rather frightening to the inexperienced abuser, inducing a panic reaction. Other reported symptoms include disorientation, confusion, assaultiveness, irritability, depression (which might reach the level of suicidal thinking/ acts), and paranoia. As the list of PCP-induced effects would suggest, many of these effects are not desired by the abuser, who might attempt to control them through simultaneous use of other compounds.

The Pharmacology of PCP

Because it is an illicit compound in this country, the phenomena of PCP abuse, dependence, or the PCP withdrawal syndrome have not been studied in detail (Zukin et al., 2005). Much of what is "known" about PCP and its effects is based on anecdotal case reports involving PCP abusers, or through the limited experience with PCP as an experimental anesthetic agent.

Chemically, PCP is a weak base, soluble in both water and blood lipids. Because it is a weak base, it will be absorbed through the small intestine when ingested orally, a process that will result in a slower onset of the drug's effects as compared to when it is smoked (Zukin et al, 2005). Orally administered doses of PCP begin to manifest in 20–30 minutes after the drug was ingested, but there is a great deal of intraindividual variability in both the onset of the drug's effects in the oral abuser and the duration of its effects after ingestion. When smoked, the effects begin to manifest in 2–3 minutes (Schnoll & Weaver, 2004). The effects of a small dose of orally administered PCP usually last 3–4 hours, whereas the peak effects of smoked PCP are achieved in 15–30 minutes and last for 4–6 hours after a single dose (A. J. Jenkins, 2007). Much of the PCP that is smoked is destroyed in the smoking process, with the result being that only 30–50% of the available PCP smoked actually reaches the circulation.

Because of its lipid solubility, PCP tends to accumulate in body tissues with a high concentration of lipids, such as the brain (Scholl & Weaver, 2004). Indeed, the levels of PCP in the brain might be 10–113 times as high as the blood plasma levels (Zukin et al., 2005). Once in the blood, PCP interacts with a number of different neurotransmitter receptor sites, acting as an antagonist for N-methyl-D-aspartic acid (NMDA) (A. J. Jenkins, 2007; Zukin et al., 2005). PCP also functions as a sigma opioid receptor agonist, and because activation of this receptor site causes dysphoric effects, this seems to be the mechanism through which PCP causes such unpleasant effects (Brust, 2004; Drummer & Odell, 2001). It also binds at some of the endogenous cannabinoid receptor sites, causing hallucinations through this process (Glennon, 2004).

The effects of PCP on the user's brain vary, depending on such factors as the abuser's experience with the drug and the drug concentration in the abuser's brain. At about 10 times the minimal effective dose, PCP begins to function as a monoamine reuptake blocker, blocking the action neurotransmitters such as dopamine and norepinephrine. This is one mechanism through which PCP might induce euphoria. Thus depending on the concentration of PCP in the brain, it might function as an anesthetic, stimulant, depressant, or hallucinogenic compound. Depending on the concentration of PCP in the brain, it also may alter the normal function of the NMDA/glutamate receptor[22]

---

[22]See Glossary.

in the brain, which might account for the excitement and agitation seen in some PCP abusers (Traub, 2009).

PCP is biotransformed into a number of inactive metabolites, which are then excreted by the kidneys. Following a single dose of PCP, only about 10% is excreted unchanged (S. G. Karch, 2009). There is significant intraindividual variability in the PCP half-life, but R. T. Jones (2005) offered a figure of 20 hours as the average for this compound. If the individual has used an exceptionally large dose, however, this may be extended to as long as 72 hours, and following a PCP overdose might be as long as several weeks. One reason for this is the affinity of the PCP molecule for lipid molecules, which allows for significant stores of PCP to accumulate in the body's fat tissues only to slowly "leak" back into the general circulation over time. Further, if abusers should engage in heavy exercise, diet, or experience major trauma, they might experience a PCP "flashback" as significant amounts of PCP are released back into the circulation (Schuckit, 2006a). In the past, physicians believed that it was possible to reduce the half-life of PCP by making the urine very acidic. This was accomplished by having the patient ingest large amounts of ascorbic acid or cranberry juice. However, it has since been discovered that this practice may cause myoglobinuria and possible kidney failure, and so is no longer recommended as a treatment for PCP overdoses (Brust, 2004).

Tolerance to PCP's euphoric effects develops rapidly (Javitt & Zukin, 2005). The typical illicit-drug dose is approximately 5 mg; however because of the myriad amounts of PCP in different preparations, it is impossible to predict in advance how much drug is being ingested without special testing. In the next section we will look at some of the known complications of PCP abuse.

Complications of PCP Abuse

Some of the complications of PCP abuse are reviewed in Table 12-1.

Following even mild levels of PCP intoxication is a period of adjustment that may last 24–48 hours, which may be prolonged in cases where the person ingested an exceptionally large dose. During this adjustment period, the individual will gradually "come down," or return to a normal level of function. Chronic PCP abusers report social withdrawal and feelings of depression following their last episode of PCP abuse. A mild withdrawal syndrome following periods of prolonged PCP abuse has been reported, and many abusers report

TABLE 12-1 KNOWN COMPLICATIONS OF PCP ABUSE DOSE		
1–5 mg	**5–10 mg**	**10–25 mg OR HIGHER**
Alcohol-like intoxication	Aggression	Analgesia/anesthesia
Aggression	Analgesia	Arrhythmias (possibly fatal)
Anxiety	Anxiety (may be severe)	Coma (possibly with the eyes open)
Ataxia	Depersonalization	Encopresis
Body image distortion	Euphoria	Hallucinations (both visual and tactile hallucinations reported)
Confusion	Hypersalivation	
Distorted sense of time	Increased muscle strength	Hypertension (possibly causing strokes or other damage to user's body)
Euphoria	Lethargy	
Hallucinations (usually visual, but other forms of hallucinations also reported)	Memory impairment	Paranoia
	Nystagmus	Reduced reaction time
Nystagmus	Paranoia	Respiratory depression/arrest
Periods of rage	Psychosis (drug induced)	Rhabdomyolysis
	Sweating	Seizures

NOTE: Based on information in Javitt and Zukin (2005), Mozayani (2009), Sadock and Sadock (2007), and Tomb (2008).

having problems with their memory, which seem to resolve after they stop abusing this compound. This is consistent with evidence that PCP can cause neural necrosis[23] in the hippocampus (Javitt & Zukin, 2005). It is not known at this time what degree of recovery, if any, is possible from PCP-related brain damage.

Another possible complication of PCP abuse is a drug-induced psychosis. In the case of PCP, this psychosis appears to progress through three different stages. The first stage of the PCP-induced psychosis is the most severe, and includes symptoms such as paranoid delusions, anorexia, insomnia, and unpredictable assaultiveness. During this phase, the individual is exceptionally sensitive to external stimuli such as bright lights or loud sounds, and the "talking-down"

---

[23]See Glossary.

techniques so effective with LSD bad trips will not work with patients in a PCP-induced psychosis. Restraints are occasionally necessary to prevent patients from harming themselves or others during this phase.

The second stage of the PCP psychosis is marked by continued paranoia and restlessness, but users are usually more calm and in intermittent control of their behavior. This phase usually lasts around 5 days and gradually blends into the final phase of the PCP psychosis. In the final phase, which may last 7–14 days in the typical case, users gradually return to a normal stage of mind, although possibly they are depressed for a period of time as part of the post-PCP adjustment process. Although the PCP psychosis is usually time limited, in some cases recovery might take months or even years.

PCP Abuse As an Indirect Cause of Death

The PCP-induced hypertensive episodes noted earlier might last for as long as 3 days after the individual's last use of PCP, placing stress on the cardiovascular system during that time (Brust, 2004). Also, PCP-related periods of aggression have been identified as a factor in drug-related homicides in which either the perpetrator or the victim is under the influence of PCP when the homicide was committed. PCP-induced seizures present the same potential for death as those found in typical seizures and thus might indirectly cause the user's death. Finally, the dissociative and anesthetic properties of PCP can cause or exacerbate traumatic injuries for abusers, possibly contributing to their death. Given this litany of undesirable effects, it is a mystery as to why people might choose to abuse this compound. However, as noted earlier in this chapter, PCP continues to lurk in the shadows and may again become a popular drug of abuse.

ECSTASY (MDMA)

A Short History of Ecstasy (MDMA):

The compound N, alpha-Dimethyl-1,3-benzodioxole-ethanamine (MDMA) was first isolated in 1912, with a patent on the compound being issued in 1914 (Schuckit, 2006a). Chemists had hoped that the compound would help as an appetite suppressant, but when subsequent research failed to support this theory researchers quickly lost interest in MDMA. It remained a laboratory curiosity until the early 1950s, when the U.S. Army asked the University of Michigan to determine its toxicity, as part of a preliminary assessment of this compound as a possible chemical warfare agent (S. B. Karch, 2009). However, the decision was made not to pursue further research into this compound by the Army, and it returned to chemical obscurity.[24]

In the mid-1960s, a small number of psychotherapists suggested that it might be useful as an adjunct to psychotherapy, and for a brief period of time there was limited research into this application of MDMA (Batki, 2001; Gahlinger, 2004; Shulgin & Shulgin, 2007). Like LSD, in the 1960s MDMA also escaped from the laboratory to become a drug of abuse, but it was quickly overshadowed by LSD, which both was more potent and did not induce the nausea or vomiting experienced by MDMA abusers. Indeed, MDMA was of so little importance as a drug of abuse that it was not included in the Comprehensive Drug Abuse Prevention and Control Act of 1970 classification system.

Illicit-drug abusers began to become interested in MDMA in the mid-1970s, in part because it was not then classified as an illegal substance. Drug suppliers began to market it as a commercial venture, engaging in premarketing discussions about possible product names much as an automotive company would for a new vehicle. The name "ecstasy" was eventually selected for this compound, a demand for the product was generated, and a supply/distribution network was set up to meet the demand (S. B. Karch, 2009; McDowell, 2004). The original samples of MDMA even contained a "package insert" (S. B. Karch, 2009) that was filled with psycho-babble and that gave suggestions as to how MDMA might best be used. Within the span of a few years, MDMA became a popular drug of abuse in both Europe and the United States. The Drug Enforcement Administration (DEA) soon corrected its earlier oversight and classified MDMA as a Schedule I compound under the Comprehensive Drug Abuse Prevention and Control Act of 1970 classification system.

MDMA has remained a popular drug of abuse, as evidenced by the fact that worldwide production of this illicit compound is thought to exceed 8 metric *tons* per year (United Nations, 2008). Another measure of the popularity of MDMA as a drug of abuse is the fact that there are more than 150 "street" names for this compound (Kilmer, Palmer & Cronce, 2005). Historically, MDMA has been a popular drug of abuse in dance

---

[24]It has emerged, however, as a *possible* adjunct to the treatment of at least some forms of posttraumatic stress disorder (PTSD) (Mithoefer, Mithoefer, & Wagner, 2008). Further research into this possible medical application of MDMA is under way at this time.

clubs, although it is also abused in other venues as well (Gahlinger, 2004).

Scope of MDMA Abuse

Globally, 9 million people between the ages of 15 and 64 years are thought to have used MDMA at least once in the preceding 12 months (United Nations, 2008). In the United States, an estimated 8 million people are thought to have abused MDMA at least once, and 2.2 million people are thought to have done so in the past 12 months (Gwinnell & Adamec, 2006; United Nations, 2008). MDMA is most popular in the young-adult population, with 15% of 19- to 30-year-old adults in the United States admitting to having used this compound at least once (Kobeissy et al., 2007). In Europe, MDMA is the second most popular illicit drug of abuse, exceeded only by marijuana (Morton, 2005).

It was originally thought that MDMA was harmless, a myth that helped it to find widespread acceptance (Ramcharan et al., 1998). It found willing acceptance by a subculture devoted to loud music and parties devoted to the use of MDMA, similar to LSD parties of the 1960s. Such parties, which had come to be called "raves," first began in Spain, spread to England and across Europe, and then came to the United States (McDowell, 2004; Rochester & Kirchner, 1999). Although these parties have become less common by the end of the first generation of the 21st century, MDMA has moved into mainstream nightclubs, especially those popular with older adolescents and young adults (Morton, 2005).

Patterns of MDMA Abuse

Typical MDMA abusers will ingest 60–120 mg[25] at a time. Binge abusers might take as many as 5–5 tablets[26] at one time in an attempt to enhance the euphoria found in a lower dose (Outslay, 2006). Ecstasy abusers tend to engage in episodic MDMA abuse, interspacing periods of abstinence from MDMA use to allow themselves to recover from the drug's effects[27] with episodes of active drug abuse (Commission on Adolescent Substance and Alcohol Abuse, 2005; Gouzoulis-Mayfrank et al., 2000). This pattern of abuse reflects the pharmacokinetics of MDMA, because prolonged use or the ingestion of large doses makes it less likely that the abuser will experience MDMA-related euphoria. MDMA demonstrates a "plateau effect," beyond which the individual will not achieve more euphoria but will be vulnerable to the negative effects of this compound (Bravo, 2001).

Although MDMA abusers tend to engage in episodic use of this compound, very heavy abusers might ingest up to 40,000 tablets in their lifetime (Lawton, 2009).

Pharmacology of MDMA

Technically, MDMA is classified as a member of the *phenethylamine*[28] family of compounds, but its chemical structure is also very similar to that of the amphetamines, and some neuropharmacologists classify it as a hallucinogenic amphetamine. For the sake of this chapter, it will be classified as a hallucinogenic compound, because this is the context in which it is most commonly abused. It is usually abused in tablet form, although there is a growing tendency for MDMA powder to be sold because it is easier to produce the powder than to form it into a tablet (Boyer, 2005). The use of such powder raises the potential for a lethal overdose, however, because it is harder to judge the total dose being used (Lawton, 2009).

The pharmacokinetics of MDMA is complicated by the fact that there are mirror images of the molecule that might be produced,[29] known as the *left-handed* and the *right-handed* form ("Pharmacokinetics of MDMA (Ecstasy) Studied," 2008). The effects of each molecule on the body may vary, depending on which form of MDMA was produced by the illicit laboratory that supplied that batch of MDMA ("Pharmacokinetics of MDMA (Ecstasy) Studied," 2008). So the information that follows is tentative, and may be revised as scientists discover more about the pharmacokinetics of each form of MDMA.

Ecstasy is well absorbed from the gastrointestinal tract, and thus the most common method of use is through oral administration. The effects begin within about 20 minutes of ingestion of a single dose and peak within 1–4 hours following the ingestion (de la

---

[25]Although this is based on the theory that the MDMA ingested is pure. Many illicit-drug samples are adulterated with various compounds, making it difficult to estimate the actual amount of MDMA ingested by any given abuser.

[26]The potency of illicit MDMA tablets varies from one batch to the next, and there is no standardization between manufacturers.

[27]Although polydrug abusers might continue to abuse other compounds during these periods of abstinence.

[28]Discussed in Chapter 37.

[29]Technically a *chiral* molecule.

Torre et al., 2004; Gonzalez et al., 2009; McDowell, 2004, 2005). However, Karch (2009) suggested that the peak blood levels following a single dose of MDMA are achieved in 2–4 hours, suggesting that there is some disagreement as to the exact time that peak blood levels are achieved following the ingestion of a single dose. The estimated half-life following ingestion of a single dose is estimated to be 4–7 (S. B. Karch, 2009) and 8–9 (de la Torre et al., 2004; Gahlinger, 2004; Klein & Kramer, 2004) hours.

It has been suggested that MDMA is extensively biotransformed in the liver, and the elimination half-life has been estimated to be 8 hours (Tacke & Ebert, 2005). There are two main metabolic pathways for MDMA, which is to say that the compound might be broken down in the liver by two of the four different mechanisms discussed in Chapter 3. About 9% of a single dose of MDMA is biotransformed into the metabolite MDA, which is itself a hallucinogenic (de la Torre et al., 2004). One study using a human volunteer subject found that three-fourths of the MDMA ingested was excreted unchanged in the urine within 72 hours, suggesting that there is variation between individuals as to the elimination half-life of MDMA and whether it requires biotransformation prior to elimination.

Because MDMA is highly lipid soluble, it is able to easily cross the blood–brain barrier (BBB) and enter the brain without significant delay. In the brain, MDMA functions as an indirect serotonin agonist, first forcing the release, and then blocking the reuptake, of serotonin and to a lesser degree norepinephrine and dopamine (Gahlinger, 2004; McDowell, 2004, 2005; Parrott et al., 2004). This process appears to take place in the limbic system of the brain (Erickson, 2007). However, there is very little objective research into its effects, and virtually all that is known about the pharmacokinetics of this compound is based on individual case reports involving illicit-drug abusers.

It should be observed that the aforementioned is based on the assumption that the person ingested only one dose of MDMA. Many individuals consume multiple doses over extended periods (8–12 hours), which alters the pharmacokinetics of this compound. Higher doses result in higher plasma levels of MDMA, for example, producing both stronger effects and greater exposure to contaminants in the compound ingested (Ricaurte et al., 2008). In cases where the MDMA abuser dies (which, as will be discussed later in this chapter, is a distinct possibility), the residual MDMA molecules in the abuser will be extensively redistributed around the body. This is to say that postmortem blood levels of MDMA may not be the same as the blood levels of this compound at the time of the abuser's death ("Pharmacokinetics of MDMA (Ecstasy) Studied," 2008). As the information in this section suggests, there is limited information about the pharmacokinetics of MDMA and much that remains to be discovered about this compound.

Subjective and Objective Effects of MDMA Abuse

Currently, there are at least six different identified methods for making MDMA, with specific instructions on how to make MDMA available on the Internet (Rochester & Kirchner, 1999). Specialized equipment and training in organic chemistry are both required to avoid the danger of contaminating the illicit MDMA being manufactured by toxins. Beyond these requirements, MDMA is easily synthesized. Much of what is known about MDMA's effects is based on observations made by illicit-drug users and a limited number of research studies involving volunteer subjects receiving a measured dose of MDMA under controlled circumstances (Outslay, 2006).

The subjective effects of MDMA can be divided into three phases: (a) acute, (b) subacute, and (c) chronic (Outslay, 2006). The subjective effects of MDMA during the acute phase are dependent on such factors as the setting in which the drug is used, the dose ingested, and the individual's expectations for Ecstasy. At a dose of between 75 and 100 mg, abusers report experiencing a sense of euphoria, closeness to others, increased energy, mild perceptual disturbances such as enhanced color/sound perception, a sense of well-being, reduced defensiveness, and improved self-esteem (Bravo, 2001; de la Torre et al., 2004; Outslay, 2006). These effects begin to manifest about 30–60 minutes after MDMA is ingested, peak at about 75–120 minutes after it is first ingested, and last for 6–12 hours (Outslay, 2006). Some of the reported desirable effects of MDMA are identified in Table 12-2 (de la Torre et al., 2004; Kobeissy et al., 2007; Outslay, 2006; Passie, Hartman, Schneider, Emrich, & Kruger, 2005).

However, these effects are achieved at a cost, for MDMA can also induce many undesirable effects, which are reviewed in Table 12-3 (Bravo, 2001, 2005; de la Torre et al., 2004; Grob & Poland, 2005; McDowell, 2005; Kobeissy et al., 2007).

The individual is more likely to experience one or more of these undesirable effects at higher dosage

TABLE 12-2 PERCEIVED BENEFITS OF MDMA USE
Euphoria
Increased empathy toward others
Emotional openness
Increased psychomotor energy
Increased self-confidence
Enhanced mood
Increased sex drive
Feelings of intimacy
Increased feeling of personal desirability as sexual partner
Belief that individual has improved self-awareness/insight
Intense feelings
Different state of mind/perceptions

TABLE 12-3 POSSIBLE CONSEQUENCE OF MDMA ABUSE
Nausea/vomiting
Headaches
Bruxism (grinding of the teeth)
Hypertension
Heart palpitations
Sudden cardiac death
Anorexia
Urinary incontinence
Ataxia
Muscle tension
Blurred vision
Motor tics
Loss of consciousness
Hyperthermia
Hypothermia
Seizures, possibly leading to status epileptics (potentially fatal)
Subarachnoid hemorrhage
Central venous sinus thrombosis

levels, although unpleasant effects are possible even at low doses (Grob & Poland, 2005). Many abusers experience bruxism, which abusers attempt to control by using a baby pacifier or candy to suck on after ingesting MDMA (Gahlinger, 2004; Klein & Kramer, 2004).

Surprisingly, although MDMA induces enhanced feelings of sexual arousal and attractiveness, habitual MDMA abuse has also been implicated as the cause of decreased sexual desire, and for men inhibition of the ejaculatory reflux as well as erectile dysfunction (Finger et al., 1997; McDowell, 2004). Research has also found that MDMA abusers are more than *eight times* as likely to experience episodes of sleep apnea as are nonabusers (McCann, Sgambati, Schwartz, & Ricaurte, 2009). McCann et al. suggested that this increased incidence of sleep apnea might be due to MDMA's ability to function as a selective serotonin neurotoxin, because serotonin is implicated in the maintenance of normal respiration during sleep.

Following the period of acute MDMA abuse, there is an extended withdrawal period. The subacute phase begins 6–2 hours after the individual has ingested MDMA and in most cases lasts 1–7 days, although in extreme cases it can last for up to a full month (Outslay, 2006). This phase is also called *coming down* or the *hangover phase* by drug abusers (Outslay, 2006). Some of the symptoms experienced during this phase include fatigue, dry mouth, anorexia, insomnia, irritability, drowsiness, difficulty concentrating, and headache (de la Torre et al., 2004; McDowell, 2005). It was once thought that the subacute phase of MDMA might also include feelings of depression, but this has not been proven. This would cast doubt on the belief that the subacute stage of MDMA includes depression.

As the subacute phase tapers into the chronic phase, the abuser will experience symptoms such as anxiety, depression, confusion, cognitive dysfunction, insomnia, irritability, low energy, and suspiciousness/paranoia (Outslay, 2006). These effects usually last for between 1 and 7 days, although in extreme cases they might continue for up to a month after the individual's last MDMA abuse.

Complications of MDMA Abuse

MDMA has a reputation on the streets as a "safe" drug, an illusion supported by the lack of obvious consequences of abuse observed in people who have abused methamphetamine, for example (Yudko & McPherson, 2009). The illusion of safety belies the fact that there is a significant overlap between the effective dose and the toxic-dosage range of MDMA (S. B. Karch, 2009; Outslay, 2006). For example, animal research suggests that the lethal level of MDMA in humans is approximately 6000 mg (Rosenthal & Solhkhah, 2005), a dosage level that, given the potency of some illicit MDMA samples, might be achieved after ingesting only 20–30 tablets (Lawton, 2009). However, fatal reactions to MDMA have been noted at doses far lower than this (Lawton, 2009).

Some of the symptoms of MDMA toxicity include nausea, vomiting, dry mouth, dehydration, sweating, restlessness, tremor, exaggerated reflexes, irritability, bruxism, cardiac arrhythmias, confusion, panic attacks, a drug-induced psychosis, hypertension, extreme (possibly fatal) elevations in body temperature, delirium, coma, hypotension, rhabdomyolysis,[30] and possible renal failure (de la Torre et al., 2004; Morton, 2005; Parrott et al., 2004; Rosenthal & Solhkhah, 2005; Zevin & Benowitz, 2007). As these symptoms clearly suggest, *any* real or suspected overdose of MDMA is a medical emergency that requires immediate medical intervention to avoid the danger of the patient's death. In the following section, we will examine some of the more specific dangers of MDMA abuse in detail.

MDMA-Related Cardiac Problems

It is now known that MDMA abuse can cause an increase in the heart rate, in blood pressure, and in the rate at which the heart muscle uses oxygen (Grob & Poland, 2005). MDMA abuse is a cause of cardiac arrhythmias such as the potentially fatal ventricular tachycardia (Klein & Kramer, 2004; Gahlinger, 2004; Grob & Poland, 2005; S. B. Karch, 2009). One study of the hospital records of 48 patients who had been admitted to a hospital accident and trauma center following MDMA use found that two-thirds had heart rates above 100 beats per minute, or 38% higher than normal (H. Williams et al., 1998). It has been recommended that MDMA overdoses be treated with the same protocols used to treat amphetamine overdoses, with special emphasis placed on assessing and protecting cardiac function (Gahlinger, 2004; Rochester & Kirchner, 1999).

Animal research also suggests that MDMA functions as a cardiotoxin, causing inflammation of the heart muscle and damage to the left ventricle of the heart (Badon et al., 2002; Shenouda, Lord, McIlwain, Lucchesi, & Varner, 2008). In another study, the team of Patel et al. (2005) compared the heart muscle tissue samples of a group of deceased MDMA abusers (as confirmed by toxicology tests) with those of deceased people of a similar age who did not have evidence of MDMA in their systems at the time of death, and found that hearts of the MDMA abusers were 14%

heavier than those of nonabusers. This would appear to reflect the development of fibrous tissue within the cardiac muscle, which could interfere with the transmission of electrical signals in the heart necessary for maintenance of a normal cardiac rhythm. The development of fibrous tissue within the cardiac tissues would appear to reflect the cardiotoxic effects of MDMA (Klein & Kramer, 2004).

There is also evidence that chronic MDMA use can result in damage to the valves of the heart (Setola et al., 2003). Setola et al. examined the impact of MDMA abuse on tissue samples in laboratories and found many of the same changes in heart valve tissue seen in the now-banned weight loss medication fenfluramine.[31] Given the widespread use of MDMA, these research findings suggest the possibility of a future epidemic of MDMA-induced heart problems in habitual abusers. Animal research does suggest that chronic MDMA abuse was associated with cardiac damage and potentially sudden cardiac death. The authors found that intracellular calcium levels were significantly higher in the hearts of MDMA-exposed rats than in MDMA-naive rats. The concentration of calcium within the heart muscle cell helps to determine the rate and force at which it can contract. This appears to be the mechanism by which MDMA abuse can induce sudden cardiac death, or at least damage the heart muscle, according to the authors.

MDMA-Related Neurological Problems

MDMA abuse is thought to be a causal agent in a wide range of neurological problems. Case reports indicate that some abusers have suffered intracranial hemorrhage, whereas others have suffered occlusive strokes.

Animal research suggests that MDMA induces the body to secrete abnormal amounts of the antidiuretic hormone (ADH) (Gahlinger, 2004; Henry & Rella, 2001; Tacke & Ebert, 2005). This hormone reduces the production of urine and promotes the reabsorption of water by the kidneys. If abusers ingest large amounts of fluid in an attempt to avoid possible MDMA-induced dehydration, they could be vulnerable to developing abnormally low blood sodium levels,[32] which in turn can cause or contribute to the cardiac arrhythmias discussed earlier in this chapter, as well as to seizures or other physical problems (Grob & Poland,

---

[30]See Glossary.

[31]Also known as "fen-phen." After it was introduced, scientists discovered that this medication induced degeneration of heart valve tissue, prompting the manufacturer to withdraw it from the market.

[32]Known as *hyponatremia*.

2005; McDowell, 2005; Parrott et al., 2004). Unfortunately, many MDMA abusers believe that the best way to avoid MDMA-related dehydration is to ingest large amounts of fluid, which as noted in the last sentence might cause or exacerbate various health problems.

There is a growing body of literature from both animal and human studies that suggests that MDMA can cause memory problems that may persist for weeks, or even months, after the individual's last use of Ecstasy (McDowell, 2005; Morton, 2005; Yudko & McPherson, 2009). A rather frightening study conducted by Schlit et al. (2007) examined new (<2 months) MDMA abusers and found small, but measurable, cognitive deficits on the neuropsychological tests administered, and cognitive deficits are noted in patients who have ingested MDMA as infrequently as 20 times (Lawton, 2009). The cognitive deficits appear to be dose related, with abusers who report higher levels of abuse being found to have higher levels of cognitive dysfunction in such areas as memory and verbal learning, as well as increased distractibility and a general loss of efficiency (Lawton, 2009; Lundqvist, 2005; Quednow et al., 2006).

There is controversy over whether or not extended periods of MDMA abuse can result in permanent cognitive impairment. The team of Schlit et al. (2007) concluded that extended periods of MDMA abuse can result in cognitive decline. However, Krebs and Johansen (2008) challenged this conclusion on methodological grounds, pointing out that longitudinal research studies should answer this question more definitively than retrospective studies, which are commonly utilized in research involving MDMA's effects on memory function.[33] Lawton (2009) observed that most MDMA abusers also abuse other compounds, making the isolation of MDMA's effects rather difficult.

MDMA abuse has been identified as a cause of the serotonin syndrome.[34] Because temperature dysregulation is one of the observed consequences of the serotonin syndrome, this might be the mechanism through which MDMA is able to induce hyperthermia and dehydration following use of this compound (Klein & Kramer, 2004). MDMA-related serotonin and dopamine release might also be a temperature-sensitive effect, with higher ambient temperatures being associated with higher levels of these neurotransmitters. Unfortunately, these neurotransmitters are involved in the euphoric sensations that many MDMA abusers seek, with the result that being in an area with a high ambient temperature might increase MDMA-induced pleasure while simultaneously placing the abuser's life at greater risk (O'Shea et al., 2005).

For reasons that are not well understood, MDMA appears to be able to lower the seizure threshold in abusers, possibly resulting in fatal seizures (Henry & Rella, 2001; S. B. Karch, 2009). This might reflect genetic vulnerability on the part of the patient experiencing an MDMA-related seizure, as there is evidence that patients who have inherited two copies of what is known as the "short" serotonin transporter gene may be at greater risk for MDMA-related neurotoxicity (Roiser, Cook, Cooper, Rubinsztein, & Shakian, 2005). MDMA-related seizures also tend to be seen at higher dosage levels, although this is not a guarantee that lower doses will avoid the risk of seizures (Brust, 2004; J. P. Thompson, 2004).

As if all of this were not enough, there is strong evidence that MDMA functions as a selective neurotoxin that targets serotonergic neurons (Bauman & Rothman, 2007; Brust, 2004; McDowell, 2005). Animal research suggests that this effect can be seen at dosage levels utilized by human abusers (Ricaurte, Yuan, Hatzidimitriou, Branden, & McCann, 2002). Although the MDMA-related brain damage is more likely in people who have ingested large doses of this compound, it is possible even on the occasion of the first dose (McDowell, 2005). The mechanism through which MDMA might function as a serotonin-specific neurotoxin is still not known, but preliminary evidence suggests that fluoxotine might protect the serotonin-based neurons from damage, if ingested within 24 hours of the time that MDMA was ingested (Walton, 2002).

Although it was once thought that MDMA would place the abuser at increased risk for Parkinson's disease later in life, this theory was later retracted (Brust, 2004; Yudo & McPherson, 2009). There is little evidence that supports earlier beliefs that there was a relationship between MDMA abuse and subsequent development of Parkinson's disease (Morton, 2005; Yudko & McPherson, 2009). However, there is research data suggesting that MDMA might weaken the blood–brain barrier[35] for months, possibly even years, after the last period of abuse (Vollmer, 2006). This would place the abuser at increased vulnerability to various

---

[33]Asking people who have been abusing MDMA for 3 years, for example, to estimate how often they have used this compound might yield less accurate results than a longitudinal research study that examined how often they abused MDMA on a week-by-week or month-by-month basis carried out over a 3-year period of time.

[34]See Glossary.

[35]See Glossary.

toxins, and pathogenic organisms normally blocked by the BBB.

MDMA-Related Emotional Problems

There is evidence that MDMA abusers might experience flashback experiences similar to those seen after LSD abuse in the days following the MDMA use. MDMA abusers are also sometimes forced to relive past experiences that they might not wish to face. This is the effect that made psychiatrists consider MDMA as a possible adjunct to psychotherapy in the 1960s. But when an MDMA abuser is forced to reexperience these memories, there is usually no therapist to provide guidance and support, and this effect might be detrimental to the abuser's mental health.

MDMA abuse has also been linked with postabuse anxiety attacks, persistent insomnia, irritability, rate reactions, and a drug-induced psychosis (Commission on Adolescent Substance and Alcohol Abuse, 2005; Gahlinger, 2004; S. B. Karch, 2009; McDowell, 2005). Finally, as MDMA's effects wane, the individual might experience a depressive reaction that might range from mild to quite severe, which will last 48 hours or more (Gahlinger, 2004).

MDMA-Related Gastrointestinal Problems

In Europe, where MDMA abuse was common in the 1990s, there were reports of MDMA-related liver toxicity and hepatitis. The exact relationship between MDMA abuse and the development of these liver problems is not known at this time. This might be the result of an idiosyncratic reaction on the part of a small number of people, or a reaction to one or more contaminants mixed with the MDMA that was abused (Grob & Poland, 2002; Henry & Rolla, 2001).

Other MDMA-Related Problems

There are reports of MDMA-related rhabdomyolysis,[36] possibly induced by heavy MDMA-induced exercise such as prolonged dancing (Gahlinger, 2004; Grob & Poland, 2005; S. B. Karch 2002; Klein & Kramer, 2004). Although MDMA-related deaths are rare, they still are not unknown. MDMA abuse has been identified as a cause of death, with the causal agent of death being strokes associated with MDMA-induced hypertensive episodes, seizures, liver failure, or cardiac arrhythmias. The danger of MDMA-related death is increased if the abuser has ingested either multiple compounds or high doses of MDMA. Kalantar-Zaden, Nguyen, Chang, and Kortz (2006) discussed a case in which an otherwise healthy 20-year-old female college student, who had a history of MDMA abuse, was transported to the hospital with abnormally low blood sodium levels. In spite of aggressive medical care, she died about 12 hours after her arrival at the hospital.

Medication Interactions Involving MDMA

In the past, physicians thought that beta adrenergic blockers (ß-blockers or "beta" blockers) were helpful in treating MDMA toxicity, but the team of Rochester and Kirchner (1999) challenged this clinical belief on the grounds that the alpha adrenergic system would remain unaffected, and this could impact on blood pressure in spite of the use of ß-blockers. The use of haloperidol was also not recommended, as the interaction between MDMA and haloperidol might interfere with body temperature regulation (Brust, 2004). The best treatment for MDMA toxicity is thought to be supportive treatment, with maintenance of normal body temperature, airway and cardiac support, as well as the judicious use of a benzodiazepine to control anxiety, if necessary (Schuckit, 2006a). There have been case reports of interactions between MDMA and the antiviral agent Ritonavir (Concar, 1997). Each agent affects the serotonin level in the blood, and the combination of these two compounds can result in a three-fold higher MDMA level in the blood. Some fatalities have been reported in abusers who have mixed these compounds (Concar, 1997).

Salvia Divinorum

Although *Salvia divinorum* has been used for generations in central Mexico and South America during religious and healing ceremonies, it is a relatively new arrival in the hallucinogenic market in this country. Media attention on the abuse of *Salvia divinorum* as the "next LSD" has helped fuel curiosity about this plant in the United States. The leaves are obtained from the plant. It remains legal in most states, although both state and federal regulations against its cultivation, sale, and use are pending. Because it is a recent arrival on the drug abuse scene, the pharmacokinetics of *Salvina divinorum* remain unclear at this time. It has been discovered that the active agent of this plant is *salvinorin A,* which has a strong effect on the kappa opioid receptors[37] in the brain (NIDA Info Facts,

---

[36]See Glossary.

[37]Discussed in Chapter 11.

2007). Traditional users will chew the leaves, although abusers will also smoke the leaves or crush the leaves and drink the extract either alone or when mixed with soda.

The effects last for between 30 seconds and 30 minutes, depending on the potency of the leaves and the individual's history of *Salvina divinorum* use. This would suggest that, like LSD, tolerance to the effects of this compound develops rapidly. Subjective effects begin in about 30–60 seconds and include perceptual distortions of the body and the environment. Abusers might demonstrate slurred speech, dizziness, mood swings, and a feeling of detachment from their surroundings. There has been a case report of a persistent psychotic reaction in a 21-year-old male who had abused *Saliva divinorum* (Przekop & Lee, 2009). It was suggested by the authors that the patient has a genetic predisposition for schizophrenia and that the clinical manifestations of this disorder were exacerbated by the abuse of *Saliva divinorum;* however, the accuracy of this theory is not known at this time.

Chapter Summary

The phenomenon of hallucinogen abuse has waxed and waned over the years, with abusers rushing to embrace first one compound and then another. The compound LSD, the prototype hallucinogen, was popular in the 1960s, whereas PCP became popular in the 1970s and 1980s. Currently, MDMA is a popular hallucinogen of abuse. All of these compounds continue to be abused, although one is more common than the other. The phenomenon of hallucinogen abuse appears to reflect an inborn desire on the part of some people to alter their perception of reality and possibly achieve euphoria from the drug's effects. As we stand on the brink of molecular pharmacology, it is logical to expect that the techniques used to develop more effective pharmaceuticals will eventually be used by illicit-drug manufacturers to produce even more potent pharmaceuticals, ensuring that the abuse of these compounds will remain a problem well into the 21st century.

CHAPTER 13

Abuse of and Addiction to Inhalants and Aerosols

Introduction

The term *inhalant* does not refer to a specific compound, but to a *method of substance use* that introduces any of a wide variety of compounds into the user's body. Many such compounds are toxic, including various cleaning agents, herbicides, pesticides, gasoline, kerosene, certain forms of glue, lacquer thinner, and some of the chemicals used in felt-tipped pens. None of these compounds was intended to be introduced into the human body. However, when inhaled each of these compounds alters normal brain function and may induce a sense of euphoria. It is possible for children and adolescents to purchase any of dozens, perhaps hundreds of potential inhalants without parental permission. Inhalant abuse is normally a time-limited phase for children and adolescents, and after a year or two they grow tired of this process and discontinue it. However, on occasion the child or adolescent will continue to abuse inhalants, and it is not unheard of for an adult to enter treatment for inhalant abuse. Because these compounds are so widely abused, and have a terrible potential for harm to the abuser, we will focus on the problem of inhalant abuse in this chapter.

A Brief History of Inhalant Abuse

The use of inhaled compounds to alter the user's perception of reality might be traced back at least to ancient Greece and the Oracle at Delphi (Hernandez-Avila & Pierucci-Lagha, 2005). Historians believe that the Oracle would inhale fumes from a volcanic vent and then, while in a state of delirium, deliver prophetic statements that the recipient was supposed to interpret. More recently, the use of anesthetic gasses for recreational purposes became popular in the 19th century. In the 20th century, when various industrial solvents became available,

they quickly became compounds that were abused by inhalation (Commission on Adolescent Substance and Alcohol Abuse, 2005; Hernandez-Avila & Pierucci-Lagha, 2005; C. W. Sharp & Rosenberg, 2005).

The mainstream media paid little attention to the problem of inhalant abuse until the 1950s and 1960s, when the practice of "glue sniffing" became popular (Brust, 2004). The glue used to hold model ships, planes, and automobiles often contained the compound toluene,[1] which when inhaled can alter the individual's consciousness. It is not known why the practice of glue

---

[1]This compound has since been removed from model airplane glue.

sniffing began, but historical evidence suggests that it began in California. The first known reference to glue sniffing was in a Denver newspaper (Brust, 2004; C. W. Sharp & Rosenberg, 2005). Other newspapers began to cover the story of inhalant abuse, in the process explaining exactly how children or adolescents should use airplane glue to become intoxicated and what effects they should expect. Although the media stories first appeared in the U.S. newspapers, the problem of inhalant abuse is now recognized as a worldwide one. In many "third world" countries, the abuse of inhalants helps to dull the individual's awareness of hunger, for example (M. Weiss, 2007). It is especially popular in Europe and Japan for recreational purposes rather than to dull the pangs of hunger (Brust, 2004; S. B. Karch, 2009).

The Pharmacology of the Inhalants

As was discussed in the introduction, *inhalants* are not a drug but a range of compounds that share a common method of abuse. Whereas cocaine or heroin my be "snorted," this does not place them in the category of an "inhalant" because the goal of this process is to deposit the powder in the blood-rich tissues of the sinuses, not the lungs, for absorption. A true "inhalant" is absorbed through the lungs and passed into the general circulation from there.

Inhalation is one of the most effective means to introduce a compound into the general circulation. Many molecules are able to cross over from the lungs into the circulation quickly and effectively, a trait that physicians often rely on to introduce anesthetic gasses into a patient's body to induce unconsciousness for major surgery. Inhalant abusers also rely on this rapid means of introducing a compound into the circulation to induce pleasure. Unfortunately, this process is perhaps the most neglected research area of modern medicine, leaving more questions than answers (McGuinness, 2006).

A number of different classification systems of inhalants have been suggested, two of which are reviewed in Table 13-1.

Of these four categories in Espeland's (1997) classification system, children and adolescents will usually abuse compounds that fall into the first two but will have limited access to the third category. The abuse of surgical anesthetics is usually limited to health care

TABLE 13-1 COMPARISON OF TWO INHALANT CLASSIFICATION SYSTEMS		
	BRUST (2004), CROWLEY AND SAKAI (2005)	**ESPELAND (1997)**
1	solvents	organic solvents
2	propellants (used in spray cans)	aerosols (used in spray cans)
3	paint thinners	volatile nitrites (Amyl nitrite or butyl nitrite)
4	fuel fumes	general anesthetic gasses

professionals, or medical school students, who have access to such compounds (Hernandez-Avila & Pierucci-Lagha, 2005).

The most common inhalants are simple, carbon-based molecules such as benzene, toulene, hexane, acetone, butane, and ethyl chloride (Ricaurte et al., 2008). All of these compounds, plus gasoline fumes (another favorite inhalant in some regions of the world), are able to enter the bloodstream without their chemical structure being altered in any way (Bruckner & Warren, 2003). The compounds most commonly abused as inhalants are very lipid soluble, a characteristic that allows those molecules to rapidly cross the blood–brain barrier (BBB) into the brain within seconds of their use (Commission on Adolescent Substance and Alcohol Abuse, 2002; Crowley & Sakai, 2004).

Parents will often ask why, if children are abusing various compounds through inhalation, the government does not just outlaw these products. The answer to this question is that this is impossible. It has been estimated that there are over *1000* common household or industrial products that might be abused as an inhalant (McGuinness, 2006; Wolfe, 2009). Further, children and adolescents are adept at finding compounds around the house that might be abused as an inhalant. For example, the team of Feuillet, Mallet, and Spadari (2006) presented a case history in which twin sisters were inhaling mothball fumes to become intoxicated.

Virtually no information is available effects of the compounds abused by inhalation at the cellular level (McGuinness, 2006). Indeed, most of the compounds abused as inhalants were never intended to be introduced into the human body. Even where such research has been conducted, abusers often use concentrations of the compound(s) of choice that are orders of magnitude beyond those achieved when that compound is used as directed (Bruckner & Warren, 2003). For example, the maximum permitted exposure level for toluene fumes in the workplace is 50–100 parts per million (ppm) (Crowley & Sakai, 2005). The concentration used by those who choose to abuse this compound through inhalation are 50–100 times as high as the maximum permitted industrial exposure level. At best there is only limited research into the effects of toluene on the body at such levels. To further complicate matters, abusers might use a compound in which the desired substance is a secondary ingredient, exposing themselves to the effects of the primary compound in that product as well as the desired substance (Hernandez-Avila & Pierucci-Lagha, 2005). Finally, toxicological information on the effects of the majority of products inhaled in adults is limited, at best. There is virtually *no* information available as to the effects of these compounds on children or adolescents (Bruckner & Warren, 2003).

To further complicate matters, the effects of the chemical being abused are dependent on (a) the chemical(s) being abused, (b) the intensity of exposure, (c) the body size of the abuser, (d) the abuser's expectations for the effects of that compound, and (e) the setting in which the inhalant abuse takes place (Wolfe, 2009). Another factor is the abuser's general state of health. Given the interaction between these variables, and the wide variety of compounds that might be abused as an inhalant, it is impossible to speak of a class-specific "pharmacology" or "toxicology" of these compounds. However, many of the commonly abused inhalants do share some common toxicological characteristics. For example, many of these compounds must be biotransformed by the liver before the process of elimination (usually by the kidneys) can begin (Bruckner & Warren, 2003). There are exceptions to this rule, however: The anesthetic gases are exhaled without extensive, or in some cases any, biotransformation taking place (Crowley & Sakai, 2004).

Scientists do not fully understand the mechanism(s) by which the inhalants alter the normal function of the brain (Commission on Adolescent Substance and Alcohol Abuse, 2005; McGuinness, 2006). An example of this is the ongoing debate over how the surgical anesthetics work and whether a patient under the effects of an anesthetic can still feel pain. As a group the compounds abused by inhalation are thought to alter the normal function of the gamma-amino-butyric acid (GABA) and/or the N-methyl-D-aspartate (NMDA) neurotransmitter systems (Crowley & Sakai, 2004).

Because of all of these various variables, there are no standard formulas by which to estimate the biological or elimination half-life of a compound being abused as an inhalant. The elimination half-life of different inhalants might range from hours to days, depending on the specific compound being abused (Brooks, Leung, & Shannon, 1996). It should be noted, however, that the half-life of most solvents is longer in obese abusers, because these compounds bind to lipid molecules. Given the current epidemic of childhood obesity in the United States, this is a matter of some concern for health care professionals who work with inhalant abusers.

Either directly or indirectly the inhalants are toxic to the body through a variety of mechanisms. Behavioral observations on animals exposed to an inhalant suggests that their effects are similar to those of alcohol or the barbiturates (Commission on Adolescent Substance and Alcohol Abuse, 2005; Hernandez-Avila & Pierucci-Lagha, 2005). Further, it has been observed that some inhalants potentiate the effects of central nervous system (CNS) depressants used concurrently, such as alcohol and the benzodiazepines, possibly with fatal results. Thus there is no standard "pharmacology" of those compounds being abused as an inhalant, and this complicates the problem for health care professionals who must treat inhalant abusers.

Scope of the Problem of Inhalant Abuse

When the mass media in the United States focus their attention on the problem of inhalant abuse in this country, they ignore the fact that this is a worldwide problem (Spiller & Krenzelok, 1997). Researchers disagree about the scope of inhalant abuse among children and adolescents in the United States. One report suggested that approximately 4.5% of children or adolescents admit to the abuse of an inhalant at some point in their lives and that the phenomenon of inhalant abuse involved approximately equal numbers of males and females ("Patterns and Trends in Inhalant Use by Adolescent Males and Females: 2002–2005," 2007). In contrast to this, Brust (2004) suggested that boys were more likely to abuse inhalants than girls by a ratio of 10:1, whereas Spiller and Krenzelok (1997) suggested that boys who abused an inhalant outnumbered girls by a ratio of 3:1. There obviously is a need for more research into this area to determine the exact prevalence of inhalant abuse.

It is frightening to note that many who abuse compounds via inhalation do not view this as a form of "drug" abuse (Wolfe, 2009). It is thought that 2 million people in the United States have abused an inhalant in the preceding 12 months ("Agency: More Teens Abusing Inhalants," 2005; Hernandez-Avila & Pierucci-Lagha, 2005). Inhalant abuse for the most part is limited to experimental use that occurs a few times and then is discontinued, without the child or adolescent going on to develop other drug problems (Crowley & Sakai, 2005). Of the estimated 2 million people who have abused an inhalant in the preceding 12 months, 1 million did so for the very first time ("Agency: More Teens Abusing Inhalants," 2005). If children and/or adolescents were to engage in prolonged periods of inhalant abuse, the number of abusers in the past year would be much higher than it is.

The mean age at which abusers begin substance-centered inhalation is about 13 years, and the mean age of inhalant abusers is thought to be 16.6 years of age (C. E. Anderson & Loomis, 2003; Spiller & Krenzelok, 1997). These figures would seem to suggest that inhalant abuse is an episodic phenomenon during the teen years, an observation supported by the fact that inhalant abuse appears to be most common in the 11- to 15-year age group, after which point most adolescents mature out of this practice (Commission on Adolescent Substance and Alcohol Abuse, 2005). There are reports of children as young as 3 years of age abusing inhalants, however, and so it is important to keep in mind the fact that children do abuse inhalants on occasion (Crowley & Sakai, 2005).

It has been estimated that only about 4% of inhalant abusers become dependent on a compound abused through inhalation (Brust, 2004). Hernandez-Avila & Pierucci-Lagha (2005) identified four patterns of inhalant abuse:

1. Transient social use: This occurs for a brief period of time in response to social situations, usually involving individuals 10–16 years of age.
2. Chronic social use: The individual abuses an inhalant for 5 or more years with others; usually seen in individuals 20–30 years of age. These individuals demonstrate signs of brain damage and usually have minor legal problems in their histories.
3. Transient isolated use: These individuals are usually 10–16 years of age and have a short history of inhalant abuse.
4. Chronic isolated use: These individuals have a history of continuous solo abuse of inhalants lasting for 5+ years, with a history of serious legal problems and possible evidence of brain damage.

There is lively debate over whether inhalants serve as a "gateway" to further drug abuse. It has been found, for example, that 23% of cocaine abusers had a history of prior inhalant abuse (Worchester, 2006). It has been found that people who admit to a history of inhalant abuse were 45 times more likely to engage in the practice of self-injected drug abuse, whereas those individuals who admit to the use of inhalants *and* marijuana use were 89 times as likely to have used injected drugs as the general population (Crowley & Sakai, 2005). These figures, although disturbing, raise an interesting question: Does the inhalant abuse pave the way for further drug abuse, or do those people who are more likely to abuse drugs begin with inhalant abuse and then "graduate" on to other forms of substance use later in life? This debate over whether inhalants serve as a "gateway" to later drug abuse has not been resolved and continues to this day.

Methods of Inhalant Abuse

There are a number of ways that inhalants might be abused, and the specific method of abuse is dependent on the specific compound being abused (C. E. Anderson & Loomis, 2003; Wolfe, 2009). Some compounds may be inhaled directly from its container, a practice called *sniffing* or *snorting*. Other compounds are poured into a plastic bag, which is then placed over the abuser's mouth and nose so that the individual can inhale concentrated fumes, a practice called *bagging* (C. E. Anderson & Loomis, 2003; T. Nelson, 2000). Still other compounds are poured onto a rag, which is then placed over the individual's mouth and nose, which allows the fumes to be inhaled along with air, a process called *huffing* (C. E. Anderson & Loomis, 2003; T. Nelson, 2000).

Fumes from aerosol cans may be directly inhaled, or sprayed into the mouth. An example of those fumes that are directly inhaled are cigarette lighters. Abusers will activate the cigarette lighter without lighting it, allowing the fumes to escape the container for inhalation. Finally, there are those compounds that might be heated, releasing the fumes that are then inhaled (T. Nelson, 2000). Obviously, if the compound being abused should be flammable, there is a significant risk of fire should the compound being heated be exposed to open flame or a spark, but this is a risk that inhalant abusers either are not aware of or dismiss as a cost of their abuse of inhalants.

Subjective Effects of Inhalants

The initial effects of an inhalant begin with seconds to, at most, minutes and last for approximately 45 minutes per episode of abuse (Schuckit, 2006a; Zevin & Benowitz, 2007). The desired effects from inhalants include a hazy euphoria somewhat like that produced by alcohol, as well as a sense of spinning, numbness, hallucinations, and loss of inhibitions (C. E. Anderson & Loomis, 2003; Brust, 2004; C. W. Sharp & Rosenberg, 2005; Wolfe, 2009; Zevin & Benowitz, 2007). Some of the less desirable effects of inhalants include nausea, vomiting, amnesia, slurred speech, excitement, double vision, ringing of the ears, agitation, and violence (Hernandez-Avila & Pierucci-Lagha, 2005; Schuckit, 2006a; C. W. Sharp & Rosenberg, 2005; Tekin & Cummings, 2003). Following the initial stage of euphoria, CNS depression develops, which may be followed by a drug-induced "hangover" experience that can last between a few minutes to a few hours, depending on the exact substance being abused and the intensity with which it was abused (C. W. Sharp & Rosenberg, 2005). Abusers also report a residual sense of drowsiness and/or stupor, which will last for several hours after they abused an inhalant (Commission on Adolescent Substance and Alcohol Abuse, 2005).

Complications Induced by Inhalant Abuse

When inhalant abuse first emerged in the 1950s and 1960s, most health care professionals did not think that there were any serious health consequences that might be induced by this practice. However, in the last quarter of the 20th century scientists concluded that depending on (a) the substance being abused, (b) the method of abuse, and (c) the frequency of abuse, the abuser might experience significant health problems and possible death (Worchester, 2006). A partial list of potential consequences from inhalant abuse includes those listed in Table 13-2 (C. E. Anderson & Loomis, 2003; Brust, 2004; Crowley & Sakai, 2004, 2005; Filley, 2004; S. B. Karch, 2009; C. W. Sharp & Rosenberg, 2005; M. Weiss, 2007; Wolfe, 2009; Worchester, 2006; Zevin & Benowitz, 2007).

It should be noted that inhalant-induced death can occur the first time that an individual abuses a compound via inhalation or the 200th time ("Huffing can kill your child," 2004). Approximately 50% of inhalant-related deaths are the result of inhalant-induced

TABLE 13-2 POSSIBLE HEALTH CONSEQUENCES OF INHALANT ABUSE

CARDIOPULMONARY SYSTEM

anoxia and/or respiratory depression, possibly to point of death

aspiration of vomited material (may result in death, especially if abuser is unconscious)

bone marrow damage resulting in reduction in red blood cell production

cardiac arrhythmias (may prove fatal)

RESPIRATORY SYSTEM

cough/wheezing

erosion of nasal mucosa, formation of ulcers in nose, mouth, and throat

exacerbation of preexisting asthma

lung function changes, possible chronic lung disease

sinusitis (irritation of sinus tissues)

CENTRAL NERVOUS SYSTEM

cerebellar ataxia

deafness or loss of hearing (may become permanent)

encephalopathy

nystagmus

organic brain damage (including possible drug-induced dementia)

Parkinson's disease–like movement disorder

peripheral neuropathies

seizures

tremor

visual impairment (may become permanent)

PSYCHIATRIC

Psychosis (drug induced) (may be permanent)

OTHER COMPLICATIONS

chemical burns to skin, especially around mouth/nose

death (variety of mechanisms, noted above)

kidney damage (might be permanent)

laryngitis

liver damage (possibly permanent)

muscle tissue damage secondary to rhabdomyolysis

vomiting, possibly leading to aspiration-induced death

ventricular fibrillation,[2] or *sniffing death syndrome* (McGuinness, 2006). Further, depending on the substance being abused, abusers might introduce various heavy metals such as copper or lead into their body, which will have lifelong consequences (Crowley & Sakai, 2005). Gasoline was a common cause of lead poisoning when it was abused as an inhalant, although in the United States lead has been removed from gasoline and this is rarely a problem now. If the compound being abused is a propellant-propelled substance (such as spray paint, for example), the abuser runs the risk of coating the inside of the lungs with the compound itself, although the propellant was the desired substance to be abused via inhalation. This may interfere with the normal function of the lungs, if not block it entirely, resulting in the abuser's death.

Although a standard neurological examination is often unable to detect solvent-induced organic brain damage until it is relatively advanced, sensitive neuropsychological tests often detect signs of inhalant-induced brain damage even in industrial workers who are exposed to levels far lower than those utilized by inhalant abusers. Toluene is a prime example of this, and chronic toluene exposure can induce intellectual impairment, as well as leukoencephalopathy and atrophy of the optic nerves (Crowley & Sakai, 2004, 2005; Ricaurte et al., 2008).

Upon the cessation of an episode of inhalant abuse, the abuser will go through a withdrawal syndrome very similar to that seen in the alcohol-induced delirium tremens (DTs) (Hernandez-Avila & Pierucci-Lasha, 2005). The exact withdrawal syndrome will depend in large part on the exact compound(s) being abused, the length of exposure, the concentration of the compound(s) used by the abusers, and whether they are abusing other compounds beyond the inhalants. Some of the symptoms observed during inhalant withdrawal include muscle tremors, irritability, anxiety, insomnia, muscle cramps, hallucinations, sweating, nausea, a foul odor on the abuser's breath, loss of vision, and possible seizures (Worchester, 2006).

Inhalant Abuse and Suicide

There is a strong correlation between inhalant abuse, depression, and suicidal behavior (McGuinness, 2006). This is not to say that every inhalant abuser will attempt suicide, but that because depression is a risk factor for suicidal behavior, and depression is a consequence of inhalant abuse, there is a potential for adolescent suicidal behavior as a result of inhalant abuse. Thus the more intense the frequency and duration of inhalant abuse, the greater the risk for suicidal behavior (Espeland, 1997; Freedenthala, Vaugh, Jensona, & Howard, 2007). It is often difficult to determine whether adolescents intended to end their lives as some of the methods of inhalant abuse utilized by adolescents lend themselves to ambiguity as to whether it was an intentional or accidental death. For example, if abusers insert an inhalant into a plastic bag, then insert their head and close the bag around the head and neck, and then begin to inhale the fumes until they lose consciousness and eventually die, it is difficult to determine whether this was an actual suicide or just an accident unless they left a suicide note behind. However, suicidal behavior is an additional consequence to inhalant abuse.

Anesthetic Misuse

The first two anesthetics used, nitrous oxide and ether, were first recreational substances (Hernandez-Avila & Pierucci-Lasha, 2005). Their potential as surgical anesthetics were recognized only when Horace Wells attended a party in which people were indulging in nitrous oxide abuse and observed a person under its influence injure himself without apparent pain. Unfortunately, the first planned exhibition of nitrous oxide as an anesthetic agent was something less than a success.[3]

The pharmacological effects of general anesthetics are similar to those induced by the barbiturates (Hernandez-Avila & Pierucci-Lagha, 2005). There is a dose-dependent response ranging from sedation, through sleep, and, as the dose increases, to analgesia and unconsciousness. At extremely high doses, the anesthetic gasses can cause death. Following is a discussion of one of the most commonly abused anesthetic gasses: nitrous oxide.

Nitrous Oxide

All of the surgical anesthetic gasses are able to induce a loss of consciousness, during which time the patient is less responsive to painful stimuli. Nitrous oxide presents both the physician using it as a surgical anesthetic, or the abuser, with certain dangers. First, special precautions must be taken to maintain a proper oxygen supply to the brain. Room air alone will not supply sufficient oxygen to the person who is unconscious

---

[2]A cardiac arrhythmia.

[3]Discussed in more detail in Breakout Discussion #1 for Chapter 13.

after nitrous oxide use. To avoid hypoxia,[4] the physician (or dentist, because it is often used as an anesthetic during dental surgery) must supply supplemental oxygen at over pressure[5] during the procedure. Abusers often do not know about this characteristic of nitrous oxide, and very few have access to the equipment necessary to supply oxygen at over pressure. Thus nitrous oxide abusers run a substantial risk of hypoxia-induced brain damage or even death.

Anesthetic-induced hypoxia is not limited to nitrous oxide. Virtually all of the inhalants, including nitrous oxide, can interfere with the delivery of oxygen to the brain and induce hypoxia-related brain damage. In the case of nitrous oxide, abusers report feelings of euphoria, giddiness, hallucinations, and a loss of inhibitions. Medical and dental students, who have access to nitrous oxide through their professional training, will occasionally abuse nitrous oxide, as well as such anesthetic agents as ether, chloroform, trichlorothylene, and halothane.

Children and adolescent will occasionally abuse nitrous oxide, which is still used as a propellant in certain spray cans of various products. They must take special precautions to release *only* the nitrous oxide.[6] In very rare cases abusers will actually manufacture nitrous oxide, although this process may then expose abusers to impurities found in the product that they manufactured. There is little information available about the dangers of this practice, the effects of prolonged abuse, or the effects of the impurities on the abuser's body.

The volatile anesthetics are not extensively biotransformed by the body, but enter and leave the body virtually unchanged. Once the source of the anesthetic is removed, such as when the surgical procedure is completed, the concentration of the anesthetic in the brain will begin to drop, and eventually the patient is able to regain consciousness to begin the process of recovery.

The Abuse of Nitrites

There are different forms of nitrites commonly abused: (a) the pharmaceutical compound amyl nitrite, which is used in certain heart conditions, (b) butyl nitrite, and (c) isabutyl nitrite. Although inhaled, all of these compounds function as a coronary vasodilator, allowing more blood to flow to the heart. This is why amyl nitrite is used in the control of angina pectoris: When administered it allows the coronary arteries to dilate, increasing the blood flow to the heart for a period of time. Amyl nitrite is administered in small glass containers embedded in layers of cloth. When needed, users will "snap" or "pop"[7] the container in their fingers and inhale the fumes to achieve the desired effect.

With the introduction of nitroglycerine preparations, which are as effective as amyl nitrite but lack many of its disadvantages, amyl nitrite has fallen into disfavor and is now only rarely used (Hernandez-Avila & Pierucci-Lasha, 2005). Still, it does have a limited role in medicine, such as in certain diagnostic procedures and the treatment of cyanide poisoning. Nitrite abusers prize these amyl nitrite capsules, using them in much the same manner that they abuse butyl nitrite or isabutyl nitrite. These compounds are available from mail order houses or specialty stores, depending on the state regulations for that specific area. In many areas, butyl nitrite is sold as a "room deodorizer" in small bottles that usually cost more than $10. Abusers believe that butyl nitrite will induce a prolonged, intense orgasm if inhaled just before the abuser achieves orgasm.[8] Because amyl nitrite is known to induce delayed orgasm and impotence in male users, it is not unreasonable to expect that its close chemical cousins would also induce these effects. Further, after-effects of the use of these compounds include an intense, sudden headache, increased pressure in the fluid in the eyes (a danger for patients with glaucoma), possible weakness, nausea, and cerebral hemorrhage induced by nitrite-induced increased blood pressure. In addition, the nitrites appear to suppress the action of the body's immune system, especially the natural killer cells, possibly increasing risk for acquisition of an infection while under the effects of the nitrites. But abusers are willing to run the risk of these adverse events, in spite of the fact that most people wonder why anyone would be willing to run these risks just for a few seconds of pleasure.

---

[4]See Glossary.

[5]See Glossary.

[6]The author of this text is aware of at least one case where the abuser tried to release the nitrous oxide that was used as a propellant in a can of whipped cream, but accidentally released the whipped cream directly into the nose and sinuses.

[7]Thus the name "poppers" or "snappers" used by illicit users.

[8]The author of this text has met butyl nitrite abusers who claim that rather than enhance sexual pleasure, butyl nitrite actually interfered with their enjoyment of the sexual encounter.

Chapter Summary

Inhalant abuse appears to be a phase through which many children and adolescents pass. For the most part, the individual engages in a few episodes of inhalant abuse over a period of 1–2 years and then discontinues the practice. But a small percentage of abusers go on to abuse other compounds, and an even smaller percentage of abusers continue to use inhalants for extended periods. The effects of these compounds are short-lived, although this depends on the specific compound(s) being abused and the intensity with which the abuser inhales this compound(s). Because there are literally thousands of commercial products that may be abused as an inhalant, these compounds are easily available to children and adolescents, a fact that may contribute to their attractiveness as a drug of abuse. However, inhalant abuse also exposes the abuser to compounds, the effects of which are unknown to toxicologists, or in dosage levels that have not been studied by toxicologists. Death or organic damage to various body organs is possible from inhalant abuse, making these compounds a dangerous "high" for children or adolescents.

CHAPTER 14

The Underrecognized Problem of Steroid Abuse and Addiction

Introduction

Anabolic steroids are often classified as "performance-enhancing" drugs, and as such are often abused by athletes who seek a competitive edge. However, they are not the first such compounds to be used for this purpose. Ancient Greek warriors would eat deer muscle to increase their speed, and lion heart muscle to increase their bravery (M. Stephens, 2008). The gladiators of ancient Rome used a wide variety of potions in the hope of being able to gain a competitive edge over their opponents (Botre & Pavan, 2008). It is not known how effective these compounds were, but the users believed in them, which may have enhanced their fighting or athletic ability if only through the placebo effect.

In the present era, when the words *performance-enhancing compounds* are uttered, people think of the anabolic steroid abuse, often by world-class amateur and professional athletes. They are rarely aware of, and are often shocked to learn that these compounds are extensively abused on the local level for a variety of reasons. Surprisingly, abuse of testosterone and its derivatives carries a significant risk of harm to the abuser, and although they do appear to be able to induce a mild euphoria, they are most often abused to improve athletic performance.

In a sense, anabolic steroid abuse reflects a two different social diseases. First is the emphasis on appearances. This is perhaps most clearly illustrated by the trend for advertisers to describe their product as being "on steroids," giving the impression of enhanced speed, durability, and attractiveness (H. G. Pope & Brower, 2008; Rylkova, Bruijnzeel, & Gold, 2007). The second social disease is the belief that it is acceptable to "win at any cost," even if this involves the use of illegal and potentially lethal compounds. Because of this belief many athletes will look for something—anything—that will give them an "edge" over the competition. In the face of persistent rumors that certain athletes have been using anabolic steroids to enhance performance, an "arms race mentality"

(Joyner, 2004, p. 81) has evolved in both amateur and professional athletics.[1] Believing that the opposition is abusing these compounds, other athletes also begin to use performance-enhancing compounds to overcome what they perceive as an unfair advantage and to level the playing field.[2,3]

To meet the demands of both those who wish to enhance athletic performance and those who wish to improve their appearance, a whole industry has evolved. Because of the widespread abuse of these compounds, it is of value for the substance abuse counselor to have a working knowledge of these compounds and their effects.

An Introduction to the Anabolic-Androgenic Steroids

The term *anabolic* refers to the ability of these compounds to increase the speed of tissue growth or repair, possibly through the retention of nitrogen molecules within muscle tissue. The term *steroid* refers to the fact that these compounds are structurally similar to testosterone, the male primary sex hormone. Because of their chemical similarity to testosterone, steroids have a masculinizing (androgenic) effect on the user (H. G. Pope & Brower, 2008). This natural effect is seen when boys reach puberty and their bodies start to produce significant amounts of testosterone: Suddenly muscle growth is seen, along with various other masculinization effects. The adolescent may have been exercising prior to the onset of puberty, but it is only after puberty that their efforts result in significant muscle growth. Thus at times, the anabolic steroids are referred to as the *anabolic-androgenic* steroids.[4]

[1]The team of Thevis, Thomas, Kihler, Beuck, and Schanzer (2009) identified a wide range of compounds beyond the anabolic steroids that are being abused for their performance-enhancing effect, including a range of nonsteroid compounds, many of which are quite difficult to detect using current methods. However, the anabolic steroids are still being abused, and thus their abuse should be understood by health care professionals.

[2]Rylkova et al. (2007) estimated that up to 95% of professional football players and 80–99% of other professional athletes use anabolic steroids to enhance performance.

[3]The article "Drugs in Sports: New Problems in Doping Detection" (2009) provides a very good summary of the nonsteroidal compounds being used and developed, or that have the potential for abuse by professional athletes for performance enhancement purposes. Their use lies outside of the scope of this chapter, and they will not be discussed here, because they are rarely if ever abused by amateur athletes.

[4]For the sake of this chapter, the terms *steroids* or *anabolic steroids* will be used.

Medical Uses of Anabolic Steroids

Although the anabolic steroids have been in use since the 1950s, there are few approved uses for these compounds (H. G. Pope & Brower, 2005, 2008). The anabolic steroids share a common core chemical structure[5] to progesterone, adrenocortical hormones,[6] and bile acids found in the human body. They are also similar in structure to the poison manufactured by the skin of several species of toads, and a range of compounds that are known to be carcinogenic. Physicians will prescribe corticosteroids to suppress the immune system as an adjunct to the treatment of various diseases, but these are the *corticosteroids*, not anabolic steroids. This is an important distinction for the reader to keep in mind.

Anabolic steroids are occasionally used to treat delayed puberty in adolescents and as an adjunct to the treatment of certain forms of breast cancer (Congeni & Miller, 2002). They promote the growth of bone tissue following injuries in certain cases and might be useful in the treatment of osteoporosis (Congeni & Miller, 2002). Their close chemical cousins, the corticosteroids, have been found to be useful in treating a range of conditions. Evidence suggests that although the anabolic steroids might be of value in treating AIDS-related weight loss, there are few other legitimate applications for the anabolic steroids at this time.

Why Steroids Are Abused

As the information in the last section would suggest, there are few approved applications for anabolic steroids. Because the anabolic steroids can (a) increase lean

[5]Technically known as a hydrogenated cyclopentophenanthine ring.

[6]Also known as *cortiosteroids*.

muscle mass, (b) increase muscle strength, and (c) reduce the period of recovery time necessary between exercise periods, athletes are often drawn to them (S. B. Karch, 2009; H. G. Pope & Brower, 2008). They also are able to induce a sense of euphoria (Eisenberg & Galloway, 2005; Hildebrandt, Langenbucher, Carr, Sanjuan, & Park, 2006). In contrast to alcohol or the other drugs of abuse, anabolic steroid abusers are often rewarded for their athletic performance, especially if the steroid use is undetected by urine or blood toxicology testing. Even the team physician might not suspect or detect anabolic steroid use on the part of the player(s), in part because most physicians receive relatively little training in the recognition and treatment of anabolic steroid abuse (H. G. Pope & Brower, 2008).

Once the cycle of steroid abuse is initiated, many abusers continue because these compounds can induce a state of "reverse anorexia nervosa" (Kanayama, Barry, Hudson, & Pope, 2006, p. 697). Individuals with this condition, which is more descriptive than a diagnostic category, become obsessed with their body image and fear that they might look "small" to others. This condition is usually seen after the individual has been abusing anabolic steroids on an extended basis, and it functions as an incentive for further steroid abuse. However, there is some evidence suggesting that body image disorders predate the abuse of anabolic steroids in many people (Kanayama et al., 2006). It is thus not surprising to learn that nonathlete steroid abusers believe that these compounds will help them look more attractive (Kanayama et al., 2006; H. G. Pope & Brower, 2004, 2005, 2008).

Another subgroup of steroid abusers is composed of law enforcement and security officers, who believe that these compounds will increase their strength and aggressiveness (Eisenberg & Galloway, 2005; Galloway, 1997). These individuals hope that their use of steroids will give them an advantage when confronting a potential lawbreaker. A small subgroup of adolescent girls believe that these compounds will help them lose body fat and help them look more "toned" or attractive ("Girls Are Abusing Steroids Too," 2005). Thus there is no "standard" steroid abuser, but various subgroups who share the characteristic of anabolic steroid abuse in common.

The Legal Status of Anabolic Steroids

In the United States, anabolic steroids have been classified as a Category III controlled substance[7] since 1990.

This means that at least 28 different chemical compounds in the anabolic steroid group have been classified as illegal, and their use for nonmedical purposes, or their sale by individuals not licensed to possess and distribute them, is a crime punishable by a prison term of up to 5 years (10 years if the steroids are sold to minors).

Scope of the Problem of Steroid Abuse

Anabolic steroid abuse is a silent epidemic, and the true scope of the abuse of these compounds is not known (Eisenberg & Galloway, 2005; S. B. Karch, 2009). There is little information about the use of performance-enhancing compounds (including anabolic steroids) by preadolescent athletes, although there have been such cases found in Europe (Laure & Binsinger, 2007). In the United States, urine toxicology testing for performance-enhancing drugs in athletes does not begin until high school, and so the abuse of such compounds in preadolescents is unlikely to be detected and thus might be more widespread than suspected, according to Laure and Binsinger.

In the United States, it is thought that approximately 7% of high school seniors have abused anabolic steroids at least once (Kanayama et al., 2006; Rylkova et al., 2007; M. Stephens, 2008). Although earlier studies suggested that adolescent girls might be abusing anabolic steroids in large numbers, H. G. Pope and Brower (2008) discounted this theory on the grounds that these medications have an androgenic effect, which would be most unwelcome for the typical adolescent girl. In spite of this fact, there is preliminary evidence suggesting that the number of girls who are abusing an anabolic steroid is increasing ("Girls Are Abusing Steroids Too," 2005). Although anabolic steroid abuse was seen most often in older adolescents, there is a disturbing trend for younger adolescent athletes to abuse these compounds, both to improve their appearance and to improve athletic ability (Calfee & Fadale, 2006; Rylkova et al., 2007).

It has been estimated that there are 400,000 current abusers of anabolic steroids in the United States at this time, and that at least 1 million people have abused an anabolic steroid at some point in their lives (Kanayama et al., 2006; H. G. Pope & Brower, 2008). The median age for anabolic steroid abusers is 18 (S. B. Karch, 2009), which is consistent with the observation that college-aged steroid abusers frequently report that they did not begin to use these compounds until just before or shortly after starting college (Dickensheets, 2001).

---

[7]See Appendix 4.

Further, although the popular image of a steroid abuser is that of a professional athlete, J. Cohen, Collins, Darkes, and Gwartney (2007) found that the typical male steroid abuser in their research sample was a well-educated, Caucasian 30-year-old who held a "white-collar" job.

Pharmacology of Anabolic-Androgenic Steroids

The anabolic steroids are members of a group of biologically active compounds that share a basic element to their chemical structure.[8] Other members of this group of compounds include progesterone, adrenocortical hormones, bile acids, some poisons produced by various toads, and some carcinogenic compounds. It is thought that the steroids force the body to increase protein synthesis and inhibit the action of a group of chemicals known as the glucocorticoids, which cause tissue break down (Casavant, Blake, Griffith, Yates, & Copley, 2007; Congeni & Miller, 2002; Rylkova et al., 2007).

The anabolic steroids might be broken down into two subgroups: (a) those compounds that are active when administered orally and (b) those compounds that must be injected into muscle tissue to become active. The orally administered steroids are more easily administered, but have a shorter half-life and are more toxic to the liver than steroids administered parenterally. It has been hypothesized that in the brain the neurosteroids might modulate the action of the GABAa receptor through an unknown mechanism, which then allows the neurosteroids to alter the user's emotions. The GABAa receptor is found in the brain regions involved in the aggression response, anxiety, and reproduction (Rylkova et al., 2007). As will be discussed later in this chapter, anabolic steroid abusers have been found to experience a wide range of behavioral problems, suggesting that they cross the blood–brain barrier and bind at some of the same receptor sites that are utilized by the neurosteroids.

As noted previously, the anabolic steroids are similar in chemical structure to testosterone. At puberty testosterone triggers not only the development of secondary sex characteristics in boys, but also the muscle growth that separates them from preadolescent children. Thus it makes clinical sense for athletes to abuse anabolic steroids to add to their muscle mass, although this muscle strength is achieved at a terrible cost.

Naturally, men develop various forms of cardiovascular disease at an earlier age than the average woman, who are protected from many of the harmful effects of testosterone until menopause. When abused, the progression to cardiovascular disease is enhanced, as will be discussed later in this chapter.

Sources and Methods of Steroid Abuse

Because anabolic steroids have few recognized medical uses, and strict controls are in place to limit the amount(s) prescribed by physicians, most anabolic steroids used in the United States are obtained from illicit sources (Eisenberg & Galloway, 2005). This sources include legitimate pharmaceuticals that are diverted to the illicit market, steroids intended for the veterinary market, and compounds smuggled into the United States by a variety of means. Internet pharmacies are an increasingly popular source of anabolic steroids abused in the United States, as the shipment of pharmaceuticals from the supplier to the "patient" is unlikely to be intercepted. Anabolic steroids might also be purchased in other countries and then smuggled into the United States. These compounds then move through an informal distribution network centered around health clubs or gyms (Eisenberg & Galloway, 2005; S. B. Karch, 2009; Mahoney, 2006).

In the world of professional athletics, there is also a thriving market for what are known as "designer" steroids (Knight, 2003, p. 114). These substances are steroid compounds that are manufactured in secret and supposedly are undetectable by the current generation of urine or blood toxicology tests. Given the fact that there are *more than 1000* known derivatives of the basic testosterone molecule, it is easy to understand the potential for developing a steroid that is not detectable by the current generation of laboratory tests. One such example of a "designer" steroid is the compound tetrahydrogestrinone (THG). This compound was reported to have "all the hallmarks of an anabolic steroid, crafted to escape detection in urine analysis tests" (Kondro, 2003, p. 1466). THG was not detectable by urine toxicology tests until a new test was developed for it in 2003, at which time there was a "flurry" of reports that THG was found in the urine of a number athletes ("Athletes Caught Using a New Steroid—THG," 2003; Knight, 2003). The development of tests to detect THG is only the latest round in an ongoing race between those who wish to abuse these compounds and those who wish to detect their abuse.

---

[8]Technically, a hydrogenated cyclopentophenanthrine ring.

TABLE 14-1 TERMINOLOGY USED BY STEROID ABUSERS

TERM	DEFINITION
Blending	Mixing different steroids for use at the same time; might involve both oral and injected forms of steroids
Bulking up	Increasing muscle mass through steroid use and an exercise program; follows a fixed schedule, with the abuser also using a special diet along with anabolic steroids
Cycling	Taking multiple doses of steroid(s) over time, with drug-free holidays intermixed with periods of active steroid abuse
Doping	Using any of a range of compounds to improve athletic performance
Injectables	Steroids designed for intramuscular injection(s)
Mega-dosing	Taking massive doses (possibly by *blending*)
Orals	Steroids designed for oral use
Pryamiding	Process of slowly increasing the daily dose of anabolic steroids over time, then when a target dose is reached, slowly reducing the dose over time; often done so that the individual will not test "positive" on urine or blood tests for steroids after competition
Shotgunning	Taking steroids on an inconsistent basis
Tapering	Slowly reducing one's daily dose of steroids over a period of time

As noted earlier, anabolic steroids might be ingested orally or injected into muscle tissue, and some abusers take both forms of steroids at once for an enhanced effect. This is hardly a practice that a physician would recommend that a patient follow. Steroid abusers also have developed their own language for steroid abuse, which is summarized in Table 14-1.

Many of these practices are quite common among steroid abusers. For example, 61% of steroid-abusing weight lifters were found to have engaged in the practice of "stacking" their steroid dose (H. G. Pope & Brower, 2004, 2005; Porcerelli & Sandler, 1998). Some of those who "pyramid" steroid doses are, at the midpoint of their cycle, taking massive doses of one or more compounds, although it should be noted that many abusers who "pyramid" also interspace periods of active steroid use with periods of total abstinence which might last weeks, months, or even as long as a year.[9]

Unfortunately, these periods of abstinence might be marked by the loss of much of the steroid-induced muscle mass, resulting in the abuser returning to the abuse of anabolic steroids to recapture the lost muscle mass.

The Unknown Hazards of Steroid Abuse

The long-term effects of anabolic steroid abuse have not been studied in detail, and much of the clinical literature on their effects is based on their effects when used at therapeutic doses to treat disease (H. G. Pope & Brower, 2008). At therapeutic dosage levels, anabolic steroids can induce such side effects as sore throat, fever, vomiting (with or without blood being mixed with the material regurgitated), dark-colored urine, bone pain, unusual weight gain, headache, and a host of other effects (Congeni & Miller, 2002). However, anabolic steroid abusers have been known to utilize dosage levels that are 40–100 to perhaps as much as 200 times (Congeni & Miller, 2002; Eisenberg & Galloway, 2005; H. G. Pope & Brower, 2008; Tomb, 2008) the maximum recommended dosage level for these compounds. There is virtually no systematic information available about the effects of such dosage levels, and what little is known is based on antidotal case reports of steroid abusers.

It is known that the effects of anabolic steroids on muscle tissue will last for several weeks after the drug(s) were last administered, a characteristic that athletes often rely on to avoid having a "positive" urine toxicology test for performance-enhancing compounds after competition (Knight, 2003). It is also known that the adverse effects of anabolic steroid abuse depend on (a) the route by which the compound was administered, (b) the specific compound utilized, (c) the dosage level(s) utilized, (d) the frequency of steroid use, (e) the general health of the abuser, and (f) the age of the steroid abuser. To complicate matters, many steroid abusers view themselves as being more knowledgeable about the adverse effects of the compounds being abused than physicians,[10] often seeking to control these adverse effects without medical treatment (Hildebrandt et al., 2006; H. G. Pope & Brower, 2008). This is due, in part, to the steroid abuse fiasco of the 1970s, in which physicians tried to discourage anabolic steroid abuse by attempting to convince athletes that they were

---

[9]This then makes the individual vulnerable to the "reverse anorexia nervosa" effect that was discussed earlier in this chapter, as the steroid-induced muscle mass is lost over a period of time.

[10]Often for good reason, because most physicians are not trained to detect, or treat, steroid abusers.

ineffective as muscle growth agents. Steroid abusers knew differently from personal experience, and thus the credibility of physicians as a source of information about steroid abuse and its consequences has been destroyed (H. G. Pope & Brower, 2008; M. Stephens, 2008). Unfortunately, many anabolic steroid abusers now accept information from their drug dealers about the effects of anabolic steroid rather than seek a physician's opinion (H. G. Pope & Brower, 2008).

Known Adverse Effects of Anabolic Steroids When Abused

On the Reproductive System

Male steroid abusers even at therapeutic dosage levels might experience an enlargement of the breasts[11] as the body converts the excess testosterone into estrogen (Botre & Pavan, 2008; H. G. Pope & Brower, 2009). This effect is more pronounced when the individual uses exceptionally high doses of steroids. Male steroid abusers might also experience an increased frequency of erections, or a continual erection (known as *priapism*, which is a medical emergency). Male steroid abusers might experience unnatural hair growth or loss, reduced sperm production, and an increased frequency of the urge to urinate, as well as degeneration of the testes, prostate gland enlargement, problems in urination, changes in libido, impotence, and sterility (Botre & Pavan, 2008; Eisenberg & Galloway, 2005; H. G. Pope & Brower, 2008; Schuckit, 2006a). Long-term steroid abuse might be a causal agent in the development of prostate cancer in some abusers (H. G. Pope & Brower, 2005).

Women who abuse anabolic steroids might become infertile, and remain so for a period of months, to possibly years, after their last use of steroids (Casavant et al., 2007). They might also experience an abnormal growth of the clitoris, irregular menstrual periods, unnatural hair growth or loss, a deepening of the voice, atrophy of the uterus, and a possible reduction in breast size (Botre & Pavan, 2008; Casavant et al., 1997; H. G. Pope & Brower, 2004, 2008; Schuckit, 2006a; Volkow, 2006b). The menstrual irregularities seen in female steroid abusers may become permanent, as is true for many of the masculinizing effects induced in women who abuse steroids (H. G. Pope & Brower, 2005; Volkow, 2006b).

Effects of Anabolic Steroid Abuse on the Liver, Kidneys, and Digestive System

Steroid abusers may experience altered liver function that may be detected by blood tests such as the serum glautamic-oxaloacetic transminase (SGOT) and the serum glautamic-pyruvic transaminase (SGPT) tests (S. B. Karch, 2009; Sturmi & Diorio, 1998). Elevations on these tests are a sign of hepatoxicity.[12] There is evidence suggesting that, when abused for periods of time at high dosage levels, steroids might contribute to the formation of both cancerous and benign liver tumors (Eisenberg & Galloway, 2005; S. B. Karch, 2009; H. G. Pope & Brower, 2005, 2008; Sturmi & Diorio, 1998). There is evidence that the form of liver tumor known as an adenoma may redevelop, or at least start to regrow, following steroid cessation (N. M. Martin, Abu Dayyeh, & Chung, 2008). This strongly suggests that steroid use "holidays"[13] do not affect the growth of such liver tumors to a significant degree. Finally, anabolic steroid abuse might contribute to fluid retention in the body, increasing the workload on the heart (Botre & Pavan, 2008).

Anabolic Steroid Abuse and the Cardiovascular System

The heart is composed of muscle tissue and is strongly affected by the anabolic steroids ("Steroids and Growth Hormones Make Users 'Really Ripped,'" 2003). There appears to be a dose-related cardiotoxic effect from anabolic steroids, and it is estimated that habitual steroid abusers have a four to six times higher incidence of sudden cardiac death as age-matched nonabusers (Belhani et al., 2009). The authors based their research on animals, which were later sacrificed and their hearts were examined. The authors found that those animals that received monthly supplemental doses of testosterone had severe lesions in the muscle tissue of the heart, whereas the control sample did not. The exact mechanism through which testosterone or its derivatives might induce such lesions remains unknown (Casavant et al., 2007). However, such lesions might be a causal mechanism through which anabolic steroid abusers become more vulnerable for sudden cardiac death (Fineschi et al., 2005).

Although not seen in every abuser of anabolic steroids, the abuse of these compounds is also associated

---

[11]Technically, this condition is known as *gynecomastia*.

[12]See Glossary.

[13]Periods of time in which the individual does not abuse a given compound.

with the development of conditions such as hypertension, cardiomyopathy, myocardial infarction, or chronic heart disease (Casavant et al., 2007; Eisenberg & Galloway, 2005). Because of steroid-induced water retention, many anabolic steroid abusers develop edema in the hands and/or feet, which they often attempt to control by taking diuretic medication(s) (Eisenberg & Galloway, 2005; Schuckit, 2006a). Steroid abusers have been known to experience a drug-induced reduction of high-density[14] lipoprotein in the blood, while simultaneously increasing the low-density lipoprotein levels by as much as 36%. This contributes to accelerated atherosclerosis of the heart and surrounding blood vessels (Kanayama et al., 2006; H. G. Pope & Brower, 2005). Further, anabolic steroid abuse is associated with thrombotic stroke (Botre & Pavan, 2008; S. B. Karch, 2009). Such strokes are caused by the ability of steroids to cause blood cells to clump together, increasing the danger of blood clot formation.

Steroid Abuse and the Central Nervous System

For many years scientists disputed the claim that anabolic steroid abuse can cause behavioral changes in the individual. However, it is now accepted that anabolic steroid abuse can induce behavioral changes for the abuser. The massive doses of steroids utilized by some athletes has been associated with changed in the GABAa receptor site, as well as dopamine and serotonin receptor sites in the mesolimbic region of the brain. These findings are consistent with reports of increased aggression by some steroid abusers.

Most abusers are reluctant to admit to neuropsychiatric problems induced by their steroid abuse in spite of the strong evidence to the contrary (H. G. Pope & Brower, 2008; H. G. Pope, Kouri, & Hudson, 2000). There are no premorbid signs that would warn abusers that they were at risk for neuropsychiatric problems as a result of anabolic steroid abuse (H. G. Pope, Kouri, & Hudson 2000). Some regular anabolic steroid abusers experience a sense of dysphoria[15] or even depressive reactions, especially during the withdrawal phase (Kilmer et al., 2005; H. G. Pope & Brower, 2004, 2005, 2008; Schuckit, 2006a). Steroid-related depression appears to respond well to a simple discontinuation of steroid abuse, but if prolonged responds well to psychotherapy and the use of selective serotonin reuptake inhibitors (SSRIs) by physicians (H. G. Pope &

Brower, 2008). It is important to keep in mind that approximately 4% of steroid abusers have made at least one serious suicide attempt (H. G. Pope & Brower, 2008).

Anabolic steroid abusers are at risk for a drug-induced psychosis and the development of a condition known as "roid rage" (Botre & Pavan, 2008; Eisenberg & Galloway, 2005; H. G. Pope & Brower, 2004, 2005). In rare cases, steroid-related violence has resulted in the death of the user or another person (H. G. Pope, Phillips, & Olivardia, 2000). So common is the relationship between steroid abuse and violence that it has been suggested that large, muscular perpetrators of interpersonal violence be screened for steroid abuse upon abuse (H. G. Pope & Brower, 2004). Other psychiatric symptoms observed in steroid abusers include impulsiveness, irritability, and antisocial behavior.

Although these reactions are attributed to steroid abuse, there is also the possibility that individuals who become violent while taking steroids might have a history of criminal thinking and antisocial behavior that predates their steroid abuse (Klotz, Garle, Granath, & Thiblin, 2006). Such individuals would be at risk for impulsive behaviors such as reacting with violence, which then would be attributed by researchers to their steroid use rather than their predisposing personality, according to Klotz et al. Although this hypothesis is interesting, it has not been proven and thus is but one possibility for the apparent connection between steroid abuse and violent behavior.

Other Steroid-Related Disorders

Patients with medical conditions such as certain forms of breast cancer, diabetes mellitus, blood vessel disease, kidney, liver or heart disease, and men with prostate problems, should not use anabolic steroids except if directed to do so by a physician who is aware that the patient has these problems (Eisenberg & Galloway, 2005). There is evidence that anabolic steroid use contributes to, if not causes, cancer, and their use is not recommended for patients with either active tumors or a history of either benign or cancerous tumors, except if directed to do so by a physician who supervises the patient during the period of steroid use.

Other side effects caused by steroid abuse include severe acne, especially across the back ("steroid acne"), which some patients attempt to control by taking illicit antibiotics, and oily skin (Botre & Pavan, 2008). The abuser might develop a foul odor on the breath (Casavant et al., 2007). There was one case report of unnatural bone degeneration that was attributed to the abuse of steroids. Further, animal research

---

[14]The so-called "good" cholesterol.

[15]See Glossary.

suggests that anabolic steroid abuse may contribute to tendon degeneration, possibly to the point where the tendon might rupture under stress (Casavant et al., 2007; Eisenberg & Galloway, 2005). Adolescents who abuse anabolic steroids are vulnerable to premature cessation of bone growth as the "growth plate" at the end of the bone prematurely fuses (Casavant et al., 2007).

It has also been suggested that anabolic steroids might prove to be a "gateway" to other drug abuse as the abuser attempts to cope with muscle-related pain, acne, and other steroid-related problems (Kanayama, Cohane, Weiss, & Pope, 2003). Further, if abusers should share needles with other steroid abusers, an all too common practice, they are vulnerable to the acquisition of various blood-borne infections from those who shared that needle earlier (Eisenberg & Galloway, 2005).

Drug Interactions Between Anabolic Steroids and Pharmaceuticals

The anabolic steroids interact with a wide range of medications used to treat disease states and also with many of the drugs of abuse. There is evidence of an interactional effect between acetaminophen[16] and anabolic steroids. Further, alcohol-dependent patients on Antabuse (disulfiram) should not take anabolic steroids, nor should patients who are taking the medication naltrexone or the anticonvulsant medications such as phenytoin, valproic acid, or any of the phenothiazine class of antipsychotic medications.

Are Anabolic Steroids Addictive?

A quarter of a century ago, most physicians would have said, "No, anabolic steroids are not addictive." Even now the question is debated (H. G. Pope & Brower, 2008). Clinical evidence would suggest that anabolic steroid dependence rests on three pillars: (a) the individual's *psychological* reliance on steroids ("I need steroids to bulk up"), (b) the individual's perceived past benefit from past steroid abuse, and (c) ultimately the development of physical withdrawal symptoms. The psychological dependence on anabolic steroids rests upon the belief that users need steroids to avoid the loss of muscle mass or maintain their attractiveness to the opposite sex.

The second factor, perceived benefit, rests on a foundation of external feedback ("you look *great*" or "your endurance is improving"), functions to encourage continued steroid abuse. Some abusers also report a mild sense of euphoria from anabolic steroids, which serves as an additional incentive to continue abusing these compounds. The euphoric effects of anabolic steroids are assumed to be approximately the same as caffeine, nicotine, or possibly the benzodiazepines (Wood, 2004). Steroid-induced euphoria may reflect the impact of these compounds on the mesolimbic system, especially the dopamine neurotransmission system (H. G. Pope & Brower, 2005; Wood, 2004).

Chronic steroid abusers do experience a protracted withdrawal syndrome upon discontinuation of these compounds, with symptoms such as loss of muscle mass and the development of a depressive reaction that might reach suicidal proportions (H. G. Pope & Brower, 2005). Other symptoms experienced by the steroid abuser during withdrawal include insomnia, fatigue, dysphoria, restlessness, anorexia, headaches, and lowered libido (Kilmer et al., 2005). Gradual detoxification from steroids and intensive psychiatric support limit the impact of the withdrawal syndrome on the individual's life.

Some of the diagnostic signs that help to identify the person with a steroid addiction include (a) use of higher doses than intended, (b) loss of control over the frequency of steroid use, (c) preoccupation with further steroid use, (d) continued use of steroids in spite of the individual's awareness of problems caused by their use, (e) development of tolerance to steroids, resulting in the use of larger doses to achieve the same effects once achieved at a lower dose, (f) the disruption of normal daily activities by steroid abuse, and (g) continued use of steroids to control or avoid withdrawal symptoms. As the reader can appreciate, the diagnostic signs of steroid addiction are virtually the same as those for other drugs of abuse, suggesting that steroids indeed are addictive.

Chapter Summary

The anabolic steroids emerged as drugs of abuse in the latter part of the 20th century, with several subgroups of abusers emerging over the years. But the dynamics of steroid abuse differ from those of other, more traditional drugs of abuse. The primary reason why anabolic steroids are abused is not for their euphoric effects, although many abusers report that anabolic steroids do induce euphoria, but for their effects on muscle

---

[16]Discussed in the next chapter.

development. Some adolescents and young adults believe that the steroids will help them achieve a better physical appearance, whereas athletes believe that because the competition is using steroids, they must do so in order to "level the playing field." Both groups continue to engage in anabolic steroid abuse in spite of the knowledge that these compounds alter the normal function of the central nervous system and can cause premature termination of bone growth and cardiovascular damage that will be with them for the rest of their lives. The identification and treatment of steroid abusers is primarily a medical issue, although substance abuse rehabilitation professionals play an important adjunctive role in this process and thus should have a working knowledge of anabolic steroid abuse.

CHAPTER 15

Over-the-Counter[1] Analgesics: Unexpected Agents of Abuse

Introduction

At first glance, the reader might question why the over-the-counter (OTC) analgesics are included in a book on substance abuse. These compounds do not induce a sense of euphoria and are never utilized as "recreational" drugs. Yet the OTC analgesics are ubiquitous: Seventy percent of adults over the age of 65 take an OTC analgesic at least once a week (Stillman & Stillman, 2007). Further, many drug abusers will also use an OTC analgesic either during the period of active drug abuse or immediately after these periods of substance use.

However, the OTC analgesics are not innocuous compounds in spite of their widespread use. Each year in the United States an estimated *103,000* people are hospitalized because of complications induced by OTC analgesic use, and 16,500 people die from these OCT-induced problems (Savage et al., 2008; Stillman & Stillman). Although some of these compounds may be used during the acute withdrawal phase of various drugs of abuse, it is imperative that substance abuse counselors have at least a working knowledge of the side effects of these compounds and their potential for harm to better meet the needs of their clients.

A Short History of the OTC Analgesics

Folk healers have long used various plants or extracts from different plants to treat disease, especially disease and fever. One such plant extract is the bark of the willow tree, which contains *salicin* (from the Latin word *salix*, which means "willow") for pain relief and relief from fever for more than 2000 years (Jeffreys, 2004; Stimmel, 1997a). Around the year 400 BCE, the Greek physician Hippocrates recommended that patients experiencing mild levels of pain, or fever, or women in labor, chew the bark of the willow tree. But the bitter taste, limited availability of the bark, and the inconsistent effect forced physicians of the era to turn to opium as a way to control even mild levels of pain.

Then in the 1880s the active agent of willow bark, *salicin*, was isolated and ways were found to synthesize large amounts of the compound for commercial use. Then chemists learned how to produce salicylic acid, which had the same properties as its chemical cousin

---

[1]Over-the-counter medications are available without a prescription. Thus the term *over-the-counter medications*.

salicin but was easier to produce. However, salicylic acid, like salicin, was found to cause a great deal of gastric distress when ingested. So chemists continued their search for a compound with the advantages of salicin, but without its harsh effects. In 1898 Bayer Pharmaceuticals introduced the compound acetylsalicylic acid under the brand name *Aspirin*.[2] Like its chemical cousin salicin, Aspirin was found to be effective in controlling mild to moderate levels of pain, without the harsh gastrointestinal irritation produced by salicylic acid or the danger of addiction inherent in the use of narcotic analgesics.

Because of its multiple effects, aspirin[3] has become *the* most frequently used medicinal compound in the world. It has been found to reduce fever and control inflammation, with approximately 50 billion doses being consumed around the world each year (Page, 2001). A quarter of this amount is consumed in just the United States alone (Page, 2001). Aspirin's side effects were found to be less intense to those of salicylic acid, but it still has a significant potential to harm the abuser. This is why pharmaceutical companies embarked on a search for compounds with the benefits of aspirin without its side effects. This resulted in the discovery of a class of compounds known as the *propionic acids* from which the compounds naproxen and ibuprofen were developed.[4]

Acetaminophen was introduced as an OTC analgesic in the 1950s. The term *acetaminophen* is a form of chemical shorthand for the compound *N-acetyl-para-aminophenol*. This compound was first isolated in 1878, and although it was recognized that it could lower fever, it was feared that acetaminophen had the same dangerous side effects as a close chemical cousin, para-aminophenol. So it remained a footnote in the chemistry textbooks until the early 1950s (C. C. Mann & Plummer, 1991). By that time sufficient evidence had accumulated to show that acetaminophen was much safer than para-aminophenol and that it did not have the same potential for gastric

distress found in aspirin. A massive advertising campaign followed the introduction of a brand name of acetaminophen, which placed emphasis on how this compound was not irritating to the stomach, as was aspirin. This advertising campaign, combined with a growing awareness of aspirin's potential for gastric distress, made it the most commonly used compound for fever control on this planet at the start of the 21st century (Sharma, 2003).

This is not to imply that acetaminophen has entirely replaced aspirin, as aspirin remains a popular OTC analgesic (Jeffreys, 2004). Indeed, more than a century after its discovery scientists continue to find new applications for aspirin, and it has been suggested that if it were to be discovered today, it would be classified as a prescription-only medication. However, aspirin does present the user with various potential side effects, some of which are potentially deadly to the user.

The Origins of the Term NSAID

As is true for the adrenocortical steroids, endogenous compounds produced by the body in response to stress, aspirin and the propionic acid derivatives have an anti-inflammatory effect. However, because these compounds have a different chemical structure than the adrenocortical steroids, they are classified as *nonsteroidal* anti-inflammatory drugs (or NSAIDs). There are approximately 20 NSAIDs currently in the United States, although most are available only by prescription. The exceptions to this rule are aspirin and the propionic acid derivatives ibuprofen, ketoprofen, and naproxen. The COX-2 inhibitors, which were introduced in the 1990s, are available only by prescription and have been classified as NSAIDs (D. Jackson & Hawkey, 2000).

Medical Uses of the OTC Analgesics

Aspirin

Aspirin was first introduced in 1897, and in spite of this fact scientists are still discovering applications for this compound. The most common application for aspirin is the control of mild to moderate levels of pain from conditions such as common headache, neuralgia, pain associated with oral surgery, toothache, dysmenorrhea, and various forms of pain in the muscles and joints. Further, it has been discovered that just one regular aspirin tablet every second day will reduce

---

[2]Aspirin is a member of a family of closely related compounds, many of which have analgesic, anti-inflammatory, and antipyretic action. However, because all of these compounds are less powerful as aspirin, they will not be discussed further in this chapter.

[3]The word *aspirin* is a historical accident, discussed in detail in C. C. Mann and Plummer's 1991 text. It is far too complex to be discussed in this chapter, but from this point on the word *aspirin* with a small *a* will be used.

[4]Other compounds, such as ketoprofen, were also developed from the propionic acids, but will not be discussed further in this chapter.

the frequency of migraine headaches by 20% in a subset of migraine patients.

Aspirin is able to reduce fever by causing the blood vessels in the peripheral regions of the body to dilate and to encourage sweating. This remains a common application of aspirin. Although this effect will reduce fever, it will not reduce the body temperature below normal. Aspirin has also been found to interfere with the production of a family of compounds known as the *prostaglandins*[5] (B. A. Wilson et al., 2007). In the closing decade of the 20th century, it was discovered that regular low-dose aspirin reduces the incidence of myocardial infarctions[6] in both men and women (J. S. Berger et al., 2006; Buring & Ferrari, 2006; Chan, Manson et al., 2007). Physicians have also found that aspirin is of value *during* a myocardial infarction, helping to dissolve blood clots that have blocked essential blood vessels, starving the heart for blood (Dajer, 2005; Hung, 2003). Paradoxically, extended periods of aspirin use at high dosage levels appear to *increase* the individual's risk for heart disease and what are known as "microbleeds" or microscopic strokes (D'Arcy, 2007; Vernooij et al., 2009).

There are several mechanisms through which aspirin use can reduce the individual's risk for an initial, or subsequent, myocardial infarction. Aspirin is able to reduce the blood levels of the *C-reactive protein*, and higher levels of this compound have been found to be associated with an increased risk of either a myocardial infarction, an occlusive stroke, or a blood clot that might block a vein (a venous thrombosis). However, for reasons that are not clear, this beneficial effect is noted only for individuals older than 50 years of age and is strongest in people with lower blood cholesterol levels.

Another mechanism by which aspirin is thought to reduce the incidence of heart attack is that it can inhibit the action of a form of prostaglandin known as *thromboxane A2*, which is found in blood. Thromboxane A2 is involved in the formation of blood clots (Hutchison, 2004; Jeffreys, 2004; Page, 2001). However, there is a great interindividual variation between the ability of low-dose aspirin to block thromboxane A2, and each individual's aspirin requirements should be assessed by a physician. Further, because blood platelets have a normal life span of 8–10 days, the body is constantly replacing old blood platelets with new ones,

which have stores of thromboxane A2. Thus it will be necessary for the individual to take aspirin at least every day, or possibly every second day, to provide the desired inhibition of blood clot formation.

Currently, there is an ongoing controversy in the medical field about whether some patients are resistant to the antithrombotic[7] effects of aspirin. Some physicians argue that the "resistance" is due to medication noncompliance. Others argue that some individuals are indeed more resistant to aspirin's antithrombotic effects than are others (Dalen, 2007; Halushka & Halushka, 2002; Krasopoulos, Brister, Beattie, & Buchanan, 2008). This debate continues until the present time.

Scientists have also found that low doses of aspirin are effective as an adjunctive treatment for a rare neurological disorder known as the *transient ischemic attack* (TIA). At higher dosage levels, it has been found to be an effective anti-inflammatory agent, thus making it of value in the treatment of such disorders as rheumatoid arthritis and osteoarthritis (Jeffreys, 2004). There is also an impressive body of evidence suggesting that regular low doses of aspirin might interfere with some forms of cancer, such as cancer of the breast (Terry et al., 2001). This is especially true for the form of breast cancer known as hormone receptor-positive cancer (Terry et al., 2004). There is also preliminary evidence suggesting that regular low-dose aspirin use is associated with a lower incidence of esophageal cancer and ovarian cancer (Page, 2001). The regular use of aspirin, or another NSAID, might reduce the risks of a man developing prostate cancer. However, recent research by E. A. Singer, Palapattu, and Van Wjingarrden (2008) raised questions about whether regular NSAID use might not lower the results of a blood test known for the prostate-specific antigen (PSA), used to detect early prostate cancers. This is a matter of some concern because lower PSA levels might reflect the effects of the NSAIDs rather than the absence of cancer, Singer et al. suggested, preventing the detection of the tumor until it is more advanced and thus more difficult to treat.

Surprisingly, aspirin use has been found improve the blood flow to capillaries that feed the retina, thus inhibiting the development of diabetic retinopathy (Adler & Underwood, 2002; R. Q. Roberts et al., 2002). Further, there is evidence that regular low-dose aspirin use slows the process by which the eye forms cataracts and might protect the sensitive

---

[5]See Glossary.

[6]Also known as a "heart attack."

[7]See *thrombosis* in the Glossary.

structures of inner ear from damage during the normal aging process or from certain medications (Coghlan, 2006a).

Acetaminophen

There is some disagreement in the medical world as to whether acetaminophen should be classified as an NSAID. In spite of the fact that most researchers do not classify acetaminophen as an NSAID, it is quite useful. It is as effective as aspirin in the control of fever (American Society of Health System Pharmacists, 2008). As an OTC analgesic, it is as potent as aspirin and may be used to treat virtually every pain condition that aspirin does, except those induced by inflammation. Acetaminophen has no significant anti-inflammatory action.

The Propionic Acids

This class of NSAID compounds includes ibuprofen, naproxen, and ketoprofen, all of which are available over the counter.[8] As a group, the propionic acids are used to control fever, mild to moderate levels of pain, and inflammation. The anti-inflammatory action of these compounds makes them useful in treating conditions such as rheumatoid arthritis, dysmenorrhea, gout, tendonitis, bursitis, headaches, and the aches and discomfort of the common cold. When used with narcotic analgesics, scientists have found that the NSAIDs increase the analgesic potential of the latter compounds, allowing for a greater range of pain control without the need to increase the dosage of the narcotic. There is mixed evidence suggesting that the regular use of NSAIDs (including aspirin) may slow the progression of Alzheimer's disease and vascular dementia (Adler & Underwood, 2002; Veld et al., 2001; Vlad, Miller, Kowall, & Felson, 2008). In addition to these general benefits, researchers have found specific applications for each compound.

The NSAIDs all present the user with some risk of cardiovascular problems. This risk is thought to be lower when the patient uses ibuprofen or naproxen, but these compounds still carry some risk of cardiovascular complications as a result of their use, including myocardial infarction and/or stroke (D'Arcy, 2007). Further, the NSAIDs all function as nonselective cyclooxygenase[9] inhibitors, presenting the user with both benefits and the potential for harm. This will be discussed later in this chapter.

Normal Dosage Levels of the OTC Analgesics

Aspirin

A standard dose of two 325 mg aspirin tablets provides an analgesic effect equal to that of 50 mg of the narcotic analgesic meperidine (Demerol), 32 mg of codeine, a 50 mg oral dose of pentazocine (Talwin), or 65 mg of propoxyphene (Darvon) (McGuire, 1990). Although some people easily dismiss aspirin as an analgesic, these data demonstrates that it is indeed a potent compound.

Pharmacists and physicians are still unsure of the optimal dose of aspirin for analgesia. There does appear to be a "ceiling" effect that is encountered at doses of around 1000 mg every 4 hours, after which larger doses will not bring about any more analgesia but do increase the possibility of an adverse reaction. The American Society of Health System Pharmacists (2008) recommends that the normal adult oral dose of aspirin should be 325–650 mg every 4 hours as needed for pain. Furthermore, it is recommended that aspirin should not be used on a continuous basis for more than 10 days by adults, or 5 days by children, except under a physician's orders.

Acetaminophen

The usual adult dose of acetaminophen is 325–650 mg every 4 hours as needed for the control of pain (American Society of Health System Pharmacists, 2008). Acetaminophen's analgesic potential is approximately the same as aspirin's, and it has an antipyretic[10] effect that is approximately the same as aspirin's. However, like aspirin, acetaminophen has a "ceiling" effect that is reached when the individual ingests approximately 1000 mg every 4 hours. Like aspirin, it is recommended that the individual not use acetaminophen for longer than 10 days unless advised to do so by a physician.

Ibuprofen

In its OTC form, the recommended dose of ibuprofen is 200–400 mg every 4 hours for the control of pain. At these dosage levels ibuprofen has an analgesic potential

---

[8]These were all prescription-only medications at first, but were introduced as over-the-counter analgesics in modified dosage from the prescription form of these same compounds.

[9]See Glossary.

[10]See Glossary.

that is equal to that of aspirin or acetaminophen. When prescribed for a patient, dosage levels of 400–800 mg three or four times a day are usual (B. A. Wilson et al., 2007). Four hundred milligrams every 4–6 hours is recommended for the control of mild to moderate levels of pain (B. A. Wilson et al., 2007). Even when used in its prescription dosage forms, it is recommended that the individual not ingest more than 3200 mg of ibuprofen in 24 hours (B. A. Wilson et al., 2007).

Naproxen

As an OTC analgesic, patients are advised to take one tablet every 12 hours. Prescription dosage levels are somewhat higher than the OTC analgesic dosage levels, but the patient is still advised to take the medication only twice daily.

Pharmacology of OTC Analgesics

Although all of the OTC analgesics are effective in controlling mild to moderate levels of pain and fever, it is important to point out that before these compounds are used, the *cause* of the fever, or pain, should be identified, lest the OTC analgesic being used mask the appearance of a serious medical condition. Further, patients are warned to follow dosing instructions for that specific OTC analgesic to minimize the risk to their life.

Aspirin

Aspirin is well absorbed from the gastrointestinal tract after oral ingestion. If ingested with food, all of the aspirin will still be absorbed, but it will take 5–10 times longer than if the patient ingested the aspirin on an empty stomach. This provides a 'buffering" effect that might help protect the stomach lining from aspirin-related irritation, at the cost of slower absorption. To avoid the problem of aspirin-induced stomach irritation, it is often sold in combination with antacids or an enteric coating. However, these also result in erratic absorption rates, possibly contributing to the patient's pain (B. A. Wilson et al., 2007). Antacids also reduce the amount of aspirin that reaches the patient's circulation by 30–70%, a matter of some concern for patients who wish to control some form of pain.

When taken on an empty stomach, the absorption of aspirin depends on the speed with which the tablet(s)

crumble, allowing individual aspirin molecules to pass through the gastrointestinal tract into the circulation. Peak blood levels of aspirin are achieved between 15 (B. A. Wilson et al., 2007) and 60–120 minutes (Stimmel, 1997a) after a single dose. Between 80 and 90% of a single dose of aspirin is bound to plasma proteins, providing a reservoir of aspirin that might slowly be released back into the user's circulation over a period of time (Stimmel, 1997a). The therapeutic half-life of aspirin is 2–3 hours following a single dose, although this may be increased to 8–15 hours when aspirin is used on a regular basis. It is rapidly biotransformed into water-soluble metabolites, which are then removed from the circulation and excreted in the urine. Only about 1% of a single dose of aspirin is excreted unchanged. Tolerance to the analgesic effects of aspirin only rarely develops (Stimmel, 1997a).

Unlike narcotic analgesics, which work mainly within the brain itself, aspirin appears to work both at the site of injury and in the hypothalamus. There is also evidence that it works at unidentified sites in the spinal cord. To understand how aspirin works at the site of injury, it is necessary to investigate the body's response to injury. Every cell in the body contains a variety of chemicals, some of which alert the body to cellular injury and death. Some of these chemicals include *histamine, bradykinin*, and a group of chemicals known as the *prostaglandins*. Aspirin inhibits prostaglandin production, thus limiting the inflammation and pain that develops in response to cellular injury.

Unfortunately, prostaglandin production is also necessary for the compound cyclooxygenase, which has two subtypes: COX-1 and COX-2. A third subtype, tentatively classified as COX-3, has been identified, although its role in the body is still unclear at this time. COX-1 is involved in normal cellular maintenance, especially in the stomach and kidneys. COX-2 is released only when body tissues are damaged, contributing to the inflammation response. Unfortunately, COX-1 and COX-2 share 60% of the same chemical structure, and it is through the shared elements of their chemistry that aspirin and the other NSAIDS act. Thus all of the NSAIDs could be classified as nonselective COX inhibitors, which provides both a benefit (reducing COX-2 production) and a danger (reduction of COX-1 production) for the patient (Stillman & Stillman, 2007).

The inhibition of COX-2 appears to be the mechanism through which aspirin is able to impact the development of colorectal cancer (J. Baron et al., 2003;

Kreeger, 2003). But this involves only those forms of colorectal cancer that overexpress COX-2 and not all forms of colorectal cancer (Chan, Obino, & Fuchs, 2007). However, the routine use of aspirin to protect against colorectal cancer was discouraged by C. Dube et al. (2007) on the grounds that any potential benefit gained from the use of an NSAID such as aspirin is outweighed by the dangers associated with the use of these compounds.

Further, it has been discovered that taking just one 325 mg aspirin tablet a day for an extended period of time provides a modest degree of protection against prostate and breast cancer, but the operational mechanisms by which these effects are achieved or the risk/benefit ratio for regular aspirin use as a protection against these conditions has not been calculated (Jacobs et al., 2007).

Acetaminophen

Acetaminophen is easily administered orally, in tablet, capsule, and liquid forms. It may also be administered in the form of a rectal suppository. After oral ingestion, virtually 100% of a single dose is absorbed through the gastrointestinal tract (B. A. Wilson et al., 2007). The peak effects are achieved in between 30 and 120 minutes, and acetaminophen is extensively biotransformed by the liver before excretion, although small amounts are possibly found in the breast milk of a lactating mother.

In terms of its analgesic and antipyretic potential, acetaminophen is as potent as aspirin. But acetaminophen is toxic to the liver, and doses greater than 4000 mg/day or for longer than 10 days must not be used to avoid danger to the liver. Individuals who are alcohol dependent must not use alcohol except under the supervision of a physician, in order to avoid the danger of liver damage brought on by the concurrent use of these two compounds. However, unlike the NSAIDs, acetaminophen does not interfere with the normal clotting mechanism of the blood, nor does it induce an allergic reaction as is possible with aspirin use.

Scientists speculate that acetaminophen might block the synthesis of the COX-3 enzyme, as it is not an inhibitor of either COX-1 or COX-2. COX-3 synthesis is limited to the central nervous system (CNS), and thus if acetaminophen does inhibit COX-3, it does so in a yet-to-be-discovered region of the brain. The mechanism by which acetaminophen is able to reduce fever is also unknown at this time.

Ibuprofen

Ibuprofen is usually administered orally. About 80% of a single dose of ibuprofen is absorbed from the gastrointestinal tract. Peak plasma levels are achieved in between 30 and 90 minutes, and the half-life of a single dose is between 2 and 4 hours (B. A. Wilson et al., 2007). About 99% of ibuprofen molecules become protein bound after absorption, providing a reservoir of ibuprofen that is slowly released back into the circulation over time. Ibuprofen and its metabolites are mainly eliminated through the kidneys, although a small amount is eliminated through the bile.

Like aspirin, ibuprofen is a nonselective cyclooxygenase inhibitor. Unlike aspirin, ibuprofen requires 2-4 weeks before the full anti-inflammatory effects are seen. When used at dosage levels of 2400 mg/day, it appears to be about as effective as aspirin in controlling inflammation if used for a sufficient period of time. Unfortunately, patients cannot use aspirin for short-term inflammation control until the full effects of ibuprofen develop, as one compound interferes with the anti-inflammatory action of the other.

Ibuprofen is about one-fifth to one-half as irritating to the stomach as aspirin. Although this is an impressive improvement over aspirin, it still must be recalled that 4–14% of patients taking ibuprofen will experience drug-induced gastrointestinal irritation, and 3 of every 1000 long-term users will experience an ibuprofen-related gastrointestinal bleed. Researchers have found that 27% of patients who had used ibuprofen on an extended basis had evidence of gastric ulcer formation, even if they had not experienced physical distress from this compound at the time.

Naproxen

Naproxen is another member of the propionic acid family, and is also a member of the NSAID family of compounds. There is evidence suggesting that naproxen's anti-inflammatory action may be stronger than that of aspirin, and it also has an antipyretic effect, possibly by inhibition of prostaglandin inhibition in the hypothalamus region of the brain. But because naproxen X has only a limited antiplatelet effect, it is of limited use in the treatment of cardiovascular disease or preventing heart attacks (Hutchison, 2004; D. H. Solomon, Glynn, Levin, & Avorn, 2002).

When ingested orally, naproxen begins to work within 1 hour, and its analgesic effects last for 7–8 hours. In the circulation, naproxen binds to blood proteins, which can absorb only so many naproxen molecules before they are saturated; the other molecules float in the circulation without binding to a protein. When prescribed by physicians, it was found that the steady-state blood level was achieved when the patient took 500 mg twice a day for 2–3 days (American Society of Health System Pharmacists, 2008). The elimination half-life of naproxen in the health adult is 10–20 hours. About 30% of a given dose is biotransformed by the liver into the inactive metabolite 6-desmethylnaproxen, and only 5–10% of a single dose is excreted unchanged.

Complications Caused by OTC Analgesic Use

The OTC analgesics are hardly "safe" medications, and they account for almost a quarter of the adverse drug reactions reported to the Food and Drug Administration (FDA). As noted earlier, the OTC analgesics are responsible for 103,000 hospitalizations and 16,500 deaths each year in just the United States. Thus although the OTC analgesics are available without a prescription, they do pose a potential for harm. In the sections that follow, we will discuss some of the complications caused by each of the OTC analgesics.

Acetaminophen

There is little known about the phenomenon of cumulative-dose toxicity induced by the chronic use of acetaminophen (D. M. Smith, 2007). Acetaminophen has cumulative effects on the liver, and to avoid this the patient is warned not to use this compound for more than 10 days, unless directed to do so by a physician. Acetaminophen has also been implicated as the cause of anaphylactic reactions on rare occasions. The mechanism through which acetaminophen might trigger such a massive allergic response is not known at this time. It is also *nephrotoxic*, which is to say that its continued use at too high a dosage level might prove to be toxic to the cells of the kidneys. Its use was also once thought to be associated with the development of ESRD,[11] but this possibility has been ruled out (Fored et al., 2001; Rexrode et al., 2001). However, as with all medications, acetaminophen

should be used only when the potential benefits outweigh the possible risks associated with its use.

Aspirin

Aspirin is the most commonly used compound in the United States, and each day 35,000 kilograms of aspirin are consumed there, whereas an additional 6000 kilograms are consumed each day in the United Kingdom (Halushka & Halushka, 2002). To express how frequently aspirin is used in the United States, Steele and Morton (1986) estimated that *30–74 million pounds* were consumed each year. This is in spite of the fact that up to 15% of aspirin users will have one significant, possibly fatal, adverse reaction. For example, therapeutic doses of aspirin have been found to destroy up to 75% of the melatonin in the brain, which can potentially contribute to insomnia, especially in the elderly (Pettit, 2000). Even at recommended dosage levels, aspirin can induce minor amounts of bleeding in the gastrointestinal tract, and the chronic use of aspirin even at therapeutic dosage levels can induce anemia. Aspirin has been identified as the cause of between 500 and 1000 deaths each year from aspirin-induced hemorrhage.

It has been found that 4% of patients who use an NSAID such as aspirin for an extended period of time will develop gastric ulcers, and up to 40% of frequent aspirin users develop an erosion of the lining of their stomachs (D. A. Marcus, 2003). Even doses as low as 75 mg/day can significantly increase the user's risk for damage to the lining to the gastrointestinal tract. Aspirin users who ingest it with acidic compounds such as coffee, fruit juices, or alcohol increase their risk of gastrointestinal irritation, as the irritating effects of each compound enhances those of the other.

When used at recommended dosage levels, aspirin is thought to be a factor in 20–41% of "bleeding" ulcers, which is another measure of how dangerous it can be to the user. These gastric ulcers are thought to reflect aspirin's ability to block the normal action of COX-1. Up to 33% of patients who use aspirin for an extended period of time develop breathing problems of various degrees, which also appears to reflect the ability of aspirin to interfere with the normal actions of COX-1. For these reasons, aspirin is not recommended for patients who have a history of ulcers, bleeding disorder, or other gastrointestinal disorders (American Society of Health System Pharmacists, 2008).

---

[11]End-stage renal disease, briefly discussed later in this chapter.

Aspirin can induce allergic reactions in the user. Although aspirin allergy is rare in the general population (0.2%), approximately 20% of those individuals with *any* kind of an allergy will be allergic to aspirin. These patients are also likely to demonstrate cross-sensitivity to the other NSAIDs (B. A. Wilson et al., 2007). Those individuals with the "aspirin triad," that is to say nasal polyps, asthma, and chronic rhinitis, should not use aspirin or any other NSAID except under a physician's supervision (B. A. Wilson et al., 2007). The "aspirin triad" identifies individuals who potentially will have a serious adverse reaction to aspirin. Between 5 and 15% of asthma patients who use aspirin will experience a serious adverse reaction, and if the individual should also have a history of nasal polyps, this could increase to as high as 40%.

Between 4 and 11% of asthma patients who use aspirin on a regular basis will experience an aspirin-induced bronchial spasm at some point (R. G. Barr et al., 2007). Paradoxically, regular use of aspirin can have a mild protective effect against the development of asthma in later life. This is surprising in light of the fact that NSAIDs can exacerbate asthma by their ability to interfere with COX-1 production in the body, and illustrates how there is much more to be discovered about how the NSAIDs such as aspirin function in the body.

Aspirin (and the other COX inhibitors) can block the immune response following an inoculation against various viral infections, such as the one for influenza (Ryan, Malboeuf, Bernard, Rose, & Phipps, 2006). Further research is necessary to support this finding, but it does seem to account for why older individuals, who frequently use COX-2 inhibitors for a variety of problems, do not seem to respond as well to inoculations as do younger patients. It also may account for the observation that aspirin use for symptomatic relief while the patient has a rhinovirus seems to extend the duration of the "cold" by a small degree.

Aspirin can induce other side effects, including anorexia, nausea, and vomiting. As is true for all NSAIDs, aspirin should not be used by people with a bleeding disorder such as hemophilia (American Society of Health System Pharmacists, 2008; B. A. Wilson et al., 2007). For similar reasons, patients on anticoagulant therapy involving compounds such as heparin or warfarin should not use aspirin except if directed by a physician to do so. The combined effects of aspirin and the anticoagulant medication might result in significant unintended blood loss if the patient were to have even a minor accident, and might even contribute to a hemorrhagic stroke (He, Whelton, Vu, & Klag, 1998). Thus the attending physician must weigh the potential benefits from the use of aspirin against the dangers for such patients.

The combination of NSAIDs is dangerous and should not be attempted except under a physician's supervision. All NSAIDs can induce *tinnitus*[12] in high doses or if used simultaneously. A very rare but potentially deadly side effect of aspirin is *hepatoxicity*, and the liver begins to fail to filter the blood properly if it cannot recover from this trauma. Also, aspirin has been known to induce clinical depression in rare users, and in the elderly has been known to induce or exacerbate anxiety states.

Because of age-related changes in blood flow and liver function, elderly NSAID users are at higher risk for toxic reactions to any of the NSAIDs. These normal age-related changes make it more difficult for the body of an older NSAID user to biotransform and then excrete these compounds, adding to the danger of toxicity from the NSAID being used. Further, because of its ability to interfere with COX-1 in the renal system, aspirin can contribute both to kidney failure in rare cases and to ESRD (Fored et al., 2001).

In the last quarter of the 20th century, scientists discovered that the use of a NSAID such as aspirin to treat the symptoms of a viral infection was a two-edged sword. Although aspirin might provide some symptom relief, it might also contribute to the development of Reye's syndrome in children who have a viral infection (Jeffreys, 2004; Stimmel, 1997a). Acetaminophen is often suggested as an alternative to aspirin or other NSAIDs if children should need symptomatic relief.

Surprisingly, the anti-inflammatory effect of the NSAIDs, especially aspirin, appears to interfere with the effectiveness of the intrauterine devices used to prevent pregnancy. Aspirin appears to cause fertility problems, inducing reduced sperm motility by up to 50% when used at therapeutic doses. This is not to suggest that aspirin should be thought of as a form of birth control. But it might make it harder for a couple to have a child, should they wish to do so. Finally, it should be noted that an aspirin overdose can result in permanent organ damage or even.

---

[12]See Glossary.

Medication Interactions Involving Aspirin[13]

Individuals who are being treated for high levels of uric acid in the body should not use aspirin except as directed. Even at normal dosage levels, aspirin can interfere with the body's ability to excrete uric acid and block the action of the medication probenecid, which is used to treat high blood uric acid levels. Acetaminophen is often suggested as an alternative to aspirin if the patient should require analgesia during this period of time (B. A. Wilson et al., 2007).

Because of its ability to interfere with the normal function of COX-1, aspirin should not be used by patients with hypertension except as directed by a physician. Aspirin-induced COX-1 inhibition interferes with normal kidney function and may contribute to fluid retention, increasing the workload on the heart. Also, patients using low-dose aspirin should not take vitamin E, which also has an anticoagulant effect, to minimize the danger of excessive bleeding (Harkness & Bratman, 2003). Further, *any* of the NSAIDs can interfere with the body's ability to metabolize folate (Harkness & Bratman, 2003). High folate levels pose a health risk for the individual, thus making the concurrent use of these compounds a dangerous practice.

Patients taking the prescription medication valproic acid will experience higher than normal levels of this compound if they are simultaneously using aspirin, because the aspirin molecules will bind at the blood protein binding sites normally utilized by the valproic acid molecules (DeVane & Nemeroff, 2002). To avoid the potential for a dangerous interaction, patients taking valproic acid should discuss whether it is safe for them to also use aspirin.

Individuals who plan to consume alcohol should not use aspirin immediately prior to or during the period of active alcohol use. There is strong evidence to suggest that aspirin interferes with the activity of the enzyme gastric alcohol dehydrogenase, which starts to break down alcohol in the stomach before it reaches the circulation. Finally, people who are using aspirin should not use the herbal medicine ginkgo biloba, because the combination of these two compounds can result in excessive bleeding (Cupp, 1999).

---

[13]It is not possible to list every possible interaction between aspirin and other compounds. A physician or pharmacist should be consulted before the simultaneous use of two or more compounds, even if one is "only" an OTC analgesic.

Ibuprofen

As an NSAID, ibuprofen shares most of the same complications caused by aspirin use. It also has a number of drug-specific complications, some of which will be reviewed here.

Ibuprofen has been identified as causing blurred vision in a small percentage of users. This condition usually clears up after the person stops taking ibuprofen. Patients who experience any change in their vision should contact their physician immediately. It has also been implicated in the formation of cataracts, and so patients with preexisting cataracts should use ibuprofen only if directed to do so by a physician.

Ibuprofen has been identified as the cause of a skin rash in 3–9% of users and can cause migraine headaches in both men and women. Other identified side effects include (but are not limited to) heartburn, nausea, diarrhea, vomiting, nervousness, hearing loss, congestive heart failure in people with marginal cardiac function, and like aspirin, elevated blood pressure (Thompson PDR, 2007). This latter effect is caused, in part, by ibuprofen's ability to interfere with normal prostaglandin production in the body, especially the kidneys. Acetaminophen has been suggested as an alternative to ibuprofen in patients with hypertension, unless directed otherwise by a physician.

Patients who suffer from an autoimmune disease such as systemic lupus erythematosus ("lupus" or SLE) should not use ibuprofen except under a physician's direction. Further, ibuprofen has been identified as a cause of *aseptic meningitis*, especially in patients with SLE (Rodriguez, Olguin, Miralles, & Viladrich, 2006). It is also possible for patients with no identified autoimmune disorder to develop aseptic meningitis after ibuprofen ingestion.

Drug Interactions Involving Ibuprofen

Patients with what is known as a bipolar affective disorder ("manic depression" was an earlier term for this condition) are often prescribed lithium. When a patient taking lithium also ingests ibuprofen, the blood levels of lithium could increase as much as 25–60%, a matter of some concern in that lithium has only a very narrow therapeutic window (Pies, 2005). Ibuprofen-related lithium toxicity is more pronounced in older patients, but is possible with younger patients who take these two compounds simultaneously. All patients on lithium should discuss their use of ibuprofen, or any OTC analgesic, with their physician, to avoid the danger of drug interactions.

Patients receiving the medication methotrexate should not take ibuprofen except under a physician's supervision, because this drug reduces the rate at which methotrexate is excreted by the body. This may contribute to toxic levels of methotrexate building up in the patient's body. Acetaminophen has been suggested as an alternative to the use of NSAIDs by patients on methotrexate. Further, ibuprofen has been found to block the actions of aspirin in controlling blood clot formation, a matter of concern for patients who use aspirin to avoid a heart attack or blood clot formation (Hutchison, 2004). As before, concurrent use of different NSAIDs should be avoided, unless ordered by a physician.

Naproxen

Much of the information that is available about naproxen and its effects is based on experience with the prescription strength form of this compound. Naproxen is an NSAID, and like aspirin should not be used in patients who have any of the symptoms in the "aspirin triad" (discussed earlier) except under a physician's supervision. Because it is also a nonselective COX inhibitor, naproxen might interfere with the action of COX-1 in the body, resulting in the possible formation of gastric ulcers and gastrointestinal bleeding. Because of its ability to inhibit the function of COX-1, which serves a protective function in the stomach, patients with a history of gastrointestinal bleeding are advised not to use naproxen except as ordered by a physician.

On occasion, male users have experienced naproxen-induced erectile problems and problems with the ability to ejaculate. As with any medication, the longer the patients use the medication the more likely they are to develop one or more complications induced by that compound. Other known side effects of naproxen include (but are not limited to) drowsiness, dizziness and/or vertigo, depression, diarrhea, heartburn, constipation, abdominal pain, and possible vomiting (Qureshi & Lee-Chiong, 2004). On rare occasions patients taking naproxen have experienced side effects such as skin rash, headache, insomnia, loss of hearing, and/or tinnitus. All NSAIDs have been implicated as a possible cause of ESRD, and there have been rare reports of patients taking naproxen developing aseptic meningitis (Rodriguez et al., 2006). Although this list does not identify every possible consequence of naproxen use, it does serve to identify this compound as a potent one, with great potential for danger to the user.

OTC Analgesic Overdoses[14]

Acetaminophen

When used as directed, acetaminophen has been called "the safest of all analgesics" (Katz, 2000, p. 100). However, acetaminophen does have significant risks associated with its use. There are more than 100,000 cases of acetaminophen overdoses each year in just the United States (Fontana, 2008). Surprisingly, approximately 57% of these acetaminophen overdoses are unintended. It is surprisingly easy to ingest an acetaminophen overdose, as one would need to ingest only 4000 mg (eight extra-strength tables) at one time, or less if one were drinking or on a "starvation" diet ("Scientists Call for Stronger Warnings for Acetaminophen," 2002).

Because acetaminophen is an ingredient in so many different products, and so few people check the table of ingredients prior to ingestion, there is a significant pool of people who unintentionally overdose on this compound (Fontana, 2008; Russo, 2006). This is unfortunate, as 20% of the patients who suffer an unintentional acetaminophen overdose will die, usually from acute liver failure (Fontana, 2008). Although it might be possible to perform a liver transplant on an emergency basis, liver transplants are difficult, in part because the demand exceeds the supply, and even if an emergency liver transplant is performed, 30% of those patients who receive a liver on an emergency basis following acute liver failure die within a year of the procedure (Fontana, 2008; Russo, 2006).

A second group of people who are at risk for unintentional acetaminophen overdoses are those who ingest very large doses of vitamin C while using acetaminophen (Harkness & Bratman, 2003). The high dose of vitamin C appears to interfere with acetaminophen biotransformation, possibly to the point where the individual's blood levels of acetaminophen might reach toxic levels. Again, it is imperative for people taking any herbal medicine or vitamin supplement to consult with a pharmacist or physician about the relative safety of the compounds that they are ingesting.

Although there is an antidote that can be used in an acetaminophen overdose known as N-acetylcysteine (NAC), it must be administered in the first 48 hours following the ingestion of the overdose to be effective, and its full effectiveness is seen only if administered in the first 12 hours following the overdose

---

[14]Any known *or suspected* drug overdose should be assessed by a physician immediately.

(D. M. Smith, 2007). Because so many patients unknowingly overdose, they are unlikely to seek medical attention during the critical 48-hour period. By the time the cause of their symptoms is identified, it is far too late for anything but an emergency liver transplant.

Another group of acetaminophen overdose patients are those who have intentionally ingested an overdose as part of a suicide gesture or suicide attempt. Acetaminophen is involved in approximately 94%[15] of all intentional drug overdoses. Adolescents who ingest an overdose of acetaminophen usually are making a suicide gesture, and because the first objective evidence of acetaminophen toxicity does not develop until 12–24 hours after the overdose was ingested, adolescents are often initially assured that they did no harm in the suicide gesture. By the time that the adolescent is brought in to the hospital, hours or even days after the overdose was ingested, it is far too late for NAC to be administered, because it must be administered *within 12 hours* of the overdose to be fully effective.

The mechanism by which acetaminophen destroys the liver is found in the fact that when ingested at normal dosage levels, about 4–5% of the acetaminophen is biotransformed into a toxic metabolite known as N-acetyl-p-benzoquinoneimine (Peterson, 1997). Under normal conditions this is not a problem, as it is rapidly biotransformed into other, safer metabolites by the enzyme glutathione. However, chronic alcohol abusers, people who suffer from malnutrition, those who have liver damage, or those who ingest an acetaminophen overdose rapidly deplete their livers of glutathione, leaving it vulnerable to acetaminophen-induced liver damage.

The untreated acetaminophen overdose will progress through four different stages: Phase 1 begins within 30 minutes to 24 hours depending on the size of the dose ingested, during which time the individual will experience vague symptoms of distress, including anorexia, nausea and/or vomiting, and diaphoresis[16] (D. M. Smith, 2007). Phase 2 starts 24–72 hours after the overdose and is marked by symptoms such as abdominal pain, oliguria, and a swollen, painful liver. Blood tests will demonstrate abnormal liver function, and the kidneys may show signs of dysfunction (D. M. Smith, 2007). In Phase 3, which begins 72–96 hours after the overdose was ingested, the individual will demonstrate nausea, vomiting, jaundice,

and overt symptoms of liver failure (D. M. Smith, 2007). Other possible symptoms include hemorrhage, hypoglycemia, renal failure, and hypotensive episodes. It is during this phase that acetaminophen overdoses prove fatal. If individuals survive Phase 3, they will enter the final phase, which begins between 2 days and 4 weeks after the overdose.[17] During this phase, the liver begins to repair itself, a process that can last for months or even years after the overdose (D. M. Smith, 2007).

Aspirin

Aspirin is frequently ingested as part of a suicide gesture or attempt. The estimated toxic dose is about 10 grams for an adult, and about 150 mg/kg for children. Symptoms of an aspirin overdose include headache, thirst, dizziness, tinnitus, confusion and/or delirium, hallucinations, diaphoresis, visual problems, and hearing impairment. Other symptoms include restlessness, excitement, apprehension, tremor, seizures, stupor, coma, hypotension, and possible death (B. A. Wilson et al., 2007). Aspirin overdoses are also associated with bleeding problems as a result of its ability to block the ability of the blood to clot.

Ibuprofen

Symptoms of an ibuprofen overdose include seizures, acute renal failure, abdominal pain, nausea and/or vomiting, drowsiness, and metabolic acidosis. There is no specific cure for an overdose of ibuprofen other than general supportive medical care at this time. Like aspirin, another NSAID, ibuprofen overdoses can result in a tendency on the part of the patient to bleed excessively.

Naproxen

The lethal dose of naproxen in humans is not known at this time. Some of the symptoms of a naproxen overdose include (but are not limited to) lethargy, drowsiness, nausea and/or vomiting, epigastric pain, respiratory depression, coma, hypotension and/or hypertension, as well as convulsions. Like the other NSAIDs, naproxen overdoses can induce a tendency for excessive bleeding (Thompson PDR, 2007). Treatment is supportive, as there is no specific treatment for the naproxen overdose.

---

[15]It is also imperative to keep in mind that multiple agents may have been ingested as part of the suicide attempt.

[16]See Glossary.

---

[17]The exact point at which Phase 4 starts is dependent in part on the amount of acetaminophen ingested.

Chapter Summary

Over-the-counter (OTC) medications, especially the OTC analgesics, are often discounted as not being "real" medicine. In reality they are potent compounds that are quite popular with the general population. Each year in the United States alone, more than 20,000 tons of aspirin are manufactured and consumed, and aspirin accounts for only about 28% of the OTC analgesic market. This is a good measure of the popularity of these compounds.

The OTC analgesics are quite effective in the control of mild to moderate levels of pain, and it has been discovered that when added to the narcotic analgesics in certain circumstances they might actually enhance the analgesic effects of these more potent compounds as well. Many of the OTC analgesics have been found to control inflammation associated with autoimmune disorders. Some members of the OTC analgesic family of compounds are thought to suppress certain forms of cancer, or lead to their early detection. In spite of the fact that aspirin, the oldest OTC analgesic, is more than a century old, researchers are still discovering new applications for this potent medication, acetaminophen, and the propionic acid compounds sold as OTC analgesics.

CHAPTER 16

Tobacco Products and Nicotine Addiction

Introduction

Biologists suggest that nicotine, what would become known as the active agent in tobacco, emerged as a natural form of insect repellant. It is quite effective in this role, as only one known species of insect will consume the tobacco plant. Unfortunately, the first settlers in what would come to be called the New World began to experiment with tobacco use, and by 6000 BCE[1] its use was widespread throughout the two continents. By the year 5000 BCE, the people living in what are modern-day Peru and Ecuador were actively cultivating tobacco (E. Burns, 2007). It was used in religious and social ceremonies, and when the smoke of the tobacco plant was delivered rectally, it was thought to be a useful medicine (E. Burns, 2007). The first written reference to tobacco was found in a Mayan carving thought to have been made around 600 BCE (Schuckit, 2006a).

Then the first European explorers arrived, and for all concerned the world changed. The art of tobacco smoking was carried across the Atlantic by the early European explorers, who had adopted the habit of smoking while in the New World. But in Europe this practice met with some skepticism, if not outright hostility. In Germany, public smoking was deemed a crime that could be punished by the death, whereas in Russia, castration was the sentence for same offense (Hymowitz, 2005).[2] In Asia, the use of or distribution of tobacco was a crime punishable by death, whereas smokers were executed as infidels in Turkey. In spite of these sanctions, the practice of smoking tobacco continued to spread across Europe and into Asia (Schuckit, 2006a).

Because of its ability to alter body function, European physicians came to view tobacco as having medicinal properties, in part because they had so few medications that worked. Further, the practice of smoking tobacco products gained acceptance as a social practice and a sign of sophistication, in both Europe and the Americas. Its use was widespread in the 16th, 17th, 18th, and

---

[1]Which stands for "Before the Common Era."

[2]The readers may decide for themselves which punishment was the greater incentive for smoking cessation.

19th centuries. But in the last half of the 20th century, physicians began to identify long-term consequences of tobacco smoking, and a campaign against its use began in spite of efforts on the part of the tobacco industry to disprove any claims of harm from its products. By the end of the first decade of the 21st century, tobacco use remains widespread, controversial, and the subject of much debate. In this chapter, the practice of using tobacco, and the complications associated with its use, will be reviewed.

History of Tobacco Use in the United States

Anthropologists now believe that tobacco was actively being cultivated in South America as early as 8000 years ago (E. Burns, 2007; Walton, 2002). But this is not the same form of tobacco that we know today. The original strain(s) of tobacco were more potent and may possibly have contained hallucinatory compounds, which are not found in today's tobacco (Schuckit, 2006a; Walton, 2002). European smokers preferred the milder *Nicotiana tabacum* as opposed to the more potent *Nicotina rustica* used by the natives of the New World, and this is the form of tobacco that was cultivated by the first settlers from Europe (E. Burns, 2007). Indeed, it can be argued that the establishment of the first colonies of Europeans in the New World was fueled, in part, by the demand for tobacco in Europe. Tobacco use was also popular in the colonies established by various European powers, and at times it actually functioned as a form of currency in certain colonies (E. Burns, 2007). Ultimately, the establishment of the original 13 colonies, and their eventual rebellion, could be traced back to European demand for tobacco.

At the time, the preferred method of tobacco use was by smoking, although there were those who insisted on chewing the tobacco leaf, either spitting the expectorant out or, if they were from the upper classes, swallowing it. No less a person than John Hancock himself chewed tobacco, and he went on to prove that he was a nonconformist by later being the first person to sign the Declaration of Independence in 1776.

Tobacco played an interesting role during the Civil War, when soldiers from both sides would arrange for an informal truce from time to time to barter tobacco for coffee and sugar. By the mid-19th century, several forces combined to change the shape of tobacco use.

First, new varieties of the tobacco plant were developed, providing for greater yields. New methods of curing the curing the leaves from the tobacco plant were developed as well, allowing for a more rapid transit from harvest to arrival at the manufacturer's. Simultaneously, the advent of the Industrial Age allowed the development of machinery capable of manufacturing the cigarette, a smaller, less expensive, and neater way to smoke in large numbers than was possible with cigars. Just one machine invented by James A. Bonsack could produce 120,000 cigarettes a day, far in excess of what could be made by hand.

The introduction of machinery to the manufacturing process allowed for the sale of cigarettes to members of the lower social classes, as the cigarette was now affordable to virtually everybody. This was seen as a social danger, and by 1909 no fewer than 10 different states had laws prohibiting the use of cigarettes. These laws did little to stem the tide of cigarette smoking. At the same time, it was discovered that the practice of chewing tobacco and spitting the expectorant into the ever-present cuspidor contributed to the spread of tuberculosis and other diseases. In a piece of historical irony, public health officials began to endorse cigarette smoking as a safer, more sanitary, relatively inexpensive substitute for tobacco chewing. Unlike pipe or cigar smokers, cigarette smokers discovered that the smoke from their cigarettes was so mild that it could be inhaled. The practice of cigarette smoking quickly became the preferred method of tobacco use in the United States, although there were (and remain) those who preferred to chew tobacco rather than smoke it.

Scope of the Problem of Tobacco Use

Globally, it has been estimated that 1 billion men and approximately 250 million women smoke (Levitz, Bradley, & Golden, 2004; J. E. Rose et al., 2003).

One-third of the world's smokers are thought to be Chinese men ("China's Healthcare Woes," 2008; Tobacco, 2009). So popular is the practice of cigarette smoking around the world that the per capita consumption of cigarettes is estimated at 1000 for every man, woman, and child on earth, with an estimated *15 billion* cigarettes being smoked each day on this planet (Sundaram, Shulman, & Fein, 2004). Globally, cigarette smoking is a $400 billion per year industry.

In the United States, an estimated 387.6 billion cigarettes are consumed each year (M. Kaufman, 2006). In contrast to the 1950's, when approximately half of the adult population smoked cigarettes, 20.6% of the population now smokes (S. R. Dube et al., 2009). Statistically, a small minority of cigarette smokers abuse other compounds, but it is not uncommon for the subpopulation of individuals with a substance use disorder (SUD) to also be cigarette smokers. The prevalence rate for cigarette smoking among people with an SUD has been estimated at between 71 and 100% (el-Guebaly, Cathcard, Currie, Brown, & Gloster, 2002).

Although childhood is not often viewed as part of the problem of cigarette smoking, researchers have found that individuals' prosmoking attitudes are often formed during the childhood years, and that children begin to experiment with cigarettes either in late childhood or early adolescence. This is clearly seen in the finding that one-third of 9-year-old children in the United States have taken at least one experimental "puff" on a cigarette (Hymowitz, 2005). The median age at which individuals begin to experiment with regular cigarette use is around 15 years (Patkar, Fergare, Batra, Weinstein, & Leone, 2003). These facts have not been lost on the tobacco industry, who have experimented with such things as "flavored" cigarettes that might be attractive to smokers in their childhood years. Unfortunately, as will be discussed later in this chapter, there is evidence that suggests that the physical addiction to nicotine develops within just a few days of the initiation of cigarette use, something that younger smokers might not understand when they begin to smoke (DiFranza et al., 2007).

The Pharmacology of Cigarette Smoking

The primary method of tobacco use is through cigarette smoking, although chewing tobacco and cigar smoking is gaining popularity in some circles (Schuckit, 2006a). Chemically, cigar smoke is very similar to tobacco smoke, although it does contain a higher concentration of ammonia (Jacobs, Thun, & Apicella, 1999). It also is too alkaline for the smoker to comfortably inhale the tobacco smoke very deeply, and so absorption of nicotine (and the various other compounds found in tobacco smoke) occurs in the upper airway of the cigar smoker (E. Burns, 2008).

The primary method of tobacco abuse is cigarette smoking, and for this reason the words *smoking, cigarette,* and *tobacco* will be used interchangeably in this chapter except when other forms of tobacco (such as when tobacco is prepared for chewing) are discussed. The chemistry of tobacco smoke is influenced by a number of variables, including (a) the exact composition of the tobacco being smoked, (b) how densely the tobacco is packed, (c) the length of the column of tobacco (for cigar and cigarettes), (d) the characteristics of the filter (if any), and (e) the temperature at which the tobacco is smoked. Many studies of the composition of cigarette smoke were conducted in the 1960s, and this data is still often referenced in professional journals although the composition of today's cigarette is far different from the cigarette of the 1950s. The observed changes in the composition of cigarettes over the last half century raise questions about the relevance of research studies conducted into the contents of tobacco smoke from past generations to the modern cigarette.

Up to 40% of today's average cigarette is composed of "leftover stems, scraps and dust" (Hilts, 1996, p. 44), some of which is swept off of the floor before being added to the tobacco. Where in 1955 it took 2.6 pounds of tobacco to produce a thousand cigarettes, the use of these fillers has made it possible to produce a thousand cigarettes with only 1.7 pounds of tobacco (Hilts, 1996). These manufacturing practices allow for a 44% profit margin per pack of cigarettes sold (Fonda, 2001). As will be discussed later in this chapter, there is strong evidence that nicotine is being added to the raw cigarette by the manufacturer making it more addictive than the cigarette of 1950.

Researchers have isolated some 4700 chemicals from tobacco smoke, of which 2550 come from the unprocessed tobacco itself (Fiore, 2006; Schmitz & Delaune, 2005; Stitzer, 2003). It is possible that up to 100,000 other compounds wait to be discovered in cigarette smoke, although research in this area is limited (Schmitz & Delaune, 2005). A partial list of the compounds known to be in tobacco smoke includes:

Acetaldehyde, acetone, aceturitrile, acrolein, acrylonitrile, ammonia, arsenic, benzene, butylamine, carbon monoxide, carbon dioxide, cresols, crotono-nitrile, DDT, dimethylamine, endrin, ethylamine, formaldehyde, furfural hydroquinone, hydrogen cyanide, hydrogen sulfide, lead, methacrolein, methyl alcohol, methylamine, nickel compounds, nicotine, nitric oxide, nitrogen dioxide, phenol, polonium-210 (radioactive), pyridine, "tar" (burned plant resins). (Shipley & Rose, 2003, p. 83, boldface in original deleted)

Cigarette smoke is known to contain a small amount of arsenic, a known poison.

As briefly noted earlier, various perfumes are added to the tobacco leaves to give the cigarette a distinctive aroma (Hilts, 1996). These compounds were not intended for introduction into the human body, and toxicology studies into their effects have rarely been carried out. Other compounds found in cigarette smoke result from compounds found in the cigarette wrapper, the herbicides, fungicides, and rodenticides sprayed onto the tobacco prior to harvest, as well as various machine lubricants that come into contact with the tobacco and paper as they move along in the manufacturing process (Glantz, Slade, Bero, Hanauer, & Barnes, 1996). Although it is known that smokers will inhale these products when they smoke, there has been virtually no research into the pharmacokinetic or toxicological effects of these compounds in the human body.

In response to challenges that cigarettes were dangerous to the smoker, the tobacco industry introduced "light" or "filter" brands of established brand names, to give the illusion that they were safer. In reality these changes did little to reduce the individual's level of exposure to the toxins found in cigarette smoke (Hilts, 1994; Pennock, 2007).[3] This is seen, for example, in the research finding that smokers of "light" cigarettes have the same coronary artery problems as smokers who used regular brands, and that these cigarettes were just as addictive as regular cigarettes (ABC News, 2006; Gullu et al., 2007; Hymowitz, 2005).

Although the tobacco industry claims that it is attempting to find or develop a safer cigarette, "the search for a safer cigarette is akin to alchemists seeking to turn lead into gold" (A. Blum, 2008, p. 1646).

There simply is no "safe" cigarette. There are at least 60 known carcinogens in cigarette smoke (Levitz et al., 2004). Further, cigarette smoke contains at least 1000 times the level of radioactive gasses such as radium and polonium that were contained in the fallout from the nuclear reactor in Chernobyl, Russia, when it exploded in the 1980s (Papastefanou, 2007). These compounds, which are found naturally in the soil, are concentrated in the tobacco plant as it grows, remain in the leaves when they are harvested, and when the smoker inhales are carried into the lungs. The tobacco industry was aware of this fact more than 40 years ago, but suppressed this research to avoid alarming smokers about radioactive compounds in cigarette smoke (Muggli, Ebbert, Robertson, & Hurt, 2008). Because of this fact, it was recommended that in addition to the standard federally mandated warning labels on the side of cigarette packages, they be required to carry a radiation exposure label (Muggli et al., 2008). However, this proposal was not enacted.

Nicotine

Nicotine in tobacco plants serves as a natural insecticide, discouraging insects from attacking the tobacco plant. This compound was first isolated by chemists in 1828, and in 1889 nicotine's effects on nervous system tissue were first identified. Almost a century later, scientists are still attempting to understand all of nicotine's effects on the central nervous system (Stitzer, 2003). Such research is important because nicotine is the primary reinforcing agent in tobacco. What might loosely be called "Big Tobacco"[4] knew for decades that nicotine was the major psychoactive compound in cigarettes, and that cigarettes were viewed as little more than single-dose administration systems for nicotine (Glantz et al., 1996; Hilts, 1994, 1996). Further, there is strong evidence that cigarette manufacturers increased the nicotine content of most major brands of cigarettes by 10% between 1998 and 2004 (D. Brown, 2006).

Although well absorbed through the gastrointestinal tract, much of the nicotine ingested is biotransformed through the first-pass metabolism process, limiting its

---

[3]Another interesting public relations approach was the establishment of the so-called "Tobacco Research Institute." "Donations" were assessed on the total market share each company held (Pennock, 2007). This institute was supposed to conduct unbiased research into tobacco and its uses. However, fully 50% of the budget for this organization is devoted to public relations activities, a most curious application of research funds. Further, it devotes the majority of its activities to debunking research that suggests that tobacco smoking is dangerous.

[4]Major cigarette producers.

effectiveness.[5] However, cigarette smoking is viewed as the ideal method by which to introduce nicotine into the body because it avoids the risk of the first-pass metabolism process. Each puff of a cigarette introduces a small dose of nicotine, which then reaches the brain in a matter of seconds (Gwinnell & Adamec, 2006; Stahl, 2008). Through this process, the typical two-pack-a-day smoker self-administers approximately 400 doses of nicotine each day, without the danger of the liver interfering with the nicotine before it reaches the brain (Gwinnell & Adamec, 2006). This provides an "overlearning" process in which the smoker self-administers hundreds of thousands, or even millions, of repetitions over their life span (J. R. Hughes, 2005). These repetitions are then reinforced by the brain's reward mechanism, which is triggered by the cigarette smoke.

The lethal dose of nicotine for an average adult is estimated to be approximately 60 mg. Although the average cigarette contains 10 mg of nicotine, only about 25% of the available nicotine enters the bloodstream as a result of smoking a cigarette (Greydanus & Patel, 2005; Oncken & George, 2005; Sadock & Sadock, 2007). This is because the nicotine molecule is not able to cross from the lungs to the general circulation easily. In spite of this fact, average smokers will cumulatively introduce between 20 and 40 mg of nicotine into their body each day. This is a significant fraction of the estimated lethal dose, and this cumulative nicotine exposure impacts body function in a variety of ways.

Once in the circulation, nicotine is rapidly distributed to virtually every blood-rich organ, including the lungs, spleen, and especially the brain (Hymowitz, 2005). Nicotine is both water soluble and lipid soluble, allowing it to accumulate in the brain of the smoker, with very little of the nicotine absorbed becoming protein bound (Hymowitz, 2005). This contributes to nicotine's rapid effects on the brain. These effects are further enhanced by the coincidence that the nicotine molecule is very similar to that of the neurotransmitter acetylcholine (Schmitz & Delaune, 2005). Surprisingly, in contrast to the other identified neurotransmitter systems, acetylcholine does not appear to have a region of the brain where it is most concentrated (Swann, 2009). Acetylcholine receptors have

been identified in the thalamus, basal ganglia, cerebral cortex, hippocampus, and cerebellum of the brain, and there are 12 subtypes of the acetylcholine receptor known as of this time (Bacher, Rabin, Woznica, Sacco, & George, 2010).

By stimulating the release of dopamine in the brain, nicotine is able to activate the reward circuits (Swann, 2009). Nicotine-induced dopamine release in the brain is enhanced by its ability to reduce the levels of an enzyme known as monoamine oxidase ß in the brain. This enzyme normally helps to break down dopamine after its release into the synapse. By reducing brain monoamine oxidase ß levels, dopamine will have a stronger effect at receptor sites where it binds. Further, nicotine stimulates the release of small amounts of nitric oxide in the brain, which again has the effect of slowing down the process of dopamine reuptake. The combined action results in the neurotransmitter dopamine that is released in the brain having a stronger and more prolonged effect on the smoker (Fogarty, 2003). Other neurochemical changes induced by the binding of nicotine molecules to the acetylcholine receptors include the release of vasopressin, GABA, glutamate, beta endorphin (ß endorphin), and epinephrine[6] (Bacher et al., 2010; Fogarty, 2003; Gwinnell & Adamec, 2006; Hymowitz, 2005; Schmitz & Delaune). Many of these compounds are involved in the sensation of relaxation or pleasure, but nicotine-induced epinephrine release contributes to the smoker's sensation of alertness.

Smokers have long maintained that smoking helps them calm down during times of stress. The team of Gehricke et al. (2009) examined the mechanics of nicotine-induced relaxation through the use of the compound fluorodeoxy-glucose during PET scans, and found that individuals who had nicotine in their systems demonstrated a change in brain metabolism in such a way that it interfered with the cortical and subcortical regions of the brain responsible with the integration and expression of emotions with perceptions. This would then induce a sense of relaxation in those smokers under stress. However, it should be noted that for some unknown reason the clinical effects of nicotine are different for those people who struggle with a psychiatric disorder as compared with normal individuals (Bacher et al., 2010).

It has been found that nicotine induces a total saturation of 1 of the 12 known subtypes of the acetylcholine receptor in the brain (A. L. Brody et al., 2006;

---

[5]This is, however, a significant danger for children, who will often chew cigarettes out of curiosity and might swallow significant amounts of tobacco, possibly with lethal results. As stated elsewhere in this text, *any real or suspected overdose* should be brought to a hospital for medical attention **immediately**.

---

[6]Also known as *adrenaline*.

Stahl, 2008). Long-term binding at this acetylcholine receptor site subtype[7] induces desensitization, a process that by coincidence takes about as long as it takes to smoke just one cigarette (Stahl, 2008). The process of resensitization begins almost immediately, resulting in a state where these receptor sites are not occupied by nicotine molecules, causing or exacerbating withdrawal symptoms experienced between cigarettes and restarting the cycle as the smoker lights another cigarette (Brody et al., 2006; Stahl, 2008). This cycle takes about 45 minutes, with the result being that a one-pack-a-day smoker can keep this acetylcholine receptor subtype desensitized throughout the day (Stahl, 2008). This helps the smoker feel relaxed as a result of smoking and contributes to the experience of "craving" when the smoker quits.

Peak concentrations of nicotine are achieved in the first few minutes after smoking a cigarette, and then drops as the nicotine is redistributed to blood-rich body tissues. The biological half-life of nicotine is approximately 2 hours (J. R. Hughes, 2005; Stitzer, 2003). Because only 50% of the nicotine from one cigarette is biotransformed in the first half-life period, a reservoir of nicotine builds up in the body that has not been biotransformed or excreted. This reservoir is constantly renewed as the smoker continues to smoke. A limited degree of tolerance to nicotine does develop during the day, but is just as rapidly lost in the night hours when the average smoker abstains (J. R. Hughes, 2005). This is why many smokers report that the first cigarette in the morning has such a strong effect on them.

The majority of the nicotine absorbed into the body is metabolized before elimination, and only 5–10% is excreted unchanged (Hymowitz, 2005). The majority of nicotine is biotransformed into *cotinine,* a metabolite that in recent years has been found to have a psychoactive action of its own (Schmitz & Delaune, 2005). However, about 10% of the nicotine that is broken down is biotransformed into *nicotine-n-oxide.* Both metabolites of nicotine are then excreted in the urine. Although it was once thought that cigarette smokers were able to biotransform nicotine more rapidly than nonsmokers, research has failed to support this belief.

Acetaldehyde

Tobacco smoke also contains a very small amount of acetaldehyde. This is the first metabolite of ethyl alcohol that is produced when it goes through the biotransformation process. Research has demonstrated that acetaldehyde that is absorbed will bond with the saliva, allowing the toxin to remain in contact with oral tissues longer than would normally be the case, increasing the individual's risk of oral cancers (Melton, 2007).

Drug Interactions Between Nicotine and Prescribed Medications

Nicotine is biotransformed through the cytochrome P-450 metabolic pathway in the liver, altering the pharmacokinetics of other compounds that are biotransformed by this same metabolic pathway through a process known as enzyme induction. It is for this reason that drug interactions between nicotine and other compounds are well documented. For example, it is known that cigarette smokers will require more morphine for pain control than nonsmokers. Cigarette smokers will also have lower blood plasma concentrations of such compounds as propranolol, haloperidol, and doxepin at a given dosage level than will nonsmokers (J. R. Hughes, 2005). Tobacco smokers may experience less sedation than nonsmokers when administered a given dose of a benzodiazepine, but appear to be able to biotransform marijuana more rapidly than nonsmokers (T. Nelson, 2000).

Tobacco also interacts with many anticoagulants making it difficult to achieve adequate coagulation control. Women who use oral contraceptives and who smoke are at significantly higher risk for stroke, myocardial infarction, and thromboembolism than women the same age who are nonsmokers. Smokers who use theophylline who quit smoking may experience a significant rise in theophylline levels in the first week of abstinence. This seems to reflect the impact on the theophylline levels of various compounds in cigarette smoke such as benzopyrene, and once the smoker stops there is no further interaction effect between benzopyrene and theophylline, allowing the blood levels of the latter compound to rise. Further, the blood levels of caffeine might increase by as much as 25% following smoking cessation, causing caffeine-induced anxiety symptoms for the individual. Anxiety is also an early symptom of nicotine withdrawal, which the smoker quickly learns to self-medicate by smoking another cigarette and stopping the withdrawal symptoms before they develop.

It has been found that nicotine will decrease the blood levels of clozapine and haloperidol by as much as 30–50%, as a result of its ability to reduce the speed of the biotransformation of these compounds (Kavanagh, McGrath, Saunders, Dore, & Clark, 2002). At the

---

[7]Known as the a4ß2 nicotinic acetylcholine receptor subtype, in case you wondered.

same time, it blocks the biotransformation of the anti-depressant medications desipramine, doxepin, and nor-etriptyline, raising blood levels of these compounds. These nicotine-drug interactions can complicate the patient's treatment and interfere with the patient's response to the prescribed medication(s).

It has been discovered that 70–95% of heavy drinkers also smoke, possibly because nicotine is more reinforcing for the drinker than it is for the non-drinker.[8] This may reflect the fact that nicotine addiction is mediated by many of the same genes that are thought to trigger alcohol dependence (Le, Li, Funk, Shram, Li, & Sharam, 2006). Further, the stimulant effects of the nicotine appear to counteract some of the sedation induced by the individual's alcohol use, allowing that person to drink more or drink longer. Although the list of possible interactions between cigarette smoke and medications does not discuss every possible interaction effect, it does demonstrate that nicotine is a very potent compound, with the ability to influence the pharmacokinetics of many pharmaceuticals currently in use.

The Effects of Nicotine on the Smoker's Body

Nicotine causes a dose-dependent, biphasic response at the level of the neurons affected by this compound, and this effect is most pronounced on the acetylcholine-based neurons (Brust, 2004; Oncken & George, 2005; J. E. Rose et al., 2003). Because nicotine's chemical structure is very similar to that of acetylcholine, it initially triggers the firing of these neurons, possibly contributing to the smoker's feeling of increased alertness. However, over longer periods of time the nicotine saturates the acetylcholine receptor sites, reducing the rate at which these neurons fire. This might be one mechanism by which cigarette smoking helps to make the smoker feel relaxed.

Nicotine is quite toxic, and the estimated lethal oral dose is between 40 and 60 mg (Hymowitz, 2005). This is one reason why it is so dangerous for a child to ingest any tobacco that they might find, as the absorption rate for orally administered nicotine in children is far higher than when it is smoked by an adult. Symptoms of nicotine toxicity include nausea, vomiting, diarrhea, abdominal pain, headache, sweating, and

pallor (Hymowitz, 2005).[9] Oral overdoses can also demonstrate symptoms such as dizziness, weakness, confusion, coma, and possible death from respiratory paralysis. These symptoms are very similar to those reported by first-time smokers, suggesting that they are demonstrating nicotine toxicity as a result of their cigarette smoking. However, if the smoker persists, the stimulation of the neurotransmitter systems involved in the reward cascade will help the new smoker learn to associate the practice of smoking with pleasure and relaxation.

In the body, nicotine stimulates the release of acetylcholine, which controls many body functions. This may account, at least in part, for nicotine's effects on the cardiovascular system, such as the increase in heart rate, blood pressure, and strength of heart contractions observed after a person smokes a cigarette. Nicotine also induces a reduced rate and strength of muscle contractions in the stomach and causes the blood vessels in the peripheral regions of the body to constrict (Schuckit, 2006a). The process of smoking deposits many potentially harmful chemicals in the lungs, possibly contributing to the decreased action of the cilia[10] in the lungs. These nicotine-induced effects seem to account for at least some of the pulmonary problems seen in chronic smokers.

Nicotine Addiction

Although this information was not discussed in public for many years, researchers for various tobacco companies have known that nicotine was highly addictive since the early 1960s. This discovery was promptly suppressed (Hurt & Robertson, 1998; Slade, Bero, Hanauer, Barnes, & Glantz, 1995). Indeed, one industry memo from 1963 cited by Slade et al. illustrates how the tobacco industry knew that it was "in the business of selling nicotine, an addictive drug" (p. 228). However, it was not until 1997 that a single major tobacco company in the United States admitted in court that tobacco was addictive (J. Solomon, Rogers, Katel, & Lach, 1996).

Like the other drugs of abuse, nicotine alters the firing pattern of neurons in the nucleus accumbens region of the brain. Surprisingly, the compound that is closest to producing the same pattern of altered neural function is the opioid family of compounds (Britt & McGehee, 2008). This makes clinical sense because

---

[8]Some drinkers have reported that they smoke *only* when they are drinking and that they can abstain from cigarettes between periods of alcohol use.

[9]Any real *or suspected* overdose should always be assessed by a physician *immediately*.

[10]See Glossary.

smokers report a sense of pleasure when they smoke, suggesting that nicotine stimulates the release of endogenous opioids in the brain. The addictive potential of nicotine would seem to be higher than that of cocaine, as illustrated by the fact that whereas 3–20% of those who try cocaine become addicted to it, at least 33–50% of those who experiment with cigarette smoking become addicted[11] to the practice (Oncken & George, 2005). Further, like the other drugs of abuse, the greater people's exposure to nicotine, the higher the chance that they will become addicted to nicotine.

Scientists have documented physical changes in the brain's nerve pathways after just a few cigarettes, suggesting that even a limited exposure to nicotine may initiate the addiction process (Mansvelder, Keath, & McGehee, 2002). This might explain why 94% of those children who smoke just four cigarettes go on to become regular smokers. Still, 5–10% of smokers are not addicted and smoke just occasionally. These people are classified as "chippers," but unfortunately very little is known about this subgroup of cigarette smokers, nor is it known what percentage of "chippers" will eventually become addicted to nicotine.

The majority of those who smoke, possibly as many as 90–95%, are addicted to nicotine and demonstrate the characteristic symptoms of drug addiction: (a) tolerance, (b) a characteristic withdrawal syndrome, and (c) drug-seeking behaviors. Cigarette smokers also titrate their smoking (another characteristic symptom of addiction) to maintain a fairly constant level of nicotine in their blood (Oncken & George, 2005). This is demonstrated by the fact that when given cigarettes with a higher nicotine content, smokers will smoke less, whereas they increase the frequency of their cigarette use when given cigarettes with a lower nicotine content. Smokers of low-tar cigarettes have also been observed to inhale more deeply and hold their breath longer than do smokers of high-tar cigarettes. But there has been relatively little research into how the tar content of cigarettes influences smoking behavior. Smokers also develop individualized smoking rituals, which seem to provide them with a sense of security and contribute to the urge to smoke when they are anxious.

Nicotine Withdrawal

Withdrawal symptoms from nicotine typically begin within 2 hours of the smoker's last cigarette, peak within 24 hours (Oncken & George, 2005), and then gradually decline in intensity over the next 10 days. The exact nature of nicotine withdrawal varies from individual to individual, and in spite of the horror stories often told about nicotine withdrawal, approximately a quarter of those who smoke report no significant withdrawal distress when they do attempt to quit.

The reported symptoms of nicotine withdrawal include sleep problems, irritability, impatience, difficulties in concentration, lightheadedness, restlessness, fatigue, drowsiness, strong "craving" for tobacco, hunger, gastrointestinal upset, constipation, headache, and increased coughing. Extended withdrawal symptoms appear to continue for as long as 6 months after the individual's last cigarette, although they vary in intensity from one person to another. Although many smokers report that smoking helps them to calm down, there is strong evidence that cigarette smoking can induce or exacerbate anxiety symptoms in those individuals with a panic disorder (Isensee, Hans-Ulrich, Stein, Hofler, & Lieb, 2003).

Complications of the Chronic Use of Tobacco Products

As noted earlier in this chapter, cigarette smoking is the primary method by which nicotine is introduced into the body. Cigar and pipe smokers reflect only a small percentage of tobacco users; however, pipe and cigar smoking carry many of the same health risks associated with cigarette smoking (J. Rodriguez et al., 2010), although the complications induced by these methods of tobacco use will not be discussed further in this chapter.

The cigarette, the most common means by which tobacco is smoked, is also the "most lethal delivery system" (Erickson, 2007, p. 133) possible. Unfortunately, although many cigarette smokers acknowledge this fact, they also maintain an illusion of personal immunity from these smoking-related problems, at least until the development of such a medical disorder (R. Rogers, 2008). The most common cause of death associated with cigarette smoking is cancer. Globally, smoking is thought to cause 5 million premature deaths each year, many from various forms of cancer (Coghlan, 2009). There is some dispute as to the proportion of cancer-related deaths that are smoking related. Ezzati, Henley, Lopez, and Thus, (2005) suggested that 21% of all cancer deaths are smoking related, although in some regions of the country where there is a strong tradition

---

[11]Leamon et al. (2008) suggested that one-third of those people who smoke just one cigarette will go on to become addicted to nicotine.

TABLE 16-1 PROPORTIONS OF CANCER CASES ASSOCIATED WITH SMOKING	
Lung cancer	87%
Esophageal cancer	75%
Bladder cancer	30–40%
Pancreatic cancer	30%

NOTE: From Hymowitz (2005) and World Health Organization (2006).

of smoking, this is possibly as high as 40%. In contrast to this, the team of Leistikow, Kabit, Connolly, Clancy, and Alpert (2008) used a different methodology and concluded that smoking was associated with 74% of all cancer deaths in the 30- to 74-year-old age bracket. The authors went so far as to suggest that smoking was responsible for most premature cancer-related deaths in the United States each year.

In the United States smoking is thought to be associated with a various of forms of cancer, the most common of which are reviewed in Table 16-1 (Bacher et al., 2010).

To put the relative risk of premature death into perspective, the body of a cigarette smoker appears to be 5–10 years older than their chronological age (Woloshin, Schwartz, & Welch, 2008). It has been estimated that the typical male smoker in the United States will lose 13.2 years of potential life because of a smoking-related illness, whereas the average female smoker is thought to lose 14.5 years of potential life as a result of smoking-induced illness (Carmona, 2004; Sundaram et al., 2004). In addition, nonsmokers enjoy a better quality of life than do cigarette smokers in middle age and beyond (Strandberg et al., 2008). The various complications induced by cigarette smoking are thought to account for 19–25% of all deaths in the United States each year, which in terms of real numbers is approximately 443,000 deaths per year ("Cigarette Smoking Among Adults—United States," 2007). This number includes the estimated 15,000 nonsmokers who are estimated to die each year as a result of "passive" or "secondhand" smoking (discussed later in this chapter). In Table 16-2, we will look at the exact distribution of smoking-related deaths each year.

Although the relationship between cigarette smoking and cancer has been well documented, the causal mechanism has not been isolated as of this time. There are known carcinogenic chemicals in cigarette smoke, as evidenced by the fact that abnormal bronchial cells have been found in 98% of current smokers, as opposed to just 26% of nonsmokers (Wadland & Ferenchick, 2004). Nationally, cigarette smoking is thought to cause 17–30% of all deaths from cardiovascular disease each year, 24% of all deaths from pneumonia/influenza, and 10% of infant deaths can be attributed to cigarette smoking (D. M. Burns, 2008; J. R. Hughes, 2005; N. S. Miller, 1999).

There is a known relationship between cigarette smoking and breast cancer, although the mechanism for this relationship is not clear. However, the team of Guo et al. (2008) presented a theory that might explain the relationship between cigarette smoking and cancer. The authors suggested that even the reduced levels of nicotine found in secondhand smoke[12] interact with receptors in breast tissue cells, signaling the cells to begin uncontrolled replication and migration. This theory is based on only a preliminary interpretation of the research data, and if true would seem to offer a major insight into how smoking induces cancer.

This theory is hardly insignificant, because the cost of smoking-related health care problems and economic costs in the Untied States alone is estimated at $400 billion per year (T. P. George & Weinberger, 2008). The cost of cigarette smoking to society has been estimated to be $3,000 for every man, woman, and child in the United States (Centers for Disease Control and Prevention, 2004). Smoking also results in indirect economic loss each year in the United States. For example, cigarette smoking is a known risk factor for residential fires, causing an estimated 187,000 each year. Thus the practice of cigarette smoking produces a significant economic drain on the economy of this country. For the individual, cigarette smoking results in significant health risk from a variety of disorders, which are discussed in more detail in the next few paragraphs.

The Mouth, Throat, and Pulmonary System

Cigarette smokers are at increased risk for respiratory disorders during sleep, such as snoring and obstructive sleep apnea. The smoker is also 10–15 times as likely to develop lung cancer as the nonsmoker (Kuper, Boffetta, & Adami, 2002). Smokers are also thought to be 27 times more likely to develop laryngeal cancer than nonsmokers, and the risk for these forms of cancer is dose related (World Health Organization, 2006). Cigarette smokers are also at increased risk for chronic bronchitis, pneumonia, and chronic obstructive pulmonary

---

[12]Discussed later in this chapter.

TABLE 16-2 CAUSES OF ANNUAL SMOKING RELATED DEATHS IN THE UNITED STATES

CAUSE OF DEATH	PERCENTAGE OF DEATHS FROM THIS DISEASE RELATED TO SMOKING	TOTAL NUMBER OF ANNUAL DEATHS FROM THIS CONDITION INDUCED BY SMOKING
Lung cancer	28%	120,000/year
Coronary artery disease	23%	98,990/year
Chronic lung disease other than cancer	17%	73,100/year
Other forms of cancer	7%	30,100/year
Strokes	6%	25,800/year
All other forms of illness	19%	81,700/year

disease (COPD) (Brust, 2004). It has been estimated that 80–90% of deaths from COPD might be traced to the cigarette smoking (Anczak & Nogler, 2003). The individual's vulnerability for developing COPD is based in part to their genetic heritage, and it is a potentially fatal complication for smokers who continue to smoke after it develops (Sadeghejad et al., 2009).

Ten percent of those individuals over the age of 65 who manifest COPD symptoms continue to smoke (Gwinnell & Adamec, 2006). It is not uncommon for these people to rationalize their continued smoking on the grounds that because the damage has already been done, there is no sense in quitting cigarettes. In reality there are benefits to quitting, even for the elderly. For example, 3 months after quitting cigarettes, lung function will have improved by about one-third, which is a matter of importance for patients with COPD (Gwinnell & Adamec, 2006).

The Digestive System

Cigarette smoking is the cause of approximately half of all cases of gum disease and tooth loss (Centers for Disease Control, 2004). As noted earlier, smokers are also at increased risk of developing cancer of the mouth or throat. This effect is multiplied if the smoker is also a heavy drinker. Where heavy smokers have been found to have a sevenfold higher incidence of cancer of the mouth and pharynx than nonsmokers, and heavy drinkers have a sixfold higher incidence of these forms of cancer, the heavy smoker who is also a heavy drinker has a *38-fold* higher incidence of cancer of mouth and pharynx ("Alcohol and Tobacco," 1998).

Cigarette smoking contributes to the formation of gastric ulcers, especially peptic ulcers, and cancer of the stomach, and is a factor in the development of some forms of cancer of the pancreas (Carmona, 2004). For reasons that are not understood, cigarette smokers are also at increased risk for the development of type 2 diabetes (Willi, Bodenmann, Ghali, Faris, & Cornuz, 2007; Yeh, Duncan, Schmidt, Wang, & Brancati, 2010). The reason for this association is not known, although lifestyle factors such as a lack of exercise and poor diet are possibilities, and the increased risk for type 2 diabetes does not appear to decrease with smoking cessation (Yeh et al., 2010). Again, the reason for this is not known.

The Cardiovascular System

Cigarette smoking has been identified as the leading risk factor for heart disease, which results in a death every minute in the United States (Committee on Secondhand Smoke Exposure and Acute Coronary Events, 2009). Cigarette smoking is thought to account for approximately 30% of these deaths.

The mechanisms by which cigarette smoking contributes to deaths from cardiovascular disease are varied. Smoking even a single cigarette has been shown to alter the cardiac rhythm (McClain, 2006). In addition to this, the coronary arteries of the heart briefly constrict when a person smokes. Because the coronary arteries are the main source of oxygen and nutrients to the heart, anything that causes even a transitory constriction of the coronary arteries is a matter of concern. If the artery is also partially blocked by atherosclerotic plaque, the reduction in blood flow might be so severe that parts of the heart muscle begin to die for want of oxygen and nutrients. Heart attack survivors who continue to smoke are at increased risk for a second heart attack, bringing with it the risk of premature death from heart disease. This risk can be reduced by a reduction in cigarette use: If the smoker were to cut back just five cigarettes per day, they would reduce their chances of premature mortality by 18% (Gerber et al., 2009). If smokers quit after having the first heart attack, their risk of experiencing a second heart attack begins to drop within 6–12 months of their last cigarette.

Cigarette smokers have been found to be at increased risk for hypertension,[13] the development of aortic aneurysms, and atherosclerotic peripheral vascular disease, than are nonsmokers. Smokers are also at increased risk for strokes, and smoking is thought to be the cause of approximately 26,000 fatal strokes each year in the United States (Carpenter, 2001). Further, cigarette smoking introduces large amounts of carbon monoxide into the blood, blocking its ability to carry oxygen to the body tissues. The blood of a cigarette smoker might lose as much as 15% of its oxygen-carrying potential as smoking-induced carbon monoxide binds to the hemoglobin in the blood (A. Parrott et al., 2004; Tresch & Aronow, 1996).

The Skin

The various smoking-related problems previously noted will ultimately impact on the smoker's skin, causing a process of "premature aging" (A. Parrott et al., 2004). Drawing on the data obtained from a research sample of 82 subjects aged 22–91 years, the team of Hefrich et al. (2007) attempted to develop an objective scale to assess adult skin aging. They found that cigarette smoking was associated with a dose-related premature aging of the skin of the face, as expected, but also found that this premature aging process involved the entire skin, not just the skin of the face, as had long been believed.

The Central Nervous System

Smoking appears to be related to a higher incidence of cataract formation in the eyes of smokers, although the exact reason for this is not clear at the present time (Centers for Disease Control, 2004). Cigarette smokers also appear to be at higher risk for the development of macular degeneration than are nonsmokers the same age (J. S. L. Tan et al., 2008). There is also an emerging body of evidence, based on animal research, that a compound known as NNK,[14] a carcinogen found only in tobacco, appears to cause the release of proteins that contribute to inflammation as well as damage to the neurons of the brain (Ghosh et al., 2009). The possibility that a similar process might cause brain damage in human cigarette smokers has not been confirmed or

ruled out. There is, however, strong evidence that smoking might speed up the progression of damage seen in multiple sclerosis, although this is still uncertain because of conflicting research findings (Healy et al., 2009). After periods of debate and contradictory research findings, cigarette smoking has been accepted as a risk factor for at least some forms of amyotrophic lateral sclerosis (ALS) (Armon, 2009).

The Reproductive System

The impact of cigarette smoking on the women's health is discussed in detail in Chapter 18. It is sufficient to point out here that cigarette smoking has a significant impact on the woman's reproductive system.

Male smokers are at increased risk for various reproductive system problems, including smoking-related erectile dysfunction. The causal mechanism for this might be cigarette-related vascular damage to the blood vessels involved in the erectile response (Bach, Wincze, & Barlow, 2001). Surprisingly, although cigarette smoking does not appear to raise the individual's risk for cancer of the prostate, men who smoke appear to have a higher mortality rate from prostate cancer than nonsmokers, for unknown reasons (Carmona, 2004). It is possible that men who smoke also engage in other behaviors that increase the risk of mortality from prostate cancer, such as poor diet for example, but this is only a theory.

Other Complications Associated with Cigarette Smoking

For reasons that remain unclear, cigarette smoking is thought to either cause, or at least exacerbate, psoriasis. There is also strong evidence that cigarette smoking might exacerbate rheumatoid arthritis in people with the genetic predisposition for this disorder (Lundstrom et al., 2009). Cigarette smokers have a higher incidence of kidney cancer as compared with nonsmokers, and there appears to be a relationship between cigarette smoking and the development of a condition known as *Grave's disease*[15] (Carmona, 2004). There is also an apparent relationship between cigarette smoking and bone density loss in postmenopausal women (Carmona, 2004). Other effects of smoking on the women's body are discussed in Chapter 18.

Cigarette smokers are twice as likely to admit to having suicidal thoughts as were nonsmokers the same age (Bronisch, Hofler, & Lieb, 2008). This may

---

[13]Itself a known risk factor for stroke.

[14]If you must know: 4-Methylnitrosamino-1(3-pyrdyl)-1-butanone.

[15]See Glossary.

or may not be associated with the altered brain function in former smokers that continues for an extended period of time after the smoker's last cigarette. Many former smokers will report that they "never felt quite right" after they gave up cigarettes, suggesting that smoking-induced cognitive changes might linger for many years after the smoker's last cigarette.

A surprising complication of cigarette smoking is what Cutler-Triggs, Fryer, Miyoshi, and Weitzman (2008) termed "food insecurity," or the inability to obtain sufficient supplies of food. There are an estimated 13 million children in the United States who grow up in homes where there are not always sufficient levels of food, and the authors found that 17% of those children who had at least one smoking parent could be classified as living in such a home, as opposed to just 9% of those children who were living in a home where the parents did not smoke. It was noted that in some families up to 20% of the family income was spent on tobacco rather than on other, more healthy products such as food, according to the authors. This drain on the family income then contributes to a reduction in food availability, which then can contribute to nutrition-based developmental problems for the child.

At one point in time, it was thought that cigarette smoking might provide some protection against the later development of Alzheimer's disease. Subsequent research failed to support the initial study that suggested this, and at this time cigarette smokers are thought to be at *increased risk* for the development of dementia later in life (Sundram et al., 2004).

Degrees of Risk

There is no such thing as a "safe" cigarette. Smoking cessation is the only known way to reduce the risk of or avoid smoking-induced health problems (Carmona, 2004). "Low-tar" or "light" cigarettes appear to offer the same degree of risk as regular cigarettes (Carmona, 2004). Smoking as few as three cigarettes a day has been found to increase the individual's risk of cardiovascular disease by 65% (C. A. Pope et al., 2009). This data suggests that the individual's risk for cardiovascular disease increases with minimal exposure to cigarettes.

Chewing Tobacco

There are three types of "smokeless" tobacco in use today: (a) moist "snuff," (b) dry snuff, and (c) chewing tobacco (often called "spit tobacco"). In the United States, only an estimated 3.5% of tobacco users (or, 8.7 million people) use "smokeless" tobacco products (Substance Abuse and Mental Health Services Administration, 2009). Many of these people use chewing tobacco on the assumption that it is safer than smoked tobacco and exposes them to lower levels of nicotine. Unfortunately, research has demonstrated that using chewing tobacco 8–10 times a day will result in blood levels of nicotine similar to those seen in a 1½-to-2-pack-a-day cigarette smoker (Shipley & Rose, 2003). Further, some of the compounds found in chewing tobacco have been linked to hypertension, and there are at least 16 carcinogenic compounds in the typical sample of chewing tobacco (Hecht & Hatsukami, 2005). This places those who use chewing tobacco at higher risk for cancer of the mouth and throat as nonusers (Hecht & Hatsukami, 2005). Indeed, the team of Hecht et al. (2007) found *higher* levels of one known carcinogen[16] in the urine of those who used chewing tobacco than was found in the urine of cigarette smokers.

Although many of those who use "smokeless" tobacco, as chewing tobacco is also called, believe that it is safer, recent research shows that tobacco chewers are actually at *higher* risk for a fatal myocardial infarction and/or stroke than are cigarette smokers (Boffeta & Straif, 2009). This might reflect tobacco's ability to increase heart rate and blood pressure, according to Boffeta and Straif. This is consistent with the known greater incidence of coronary artery disease as compared to nonsmokers. Those who use "chewing" tobacco also have a higher risk of cancer of the pancreas in addition to a higher risk of oral and throat cancers (Boffetta, Hecht, Gray, Gupta, & Straif, 2008). Those who chew tobacco often experience problems controlling their blood pressure as well. Thus although chewing tobacco is often viewed as the "lesser of two evils" by those who use it, this product is certainly not without its risks.

Secondhand Smoke[17]

Nonsmokers who associate with smokers are exposed to many of the same toxins found in cigarette smoke, some of which cling to smokers' clothing if they were to smoke outside and then come indoors. Because

---

[16]Which was the compound 4-(methylnitrocamine)-1-(3pryidyl)-1-butanol, and its metabolites.

[17]Also called "passive smoking" or "environmental tobacco smoke." All three terms will be used in this chapter.

toxins found in cigarette smoke do not disappear when the smoker exhales, a nonsmoker is thought to be exposed to these same toxins. Research has found, for example, that almost *88% of nonsmokers* demonstrated cotinine, a metabolite of nicotine, in their blood. This exposure to cigarette smoke has come to be called "secondhand" or "environmental" smoke, and research has found that it presents significant danger to the nonsmoker.

There is also strong evidence that the tobacco industry tried to discredit research that associated exposure to secondhand or environmental tobacco smoke to heart diseases (Tong & Glantz, 2007). In spite of such denials, research has demonstrated that the coronary arteries of those exposed to secondhand smoke experience short-term coronary artery disease constriction after their exposure to cigarette smoke just as do cigarette smokers (Gullu et al., 2007; Otsuka et al., 2001). Exposure to environmental tobacco smoke also is thought to speed up the formation of atherosclerotic plaque by 20%, as opposed to 50% faster for the active smoker.

Nonsmokers exposed to significant amounts of environmental tobacco smoke are at higher risk for developing pulmonary disorders such as lung cancer or tuberculosis (Leung et al., 2010). Between 3000 and 8000 nonsmokers die each year from cancer induced by environmental tobacco smoke in just the United States (Fiore, 2006). An interesting test of the theory that environmental tobacco smoke exposure could cause disease for nonsmokers was carried out by Stark et al. (2007). The authors compared data from a sample of 52 nonsmoking restaurant workers from bars where smoking was permitted against 32 bars where smoking was prohibited. They found that the former group had six times the level of the compound NNAL[18] in their urine than did those bar workers from bars where smoking was not permitted. The importance of this study is in the fact that both sample groups were nonsmokers, and NNAL is a smoking-specific carcinogenic compound, thus suggesting that those bar workers in smoking-permitted bars were receiving significant exposure to toxic environmental tobacco smoke.

It has been concluded that exposure to secondhand smoke increases the individual's risk of an initial myocardial infarction, and if the individual survives, subsequent myocardial infarctions. The team of

Pell et al. (2008) examined the hospital admission records of nine hospitals in Scotland after a law was passed banning cigarette smoking in bars, restaurants, and other public places. The authors discovered that the number of admissions to these hospitals for acute coronary syndrome dropped 17% in the first year following the start of this ban, which is a significant, and not isolated, measure of the dangers of secondhand cigarette smoke. The team of Meyers, Neuberger, and He (2009) also concluded that the risk of acute myocardial infarction drops by 17% in the first year of a public smoking ban, and that it is even higher in subsequent years. In the city of Pueblo, Colorado, hospital admissions for acute myocardial infarctions dropped by 41% after implementation of smoking ban in public places ("Reduced Hospitalizations for Acute Myocardial Infarction," 2008). These and similar studies suggest that those exposed to environmental tobacco smoke suffer a higher risk of cardiac disease as a result of their inadvertent exposure to cigarette smoke.

Adults who are exposed to secondhand smoke are also at higher risk for cognitive impairment than are those who are not exposed to cigarette smoke (Llewellyn, Lang, Langa, Naughton, & Matthews, 2009). Llewellyn et al. found that those adults with the highest level of exposure to environmental tobacco smoke were more likely to fall in the lowest 10% of cognitive testing, as compared with adults with lighter levels of exposure to environmental tobacco smoke. Further, children are also vulnerable to environmental tobacco smoke.

Researchers believe that secondhand smoke causes approximately 6100 deaths in children each year in the United States. For example, children exposed to environmental tobacco smoke are at increased risk for developing asthma, which may be fatal if medical assistance does not arrive in time (Guilbert & Krawiec, 2003). The team of Kwok et al. (2008) concluded that infants exposed to secondhand smoke in the first 3 months of life were twice as likely to develop an infectious disease(s), some of which were severe enough to require hospitalization, during the first 8 years of their lives. Another measure of the vulnerability of children to environmental tobacco smoke was provided by Kerrigan (2008), who utilized data from the state of Wisconsin infant follow-up studies, where it was suggested that 56% of those infants who died after discharge from the hospital following birth had been exposed to environmental tobacco smoke.

---

[18]Chemical shorthand for: 4-(methylitrosamino)-1-(3-paridyl)-1-butanol.

Childhood exposure to secondhand smoke is, surprisingly, an apparent risk factor in the development of pulmonary diseases such as emphysema (Lovasi et al., 2010) or lung cancer (Oliva-Marston et al., 2009) for that individual later in life. Lovasi et al. (2010) hypothesized that early damage to the alveolar walls might increase that child's chances of developing emphysema in middle to late adulthood. However, although the results of these studies are suggestive, they are not proof that such a relationship exists, and there is a need for further research into childhood exposure to secondhand smoke and adult pulmonary disease. As these studies and those cited in earlier paragraphs suggest, environmental tobacco smoke is a serious health risk for those who are around the smoker, and a factor in premature illness or death for a significant number of infants or children who were in effect involuntary smokers.

It has even been suggested that exposure to tertiary, or "third-hand" tobacco smoke could be harmful, although this claim is controversial (D. Robson, 2009). Tertiary tobacco smoke exposure occurs when the nonsmoker is exposed to the residue of cigarette smoking found on the individual's clothing and on environmental surfaces. However, the scientific validity of such claims has been challenged not from the tobacco industry but from a small group of independent scientists (D. Robson, 2009). For example, antismoking groups have seized on a research study that concluded that breathing secondhand smoke for 30 minutes increased one's risk of a heart attack as compared to that of an active smoker. However, the research data supporting this claim has been limited, and most physicians believe that such exposure will result in a heart attack only if the nonsmoker was on the brink of a coronary event.

Although antismoking groups have trumpeted the fact that "Big Tobacco" interfered in scientific research in the 1960s and 1970s by paying scientists to conduct research contradicting those that found that cigarette smoking was dangerous, they remain mute about the fact that many scientists conducting research into the dangers of cigarette smoking receive funding from companies that make nicotine replacement products (D. Robson, 2009). This is not to imply that cigarette smoking or environmental tobacco smoke are not dangerous. It does, however, underscore the need for a careful, *unbiased* examination of the evidence before claims of dangers of or the extent of such dangers from either direct or indirect exposure to cigarette smoke are made.

Smoking Cessation

It is difficult to quit smoking, yet the majority of smokers make determined efforts to do so. J. R. Hughes (2005) found that only 19% of cigarette smokers had *never* tried to quit smoking, which means that more than 80% of smokers have tried to quit at least once. In spite of this fact, however, the success rate for smoking cessation programs, even those that utilize pharmacological support, remains quite low. Average cigarette smoker will require 5–10 serious attempts to quit smoking before they achieve success. However, success is possible, as evidenced by the fact that there are more former smokers in the United States today than current smokers (Fiore, Hatsukami, & Baker, 2002; J. R. Hughes, 2005).

In spite of public media advertisements suggesting that smokers require pharmacological support to quit, it has been found that between two-thirds and three-quarters of former smokers were able to quit without pharmacological support (S. Chapman & MacKenzie, 2010). Chapman and MacKenzie also found that most former smokers reported that quitting was easier than expected. However, this assertion is not supported by the finding that there is an inverse relationship between the frequency with which people smoke and their probable success in giving up tobacco use with any single attempt. Light smokers, defined as individuals who smoke 20 cigarettes a day or less, appear to be more capable of stopping on their own, whereas heavy smokers are more likely to require professional assistance. In either case, the individual's *expectations* for nicotine withdrawal and smoking cessation influence their success rate. Those people who expect the most withdrawal distress or a higher number of problems when they attempted to quit are more likely either to not attempt to quit or to fail in their efforts to quit.

There is preliminary evidence to suggest that individuals' ability to quit smoking is mediated by their genetic inheritance (Uhl et al., 2008). However, the authors pointed out that smoking cessation was probably polygenetic, which is to say that multiple genes are involved, providing a range of potential responses to the individual's attempt to give up cigarette smoking.[19] Uhl et al. also noted that the genes that they identified were similar but not identical to those suspected of

---

[19]This is also in addition to the social supports system(s) that the smoker might have for smoking cessation and the like. So, again, individuals' genetic heritage does not *rule* their behavior. It just helps to define the limits within which they might respond to a behavioral challenge.

being involved in other addictive behaviors in other studies. Indeed, the authors found much less of an overlap between these two sets of genes than they had anticipated, suggesting that different genetic mechanisms might be at work between cigarette smoking and the other addictive behaviors.

To complicate matters even further,[20] there is strong evidence suggesting that smokers' dietary choices might influence their success in quitting. The team of McClemon, Westma, Rose, and Lutz (2007) found that smokers who consumed meat, coffee, and alcohol experienced greater pleasure from cigarette use, whereas products such as dairy products, celery, and other vegetables reduced smokers' sense of pleasure from smoking. Thus those who wish to quit smoking must review their dietary habits and change their diet to give themselves the best possible chance of quitting.

Older smokers cited health concerns as the motivating factor in their efforts to quit, according to Reichert et al., these findings suggest that the individual's desire to quit might vary depending on the smoker's age. While one-to-one counseling is of value to those who wish to quit smoking, those who attend smoking cessation support groups have been found to be twice as likely to succeed as those who only have one-to-one counseling (Bauld, Chesterman, Ferguson, & Judge, 2008).

In terms of the mechanics of smoking cessation, the most common and possibly least effective method of smoking cessation is the "cold turkey" method in which the smoker just quits smoking (Patkar et al., 2003). The sudden discontinuation of cigarettes tends to result in high relapse rates, as opposed to those methods of smoking cessation that utilize a nicotine replacement component and psychosocial support (Patkar et al., 2003). The various pharmacological supports for smoking cessation are reviewed in Chapter 33.

Former smokers are vulnerable to "relapse triggers" that they encounter in the environment, the most important of which is being around people who are still smoking. Watching others smoke cigarettes, and smelling tobacco smoke from a distance, will trigger thoughts of returning to active smoking for the individual. These relapse triggers are a factor in more than 50% of the cases where the former smoker relapses (Ciraulo, Piechniczek-Buczek, & Iscan, 2003). Thus like other forms of drug addiction, recovering smokers much change their friendships, avoid high-risk situations, and be aware that environmental triggers will make them think about smoking.

There is a poorly understood relationship between depression and cigarette smoking. Evidence suggests that depressed smokers experience more reinforcement from cigarettes than do those who are not depressed and are vulnerable to possible relapse because of this (Patkar et al., 2003). This is not to say that cigarette smoking caused the depression. Rather, depression and cigarette smoking appear to be two separate conditions that appear to overlap, with depression possibly serving as a relapse trigger for recovering smokers. Other emotional states such as boredom or anxiety also can serve as relapse triggers, as many smokers have learned to cope with these emotions through smoking.

Cigarette Cessation and Weight Gain

Many smokers cite their fear of gaining weight as an obstacle to smoking cessation. Admittedly about 80% of former smokers will gain *some* weight in the early stages of recovery (Centers for Disease Control, 2004). But this statistic is misleading: 57% of those who continue to smoke also gain weight during the same period of life, suggesting that some of the weight gain might be falsely attributed to smoking cessation rather than just a tendency on the part of smokers to gain weight as they age. Still, individuals in the early stage of smoking cessation do need to watch their diets. Average smokers increase their caloric intake by about 200 calories a day, or the equivalent of about one sandwich per day (Stitzer, 2003). Over the course of a week, the extra accumulated caloric intake would amount to 1400 calories, which means that the former smoker would be ingesting 8 days' worth of calories every 7 days. This obviously will expose the former smoker to the danger of weight gain, at least in the short term.

Another factor that contributes to weight gain in the former smoker is that nicotine stimulates the body's metabolism by about 10%, forcing the body to "burn" calories faster than normal (Stitzer, 2003). Finally, many cigarette smokers are underweight because of nicotine-induced anorexia. When they stop smoking, their bodies will attempt to "catch up" and add weight to achieve the appropriate weight level for their body frame. Finally, smokers are often fluid deficient, and when they stop smoking the body will ingest extra fluids to achieve the appropriate fluid levels. These factors may contribute to cessation-related weight gain in the former smoker, which in a sense is true.

Following smoking cessation, the average individual gains about 5 pounds (Centers for Disease Control, 2004), although in about 10% of former smokers this weight gain might be as much as 25 pounds. Surprisingly,

---

[20]Is anything in life ever simple?

TABLE 16-3 SUMMARY OF BENEFITS OF SMOKING CESSATION

CONDITION	BENEFIT
Stroke	Within 5-15 years, the former smoker's risk of stroke will be about the same as that of a person who never smoked.
Cancer of the mouth, throat and esophagus	After 5 years of abstinence, the former smoker's risk developing one of these cancers is 50% lower.
Coronary artery disease	After 1 year of abstinence the former smoker's risk of coronary artery disease will drop by 50% of 15 years of abstinence it will be about the same as that of a nonsmoker.
Lung cancer	The risk for this form of cancer will drop 50% in the first 10 years of abstinence.
Hypertension	Smoking cessation is associated with a linear improvement in arterial wall flexibility over the first 10 years of abstinence, resulting in lower blood pressure.
Life expectancy	Former smokers add between 2.5 and 4.5 years of life to their predicted life expectancy.
Recovering cardiac patients	Former smokers are less likely to suffer a 2nd heart attack (reinfarction) than current smokers.

NOTE: From Centers for Disease Control (2004).

there is evidence suggesting that those individuals who gain more weight are also more likely to abstain from cigarettes. Further, although this weight gain is often distressing to the former smoker, there is evidence that after 6 months or so the individual's body weight will return to precessation levels. Thus, cessation-related weight gain may be a transitional step in the former smoker's adjustment to life without cigarettes.

Although obesity is a known risk factor for cardiovascular disease, the health benefits that accrue following smoking cessation usually far outweigh the potential risks from smoking cessation related weight gain. Former smokers would need to gain 50–100 pounds to place the same stress on their cardiovascular system as they did by smoking one pack a day. Thus the postcessation weight gain is not as dangerous as continued cigarette smoking. Table 16-3 lists some of the benefits of smoking cessation.

Chapter Summary

Tobacco use, which was once limited to what European explorers would come to call the New World, was first introduced into Europe by explorers who learned the practice of smoking during their travels. Once the practice of smoking tobacco reached Europe, it spread rapidly in spite of rather draconian measures by authorities to try and stop its spread. By the end of the 19th century, tobacco chewing had become a common practice, whereas the concurrent development of machines that allowed for the rapid production of cigarettes allowed health providers to suggest cigarette smoking as a less offensive and more sanitary substitute for chewing tobacco.

In the time since its introduction into society, nicotine, the main psychoactive agent in tobacco, has been found to have an addiction potential similar to that of narcotics or cocaine. Significant numbers of people have become addicted to cigarettes, and each year 34% of current smokers attempt to quit. Unfortunately, only 2.5% of smokers are able to discontinue the use of cigarettes each time they attempt to quit, in spite of the best of pharmacological support. This fact is a testament to the addictive potential of nicotine, but also reflects the sad fact that the majority of those who smoke will continue to expose themselves to the dangers associated with tobacco use.

CHAPTER 17

Chemicals and the Neonate:

The Potential Consequences of Drug Abuse During Pregnancy[1]

Despite information received by the general public on the adverse effects of substance abuse in pregnancy, there is still significant substance abuse among pregnant women in the U.S.

—*Goler, Armstrong, Taillac, and Osejo (2008, pp. 3–4)*

Introduction

Maternal substance use, even the use of some prescribed medications, may have dire consequences for both a woman and her unborn child if she is pregnant. A predinner cocktail by a pregnant woman, for example, may disrupt fetal growth and development in a multitude of ways. Indeed, the use of many prescription and over-the-counter medications might disrupt normal fetal growth and development. Unfortunately, recreational drug abuse is most prevalent in the age cohort actively involved in reproduction (Bolnick & Rayburn, 2003). In this chapter the effects of maternal substance use during pregnancy will be explored.

Scope of the Problem for Women

Maternal substance use during pregnancy is not an uncommon problem. Alcohol use during this phase is most common, with 5.1% of pregnant women questioned admitting to the abuse of an illicit substance in the previous 30 days (Substance Abuse and Mental Health Services Administration, 2009). Although alcohol use is legal, it still has the potential to cause terrible harm to the developing fetus. Further, 10.6% of pregnant women between the ages of 15 and 44 admitted to drinking alcohol in the previous 30 days, and 4.5% of the women surveyed admitted to binge drinking in the past 30 days (Substance Abuse and Mental Health Services Administration, 2009). It is important to remember that this study addressed the past 30 days. Finnegan and Kandall (2008) estimated that 18.8% of women will consume alcohol at least once during pregnancy (although many do so before they become aware that they are pregnant). In spite of these facts, there has only been limited research into the impact of maternal illicit alcohol or drug use on fetal growth and development.

Until recently physicians usually had to rely on maternal self-report to identify babies who were exposed to alcohol or drugs in utero. If meconium[2] testing was conducted, the results were usually not available for many days, in part because the physician might be forced to wait that time for the meconium to be expelled following birth. However, Montgomery et al. (2008) have suggested that the umbilical cord can be tested for fetal

---

[1]Technically, the study of how chemical compounds affect neonatal development is the field of *teratogenicity*. A compound that can harm the fetus is called *teratogenic*.

[2]See Glossary.

exposure to many compounds commonly abused. The authors found that of 498 umbilical cord tissue samples tested, 32% were "positive" for compounds such as methamphetamine, cocaine, marijuana, and phencyclidine.[3] The authors suggested that umbilical cord tissue testing might provide a rapid identification of infants who might be at risk for complications as a result of prenatal exposure to these compounds. This would also avoid the problem of maternal dissimulation.[4]

Substance abuse treatment as an integrated component of prenatal care has been found to reduce the number and severity of drug-induced consequences during pregnancy (Armstrong et al., 2008). Although prenatal health visits present a good opportunity to refer the woman with an SUD to treatment or to correct nutritional deficiencies, health care providers are often hesitant to discuss substance use disorders with pregnant women (J. C. Chang et al., 2008).

Scope of the Problem for the Infant

A Period of Special Vulnerability

Women who abuse alcohol or an illicit drug during pregnancy should automatically be classified as having a high-risk pregnancy in the opinion of Finnegan and Kandall (2008). The very nature of prenatal growth makes this a time of vulnerability for the fetus, with the first trimester being especially important to subsequent growth and development. Unfortunately, many women in the first trimester of pregnancy either will be unaware of their status or will not even attempt to alter their substance use patterns until after their pregnancy has been confirmed (Bolnick & Rayburn, 2003). Even worse, some substance-abusing women will not attempt to modify their drug or alcohol use behavior(s) until relatively late in pregnancy after much of the damage has already been done (Bolnick & Rayburn, 2003). Not surprisingly, women who knowingly continue to abuse alcohol or drugs during pregnancy were raised by parents who also had substance use problems (Gwinnell & Adamec, 2006).

Prenatal exposure to radiation or a number of compounds, including alcohol and the drugs of abuse, can have profound, possibly lifelong, consequences for the developing fetus. The process of organ differentiation, for example, takes place during the weeks 3–8 of pregnancy, often before the mother-to-be is even aware that she is pregnant. If the toxic exposure is to a chemical, the danger is compounded by the fact that only 60% of the blood that the fetus receives is processed by the liver before proceeding on to the rest of the body. The other 40% of the blood, and any toxins that it might contain, enters the general circulation of the fetus.

Further, the fetal liver and excretion systems are poorly developed in the fetus at this stage, with one result being that compounds that are routed to the liver are not always biotransformed at the same rate as would be found in the mother's body. This can both allow the toxins more time in the body of the fetus and allow the buildup of potentially fatal levels of some compounds in the fetal circulation. In addition to this, the fetal blood–brain barrier is still developing, allowing many compounds easy access to the fetal nervous system (Barki, Kravitz, & Berki, 1998). Finally, the circulatory system of the fetus has lower blood protein levels than are found in the adult's blood, providing fewer binding sites for protein-bound compounds and thus a higher concentration of these molecules in the fetal circulation. All of these factors combine to magnify the effects of a toxin(s) in the fetus. Researchers have generally found lasting, but usually subtle, effects of prenatal drug exposure in children exposed to chemicals in utero (Malanga, 2009).

In this era of polydrug abuse, it can be difficult to isolate the effect of one specific compound of the fetus (Mendelson et al., 2006). To further complicate matters, factors such as the quality of prenatal medical care and maternal malnutrition influence neonatal growth. Following birth, factors such as being raised in an adverse social environment or poor postnatal caregiving also influence the baby's growth and development. This constellation of risk factors makes it virtually impossible to isolate the effects of maternal abuse of one compound on prenatal growth and development. However, each year in the United States almost 10% of the women of childbearing age meet the criteria for treatment admission for a substance use disorder, although 85% of these women do not perceive the need for such treatment or are never referred to a treatment program (Zilberman, 2009). Thus although the effects of specific compounds on neonatal growth and development are often difficult to isolate and study, there is a significant need for a better understanding of drug

---

[3]Each of which is discussed in the appropriate chapter of this text.

[4]See Glossary.

exposure on fetal growth and for appropriate referrals for the mother to treatment centers that specialize in working with pregnant drug abusers.

Following birth, maternal substance abuse will continue to affect the infant's life. Maternal preoccupation with drug use, the effects of poverty, the impact of maternal depression on the parent-child relationship, the need to compete with siblings for parental attention, maternal anxiety, the intense needs of the drug-exposed infant for nurturance and care, all can combine to cause a poor developmental outcome in the infant, child, and adolescent. However, because there are so many variables involved, scientists have for the most part failed to find a pattern, or syndrome, that is specific to the infant or child that was exposed to the drugs of abuse during gestation.[5]

Although technically postpartum depression is not a complication of fetal exposure to a substance of abuse, there is a relationship between maternal substance use, depression, and attempted suicide following birth. The team of Comtois, Schiff, and Grossman (2008) examined the hospital records of women who gave birth in Washington State between the years 1992 and 2001. The authors found that substance-abusing mothers who developed postpartum depression were six times as likely to attempt suicide in the first year following the child's birth than were nonabusing women. Given the central role of the mother as the primary caregiver in the first years of the infant's life, it is clear that such actions on the part of the mother would certainly impact the growth and development of the child.

The discussion that follows must be interpreted as the current understanding of how maternal substance use affects the infant's growth and development. There is still much to learn in this area, and new information is being added to the existing database on a daily basis. In the following sections we will examine the latest information on the effects of many compounds of abuse on fetal growth and development.

Alcohol

Each year in the United States 757,000 women will consume alcohol at least once during pregnancy. Researchers estimate that 12–18.8% of pregnant women use alcohol at some point during pregnancy, and that 2–4% binge-drink during this time (Bhuvaneswar & Chang, 2009; Finnegan & Kandall, 2008; Centers for Disease Control, 2009b). Surprisingly, in spite of the well-publicized risks associated with maternal alcohol use during pregnancy, there has been little change in the frequency or amount of maternal alcohol use since 1991 (Centers for Disease Control, 2009b). It should be noted that these figures may underestimate the scope of the problem, because many women do not report the frequency or amount of their alcohol use during pregnancy (G. Chang, 2006).

Maternal alcohol use during pregnancy is important because (a) alcohol easily passes across the placenta into the fetal circulation, (b) fetal blood alcohol levels reach the same level of the mothers in a matter of *15 minutes,* and (c) alcohol is a known teratogenic[6] compound (Fryer et al., 2009; Rose, 1988). This makes the fetus an unwilling participant in the mother's alcohol use. This is clearly illustrated by the fact that if the mother were drinking immediately prior to childbirth, it is possible to detect alcohol on the breath of the infant (I. M. Rose, 1988). If the mother were alcohol dependent, then the infant will begin to go through the alcohol withdrawal syndrome 3–12 hours after delivery (American Academy of Pediatrics, 1998).

In early 1973, maternal alcohol use during pregnancy was identified as a major causal agent for birth defects in this country (Sokol, Delaney-Black, & Nordstrom, 2003). The pattern of developmental problems identified in infants born of alcohol abusing mothers was called the fetal alcohol syndrome (FAS). FAS is the third most common cause of birth defects in developed countries and is the most preventable (Getzfeld, 2006; J. Glasser, 2002; Kruelwitch, 2005; Sadock & Sadock, 2007; Swift, 2005). In the time since FAS was first identified as a separate disorder, it has been discovered that it is the end point of a spectrum of complications induced by alcohol in infants born to women who used alcohol during pregnancy. Many children who were exposed to alcohol in utero will have some but not all of the symptoms of FAS (Cunniff, 2003; Rourke & Grant, 2009). These children were said to have *fetal alcohol effects* (FAE). Although the terms *fetal alcohol syndrome* is still being used in some journals, physicians are increasingly using the term *fetal alcohol spectrum disorder* (FASD) to identify children who were exposed to alcohol in utero (Sokol et al., 2003). However, it is important to point out that

---

[5]Some might argue that the fetal alcohol syndrome (FAS), discussed later in this chapter, is an exception to this rule. However, how many infants are exposed to alcohol in gestation who do not develop this condition because they lack the genetic heritage necessary to produce FAS?

---

[6]See Glossary.

FASD is not a recognized diagnostic category, and it remains a theoretical construct (D. Brown, 2006).

Mechanisms by Which Maternal Alcohol Use Impacts Fetal Development

There are multiple mechanisms by which maternal alcohol use can disrupt normal fetal development (Fryer et al., 2009). One is the maternal use of alcohol inhibiting the production (biosynthesis) of a family of compounds known as *gangliosides* in the developing fetal brain. These enzymes are most active during the first trimester of pregnancy, playing a role in fetal brain development. By blocking the biosynthesis of the gangliosides during the first trimester of pregnancy, maternal alcohol use can prove especially destructive to the growing fetal central nervous system (CNS). Unfortunately, the woman might not even know that she is pregnant until well into the first trimester, or even later, and by then the damage has been probably been done.

If the woman should know or suspect that she is pregnant, it is important to remember that there is *no safe level of alcohol use* during pregnancy[7] (G. Chang, 2006; Cunniff, 2003; Kruelwitch, 2005; Sokol et al., 2003). Although few heavy drinkers would consider four to six drinks per day a significant level of alcohol intake, research has shown that even this level of alcohol use will result in two-thirds of the children developing some degree of FASD.

Consequences of Maternal Alcohol Use

It is often difficult to isolate the effects of the mother's use of one substance (alcohol, in this case) from the concurrent abuse of other compounds (cigarettes, for example). Although it is thought that maternal alcohol use can induce FASD this condition is often difficult to identify in its less severe forms because there are no disorder-specific tests that might identify such children. However, this does not mitigate the danger of fetal exposure to alcohol through maternal alcohol use during pregnancy. It has been estimated, for example, that 17% of FAS infants are either stillborn or die shortly after birth (Fryer et al., 2009; Renner, 2004b).

In the United States, it is estimated that 24 children are born each day with FAS, and an unknown number are born with some degree of FASD (Finnegan & Kandall, 2008; Peters, 2007; Sokol et al., 2003; Wattendorf & Muenke, 2005). In South Africa, which has the dubious distinction of having the highest rate of children born with FAS, 6.66%, or 1 in every 15 live births, is a child with FAS (J. Glasser, 2002).

There is an emerging body of evidence suggesting, for example, that different structural components of the developing brain of the fetus are especially vulnerable to alcohol's effects at different points in gestation. Structures such as the corpus callosum, caudate nucleus, and cerebellum appear to be especially vulnerable to the effects of maternal alcohol use (Fryer et al., 2009). These findings are important because the corpus callosum is the region of the brain that transfers information from one hemisphere to the other, whereas the caudate nuclear and the cerebellum are involved in the coordination of muscle movements. Radiographic studies of the brains of infants born to alcohol-abusing mothers have found structural damage to the corpus callosum, if not the absence of this vital brain structure (a condition known as *agenesis* of the corpus callosum).

There is also a mounting body of evidence that suggests that maternal alcohol use during pregnancy will increase the child's risk of developing acute lymphoid leukemia later in life (Menegaux et al., 2006). There is also a growing body of evidence suggesting that maternal alcohol use during pregnancy can cause, or at least exacerbate, the later development of an attention deficit disorder in the child (Peters, 2007). Unfortunately, most heavy drinkers also smoke cigarettes, and as will be discussed later in this chapter, there is a relationship between cigarette use and the development of attention deficit disorders in children later in life. Finally, there is evidence that maternal alcohol use during pregnancy increases the chances that the child will grow up to have an alcohol use disorder in later life (Alati et al., 2006). It should be noted that all of these problems might develop in infants exposed to alcohol in utero even if they do not develop a clinical FASD.

Characteristics of Children with Fetal Alcohol Spectrum Disorder

Of those infants who do survive, one in five will have a major birth defect, whereas many of the others will have more subtle birth defects such as cognitive deficits (Renner, 2004b). Infants who are born with severe FASD usually have a lower than normal birth weight

[7]Some women, having been told that they should ingest *no more than* one standard drink in 24 hours, believe that they can "save up" each day's acceptable level of alcohol intake so that they can go on a binge at a later time. Unfortunately, research has found that even one such binge will place the fetus at risk for FAS/FASD as well as later developmental problems (D. Brown, 2006).

and often demonstrate a characteristic pattern of facial abnormalities. Many infants demonstrate microcephaly[8] at birth, reflecting a smaller brain size than is normal. Noninvasive neurodiagnostic imaging of the brains of children exposed to alcohol in utero often reveals damage to the cortex, cerebellum, basal ganglia, hippocampus, and corpus callosum (Cunniff, 2003).

In later life these children experience behavioral problems that possibly are more severe than those children with attention deficit hyperactivity disorder (ADHD) (Greenbaum et al., 2009). These children have been found to have weaker emotional processing and social cognition skills than do normal children, and although behaviorally children with FASD appear similar to children with ADHD, it has been hypothesized that there are different neurological mechanisms between the two disorders (Greenbaum et al., 2009). This theory is based, in part, on the discovery by Greenbaum et al. that their sample of children with ADHD had normal social processing skills. The authors suggested that although children with FASD often appear to behave like children with ADHD, their behavior might reflect damage to the orbitofrontal region of the brain rather than those regions of the brain involved in ADHD. Children with FASD also experience short attention span, anger control issues, impulsiveness, self-abusive behaviors, poor coordination, cardiac, renal, and visual system disturbances, learning disabilities, and a variety of other developmental delays (Bhuvaneswar & Chang, 2009; Grinnell & Adamec, 2006; Peters, 2007). The annual cost to society for providing remedial services to children with FAS/FASD in the United States is estimated to be approximately $700 million per year (Bhuvaneswar & Chang, 2009).

The low–birth weight characteristic of FAS children at birth appears to at least partially resolve itself by adolescence, with the result being that children with FASD usually fall within the normal height and weight range for adolescents and adults their age (Peters, 2007). This does not alter the fact that these children often need lifelong social service support(s) in order to function in society. There is also strong evidence that children exposed to alcohol in utero are at increased risk for developing an alcohol use disorder of their own later in life[9] (Gilman, Bjork, & Hommer, 2007).

---

[8]See Glossary.

[9]Raising an interesting question: Is the child's later increased risk for an alcohol use disorder brought about by the exposure to alcohol in utero, because of their genetic heritage, or due to environmental forces, if not all three?

Breast Feeding and Alcohol Use

Alcohol in the mother's circulatory system passes freely into her breast milk in concentrations similar to that found in her body. Fortunately, even if the infant were to nurse while the mother was quite intoxicated, the amount of alcohol ingested by the infant along with the mother's milk would be diluted throughout the baby's system, resulting in a lower blood alcohol level for the infant than that for the mother (Heil & Subramanian, 1998). But even this limited alcohol exposure is associated with abnormal gross motor development for the infant, with a dose-dependent relationship between the mother's alcohol use and infant psychomotor problems. Further, it theoretically is possible that maternal alcohol use during nursing might interfere with the development of the infant's immune system, just as it interferes with the normal function of the immune system in the adult. For these reasons, maternal alcohol use during the time when the mother is breast-feeding is not suggested (Sadock & Sadock, 2007).

Disulfiram Use During Pregnancy

Disulfiram is often used as an adjunct to the treatment of alcohol addiction. It has been discovered that during gestation a metabolite of disulfiram, diethyldithiocarbamate, can bind to lead and might bring that lead across the placental barrier. Fetal exposure to lead is known to disrupt normal neurological growth and development for the fetus, and so the use of disulfiram during pregnancy is not recommended.

Abuse and Addiction to Amphetamines and Amphetamine-Like Compounds During Pregnancy

In spite of the media emphasis on the methamphetamine "epidemic" in this country, there is surprisingly little research into the specific effects of maternal amphetamine use on fetal growth and development (Finnegan & Kandall, 2005). It is assumed that the effects of maternal amphetamine abuse are similar to those of maternal cocaine abuse, however this is an unproven assumption (Finnegan & Kandall, 2005). It *is* known, however, that unlike babies born to mothers who are actively drinking or abusing opioids, babies born to a mother who is abusing an amphetamine compound are *not* born "addicted" to the amphetamine[10] (Erickson, 2007).

There is evidence that women who abuse methamphetamine during pregnancy are more likely to be younger, live alone, have a lower income, have a lower educational level, and receive less prenatal care than their nonabusing counterparts (Winslow et al., 2007). These are all factors that can influence maternal, fetal, and (following birth) infant health. Preliminary evidence suggests that infants exposed to amphetamine compounds in utero are more likely to experience premature birth, suffer from congenital brain lesions, and have a visual cortex dysfunction (Brust, 2004; Cloak, Ernst, Fujii, Hedemark, & Chang, 2009; Rawson & Ling, 2008). There is also evidence that infants exposed to methamphetamine in utero have altered neurological function in the frontal cortex region of the brain (L. M. Smith et al., 2001). The infant's risk of neurological harm appears to be dose related, with those infants with a greater degree of exposure having the highest degree of risk for neurological damage (Erickson, 2007). However, further research is needed to confirm these initial findings.

A recent, rather disturbing finding is that maternal starvation might alter fetal DNA expression through a process known as *epigenesis*.[11] If the mother should be a heavy amphetamine abuser, she is likely to neglect her daily dietary requirements, which will affect both the mother and the fetus. This, in turn, can cause long-term (possibly lifelong) changes in DNA expression for the mother and the infant. Such changes might leave the infant vulnerable to diabetes or cancer later in life ("Hunger Leaves Its Mark on Fetal DNA," 2008). Animal research would also suggest that prenatal exposure to methamphetamine might predispose the infant to the neurotoxic effects of this compound later in life (Heller, Bubula, Lew, Heller, & Won, 2001). It is not known whether this occurs in humans at this time, but the study results do suggest a possible methamphetamine neurotoxic prior to birth and a vulnerability to methamphetamine neurotoxicity later in life. Again, further research is necessary both to confirm these theories and to trace the implications of these findings across the life span for both the mother and the infant.

There is a strong body of evidence suggesting that maternal use of methamphetamine is associated with such problems as anemia, premature birth, poor intrauterine growth, and a tendency for the placenta to separate from the wall of the uterus (Winslow et al., 2007). Other possible consequences of maternal methamphetamine abuse might include meconium aspiration, infection of the amniotic cavity, placental hemorrhage, and neonatal anemia. Following birth, there is evidence suggesting that the infant is vulnerable to psychosocial development problems and frontal lobe dysfunction, as well as sleep abnormalities and birth defects such as a cleft lip (Brust, 2004). It is not known what percentage of methamphetamine-exposed infants will experience these (or other) problems, and Erickson (2007) suggested that the majority of infants exposed to methamphetamine in utero will reach most normal developmental milestones on time and that there is little evidence suggesting long-term damage to the fetus if they (a) receive proper postdelivery medical care, (b) receive adequate parenting, and (c) are allowed appropriate social interactions with other children.[12]

Unfortunately, most women who are pregnant and who abuse methamphetamine also engage in polydrug abuse, making it exceptionally difficult to isolate the effects of maternal methamphetamine abuse from the combined effects of the other drugs of abuse. Thus the issue of whether there are methamphetamine-specific consequences to the fetus remains unclear at this time.

Barbiturate and Barbiturate-Like Drug Abuse During Pregnancy

Fortunately compounds such as the barbiturates glutethemide, meprobamate, and ethchlorvynol are only rarely prescribed, and they are not very widely abused now, although they were common drugs of abuse in the 1950s and 1960s. All of these compounds can cross the placenta into the fetal circulation, and if abused in high doses by the mother will induce a neonatal withdrawal syndrome similar to that induced by alcohol withdrawal for the infant. The infant neonatal withdrawal syndrome for compounds such as the barbiturates, glutethemide, meprobamate, and ethchlorvynol might require up to 4 days to develop, depending on the

---

[10]However, because of the problem of polydrug abuse, it is still possible for the infant to be addicted to another compound(s) that the mother was abusing.

[11]See Glossary.

---

[12]Unfortunately, if the mother continues to abuse methamphetamine, her ability to provide these things would be compromised, leaving the child to suffer.

exact compound(s) being abused and the total dose ingested by the mother.

This neonatal withdrawal syndrome could be mistaken for hypoglycemia, sepsis, a range of cardiovascular disorders, or meningitis, if the mother's substance use disorder was not known by the attending physician. Physicians have found that phenobarbital, a long-term barbiturate, will allow for the gradual withdrawal from these compounds for the infant. Because these compounds are so rarely prescribed, and even less likely to be abused in today's world, they will not be discussed again in this chapter.

Benzodiazepine Use During Pregnancy

There are numerous antidotal case reports suggesting that benzodiazepine use during pregnancy can result in facial abnormalities such as cleft palate, congenital heart defects, hernias, and pyloric stenosis. But research has failed to support the contention that benzodiazepine use caused these effects (Iqbal, Sobhan, & Ryals, 2002). The teratogenic potential of benzodiazepines thus remains unclear at this time. It is recommended that when used during pregnancy the prescribing physician use the lowest possible dose for the shortest period of time (Iqbal et al., 2002; Raj & Sheehan, 2004). As with any medication, they should be used only when the potential benefits are thought to outweigh the possible risks of their use.

Benzodiazepine Use During Breast Feeding

All of the known benzodiazepines will cross over from the maternal circulation into the milk. In spite of this, Hale (2003) concluded that the short term use (that is, 1–2 weeks) was acceptable, although the longer-term risks remain unknown. Maternal diazepam use has been identified as a possible cause of neonatal sedation and lethargy (Iqbal et al., 2002). The benzodiazepines are biotransformed in the liver, an organ that is not fully developed in the neonate, and so the prescribing physician must weigh the potential benefits of the benzodiazepine to the mother against the risks to the nursing infant.

Buspirone Use During Pregnancy

It is not recommended that the expectant mother use buspirone unless a physician determines that the anticipated benefits outweigh the potential risks to the fetus.

Animal research has suggested that there is an increased risk of stillbirth, but little evidence of long-term cognitive deficits in rats exposed to buspirone in utero.

Cigarette Smoking During Pregnancy

Each year in the United States between 16 and 20% of the estimated 4 million women who give birth annually smoke cigarettes during their pregnancy (Finnegan & Kandall, 2008). However, given the fact that approximately 27.3% of nonpregnant women smoke, this would suggest that a significant percentage of women discontinue the use of cigarettes when they discover that they are pregnant (Substance Abuse and Mental Health Services Administration, 2009).

Unfortunately, many of the compounds found in cigarette smoke are able to cross the placenta into the fetal circulation (Buka, Shenassa, & Niaura, 2003). Researchers are still unsure how these chemicals impact on the smoker's body, and even less is known about how these compounds affect fetal growth and development. Some of the consequences of maternal smoking during pregnancy include premature rupture of the membranes, abrupto placentae, myocardial infarction,[13] venal and arterial thrombosis, vitamin and mineral absorption problems, and placenta previa (Bhuvaneswar & Chang, 2009; D. M. Burns, 2008).

Infants born to smoking mothers tend to have lower birth weights than infants born to nonsmoking women (Brust, 2004; Centers for Disease Control, 2004). However, emerging evidence would suggest that if the woman stops smoking early enough, the impact of her previous cigarette smoking might be overcome and the fetus become less likely to be an underweight child at birth (McGowan et al., 2009). McGowan et al. found that those pregnant women who stopped smoking before the 15th week of pregnancy were significantly less likely to experience premature delivery or have an underweight infant at birth. The causal mechanism for premature labor and for underweight infants is caused by nicotine-induced constriction of the blood vessels in the placenta, reducing the flow of blood to the fetus. The reduction in placental blood flow might also account for the observation that maternal cigarette smoking might contribute to *congenital limb deficiency*

---

[13]Admittedly a rare complication of pregnancy, being seen in only 1 in every 35,000 cases of pregnancy.

(a failure of the limbs to develop properly). However, much research is needed in this area.

Research has also suggested that maternal cigarette smoking during pregnancy might be associated with behavioral problems (especially substance abuse such as cigarette smoking) during the child's adolescent years (Buka, Shenassa, & Niaura, 2003; Keyes, Legrand, Iacono, & McGue, 2008). The causal mechanism for this association is not clear, although both parental and subsequent adolescent substance use behaviors reflect a possible common genetic factor (Keyes et al., 2008). There also is evidence suggesting that infants born to mothers who smoke have reduced lung capacity and are themselves more likely to grow up to become cigarette smokers. Maternal cigarette use is thought to account for 20% of the problem of low-birth weight children, as well as 8% of the cases of premature labor and 5% of the cases of perinatal death each year in the United States.

Women who smoke or who are exposed to second-hand smoke are more likely to suffer spontaneous abortion and an increased risk of vaginal bleeding (Centers for Disease Control, 2004). Further, maternal cigarette use appears to increase the odds that the infant will develop asthma in later life (Guilbert & Krawiec, 2003). As if this were not enough, there is a body of evidence suggesting that infants born to mothers who smoke are at risk for impaired cognitive performance later in life. Nicotine is a known teratogen,[14] which increases the odds that the child will develop ADHD (T. J. Spencer, 2008). Finally, there is an impressive body of evidence that suggests that maternal cigarette smoking raises the risk that the infant will die of sudden infant death syndrome (SIDS) by 300–400% (Brust, 2004; Centers for Disease Control, 2004; Pendlebury et al., 2008). As these findings suggest, maternal cigarette smoking can extract a terrible cost from the fetus, who is an unwilling participant in the mother's smoking.

Smoking and Breast Feeding

It is recommended that the mother abstain from cigarette smoking if she plans to breast-feed her infant. Nicotine tends to be concentrated in breast milk and has a half-life in breast milk of about 1.5 hours. The total nicotine concentration in the breast milk depends on the number of cigarettes that the mother smokes and the time between her last cigarette and the time that she breast-feeds the infant. Because nicotine is a

stimulant, and stimulants tend to have an anorexic side effect, it is not surprising to learn that infants born to smoking mothers who breast-feed tend to gain weight more slowly than other infants.

Nicotine Replacement Therapy During Pregnancy

It is strange to think that a physician might prescribe a nicotine replacement therapy for a pregnant woman in light of the preceding information. Such therapies would seem to be contraindicated for the pregnant woman. However, in reality this is helpful to the fetus, because there are over 4000 known compounds in cigarette smoke, many of which hold the potential to interfere with normal fetal growth and development. The nicotine replacement therapy will thus reduce fetal exposure to chemicals from over 4000 to just 1, and thus the benefits outweigh the potential hazards to the fetus.

Bupropion Use During Pregnancy

Bupropion is often used as an aid to smoking cessation. Its safety during pregnancy has not been established, however, and the effects of this compound on fetal growth and development have not been studied in detail.

Cocaine Abuse During Pregnancy

It has been estimated that 5–10% of pregnant women in the United States abuse cocaine at least once during pregnancy, although for the most part this is part of a pattern of polydrug abuse or addiction rather than an isolated cocaine use disorder (Zilberman, 2009). However, the implications of such maternal cocaine abuse on fetal growth and development remain unclear at this time. During the wave of cocaine abuse that swept across the United States in the 1980s, the mass media gleefully reported that scientists had warned of an epidemic of "crack" (cocaine) babies about to descend on society, bringing with them a need for huge expenditures for special education and social service supports (Malanga, 2009). The media warned that a generation of "crack [cocaine] babies" would overwhelm the educational system with special-needs children, and a generation of cocaine-damaged children who were "inevitably and permanently damaged" (Zuckerman, Frank, & Mayes, 2002, p. 1991). In a number of states, laws were

---

[14]See Glossary.

passed to the effect that the mother might be charged with criminal assault or child abuse if she abused cocaine while pregnant.

However, the much anticipated and feared wave of special-needs children spawned by maternal cocaine abuse during pregnancy did not appear. This is not to say that maternal cocaine abuse during pregnancy is entirely safe, only that for the most part the effects on the neonate are limited. However, the infant will have "lasting, albeit subtle, effects of prenatal drug exposure on brain structure" (Malanga, 2009, p. 2062.) Stanwood and Levitt (2007) found, for example, evidence of permanent structural changes in the brains of animals exposed to cocaine in utero. But the existence of a "prenatal cocaine exposure syndrome," or the form that such a hypothetical construct might take, remains unproven.

Virtually every effect once attributed to prenatal cocaine exposure has subsequently been found to be caused by such factors as instability within the family unit, poor maternal nutrition, maternal depression, concurrent abuse of other compounds, lack of prenatal care, and so on (Ackerman, Riggins, & Black, 2010; Finnegan & Kandall, 2005; Juliana & Goodman, 2005; "Prenatal Cocaine Exposure Not Linked to Bad Behavior in Kids," 2006). These discoveries made it difficult to identify the prevalence or impact of just prenatal cocaine abuse on the fetus (S. B. Karch, 2009). For example, it was once believed that maternal cocaine abuse induced a condition of placenta previa.[15] However, most cocaine abusers also smoke cigarettes, and cigarette smokers have a 2.3-fold higher incidence of placenta previa than nonsmokers. Further, research has demonstrated that half of pregnant cocaine abusers also consumed alcohol, a known toxin.

In the 1980s, many states enacted laws that mandated incarceration for the expectant mother who abused cocaine to protect the fetus. In response to these laws, pregnant cocaine-abusing women stopped seeking prenatal health care to avoid the danger of having their names turned in as cocaine abusers and then being incarcerated. This process then resulted in the mother receiving poor prenatal care, which is itself a risk factor for various complications during pregnancy. For many women, the first medical care that they received during pregnancy was when they arrived at the hospital in labor. Early research studies then concluded that the observed deficits following the infant's birth *must* have been caused by her cocaine abuse, rather than the lack of prenatal care.

Scope of the Problem

Maternal self-report, a popular method by which substance abusers are identified, tends to underestimate the prevalence of prenatal cocaine abuse (Lester et al., 2001). Some women fear criminal prosecution and thus do not admit to prenatal cocaine abuse, whereas others forget the timing of their cocaine use as compared to that of their pregnancy. Some women fear that stigma associated with prenatal cocaine abuse and thus do not admit to the abuse of cocaine when asked (Zilberman, 2009). For these, and possibly other factors, maternal self-report of prenatal cocaine use is a poor measure of the actual abuse of this compound by women during pregnancy.

Maternal blood cocaine levels are a poor indicator of potential effects on the fetus. It has been discovered that the concentration of cocaine in the amniotic fluid might be higher than that found in the maternal circulation (J. R. Woods, 1998). This finding is of importance when one considers that the skin of the fetus does not develop the ability to block passive absorption of cocaine from the amniotic fluid until the 24th week of pregnancy (J. R. Woods, 1998). In theory, this can magnify the effects of maternal cocaine on the fetus, although there has been little research into this possibility.

Known and Suspected Effects of Maternal Cocaine Abuse

There is much that remains to be discovered about the effects of maternal cocaine abuse on fetal growth and development. For example, cocaine is known to interfere with the normal transfer of amino acids in the placenta, but the significance on the fetus remains unknown (S. B. Karch, 2009). Because of the developmental immaturity of the infant's body however, the cocaine that is absorbed will remain in infants' blood for days after birth because they lack the adult's ability to rapidly biotransform cocaine (S. B. Karch, 2009).

The impact of this cocaine exposure on the fetal growth remains unknown. The possibility that there is a "threshold" effect beyond which maternal cocaine use might cause damage to the fetus has been suggested (S. L. Johnson, 2003), although this remains an unproven theory.

Efforts to identify such a pattern of symptoms specific for prenatal exposure to cocaine have met with

---

[15]A condition involving the placement of the placenta in the uterus that can cause very severe bleeding during labor and delivery.

failure. For example, the team of Myers et al. (2003) attempted to identify a fetal cocaine exposure syndrome by using the Brazelton Neonatal Behavioral Assessment Scale to compare infants who were and were not exposed to cocaine in utero and failed to find any significant differences between these two groups of infants. Where researchers *have* identified differences between infants who were and were not exposed to cocaine in utero, the differences have been small in magnitude. For example, the team of Butz et al. (2005) measured the head circumference of infants exposed to cocaine and heroin prior to birth. At age 3, the authors administered a standardized IQ test to the infants. The 204 infants who had been exposed to heroin and/or cocaine had smaller head circumference(s) at birth, but by the age of 3 years this difference had disappeared. Further, the authors found that both groups of children had similar IQs. These findings were similar to those of Ackerman et al. (2010), who found that observed differences between infants who were and were not exposed to cocaine in utero were both small and strongly influenced by environmental factors. Although the authors identified a pattern of the 6-year-old children studied having trouble focusing attention on problems and also behavioral self-control problems, it was not proven that such problems would result in permanent behavioral or cognitive problems according to the authors.

There is limited data that does suggest that children exposed to cocaine in utero might suffer developmental delays in such areas as psychomotor skills, language use, and overall mental development (Finnegan & Kandall, 2004; B. A. Lewis et al., 2004). There is also evidence that prebirth cocaine exposure might be associated with spontaneous abortion, abrupto placentae, low birth weight, strokes in the fetus, disruption in normal uterine blood flow patterns (which may initiate premature labor in some cases), increased frequency of respiratory distress syndrome following birth, malformations of the genitourinary tract, and infarction of the arteries providing blood to the bowels (Acosta et al., 2005; Finnegan & Kandall, 2005; Gold & Jacobs, 2005; S. L. Johnson, 2003; S. B. Karch, 2009; R. W. Keller & Keller-Snyder, 2000; Moffett, 2006; Oehmichen et al., 2005).

There is also mixed evidence suggesting that the infant exposed to cocaine in utero might be at increased risk for the subsequent development of SIDS (Finnegan & Kandall, 2005). Thus the relationship between maternal cocaine abuse and SIDS for the infant remains unknown. S. B. Karch (2009) reported that approximately 20% of infants exposed to cocaine in utero will grow up to develop ADHD. Cocaine abuse is also not without its dangers for the mother as well, which are discussed in the next chapter.

Cocaine and Breast Feeding

There is limited data on the effects of maternal cocaine use during the period of time that she is breast feeding (Zilberman, 2009). The cocaine molecule is highly lipid soluble, and it may be stored in breast milk and then passed on to the infant by the mother during breast feeding. The cocaine concentration might be *eight times* as high in breast milk as it is in the mother's blood, and for this reason maternal cocaine abuse during the period when she is breast feeding is to be discouraged.

Hallucinogen Abuse During Pregnancy

There is only limited research into the effects of maternal hallucinogen abuse on fetal growth and development (Kandall, 1999). What will follow is a brief description of the effects of the most commonly abused hallucinogens on the fetus. It is important to keep in mind that other hallucinogens might also be abused, and it is impossible to list every possible hallucinogen and every possible effect of each on fetal growth and development. However, because so little is known about the pharmacokinetics of the hallucinogens, the use of these compounds by the nursing mother is *not* recommended.

PCP Abuse During Pregnancy

At most, there is limited information on the effects of phencyclidine on the fetus. The available evidence would suggest that infants exposed to PCP in utero are at increased risk for conditions such as hydrocephalis, sleep respiratory problems, and abnormal development of different body organs such as the heart, lungs, urinary system, or the musculoskeletal system (Brust, 2004). Immediately following birth, infants born to PCP-abusing mothers demonstrate abrupt changes in their level of consciousness, fine motor tremors, sweating, and irritability. There is a possibility that some or all of these effects are caused by polydrug abuse rather than the abuse of PCP alone.

MDMA Abuse During Pregnancy

Preliminary research into the effects of MDMA on the fetus would suggest that congenital growth problems are five times more common in the infants of MDMA-abusing mothers than is normal. The mechanism by which MDMA might cause or contribute to congenital birth defects is not known at this time.

LSD Abuse During Pregnancy

Virtually nothing is known about the effects of LSD abuse on fetal growth and development. It is, however, not recommended that nursing mothers use this compound, if only because its effects remain unknown.

Salvia Divinorum Use During Pregnancy

Because so little is known about the pharmacokinetics of this compound, its use during pregnancy is *not* recommended. Further, women who are attempting to become pregnant should not use this compound for a minimum of 3 months before conception to minimize the potential risk to the fetus. Because of the lack of information about the impact of maternal *salvia divinorum* use during pregnancy, it is recommended that nursing mothers *not* use *salvia divinorum* at this time.

Inhalant Abuse During Pregnancy

Each year in the United States, 12,000 pregnant women are thought to abuse an inhalant at least once during the course of their pregnancy (Brust, 2004). However, in spite of this fact there has been virtually no research into the effects of inhalants on fetal growth and development. Current evidence does suggest that inhalant abuse is a cause of growth retardation in utero, fetal death, tremor and ataxia following birth, as well as smaller birth weight (C. W. Sharp & Rosenberg, 2005). The effects of toluene, which is known to cross the placenta, are unknown because the liver of the fetus and newborn is still quite immature and unable to metabolize this compound. There is preliminary evidence to suggest, however, that toluene exposure during pregnancy can cause a syndrome similar to FASD (discussed previously). Bowen, Batis, Mohammadi, and Hannigan (2005) exposed pregnant rats to toluene fumes and found that the "pups" suffered from growth restriction as well as a range of physical abnormalities. These are only preliminary results, but until proven otherwise toluene exposure by pregnant women should be avoided.

Marijuana Use During Pregnancy

There is only limited research data on the effects of maternal marijuana use on fetal growth and development (Bhuvaneswar & Chang, 2009; Finnegan & Kandall, 2004). The placenta is able to provide the fetus with some degree of protection against marijuana, and fetal blood levels of THC are estimated to reach only one-sixth those of the mother (T. Nelson, 2000). However, even these low levels of THC potentially can have dire consequences on the fetus. There is evidence based on animal research that the endocannabinoid anandamide helps to guide both the specification of what are known as pyramidal cells in the brain and the pattern of axon growth in neurons as the brain develops (Mulder et al., 2008). During the process of corticogenesis,[16] the endocannabinoid molecules help to guide the movement of the pyramidal cells and the growth of neural axons as cortical neural networks are established. This makes maternal marijuana use of special concern because there is an emerging body of evidence that suggests that marijuana abuse during pregnancy might interfere with the normal endocannabinoid function of guiding neural growth in the fetal brain, possibly causing long-term (if not permanent) changes in the brain's physical structure (Gold & Dupont, 2008). This might be the mechanism through which the subtle neuropsychological deficits reported by Zilberman (2009) develop.

Admittedly, it is difficult to isolate the effects of maternal marijuana abuse from the effects of tobacco or other drugs of abuse. It is rare for a mother-to-be to abuse only marijuana, and concurrent cigarette smoking is a complicating factor. Other variables that must be considered include (a) the potency of the marijuana being smoked, (b) the frequency of maternal marijuana use, (c) how deeply the mother inhaled when she did smoke marijuana, and (d) what other compounds (pesticides, for example) are intermixed with the marijuana smoked. Finally, although it is assumed that THC is the only compound that will impact fetal growth and development, marijuana smoke contains a number of different compounds and their impact on fetal growth and development has not been studied.

In spite of these unknown variables, scientists have tentatively concluded that children whose mothers abused marijuana during pregnancy are at higher risk for maladaptive social behaviors, cognition, and

---

[16]Growth and development of the cortex.

psychomotor skills following birth (Gold & Dupont, 2008). They were also found to have lower reading comprehension skills at 10 years (Goldschmidt, Richardson, Cornelius, & Day, 2004). This finding must be interpreted with caution however, because there are numerous other variables that might also affect the child's reading comprehension skills at the age of 10 besides maternal marijuana use. There is also evidence that children exposed to marijuana smoke in utero demonstrate abnormal tremors, startle reflexes, and eye reflex problems. Women who have smoked marijuana at least once a month are also thought to be at higher risk for premature labor and for having children with lower birth weights, who have a higher risk of ventricular septal defects, and who were smaller than normal for their gestational age (Bhuvaneswar & Chang, 2009). However, again, the separation of the effects of possible maternal cigarette smoking from maternal marijuana use makes these conclusions quite tentative.

In Jamaica, where heavy maternal marijuana use is common, researchers have failed to find any major differences between a group of infants exposed to marijuana in utero and a group of infants who were not exposed to marijuana during gestation (Dreher, Nugent, & Hudgins, 1994). Where Dreher et al. did find differences between these two groups, it was noted that they could be attributed to the mother's social status, the number of adults living in the household, the number of other children competing for the mother's attention, or other environmental factors rather than maternal marijuana use.

It is not known whether the effects of maternal marijuana use will manifest shortly following birth or later in the child's life. Given the crucial role of anandamide in guiding neural growth and development during corticogenesis, it should not be surprising to discover that there is evidence of prefrontal lobe dysfunction in children exposed to marijuana in utero that did not manifest until the child was 6–9 years of age. But there is much to be discovered about the effects of marijuana use during pregnancy and the long-term outcome for the child exposed to marijuana in utero.

Marijuana and Breast Feeding

There is no data suggesting that maternal marijuana abuse during breast feeding has any effect on the infant. Prior to birth the placenta provides some degree of protection against THC absorption. However, this compound is concentrated in breast milk and will be passed on to the infant during breast feeding. The THC level in breast milk has been found to be six times higher than that in the mother's blood levels (Nelson, 2000). Given the small size of the infant and the higher concentration of THC in the breast milk, the possibility exists that the infant will be exposed to significant levels of THC at a time when corticogenesis is still progressing. Thus maternal marijuana use both during pregnancy and following birth is to be avoided.

Narcotic Analgesic Abuse During Pregnancy

Each year, approximately 7000 babies are born to women who abused narcotics during pregnancy (Bhuvaneswar & Chang, 2009). However, this might underestimate the problem of narcotics abuse during pregnancy because (a) it is standard practice to administer narcotic analgesics during labor, making it impossible to identify cases of predelivery opioid abuse from those cases where narcotic analgesics were administered during labor and delivery, and (b) it is not unusual for the pregnant opioid abuser to switch to fentanyl because its potency makes it hard to detect on standard urine toxicology tests (Bhuvaneswar & Chang, 2009). Their continued opioid abuse during pregnancy might then remain undetected possibly throughout the duration of their pregnancy unless a health care professional were to request a test specifically to detect fentanyl.

In addition, a number of women are directed to use a narcotic analgesic by their physician at least once during the period of pregnancy. Although limited exposure to opioids under a physician's supervision appears to present minimal danger to the fetus, long-term exposure to this class of drugs, interspaced with periods of abstinence when the mother was unable to obtain drugs to abuse, holds the potential to harm the fetus. Notice that the word *potential* was used in the last sentence: There is little research into the possible long-term consequences of maternal opioid use or abuse immediately prior to and during pregnancy (Bhuvaneswar & Chang, 2009).

Statement of the Problem

For the woman with an opiate use disorder, many of the early symptoms of pregnancy, the feelings of fatigue, nausea, vomiting, pelvic cramps, and hot sweats, might be interpreted as early withdrawal symptoms rather than early symptoms of pregnancy

(Bhuvaneswar & Chang, 2009; Kieser, 2005; "Medication-Assisted Treatment (MAD) During Pregnancy—Part 1," 2009). Unless the woman were to confirm the possibility of pregnancy through one of the commercially available in-home pregnancy tests or medical examination, there is a danger that the opiate-dependent woman will attempt to self-medicate what is perceived to be early withdrawal symptoms by taking even higher doses of narcotics. This results in higher levels of fetal exposure to both the compound(s) being abused as well as the adulterants that are often mixed in with illicit drugs, plus an increased risk for the various infections inherent in the practice of illicit-drug abuse.[17]

If the woman were to request a medical examination to determine whether she is pregnant, she will find that even physicians experienced in the treatment of narcotics addiction often find it difficult to diagnose early pregnancy in this subgroup of women. The decision to seek out a medical examination is fraught with danger however, because in many communities the physician is required to report the woman's pregnancy to the authorities so that appropriate steps might be taken to protect the fetus during this all-important developmental period.

To complicate matters, even under the best of conditions pregnancy carries with it the potential for life-threatening complications for the woman. If she has a history of narcotics abuse, the potential for developing one or more of these complications is increased. Some of the medical problems that might develop during pregnancy in the narcotics-addicted woman include those listed in Table 17-1 (Bhuvaneswar & Chang, 2009; Finnegan & Kandall, 2005, 2008; Kieser, 2005).

If the mother should have or acquire an infection during pregnancy, there is a strong chance that she will pass the infection on to the fetus prior to birth. Approximately 30% of those women who abuse illicit opiates, are pregnant, and develop bacterial endocarditis will die from complications of this infection. Approximately the same percentage of pregnancies end in fetal death (Bhuvaneswar & Chang, 2009), for example. A high percentage of women who have viral hepatitis or HIV pass the virus on to their infant either during gestation or during the process of giving birth, a process known as *vertical transmission*.

Maternal addiction to narcotics means that the infant will also be addicted to these compounds following birth. The infant will then go through the neonatal

TABLE 17-1 POTENTIAL COMPLICATIONS FOR MOTHER AND/OR INFANT WHEN MOTHER IS OPIATE DEPENDENT
Potential Complications for Mother and/or Fetus
anemia
stillbirth
breach presentation during delivery
placental insufficiency
spontaneous abortions
premature delivery
neonatal meconium aspiration syndrome (which may be fatal to the infant)
amenorrhea
postpartum hemorrhage
neonatal infections acquired from mother
lower birth weight
neonatal narcotics addiction/withdrawal
maternal diabetes
increased risk of SIDS

opioid withdrawal syndrome, which starts within 24–72 hours of birth (depending on the specific compounds being abused by the mother). The acute phase of the neonatal opioid withdrawal syndrome will last as long as 3–6 weeks.[18] During this time, the infant will demonstrate such symptoms as yawning, wakefulness, watery eyes, fever, shrill or high-pitched cry, stuffy/runny nose, salivation, hiccups, vomiting, diarrhea, poor weight gain, apnea, sneezing, tremors, and seizures (Finnegan & Kandall, 2008, 2005; Kieser, 2005). Before the development of effective treatments for the neonatal opioid withdrawal syndrome, up to 90% of these infants failed to survive this process (Brust, 2004). The risk of premature death has dropped significantly since effective treatments were developed, but has not been eliminated entirely.

The acute stage of the neonatal withdrawal syndrome blends into the second phase: extended withdrawal. This phase might last for 4–6 months, during which time the infant might demonstrate such symptoms as restlessness, agitation, tremors, and sleep disturbance. These behaviors will add stress on the mother, who might be in the early stages of recovery from a

---

[17]Discussed in Chapter 36.

[18]Depending on the opioids being abused by the mother, Bhuvaneswar and Chang (2009) suggested that the first phase of the neonatal opioid withdrawal syndrome might last as long as 10 weeks.

substance use disorder, thus serving as a relapse trigger for the mother. Such infant behaviors also might interfere with the "bonding" process between mother and infant at a time when it is of critical importance (Kerrigan, 2008).

To limit the risk to both the mother and neonate, physicians now believe that the mother should *not* be withdrawn from opiates during pregnancy. It is recommended that the mother be stabilized on methadone[19] to normalize the intrauterine environment (Bhuvaneswar & Chang, 2009; "Medication-Assisted Treatment (MAT) During Pregnancy—Part 1", 2009; Polydorou & Kleber, 2008). This reduces the incentive for the mother to abuse other drugs, and there is evidence that suggests that children whose mother had been stabilized on methadone experience longer gestation periods and are heavier at birth (Finnegan & Kandall, 2005). A little known fact is that the half-life of methadone is reduced by about one-third in the mother, possibly as a result of hormone-related changes in the mother's body during pregnancy (Stout, 2009). Thus methadone stabilization should be attempted only by a physician experienced in this process. Following birth, the infant and mother can then safely be detoxified from opiates. In the case of the infant, morphine is the medication of choice neonatal opiate withdrawal. Some physicians also like to use a barbiturate during the withdrawal process, to avoid possible withdrawal-related seizures (Kieser, 2005).

Maternal Narcotics Abuse and Breast Feeding

The narcotics, including heroin, do pass into breast milk, and thus the infant is exposed to the mother's narcotics abuse if she should breast feed her children. During this phase of life, the infant's liver is still rather immature and not fully functioning, theoretically allowing narcotics to build up in the infant's body between periods of active feeding. Theoretically, prolonged periods of maternal narcotics abuse during the time that the mother is breast feeding might cause the infant to become sleepy, eat poorly, and possibly develop respiratory depression from the trace amounts of the opioids being abused found in maternal milk.

Research has demonstrated, however, that breast-feeding mothers who are using morphine under a physician's supervision can do so safely because only a minimal amount of morphine is concentrated in breast milk, and an even smaller proportion of the morphine ingested by the infant will actually reach the baby's circulation (Hale, 2003). A similar situation is true for breast-feeding mothers who are using codeine: The level of codeine in the breast milk will be only 5% of the mother's blood level, with the result being that only minimal amounts are absorbed by the infant if the mother is using low to moderate levels of codeine (Hale, 2003). The concentration of methadone in breast milk is between 1% (Kieser, 2005) and 3% (Schottenfeld, 2008) of the mother's blood level, which is far too low a dose to have much of an effect on an infant being breast-fed. There is evidence that suggests that breast feeding during the first days following birth may help the physical distress experienced by the infant going through the opiate withdrawal syndrome (Paradowski, 2008). However, it is recommended that mothers using meperidine not breast-feed, as this medication can cause the infant to become oversedated (Hale, 2003).

Over-The-Counter Analgesic Use During Pregnancy

Aspirin

Aspirin has been found to cross the placenta and thus enter the fetal circulation. Because of this, women who are, or who suspect that they might be, pregnant should not use aspirin except under a physician's supervision (R. A. Black & Hill, 2003; B. A. Wilson et al., 2007). There is a body of evidence that suggests that aspirin use during pregnancy might be a cause of stillbirth and increased perinatal mortality. Further, aspirin use by the mother might be a factor in the development of fetal anemia, retarded intrauterine growth, and antepartum and or postpartum bleeding, especially if the mother should ingest the aspirin the week prior to delivery. The risk of bleeding is not limited to the fetus, for aspirin will also interfere with the mother's ability to form blood clots, which may place her life at risk during labor and delivery.

---

[19]Buprenorphine can be used as an alternative in some cases, such as where the woman was already participating in a buprenorphine treatment program, or in cases where it is not possible for her to participate in a methadone maintenance program because of geographic restrictions. However, in such cases it is recommended that the attending physician discuss the benefits and risks of this to the woman and have her sign a consent form indicating that she chooses to use buprenorphine during pregnancy.

Acetaminophen

Physicians have recommended acetaminophen as an alternative to the use of aspirin during pregnancy (R. A. Black & Hill, 2003). However, there is preliminary evidence suggesting that exposure to acetaminophen in utero might increase the infant's risk of developing asthma in childhood (Beasley et al. 2008). Obviously it will be necessary to examine this issue in more detail, and for now it is recommended that acetaminophen be used only under a physician's supervision.

Although low levels of acetaminophen are found in breast milk, there is no evidence at this time suggesting that this exposure has an adverse effect on the fetus, as long as the acetaminophen is used in appropriate doses. However, as always, the breast-feeding mother should contact her health care provider to discuss whether it is safe to use any medication while she is nursing.

Ibuprofen

There has been limited research into the effects of the proprionic acids on fetal growth and development (R. A. Black & Hill, 2003). Black and Hill recommended that ibuprofen or similar compounds be used during pregnancy only upon the advice of a physician, because there is some research data that suggests that these compounds may prolong labor and possibly cause other effects on the developing fetus.

There is little evidence suggesting that ibuprofen enters human breast milk in sufficient quantities to cause problems for the newborn, when used at appropriate dosage levels (Hale, 2003). However, as always,

the breast-feeding mother should contact her health care provider to discuss whether it is safe to use any medication while she is nursing.

Chapter Summary

If a woman with a substance use disorder were to become pregnant, the fetus that she carries would become an unwilling participant in the mother's SUD because the majority of the drugs of abuse cross the placenta and enter the fetal circulation. These compounds are often teratogenic, thus holding the potential to harm the fetus during gestation. This is especially true in the first trimester of pregnancy, which is a period of special vulnerability for the fetus. It is during this trimester that organ differentiation and the process of corticogenesis are under way. Disruption of these processes would potentially have lifelong consequences for the infant following birth.

If the mother were physically addicted to a compound(s), the infant might very well be born with a physical addiction to these same compounds. Indeed, if the mother were to have been drinking alcohol immediately prior to birth, it may be possible to smell alcohol on the infant's breath following delivery. Each compound presents a special range of potential dangers to both the mother and fetus, and even the over-the-counter analgesics have been found to have a significant teratogenic potential in some cases. The more significant of these risk factors, and the compounds that might cause these complications, are reviewed in this chapter.

CHAPTER 18
Gender and Substance Use Disorders

Until very recently, drug abuse has been viewed as a marginal issue for women and portrayed largely as a male problem.

—*Fox and Sinha (2009, p. 65)*

Introduction

The issue of substance use disorders in women has long been overlooked by society. This is unfortunate because epidemiological data suggests that 13.8% of men and 7.1% of women will struggle with a substance use disorder at some point in their lives. At this time, the SUDs appear to be approximately half as common in women as they are in men, hardly a "marginal" issue. It is the goal of this chapter to try to dispel some of these stereotypes and to examine the forces that help shape the growth of substance use disorders in women.

Gender and Addiction: The Lessons of History

It is unfortunately true that the lens of history distorts events from the distant past and only rarely allows us to identify the parallels between a past situation and an evolving problem in time to avoid re-creating the same mistake(s) that fill our history books. An example of how the lens of history distorts images from the past is the social belief that most of those who were addicted to "patent" medicines at the turn of the 19th century were women. In reality, one-third of the total number of those people who had become addicted to a "patent" medicine before the year 1900 were men, a fact that is often overlooked by the history books. The fact that there was a double standard for men and women with an SUD during this era was also overlooked for the most part by historians. Women who abused or were addicted to a drug of abuse were subjected to a greater degree of social condemnation than were men (W. J. Lynch, Potenza, Cosgrove, & Mazure, 2009). Further, their substance use disorder was viewed as being less

important than that of men (M. Cohen, 2000; Jerslid, 2001). The net result of this process was that information on the natural history, clinical presentation, physiology, and treatment of substance use disorders in women is limited (Work Group on Substance Use Disorders, 2007, p. 44).

This is unfortunate because there is limited clinical data on how the various drugs of abuse effect women and on the fact that many of the social prohibitions against substance abuse by women have weakened, or disappeared entirely (S. B. Blume & Zilberman, 2004). This has resulted in an increasing number of women seeking substance abuse treatment at a time when only 40% of rehabilitation programs provide any form of gender-specific treatment for women with substance use disorders. Regrettably, advertising companies now view women as an untapped market for alcohol consumption and have started to target this population with gender-specific advertisements. Alcohol use is portrayed as a sophisticated way to enjoy the company of friends, and its use is encouraged. Many women then engage in heavier alcohol use than they would otherwise, increasing their chance of developing an alcohol use disorder (AUD). A concurrent historical force was that the other drugs of abuse became easily available in spite of efforts to interdict them or suppress the illicit-drug trade. These factors all contribute to a growing substance abuse problem for women.

Statement of the Problem

For generations, society's response to the problem of substance abuse by women has been to hide the issue, protect the individual, or totally isolate her from social and/or family support (S. B. Blume & Zilberman, 2005b; M. Cohen, 2000). This attitude is slowly changing, which is a welcome change in social attitudes in that one in every three people with a substance use disorder is a woman (Work Group on Substance Use Disorders, 2007). This means that approximately 4.4 million women are addicted to alcohol, whereas another 2 million women are thought to have an addiction involving a compound other than alcohol in the United States alone (Greenfield, 2003).

Alcohol or substance use by a woman does not automatically mean that she is addicted: Over 63% of women in the United States will use alcohol,[1] and 12.5% of women will abuse an illicit drug each year. As one would expect, the odds that a woman would become addicted to a substance reflects the frequency with which she uses that compound as well as the age cohort that the woman belongs to, as evidenced by Table 18-1.

Although Table 18-1 would suggest that SUDs in women are found in a minority of women, they are not always recognized by physicians (Brady, Tolliver, & Verduin, 2007). This failure at diagnostic recognition contributes to the terrible toll untreated SUDs extract on the individual and society. Women with an AUD, for example, are thought to be 23 times more likely to commit suicide as their nondrinking counterparts (Markarian & Franklin, 1998), whereas women with a drug use problem are 50–100% more likely to die as a result of their SUD (Fox & Sinha, 2009).

The addictions have never been a popular area for clinical research, and for much of the 20th century what little research that existed in the field of the addictions focused exclusively on *male* subjects, then were applied to women in treatment on the assumption that they will also work for this population as well.

---

[1]This percentage reflects *all* of those women who consume alcohol in the United States each year, not just those with an alcohol use disorder.

TABLE 18-1 AGE COHORT DISTRIBUTION OF SUBSTANCE USE DISORDERS IN WOMEN

AGE COHORT	PERCENTAGE OF WOMEN ABUSING ALCOHOL OR DRUGS
18–25 years	15.70%
26–34 years	8.90%
35–49 years	5%
50 years and above	1.50%

NOTE: Based on "Substance Abuse and Dependence Among Women" (2005).

Only now is it being acknowledged that hormonal, pharamacokinetic, neurochemical, and social factors alter a woman's vulnerability to and recovery from substance use disorders (W. J. Lynch et al., 2009). Although gender-specific treatment programs are of value in the rehabilitation of the substance-abusing woman, there is limited access to such programs in many parts of the country (Sinha, 2000).

The "Convergence" Theory

The "convergence" theory holds that the percentage of women with an SUD is slowly approaching that of men. There are many reasons for this convergence in substance use disorder rates. The convergence theory is based, for example, on the mistaken assumption that substance use disorders for women at the start of the 20th century were rare and only became more common during the last quarter of the past century. Yet as was discussed earlier in this text, the majority of those who were addicted to a "patent" medication at the start of the 20th century were women. This raises the question whether substance use disorders in women were uncommon during that era or simply took on different forms for men and women in this period of history.

As was noted earlier, a woman with a substance use disorder such as alcohol abuse or dependence is less likely to be identified than a man with a similar SUD. This raises questions about the accuracy of the data on which the convergence theory is based, although the theory has strong adherents in many areas (W. J. Lynch Zilberman, 2009). The adherents to the convergence theory point to findings that 8.1% of adolescent girls and 8.0% of adolescent boys will develop a substance use disorder at some point during adolescence (Upadhyaya & Gray, 2009) and that the number of fatal car accidents involving 19- to 24-year-old women has increased in the past few years (Tsai, Anderson & Vaca, 2010) to support their claims. Thus there does appear to be evidence supporting the convergence theory, especially for younger age cohorts.

Does Gender Affect the Rehabilitation Process?

For a variety of reasons the answer to this question is: Yes! Women who enter substance abuse rehabilitation are more likely to suffer from a psychiatric disorder that predates the development of their SUD (Brady & Back, 2008). Further, sexual dimorphism in brain development and function exists from the fetal period of development. It has been assumed for years that the neurological mechanisms of substance-induced reward are the same for men and women, but current evidence suggests different brain activation patterns for each sex when exposed to the drugs of abuse (Pigott, Walker, Tietelbaum, & Lu, 2009). For example, the liver's P-450 metabolic pathway is involved in the biotransformation of approximately 80% of all drugs (DeVane, 2009). However, there are differences between the sexes in how the P-450 pathway functions, as well as wide interindividual variability, all factors that influence the biotransformation of various compounds (DeVane, 2009). Finally, hormonal changes in the woman's menstrual cycle may alter the reinforcement potential of a drug(s) of abuse, enhancing or detracting from the reinforcing effects of that compound (W. J. Lynch et al., 2009).

There are neurological differences between how each sex responds to the various drugs of abuse, very few of which have been explored. The possibility that THC has different effects on the brains of men and women has not been studied in detail, for example (Pigott et al., 2009). It is known that the brain of a woman has a different pattern of dopamine transporter molecules in certain regions of the brain as compared to those of a man, which alters the reinforcement potential of a given drug of abuse for women. Because of this process, it has been suggested that women might become addicted to a drug(s) of abuse after less exposure to that compound than would be true for a man (W. J. Lynch et al., 2009).

Then there are the social factors that influence how a person of either sex would fare in a treatment program. Women are less likely than men to enter a substance abuse rehabilitation program, in part because of social barriers that prevent them from

doing so (S. M. Gordon, 2007). Social stigmatization is another factor that affects how women and men view entry into drug rehabilitation treatment, although the stigma against SUDs in women is less in younger age cohorts (W. J. Lynch et al., 2009). External barriers to treatment admission include having sole possession of children following divorce (or termination of a relationship), limited funding for treatment, or a spouse who also has an SUD, making recovery more difficult for the woman (S. B. Blume & Zilberman 2004, 2005a, 2005b; S. M. Gordon, 2007). Although it is recognized that single parenthood is a barrier to treatment, few treatment programs have provisions for a woman who is pregnant or who has custody of children (S. B. Blume & Zilberman, 2004; Ringwald, 2002). The financial cost of substance abuse rehabilitation also serves as an external barrier to treatment for women who are divorced because they frequently lack access to health care insurance after their divorce.

Another barrier to treatment is that women who enter a rehabilitation program tend to have a smaller social support circle, often discovering that friends, family, employers, and society are less tolerant of a woman with an SUD than a man with the same problem (S. M. Gordon, 2007). Intuitively, it would be expected that an important source of social support for the woman with an SUD would be the spouse or significant other. Consistent with this expectation is the finding that being divorced is a risk factor for SUDs for women between the ages of 30 and 40. Surprisingly, being married is a risk factor for women between the ages of 40 and 50! This apparently reflects the fact that unhappy marriages contribute both to the initial problem of substance abuse and to possible relapse for the woman with an SUD. For both age groups, women with an SUD usually receive less support from their partner for efforts to recover than do men, which is a risk factor for the initial development of an SUD or relapse after treatment for women (C. A. Green, 2006). Marital therapy is often a useful adjunct to the woman's treatment program for this reason (Fals-Stewart, Lam, & Kelley, 2009).

Where men are most often introduced to drug(s) of abuse by peers, women report that they were introduced to drug(s) of abuse by their partner, who then serves as their main source of supply for the desired compound(s) (S. B. Blume & Zilberman, 2005a, 2005b; S. L. Johnson, 2003). This is one of the mechanisms through which a woman's substance use disorder might be rendered "invisible" to others, because the woman would not need to go out to obtain the desired compound(s). Another manner in which SUDs in women are rendered invisible is the fact that many women obtain desired medications from physicians. Thus they are not viewed by society as "addicts" but as "patients."

Men and women tend to follow different pathways into treatment. Women are more likely to utilize the resources of a health care, clergy, or mental health professional at first, and only if their SUD is identified are they referred to a rehabilitation program (S. B. Blume & Zilberman, 2005b; Friemuth, 2005; C. A. Green, 2006). The tendency for women with SUDs to seek assistance from mental health professionals might be explained, at least in part, by the tendency for women to suffer from depression and/or anxiety disorders more often than do men, conditions that result in referrals to health care or mental health workers (S. B. Blume & Zilberman, 2005a, 2005b; Dixit & Crum, 2000; C. A. Green, 2006). Women who have an AUD are seven times as likely to suffer from depression as are men with an AUD, for example (Brady & Back, 2008). Although these referrals to mental health professionals are useful, such "indirect" treatment of the SUD is rarely effective, and the substance use disorder itself must be addressed (C. A. Green, 2006).

In contrast to this process, men are more likely to enter treatment because of legal, marital, social, employment, or familial pressure. Thus there are different pathways into rehabilitation. Further, after entering treatment men and women relate to their SUD differently: Men tend to externalize responsibility for their SUD, whereas women tend to blame themselves for having developed an SUD. This is clearly seen in the observation that women with an alcohol use disorder have lower self-esteem as compared to men with a similar SUD (M. Cohen, 2000; Sinha, 2000). Another excellent example of how the dynamics of substance use disorders differ between men and women is that for the woman, the symptoms of depression are likely to serve as a relapse trigger for continued further substance abuse. In contrast to this, depression in the substance-abusing man often triggers a reduction in substance abuse levels in an attempt to reduce his level of depression. This is not to say that men with substance use disorders might not suffer from clinical depression. Rather, this illustrates the different dynamics that are at work for men and women with a concurrent SUD and depressive disorder.

Whereas men most commonly support their drug use disorder through the sale of drugs to others, women with an SUD frequently have to resort to prostitution to support their addiction. These women also experience significant shame issues, but are hardly likely to admit to their past in a mixed-gender program. Even in gender-specific treatment programs, special issues must be addressed in different ways by rehabilitation center staff. The role that alcohol or drugs play in the woman's life will differ in response to her social status (Norton-Hawk, 2009). Imagine, if you will, two women who have resorted to prostitution as a means of supporting their addiction. Even here a "one size fits all" approach for these two hypothetical women ignores the reality of social-class differences within the world of prostitution (Norton-Hawk, 2009). Upper-class women who engage in prostitution are called "escorts," whereas lower-class women who work as prostitutes are "streetwalkers," with different sets of values and life experiences than their more affluent peers.

Work, Gender, and Substance Use Disorders

There is a complex relationship between the individual's work status and the development of SUDs. Women who are less happy with their jobs or who work in male-dominated professions tend to use alcohol more heavily (Jerslid, 2001). The importance of this observation becomes apparent when one stops to consider the fact that most women in the workforce are working below their capacity, often in low-status, high-frustration positions. Still, work offers the woman increased social status, social support, and improved self-esteem, factors that help protect her against the development of an SUD.

As noted earlier, women with an SUD are usually solitary users and less likely to come to the attention of authorities (or employers) because of substance-related behavioral problems than are men (S. L. Johnson, 2003). Further, because women tend to be underemployed, their chemical abuse is less likely to result in underperformance or unacceptable job performance than is the case for a male worker (S. B. Blume & Zilberman, 2004). Even if the woman's substance use is identified, the low-status jobs that women usually hold do not generally allow for easy access to employee assistance program counselors, who act as "gatekeepers" to treatment programs. Also, the threat of loss of employment for a woman in such a low-status position is not as effective an incentive to enter treatment as it is for men. The majority of women can simply quit their job if threatened with termination unless they enter treatment. If the woman is the primary breadwinner in the family, then the referral to treatment is blocked by other barriers that stand between a woman and substance abuse rehabilitation programs (discussed earlier).

Dual Diagnosis/Victimization Issues

There is a significant overlap between SUDs in women and a history of past or current victimization. This is seen in the relationship between being abused in childhood and the development of posttraumatic stress disorder (PTSD) and an SUD later in life (L. R. Cohen & Hien, 2006). Whereas 20% of substance-abusing men have experienced some form of trauma, between 30 and 60% of substance-abusing women have been exposed to some form of physical or sexual violence and have PTSD (Finnegan & Kandall, 2008; S. Ross, 2008). Research has also demonstrated that 83% of women entering a substance abuse rehabilitation program had at least one parent with a substance use disorder and that 67% had suffered a sexual assault at some time in their lives (Finnegan & Kandall, 2008).

It will be necessary for these individuals to come to terms with their abuse history as part of their recovery program (M. Cohen, 2000; Sinha, 2000). However, the substance abuse rehabilitation program to which the individual is admitted might lack the resources, time, or treatment staff with sufficient training to help the individual address this vital aspect of her recovery program (D. Blum, 1998; L. R. Cohen & Hien, 2006).

It is a mistake, however, to assume that the victimization *caused* the SUD. The relationship between victimization and SUDs is complex, and to think that an SUD is automatically the result of having been victimized by a significant other is "not only damaging but also anti-therapeutic and disempowering" (Jerslid, 2001, p. 35). In some cases, the SUD preceded the individual's victimization (J. S. Brook, Pahl, & Rubenstone, 2008). Because there are many factors that can cause or exacerbate an SUD, staff must carefully access the relationship between the individual's SUD and victimization. This further underscores the need for gender-specific treatment programs. Many women feel inhibited in a mixed-group setting, especially if they have been victimized by a male (McCrady, 2001). Further, the language used by many men in treatment is often offensive, if not demeaning, to women, contributing to a higher dropout rate for women in mixed-group settings as opposed to gender-specific programs. Further,

traditional substance abuse rehabilitation programs, following the example set by 12-step programs such as Alcoholics Anonymous,[2] place great emphasis on surrender and submission. Women with victimization issues find this approach to be difficult, if not impossible, to accept.

Differing Effects of Common Drugs of Abuse on Women

It has been discovered that a given compound does not automatically have the same effect on a woman as on a man. For decades much of what was assumed to be true about the effects of the drugs of abuse on women was extrapolated from studies using exclusively men, possibly men in Veterans Administration hospital settings. Such studies totally ignore the possibility that these compounds might have far different effects on women. It has long been known that there are sexual differences in brain structure and function, but how these affect the woman's responses to the drugs of abuse as compared to those of men has not been explored (J. L. Newman & Mello, 2009).[3]

The hormonal changes involved in women's monthly menstrual cycle has been found to alter their sensitivity to the effects of many drugs of abuse (J. L. Newman & Mello, 2009; Reed & Evans, 2009). A related issue is that research suggests that 20–40% of women of childbearing age utilize hormone-based methods of contraception. However, there has been no research into how such methods of birth control might influence the woman's response to a drug(s) of abuse (Reed & Evans, 2009).

There is a growing body of evidence that suggests that substance abuse by women might result in an earlier entry into menopause than for women who do not abuse chemicals. This raises the possibility that pre-menopausal women might react to a drug(s) of abuse in a different manner than postmenopausal women. The issue of the differences between the factors that initiate, maintain, and help the rehabilitation from the drugs of abuse is thus quite complicated. In this section we will examine some of the known differences in the effects of various compounds on women as compared to men.

---

[2]Discussed in Chapter 35.

[3]People who wish to learn more about this topic might wish to begin with C. A. Munro et al. (2006). Sex differences in striatal dopamine release in health adults. *Biological Psychiatry, 59,* 966–974.

Alcohol Use Disorders in Women

There is controversial evidence suggesting that moderate alcohol use might provide a neuroprotective effect for women. Strandberg et al. (2008) concluded on the basis of their research that women with a low to moderate alcohol intake level (defined by the authors as one to seven standard drinks a week) seem to demonstrate a slower rate of cognitive decline as they age than do men with the same alcohol intake level. The authors speculated that the causal mechanism for the observed findings might reflect the protective effects of estrogen rather than the level of alcohol intake, but they found clear evidence of significant differences in the rate of cognitive decline over time.

Unfortunately, women are more vulnerable to the negative effects of alcohol, including such factors as lower body mass, different fluid content, and lower levels of gastric alcohol dehydrogenase in the stomach and liver (Myrick & Wright, 2008; Payne, Back, Wright, Hartwell, & Brady, 2009). Women also have a lower muscle mass to body weight ratio and lower body fluid ratios. As a result of these factors, the average woman needs to ingest 40% less alcohol to achieve the same blood alcohol level as a man (S. B. Blume & Zilberman, 2005b; R. L. Collins & McNair, 2002; Reed & Evans, 2009). To further complicate matters, the normal variations in estrogen levels during the menstrual cycle affect the speed that alcohol is absorbed and its effects on the woman (Reynolds & Bada, 2003).

It is important to avoid oversimplification when discussing alcohol use disorders among women. Different age cohorts have different norms for alcohol use, and their peak period of alcohol ingestion varies from age cohort to age cohort. Women between the ages of 18 and 24 appear to develop an alcohol use disorder earlier in life than do women in the 25- to 49-year age bracket, which might reflect the different norms for substance use between these two age groups.

Statistics demonstrate that women are less likely to develop an alcohol use disorder (AUD) then are men (Erickson, 2007). However, in those cases where the woman *does* develop an AUD, she is less likely to be identified as having an SUD. This is due in part because women tend to be solitary drinkers and only rarely engage in the problematic behaviors that commonly identify male drinkers (Myrick & Wright, 2008; Nichol, Krueger, & Iacono, 2007). Solitary drinking by women might reflect the different dynamics for alcohol abuse between men and women. Men who drink abusively do so more to achieve the euphoric effects of alcohol, whereas the majority of women who abuse alcohol tend to do so to self-medicate emotional pain (Grahm, Massak, Demers, & Rehm, 2007; Payne et al., 2009). One danger of this trend is that women with alcohol use disorders are more likely to plan and attempt suicide (Payne et al., 2009).

Physical Complications

Because of the process known as "telescoping," women begin to experience physical complications from abusive alcohol use more rapidly than do their male counterparts (S. B. Blume & Zilberman, 2005a, 2005b; Brady & Back, 2008; Myrick & Wright, 2008; Payne et al., 2009). Women are more sensitive to the toxic effects of alcohol on the striated muscle tissue than are men, for example (S. B. Blume & Zilberman, 2005a, 2005b). Such damage to the striated muscle tissue is seen after the average woman has ingested a lifetime total of about 60% that is necessary to produce such muscle damage in men (Kinsella & Riley, 2007). It has also been found that the consumption of just two or more standard drinks per day increases the risk that the woman will experience cardiac arrhythmias such as atrial fibrillation (Conen et al., 2008).

Women with alcohol use disorders also appear to be at increased risk for central nervous system damage as compared with male drinkers, but they develop this damage after a shorter drinking history (Rourke & Grant, 2009). The pattern of brain damage is slightly different between the sexes, however. Hashimoto and Wiren (2007) discovered, for example, that female mice demonstrated a *higher* level of neuronal death during alcohol withdrawal than did male mice. It is not known whether this is true for humans as well, but these results were suggestive of a sex-specific pattern of neural death during the alcohol withdrawal process.

The average woman with an AUD who enters treatment will have more severe medical problems than the typical male drinker entering treatment (C. A. Green, 2006; Sinha, 2000). The woman with an AUD, for example, usually requires just half the time to develop cirrhosis of the liver as a male drinker, and the cirrhosis is more likely to prove fatal for the woman with an AUD than for the man (Myrick & Wright, 2008). Further, if the woman has a concurrent hepatitis C infection, she typically will die 10 years earlier than a man with both conditions. Women with an AUD are vulnerable to reproductive system dysfunctions such as amenorrhea, uterine bleeding, dysmenorrhea, and abnormal menstrual cycles, as well as a reduction in ovarian size, reduced infertility, and an increased rate of spontaneous abortions or miscarriages if she should be pregnant (Myrick & Wright, 2008; Payne et al., 2009; Schuckit, 2008a). They are also at increased risk for osteoporosis and breast cancer (Kovalesky, 2004; Myrick & Wright, 2008; Sampson, 2002). It has been found that women taking birth control pills have a lower rate of alcohol biotransformation than women who do not use this method of contraception, extending the effects of alcohol in these women (Erickson, 2007). Finally, if the woman should suffer from a concurrent eating disorder, her alcohol use might exacerbate the electrolyte imbalances induced by the eating disorder, increasing the risk to her life (Benton, 2009).

Although the phenomenon of "telescoping" is well established for women with alcohol use disorders, there is only limited research data at this time supporting the possibility that the same phenomenon applies to women who abuse the other drugs of abuse (Brady & Back, 2008).

Interpersonal Resources

Women with an AUD tend to be involved in less supportive relationships than men with a similar disorder, a factor that might contribute to the higher levels of depression seen in alcohol-abusing women. Women with an alcohol use disorder are *four times* as likely to be living with a substance-abusing partner than are men, in part because men are more likely to seek a divorce from a substance-abusing partner than is a woman (S. B. Blume & Zilberman, 2005b). Depressed women also tend to consume more alcohol per episode of active drinking, exacerbating the risk of alcohol-induced physical problems. Women with a substance use disorder, and especially with an alcohol use disorder, tend to experience more social stigma then do men with the same addiction. Further, they encounter barriers to treatment such as child care, child custody issues,[4] and issues associated with pregnancy. Many rehabilitation centers refuse to work with a woman who has children or who is pregnant for example, and few residential treatment programs have facilities for child care while the woman is in treatment.

A Positive Note

Although a great deal remains to be discovered about the impact of gender on the substance use disorders and their treatment, there are also hopeful signs emerging from the research data. Women, for example, appear to be more aware of their substance use disorders and to respond more positively to intervention(s) aimed at treating these problems. Thus the treatment outcome for women with an alcohol use disorder is at least as good as, if not better than, men with similar disorders who entered treatment (Payne et al., 2009). Women who successfully completed treatment were found to be nine times as likely to abstain from recreational drug use than those who failed to successfully complete treatment (C. A. Green, 2006).

A Cautionary Note

Although Alcoholics Anonymous (AA) is often suggested as an adjunct to recovery, it has been alleged that such programs also present the woman in recovery with a subtle form of sexism (Coker, 1997). In her essay on the subject, Jerslid (2001) noted that the program, "which confronts the false pride of the alcoholic, may not be helpful to a woman who needs to build her self-esteem from the ground up (p. 6). This is clearly seen in the fact that as a group women tend to feel higher levels of shame than do men. It is for this reason that women are more likely to be solitary drinkers than are men with AUDs. But the AA program places great emphasis on uncovering the sources of shame, a characteristic that may make women feel uncomfortable or unwanted at these meetings (S. B. Blume & Zilberman, 2004; Jerslid, 2001). Complicating matters is that women now start to drink at a younger age and to consume far greater quantities than did earlier generations (Greenfield, 2003; Grucza, Norberg, Bucholz, & Bierut, 2008; Sinha, 2000). Thus the challenge to AA at this time is to both eliminate the sexism inherent in the 12-step program as well as make the program relevant to all age cohorts of women. Whether this self-help program can accomplish this during the process of remaking itself to meet the needs of women with an AUD in the 21st century remains to be seen.

Amphetamine Use Disorders in Women

Methamphetamine is one of the family of the amphetamine compounds, but it has received the most publicity as a stimulant of abuse and thus will be the focus of this section. The ratio of male to female

---

[4]The woman's AUD is often used against her in child custody disputes, for example.

methamphetamine abusers is nearly 1:1 (Rawson & Ling, 2008), however the dynamics of the methamphetamine use disorders are not the same for men and women. Male methamphetamine abusers tend to be drawn to the drug for its euphoric effects, whereas women are drawn to methamphetamine because of its ability to induce anorexia, and to self-medicate depression (Rutkowski & Maxwell, 2009). Unfortunately, animal research suggests that women are more vulnerable to the addictive potential of central nervous system stimulants than are men (Torregrossa & Kalivas, 2009).

Women who are forced to work in the illicit sex trade are at increased risk for methamphetamine abuse because of its ability to allow the woman to work longer hours (Rutkowski & Maxwell, 2009). This establishes a vicious circle in which the woman becomes addicted to an amphetamine compound such as methamphetamine and in many cases is ultimately forced to work in the illicit sex trade to obtain the funds to support her addiction to the amphetamine compound(s) being abused. Further, because 70% of women who abuse methamphetamine report a history of physical and/or sexual abuse in their lives (Rawson, & Ling, 2008), the mild antidepressant effect of methamphetamine helps to explain understand the lure of this compound for women who have been abused or forced to work in the illicit sex trade. This might account for the fact that when an adolescent girl or woman is admitted to a substance abuse rehabilitation program for a methamphetamine use disorder, she will usually report higher levels of use than is true for the average adolescent male.

There is a relationship between the abuse of amphetamine compounds and anxiety. Approximately one-third of women who abuse methamphetamine report having an anxiety disorder before they began to abuse methamphetamine. Two-thirds report symptoms of an anxiety disorder after starting to abuse methamphetamine (Brady & Hartwell, 2009). This raises the question whether anxiety symptoms might not serve as a relapse trigger for the woman with a methamphetamine use disorder, however research on this topic is lacking at this time. There is preliminary evidence, however, suggesting that women might be less vulnerable to the neurotoxic effects of methamphetamine due to the limited protective action of estrogen.

Currently, methamphetamine has the dubious distinction of being the most commonly abused illicit substance for pregnant women seeking treatment admission, accounting for 24% of all treatment admissions in 2006[5] (Terplan, Smith, Kozloski, & Pollack, 2009). Terplan et al. found that the majority of women decrease their frequency and level of methamphetamine abuse during pregnancy, if not stop it entirely, in part because of the fear that they might lose their children, but are reluctant to seek prenatal care because of their fear of legal sanctions or the stigma associated with methamphetamine abuse. The authors called for a more comprehensive screening process by health care professionals during pregnancy to identify high-risk cases and make appropriate referrals for treatment.

All of these gender-specific dangers are in addition to the physical and emotional risks of amphetamine abuse by both men and women discussed in Chapter 8. Although there is still a great deal to be discovered about the effects of the amphetamine compounds on women, it should be clear from the information reviewed in this section that the dynamics and consequences of methamphetamine use are different for each sex.

Cocaine Use Disorders in Women

Not surprisingly, the phenomenon of cocaine abuse is not the same between men and women. There is evidence that the woman's gonadal hormones might influence her subjective response to cocaine (J. L. Newman & Mello, 2009). Higher progesterone levels have been found to mute the woman's sense of euphoria after using cocaine (Elton & Kilts, 2009; Lukas, 2006). Unfortunately, progesterone is involved in the maintenance of pregnancy,[6] and this may add to the incentive for the pregnant woman to use *more* cocaine in an attempt to achieve the same degree of euphoria that she achieved before becoming pregnant, increasing the risk to both the mother and the fetus. A second danger is that because progesterone is a component in many hormone-based methods of birth control, there is a danger that women using such methods of

---

[5]The last year that data was available for analysis.

[6]The use of progesterone in birth control pills acts on the principle that this compound, normally found in high concentrations when the woman is pregnant, forces the body to assume that the woman is already pregnant. A fertilized egg will then be blocked from implanting itself in the wall of the uterus.

birth control might feel tempted to use more cocaine in an attempt to achieve the desired level of euphoria, again increasing her risk of an adverse reaction to the cocaine.

It has been observed that female rats appear to be willing to work harder for cocaine than are male rates, although the applicability of this finding to humans remains unclear. Human female cocaine abusers appear to be at increased risk for developing the adverse effects of cocaine then is true for male cocaine abusers. Some of the adverse effects for cocaine abuse by a woman include not just those identified in Chapter 9, but also include such problems as galactorrhea,[7] amenorrhea, and infertility (Mendelson & Mello, 2008). However, clinical research does suggest that women who abuse cocaine develop a lower number of cerebral perfusion defects and lower levels of damage to the frontal cortex than do male cocaine abusers (Brady & Back, 2008).

There is preliminary evidence suggesting that women who smoke cocaine over the course of their menstrual cycle have a different response to it than men who smoke cocaine (J. L. Newman & Mello, 2009; Reed & Evans, 2009). Women who abuse cocaine begin to do so at an earlier age than do male cocaine abusers, and there is evidence that they are also more vulnerable to the addiction potential of cocaine (W. J. Lynch et al., 2009). This in turn results in women with cocaine use disorders entering treatment at a younger age than does the average man. Male cocaine abusers are more likely to support their cocaine dependence through participation in illegal activities such as drug sales, whereas women are more likely to receive cocaine from a sexual partner or be forced to engage in prostitution to support their addiction.

One surprising route of exposure to low levels of cocaine for a woman is through the semen of a male partner who is a cocaine abuser (S. B. Karch, 2009). It is not clear at this time whether the exposure to the small amount of cocaine in the ejaculate could induce any form of physical reaction in the woman or serve as a relapse "trigger," although this is unlikely because the amount of cocaine in the semen would be quite small. All of this information underscores the vast differences between how men and women react to cocaine and how little is known about this problem.

Hallucinogen Abuse in Women

Ecstasy (MDMA)

There is little research into how the different hallucinogens, especially MDMA, affect men and women. There is preliminary evidence suggesting that for unknown reasons women are more vulnerable to MDMA-related neurological damage than are men (Greenfield, 2003). However, the findings of a study by Medina, Price, Harper, Logan, and Shear (2008) would argue just the opposite. The authors attempted to examine the effects of MDMA on executive functioning[8] and found that there was a dose-dependent relationship between the abuse of MDMA and lower working memory ability scores. Although the authors found a significant gender effect, male MDMA abusers were found to be more likely to demonstrate impulsiveness and impaired memory function as compared to female MDMA abusers. Thus the issue of whether there are sex-related differences in the pattern of neurological damage remains unclear at this time.

Yudko and McPherson (2009) suggested that lower-functioning males appear to be at increased risk for MDMA-induced neurological deficits in the areas of verbal and visual memory, but not women or higher-functioning men, suggesting that premorbid level of function might be another variable besides gender that influences MDMA's impact on neurological function.

LSD and Phencyclidine

There has been virtually no research into how gender might affect the individual's response to these compounds or how these compounds might impact on the user's neural function.

Marijuana Use Disorders in Women

Statistically, women are more likely to begin to abuse marijuana at an older age than are men, with the mean age of first marijuana use being 17.6 years for adolescent girls as compared with 16.4 years for adolescent boys (McRae-Clark & Price, 2009). It is known that men are about three times as likely as women to use marijuana daily, and there is limited evidence suggesting that women progress to marijuana dependence

---

[7]See Glossary.

[8]See Glossary.

more rapidly than do men who become dependent on this compound (McRae-Clark & Price, 2009). There has been virtually no research into the possible gender-based differences in the path to marijuana use or possible gender-related differences in the user's physiological reaction to marijuana.

Preliminary evidence does suggest that women who suffer from social anxiety disorder are more likely to turn to marijuana to self-medicate some of their distress than men, but further research is needed to explore this topic (McRae-Clark & Price, 2009). Although marijuana abuse can induce anxiety, especially in inexperienced users, it does not appear to do so more often in women than it does in men (Brady & Hartwell, 2009). At first the assertion by McRae-Clark and Price (2009) to the effect that 32% of women but only 13% of men experience marijuana-induced panic at some point in their marijuana use careers would seem to contradict the assertion made by Brady and Hartwell (2009), but it is necessary to remember that there is a difference between the experience of *anxiety* and that of pure *panic* to see where both statements might be correct.

Marijuana abusers are at increased risk for depression, but the causal mechanism for this effect or whether it is the same causal mechanism for men and women has not been explored (McRae-Clark & Price, 2009). It has been demonstrated that the woman's reaction to alcohol ingestion will differ at various points in the menstrual cycle. Unfortunately, there has been virtually no research to determine whether a similar hormonal-specific difference in the physiological response exists for women who abuse marijuana (McRae-Clark & Price, 2009). It is known that some women abuse marijuana to self-medicate premenstrual dysphoria, however there is no research data demonstrating the prevalence of this practice (J. L. Newman & Mello, 2009). There is preliminary evidence suggesting that men might be more sensitive to the positive effects of marijuana smoking than are women, but further research is needed to confirm this finding (Reed & Evans, 2009). As was discussed in Chapter 10, the use of marijuana often predates the onset of schizophrenia (M. T. Compton & Ramsay, 2009). However, women who abused marijuana and then went on to develop schizophrenia did so about 4 years later than did men (M. T. Compton & Ramsay, 2009). Whether this is a reflection of some kind of marijuana-induced partial protection against psychosis or of another, undiscovered factor remains unknown.

Narcotics Abuse and Women

To date only a handful of studies have examined the possibility that men and women will react differently to a narcotic analgesic. Neuropharmacologists have discovered that women appear to be slightly more sensitive to the analgesic effects of morphine as compared to men, but that they also seem to require more time before experiencing the morphine-induced analgesia (J. L. Newman & Mello, 2009). Research based on animal studies suggests that female rats will self-administer more opiates when given the opportunity to do so than will male rats, although the applicability of this data to humans remains uncertain (Brady & Back, 2008).

The problem of prescription diversion is an ongoing issue, and the limited data that is available would suggest that whereas 1.4% of men 18–25 years of age have abused a prescription narcotic, 1.1% of women in this same age bracket have done so (Brady & Back, 2008). This difference in incidence is more pronounced in older age cohorts because illicit-drug use was either less socially acceptable or at least less frequently reported in earlier generations. Further, the limited data available at this time suggests that approximately 57% of women who are addicted to opioids are addicted to prescribed medications, whereas only 37% men become addicted to prescribed opioids (Back & Payne, 2009).

As a group, women who abuse narcotics tend to begin to abuse these compounds at an older age than do men, but the average woman will enter treatment for her SUD at about the same age as male opioid abusers. This suggests that women's opioid use disorder is "telescoped" into a shorter period, as compared with male abusers. Further, there is evidence of a difference between how the average woman abuses an opioid as compared with men. Whereas men are more likely to inject narcotics, women tend to use inhalation as the preferred method of administration, although there are exceptions to this rule. Finally, it has been found that women opioid abusers were more likely to be involved in a sexual relationship with another drug abuser than were male opioid addicts. More than half report having received drugs as a present from their partner on occasion, a pattern rarely seen in male opioid addicts.

There is also limited evidence that hormonal changes seen in the menstrual cycle might increase the woman's sensitivity to pain, which might then become a relapse risk for her during the early stages of recovery. However, as noted earlier there is a paucity of data concerning the opioid use disorders and gender,[9] and much remains to be learned about how gender affects the rehabilitation of opioid abusers.

Nicotine Use Disorders in Women

The various complications of cigarette smoking result in this practice being the leading cause of lung cancer in women (J. L. Newman & Mello, 2009). The effect of cigarette smoking on women is sparse and often limited by methodological errors such as ignoring the woman's menstrual cycle when such research is carried out. Another factor that has been ignored in many research studies exploring the effects of nicotine on women is the method of birth control that they are using. Hormone-based methods of birth control alter nicotine metabolism, although most research studies in this area fail to assess whether the woman uses birth control, and, if so, the method utilized (J. L. Newman & Mello, 2009).

There are both sexual dimorphic differences in the neural activation pattern of smoking for men and women, and differences within a given woman as a result of the hormonal changes associated with her menstrual cycle. The team of Fallon, Keator, Mbogori, Taylor, and Potkin (2005) examined the brains of men and women (smokers and nonsmokers) using positron emission tomography (PET) technology. They found a *decrease* in measured brain metabolism of the women in their study who were using transdermal nicotine patches, whereas the men in the study demonstrated an *increase* in brain metabolism. The exact ramifications of these findings remain unclear at this time, but might account for those of Caspers, Amdt, Yucuis, McKirgan, and Spinks (2010), who found that middle-aged women who smoked demonstrated greater deficits in visuospatial abilities, cognitive processing speed, and executive functioning functions than middle-aged men with a history of tobacco use or similarly aged women who never smoked cigarettes. The results of this study are also consistent with those of the study reviewed in the next paragraph.

In an effort to identify nicotine's effects on men and women, Sofuoglu and Mooney (2009) administered intravenous doses of nicotine to volunteer subjects and found that the women in their study reported a stronger "rush" effect and were more likely to respond positively to a specific nicotine dose than were the men in the study. However, the women were also more sensitive to the negative effects of nicotine. The authors called for further research into how men and women might have different subjective effects from nicotine. There also is strong evidence that nicotine metabolism is different for men and women. Women appear to metabolize nicotine more rapidly than do men, but seem to be more sensitive to the rewarding effects of nicotine (Brady & Back, 2008; Reed & Evans, 2009). Women appear to also follow different pathways to nicotine use disorders than do men. For example, adolescent girls are more likely to initiate tobacco use, and less likely to stop smoking, than are adolescent boys (Wunsch, 2007).

Cigarette smoking is known to cause health care problems specific to women. The average woman who smokes is thought to lose approximately 14 years of potential life due to health care problems either brought on by or at least exacerbated by cigarette smoking. Chronic obstructive pulmonary disease (COPD) is more common in women who smoke as compared with men (J. L. Newman & Mello, 2009). Under normal conditions, women tend to experience their first heart attack about 10 years later than do men, which is known as the "myocardial infarction gender gap." However, this decade of protection is lost if the woman should smoke cigarettes (Herzog, Aversano, & Atlantic CPORT Investigators and Coordinators, 2007). Women who smoked were twice as likely to present to a hospital with symptoms of a specific form of heart attack[10] than their nonsmoking counterparts (Herzog et al., 2007). However, the authors also found that if the female smoker were to stop smoking, her risk for cardiac disease dropped to that of her nonsmoking counterpart within 6 months, thus providing another incentive for the woman who smokes to quit.

Cigarette smoking has been identified as a cause of reduced fertility in women and as a causal factor in fetal death or stillbirth (Carmona, 2004; Reichert et al., 2005). Cigarette smoking has also been identified as a risk factor for the development of various forms of cancer in women, including cervical cancer and cancer of the esophagus, pancreas, kidney, bladder, breast, and pharynx. If the woman who smokes should quit, her risk of cancer slowly declines over the next few

---

[9]If somebody is looking for a good master's degree thesis or doctoral dissertation topic, you are welcome to develop this idea further.

[10]Technically known as the *ST-segment elevated myocardial infarction.*

years. There is even evidence that smoking cessation may result in a reduction in the size of some cancers for women after these tumors develop. Cigarette smoking has been identified as a cause of bone density loss in postmenopausal women (Carmona, 2004). Women who smoke cigarettes are at higher risk for developing rheumatoid arthritis, and as a group, women who smoke have been found to have less strength and less psychomotor coordination than nonsmoking women the same age. The causal mechanisms for these effects remain unknown.

Unfortunately, an emerging body of evidence suggests that "Big Tobacco" has focused advertising efforts on women and young girls ("'Deadly in Pink' Report Targets Big Tobacco," 2009). At least two major cigarette companies, Philip Morris USA and R.J. Reynolds Tobacco, have devised advertising campaigns designed to convince women that cigarette smoking is both fashionable and a sign of femininity ("'Deadly in Pink' Report Targets Big Tobacco," 2009). Given the gender-specific dangers of cigarette smoking, one must question the morality of these apparent advertising campaigns.

Smoking Cessation

Although few physicians would argue against the benefits of smoking cessation, it has been found that the gonadal sex hormones involved in the woman's monthly menstrual cycle influence the subjective level of distress that she experiences in the early stages of smoking cessation (J. L. Newman & Mellow, 2009). The observed benefits of smoking cessation might differ for men and women. Admittedly both groups benefit from smoking cessation, but the pattern of recovery follows a slightly different path for each sex. For example, there is evidence suggesting that women are less likely to benefit from the pharmacological effects of bupropion during smoking cessation (W. J. Lynch et al., 2009). Nicotine replacement therapies also appear less effective for women who smoke and attempt to quit with the assistance of this pharmacological support as compared to men. Finally, the factors that enhance the individual's risk for relapsing are different between men and women, in part because of the hormonal changes associated with menstruation.

As this information suggests, there is a great deal to be discovered about how nicotine affects women and whether smoking cessation treatment methods need to be altered to accommodate the woman's menstrual cycle status.

Other Compounds
Aspirin

Although aspirin is not a drug of abuse in the traditional sense, it is often used to provide a degree of protection against heart attacks and to treat a heart attack once it has started, as discussed in Chapter 15. However, aspirin appears to have different effects on women as compared with men (Steinhubl et al., 2009). Men who take aspirin to prevent cardiovascular events appear to have fewer heart attacks, whereas women who take aspirin appear to have fewer strokes. The possibility that aspirin might reduce the woman's risk of a heart attack remains unclear at this time, although it is still recommended for the treatment of a heart attack once one has started. But recently scientists began to question whether women were able to benefit from daily aspirin use as much as men (Chan et al., 2007).

There has been virtually no research into how the woman's menstrual cycle might influence her response to the other NSAIDs.[11]

Chapter Summary

The relationship between gender and the substance use disorders (SUDs) has moved through several stages in the 20th century. At first, it was hidden from polite society. If acknowledged at all, the victim was viewed as a "fallen" woman whose morals were suspect. As society moved into the middle of the 20th century, the face of SUDs changed, with physicians prescribing many drugs of abuse to women for various complaints such as anxiety or insomnia. This again rendered a large part of the problem of substance abuse among women hidden from society, and to a certain degree legitimized it because the woman in question was taking only a prescribed medication.

In the last quarter of the 20th century, there was a growing awareness that a large percentage of women suffered from substance use disorders, as was true for men. When treatment was attempted, the treatment methods utilized were those that had been developed for male addicts years earlier on the assumption that they would also work for women. But this was a mistaken assumption, and by the last decade of the 20th century researchers had started to understand that the

---

[11]Discussed in Chapter 15.

course of the substance use disorders, the roads by which each sex traveled to develop their SUD, and the role that the substance use played in their lives differed between men and women. In the last decade of the 20th century, researchers began to discover that there were subtle and often significant differences in how a given compound affected men and women. This chapter explored what is currently known about how gender changes the individual's response to various drugs of abuse and identifies several areas where further research is needed to better understand this phenomenon.

CHAPTER 19

Hidden Faces of Substance Use Disorders

Introduction

It would be nice if substance use disorders (SUDs) were to present with a singular set of signature symptoms, as this would make the identification of these problems easier. Many of the stereotypical images of a person with an SUD are familiar: The "skid row" alcoholic, drinking a bottle of cheap wine wrapped in a plain brown paper bag, for example. Another popular image is that of the male heroin addict, with a belt wrapped around his arm and a needle in hand, about to inject himself with illicit heroin. Such stereotypes heighten our awareness of the problem of SUDs, while simultaneously blinding us to the fact that SUDs do not always follow these familiar pathways. Who, for example, would recognize the white, middle-class heroin addict working in an office setting, or the cocaine-dependent mother who stops off to buy some "crack" cocaine after finishing her shopping trip? How many people would recognize the benzodiazepine dependency behind the smiling face of a day-care worker? It is the goal of this chapter to help the reader become aware of some of the hidden faces of the SUDs.

Substance Use Disorders and the Homeless

It has been estimated that there are between 2 and 3 million people in the United States, or about 1% of the total population, who are homeless (Joseph & Langrod, 2005). Single men make up 41% of this number, whereas families (usually headed by women) comprise 41%, single women comprise 13%, and children or adolescents make up about 5% of this population. In spite of the popular stereotype of the homeless person having an SUD, there is a surprising relationship between homelessness and the SUDs. Researchers have found that 45-78% of homeless people have a SUD, but that the incidence of substance use disorders does not increase after the person

becomes homeless (Arehart-Treichel, 2004; J. E. Smith, Meyers, & Delaney, 1998). Indeed, the experience of losing one's home appears to act as an incentive for the individual to *stop* abusing chemicals in some cases (Arehart-Treichel, 2004).

The role of people's substance use in the loss of their home is complex, and there is not always a causal relationship. The causes of homelessness might be traced to (a) high rates of poverty, (b) chronic unemployment or underemployment, (c) low-paying jobs, (d) loss of benefits, and (e) lack of affordable housing (Joseph & Langrod, 2005). It should be noted that Joseph and Langrod did not identify SUDs as a major cause of homelessness, although substance abuse and mental illness do indirectly contribute to the problem of homelessness. Alcohol is a common substance of abuse among the homeless, reflecting the substance pattern of the culture in general. Methamphetamine is a significant problem for the homeless (Rutkowski & Maxwell, 2009). However, it is not known whether the homelessness is the cause of the methamphetamine abuse, if the reverse is true, or if both conditions reflect some common, undiscovered factor. If substance abuse rehabilitation is attempted, homeless individuals present special challenges to the treatment program staff. Issues such as medical problems (increased incidence to tuberculosis,[1] for example), keeping appointments, attending 12-step group meetings, or obtaining prescribed medications all become barriers to rehabilitation. If the homeless person also has a child or children, these barriers to treatment are compounded by many orders of magnitude. These are all social problems that must be addressed, but there does not appear to be any easy solution, especially during these financially troubled times.

SUDs and the Elderly[2]

The problem of SUDs among older people has received very little attention from researchers, but this situation is rapidly changing. More than 75 million "baby boomers" are reaching retirement age, and untold millions of them experimented with drugs while they were teenagers or young adults and found that they liked the effects so much they continued to use them (Kluger, 2006). A wave of older drug abusers is about to crash into the medical system, which is ill prepared to deal with such issues (Dowling, Weiss, & Condon, 2008).

The warning signs have been there: The alcohol use disorders (AUDs) are the third most common psychiatric problem found in older persons (Luggen, 2006). Further, there is a misperception among the general public that suggests that older people do not abuse drugs. It was once thought, for example, that the AUDs were self-limiting in older people because the physical effects of alcohol would prevent the drinker from reaching older age. This is hardly true, as not only are individuals with SUDs reaching retirement age and beyond, they remain underrecognized

as substance abusers by physicians (Zimberg, 2005; Zisserman & Oslin, 2004).

Research suggests that as the baby boomers continue to age, they continue to engage in recreational drug abuse. This is the age cohort born between 1945 and 1965, who came of age in the 1970s and 1980s when there was a more permissive social environment, which tolerated substance use (Colliver, Compton, Gfroerer, & Condon, 2006; Gomberg, 2004, Zimberg, 2005; Zisserman & Oslin, 2004). This trend is not expected to change in the next decade. For example, whereas 4.5 million teenagers smoked marijuana in 2008 (the last year for which data is available), it is estimated that 4.42 million Americans over the age of 45 did as well (Raw Data, 2010). Further, marijuana abuse was found to be more common than nonmedical use of prescription drugs for adults aged 50–54 years of age, although for people older than age 65 the abuse of prescription drugs was more common than marijuana abuse ("Illicit Drug Use Among Older Adults," 2009). Unfortunately, research into the methods of identification and treatment of SUDs in older people has progressed very slowly at best (Zimberg, 2005).

Scope of the Problem

Fully 20% of the men and 6% of the women over the age of 50 admit to binge-drinking at least once in the past year (Glazer & Wu, 2009). These people might be called "late middle-aged adults" because it is assumed that they would object to the classification of "elderly." However, these late middle-aged adults are not far from becoming part of the elderly segment of the population, and so alcohol or drug use trends in this subgroup are likely to be carried over into their later years.

As a group, the elderly, or those people above the age of 65 years, make up about 12% of the general population. Many of these people will bring an established SUD with them into the older age cohorts, however others will develop an SUD only after they reach the age of 65 years. Thus alcohol or substance misuse either is or will be a problem for at least 19% of those above the age of 65 years (Blow, Serras, & Barry, 2007; Glazer & Wu, 2009). Although it used to be thought that older people would "mature out" of their SUD, researchers have found out that the baby boomer generation has not turned away from drug or alcohol abuse, as evidenced by the fact that an estimated 1.7 million people over the age of 50 are addicted to a drug(s), a number that is expected to reach 4.4 million by the year 2020 (Kluger, 2006).

---

[1]Discussed in Chapter 36.

[2]Defined, for the sake of this text, as postretirement age or after the age of 65, although some studies use a cut-off age of 50. Thus there is some confusion about how *elderly* might be defined between different researchers.

Researchers believe that 1% of the elderly have used an illicit drug in the past 30 days and that between 13 and 19% of the men and 9% of the women over the age of 60 have an established AUD (Brust, 2004; Gwinnell & Adamec, 2006). Fifteen percent of older drinkers also have a concurrent drug abuse disorder (Greenfield, 2007).

Although SUDs, and especially drug overdoses, are thought to be most common in the young-adult population, one study of 3700 drug-related deaths in California found that only 51 involved victims under the age of 20 and that more than half were involved victims between the ages of 35 and 54 years (Sherer, 2006). There are several possible reasons for these overdoses. First, because of age-related changes in the body, the individual becomes more vulnerable to the negative effects of alcohol or other drugs of abuse (Drew, Wilkins, & Trevisan, 2010; Gomberg, 2004; Stevenson, 2005). An example of the effect of these age-related changes on the body might be seen in the fact that just 3 standard cans of beer or mixed drinks by a 60-year-old has the same impact on the body as the consumption of 12 standard beers or mixed drinks by a 21-year-old (D. J. Anderson, 1989). Because of these factors, the level of "moderate" alcohol consumption in the elderly is now defined as just one standard drink or can of beer in a 24-hour period (Rigler, 2000; Zisserman & Oslin, 2004). Hazardous alcohol use is now defined as more than three drinks in one sitting or more than seven drinks in a 7-day period (Drew et al., 2010).

As a group, the elderly population use one-third of prescription medications and one-half of all over-the-counter medications sold each year in the United States (Gross, 2008; "U.S. Face of Drug Abuse Grows Older," 2006). Unfortunately, many of the more popular drugs of abuse, including alcohol, can interact with pharmaceuticals used to treat many diseases such as arthritis and heart disease, as evidenced by the fact that at least 19% of older individuals who drink alcohol will experience at least one adverse alcohol–drug interaction (Brust, 2004). If the individual were to also have an SUD, the risk of an adverse drug–drug interaction is multiplied, possibly with fatal results (Gwinnell & Adamec, 2006; Stevenson, 2005; Zimbert, 2005). The abuse of alcohol or other illicit substances also can exacerbate many medical disorders, adding to the tendency for this age group to use health care resources more often than younger people (Stevenson, 2005). This is clearly seen in the fact that 25–30% of the men and 5–12% of women who are hospitalized are thought to have an AUD (Stevenson, 2005).

Why Is the Detection of SUDs in the Elderly So Difficult?

There are several reasons for this problem. Older adults tend to have more medical problems than do younger people, and in the earlier stages SUDs often mimic the symptoms of other disorders, making the differential diagnosis very difficult for the physician. Also, older substance abusers tend to attribute physical complications caused by their SUD to the aging process, a form of denial aided by physicians, who rarely inquire about possible substance abuse in older people (Drew et al., 2010; Stevenson, 2005). Physicians might also fail to look for an SUD in an older patient, based on the assumption that this person *deserves* to use alcohol (or, less often, illicit drugs) as a reward for a lifetime of hard work (Stevenson, 2005; Zimberg, 2005). Further, because some physicians believe that the older person with an AUD is unlikely to respond to treatment, they do not look for SUDs in their patients.

Social isolation might also make it difficult for such individuals to be identified as having an SUD, especially if the person lives alone. Further, older people with an SUD rarely demonstrate the traditional warning signs of an addiction such as the substance-related legal, social, or occupational problems found in younger adults with SUDs (Drew et al., 2010). If an older person with an SUD who is in the workforce should miss work because of an SUD-related problem, it is easily explained away as age-related problems or of taking care of a sick spouse. If family members should suspect that their older family member(s) have an SUD, familial shame might demand that the issue remain hidden.

What Are the Consequences of an SUD in the Elderly Person?

Even under normal circumstances, older individuals are at increased risk for falls that might cause bone fractures. This risk is compounded by the presence of an SUD. Older people with AUDs have also been found to be at increased risk for depression, memory problems, liver disease, cardiovascular disorders, and sleep problems (Luggen, 2006; Rigler, 2000; Zisserman & Oslin, 2004). Because the age-related decline in reaction time is compounded by the effects of various compounds of abuse,[3] older people with an SUD are also at increased risk for motor vehicle accidents.

---

[3]This increased reaction time might also be caused by many prescribed medications.

A very real problem is that a lifetime of substance abuse results in cumulative health problems that manifest when the person is in their 60s or 70s (Kluger, 2006). Older people with an SUD are known to be at increased risk for dementia, or pseudo-dementia caused or exacerbated by vitamin absorption deficiencies often seen in people with SUDs. Other complications of just the AUDs in older people include myopathy, cerebrovascular disease, gastritis, diarrhea, pancreatitis, cardiomyopathy, hypertension, diminished immune response to infections, peripheral muscle weakness, electrolyte and metabolic disturbances, and hypotension. The implications of the abuse of other compounds by older people have not been addressed by researchers; however, it is fair to assume that these compounds also place the abuser at higher than expected risk for various adverse outcomes.

Depression is a common problem in older adults, in part because of vitamin malabsorption syndromes that develop with age. These vitamin malabsorption syndromes are exacerbated by SUDs, which then contribute to depressive states in the person. Depression is also interrelated with suicide, and it has been estimated that 25–50% of all older suicide victims have used alcohol prior to their attempted suicide. Further, there is evidence that AUDs in early or middle adulthood is associated with the development of depression later in life. If the individual's SUD is not recognized, then the depression might not be appropriately treated, compounding these problems.

Different Patterns of Alcohol/Drug Abuse in the Elderly

The problem of SUDs in the elderly is complicated by the issue of age. Older drinkers (defined in this study as people between the age of 50 and 74) are more likely to misjudge their level of impairment at low to moderate levels of intoxication than younger adults (Gilbertson, Ceballos, Prather, & Nixon, 2009). Whereas younger adults are more likely to be polydrug abusers, mixing alcohol with cocaine for example, older adults are more likely to have just an AUD (Gross, 2008). It is not known whether the baby boomer generation will follow this pattern.

There are subtypes of older people with alcohol use problems. The first subgroup is comprised of those individuals who had no evidence of an AUD in young or middle adulthood, but who did develop an AUD in late adulthood. These individuals are said to have *late-onset* alcoholism (Mundle, 2000; Rigler, 2000). A second subgroup of older adults with AUDs are those

people who had intermittent problems with alcohol in young and middle adulthood, but who developed a more chronic pattern of alcohol abuse in late adulthood. This subgroup is called the *late-onset exacerbation* subgroup (Zimberg, 1995, 1996). Finally, there are those individuals who had problems with alcohol in young adulthood, which continued through middle adulthood into the late adult years, a pattern known as *early-onset* alcoholism (Mundle, 2000; Zimberg, 2005). This subgroup makes up two-thirds of the older population with AUDs (Stevenson, 2005).

Older individuals with early-onset alcoholism were found to come from lower socioeconomic levels, have less formal education, smoke more, socialize with other alcohol abusers more often, come from families where alcohol use was tolerated or encouraged, be single or divorced, and more often come from estranged families (Stevenson, 2005). In contrast, individuals with late-onset alcoholism tend to report more adverse life events such as retirement, illness or death of their spouse, loss of lifelong friends, deterioration in health, and depression (Stevenson, 2005).

Prescription drug misuse is often overlooked in the elderly. Drug misuse can take several forms, including (a) mixture of alcohol and prescribed medications, (b) intentional overuse of a prescribed compound, (c) intentional underuse of a prescribed medication, often to extend the duration between refills, (d) erratic use of a prescribed medication, or (e) the failure of the attending physician to obtain a complete drug history, including that of over-the-counter medications, resulting in dangerous combinations of various compounds. Surprisingly, *underutilization* of prescribed medications is the most common form of medication misuse, usually reflecting the patient's inability to afford the medication (Piette, Heisler, & Wagner, 2004).

The Treatment of Older Patients With SUDs

There are few outcome studies that focus on older patients with an SUD (Satre, Mertens, Arean, & Weisner, 2004; Zimberg, 2005). Even when the older patient with an SUD is referred to treatment, there are few specialized programs that can meet the unique needs of older substance abusers. These special needs can include (a) a *primary prevention* program to warn the individual of the potential dangers of alcohol or drug abuse, (b) an *outreach* component to identify and help serve older patients who might be overlooked by traditional social service agencies, (c) *detoxification* programs designed to meet the needs of the older patient with an SUD (who may require longer-than-normal periods to complete the detoxification process), (d) *protective environments* for older patients, including treatment components, (e) *primary treatment* for those people whose status would allow them to benefit from such treatment programs, and (f) *after-care* programs for older individuals. All of the aforementioned would be in addition to access to social work support services and long-term residential care for people who have suffered medical or psychiatric damage from their SUDs.

Given the current era of "managed care,"[4] it is unlikely that such extended treatment programs might be developed. Just the detoxification process, which in younger adults might be completed in 3–7 days, might require 28 days or more for the older adult with an SUD to complete (Gomberg, 2004; Mundle, 2004; Stevenson, 2005). Even if older patients do complete the detoxification process, they will often present treatment staff with a range of sensory deficits not seen in young-adult patients and often dislike the profanity commonly encountered in mixed-age groups. Unless these special needs are addressed, older patients with an SUD are unlikely to be motivated to remain in treatment or might resist a referral to treatment following relapse (Zimberg, 2005). It is imperative for treatment program staff to be aware of the age-specific stressors that older people will present when they are in a rehabilitation center setting, such as bereavement, loneliness, and the effects of physical illness (Zimberg, 2005, 1996). On a positive note, there is evidence that older adults with an SUD respond better to an age-specific treatment program than do younger substance abusers (Drew et al., 2010). Older patients were found to remain in primary treatment longer and to respond to psychosocial interventions such as Alcoholics Anonymous (AA) with more enthusiasm, while presenting a lower risk of relapse than seen with other subgroups of drinkers (Satre et al., 2004).

Homosexuality and SUDs

A great deal of research has addressed the role of alcohol and drugs of abuse among men who desire sex with other men (T. L. Hughes et al., 2006). By contrast, the problem of alcohol or drug misuse among women whose sexual preference is other women, or bisexual individuals of either sex, has received relatively little clinical attention (T. L. Hughes et al., 2006; Trocki, Drabble, & Midanik, 2009). It is thought that SUDs are more prevalent in the gay/lesbian/bisexual (GLB) population than in the general population, including tobacco use (Cabaj, 1997, 2005; M. King et al., 2003; Trocki et al., 2009). This is clearly seen in the level of methamphetamine abuse within the gay and lesbian community (Ling, Rawson, & Shoptaw, 2006). But although the gay or lesbian client with an SUD presents special needs, many substance abuse rehabilitation professionals do not feel qualified to work with these individuals (Cabaj, 1997, 2005).

Statement of the Problem

It is estimated that sexual minority-group members comprise between 2 and 9% of the general population (Trocki et al., 2009).[5] This subpopulation has been found to have higher rates of illicit drug and alcohol use than the general population. For example, it has been estimated that 28–35% of the gay and lesbian population has engaged in noninjection drug abuse, as compared with just 10–12% of the general population (Cabaj, 2005).

There are many reasons for this increased vulnerability for SUDs in the GBL community. Individuals who announce their sexual orientation at an earlier age tend to experience more negative feedback from friends and family, adding to their stress level. Alcohol and drugs then offer the possibility of escaping from this stress, if only for short periods of time. Further, living on the fringes of a society that is, at best, only slowly coming to accept homosexuality as a possible variant of human relationships, opportunities for socialization within the GBL community are limited. It is for this reason that the gay bar has come to play such a central role in the gay or lesbian community. It is a place where one might go to socialize without fear of ridicule, to meet potential partners, or simply to relax. The gay bar also may play a major role in the process of learning about one's sexuality and its implications for daily life.

---

[4]Discussed in Chapter 34.

[5]The lower estimates reflect those individuals who *report* a sexual identity that would place them in a sexual minority, whereas higher estimates reflect the percentage of the population that has actually engaged in behaviors typically seen in people who belong to a sexual minority (Trocki et al., 2009). Within this context, recreational drug use might provide an excuse for individuals to engaging in otherwise unacceptable behaviors to blame their state of intoxication for their "deviant" behavior(s) (Cabaj, 2005).

Given that the sexual behaviors of homosexual males are obviously different than those of lesbian women, the role of chemicals would also differ between the two sexes. For homosexual males, methamphetamine is frequently used for both its arousal and disinhibition effects (Rutkowski & Maxwell, 2009). Homosexual males have been found to utilize medications intended to treat erectile dysfunction more often than heterosexual males of the same age (N. A. Graham, Polles, & Gold, 2007). Finally, homosexual males have utilized compounds such as amyl or butyl nitrite at the moment of orgasm, in the belief that these chemicals enhance the intensity of the orgasm.[6]

Early research suggested that more than half of all lesbian women had an AUD, a rate that is five to seven times as high as the norm for nonlesbians the same age. However, the methodology on which these estimates are based has been challenged (Cabaj, 2005). The early research studies used samples drawn from volunteers gathered together at a gay bar, which may erroneously inflated the percentage of women with an apparent AUD, according to Cabaj (2005). Statistically those people most likely to be in a gay bar on any given night are going to be those with an SUD, establishing a strong bias against those gay or lesbian individuals who do not have an SUD. However, this challenge to the methodology of the early research studies does not alter the fact that 15% of lesbians will seek treatment for an SUD at some point in their lives, as opposed to only 1.6% of heterosexual women (T. L. Hughes et al., 2006).

The true scope of SUDs among lesbians remains unknown at this time. This is, in part, because many estimates were extrapolations of studies conducted on homosexual males. This obviously is inappropriate, in that it will provide a distorted view of the problem. In addition there has been little research into the health care needs of bisexual or lesbian women and virtually no research into the treatment method(s) that may be most effective for either gay men or lesbians (Cabaj, 1997, 2005). There are few dedicated treatment programs for GBL clients, and those few programs that do exist are usually located in major cities where there is a significant GBL population. This puts a geographic barrier in place for those gay, bisexual, or lesbian people who live in more rural areas and who do not have access to these programs.

In the last decade of the 20th century, there was a movement to establish special AA group meetings oriented toward the specific needs of bisexual or homosexual people. But like the specialized treatment centers for bisexuals or homosexuals, these dedicated AA meetings are usually found in major cities. Further, because formal religions often persecute or reject homosexual men and women, the heavy emphasis of AA on spirituality may make gay or lesbian members uncomfortable. If gay men or lesbian women were to enter a traditional treatment center, they are likely to encounter staff who feel inadequately trained to meet their needs, reflecting the need for substance abuse rehabilitation professionals to be trained in working with these clients.

Substance Abuse and the Disabled

It has been estimated that 19% of the population, or just under one-fifth of the entire population of the United States, has a disability. The exact form of these disabilities is reviewed in Table 19-1 (Pearson, 2009).

This data does not include every form of disability possible. For example, it does not include those people living with some degree of hearing impairment or many forms of developmental dysfunction such as congenital limb malformation syndromes. However, it does illustrate the fact that a significant number of people in this country are living with a long-term disability. Unfortunately there is only a limited body of information about the relationship between physical disability and the SUDs. It is known that SUDs are more common among people with a disability than

TABLE 19-1 PEOPLE AFFECTED BY A FORM OF DISABILITY IN THE UNITED STATES	
FORM OF DISABILITY	**NUMBER OF PEOPLE**
Spinal cord injury	400,000
Cerebral palsy	500,000
Poststroke disability	3 million
Learning disabilities	3.5 million
Alzheimer's disease	4.0 million
Serious persistent mental illness	5 million
Traumatic brain injuries	5.3 million
Mental retardation	7.3 million

---

[6]And significantly increase the abuser's risk of a stroke at that critical moment because of the extremely high blood pressure levels achieved through this practice.

the general population (J. D. Corrigan, Bonger, Lamb-Hart, Heinmann, & Moore, 2005; Pearson, 2009). This is clearly seen in the fact that 62% of those people who are disabled also have an AUD (Heinmann & Fawal, 2005).

Unfortunately, even if a disabled person is identified as having an SUD, treatment resources for these individuals are very, very limited. For example, if the person is hearing impaired and uses sign language, many treatment programs must rely not on professional sign language interpreters, but on friends and family members to translate questions and comments into sign language (Heinemann & Rawal, 2005). Even if treatment programs have videotapes of lectures that are closed captioned, or utilize sign language interpreters to translate group therapy sessions for the hearing-impaired client, few programs can provide such sign language interpreters outside of group or individual therapy sessions. This prevents the client from participation in informal give-and-take discussions outside of group or individual psychotherapy sessions and can make the client feel isolated.

In contrast to this lack of treatment resources for patients with physical disabilities, *drug dealers* are quite happy to offer their "services" to the disabled. Some drug dealers have gone so far as to learn sign language in order to communicate with hearing-impaired clients, providing a service lacking in many rehabilitation programs. To complicate efforts at rehabilitation, many family members believe that hearing-impaired people (or people with other disabilities) are entitled to use recreational chemicals because of their disability. In this manner, significant others might overlook signs of an SUD that requires professional intervention. As this section has demonstrated, the physically disabled population forms a hidden subgroup in the United States, which is underserved and often hidden from view.

Traumatic Brain Injuries

As is noted in Table 19-1, the number of people living with the aftereffects of a traumatic brain injury (TBI) is slightly higher than the number of people living with a serious and persistent form of mental illness (Pearson, 2009). This fact often surprises the health care professional, who is generally unaware of this fact or of the interrelationship between SUDs and people living with a TBI. As noted earlier in this text, many people suffer a TBI while under the influence of one or more chemicals (usually alcohol). However, between 10 and 20% of those

people who struggle to live with the impact of a TBI on their lives did not have an SUD at the time of their admission to a rehabilitation program (Pearson, 2009). These individuals appear to turn to alcohol or illicit drugs to self-medicate their frustration after reaching a point where hope for further recovery is unrealistic.

Individuals who suffer a TBI often resort to the same coping mechanisms that they utilized prior to their injury. Thus one challenge that faces the substance abuse rehabilitation professional who works with post-TBI patients is determining whether the SUD *predates* the injury or develops after the injury. The substance rehabilitation of both groups of individuals is exceptionally difficult. However, the role that the chemical plays in their lives might be far different, and so the rehabilitation professional must identify this role to even begin to successfully plan a rehabilitation program. To further compound the problem, personality-disordered individuals comprise a significant percentage of those who have suffered a TBI. This forces the rehabilitation professional to try and address the issues of the personality disorder while helping the patient recover from and adjust to the aftereffects of the TBI, *and* deal with the SUD. Most substance abuse rehabilitation professionals, at best, have been poorly trained to do all of these tasks (J. D. Corrigan, Bonger et al., 2005).

Treatment guidelines for working with the patient with a TBI who has an SUD are lacking, although there is evidence suggesting that duration of treatment is one predictor of treatment success (J. D. Corrigan, Bonger et. al., 2005). In order to keep these patients in treatment longer, financial incentives might be helpful in working with TBI patients who also have an SUD. But these patients are perceived as a source of frustration for most treatment program staff, especially those programs that do not normally work with patients who have suffered a TBI.

Ethnic Minorities and SUDs

Substance abuse rehabilitation professionals who work with members of various ethnic minority groups are faced with a conundrum: Rehabilitation programs appear to be as effective for ethnic minority members as they are for the general population (A. W. Blume & de la Cruz, 2005). However, ethnic minorities have limited access to general health care and substance abuse rehabilitation programs, and there is a paucity of research into the outcome of treatment for minority-group members (Niv, Pham, & Hser, 2009).

The relationship between SUDs and ethnic-minority status is quite complex. One variable is the process of acculturation for the individual (R. L. Collins & McNair, 2002; el-Guebaly, 2008). Each successive generation moves closer to the social norms of the dominant culture in the United States. Yet in so doing, members of many ethnic groups become more vulnerable to SUDs as cultural prohibitions that once protected individuals are discarded (R. L. Collins & McNair, 2002; el-Guebaly, 2008). There are thus intergenerational differences in the development of SUDs in minority groups. There are also significant intergroup differences between various ethnic groups, preventing the development of a substance abuse rehabilitation model that might be applied to all ethnic-minority groups in this country. What follows is a brief summary of the substance abuse patterns of some of the larger ethnic groups in the United States (Niv et al., 2009).

Native Americans

The Native American population in the United States is subject to numerous misperceptions. First, there is no standard definition of "Native American". Some researchers include Alaskan natives with American Indians, as if these diverse groups might share similar cultural and social traditions ("Alcohol and Minorities: An Update," 2002). Other researchers classify members of each subgroup as falling in a different population. This lack of a standard definition only serves to cloud the issue of the impact of SUDs on the Native American population.

The Native American population is not a single, cohesive group, but a heterogeneous population of approximately 2 million people belonging to between 200 (Markarian & J. Franklin, 2005) and 500 (R. L. Collins & McNair, 2002) different tribes. Even within the population of Native Americans, there are many differences. For example, only about one-third of the identified members of the various tribes live on reservations, whereas the majority live outside of identified reservations (Beauvais, 1998). Just the fact that they live on or outside of an identified reservation makes these two subgroups different even if, technically, they are members of the same tribal unit. One cannot assume that they are exposed to the same alcohol or drug use "cues," that the use or abuse of the same compound has the same meaning for those who live on the reservation as it does for their cousins who live outside of identified reservation boundaries, and so on.

The different tribes have an estimated 200 distinct languages, as well as different cultural and social histories. This makes generalizations from research conducted on one tribal group to the next difficult, if not impossible. For example, in some tribes in the northeastern United States, 111 of every 1000 people meet the criteria for a formal diagnosis of an AUD, whereas in some tribes of the Southwest, only 11 of every 1000 members would qualify for the same diagnosis. Obviously, there are different forces at work within these different tribes to cause such a discrepant rate of alcoholism. There is also marked intergenerational variation within tribal units, with younger members tending to abuse alcohol and being drawn to the abuse of methamphetamine more often than their elders (Beauvais, 1998; Rutkowski & Maxwell, 2009).

Although all of these issues make research into the interrelationship between SUDs and tribal membership difficult, there are a few facts that are known. For example, the alcohol-related death rate for Native Americans is estimated to be 440% higher than it is for the general population in the United States (Ringwald, 2002). There is also an apparent relationship between alcohol use and suicide within the Native American population (Crosby et.al., 2009). Approximately 37% of Native Americans who committed suicide in the 2005–2006 period met the legal definition for intoxication at the time of their death, whereas an unknown percentage had ingested smaller amounts of alcohol before their suicide (Crosby et al., 2009).

Statistically, Native American males have an AUD twice as often as do women ("Alcohol and Minorities: An Update," 2002). There are exceptions to this rule however, as evidenced by the fact that approximately equal percentages of men and women in the Sioux nation have AUDs (R. L. Collins & McNair, 2002). Nor can the abuse of a given compound such as alcohol be viewed in the same context in Native American cultures as compared with the larger society around them. There is evidence that Native Americans might develop an SUD for different reasons than people from the mainstream culture, although both groups might abuse the same chemical(s) (Schmidt, Greenfield, & Mulia, 2006).

There is virtually no research about which treatment modalities might work best when the rehabilitation professional is working with a Native American substance abuser. Preliminary data suggests that substance-abusing Native Americans might have a better recovery rate if they are referred to a specialized program that specializes in working with Native American clients (Schmidt et al., 2006). However, this is not always possible due to geographic and funding limitations, and so the client is referred to a treatment center that is probably not equipped to deal with Native American substance abusers but that is more accessible geographically or is funded by a given health care insurance provider. Unfortunately, only 20 % of substance abuse rehabilitation programs offer specialized program components for Native Americans (Schmidt et al., 2006), an issue that is rarely considered when treatment recommendations are made. The substance abuse rehabilitation professional is then faced with the need to develop skills necessary for working with substance-abusing Native Americans when there has little research into the specific treatment skills necessary to work with these individuals. Native Americans are, for example, likely to withdraw into themselves and fail to participate in treatment if subjected to harsh confrontation, an observation that has implications for rehabilitation programs serving Native Americans. Rehabilitation center staff working with Native Americans need to be sensitive to the cultural differences and beliefs of these clients both within a single tribe and between tribes.

One popular misconception that cuts across tribal boundaries is that Native Americans are more sensitive to the effects of alcohol than are members of other ethnic groups. But there is little factual evidence to support this belief (Caetano, Clark, & Tam, 1998). Further, although it is widely believed that European explorers introduced alcohol to Native Americans, there is historical evidence suggesting that at least some tribes used alcohol in religious ceremonies, as a medicine, and as a way to prepare for warfare, before the arrival of European explorers (R. L. Collins & McNair, 2002). So at least some tribes were aware of alcohol and its effects before the arrival of European explorers, and much of what we thought we knew about the SUDs in this population has been proven to be inaccurate. So there is much to be discovered about the history of alcohol use within the Native American population, the treatment modalities that are most effective in the rehabilitation of substance abusing individuals, and what treatment methods might be counterproductive in the treatment of Native Americans with an SUD.

Hispanic (Latino) Clients

It is estimated that approximately 11% of the entire population of the United States is Hispanic. However, there is a problem when speaking of a single Hispanic or Latino population in that individuals normally classified as Hispanic in surveys might in reality come from any one of 20 different countries (el-Guebaly, 2008). About 60% of the Hispanic population traces their roots to Mexico, 15% came into this country from Puerto Rico, 5% from Cuba, and the rest from various other countries. Each of these social groups has different attitudes, different cultures, and different attitudes toward alcohol and drug use (Markarian & Franklin, 2005). To illustrate the differences between these subgroups, on occasion a word that holds one meaning in one Latino subgroup will carry a different, possibly socially offensive meaning in another subgroup. Yet these different subpopulations are all lumped together under the rubric of Hispanic or Latino by researchers, a mistake that introduces many variables into treatment effectiveness research that are not controlled for at the time of the research study.

Traditionally, alcohol use, especially heavy alcohol use, is a male activity within the Hispanic cultures (R. L. Collins & McNair, 2002). However, there are significant differences in the prevalence of substance abuse between the various Hispanic subgroups noted earlier. Eighteen percent of Mexican Americans are considered heavy drinkers, for example, whereas only 5% of Cuban Americans engage in heavy alcohol use. In both subgroups it is rare for a woman to use alcohol, and an even smaller percentage engage in heavy alcohol use (R. L. Collins & Mc-Nair, 2002).

In spite of the demonstrated need, the need for treatment resources exceeds demand. Only about one-third of substance abuse rehabilitation programs offer specialized components for Hispanic clients (Schmidt et al., 2006). Language barriers, perceived stigma, and legal concerns over notification of authorities if the individual is an illegal immigrant all might limit access to treatment even if such resources are available (Niv et al., 2009). Many treatment programs, unused to working with Hispanic clients, offer only generic treatment materials that are not specific to individuals or their subculture. To complicate matters, in many cases the Hispanic family is a single-parent household, especially in families at the lower end of the socioeconomic spectrum (Conner, Le Fauve, & Wallace, 2009). The parent, usually the mother, is often forced to work outside of the home in a job that rarely provides adequate health care insurance (Conner et al., 2009). If the substance abuser is the mother, provisions must be made for child care and education while she participates in treatment, and adequate financial resources must be found for the treatment program, requirements that make participation virtually impossible for the mother. If the substance abuser is a family member other than the mother, then the financial burden still might prevent that person from entering treatment.

Hispanics also often experience longer delays in receiving care for their SUD, receive less active treatment for it, and are less likely to be referred to residential treatment programs (Dunigan, 2009; Niv et al., 2009). These delays result in increased risk to life. Approximately 29% of Hispanics who ended their lives during the time covered by the study period were legally intoxicated at the time of their death, for example (Crosby et al., 2009). This figure does not include people of Hispanic heritage who ended their own lives, often after ingesting some alcohol but who were not legally intoxicated at the time of their death. Thus there is a need for substance abuse rehabilitation programs to develop not just a sensitivity for working with Hispanic clients, but also an awareness of the differences between various Hispanic subgroups and equality in treatment services offered.

Asian Americans

This term is misleading, in that it is used to include Chinese Americans, Filipino Americans, Asian Indians, Korean Americans, Japanese Americans, and Vietnamese Americans, to name some of the different subgroups included under this umbrella term. The term is also frequently applied to people from Hawaii, Micronesia, Polynesia, and Hawaii ("Alcohol and Minorities: An Update," 2002; Conner et al., 2009). Each of these subgroups has its own diverse culture, traditions, and in many cases language (Markarian & Franklin, 2005).

In general, women from an Asian American culture are more likely to abstain from alcohol or drink only on special occasions than are their male partners. But even this rule must be tempered with the observation that women from various subgroups have widely disparate alcohol use patterns. For example, only 20% of Korean American women admitted to the use of alcohol on occasion, whereas more than 67% of Japanese American women admitted to using alcohol at some point (Caetano et al., 1998). Little is known about the needs of these subgroups or the treatment methods that might be most effective when they are admitted to a rehabilitation facility.

African Americans

There has been virtually no research into the impact of illicit-drug use on the African American population, although there is a slowly growing body of literature

addressing the issue of the AUDs in this subpopulation. Such research has found that African American males with AUDs were more likely to initiate heavy drinking later in life than Caucasian males, but were more likely to experience physical complications from alcohol use earlier in life (Edlund, Booth, & Feldman, 2009; Markarian & Franklin, 2005). This data suggests that alcohol use patterns differ between the African American and the Caucasian population in this country.

To complicate matters[7] there is also evidence suggesting that intergenerational differences in substance use patterns within African Americans exist. African American women in the 18- to 29-year age cohort are significantly more likely to have an AUD than are their older peers, with 3.8% of the younger age cohort meeting diagnostic criteria for an AUD as opposed to only 2.1% for older age groups (Payne et al., 2009). The path into a rehabilitation program(s) is often different than that seen in the Caucasian population. For example, African American women are 10 times as likely to be involved with the court system for a substance-related problem than are Caucasian women (Schmidt et al., 2006).

Regrettably, there is preliminary evidence to suggest that African Americans with an SUD will receive a different quality of treatment than Caucasians with an SUD (Schmidt et al., 2006). African Americans tend to remain in treatment for shorter periods of time as compared with Caucasian clients, for example, and are more likely to be discharged before successful completion of the rehabilitation program (Niv et al., 2009). The reason(s) for this difference is not known at this time, but might reflect the fact that African Americans with an SUD are less likely to perceive a need for treatment than are Caucasians with a similar chemical abuse problem (Edlund et al., 2009), possibly combined with a lower quality of treatment services. As this data suggests, there is much to be discovered about this subpopulation and the treatment methods that might be most effective in helping individuals from this subpopulation recover from SUDs.

Chapter Summary

As this chapter has attempted to demonstrate, there are many subpopulations within this country with members who might have an SUD, but there is very little known about the factors that might initiate the substance abuse

---

[7]Do you not hate it when I use that phrase?

disorder, the factors that might maintain it, or the treatment methods that might be most effective with each subpopulation. All too often research studies that have been conducted in this area have utilized exclusively male samples, with the result being that virtually nothing is known about the factors that might initiate or maintain the SUDs in the women from each subgroup.

In general, people have a stereotypical image of what the "typical" person with an SUD looks like. Although these images are often correct, they also serve to blind us to the fact that there are many hidden subpopulations with their own unique cultures, histories, and avenues toward the initiation of, maintenance of, and recovery from SUDs. Even at the start of the 21st century, these subgroups are rarely recognized by treatment professionals as being different, and their needs in rehabilitation programs are often not met.

CHAPTER 20

Substance Use and Abuse by Children and Adolescents

Introduction

Childhood and especially adolescence are periods of "rapid physical, cognitive, emotional, social and behavioral changes" (Upadhyaya & Gray, 2009, p. 421). However, researchers disagree about such basic issues as when childhood ends and adolescence begins. Windle et al. (2009) suggested that early adolescence might begin as early as the age of 10, with the onset of puberty. The authors did admit there is significant interindividual variability in this developmental landmark, but noted that during this phase of life the individual moves from elementary school on to middle or junior high school, a process that brings with it developmental demands not encountered earlier in life.

It is important to keep in mind the fact that the developmental changes in childhood and adolescence are tied to the individual's age, but they are not synonymous with the aging process (Masten, Fade, Zucker, & Spear, 2009). This makes it difficult to make broad statements about the impact of alcohol or drug use on people of a given age. Children or adolescents of the same biological age might be working their way through different stages of biopsychosocial growth (Masten et al., 2009). Ultimately, it is the duty of the assessor to place the substance use disorder (SUD) in the context of a given child's or adolescent's life, a process that is complicated by the fact that substance abuse potentially can disrupt the growth process for that individual, possibly with lifelong consequences. The issue of substance abuse by children and adolescents is thus complex and influenced by a variety of factors, many of which will be discussed in this chapter.

The Problem of Substance Abuse in Childhood and Adolescence

SUDs in childhood and adolescence are not recent developments but have been a social problem for generations. During the 19th century, alcohol dependence was rampant among children and young adolescents in England, for example (Wheeler & Malmquist, 1987). This helped to spark a period of social reform movement in that country that pushed underage substance abuse underground, although it never really disappeared. Unfortunately some segments of society (such as what might be called "Big Tobacco," for example) appear to encourage the use and abuse of some substances by children and adolescents.

Currently, it is estimated that the economic cost to society by underage alcohol use alone is $62 billion per year (Spoth, Greenberg, & Turrisi, 2009). This fact alone would suggest that a complete understanding of the problem of child and adolescent SUDs is of importance. Further, research has repeatedly demonstrated that SUDs most commonly develop during adolescence, although there is anecdotal evidence of substance abuse by children (Crowley, 2007; Substance Abuse and Mental Health Services Administration, 2005; Zucker, Donovan, Masten, Mattson, & Moss, 2009). Children begin to form personal attitudes toward alcohol use early in life, as evidenced by the fact that by preschool children have at least a rudimentary knowledge of alcohol, its effects, and the social norms that govern its use (Zucker et al., 2009).

Complicating Factors

Unfortunately, many people believe that "childhood" and "adolescence" are unitary constructs. Both childhood and adolescence have multiple subphases, each with stage-specific developmental issues that the individual must address to achieve optimal growth and development. To say that a specific individual began to abuse alcohol or illicit chemicals during "childhood" or "adolescence" does not communicate the nuances of stage-specific effects of such chemical abuse on development. To understand this point, it is only necessary to compare the cognitive, social, and physical status of a 7-year-old child and those of a 10-year-old. The body, brain, and social skills of the 10-year-old are, hopefully, more advanced than those of a 7-year-old child. Along parallel lines, the social skills and brain of a 13-year-old adolescent should be more advanced than those found in the 10-year-old child.[1]

The developmental processes and transitions that the adolescent must pass through include puberty, identify formation, transition to middle and then high school as appropriate, peer group selection, initial dating relationships, and evolution of the parent–child relationship pattern (Wagner, 2009). Yet virtually nothing is known about how these (or other) developmental issues might influence the process of treatment for the substance-abusing adolescent (Wagner, 2009). To complicate matters, the face of childhood and adolescence itself is changing. The age of puberty for the current generation, when compared with earlier generations, has been steadily decreasing, possibly as a result of improved diet and health care (Masten et al., 2009). This is in itself a stressor that might contribute to the development of SUDs in children and adolescents, a possibility consistent with research findings that those individuals who enter adolescence at an earlier age are more vulnerable to the development of an SUD than are their peers who reach puberty at a more appropriate age (S. A. Brown et al., 2009; Wagner, 2009).

Wunsch (2007) suggested that there were three different subphases of adolescence: (a) early, (b) middle, and (c) late stage. Early adolescence is thought to begin at about the age of 10 and end around the age of 14. The developmental task during this phase of life is for the individual to come to terms with the pending and ongoing process of physical growth and development. Not surprisingly, the physical changes experienced during this phase are independent of, but intertwined with, the ongoing process of the maturation of the brain, which will be discussed later. Middle adolescence is thought to begin at about the age of 15 and continue for approximately 2 years (Wunsch, 2007). The developmental tasks during this phase include issues of self-acceptance and identity formation. Finally, during the stage of late adolescence (17–21) adolescents' focus must shift to the psychosocial realm as they explore possible adult roles, interpersonal relationships, vocational opportunities, and their relationship within society (Wunsch, 2007). If, as many clinicians suspect, alcohol or drug abuse can alter or block normal development, then it becomes apparent that these chemicals will have varying effects as a result of individuals' age and psychobiosocial maturational level at the time and duration of their abuse (Jorgensen, 2008; Masten et al., 2009; Wagner, 2009).

---

[1]Although this point might be disputed by some parents.

To further complicate matters, adolescence in industrialized societies has been extended to allow the individual additional time for vocational training and educational experiences. This results in the evolution of a new phase of life not found in earlier generations called "emerging adulthood" (Masten et al., 2009, p. 5). During this phase of life individuals enjoy greater freedom than they had in adolescence, but still do not enjoy the full rights and obligations of adulthood. Even before the social sciences have fully determined the implications of this new phase of life, they are being called upon to determine the impact of the SUDs on people in this new era.

Scope of the Problem of Substance Abuse in Childhood and Adolescence

It is quite difficult to provide firm data about the scope of the problem of substance abuse in childhood and adolescence. As noted earlier, the definitions of *childhood* and *adolescence* have become rather unclear. Further, the distinctions between substance *use, abuse,* and *dependence* are not clearly defined. Different researchers use the terms *substance use, abuse,* and *dependence* interchangeably, which is another source of confusion. Because alcohol and illicit drugs are illegal[2] by definition, many clinicians believe that *any* substance use during childhood or adolescence is a sign of a serious problem. Other clinicians maintain that *experimental* substance use, especially of alcohol and marijuana, is just one aspect of adolescence (Greydanus & Patel, 2005; Y. Kaminer & Tarter, 2004). The essential question, Greydanus and Patel suggested, "is not whether most teenagers will use drugs, but which one(s) they try" (p. 392), how often they do so, and when. Given this information, how does a parent determine what is experimental substance use as opposed to problematic use?

For example, the phenomenon of inhalant abuse rapidly waxes and wanes in a local region. All of these factors make it virtually impossible to develop a comprehensive picture of the problem of child or adolescent substance use patterns, much less address them adequately. In the sections that follow are the best estimates of the scope of the problem of child and adolescent substance abuse.

Childhood Chemical Abuse Patterns

The database on the scope of child substance abuse behaviors is exceptionally limited at best (Parekh, 2006; Zucker et al., 2009). This is clearly seen in the assertion by Wagner (2009) that 85% of all adolescents included in research studies addressing alcohol abuse by adolescents were younger than 15 years of age and none were younger than 12 years of age. This age bias might reflect the significant degree of denial associated with the problem of alcohol use disorders (AUDs), which most people find to be rather disturbing. Such denial is ill founded in light of research findings that just under a quarter of 9-year-old students have used alcohol at least once, whereas just under half of 11- to 14-year-old students have used alcohol (Fetro, Coyle, & Pham, 2001). Minkoff (2008) suggested that for many children, the initial substance use was well before the age of 9, possibly as early as 6 years; however this has not been proven by clinical research. Many children between the ages of 6 and 14 will admit to the abuse of inhalants, cigarettes, alcohol, or possibly other compounds, if asked. Ten percent of 9-year-old children when asked admitted to having at least sipped alcohol on at least one occasion, a number that translates into approximately 427,000 children in the United States alone (Millar, 2009). Of those children between the ages of 8 and 11 who do drink, 78% obtain alcohol from either their parents or other family members (Zucker et al., 2009). Few children below the age of 9 consume alcohol without their parents being aware of this fact (Zucker et al., 2009). It has been suggested that children appear to be drawn to alcohol use because it helps make them feel as if they were older (Millar, 2009), however this hypothesis has not been proven.

An especially distressing discovery is the evidence of children abusing prescription opioids (obtained from prescriptions for parents, siblings, and so on found in the medicine cabinet) and heroin (Sadock & Sadock, 2007). Because of their small body volume, children and to a lesser degree adolescents are at risk for overdosing on these compounds, possibly with fatal results (J. E. Bailey et al., 2008). As frightening as these statistics are, there is no mechanism in place to track the problem of childhood drinking or substance abuse (Millar, 2009).

Adolescent Substance Abuse Patterns

The database for adolescent substance use behaviors is marginally better than that for childhood alcohol and drug abuse. In one of the few realistic surveys, the

---

[2]Remember, in most states alcohol cannot be purchased until the age of 21.

Substance Abuse and Mental Health Services Administration (2009) estimated that in 2008:

- *9.3% of 12- to 17-year-olds were current illicit-drug abusers.*
- *6.7% of 12- to 17-year-olds had abused marijuana in the past 30 days.*
- *2.9% had abused prescription drugs in the past 30 days.*
- *1.1% had abused some kind of inhalant in the past 30 days.*
- *1.0% had abused a hallucinogenic in the 30 days preceding the survey.*
- *0.4% had abused cocaine in the 30 days preceding the survey.*

Another useful data source are surveys conducted on student populations from various schools. However, many high-risk students do not attend classes or at most do so on an inconsistent basis. Statistically, these students are likely to be underrepresented in such surveys (Commission on Child Health Care Financing and Committee on Substance Abuse, 2001). Further, national surveys blur regional variations in child or adolescent substance use patterns. Adolescent substance use patterns reflect geographic location, regional availability of certain substances, peer group pressure(s), parental guidance (or lack thereof), current substance use trends, and the like. Thus the information that follows should be accepted as conservative estimates of the scope of the problem of substance abuse prior to the start of adulthood.

With these problems in mind, L. D. Johnston, O'Malley, Bachman, and Schulenberg (2009) reported that their survey of high school seniors in 2008[3] revealed that 71.9% in the class of 2008 reported having abused alcohol at least once. There has been a gradual downward trend in the number of high school seniors reporting alcohol use in the past decade. As Figure 20-1 demonstrates, marijuana was the most commonly abused compound by students who graduated in the year 2008 (based on L. D. Johnston et al., 2009).

By the time of graduation, approximately 5–8% of high school seniors will meet the diagnostic criteria for a formal diagnosis of an AUD (L. D. Johnston et al., 2009; Parekh, 2006; "Young Adult Drinking," 2006). As a group, adolescents are estimated to make up 12–20% of the entire alcohol market in the United States, with 4.3 million adolescents consuming alcohol each year (Pumariega & Kilgus, 2005; Rosenbloom,

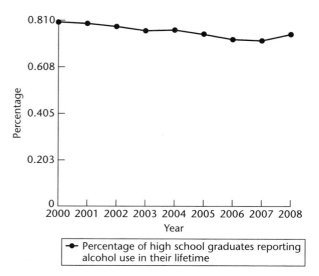

FIGURE 20-1 Percentage of High School Seniors Reporting Alcohol Use
Source: Johnston, L.D., O'Malley, P.M., Backman, J.G., & Schulenberg, J.E. (2010). *Monitoring The Future: National Results on Adolescent Drug Use.* Bethesda, MD: National Institute on Drug Abuse.

2005; Wu & Ringwalt, 2006). There is evidence that alcohol advertisements are broadcast at times when children or adolescents are more likely to be watching television, an observation that, if proven, raises disturbing questions about the role of advertising in the development of AUDs in these age cohorts (P. J. Chung et al., 2009). Beer is the most popular alcohol-containing beverage for adolescents, although there is growing evidence that liquor is becoming increasingly popular in part because it is more easily hidden from adults by mixing it with soft drinks (Centers for Disease Control, 2007). There has been a very slight, gradual downward trend in the level of high school student alcohol use. However, as the aforementioned data demonstrates, alcohol use is prevalent in both populations.

But adolescents do not abuse just alcohol. As Figure 20-2 demonstrates, for the seniors of the class of 2008 marijuana was the compound most commonly abused (based on L. D. Johnston et al., 2009).

Although marijuana is the most commonly abused illicit compound for high school students, methamphetamine and prescription medications that are diverted by the adolescent for illicit use are also growing problems for adolescents (Millar, 2009). When asked which prohibited substance was easiest for them to obtain, 15% of

---

[3]The most current data available at this time.

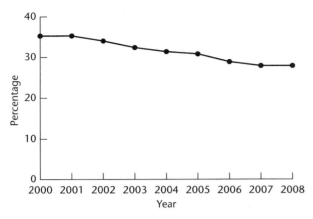

FIGURE 20-2 Comparison of Child/Adolescent Marijuana Abuse Against Total Illicit Drug Use

the students surveyed said beer, whereas 23% said marijuana, although the abuse of diverted prescription medications, especially opioids, has become more common (L. D. Johnston et al., 2009; Wunsch, 2007). Approximately 10% of adolescents report having used a medication prescribed for somebody else. Girls being more likely to share medications with other girls, whereas boys are more likely to share prescribed medications with other boys (M. C. Miller, 2007).

This switch in substance abuse patterns might reflect the fact that adolescent abusers often do not realize both that these compounds can be addictive and that their use carries with it a high potential for overdose and possible death (Heymann, 2008). Adolescents often believe the myth that you can become addicted to narcotic analgesics only if you inject them. Thus they believe that it is safe to use intranasal methods of administration; and then as their abuse evolves into an addiction, they are forced to turn to injected narcotics to achieve the same results once achieved with lower doses or less intense methods of abuse (G. B. Collins & Leak, 2008; Marsch et al., 2005).

The diversion of CNS stimulants such as methylphenidate or one of the amphetamine compounds is also of growing concern, with 23% of adolescents admitted to a substance abuse rehabilitation program admitting to the abuse of such compounds (Croft, 2006). As the number of prescriptions for CNS stimulants aimed at controlling the symptoms of ADHD increases, there is evidence of an increasing problem of stimulant abuse and diversion as well (Setlik, Gond, & Ho, 2009). The usual method of abuse is by oral ingestion or intranasal use.

In contrast to the preceding information are those compounds that might be administered intravenously. The intravenous use of any compound is so rare during adolescence that it should automatically be seen as a sign of a serious SUD.

Why Worry about SUDs In Childhood and Adolescence?

There are many reasons why the abuse of alcohol or drugs by children or adolescents is of special importance. First, there is good evidence that adolescent cigarette smokers are 50% more likely to develop an AUD later in life than nonsmoking adolescents (Grucza & Bierut, 2006). Further, SUDs are the leading cause of mortality for older adolescents, contributing to accidental death, suicidal thoughts and attempts, interpersonal violence, motor vehicle accidents, and the problem of having unprotected sex (Y. Kaminer & Buckstein, 2005; T. R. Miller, Levy, Spicer, & Taylor, 2006; J. P. Shepard, Sutherland, & Newcombe, 2006; Windle et al., 2009). Cumulatively, the estimated financial cost of alcohol-related rape, homicide, assault, larceny, burglary, motor vehicle theft, loss of employment, and medical care for underage drinkers to society is $3 per mixed drink, a cost that far outweighs the estimated 10¢ in taxes generated by that drink.

Adolescent substance abuse is also part of the health care problem facing the United States at this time. Complaints of chest pain is the third most common reason why adolescents seek health care, for example. Research has demonstrated that 17% of adolescents in a hospital setting for assessment of their chest pain had ephedrine in their urine in spite of often strident denials that they had not abused this compound (James et al., 1998). The cost of the medical evaluation for a possible cardiac condition in the adolescent is both labor and resource intensive. If the adolescent's chest pain is found to reflect not a cardiac disorder but unsuspected drug use, then these health care resources become part of the health care problem in the United States.

The Neurological Factor

Developmental neurologists have determined that childhood and adolescence are periods of dynamic growth in the central nervous system that continue well into early adulthood if not beyond (Jorgensen, 2008; Parekh, 2006).[4] Researchers now believe that as a result of the ongoing development process of the central nervous system, children and adolescents have different responses than adults to alcohol or the drugs of abuse (McVoy & Findling, 2009). Further, there is an emerging body of evidence suggesting that the effects of the various drugs of abuse on neurological maturation are dependent on (a) when the individual begins to abuse the compound(s) in question, (b) the duration, and (c) the frequency of abuse, among other factors.

To illustrate the process of neurological maturation, it is necessary only to consider the fact that the development of what is known as the "gray matter" in the human brain normally peaks at about the age of 11 in girls and about a year later for boys (Windle et al., 2009). After that point there is a gradual reduction in the volume of "gray matter" within the brain as the brain eliminates neural pathways[5] that are unused or redundant, possibly because of the metabolic cost of maintaining such pathways over the individual's life span (Windle et al., 2009). A preliminary research study has found, for example, that binge drinking in adolescents results in altered fiber coherence in the "white matter"[6] of the brain (McQueeny et al., 2009). Research has suggested that moderately heavy alcohol use during adolescence, such as that necessary to produce a "hangover" in the drinker, may affect neurological growth (Squeglia, Spandoni, Infante, Myers, & Tapert, 2009). To date, a similar process among adult drinkers has not been identified, suggesting that this sign of neurological injury might be stage-specific to adolescence, although the implications of this alteration in gray-matter fiber coherence are not known at this time.

This ongoing process of neurological maturation might explain why children and adolescents are at *increased* vulnerability to many of the harmful effects of alcohol and illicit drugs (Nutt, Robbins, & Stimson, 2005). The adolescent brain is thought to be four to five times more vulnerable to alcohol-induced brain damage as is the adult brain (Tappert, Caldwell, &

Burke, 2004/2005; Wuethrich, 2001). During adolescence the *hippocampus*[7] appears to be especially vulnerable to alcohol-related damage (De Bellis et al., 2000; Tappert et al., 2004/2005). This might account for the small (7–10%) but still significant decline in psychological test performance in adolescent alcohol abusers as compared with nondrinkers (Strauch, 2003). This decline in measured cognitive abilities appears to be enhanced by concurrent use of marijuana and appears to be permanent (Wagner, 2009). In theory, this reduction in cognitive abilities might reflect alcohol-induced damage to the hippocampus and possibly other regions of the brain.

When compared with adult drinkers, adolescents appear to experience less sedation from a given dose of alcohol (Strauch, 2003; Upadhyaya & Gray, 2009; Varlinskaya & Spear, 2006). This lack of equal sedation can contribute to adolescent overuse of alcohol, which in turn can overwhelm constraints against high-risk behavior(s) such as driving while intoxicated or engaging in unprotected sex. Further, where adults attend to and interpret novel stimuli through the prefrontal regions of the cortex, adolescents appear to attend to the same stimuli through the activation of the amygdala region of the brain (Thatcher & Clark, 2008). The amygdala[8] is part of the limbic system, a system in the brain involved in the emotional response to external reality. This explains why adolescents respond to life differently than adults: They process information differently. Because memories associated with strong emotions are stronger and are more deeply entrenched in the mind, substance abuse during adolescence exposes users to the risk of establishing strong positive memories of the effects of a compound(s) of abuse, making it more likely that they will want to repeat that experience later. This is consistent with animal research studies that suggest that adolescents might be more vulnerable to urges to return to the place where they abused a compound(s). This in turn would place them at greater risk for relapse because of the environmental drug use cues (Brenhouse & Anderson, 2008).

This helps to explain why substance abuse in adolescence, especially early adolescence, raises the individual's lifetime risk for an SUD (Rosenbloom, 2005). Fifteen percent of those individuals who become alcohol dependent begin to drink before the age of 18, for

---

[4]The topic of developmental neurology is rather fascinating. However, it lies outside of the scope of this chapter and must be referenced only in passing. Readers are referred to any of a wide range of textbooks on the subject if they are interested in learning more about this subject.

[5]A process called "synaptic pruning" by neurologists.

[6]See Glossary.

[7]See Glossary.

[8]See Glossary.

example, whereas another 32% begin to drink between the ages of 18 and 22 years (R. Nelson, 2007). Thus almost half of those people who become alcohol dependent do so before they are legal adults and entitled to buy alcohol (R. Nelson, 2007). In contrast to this, only about 20% of those individuals who develop an AUD at some point in their lives do so after the age of 30 (R. Nelson, 2007). These figures illustrate one reason why adolescence is a period of special vulnerability for the later development of an SUD.

The "Gateway" Theory

This controversial theory was espoused by Henry Anslinger, the then U.S. Commissioner of Narcotics, to justify making marijuana illegal after the end of Prohibition, thus providing a rationale for the continued existence of the Bureau of Narcotics (McPherson et al., 2009). Anslinger provided Congress with lurid tales of depraved behavior by marijuana abusers, many of which were fabrications, to justify making marijuana illegal. As part of this campaign, Anslinger also proposed (with remarkably little evidence) that marijuana abuse would prove to be a "gateway" to the abuse of more serious compounds. Since then, the gateway theory has become part of clinical lore (McPherson et al., 2009).

This theory has generated controversy for more than 70 years now. The team of Walker, Venner, Hill, Myers, and Miller (2004) found that there appeared to be a progression in adolescent substance abuse starting with alcohol to tobacco, then the inhalants, marijuana, and then other drugs of abuse. In another test of the gateway theory, the team of Ellgren, Spano, and Hurd (2006) administered cannabis to adolescent rats and then offered the rats the opportunity to use heroin. The authors found that the marijuana-exposed rats were more likely to self-administer heroin than were marijuana-naive rats. The authors interpreted this as evidence of the gateway theory.

In contrast to this conclusion, Rosenbloom (2005) suggested that the gateway theory is just an illusion and that the progression from one compound to another is not automatic. Several groups of researchers have concluded that personality characteristics such as conduct disorder (CD) childhood or adolescence might be more predictive of subsequent SUDs than simple marijuana abuse in adolescence (D. B. Clark, Vanyukrov, & Cornelius, 2002; Watson et al., 2000). More doubt on the gateway theory was generated by the study conducted by Tarter, Fanyukov, Kirisci, Reynolds, and Clark (2006). The authors reported that about 25% of the 200 male subjects who admitted to the use of marijuana did abuse this compound *before* using alcohol or tobacco products, but that the majority of those who abused marijuana did not progress to the abuse of other drugs.

Another challenge to the gateway theory of substance abuse came from Kandel and Chen (2000), who examined the marijuana use patterns of a community-based sample of 708 marijuana abusers (364 male and 304 female abusers) and found that the early abuse of marijuana was not found to predict later problems with chemicals or a progression to later substance abuse. This study was supported in part by the study conducted by Perkonigg et al. (2008). The authors followed a sample of 3021 adolescents over a 10-year period, with interviews at 4 years and 10 years after the initial survey. The authors found that 7% of their sample reported that they had used cannabis only once, 11% of their sample reported using it two to four times, and only a minority of their sample (approximately 13%) met the criteria for a diagnosis of cannabis dependence at the start of their study, at the 4-year follow-up interview, and at the end of the study. They also concluded that those adolescents who reported five or more episodes of marijuana use were the most likely to continue to use marijuana during the early years of adulthood, but the majority of their subjects did not continue to abuse marijuana.

One class of compounds that is frequently overlooked in the debate over the "gateway" theory of marijuana abuse are the inhalants. These compounds are often the first mood-altering chemical that children or young adolescents experiment with (Hogan, 2000). For most children or adolescents, inhalant abuse is usually a transient phase, and so the individual's risk for inhalant-induced brain damage is limited. Such abusers usually engage in episodic inhalant abuse for 1–2 years, after which time they gradually discontinue it. A very small minority of children or adolescents become long-term, possibly lifelong, inhalant abusers, and an unknown percentage of childhood or adolescent inhalant abusers go on to abuse other compounds. The role of inhalant abuse by these children or adolescents is open to debate: Were these individuals unwittingly ensnared by the effects of the inhalants and then turned to the abuse of other compounds, or were those children or adolescents who abused inhalants the most likely to develop other SUDs? At this point there is no clear answer to these questions, and debate surrounding the very concept of the gateway theory of the SUDs continues.

Tobacco Abuse by Children and Adolescents

Cigarettes and other tobacco products occupy a unique place in society: They are known to be addictive and destructive, yet can be legally purchased by adults. In contrast to this, children and adolescents are forbidden by law to purchase or use tobacco products. In spite of the legal restrictions against tobacco use, they are a very real part of childhood and adolescence, with an estimated under-aged 3 million cigarette smokers in the United States being under the age of 18 (Rosen & Maurer, 2008). In the United States, the *average* age at which a smoker begins to use cigarettes is 12, and most of those who begin to smoke at this age are regular smokers by the age of 14 (Hogan, 2000). This may reflect the fact that the adolescent brain, which is still maturing, seems especially vulnerable to the addictive effects of many compounds (Di Franza, Savageau, Fletcher, Pbert et al., 2007; Strauch, 2003).

Each day in the United States approximately 4400 children or adolescents smoke their first cigarette (Rosen & Maurer, 2008). It is not known how many of these adolescents will continue to smoke after that first cigarette, but it is known that cigarette smoking is growing in popularity in the adolescent age pool (Rimsza & Moses, 2005). Unfortunately, there are at best only limited resources to help the adolescent smoker quit (K. Blum, 2006). To complicate matters, at least one major tobacco company has conducted research into the phases of cigarette smoking in adolescents (Hilts, 1996). Another tobacco company referred to adolescents in an internal memo as an "up and coming new generation of smokers" (Phelps, 1996, p. 1A). The R.J. Reynolds Tobacco Company, most certainly a major cigarette producer, went so far as to refer to 12-year-olds as a "younger adult" generation of smokers ("Big Tobacco's Secret Kiddie Campaign," 1991).

The neurological and behavioral immaturity of adolescents makes it difficult for them to accurately assess the risks associated with various behaviors, including cigarette smoking (Pumariega & Kilgus, 2005; Strauch, 2003). Indeed, there is evidence that for adolescents who smoke to help build their self-esteem, the warnings on the side of cigarette packages serve as an enticement to continue to smoke because this would then prove their courage (Hansen, Winzeler, & Topolinski, 2010). Thus the traditional method(s) of providing adolescents with information about the dangers of cigarette smoking might prove to have the opposite effect.

Also, the natural rebelliousness of adolescents makes them vulnerable to the image of cigarette smoking as a way to rebel against parental authority (Dickinson, 2000; Greydanus & Patel, 2005). This image is encouraged by tobacco companies. Given that the typical adolescent spends 6–7 hours a day listening to or watching some form of mass media, it might be called a "super-peer" (Hogan, 2000, p. 937) for this age group (Windle et al., 2009). Another influence on adolescent smoking behavior is whether the parents smoke. This is supported by the observation that the majority of adolescent smokers have parents who also smoke cigarettes.

Stages of Childhood/Adolescent Smoking

The child or adolescent's transition from a nonsmoker to active cigarette smoking passes through four phases: (a) the *preparatory phase,* during which time the individual forms attitudes accepting of cigarette smoking, (b) the *initiation phase,* when the individual smokes for the first time, (c) the *experimentation phase,* when the smoker learns how to smoke after the first tentative smoking efforts, and (d) the *transition phase* to regular smoking (Holland & Fitzsimons, 1991).

Why Do Children and Adolescents Abuse Chemicals?

SUDs in childhood and adolescence do not arise in isolation but are influenced by the individual's (a) constitutional predisposition (genetic heritage), (b) environmental factors (lack of parental supervision, exposure to substance-abusing parents, peer groups, and so on), and (c) life events (child abuse, victimization, etc.) (Upadhyaya & Gray, 2009). Further, there are the ongoing processes of physical, emotional, and neurological development during childhood and adolescence. As any parent will attest, children and especially adolescents will tell you that they know what is right and wrong and that they do not need to be told what to do. Unfortunately, a consequence of the process of neurological maturation is that individuals are unable to adequately assess the risks inherent in behaviors such as substance abuse. They tend to underestimate the negative consequences of high-risk behaviors, such as substance abuse, occasionally with dire results (Hogan, 2000; Pumariega & Kilgus, 2005).

Hogan (2000) offered five basic reasons why children and adolescent abusers use chemicals: (a) to feel grown up, (b) to take risks or rebel against authority, (c) to fit into a specific peer group, (d) to relax and feel good, and (e) to satisfy curiosity about the effects of that compound(s). Further, some adolescents view various chemicals as an acceptable way to self-medicate negative feelings such as depression or stress (Wills, Sandy, Yaeger, Cleary, & Shinar, 2001) or to demonstrate sexual prowess (A. Barr, 1999). As this list indicates, there is really no simple answer to why children and adolescents abuse chemicals. There are also other factors that will influence childhood and adolescent substance use patterns, which will be discussed in the following sections.

Parent–Adolescent Relationship Patterns and SUDs

Parents often forget that children (and adolescents) learn by interacting with and observing their parents, especially the behavior of the same-sex parent (Patock-Peckham & Morgan-Lopez, 2006). Later, they also begin to observe other adults as well for alternative behavioral models, although in most cases the parents retain primary responsibility for modeling behaviors. These early learning experiences are so important that research suggests that the pattern of parental interactions, especially how they resolve conflict, might affect the child's mental health as much as 30 years later ("Deteriorating Home Life Puts Kids at Risk," 2009). Unfortunately, parents often dismiss their influence on the developing child or adolescent, especially during the latter period of life. The truth is that parent–child relationship influences are stronger than those of adolescent peer groups, and it is within the context of the parent–child relationship that children primarily learn about the negative effects of alcohol and parental attitudes toward other forms of drug abuse (J. E. Donovan, Molina, & Kelly, 2009; Thatcher & Clark, 2008).

This is a two-edged sword as there is also a strong relationship between *parental* substance use patterns during the childhood years and the subsequent substance use behavior of the adolescent (Chassin, Flora, & King, 2004; K. G. Hill, Hawkins, Catalano, Abbott, & Guo, 2005). This is a fact that is especially disturbing because by the age of 17, 51% of adolescents would have seen one or both parents intoxicated after drinking (National Center on Addiction and Substance Abuse at Columbia University, 2009b). During the transition from childhood to adolescence, the individual adopts parental attitudes and values, including

those toward the positive effects of alcohol (S. A. Brown et al., 2009). Thus the experience of viewing parental intoxication in the face of parental admonitions against drinking provides conflicting information to the child or adolescent[9] (J. E. Donovan et al., 2009; National Center on Addiction and Substance Abuse at Columbia University, 2009b). It is not known whether the same social learning process is present for the other drugs of abuse, but parental influence does indeed play a strong role in the child's adoption of social expectations for alcohol's effects for both boys and girls (J. E. Donovan et al., 2009).

One element of people's relationships with their parents is the quality of the *attachment bonds* that develop with the parents in childhood (Bell, Forthun, & Sun, 2000; Hogan, 2000). Children with positive attachment bonds tend to be resistant to the urge to engage in substance use, have more positive peer relationships, are more socially competent, and demonstrate better coping skills than adolescents who go on to abuse chemicals. Such strong attachment bonds are expressed by such parental behaviors as consistently spending time with their children, positive parental substance use modeling behavior, and the degree of parental emotional involvement in the lives of their children (Y. Kaminer & Buckstein, 2005). Children whose parents spend more time with them[10] and who make a greater effort to communicate with them report lower rates of alcohol and tobacco use.

An overlapping factor that influences adolescents' substance use patterns is parental *control* or supervision (Patock-Peckham & Morgan-Lopez, 2006). Adolescents who report the highest levels of parental monitoring and enforcement of rules have lower levels of misconduct, delinquency, and substance abuse[11] (Patock-Peckham & Morgan-Lopez, 2006; Tildesley & Andrews, 2008). Parental supervision allows for the parents to monitor who their adolescents are spending time with and the activities they might engage in away from the parents (Y. Kaminer, 2008). This degree of parental supervision then allows for intervention should the adolescent start to "stray" into dangerous

---

[9]"Don't do as I do, but do as I say!"—a behavioral stance that adolescents are quick to dismiss on the basis of parental hypocrisy.

[10]Such as having a common hobby, for example.

[11]This is not to say that strict parental rules will *prevent* adolescent substance abuse. But high levels of parental monitoring and enforcement of established rules are generally associated with lower levels of deviant behavior(s), including alcohol or illicit-drug abuse.

territory. A related factor is children's ability to *communicate* with the parents, to ask questions and express concerns about their exposure to individuals who abuse alcohol or drugs. This also serves as a protection and would seem to explain why children whose parents have an AUD also tend to have higher rates of alcohol abuse (Tildesley & Andrews, 2008). These are behaviors that are unlikely to be seen in the home where one or both of the parents have an SUD such as alcoholism, thus providing a multigenerational effect for SUDs.

A reflection of parental control or supervision is their awareness of the substance use pattern by their child or adolescent. Fifty-five percent of parents were aware of cigarette smoking by their adolescent, and 50% were aware of the adolescent's alcohol use (Fisher et al., 2006). They are less aware of the adolescent's substance-related problems such as marijuana dependence according to Fisher et al. This claim is supported by the observation that 80% of parents expressed a belief that recreational chemicals were not at parties that their children attended, in contrast to the 50% of adolescents who reported that both alcohol and drugs were freely available at these parties (Sheff, Warren, Ketcham, & Evan, 2007). As a group, parents underestimated teenage alcohol consumption by a factor of 4:1, inhalant abuse by a factor of 4:1, and illicit-drug abuse by a factor of 2:1 (Center for Substance Abuse Research, 2006). However, this lack of parental awareness appears to be strongest during early adolescence (McGillicuddy, Rychtarik, Morsheimer, & Burke-Storer, 2007). The reason for this observed discrepancy is not known at this time but might reflect a tendency for parents to underestimate the possibility that their child is engaging in substance use behavior (McGillicuddy et al., 2007). Parents who struggle with psychosocial adjustment issues of their own are also less likely to be aware of their child's substance abuse pattern, according to McGillicuddy et al.

Vocational/Occupational Choices

There is strong evidence of an association[12] between time spent working and tobacco or alcohol use for adolescents in school. Those students who spent more time at work than they did on study were more likely to engage in alcohol and tobacco use (Wagner, 2009).

The individual's initial occupational choice(s) following graduation also is associated with substance use behaviors. Adolescents who enlist in the military, for example, both sever traditional sources of support such as peers and parents while simultaneously entering a subculture in which heavy alcohol use is accepted (Ames, Duke, Moore, & Cunradi, 2009; Benton, 2009; Zucker et al., 2009). In both the military and other occupations, heavy-drinking subgroups develop, which provide a sense of belonging (Benton, 2009). It is within these subcultures that the adolescent completes the transition from adolescence into the first stages of adulthood. Behavioral choices made during this transitional period often are continued into adulthood.

Adolescent Affective Disorders

Depression is a risk factor for adolescent substance abuse (Y. Kaminer, 2008; Kriechbaum & Zernig, 2000). But the correlation between these two conditions is a modest one at best and is strongest for girls as opposed to boys (C. B. Fleming, Mason, Mazza, Abbott, & Catalano, 2008). The authors found that depression in early adolescence was positively correlated with alcohol, marijuana, and cigarette use for adolescent girls but only for marijuana use for boys. This might reflect the fact that few adolescent boys, like their adult counterparts, recognize the existence of their depression or other negative emotional states (Mayeda & Sanders, 2007). Adolescent girls tend to be more in touch with feelings such as depression or anxiety, and it is for this reason that the affective disorders on substance use behaviors differs between adolescent boys and girls.

One interesting study was conducted by Rao, Hammen, and Poland (2009). The authors measured the cortisol[13] levels in 151 adolescents (a process that required the collection of urine for 24 hours from each individual for testing). The authors found that adolescents who had higher levels of cortisol in their urine (an indication of stress, often a precipitant of depression in adolescents) were more vulnerable to the development of SUDs. The results of this study confirm the relationship between depression and subsequent SUDs in adolescents.

It is often surprising for parents to learn that behavioral extremes are often problem signals for the adolescent (Lundeen, 2002). Total abstinence from any substance use during adolescence has actually been identified as a signal of impending problems. The critical

---

[12]As before, associational relationships are not the same as *causal* relationships.

[13]See Glossary.

point to Lundeen (2002) is not whether the adolescent abuses alcohol or illicit drugs so much as *which compounds, how often,* and *in what quantities.* Adolescents who frequently abuse alcohol or drugs tend to have poor impulse control, be socially alienated, and experience high levels of emotional distress, all warning signs that they may lack the social skills necessary to cope effectively. In contrast to this, adolescents who are totally abstinent from alcohol and illicit drugs may be anxious, emotionally constricted, lack self-confidence, and may lack the social skills necessary to cope with life's demands. Thus adolescents' substance use pattern must be viewed within the context of their emotional adjustment.

Conduct Disorder/Oppositional Defiant Disorder

Conduct disorder (CD) and the oppositional defiant disorder (ODD) are two behavioral disorders that first appear in childhood and continue through adolescence. The diagnostic criteria for either condition lie beyond the scope of this text, but are listed in the *Diagnostic and Statistical Manual of Mental Disorders* (4th edition, text revision) (American Psychiatric Association, 2000). Both of these disorders share the common traits of impulsiveness and limited behavioral control, increasing the individual's risk for the development of an SUD (D. B. Clark et al., 2002). Behavioral problems usually proceed the development of adolescent SUDs, possibly reflecting a common neurological basis for these conditions (D. B. Clark et al., 2002; Newcorn & Ivanov, 2007). This theory is supported by the observation that 50–80% of adolescents with a diagnosis of CD will develop an SUD at some point in their lives (Y. Kaminer & Buckstein, 2005).

The prefrontal cortex of the brain is actively involved in the process of assessing potential risks and of behavioral control. Preliminary evidence suggests that individuals with CD and ODD, as well as adults with antisocial personality disorder, have altered neurological function in this region of the brain, possibly contributing to the behavioral problems central to either disorder. The presence of these disorders will reduce the chance of treatment being successful. In order for treatment to be effective, it is necessary to develop a program that addresses the issues of behavioral control in the SUD rehabilitation program (D. B. Clark et al., 2002).

Peer Group Influences

Parents often dismiss their ability to influence the adolescent's decisions about substance abuse and point to

the peer group as being more influential than they are at this stage of the individual's life (Thatcher & Clark, 2008). Admittedly, adolescent peer groups may serve as either a protective or negative influence on adolescent substance use behaviors (J. S. Brook et al., 2008; G. R. Ross, 2002; Simkin, 2002). However, peer group influences peak between the ages of 11 and 13, and in spite of parental perceptions parents still retain a strong influence on fundamental issues such as morality, religion, and perceived importance of education in adolescents (Windle et al., 2009).

Further, peer group influences are not always negative. Peer approval (or disapproval) might prove to be more important to the individual than the pharmacological reward potential of a compound(s) that might be abused. However, the relationship between adolescents and their peer group is quite complex. Peers provide feedback to the adolescent that might either parallel or contradict that provided by the parents, reinforcing or reducing the individual's desire to abuse alcohol or drugs. In those cases where the peer group does support substance use, peers strongly influence the *initiation* of substance use behavior(s) but not automatically its continued use (Rhee et al., 2003). At this point other factors, such as the pharmacological reward potential of the compound(s) being abused, possible parental intervention, and individuals' expectations for continued substance abuse, help determine whether they might desire additional exposure to the chemical(s) in question. As a result of this process, adolescents tend to gravitate toward peer groups with views toward substance abuse, values, expectations, and behavioral demands similar to their own (Pumariega & Kilgus, 2005; Simkin, 2002). Thus peer group selection is the *last* step in the chain of events leading up to the adolescent's abuse of a chemical(s).

Music Selection

The typical adolescent spends approximately 2 hours each day listening to music, often on a personal music system controlled by a microchip system. The team of Primack, Dalton, Carroll, Agerwal, and Fine (2008) examined the content of the music that adolescents listen to and found either implicit or explicit references to substance use in a significant percentage of songs examined. The authors found that alcohol was the most commonly referenced substance, followed by marijuana. They also found that rap music contained the greatest percentage of references to substance abuse (more than three-quarters of songs sampled), whereas pop music had the least (10% of songs sampled). This disturbing finding is made even more frightening by the content of the references to alcohol or substance use: They glorified the use of the compound(s) in the content of that song, associating the use of these compounds with sexual, emotional, and/or financial gains for the user (M. C. Miller, 2008). It is not clear at this time whether adolescents' choice of music is a response to their abuse of chemicals, whether it is just a phase through which adolescents must pass,[14] or, whether their alcohol or drug abuse might predate the abuse of chemicals. In any case, these findings are disturbing.

Personal Values

An often overlooked aspect of SUDs are the individual's values. These may carry out a protective function against substance abuse or may facilitate the development of adolescent SUDs. There is a negative correlation between such factors as academic achievement, church attendance, the individual's beliefs about the importance of academic achievement, and substance abuse (Van den Bree & Pickworth, 2005). However, it is not clear whether these factors help to protect the adolescent from SUDs, because correlation does not imply causality.

Rebellion

A factor that is closely intertwined with personal values is the adolescent's attempts to rebel against perceived parental authority. Substance abuse appears to many adolescents to be an avenue through which they can express their rebellion because the use of such substances is illegal and thus using them is viewed as being especially daring in the eyes of their peers (A. Barr, 1999). However, there is a difference between rebellion and delinquency or CDs. In these latter groups, periods of heavy drug abuse appear to serve as a catalyst for subsequent criminal activity (Heyman, 2009). These are behaviors that are not seen in adolescents who are engaging in rebellious behaviors as a part of establishing personal identity but are more characteristic of adolescents with a CD.

Insomnia

An interesting theory was recently introduced suggesting that those adolescents who suffer from insomnia are at higher risk for later depression and SUDs ("Adolescents With Insomnia Are at Risk for Future Substance Abuse and Depression," 2008). The average adolescent requires between 8.5 and 9.25 hours of sleep per night, although their sleep pattern shifts to one where they go to sleep later and wake up later than do their older peers (S. A. Brown et al., 2009). Adolescents who sleep for shorter periods force sleep deprivation states on themselves in spite of "catch-up" opportunities for extra sleep on the weekends (S. A. Brown et al., 2009).

Researchers have not determined whether sleep deprivation is a causal agent in adolescent SUDs; however the available evidence does suggest that it can become a separate, coexisting problem for adolescents who later develop an SUD (Roane & Taylor, 2008). A surprising problem, once thought to be seen only in adults, is the possibility that the adolescent might suffer from obstructive sleep apnea,[15] a medical condition that appears to raise the adolescent's risk for an SUD, in part through its ability to induce depression.

Abuse History/Victimization

There is a body of evidence suggesting that physical, sexual, and emotional abuse during childhood and adolescence might be associated with the development of SUDs later in life (Clay et al., 2008). About 30–60% of women in primary substance abuse rehabilitation report having experienced such severe levels of abuse that they meet the diagnostic criteria for posttraumatic stress disorder (PTSD). Although the exact causal mechanism(s) for this association have yet to be identified, it is thought that severe abuse could cause a dysregulation of the normal stress response mechanisms in the body, which in turn could block normal maturation of the brain in adolescence and early adulthood, especially in the frontal and prefrontal cortex, those regions that govern behavior and also anticipate the consequences of behavior. More research is necessary to confirm whether this theory is accurate, but it does seem to be a mechanism through which physical, emotional, and sexual abuse might be associated with later SUDs.

Part Summary

Although it is tempting to blame peer group influences on child or adolescent substance abuse, in reality such a belief is too simplistic. People's decision to begin to abuse alcohol, tobacco, or drugs is the result of the

---

[14]In the sense that the adolescent finds such music exciting for a period of time and then discards this form of entertainment in favor of another form of music.

[15]See Glossary.

interaction between such factors as the quality of parent–child relationships, parental drug or alcohol use patterns, individuals' affective state, and their stage-specific struggle for autonomy. Adolescence substance abuse takes place during a period of neurological vulnerability, as well as being a factor for later alcohol or drug use disorders for the individual (Fiellin, 2008).

Substance Abuse: How Much and When Does It Become Too Much?

Childhood

The issue of childhood substance abuse is both more clear and more difficult for clinicians. The issue of experimental substance use by children is self-evident: Any use of alcohol or illicit compounds is potentially dangerous. The regular abuse of such compounds are certainly signs of a serious problem. However, even if children have been appropriately identified as having an SUD, treatment resources for these children are virtually unknown (Millar, 2009).

It has been hypothesized that early-onset alcohol use by children (defined as before the age of 13) might reflect a genetic predisposition toward alcohol dependence within the child (Agrawal et al., 2009). This conclusion is partially supported by the work of R. W. Hingson, Heeren, and Winter (2006), who found in their study of 43,000 adults in the United States that 47% of those who began to drink before the age of 14 years were alcohol dependent when interviewed, as opposed to just 9% of those who began to drink after the age of 21 years. Although of interest, clinicians lack both access to highly reliable genetic-testing techniques or knowledge of which genetic traits to look for in the child at risk for developing an AUD.

Adolescence

Adolescence is a time of exploration as the individual establishes the foundation for personal identity in later years. Experimental substance use, especially of alcohol and marijuana, can be a part of this process of exploration. Unfortunately, there are no firm boundaries between experimental use, substance abuse, and substance addiction (Y. Kaminer, 2008). *Total* abstinence from alcohol and the drugs of abuse during adolescence is rare, with only 11% of adolescents abstaining from all chemicals throughout adolescence (Chassin et al., 2004). Thus for the majority of adolescents, the experimental abuse of

alcohol and marijuana appears to be the norm. The implications of substance use behavior, however, need to be interpreted in light of the adolescent's age and developmental level (Wagner, 2009).

It is important to keep in mind that substance *abuse* in adolescence is not always a prodrome to substance *addiction* later in life (Heyman, 2009; Y. Kaminer, 2008). Admittedly, some adolescent substance abusers do go on to become addicted to alcohol or drugs. The majority do not. This is supported by the study conducted by Knight et al. (2007), who found that whereas 44% of the 2133 12- to 18-year-olds screened were identified as having either a past or current history of alcohol and/or drug abuse, the majority of these individuals did not progress to substance dependence later in life.

Clinicians lack definitive criteria to identify adolescents with an SUD, how to assess their motivation to participate in a treatment program, age-appropriate rehabilitation techniques, or the effectiveness of the rehabilitation program (Y. Kaminer, 2001; Knight, 2000; Wagner, 2009). These problems may explain why about half of the adolescents who successfully complete treatment relapse within 90 days of discharge, and why two-thirds relapse within 6 months following discharge from a treatment program (Wagner, 2009). Unfortunately, research evidence suggests that adolescents appear to be more vulnerable to the addictive potential of alcohol or drugs than are adults. Where adults might require 2–7 years of habitual substance abuse before they become addicted to that substance, adolescents might become addicted to the same compound in as little as 12–18 months (Freimuth, 2005). Thus relapse following treatment is especially serious for adolescent substance abusers.

Problems in Diagnosis and Treatment of Adolescent SUDs

Over 1.1 million adolescents appear to meet the criteria for admission to a substance abuse rehabilitation program, but less than 1 in 10 is admitted to such a program (Griswold, Arnoff, Kernan, & Khan, 2008; Wagner, 2009). There are many reasons for this. For example, each state varies as to the legal requirements under which an assessment of adolescent SUDs might be carried out. Parental consent might be required in some states whereas in others it is not required, a factor that might contribute to parental denial.[16] In some states the adolescent has the right to refuse to

---

[16]"If we do not allow the assessment to be done, we will not have to face the possibility that our child is abusing alcohol or drugs."

participate in the assessment, whereas in other states the adolescent lacks this privilege because they are juveniles. It is imperative that assessors be familiar with the legal requirements of their area of practice to avoid violating the law.

One immediate challenge facing the assessor working with adolescents is that many people in this age group view substance abuse as a sign of moral weakness, making it difficult for them to admit to the abuse of chemicals (Corrigan, Lurie et al., 2005). Another challenge facing the assessor is the fact that self-report of individual substance use is unreliable, as evidenced by the fact that so many adolescents admitted to hospital emergency rooms for chest pain deny the abuse of cocaine in spite of having cocaine metabolites in their urine.

Further, the standards for assessment, diagnosis, or treatment decisions are still in their infancy at best (Wagner, 2009). For the most part, the diagnostic criteria used for adolescents are based on standards used for adults, which are not applicable to this special subpopulation of substance abusers (Y. Kaminer & Buckstein, 2005; Myrick & Wright, 2008; Wagner, 2009). Adolescent substance abusers, for example, are less likely to report tolerance to their drug(s) of choice than are adults because they have not had sufficient time for significant levels of tolerance to develop (Myrick & Wright, 2008). Yet tolerance to a chemical(s) is often viewed as a diagnostic milestone by assessors who work with adolescent substance abusers.

Adolescents present a special challenge to health care professionals, which might be why less than half of the pediatricians surveyed reported that they screen adolescent patients for tobacco, alcohol, or drug use disorders (Winters & Kaminer, 2008). This may reflect what Van Hook et al. (2007) identified as the "Six T's" that block physician identification and referral of adolescent substance abusers: (a) lack of time, (b) lack of training, (c) presence of competing medical problems that require treatment, (d) lack of treatment resources, (e) tendency for parents to remain in the exam room, making the adolescent less likely to reveal substance abuse, and (f) tendency for physicians to not have an awareness of screening tools available to the them. Less than a quarter of pediatricians surveyed reported that they felt comfortable assessing an adolescent for an SUD or making a referral to a treatment program, and this issue is often not discussed with the adolescent during a visit to the physician ("Doctors Often Skip Health Behavior Conversations With Teens," 2008). This is unfortunate because research has found that

up to 65% of adolescents would like to discuss their substance use with their physician (Griswold et al., 2008).

Myrick and Wright (2008) suggested that assessors working with adolescents review their (a) educational status (including school attendance, academic performance, and disciplinary actions, if any), (b) the possibility of loss of control over the substance(s) being abuse, (c) familial relationships (including possible conflict within the family), (d) peer relationship patterns (substance-abusing peers or nonusing peers, for example), (e) legal status (including history of underage drinking citations, arrests for possession of marijuana, and so on), (f) how they use their free time, and, (g) history of physical or sexual abuse. These are potential markers for the adolescent substance abuser, according to the authors.

One way to improve the accuracy of an assessment of adolescents with a possible SUD is to establish an extensive database of the individuals and their possible substance use patterns (Evans & Sullivan, 2001; Juhnke, 2002). The pediatrician who asks the parents about their impressions of their adolescent's growth, maturation, and substance use behaviors would form a far different clinical impression of the adolescent than would the physician who asked the adolescent directly and in private about possible substance abuse. However, even in situations where the adolescent is promised confidentiality they still might underreport their substance abuse (Stein & Rogers, 2008). Thus the assessor must seek to obtain as wide a database as possible in the time allotted for the assessment.

Screening/Assessment Tools[17]

In the last decade of the 20th century and the first decade of the 21st century, a number of well-designed substance abuse screening and assessment tools for use with children and adolescents were introduced. In this section, we will look at some of the instruments that have been developed or adapted for use with this population.

One of the more popular instruments is the *CRAFFT*, which is a short verbal instrument. This assessment tool includes questions about whether adolescents have ever been a passenger in a vehicle where the driver was under

---

[17]It is not possible to review every screening or assessment instrument available. This summary is limited to some of the more popular or, in the opinion of this author, better designed instruments.

the influence of chemicals, used chemicals to relax, or used chemicals when alone. Other issues addressed are whether they have used chemicals to help them relax or to forget problems, or if their substance use has ever resulted in psychosocial problems for the individual.

At the beginning of the last decade of the 20th century the *Drug Use Screening Inventory-Revised* (DUSI-R) was introduced (Kirisci, Mezzich, & Tarter, 1995). This copyrighted 159-item instrument was designed for adolescents (or adults) who are suspected of having an SUD. The DUSI-R requires only about 10 minutes for the individual to complete, and it assesses such potential problem areas as the individual's (a) substance use behavior, (b) general behavior patterns, (c) health status, (d) psychiatric health status, (e) social skills level, (f) peer relationships, and (g) leisure/recreational habits. The DUSI-R is not diagnostic in itself, but does identify problem areas that might be addressed in a clinical interview.

The *Drug and Alcohol Problem (DAP) Quick Screen* (R. H. Schwartz & Wirth, 1990) was designed for use by physicians in the office setting in approximately 10 minutes. One advantage of this instrument is that it attempts to identify adolescent suicidal thinking, an area of growing concern because the number of adolescent suicides is so high.

One instrument that is in the public domain is the *Problem Oriented Screening Instrument for Teenagers* (POSIT), developed by the National Institute on Drug Abuse (NIDA) and the National Institutes of Health (NIH). This instrument is composed of 139 questions that are answered either "yes" or "no" by respondents 12–19 years of age. Individuals' response pattern provides information on their (a) substance abuse patterns, (b) physical health, (c) mental health, (d) family relations, (e) peer relations, (f) educational status, (g) social skills, and (h) aggressive behavior/delinquency tendencies. Identified problem areas are then examined in more detail through clinical interviews with the client.

One of the more popular instruments used when assessing an adolescent is the adolescent version of the *Substance Abuse Subtle Screening Inventory-3* (SASSI-3) (Juhnke, 2002). This instrument is used with adolescents 16 years of age or older who have at least a fourth-grade reading level. The SASSI-3 is discussed in more detail in Chapter 28, but the reader should know that an adolescent version of this instrument does exist and might be used to help assess the adolescent client.

The *Adolescent Drinking Index* (ADI) is occasionally utilized by assessors, although there is limited data on

its effectiveness with adolescents who attempt to minimize their substance use behaviors (Stein & Rogers, 2008). Another instrument that is occasionally used when assessing adolescents for possible SUDs is the *Adolescent Drug Abuse Diagnosis* (ADAD) test. It attempts to measure nine different areas of the adolescent's life and then rate the degree of distress caused by substance abuse in each of these domains. This instrument can also be used to assess pretreatment and posttreatment changes for the adolescent (S. L. Johnson, 2003).

A rapidly administered verbal screening instrument is the *TWEAK*, which asks adolescents about Tolerance, whether others have ever been Worried about their substance use, whether they have ever used an Eye opener in the morning, whether they have ever experienced Amnesia during periods of substance use, and K (cut) their attempts to cut down on substance use (S. L. Johnson, 2003). This instrument may also be used with adults and is a useful mnemonic[18] device for the assessor to use with both adolescents and adults.

A simple screening tool for smoking in preadolescents was offered by Doubeni, Li, Fouayzi, and DiFranza, (2008). The authors suggested two simple questions:

1. Would it be easy for you to obtain a cigarette?
2. Do you have friends who smoke?

A "yes" answer to either question identified a child who was at high risk for cigarette smoking, and appropriate intervention procedures should be initiated, the authors suggested. Finally, the *Teen Addiction Severity Index* (TASI) is occasionally used by assessors attempting to interpret the adolescent's substance use pattern. However, the normative samples for this instrument were small, and generalizability to the general adolescent population is open to question (Stein & Rogers, 2008).

As this section has demonstrated, although there are a number of instruments used in the screening and assessment of substance abuse, each has serious flaws or limitations, and the data provided by each test should be interpreted with caution.

Adolescent rehabilitation programs

Having identified an adolescent with an SUD, an assessor is then faced with a dilemma: There are few

---

[18]See Glossary.

programs tailored to adolescents available (Y. Kaminer, 2008). It was found that less than one-third of rehabilitation programs offered a program specific for adolescents, and the quality of such programs is, on average, only fair (Knudsen, 2009). Inpatient adolescent rehabilitation programs tend to have a greater number of the ancillary services necessary for a successful outcome compared to adolescent outpatient programs. Thus treatment resources for the adolescent abuser are often less than desirable.

Referrals for substance abuse treatment come from many different sources. The juvenile court system, and especially the emerging "drug court" program, will often refer an offender for evaluation with the stipulation that the adolescent also follow treatment recommendations. School officials will often refer a suspected substance abuser for assessment, and it is not unusual for parents to make such referrals, especially in strict homes where even the first hint of substance abuse is not tolerated. The phenomenon of home urine drug tests has contributed to this process, although possibly at the cost of damaging parent–child trust. Parents rarely understand that a "positive" urine toxicology test, which is to say a urine sample with evidence of drug metabolites in it, does not in itself prove that the child or adolescent is *addicted* to a compound, a point that might result in further conflict (Winters & Kaminer, 2008). There are also "false positive" results, which will be discussed further in Chapter 34.

During the rehabilitation process, treatment center staff need to consider adolescents' level of cognitive maturity when working with them. Adolescents and adults process environmental stimuli through different cognitive mechanisms, making their rehabilitation problematic because treatments developed for adults will not automatically be applicable to adolescents. As a group, adolescents tend to have a rather immature view of life and the consequences of their decisions. Unfortunately, this simplistic oversimplification may result in treatment center staff interpreting cognitive immaturity as a sign of denial or resistance.

It is not unusual for adolescents to view substance abuse in a different light than to their parents. For example, many adolescents do not view "sipping" liquor or beer as actually "drinking," although their parents might have a far different opinion (Rosenbloom, 2005). Further, like their adult counterparts, adolescents who do abuse alcohol or illicit drugs may minimize their substance abuse. They might admit to the use of "one or two beers," for example, without revealing that the beer cans are 40 ounces[19] in size, and not the more traditional 12 ounces (Rosenbloom, 2005). Finally, it is not uncommon for treatment center staff to interpret age-specific rebellion as an "acting-out" behavior rather than adolescent self-medication of emotional trauma (Jorgensen, 2001). This underscores the need for a multidisciplinary assessment of adolescents to allow for an accurate identification of their strengths, weaknesses, their stage of substance abuse, and their level of maturity and adaptive style, so the staff might better understand how to work with them.

Stages of Adolescent Substance Abuse

There are a number of paths that adolescents might follow once they begin to abuse chemicals. Two examples are the models suggested by Greydanus and Patel (2005) and Parekh (2006). Each suggests that adolescent substance abuse proceeds through five stages and are contrasted in Table 20-1.

As has been stated before, the adolescent's progression from one stage to the next in either model is *not* automatic. Social forces and the normal developmental process during adolescence can either facilitate or block the progression from one stage of substance abuse to another. In extreme cases however, the time between entering Stage 0 and the start of Stage 4 can be just a matter of a few months (Greydanus & Patel, 2005).

Both models require that the adolescent must be exposed to a drug(s) of abuse and then learn what to expect from the substance(s) in question. In each model, adolescents who develop an SUD also experience a change in friendship patterns as they begin to drift away from nonusing peers to a new peer group more accepting of substance use. After extended periods of abuse, adolescents might reach the "burnout" point, where they abuse chemicals not to enjoy the effects but to avoid withdrawal and feel "normal"[20] again. It is during this stage that abusers also begin to experience any of the various biopsychosocial complications induced by constant substance abuse, which can include memory loss, memory "flashback" experiences, paranoia, anger, guilt, shame, depression, possible suicide attempts, cognitive impairments, and so on.

---

[19]Sometimes referred to as "silos" or "tall boys" by the drinker.

[20]"Normal" in this sense of the word connotes a state of mind where the person is not exposed to the emotions normally suppressed by the abuse of the drugs, which the individual has now come to believe is the normal state of mind.

TABLE 20-1 COMPARISON OF TWO MODELS OF ADOLESCENT SUBSTANCE ABUSE

PAREKH (2006)	GREYDANUS AND PATEL (2005)
(1) Initiation: first use of a mood-altering chemical (either alone or with peers).	Stage 0: No substance abuse, but is very interested in learning more about them, suffers low self-esteem, and is vulnerable to peer pressure.
(2) Learning the mood swing: Adolescent is taught (by experience or by others) what to look for in the abuse of a chemical(s).	Stage 1: Experimentation. No real negative consequences encountered, yet.
(3) Regular use/seeking the mood: Continued abuse to maintain substance-induced pleasure.	Stage 2: Adolescent actively seeks drug's effects; centers life more and more around use of chemicals.
(4) Abuse/harmful consequences: Adolescent begins to encounter academic performance problems, etc., but continues to abuse chemicals.	Stage 3: Preoccupation with substance use by adolescent. Mood swings and acting-out behaviors noted in this stage. First negative consequences of substance abuse encountered.
(5) Adolescent is now physically addicted to a chemical(s) and is trapped in a cycle of compulsive use to avoid withdrawal.	Stage 4: Continued consequences. Substance use continues so that abuser can feel "normal" again.

Adolescent Addiction to Chemicals

The question of whether the adolescent substance abuser might become physically addicted to a compounds(s) is quite controversial (Commission on Adolescent Substance and Alcohol Abuse, 2005). This is because the signs of addiction normally encountered with adults who are dependent on a drug are not always seen in the adolescent substance abuser (Evans & Sullivan, 2001; Pumariega & Kilgus, 2005). Because of the relatively short duration of their alcohol use, adolescents do not always demonstrate the alcohol withdrawal symptoms suggestive of an AUD in adults. Adolescent substance abusers also rarely develop characteristic patterns of organ damage seen in adults addicted to these same chemicals, however they might admit to the development of *tolerance* to their drug of choice. Further, because the dynamics and consequences of SUDs are different between adolescent and adult substance abusers, adults with an SUD who die usually do so because of substance-related illness. Adolescents with an SUD who die usually do so because of their involvement in risky behaviors such as driving while under the influence of chemicals, homicides, accidents, and suicides (D. B. Clark, Martin, & Cornelius, 2008).

A common misconception is that adolescents who abuse substances will "mature out" of their SUD. The difference between those adolescents who will "mature out" of their SUD and those for whom it is only a passing phase is difficult to determine, at best. Some adolescents who drink heavily have been found to continue this pattern of alcohol use into early adulthood, hardly evidence that they rapidly "mature out" of their

alcohol use (Rohde, Lewinsohn, Kahle, Seeley, and Brown, 2001; J. E. Wells, Horwood, & Fergusson, 2006). Fully 40% of 12-year-old alcohol abusers appear to meet diagnostic criteria for alcohol dependence for the rest of their lives, suggesting that 60% do "mature out" of this problem behavior (Larimer & Kilmer, 2000). However, Larimer and Kilmer did not provide a time line for this maturational process.

Adolescent Substance Abuse Treatment: A Cause for Optimism?

There is strong evidence suggesting that adolescents with AUDs will respond to treatment better than do adults referred to a rehabilitation program (Kriechbaum & Zernig, 2000). In many cases, the psychological trauma that motivates adolescents to abuse chemicals is easier to access through psychosocial interventions than in adults, because they lack the layers of defenses surrounding those memories (Jorgensen, 2001). Further, although many parents fear the worst, the heavy abuse of alcohol or illicit drugs is often limited to just adolescence (Y. Kaminer, 1999). Research suggests that only a minority of those adolescents who briefly abuse a chemical continue on to become dependent on drugs later in life (Kriechbaum & Zernig, 2000; Larimer & Kilmer, 2000). There is also evidence that for every year that adolescents avoid the abuse of prescription drugs, the risk for developing a future prescription drug use disorder drops 5% (McCabe, West, Morales, Cranford, & Boyd, 2007). Further, the Commission on Adolescent Substance and Alcohol Abuse (2005) concluded that adolescents who began to drink before the age of 15 years were four to six times as likely to develop an AUD as were those who waited until after 21 years of age before drinking.

Is There a Financial Incentive for Overdiagnosis?

It is often surprising to the average person to learn that many treatment programs for substance-abusing adolescents are "for profit," which means that their financial status rests on how many individuals are in treatment there at any given moment. Substance abuse rehabilitation programs have become a "lucrative industry" (T. Bell, 1996, p. 12), and in order to maximize profits many admissions professionals blur the line between use, abuse, and addiction, offering a "one-size-fits-all" style of treatment (Weiner, Abraham, & Lyons, 2001). Not surprisingly, the admissions officers of many of these same treatment centers hold that *any* substance use by adolescents automatically means that there is a drug abuse problem present. Treatment is recommended at the first sign of an SUD in the adolescent on the grounds that because the use of *any* substance is by definition against the law for adolescents, it is a sign of an SUD (Harrison, Fulkerson, & Beebe, 1998).

Many adolescent treatment professionals maintain that treatment for the adolescent is automatically a positive, growth-enhancing experience. This ignores the reality that an unknown percentage of adolescents are *harmed* by intervention or treatment programs (Szalavitz, 2006). The analogy of surgery might not be out of place here. If surgeons were to advocate abdominal surgery, stating that it is automatically a healthy thing for people to do, they would be charged with criminal intent and malpractice in short order. Yet many programs force the adolescent into treatment in spite of possible violation of the rights of the adolescent under the laws of that state, even if this forced treatment admission is at the parents' request (Evans & Sullivan, 2001).

There are adolescent treatment programs where the staff attempt to convince parents that adolescents will be permanently impaired because of the assumed SUD and that they can never be emotionally "whole" without treatment. Lamentably, there is no research to support this philosophy, just as there is no evidence that telling adolescents they are a lifelong addict is either true or healthy for adolescents. Such programs ignore the research evidence, which suggests that the majority of adolescents identified as having an SUD do not continue down the path to chemical addiction (Y. Kaminer & Buckstein, 2005). But the continued existence of the

treatment program, not to mention the paycheck for the treatment center staff, depends on keeping as many adolescents in treatment as possible. This provides an incentive for overdiagnosis of adolescent SUDs.

The Danger of Underdiagnosis

There is strong evidence that the majority of substance-abusing adolescents are never identified as such (Evans & Sullivan, 2001; M. T. Lee, Garnick, Miller, & Horgan, 2004). The implications of this failure are staggering: For example, SUDs are a significant part of the problem of adolescent suicide (T. R. Miller et al., 2006; Simkin, 2002; Weiner et al., 2001). Some of the other risk factors for adolescent suicide include[21] (a) adolescent affective disorders, (b) thoughts of suicide by the adolescent, (c) a family history of depression or suicide, (d) impending court or legal problems, (e) thoughts about joining a deceased loved one, and (f) having easy access to a handgun (Simkin, 2002; Sorter, 2010).

Adolescent substance abuse contributes to disinhibition and high-risk behavior(s), which are in turn a major factor for adolescent accidental injuries (T. R. Miller et al., 2006). Approximately 40% of adolescents treated in one hospital emergency room had evidence of drugs or alcohol in their urine (P. F. Erlich, Brown, & Drongowski, 2006). It has been hypothesized that these behaviors reflect the belief by adolescents that they are invulnerable, or that bad things do not happen to them but always to somebody else. However, Borowsky, Ireland, and Resnick (2009) suggested that for about 15% of adolescents, engaging in high-risk behaviors reflects a belief that they will die at an early age. The authors found that almost 11% of their sample thought that they had only a 50% chance of living to the age of 35, for example. However, although this information was used to guide medical treatment for the injured adolescent, it was found to rarely result in a referral for assessment and possible treatment. Nevertheless, an accidental injury or other high-risk behaviors for the adolescent might be one of the first signs that the adolescent might have an SUD.

The substance abuse rehabilitation professional must find a middle ground between overdiagnosis and underdiagnosis, a process that is difficult at best and possibly impossible. However, this dilemma does underscore the need for accurate diagnostic criteria to identify adolescent substance abusers.

---

[21]This list is hardly comprehensive. The topic of adolescent suicide is the subject of many books, and the reader is referred to one of the many books or research papers on this subject.

Possible Diagnostic Criteria for Childhood and Adolescent SUDs

Children

Zucker et al. (2009) warned that the "predictors" of possible SUDs in children or adolescents must be viewed as probabilities rather than firm indications of the existence of an SUD in either age group. With this warning in mind, some of the identified risk factors for childhood alcohol use include (Millar, 2009; Zucker et al., 2009):

- *Having a friend or close sibling who uses alcohol or drugs*
- *Internalizing feelings instead of expressing them*
- *Externalization of feelings*
- *Social problems*
- *Poor impulse control*
- *Engaging in risk-taking behavior(s)*
- *Poor parental supervision and/or inconsistent discipline*
- *Trauma (including parental divorce)*
- *Victimization*
- *Poor academic performance*
- *Problems controlling the child's temper outbursts*
- *Parental alcoholism*
- *Caucasian heritage*

The issue of internalization versus externalization as a predictor of a possible SUD by children would initially appear to be contradictory. However, each identifies a different pattern of risk factors applied to different subpopulations of children (Zucker et al., 2009). Externalizers tend to demonstrate poor emotional and behavioral self-control, possibly finding full expression in those children diagnosed as having a CD according to Zucker et al. (2009). In contrast, children who are internalizers tend to have experience anxiety, depression, shyness, and excessive inhibition, according to the authors.

Adolescents

There is no single characteristic profile to warn parents that their adolescent child is at high risk for abusing alcohol and/or drugs. Every adolescent is unique and thus will present the assessor with a unique combination of strengths, needs, and weaknesses (Weiner et al., 2001). As noted earlier, adolescent affective disorders, CDs, and a history of sexual abuse are all indicators of a possible SUD (D. B. Clark et al., 2002; Crowley, 2007; Evans & Sullivan, 2001; S. L. Johnson, 2003; Thatcher & Clark, 2008). Although not definitive, following is a list of diagnostic hints of possible SUDs in a given adolescent (S. L. Johnson, 2003; Y. Kaminer, 2008; Kirisci, Vanyukov, & Tarter, 2005; Kriechbaum & Zernig, 2000; L. Miller, Davies, & Greenwald, 2000; Parekh, 2006; Wills et al., 2001):

1. Family history of SUDs
2. Affective illness
3. History of suicide attempts
4. Loss of loved one(s)
5. Low self-esteem
6. High levels of stress
7. Poor social skills, maladaptive coping skills, social isolation
8. Troubled relationship with parents (either items 9 or 10)
9. Parents with permissive attitude toward deviant behavior
10. Parents with overly strict attitude toward deviant behaviors
11. Adolescent coming from a single-parent or blended family
12. Feelings of alienation or running away from home
13. Low commitment or low expectations for school
14. Early use of cigarettes
15. High levels of involvement with drug-using peers
16. Antisocial behavior
17. Poor impulse control
18. Early sexual experience
19. Early experimental substance use
20. Legal problems during adolescence
21. Absence of strong religious beliefs
22. Unsuccessful attempts to stop or cut back on substance use
23. History of substance withdrawal
24. Having experienced one or more alcohol-induced "blackouts"
25. Continued substance abuse in spite of consequences
26. Use of chemicals prior to or during school

The greater the number of the preceding criteria that individuals have experienced, the higher the odds are that they have an SUD. But just concluding that the adolescent has an SUD is insufficient. Suris, Akre, Berchtold, Jeannin, and Michaud (2007) found that there were different subgroups of adolescent marijuana abusers. Surprisingly, the authors found that some adolescent marijuana abusers did not use tobacco products at all. Such adolescents were (a) more likely to be involved with sports activities, (b) be on an academic track, and (c) have higher academic achievement levels, as compared with adolescents who abused both marijuana and tobacco products.

Surprisingly, many adolescents who abuse alcohol do so, at least in part, because their *parents* supplied them with the alcohol ("Underage Alcohol Use," 2008). At least 1 adolescent in 16 (6.25% of the total) received alcohol from a guardian or parent, whereas more than 40% of those surveyed obtained the alcohol used in the past 30 days from an adult, who usually supplied it at no cost ("Underage Alcohol Use," 2008).

Whereas *loss of control* over substance abuse is one factor that clinicians look for when working with adult substance abusers, it is important to keep in mind that the loss of control expresses itself differently for adolescents. Individuals in this age group who have an SUD usually express loss of control through a violation of personal rules ("I will drink only on weekends," or "I will not use marijuana tonight," for example). Thus the assessor must be aware of adolescent expressions of loss of control over substance use and not rely on the adult criteria for this problem. In the next section we will review some of the screening instruments used to detect SUDs in adolescents.

Screening Instruments

The diagnostic process is often aided through the use of one or more screening instruments, such as those discussed next. A useful screening instrument is the CRAFFT (Knight, 2005; Parekh, 2006). This copyrighted instrument is administered in less than 5 minutes and addresses domains such as whether the individual has ever been a passenger in a car where the driver was intoxicated, use of chemicals to relax, use of chemicals while alone or to forget pain issues, having been confronted by family or friends about one's substance use, or psychosocial trouble because of substance use. A positive answer on two or more of these items suggests the need for a more in-depth assessment of the individual's substance use pattern (Knight, 2005). A "yes" answer to three or more items correctly identified approximately two-thirds of adolescent substance abusers (Knight, 2005).

Although the CAGE, TWEAK,[22] and AUDIT are established screening tools when working with adult

clients, they are of limited effectiveness when working with adolescents or college students (Boyd, McCabe, & Morales, 2005; Parekh, 2006). The former two instruments are relatively insensitive to adolescent alcohol abuse, although the AUDIT might be modified to be more useful in working with this population (Boyd et al., 2005). The SASSI-3[23] has been found useful in the identification of adolescents who might have an SUD, and might present a more suitable alternative to the CAGE, TWEAK, and AUDIT for assessing possible adolescent substance abuse problems.

The team of R. L. Brown, Leonard, Saunders, and Papasoulioutis (1997) suggested a simple, two-question screening instrument:

1. In the last year, have you ever drunk or used drugs more than you meant to?
2. Have you felt that you wanted or needed to cut down on your drinking or drug use in the past year?

A "yes" response to either question suggests a need for a further in-depth assessment, according to the authors, whereas a "yes" response to both questions is thought to be 75% accurate in identifying substance abusers.

Consequences of Child/Adolescent Substance Abuse

Perhaps the most serious consequence of substance abuse in childhood or adolescence is the abuser's death. This might be the result of any of a wide variety of mechanisms, many of which are discussed in this or earlier chapters. However, another apparent consequence of substance abuse before the age of 19 years appears to be impaired psychosocial functioning as an adult (Rohde et al., 2007). The authors followed a sample of 773 individuals who were substance abusers as adolescents and found that the former substance-abusing adolescents tended to have less formal education, poor coping skills, and low global functioning, as well as a higher incidence of suicide attempts. Indeed, Sorter (2010) identified substance abuse as a major factor in adolescent suicide attempts. These findings suggest that substance use during childhood or adolescence might have lifelong consequences.

---

[22]See Chapter 28.

[23]Discussed in Chapter 28.

Substance Abuse Rehabilitation for Children or Adolescents SUDs

It has been estimated that 6% of adolescents aged 12–17 years should be in a treatment program for an AUD, whereas 5.4% need treatment for an SUD other than alcohol (Winters & Kaminer, 2008). The percentage of children and adolescents who are abusing a substance but whose abuse has not reached the point where treatment supervised by a substance abuse rehabilitation professional is not known. This data underscores the need for adolescent substance abuse rehabilitation programs, as the approximately 180,000 adolescents who enter a substance abuse treatment program each year represent only the tip of the iceberg, so to speak (Crowley, 2007).

Even after admission to treatment, it is important to keep in mind that there are many factors that can interfere with the effectiveness of treatment. Some of these include: (a) unrealistic parental expectations for treatment, (b) hidden agendas for treatment by both the adolescent and parents, (c) parental psychopathology, and (d) parental substance use. Although it is useful to include the parents and family members in the treatment program, often they refuse to participate in the rehabilitation efforts. An example of points "c" and "d" just listed is found in the observation that even parental smoking has been found to influence the substance use patterns of the adolescent, suggesting that parents lose credibility when they try to prevent adolescent SUDs if they are themselves engaging in the use of a substance (Keyes et al., 2008). In other words, it is hard to argue that drugs are not good for you when you have a cigarette hanging from your lips.

The Special Needs of the Adolescent in a Substance Abuse Rehabilitation Programs

Adolescents in treatment programs present special challenges to the rehabilitation program staff. First, the developmental process continues even while the adolescent is in a rehabilitation program, and thus the adolescent's cognitive abilities, strengths, weaknesses, and defensive style will possibly change over the course of treatment if it is carried out over extended periods of time. Further, treatment must address ancillary issues such as sexually transmitted diseases, birth control, and vocational needs. Another issue that should be addressed by rehabilitation center staff is the adolescent's

cultural heritage. A diverse treatment program staff will enable the adolescent to find at least one person to identify with during treatment.

The format of group therapy, a mainstay in most rehabilitation programs, must be modified for adolescents. First, such groups should not be mixed-gender groups, but rather, restricted to single gender because of the developmental issues for each sex during this phase of life (D. W. Brook, 2008). Such groups should also include problem-solving training and a family therapy component (D. W. Brook, 2008). Adolescents benefit from a here-and-now focus, rather than on possible long-term consequences from their substance use, and confrontation is more readily accepted if it comes from a peer rather than a staff person (D. W. Brook, 2008). The group leader must also focus on limit-setting issues more than would be typical for a group with adults (D. W. Brook, 2008).

Adolescent involvement in the juvenile criminal justice system presents an issue that should be addressed, and treatment staff should include child welfare and social service agencies as necessary for the individual's rehabilitation. Finally, the adolescent's social needs must be addressed. Adolescents who had at least one nonusing peer, and who remained in treatment or aftercare for approximately a year were found to be less likely to relapse (Latimer, Newcomb, Winters, & Stinchfield, 2000). If there are 12-step programs for adolescents, this might be a useful adjunct to the rehabilitation program. Al-Anon might prove to be a valuable support for the family members of the adolescent in rehabilitation. Thus the rehabilitation process should be sufficiently long and intense enough to allow for these issues to be adequately addressed during recovery. Finally, the rehabilitation center staff should be aware of the unique effects of the drugs of abuse on the adolescent. In the following sections, we will look at the effects of some of the more common drugs of abuse on child and adolescent growth and development.

Alcohol

Research evidence strongly suggests that alcohol dependence, as diagnosed by the *Diagnostic and Statistical Manual of Mental Disorders* (4th edition, text revision), peaks at around the age of 18 years and declines over the next 30 years (Crowley, 2007). This is consistent with the observation that approximately three-quarters of high school seniors will admit to the use of alcohol at least once. Adolescents under the age of 21 are thought to consume 17–20% of all alcoholic beverages sold each year in the United States

(Commission on Adolescent Substance and Alcohol Abuse, 2005; Kaminer, 2008). In spite of this fact, there is a lack of data on how child/adolescent alcohol use might affect the physical or emotional growth of the individual.

Marijuana

Researchers believe that 4.5 million teenagers used marijuana in 2008,[24] exposing them to the endocannabinoid-like chemical THC. One function of the endocannabinoids[25] is to guide neural growth during the development of the cortex. This region of the brain is still in development during childhood and adolescence, and thus adolescent marijuana abuse holds the potential to interfere with normal neurocognitive development in the adolescent abuser (Gold & Dupont, 2008). The long-term implications of adolescent marijuana abuse are still being explored, but animal-based research suggests that marijuana abuse during adolescence might permanently alter serotonin and norepinephrine levels in the adult brain (Bambico, Nguyen, Katz, & Gobbi, 2009). Theoretically this could lead to increased anxiety and depression in humans who engage in daily marijuana abuse in adolescence, however this has not been proven. Further, between 33 and 40% of adolescents who smoke marijuana daily will become addicted to it (Crowley, 2007; Gruber & Pope, 2002). Many of these individuals continue to use marijuana in part to avoid withdrawal symptoms,[26] a fact that may have lifelong consequences for that individual's cortical development during this critical period of life.

The adolescent brain is still developing well into the early 20s. This developmental process contributes to the fact that a marijuana use disorder (MUD) in the 15-year-old manifests itself differently, follows a different path, and might have different neurobehavioral consequences, than an MUD in a young adult (Ellickson et al., 2004). Clinicians who attempt to identify adolescent marijuana addiction must keep in mind that this disorder might manifest itself differently in adolescents than in adults. One characteristic that might identify adolescents with a marijuana addiction is that they started to use it prior to the age of 16 and that they report having positive experiences when they first used it (Fergusson, Horwood, Lunskey, & Madden, 2003).

Tobacco

The purchase of tobacco products by people under the age of 21 is illegal in many stages, which automatically means that it is illegal for children to smoke at all. By the age of 18 years, 66% of adolescents in the United States have tried cigarettes, and 13% smoke at least two packs of cigarettes a day (Y. Kaminer & Tartar, 2004). In Russia, it is not unknown for children as young as 10 years of age to be cigarette smokers (Tobacco, 2009).

Unfortunately, there is an emerging and quite impressive body of evidence that supports the argument that the tobacco industry was actively manipulating the menthol levels in cigarettes with the intention of enticing adolescents and younger adults to begin smoking. Menthol levels were used to cover the harsh taste of cigarette smoke and were found to be more attractive to adolescents than nonmenthol brands, thus acting as an incentive for the adolescent or young adult to begin smoking, Kreslake, Wayne, Alkpert, Hoh, and Connolly (2008) suggested.

Opioids

The diversion of prescribed narcotic analgesics has become a major problem in the past two decades. This should not be surprising: On the basis of their animal research, Zhang et al. (2008) examined the rate of self-administration of oxycodone by adolescent and adult mice. The authors found that the lowest levels of oxycodone that resulted in increased self-administration in adolescent mice did not interest adult mice in their sample group, suggesting that there are differences between how the adolescent and adult mice responded to this compound. This might explain why oxycodone is a popular drug of abuse among adolescents, with approximately 4% of adolescents surveyed admitted to having abused it at least once. An additional 9.7% of adolescents surveyed admitted to the abuse of Vicodin at least once, although it is not clear what degree of overlap exists between these two groups of adolescents (Wunsch, 2007).

Unfortunately, children and adolescents seem to believe the myth that narcotic analgesics are not addictive if ingested orally, only to find that the reverse is true. It is not uncommon then for adolescents to turn to heroin to avoid opioid withdrawal symptoms when they are unable to obtain their drug of choice.

The issue of child and adolescent abuse of opioids is of special concern because the abuse of these compounds in growing in popularity. In cases of adolescent opioid addiction, the standard treatment has been counseling coupled with a 2-week "taper" from opioids

---

[24]The last year for which data is available.

[25]See Glossary.

[26]Discussed in Chapter 10.

through the use of a buprenorphine[27] or naloxone[28] compound (Woody et al., 2008). Woody et al. examined the use of longer-term (12-week) use of buprenorphine-naloxone followed by detoxification and concluded that this approach was more effective than the standard 2-week detoxification sequence combined with substance abuse rehabilitation counseling, as measured by the number of opioid-free urine toxicology tests and patient retention in treatment. However, the authors also found that by the end of 12 weeks the number of adolescents who remained in treatment following the extended treatment was approximately the same as those who received the standard treatment.

Hallucinogens

There is no known data at this time. However, it is observed that compounds like MDMA are capable of causing memory disturbances, which may be permanent.

Inhalants

There is no additional data beyond what is discussed in Chapter 13.

Cocaine

It is estimated that by the age of 18 years, 8% of adolescents will admit to the use of cocaine at least (Y. Kaminer & Tarter, 2004). The risks of adolescent cocaine abuse appear to parallel those of cocaine abuse in adults. No age-specific dangers have been identified, although it should be pointed out that cocaine-induced strokes or heart attacks will have lifelong consequences. Sudden cardiac death will have lifelong consequences for adolescents, at least for the few moments that they remain alive after the cessation of cardiac activity.

Other CNS Stimulants

There is an impressive body of evidence suggesting that methcathinone, which has virtually disappeared in the United States, has been resurrected as a drug of abuse in England. The core methcathinone molecule is often modified, forming a variety of methcathinone-like compounds that are also found in England. The effects of these compounds on childhood or adolescent growth and development are not known at this time.

Other Compounds Abused by Children and Adolescents

There are clinical examples of children mixing nail polish remover with soda then drinking the obtained mixture to induce a state of euphoria (Brust, 2004). The extent of and long-term consequences of this practice are not known at this time.

Chapter Summary

Although society has reawakened to the problem of child and adolescent substance abuse or addiction, there remains a lack of serious research into the problem or its solution(s). It is known that peer pressure, the media's portrayal of substance use, parental substance use, and self-esteem are all intertwined and play a role in the adolescent's decision to begin and continue substance abuse, but the exact role of these forces is not known. Yet child or adolescent substance abuse can have lifelong consequences. A cocaine-induced stroke at the age of 17 does not resolve when the adolescent turns 18 and becomes a legal adult, for example. Injuries sustained in an alcohol-related motor vehicle accident, even if the adolescent was only a passenger, will have lifelong implications for the individual's health and potential for advancement.

In the face of a dearth of clinical research to guide the treatment professional, it is necessary to steer a cautious path between overdiagnosis and underdiagnosis of an SUD. Just as is true for surgery, the treatment professional must weigh the potential benefits against the possible harm from this process, and there is indeed a potential for harm from an intervention effort that is poorly executed or forced on an adolescent who has engaged only in experimental substance use. Many adolescents "mature out" of their substance abuse as they reach young adulthood (Szalavitz, 2006). Others continue to abuse chemicals in a problematic way. The diagnostic criteria to identify those who are more likely to continue to develop an SUD are still lacking. Thus treatment professionals have no established principle to guide them in their efforts to identify, assess, or treat children or adolescents with SUDs. This is an evolving area of pediatric medicine, and health care professionals must attempt to assess and treat child and adolescent substance abusers while the guidelines for assessment and treatment are still being developed. It is a daunting challenge.

---

[27]Discussed in Chapter 33.

[28]Discussed in Chapter 33.

CHAPTER 21

Substance Use Disorders in College Students[1]

Introduction

The college experience is a unique experience that, although becoming increasingly common among late adolescents, is still not shared by all late adolescents or young adults. Whereas in 1970 37% of people in the 18- to 19-year-old cohort entered college, in the year 2008 fully 49% of people in this age cohort started college. In spite of this increase in enrollment, only 20–24% of adults over the age of 25 will graduate from college (Furstenberg, 2010). These facts underscore the fact that entry into and especially graduation from college is unique for young adults. It is becoming increasingly clear that behavioral observations of young adults do not automatically apply to this subpopulation and that they are worthy of study as a special subgroup of recent high school graduates. In this chapter, we will examine the emerging evidence suggesting that substance use patterns for those who pursue postsecondary education are different than those seen in high school graduates who do not go on to college.

A Special Environment

The college[2] experience provides late adolescents or young adults[3] a unique environment that is, to some degree, protected from the larger society within which it exists. Within the sheltered environment of a postsecondary educational facility, a sense of community membership evolves for students who reside in both on-campus[4] and off-campus housing.[5] The institution provides an isolated environment in which there is minimal parental supervision for the most part, but in which students are faced with unique academic, behavioral, interpersonal, developmental, and financial

---

[1]In the original editions of this text, this topic was included as a subsection of the chapter on adolescence. However, given the relative importance of this topic, the decision was made to review this material in a separate chapter.

[2]A term that for the sake of this chapter includes college, junior college, or vocational-technical institutions.

[3]For the sake of this chapter, young adult is defined as between 17 and 23 years of age.

[4]A term that includes those who live in fraternity or sorority ("Greek") houses, as well as college dormitory units.

[5]Apartments shared with others, or living with parents and commuting to college, for example.

demands. Their ability to adapt is both tested and often rewarded with opportunities that do not exist outside of the postsecondary environment.

The college experience forces the high school graduate to attempt multiple tasks simultaneously: (a) learning to function independently in a challenging academic environment, (b) developing social networks that might prove supportive (or distracting) from the first task, and (c) possibly dealing with the feelings that follow separation from home for extended periods. During this phase of life, young people's relationship with their parents will also evolve, and often areas of conflict are outgrown as parents assume the new role of mentors in young adults' lives (S. A. Brown et al., 2009). As college students make this transition, they must reexamine their relationship with alcohol and the other drugs of abuse, a process that will continue throughout the college years and that overlaps with the other tasks outlined earlier.

Upon entering college, students begin the process of building a peer relationship support system consistent with their expectations and goals for college. Those students with the strongest motives for attending college are typically more likely to reach out to others with similar values and least likely to abuse alcohol or recreational drugs because this would interfere with their academic goals. This is seen in the fact that although 17.6% of young adults have abused an opioid, only 1.9% of college students report doing so (Schuckit, 2010b). There is, however, a subpopulation of undergraduates who turn to alcohol or other drugs as a means of dealing with the pressure to meet academic expectations (Vaughan, Corbin, & Fromme, 2009). Although alcohol or the other recreational drugs might relieve some of the stress and anxiety experienced by these students during the academic years, such substance abuse also can contribute to a vicious cycle of substance related to poor academic performance, increased stress, increased use of chemicals to address that stress, and then further deterioration in academic performance. Johnson (2010) reported, for example, that one-quarter of college students admitted that their alcohol use had caused drinking-related academic problems such as missing classes, poor grades, or failing to keep up with assigned materials.

In contrast to the student population with strong academic goals, some undergraduates find that heavy alcohol use facilitates the establishment of social relationships with other heavy alcohol users and is a strong motivating factor for continued heavy alcohol use. Unfortunately, there is an inverse relationship between the individuals' level of alcohol use and academic performance, as many students discover to their dismay[6] (Vaughan et al., 2009).

An Evolving Relationship

Alcohol's role in the college environment does not remain static. Over the course of their academic careers, students who were most heavily invested in heavy alcohol use might actually turn their attention to academic studies.[7] This change in priorities might be motivated by the discovery that students are moving closer to graduation and soon will enter the workforce and seek a position in their chosen field (Vaughan et al., 2009). Students also frequently find that upon reaching the status of legal adulthood the thrill of drinking is lost because it is no longer a prohibited activity for them. Some students find that their initial choice of a field of study no longer holds their interest, discovering a passion for an unexpected academic pursuit that they then explore. This change in academic focus[8] forces the student to develop new social networks, possibly establishing social networks with students who are more heavily invested in academic performance rather than alcohol or drug use.

Within the college environment, students discover that there are rewards for their efforts and that life can be unfair, as the whims of fortune dictate. The distinctive demands of postsecondary education may conspire to prevent individuals from completing their chosen program of study for a variety of social or financial reasons. Some students, faced with overwhelming financial demands, either drop out of school, transfer to institutions where the tuition is more affordable, or elect to pursue part-time studies intermixed with employment, to pay for their educational careers. Some students fail to graduate because of illness, accidents, disease, or the unplanned demands of parenthood.[9] Each course of action forces students to establish new social network systems with similar or

---

[6]It is not unusual to discover that those freshmen who were most heavily invested in the party scene in the fall semester are either on academic probation during the spring semester or have been dismissed from college for their poor academic performance in the preceding semester. Unfortunately, this phenomenon is not limited to first-year college students.

[7]Well, it *has* been known to happen, on occasion.

[8]Also known as "switching 'majors.'"

[9]Which itself might be a result of the disinhibition effects of alcohol abuse in the early years of college, and high-risk sexual activity encouraged by alcohol's effects.

different social relationships and to reexamine their substance use pattern.[10]

Students' relationship with alcohol is influenced by their ethnic heritage. Many Latino and African American students are the first members of their family to attend college, thus introducing the possibility that familial pressures to perform well in the college environment and advance socially following graduation are strong factors that might inhibit the use of alcohol by these students (Vaughan et al., 2009). Asian American students often enter college with strong social and familial pressure to succeed in their studies even if they are not the first members of their family to attend college (Vaughan et al., 2009). In contrast, Caucasian students often bring their expectation that heavy alcohol use is an integral part of the college experience, contributing to alcohol abuse by this population of students (Vaughan et al., 2009). Women in all subgroups tend to be more academically oriented, especially during the early stages of the college experience, which tends to protect them from alcohol abuse problems in college (Vaughan et al., 2009).

Although it has not been proven, hypothetically the protected college environment might be one reason why college students are more likely to engage in binge drinking as opposed to their noncollege peers. College students typically were less likely to be binge drinkers in high school than their noncollege peers, a pattern that reverses itself after they enter college. Forty percent of college students surveyed indicated that they had engaged in binge drinking compared with 35% of their noncollege peers, who logically would be assumed to have assumed work and parenting responsibilities (S. A. Brown et al., 2009; Lambert, Fincham, Marks, & Stillman, 2010). College students are also more likely to drink with the goal of intoxication as opposed to their noncollege peers. People who did not enter the college environment report more frequent alcohol use and are more likely to be daily drinkers than their noncollege peers, but tend to also drink less per occasion as well. This fact underscores the differences between these two subgroups of late adolescents or young adults.

One aspect of the college experience is the continuing development of dating relationships and the possibility of encountering a future life partner. Courting rituals might be initiated either to immediately progress to the anticipated goal, or the goal is acknowledged but by agreement is postponed until after graduation.

Couples who wait until after college graduation, an event that takes place in the early to mid-20s, to be married experience a lower divorce rate than do groups who marry before this (Furstenberg, 2010). As is noted elsewhere in this text, partner selection tends to focus on finding a partner whose substance use behavior (and other values) is similar, to minimize the possibility of conflict within the relationship. Alcohol and to a lesser degree other drugs are often intertwined with all of these processes, including those of actual class work, of course.

Scope of the Problem

Substance use by college students is hardly a new phenomenon. In 1354, for example, there was a drunken brawl between students of Oxford University in England and the local townspeople that left 63 students dead (Boyd et al., 2005). Currently, alcohol use remains ubiquitous in the college environment; and with the "chemical revolution" that started in the late 19th century, a growing number of new potential compounds of abuse became available to students in postsecondary institutions. For example, medical and dental school students have on occasion been known to abuse surgical anesthetic agents such as ether for recreational purposes.

The use of stimulants to help the student cram for final examinations is pervasive, and college health center staff members are amazed at how many students discover that they have attention deficit hyperactivity disorder (ADHD) just before final-exam week. However, research has revealed that the percentage of young adults admitting to the abuse of an amphetamine compound is slightly higher for adults who do not go on to attend college as opposed to college students. Further, many students experiment with marijuana, hallucinogens, or other drugs of abuse out of curiosity, and some go on to create an informal program of study through the abuse of such compounds. For the majority of these students such substance use reflects exploratory or experimental use. However in some cases the student's substance use pattern reflects a growing substance use disorder.

Although it is illegal for students under the age of 21 years to drink, just under 90% of college students view alcohol as a central component to their social lives and consume alcohol. Approximately 40% of college undergraduates "engage in heavy episodic drinking at least once every two weeks" (Leeman, Toll, Taylor, & Volpicelli, 2009, p. 553). At many colleges, certain nights are identified as "party" nights, with alcohol use being more

---

[10]Which for some college students begins on Thursday night, depending on their class schedule.

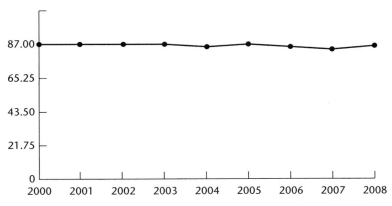

FIGURE 21-1 Percentage of College Students Reporting Lifetime Alcohol Use

common, if not expected, on these nights (Benton, 2009). "Student alcohol use also is very common during special events such as holidays and spring break" (C. M. Lee et al., 2009), and certain colleges are, in spite of their academic credentials, also known as party schools.

Each year the team of L. D. Johnston et al. (2009) conducts a survey of substance use among students and found that the prevalence of alcohol use by college students during the first 8 years of the 21st century has remained relatively steady (see Figure 21-1).

One subpopulation where alcohol use is very common is the college fraternity, although this varies from fraternity (or sorority) to fraternity (or sorority). Students often self-select to gain admission to Greek houses with alcohol use patterns more consistent with their desired level of alcohol intake (Park, Sher, & Krullet, 2009). For example, Benton (2009) found that 86% of fraternity members binge-drink, a figure that is approximately 35% higher than for college students who are not fraternity members. On a similar note, 80% of sorority members who live in a sorority house binge-drink, a figure that is approximately twice that for women who are not sorority members (Benton, 2009). There are many possible explanations for these findings. As noted earlier, the fraternity and sorority system might attract people more likely to engage in abusive drinking, for example. In certain fraternities (or to a lesser degree sororities) alcohol (or other substance) use might be viewed as a rite of passage for the new member.

The Substance Abuse and Mental Health Services Administration (2009) reported that 61% of college students were current alcohol users, 40.5% were binge drinkers,[11] and 16.3% were identified as being heavy

drinkers. Although there has been a slight increase in the percentage of college students who engage in binge drinking in the past decade, this increase was found in the 21- to 24-year age bracket[12] rather than the 18- to 21-year age group (R. W. Hingson, Zha, & Weigzman, 2009). Such binge drinking is, at least in theory, supported by the tradition of happy hour(s) at bars near the college campus, and there is an initiative to stop specialized events at local bars that encourage heavy drinking. It has been found, however, that even if such intervention efforts were successful, college drinkers simply turn to other sources of cheap alcohol and that the frequency of intoxication remains relatively unchanged in this age group (S. K. Wells, Graham, & Purcell, 2009).

Certain colleges have reputations as being party schools, and the rate of alcohol use by students at these institutions tends to be higher than at other colleges in the United States. T. F. Nelson, Xuan, Lee, Weitzman and Wechsler (2009) found that 85–88% of students at these colleges engaged in alcohol use, with 53–58% engaging in heavy, episodic alcohol use, percentages that are significantly higher than the national averages for college alcohol use. To combat this problem there has been an intense effort to curb alcohol use at the 18 colleges with the highest rate of alcohol use, but researchers have found that in the period from 1993 to 2005, the amount of alcohol use on each campus has been virtually the same each year (T. F. Nelson et al., 2009). Further, within the college environment there is a self-selection process through which students seek admission to specialized microenvironments (smoking permitted versus smoking prohibited dormitory units,

---

[11]Defined as the consumption of five 12-ounce cans of beer or standard mixed drinks in a period of drinking.

[12]Student age group for returning students or graduate school students.

for example). The known relationship between cigarette smoking and alcohol use would suggest that some dormitory units are more attractive to smokers or drinkers, encouraging the incoming student to seek admission to these housing units.

An estimated 20.2% of college students abuse illicit drugs (usually marijuana), a rate that was similar to that found in their non-college-bound peers. An estimated 2.1% of college students are thought to have abused a hallucinogenic in the past year, with 1.2% abusing MDMA and 0.6% abusing LSD at some point during the month preceding the survey conducted by the Substance Abuse and Mental Health Services Administration (2009).

One frequently overlooked aspect of college students with SUDs are those students who utilize a performance-enhancing compound such as anabolic steroids, CNS stimulants, and nutritional supplements. The team of Buckman, Yusko, White, and Pandina (2009) examined this student subpopulation and found that students who used performance-enhancing compounds tend to demonstrate more problematic alcohol use patterns, are more likely to engage in tobacco abuse, and are more likely to use cocaine, marijuana, and hallucinogens and abuse prescription drugs. The authors also found that this subpopulation of students was also more likely to engage in risk-taking and sensation-seeking behaviors than age-related college peers who do not use performance-enhancing compounds. Surprisingly, many of the compounds being abused, such as tobacco products or alcohol, detract from athletic performance. This raises the question whether the abuse of performance-enhancing compounds by this subgroup of college students might reflect a more general tendency to abuse chemicals rather than a desire on their part to improve athletic performance. There is a need for further research into the substance use patterns of this group of college students according to Buckman et al. (2009).

If it Is Statistically Normal, Why Worry About College Substance Abuse?

The answer to this question is relatively straightforward:

- *40% of college students admit to having been a passenger in a motor vehicle where the driver was known to be under the influence of alcohol in the past month.*

- *Over 70,000 college students are the victims of alcohol-related sexual assault or "date rape" experiences each year. In student-related rape situations, over 90% knew the perpetrator.*
- *Over 500,000 college students suffer accidental injuries each year while intoxicated.*
- *An estimated 600,000 college students are involved in an alcohol-related fight each year, with the injuries sustained often becoming badges of honor or the source of bragging rights.*
- *59% of off-campus fires involve alcohol, with approximately 10 students per year losing their life in these fires.*
- *Approximately 25% of students admit that their alcohol use has negatively affected their academic performance.*

This is only a short summary of the damage done each year by alcohol or drugs to the college student population. Unfortunately, alcohol use is often viewed as a rite of passage within the college community, a fact that might contribute to the observation that alcohol abuse and dependence is *three times that of the general population,* although noncollege young adults tend to drink slightly more often (Benton, 2009). The relative proportions of college and noncollege drinkers in young adulthood are reviewed in Figure 21-2.

The apparent conflict between the information provided thus far is easily reconciled: College students, although they are less likely to drink on a regular basis than their non-college-bound peers, are more likely to engage in heavy alcohol use when they do drink. The relationship between heavy drinking in young adulthood is shown in Figure 21-3.

There are many reasons for this disparity between the heavy use of alcohol by college students as opposed to their noncollege peers. First, a group of college students tends to *overestimate* their peers' acceptance of drunken behavior, and second they overestimate the number of their peers who are engaging in heavy alcohol use (Park et al., 2009; H. R. White & Johnson, 2004/2005). Unfortunately, because college students place great emphasis on peer group acceptance, this misperception becomes one of the strongest factors in shaping their alcohol use patterns as a student (Marlatt et al., 1998). College students also both overestimate the frequency with which their peers suffer negative consequences from their drinking and come to believe that such negative consequences are not a sign of unhealthy alcohol use but are the norm for their age cohort (Lee, Geisner, Patrick, & Neighbors, 2010). In

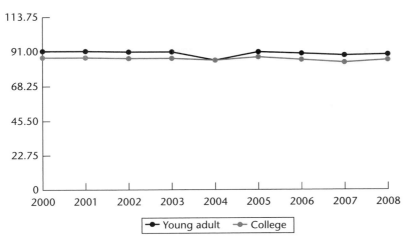

FIGURE 21-2 Relative Percentage of Lifetime Alcohol Use in Young Adults: College Students Versus Noncollege Adults

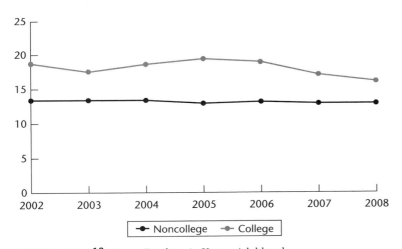

FIGURE 21-3[13] Heavy Drinking in Young Adulthood

other words, students tend to compare their alcohol-related negative consequences with their peers, and rather than experience them as aversive come to view them as typical rather than unhealthy. Through this process, alcohol-related adverse consequences become the expected norm rather than an outcome to be avoided for many college students and thus lose their power to inhibit further alcohol use. Further, there is a relationship between students' living environment and their alcohol use level. College students experience a closed environment, or what is known as "group insulation" (Neighbors, Pedersen, & Roberts, 2009, p. 14). As a result of this process, they are protected against all

but the most severe repercussions of their alcohol use (Neighbors et al., 2009). This process tends to isolate college students from external influences on their behavior, especially alcohol use, with external norms being ignored, classified as irrelevant, or discounted (Neighbors et al., 2009). The outcome of this process holds the potential to be fatal for the student drinker.

Consequences of Substance Use Disorders in the College Age Population

The college student who abuses alcohol or any of the drugs of abuse has the potential to develop any of the adverse consequences for alcohol use/abuse identified

---

[13]Table based on data contained within the report by the Substance Abuse and Mental Health Services Administration (2009).

earlier in this text. In addition to these consequences, however, is the impact of alcohol use on the college student's brain. Neurologically, the individual's brain is in an ongoing state of transition during the college years, as the frontal lobes become fully integrated into the brain's structure and assume their duty in assessing and planning behaviors. It is within this sheltered environment, one where alcohol use is common, that late adolescents or young adults are thrust as they begin their college career.

Unfortunately, the developmental immaturity of the student's brain during the early college years might *predispose* individuals in this age group to alcohol's reinforcing effects in spite of its potential for harm (Spear, 2002). In addition, during the time between when a student is admitted to a college or university and the time of graduation, there is an ongoing process of physical and neurological maturation (De Bellis et al., 2000; Tappert et al., 2004/2005). This process often is difficult to detect, as average college students have achieved the majority of their total height before entering a community college, college, or university. However, although the body is nearing maturation, it has not reached its full growth potential until the mid-20s. The mind of the 18-year-old freshman is most certainly less mature than the mind of the 22-year-old college graduate, for example.[14] If, during the college years, individuals should abuse alcohol or drugs, their response to that chemical(s) will be influenced in part by their maturational stage (Jorgensen, 2008).

Research has suggested that the adolescent brain is thought to be four to five times more vulnerable to alcohol-induced brain damage than the adult brain (Tappert et al., 2004/2005; Wuethrich, 2001). The implications of this are noteworthy, because researchers have found a small (7–10%) but marked decline in psychological test performance in adolescent drinkers (Strauch, 2003). This decline in measured cognitive abilities appears to be permanent, suggesting that the alcohol abuse that college students engage in might have lifelong consequences. Alcohol-induced damage to the *hippocampus,*[15] a region of the brain involved in the process of memory formation and information retrieval, thus holds the potential for lifelong consequences for the college drinker.

Even binge drinking is not without its dangers. An emerging body of evidence suggests that even binge drinking can contribute to apparent neurological dysfunction. The team of Crego et al. (2009) identified a sample of college students who engaged in binge drinking, as opposed to those who did not binge-drink, and administered neuropsychological tests. The authors found that although the binge drinkers were able to complete the subtest tasks, they required higher levels of attentional effort needed to do so. The authors interpreted this as evidence that even binge drinking might result in subtle neurological deficits.

Heavy alcohol abuse has been identified as one factor that appears to facilitate the development of a compound known as *C-reactive protein*[16] in the body. This compound is thought to be associated with the development of heart disease later in life (Gupta, 2007). If this theory is correct, then the individual's abuse of alcohol during the college years might have lifelong consequences for the drinker. Fortunately, only a minority of college students appear to continue to drink abusively after graduation, which would limit the production of C-reactive protein following graduation. Still, alcohol use by college students comes with a terrible price: Each year in the United States alcohol use is a factor in the death of 1,800 college students, 599,000 nonfatal injuries, 696,000 physical assaults, and 97,000 sexual assaults (R. W. Hingson, Zha, & Weigzman, 2009). It has been estimated that male college students were 19% more likely to suffer an injury for each day that they consumed more than eight drinks, whereas female college students were 10% more likely to suffer an injury while intoxicated for each day that they consumed five or more drinks (Mundt, Zakletskala, & Flemming, 2209).

There is an interesting relationship between educational levels and use of tobacco products. An estimated 34% of young adults who did not graduate from high school smoke cigarettes, as opposed to 26.6% of individuals with some college experience and 14.0% of college graduates (Substance Abuse and Mental Health Services Administration, 2009). This data is interesting, but it is the abuse of illicit substances that carries the most significant list of potential consequences for college students: The acquisition and possession of illegal substances are grounds for legal sanctions, which might include incarceration and loss of access to financial assistance programs for the student. As this data suggests, alcohol and illicit-drug use is not a harmless pastime for college students, bringing with it a range of potentially life-altering consequences for the student.

---

[14]With apologies to college freshmen.

[15]See Glossary.

[16]See Glossary.

One area of special concern is the tradition in which college students celebrate their 21st birthday with the consumption of alcohol, which is involved in between 80 and 90% of college students' celebrations upon achieving that milestone (Day-Cameron, Muse, Hauenstein, Simmons, & Correia, 2009). This landmark is often marked by drinking rituals, many of which are sponsored or at least encouraged by the students' expectations and drinking establishments near the campus. The consumption of 21 drinks by students upon their 21st birthday, sometimes with the stipulation that they do so within an hour's time, is not uncommon. Having reached their 21st birthday, many students feel the need to prove that they are able to accomplish this self-imposed task, with the result being that students play a "chemical equivalent of Russian roulette" (Neighbors et al., 2009, p. 14). The outcome is often the need for emergency hospitalizations for acute alcohol poisoning or even death for the student in many cases.

Finally, one current myth that is frequently believed by college drinkers is that they can mitigate the effects of their alcohol use by interspacing periods of drinking with the ingestion of "energy drinks." Approximately one-quarter of college student drinkers believe this myth (Spear, 2010). However, the team of Thombs et al. (2010) obtained blood alcohol levels from 802 college students who were selected at random when they exited a bar at the end of the night and found that those students who had consumed energy drinks were 300% more likely to leave the bar highly intoxicated and 400% more likely to plan to drive home in spite of their level of intoxication than were those students who did not consume energy drinks that evening. Thus rather than mitigating the effects of the alcohol consumed, such behavior appears to encourage the overuse of alcohol with the concomitant dangers associated with excessive alcohol use.

Graduate School

Graduate studies are a prerequisite for entry into some professions, such as the law, psychology, and medicine.[17] For some individuals, graduate school is simply a way to escape from the responsibilities of adulthood for a few more years (Benton, 2009). For both groups, substance use and abuse are potential problems. Some individuals continue the substance use pattern(s) established in their undergraduate program into their graduate program, whereas others begin to "mature out" of the substance use patterns established in their undergraduate years.

For some professionals-in-training, heavy alcohol use in social settings allows for professional "networking" in which both opportunities for clerkships or summer study programs might be discussed and where the foundation for later professional relationships might be established. Alcohol use during these competitive graduate programs also provides students with a chance to "decompress," often with surprising results. A survey of medical school students found, for example, that 11% were excessive drinkers, whereas 18% met the criteria for a diagnosis of alcohol abuse (Benton, 2009). Surprisingly, these students appeared to perform better academically than their nondrinking peers (Benton, 2009).

Following graduation, students encounter two nasty realities already discovered by their undergraduate friends: First, the sheltered environment of college does little to prepare individuals for the hustle and demands of the work environment. Department supervisors do not care whether their employees had competing deadlines for different projects: They will want assigned projects on time and within budget. Employees do not get an extension on the work assigned, as students might have received for a term paper that was not quite finished, for example. Second, students often discover with some degree of shock that the career that they prepared for over such a long period of their lives might not be the panacea that they had hoped for (Benton, 2009).

In the face of these discoveries, most former students either modify or discontinue the use of the substances abused in college or graduate school, to help them face the demands of their work career. Personal expectations are adjusted, and career goals are either modified or possibly dropped entirely. For a minority of graduate school students, alcohol or the other drugs abused during college and graduate school might serve as an "anchor" to hold on to during this transition period (Benton, 2009). Alcohol consumed during graduate school will have the same effect as alcohol consumed while in the workplace, providing a familiarity and predictability, not to mention escape from bruised emotions, which provides a strong incentive for the person to continue to abuse alcohol or other chemicals. Further, if heavy alcohol or drug use was the expectation during the "decompression" and networking periods after the week's studies, former students might carry these expectations with them into the work environment. Unfortunately, there is evidence suggesting that

---

[17]Which might be viewed as a form of graduate school.

upscale men's clothing stores are using alcohol as a possible way to entice customers, adding to the allure of alcohol during what is for many young adults a difficult transition.

Are There Forces That Help Protect the Student from Substance Use Disorders?

The answer to this question is an unqualified "yes." College students share the same risk factors and protective mechanisms that are found in the general population. Active religious involvement, for example, has been found to reduce the student's risk for developing an alcohol use disorder by 40% (Lambert, Fincham, Marks, & Stillman, 2010). Peer group affiliation and personal goals and aspirations might also both be viewed as mitigating factors. Parental influence, although not as strong as during the childhood and adolescent years, still can help to shape the student's substance use pattern. Role models also help to shape the student's substance use behaviors as well. Finally, an often overlooked factor that occasionally helps to protect the student from developing a substance use disorder is plain old common sense.

Chapter Summary

In late adolescence individuals are faced with a number of choices that will influence the rest of their lives. One such decision is whether to pursue a college degree in the hopes of enhanced earning potential later in life or to enter the workforce immediately. Slightly under half of people in the 18- to 19-year old age cohort do enter an institution of higher learning, although in many cases they do not complete more than a semester or two before dropping out of school because of financial, social, or familial factors that prohibit further participation in higher education. The role of alcohol and illicit drugs for those who continue with their educational careers beyond high school is often similar to and in many ways different from the substance use behaviors of people in the 18- to 19-year-old age cohort who decide not to pursue a degree from a college, community college, or vocational-technical school.

CHAPTER **22**
Codependency and Enabling

Introduction

Health care professionals who specialize in the behavioral sciences are often faced with a bewildering array of behaviors that they must both categorize and try to understand. To help them in this task, behavioral scientists utilize *constructs* or a form of professional shorthand that allows them to rapidly share complex information. A weather front is an excellent example of a construct. In reality there are no lines that connect different weather cells, or firm boundaries between different bodies of air. By using the analogy of the battle lines of World War I, it was possible for meteorologists to develop a system that allowed them to portray complex data about the changing weather patterns in a visual medium that others could understand.

As mental health professionals began to explore the interpersonal dynamics within the family of a substance abuser, they developed a number of new constructs to help them both understand and explain the impact of substance use disorders (SUDs) both within the family and to others. Two of these constructs, *Codependency* and *enabling,* were quite popular in the 1980s and early 1990s. They have become less popular in the early years of the 21st century, but are still occasionally utilized to summarize the complex dynamics within the family of a substance abuser. In this chapter these constructs will be examined in more detail.

Enabling

To *enable* a person with an SUD is to *knowingly* behave in such a manner as to make it possible for that person to continue to abuse chemicals. This protects substance abusers from having to pay the natural consequences for their substance abuse. This concept emerged in the early 1980s, when it was suggested that within some families there seemed to almost be a conspiracy in which for a variety of reasons family members supported the addicted person's continued chemical abuse.

Some family members feel threatened by the realization that substance abuse has found its way into their home, and they enter a stage of *denial* in order to avoid recognizing that this problem exists. Denial might be motivated by a desire on the part of the affected family members to avoid perceived blame for the dysfunctional member's behavior (Sadock & Sadock, 2007). This is a powerful motivator, although as discussed in the next chapter there are times when family members come to enjoy the power and responsibility given up by the dysfunctional family member, providing an incentive for the family to deny that there is indeed a problem. This overlaps with the tendency of some people affected by the individual's SUD to become *overly protective*, which is often thought to be an expression of love (Ruben, 2001). If the substance abuser should be unable to go to work or school because of intoxication or postintoxication recovery, for example, a parent or partner might call to report the substance abuser as being "sick," hiding the true nature of the dysfunctional family member's problem.

Enabling behaviors might be motivated by a variety of factors, including social pressure to be a "good" spouse or to support one's partner, or by pathological interdependency (Sadock & Sadock, 2007). These behaviors are found not only within the context of a family unit. An "enabler" might be a parent, sibling, coworker, neighbor, supervisor, friend, neighbor, or even a health care professional. Any person who *knowingly* acts in a way that protects addicted people from the consequences of their might be said to have enabled the substance abuser. Many health care professionals, for example, will not add a diagnosis of alcohol or drug dependence to a patient's file, for a variety of reasons. Some physicians rationalize this as being a way to protect the individual from the condemnation of society or possible denial of insurance benefits at a future date. Others might wish to protect the family of the substance abuser from the shame of having to acknowledge that such a problem existed in their home, and so forth. The essential point here is that *enablers* are any people who act to protect substance abusers from the full consequences of their behavior.

Enabling behaviors are not limited to those who are in the dysfunctional family member's immediate environment. Witnesses who refuse to testify against a criminal because they do not wish to become involved, or because of the inconvenience or fear of reprisal, might be said to have enabled the criminal. For the purpose of this text, we will focus just on those forms of enabling that apply to substance abusers.

Codependency

The concept of *Codependency* emerged in the latter quarter of the 20th century. It has become both a popular construct used in "pop" psychology and one of the cornerstones of rehabilitation programs. In spite of the fervor with which some rehabilitation professionals preach that many of us are Codependent, it is important to keep in mind that this is a *construct*, not reality. Indeed, this is seen in the fact that there is no standard

definition of Codependency, and various rehabilitation professionals argue over whether it should be spelled as one word (*Codependency*) or possibly hyphenated (*Co-dependency*), although the former spelling appears to slowly be winning out (Jaffe & Anthony, 2005; Sadock & Sadock, 2007). Another controversy is whether it should be spelled with a capital *C* (*Codependency*[1]) or a lowercase *c* (*codependency*). As will be discussed later in this chapter, there has even been strong disagreement between professionals about the validity of this construct (A. W. Blume, 2005).

Codependency Defined

For decades, family members have been quietly discussing how they had suffered, and often continued to suffer, from ongoing relationships with a dysfunctional (often substance-abusing) person. Gwinnel and Adamec (2006) defined *Codependency* as an "unhealthy relationship in which a person who is closely involved with an alcoholic or addicted person … [and] acts in such a way as to allow the addict to continue the addicted behavior" (p. 68). This relationship pattern usually is seen in a familial unit, although it might also exist between close friends, between an employer and an employee, or even between a police officer and a person driving while under the influence of chemicals![2]

Another definition of Codependency was offered by S. L. Johnson (2003), who suggested that it was a relationship in which "[there is a] continued investment of self-esteem in the ability to influence-control feelings and behavior, both in oneself and in others, in the face of serious adverse consequences" (p. 133). In contrast, A. W. Blume (2005) suggested that Codependency might be viewed as "loosely an emotional dependence upon the person with a drug problem" (p. 168). But perhaps the most inclusive definition of Codependency is offered by Zelvin (1997), who suggested that "Codependency [is a] problematic or maladaptive seeking of identify, self worth, and fulfillment outside of the self" (p. 50). Each of these definitions seeks to identify core aspects of Codependency: (a) the overinvolvement of family members with a dysfunctional member, (b) obsessive attempts on the part

---

[1] The upper case *C* will be used throughout this text, as in *Codependency*.

[2] In some communities, the police will simply escort drivers home, with the warning that they should not drive again until they are sober. This places both the police officers and the community that employs them at risk for liability should the intoxicated individual not heed this warning and have an accident.

of the Codependent person to control the dysfunctional person's behavior, (c) a tendency to base self-esteem on external sources of feedback, rather than on internal feelings, and (d) the tendency to make personal sacrifices in an attempt to "cure" (or at least limit) the dysfunctional member's problem behavior. It is important to note that all of these definitions of Codependency identify another core characteristic of the Codependent relationship: They are all externally focused, which is to say that the focus is on only the dysfunctional member.

The Relationship Between Enabling and Codependency

These two constructs are intertwined. To confuse matters, they both might be found in the same person, although this is not always the case. *Enabling refers to specific behaviors* that protect people with a substance use disorder from the consequences of their SUD. *Codependency refers to a relationship pattern* between one person and the person with the SUD. Giving money to a beggar on the street might enable that person to buy more alcohol or drugs. The donor does not need an ongoing relationship with the individual who has an SUD, and in the example here might never see that person again. There is no meaningful relationship, just a single act of enabling. Codependency and enabling do overlap, and a diagram of the relationship between the two might look something like that in Figure 22-1.

Enabling is often motivated by a variety of factors, including social pressure (a priest who admonishes a child that "you should honor your father and mother" in spite of their alcohol dependence and physical abuse of the child, for example), a desire to protect the family member with an SUD (for example, "if I tell your supervisor the truth, you might lose your job, and then how could we cope?"), or pathological interdependency between the people involved (Sadock & Sadock, 2007). Codependency and enabling might overlap, and at

times even be found in the same person, but they are also independent constructs that are used to help the clinician better understand the interpersonal dynamics both within the family and between the person with the SUD and others.

The Dynamics of Codependency

In an early work, Beattie (1987) spoke of Codependency as being a process in which the lives of those involved become unmanageable because they are involved in a committed relationship with a person who is addicted to chemicals. Codependent people interpret the commitment as preventing them from leaving the dysfunctional members or even confronting them about their behavior. Further, because of a blurring of boundaries within the family unit, Codependents begin to believe that the behavior of the dysfunctional member is somehow a reflection on themselves. This process of extreme involvement in the life of another person illustrates the boundary violations often seen in Codependency known as *enmeshment.*

Enmeshment, or its polar opposite *fusion,* is based on the individual's unconscious fear of abandonment (Dayton, 2005). The Codependent person's self-esteem is threatened by the dysfunctional person's behavior. To avoid this risk, the Codependent person often places personal aspirations and desires aside, becomes obsessed with the need to control the behavior of the dysfunctional person's behavior, and may assume control over aspects of that person's life not normally seen in more healthy families (Beattie, 1987; S. L. Johnson, 2003). An extreme example of this is when Codependent people assume responsibility for the dysfunctional person's recreational substance use, blaming themselves for the other person's substance abuse ("I made them so upset that they drank!"). "It is all my fault" is a common belief on the part of the Codependent person.

To avoid this painful dilemma, the Codependent person often becomes preoccupied (Wegscheider-Cruse, 1985) or obsessed (Beattie, 1989) with controlling the dysfunctional member's behavior. An extreme example of this attempt to control the behavior of the dysfunctional person is found in the experience of a prison psychologist who received a telephone call from the elderly mother of an inmate. She asked the psychologist to "make sure that the man who shares my son's cell is [going to be] a good influence on my son," because "there are a lot of bad men in that prison and I don't want him falling in with a bad crowd." This request ignores the grim reality that her son was not in prison for singing off key in choir practice on this

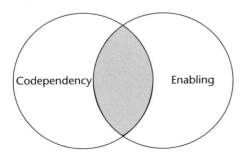

FIGURE 22-1 The Relationship Between Codependency and Enabling Behaviors

occasion, and that he had a history of multiple arrests in the past.

The mother in this case might be said to be in serious denial about her son's behavior, as well as so involved in her son's life that she was still trying to control and "cure" him in spite of the thick walls and armed guards. She became quite disturbed when it was gently suggested to her that she needed to *detach* from her son and his dysfunctional behavior. *Detachment* is one of the cornerstones of recovery from Codependency (S. Brown & Lewis, 1995). Through this process the Codependent person learns to "let go" and stop attempting to control the dysfunctional person's life. But it is a difficult lesson for many Codependent people to learn, as in the earlier example. Perhaps the mother's intentions were good, but her efforts reflected an overinvolvement with her son's life.

The goal of Codependency is *control.* Through various adaptive behaviors, Codependent people are viewed as attempting to achieve a sense of control over their own inner turmoil and over the dysfunctional person. Sometimes, Codependent people set the goal of "fixing" the dysfunctional people, so that they will no longer engage in inappropriate behaviors. A secondary goal is that the dysfunctional person will then come to appreciate the Codependent's efforts and possibly come to love them (Knauer, 2002; Ruben, 2001). However, this attempt at control often results in the dysfunctional person (or possibly others) criticizing the Codependents that they do not understand (or appreciate) the abuser.

Some individuals who find themselves in a relationship with a dysfunctional person adopt a rigid, controlling approach. They seek to stabilize the home through rules and repetition, to limit (if not eliminate) the dysfunctional behavior(s) by the other (S. L. Johnson, 2003). On other occasions, the Codependent person adopts a self-pitying approach, attempting to manipulate the dysfunctional person through guilt ("If you really loved me, you would stop") (S. L. Johnson, 2003).

The Rules of Codependency

Although Codependent people often report that they feel as if they were going crazy, an unbiased outside observer will carefully note that there are certain unspoken rules within the family unit. Beattie (1989) identified several of these rules:

1. It is not OK for me to feel.
2. It is not OK for me to have problems of my own.
3. It is not OK for me to have fun or a life of my own.
4. I'm not lovable.
5. I'm never good enough.
6. If people act crazy, I am responsible.

These rules are actively transmitted within the family, setting the foundation for Codependency: For example, "If you did what I told you, I would not have gone out drinking last night!" is an example of rule number 6. "College! Don't even waste your time by applying, you'll never make it!" is an example of rules 2, 3, 4, and 5. Through the transmission of these rules, Codependent people's will is broken, and they become so unwilling to assert an independent will that dysfunctional people do not need to fear being confronted about their inappropriate behavior.

There is an inherent power struggle between the dysfunctional family member and a Codependent: The Codependent person wants to control the behavior of the dysfunctional person to keep peace within the family and avoid conflict. Dysfunctional family members want to shape Codependents so that they will not challenge their inappropriate behavior(s). An all-too-common experience for family and marriage therapists is for one partner to set up an appointment to ask that the therapist "fix" the other person, when she or he does not want to be fixed. For example, the cocaine-abusing husband enters marital therapy with the demand that the therapist "make her stop nagging me" while having no intention to stop abusing cocaine and causing the financial hardship for the family that causes the wife to "nag" him.

Are Codependents Born or Made? Proponents of the concept of Codependency suggest that it is a *learned relationship pattern,* which may result from physical/sexual abuse during childhood (Knauer, 2002). As a result of such boundary violations, the Codependent person learns to tolerate boundary violations as the price of temporary peace. Through this and other boundary violations, Codependent individuals are taught that they are "less than" others and not worthy of ordinary levels of respect or independence (Knauer, 2002). Abused children also learn to tolerate boundary violations and to accept responsibility for familial problems beyond their control. Over time the child learns to accept the dysfunction as the norm and is socialized into accepting the role of a Codependent (Zelvin, 1997).

It is on this flawed foundation that the Codependent person attempts to build adult relationships. Communication within relationships grinds to a halt and is limited to "safe" topics that will avoid confronting the dysfunctional person's behavior. The children quickly learn that *nobody* mentions the inappropriate behavior on the part of the dysfunctional person. "Don't say anything about (insert the inappropriate behavior), or else (the dysfunctional person) will become upset!" is a common message of the Codependent parent. In cases of child sexual abuse, the child is taught not to mention it so as to maintain family cohesion and peace. To survive, these children learn *emotional constriction,* to avoid facing such negative feelings within themselves, and learn to live a rigid, compulsive lifestyle focused on the other person's life (Craig, 2004). Through this process, the child learns the *no-talk rule,* which is the foundation of the Codependent's lifestyle.

Codependency and Self-Esteem

In an attempt to maintain peace within the family, Codependents learn that their emotional pain is subservient to maintaining peace within the family. They are taught that they should never express their own emotional pain, as it is unimportant when compared with the goal of familial peace. The Codependent's self-esteem might be damaged, or shattered, but as long as the secret is maintained this is unimportant from the perspective of the family unit. Denial is often utilized by the Codependent to avoid feelings of blame for the other's dysfunctional behavior(s) and to quell internal struggles. The unfortunate result of this is that

> Co-dependents frequently appear normal, which in our culture is associated with a healthy ego. Nevertheless they also describe themselves as "dying on the inside", which is indicative of low self worth or esteem. (Zerekh & Michaels, 1989, p. 111)

Because of low self-esteem, Codependents learn to measure self-worth by how successful they were in their caretaking behaviors. In a sense, Codependents learn to measure their self-worth through external standards (often set by the Codependent family member) rather than by internal standards.

Although external observers will quickly identify the unhealthy expectations and goals of Codependents, they seem to be *locked into* this lifestyle. In reality, they cannot envision another way of living. They often take pride in how much they have suffered, a behavior learned in childhood, and interpret their suffering at the hands of another as a form of moral victory, if not an affirmation of their love. Because they are unable to envision any other way of living, these trials become almost a badge of honor and a defense against the sense of worthlessness sensed within.

The Cycle of Codependency

Once the cycle of Codependency has started, it takes on a life of its own. A graphic representation of the cycle of Codependency might appear something like that in Figure 22-2.

In Figure 22-2, there are two essential elements. First, the Codependent person must suffer from fragile or low self-esteem. If they have adequate self-esteem, then they would be able to affirm "self" without external validation, and thus not be vulnerable to the dysfunctional member's threats to withdraw affection or support. The self-affirming person would draw away from the dysfunctional member, thus blocking the unhealthy relationship from evolving in the first place.

Equally important is that the partner be dysfunctional. The dysfunctional other is necessary to draw in the Codependent person. This is why Codependent people seem to be attracted to dysfunctional partners. If the dysfunctional partner were to be healthy instead of dysfunctional, the cycle falls apart. But it is equally important to remember that this cycle reflects the Codependent person's attempt to resolve conflicts left over from childhood through their adult relationships. A common experience for substance abuse rehabilitation professionals is to see where the Codependent spouse has replaced the dysfunctional family member from childhood with the same type of person as a marital partner. Freud called this the "repetition compulsion," a construct that suggests that individuals continue to struggle with unresolved issues from childhood until they are resolved. To the believer in Codependency however, this same construct is interpreted as if the Codependent is "addicted" to the dysfunctional style of the partner.

Patterns of Codependency

In the last quarter of the 20th century, substance abuse professionals attempted to identify common coping styles that might identify different varieties of Codependent people. A number of such coping styles have been suggested, including those listed in Table 22-1 (Capretto, 2007; Craig, 2004; Ellis, McInerney, DiGiuseppe, & Yager, 1988; S. L. Johnson, 2003).

Health care professionals often work with family members of a dysfunctional person who demonstrate some or all of these behavioral patterns. An example of the "coconspirator" might best be seen in the spouse of a cocaine addict who wanted marital counseling because the addicted partner would not limit her or his cocaine use to the $100 per week that was budgeted for

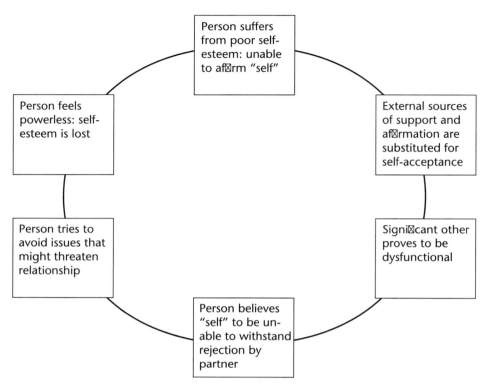

FIGURE 22-2 The Circle of Codependency

this. Another example of the coconspirator might be seen in the couple who requests marital counseling for the anger outbursts of the dysfunctional partner, without ever discussing the partner's continued substance use disorder. Another example of this coping style might be seen in the partner who goes to the bar with the dysfunctional partner to "try and show the abuser how to drink in a responsible manner." These efforts to change the dysfunctional family members behavior from within the family unit are usually doomed to failure.

A very good example of the messiah is the father of an opiate-dependent young adult who is in a therapy group for family members. The father tearfully discussed the litany of problems that the addicted child had caused, and how the mother and father had to take out personal loans on several occasions to pay off their child's drug debts. Another group member suggested that the mother and father just force the wayward child to pay those bills and be responsible for him or herself. The father thought for a long moment and then said that if he did this, their child, now an adult, "might leave us." When several family group members suggested that this would not automatically

be bad, because it would allow their child to "hit bottom" and see the need to address the addiction, the father quickly replied, "Oh, I couldn't do that, (child's name) is not ready to assume responsibility for (his or her self) yet!" Thus the parents continued to support their child's addiction, to avoid the short-term consequences of having the child become angry at them.

The Relationship Between Codependency and Mental Health

Although this model of the interactional pattern within the home where there is a substance abuser appears to make sense, there is a very real tendency for rehabilitation professionals to overidentify with the concept of Codependency. Even if the individual were to be Codependent, there are degrees of Codependency, just as there are degrees of heart failure or obesity. It is not (as some would have us believe) an all-or-nothing condition. Because of these degrees of Codependency "anyone is Codependent" (Beattie, quoted in Tavris, 1992, p. 194).

This stance overlooks the fact that many of the same behaviors that were outlined earlier are also found in healthy family relationships. Codependency, according

TABLE 22-1 IDENTIFIED PATTERNS OF CODEPENDENCY

COPING STYLE	GOAL OF COPING STYLE
Apathetic partner	(might also be called "silent sufferer") The partner simply stopped caring (emotional shutdown often seen with this pattern of coping).
Approval seeker	Constantly seeks the approval/acceptance of the dysfunctional partner (for external validation)
Caretaker	Devotes his/her life to caretaking of the dysfunctional partner
Coconspirator	Consciously or unconsciously joins with the dysfunctional member to maintain pseudo-stability within the family unit (also called the "joiner")
Controller	Engages in manipulative behaviors in an attempt to control every aspect of the life of the entire family, as they feel (often with some justification) that their own life is out of control
Family mascot/ clown	More often seen of family members who attempt to deflect attention from the dysfunctional family member on to themselves (thus avoiding conflict)
Martyr	Self-righteous partner will receive support for being the "good" partner, allowing for affirmation in the face of lack of self-esteem
Messiah	Fights against the dysfunctional behavior(s) in such a way that the abusers are never forced to face consequences of their behavior (also called *chief enabler*)
Protector	Seeks to maintain familial peace at any cost, even if it allows dysfunctional behaviors to continue
Persecutor	Blames everybody *but* the dysfunctional member for familial problems (may be called *get even* pattern of relationships)
Separator	Over time spends less and less time at home, avoiding conflict that might otherwise exist in family unit

to Wegscheder-Cruse and Cruse (1990), "is an exaggeration of normal personality traits" (p. 28). Only a few "saints and hermits" (Tavris, 1990, p. 21A) fail to demonstrate at least some of these behaviors on occasion. It is a matter of the adaptability of the individual's coping style. If Codependents are consistently using one of the coping styles mentioned earlier to the exclusion of

other, healthier coping styles, their adaptive potentials are limited and they are trapped in an unhealthy relationship pattern.

To complicate matters, there is a strong overlap between love and Codependency because of how love relationships are viewed within this society (Zelvin, 1997). Love is viewed as allowing for the blending of identities and the loss of ego boundaries. This is perhaps a strength of love, but it also allows for Codependency to develop if it is taken to an extreme. Between the extremes of total independence (the "hermit" noted earlier) and total dependence on the other (the Codependent), is an *interdependency,* which is the hallmark of healthy relationships.

Reactions to the Concept of Codependency

It is important to remember that Codependency is a *construct,* which in this case might be traced to M. L. Lewis's (1937) theory that the spouse of a person with an alcohol use disorder (usually the wife) had a disturbed personality and was trying to resolve her own inner conflicts through a marriage to a person with an AUD. Suddenly, the partner was classified as being dysfunctional, although in a different way than the spouse with the substance use disorder. From this point on, mental health professionals have struggled to determine whether Codependency is a legitimate form of psychopathology, a struggle that has not been helped by the fact that Codependency has been characterized as "an addiction, a personality disorder, a psychosocial condition, and an interpersonal style" (Hurcom, Copello, & Orford, 2000, p. 487). As this last comment would suggest, Codependency is not a useful diagnostic category and is not recognized by the American Psychiatric Association as such in the *Diagnostic and Statistical Manual of Mental Disorders* (4th edition, text revision) (American Psychiatric Association, 2000; S. L. Johnson, 2003).

There is little evidence that Codependency even exists (A. W. Blume, 2005). Rather, it is the opinion of many professionals that Codependency is a pseudo-problem more than an area of legitimate therapeutic inquiry. This stance is supported by the fact that research into Codependency and enabling has all but disappeared by the end of the first decade of the 21st century. If it were a legitimate problem, such as coronary artery disease, for example, why has it virtually disappeared from the professional literature over the past two decades? Again, using the analogy of coronary artery disease, the issue of disease involving these important structures of the heart has not disappeared from the medical literature.

Many health care professionals are uncomfortable with the concept of Codependency because it transforms the relationship style, even if it is an unhealthy one, into a medical problem (Hurcom et al., 2000). The application of the label of a "Codependent" to a marital partner *disempowers* the individual. Further, the concept of Codependency is based on traditional 12-step programs, which suggest that the "disease" of Codependency is progressive and can be addressed only by attending the appropriate self-help group (Randle, Estes, & Cone, 1999). This position rests on the assumption that "a knife wound to the chest will heal but an injury to the mind will never repair itself" (Sherwood, 2009, p. 286), a stance that further disempowers the individual.

There is a strident, ongoing debate over whether Codependent people have similar life experiences and personality traits, or if such uniformity in patient histories and presenting symptoms might be an artifact of the therapeutic relationship. The therapist, expecting certain characteristics in the patient, selectively attends only to those patient characteristics that conform to the preconceived construct of Codependency. Further, because of the vague, ill-defined nature of the characteristics of Codependency, virtually every person will meet at least one of the defining characteristics. At what point, for example, does a mother's natural protectiveness for her child become "overprotective"? How do you define "just protective enough" without going over that hypothetical line?

Another challenge to the validity of the Codependency construct is the observation that up to 99% of the adults in this country could be said to have been raised in a "dysfunctional" home.[3] The majority of parents provide a "good enough" home environment, although there is always room for improvement. Statistically, only a small minority of parents might be said to provide a fully dysfunctional, unhealthy home environment. Further, the family is not (as is often suggested) an "incubator of [psychological] disease" W. Kaminer, 1992, p. 12). Within this hypothetical incubator of adult problems, children are thought to be infected with one or more dreaded conditions that they will have to struggle against for the rest of their lives (unless they join the appropriate self-help group).

Within the paradigm of Codependency, problems are never viewed as an incentive for adaptive changes and growth for children, but as lifelong obstacles to their emotional growth. Yet there is little research that supports the thesis that a child raised in a "dysfunctional" home is automatically doomed to a lifetime of suffering. Indeed, adversity often serves as a stimulus for personality growth (Sherwood, 2009). This is not to dismiss the deep, perhaps lifelong emotional scars of childhood trauma for some people. But there are also many people who were raised in equally unhealthy environments but who found ways to cope and possibly even grow in spite of their childhood environments. One reason for this appears to be the natural resilience of children (Masten, 2001; Wolin & Wolin, 1993, 1995). Proponents of the Codependency construct often overlook this protective factor, which appears to actually be quite common in childhood (Bonanno, 2004).

It has been suggested that self-help groups for Codependency misrepresent the promise of recovery while actually fostering dependence on the self-help group. The group member is expected to recover memories of parental behaviors consistent with the group's expectations, which is to say to continue to recall material and behave in a "Codependent" manner (Randle et al., 1999). Individuals who fail to follow the group's expectations are said to be in "denial." If individuals reject the insights offered by various books on Codependency, they are also said to be in "denial." Further, no matter how serious or slight the parental misbehavior, there is just one model for recovery: the Codependency model. All emotional trauma is viewed within this model as being equally as destructive.

Critics of the model of Codependency point out that this construct seems to excuse individuals from responsibility for their behavior. Through the "disease" of Codependency, blame is shifted from the substance-abusing individual to the significant other, who is automatically said to "enable" the partner's dysfunctional behaviors. Unfortunately, Codependents' behavior are automatically deemed pathological by many mental health professionals. Such a stance denies the possibility that the individual's behavior might be health and role specific, or a response to the partner's substance use disorder (Hurcom et al., 2000).

Further, the Codependency model reflects the *family disease model* concept utilized by family therapists. This therapeutic model suggests that "the solution is for each family member to recognize that he or she has a disease" (Fels-Stewart, O'Farrell, & Bircher,

---

[3]The concept of Codependency has been extended to include entire communities, states, and countries (Hurcom et al., 2000).

2003, p. 148). In this case, family members have either a substance use disorder or the disease of Codependency, and are judged not on their own accomplishments, but on whether the abusers with the SUD are able to abstain from chemicals. Family members feel guilty because of familial bonds with the substance-abusing member, and the "problem" becomes not that of substance abuse, or sexual misbehavior, or physical violence on the part of the dysfunctional person, but on *family* members who suffer from the disease of Codependency!!!

Although M. L. Lewis's (1937) work was advanced more than a century ago, it was resurrected in the 1950s as a popular theory that the spouse was a coalcoholic (Sadock & Sadock, 2007; Simmons, 1991; Sher, 1991). This theory assumed that the spouse was as much in need of professional treatment as was the substance-abusing partner, because he or she (a) helped to cause the other's alcoholism, (b) continues to support it, and (c) thus obviously must be disturbed. These beliefs reflect the fact that throughout history the spouse of the alcoholic has "been blamed and pathologized for their partner's drinking" (Hurcom et al., 2000, p. 473). The fact that there has been little clinical evidence presented to support this theory or to suggest that the spouse of an alcoholic has any consistent form of psychopathology does not prevent the theory of coalcoholism from being resurrected under the name of "Codependency."

Another challenge to the Codependency concept was offered by Jaffe and Anthony (2005). The authors observed that this construct has been so watered down, and misused that it has lost any possible hint of diagnostic specificity. This is seen in the definition of Codependency offered by Peck (1997) in which Codependency is viewed as "a relationship in which partners cater to—and thereby encourage—each other's weaknesses" (p. 180). This definition could be applied to virtually every relationship, because we all make provisions for another person's unhealthy behavior on occasion! Spouses who know that their partner is always a half hour late and make plans accordingly could be said to have engaged in a Codependent behavior by Peck's (1997) definition.

Many critics of the Codependency construct point out that it rests on little more than "new age" rhetoric. For example, the husband and wife team of Wegscheider-Cruse and Cruse (1990) speak knowingly about how Codependency results from the "interactions between one's own manufactured 'brain chemicals' (having to do with our reinforcement center) and

one's behavior that stimulates the brain to establish compulsive and addictive behavior processes" (p. 12). The authors go on to conclude that Codependency is a brain disease on the assumption that "we have a brain that gives us an excessive rush, [and] we get into self-defeating behaviors that keep the rush coming (Codependency)" (pp. 12–13).

Admittedly, there is strong evidence to suggest that the human brain evolved in such a way as to help us cope in a social environment (Gazzaniga, 2008). Further, the author suggests, interpersonal relationships affect the neurochemical balance within each individual's brain. But what Wegscheider-Cruse and Cruse (1990) overlook is that there is no scientific evidence to support their position. There is no evidence that a relationship can cause an "excessive rush.[4]" Nor has science found evidence that we get into "self-defeating behaviors that keep the rush coming." Indeed, this stance tends to be self-defeating, in the sense that if human beings were to engage in self-defeating behaviors for personal pleasure, how would the species have ever survived?

This is not to dismiss the fact that there are many people who have suffered terrible psychological, and on occasion physical, injury from their involvement with an addicted partner. However, to automatically classify them as Codependent without an investigation into the dynamics of the relationship is unfair. Further, the Codependents are expected to come to terms with their pain and achieve healing without blaming addicted partners for virtually anything that they have done. In other words:

According to adherents of [the theory of Codependency], families of alcoholics cannot ... hold them [the addicted person] responsible for the abuse. Somehow the victim must get well by dint of pure self-analysis, meditation and prayer, without reference to the social, economic, legal and psychological forces that create[d] [the] dysfunctional families. (Codependency," 1990, p. 7)

For many people, this is an impossible task.

Chapter Summary

In the 1970s, a pair of new constructs were introduced that allowed professionals to view addicted people and their support system in a different manner than

---

[4]Which begs the question: What would be a sufficient "rush"? If something exists in excess, does this not imply that it also exists in a form where there is a sufficient supply, without being present in excess?

had been used previously. The construct of enabling was introduced to explain how others might behave in a manner that supported the continued dysfunctional behavior of a person with a behavioral disorder. Family members who maintain silence with full knowledge of an incestuous relationship within their home might be said to be engaging in enabling, for example. The construct of Codependency, which was an extension of the 1950s theory that the spouse of the alcohol-dependent person was a "coalcoholic" was introduced. Through Codependency, family members, friends, employers, and others might be said to enter into a relationship that supported the continued abuse of chemicals by the identified patient. Proponents seized upon these constructs as proof that the disease of alcoholism (and, by extension, the other drugs of abuse) included not just the alcohol-dependent person, but others who also needed "treatment." Self-help groups also evolved to meet the perceived need for rehabilitation by those who "suffered" from Codependency.

After a spell of initial enthusiasm, support for these constructs has faded somewhat. Currently a battle rages about whether these are real diagnostic entities, just as constructs characterize certain behaviors, or pseudo-issues that cloud the problem of substance abuse rehabilitation.

CHAPTER 23
Addiction and the Family

> Outside of residence in a concentration camp, there are very few sustained human experiences that make one the recipient of as much sadism as does being the close member of an alcoholic.
>
> —*Vaillant (1995, p. 22)*

Introduction

A conservative estimate suggests that there are at least four to five people hurt by the behavior of a person with a substance use disorder (SUD) (Capretto, 2007). The most common source of such pain is through parental alcoholism. Yet in spite of this fact there has been little research into the issue of how parental alcoholism might alter family dynamics or the interaction pattern within that family (C. A. Green, 2006). Further, in spite of the awareness of the widespread problem of adolescent SUDs,[1] there has been virtually no research into how parental SUDs impact the family in which the child lives. There are many theories and personal beliefs, but little hard data on which to view the impact of the SUDs on the family unit or to guide intervention efforts. In this chapter, the theory and supporting evidence of addiction's impact on the family will be reviewed.

Scope of the Problem

Researchers believe that at this moment approximately 9.6 million children are living in a home where at least one parent currently has an active SUD (Capretto, 2007). Because the individual's alcohol or drug abuse tends to alternate between periods of more and less abusive drinking, perhaps twice this number of children are living in a home where one or both parents have abused a chemical(s) in the past year (Capretto, 2007). By the time that they reach adulthood, more than one-half of adults in the United States will have lived in a family where one member has or at least

had, an alcohol use disorder (AUD)[2] (B. F. Grant et al., 2006).

Addiction and the Family Unit

Although it is understood that the relationship between the SUDs and family dynamics is extremely complex, it is also poorly understood. It has been found, for example, that in marriages where there is a wide discrepancy in the alcohol use pattern of the partners, there are usually lower levels of intimacy than in marriages where

---

[1] Discussed in Chapter 20.

[2] The differences between these two estimates reflect, in part, how "family" is defined in either study. For example, would a second cousin with an alcohol use disorder who lived 1,000 miles away be defined as a "family" member in both studies or only in one study?

the alcohol use pattern of the partners is more similar. There are two possible explanations for this pattern: First, this might be a side effect of the individual's AUD. A second possibility, however, is that those individuals who are drawn to heavy alcohol use have fewer intimacy skills. Which (if either) of these theories is correct is not known at this time. It is virtually impossible to find a specific area in a marriage or family unit that is affected by just the SUD. Most families with a parental SUD also suffer from a wide variety of other issues, making it impossible to isolate the impact of just the parental SUD. Further, over time problems within the marital unit become intertwined, with each issue impacting almost every other aspect of family life. In spite of this lack of specificity, there appears to be a relationship between the SUDs and marital or familial problems.

Alcohol is the substance most commonly abused in this society, and clinicians are often asked by spouses of substance abusers how, when they seemed so normal during courtship, they now have an AUD. The answer is that during the courtship phase and the first year of marriage, alcohol abusers commonly reduce their level of alcohol intake (Leonard & Mudar, 2003). There is also a shift in relationship patterns following marriage. Husbands tend to discontinue friendships in which the friend's alcohol use does not correspond with their own, and spend less time in non-marriage-centered social activities (or spend more time with their partners, depending on how you look at it) (Leonard & Mudar, 2003). Further, either consciously or unconsciously, people's substance use pattern plays a role in their choice of relationship partners. In many cases, people with an AUD select a partner whose alcohol use pattern is very similar to their own (I. Grant et al., 2007). It is logical to assume that this is also true for the other drugs of abuse, although there has been minimal research into this aspect of mate selection. If there is a discrepancy between alcohol use patterns, there are several possible adjustments that might be made to the relationship:

1. Most commonly both partners adjust their alcohol use pattern until it is more consistent with that of their partner.
2. However, one partner might engage in "secondary denial" (Benton, 2009, p. 109) and avoid conscious awareness that his or her partner's AUD is as serious as an objective observer would suggest.
3. Finally, if there is a wide discrepancy in alcohol use patterns, the relationship might be terminated

either during courtship or after marriage. This course of action requires that the individual have sufficient ego strength to end the relationship, which as seen in the last chapter might not always be the case.

The Family Systems Perspective

This theory holds that people tend to select partners who have achieved similar levels of "differentiation of self" (M. Bowen, 1985, p. 263). From this perspective each partner has achieved a similar level of emotional growth or maturity, although each partner follows a separate path in his or her quest to accomplish this developmental task. There is no single path to growth: Some paths are more adaptive and healthy, and others just the reverse, but the process of growth is still under way at all times.

For the child, the main developmental goal calls for the individual to separate emotionally from one's parents (*individuation* or *differentiation*), resolving the emotional attachments to the parents that evolved in childhood (Cozolino, 2002). In the healthy family, children gradually learn to identify both the needs of the self and those of others, while growing in their ability to self-regulate their own emotions and be available to nurture others (Cozolino, 2002).

In the dysfunctional home, familial rigidity and loss of focus play havoc with this process. During the first year of life, for example, the infant is almost totally dependent on the parents, becoming less and less dependent on the parents over time. This ego growth is demonstrated through behaviors such as independent play, spending time with friends, and so on. In the healthy family, the parents recognize this, and gradually withdraw control as the child becomes more capable of independent living and self-nurturance. However, in the dysfunctional home, this growing independence threatens the pseudo-stability achieved through the loss of independent identities and rigidity. In response to this perceived threat, the parents might respond not with encouragement but with a reinforcement of control, forcing the child to identify with the rules of the family system no matter what the cost (Cozolino, 2002).

The primary means by which parents attempt to maintain control and discourage emotional independence is through *anxiety* and *threats of abandonment* (Cozolino, 2002). Children are threatened with possible abandonment on both a conscious and unconscious level if they should express an opinion or engage in a behavior that threatens the pseudo-stability within the family unit.[3] Guilt is another weapon that is employed in this process. For example, at the funeral of a hypothetical 18-year-old boy who had died in a motor vehicle accident, the mother might turn to the older sister and say, "This would never have happened if you were here to keep an eye on him." It is a rare individual who is able to break through these bonds of guilt and shame and establish a healthy independent emotional identity. Rather, through the repetition compulsion first identified by Sigmund Freud, children often grow up to find people with similar levels of emotional differentiation as their parents, in an effort to resolve this conflict now that they are an adult.

Parental Rules

In many dysfunctional families, three "rules" evolve to maintain the pseudo-stability that the family attempts to establish:

1. Don't talk about the problem.
2. Don't have feelings about the problem.
3. Don't trust anybody. (Capretto, 2007).

Within the framework of these rules, children are forced to rely on only the parents for guidance and support in spite of the fact that their parents might be unable to provide these things to them. Further, the natural predilection for children to mature might be a threat to the pseudo-stability of the family as the children learn that these rules are rarely found outside of their own family. To avoid this, the parents might become smothering, crushing the children's move for independence under layer upon layer of parental control to ensure that the family environment does not change.

As a result of this process, the child's natural quest for emotional autonomy becomes a source of shame, as the parents instill the family "rules" discussed in the last paragraph into the child. Shame is a powerful, painful emotion. If it is experienced for too long or too intensely, it becomes so painful for children or adolescents that they begin to detach from their own emotions to survive. In this manner the child learns to follow the family's rules to escape from the layers of

shame and guilt that they are taught is rightfully theirs if they should deviate from the familial rules noted previously.

Failing to receive positive feedback and parental support for their quest for emotional independence, children might come to view themselves as being weak, incompetent, and incapable of standing alone. The family might reinforce this assessment of the "self," which then discourages further moves toward autonomy. The child comes to believe "I am not worthy . . . I am damaged . . . unable to cope on my own." Failure to learn how to nurture the "self," a task that in this family environment would be virtually impossible, the child turns to external sources of feedback: the very dysfunctional people who brought the child to this pass in the first place.

The Marriage with a Partner with an SUD

There are three common forces found in families where there is an SUD: (a) the desire for stability, (b) the threat to the family stability that results from the SUD, and (c) how the marital partners cope with issues (a) and (b). To complicate matters, individuals with an SUD do not have the same priorities as their partner: Their priorities revolve around the continued use of the chemical(s) in question, not the marital or familial unit. The SUD becomes a "silent partner," first of the marriage and then of the entire family. Those who threaten to break the "no talk/no trust" rules identified earlier face possible emotional expulsion from the family (Dayton, 2005). This family relationship style is then passed from one generation to the next. Children are taught not to trust their own perception(s) but to turn to others for guidance and support, even if these individuals are dysfunctional and do not have the child's best interests at heart.

It is often surprising to learn that although society demonizes SUDs, they do actually serve as a *stabilizing influence* in some marriages. The partner with the SUD might use the chemical(s) to cope with the demands not only of marriage, but also of life in general (Hurcom et al., 2000). Nonabusing partners, or their children, might assume roles that substance-abusing partners either do not feel capable of filling or that they willingly relinquish to focus their attention on continued substance use. As a result of the assumption of these roles, marital partners or family members may find themselves holding powerful positions within the family that they are unwilling to give up should the

---

[3]For example, a mother might make the observation to a daughter about to leave for college that "Your father and I want you to do the very best that you can while at college" on one occasion, and later say "It is breaking your heart that you will be living so far away," setting up a conflict in the daughter's mind as to the wisdom of moving away to college.

substance-abusing parent learn to face life without the chemical(s). This will then become a "relapse trigger" for the parent in the earliest stages of recovery.

This sets the stage for control issues to surface as the marital partners or family members work at cross-purposes. *Conditional love* becomes a weapon used by one or both sides to impose their will on the other. This conditional love threatens the nonabusers with a withdrawal of affection and support unless they adhere to the demands of the abuser. It also becomes a justification for continued substance use by substance-abusing partners, because they are obviously misunderstood, mistreated, and not loved (at least in their own eyes).

The family then seeks to establish at least a pretense of stability, in spite of boundary violations and continued substance abuse by important members of the family unit. To protect this pseudo-stability achieved in dysfunctional families, the unhealthy behavior(s) by the dysfunctional partner are exempted from scrutiny. "We came here for *marital* counseling," the couple screams, "not to discuss alcoholism!!!" Parents who bring their child in for the treatment of depression might stomp out of the session in anger if their incestuous behavior is revealed, and the parents might refuse to pay for services rendered because this was not why they brought the child in to see a mental health professional![4]

It must be recalled that dysfunctional partners seek to build a support system that will enable them to continue to engage in their dysfunctional behavior(s) (Capretto, 2007). Because the core problem is except from discussion, the family is forced to choose between (a) confronting the problem directly, at the possible risk of destroying the marriage or family, or (b) finding an alternative, less threatening way to cope. Silence[5] may be viewed as a safer alternative than confronting the problem. *Emotional withdrawal* also becomes a weapon utilized in the quest for control. Hurcom et al. (2000) discovered that almost 50% of spouses without an SUD admitted to using this tactic at least on occasion. Although the goal is to help the partner with the SUD reduce or stop the substance abuse, more often than not it has the opposite effect. "A bottle," it is often said at Alcoholics Anonymous meetings "will never reject you."

All of this takes place during a time when the children's neural networks are still in a stage of growth and development (Sheff et al., 2007; Teicher, 2002). Thus the impact of parental SUDs may hold lifelong consequences for children, especially during critical periods of growth and development. For example, when children are developing "core beliefs about security and safety" (Sheff et al., 2007, p. 7), they might be engaged in such behaviors as staying awake while the parent is out drinking, checking on the safety of sleeping siblings, cooking meals for their siblings because the parent is unable or unwilling to do so, and developing elaborate coping plans in case of emergencies. These children or adolescents are likely to be viewed as overly mature, serious, and well organized, characteristics that unfortunately mask the true nature of their home environment because they are viewed as signs of emotional maturity (Dayton, 2005; Ruben, 2001).

In parental dyads in which one parent has an SUD and the other does not, conflict between the two might distract either one from providing emotional support when their child needs comfort and security (Sheff et al., 2007). Extremes of abuse and neglect, fostered by parental substance abuse and preoccupation about further substance use, may predispose the child to depression, anxiety states, suicidal thoughts, or attempts at self-harm, as well as impulse control disorders and later substance abuse on the part of the growing child[6] (Anda et al., 2000; S. R. Dube et al., 2001; Teicher, 2002).

Another consequence of parental alcoholism is a state of chronic stress for the child, which then results in higher levels of illness (Wyman et al., 2007). Although the work of Wyman et al. did not directly address the issue of parental alcoholism, the findings that chronic stress alters the body's immune response implies that parental SUDs might strongly influence the child's growth and health. Some of the forms of stress include children or adolescents blaming themselves for their parents' drinking and living in fear that their parents might divorce (Ruben, 2001).

Growing up in a home where there is a substance-abusing parent has also been suggested as a possible contributing cause to those who grow up and seem to be "addicted" to excitement (Ruben, 2001). According to this theory, children might engage in dysfunctional

---

[4]Mandatory reporting laws in most states will also result in the parent being reported to the authorities, possibly eliciting threats against the therapist from the parent.

[5]Expressed as *avoidance, rationalization,* or *denial.*

[6]After all, who is going to help the child learn to control internal impulses or develop healthy attitudes about substance use in a family such as this?

behaviors such as fire setting, and later in life seek out partners who are likely to provide the desired level of excitement, to re-create the family environment and allow them to feel "normal." Adolescents raised in such a dysfunctional home might be forced to spend so much time and energy meeting their basic survival needs that they are unlikely to have time to establish a strong self-concept or attend to other developmental issues of adolescence (Juliana & Goodman, 2005; Sheff et al., 2007). This then contributes to the tendency for children to grow up and become involved in a dysfunctional relationship when they do achieve adulthood, as noted in Chapter 22. Thus the family environment contributes later in life to the problem of Codependency.

Surprisingly, growing up in a home where there is a substance-abusing parent does not *automatically* result in problems for the growing child. There are a number of factors that influence the impact of parental SUDs on the child. For example, the sex of the substance-abusing parent influences the impact on the child. A second factor is the duration of time during which the parent was abusing chemicals. A parent who was abusing or addicted to a chemical(s) for "only" 3 years will have a different impact on the child's growth and development than a parent who has been physically dependent on a chemical for the child's entire life, for example. Another factor that might mute the impact of parental SUDs is the family constellation. A child raised in a home where parental substitutes in the form of older siblings will be protected to some degree from the impact of parental substance abuse. If the child can also find parental surrogates in the form of an uncle, neighbor, real or imagined hero, and so on, it is possible for the child to escape the worst of parental substance abuse.

It is necessary for the child to find a way to cope or adjust to parental SUDs. It is often surprising for readers to discover that *detachment* is paradoxically a reflection of *unconditional love* on the part of family members. In effect, the child or spouse learns that "your behavior is *not* a reflection on me" and that "I love you enough to let you be independent, even if this means that you choose a path of destruction." As part of this process, the individual learns to establish and maintain interpersonal boundaries (C. Black, 2003). This growth process can take many years, but in the end it blocks the unnatural enmeshment that had existed between family members and makes dysfunctional members responsible for their own behavior(s).

The Cost of Adolescent SUDs

Until now the discussion has focused on parental SUDs. However, the substance-abusing family member might also be a child or adolescent. Surprisingly, there has been virtually no research into how adolescent SUDs impact familial life. The authors did find that families with an adolescent substance abuser evidenced (a) a lack of trust in the adolescent on the part of all family members, (b) threats, abuse, and violence within the family, (c) siblings often angry with the substance-abusing adolescent for disturbing the familial tranquility, (d) a tendency for family members to isolate the substance-abusing adolescent, and (e) a tendency for parents to be blamed for the adolescent's substance abuse. There has been virtually no research into how adolescent substance abuse might impact the mental health of brothers or sisters of the adolescent substance abuser.

Interventions

The family in which there is a substance abuser or addict often does not know how to cope. However, there are a number of therapeutic interventions that might help the family. The most effective of these interventions is *coping skills training.*

Coping skills training (CST) does not attempt to identify why a certain family member has an SUD, and might not even include that person in the training sessions. The focus on CST is to help the affected family members learn how to cope with the afflicted member's behaviors. For example, if the identified patient has routinely asked for "loans" that were used to pay for alcohol or drugs, the CST program might focus on helping family members learn refusal skills. If the identified client should have a history of violence, and between one-third and one-half of male substance abusers have been violent toward their partner in the past year, the focus of the CST sessions might be on helping the spouse identify available resources and explore legal options to deal with this violence. Although the focus of CST is not to force the afflicted person into treatment, one common result of such training programs is that the alterations in clients' support group prove to be an incentive for them to enter a rehabilitation program. Further, CST training helps family members make the transition from being victims of the afflicted person's addiction to actively taking protective steps to cope with the individual's SUD.

The Adult Children of Alcoholics (ACOA) Movement

In the latter part of the 20th century, a number of adults stepped forward saying that they were suffering from emotional dysfunctions that they claimed were due to parental substance abuse. Because parental alcoholism is more prevalent than the abuse of other chemicals, these individuals came to be known as "adult children of alcoholics" (ACOAs). Although the therapeutic focus has shifted away from the ACOA model, health care professionals will still occasionally hear from patients who believe they were harmed by parental alcoholism.

Surprisingly, there has never been a single, accepted definition of the "adult child" of an alcoholic parent. But Ruben (2001) suggested that the term "carries a double meaning: an adult who is trapped in the fears and reactions of a child, and the child who was forced to be an adult without going through the natural stages that result in a healthy adult" (p. 8).

Proponents of the ACOA model hold that children raised in a home with parental alcoholism are emotionally scarred for life (Ruben, 2001). Because of the parental alcohol dependence, children would (a) have to guess at what normal behavior was in social situations, (b) have trouble forming intimate relationships, (c) have difficulty following a project through from start to finish, (d) tend to lie in situations where it was just as easy to tell the truth, (e) not feel comfortable with the "self" but constantly seek affirmation from others, (f) have trouble relaxing and having fun, (g) judge themselves harshly, (h) handle conflict situations poorly and try to avoid conflict if possible, and (i) be loyal to others, even if that loyalty is misplaced (such as when they are physically or sexually abused, or their partner has failed to respect their loyalty) (Ruben, 2001; Woititz, 1983).

Other characteristics of the "adult child" might include a tendency to self-sabotage (Ruben, 2001), that is, to express internal distress through conduct disorder or SUDs in childhood or adolescence (Fals-Stewart, O'Farrell, & Birchler, 2003, 2004). There is a danger that they will not allow themselves to exceed their parents' level of competence or achievement in life, lest they seem disloyal to their parents (Ruben, 2001). It has also been suggested that the traditional view of ACOAs is too narrow, and that some "adult children" develop personality traits that are the opposite of those expected of a child raised in a dysfunctional home. Thus whereas some "adult children" to

have trouble following through with activities, it has been suggested that others become overly responsible, compulsive workaholics and possibly overachievers (Ruben, 2001). It is possible to see from the last few paragraphs how parental SUDs (discussed in the Chapter 22) might result in a new generation of Codependent people, if you believe the ACOA model.

The team of K. E. Hart and Fissel (2003) explored the impact of growing up in a home where there was an alcohol-dependent parent on the later adjustment on children and found that the children of alcohol-dependent parents might be vulnerable to later physical illness as an adult, although the exact reason for the relationship is not clear at this time. It has also been suggested that being raised in a home where there was an alcohol-dependent parent might predispose children to problems such as dysthymia, phobias, and anxiety disorders.

The Growth of ACOA Support Groups

It is not possible to examine the self-help ACOA movement in detail. Historians will note, however, that ACOA support groups emerged and then grew more numerous at a phenomenal rate. At one point it was estimated that 40% of adults in the United States were a member of some kind of 12-Step support group, of which the ACOA groups were the most numerous (Garry, 1995). This phenomenal growth was fueled by many different factors, such as the large number of adults who thought that they had been hurt by parental AUDs, and the desire of many people to find peace and resolution by working through their feelings about their childhood experience(s) growing up with a parent with an AUD.

Criticism of the ACOA Movement

Perhaps the most revealing fact about the ACOA movement is how short-lived it was. There has been a significant reduction in both the number of ACOA groups and the number of participants in these groups. In some areas of the country, there has been a 9% decline in the membership of ACOA groups, and once-thriving groups now struggle to muster 10–20 members (Gillham, 2005). There are number of possible reasons for this phenomenon. First, it has never been proven that growing up in a home with a parent with an AUD *in itself* is sufficient to cause psychosocial problems for the children in that home, or for these same children when they grew up to become adults (Bijttebier, Goethals, & Ansoms, 2006).

Further, the philosophical grounds on which the ACOA movement is based has been challenged because it is essentially:

> *an enterprise wherein people holding the thinnest of credentials diagnose in basically normal people symptoms of inflated or invented maladies, so that they may then implement remedies that have never been shown to work. (Salerno, 2005, p. 2)*

The ACOA movement is a natural reflection of the American culture at the end of the 21st century, in which there is a "popular assumption that . . . without professional help most people are incapable of dealing with adversity (Sommers & Satel, 2005, p. 6). This assumption is wrong, and has been called "therapism" (Sommers & Satel, 2005, p. 6). This process has spawned an entire industry that, in order to continue to exist, must negate the possibility of resilience or that people might find a way to cope with adversity without professional intervention. This industry maintains that to cope with trauma, it is first necessary for individuals to express their feelings (with the assistance of a trained helper, who is often paid for this assistance) and then banish it from consciousness. Such techniques are supported by anecdotal evidence rather than scientific research, raising the possibility that any "cures" achieved through this practice may be just "placebo" cures.

This is perhaps epitomized by a conversation overheard by the author of this text in which a woman called in to a radio talk show that was hosting the author of a book on rape trauma. The caller reported that she had been raped when she was a certain age, and the rape trauma author interrupted her to immediately say, "You are a victim, and don't let anybody tell you otherwise!" Imagine this process being repeated a thousand times, and suddenly you have a demand for a new self-help book or therapeutic intervention, even if the consumer does not need such "assistance." Other examples include school districts that threaten to file criminal-neglect charges against parents who refuse psychoactive medications for children identified as having attention deficit hyperactivity disorder, although most states also have laws stating that patients (or their representatives) can refuse any medication that they do not wish to take.

Therapism has become big business, and virtually the only "research" being conducted is by publishing companies who want to identify and anticipate emerging market trends so that the next wave of "self-help" books might reach the largest number of people without helping them do more than spend their money on the latest craze in the self-help book market (Salerno, 2005). Such self-help books help readers relive traumatic events (possibly long forgotten) under the guise of helping them, while informing them of their victimhood status and weakening their coping abilities rather than assisting them in further growth (Salerno, 2005; Zur, 2005). Salerno supported this argument with the observation that self-help books have been on the market since the 1950s, if not longer, and there is little evidence that the rate of psychopathology in the United States has appreciably declined in that time.

It has even been suggested that the ACOA movement reflects the baby boomer generation's attempt to hold on to a portion of their childhood by repeatedly recalling or generating resentments from their own childhood while blaming the previous generation for perceived misdeeds. It is "fashionable to be a victim" (Zur, 2006, p. 49), and thus we can feel justified in failing to accomplish everything that we wanted when we were young adults while blaming our parents, or so it has been argued. Some individuals hold to this position so tenaciously that it is almost as if they were "addicted" to being in an ACOA or similar recovery group (Salerno, 2005).

The ACOA movement is based on what clinicians call the *damage model.* Proponents of this position hold that "all children are affected" by parental alcoholism, for example (C. Black, 1982, p. 27; see also C. Black, 2003). Yet in spite of strident, vocal advocates, the damage model has not been supported in the clinical literature. People find ways to cope with trauma. Bijttebier et al. (2006) examined data from a community sample of 10- to 14-year-old children from the Netherlands and Belgium, and found that they did not demonstrate higher levels of anxiety or depression when compared with a control group of children. The children did report lower levels of familial cohesion, which could contribute to the lower feelings of self-worth reported by the children, although it was not clear whether the lower self-esteem contributed to lower self-esteem or just the reverse. Further, it was discovered by the authors that parental support by the nondrinking parent and peer group relationships helped to mediate the impact of parental alcoholism.

Admittedly, some children are raised in terrible, abusive environments. But the assumption that growing up in such an environment *automatically* results in lifelong psychological pain for everybody has not been proven (Bijttebier et al., 2006). Using the criteria advocated by proponents of the ACOA movement, virtually all children are raised in a dysfunctional home, because the "healthy," conflict-free family is a myth. There has been little research into what constitutes a "normal" family, or the limits of unhealthy behavior(s)[7] that a family might tolerate and still provide a health environment for the children. Yet it is on this weak foundation that proponents of the ACOA model claim that 96% of the population was raised in a "dysfunctional" home (Salerno, 2005). This 96% figure has never been proven, but proponents of the ACOA model quote it as if it were an established fact.

People have been coping with what we would now call unhealthy environments for generations, and yet the species has survived. This reflects the effects of resilience, which is overlooked by the ACOA construct. There is evidence that resilience involves a gene that is involved in the synthesis of serotonin ("Resilience," 2006). This raises the question as to whether the "damage" done by parental AUDs is caused by their AUD or by possible genetic predisposition for depression and anxiety. Resilience does not mean that individuals are invulnerable to trauma, but that there is a natural development of the adaptive systems in childhood that may help children resist the damaging effects of their environment (D. Blum, 1998; Masten, 2001). It is only when these protective mechanisms are overwhelmed by extreme events that their normal growth is disrupted. However, resilient children are adept at finding ways to cope with parental AUDs through the use of parental surrogates or peer group support(s), and a focus on future goals rather than current familial disruptions.

It has also been suggested that the ACOA construct reflects an oversimplification of the developmental process (Zweig & Wolf, 1997). Simply naming a process does not imply that one understands it. An excellent example of this is cancer. Calling it "cancer" does not mean that its causes, controls, development, or suppression are understood in their entirety. Further, it has been suggested that the ACOA model often leaves the reconstructive process unfinished, having failed to proceed to the deepest levels necessary for complete healing (Zweig & Wolf, 1997).

Other detractors of the ACOA construct point to the emphasis of this model on what is called the "inner child," a phrase that has found its way into popular culture. The inner child is not a part of any established clinical theory, but reflects a complex blend of "[Carl] Jung, New Age mysticism, holy child mythology, pop psychology, and psychoanalytic theories about narcissism and the creation of a false self" (W. Kaminer, 1992, p. 17).

ACOA proponents focus on the problems of their childhood rather than those of adulthood. Even if this elusive creature existed, the "inner child" reflects a phase of life when the individual was emotionally, developmentally, cognitively, and socially immature. These conditions no longer exist for the individual, who has grown into adulthood even if the ACOA insists on focusing on perceived past trauma.

Finally, it has been suggested that the ACOA model is a white, middle-class invention. There has been virtually no application of this construct to inner-city children, for example, nor has this model been applied to substances other than alcohol. Yet there are children who have been raised in homes where the parents abused compounds such as cocaine or narcotic analgesics, and the literature that explores how being raised in such a home is quite limited.

Given these challenges to the ACOA model, one must wonder whether the personality characteristics identified as having been caused by being raised in a home where there was an alcoholic parent reflect not psychopathology but everyday problems in living. But now, thanks to an overabundance of self-help books, we have a language through which we might blame earlier generations for the problems in life that we might encounter, rather than take steps to address them.

Chapter Summary

This chapter addressed the impact of parental SUDs on the family. Although this topic is a popular one for general discussion, there are few clinical studies that explore the impact of parental SUDs on the family. Further, it has been revealed that much of what is true about the impact of parental alcoholism on the family is based on theory or personal beliefs, not on established fact. On the surface, it would appear that parental SUDs result in the child being "trained" to become dependent on external feedback, which then contributes to the development of Codependency.

It has been suggested that whereas proponents of the dysfunctional family model suggest that this is the cause of psychopathology in family members, the

---

[7]If the truth be told, we all have some unhealthy behaviors. Well, most of us have unhealthy behaviors.

"adult child" concept has met with considerable criticism and has almost disappeared from the research agenda. Health care professionals point out that the damage model dismisses the possibility of individual resilience. This model automatically assumes that the experience of growing up in a home with a parent who has an SUD will result in trauma, a theory that has not been proven. Health care professionals also suggest that the "adult children" concept of parents with SUDs places too much emphasis on perceived past slights during childhood, at the expense of current life problems for the adult.

CHAPTER **24**

The Dual-Diagnosis Client: Substance Use Disorders and Mental Illness

Introduction

Two generations ago many psychiatric textbooks suggested that substance use disorders (SUDs) in patients with mental illness were rare. This claim, based on clinical lore and a lack of research data, was found to be wrong. When epidemiological studies on SUDs among those with mental illness were conducted, health care professionals became increasingly aware of the fact that not only do the two conditions often exist in the same individual, but that the majority of psychiatric patients also have a co-occurring SUD (Buckley, 2006; Minkoff, 2008; Seppala, 2004). This knowledge was only the first step, as health care professionals still struggle to understand the complex relationship between SUDs and mental illness. Their confusion is perhaps best epitomized by the fact that clinicians have yet to even agree on whether to call these individuals dual-diagnosis clients, mentally ill substance abusers, or mentally ill/chemically dependent (MI/CD) patients.[1,2]

Although health care professionals now accept that dual-diagnosis patients are the norm rather than the exception, they still tend to view these patients as a single diagnostic category (for example, "mentally ill substance abusers") as opposed to a heterogeneous population with multiple pathways to both SUDs and expressions of their mental illness (Hesselbrock & Hesselbrock, 2007). Thus clinicians lack knowledge of such factors as those that (a) initiate and (b) maintain an SUD in those people who have a mental illness (Drake, Mueser, Brunette, & McHugo, 2004; Petrakis et al., 2002). As one would expect in such a state of confusion, there is limited research into what treatment methods might be most effective for the dual-diagnosis patient, how the effects of the drugs of abuse might help to suppress (or exacerbate) psychiatric symptoms, and whether substance abuse can simulate the symptoms of mental illness.

---

[1]A term that ignores the possibility that the mentally ill individual might be only a substance *abuser* and not be physically dependent on it.

[2]For the purposes of this text, the terms *dual diagnosis* or *MI/CD* will be used. It is recognized that each term is limited in scope, but we have to begin somewhere, do we not?

In this chapter the unfolding issue of how to identify and treat dual-diagnosis patients will be reviewed.

Definitions

Dual-diagnosis patients are said to suffer from a concurrent form of mental illness and an SUD. Unfortunately, there is little consensus about the forms of mental illness that should be used to define the dual-diagnosis client. It has been suggested that coexisting conditions such as SUDs and (a) anorexia, (b) bulimia, (c) gambling, (d) spousal abuse, (e) compulsive shopping, (f) compulsive sexual behaviors, (g) AIDS, and even (h) other physical disorders qualify as dual-diagnosis clients (Minkoff, 2008). This text will limit this term coexisting to psychiatric disorders as defined by the American Psychiatric Association (2000) and an SUD.

It is important to keep in mind that active substance abuse or the withdrawal from many drugs of abuse can magnify or simulate symptoms of psychiatric disorders (Buckley, 2006; S. Ross, 2008; Schuckit & Tapert, 2004). An excellent example of this is the anxiety often experienced by alcohol- or benzodiazepine-dependent people during the withdrawal process. This anxiety is usually drug induced and will usually diminish or disappear entirely when the individual recovers from the withdrawal process or the effects of acute substance abuse, and thus does not qualify for the term dual diagnosis (Minkoff, 2008).

Coexisting disorders are not difficult to understand. Patients often have more than one medical disorder: For example, a patient might suffer from hypertension and obesity, conditions that may be interrelated and that may interact (for instance, if you lose weight, your blood pressure will probably drop). When discussing dual-diagnosis clients, it is important to keep in mind that the SUD did not cause the psychiatric disorder, although it might be intertwined with it. An example of this might be a patient with a bipolar disorder who also abuses alcohol. Each disorder can influence the progression of the other, a fact that complicates the treatment of both conditions (Drake et al., 2001).

Theoretical Models

S. Ross (2008) suggested four possible models for dual-diagnosis conditions. In the first, it was suggested that

rather than a causal relationship between one and the other, both reflected a third, undiscovered factor. At best there is limited research evidence suggesting this possibility. Ross's second theory is that substance use by people with a mental illness reflects an attempt at self-medication. Although there is limited evidence suggesting that people with mental illness might use chemicals to self-medicate the dysphoria[3] commonly experienced in mental illness, there is little evidence of condition-specific substance abuse. The theory that substance abuse is secondary to another form of psychopathology and thus should resolve when the "primary" condition is the third theoretical model suggested by S. Ross. Although this theory was popular in the latter half of the 20th century, there is virtually no research evidence that supports this perspective.

The final model suggested by S. Ross (2008) was that individuals with mental illness might be exceptionally sensitive to the effects of the drugs of abuse. This "supersensitivity" model has some research evidence supporting it. However, it should be pointed out that no single model explains the problem of substance abuse by patients with mental illness.

Dual-Diagnosis Clients: A Diagnostic Challenge

Dual-diagnosis clients, or at least a client who possibly is a dual-diagnosis patient, offer a challenge to health care professionals. The assessor must have "the ability to distinguish the signs and symptoms of the primary psychiatric illness from those caused or exacerbated by a primary SUD" (Geppert & Minkoff, 2004, p. 105). This is a daunting task. The majority of patients admitted to a substance abuse treatment program will have symptoms of a psychiatric disorder at the time of admission. Many of these symptoms are substance induced or withdrawal induced, and will subside after a period of abstinence. Thus the assessor might have to wait for as long as 2–8 weeks for the diagnostic picture to clear (E. M. Jones et al., 2004; S. Ross, 2008; Work Group on Substance Use Disorders, 2007).

---

[3]See Glossary.

Minkoff (2008) pointed out that a careful clinical history might help differentiate substance-induced from actual psychiatric problems. For example, if a patient (and family members) attest that the depressive symptoms appeared months before the individual started drinking heavily, it would be safe to assume that the observed symptoms of depression reflect a preexisting disorder that now coexists with the SUD. The depression is not substance induced in spite of the apparent causal relationship. An accurate clinical history is thus of critical importance in the determination of actual dual-diagnosis clients as opposed to substance-induced psychiatric problems (Washton & Zweben, 2006).

Unfortunately, it is not uncommon to encounter patients who have the label of being dual-diagnosis patients who report that a careful clinical history was not carried out when they were admitted to other treatment centers. More than one patient has reported having been diagnosed as having a "transient psychosis" and started on antipsychotic medication, without any health care professional inquiring as to possible substance abuse. In addition to having been exposed to potent medications without need, these individuals now have to cope with the diagnosis of having a "transient psychosis" on their medical record, possibly for the rest of their lives. To complicate matters, the withdrawal syndrome from a chemical(s) might simulate the signs of virtually every known form of mental illness, and it is often necessary to wait 6–8 weeks to determine whether or not the psychiatric disorder is present.

The material in the last paragraph should not be interpreted as suggesting that every patient must wait 6–8 weeks before treatment of an apparent psychiatric disorder be started. If the symptoms are severe, the attending physician should immediately institute appropriate pharmacological treatment even if those symptoms are later determined to have been caused by a substance withdrawal syndrome (Busch, Weiss, & Najavits, 2005; Watkins, Burnam, Kung, & Paddock, 2001; Work Group on Substance Use Disorders, 2007). However, it should also be recognized that the diagnosis of a dual-diagnosis client is an ongoing process and might need to be modified as the patient recovers from the acute substance withdrawal syndrome.

Shivani, Goldsmith, and Anthenelli (2002) identified three subgroups of alcohol-abusing dual-diagnosis clients: (a) individuals with alcohol-related psychiatric symptoms, (b) individuals with alcohol-induced psychiatric syndromes, and (c) individuals with comorbid alcohol and psychiatric disorders. The first group experienced an alcohol-induced disruption of normal brain function according to the authors, resulting in the person demonstrating symptoms of a psychiatric disorder. In contrast to this subgroup were those drinkers who demonstrated symptoms of a psychiatric syndrome either caused or exacerbated by their use of alcohol. Admittedly the difference between these two subgroups is vague, and in both subgroups the symptoms usually clear with extended abstinence. However, the third group clearly has co-occurring psychiatric and alcohol use disorders, according to the authors.

Accurate diagnosis of either an SUD or any form of mental illness is complicated by the fact that each condition is viewed by some parts of society as a stigma (Pies, 2003). Like their normal peers, dual-diagnosis clients often utilize the defense mechanisms of denial and minimization, although in the latter case these defenses are utilized to protect to both their SUD and their mental health disorder (Minkoff, 2008; Shivani et al., 2002). Forceful questioning about either the possibility of an SUD or a mental health problem may (a) cause patients to experience significant levels of shame or (b) awaken fears in patients that by admitting to having an SUD they might lose entitlements (Social Security disability payments, for example). Some dual-diagnosis clients fear that their admission that they have an SUD could result in a refusal for access to psychiatric care. Also, because many dual-diagnosis clients feel so hopeless, they have little motivation to stop abusing drugs that might bring them some degree of relief from their emotional pain.

As the material reviewed so far suggests, the diagnosis of a psychiatric disorder in a substance abuser or the diagnosis of a substance abuse problem in a psychiatric patient can be extremely complicated. This raises the question that the next section attempts to answer.

Why Worry about Dual-Diagnosis Clients?

Perhaps the most eloquent answer to this question was provided by Geppert and Minkoff (2004), who suggested that:

As a whole this population has worse treatment outcomes, higher health care utilization; increased risk of violence, trauma, suicide, child abuse and neglect, and involvement in the criminal justice system; more medical comorbidity, particularly of infectious diseases; and higher health care costs than people with a single disorder. (p. 103)

As mentioned previously, there is a significantly higher risk of suicide in dual-diagnosis clients (Geppert, & Minkoff, 2004; Mueser et al., 2003; S. Ross, 2008), which has been estimated to be 60- to 120-fold higher than for the general population (Nielson et al., 1998). Further, dual-diagnosis clients are at increased risk for incarceration, less able to handle personal finances, and more prone to depression and feelings of hopelessness. They tend to have a weaker support system than does the normal person.

Because of their fragile brain chemistries, dual-diagnosis clients run the risk of exacerbating their psychiatric disorder through their abuse of recreational chemicals. This "sensitization" effect is especially noticeable in patients with schizophrenia (S. Ross, 2008). Even social use of alcohol, for example, can destabilize the dual-diagnosis client and result in a greater need for rehospitalization (Mueser et al., 2003; Patrick, 2003; J. J. Prochaska, Gill, Hall, & Hall, 2005). Further, untreated psychiatric symptoms can serve as a "relapse trigger" for renewed substance abuse (E. M. Jones et al., 2004; Washton & Zweben, 2006). This in turn can result in the need for rehospitalization.

Dual-diagnosis clients are also at increased risk of being assaulted and of being homeless (Brekke, Prindle, Woo Bae, & Long, 2001; Pankiewicz, 2008; S. Ross, 2008). Their need for repeated hospitalizations imposes an increased financial burden imposed on society and often on their families. They face a 300% higher chance of contracting the virus that causes AIDS,[4] a 170% higher risk for contracting the hepatitis B virus, and a 250% higher chance of contracting the hepatitis C virus,[5] the treatment of which is often carried out at public expense. Finally, clients who have developed posttraumatic stress disorder (PTSD) after psychological or physical trauma have higher rates of SUDs and are at increased risk for retraumatization (Mueser et al., 2003). Thus there are significant social and personal financial losses either caused or exacerbated by substance use by psychiatric patients (Pankiewicz, 2008). All of these issues make the need to address dual-diagnosis issues undeniable.

Scope of the Problem

With the introduction of the first generation of antipsychotic medications in the late 1950s, society began to call for the "deinstitutionalization" of patients formerly hospitalized in private and state facilities. However, support services in the community were overwhelmed or did not exist, and patients released into the community often refused to take prescribed medications because of their harsh side effects. At the start of the 21st century, many people who would have been sent to state hospitals in earlier generations are now homeless or incarcerated (S. Ross, 2008). Indeed, so many people with mental illness are now incarcerated that some authorities view the prison system to be the new state hospital system for the mentally ill.

An estimated 4 million individuals are thought to have a concurrent substance abuse and mental illness problem in the United States (S. Ross, 2008). Unfortunately, only 8% of MI/CD clients received treatment for both disorders in the past year, and 72% have never had both issues addressed in a treatment setting (J. J. Prochaska et al., 2005). Where treatment is offered, it is most often for either the mental illness problem or the SUD, but not both disorders (Buckley, 2006). In the correctional system, "treatment" is usually limited to pharmacological control of the mental illness problem alone.

Health care professionals were once taught that substance abuse was rare in psychiatric patients, or, if it did exist, it was secondary to the "primary" psychiatric disorder. Further, it was mistakenly believed that if the primary psychiatric disorder could be resolved, the individual's motivation for further substance use would disappear and the SUD would resolve itself (Washton & Zweben, 2006). It is now understood that these are separate, each potentially deadly, disorders that might coexist in the same individual, if not predispose the person to the other disorder. It has been found, for example, that if patients have any form of mental illness, they are 270% more likely to have an SUD than the average person (Volpicelli, 2005). Various estimates suggest that between 30 and 80% of patients with a form of mental illness also have an SUD (Minkoff, 2008; Patrick, 2003; S. Roberts, 2004; Watkins et al., 2001). Table 24-1 summarizes the estimated concordance rate between the SUDs and various psychiatric disorders.

The relationship between a mental illness and a concurrent SUD is quite complex. There is evidence, for example, suggesting that the more serious the form of psychopathology, the more difficult it might be for the individual to abstain from drug abuse (Ritsher, Moos, & Finney, 2000). This is consistent with the findings of the team of Chambers et al. (2007), who concluded that rats that had suffered damage to the amygdala region of the brain were more responsive to novel stimuli, less

---

[4]These viral infections are discussed in Chapter 36.

[5]Often at public expense through Medicare and similar programs.

CONDITION	ESTIMATED LIFETIME SUD PREVALENCE RATE
Depression	17–32%
Bipolar affective disorder	56–64%
Anxiety disorder	15–36%
Antisocial personality disorder (ASPD)	84%
Attention deficit hyperactivity disorder (ADHD)	23%
Eating disorders: Anorexia	17%
Bulimia	46%
Posttraumatic stress disorder (PTSD)	30–75%
Schizophrenia	50%
Somatoform disorders	Unknown

TABLE 24-1 ESTIMATED CONCORDANCE RATE BETWEEN SELECT FORMS OF PSYCHOPATHOLOGY AND SUDS

NOTE: Based on Hartwell, Tolliver, and Brady (2009), S. Ross (2008), and Ziedonis and Brady (1997).

responsive to dangerous stimuli, and more prone to cocaine addiction. Although suggestive, the assessment of amygdala function in the human brain is difficult, making it virtually impossible to determine whether this is a factor in human cocaine abuse or SUDs in general.

Unfortunately, physicians are rarely trained to detect and treat SUDs in psychiatric patients. It has been found, for example, that emergency room physicians will, when confronted with a dual-diagnosis client, commonly attribute the observed symptoms to the patient's psychiatric disorder to the exclusion of a possible SUD[6] (Schanzer, First, Dominguez, Hasin, & Caton, 2006). This underscores the need for training for professionals to better understand and properly diagnose dual-diagnosis patients.

Psychopathology and Drug of Choice

For many years, clinicians were taught that there was a relationship between patients' psychiatric disorders and their drug of choice. This hypothesis, although it continues to echo through the academic halls where health care professionals are trained, has not been supported by the clinical literature (Drake, 2007; Drake & Mueser, 2002). Part of the confusion might be traced to the fact that much of the clinical data is drawn from research studies that perhaps unknowingly intermixed substance abusers and individuals who are addicted to a chemical(s) as subjects. It has been assumed that both abusers and addicted people with mental illness engage in substance abuse for the same reasons, an unproven assumption at best. It is possible that a substance abuser might engage in chemical use (possibly to self-medicate emotional distress), whereas a mentally ill person with a physical addiction to a drug continues to abuse chemicals for other reasons (avoidance of withdrawal effects, association with a peer group, and so on) (F. Weiss, 2005). The results of intermixing substance abusers with addicted people with psychiatric conditions might have failed to support what is actually a very defendable hypothesis: that substance abusers seek to self-medicate their emotional pain by abusing alcohol and drugs.

Proponents of the self-medication hypothesis often point to the apparent tendency for people who have developed PTSD to engage in substance abuse (Cross & Ashley, 2007; Khantzian, 2003b; Preuss & Wong, 2000). This is a complicated matter, for the course of PTSD varies over time.[7] People's goal in self-medication is also thought to vary over the course of time, depending on whether they were attempting to cope with the intrusive memories of the trauma or with the emptiness of emotional numbing (Khantzian, 2003b).

It has been suggested that although the self-medication hypothesis has significant appeal to clinicians because it seems to have face value, there is little clinical research supporting this theory (Mueser et al., 2003; S. Ross, 2008). Perhaps some people with a mental illness are drawn to substance use for the same reason as are other people: It is "cool" and a sign of rebellion (M. J. Sharp & Getz, 1998, p. 642). At the same time, substance abuse may offer the abuser an identity of sorts and on some level aid in the development of a social network (Busch et al., 2005; Drake & Mueser, 2002). Finally, in the minds of many dual-diagnosis clients, the stigma associated with substance abuse is less severe than is that associated with mental

[6]In defense of the attending physician, in many cases the emergency room doctor has limited historical data on the patient, who may be unable or unwilling to provide a history. This makes it difficult to differentiate between psychiatric dysfunction and substance-induced problems. However, it should also be noted that a misdiagnosis can have lifelong implications for the client (Schanzer et al., 2006).

[7]The issue of PTSD and its manifestations are discussed in more depth in Breakout Discussion #1.

illness, motivating many dual-diagnosis clients to substitute the less severe stigma of having an SUD for that of mental illness (M. J. Sharp & Getz, 1998).

Substance abusers, including those with a form of mental illness, tend to be more impulsive and interested in new sensations (Dervaux et al., 2001). This would suggest that mentally ill substance abusers might not be engaging in self-medication so much as seeking new sensory sensations for entertainment. Further, the availability of alcohol or drug(s) impacts on individuals' substance use pattern both for those with a mental illness and for those who do not have such a disorder (Drake, 2007). Because alcohol is the most common substance available in society, it stands to reason that mentally ill substance abusers will more commonly abuse alcohol than other compounds. This hypothesis is supported by the study completed by Swartz et al. (2006), who concluded that the pattern of substance abuse by schizophrenic patients studied was similar to those found in the general community. A similar finding was reported by Lybrand and Caroff (2009), who observed that cocaine abuse by people with schizophrenia was rare in rural areas of the country, but more common in urban areas, where it is more easily obtained.

The factor of drug availability may have confounded early studies that attempted to find a correlation between the form of mental illness and the substance(s) being abused. Most certainly there is little evidence to support a condition-specific pattern for substance abuse by those with mental illness who also have an SUD, although Miles et al. (2003) did find a positive relationship between CNS stimulant abuse and violence. But it is not clear whether the observed violence was the result of CNS stimulant abuse, which in itself can contribute to violent behavior by the abuser, or was the result of the individual's mental illness. Still, because the self-medication hypothesis has so many supporters, we will examine the relationship between various forms of mental illness and SUDs.

Attention Deficit Hyperactivity Disorder (ADHD)

In the final years of the 20th century, ADHD emerged from the depths of controversy to become an accepted diagnostic entity. Currently, it is thought that ADHD is about as prevalent as asthma, affecting 4–5% of the population (Khurana & Schubiner, 2007).

A relationship between ADHD and SUDs was first suggested approximately a decade ago (Diller, 1998;

B. H. Smith, Molina, & Pelham, 2002). For example, 21% of adults with ADHD are thought to have a concurrent cocaine use disorder (Acosta et al., 2005). It is not clear whether the ADHD caused the SUD, whether both conditions reflected a third unidentified factor, or whether the observed findings were just a chance finding of no clinical significance. However, scientists do know that both conditions reflect a dysfunction of the dopamine neurotransmission system of the medial forebrain region of the brain, which appears to be the common factor.

There was a popular myth in the 1990s and early part of the 21st century that adolescents with ADHD were at increased risk for CNS stimulant abuse. The truth is just the opposite: If the adolescent's ADHD is adequately controlled, the individual appears to be at lower risk for the development of an SUD later in life (Work Group on Substance Use Disorders, 2007). However, it is still recommended that parents control access to the medication(s) being used to treat the ADHD to minimize potential abuse problems (Biederman et al., 2008; Knight, 2005).

The exception to this rule are those children who suffer from one of the conduct disorders,[8] such as the oppositional defiant disorder.[9] These children do appear to be at increased risk for the later development of an SUD (August et al., 2006; Disney, Elkins, McGue, & Iacono, 1999; Lynskey & Hall, 2001). This apparent association between children with a conduct disorder and subsequent substance abuse might reflect the fact that between 35 and 50% of children diagnosed with ADHD also have a conduct disorder and thus is an artifact rather than a real clinical issue (Smucker & Hedayat, 2001).

There has been a great deal of research on childhood ADHD, and it has been discovered that in about 85% of cases this condition does carry over into adulthood[10] (Khurana & Schubiner, 2007; Wilens, 2006). Between 15 and 25% of adults with ADHD will also have an SUD, and active substance abuse can make the diagnosis of ADHD difficult (Wilens, 2006). In cases of proven adolescent ADHD, CNS stimulants such as methylphenidate or the amphetamines should not be the treatment of choice (Riggs, 2003). Rather,

---

[8]See Glossary.

[9]See Glossary.

[10]It should be pointed out that most substance abuse rehabilitation professionals are not trained in the diagnosis of ADHD. Suspected cases should be assessed by a psychologist or physician who specializes in the diagnosis of such cases.

compounds such as bupropion, pemoline, and atmoxetine have been found to be both safe and effective in treating adolescent ADHD without the high abuse potential of the CNS stimulants.[11]

There is preliminary evidence suggesting that individuals with ADHD are more vulnerable to the disinhibiting effects of alcohol than people without ADHD (Weafer, Fillmore, & Milich, 2009). Weafer et al. found that adults with ADHD appear to demonstrate less behavioral control in response to a given amount of alcohol than did the control subjects, and that there was a dose-dependent loss of inhibition in both groups that was most pronounced in the ADHD group of subjects. The authors of this study call for further research into this area, which hints that adolescents and adults with ADHD might not respond to alcohol in the same manner as normal people will, possibly making them more vulnerable to AUDs although this has yet to be proven.

The issue of ADHD has been controversial, and the construct has even been challenged in the clinical literature. However, cutting-edge research using functional magnetic resonance imaging (fMRI) hints at abnormal regional brain activation patterns in adolescents or adults with ADHD as compared with age-matched normal clients, suggesting that accurate tests to identify such patients can be developed in time. If such tests are developed, the client should be substance free at the time of assessment because these compounds can also cause abnormal regional brain activation patterns.

Schizophrenia

Between 40 and 50% of patients with schizophrenia also have a concurrent SUD (Lybrand & Caroff, 2009; Pankiewicz, 2008; Roberts, 2004). Statistically, the most commonly abused substance was alcohol (used by 34% of people with schizophrenia), although about 13% will develop an SUD involving a compound(s) other than alcohol (S. Ross, 2008). Substance abuse by patients with schizophrenia is associated with an earlier onset of schizophrenia, a poorer response to psychiatric treatment, higher rates of rehospitalization due to a resurgence of psychiatric symptoms, greater likelihood of being noncompliant with medications prescribed for their psychiatric disorder, and greater likelihood of engaging in suicidal behavior, increased

violence, greater likelihood of being victimized, increased homelessness, and greater likelihood of being incarcerated than schizophrenic patients who do not abuse recreational chemicals (Lybrand & Caroff, 2009; Pankiewicz, 2008). The association between schizophrenia and SUDs is so strong that Fazel, Långstrom, Hjern, Grann, and Lichtenstein (2009) concluded that the observed link between schizophrenia and violent crime might be limited almost exclusively to those people with both an SUD and schizophrenia.

Higher-functioning patients with schizophrenia are more likely to have a concurrent SUD. Upon reflection this becomes apparent: Because of their higher level of function they have the interpersonal skills necessary to access alcohol or illicit drugs (Swartz et al., 2006). Although there is no apparent relationship between schizophrenia and the individual's substance of choice, it should be pointed out that availability is a significant factor in the patient's substance use behaviors. Surprisingly, many patients with schizophrenia will seek out hallucinogenic compounds to use. Given that hallucinations are a primary symptom of schizophrenia, intuitively one would expect that patients with schizophrenia would avoid these compounds. However, many of these patients defend their abuse of hallucinogens because these compounds at least give them some degree of control over when they experience hallucinations, which provides an insight into their motivation to abuse these compounds and the magnitude of emotional discomfort experienced by many patients with schizophrenia.

There is a significant interactional effect between schizophrenia and nicotine dependence. It has been estimated that at least 90% of patients with schizophrenia also smoke cigarettes, and many are heavy cigarette smokers (Pankiewicz, 2008). Fully 44% of all cigarettes consumed in the United States are consumed by people with a mental illness, which exposes them to all of the dangers associated with cigarette smoking[12] ("Why Do the Mentally Ill Die Younger?", 2008). In the case of schizophrenia, it is thought that the nicotine in cigarettes helps to reverse many of the cognitive deficits associated with the disorder or the medications used to treat it (Pankiewicz, 2008). However, the health risks associated with tobacco use mitigate any possible benefit from cigarette smoking in this population, and smoking cessation in this population is recommended (Hitsman, Moss, Montoya, & George, 2009).

---

[11]The clinician's suspicion that patients might also have a concurrent SUD should be raised if the patients suggest that the *only* compounds that have worked for them are the CNS stimulants, with higher abuse potentials.

---

[12]Discussed in Chapter 16.

Patients with schizophrenia who abuse cocaine experience a different cocaine withdrawal syndrome than is normally seen (G. Carol, Smelson, Losonczy, & Ziedonis, 2001). Further, individuals who suffer from schizophrenia and who habitually abuse cocaine are at higher risk for developing tardive dyskinesia[13] than those people with schizophrenia who do not abuse this compound (Lybrand & Caroff, 2009). These disorders all reflect a dysfunction of the dopamine neurotransmission system, and this might be the reason why schizophrenic patients appear to experience more intense craving for cocaine than do nonschizophrenic patients during cocaine withdrawal. This suggests that there is a need for intensive intervention, including possible modification of medications, to help these individuals cope with the symptoms of cocaine withdrawal.

There has been little formal research into the issue of which medications might be most effective in treating substance-abusing clients with schizophrenia (San, Arranz, & Martinez-Rega, 2007). Anecdotal reports suggest that the "second generation" or "atypical" antipsychotic medications are more effective in controlling the symptoms of schizophrenia in such patients than the older medications used to treat this condition, but there has been little formal research into this area (San et al., 2007).

Anxiety Disorders

The relationship between SUDs and anxiety disorders is quite complicated (Maremmani et al., 2010). Many of the drugs of abuse can induce anxiety either as a side effect of their use or during the withdrawal process. To complicate matters, it is quite common for individuals to turn to alcohol or other drugs of abuse to self-medicate anxiety (Encrenaz et al., 2009). Thus it is imperative that the health care professional(s) working with individuals determine whether they are experiencing substance-related anxiety, or if they have a concurrent anxiety disorder, to assist in the proper treatment of patients.

One point that assists in the differentiation between substance-induced anxiety and anxiety disorders is that the anxiety disorders are thought to predate the development of the SUD (Cheng, Gau, Chen, Chang, & Chang, 2004). However, this does not negate the need for a case-by-case evaluation to determine the exact relationship between individuals'

anxiety disorders and their SUD. For example, as was noted in Chapter 5, one symptom of the alcohol withdrawal syndrome is anxiety (Driessen et al., 2001). Such withdrawal-related anxiety usually disappears in the first days or weeks following alcohol cessation.[14] It is only if individuals continue to experience moderate to severe levels of anxiety or depression after 3 weeks of abstinence that the possibility they have a concurrent anxiety disorder should be considered (Driessen et al., 2001).

The anxiety disorders, at least in theory, provide a clear example of the self-medication hypothesis advanced by psychoanalytic theorists (Khantzian, 2003b). Thus according to this theory, the individual would be drawn to the abuse of alcohol, opioids, or benzodiazepines, all compounds with an anxiolytic effect. This theory is supported by the research finding that up to 20% of individuals with a primary anxiety disorder also have a concurrent SUD (Preuss & Wong, 2000). It is thought that about 15% of people with an AUD will demonstrate social anxiety, whereas 20% of those people in treatment for social anxiety will also have a concurrent alcohol use problem (Book & Randall, 2000).

There are a number of effective medications as well as psychotherapies for social anxiety disorder, and some medications that are contraindicated for use with substance-abusing patients with an anxiety disorder. For example, although the monoamine oxidase inhibitors (MAOIs) have been found to be very effective in treating social anxiety disorder, these medications are contraindicated for patients with an SUD because of the risk that they will use alcohol, exposing them to the risk of a potentially fatal hypertensive crisis as the MAOI interacts with some of the compounds found in some forms of beer, wine, and liquor (Book & Randall, 2000). Further, whereas the benzodiazepines have been found to be useful for the short-term relief of anxiety, their abuse potential prohibits their use in treating patients with a social anxiety disorder and an SUD (E. M. Jones et al., 2004; Riggs, 2003). The selective serotonin reuptake inhibitors (SSRIs) are now viewed as the most appropriate treatment for this subgroup of patients (Book & Randall, 2002; E. M. Jones et al., 2004; S. Ross, 2008).

---

[13]See Glossary.

[14]This is not to imply that the individual's anxiety should not be addressed during the alcohol withdrawal syndrome. Rather, the issue being considered here is whether or not the individual has a concurrent anxiety disorder.

The Dissociative Disorders[15]

The dissociative disorders represent a series of related conditions in which the individual essentially is able to "detach" from reality for periods of time to escape from extreme psychological stress. One man, upon being told of the death of his spouse, recalls the sensation of watching himself from across the room as he lost consciousness, slamming his head against a concrete wall and a cement floor on the way down, while thinking "that's gonna hurt". This short period of dissociation illustrates how dissociation can help the person escape from psychological stress, although the man in this case was the first to admit that the emotional numbing did not last long enough.

It should be noted that dissociation does not involve the use of psychoactive chemicals. This state is achieved by the mind itself. In its most extreme form, the individual might manifest more than one personality, a condition that was once called multiple personality disorder and is now called the dissociative identity disorder (DID). There are differences between the "normal" patient with an SUD and a patient with a coexisting DID and SUD. First, such patients usually do not report reduced discomfort at the end of detoxification, but may report continued distress or even higher levels of distress. From the observer's standpoint, patients with these comorbid disorders will appear to relapse at times of apparent stability.

It has been estimated that approximately one-third of patients with DID will also have a coexisting SUD (Putnam, 1989). CNS depressants such as alcohol or the benzodiazepines are more commonly abused by patients with DID, although on occasion the CNS stimulants are also abused. Hallucinogens do not seem to be a popular class of drugs to be abused for this subpopulation, possibly because of the impact of these compounds on the abuser (Putnam, 1989). Substance abuse by patients with DID appears to be an attempt to self-medicate their emotional distress (Putnam, 1989).

Obsessive-Compulsive Disorder (OCD)

This is the fourth most common psychiatric disorder found in the United States. Researchers disagree about the percentage of patients with OCD who have a concurrent SUD. Encrenaz et al. (2009) offered an estimate of 11.5% of men and 5.5% of women with OCD having a concurrent SUD. Drawing on another sample, Goldsmith and Garlapati (2004) estimated that up to 36% of those people with OCD will have a concurrent SUD. There does not appear to be a specific compound favored by individuals with OCD, although theoretically patients with OCD might be drawn to the CNS depressants such as alcohol or the benzodiazepines because of their anxiolytic properties.

Bipolar Affective Disorders[16]

The bipolar affective disorders might be exacerbated by the abuse of some compounds, especially the amphetamines, alcohol, and cannabis (Maremmani et al., 2010). Further, the process of withdrawing from the drugs of abuse can induce either mania or depression (Sonne & Brady, 2002; Suppes & Keck, 2005). Such treatment often involves the use of mood-stabilizing medications, which have been proven to be safe and effective in controlling the symptoms of this condition (Maremmani et al., 2010).

It has been estimated that between 40 and 70% of patients with a bipolar disorder will also demonstrate symptoms of an SUD at some point in their lives (E. S. Brown, 2005; Ostacher & Sachs, 2006; Vornik & Brown, 2006). Substance abuse by these dual-diagnosis patients appears to be a factor in the need for more frequent hospitalizations, less effective symptom control, and an increased failure rate for therapeutic intervention for either condition (Maremmani et al., 2010; Sadock & Sadock, 2007; Sonne & Brady, 2002). One reason for the increased rate of treatment failures is the possibility that the sense of confidence and enthusiasm often seen during the manic stage is frequently interpreted by rehabilitation center staff as treatment progress rather than a symptom of mania (Maremmani et al., 2010).

Clinical research suggests that substance abusers with a bipolar disorder tend to use more drugs of abuse during the manic phase of their condition, although an exception to this rule is the alcoholic with a bipolar affective disorder (Maremmani et al., 2010). In the latter case it would appear that alcohol-dependent people who are in the depressed phase of a bipolar disorder drink more than they do at other times (Maremmani et al., 2010). It has been hypothesized that some patients might use CNS stimulants such as cocaine to simulate the manic phase of a bipolar disorder, to prolong the sense of power and invulnerability experienced during the earlier phases of mania.

---

[15]Discussed in more detail in Breakout Discussion #2.

[16]This condition was once referred to as *manic depression*.

As was discussed earlier in this text, there are characteristic withdrawal syndromes for each class of the drugs of abuse, and in many cases depression is a symptom experienced during drug withdrawal. In dual-diagnosis people however, the depression that often accompanies the withdrawal from many recreational compounds may serve as a relapse "trigger," contributing to urges to return to substance abuse (F. Weiss, 2005).

The relationship between the bipolar affective disorders and the SUDs is quite complicated. It is imperative that the clinician have an accurate clinical history to help determine whether the observed symptoms predate or emerged after the patient started to abuse chemicals (Minkoff, 2008). Collateral information is often of value in the assessment process and during the formulation of a differential diagnosis, and appropriate treatment for the patient should be initiated immediately (Minkoff, 2008; Ostacher & Sachs, 2006).

Depression

Although the experience of depression is often seen in patients with a bipolar disorder, depression is also a disorder in its own right and thus here it is appropriate to discuss both the depressed phase of a bipolar disorder and depression as a separate condition. Depression spans a range of conditions ranging from the depressed phase of a bipolar disorder through the various forms of major depression (both with and without psychotic features) to dysthymia.[17]

Research has shown that depressed individuals are at increased risk for the development of an SUD: 21% of those who have experienced depression in the last year also have an AUD, and 9% met the diagnostic criteria for a drug use disorder (K. E. Wells, Paddock, Zhang, & Wells, 2006). This is just within the past year: Over the course of their lifetime, 27% of patients with a major depression and 31–43% of patients with dysthymia will also have an SUD (Evans & Sullivan, 2001; Goldsmith & Garlapati, 2004; McIlveen, Mullaney, Weiner, Diaz, & Horton, 2007). Fourteen percent of men who are depressed also have an SUD, as opposed to just 5.8% of depressed women (Encrenaz et al., 2009). This discrepancy might reflect the tendency for women to seek professional help with depression more often than do men.

The treatment of concurrent depression and substance abuse is rather complicated in that the abuse of chemicals within this patient population can either exacerbate their depression or negate the effects of prescribed medications that are designed to help them recover from depression. The reverse is also true: Untreated depression complicates the treatment of SUDs (K. E. Wells et al., 2006). There is a financial incentive to identify and effectively treat patients with concurrent depression and SUDs. It has been found that the amount of money spent treating patients with comorbid dysthymia and an SUD was five times higher than that necessary to treat a patient with only an SUD (Westermeyer, Eames, & Nugent, 1998). Further, untreated depression is a possible "relapse trigger" following detoxification for patients with comorbid depression and SUDs (McIlveen et al., 2007; Nunes & Levin, 2006). Although clinical lore holds that people with an AUD are more prone to major depression, a more common pattern is that individuals with major depression are at increased risk for the development of an AUD (Fergusson, Boden, & Horwood, 2009).

To identify individuals with a primary depression,[18] it is necessary to obtain a detailed, comprehensive psychiatric history (Minkoff, 2008; Nunes & Levin, 2006). This history will reveal whether the depression predated the SUD or developed after the individual began to abuse chemicals. However, in cases where the individual has a long-standing SUD, this differentiation might not be possible. In all cases the SUD should be addressed immediately, while the health care professional(s) continuously monitors the patients' status against the possibility that they have a primary depression that might have been masked by the SUD (Minkoff, 2008).

Eating Disorders

Although eating disorders are predominantly found in girls, adolescent girls, or women, there is a small subgroup of men who also have one or another form of an eating disorder.[19] There is a known relationship between eating disorders and AUDs, and each complicates the treatment of the other (L. R. Cohen & Gordon, 2009). The relationship between eating disorders and other forms of drug abuse is not clear at this time. But it is known that people with an eating disorder often use alcohol to suppress their appetite and to avoid or suppress food "urges" (L. R. Cohen & Gordon, 2009).

---

[17]See Glossary.

[18]As opposed to a substance-induced depression.

[19]There are several subtypes of eating disorders. The topic of eating disorders and the recognition of each subtype is beyond the scope of this text. The reader is referred to any of a growing number of books on the topic of eating disorders for more information.

Because many of the other drugs of abuse suppress appetite or make the user "numb" to the sensation of hunger, it is not unreasonable to expect that some people with an eating disorder use these compounds for the same reasons.

It has been suggested that the eating disorders are a form of self-medication of emotional distress, although this theory has not met with universal acceptance (L. R. Cohen & Gordon, 2009). It has also been suggested that AUDs and eating disorders are different manifestations of a self-regulatory mechanism(s), although the exact causal mechanisms for either condition remains uncertain. It has been found that less than 20% of publicly funded substance abuse rehabilitation programs screen for eating disorders, and that only a small percentage of treatment programs have the ability to treat people with co-occurring eating disorders and SUDs (L. R. Cohen & Gordon, 2009). As should be obvious by now, there is much to be discovered about the relationship between eating disorders and SUDs, as well as the treatment of these conditions when they are both found in the same person.

Compulsive Gambling

Gambling in itself is not a sign of psychopathology. The vast majority of the population will gamble at one time or another, even if the stakes are as small as a can of soda. However, about 2–7% of those who gamble do so compulsively, possibly in spite of past negative experiences while gambling (J. E. Grant, Kushner, & Kim, 2002; Potenza, Fiellin, Heninger, Rounsaville, & Mazure, 2002; Potenza, Kosten, & Rounsaville, 2001).

Pathological gambling frequently coexists with SUDs. Researchers have found that up to 44% of those individuals who have a compulsive-gambling problem will also have an AUD at some point in their lives (J. E. Grant et al., 2002). Compulsive gamblers are thought to be two to four times as likely to have an AUD as the average person (J. E. Grant et al., 2002). This shared vulnerability appears to reflect the fact that each disorder activates the brain's reward circuitry, which in turn can serve as a relapse trigger for the other disorder. Another possible relapse trigger is that the negative experiences (financial losses) incurred while gambling entice individuals to use chemicals to make themselves "numb" to the emotional pain of their financial distress.

Further, there appears to be a relationship between depression and compulsive gambling; however, there is little correlation between the amount of money lost and the intensity of the individual's depression (Unwin, Davis, & De Leeuw, 2000). If the individual has lost a

significant amount of money, then there is a danger of suicidal thinking by the client. Long-term rehabilitation involves confronting the individual's irrational beliefs about both substance use and gambling, and helping the gambler develop a coping style that negates the urges to engage in gambling. Self-help groups such as Gamblers Anonymous (GA), modeled after similar groups for alcohol and other drugs, are often of value in this effort. However, clinicians must keep in mind that compulsive-gambling disorders frequently coexist with SUDs, and that each can complicate the treatment of the other.

Personality-Disordered Clients

It has been estimated that 50–60% of clients with an SUD have a concurrent personality disorder[20] (Work Group on Substance Use Disorders, 2007). Individuals with a personality disorder and an SUD are overrepresented in the population of patients with SUDs, as compared to 40% of individuals with an AUD, but only 6% of the control sample were found to have a personality disorder (Echeburua, de Medina, & Aizpiri, 2005). The most common subgroup were those individuals with a dependent personality disorder (13% of Echeburua et al.'s research sample), followed by the paranoid personality disorder and the compulsive personality disorder (10% each), according to the authors.

Antisocial Personality Disorder and SUDs

The most common personality disorder found in the substance-abusing population is the antisocial personality disorder (ASPD). In the general population, just under 6% of men and 1.2% of women will meet the diagnostic criteria for this condition at some point in their life (Daghestani, Dinwiddie, & Hardy, 2001). However, this subgroup of the population tends to engage in alcohol abuse at an earlier age, and to be much more likely to have an AUD later in life (Moeller & Dougherty, 2001). It has been estimated that between 15 and 50% of men with an alcohol dependence problem and 1% of women with an alcohol dependence problem have a concurrent personality disorder, most commonly ASPD (McCrady, 2001; Shivani et al., 2002). It has also been estimated that up to 48% of those individuals with a cocaine use disorder, up to 48% of those with an opiate

---

[20]To learn more about the concept of personality disorders, the reader is referred to the *DSM-IV-TR* (American Psychiatric Association, 2000) or a good psychopathology textbook.

TABLE 24-2 SUBGROUPS OF ANTISOCIAL PERSONALITY-DISORDERED CLIENTS

SUBGROUP	PERCENTAGE OF TOTAL SAMPLE	CONDUCT DISORDER IN CHILDHOOD?	CHARACTERISTICS
Early onset, strong ASPD features	10%	Yes	Meets *DSM-IV-TR* criteria for diagnosis of ASPD
Late onset, strong ASPD features	12%	Yes, but not as often as the preceding group	ASPD symptoms do not appear until adulthood, with minor conduct problems as a child observed.
Emotionally unstable ASPD subgroup	18%	Moderate history of childhood conduct disorder	Hostility, guilt, dependent behaviors, avoidant features all begin to manifest in adulthood
Non-ASPD/substance-induced features	17%	Rarely	Substance-induced ASPD features
Moderate substance abuse/moderate ASPD features	15%	Rarely	Strong ASPD features intermixed with low levels of guilt or depression, some substance-induced distress
Low ASPD	28%	Rarely	Rare reports of antisocial behaviors in adulthood

NOTE: Based on Alterman et al. (1998).

use disorder, and up to 62% of polydrug abusers have ASPD (Vaglum, 2003).

This single personality disorder accounts for 23% of the overlap between personality-disordered clients and substance-abusing clients (Grekin, Sher, & Wood, 2006). Alterman et al. (1998) examined the relationship between ASPD and opioid use disorders and found that in their sample of 252 individuals in a methadone maintenance program diagnosed with ASPD, there were six subgroups of patients, as shown in Table 24-2.

As was noted in Table 24-2, for at least some people the observed ASPD features may be a reflection of a substance-induced condition rather than a true personality disorder (Alterman et al., 1998; Evans & Sullivan, 2001). The lifestyle imposed on the individual by the continued substance abuse may induce what at first glance appears to be an ASPD. The concept of an "acquired" personality disorder might explain the clinical observation that those individuals with ASPD who experience psychiatric distress such as anxiety and/or depression might be able to benefit from substance abuse rehabilitation programs (Evans & Sullivan, 2001; Modesto-Lowe & Kranzler, 1999).

Borderline Personality Disorder and SUDs

The borderline personality disorder (BPD) is often an enigma to both the mental health professional and the layperson. Clinically, individuals with BPD alternate

between overidealization of significant others and total rejection and distrust of the same person after a perceived slight or rejection.[21] They do, however, share the characteristic of impulsiveness and overemphasis on their own perceived "rights," as does the antisocial personality-disordered client, and thus are often misdiagnosed as such. Perhaps 30–50% of people with an SUD will also have BPD (Work Group on Substance Use Disorders, 2007). The role of the chemical(s) varies from person to person with BPD, but for many alcohol or drugs of abuse help to make them "numb" to the emotional fires within and provide a way to distract them from their emotional pain. Substance abuse rehabilitation for people with this disorder is often difficult, is both time and labor intensive, and requires a commitment on the part of the therapist to continue to work with the client in spite of problems that develop along the way.[22]

Mixed Personality Disorders

There are a number of personality disorders identified in the American Psychiatric Association's Diagnostic

---

[21]A therapist arriving 5 minutes late for a session might serve as sufficient provocation for a person with BPD to mistrust others, for example.

[22]The author has found that the *Addiction Treatment Planner* by Robert R. Personson and Arthur E. Jongsma provides many useful treatment goals for the counselor with a client with BPD.

and Statistical Manual for Mental Disorders (4th edition, text revision; DSM-IV-TR) (American Psychiatric Association, 2000), and we do not have room here to discuss all of the different subtypes of personality disorders. The DSM-IV-TR provides clear diagnostic criteria for each of the personality disorders identified in this text. Surprisingly, the most common diagnosis is that of a mixed personality disorder, which is to say that the client has personality traits from more than one personality type. A person with histrionic personality disorder might have some ASPD traits (such as impulsiveness and lack of empathy for others, for example) and some narcissistic personality traits (such as a sense of entitlement, for example) mixed into what is predominantly a histrionic personality pattern, to cite one possible pattern. Experienced clinicians usually have seen many different combinations of personality traits intermixed in substance-abusing clients and will tell you that it is uncommon to encounter a "pure" personality-disordered individual.

Posttraumatic Stress Disorder

The individual who suffers from PTSD presents a difficult challenge to the treatment team. Such clients often turn to alcohol or illicit drugs to self-medicate their condition, which is marked by intrusive thoughts about the traumatic event, emotional "numbing," nightmares, and mood swings.[23] Systematic research on patients with PTSD who attempt self-medication through the use of these agents (or by diversion of medications prescribed by others) is lacking, however. It is recommended that the therapist(s) working with these clients have special training in working with PTSD clients because of this fact. Pharmacotherapy with clients with PTSD is difficult. The benzodiazepines are thought to either have no effect on posttraumatic anxiety or possibly even contribute to the development of the disorder because of the dissociative effect induced by this class of medications (Shalev, 2009). In theory, blocking the beta-adrenergic system after the trauma should reduce the chances of an individual developing PTSD, but use of agents such as the mood-stabilizing agent gabapentin or the beta-blocking agent propranolol has proven effective in this capacity (Shalev, 2009).

Cognitive-behavioral therapies (CBT), possibly combined with relaxation training and coping skills training, have shown promise in assisting individuals with PTSD;

however, the research evidence for the effectiveness of such interventions is mixed (Shalev, 2009). Thus these clients will continue to present unique challenges to health care professionals, and rehabilitation workers must keep abreast of the latest developments in PTSD treatment to be able to assist their clients.

Problems in Working with the Dual Diagnosis Client

The dual-diagnosis client is often difficult to work with. Their motivation for substance abuse rehabilitation will vary from individual to individual, but as a group they tend to request substance abuse treatment only as a result of personal/family/legal problems (Goldsmith & Garlapati, 2004). Often, they present with combinations of problems. The most effective treatment model for those who work with the dual-diagnosis client is often the medical model (Patrick, 2003). Unfortunately, treatment resources (such as dedicated treatment programs for dual-diagnosis clients, financial support for treatment, and so on) are "woefully scarce" (Pepper, 2004). Dual-diagnosis clients also often have fragile support systems, and 12-step support groups frequently are intolerant of the special needs of this population of clients. For example, many 12-step support groups view the use of prescribed mood-altering medications, often used to help control the emotional distress of dual-diagnosis clients, as an indication that the client is substituting one addiction for another (Evans & Sullivan, 2001). Further, dual-diagnosis clients often feel out of place in 12-step groups, especially in the earlier stages of rehabilitation (Petrakis et al., 2002). Thankfully, however, there is a move to establish "double trouble" or dual-diagnosis 12-step support groups in many communities.

As is true for many substance-abusing individuals, dual-diagnosis clients often demonstrate significant levels of denial. But the denial seen in many dual-diagnosis clients often takes a different form than is seen in the "typical" substance-abusing client. The free floating or interchangeable denial often seen in dual-diagnosis clients involves the utilization of one problem to defend the other. Thus if a health care professional should attempt to focus attention on patients' psychiatric condition, they will express a desire to talk about their SUD. If a substance abuse rehabilitation professional should attempt to address clients' SUDs, they will talk about their mental illness issues. A variation of this process is encountered when patients with a dissociative disorder attribute their loss of memory (experienced when one personality is forced out of the seat of

---

[23]The reader is referred to the current edition of the *Diagnostic and Statistical Manual of Mental Disorders* for a full listing of the diagnostic criteria for this condition.

consciousness so that another might take over) to chemicals rather than to the process of dissociation.

To complicate matters, many health care professionals view dual-diagnosis clients as being primarily substance-abusing patients who require substance abuse treatment. At the same time, many substance abuse treatment professionals view these same individuals as being psychiatric patients. The deplorable outcome of this professional blindness is that the patient might be bounced between chemical dependency and psychiatric treatment programs (Minkoff, 2008). This is a legacy of the federal drug treatment initiatives of the 1970s and 1980s, which established a number of different agencies focused on the identification and rehabilitation of substance abusers (Osher & Drake, 1996). Responsibility for supervision and development of psychiatric treatment programs was assigned to a different series of federal agencies, and for the most part interdepartmental communication and cooperation was virtually nonexistent.[24] As a result of this process, it is the rare staff psychiatrist in a treatment facility that understands that intense emotions generated by psychiatric distress can serve as relapse triggers for the dual-diagnosis patient (Goldsmith & Garlapati, 2004). Further, in their efforts to ease the client's distress, attending physicians might administer potentially addictive compounds to clients with the best of intentions, but with little insight into how these same compounds might complicate their recovery from their SUD.

Traumatic Brain Injury and SUDs[25]

One exceptional subgroup of dual diagnosis clients that deserves discussion are those individuals who have suffered a traumatic brain injury (TBI) who also abuse alcohol and/or drugs. The TBI might have been caused by the individual's abuse of chemicals, or it might be a coexisting disorder that is intertwined with the SUD. The effects of the TBI vary from one individual to the next, depending on the (a) cause of the brain injury, (b) location of the injury, (c) extent of the injury, and (d) the individual's level of function prior to the injury. A patient with a meningioma[26] will have different presenting symptoms than a patient who suffered a TBI in a motor vehicle accident with massive damage to the frontal lobes, for example. Further, the degree of

recovery will vary from one patient to the next, and the patient only rarely returns to the preinjury level of function. Recovery from a TBI often continues for months or years after the original neurological insult.

When working with the patient with both a TBI and an SUD, it is important for treatment staff to remember that the client's apparent "denial" might reflect the effects of the TBI itself. Some degree of retrograde amnesia[27] might follow a TBI, with the result being that the patient does not remember consuming alcohol or illicit drugs prior to the injury and does not believe family members who tell them otherwise. This process is complicated by the fact that some memories might return over time but that this recovery of memory function is neither uniform nor is it predictable. The individual's ability to remember events prior to the TBI might remain limited and inconsistent. This inconsistent return of memory might result in treatment staff interpreting the TBI clients' inability to recall using alcohol or drugs, while being to recall being transported to the hospital in an ambulance a few minutes later, as frank denial of their drug use rather than an incomplete return of memory, for example.

Traumatic brain injuries are not static entities. The recovery process might require weeks, months, or even years and is often aided by physical and speech therapy exercises. Even with the best of treatment, the patient might be left with permanent deficits. TBI patients often find this to be quite frustrating, especially if they can remember the skills that they no longer possess and turn to alcohol or drugs as a way to self-medicate their frustration. These compounds, unfortunately, appear to have a stronger effect on people with a TBI as opposed to the normal person, a point that is difficult for many TBI patients to understand. Further, TBI patients, often with justification, feel that they are "different," and alcohol and/or illicit drug abuse offers them one avenue through which they can associate with peers. An unfortunate social attitude is that people with a TBI are entitled to abuse alcohol or illicit drugs because of what they have endured as a result of their TBI.

Dual-Diagnosis Clients and Medication Compliance

Medication compliance is a problem for psychiatric patients in general, especially for dual-diagnosis clients (Goldsmith & Garlapati, 2004). As a group, dual-diagnosis clients are 8.1 times more likely to be

---

[24]All of which, by the way, was done at taxpayer expense because both groups of agencies are funded through taxes.

[25]The subject of TBIs is discussed in further detail in Breakout Discussion #5 for this chapter.

[26]See Glossary.

[27]See Glossary.

noncompliant with their medication(s) as are tradi-tional psychiatric clients (Drake, 2007; RachBeisel, Scott, & Dixon, 1999). Unfortunately, this complicates the treatment of both their psychiatric and their sub-stance use disorders. Medication noncompliance might be expressed in a variety of ways, such as (a) refusing to take prescribed medications, (b) continuing to use alcohol and/or illicit drugs even after being admitted to a psychiatric treatment facility, or (c) selectively taking only those medications that will provide the desired effects. To avoid potentially dangerous interactions, some dual-diagnosis clients will go so far as to discontinue psychiatric medications in anticipation of recreational drug use. The most common reason for these behaviors is not to self-medicate psychiatric distress or avoid unpleasant side effects, but simply to enjoy the "high" experienced through recreational chemical abuse.

It was noted in the last paragraph that sometimes dual-diagnosis clients will selectively refuse certain medications while taking others. It is important to keep in mind the fact that many psychiatric medica-tions have a significant abuse potential of their own. For example, anticholinergic medications[28] have a significant abuse potential, and it is not unknown for clients to hoard a number of pills and then ingest them all at once for their psychoactive effects (Buhrich, Weller, & Kevans, 2000). These same medi-cations may potentiate the effects of the amphetamine compounds. Dual-diagnosis clients may substitute their psychiatric medications when they are unable to access more desired drugs of abuse. Thus urine toxicology testing to identify clients who fail to have prescribed medications in their urine or who have metabolites of recreational drugs in their urine is often of value in such cases.

Treatment Approaches with Dual-Diagnosis Clients

Although health care and substance abuse rehabilita-tion professionals have long denied the reality of dual-diagnosis patients, treatment approaches are start-ing to emerge to guide professionals in their work with these clients. However, it should be noted that many of these treatment approaches rest not on a foundation of clinical research but on expert opinion. Indeed, there is a "dearth of empirically sound interventions" for dual-diagnosis clients (Bellack, Bennett, Gearon, Brown, &

Yang, 2006, p. 427). To complicate matters, there is strong evidence that access to psychiatric care for substance-abusing clients is becoming more difficult as many treatment centers cut staff to reduce program costs (Knudsen, Roman, & Ducharme, 2004).

The ideal treatment setting for dual-diagnosis cli-ents is an integrated treatment program, in which both the SUD and the individual's psychiatric pro-blems might be addressed simultaneously by treat-ment professionals from various fields of training who work as a team to help the patient (Busch et al., 2005; Pankiewicz, 2008). Such treatment programs achieve long-term abstinence rates of about 15%, which approximates the abstinence rate achieved in normal clients who enter rehabilitation (Pankiewicz, 2008). Surprisingly, R. D. Weiss, Potter, and Iannucci (2008) suggested that there is little research supporting the advantages of integrated treatment approaches. Even if this data is incorrect, very few treatment pro-grams, perhaps less than 10% of the total number, offer such combined or integrated treatment formats (Patrick, 2003; Renner, 2004b).

More commonly, dual-diagnosis clients are referred to treatment facilities that address both psychiatric and SUDs that utilize a serial treatment approach (Goldsmith & Garlapati, 2004). In such a program the most serious issue is addressed until that condition is stabilized, and then the client is transferred to a different unit so that the second disorder might be addressed. This might be either a different unit within the same facility or one at a different rehabilitation facility entirely. A serious weak-ness of this treatment approach is that clients rarely follow through and enter the second program (Busch et al., 2005; Mueser et al., 2003). To complicate matters, the "managed care" initiatives of the middle and late 1990s[29] have made admission to one treatment facility difficult at best and referrals from one facility to another almost impossible (Evans & Sullivan, 2001; Mueser et al., 2003; Patrick, 2003). Even if sequential admissions are accomplished, treatment stays allowed under man-aged care programs are often inadequate for either condition. Pankiewicz (2008) estimated that only 5% of dual-diagnosis patients treated in such a series of pro-grams will achieve long-term abstinence.

An alternative to the serial treatment model is the parallel treatment model, in which both conditions are addressed simultaneously but in different sections of the same facility (Busch et al., 2005). Hypothetically, the client's SUD might be addressed on the second

---

[28]Often prescribed to help control the unpleasant side effects of psy-chotropic medications being used to treat the mental illness.

[29]Discussed in Chapter 34.

floor of the east wing of a hospital setting, whereas the psychiatric illness is addressed on the fourth floor of the west wing of the same facility. There are numerous drawbacks to this approach, including poor communication between treatment staff on each unit and the act of physically moving patients from one floor to another (where they must adjust to the therapeutic mileau of the new unit during a time of special vulnerability). Yet another drawback is that this model interferes with the development of a firm therapeutic relationship between the therapist on one unit and the patient who, upon stabilization, will be transferred to another unit (Drake & Mueser, 2002). Obviously, this makes for an inefficient treatment process, and this model is the least effective of the three programs discussed thus far (Drake et al., 2004; S. Ross, 2008).

The Stages of Treatment

Substance abuse rehabilitation with dual-diagnosis clients is more complicated than with substance-abusing/addicted patients without a concurrent mental illness. The first goal in working with the dual-diagnosis client is the establishment of a good therapeutic relationship (Drake & Mueser, 2002). This task might take a protracted period of time, and the therapist must make every effort to be nonconfrontational, optimistic, and empathetic, avoid making moralistic judgments, and work on establishing a therapeutic relationship (Patrick, 2003).

The second phase of treatment is that of persuasion (Drake & Mueser, 2002), or engagement or motivational enhancement/engagement (Geppert & Minkoff, 2004). During this phase of rehabilitation, the rehabilitation staff works to help clients understand the relationship between their SUD and psychiatric problems. Issues such as medication noncompliance and its relationship to decompensation and rehospitalization are addressed during this phase. Breaking through the client's denial without causing increased psychiatric distress is also carried out during this phase so that the client might see that abstinence helps to reduce need for rehospitalization and avoids destructive effects of the drug(s) being abused (Geppert & Minkoff, 2004; Patrick, 2003).

The third phase of rehabilitation is that of active treatment, during which time the staff teach clients coping skills, helping them find sources of support and manage their illness (Drake & Mueser, 2002). This stage has also been called that of prolonged stabilization: active treatment/relapse prevention (Geppert &

Minkoff, 2004). The client is at high risk for relapse during this stage, if only because the motivation inherent in a psychiatric emergency has eased (Drake, 2007). The use of group therapy is often of value during this phase, although because of the perceived stigma associated with mental illness in the eyes of the clients, it is best that these therapy groups be held on the psychiatric ward of the treatment facility.

One of the advantages of therapy groups is that more experienced patients might share their experience(s) about how even limited alcohol or drug abuse contributed to their psychiatric decompensation and the problems in living that they encountered the last time that they had finished rehabilitation and returned to independent living. Such groups may reduce rehospitalization rates, although research has demonstrated that dual-diagnosis clients tend to continue to abuse chemicals after discharge from treatment.

During the third phase of treatment, relapse prevention becomes a major focus. The patient and treatment staff identify relapse "triggers" that contribute not only to renewed substance use but also to psychiatric decompensation. Another focus is on helping the client learn how to build a substance-free support system, as a failure to establish such a substance-free support system is a major factor contributing to relapse for this population (Swartz et al., 2006).

It should be pointed out that although many of the same techniques developed for use with the average substance abuse client will work with dual-diagnosis clients, there is no single treatment method or intervention that is equally effective with each individual client (Geppert & Minkoff, 2004). Thus treatment methods and interventions should be individualized, taking into account where patients are in the recovery process, their psychiatric status, and their willingness to change (Geppert & Minkoff, 2004). It should be noted that confrontational techniques often used with substance-abusing clients are rarely effective with dual-diagnosis patients and may even be counterproductive (S. Ross, 2008). When confrontation is needed, it should be less intense than that used with more traditional substance-abusing patients.

Once individuals' psychiatric problems have been brought under control, their substance-related defenses again begin to operate and they will then return to the position of protecting their substance use. Dual-diagnosis clients often believe that once their psychiatric problems are controlled, they are no longer in danger of becoming addicted to the chemical(s) being abused. Clients might try to tell counselors "what they want to hear" rather than what they need to say to address their SUD, or to avoid confrontation that is viewed as being harsh, rejecting, and confrontational by the client. This is why group therapy is so useful during this phase of treatment: Patients are often more willing to listen to other patients who share their experiences with substance abuse following an earlier hospitalization than they are to a counselor. Also, group members are able to problem solve together, with patients being able to share their wisdom with others as they discuss life's problems.

The Outcome of Treatment

One variable that has been found to affect treatment outcome was the home environment into which the patient was discharged (Stahler, Mennis, Cotlar, & Baron, 2009). Discharging patients into the environment where they abused chemicals will activate location-triggered substance use cues, and the effects of this is compounded if patients live a great distance from 12-step support groups (Stahler et al., 2009). This topic has opened a new avenue for clinical research that might offer insights into improving treatment outcomes.

Although complete abstinence is the desired goal, the program staff must also accept that for most dual-diagnosis clients, a major reduction in substance abuse levels might be a more realistic outcome, at least at first. This "harm reduction" approach will at least limit the amount of damage and suffering that individuals suffer until they can realize the need for abstinence. Progress in working with dual diagnosis clients is often slow, with frequent regressions to an earlier level of functioning. With continued patience, it is often possible for dual-diagnosis clients to discontinue recreational drug and alcohol use over time. But this is the end point of a long, difficult process for both the client and treatment staff.

Chapter Summary

The dual-diagnosis clients present a difficult challenge for health care professionals. Once thought to comprise only a small fraction of psychiatric patients, it is now accepted that dual-diagnosis clients are perhaps a majority of those seen in a psychiatric setting. However, diagnosis of concurrent psychiatric and SUDs problems is complicated by the fact that virtually every symptom of mental illness can be simulated by active substance use or the various withdrawal syndromes. A careful clinical history often is of value in identifying those patients who have a preexisting mental illness as opposed to those whose psychiatric symptoms are induced by the substance abuse or withdrawal.

Clinical evidence suggests that dual-diagnosis clients often use the problems induced by one disorder to protect the other, a process called free-floating denial. If health care professionals attempt to focus on clients' health or psychiatric problems, the clients will shift the focus onto their SUD. If substance abuse rehabilitation professionals attempt to focus on clients' SUDs, the clients will try to discuss their health issues, thus blocking therapeutic inquiry into areas that might induce change. However, it is possible to work with dual-diagnosis clients if the therapist is willing to endure extended periods of minimal progress on the part of the client, if not outright regression. But over time it is possible to assist many dual-diagnosis clients to commit to abstinence.

CHAPTER 25

The Medical Model of Substance Use Disorders

Treat the person with the disease, not the disease in the person.

—*Sir William Osler (1910)*

Introduction

In 1956 the American Medical Association voted to accept alcoholism not as a moral failing by the individual afflicted with this condition, but as a disease state that expressed itself through habitual heavy alcohol abuse that fell within the purview of medicine (S. M. Stein & Friedmann, 2001). By extension, the same reasoning has been applied to the other drugs of abuse. In the time since alcoholism was accepted as a disease state by physicians, they have struggled to better understand the forces that help initiate, maintain, and treat substance use disorders on the assumption that they too reflect disease states. In this chapter, the medical perspective[1] on substance use disorders will be examined.

Introduction to the Medical Model

To understand the medical model of substance use disorders, it is necessary to understand the assumptions on which this model rests. The medical model rests on the assumption that disease states are the result of a biological dysfunction, possibly one on the cellular or even molecular level. Human behavior is viewed as reflecting the interaction between the individual and the environment, a process that triggers the expression of certain genetically inherited traits while suppressing others. The concept of "free will" is viewed by many medical-model adherents as an illusion, and they maintain that much of human behavior is based on the interaction between the individual's biological predisposition and the environment. An example of this is seen in cases where the individual enters a state of anaphylactic shock after exposure to an antigen such as bee sting venom. The individual with the potential for an episode of anaphylactic shock who is never exposed to that antigen will not experience this life-threatening condition, in contrast to those individuals who are exposed to the antigenic agent.

Jellinek's Work[2]

The acceptance of alcoholism as a disease state rests, in large part, upon the work of E. M. Jellinek (1952, 1960), who argued that alcoholism was a disease, like cancer or pneumonia. He reasoned that like other disease states, alcoholism presented a specific pattern of symptoms, including (a) a loss of control over one's drinking, (b) a progression of symptoms, and (c) if left untreated, the potential to cause the drinker's death. Further,

---

[1]This perspective is also often called the *biological* or *disease* model.

[2]It is important to note that Jellinek's work addressed only the addiction to alcohol. Although it has been applied to other forms of chemical dependency by other clinicians, Jellinek did not develop his theory for substance use disorders other than alcohol.

Jellinek (1952) argued that the addiction to alcohol progressed through four different stages:

1. The *prealcoholic* stage is marked by individuals' use of alcohol to self-medicate social tension, frustration, and anxiety. They are no longer drinking on a purely social basis but have started to engage in what is called "relief drinking."

2. As individuals continue to engage in "relief" drinking, they slip closer to and eventually enter the *prodromal stage* of alcohol use. During this phase, individuals begin to demonstrate such alcohol-related problems as "blackouts," guilt over their behavior while intoxicated, and the urge to hide their drinking from others.

3. With the continued use of alcohol, individuals eventually become physically dependent on alcohol. Their self-esteem suffers from their alcohol use, and social activities that do not involve the use of alcohol are shunned in favor of alcohol-centered activities. At times, individuals will make an effort to reassert control over alcohol, only to return to abusive drinking again after a period of time.

4. Finally, with continued alcohol use the individuals enter the *chronic* stage of alcohol use. During this phase, they will demonstrate symptoms such as a deterioration in morals, the use of alcohol substitutes when ethyl alcohol is not available,[3] the development of psychomotor "tremors" after drinking, and possibly drinking with their social inferiors.

Jellinek went on to both extend and revise this earlier work, and in 1960 suggested that there were different patterns of alcohol dependence following a perspective first advanced by Dr. William Carpenter in 1850 (Lender, 1981). However, where Dr. Carpenter suggested that there were three different forms of alcohol dependence, Jellinek (1960) suggested five subforms of alcohol dependence.

Advanced when the majority of people in this country viewed alcoholism as a moral weakness,[4] Jellinek's (1960) model offered a new paradigm for physicians to use when assessing people with an alcohol use disorder (AUD). It also offered many advantages over the moral model within which most people had viewed the AUDs:

1. It provided a framework within which physicians could classify different patterns of alcohol abuse, as opposed to the more restrictive dichotomous view that the person was either an alcoholic or not.

2. Jellinek's model also made the AUDs worthy of study by science.

3. The Jellinek model suggested that the individual with an AUD was worthy of "unprejudiced access" (Vaillant, 1990, p. 5) to medical care.

4. Finally, the Jellinek model attributed the individual's AUD not to a lack of willpower, but to a physical disease state over which the individual had no control.

Although initially embraced with great enthusiasm, in the last half century many researchers have since come to question the Jellinek (1960) model. There are significant variations in drinking patterns over time, and the single path leading to destruction suggested by Jellinek (1960) has since come to be viewed as one of a number of trajectories that the drinker might follow. Research has found that once alcoholism is established, for example, its course is usually one of periods of abusive alcohol use intermixed with reduced alcohol or even abstinence over periods of time (Schuckit, 2006b; Vaillant, 1995). Thus clinical research does not support the Jellinek (1960) model, which has long been the mainstay of substance abuse rehabilitation.

The Genetic Inheritance Theories

At the start of the 21st century, the "medical model" of the addictions is almost synonymous with the belief in some quarters that there is a genetic predisposition(s) toward addiction. Unfortunately, the average person (and many physicians) share two basic misconceptions about genetic inheritance: (a) the belief that genetic evolution stopped with the development of human culture and, (b) the belief that genetic *predisposition* is the same thing as genetic *predestination*. The former misconception is understandable when one stops to consider that the pace of genetic change is much too slow for people to see over the course of their lifetime. Indeed, in most cases even a period of several centuries would not demonstrate much biological change due to evolution, if any.

The second belief is also easily proven to be a misconception: If people were to have a genetic predisposition to be vulnerable to an infectious disease (tuberculosis, for example), but were never exposed to such bacteria, then they would not develop the disease. The same is true for the SUDs: If people with the genetic predisposition to make them vulnerable to an addiction never begin to abuse alcohol or drugs, it is

---

[3]Discussed in Chapter 5.

[4]A perspective that, unfortunately, most people in the United States continue to believe (Brust, 2004).

unlikely that an SUD would develop. Thus life experiences help to determine which genes are or are not expressed[5] in spite of the individual's genetic heritage. Unfortunately, there still remains a strong belief by the general public that genetic inheritance means inexorable outcome. This is often seen at treatment program case reviews where it is mentioned that one or both of a given patient's parents were addicted to alcohol or drugs. Upon hearing this, staff members will look at each other knowingly, and somebody will say something to the effect of "well, there is the genetic link" to the SUD, as if the patient had inherited the addiction from their parent(s).[6]

The etiology of even the most common SUD, alcoholism, remains elusive. In reality, "there is no evidence whatsoever that a variance in any particular gene can turn someone into an addict" ("Is There a Genetic Basis for Drug Addiction?", 2008). However, the author admits it would not be unreasonable to expect that variations in genetic heritage might *predispose* the individual to substance use disorders. However, some genetic variations also have been found to have a *protective* function, reducing the individual's vulnerability for an SUD ("Is There a Genetic Basis for Methamphetamine Resistance?", 2008). This would suggest that genetic heritage is one factor in the individual's ultimate potential for developing a substance use disorder, but not the sole determining factor.

There is indirect evidence of a genetic predisposition toward the alcohol use disorders (Tomb, 2008). For example, the gene called *slo-1* controls the activity of a protein that forms an ion channel in the neural wall. Evidence would suggest that when the alcohol molecule binds at a receptor site, it forces the ion channel to remain open longer than normal, thus showing the rate at which that neuron can "fire" (Lehrman, 2004). This line of research suggests that the *slo-1* gene might be involved in the development of alcohol use disorders, although the exact mechanism remains unclear.

A neurochemical that seems to be involved in the development of substance use disorders is called the *cAMP response-element-binding protein* (CREB) (Grens, 2007). CREB is involved in a multitude of neural functions in the normal brain, and scientists are

unsure of its role in the development of SUDs. But the current evidence would suggest that CREB is involved in the subjective adverse withdrawal effects after a drug is discontinued, whereas another neurochemical, ΔFosB,[7] is involved in the reward cascade that promotes drug abuse (Grens, 2007).

ΔFosB, has garnered a great deal of clinical interest of late. Neurons produce a little ΔFosB every time an individual uses a drug of abuse, and its effects are long lasting (Brust, 2004; Doidge, 2007; Whitten, 2008a). It is thought that at some point the accumulated ΔFosB triggers the activation (or possibly the *de*-activation) of a gene in the neuron, altering the individual's response to the neurotransmitter dopamine. Dopamine is intimately involved in the reward process cascade that makes the use of certain chemicals so enjoyable for some people. This process would seem to make individuals more sensitive to the rewarding effects of that compound, reinforcing the tendency for them to abuse that compound in the future (Brust, 2004; Doidge, 2007).

The team of Vadez et al. (2007) concluded that the Gm7 gene seems to play a role of alcohol consumption of mice in a laboratory setting. Those mice with an identified genetic variant of this gene were found to consume more alcohol than a strain of mice lacking this gene, according to the authors. Although this study is suggestive, it is not known whether humans possess the *Gm7* gene. It is possible that a similar process might exist in humans even if they do not possess the *Gm7* gene complex found in mice, but further research is needed in this area. Another study that seemed to find a biological foundation for SUDs was conducted by C. S. Barr et al. (2007). Using animal research, the authors concluded that a variant of the μ opioid receptor site in the brain[8] seemed to make alcohol more rewarding to some monkeys as compared to others. This variant of the μ opioid receptor site is very similar to one observed in human subjects, suggesting that this might be at least partly why some people are at risk for the development of an alcohol use disorder.

Both genetic and environmental forces appear to interact to predispose persons to the abuse of entire classes of drugs rather than a specific compound. Patients will tell of how they tried methamphetamine and cocaine, for example, but that once they injected heroin, "I was home!" Unfortunately, we still do not know enough about the genetics of the addictions to identify

---

[5]Another way to say this is *"environmental influences,"* right?

[6]This is not to deny that the patient *might* have inherited a genetic predisposition toward an SUD. But until scientists can identify which gene(s) are the basis for this predisposition and then develop tests to determine if a given patient has actually inherited those genes, it is improper to engage in what might be called a "guilt by genetic association" process.

[7]Δ is the Greek symbol for Greek letter "delta."

[8]Discussed in Chapter 7.

which genes might predispose a given individual to a specific class of compounds. Indeed, we still do not know which genes might predispose a given individual to *any* form of an SUD, although that does not prevent the mass media from talking about how the addictions are based on genetic heritage.

Admittedly, genetic factors were found to account for 44% of the risk factor for marijuana abuse (Gruber & Pope, 2002). "Family environmental factors" (p. 392) accounted for an additional 21% of the risk for a marijuana use disorder according to the Gruber and Pope, whereas the pharmacodynamic reward potential of marijuana, cultural influences, peer influence, and individual expectations would account for an unknown percentage of the total risk for the development of a marijuana use disorder. The influence culture is hardly insignificant and is clearly demonstrated in the differences in the individual's perception of the amphetamine compounds in England and the United States in the 1930s. In the United States, great emphasis was placed by the manufacturer on how these compounds would increase the individual's energy level, making the user more productive and ambitious, both qualities associated with the "American Dream" of affluence. In England the effects of these same compounds were interpreted as making the user more self-confident, a trait much valued in the English culture (Rasmussen, 2008).

Another example might be seen in the ongoing social experiment taking place in Sweden. As the social restrictions against the use of tobacco products by women in that country relax, a greater and greater number of younger women are taking up the habit of smoking cigarettes (Kendler, Thornton, & Pederson, 2000). There is no evidence of a massive shift in genetic inheritance in that country, so it is logical to expect that cultural/social factors were acting as a balance to the individual's genetic inheritance up until the recent past, when these sanctions began to ease.

The work of Cloninger et al. (Cloninger, Bohman, & Sigvardsson, 1981; Cloninger, Sigvardsson, & Bohman, 1996) opened new avenues for investigating the possible relationship between genetic inheritance and the alcohol use disorders. The authors drew on the extensive adoption records of 3000 boys whose parents had an AUD, who were adopted shortly after birth. Their findings startled the world of psychiatry. Even in cases where the adoptive parents did not have an AUD, many of the research subjects went on to develop an AUD in later life. Some of these adoptees fell into a group marked by moderate use of alcohol in young adulthood, minimal involvement in antisocial behaviors, dependence on social approval, avoidance of high-risk and novel situations, but they developed an AUD later in their lives (Hesselbrock & Hesselbrock, 2007). These individuals were classified as "Type I" (or "late-onset") alcoholics by Cloninger et al. (1981, 1996).

The second group were individuals whose birth parents had AUDs. The children in turn demonstrated AUDs before the age of 25 years, were risk takers, tended to seek out novelty (a characteristic that often resulted in at least experimental drug use on their part), and engaged in violent behaviors (Hesselbrock & Hesselbrock, 2007). These individuals were classified as "Type II" (or "early-onset" alcoholics Cloninger et al. (1981)). Heritability for Type II alcoholism was higher than Type I alcoholism, suggesting at least some genetic vulnerability that was transmitted from natural father to the son. A smaller subset of female adoptees also appeared to follow this pattern.

The concept of Type I/Type II alcoholism stimulated research efforts to identify risk factors that might predict or contribute to the development of these different forms of alcohol use disorders. However, the alcohol use disorders are more complicated than this theory would suggest (Hesselbrock & Hesselbrock, 2007). Other factors such as drinkers' age, sex, and whether they internalize stress or externalize blame and responsibility were all found to play a role in their drinking pattern (Hesselbrock & Hesselbrock, 2007). To further complicate matters, in 1996 the team of Cloninger et al. (1996) again explored the prevalence of AUDs in 557 boys and 600 girls adopted as children, using the extensive records kept by authorities in Gothenburg, Sweden. As before, the adopted children had at least one parent who had an AUD, and they were not adopted by a relative. The data suggested that the Type I/Type II dichotomy of drinkers did appear to be separate but possibly related forms of alcoholism.

Although these studies are suggestive, and possibly meet the criteria for research, it is not always clear that the distinctions found in research studies help clinicians in the process of forming a diagnosis (Hesselbrock & Hesselbrock, 2007). Furthermore, as Hesselbrock and Hesselbrock observed, many research studies exclude "atypical" subjects, forcing an artificial dichotomy between subgroups of research subjects. Also, as the authors observed, there has been virtually no research into long-term posttreatment outcomes to determine whether the observed subgroups provide insight into how individuals will fare in a rehabilitation setting.

At the end of the first decade of the 21st century, it is generally accepted that genetic inheritance appears to account for about 60% of the individual's risk for developing a substance use disorder (Brust, 2004). However, beyond this general statement, researchers have yet to identify an alcohol/drug dependency "gene" or combination of genes that would seem to account for the individual's increased risk for developing an SUD.

The Biological Differences Theories

In the 20th century, researchers tried to identify and isolate a biological difference between those individuals who were alcohol dependent and those who were not. Perhaps, it was reasoned, there was a difference in how people with an AUD metabolized alcohol, that they biotransformed alcohol more rapidly or that they reacted differently to alcohol than did the nonalcoholic person. There *are* hints that possible differences do exist, although it is not clear whether these are enough to account for any additional risk for the individual developing an SUD. Nurnberger and Bierut (2007) found that when individuals were connected to electrodes that measured brain wave activity and then exposed to a standard stimulus (a strobe light), there was a short spike in electrical activity in the brain between 300 and 500 milliseconds after the stimulus began.[9] As a group, it was found that individuals with an AUD and their children had a weaker response in that region of the brain responsible for inhibition of neural activity. It was suggested that alcohol would serve as an additional inhibitory agent to enhance the effects of the neurotransmitter gamma aminobutryric acid (GABA),[10] which normally serves as an inhibitory agent in the brain (Nurnberger & Bierut, 2007). However, it is not known whether these findings are specific to AUDs or if they would apply to individuals with all forms of SUDs.

An interesting, ongoing research project was recently started at the University of Nottingham, England. Based on the observation that a large number of people will experiment with drugs or alcohol, but that only approximately 15% become addicted, Dr. Lee Hogarth has initiated a study to examine whether abnormalities in the frontal cortex might predispose the individual to a substance use disorder. This research project, which will utilize MRI studies of both addicted and nonaddicted individuals, will attempt to identify abnormalities in the structure of the prefrontal lobe of substance abusers as compared with nonusers, with the goal of completing the study in the year 2011 ("Could Brain Abnormality Predict Drug Addiction?", 2008).

The team of R. Z. Goldstein and Volkow (2002) also tried to identify a biological difference between those with an SUD and those without, using neuroimaging technology. The authors found that the orbitofrontal cortex and the anterior cingulate gyrus, both of which are interconnected with the limbic system, become active when individuals abuse a compound. These regions of the brain are thought to be involved in the process of cognitive-behavioral integration of goal-directed behavior and motivation. It was hypothesized that repeated exposure to drug use cues would lead individuals to learn to expect certain effects from the use of a chemical, while they also become less and less responsive to normal reward experiences. The authors suggested that individuals with an SUD might overvalue the reinforcing effects of a substance(s), focusing more and more time and energy on reacquiring the rewards seemingly offered by the abuse of alcohol or drugs. Although this theory is still in its formative stages, it does appear to account for many of the facets of SUDs.

In recent years, it has become possible to peer into the working brain to determine how the drugs of abuse alter normal biological functioning. Individuals who have become addicted to a drug(s) of abuse demonstrate altered function in such regions of the brain as the amygdala, orbitofrontal cortex, ventral tegmental area, and locus ceruleus[11] (Trafton & Gifford, 2008). Although Trafton and Gifford suggest that these changes account for the behaviors seen in individuals with a physical addiction to a drug(s), it is also possible that many of these changes predate the development of the addiction. In effect, many of these changes might reflect biological predispositions to the rewarding effects of the drug(s) of abuse, making those individuals more likely to engage in repeated use of these compounds if they should be exposed to them. To resolve this issue, it would be necessary to have pre/post-SUD development functional brain-imaging studies from the same individuals to determine what their baseline level of brain function was before they began to abuse drugs.

---

[9]Technically, this is called the *P-300* response.

[10]See Glossary.

[11]Essentially regions of the human brain involved in executive functions, and the limbic system, which is involved in the reward process.

The Dopamine D2 Hypothesis

The dopamine D2 hypothesis overlaps with the "biological differences" school of thought (discussed in the last section). There are at least five subtypes of dopamine receptor in the human brain (Ivanov et al., 2006). The distribution and function of these subtypes of dopamine receptors is still being explored by neuroscientists, and there is evidence suggesting that each subtype of dopamine carries out a different function in specific regions of the brain. But there is a growing body of evidence that suggests that individuals with an SUD have a reduced number of the dopamine D2 receptor subtype, which in theory would make them less sensitive to normal reinforcers such as food, water, and sex (Ivanov et al., 2006). This also would make them sensitive to a compound(s) that would force more dopamine into the dopamine D2 receptor sites, increasing the level of activation to a more normal level of activation. This theory is supported by the observation that cocaine administration increases the level of dopamine in such regions of the brain as the nucleus accumbens[12] by 400–500%, whereas dopamine levels drop below normal in this same region of the brain during cocaine withdrawal (Ivanov et al., 2006). The reduced number of dopamine D2 receptor sites is thought to predate the individual's exposure to any of the drugs of abuse (Commission on Adolescent Substance and Alcohol Abuse, 2005).

Applications of the Medical Model of the Addictions

As a theory, the medical model of SUDs does appear to make sense under certain circumstances. However, the true applicability of a theoretical model is when it is applied to a specific problem to determine whether it is viable or not. The decision to use the cowpox virus to protect people from smallpox provides an excellent example of how a theory (that having been exposed to the cowpox virus protects the individual from smallpox) is put into practice. The application of the medical model to the problem of the substance use disorders appears to have taken two general routes. First, physicians have searched for a compound(s) that might moderate or eliminate the individual's desire for a drug(s) of abuse.[13] Failing this, they have also searched for a medication(s) that might ease the patient's withdrawal symptoms from the drug(s) of abuse.[14] Each avenue of treatment has met with limited success, at best.

However, scientists have started to use the body's own defenses against drug(s) of abuse (Giles, 2008). Experimental vaccines that prime the immune system to attack cocaine molecules in the circulation, for example, appears to block the euphoric effects of this compound, thus eliminating the reward potential for further cocaine use. It is not clear, however, whether individuals who had received a "cocaine vaccine" might switch to another drug of abuse, such as the amphetamines, or simply discontinue the abuse of CNS stimulants entirely. One possibility is that patients who have received the appropriate antidrug vaccine might be more receptive to psychosocial interventions, which have been the mainstay of rehabilitation efforts to date. However, other possibilities include unforeseen consequences of the vaccine use, as have been found when other medications were first introduced for use by patients. Thus the viability and safety of this experimental treatment approach remains to be proven.

Reaction Against the Disease Model of the Addictions

It is of great surprise to many people to learn that there are competing models that fall under the rubric of the "medical" or "disease" model. There is no single, universally accepted "disease" model of SUDs. Rather, what is called the "medical" model reflects a group of loosely related theories that suggest that SUDs are the outcome of an unproven "disease" process. Depending on the individual researcher's perspective, SUDs are thought to reflect abnormal psychobiological or biopsychosocial processes, the treatment of which rested not with physicians but with substance abuse counselors and mental health professionals for much of the 20th century (S. M. Stein & Friedmann, 2001). At the start of the 21st century, there are those who challenge the medical model of SUDs for a wide range of reasons, many of which will be discussed in the following sections.

Methodological

Many critics of the disease or medical model center their attack on weaknesses in the Jellinek (1960) model[15] itself. Jellinek's model was based on flawed methodology, in that he had mailed out 1600 surveys

[12]As discussed in the Glossary, this region of the brain is involved in the reward cascade in the brain.
[13]Discussed in Chapter 33.
[14]Again, discussed in Chapter 33.
[15]See Appendix 2.

to members of Alcoholics Anonymous (AA). However, of the 1600 surveys sent out, only 98 were returned: (a) a response rate of just 6%. Few research studies would be carried out on the basis of such a limited participation rate now. Further, (b) Jellinek assumed that AA members were the same as nonmembers. This is a dangerous assumption, because by the very fact that they attended AA participants had identified themselves as being different in at least one aspect from nonmembers. Finally, Jellinek (c) assumed that those participants who returned his surveys were the same as those who had not returned his survey. Again, this assumption is a rather dangerous one on which to base a research study, because by returning the survey, the 6% who did so marked themselves as being different from the 94% who did not.

It should also be noted that Jellinek (1960) utilized a cross-sectional design. Although this does not violate any known research rule, cross-sectional studies might not yield the same results as a life span (longitudinal) research design. Bentall (2009) warned that psychiatric diagnoses, which would include the substance use disorders, "have almost no scientific or prognostic value" (p. 267). This observation is consistent with findings that the Jellinek's (1960) model has not been found to apply to predict alcohol use patterns over the course of an individual's lifetime (Vaillant, 1995). For example, the typical individual with an AUD alternates between periods of more or less problematic alcohol use over time (Vaillant, 1995). Individuals who abuse illicit drugs also tend to follow a variable course rather than an automatic downward spiral (Toneatto, Sobell, Sobell, & Rubel, 1999).

Further, the concept of *loss of control* over alcohol use, a central feature of Jellinek's (1960) theory, has been challenged (Heyman, 2009; Schaler, 2000). Research and clinical experience both suggest that when individuals with an AUD drinks, they do so to achieve *and maintain* a desired level of intoxication, which would suggest that they do indeed have some measure of control over their alcohol use. Rather than speak of loss of control, clinicians now speak of *inconsistent* control over drinkers' level of alcohol intake (Vaillant, 1990, 1995). Thus as should be evident by now, Jellinek's work, which forms part of the foundation of the medical model, has been found to be flawed.

The Genetic Inheritance Theories: Do Genetics Rule?

It would not be unreasonable to argue that people have almost been "programmed to believe [that] genetics

rule" (Lipton, 2008, p. 186). To the average person, this means that the individual's genetic heritage is an inalterable fate (Watters, 2006). This belief has been called "neurogenetic determinism" (Begley, 2007, p. 252), a belief that suggests that humans are no more than a slave to their genes or current pattern of neurotransmitter activation (Begley, 2007). An extreme interpretation of this position is that people are then absolved of responsibility for their behavior because they did not select their genetic inheritance! In reality, people's genetic inheritance *influences* but does not control behavior (Gelernter & Kranzler, 2008).

This is perhaps best understood by the observation that only 100 of the 30,000 genes in the human genome are thought to be involved in the susceptibility to alcohol or drug use disorders ("Genetics of Drug Addiction: The Memory Connection," 2009). This number sounds impressive, until one stops to consider that it is only 0.00333% of the entire human genome! Our state of ignorance about biogenetics is such that:

We can now read the entire human genome, all 3.5 billion base pairs[16] of DNA, in which the recipe for Homo sapiens *is written. Within this genetic tome, scientists have identified about 18,000 genes, each of which encodes proteins that build our bodies. And yet scientists have no idea what a third of those genes are for and only a faint understanding of most of the others.* (Zimmer 2008, p. 3)

So naturally people start making important noises about how the addictions are a biogenetic disorder. In reality the individual's genetic heritage will establish certain potentials on which the environment and personal experience act to determine whether this genetic potential is activated. A crude but effective example is provided by the humble honey bee. All female honey bees develop from larvae that are genetically identical. However, only those larvae fed a special food known as the "royal jelly" will grow to become a queen bee, whereas others simply become sterile worker bees (E. Young, 2008).

Admittedly, human beings are a bit more complex than honey bees; however, this example does illustrate how external forces (in this case, diet) can influence the growth of the individual organism (in this case,

---

[16]Each gene is composed of strands of DNA, which are, in turn, composed of many pairs of molecules arranged in a long string. Zimmer is referring to the fact that we have yet to "read" all 3.5 billion base pairs that combine to make up the 30,000 genes in the human genome.

the queen bee). Thus the genetic heritage establishes only a range of responses to the environment, and then environmental forces determine which of those potential responses are activated or suppressed (Begley, 2007; G. Lynch & Granger, 2008). This process was clearly demonstrated in an experiment discussed by Tabakoff and Hoffman (2004), who sent a number of genetically identical rats to researchers in different laboratories. The rats then received standard doses of alcohol under closely controlled conditions. Surprisingly, rather than respond to the alcohol in a consistent manner, the rats in the various laboratories demonstrated significantly different responses to the same dose of alcohol. Because the rats were genetically identical, their response to the alcohol was not controlled by their genetic heritage. It was discovered that the environment in each laboratory differed from the others in significant ways.[17] The results of this study support the contention that environmental forces are at least as important as genetic heritage in shaping the individual's vulnerability for alcoholism (and, by extension, the other SUDs).

Advocates for the disease model of the addictions often overlook a position that because of evidence suggesting a genetic predisposition towards the addictions that these disorders are automatically *medical* disorders. (Marlowe & DeMatteo, 2003). People's eye color or hair color are also genetically predetermined, yet these are hardly viewed as medical disorders. Further, it is possible to view SUDs as a form of reckless misconduct such as speeding, and that perhaps these issues are best addressed through the criminal justice system (Marlowe & DeMatteo, 2003). Further, Heyman (2009) pointed out that the substance use disorders remit at double the rate of other psychiatric disorders, a difference that raises questions about the comparison with persistent medical conditions. Scientists now view the addictions as a form of a *disorder of neuroplasticity* (Salzman, 2008). In brief, this theory suggests that the brain's neural pathways are constantly rewiring themselves in response to environmental changes. This process is shaped by both the individual's genetic inheritance and the environment. The genetic heritage establishes adaptive limits for the neural circuits in the brain,[18] which responds to environmental changes by building new neural pathways. However, environmental stressors (which might include alcohol and the drugs of abuse) might press the neural structure of the brain beyond these adaptive limits. In such cases the individual's brain attempts to compensate in ways that are to a greater or lesser degree dysfunctional.[19]

Admittedly, there is an impressive body of evidence suggesting a strong role for the individual's genetic inheritance in the development of an SUD. However, it is much more complicated than the popular theory that there is a single "alcohol gene" (Nurnberger & Bierut, 2007). There is, after all, no "fast ball" pitching gene or a "scuba diving" gene, so why should a disorder as complex as the SUDs rest on a single gene? This question is consistent with clinical research that suggests that the addictions are *polygenetic* in nature. Heyman (2009) went so far as to state that even now, 70 years after alcoholism was classified as a disease state, researchers have yet to identify a pathogen or genetic combination that causes the AUDs. Research has demonstrated that no single gene has a very large effect on the possibility that the individual will develop an SUD. G. M. Miller (2008) suggested that the progression to a drug addiction is not the result of a single gene, but of a number of genes that indirectly contribute to the individual's risk of developing an SUD in combination with environmental and social influences that also play a role in the possible development of an SUD.

Although it is comforting to blame people's genetic heritage for their substance use disorder, "we are still a long way from being able to interpret that sequence [of genes] in relation to risk for psychiatric illness" (Austin, quoted in Arehart-Treichel, 2008, p. 20). It has been estimated that for the alcohol use disorders, a person's genetic predisposition might involve as many as 51 different *regions* of genes, many of which are involved in the process of intercellular or intracellular signaling, regulation of gene expression, and cellular development (C. Johnson et al., 2006). Each of these regions of genes contributes a greater or reduced degree of risk for the subsequent development of an SUD, all of which are then influenced by various psychosocial forces[20]

---

[17]For example: How much time did the researchers spend touching or petting the rats? Were they housed in individual cages or in small groups kept in larger cages? What was the noise level in each laboratory? Was the environment for the rats "enriched" (providing toys) or "barren" (bare cages)? And so on and so on.

[18]The number of neural circuits in a single person's brain is estimated to be more than the number of grains of sand on all of the beaches on the planet Earth.

[19]An excellent example of this process is the formation of scar tissue in the central nervous system following trauma, a process known as *gliosis*, in which the brain's ability to reestablish damaged neural pathways is prevented.

[20]Some of these life experiences would include community attitudes toward substance use, peer pressure(s), role models, religious belief(s), academic goals and performance, past psychiatric history, and past substance use exposure (G. M. Miller, 2008).

(C. Johnson et al., 2006; G. M. Miller, 2008). To further complicate matters,[21] there is strong evidence that certain genes are involved in the process of *initiating* substance use behaviors and others in *maintaining* them ("Addiction and the Problem of Relapse," 2007). Yet it is on this foundation of ignorance that addiction counselors (physician, psychologist, social worker, nurse, and so on) knowingly speak of people's genetic predisposition toward an addiction as if they were doomed to develop such a disorder in spite of our state of ignorance about biogenetics.

Challenges to the Medical Model of the Addictions
The Dopamine D2 Receptor Site Hypothesis

The dopamine D2 receptor site hypothesis does seem to be the most promising of the medical models of the addictions. Animal research suggests that rate that are deficient in the dopamine D2 and D3 receptor sites appear to be at increased risk for cocaine abuse, for example (Dalley et al., 2007). Thus the dopamine D2 hypothesis does seem to suggest a biological predisposition for both impulsive behavior(s) and a possible mechanism that supports continued cocaine use. However, research studies appear to focus only on those people with an identified SUD rather than general-population studies that would determine whether individuals with dopamine D2 receptor site deficiencies are drawn to substances, or if there is a sizable percentage of the population with a similar dopamine D2 receptor site deficiency that is not drawn to substance use disorders.

Other Biological Vulnerability Studies

There have been a series of studies in the last half of the 20th century that identified a possible biological predisposition toward SUDs. Schuckit's (1994) study is often cited as evidence of this hypothetical biological vulnerability. This study identified 223 men who were found to have an abnormally low physical response to a standard dose of alcohol. Forty percent of those men who were raised by a parent with an AUD, but only 10% of the control group, demonstrated this reduced response to a standard dose of alcohol when first tested.

A decade later, the author went back and found that 56% of the men who had been found to have an abnormally low response to alcohol had developed an AUD (Schuckit, 1994). This was interpreted as evidence that a low physical response to a standard dose of alcohol might serve as a biological "marker" for the later development of an AUD.

However, proponents of the biological differences perspective overlook the fact that only 91 men in the original research group of 227 men had the abnormally low response to alcohol in the first study. Fifty-six percent of this group, or just 62 men, had progressed to develop an AUD at the time of the follow-up study. Although this study does illustrate that there does appear to be a possible biological predisposition for an AUD, it also demonstrates that this biological predisposition does not *predestine* the individual to develop the AUD, in that many individuals with the same abnormally low response to the test dose of alcohol at the time of the initial testing did *not* have an AUD at the follow-up study.

Challenges to the Neuroplasticity Aspects of the Disease Model

It is of interest to observe that those who advocate the medical model are quick to point to the concept of neuroplasticity[22] to support the disease model of the addictions. Proponents of this position suggest that the repeated use of a recreational drug of abuse causes the neurons in different regions of the brain to alter their structure and function to the point where the individual no longer can exercise free will (Geppert, 2008). The addictions are "brain diseases," it is argued, because the persistent use of the drugs of abuse induce changes in the structure and function of the brain through the process of neuroplasticity. A counterpoint is offered by Heyman (2009), who suggested that "drug-induced brain change is not sufficient evidence that addiction is an involuntary disease state. Drugs change the brain, but this does not make addiction a disease" (p. 97). Diet, exercise, and even learning to play a musical instrument all indirectly change the structure of neurons in the brain, but in spite of strident claims to the contrary this does not make them "diseases." They are voluntary behaviors.

The brain is constantly altering neural connections in response to internal and external forces. The acquisition of a new skill will require the brain to make minor or major alterations in the existing neural

---

[21]As if the author of this text would *ever* want to do that to you, gentle reader.

[22]See Glossary.

networks. An infant who starts to walk or a child who attempts to ride a bike is able to do so because of the brain's ability to rewire itself in response to changing demands being placed on it. The joy that children feel at taking their first steps hardly reflects an ongoing addictive process, and there are few who would assert that learning to ride a bike is an addiction, although both meet the same criteria by which the proponents of the "addictions-as-a-brain-disease" model use to support their position. In reality scientists know very little about the factors that initiate, maintain, or inhibit neuroplasticity, and thus we do not know the relationship between the SUDs and recovery. Torregrossa and Kalivas (2009) noted that the process of neuroplasticity might be active in both the development of and recovery from addictions to various chemicals. This makes sense. If neuroplasticity is involved in the maintenance of a substance use disorder, why can it not also be involved in the process of recovery?

Challenges to the Brain-Imaging Studies

Proponents of the medical model will often point to dramatic brain scan pictures obtained from PET scan procedures in which certain regions of the brains of people with an SUD become very active when they are exposed to drug use cues as evidence that the addictions are brain disorders. It is very easy to read too much into brain scans (Noe, 2009; Shermer, 2008). Although dramatic, these brain scans are obtained in an unnatural environment (crammed in a neuroimaging machine and being exposed to photographic drug use cues is hardly the same as being in a street environment where the individual might be exposed to drug use cues) (Shermer, 2008).

Peter Breggin (2008), a critic of the pharmaceutical approach to treating mental health problems, argues that:

Health care providers and the general public have...been bamboozled by the much advertised speculation that brain scans can demonstrate the existence of mental disorders, or even diagnose them. In reality, no psychiatric disorder is demonstrable or diagnosable by brain scan, or by other medical or biological tests. (p. xxx)

The relevance of this quote is that the addictions are identified as a psychiatric disorder. There is strong evidence suggesting that the cerebral blood flow process is more complex than a simple person-views-drug-use-cue = increased blood flow to certain regions of brain

(Sirotin & Das, 2009). Sirotin and Das found that the blood flow pattern in the cortex might include an anticipatory element in which additional blood is sent to certain regions of the visual cortex *in anticipation* of expected visual stimuli, not in response to it. Although the authors observed that their findings do not negate previous fMRI-based research, they do suggest that the results of such studies be interpreted with caution. Neuroscientists do not know how to define normal consciousness, much less the increased activity in certain regions of the brain observed in fMRI or the meaning of normal neural activity observed in such tests, and thus their interpretation of fMRI or PET scan images that show increased activity in certain regions of the brains of people with SUDs is suspect (Eagleman, 2007).

It is also important to keep in mind that the dramatic differences in the level of neural activity in different regions of the brain seen in these fMRI images represent not massive differences in the level of neural activity, but color enhancement of what are often only minimal differences in neural activity between adjacent regions of the brain added to the image by technicians (Shermer, 2008; Vul, Harris, Winkielman, & Pashler, 2009). The images presented in textbooks and at public discussions are actually statistical compilations of individual brains, not actual representations of a given individual's (or group of individuals') brain (Shermer, 2008). There is evidence that many such studies used a procedure that inflated the apparent strength of the identified link (Giles, 2009a; Noe, 2009), reinforcing the conclusion that the interpretation of an fMRI or PET scan at this time is as much an art as a science (Shermer, 2008; Vul et al., 2009).

The neurological activity within various regions of the brain transpires within a matter of hundredths of a second, whereas the process of building up a fMRI or PET scan image requires a matter of minutes (Noe, 2009). Thus it is difficult to extrapolate from the obtained images that increased activity in the identified regions of the brain are due to substance use cues. The state of the science is just not developed to the level where such generalizations might be made (Noe, 2009). Finally, these areas of increased brain activity are not distinct regions of the brain but part of an integrated whole. How these integrated brain structures might function as part of the whole is not clear (Vul et al., 2009). In spite of their dramatic appearance at conferences or in medical textbooks, these brain scan images never permit the scientist to predict whether the individual subject will or will not resist the urge to use drug(s) in spite of brain activity levels (Sommers & Satel, 2005). As Sommers and Satel observe, brain scans of individuals with an SUD who are experiencing a craving *but who do not give in to it* show activation in the same regions of the brain as those who do give in to the impulse to abuse chemicals. Surprisingly, they show *more* activity in these regions of the brain than do those individuals who give in to the impulse to use a drug(s), a fact that is seldom mentioned in textbooks or public discussions.

Indeed, the medical model holds that an *urge* to use a chemical is a compulsive, uncontrollable craving that must be satisfied. In reality this is not true (Heyman, 2009). Substance use "cravings" or "urges" are one of a number of factors that might trigger a relapse to active substance use, but they are "not an obligation" (Heyman, 2009, p. 111). Any person who has been on a diet can testify that although difficult, the urge to eat can be resisted.[23] Many addicted individuals will admit that they can indeed resist the urge to use a compound *if the reward for doing so is high enough*. Substance use becomes a behavioral choice for individuals: Which do they value more, the perceived pleasure brought on by a chemical or the benefits of an identified reward? Many persons in their early 20s who have an identified SUD will modify or discontinue the use of chemicals after they realize the SUD interferes with their life goals. This would suggest that perhaps the issue of free will is not so easily dismissed after all. The urge is not irresistible for all people with an SUD. Further, many individuals with an SUD will successfully resist urges to use a chemical for days, weeks, months, or even years, further casting doubt on the theory that the various drugs of abuse induce a total loss of control over further substance use by the abuser. Yet it has been demonstrated that this is not true. The ability of the person with an SUD to resist urges to use chemicals places the SUDs in a different category than such disorders as breast cancer[24] or a brain tumor.

---

[23]Or the person might substitute a less destructive piece of food, such as a piece of fruit, in place of a more fattening item such as a piece of candy.

[24]In response to those readers who are ready to scream that the author is a sexist pig, it should be pointed out 3–4% of all cases of breast cancer involve men. As for the "pig" part, it should be pointed out that the author had neurosurgery that involved, in part, the use of a "porcine dura graft" (a dura tissue graft obtained from pig dura, to guide the regrowth of the natural dura tissue). So that part of the charge is accurate: The author is pig-headed.

The Media Challenge to the Medical Model

Yet another challenge to the disease model of the addictions is found in the fact that the alcohol "industry" spends an estimated $1 billion per year in the United States to promote their product. If alcohol were indeed the causal agent in the disease of alcohol use disorders, why is it promoted through commercial advertising? For example, when was the last time that you saw an advertisement for the bacillus that causes bubonic plague? The answer(s) to this question raises some interesting questions about the role of alcohol within this society and the rush to classify excess alcohol use as a "disease."

The Medical Model and Individual Responsibility

As Gunn (2003) noted:

Thinking that diseases as entities that invade or take hold of people tends to lead to the kind of medicine patients often complain about. They notice when a doctor is more interested in some abstraction he or she calls a "disease" than in them and their suffering. (p. 33)

In other words, the admonition made by Sir William Osler quoted at the beginning of this chapter is totally ignored. The health care professional now treats the disease entity and not the person. Preconceptions about the addictions (or any other disease state) may distort the health care professional's perception that the disorder exists in a *person*.

Because physicians are as a group rather pessimistic about the treatment of SUDs, they "exempt addiction from our beliefs about change. In both popular and scientific models, addiction is seen as locking you into an inescapable pattern of behavior" (Peele, 2004a, p. 46). This is a social myth that allows for the misperception that a person's biology will always provide an excuse for unacceptable behavior. Biology in this culture provides "the perfect alibi, the get-out-of-jail-free card, the ultimate doctor's excuse" (Pinker, 2002, p. 49). If you skip a day of work and the boss demands to know where you were, and reply that you were "home sick" you are instantly excused for missing a day of work. An excellent example of how the disease model exonerates individuals for their behavior is seen in the following case:

The parents, identified as the "Lowells" in the article were: well-versed in the clinical aspects of substance abuse [but were] ... outmaneuvered by the cunning that so often accompanies [an] addiction. (Comerci, Fuller, & Morrison, 1997, p. 64)

Notice that it was not that the parents were possibly inadequate as parents, or that the adolescent was a difficult, manipulative child. Rather, it is the *addiction* that is responsible for the misdeeds carried out within that home. Neither the parents nor the adolescent are held accountable. The issue of responsibility for one's behavior is totally pushed onto the substance use disorder and not onto the person engaging in the substance use behavior, which Heyman (2009) challenges as a misperception forced on us by the medical model.

Another example of how the medical model absolves the individual of responsibility is the addiction to heroin. Heroin addicts must (a) perceive the need for the drug, (b) find somebody who is willing to sell it, (c) complete the financial transaction to buy it, (d) find a safe place in which to prepare the heroin for injection, (e) mix the powder with water, (f) heat the mixture in a teaspoon, (g) pour it into a syringe, (h) find a vein into which to inject the mixture, and then (i) inject the drug into their body. This is a rather complicated chain of events, each of which involves the active participation of the individual, who is then said to be a "victim" of the disease process. If we all had to go through this much work to become "sick," it is doubtful that anybody would ever be ill again!

Yet another challenge to the medical model of the addictions is a closely guarded secret: The majority of those people with an SUD come to terms with it, not with the assistance of a medical professional, or even a professional counselor, but on their own (Heyman, 2009; Peele, 2004a). This suggests an inherent contradiction in the disease model of the addictions, because patients with other disease states are not expected to deal with the disorder on their own, but to submit to the proper treatment at the hands of the appropriate health care professional. How often do you hear of people with a life-threatening illness curing themselves as opposed to being healed by a health care professional(s)? Yet it has been estimated that up to 95% of those with an SUD stop abusing chemicals on their own.

A very real shortcoming of the medical model as practiced today is that it prevents human contact by placing one person into the role of the physician and the other into the role of the patient (Frattaroli, 2001). The medical model focuses attention on only one aspect of the individual, the addiction, to the exclusion of the individual as a whole (Frattaroli, 2001). In the process the practitioner who follows the medical model loses sight of the role that the addiction might play in the individual's life, the forces that maintain the addiction, and those intra- and interpersonal forces that might help the individual maintain abstinence. If this perspective is true, then one must ask how an impersonal medical relationship can ever hope to heal a very personal, painful disease state known as the addictions. The individual's *behavioral choices* influence the course of the disease, as is true for other persistent disease states such as diabetes. If patients with adult-onset diabetes were to lose 10% of their body weight, begin to exercise on a regular basis, and make certain changes in their diet, the course of the disease would not be the same as it would be for those patients who did none of those things. The same logic applies to those individuals who discover that they have a substance use disorder: They remain responsible for the behavioral choices that they make in response to this discovery and its treatment (Washton & Zweben, 2006).

Chapter Summary

What has come to be called the "medical" or "disease" model has emerged to dominate the way in which the substance use disorders are viewed and, as will be discussed in later chapters, treated. However, there is controversy as to the degree to which the individual's genetic heritage actually serves to predispose the individual to a substance use disorder, and how much of this is the result of psychosocial factors. Further, it was discussed how our present state of understanding of the possible genetics of an SUD is still so limited that we cannot identify whether there are genetic combinations that will make the individual more or less likely to develop an SUD or, if so, how to test for them. Thus the medical model of the addictions has been both acclaimed as providing a comprehensive viewpoint for the SUDs and attacked as being too limited in scope.

CHAPTER **26**

The Psychosocial Models of Substance Use Disorders

Introduction

Many proponents of the medical/disease model of the addictions will (if only reluctantly) admit that there is a major psychosocial component to the addictions. Indeed, "lively debate still abounds about whether addiction is truly a disease at all or under what circumstances it may be conceptualized in that manner" (Gendel, 2006, p. 650). A contrast to the medical or disease model of addictions, proposed by the psychosocial schools, holds that the addictions are learned behavior(s), poor psychosocial functioning, or the result of maladaptive thinking (Work Group on Substance Use Disorders, 2007). Unfortunately, many view the psychosocial and disease models as being mutually exclusive. Although they are indeed discussed in separate chapters in this text, this is only for the sake of clarity. In reality the psychosocial and medical models of the addictions are intertwined with each other in a manner similar to that seen in the DNA of a cell. In this chapter we will review some of the more important aspects of the psychosocial models of the addictions.

A Matter of Perspective

Proponents of the medical or disease model often point out that Dr. Benjamin Rush first suggested that alcoholism was a disease more than 260 years ago. When he made this proposal, a "disease" was classified as something that is able to cause an imbalance in the nervous system (R. E. Meyer, 1996). By this standard, SUDs would appear to meet the definition of a "disease" state. What is overlooked is that in the time since Benjamin Rush made his suggestion, the very definition of an "addiction" has changed. Thus where it was clear to Dr. Rush that alcoholism was a disease in the 1770s, at the start of the 21st century psychiatrists are still debating what is and is not a manifestation of a

psychiatric or behavioral disorder (Bloch & Pargiter, 2002; Schaler, 2000).

At what point does an atypical trait, or an extreme example of a normal trait, become evidence of a "disease"? This debate is contaminated by the intrusion of the pharmaceuticals industry, which has a vested interest in helping society define "disease" in a manner that will justify the sale of their products. The shy person of the 1960s or 1970s is now said to have a "social phobia," and just by coincidence the pharmaceuticals industry has a range of medications to treat it ("Don't Buy It," 2006). The occasional impotence of the last century has now become "erectile dysfunction," and by coincidence the pharmaceuticals industry has a range of compounds to treat a disorder that a few decades ago was called "impotence." Both of these are examples of "Disease Mongering."

An excellent example of disease mongering might be found in the historical odyssey of the amphetamines, which in the years since their introduction were advocated as agents that (a) were a treatment for asthma, (b) could treat the symptoms of nasal congestion seen in allergies or the common cold, (c) were a compound that general-practice physicians could prescribe for the "worried well," (d) were a compound to be used by people caught in the daily grind of meeting the demands of daily life, (e) were compounds that allowed those in the military to carry out their duties for longer periods of time, and (f) were antidepressants (Rasmussen, 2008). In the interim, research had been conducted on the amphetamine compounds as a possible treatment for dysmenhorrea, and in spite of clinical studies that found it inferior to adrenaline, as a vasoconstrictor, a possible adjunct to surgery (Rasmussen, 2008). With the introduction of newer, more effective antidepressants in the 1960s, the amphetamines were reclassified as *psychostimulants* rather than as the antidepressant compounds that they were called just a few years earlier, and in this capacity were touted as a treatment for attention deficit hyperactivity disorder (ADHD) (Rasmussen, 2008). The pharmaceuticals industry had a compound approved for human use. Now it just needed to find a disease to which it might be applied.

Thus the question must be raised as to whether the pharmaceuticals industry, which has a vested interest in as broad a definition of "disease" as possible to justify the sale of their products, should be allowed to also help define what a disease state is. Research studies funded by different pharmaceutical companies are more likely to be published if the results are favorable to their product or suppressed if they fail to support the use of a given company's pharmaceutical (J. E. Barnett, 2009; Rasmussen, 2008), and pharmaceutical sales representatives are hardly expected to provide an unbiased assessment of their product, citing research studies (many funded by the same company) as evidence supporting the effectiveness of their products.

It is difficult to dispute the process of disease mongering when in the behavioral sciences the question of what is or is not a true disease state has become so muddled that:

Today any *socially-unacceptable behavior is likely to be diagnosed as an 'addiction'. So we have shopping addiction, video-game addiction, sex addiction,* *Dungeons and Dragons addiction, running addiction, chocolate addiction, Internet addiction, addiction to abusive relationships, and so forth ... all of these new "addictions" are now claimed to be medical illnesses, characterized by self-destructiveness, compulsion, loss of control, and some mysterious as-yet-unidentified physiological component. (Schaler, 2000, p. 18, italics added)*

Indeed, it can be argued that through the process of blurring the distinctions between unacceptable behavior and actual disease states we have "become a nation of blamers, whiners, and victims, all too happy, when we get a chance, to pass the buck to somebody else for our troubles" (Gilliam, 1998, p. 154). However, a question that must be asked is this: Just because we are uncomfortable, is it the result of a "disease"?

One point that is often misunderstood both within and outside of medicine is that the concept of a "disease" and its treatment is fluid, and changes over time as paradigms shift and new information is uncovered. Stomach ulcers, once thought to be the consequence of stress-induced overproduction of acid, are now viewed as the site of a bacterial infection in the lining of the stomach.[1] The preferred treatment for such ulcers is now antibiotics rather than antacids and tranquilizers, for example. The very nature of the disease model makes it vulnerable to misinterpretation or misrepresentation, and partially because if this, a small but vocal minority of psychiatrists question whether the medical model should be applied to behavioral problems at all.

It should be understood that much of the neurobiology of SUDs is based on animal research. Although useful, data drawn from research conducted on animals do not fully simulate the human condition, much less SUDs (G. F. Koob, 2008). The animals in the research studies do not ingest the compounds under circumstances that simulate the normal human's daily environment, and in some cases are forced to either ingest the compound or have it injected into their bodies so that scientists can observe the reaction of their bodies to these compounds. Although useful, such studies provide only hints at possible neurological mechanisms that initiate or support the addictions, and fail to provide the interpersonal environment in which human substance use and abuse takes place.

---

[1]This is not to imply that *all* stomach ulcers are caused by a bacterial infection. A small percentage are the result of other factors, and a physician must determine the cause of the patient's complaints.

TABLE 26-1 THEORETICAL MODELS OF ALCOHOL/DRUG ABUSE

	MORAL MODEL	TEMPERANCE MODEL	SPIRITUAL MODEL	DISPOSITIONAL DISEASE MODEL
Core Element	The individual is viewed as choosing to use alcohol in problematic manner.	This model advocates the use of alcohol in moderate manner.	Drunkenness is a sign that the individual has slipped from his or her intended path in life.	The person who becomes addicted to alcohol is somehow different from the nonalcoholic. The alcoholic might be said to be allergic to alcohol.
	EDUCATIONAL MODEL	CHARACTEROLOGI-CAL MODEL	GENERAL SYSTEMS MODEL	MEDICAL MODEL
Core Element	Alcohol problems are caused by a lack of adequate knowledge about harmful effects of this chemical.	Problems with alcohol use are based on abnormalities in the personality structure of the individual.	People's behavior must be viewed within context of social system in which they live.	The individual's use of alcohol is based on biological predispositions, such as his or her genetic heritage, brain physiology, and so on.

SOURCE: Chart based on material presented by Miller & Hester (1995).

Another example of how perspective alters our view of reality is whether alcohol or drugs are viewed as being inherently evil (Shenk, 1999; Szasz, 1997). To use an analogy, is a knife evil? Knives have been in use for thousands of years. If a person were to use a knife to slice a Thanksgiving turkey, is that an evil act? If that same person were to use a knife to commit a murder,[2] is the knife an evil thing? It is important to remember that knives, alcohol, or drugs are inanimate. *It is the manner in which they are used* that determines whether an object is helpful or harmful. As a topical anesthetic, cocaine might bring welcome relief from an injury. That same cocaine, if used for its euphoric effects, might lead the individual down the road to addiction. In neither case is the chemical itself "evil." It is the purpose for which that compound is used that society uses to classify it. The antidepressant medication fluoxetine and the hallucinogen MDMA both cause select neurons in the brain to release the neurotransmitter serotonin and then block its reabsorption. Yet one is a recognized and accepted pharmaceutical, whereas the other is illegal.[3]

Multiple Models

There are a number of theoretical psychosocial models that are thought to explain at least some aspect(s) of the SUDs. One model that has many adherents in the general public is the *moral model* (Brust, 2004). From this perspective, the addictions are viewed as reflecting a weakness of character within the individual or a character flaw. For example, one recent study that utilized telephone interviews of 1012 adults living in Germany revealed that 85% of those who participated in the study thought that alcoholism was a self-inflicted disorder, whereas only 30% thought that it could be effectively treated (Schomerus, Matschinger, & Angermeyer, 2006).[4]

In contrast to the moral model, which can trace its roots back to the "demon rum" philosophy of the temperance movement, various psychosocial models of the addictions maintain that the SUDs exist because individuals have come to rely on the substance because they have *learned* to do so. Some of the more important models of the SUDs are reviewed in Table 26-1.

It should be noted that although each of these theoretical models has achieved some degree of acceptance in the field of substance abuse rehabilitation, no single model has proven to be a "grand unifying theory" of the addictions.

The Personality Predisposition Theories of Substance Use Disorders

Personality factors have long been suspected to play a role in the development of SUDs. In the case of alcohol use disorders, scientists have spent the better part of a quarter of a century searching for an "alcoholic personality," without success (Renner, 2004b). This would seem to run against clinical experience, and more than one clinician would argue that certain personality

---

[2]Jack the Ripper comes to mind here.

[3]The same point might be made about drugs used to treat "erectile dysfunction." A small but significant percentage of those who use such drugs do so not because they suffer from some degree of impotence, but because they find that it enhances sexual performance. Is this appropriate or it is a form of medication misuse?

[4]As was discussed in the previous chapter, many physicians also hold to this perspective even today.

types are associated with alcohol use disorders more often than one would expect from chance alone.

There are a number of variations to the "predisposing personality" theme, which, like the genetic predisposition theories discussed in the last chapter, are strongly deterministic in orientation. This is clearly seen in the "very word *addict* [which] confers an identity that admits no other possibilities" (Peele, 2004a, p. 43, italics in original). For example, a number of researchers have suggested that personality traits such as impulsiveness, thrill seeking, rebelliousness, aggression, and nonconformity were "robust predictors of alcoholism" (Slutske et al., 2002, p. 124).

These personality traits, however, could be viewed as different manifestations of a common genetic predisposition (Slutske et al., 2002). Within the brain, these personality traits are thought to reflect dysfunctions in the dopamine neurotransmission system. Other clinicians have suggested that the theory of the "alcoholic personality" is nothing more than a clinical myth (Gendel, 2006; Stetter, 2000). According to this theory, clinicians are trained to expect certain personality characteristics in people with an alcohol use disorder and then selectively recall those cases that meet these expectations,[5] forgetting those people who did not evidence these personality traits. If true, then the foundation on which substance abuse rehabilitation is based is again flawed. Clinicians continue to operate on the assumption that their clients are (a) developmentally immature and (b) tend to overuse certain personality defenses such as denial. Treatment is then geared to address these perceived personality flaws in the client, whether they exist or not.

In the face of this lack of supporting evidence, one must ask how the myth of the "alcoholic personality" evolved. One theory is that clinicians and researchers in the mid-20th century became confused by the high rate of comorbidity between individuals with a substance use disorder and individuals with an antisocial personality disorder (ASPD). This is understandable, because between 84 and 90% of males with ASPD will also have an SUD at some point in their lives (Preuss & Wong, 2000; Ziedonis & Brady, 1997). This is not to imply that the ASPD *caused* the SUD or the reverse! Rather, they are separate, coexisting conditions, with each interacting with and affecting the course of the other. Given that individuals with the ASPD demonstrate many of the personality traits attributed to the "addictive/alcoholic personality," it is easy to understand how one came to be confused as being synonymous with the other.

Another theory about how the myth of the "addictive personality" emerged suggests that the impact of psychoanalysis in the early 20th century might have caused clinicians to look for a hypothesized form of psychological trauma that then caused the individual to turn to alcohol or drugs (Leeds & Morgenstern, 2003). Although the various psychoanalytic schools of thought disagreed as to the specific form of trauma, they all did agree on the theory that there was an "addictive personality" that suffered from an internal conflict, which paved the way for the development of the SUD (Leeds & Morgenstern, 2003). Such theories, advanced in an era where there were few competing theories about how SUDs developed, met with widespread approval and continue to have significant support. Pinsky (2008) asserted, for example, that "if you need to see me in my addiction practice, there's almost a 100 percent guarantee you suffered childhood neglect, physical abuse, or sexual trauma" as a child (p. 46).

A central tenet of the psychoanalytic theories is that the defense mechanisms protect the individual from the immediate experience of anxiety, at the expense of long-term adjustment. An example of this process might be seen in clinical experience with marijuana abusers, who speak of the brief periods of euphoria that they experience while using marijuana, without accepting feedback from health care professionals that persistent marijuana use actually exacerbates depression (Washton & Zweben, 2006). The short-term benefits of marijuana abuse are achieved at the cost of long-term adjustment for these individuals. Another example is Khantzian's (2003b) theory that individuals with anxiety disorders might be drawn to the use of compounds such as alcohol, the benzodiazepines, marijuana, and the increasingly rare barbiturates because of their anxiolytic[6] effects. Psychoanalytic writers hold that individuals used alcohol to numb themselves to emotional pain (Frattaroli, 2001; Horney, 1964). The question has been raised, however, whether clinicians were more likely to identify people with emotional pain who also had an alcohol use disorder because it fit their theory-based preconceptions?

The behavioral psychologists did not even attempt to address the issue of a possible preexisting "addictive personality." Indeed, the issue of "personality" is not deemed relevant by behavioral theorists. The SUDs are examined in terms of reward/punishment paradigms.

---

[5]Which is also called the "illusion of correlation."

[6]See Glossary.

This school of thought suggests that humans, like all animals, work to either (a) increase personal pleasure or (b) decrease discomfort. Behaviors that accomplish one of these goals are said to be "reinforcing," whereas those that accomplish the opposite are said to be "punishment." Substance abuse offers the individual a pseudo-community, which is a positive reinforcer, induces a sense of pleasure or euphoria (again, a positive reinforcer), and helps the individual cope with unpleasant emotional states such as pain, depression (a negative reinforcer), and the like. After the development of a physical addiction to a drug(s) of abuse, further use also brings the added benefit of blocking the withdrawal discomfort (a negative reinforcer). It thus is not surprising that, for example, alcohol addiction is supported by a combination of both positive and negative reinforcers (Gilpin & Kolb, 2008).

Finally, another perspective about how the myth of the "addictive personality" came to exist was offered by Pihl (1999). The author pointed out that more than 90% of the early research studies that attempted to isolate the "addictive personality" characteristics were based on samples drawn from various treatment centers. Although such research is often of great value, it is important to keep in mind that (a) there are often major differences between those who enter a treatment center and those who do not, and (b) that there are differences in people's motivation that helped them see the need to enter a treatment center. Pihl (1999) suggested that these early research studies might have unknowingly identified a "treatment personality" more than an "addictive personality" that predisposed people to an SUD. Thus the theory that there is an "addictive personality" that predisposes the individual toward an SUD remains an interesting but unproven theory (Brust, 2004).

Substance Use Disorders and the Use of Psychological Defenses

Over the decades, proponents of the psychosocial model of the addictions have repeatedly postulated that people with an SUD have characteristic defense mechanisms used to avoid recognizing and accepting the reality of their substance use disorder. This belief has become enshrined in clinical lore to the point where it is believed that the "use and abuse of alcohol and illicit drugs has long been associated with denial and misrepresentation" (Vitacco, 2008, p. 44).

The purpose of these defense mechanisms is to protect individuals from the reality of their addiction. If faced with this knowledge, individuals would then be faced with the need to change. Some people do indeed accept this challenge. Others choose, whether on a conscious level or not, to protect their SUD and avoid the need for change. It has long been thought that the most prominent defense mechanisms used by individuals with an SUD are those of *denial, rationalization, projection,* and/or *minimization,* according to proponents of the psychosocial model.

Denial

Clinical lore suggests that the individual's SUD hides behind a wall of denial (Croft, 2006). Essentially, denial is a form of unconscious self-deception, which is classified as one of the more primitive, narcissistic defenses (Sadock & Sadock, 2007). The process of denial operates through a process of selective perception of both the past and the present, so that the individual can avoid facing painful and frightening realities from both the past and the present. The analogy of "tunnel vision" might not be inappropriate here.

Projection

Projection is the defense mechanism in which material that is unacceptable to the "self" is projected onto others (Sadock & Sadock, 2007). All defense mechanisms operate on an unconscious level, and in this case the individual attributes motives, behavior(s), and intentions that are unacceptable to the "self" to others. The young child's cry of "See what you made me do!" is not a bad example of this process. They project responsibility for their misbehavior onto others in an effort to avoid being held accountable for their misdeed(s).

Rationalization

This defense mechanism allows the individual to justify otherwise unacceptable behaviors through cognitive justifications. For example, a hypothetical 73-year-old alcohol-dependent person might give the following explanation: "The reason that I drink today is that I had pneumonia when I was 3, and the doctor told my mother to give me a teaspoon of brandy every 2 hours!" Admittedly, physicians often did make this recommendation in the first quarter of the 20th century, as the body rapidly breaks ethyl alcohol down into glucose, which the body needs to function. However, it is hard to believe that this medical treatment carried out 70 years ago would cause a person to have an alcohol use disorder today!

Many a person with an alcohol use disorder will argue that moderate alcohol use is good for the cardio-vascular system,[7] ignoring the little detail that *moderate* alcohol use appears to have some health benefit, whereas *excessive* alcohol use can cause significant damage to the drinker's body. Thus this defense mechanism allows people to justify otherwise unacceptable behavior (at least to themselves). For example, some people will argue that marijuana is not a form of *substance abuse* because it is a plant, and how can something that grows naturally be addictive or harmful?[8]

Minimization

Minimization operates in a different manner than the psychological defenses discussed thus far. In a sense, minimization operates like a form of rationalization, but it is more specific. The individual who uses minimization as a defense will either consciously or unconsciously reduce the incidence of a socially unacceptable behavior or its impact. For example, one person might explain, "I only drink on the weekends!" (ignoring the detail that for them the "weekend" begins on Friday evening and lasts until Sunday evening). Another person might admit to "experimental" use of cannabis, whereas their spouse reported that the person smokes it three times a day, every day of the week.

More than one alcohol-dependent person has been known to claim to drink "just a glass of wine each night, before bed," without mentioning that the glass is repeatedly "topped off" and that the total amount of wine consumed amounts to a full bottle. Another example of minimization might be seen in the person who claims to "only use marijuana with friends, and I never buy it." On one level this might be true: The individual might smoke marijuana with friends and might never buy it. However, does this person contribute to the cost of the marijuana that the "friends" just happen to have when he or she arrives to visit? Were the "friends" known marijuana abusers? In this case the discovery that they were using (or at least have) marijuana when the person happened to visit is hardly a coincidence.

Section Summary

Over time, the various drugs of abuse can induce characteristic patterns of behavior, or damage to the physical structure of the brain. It is entirely possible that over a period of time these physical changes in the brain might give the illusion that people with an SUD commonly utilize these defense mechanisms.[9]

Challenges to the Characteristic Defense Mechanism Theory

In recent years the assertion that people with an SUD overuse certain defense mechanisms has been challenged by a number of clinicians. Further, the theory that individuals with an SUD will *automatically* rely on the defense mechanism of denial has been challenged, and might actually do more harm than good (Foote, 2006). Indeed, W. R. Miller and Rollnick (2002) suggested that, as a group, people with an alcohol use disorder do not use denial more frequently than any other group. But because of selective perception on the part of the therapist(s), the therapeutic myth of the substance-abusing patient who uses the defenses discussed earlier in this chapter was established. To support their thesis, the authors point to what is known as the "illusion of correlation." The illusion of correlation suggests that we tend to remember events that confirm our preconceptions and to dismiss or forget information that fails to do so. According to this theory, substance abuse rehabilitation professionals are more likely to remember those clients who demonstrated the defenses of denial, rationalization, projection, and minimization. But when the client does not demonstrate these characteristics, or if the client's stage of growth and the treatment approach do not match, clinicians interpret this as evidence of the defense mechanisms identified earlier, and not as evidence of a therapeutic mismatch (W. R. Miller & Rollnick, 2002).

The Final Common Pathway Theory of the Substance Use Disorders

Although there are strong proponents of both the medical model and the psychosocial models of substance use disorders, most practitioners in the field view

---

[7]See Chapter 5.

[8]Two counterarguments present themselves: First, tobacco is also a plant, and as discussed in Chapter 16, smoking is a major cause of premature death around the world. So plants can be harmful to the user. Second, both tobacco and marijuana plants have been subjected to selective breeding experiments over the generations, with the result being that the plant that emerged from such experiments is far more potent than the original plants found in this country generations ago.

[9]For example, the extreme paranoia often seen in amphetamine or cocaine abusers. It is clinically similar to paranoid schizophrenia in many cases, but clears on its own after the person stops abusing the offending agent (cocaine or amphetamines).

SUDs as reflecting both a genetic predisposition and a social learning process (Monti et al., 2002). But to date neither the biological predisposition nor the psychosocial models of addictions have provided a "grand unifying theory" of the addictions.

But there is another perspective to consider, one called the *final common pathway* (FCP) theory. In a very real sense, the FCP school of thought is a nontheory: It holds that the substance use disorders are *a common end point* (Sommer, 2005; Stahl, 2008). But as Nurnberger and Bierut (2007) suggested of the alcohol use disorders, "there are different paths to alcoholism and different pathways underlying them" (p. 51). Further, as the authors pointed out, during the early stages of alcohol use disorders there is a remarkable amount of variation between clients and their symptoms, although in the later stages there is far less variation in symptoms between individuals. There is no reason to suspect that the process for the other SUDs is different than it is for the alcohol use disorders. Indeed, as Stahl (2008) observed, "The final common pathway of reinforcement and reward in the brain is hypothesized to be the mesolimbic dopamine pathway" (p. 945).

Thus the FCP school of thought holds that there are a multitude of individual risk factors that interact to contribute to or detract from the individual's risk for developing an SUD. In a sense, the FCP model is a *biopsychosocial model*, in that it is believed that the "addictive behaviors are complex disorders multiple determined through biological, psychological and sociocultural processes" (Donovan, 2005, p. 2). Proponents of this school of thought do not discount the possible contribution of a genetic predisposition, but also believe that life experiences contribute to a substance use disorder (Salzman, 2008).

Strong support for the FCP model of the addictions is found in the latest neurological research studies, which identify a single dopamine-based reward cascade as being the motivating factor for continued substance abuse (Ivanov et al., 2006; Salzman, 2008; Stahl, 2008). The brain's reward system evolved to help this species survive. Rewarding experiences (either natural or drug induced) increase the concentration of the neurochemical $\Delta FosB$[10] in the nucleus accumbens region of the brain. This makes clinical sense: It would be to the advantage of the individual to be able to recall cues that identified natural rewards such as food, water, or sex.

This reward potential of a substance is strongest when it is unpredictable (Fiorillo, Tobler, & Schultz, 2003). This makes clinical sense: Imagine the enthusiasm with which you would play a slot machine in Las Vegas if you were to win a consistent amount of money every time that you played. After a period of time you would become bored and search for other challenges. In the case of SUDs, the predictability of substance-induced rewards makes the use of that compound less and less rewarding over time, a process that the individual might seek to overcome through the use of larger and larger doses or through the use of new compounds.

Unfortunately, the drugs of abuse overwhelm the brain's reward system, making it fire more intensely after the use of one of these compound(s) than do natural reinforcers. Clinicians have measured a 5- to 10-fold greater level of dopamine in the nucleus accumbens region of the brain after the use of some substances than is found after exposure to natural reinforcers, for example. Further, repeated exposure to the substance-induced pleasure results in a process known as *overlearning*, in which the individual also becomes very sensitive to environmental cues associated with the substance-induced pleasure ("Addiction and the Problem of Relapse," 2007). At the same time, those regions of the brain associated with behavioral inhibition (especially the *insula* region of the brain) become less active under the influence of drug-induced rewards, enhancing the drive to use that substance(s) again (Bechara, 2006; Gendel, 2006; Volkow, 2006a). This process parallels the natural reward cascade: In the wild, it would be to the individual's advantage to be able to recall cues that identified natural rewards such as food, water, and sex.

But we do not live in a the "natural" world. We are exposed to various chemicals of our own making that now have the potential to overwhelm our natural defenses. By an accident of evolution, certain compounds are capable of creating an intense, but false signal in the brain's reward system, memory centers, and the higher cortical areas that control reward-seeking behavior(s), indicating that what the individual just did (in this case use a substance of abuse) is really, *really* important. This is the neurological basis of the *pharmacological reward potential* of a compound, which was discussed in Chapter 1 as a factor that contributed to the tendency for the individual to want to repeat the use of that compound. Strong substance use memories are formed, helping to shape behavioral decisions that lead to further drug-induced rewards (D. Brown, 2006;

---

[10]Discussed in the previous chapter.

Bruijnzeel, Repetto, & Gold, 2004; Gendel, 2006). Essentially, a normal biological process that evolved to help early humans survive has been subverted by the reward potential of compounds that humans have invented (G. Marcus, 2008).

The neurobiological steps in the substance-induced reward cascade are virtually the same for all drugs of abuse. Initially, when the drug molecules reach the brain, the nucleus accumbens releases massive amounts of dopamine, which serves to signal the cortex that the individual's recent behavior (drinking water when dehydrated, for example) was good for him or her. This information is also carried to the brain regions known as the *amygdala*[11] and the *hippocampus*[12] to establish a memory of the event that triggered the reward cascade for future reference. At the same time, the cortical control/decision-making regions use this same information to establish a hierarchy of rewards, which then help to shape future behavioral choices.[13] Over time, repeated episodes of substance-induced pleasure can induce trigger the process of neuroplasticity in the brain, so that the individual becomes sensitive to drug use cues in the environment, just as our ancestors would become sensitive to environmental cues that signaled food or water.

When these substance use cues are encountered in between periods of active substance use, the individual is motivated to consider seeking out a drug(s) to use once more (Viamontes & Beitman, 2006). At its extreme, this might become as intense as a "craving" for the chemical(s) until the desired sensation is once again experienced. Again, this parallels the natural reward process: If hungry, the organism becomes sensitive to food-related cues until it is able to obtain food to consume. Although these "craving" episodes are quite intense, they are not overpowering. Further, with

---

[11]See Glossary.

[12]See Glossary.

[13]For example: "Getting a can of soda right now would be nice, but I am starving, and so getting something to eat first sounds better!"

extended abstinence, the associational memory cues become weaker and weaker, so that the individual experiences fewer (and less intense) episodes of "craving" for a substance. Thus in the early stages of rehabilitation it is necessary to identify internal/external substance use cues and then establish a way for the individual to deal with them.

Admittedly, factors such as the *availability* of a substance, social reward systems, the pharmacological reward potential of the substance (if available), individual life goals, and the availability of substance-free alternative activities interact with the individual's genetic potential and state of health, contributing to or reducing the possibility of the decision to use a chemical(s). But the important thing is that *all* of the drugs(s) of abuse eventually activate the same nerve pathways in the brain that are normally involved in the process of learning/memory formation/reward (Correia, 2005; Salzman, 2008; Wolf, 2006). From the perspective of the FCP, the SUDs might be viewed as having multiple forms (activating chemicals) and multiple pathways, but ultimately a common etiology.

Chapter Summary

The "disease" model of substance use disorders has come to dominate the manner in which the SUDs are viewed and treated in the United States. But it is not without its critics. However, the psychosocial sciences, though able to offer valuable insights into the social and psychological factors that contribute to SUDs, have also failed to develop a "grand unifying theory" for the addictions. Each perspective appears to offer insights into the nature of the addictions, but yet each perspective fails to completely explain all of the facets of the SUDs adequately. A third perspective, that of the final common pathway, suggests that the addictions are a final common end point, but that there are multiple pathways to that end point. This perspective is supported by current neurological research, but itself also fails to provide a "grand unifying theory" to SUDs at this time.

CHAPTER **27**

The Substance Use Disorders As a Disease of the Human Spirit

Introduction

It is possible to view a select individual from a range of perspectives: The individual is or is not a taxpayer, is male or female, is in perfect health or has one of the multitude of diseases from which humankind suffers, and so on. An inconvenient truth is that people are also spiritual beings[1] who are either actively or passively involved in a relationship with a Higher Being.[2] Individuals do not suddenly stop being a spiritual being when they consult with a physician, psychologist, social worker, or other health care professional (Pargament, 2007). They remain spiritual beings in every aspect of their life, whether or not they acknowledge it.

Wade (2009) argued that "there is no church of oneself" (p. 2). Arguably, in spite of Wade's assertion, substance use disorders might be viewed as an example of a church of oneself in that the service of the individual's addiction becomes the prime focus of that person's life. The litany of the addicted person is "I want what I want, when *I* want it!!!" They then decry, "I deserve to feel this way (or in the case of the withdrawal syndromes not to feel the discomfort of withdrawal)!" Such self-centered thinking places the medical sciences in a conundrum: At its best, medical science is uncomfortable with the idea of spirituality, leaving physicians with the task of dealing with patients who are spiritual beings while lacking the conceptual paradigm within which to work with patients as spiritual beings (Pargament, 2007). This unfortunately robs the health care professional of a potentially insightful perspective into one of the forces that helps to shape the individual's response to illness. In this chapter the spiritual model of the addictions will be examined.

Modern science has been so successful at explaining the laws that govern the evolution of the universe that it is the rare theologian who can dismiss this wealth of secular knowledge as being meaningless (Wright, 2009). The reverse is, unfortunately, very true.

---

[1] It should be noted that there is a difference between spirituality and religion.

[2] Arguably, atheists, by their very rejection of the concept of a Higher Being, still could be said to be relating to that Being through this act. Otherwise, it would not be necessary to deny the existence of something that does not exist.

How the Soul Was Lost

Although René Descartes probably was not the first person to postulate that the mind and the body are separate entities, this theory forced the physical and the spiritual sciences in different directions for generations to come. The ultimate goal for each remains the same: the discovery of ultimate Truth. The theologian and scientist just disagree as to the definition of ultimate Truth. Is all that is seen and unseen part of a divine plan,[3] which in turn implies that there is a Planner, or did it just happen?[4] Would the theologian and scientist be able to accept the other's ultimate Truth?

Scientists now understand that the dichotomy between mind and body is artificial and unnecessary. Without the body, there is no "mind." Without the mind, the body cannot be perceived or inhabited by the person. However, in the journey from the unity of mind and body through separation and back to the reunification of the same, the soul appears to have been misplaced, if not lost. Yet it is the soul that is the essence of existence. Since ancient times philosophers have suggested that there exists within each of us a spark of divine light, which was called *spiritus* by the ancient Romans. Once it is extinguished the light of that individual's life is lost forever (Doweiko, 1999; Milstein, 2008). Although scientists have occasionally attempted to define or measure the spirit, it has for the most part remained ignored or viewed as a relic from the past because it is ill-defined and cannot be replicated in a laboratory. For these reasons it is rarely studied. Indeed, there are those in the scientific community who assert that the "spirit" does not exist and that it is an illusion caused by the function of the human brain. This is a rather interesting contradiction in that, at the end of the first decade of the 21st century, one of the major treatment modalities for SUDs is a program designed to facilitate spiritual growth.

Many now postulate that the "mind" reflects nothing more than the outcome of chemical interactions within and between neurons. The "mind" is nothing more than an illusion created by the brain, they argue, and as such should be subjected to the same methods of scientific study applied to other realms of existence. In time, perhaps, the neurochemical foundation(s) of the entity called "mind" will be discovered through scientific inquiry. But the act of scientific inquiry, even if it does reveal the neurochemical foundation(s) of the mind, does not explain *why* scientific inquiry came to exist. In an ironic twist of fate, at the same time that many neuroscientists deny the existence of the "mind" as a separate entity from the brain itself, pharmaceutical companies are heavily invested in the search to find compounds that might heal or at least calm troubled minds.[5]

In their search for a pharmacological treatment to emotional pain and suffering, the spiritual aspect of the individual's existence is totally ignored (Pargament, 2007). This might reflect the fact that science has "driven a wedge between faith and reason" (p. 2). Countless thousands of generations invested untold millions of man-hours in the exploration of *spiritus* and its implications for life. Further, they did so in an era when the intensity of work necessary for basic survival was far higher than it is today. Perhaps, it is argued here, one reason why these earlier generations invested so much time and effort into this search was because it was important to defining the "self" in an era where life seemed so uncertain. Does this search continue to have meaning in the first years of the 21st century?

The answers provided those living in each era a sense of common ground on which to stand and to define the "self." The search itself and the answers it revealed provided a shared reality on which to stand, from which to launch the next generation(s) onto the river of life. However, especially in the last half of a century, this spiritual "grounding" has been lost. The current generation has become "probably the first major culture in human history with no shared picture of reality" (J. R. Primack & Abrams, 2006, p. 4). In other words, the current generation has lost the roots that grounded earlier generations. Traditional rituals used by earlier generations to help define who they were and provide a sense of being "grounded" have been abandoned (Pargament, 2007). At the same time, the very concept of *spiritus* is under attack by the "pervasive doctrine of scientific materialism" (Frattaroli, 2001, p. 20). The modern reductionist views the mind as a by-product of the brain's neural activities. Everything can be understood, it is argued, if you break things down into the most elemental units.[6]

---

[3]Which would imply that there is one who made the Plan.

[4]A position that then implies that existence is meaningless, unless the individual strives to give it meaning. This would reflect a decision on the part of the individual, who assumes the role of a Planner, at least to a limited degree.

[5]See Breakout Discussion #3 for a discussion on this topic.

[6]A counterargument to this assertion might very well be: At what level of integration does the collected pool of chemical interactions between and within cells become self-aware or develop spiritual desires?

This scientific doctrine does not, however, answer the age-old questions of "who am I?" and, "why am I here?" These questions are not obsolete relics from a less sophisticated past, but reflect core questions about the human condition. Scientific materialism offers empty references to the "mind" or the "brain" as if these things were synonymous with the *soul* (Frattaroli, 2001). This contributes, in part, to a fundamental void on which individuals are expected to build their lives. Everything is a great cosmological accident, it is argued, and on that foundation you should build your life. This is both a frightening and arduous task. Alcohol and/or drugs offer what appears to be an answer to these fundamental questions: "I am here to seek pleasure," and the enticement of a reason for being (continued pleasure). It offers a form of chemical narcissism in which the desires of the "self" are made central to one's view of the universe. On this foundation, the individual is then expected to build a life, only to later discover that the chemicals offer not answers but enslavement.

One consequence of this awareness of the "self" is that individuals also becomes aware of the canyon between "self" and "other." Newborn infants begin to discern this chasm when their mother fails to instantly respond to their cries. Over the course of individuals' lives, they become aware of a sense of basic isolation from others, a chasm that will never be crossed no matter how hard one might try. Spirituality, which is part of the shared view of reality shared by earlier generations, helped to provide security in the face of this ultimate isolation.

One of the forces that helped to shatter this shared vision of reality emerged in the Middle Ages, when the philosopher Roger Bacon[7] argued that only those facts that could be observed, measured, and/or replicated were worthy of belief (Cahill, 2006). This was a radical idea at a time when the church was viewed as the ultimate authority on all matters, and eventually this viewpoint became the foundation for scientific methodology. In this we find the core of the conundrum: Although the ability of science to reproduce experimental findings and replicate the findings from one study in another gives it an air of authority, it is not (as many assume) the ultimate authority on matters of the spirit. Issues of the soul must be *experienced,* a process that does not lend itself to replication or external measurement (Frattaroli, 2001). Modern science holds that if a thing cannot be replicated or measured, then it

does not exist. Spirituality allows not for replication and measurement, but for the discovery of meaning in the face of the absurdity of life (Milstein, 2008). Each process seeks the same goal: that of finding meaning through an exploration of facts. They just differ as to the specific methodology.

A possible unintended side effect of the scientific perspective, however, is that it forced a schism between those who held that there was a spiritual foundation to life and those who espoused the scientific method. By definition God[8] is outside of creation and is not subject to the methods of scientific verification (Cahill, 2006).[9] A logical conclusion (using the perspective of modern science) is that God must not exist. To the spiritual believer, the lack of scientific verification is unimportant, for it is the search for meaning that is the journey. On such a journey, it is often comforting to accept that there is a Higher Power, although the specific name depends on the person making the journey.

Is it true that things unmeasured do not exist? Pargament (2007) suggested that spirituality is "a critical and distinctive dimension of human motivation" (p. 60). Unfortunately, large segments of society have turned away from this aspect of their lives, perhaps accounting for why many report a sense of drifting through the experience of life. If, as D. Siegel (2008) suggested, relationships shape and direct energy flow both between and within individuals, and the individual believes in nothing outside of the "self," then there is no energy flow from that individual to another. Further, without the spiritual, there is nothing against which to measure the demands of the "self." Perceptions cannot be measured, but they certainly do affect both individuals and the society within which they live. Technology[10] offers toys to entertain the masses, and science attempts to find and measure truth. Neither can provide a sense of purpose, or a direction in life.

If the individual has a spirituality centered life, then he or she will:

---

[7]See Glossary.

[8]The term here is used in the sense of a Higher Power, although the title S/He-Who-Has-No-Name might perhaps be better, because S/He would stand outside of His/Her creation.

[9]In reality, both science and spirituality seek the same thing: truth. But many lose track of this fact, and see each as antagonistic to the other. Truth is not antagonistic to itself, nor can it ever be. The methods that Francis Bacon espoused might not be the same as those selected by individuals on a spiritual journey, but each seeks to answer the same question: Who am I, and why am I here?

[10]Including the various chemicals of abuse that have emerged as a result of human creativity.

begin to build their lives around the sacred [and] the sacred can begin to lend greater coherence to disparate thoughts, feelings, actions and goals by superseding all other values, integrating competing aspirations into a unified life plan, and [provide] direction and guidance from day to day. (Pargament, 2007, p. 72)

The reverse is also true: If individuals lack a spirituality component to their lives, they are left with a void. It is into this void that alcohol and the drugs of abuse slip. Although these substances do not ultimately offer a direction in life, they *do* offer an *illusion of a purpose*, along with the *illusion of control* over one's feelings. Control, or at least the illusion of control, has been found to be one of the forces that helps to define happiness (G. Marcus, 2008; Pargament, 2007). Suddenly, one has acquired a godlike power to feel not that which is experienced, but that which is *desired*. This is a seductive power, and many are ensnared by its charms, at least until they discover that the desired control over their emotions is only an illusion and that they are now physically addicted to a chemical(s).

The Ghost in the Machine

There are some philosophers who believe that the story of the Garden of Eden, as related in the Holy Bible, might not relate to the physical act of Eve taking a bite out of an apple from the Tree of Knowledge but to the development of self-awareness (Fromm, 1956). Although other animals demonstrate at least some degree of self-awareness, in humans this awareness has reached a new level. For humans can also communicate, admittedly in an imperfect manner because we are limited to words. In gaining the gift of self-awareness, the individual also becomes aware of a terrible sense of isolation. Ultimately we are alone, a terrible and frightening reality that few can face without being scarred forever.

It is because of this sense of isolation that we strive to join with or merge with something beyond the "self." "The awareness of human separation," wrote Fromm (1956), "without reunion by love—is the source of shame. It is at the same time the source of guilt and anxiety" (p. 8). But love is a risk: We might be rejected and ultimately forced back into our isolation. For no matter how passionately we might love, or how deeply we might love, in the end we are alone. This reality proves both painful for the individual and provides the drugs of abuse an opportunity to seduce the user through the promise of effortless joy and peace. It is not by accident that many of these drugs of abuse activate the same nerve pathways activated by a strong love

relationship ... or is it? There are those who maintain that it is just by coincidence that the drugs of abuse stimulate the brain's reward system so strongly and those who maintain that they are an instrument of the Evil one.[11]

The essential point is that in humans *spiritus* not only has become aware of itself, but can communicate this awareness to others through language and to some degree shape its future. But this self-awareness comes with a price: We are no longer able to take comfort in the unknowing blending of the "self" into nature, for each is aware of one's isolation from others (Fromm, 1956). This awareness of one's ultimate isolation becomes an "unbearable prison" (Fromm, 1956, p. 7). It is our very isolation that allows the drug(s) of abuse into the lives of those who seek to escape and to join with something greater than the "self," according to the spiritual model.

Individuals' self-awareness provides them the right of self-determination, but also carries with it the *responsibility* for making choices. A bird does not choose to be a bird. A tree does not choose to be a tree. But individuals are able to choose how to behave. Fromm (1956, 1968) suggested that this ability to choose, and the responsibility that is the ultimate price that we pay, was accomplished at the cost of being aware of isolation from our fellows. If individuals were to choose to give of the "self" to another through love, they might transcend the ultimate isolation, but this is attempted only at the risk of failure.

The mid-20th century philosopher Thomas Merton (1978) took a similar view on the nature of human existence. The individual cannot achieve happiness through *any* form of compulsive behavior (Merton, 1961, 1978). Rather, the individual "self" is defined by the love that is shared openly and honestly with others (including a higher spirit). Martin Buber (1970) took an even more extreme view, stating that it is only through the relationships that the individual chooses to enter into that the "self" is defined. However, if the relationship that one enters into is not with others but with a chemical(s) to provide pleasure to the "self," is there a relationship? Love, according to Pargament (2007), reflects the ability to shift focus from the "self" to others. What if one withdraws love from others in order to invest that emotional energy and gratification into the "self"? Would this not, as the founders of Alcoholics Anonymous suggested, be a "disease" of that individual's spirit?

---

[11]Which is an interesting debate, although it is far beyond the scope of this text.

From this perspective, the individual with an SUD might be viewed as being on a form of a:

> *spiritual search. They really are looking for something akin to the great hereafter, and they flirt with death to find it. Misguided, romantic, foolish, needful, they think that they can escape from the world by artificial means. And they shoot, snort, drink, pop or smoke those means as they have to leave their pain and find their refuge. At first it works. But, then it doesn't. (Baber, 1998, p. 29)*

Admittedly, we all experience pain and a sense of discontent or being incomplete in life. Further, the stress of daily living conspires to shatter the individual's spirit in a thousand different ways. To survive, some pull within the "self." Others seek the mindless illusion of safety offered by false gods such as possessions or drugs of abuse. A minority choose to embark on a lifelong journey of spiritual growth.

The Pain of Life

To be alive, an ancient Hebrew proverb maintains, is to know pain. It is a necessary part of the human experience, and this same proverb states that not to know pain is not to be fully alive. We all begin life with "hope, faith and fortitude" (Fromm, 1968, p. 20). But in each era these traits are assaulted on a moment-to-moment basis by the trials and tribulations of life. The individual's sense of hope is shattered, and without a sense of groundedness, the individual is left with nothing but a sense of emptiness or a painful void within (Tillich, 1957). It is at this point that some recoil in horror and become spiritual narcissists: self-centered, unwilling to see any reason to deny the "self" any desire or pleasure.

This is not to say that every individual with an SUD has faced an existential crisis of the kind described here. Even in cases where people have faced such a crisis, it may have remained unconscious, hidden behind walls of self-deception and denial. Whether individuals are or are not aware of the struggle within, they are still overwhelmed by the stressors of daily living, and the various drugs of abuse offer at least the illusion of protecting them from the pain of isolation and existence.

Diseases of the Mind/Diseases of the Spirit: The Mind-Body Question

It is possible for a spiritual disorder to manifest as a physical disease? There are many answers to this question. The American humorist Samuel Clemens[12] once stated that because he was born when Halley's Comet was high in the sky in 1835, he was destined to pass from this life when Halley's Comet was again high in the sky above the Earth. This prediction did indeed come true when he died in 1910. Did he "program" himself to pass from this life? It is indeed a point that could be debated at length without a clear answer. Most health care professionals can relate a similar story in which seemingly healthy individuals predicted the time of their death in advance. At what point do these spiritual issues become a physical disease? People, having lost a deeply loved spouse, might "pine away" for their now-deceased partner and slowly fade from life. These are very real examples of how a spiritual[13] disease can manifest as a physical illness that are well known to any person involved in a patient care capacity.

The question of whether the SUDs are a brain disorder, as is suggested by proponents of the medical model, a result of a psychosocial process, as is suggested by proponents of the psychosocial models of the SUDs, or a spiritual disorder (the premise of this chapter) is one that may have implications for other disorders as well. Although many are uncomfortable in discussing spiritual matters, there is an emerging body of evidence that suggests that individuals with strong spiritual beliefs are less likely to become addicted to a chemical(s), more likely to live longer, and more likely to recover should they develop an SUD (Haber, 2008; Sterling et al., 2006).

Modern medicine struggles to adhere to an artificial mind-body dichotomy[14] that began to evolve in the 14th century. But the addictions do not fall into this neat dichotomy of mind-body. The SUDs are not totally a physical illness, nor are they exclusively a disease of the mind. Rather, they rest on a triad of supports: mind, body, *and* spirit, with the latter showing great potential to moderate the alcohol use disorders (and by implication the other SUDs as well) (Haber, 2008). This model, although it would seem to account for the observed phenomena of the SUDs, still makes many uncomfortable because of the inclusion of spirituality.

---

[12]Also known as Mark Twain.

[13]Some would argue that these are "psychological" disorders and not "spiritual" issues at all. Where the line falls between psychological and spiritual diseases is left to the reader to decide.

[14]Actually, the mind-body dichotomy is an artificial one, as each blends into the other.

The Growth of Addictions: The Circle Narrows

Alcohol use provides a very clear example of the relationship between spirituality and the alcohol use disorders. The use of alcohol is a behavioral choice. In the case of heavy alcohol use, it can be viewed as being an axis (Brown, 1985; Hyman, 2005) around which the individual's life now revolves.[15] Alcohol (and, by implication, the other drugs of abuse) assumes a role of "central importance" (S. A. Brown, 1985, p. 78) around which individuals center their life. It is often difficult for those who have never struggled with a substance use disorder to understand this point. But it is not uncommon for addicted people to choose continued substance use over family, friends, their jobs, or even personal health.

Individuals with SUDs often present others with a level of self-centeredness that puzzles, if not offends, them. Whether this is a real or pseudo-personality disorder has never been resolved. But individuals are viewed as having a form of "moral insanity" in which they:

> could not manage our own lives. We could not live and enjoy life as other people do. We have to have something different, and we thought that we found it in drugs. We placed their use ahead of the welfare of our families, our wives, husbands, and our children. We had to have drugs at all costs. (Narcotics Anonymous 1982, p. 11, italics in original deleted)

There are people whose all-consuming interest is limited only to themselves. Such people are often presented as an object of ridicule in the popular media. They care about nothing beyond that little portion of the universe known as the "self." Their only love is of the "self," which they view as being worthy of adoration or as being superior to the average person. Just as this personality type epitomizes self-love, and as such is a perversion of love itself, so the SUDs might be viewed as another form of a perversion of self-love. Individuals' initial choice to use a recreational chemical(s) might reflect curiosity or a desire to partake in a social activity. But it also could be viewed as an attempt on their part to impose their will on external reality, supporting the delusion that there is nothing as important as the "self." Unfortunately, pandering to delusions of self-importance weakens the true self and diminishes

our ability to distinguish desires from needs (Norris, 1996, pp. 14–15)

This latter point is important, for individuals who abuse chemicals often confuse their *wants* with their *needs*, a confusion that the drug(s) of abuse reinforce through their ability to overstimulate the brain's reward system. Eventually, individuals reach the point where they come to believe that continued substance use is a *need* on their part. This accounts for the tendency for the exaggerated concern of people with an SUD to maintain an adequate supply of their drug(s) of choice. For example, consider the alcohol-dependent person who, with six or seven cases of beer already in the basement, went to buy six more cases "just in case … you can never have too much of a good thing." This individual's emphasis on having 12 cases of beer as a *"good thing"* clearly reflects the manner in which they have centered their life around the continued use of alcohol. Other people are viewed as either an inconvenience to the individual's goal of continued substance use or as an object to manipulate in order to sustain access to further substance(s). However, nothing is allowed to come between individuals and their drug(s) of choice, if at all possible.

The Circle of Addiction: Priorities

As an SUD comes to dominate people's lives, they find that more and more effort must be expended just to maintain the substance use disorder. For example, many heroin or cocaine addicts have reported that they had to engage in prostitution (either heterosexual or homosexual) as well as theft in order to obtain the money necessary to buy the next day's supply of drugs. Possessions are sold or traded for chemicals, and over time individuals might even begin to deteriorate socially as more resources are directed to the maintenance of their SUD.

Some of the Games of Addiction

Given that individuals demand continued access to a desired substance(s) at the center of their life, it is only to be expected that they will attempt to build a support system that will enable them to continue to engage in the use of that chemical(s). Part of this support system is maintained through an intricate web of manipulative "games," the sole purpose of which is to protect the addiction. "I cannot risk offending Aunt

---

[15]As will be discussed in later in this text, there is evidence that many people with an evolving SUD turn aside from this path.

Clara," a person with a substance use disorder might think, "because she is old and ill, and I will lose any chance of an inheritance if I do offend her." Thus individuals choose a path that will enable them to present themselves in the best possible light.

Having a real or feigned illness is a popular manipulative "game" utilized by those who either do not wish to face the consequences of their addiction or wish to obtain desired drugs from a physician. So rather than going to work with the smell of alcohol still surrounding them because they had been out drinking the night before, they call in "sick." To block the effects of early alcohol withdrawal while at work, alcohol-dependent people might visit a physician(s) for treatment of an "anxiety" disorder, while being careful to make no mention of their alcohol use disorder. In each case, the individual's substance-related behavior is now made legitimate by the illusion of an illness, and friends/coworkers/physicians become unwitting elements of that person's substance use support system.

To protect their source of drugs and to justify its continued use, patients must often go through elaborate ruses to keep their substance use disorder hidden. They might study medical textbooks in order to learn exactly what symptoms they need to report to a physician in order to obtain a desired prescription, or even engage in "doctor shopping"[16] in order to find one willing to prescribe their desired drug(s).[17] Patients have been known to engage in feigned outrage, tears, threats of abandonment, threats to file a complaint with a regulatory board, pleading, promises to change, and even outright seduction, in order to obtain the drug(s) that they desire.

One favorite tactic is for patients to visit the local hospital emergency room in order to obtain prescriptions for desired medication(s) through real or feigned displays of distress. Some individuals have even gone so far as to have false surgical scars tattooed onto their backs, to support their claim of having back pain that was not corrected through surgical intervention. Experienced physicians are used to hearing stories about how: (a) "Nobody else has been able to help me (except you)"; (b) "My dog/horse/cat/space aliens ate my prescription"[18]; (c) "My house/apartment was burglarized,

and the only thing stolen was my prescription for _____"; or the ever-popular (d) "I lost my prescription and need it refilled or else I will go into withdrawal and it will be *your* fault!" The goal of each of these manipulative games is to obtain a prescription for a desired substance.

Some inventive patients have gone to the hospital with a report that they are passing a "kidney stone." When asked for a urine sample (which should have traces of blood it in from the damage that the kidney stone is doing to their body), they have been found to prick their finger with a pin and squeeze a drop of blood into the vial of urine to provide the necessary "bloody urine" sample to confirm their report. Others have inserted a foreign body into the urethra prior to going to the hospital, in order to irritate the urethral lining so that it will bleed when they are asked for a urine sample.[19] Finally, there are those patients who have actual injuries or illnesses, who go from hospital to hospital to obtain a prescription for a desired medication.

The point to keep in mind is that people with an SUD will either consciously or unconsciously engage in various manipulative games to support their addiction. All of these behaviors are then viewed as a reflection of the individual's spiritual illness by those who espouse the spiritual model of the addictions.

A Thought on Playing the Games of Addiction

It often surprises the nonabuser to learn the intensity with which individuals with an SUD will engage in interpersonal "games" and the indifference with which they often treat their victims. It is necessary to remind nonabusers that the addiction lifestyle is just that: a *lifestyle*. It is the abuser's whole life, and a part of that lifestyle is avoiding responsibility for one's substance use disorder or all too frequently other behaviors. Indeed, so pervasive is the tendency to be intentionally or unintentionally dishonest that an old joke from the earliest days of Alcoholics Anonymous went like this: "How do you tell if an alcoholic is lying? (pause before delivering the punch line) Their lips are moving!"

The substance use disorders, especially when at their most extreme, involve both conscious and unconscious lifestyle adjustments that often shock the nonuser. There are many variations on these lifestyle adjustments, but they share the common characteristic of

---

[16]See Glossary.

[17]This problem has become significantly more pronounced because of the Internet.

[18]Why is it that the dog/cat/horse/space aliens *never* eat amoxicillin, or antidepressant medications, or blood pressure medications, and how do they manage to survive what would be many times the lethal dose for such a small creature without any medical intervention?

[19]This tactic involves the risk of poking a hole right through the lining of the urethra, but this is seen as an acceptable risk by those individuals who use this tactic.

"a fundamental inability to be honest … with the *self*" (C. Knapp, 1996, p. 83, italics in original). Indeed, in speaking of her own alcohol use disorder, Knapp compared her relationship to alcohol to that of a love relationship. When one is in love, one will do virtually anything for the beloved. Parents will defend their child to the death. All too often, the same is true for substance use disorders: One will do almost anything for the beloved.

It is only in fleeting moments of self-examination that individuals will ask themselves: "Could it be my drinking or drug use?" But such moments of honest introspection are rare and, as the SUD continues, become less and less frequent. Nor is the addicted person immune from the deceptive tactics. It is not unusual for people with an SUD to go "on the wagon" to prove to themselves (and others) that they can "still control it." Unfortunately, by trying to prove control, they actually demonstrate that their substance use disorder is out of control. "But I can't be alcoholic" one individual might cry out when confronted with evidence to the contrary. "Why two years ago I went for six months without drinking!" Perhaps this was true … but that was six months ago, and why did this person return to the use of alcohol?

A common refrain heard from friends, family members, and medical professionals is that "they sounded so sincere." Yes, they may have sounded sincere. They might even have had an honest desire to stop abusing chemicals at that moment in time. However, the fact remains that ultimately substance use becomes a lifestyle, not just an inconvenient aspect of one's life. It requires much effort to change that lifestyle, and many choose not to pay the price for a substance-free life that they might only barely remember.

There appears to be no limit to the manipulations that people with an SUD will use to support/protect their substance use disorder. The only way to avoid being caught up in such manipulations is to maintain an attitude of quiet watchfulness and complete honesty with both the "self" and the "other."

Honesty: A Building Stone of Recovery

It is often shocking to those around people with an SUD how they could be so blind to the severity of their condition. "Well, everybody gets arrested for driving under the influence [of chemicals] three times," an alcohol-dependent people might say to defend their AUD. Others might boast, "I've been completely clean for the last two months," ignoring the fact that they are awaiting trial and that substance use would be a violation of pretrial restrictions and possibly grounds for incarceration. To make the lifestyle changes necessary to eliminate this degree of self-deception is not easy, and it requires total honesty with the "self."

An examination of people's motivation for remaining substance free is often quite revealing. One person might abstain from substances because of a fear of incarceration, whereas another might fear a threatened divorce. Although such sources of external motivation are of value at times, they do not protect the individual from responsibility for not making a choice to abstain. They are possibly "clean"; they are not "in recovery." There is still an element of deception at work if either presents as being "in recovery," although the individual with the SUD might not recognize it.

In a very real sense, many people with an SUD might be said to have lost touch with external reality. Many people with an alcohol use disorder, for example, will take the "marijuana cure," switching their substance use from alcohol to marijuana in order to avoid the legal sanctions that would result should they continue to use alcohol while under the supervision of the court. Some will even go so far as to claim extended periods of "recovery" to others, while not mentioning that they have been smoking marijuana on a regular basis (but not drinking), for example.

This is not to imply that every person with an SUD engages in conscious deception. Rather, the point being made here is that the layers of conscious and unconscious deception serve to isolate individuals from the reality of their substance use disorder, in order to protect it. People with an SUD have been known to be shocked to learn that they were unsuccessful in their attempts to deceive others about their substance abuse, and even more shocked to learn that they have become addicted to the substance that they thought that they were using on only a recreational basis. In many cases, the only person deceived for any length of time is the person with the SUD. But along the way they will lie to family members, spouses, children, probation/parole officers, judges, therapists, friends, and physicians, and then wonder why these people hold such grudges against them.

Thus one of the cornerstones of recovery is *honesty*. As people with an SUD come to understand that they were deceiving themselves along with others, they begin to question their perceptions and decisions. Where once they did not pay attention to feedback from others, recovering abusers must learn to seek out such feedback and to listen to it no matter how much it hurts them. Many fail to reach this point, and in all too many cases, their SUD claims their life.

False Pride

The Disease of the Spirit

As has been stated before, every addiction is, at its core, a disease of the spirit. People with an SUD feel entitled to their chemically induced feeling(s). The book *Twelve Steps and Twelve Traditions of Alcoholics Anonymous* (1981) spoke of addiction as being a sickness of the soul. Not surprisingly, those individuals with a stronger involvement with the church tend to have a reduced risk of SUDs (Haber, 2008). Historical evidence beyond the scope of this text would suggest that a strong spiritual life, which is the antithesis to the false pride on which an addiction rests, helps to protect the individual from SUDs.

The individual whose spirit comes to be diseased does not begin life with a damaged spirit. We "all start out with hope, faith and fortitude" (Fromm, 1968, p. 20). But for some, the accumulated insults over a lifetime become a disease in their inner world, and some turn to chemicals to fill the perceived void within or to ease their pain. Some believe that they are entitled to the chemically induced pleasure(s) of substances, whereas others find some measure of peace in the arms of a chemical lover that will ultimately betray them to the harsh reality of an addiction. This is not unique to those who have an SUD: We all face moments of supreme disappointment (Fromm, 1968). It is at this point in people's lives that they are faced with the choice of either reducing their demands to that which is attainable or turning away from the harsh light of reality to the perceived safety of the chemical's embrace. This is what existential therapists speak of as the moment when individuals realize the utter futility of existence, or their personal powerlessness. At this moment, the individuals might either accept their place in the universe or continue to distort their perception(s) to maintain the illusion of self-importance through the continued use of chemicals. Spiritual growth involves the acceptance of the pain and suffering that life might have to offer, a task that many turn away from. Some become grandiose or demonstrate the pathological narcissism so often found in people with an addiction (Nace, 2005a, 2005b).

The loss of false pride exposes the individual to despair (Merton, 1961). Through the spiritual, the individual is enabled to establish "a sense of self-transcendence and a sense of meaning construction" (Milstein, 2008, p. 2440). The counter to this is humility: an honest, realistic view of "self" worth. When one's distorted view of the "self" is forcefully ripped away, the individual experiences despair. Some turn away from this despair into the perceived warmth and comfort of a chemical. S. A. Brown (1985), for example, spoke of how alcohol provided users with the illusion of being able to control their feelings. Others invest a greater and greater amount of time and energy into maintaining the false image in spite of growing evidence to the contrary. This ego-centered personality is the antithesis of a healthy spirituality (Reading, 2007). A few choose to face their despair and their fears to learn and to grow. This honest acceptance of one's lot in life (which is humility) seems to be both the antithesis of the false pride on which the SUDs rest and the basis of psychological health.

To counter this false pride, 12-step programs such as Alcoholics Anonymous offer a chance for the individual to learn to be *humble,* a personality characteristic that might be sadly lacking in some people. It takes humility to both profess and accept to being powerless over one's drug of choice, and through an honest exploration of the "self" individuals will come to learn how much of their life has been centered around and affected by their chemical use. Many people believe that humility involves a denial of one's strengths or skills. This is hardly the truth: Humility involves an honest understanding of the "self" or of the soul. This requires psychological strength, for it is an ongoing, lifelong process. In spite of the contention by many that the substance-abusing person might be involved in a spiritual journey through the use of chemicals (Chopra, 1997), this "short-cut" comes to demand more and more of individuals' life resources, dominating their choices until they must center their life around the continued use of that chemical and abandon their search for something better. To turn aside from this path requires strength, courage, and an honest understanding of the "self."

A very real manifestation of the spiritual illness that surrounds the SUDs is found in the process of "euphoric recall." If you listen to people with an SUD discussing their substance use experiences, you will be left with the impression that they are talking about a valued friend rather than a drug of abuse (Byington, 1997). Many people with an SUD have spoken at length about the semisexual thrill they achieved through the use of cocaine, the amphetamines, or heroin, without ever mentioning that this thrill was achieved at the cost of a spouse, family members who are estranged, and perhaps the loss of tens of thousands of dollars, not to mention the risk to the user's life, for example. There is a name for this distorted form of thinking: It is called the insanity of addiction. This form of moral insanity is supported by perceptual and cognitive distortions, and propped up by the individual's false pride.

One aspect of modern society that supports this false pride is the series of media-generated illusions that the latest trend will bring happiness to the individual. This mindless search for happiness is perhaps best seen in the pursuit of happiness through the latest trend in cellular phones, cars, or clothing. "If only I had the _____, then I would be happy (or would impress people, and so on)" is a thought that flashes through the minds of countless millions when the latest model of the latest thing is revealed to the public. Perhaps the apex of this process was seen in the early days of cellular telephone service, when it was both expensive and, service was limited. Some companies started to produce fake cell phones that users could carry to try and impress others with the fact that they were both rich enough and important enough, to warrant such a service.

But to seek gratification of the "self" through externals is dangerous, for the external world is always changing. Yesterday's cutting-edge computer is now an antique, whereas the designer clothes of last week are copied and are now available in discount stores. The SUDs might be viewed as a prime example of this attempt to satisfy the "soul" without the need to compromise or work to achieve the spiritual insights necessary to attain these feelings. Just take the right combination of pills, and you will instantly be transported to nirvana (or so the drug dealers would have us believe). If the present combination of alcohol and pills does not help you to achieve your goal(s), well, let us try again. The goal is to keep you happy. Not content, but happy.[20]

Surprisingly, meditation or other spiritual techniques, which will if carried out correctly force individuals to confront their self-pride, also activate the frontal lobes of the brain. This is a region that is often underactive in the substance abuser. Meditative practices have been shown, with practice, to bring about permanent changes in brain activity and structure (Newberg & Walkman, 2009). Thus humility is one of the foundations of a good recovery program, although it can take years for a person to learn to be humble and to utilize the proper techniques, and a lifetime of learning to bring it to perfection.

The Role of Defense Mechanisms in the Spiritual Model

The traditional view of the spiritual model is that the individual with an SUD will utilize four characteristic defense mechanisms: denial, minimization, rationalization, and projection, all of which were discussed in the previous chapter. These defenses are thought to operate on an unconscious level, to protect individuals from an awareness of realities that might threaten their adjustment. Being forced to admit that what one thought was a harmless recreational drug has actually become an addiction is one of those harsh realities that the defenses strive to keep us from having to deal with. Although these defenses operate in situations other than situations where individuals have an SUD, they are a core component to the spiritual model.

Reactions to the Spiritual Model

Reactions to the spiritual model are becoming increasingly vocal. Some seek legal redress for what they view as a violation of their civil rights, with some success. The U.S. Ninth Circuit Court has ruled that patients in a government-supported treatment program cannot be mandated to attend 12-step groups, on the grounds that they are part of a religious program. Further, treatment staff at a government-funded treatment program who require this of patients in treatment might be held *personally* liable for this violation of the patient's civil rights[21] (T. Horvath, 2007).

Foote (2006) challenged the concept that the failure of an individual to abstain from a drug(s) of abuse following treatment is the patient's fault. Rather, this therapeutic failure might be viewed as a mismatch between the patient and the program staff, in the Foote's opinion. Further, the more confrontational the therapist becomes in attempting to overcome the client's "resistance," the less cooperative the client will be in the therapeutic process. Indeed, confrontation is a powerful predictor of a negative outcome, as clients are confronted over and over again about their lack of "progress" (Foote, 2006).

---

[20]The difference between these two concepts, "happiness" and "contentedness," makes for an interesting debate, does it not?

[21]The "freedom of religion" clause in the Bill of Rights also includes the freedom *from* religion, if the person should so choose.

CHAPTER **28**

The Assessment of Suspected Substance Use Disorders[1]

[The] successful treatment of substance use disorders depends on a careful, accurate, assessment and diagnosis.

—*Greenfield & Hennessy (2008, p. 55)*

Introduction

As Samuel Shem (1978) wrote in his still popular novel *The House of God*, "If you don't take a temperature, you can't find a fever" (p. 420). This dictum applies to substance use disorders as well: Many health care professionals avoid discussing the patient's substance use or abuse so they do not have to deal with this uncomfortable issue. However, when one considers the prevalence of SUDs as an unacknowledged causal factor in various disease states, as well as its contribution to the problems experienced by dual-diagnosis clients,[2] not to mention the various legal, financial, interpersonal, vocational, and personal problems either caused or at least exacerbated by SUDs, it is imperative that the health care professional obtain an accurate history of the patient's substance use patterns (S. L. Johnson, 2003). Further, in this era of "managed care"[3] initiatives, this is especially important because the health care professional must obtain "prior authorization" and justify each procedure in advance to insure maximum return for each dollar spent on health care. This is accomplished, in large part, through the process of assessment. Assessment serves the roles of (a) helping to identify those individuals who require professional assistance to help them come to terms with their SUD, (b) serves as a "gatekeeper," providing justification for admission, (c) determining the proper level of treatment and the identification of the individual's strengths and weaknesses, and (d) forms the foundation of the rehabilitation process (Juhnke, 2002). In this chapter, the process of assessing an adult with an SUD and how the assessment process relates to the process of rehabilitation will be explored.

---

[1]The assessment of suspected child/adolescent substance use disorders, and instruments used for this purpose, is discussed in Chapter 20.

[2]Discussed in Chapter 24.

[3]Discussed in Chapter 34.

The Theory Behind Substance Use Assessments

It is not uncommon for inexperienced health care professionals to cite evidence of a single episode of illicit drug use or a "dirty" urine toxicology test[4] as proof that the individual is addicted to chemicals (Washton & Zweben, 2006; Winters & Kaminer, 2008). In reality the abuse of a substance, even if that substance is illegal, does not prove that the individual is *addicted* to that compound (Gitlow, 2007). These facts simply underscore the need for a complete substance use assessment to determine whether a given individual has an SUD. This assessment process is "more than a one-time paperwork procedure conducted at the onset of treatment to simply gather minimal facts and secure a … diagnosis" (Juhnke, 2002, p. vii). It *is* the first step in the rehabilitation process, if this is necessary, and it continues throughout treatment as the individual's needs and resources are continuously assessed and addressed (Daley & Marlatt, 2006).

Life would be much easier if there were a "Holy Grail" for the detection of SUDs (M. Fleming et al., 2001, p. 321). Surprisingly, scientists have yet to agree upon a standard definition of even the basic term *addiction* (L. B. Erlich, 2001). Thus the assessor must go into the assessment process with imperfect tools, and then is asked to make a diagnosis that might have lifelong implications for the patient. For example, people's ability to purchase health care insurance at the age of 50 might be influenced by a diagnosis of an SUD made when they were only 20 years of age.

The assessment process is complicated and involves several steps. The process of *screening* a patient is carried out to identify those patients who *might* have a certain disease or condition (Knight, 2005). If all substance abusers were alike, then there would be no need for the assessment process to proceed beyond the determination of whether the individual does or does not have a chemical use problem. However, all substance abusers are not the same, and there is no one-size-fits-all presentation of substance abusers. Clients vary as to their age, gender, marital status, culture, ethnicity, degree of insight into their problem(s), legal status, medical condition, and willingness to change (Greenfield & Hennessy, 2008). Thus the assessor must consider a wide range of factors during the screening process, and if there is reason to suspect a substance use disorder is present, a complete *assessment* is performed. This is done to confirm or rule out the presence of that disorder, assess its severity, identify individual strengths, and help guide treatment (A. W. Blume, 2005; Knight, 2005). It is at this point that the assessment process enters its final phase: that of *diagnosis*. Each of these interrelated steps will be discussed in more detail in the sections that follow.

Screening

The core of the screening process is the clinical interview with the client. This clinical interview must be long enough to allow for the assessor to build a complete overview of the client's substance use pattern (Greenfield & Hennessy, 2008). This is often based on the client's responses during the clinical interview, collateral information, and a review of past records. The screening process might also involve the use of one or more paper-and-pencil instruments to help identify those individuals who might have an SUD. Although such information is valuable to the assessor, *a test score by itself does not establish whether the individual does or does not have an SUD!* The test score is but one perspective on the individual's substance use pattern. Such instruments might be filled out either by clients (known as *self-report* instruments) or by the assessors as they ask questions of the person being assessed.

Finally, an important point that must be assessed is *whether the client has ever experienced withdrawal symptoms* (or is currently going through a substance withdrawal syndrome) both at the time of the interview and in the past (Greenfield & Hennessy, 2008).

Verbal Screening Aids

A rapidly administered verbal tool that might be used with both adolescents and adults is the TWEAK. The letters serve as a useful mnemonic[5] device for the assessor to remember to ask the client whether they have developed: (a) T̲olerance to alcohol or drugs, (b) whether or not others have ever been W̲orried about their substance use, (c) whether the client has ever used an E̲ye opener in the morning, (d) A̲mnesia during periods of substance use, and (e) whether the client has made attempts to K̲ (cut) down on substance use (S. L. Johnson, 2003). A negative answer to all of these questions does not rule out an SUD but does suggest that the patient probably is at low risk for such

---

[4]Which is to say a urine toxicology test that reveals evidence of illicit drug use.

[5]See Glossary.

a problem. Alternatively, a "yes" answer to one or more of these items is suggestive of a possible SUD.

Another popular screening instrument is the CAGE questionnaire (Ewing, 1984). The CAGE questions have been in use for more than a quarter of a century. CAGE is an acronym for the four questions used in this screening tool:

- *Have you ever felt that you should **cut down** on your drinking?*
- *Have people ever **annoyed** you by being critical of your drinking?*
- *Have you ever felt bad or **guilty** about your drinking?*
- *Have you ever needed to have a drink first thing in the morning to steady your nerves or get rid of a hangover (**eye-opener**)?*

It was suggested that a "yes" response to one question suggested a need for a more thorough inquiry by the assessor, whereas "yes" responses to two or more items suggests that the individual has an alcohol use disorder. This instrument has been estimated to have an accuracy rate of 80–90% when the client answers "yes" to two or more items. Unfortunately, the CAGE questionnaire has been found to have serious problems: First, it is not sensitive to binge drinking, nor does it identify the frequency of the individual's alcohol use or the individual's level of consumption (Cooney et al., 2005). Alcohol-dependent people who are abstinent will be identified as having a problem because of past alcohol use behavior(s), not their present drinking status. Further, it also does not identify individuals who abuse substances other than alcohol. The test is also very vulnerable to deception (Stein & Rogers, 2008). Finally, it is of limited value as a screening instrument for adolescents (Knight, 2002), women, or minority members who have an alcohol use disorder ("Screening for Alcohol Problems—An Update," 2002), or for people in the earlier stages of an alcohol use disorder (Washton & Zweben, 2006). Because of these (and possibly other, yet to be identified) flaws, the CAGE is estimated to miss up to 50% of at-risk drinkers (M. F. Fleming, 1997).

To address this problem, the team of R. L. Brown et al. (1997) suggested a simple, two-question screening instrument:

1. In the last year, have you ever drunk or used drugs more than you meant to?
2. Have you felt that you wanted or needed to cut down on your drinking or drug use in the past year?

The authors suggested that, in spite of its brevity, a "yes" answer to one question indicated a 45% chance that the individual had a substance use disorder, whereas a "yes" response to both questions indicated there was a 75% chance that the individual had an SUD. However, this instrument might also yield false-positive results on occasion, warned the authors. Thus the assessor should not rely too heavily on this (or other) verbal-interview responses to rule out an SUD, but should consider those responses as one piece of information to be used in the development of a diagnosis.

Paper-and-Pencil Screening Instruments

Self-report instruments offer the advantage of being inexpensive, and may be less threatening to the client than face-to-face interviews because clients might experience feelings of shame, distrust, hopelessness, and be uncomfortable during the face-to-face interview (Greenfield & Hennessy, 2008). A disadvantage of self-report instruments is that they are more vulnerable to client attempts at deception and are designed with the assumption that the client is reasonably literate. Such instruments do not *prove* that a person has a substance use disorder (Washton & Zweben, 2006). However, when used properly such instruments provide the assessor with an additional source of data that could be incorporated into the assessment process.

One way to minimize this danger is to administer different instruments that cover the same aspect of the client's behavior. A client who denied having alcohol-related blackouts on one instrument but who admits to having blackouts on another instrument has presented contradictory information. In such cases the assessor should attempt to reconcile the two answers with each other. The same instrument might also be administered at different times, perhaps a week apart for example, and then the client's responses compared with each other. Again, there might be significant discrepancies between the two response sets, which should be explored by the assessor.

Sometimes, clients will consent to have their significant other sit in the office while the assessor reviews the results with the client. If the client had answered a test item on the Michigan Alcoholism Screening Test[6] addressing alcohol-related motor vehicle accidents negatively, the spouse might then ask, "What about that time when you drove your car into a ditch, two years ago?" In this hypothetical example, the client might

---

[6]Discussed in the next paragraph.

respond that the police had ruled that the accident was a result of ice-covered roads, but the partner might then go on to say, "But you told me that you had been drinking earlier that night!"

For alcohol use disorders, one of the most popular instruments used for screening is the Michigan Alcoholism Screening Test (MAST) (Selzer, 1971). The MAST is composed of 24 questions that can be answered either "yes" or "no" by the respondent. Test scores are weighted with a value of 1, 2, or in some cases, 5 points (Craig, 2004). A score of 7 or more points is interpreted as evidence that the individual has an alcohol use disorder (Craig, 2004). Although the MAST is a popular instrument even in the first decade of the 21st century, it does present some inherent problems. First, it can be used only in cases of alcohol *dependence* and not alcohol abuse (Vanable, King, & deWit, 2000). Second, it provides only a crude measure of the individual's possible alcohol use problem. Third, the intent of the items on the MAST is readily apparent and thus subject to dissimulation if the test taker should be less than honest (L. A. R. Stein & Rogers, R. (2008). Fourth, it is insensitive to binge drinking, and it does not address the use of compounds other than alcohol. Finally, it does not differentiate between the individual's current and past drinking history, with the result being that abstinent drinkers could be identified as having an ongoing alcohol use disorder on the basis of their response set (Schorling & Buchsbaum, 1997). Thus the MAST is best suited for the detection of individuals with a severe alcohol use disorder and should be interpreted with caution.

A paper-and-pencil screening instrument developed by the World Health Organization (WHO) is the Alcohol Use Disorders Identification Test (AUDIT). The AUDIT was standardized on samples drawn from six different countries around the world, with the intent of developing a short, easily administered screening instrument that might be used in different countries in the identification of people in the early stages of developing an alcohol use disorder (Babor, Higgins-Briddle, Saunders, & Monterio, 2001). The AUDIT is composed of 10 different questions,[7] which tap the domains of (a) hazardous alcohol use, (b) dependence symptoms, and (c) harmful alcohol use (Babor et al., 2001). To this end, it has been estimated that the AUDIT is over 90% effective in detecting people with an alcohol use disorder (Bradley et al., 2003; R. L. Brown et al., 1997). Indeed, it has been identified as being superior in performance to the CAGE and the MAST in a variety of clinical settings, and appears to be valid for both male and female respondents (Babor et al., 2001). However, the AUDIT tends to miss active drinkers over the age of 65[8] (Isaacson & Schorling, 1999) and is not appropriate for use with adolescent drinkers (Knight, 2002). Another limitation of the AUDIT is that it is designed for use in detecting AUDs and not other forms of substance abuse. It cannot isolate current drinking patterns from past alcohol use patterns, and finally, the intent of the items on the AUDIT is easily discerned, and thus the test is subject to dissimulation if this is the intent of the individual (L. A. R. Stein & Rogers, 2008).

A popular screening instrument is the *Substance Abuse Subtle Screening Inventory-3 (SASSI-3)* (Juhnke, 2002). This is a copyrighted instrument, which can be either computer or hand-scored. It is administered to individuals who are at least 16 years of age and who have at least a fourth-grade reading level. It takes about 15 minutes for the client to take the SASSI-3, and it provides measures on 10 different scales, including 2 "truth" scales. Some of the items are quite obvious in intent, whereas others are rather subtle. It can be hand-scored, although the computer-administered/scored version is becoming increasingly popular with the growing popularity of desktop computers. Although the SASSI does not provide data on which substance(s) the individual might abuse, it does provide a score that suggests that the individual is or is not likely to have a substance use disorder.

Thus far, the discussion has focused on screening instruments useful for detecting possible AUDs. A screening tool that is useful for the identification of substance abuse is the Drug Abuse Screening Test (DAST). This instrument is rapidly administered, usually in 5 minutes or less, requires a sixth-grade reading level, and excludes alcohol use. The DAST was modeled after the MAST, but focuses on illicit drug use. It is composed of 20 questions that are answered either "yes" or "no." It was originally intended for use with adults, but a modified form has been developed for use with adolescents. Scoring is easy, as 18 of the 20 items are scored as "hits" if the individual responded "yes" and the other two are scored as "hits" if the individual

---

[7]There is an abbreviated version, known as the *AUDIT-C,* which is composed of only three questions, but available evidence suggests that the full AUDIT might be more effective than the abbreviated version (Holzel, Weiser, Berner, & Harter, 2008).

[8]Remember: As was discussed in Chapter 5, even limited amounts of alcohol use by older people can have a disproportionate effect on the drinker's body.

responded "no." A score of 7+ points suggests a substance use disorder. A disadvantage of the DAST is that the intent of the items is readily apparent, allowing individuals to lie about their substance abuse, if motivated to do so.

The utility of these instruments in the detection of alcohol or drug use disorders has been challenged ("California Judges Get Tougher on Science," 1997). However, they do provide *one piece of data* that can be considered as part of a comprehensive assessment process, using multiple data points to arrive at a diagnostic formulation. One such data point might be one of the semistructured clinical interviews designed to allow the clinician to obtain the data necessary to adequately determine if there is a substance use disorder present or not. These semistructured screening instruments usually focus on the diagnostic criteria utilized by the American Psychiatric Association (2000).

An instrument often administered during the screening process is the *Beck Depression Inventory* (BDI). Although the BDI does not address substance use issues, it does provide an objective measure of the client's depression, which may form the basis for a referral to a mental health professional for both evaluation and treatment and, because the drugs of abuse can often cause or contribute to depression, further inquiry into the reasons why the client is depressed. A man with a high score on the BDI, which suggests high levels of depression, might reveal upon inquiry that his wife took the children and moved out because of substance-related conflict between them, or that he just lost his job, to cite two possible examples. The BDI is a copyrighted instrument that is easily administered and scored in just a few minutes.

One instrument that is often mistakenly considered to be a screening tool is the *Minnesota Multiphasic Personality Inventory (MMPI).*[9] The original MMPI was introduced almost 75 years ago, and the *MacAndrew Alcoholism Scale*[10] was introduced in the mid-1960s after an item analysis suggested that alcohol-dependent individuals had a tendency to answer 49 items of the 566 items differently than nonalcoholic people. A cut-off score of 24 items answered in the "scorable" direction correctly identified 82% of alcohol-dependent people in a sample of 400 psychiatric patients (J. R. Graham, 1990). In 1989, the venerable MMPI was updated, and the Minnesota Multiphasic Personality Inventory-2 (MMPI-2) was introduced. The "Mac" scale was slightly

modified but essentially retained its original form. At this point in time, the Mac scale is thought to be about 85% accurate in the detection of substance use disorders (Craig, 2004).[11]

Following its introduction, it was suggested that the MMPI-2 "Mac" scale is perhaps better able to identify personality patterns more commonly associated with substance use disorders than the actual SUDs (Rouse, Butcher, & Miller, 1999). Clients who are extroverted, who experience a blackout for any reason,[12] who tend to be more assertive, or who enjoy risk-taking behaviors, tend to score higher on the "Mac" scale even if they do not have an SUD (J. R. Graham, 1990). Further, in spite of the validity scales built into the MMPI-2, Otto, Lang, Megargee, and Rosenblatt (1989) discovered shortly after the revised MMPI was introduced that alcohol-dependent people might be able to "conceal their drinking problems even when the relatively subtle special alcohol scales of the MMPI are applied" through either conscious or unconscious denial (p. 7). Finally, taking the MMPI is time intensive, which does not make it a convenient test for screening purposes. The MMPI is, however, of use in the *diagnosis* stage of the assessment process.

Section Summary

The process of screening for a substance use disorder can involve a verbal, face-to-face interview, the use of various screening instruments, or ideally, a mixture of both. At the end of this process, the assessor should be able to determine whether or not there is evidence of a substance use disorder. If there is no evidence of an SUD, then the screening processes ends at this point. But if evidence of an SUD is detected, then the assessor moves on to the next stage, the process of *assessment*.

Assessment

During the *assessment* phase, the assessor attempts to measure the severity of the substance use disorder identified in the screening process. In conducting the assessment, the assessor must remember that the same disorder might have far different presentations as the disease progresses (Greenfield & Hennessy, 2008). The end-stage alcoholic, for example, will have

---

[9]The MMPI and the MMPI-2 are both copyrighted instruments.

[10]Also known as the "Mac" scale.

[11]Because of the shortcomings of the "Mac" scale, it should be used as one piece of data, and by itself should not be interpreted as evidence of a substance use disorder.

[12]For example, a person who has a seizure disorder.

a different clinical presentation than the young-adult drinker who is in the earlier stages of alcoholism.

There are three formats for the assessment process: (a) unstructured, (b) semistructured, and (c) structured. Often, the clinical interview is a form of unstructured assessment. Juhnke (2002) identified four benefits of the clinical interview: (a) flexibility, (b) establishment of rapport with the client, (c) reassurance to clients uncomfortable working with written tests or computers (if the test is administered on a computer), and (d) allows the therapist to watch the client's nonverbal behavior in response to question(s) so as to identify areas for subsequent exploration.

The information that the client offers (or elects not to offer) during the clinical interview is a valuable component of the assessment process. However, this data is also vulnerable to one of four different "response sets" that might distort the assessor's opinion of the client's substance use disorder (L. A. R. Stein & Rogers, 2008):

1. *Disacknowledgment:* The client offers "I don't know" or "I can't remember" responses to questions that might reveal incriminating information.
2. *Misappraisal:* The client might honestly mistake amount ingested (client reports consuming six drinks where collateral information sources report that the client had ingested eight mixed drinks).
3. *Denial:* The client might be motivated to avoid consequences of substance use behavior such as legal sanctions.
4. *Exaggeration:* The client might intentionally overreport substance use, often seen in adolescent substance abusers who use this as a "cry for help." Criminal offenders as well might utilize this form of distortion to try and establish grounds for a claim of mitigating circumstances at the time of sentencing.

Although not every client engages in such distortion(s), it is important to keep in mind that some clients might either consciously or unconsciously distort the information that they provide in response to the assessor's questions. Their responses might alter the outcome of child custody, legal problems, or employment issues. This underscores the need for the assessor to utilize collateral information sources (past treatment records, court documents, information from family members, and so on).

The first part of the interview process is the introduction by the assessor. Assessors will explain that they will be asking questions about the client's possible

substance use patterns and that *specific* responses would be most helpful. At this time assessors might want to explain that many of these questions might have been asked of the client by others in the past, but that this information is important and so the client will be asked this information again. Clients are provided with the opportunity to ask any questions that they might have, and then the interview process begins. It is not uncommon for the interview to take place within a framework provided by the *Diagnostic and Statistical Manual of Mental Disorders* (4th edition, text revision) (*DSM-IV-TR*), although other formats, such as the one utilized by the American Society of Addiction Medicine (ASAM), might also be utilized. Each of these diagnostic manuals provides certain criteria within which the individual's substance use disorder might be evaluated and provides a common language that health care professionals understand.

It is useful for the assessor to ask different questions during the interview that are designed to explore the same client response from different perspectives. This is done to provide a form of internal validity to the data obtained during the clinical interview. For example, the client might be asked, "In the average week, how often would you estimate that you use alcohol or drugs?" At a later point in the interview, the assessor might ask, "In the average week, how much would you say that you spent on alcohol or drugs?" If there is a discrepancy, the assessor will want to explore it. Clients who report using alcohol just once a week, but who claim to spend $100 a week on recreational substance use, upon inquiry might respond that they always buy drinks for their friends when they go out to drink or that they have a gambling or substance use disorder other than alcoholism.

One point that the assessor will wish to consider is the *estimated percentage of the client's income spent on alcohol or drugs of abuse.* If clients are receiving unemployment compensation checks for $200 each week, for example, but are spending $75–100 a week on alcohol or drugs, then they are spending a significant percentage of their income on substances in spite of their employment status. In contrast to this are the clients who make $2000 a week, but who spend $15 each week on beer, an example that provides evidence of a far different pattern of drinking.

Collateral information might be obtained from the client's family, friends, employer, physician (or medical record, if available), probation officer, and so on. For example, if client were to say that "alcohol is not a problem for me" but the assessor knows that they have been hospitalized six times for "detox"[13] or for medical problems caused or exacerbated by their alcohol use in the past 2 years, these two discrepant pieces of information would need to be reconciled during the interview process.

An indirect source of collateral information is *medical test data* obtained during the course of current or past medical care. There are no current blood/urine tests specific for detecting an SUD, and even if a substance is detected in individuals' urine/blood at this time, it does not mean that they are a *chronic* user. It means only that the substance was in their blood/urine at this time. However, a series of "positive" blood or urine test results makes it far harder for clients to argue that they do not abuse chemicals. Further, urine toxicology tests can also determine whether prescribed drugs that should be in the client's system are actually there, although it cannot determine the amount of that compound in the client's body. Finally, the appropriate blood or urine tests can help identify concurrent medical disorders that might complicate efforts at treating the SUD (for example, an untreated infection, or a heart problem) (Work Group on Substance Use Disorders, 2007).

Psychological Test Data

Psychological test data may directly or indirectly assist the assessment process. A number of instruments have been discussed elsewhere in this chapter that are of value in the screening and assessment process. A major disadvantage of paper-and-pencil tests is that they are subject to denial, distortion, and outright misrepresentation on the part of the client, and thus are better suited to situations where the client is unlikely to "positively dissimulate" (Evans & Sullivan, 2001).

Psychological test data might shed help identify client personality characteristics that might influence their substance use pattern. A depressed client, for example, might be using alcohol or drugs to self-medicate a depression, although the reverse is also possible: The observed depression might be substance induced. Although psychological tests other than those directly developed for screening or assessment of substance use disorders can offer little direct evidence that problems exist ("California Judges Get Tougher on Science," 1997), they can identify aspects of the problem that might have been overlooked otherwise.

Thus the assessor must not make assumptions about the client's responses. If a client reported "only this one arrest" for a drug possession charge, the assessor must not make assumptions. Rather, the assessor must ask questions such as "What about in other states or countries?" or, "Were there any substance-related charges brought against you while you were in the military?" The client's responses may be revealing.

Standardized Tests:[14,15]

Although the clinical interview forms the cornerstone of the assessment process, the assessor should also utilize standardized test results as an aid to the assessment process (Juhnke, 2002). The client's responses will become a part of the database upon which the assessor draws upon for the final stage of the assessment process: the diagnosis (discussed later in this chapter). Such self-report instruments provide a comparison between the individual's characteristics and those of patients who have been identified as substance abusers and who have benefited from intervention(s) (Samet, Waxman, Hatzenbuehler, & Hasin, 2007).

One popular instrument used for individuals over the age of 16 is the *Alcohol Use Inventory (AUI)*. This copyrighted[16] instrument is composed of 228 items, and it takes 30–60 minutes for the individual to finish. The test data then is interpreted across 24 domains to help the assessor better understand the client's alcohol use pattern. Unfortunately, the AUI is limited to alcohol use disorders. Further, the normative data for the AUI makes it inappropriate to use with certain subgroups.

The *Addiction Severity Index (ASI)* on the other hand is a "public domain" instrument that forms the core of a semistructured interview with the client. There are 161 questions on the fifth edition of the ASI, each of which the interviewer will ask clients while recording their responses. The ASI is useful in the assessment of SUDs other than alcohol use disorders and measures such areas as the client's interpersonal relationship patterns, possible medical problems, legal history, and the like (Samet et al., 2007). Clients are asked to rate their level of distress on each domain from "0" (no distress) to "4"

---

[13]A term that is often applied to clients who have to be hospitalized for treatment and observation until their bodies have been able to eliminate the alcohol and/or drugs ingested earlier.

[14]There are a number of assessment tools that have been devised for research studies, but that are not used in clinical practice. These tools will not be discussed in this text.

[15]The author is frequently asked to render an opinion as to the *best* test or instrument to use. There is no single test that is universally accepted, and each has certain strengths and weaknesses.

[16]An instrument protected by a "copyright" is privately owned, and the user must pay a royalty fee for using it.

(extreme distress), while the assessor also notes areas that should be addressed through professional intervention. Although useful, the normative population for the ASI were patients in the Veterans Administration hospital system, and this instrument has been found to have limited validity in working with special populations such as the homeless or clients with concurrent substance use and mental health problems[17] (Monti et al., 2002; Samet et al., 2007; L. A. R. Stein & Rogers, 2008).

The *Structured Clinical Interview for DSM-IV (SCID)* is an instrument available in one form for researchers and another form for clinicians (Samet et al., 2007). The clinical version of the SCID requires training as a therapist and is a semistructured instrument that will allow the assessor to explore client responses that might require clarification. It is applicable to both alcohol use and substance use disorders, but it can require up to several hours for the therapist to administer to clients, depending on their status and level of function. Fortunately, it is designed to be administered in a series of modules, and the clinician might utilize only those modules that are of relevance to that client (Samet et al., 2007).

The Drug Use Screening Inventory-Revised (DUSI-R) assesses three domains: (a) personal history, (b) a drug use screening instrument portion, and (c) a demographic, medical, and possible prevention or treatment applications (S. L. Johnson, 2003). Although this instrument provides a great deal of useful information, it is not popular at this time.

Section Summary

In this section, some of the more popular paper-and-pencil assessment instruments currently in use are reviewed. These instruments form part of the database on which assessors will base their conclusions. However, they do not take the place of a formal clinical interview, and clinicians should not base their diagnosis only on the test results.

The Assessment Format

There is no standardized format for the assessment process. Rather, the format utilized for the assessment process will vary depending on the needs of assessor and the facility for which they works. Assessments need to be sensitive to the cultural beliefs of the client, and be aware that different cultural groups might have different beliefs about substance use than the dominant

culture (Greenfield & Hennessy, 2008). However, there are some common elements to the better assessments, which will be reviewed next.

Circumstances of Referral

Why is this client here, today? Individuals with an SUD will only rarely come in for help on a voluntary basis, and are usually forced into the assessment and subsequent rehabilitation program through external pressure (Craig, 2004). Thus the manner in which clients answer the question "What brought you here, today?" will offer valuable information about their willingness to participate in the assessment process, evasiveness (or honesty), level of function, understanding of the problem(s) that they are facing, and so on.

Substance Use Patterns

The client's substance use patterns should have been identified in the assessment phase, but the assessor should identify the grounds on which the client's self-report is or is not assumed to be accurate. For example, a client who claimed to have been alcohol and drug free for the past 9 months (but who was incarcerated for that period of time) may be demonstrating some degree of denial and evasiveness, which would justify the use of collateral information sources. The assessor thus must determine the clients' current living situation, whether they are under the supervision of the courts (or incarcerated), and the clients' beliefs about their substance use. It is not uncommon for clients to proudly boast that it is only when they consume liquor that they get into trouble, so continued beer use is not a problem.

Past Treatment History

This is relevant for a number of reasons. Past research has shown that approximately half of those entering treatment for an AUD are entering treatment for the first time (LoCastro, Potter, Donovan, Couper, & Pope, 2008). First-time treatment participants for AUDs have significantly different alcohol use histories than do those being admitted to treatment for the second or third time. The social context of their alcohol use, needs, motivation for treatment, expectations, and health status will be significantly different from that of the typical individual who has been admitted to treatment for an AUD more than once (LoCastro et al., 2008).

Individuals who are entering treatment for the first time tend to drink less per occasion of drinking, are probably less knowledgeable about the nature of substance use disorders, are less likely to acknowledge the

---

[17]Discussed in Chapter 24.

severity of their SUD, and are less likely to accept total abstinence as a viable treatment goal (LoCastro et al., 2008). They are also more likely to be younger, male, and employed at the time of their admission to treatment (LoCastro et al., 2008).

Clients who have been in treatment programs in the past might be "treatment wise," an observation that is indirectly supported by the observation by LoCastro et al. (2008) that the treatment-naive group in their study appeared to have less motivation for change than did the treatment-experienced group. They were more likely to reduce their level of alcohol use prior to the admission to treatment (LoCastro et al., 2008). This suggests at least the possibility that the latter group knew the right words to say to impress staff with their willingness to "change," although it is possible that they were indeed motivated to make life changes supportive of abstinence.

Clients' past treatment history also provides an indirect measure of the severity of their SUD. Clients who claim not to have a serious substance use disorder, but who have been in a rehabilitation program three different times, both is providing information that is quite contradictory and might be signaling that they really will not be very cooperative with any efforts at rehabilitation. Thus a review of clients' past substance abuse treatment history is important.

Legal History

Increasingly, court conviction records are available through the Internet. Such records, or records provided by the Court, reveal (a) the nature of legal charges brought against the client in the past and their disposition, and possibly (b) the nature of any current charges pending against the client. It is important to keep in mind that the original charges might be reduced through the process of plea negotiation(s). Thus the client who had been arrested for possession of 6 ounces of marijuana might have been convicted of possession of less than an ounce by the court through plea negotiations. Also, a computer-based background check might reveal that clients have charges pending in another state that have yet to be resolved, or a string of previous arrests that they failed to mention. Thus clients' accuracy about their legal history provides information about the relative accuracy of their self-report.

Past Military Record

One very important and frequently overlooked source of information about clients is their past military history (if any). Some clients will report only legal convictions from their civilian record, ignoring charges/convictions from their military service. It is important to keep in mind that "reprimands" in the military often function as a form of plea negotiation, avoiding formal legal charges as would be brought against the individual by a courts martial trial.

If client should deny having ever been in the military, it might be of interest to determine *why* they never enlisted. A client who responded "I didn't want to enlist" is possibly far different from the client who responds "I couldn't enlist because I had a felony conviction on my record!" Finally, the client's discharge status should be discussed. A client who has a "general discharge under honorable conditions" might be far different from the client who received a "general discharge under dishonorable conditions" or just a "dishonorable" discharge from the military. Finally, the assessor should keep in mind that military discharges might result from medical disabilities or injuries, and thus are not automatically a sign that the individual's military service was marked by conflict with the authorities.

Educational/Vocational History

This information, based on the client's self-report and available records, provides data on clients' level of function and whether their chemical use has interfered with their educational/vocational experiences to date. Clients who report that they "just barely graduated" because they had trouble with the class work is far different from clients who report that they "just barely graduated" because they were under the influence of alcohol or drugs so often. Both types of client also present a far different clinical picture from the client who holds a bachelor of science degree from a well-known university.

The degree to which clients' substance use might have interfered with their vocational history should also be explored. Many substance-abusing clients report that they are "self-employed," which for them might be a subtle way of saying that they cannot hold a regular job because of their substance use disorder. Thus the individual's success as a self-employed worker should also be discussed. For employed or self-employed clients, their employment history should be explored in detail. Why did they leave each job? Did they leave a given job because their substance use made it impossible for them to continue to work there, or because they were offered a promotion or a better position with a different company?

Developmental/Family History

Discussion in this area is often a treasure trove of information about clients' early history and the environment they grew up in. It also provides a chance for the assessor to explore how clients feel about their parents, whether they had a substance use disorder of their own, how they addressed it (if they did), whether either parent had a handicap, or whether either parent died while the client was growing up. Clients who hesitate to say that their father was alcohol-dependent but compromise to say that he was "a problem drinker" might also be hinting that they would hesitate to apply the same term to themselves, if asked.

An exploration of the developmental history might reveal that several siblings also have SUDs, or that the client is the only member of the family unit who went on to develop an SUD. Parental alcohol/substance use disorders might hint at a genetic predisposition[18] toward an SUD on the part of the client. A discussion of clients' home environment would also suggest how permissive or strict their home was, whether they have unresolved feelings of anger toward a parent who had an SUD, and even possibly hint at self-hatred issues now that they have gone on to possibly develop an SUD.

Psychiatric History

It is amazing how often assessors overlook the client's past psychiatric history. Clients have been known to be hospitalized for such problems as a "brief reactive psychosis" or "atypical psychosis," only to later reveal that they had been abusing a hallucinogenic substance that caused a bad reaction. All too often, when asked these clients admit that nobody ever asked them whether they had abused any drug(s), and that a urine toxicology test to detect possible drug use was never performed.

There is a known relationship between substance use disorders and suicidal thinking, and it is often productive to inquire about whether the "suicidal" client had been abusing alcohol or drug(s) prior to being admitted to the hospital for suicidal thinking or an attempted suicide. *This does not imply that the client might not be a legitimate suicide risk!!!* But the client's motivation for making the suicide threat or attempt should be fully explored. If possible, the assessor should

also obtain a copy of clients' discharge summary, if not the entire treatment records, for their psychiatric treatment.

Medical History

Clients' medical history often overlaps with their psychiatric history. But the assessor needs to explore clients' medical history (Gendel, 2006). A history of a past hospitalization for treatment of internal injuries sustained in a motor vehicle accident might hint at a possible alcohol/drug-related accident that the client had not reported before. Clients might deny having any substance use disorder, but admit that they had been shot twice by rival drug dealers in the past 3 years and thus had been hospitalized on two occasions for substance-related wounds.

The assessor should inquire about any *current or recent* prescription medications. It is important to note how many different physicians are involved in the patient's care and whether these physicians are aware that the client had consulted the other(s) for care and prescriptions. Over-the-counter medication use should be discussed as well, because such medications can both exacerbate problems caused by prescription medications and alter the pharmacokinetics of those medications when used concurrently by a client. It is also important for the assessor to try and identify those clients who might have been "doctor shopping"[19] to obtain desired medications.

Finally, one area that should be addressed is individuals' *expectations* for their drug(s) of abuse. For example, Reich and Goldman (2005) found that high-risk and low-risk alcohol users appear to have different expectations for the outcome of alcohol use. As a group, high-risk drinkers tended to anticipate a more positive outcome to their use of alcohol, especially in terms of social interactions and general arousal. Low-risk drinkers, on the other hand, were more likely to expect more negative outcomes from their alcohol use, especially in terms of the level of sedation and alcohol's negative impact on their social skills.

---

[18]Although, at this point, there is no test that might identify whether this genetic predisposition is or is not present, as was discussed earlier in this text.

[19]A term applied to the process of looking for a physician who will prescribe a desired medication. Sometimes this might require that addicts see two, three, four, or even more physicians, before they find one willing to diagnose them with a condition that makes their use of a desired medication legitimate. Substance-abusing clients have been known to study what symptoms they need to report/demonstrate in order to convince the physician to prescribe a desired medication(s).

To complicate matters,[20] over time the addictions require that the individual make certain personality adjustments to allow the SUD to continue to exist within the "self." In other words, at least some of the apparent "addictive personality" illusion might be caused by the impact of the SUD on the individual's personality over time (Grekin et al., 2006). Vaglum (2003) suggested that between 20 and 40% of opiate addicts who were diagnosed as having an antisocial personality disorder actually engaged in antisocial behaviors because of their addiction, but they did not have an antisocial personality disorder prior to the development of their SUD.

Thus it is not uncommon, for example, to hear a client tell a therapist or a treatment group that "I never thought that I would reach the point where I would do _____ , but, well, I did it." In Alcoholics Anonymous[21] this is called "hitting bottom," except, as the individual repeatedly discovers, the "bottom" is lower and lower each time. In this way, the substance of choice forces the individual to engage in previously forbidden behaviors, in order to continue to engage in the abuse of that compound.[22]

Real Versus Pseudo Personality Disorders

One point that often is overlooked by assessors is that long-term substance abuse requires that the individual's personality adapt to the continued abuse of that chemical. The behaviors noted during the clinical interview or in clients' past while they were abusing chemicals might not reflect the client's core personality. The possibility of a substance-induced pseudo personality disorder must be considered by the assessor.[23]

For some personality types, such as the antisocial personality disordered client, this might involve minimal change(s). For other personality patterns, the individual might be forced into a pattern of antisocial *behavior* without having ASPD. One determining factor is whether the personality pattern that the client presents *predated* the development of the SUD or is a *consequence* of the SUD (Grekin et al., 2006). For example,

Vaglum (2003) suggested that between 20 and 40% of opiate addicts who were diagnosed as having an antisocial personality disorder actually engaged in antisocial behaviors *because of their addiction*, but that they did not have an antisocial personality disorder. The differentiation between real and substance-induced personality disorders thus is of major significance because this has profound implications for the individual's rehabilitation potential.

Clinicians have long spoken of a mystical entity known as the "addictive personality." A careful comparison of the diagnostic criteria for substance addiction and those for the ASPD would reveal a significant degree of overlap (Vaglum, 2003). This suggests that the concept of the "addictive personality" might be an artifact of the current diagnostic system rather than a real entity (Vaglum, 2003). Surprisingly, there is evidence that individuals with ASPD are more likely to seek treatment for their SUD than clients with other personality types, although the issue of court-mandated treatment[24] might confound this claim (Vaglum, 2003).

Section Summary

On the basis of the information obtained through the clinical interview, collateral information, and test data, the assessor will then be in a position to determine where, on the continuum of drug use disorders identified in Chapter 1, the client appears to fall, based on available evidence.

The Assessor and Data Privacy

The issue of confidentiality has always been a difficult issue, and recent changes in state and federal data privacy laws have served to make matters even more complicated.[25] Many clients fear, for example, that their parents, spouse, employer, law enforcement agencies, or professional licensing boards will have access to the records, making them hesitant to discuss problems or concerns openly. The assessor will need to review the data privacy laws with clients, so that they know in advance who will and will not have access to their records. It will also be necessary for the assessor to

---

[20]At this point the reader is welcome to groan in frustration or despair.

[21]Discussed in Chapter 5 and Chapter 35.

[22]An interesting point to debate is whether individuals who are unwilling to make this adjustment (unwilling to "pay the cost" for their addiction) are characteristically protected against the development of an SUD.

[23]At this point the reader is welcome to groan in frustration or despair.

---

[24]Discussed in Chapter 28.

[25]It is recommended that readers consult an attorney to discuss what data privacy regulations apply in their specific state, as well as the federal guidelines that also must be kept in mind. One federal law is the *Health Insurance Portability and Accountability Act* (HIPPA).

discuss the conditions under which information provided by the client might be released.

To further complicate matters, the data privacy rules addressing therapy or assessment sessions with a child or adolescent might be differ from the laws that apply to sessions with an adult. In some areas, adolescents above a certain age might request professional services, which, although the parent is obligated to pay for such sessions, are still protected information that cannot be discussed with the parent (Greenfield & Hennessy, 2008). Traditionally, information revealed by or about a patient is considered privileged and protected. There are exceptions to this rule, however. If patients were to reveal that they were actively abusing a child, the therapist might be obligated to report this to the authorities under what are known as "duty to report" laws. Another exception to the privilege of confidentiality are cases where individuals reveal specific plans to kill themselves or another person. In such cases, proper steps must be taken to protect the client and the potential victim(s). There are states in which the court is permitted to order that certain information be released to the court, usually when that information is relevant to an ongoing legal investigation.

Clients will frequently reveal that they have been in a treatment program on previous occasions, and these treatment records are useful adjuncts to the assessor. To obtain copies of these treatment records, it will be necessary for the assessor to obtain a *Release of Information Authorization* from the client. This is a written form signed by clients that gives their permission for one facility to release information to another facility. Clients also have the right to specify *which* information can be released by a facility. Finally, clients have the right to refuse to even talk to the assessor if they should choose to do so. The privilege of confidentiality is always the client's, except under very specific circumstances, and is not breached lightly.

When the final evaluation report is composed, the assessor should identify the exact source(s) of information utilized in the formulation of the report. Collateral information sources should be notified in advance that the client, and/or the client's attorney, has a right to request a copy of the final draft of the report, and thus their contribution to the final draft of the report might become known to the client. Further, although it is rare, on occasion the client does request a copy of the final report, and technically has a right to do so after filling out the proper Release of Information authorization forms.

Diagnostic Rules

Many individuals will resist a diagnosis of a substance use disorder, at least at first. Because of this, there are two diagnostic rules that the assessor should adhere to as much as possible. The first rule is *always gather collateral information. As a group*, alcohol-dependent people will be reasonably accurate about their substance use, especially if sober when they are asked about their substance use pattern. There are exceptions to this rule however, such as when the individual is facing the threat of legal action (Gendel, 2006). People facing the possibility of a long prison or jail sentence may exaggerate their self-report of having an SUD, not because it is true but because this might serve as a mitigating factor that might reduce the severity of their sentence. In contrast to this, dual-diagnosis clients often underreport the extent of problems caused by their substance use disorder because they fear loss of entitlements (Social Security and the like).

One advantage of collateral information data is the determination of whether the client's reported behavior(s) when under the influence of a compound is consistent with the known characteristics of that compound. Collateral information sources might support the client's claim of atypical effects from a drug(s) of abuse, or deny that the client even abused alcohol or drug(s) at times when the client claims otherwise. Every assessor has experienced the scenario in which the client claims to use alcohol "just once a week, perhaps not even that often." When asked, the spouse admits that the person uses alcohol nightly, drinking to the point of intoxication every night after work. Obviously, time constraints limit the assessor's ability to contact collateral sources of information to some degree. If the report is due in 72 hours, it might not be possible to contact collateral information sources, but an attempt should be made after obtaining the proper Release of Information authorization. Collateral information sources might include (a) the patient's family, (b) friends of the patient, (c) employer or coworkers, (d) clergy members, (e) local law enforcement officials (criminal convictions are public and might be accessed over the Internet), (f) primary-care physician, and (g) psychotherapist or family therapist (if any).

It will be of value to note whether the collateral information sources cooperate or if they refused to cooperate. It should also be noted whether clients were able to contact the collateral information source before the therapist to coach them on what to say. In more than one case the assessor has heard the client in the background, telling the collateral information source how to answer the questions asked during a telephone conversation. This information should also be noted in the assessment report.

Rule number two is *always assume deception until proven otherwise*. Clients may consciously or unconsciously distort information provided to the assessor, possibly because of their distorted way of thinking (G. R. Ross, 2002). Clients who claim to be an "infrequent" drinker but who actually consumes five to seven beers each evening with coworkers at the end of the day might be attempting to deceive the assessor or might actually believe that this constitutes "infrequent" drinking. After all, it is expected that they join coworkers at the end of the day, and they might consume alcohol only on rare occasions other than at the end of the workday with coworkers.

Unconscious deception is a very real danger during the assessment process. A wise assessor will keep in mind that even "cooperative" clients might engage in such deception. Clients might smugly report that they spend $20 a week on alcohol. When confronted with the reality that this amounts to $1040 a year, those same clients might become indigent and claim that they were spending *only* $20 a week for alcohol because their denial system will not allow them to think otherwise. It is also common for people to claim to drink "once or twice a week," until confronted with the fact that their medical problems are unlikely to have resulted from such a limited level of alcohol use.

It is important to ask about legal problems associated with clients' substance use not only in their home state but also in other states and while in the military. Clients who admit to "one" arrest for driving under the influence of alcohol might, when pressed, admit to other charges in other states, and defend their response on the grounds that they thought that the assessor "only meant this state" or that they did not think that those other convictions applied because they happened while they were enlisted in the military. Fortunately, the Internet allows access to court records from many other states, because a criminal conviction is a public document.

Other Sources of Information: Medical Test Data

There are no definitive blood or urine tests that will prove that a person is addicted to alcohol or drugs.

As will be discussed in Chapter 32, a single "dirty"[26] urine toxicology test does not, in itself, prove that the client has a substance use problem. A series of three or four "dirty" urine samples is more definitive, and it is hard for clients to claim that the urine toxicology test was done right after their first experimental use of a chemical if they had three "dirty" urine samples over 2 months!

Breath analysis might identify the blood alcohol level in the client's system, but not how long that individual has been drinking. Abnormal blood test results should serve as a warning that a patient *might* be abusing alcohol or illicit drugs. However, there are other potential causes of abnormal blood test results. For example, elevated liver function tests might reflect alcohol-related damage, or they might be caused by other medical conditions. Medical tests can often (a) confirm the presence of certain chemicals in the patient's body, (b) identify the specific compounds that are present, (c) possibly determine the level of that chemical in the patient's body, and (d) hint at how long the patient has been abusing chemicals. Further, the appropriate medical tests can identify concurrent medical disorders that might complicate efforts at substance abuse rehabilitation, such as a cardiac problem (Work Group on Substance Use Disorders, 2007).

Diagnosis: The Outcome of the Assessment Process

At the end of the assessment, the assessor should be able to answer four interrelated questions: (a) whether the individual does or does not have a substance use disorder and the evidence on which that conclusion is based, (b) the *severity* of the individual's substance use problem, (c) the client's *motivation to change*, and (d) *factors that contribute/support further substance use* (Connors, Donovan, & DiClemente, 2001). In other words, the assessor should be in a position to make a *diagnosis*. The American Psychiatric Association (2000) suggested that some of the signs of an SUD include (a) *preoccupation* with continued substance use, (b) *using more* of a substance than originally planned, (c) *development of tolerance*, (d) *characteristic withdrawal syndrome*, (e) *continued use of the chemical to avoid symptoms of withdrawal*, (f) *intoxication at inappropriate times* (at work or school, and so on),

---

[26]Meaning that metabolites of illicit drugs were apparently found in the urine.

(g) *normal activities interfered by withdrawal,* (h) *reduction in social, occupational, or recreational activities* in favor of using that time for additional substance use, and (i) *continued use* in spite of social, emotional, physical, or vocational problems caused by the substance use.

Any combination of three or more of these criteria are viewed as being sufficient to diagnosis the client as having an SUD according to the *DSM-IV-TR* criteria. Then it becomes necessary to determine whether the individual's substance use is ongoing or reflects a past pattern of use that is now either in full or partial remission.[27] If the client is abstinent at the time of the assessment, it is necessary to determine *why* the client is abstinent from alcohol or drugs. A client who claims to have abstained from all drugs of abuse for the past 4 months (while incarcerated for the last 4 months) presents a different clinical picture from the client who reports no alcohol or illicit drug use for the past 4 months while living independently. Clients who are under the supervision of the court system (or probation/parole officers) may abstain from alcohol and drugs because they are required to submit to urine toxicology testing on a random basis, for example. Thus the assessor must determine why clients have abstained from chemicals, if they report abstinence.

Although the diagnostic process is often viewed by clinicians as only a necessary step to ensure that an insurance company pays for the recommended treatment (and ensures the continued employment of the assessor!), in reality it is far more than this. It is an ongoing process against which the client's needs, strengths, and resources are measured on a day-to-day basis. A flow chart of the assessment process is depicted in Figure 28-1.

In addition to an accurate diagnosis of the client's substance use pattern, the assessor should also be able to identify the individual's *motivation for seeking the assessment.* The client who is seen after being ordered to have the assessment by a probation officer offers a different level of motivation than does a person who seeks help because of substance-related life-threatening physical illness, and both individuals present the assessor with different forms of motivation than the person who is self-motivated to stop abusing alcohol or drugs.

It should be noted that some clients seek a substance use assessment and treatment recommendations not because they wish to come to terms with their SUD, but for *impression management* purposes (Wild, Cunningham, & Hobdon, 1998). The willingness to enter treatment for a substance use disorder does not automatically translate into the willingness to change one's chemical use pattern (Connors et al., 2001). Individuals with pending court hearings on unresolved legal charges, especially drug-related legal issues, might seek admission to "treatment" without any desire to do more than "look good" before the judge ("I have been through treatment, your Honor!"). Imagine, for a moment, a person who has been arrested for the crime of selling drugs, but who does not actually abuse alcohol or drugs.[28] The question facing the assessor is whether to refer this individual to a substance abuse treatment program, when the client does not have such a disorder, or recommend that the client be referred elsewhere. Although the majority of clients referred to a rehabilitation facility are there because of external pressure (wife, employer, the court system, and so on), the person who enters treatment for the sole purpose of attempting to manipulate the court system wastes valuable treatment resources better used to treat others.

Treatment Referrals

Having established that the client does or does not have an SUD, the next step is the determination of the *appropriate level of care.* The Work Group on Substance Use Disorders (2007) suggested seven criteria that should be considered when making a decision about the appropriate level of care for the client: (a) the individual's ability and willingness to participate in treatment, (b) the individual's ability to carry out self-care activities,[29] (c) the individual's family and social environment, (d) their need for structure to assist them in achieving abstinence, (e) their need for ancillary treatment for concurrent medical or psychiatric problems, (f) the availability of treatment programs in a given area, and (g) the client's preference for a specific form of treatment.[30]

---

[27]This material is reviewed for illustrative purposes only. See the *Diagnostic and Statistical Manual of Mental Disease* (4th edition, text revision) for a complete discussion of the American Psychiatric Association's diagnostic criteria.

[28]Yes, such people exist. Their motivation for drug sales is not to support their own substance use disorder but to partake of the profits made through the sale of illicit drugs.

[29]Often called *activities of daily living,* or *ADLs.*

[30]Although the client's wishes for a specific form of treatment should not dictate the level of treatment recommended, it should be taken into consideration by the assessor, and if dismissed, a rationale for why it was dismissed should be included in the final report.

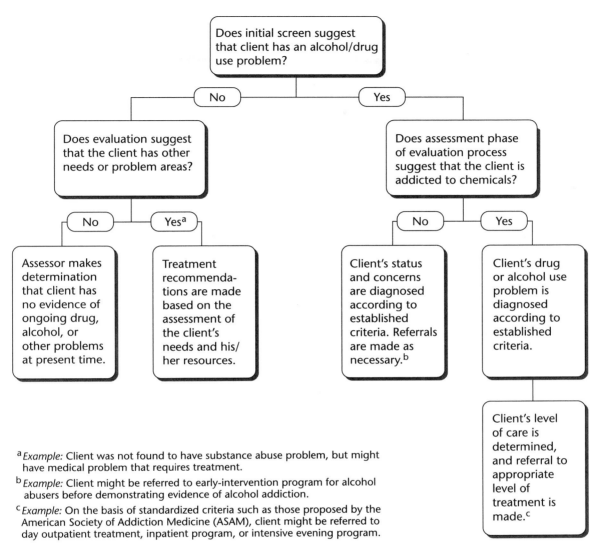

a *Example:* Client was not found to have substance abuse problem, but might have medical problem that requires treatment.

b *Example:* Client might be referred to early-intervention program for alcohol abusers before demonstrating evidence of alcohol addiction.

c *Example:* On the basis of standardized criteria such as those proposed by the American Society of Addiction Medicine (ASAM), client might be referred to day outpatient treatment, inpatient program, or intensive evening program.

FIGURE 28-1 A Flowchart of the Assessment Process

The criteria offered by the American Society of Addiction Medicine (ASAM) also provide an excellent guide to determining the appropriate level of care for a given client (American Society of Addiction Medicine, 2001). Indeed, this program guide has become the most commonly utilized system to determine client level of care needs (Gastfriend, 2004a, 2004b). The most recent revision of the ASAM patient placement criteria identifies six levels of care (eight levels for adolescents):

- *Level 0.5: Early intervention*
- *Level I: Outpatient treatment*
- *Level II: Intensive outpatient treatment/partial hospitalization*
- *Level III: Residential/inpatient treatment*
- *Level IV: Medically managed intensive inpatient treatment*
- *Level OMT: Methadone Maintenance Programs*

The ASAM patient placement criteria have been found to be effective by research studies designed to test whether they stand up to "managed care" demands for specific provisions for client level of care (Mee-Lee & Gastfriend, 2008).

Some of the factors that the assessor must keep in mind are (a) client strengths (b) client weaknesses, (c) potential for withdrawal from alcohol or drugs of abuse, (d) potential for serious medical problems during withdrawal and while in treatment, and (e) strength of the client's abstinence support system. These factors influence the assessed client need for a specific level of care. Another factor that is rarely discussed is the client's legal status. The level of care decision might have been made by the court system, which will mandate a specific level of care for the client, and failure to complete treatment at that level will result in revocation of probation/parole.

However, there are other systems available that will guide the assessor in making this determination. It is important to keep in mind one outcome of the assessment process. That is, if the client has been found to have an SUD, a determination of the proper level of care should be established. The *least restrictive treatment alternative* for meeting clients' strengths, needs, and their treatment history are then reviewed to help determine the appropriate level of care (Work Group on Substance Use Disorders, 2007).

Chapter Summary

The evaluation process consists of three phases: (a) screening, (b) assessment, and (c) diagnosis. Each of these phases rests on the one before it and closely parallels the medical diagnosis process. If there is evidence that a condition might exist (screening), it is then assessed. During the assessment process, the parameters of the condition, its duration, its intensity, factors that might reduce its severity, and others that might exacerbate it, are explored. At the end of the assessment stage, the assessor is in a position to make a formal *diagnosis* and to make treatment recommendations. Included in the treatment recommendations is the level of care that would be most appropriate for the individual client. Some of the aids available to assessors for use in each stage of the assessment process were reviewed.

CHAPTER **29**

Intervention[1]

The most promising way—perhaps the only way—to put enough addicts into treatment long enough to make a difference entails a considerable measure of coercion.

—*Satel and Farabee (2005, p. 690)*

Introduction

There are many who would challenge the validity of the chapter-opening quote, and there are also those who would defend its validity, in part because many people with substance use disorders do not perceive the need for rehabilitation (Edlund et al., 2009). The subject of intervention has become widely acknowledged as a result of often dramatic television programs in which a counselor joins a family in confronting a family member with an SUD while the camera(s) are recording every moment. Many of these televised programs show the eloquence and grace of a barroom brawl, and one must wonder how much having the television cameras present has changed the dynamics of the intervention session. However, these programs do illustrate different forms of intervention, which is the topic of this chapter.

Surprisingly, health care professionals still have no single definition of *intervention* at this time. Admittedly, there *are* benefits to treating the SUDs. Researchers have found a 26% reduction in hospitalizations for general health problems, a 25% reduction in the length of hospitalization following admission, a 38% reduction in visits to hospital emergency rooms, and a 14% reduction in physician visits, following the cessation of alcohol use, for example (F. Weiss, 2005). The average monthly medical cost for a drug abuser has been estimated at $750 per month, which is reduced to $200 per month following treatment, as compared to $100 per month for a person the same age who has never abused alcohol or drugs (Rosenbloom, 2000). Further, researchers have found that successful completion of substance abuse treatment is associated with a significant reduction in suicide attempts or completed suicides (Ilgen, Jain, Lucas, & Moos, 2007). This all translates into savings for the insurance company or state welfare system that funds that person's health care.

In spite of these obvious advantages, individuals with alcohol use disorders rarely perceive the need for treatment (Flora, 2005; Wu & Ringwalt, 2005).

---

[1]The material in this chapter is provided for illustrative purposes only. It is not intended as and should not be used as a guide to the intervention process.

It must be assumed that the same is true for individuals with other substance use disorders. Thus some form of intervention is necessary, but the methods for intervention are still in development. In this chapter, the process of intervention will be reviewed.

A Definition of Intervention

Sadock and Sadock (2007) suggested that the patient with an alcohol use disorder (the prototypical addiction) must "be brought face-to-face with the reality of the disorder (intervention), be detoxified if necessary, and begin rehabilitation" (p. 403). This is the first step—making individuals with an SUD face the reality of their addiction—that forms the core concept of intervention. However, intervention takes many forms, not just the dramatic televised events seen on so many television programs. A spouse's comment that his or her partner is drinking too much is a form of intervention. The physician's warning that if the patient continues to drink or abuse drugs she or he might die is another form of intervention. The supervisor's warning that the worker seems to have a problem and should consider going into treatment is yet another form of intervention.

But at what point does "feedback" from a friend, supervisor, spouse, or the courts become a formal intervention project? All forms of intervention begin with the same starting point: *Is it necessary for some form of intervention to be carried out?* If the answer is "no," then obviously the process stops at this point. If it is agreed that some form of intervention is appropriate, then the decision must be made about the form of intervention and who is to participate in that intervention effort. For the sake of this text, intervention will be defined as being an (a) *organized* effort by a (b) person or people who are part of the addicted person's environment, to (c) *break through the walls of denial and rationalization* that surround the addictive behavior(s), which is (d) *often supervised* by a trained professional, with the goal of obtaining an agreement from the addicted person to (e) *immediately seek admission to a designated treatment center.* In theory this process is relatively straight forward. The application of the intervention process is usually quite difficult.

A Brief History of Intervention

It was once thought that people with an SUD would not be receptive to efforts to intervene until they had

"hit bottom."[2] "Hitting bottom" was thought to be necessary for addicted people to understand that their substance use disorder was harming them and that they needed to stop abusing chemicals. An unfortunate side effect of this process was that many substance abusers might die before reaching their personal "bottom." Others find that they have a successive series of "bottoms" as they bounce from one situation to another. Other people might never accept the need for them to address their substance use disorder.

Then, Vernon Johnson (1980) challenged the concept that people must "hit bottom" before being able to accept help with their addiction. Because of the physical, emotional, social, and vocational damage that uncontrolled alcohol use could cause, he advocated early intervention rather than waiting for the person to "hit bottom." He suggested that alcohol-dependent people (with whom he had the most experience) might comprehend the reality of their alcohol use disorder *if that information was presented in a language that the drinker could understand.* Further, it was suggested that low-functioning clients (McCrady, 2001), or those individuals who were "not in touch with reality" (V. E. Johnson, 1980, p. 49) because of their substance use, were still capable of understanding some portion of the message expressed to them.

An all too common consequence of intervention efforts is that people with the SUD will resist efforts from concerned others to guide them into a rehabilitation program. To help them with this apparent misperception, a small industry emerged in the 1980s and 1990s in which trained, semitrained, self-trained, and untrained individuals offered their services to guide an intervention project. Such intervention projects have even become the focus of prime-time television programs. The well-intentioned goal of these projects was to convince a person with an SUD to agree to immediately enter treatment. Having the person simply promise not to drink or use drugs again was not perceived as

---

[2]"Hitting bottom" is a term loosely defined as the point where substance abusers have to admit to total, absolute defeat in life because of their SUD.

sufficient, as it was known that individuals with SUDs would often make such promises, only to break them the next day. The goal was for the individual to agree to and then enter treatment, and such intervention projects became enshrined in clinical lore as both useful and often necessary.

Characteristics of the Intervention Process

The characteristics of the intervention process depend, to a large degree, on the setting and the individual(s) involved. The goals of an intervention process were reviewed earlier in the section "A Definition of Intervention." The intervention process is usually supervised by a properly trained professional, although this is not always the case. The intervention process can take many forms. A spouse who informs his or her partner that "if you don't stop using _____, I am leaving!" might be said to have attempted an intervention. A physician in the consultation room who informs a patient that if she should continue to abuse chemicals that she will probably not live another 5 years, and that the physician could recommend some good treatment programs, might be said to have attempted to intervene. A friend who expresses concern about his friend's substance use, how much it scares him to see his friend following the same road that he was once following, and how much he would like to see his friend enter treatment and stop abusing drugs, could also be said to have attempted an intervention project. Legal intervention projects also exist and will be discussed later in this chapter.

The Mechanics of Intervention

At the start of the intervention effort, participants affirm their concern for the individual with the SUD. Then they express their desire that the addicted person seek a designated form of professional assistance for his or her SUD (Flora, 2005). As was noted earlier, this might be an informal discussion between friends, an employer talking to an employee, or a spouse talking to his or her partner. Familial intervention projects also may serve as a conduit through which the individual is guided into treatment.

First, as noted earlier the intervention project is carried out without malice. A second point is that the participants need to agree *in advance* about the goal of the intervention project. Given the low expectations that physicians have for the rehabilitation of

patients with an alcohol use disorder,[3] it was surprising to learn that even brief screening and intervention of patients in hospital emergency room settings had a significant impact on the patient's later alcohol use (SBIRT Research Collaborative Group, 2007). A more elaborate level of patient intervention by a physician might be seen when the physician sits down with the patient to say, "Well, your liver function tests are very elevated, suggesting that your liver has sustained major damage. You have been admitted to the hospital three times in the past year for 'detox' from alcohol, and been seen in the emergency room one more time for stitches in your scalp after you fell while intoxicated. It looks as if we have a problem here, and we need to take steps to address it." The physician, in this hypothetical example, should arrange for an immediate appointment to a specific addictions rehabilitation counselor and, if possible, walk the patient down to the counselor's office for the initial interview. A follow-up appointment with the patient and care coordination with the addictions counselor should also be arranged to ensure that the patient receives the proper treatment.

This principle reflects a cornerstone of the intervention process: Decisions about the proper response to the patient's objections and an agency to refer the individual to should be resolved *prior* to the start of the intervention project. This is true for family intervention projects, those between a physician and a patient, those between an employer and an employee, and so on. Identified patients will exploit indecision in the service of their addiction, possibly avoiding a referral to treatment entirely. Promises will be made and later broken, but by then the unified front by those involved in the intervention project will have been shattered by the demands of each individual's life. Those who participate in the intervention process should have agreed on the goal of this process in advance, avoiding debates about such questions during the meeting with the identified patient. Clients have been known to make promises for a lesser sanction, such as going to an outpatient treatment program rather than an inpatient rehabilitation facility, knowing that after a period of time the family's resolve will weaken, and they can drop out of treatment.

Paradoxically, by the time that intervention project(s) are being considered, addicted individuals will rarely deny the reality of their substance use disorder. People with an SUD are usually well aware

---

[3]Discussed in Chapter 1.

of their addiction, even if they allow this awareness into their conscious mind only on rare occasions. When confronted, however, many individuals attempt to deflect confrontation with the observation that their substance use is hurting only them, not other family members (Flora, 2005). To break through such rationalizations, the designated individual is confronted by people (family members, coworkers, and so on) whose lives have been affected by the individual's SUD. Such confrontation should involve *specific examples* of how the designated person's behavior has affected others, rather than general statements such as "Your addiction is killing us." Comments such as "I saw you taking OxyContin from your grandmother's medicine bottle a week before she died of cancer" provide both the specific data and demonstrate how the addict's behavior has affected others.

The intervention project is carried out with the goal of having clients agree to enter treatment immediately. If clients admit that perhaps their SUD has affected others, and agrees to enter treatment, they are then *immediately* escorted to the treatment center admissions office by family members. Thus when intervention is attempted, the people doing the intervention should have specific referrals in place. The identified patient has the right to refuse to enter treatment. In such cases, those who participate in the intervention project should have identified sanctions ready to put into place. These sanctions are *not* to be thought of as empty threats or as attempts to manipulate the person with the SUD into accepting the need for treatment. Rather, they are to be viewed as the first steps in the process of *detachment*. Through this process, the people imposing the sanction are saying that they will no longer be part of the individual's addiction support system. Thus a physician might say, "In this case, I can no longer in good conscience continue to prescribe [name of specific medication(s)] to you, as the risk of a fatal interaction between the medications that I prescribe and the drugs that you take is too great." A family member might inform the person with the SUD that "you are no longer welcome in my home until you have completed treatment and remain abstinent for a full year." Then these sanctions need to be maintained.

Sometimes, the identified family member will offer vague assurances that he or she will seek assistance, which is used in the service of denial, protecting the substance use disorder. "Yes, I know, you're right," the

individual might say. "But it's late. I'll call the treatment center tomorrow." However, "tomorrow" never seems to arrive, and the individual offers a thousand and one reasons for not entering treatment today or at the specified treatment center. "I can't afford to enter treatment! I have bills to pay and need to go to work!" is a common objection offered by addicted people as a reason why they cannot possibly enter a rehabilitation program at this time. Such objections might be sincere, but also deny the reality of the person's addiction. Bills might have been left unpaid, or only partially paid, but they always found the money to pay for their alcohol or drugs.

On occasion, the intervention efforts will be countered with an effort on the client's part to give the impression of compliance without acceptance of the need to fully enter the treatment process. The family intervention project had required that they enter treatment. Nobody said anything about the designated person *finishing* it, right? They offer a thousand reasons why they could not complete treatment. "I had to leave . . . they kept stuffing this 'God' crap down my throat!!!" The reality may very well be that the designated family member heard the word *God* twice in one evening, but as rationalizations go you have to work with what you have, and this is a good one. At this point it might be necessary to activate the sanctions that were put in place prior to the initiation of the intervention project, and then maintain them.

Clients have been known to drive to a treatment center, sit in the parking lot, then after a few hours drive home to say to the family, "I went there and they didn't admit me." By a subtle manipulation of the facts, addicted people imply that they do not really need treatment. To avoid such manipulation, designated family members should accompany the addicted member to the treatment center, and participate in the admissions interview so that the counselor has an honest overview of the identified patient's substance use disorder and its impact on others.

Although the intervention process has been in use for more than a generation, there is little evidence to support its effectiveness (Flora, 2005). It is possible that some families will benefit more from intervention efforts, whereas others might suffer great harm from the same process. In a very real sense the intervention process might be said to be the clinical application of a theory that has not been tested to identify either the optimal or minimal conditions where it might be applicable.

The Ethics of Intervention[4]

The process of intervention is fraught with ethical dilemmas (Scott, 2000). For example, it is based on the assumption that, through treatment, the substance-abusing person can be saved from the negative consequences of the SUD. However, the success rate of existing treatment modalities does not offer much of a guarantee that this assumption will be met (Kleinig, 2004). Further, the "judgement that a person constitutes a sufficiently significant danger to himself or others that some intervention is justified is often highly speculative" (Kleinig, 2004, p. 381). Thus the need for an intervention must be *firmly* established and documented before the process is allowed to proceed. The participant(s) need to carry out an honest, thoughtful review of the benefits and possible consequences of the intervention process, documenting that such a review took place, and what was assessed (Kleinig, 2004).

Another ethical concern is whether the designated individual wishes to participate in the intervention project. The person with the SUD must not be physically restrained, for example, except in cases where there is a danger to self or others. However, if the designated individual should express a desire to leave, she or he should be allowed to do so. The designated person is free to leave the intervention program at any time, with the exception of danger to self or others. Those who are there to conduct the intervention project should discuss the sanctions and how they plan to use them after the client leaves.

Another ethical concern is whether *informed consent* is a necessary component of the intervention project (Kleinig, 2004). Years ago, the simple authoritative assertion of a health care professional was sufficient for an intervention program to be deemed necessary. The courts now hold that the professional must offer informed consent to the client (and document that this was offered) before the client is introduced to the intervention process (Kleinig, 2004). During the intervention process, personal information about the client, or the client's behavior, might be revealed to other people who were unaware of these facts. Data privacy is of special importance in hospitals, where people might be exposed to information about the patient's substance use disorder in spite of the individual's desire to keep such information private.

A point of law holds that a patient has the right to refuse any recommended treatment. However, there are exceptions to this rule.[5] Kleinig (2004) suggested that one such exception is when harm to one person will occur because of the SUD of another person. Because a mother's cocaine abuse might harm the fetus, the courts have remanded many pregnant women into treatment in various parts of the country on the grounds that their continued substance use might harm the fetus (Kleinig, 2004).

The potential *conflict of interest* must be assessed, especially if the substance abuse rehabilitation professional should refer the client *only* to themselves or to a facility where they work (Fals-Stewart et al., 2003). Care must be taken by substance abuse rehabilitation professionals to ensure that they have *no* economic vested interest in where the client goes to treatment. Ideally the client should be offered a number of treatment options, although in reality economic and geographic realities might limit the options available to the client.

Finally, counselors' qualifications and their adherence to professional codes of ethics also need to be considered when planning an intervention project (Kleinig, 2004). Obviously, legal counsel is necessary to help substance abuse rehabilitation professionals through the quagmire that surrounds them to avoid violating state or federal laws (C. G. Scott, 2000).

Some Common Forms of Intervention:

Family Intervention Projects

There are a number of family intervention project models, the most common of which is the format advocated by V. E. Johnson (1986). Collectively, these family intervention efforts are second only to legal pressure to force the individual into treatment (O'Farrell & Fals-Stewart, 2008). However, it should be recognized that the person who is the center of the intervention project is unlikely to be enthusiastic about this process, and there is a danger for serious damage to familial relationships as a result of family intervention programs

---

[4]People planning on an intervention process are advised to consult with an attorney as to the specific laws that apply in their geographic location and what they can or cannot do to carry out the intervention process.

[5]Thus the recommendation that substance abuse rehabilitation professionals seek legal counsel as to the laws that apply in their state before attempting an intervention project.

(A. W. Blume, 2005; Flora, 2005). This danger is increased if the intervention project is poorly planned or executed. Although it is the goal that the intervention project be carried out *without malice* and in a *nonjudgmental manner* (Fals-Stewart et al., 2003; Sadock & Sadock, 2007), many family members will view the intervention project as a time to voice resentments about the individual's SUD or past behaviors, increasing the danger of a negative outcome. It must be recognized that family intervention sessions are "emotional powder kegs that can go horribly wrong" (Flora, 2005, p. 41). What follows is a brief summary of two of the more common family intervention models.

The Johnson Model

This is the model most often associated with the word *intervention*, and its original force was advanced by V. E. Johnson (1986). This form of intervention is often portrayed in many popular books, articles, and the occasional prime-time television program, usually in a positive light. Johnson model intervention projects usually involve three to four educational or rehearsal sessions before the actual intervention effort, to prepare family members, friends, or coworkers for the actual intervention session. Those people who are either actively abusing alcohol or illicit drugs, or who refuse to participate in the intervention project, should not be invited (O'Farrell & Fals-Stewart, 2008).

During the pre-effort training sessions, participants are taught about the disease model of addictions, reducing the potential for anger or malice as the participants learn that the affected person suffers from a disease and is not intentionally being mean or unsupportive. Family members are encouraged to bring written notes to the intervention session with them. Such notes should be very specific as to dates, times, and the client's behaviors that resulted in that person's decision to be part of the intervention project. Statements such as "You often come home drunk" should be replaced with specific comments such as "Last week you came home intoxicated on Monday, Wednesday, Thursday, and Saturday nights!"

Role-playing simulations are also carried out to prepare family members for possible scenarios that might emerge during the actual intervention session. If, for example, the addicted person should claim not to have driven while under the influence after going to the bar because "Mark drove me," a family member should check with Mark (if he is not a participant) to see whether this excuse is valid or not. Other possible scenarios to be addressed include what to do if the affected family member should become angry, attempts to leave, or attempts to manipulate family members into disagreement. During these pre-effort sessions family members will discuss the goal of the intervention project (usually to secure a commitment to immediately enter treatment). If successful, the participants will have prearranged admission to a treatment facility.

When all is ready, the affected family member is either invited or escorted to the intervention effort session. Such sessions often have all of the elegance and style of a hanging in the days of the wild west, and as noted there is the danger for lifelong damage to familial relationships even in the best of intervention efforts. Further, in spite of the intentions of participants, V. E. Johnson (1986) model intervention programs result in a commitment to enter treatment in only approximately 30% of the cases (O'Farrell & Fals-Stewart, 2008; W. R. Miller & White, 2007).

The ARISE Model[6]

This is a three-stage model of intervention in which the level of pressure applied by the family to encourage the affected member to enter treatment is gradually increased (Landau & Garret, 2006). This model is based on the concept of a graduated series of contact with the patient over a period of time with the goal of securing the addicted person's entry into treatment. The first stage is usually telephone contact with the client, followed by a family therapy session to explore the problem and its ramifications. In stage two, the client is invited to attend a family therapy session, and the entire family discusses options that they see available to them at that time. In the third stage, if the individual does not enter treatment within a designated period of time, a more confrontational intervention session, comparable in many ways to the "Johnson model," is then carried out. Through this process, clients are exposed to strong levels of confrontation only if they should fail to respond to more gentle feedback from family members about how their substance use disorder has affected them.

Intervention by the Legal System

Individuals who participate in court-mandated treatment arrive at this point through a variety of avenues. Some have been convicted of driving a motor vehicle

---

[6]Which stands for "A Relational Intervention Sequence for Engagement."

while under the influence of alcohol or drugs (a "DWI," as it is called in some states[7]). Others may have been arrested for possession of illicit drugs, or for any of a wide range of substance-related legal offenses. In theory, the individual retains the right to choose incarceration over treatment (Leamon et al., 2008). Essentially the individual is placed into an either/or situation: *Either* the client successfully completes treatment *or* they will go to jail. This is called *contingency management* (T. J. Morgan, 2003). Individuals who enter a rehabilitation facility under such situations are said to demonstrate *controlled motivation* (Wild et al., 1998). Unfortunately, court-mandated treatment is rarely viewed as an opportunity for growth, but instead is usually viewed as a punitive response by the legal system for past behavior(s) by the individual (Dill & Wells-Parker, 2006).

Court-mandated treatment reflects the theory that the individual might benefit from external motivation during the early stages of recovery from an SUD (DiClemente, Bellino, & Neavins, 1999; Satel, 2000; Satel & Farabee, 2005). It is hoped that eventually *internal* motivation might develop and that the individuals will apply themselves to the treatment process. There is mixed evidence suggesting that court-mandated clients work harder on treatment goals than voluntary patients and are also less likely to prematurely leave treatment if they are there because of an agreement with the court. This process offers the additional advantage that the very nature of the circumstances surrounding admission makes it quite difficult for clients to deny that they have a problem with chemicals!

Court-mandated clients have been found to have experienced fewer negative consequences to their substance use than do clients without legal pressure (J. F. Kelly, Finney, & Moos, 2006). At first this would seem counterintuitive, until one considers that the voluntary client is more likely to be older and to have experienced some of the adverse physical or social consequences of their SUD. The court-mandated client has also been found to be as likely to benefit from treatment as traditional patients (J. F. Kelly et al., 2005; Satel & Farabee, 2005). Further, there is evidence that those people who seek treatment at the invitation of the court system may remain in treatment for a longer period of time than traditional clients and are less likely to reoffend following discharge from treatment (Satel & Farabee, 2005).

In spite of the obvious benefits of court-mandated treatment, there are also some problems with this form of treatment. First, many insurance companies are, by law, able to refuse payment for court-mandated treatment (Dill & Wells-Parker, 2006). Court-mandated treatment is not a guarantee of long-term abstinence because long-term abstinence rates for those who complete treatment at the invitation of the courts appear to be the same as for voluntary patients (Leamon, Wright & Myrick, 2008). Further, some clinicians view court-mandated treatment as being coercive and consider the outcome of this process to be coerced abstinence (Jaffe & Anthony, 2005). Treatment by court order places special requirements on the treatment center.[8] Such treatment also raises interesting questions about the relationship between the law and the rehabilitation industry: If, as the medical model asserts, alcoholism is a disease, then how can the courts order it cured? Thus there is some disagreement among treatment professionals as to the value of court-mandated treatment.

Drug Court

The drug court is a concept first tried in 1989 (M. L. Taylor, 2004), and since then an ever-growing number of communities have instituted similar programs. The goal of the drug court' model is to:

> quickly identify substance abusing offenders and place them under strict court monitoring and community supervision, coupled with effective, long-term treatment services [during which] the drug court participant undergoes an intense regimen of substance abuse and mental health treatment, case management, drug testing, and probation supervision while reporting to regularly scheduled status hearings before a judge with specialized expertise in the drug court model. (Huddleston, Freeman-Wilson & Boone, 2004, p. 1)

It has been found that such programs are most effective for first-time, nonviolent offenders with the goal of avoiding the "revolving door" cycle of repeat offenses (Goldkamp, White, & Robinson, 2002). Drug court programs should (a) assess the individual's need for treatment, (b) identify the proper level of treatment for the client, (c) identify the treatment facility best suited to the client, (d) monitor client adherence to treatment through therapist reports, (e) administer

---

[7]In other states, it is called an "OWI," or "operating a motor vehicle while under the influence of intoxicants."

[8]For example, the treatment center might be expected to *immediately* notify the authorities should a client leave treatment against staff advice.

periodic urine toxicology tests, (f) provide for a reduction in legal charges if the client completes the program, and (g) provide for "aftercare" groups (Work Group on Substance Use Disorders, 2007).

There has been some dispute concerning the effectiveness of drug court programs, which are both labor and time intensive. Reuter and Pollack (2005) suggested that these programs are both cost effective and lower recidivism. For example it was estimated that New York State saved $250 million in 1 year through its drug court programs, whereas in St. Louis, Missouri, it was found that for every dollar invested in drug court, there was a savings of $6.32 in reduced welfare, medical, and law enforcement expenses (M. L. Taylor, 2004). In contrast to these claims, Eckholm (2008) suggested that drug courts reduce recidivism only 8–10%, a figure that is only slightly higher than the figure of 13% offered by Rempel (2005). Although such data is very promising, there have been few well-designed research studies into the effectiveness of drug court programs, because the very nature of the population served would make such research difficult, if not impossible (Rempel, 2005).

One problem with the drug court concept is that it is based on the theory that the substance abuse treatment programs that the clients are referred to are very effective. This is at best an unproven assumption, because it has proven virtually impossible to measure the effectiveness of individual rehabilitation programs. Further, the drug courts will place an additional demand on the already limited number of treatment beds through mandated treatment requirements. Participation in a drug court program requires an admission of guilt on the part of the client; and although the charges are dropped should the individual successfully complete the program, many potential participants opt for the possibility of being proven not guilty (McPherson, Yudo, Afsarifard, & Freitas, 2009).

Finally, the issue of the individual's motivation for participation in a drug court program must be considered. Some drug courts have admitted individuals who are not addicted to drugs but who wish to avoid prison for the sale of such compounds. Because these individuals were never addicted to the compounds that they sold, this would inflate the success rate of that drug court program[9] (Eckholm, 2008). Thus the issue of the drug court movement, its effectiveness, and when

individuals should not be referred to a drug court program is quite complicated.

Court-Mandated Involuntary Treatment

In more than 30 states, it is possible for people to be committed to a treatment facility against their will. To do this one must prove to the courts that the individual is in imminent danger of harm to self or others (Gendel, 2006). The provisions under which a person might be remanded to treatment vary from state to state, but in essence this provision of the law provides for people to be sent to treatment against their will if there is reasonable evidence to believe that they are a danger to themselves or others. Although these laws are often utilized to send one person or another to treatment, there is little evidence into the effectiveness of court-mandated involuntary treatment. There is a very real chance that clients will simply comply with treatment expectations in order to escape the court's supervision as rapidly as possible, without making any permanent changes in their substance use behaviors.

It is rare for an individual to request treatment, a phenomenon known as *autonomous motivation* (Wild et al., 1998). It is more common for individuals to admit that they would continue to abuse chemicals, if they could do so. It is for this reason that external pressure in the form of familial, legal, or professional pressure is utilized to help the addicted person see the need for treatment.

Other Forms of Intervention

T. J. Morgan (2003) suggested that *contingency management* techniques are often very effective when working with individuals with an SUD. In a sense, contingency management situations are "either/or" forms of external pressure similar to sanctions often utilized by the courts to help a certain individual find the motivation to enter treatment. A spouse might confront their partner with the warning "If you don't stop abusing alcohol or drugs, I am filing for a divorce!" If the individual should continue to abuse chemicals, then the partner should follow through with the sanction and file for divorce. A failure to do so means that warnings of further sanctions will be ignored by the addicted person, because their partner did not enforce the original sanction.

Thus a friend who had expressed a desire not to have their friend drink before or while they are playing golf might, upon seeing that the friend was drinking a can of beer, just turn around and leave. The plea from

---

[9]In the sense that this person was not abusing drugs and thus could not be counted as a "drug abuser" in that community.

the drinker that it was "only beer" should be met with the comment, "I said that if you were drinking, or appeared to have been drinking, that I would not play golf with you!" The previously stated sanction is then enforced, and should remain in place until the drinker does indeed enter treatment.

Employer-Mandated Treatment

With the advent of workplace urine toxicology testing to reduce employee accidental injuries and use of sick leave, it is not uncommon for people to seek treatment because their employer threatened to fire them if they did not. Employers justify such behavior on the grounds that employee substance use disorders cost them money. A company with just 500 employees will typically spend $133,000 in health care costs for employee alcohol-related problems each year (Brink, 2004). Further, individuals with an alcohol use disorder use more "sick" days and are five times as likely to file a worker's compensation claim as nondrinkers (Brink, 2004). Thus employers feel justified in guiding employees into treatment or out the front door. Surprisingly, there is little research into whether such employer-mandated treatment is effective or the conditions under which it is most useful. As discussed in Chapter 18, many women (or other workers in low-level jobs) often find it more convenient to just quit and look for alternative employment rather than to enter treatment as the original employer suggested.

Reactions Against the Concept of Intervention

Although few would argue against the need for assistance in extreme cases of substance abuse, cases where individuals' substance use is placing their own or the lives of others at risk, the question must be asked: *When* is coercion justified? In his discussion of this topic, Bentall (2009) argued that "paternalism and coercion could be justified *only* if doctors and other mental health professionals reliably knew what was in their patient's best interests. However their track record is appalling" (p. 273, italics added). Bentall asserts that it is the duty of a mental health professional to follow the dictum that governs medicine: *First, do no harm.* However, as the author observed, coercion has become such an accepted tool used by mental health or medical professionals that it now does not raise ethical questions for those who wield these weapons. In the

process, the individual's autonomy is swept away by those who claim to know what is in the patient's best interest.

Chapter Summary

In rare cases, clients will demonstrate autonomous motivation for treatment. However, because of the pharmacological reward potential of the drugs of abuse, most drug abusers are not interested in abstinence or recovery. Thus contingency motivation has been viewed as an appropriate manner to guide the addicted person to rehabilitation. It is hoped that while in treatment, individuals will come to see how their life was out of control and centered around continued chemical abuse, in spite of the damage being wrought to both themselves and significant others.

Intervention projects may be informal, as when a physician confronts a patient with the reality that continued substance use will result in a deterioration of health and ultimately death. Another informal intervention might be seen when friends set a limit as to what they will tolerate in the relationship, and then when the individual with the SUD continues to engage in substance-related behaviors, enforce sanctions such as ending the friendship. An employer or supervisor might confront employees with evidence that their continued substance use is harming productivity and that if they do not enter treatment and maintain continued abstinence following the completion of rehabilitation, they will be fired. Formal intervention projects involve family members and friends meeting with the identified individual, confronting him or her with evidence of how their SUD is hurting both themselves and others, and attempting to obtain a commitment from the identified individual to immediately enter treatment. If the client agrees, then appointed family members will escort the individual to an identified treatment center and participate in the admissions interview. If the client should refuse, then previously identified sanctions should be employed to help family members and friends detach from the person with the SUD and their behavior.

The rights of the individual who is the focus of the intervention process are discussed, as is the fact that the identified patient has the right to leave the intervention project should he or she wish to do so. Employer- and court-mandated interventions are discussed, as is the fact that the effectiveness of such incentives for treatment remains unproven.

CHAPTER **30**

Treatment Settings

Introduction

In the last chapter, we reviewed some of the many issues that must be addressed during the rehabilitation process. Depending on the client's assessed need for a specific level of care, the treatment process might take place on either an outpatient or an inpatient basis. There is a great deal of debate within the professional community as to the relative merits of each treatment setting, but the emerging consensus is that each offers advantages and disadvantages for both the rehabilitation center staff and the client. The advantages of rehabilitation are clear: Individuals who were involved in a treatment program or 12-step program were more likely to be abstinent 16 years after they entered rehabilitation (R. H. Moos & Moos, 2006a). In this chapter we will briefly review the different settings where the client's substance abuse disorder might be addressed.

An Introduction to Outpatient Treatment

Outpatient Treatment: A Working Definition

The outpatient substance abuse rehabilitation program might best be defined as (a) a formal treatment program involving one or more rehabilitation professionals, (b) designed to help the person with an SUD develop and maintain a recovery program, (c) which will utilize a variety of treatment approaches (psycho-educational, family and marital therapies, individual and group therapy formats), which is (d) designed to do so on an outpatient basis.

Outpatient treatment programs are quite popular, and it has been estimated that 85% of all patients who participate in a substance abuse rehabilitation program will be treated on an outpatient basis at some point in time (Tinsley, Finlayson, & Morse, 1998). Although many clients might address their SUD only through outpatient treatment, such programs might also serve

as a transitional stage for clients who originally were in an inpatient program and for whom a less intensive form of support is thought appropriate before they attempt self-directed recovery (Work Group on Substance Use Disorders, 2007).

Components of Outpatient Treatment

Outpatient treatment programs will often utilize both individual and group therapy formats to help clients address their SUD, with ancillary treatment services in the form of assertiveness training, marital and family therapy, vocational counseling, and so on. Most outpatient treatment programs follow a 12-step format, and clients are expected to attend regular self-help group meetings as part of their rehabilitation. The person who coordinates this program is a certified chemical dependency counselor or a mental health professional who specializes in the treatment of the addictive disorders.

A formal treatment plan is established at the beginning of treatment, with review sessions and appropriate goals, being scheduled on a regular basis to monitor the client's progress toward mutually agreed-upon goals. As noted, this might be done in either individual or group therapy sessions, depending on the client's identified problems. Psycho-educational lectures and bibliotherapy[1] are also often utilized in this process in order to help clients recognize the consequences of their SUD if it is not arrested. Such programs might also have a "family night" component held either once a week or once a month, where family members might ask questions or express concern about the client's progress, the nature of the addictions, and so on. As noted, ancillary rehabilitation services in the form of family and marital therapies, vocational counseling, dietary counseling, assertiveness training, and the like are utilized as indicated.

Abstinence from alcohol and illicit drugs is not only expected but is a prerequisite for participation in outpatient treatment. This is supported through the use of appropriate pharmaceutical supports,[2] and confirmed through the client's self-report, collateral information, alcohol breath testing, and urine toxicology testing. If the client should relapse, this is also addressed on an outpatient basis unless it becomes apparent that the client is unable or unwilling to abstain from chemicals while in an outpatient treatment program. In this case a referral to a more intensive level of treatment would be indicated.

In spite of the apparent advantages of outpatient treatment, research suggests that such rehabilitation programs experience high dropout rates, and many of those who are initially referred to an outpatient treatment program might be referred to an inpatient treatment program when their recovery status indicates that this might be most helpful.

Varieties of Outpatient Rehabilitation Programs

There are a number of different outpatient treatment formats, and client referral to one form of treatment or another is dependent on the available resources and the client's assessed needs for a specific level of care. Perhaps the least restrictive form of treatment is the DWI school.

Individual Rehabilitation Counseling

Depending on patients' needs and the severity of their substance use disorder, they might be seen by an addictions counselor on a one-to-one basis. Such treatment approaches are usually restricted to motivated clients who are willing to also engage in intersession assigned projects (assigned reading, for example) and utilize other existing support services (12-step groups and the like). The treatment orientation of addictions counselors will depend on their training and experience, but might include techniques oriented toward motivational interviewing, cognitive behavioral therapies, or 12-step approaches.

DWI School

These programs, called "DWI"[3] school, utilize a psycho-educational approach and are usually limited to the first-time offender who is assumed to have made a mistake by unintentionally driving a motor vehicle under the influence of alcohol or other mood-altering chemicals.[4] Individuals referred to a DWI school are not, in the opinion of the assessor, addicted to alcohol or drugs. The DWI school format involves 8–12 hours of educational lectures individual and group therapy sessions, to help the individual better understand the dangers associated with operating a motor vehicle while under the influence of chemicals.

Short-Term Outpatient Programs

These programs are usually time limited and are aimed at helping those people with a mild to moderate SUD achieve abstinence. Short-term outpatient programs utilize a blend of individual and group therapy formats, with the client being seen one to two times a week. In addition, participants might be expected to attend at least one self-help group meeting a week, are assigned material to read before the next individual or group session, and are expected to meet with their case manager at least once a week for between 1 and 2 months. Surprisingly, such programs have not been found to be effective for clients who lack an extensive substance abuse problem, although the reason for this is not clear. One possibility is that the clients are unwilling to accept the severity of their SUD and are thus dismissive of treatment efforts.

Intensive Short-Term Outpatient Programs

These programs are called by a variety of names, including "partial hospitalization," "evening treatment," or "day treatment" programs (Work Group on

---

[1]Assigned readings of specified material to assist in the rehabilitation process.

[2]Discussed in Chapter 33.

[3]Which is short for "driving while under the influence of mood altering chemicals." In some states this is called an "OWI," or "operating a motor vehicle while under the influence of chemicals."

[4]One fact that many people do not understand is that it is possible to be charged with driving while under the influence (DWI) while taking prescribed medications if those chemicals are mood-altering compounds.

Substance Use Disorders, 2007). These programs might serve either as a primary treatment intervention for the client or as a step-down level of treatment for patients who have completed a residential treatment program (R. D. Weiss et al., 2008; Work Group on Substance Use Disorders, 2007). Clients are usually seen four to five times a week. Treatment is carried out through a blend of individual and group therapy formats, and such programs last for up to 6 months. Ancillary services such as family or marital counseling are utilized as necessary, and clients are expected to participate in a community support group[5] meeting at least once a week.

Intensive Long-Term Outpatient Treatment

These programs are usually open-ended and are designed for individuals whose SUD has been assessed to be moderate to severe in intensity. Individuals referred to these programs have usually been unable to achieve lasting abstinence either on their own or after less intensive treatment(s) have been utilized. Clients are seen for a blend of individual and group therapy sessions 3–5 days or nights a week for between 12 and 18 months. Ancillary services such as vocational counseling are utilized as needed, and the client is expected to attend at least one community support group meeting a week. Surprisingly, such programs have been found to be less effective than short-term rehabilitation programs (D. S. Shepard, Larson, & Hoffmann, 1999).

Advantages of Outpatient Rehabilitation

Outpatient treatment programs are quite popular. There are a number of reasons for such popularity, not the least of which is that they are far less expensive than residential treatment programs. It has been estimated that an outpatient treatment program costs between $77 and $93 per week (Belenko et al., 2005). Unfortunately, it has been found that although residential treatment programs are far more expensive than outpatient treatment, because of insurance company copay requirements it is possible that residential treatment will cost the individual less than participation in an outpatient treatment facility. Indeed, depending on the provisions in the individual's health insurance policy, it is possible that the insurance company will not reimburse the client for participation in outpatient treatment.[6]

Outpatient treatment programs avoid the need to remove individuals from their daily environment, which allows full participation in normal family life, continued employment, and so on. This avoids the need for a reorientation period at the end of treatment, often seen after a client completes a residential treatment program. Further, such programs offer some degree of flexibility in terms of allowing alterations to accommodate the client's work schedule or family emergencies, as needed. A mixed blessing is that outpatient rehabilitation programs do not remove individuals from their environment, forcing them to confront drug use cues within the context where such cues trigger alcohol or drug use. This might allow clients to practice recovery skills learned while in treatment while still living in their home, which can result in their achieving a sense of mystery over their environment. This might also result in their relapse.

Disadvantages of Outpatient Treatment Programs

The review of outpatient treatment programs is not to suggest that such programs are a panacea, nor are they the ultimate solution to the problem of individual substance abuse or addiction. It has been found that "graduates" of outpatient treatment programs are as likely to relapse as are those who successfully complete a residential treatment program. This is not to imply that these programs are equally effective as residential treatment, as such programs tend to work with a different kind of client than do residential facilities. This fact makes comparison between the two types of programs difficult.

Another disadvantage of outpatient treatment is that such programs do not offer the same degree of structure and support inherent in a residential treatment setting. Family members might be reluctant to report substance use relapses or inappropriate behaviors on the part of the client. This indicates that such programs are of limited applicability for clients who require a great degree of support during the earliest stages of recovery. Clients are often left in the position of having to endure strong "craving" for chemicals in the very environment in which they were abusing them.

---

[5]There was a time when Alcoholics Anonymous (AA) or Narcotics Anonymous (NA) were the only community support groups available to the recovering person. In the past decade, there have been a number of faith-based and nontraditional community support groups founded, providing some alternatives to either AA or NA. These groups will be discussed in Chapter 35.

[6]The passage of insurance "parity" for mental health services, passed in 2005, may require that insurance companies reimburse the client for treatment expenses for outpatient treatment. The issue is not clear at this time.

Exposure to drug use cues can contribute to the high relapse rate seen in graduates of such programs. If clients do relapse, they will need to be reassessed to determine the proper level of treatment. These problem areas are sufficient to suggest that outpatient treatment is not the ultimate answer to substance use disorders.

Introduction to Residential Treatment Programs

Definition of Inpatient Treatment

Surprisingly, there is no standard definition of inpatient (or, as it is often called, "residential") treatment (R. D. Weiss et al., 2008). In general, residential treatment programs provide a 24-hour treatment milieu. But staffing levels vary from one program to the next, and some residential treatment programs refer patients with medical comorbidities to other facilities whereas other programs treat such medical problems in-house (R. D. Weiss et al., 2008). However, residential treatment programs share the characteristic of offering a more intensive approach than outpatient treatment programs (Work Group on Substance Use Disorders, 2007). Such programs thus usually work with the resistant client, suicidal or homicidal clients,[7] or clients who are unable to abstain in the less restrictive outpatient treatment programs (Work Group on Substance Use Disorders, 2007).

Many residential treatment programs have a strong 12-step group orientation, with clients being expected to attend multiple 12-step meetings during the week. They utilize a large number of group therapy meetings within each week, supplemented by individual therapy sessions with specialized treatment professionals as indicated. The client will meet with the case manager at least once a week, and usually more often than this as treatment issues are identified. Barriers to recovery are identified, including an assessment of the client's support system, client's level of motivation, and past treatment history.

Clients who are referred to a residential treatment program are:

> [Those who] do not meet clinical criteria for [medical] hospitalization, but whose lives and social interactions have come to focus exclusively on substance use and who ... lack sufficient motivation and/or substance free social supports to remain abstinent

in an ambulatory setting. (Work Group on Substance Use Disorders, 2007)

The decision to utilize inpatient treatment as opposed to an outpatient treatment program is based on the assessed need for a specific level of care.[8] Such programs might be offered by a general hospital, a freestanding facility, or in a therapeutic community setting. We will look at many of the residential treatment formats in the sections that follow.

"Detox" Programs

"Detoxification" ("detox") programs are *not* a form of treatment, and many people confuse the two. Although designed to assist clients in reducing their daily drug use levels until they are abstinent while minimizing the risk of medical complications, detoxification programs suffer significant dropout rates. Clients who begin a "detox" program in response to external motivation or to reduce their daily drug requirement to a level that they can more easily afford are more likely to drop out of a "detox" program than are those who are highly motivated to quit the use of chemicals (Connors et al., 2001).

Detox programs both assist the client in discontinuing the use of a chemical(s) in a safe, controlled manner, and often make referrals to the appropriate rehabilitation program, usually a residential facility (R. M. Swift, 2005). If clients elect to enter treatment at the same hospital where they are going through "detox," it will be possible for them to begin to participate in rehabilitation program activities while still in the last stages of detoxification from alcohol or drugs.

Hospital-Based Residential Treatment

Hospital-based rehabilitation programs offer a range of services, including (but not limited to): medical stabilization for ongoing (often untreated) medical problems; group, individual, marital, and family therapy programs; as well as psycho-educational programs and social service support as needed (Work Group on Substance Use Disorders, 2007). Clients will also have assigned "homework" projects, and bibliotherapy[9] is encouraged. Although many of these programs utilized the "Minnesota Model,"[10] managed care initiatives[11] have made this less common as insurance companies

---

[7]This is not always true. Some residential programs lack the resources to help the suicidal or homicidal client and will refer clients with such problems to psychiatric treatment units if necessary.

[8]Discussed in Chapter 28.

[9]See Glossary.

[10]Discussed in the last chapter.

[11]Discussed in Chapter 34.

have demanded shorter stays for clients. There is usually a strong emphasis on 12-step group participation, and clients are expected to participate either in 12-step group meetings held at the hospital or are escorted to community-based 12-step group meetings.

There is no set duration for residential community treatment, although the goal is to help clients reach a point where they can abstain from alcohol or drugs with the support of less restrictive outpatient treatment programs. A second consideration is the length of time that the insurance company is willing to fund, and whether the client is willing to pay for additional residential treatment out-of-pocket. These topics will be discussed in the next chapter.

Therapeutic Communities

The therapeutic community (TC) concept originated in the 1960s as a self-help alternative to traditional treatment programs for drug addiction. The original TCs were marked by harsh ego-stripping confrontation techniques that included 24-hour "marathon" group sessions as well as a "hot seat" in the center of a group circle where a person was expected to sit while group members confronted him or her with perceived personality flaws. All staff positions were held by former residents, with minimal input from health or mental health professionals. Some TCs expected a lifetime commitment from the client, who was viewed as unable to live independently without substances and therefore must remain within the therapeutic community.

The TC movement has moved away from these early techniques to become a more generic term for a range of programs that include short-term residential, long-term residential, and day treatment forms of treatment. Some TCs also have made provisions to work with women who have children or patients with HIV/AIDS[12] (DeLeon, 2008).

However, all of these modifications of the original TC program concept retain the core concept that the SUDS reflect deviant behaviors that indicate an immature personality (DeLeon, 2008; Satel & Farabee, 2005). According to this theory, reflections of this immature personality might be seen in the mood disturbances, unrealistic thinking, educational, and social and moral deficits often seen in people addicted to drugs. In response to the arrested development of the addicted person, the TC attempts to bring about a global lifestyle change to help the individual live without the drugs of abuse (DeLeon, 2008). Unlike the original therapeutic communities, current TCs now prescreen applicants, excluding those people from admission who have a history of attempted suicide or homicide, attempted arson, or severe uncontrolled psychiatric disorders (DeLeon, 2008). Another reason that applicants might be excluded from admission is the belief that they can "do it on my own," as this attitude reflects an unwillingness to accept the need for treatment (DeLeon, 2008). A final exclusionary criterion is an unwillingness to make the commitment to remain in the entire program (DeLeon, 2008).

Therapeutic communities are usually freestanding[13] programs that, although initially are quite resistant to the use of 12-step community support groups, have started to integrate these self-help groups into the program (Ringwald, 2002). TCs utilize a highly structured daily program that usually starts at 7 a.m. and continues until 11 p.m. This structure and the belief that it is the *community* that is the agent of change or healing are thought to assist in the desired personality change. In a sense, the TC might be viewed as providing an extended family for the program participant. The TC program format has evolved to the point where it has been integrated into some penal institutions to work with convicted felons who have an SUD, and used with people who have addictions to multiple compounds (DeLeon, 2004).

Clients are viewed as passing through three different stages during treatment: (a) compliance, (b) conformity, and (c) making a personal commitment for change (Satel & Farabee, 2005). To assist the individual in moving through these stages, the TC retains a strong emphasis on self-examination as well as public confession of past misbehavior in both group and individual counseling sessions. More advanced clients are presented as role models for initiates, and although there are a small number of professional staff in most modern TCs, it is the process of "supportive confrontation" (DeLeon, 2008, p. 465) from other residents that is viewed as the main vehicle of personality change. Participants are expected to carry out assigned work projects, first within the TC itself and later in the outside community, which is considered a privilege that program participants earn through their progress in the TC program.

---

[12]Discussed in Chapter 36.

[13]Is not associated with a hospital program and is funded either through donations or monies earned by participants who work in various capacities in the community.

DeLeon (2008) also suggested a three-stage model for long-term TC programs: (a) orientation/introduction, (b) primary treatment, and (c) reentry. During the first phase, orientation/introduction, which lasts for approximately the first 60 days, the person is confronted with the tasks of being oriented and assimilated into the program, while staff continue to assess the individual to determine whether participation in the TC is appropriate. The second stage, primary treatment, lasts from the 2nd until the 12th month, during which time the individual learns to become more autonomous, gets more desirable job assignments within the TC, and begins to teach others. The final stage, reentry, lasts from the 13th until the 24th month and focuses on helping the individual strengthen skills for maintaining abstinence, autonomous decision making skills, and vocational skills. During this phase the individual might find a job outside of the TC to both earn a salary and begin the transition to independent living.

Some components of the TC program include *encounter groups*, which are peer led, meet three times weekly, and last approximately 2 hours each. *Tutorial* sessions include training and educational experiences for the clients. Individual therapy sessions are also held, and a small minority of TCs still hold *encounter groups*, which are extended groups aimed at helping individuals resolve life experiences (a history of sexual or physical abuse, for example) that are thought to have contributed to the individual's substance abuse (DeLeon, 2008). Unannounced urine toxicology testing is also carried out on a random basis, with decisions concerning the retention of the client, in-house job assignments, or whether to allow the client to progress from one level to the next being made in part on the basis of the results of these tests (DeLeon, 2008).

Whereas the original TCs would accept only self-referrals to the program, at this time approximately two-thirds of program participants are under the supervision of probation or parole agents (Hiller, Knight, Rao, & Simpson, 2002). This element of legal coercion is viewed as providing an additional incentive for individuals to remain in the TC until they have started to internalize the recovery philosophy and lifestyle (Satel & Farabee, 2005). Unfortunately, both self-referred and legally mandated clients often fail to successfully complete the treatment program, and such programs suffer from significant dropout rates (Satel & Farabee, 2005; Work Group on Substance Use Disorders, 2007). DeLeon (2004) suggested that 30–40% of those admitted to a TC will drop out of treatment in the first 30 days, and that only 10–15% will complete the typical 2-year program. Many clients are asked to leave the TC because of accumulated rules infractions.

Therapeutic communities are not without their detractors. Over the years lawsuits have been brought against various TCs alleging physical or emotional harm to the residents. Therapeutic communities are also viewed with suspicion by many who were trained in the more traditional substance abuse rehabilitation model. In spite of these facts, proponents of TCs point to studies that suggest that more than 90% of those who complete the program remain drug free in the first year after discharge, and that 5 years after completion of the TC program 70% percent will still be abstinent.

However, this is an excellent example of how statistics can often be misleading. Retention is a problem for therapeutic communities, just as it is for every other form of substance abuse rehabilitation. Between 30 and 40% of new residents drop out of the program in the first 30 days and are thus lost to follow-up (DeLeon, 2008). Such premature termination carries with it a risk of a relapse back to active substance use. Just 25% of those who drop out of the program in less than a year were found to be drug free at the end of a 2-year follow-up period, and 50% of those who drop out of treatment after remaining in the TC for a year were found to have relapsed in the first 2 years after they left the program (DeLeon, 2004). Although proponents of the therapeutic community concept point out that 90% of program graduates might remain substance free for the first year following graduation, only 10–15% of those who begin the program actually graduate (DeLeon, 2004). Only 10 of every 100 patients originally admitted are substance free at the end of the first 5 years following graduation. These figures suggest that even TC graduates do relapse on occasion. The picture for those who drop out of the TC is even more bleak, with the rate of relapse being inversely related to the length of time that the individual was in the TC. Those persons with the shortest stay at the TC were the most likely to relapse, etc.

One follow-up study suggested that 3 years following successful completion from a TC, half of those graduates who were still alive were either working full-time or in a training program to prepare them to begin full-time work (Berg, 2003). This would suggest that the therapeutic community concept is exceptionally useful in treating the substance abuser. However, detractors of the TC program movement point out that as these figures suggest, the TC movement is not a panacea for the treatment of SUDs.

Is There a Legitimate Need for Inpatient Treatment?

Unfortunately, the debate over whether inpatient or outpatient rehabilitation programs are most effective is often fueled by financial or political considerations, not by scientific research (R. D. Weiss et al., 2008). Some critics of residential treatment point to the Project MATCH Research Group findings in the mid-1990s, which concluded that inpatient treatment is not automatically superior to less intensive treatment methods. The purpose of Project MATCH was to isolate patient characteristics that might predict a better outcome in an outpatient or an inpatient treatment setting, but failed to accomplish this goal (Rychtarik et al., 2000). Indeed, research has failed to demonstrate a clear advantage of inpatient treatment over outpatient treatment, or the reverse (Mee-Lee & Gastfriend, 2008).

Although clear advantages over outpatient treatment have not been demonstrated by research studies, it has not been recommended that inpatient treatment programs be abolished. For example, although most patients start out with outpatient treatment, three-quarters of patients with an AUD eventually require a residential treatment program. Clients with other forms of SUDs might benefit more from residential treatment because of the intensity of their addiction. In both cases, one factor that appears to predict whether a given inpatient rehabilitation program will be effective is the client's willingness to participate in follow-up or aftercare programs. There is strong evidence suggesting that over time the benefits of residential treatment accrue not only for alcohol-dependent people, but also for people with other SUDs. Further, there is evidence of a "threshold effect," with those people who remain in residential treatment for longer than 14 days being more likely to benefit from residential treatment than those who remain in residential treatment for a shorter period than 14 days.

Aftercare Programs

Health care professionals view the SUDs as chronic, relapsing disorders, and the *continuing-care* or *aftercare* program was introduced as an aid to abstinence. Such programs have been found to significantly reduce client relapses and increase total days of abstinence (Ritsher et al., 2000; G. R. Smith et al., 2006). The focus

of such groups should be on such issues as (a) maintenance of gains made in treatment and (b) helping to prevent a relapse back to active substance abuse. Such groups provide the client with a safe environment in which to discuss "urges" to use chemicals again, thoughts triggered by environmental stimuli, and "using" dreams, all of which appear to contribute to relapse, and to receive encouragement from other group members in their efforts to abstain.

As part of the last goal, irrational client beliefs (for example, "I can't cope without a drink!") should be identified and addressed, thus reducing the possibility of a relapse. Clients receiving pharmacological support for their efforts to abstain (discussed in Chapter 33) should be encouraged to take their medications as prescribed as well. Clients who report in group that they have not renewed their prescription for disulfiram[14] might be telegraphing an intention to return to active alcohol use, and group members should discuss this with the wayward individual. Client behaviors that might contribute to relapse, such as maintaining a supply of alcohol in one's home ("but it's just for friends when they come to visit!") or frequenting a bar ("but everybody knows that the bars have the best pool tables!"[15]) or the places where one used to go to obtain chemicals, need to be identified and addressed.

Partial Hospitalization Options

The *partial hospitalization* option offers several advantages over traditional residential treatment programs, while addressing the costs of inpatient treatment. Such programs allow the client to live at home but to report to the residential treatment center during the day. The advantage of partial hospitalization is that it allows for a greater intensity of treatment than is possible through an outpatient treatment, while still avoiding the need for expensive residential treatment programs. It also allows the client to start to rebuild strained familial relationships while still having the benefit of the intensive support of the day hospitalization staff. For partial hospitalization programs to be effective, the client should have a stable, supportive home environment. If the client's spouse or another family member should also have an SUD, or a serious, untreated psychiatric problem, then partial-day hospitalization is not an option. If the home environment is

---

[14]See Chapter 33.

[15]Although nobody has ever explained how having a 350-pound intoxicated person violently vomit on the felt on the pool table has ever helped the play on that specific table.

indeed supportive, then partial-day hospitalization may be a viable option for a recovery program.

The goal of the aftercare program is to provide support during the client's transition from intensive treatment to self-directed recovery. Such programs are usually conducted on an outpatient basis and include individual and sometimes group therapy sessions as well as specialized adjunctive programs such as a continuation of marital therapy started while the patient was in a more intensive form of treatment.

Aftercare programs are part of the continuum treatment services (Work Group on Substance Use Disorders, 2007). These programs are often automatically offered to clients following treatment, but recent research evidence suggests that they should not be mandatory for people following discharge from treatment. Berg (2003) identified a subgroup of former drug abusers who were (a) stable at the time of follow-up, but who (b) refused to participate in aftercare programs because they did not wish to reawaken memories of their behavior while actively abusing drugs. For this subgroup of patients, participation in an aftercare program, especially if it includes group therapy, might be counterproductive. Thus careful screening of each client before making a referral to an aftercare program is necessary to determine which individuals would and would not benefit from an aftercare program.

Halfway Houses

The halfway house concept emerged in the 1950s, providing an intermediate step between inpatient treatment and independent living. If the client should lack a stable support system, a halfway house might bridge the gap between residential and independent living. Halfway houses share several characteristics: (a) small population (less than 25 residents), (b) short patient stay (less than a few months), (c) emphasis on the use of community support groups, (d) minimal rules, (e) a small number of professional staff members, and (f) expectation of total abstinence from alcohol or drugs of abuse. Clients are also expected to work and are assigned tasks within the halfway house (cleaning the dishes, housekeeping activities, and so on).

There is mixed evidence about the effectiveness of halfway houses. This might reflect the different treatment philosophies of different halfway houses. Some facilities place strong emphasis on continued abstinence, whereas others make little or no attempt to continue the treatment process. However, because research has repeatedly demonstrated that the longer that a person remains involved in treatment activities and community-based support groups, the less chance they have of relapsing. This would indirectly support the need for halfway houses (R. H. Moos, Moos, & Andrassy, 1999).

The Advantages of Inpatient Treatment

It is a mistake to compare those who enter an outpatient substance abuse rehabilitation program with those who are referred to a residential treatment program. These are two distinct subgroups of substance abusers. People referred to a residential program are assessed as needing a *more comprehensive level of care* than those people who might be referred to an outpatient treatment. R. D. Weiss et al. (2008) observed that the combination of detoxification and residential treatment programs offers the additional advantage of taking people who support their addiction through violent crime off the streets. Hopefully, once their addiction has been addressed, the motivation to engage in violent behavior will also be minimized, if not eliminated.

Residential treatment programs also offer the advantage of allowing intensive focus on environmental issues that contributed to the maintenance of the substance use disorder. Client might be taught "refusal skills" or learn alternative behaviors that will help them abstain from further substance abuse while building a substance-free support system. For example, research has shown that people with an SUD tend to live alone or lack close interpersonal supports. The inpatient treatment "community" can function as a pseudo-family, guiding the person in acquiring those skills necessary to establish close, non-substance-centered interpersonal supports.

Further, people referred to residential treatment programs tend to have more medical problems than those referred to outpatient treatment. Inpatient programs allow for proper treatment of these medical problems (untreated hypertension, or diabetes, for example). Malnutrition is a common problem among substance abusers, and inpatient residential treatment programs allow medical professionals to address the long-term effects of malnutrition. Further, the level of staff control over the client's environment helps to discourage continued substance use. A visitor who is a known drug dealer, for example, not only might be refused admission to the treatment facility, but also might be informed that the police will be called should he or she attempt to "visit" former customers again.

If a client should attempt to use alcohol or drugs while in treatment, staff members in a residential facility are more likely to detect this than are those people who work in an outpatient treatment program. Staff members are able to establish a routine of individual and group therapy sessions, combined with spiritual counseling, vocational counseling, and ancillary services, to counteract the chaotic lifestyle often seen in substance abusers. This external structure may be internalized by recovering substance abusers, providing some degree of structure once they leave treatment and begin to live on their own. Programs that require participation in community support groups might expose a client to these external support groups for the first time in the person's life, and serve as a bridge between the residential treatment program and the client's use of such community supports after discharge.

Disadvantages of Residential Treatment

First, there is mixed evidence about the effectiveness of residential treatment (R. D. Weiss et al., 2008). Some residential treatment programs become a "revolving door," admitting and discharging the same client(s) time after time. Also, residential treatment is quite expensive, with estimated average costs of $525–$792 per week not being uncommon (Belenko et al., 2005). It is disruptive to people's established life routine to have to enter residential treatment, and this will interfere with their ability to go to work and earn a living while they are in treatment (Polydorou & Kleber, 2008). Another disadvantage of residential treatment is that patients are usually not stratified as to intensity of need, with the result being that more severely disturbed individuals are often housed with those people whose requirements are less intense (Larimer & Kilmer, 2000). Residential treatment has often been compared to a concentration camp, but given the client's level of dysfunction and substance-induced harm, this comparison is hardly fair. Finally, residential rehabilitation programs may be geographically isolated, preventing appropriate contact between clients and their family.

Chapter Summary

There is significant evidence that inpatient or residential treatment is not *always* required to help people learn how to abstain from further substance abuse. A significant percentage of those people with an SUD come to terms with that disorder without professional intervention or assistance. People who do require assistance often encounter the problem that most therapists or rehabilitation programs offer only one philosophical

model to clients, a process that might not meet the client's needs (Mee-Lee & Gastfriend, 2008).

Treatment itself might be carried out on either an inpatient or outpatient basis. Outpatient treatment programs offer an alternative to residential treatment, especially for individuals who have a strong social support system and for whom there is no coexisting psychiatric or medical illness that might complicate the individual's treatment. An advantage of outpatient treatment programs is that individuals can remain in their home environment and possibly even continue to work on a full-time basis depending on when the rehabilitation program activities are carried out. This avoids the need for a reorientation program following residential treatment.

Outpatient treatment programs also offer the advantage of long-term therapeutic support, an option that is not always possible with a short-term residential rehabilitation program. Such therapeutic supports include individual and group therapies, ancillary services such as vocational counseling, spiritual counseling, urine toxicology testing to detect continued substance use, and so forth. Outpatient treatment appears to be about as effective as residential treatment programs, but usually works with people who have not abused chemicals for as long those referred to residential facilities. However, outpatient treatment programs do suffer from high dropout rates, and a significant number of those people who are initially treated in an outpatient facility eventually require residential treatment.

Residential treatment facilities, in turn, offer advantages and disadvantages over outpatient treatment programs. Residential treatment is viewed by many as a drastic step, yet for many people this is necessary if they are ever to regain control over their life. The inpatient rehabilitation program offers a depth of support beyond that which might be achieved in an outpatient setting. Such services, including referrals for ancillary treatment as indicated, are often the individual's only realistic hope for recovery from SUDs. Although questions have been raised concerning the need for residential treatment, these programs do seem to offer a glimmer of hope for those whose SUD is deeply entrenched. Further, evidence suggests that the length of time that the individual remains involved in treatment or aftercare counseling increases the odds of achieving lasting sobriety, which is the goal of both inpatient and outpatient treatment.

CHAPTER 31

The Treatment of Substance Use Disorders

Introduction

There are many misperceptions about substance abuse treatment and its effectiveness. For example, the public often views "treatment" as if it were a single entity rather than a generic term for a variety of rehabilitation formats and intensities of therapy (Mee-Lee & Gastfriend, 2008). Further, the public often views treatment as having a fixed duration rather than as a process in which the patient's progress and needs help to determine the duration and focus of the rehabilitation effort (Mee-Lee & Gastfriend, 2008). Finally, many people seem surprised at the whole concept of an aftercare[1] program, believing that once the intensive portion of treatment is finished, the entire rehabilitation program is at an end.

Because of these misperceptions, the question of whether rehabilitation is effective or not has sparked fierce debate in the health care community. Admittedly treatment for the SUDs is not universally effective. The same might be said for surgical interventions for heart disease or cancer. The SUDs present the same clinical picture as other chronic, relapsing disorders similar to diabetes, hypertension, or multiple sclerosis (McLellan, 2001). When seen in this light, however, arguments that rehabilitation is not effective break down in the face of studies that have found that for every dollar invested in treatment, the community saves from $4 to $12 (Breithaupt, 2001; Dobbs, 2007; Mee-Lee, 2002), to possibly as much as $50 (Garrett, 2000).[2] For example, in the late 1990s the state of California conducted a research study that found that an investment of $209 million for substance abuse rehabilitation resulted in a savings of $209 *billion* in reduced criminal activity and health care costs (Craig, 2004). It has been found that alcohol-dependent people require *10 times* the health care expenditure as the nonalcoholic, whereas members of their families require five times the health care expenditure as families of

---

[1]Discussed in this chapter.

[2]These various estimates reflect, in part, different variables included from study to study. For example, one study might include long-term reductions in health care costs that another study does not include in its estimates of the savings that result from treatment.

nondrinkers (McLellan, 2001). Still the debate over whether rehabilitation is effective rages on.

It has been suggested that treatment programs are unlikely to resolve the problem of drug abuse in the United States (Reuter & Pollack, 2006). This conclusion is supported by the observation that rehabilitation formats currently in use were not guided by scientific guidance seeking to identify and apply the most effective forms of treatment (Miller & Brown, 1997). Many of the treatment methods that are *least* effective appear to be the most deeply entrenched in the rehabilitation system (W. R. Miller & Brown, 1997). For example, using alcohol as the prototypical addiction, it has been suggested that "most alcoholics who become abstinent do so *in spite of* treatment, not because of it" (Tomb, 2008, p. 151). Yet legal sanctions, often suggested as an alternative to treatment, also do not appear to be the answer.[3] It is within this debate that efforts at rehabilitation are attempted. In this chapter, the benefits, advantages, and disadvantages of different forms of substance abuse treatment will be discussed.

Characteristics of the Substance Abuse Rehabilitation Professional

It is through the therapeutic relationship that healing takes place. Thus the therapeutic relationship is of critical importance to the healing process, and to effectively work with clients with SUDs, it has been suggested that the rehabilitation professional have certain characteristics. For example, individuals who are dealing with their own substance use or serious psychological issues of their own should be discouraged from actively working with clients in treatment, at least until they have resolved their own problems. This makes sense: If counselors are preoccupied with personal problems, they will be unable to help clients advance in terms of their own personal growth.

The therapist who works with individuals with SUDs must "possess many characteristics, some of which include genuineness, empathy, modeling of the desired behaviors, and an appropriately humorous outlook" (Shea, 2006, p. 13). Further, the therapist should be adept at *guiding* the client toward recovery rather than telling them what to do. Most people have the resources to solve their own problems, if they are assisted in finding that solution (Shea, 2006). Thus the

therapist's job is to assist and guide, not to demand or order clients about in their search for the answer(s). These skills are especially important during the early stages of treatment, when the client's commitment toward a major life change is still tentative and weak (D. D. Simpson, 2004).

It must be understood that clients who enter treatment do so with different levels of motivation and problem severity (D. D. Simpson, 2004). In many cases, clients who enter a rehabilitation program are admitting that they are unable to change their own lives, although as was discussed in the last chapter many individuals who enter treatment do so under external motivation. Therapists with strong interpersonal skills would be better equipped to help the client change. Clients' acceptance of the therapist's efforts to assess them in making this change is one of the most essential characteristics of a successful therapeutic relationship. These relationships are based on mutual trust and openness, as well as the client's ability to accept external help. Miller (2003) identified several factors that seem to facilitate or inhibit recovery from substance use disorders (Table 31-1).

One common misperception of substance abuse professionals is that they are "bleeding hearts" who will excuse virtually any misdeed by clients on the grounds that they have a SUD. Indeed, may therapists in the early stages of their careers attempt to "buy" client approval through such permissiveness. It is important to keep in mind the fact that *caring for clients*

---

[3]Discussed in Chapter 37.

TABLE 31.1 FACTORS THAT FACILITATE OR INHIBIT RECOVERY FROM SUDS

FACTORS THAT FACILITATE CHANGE	FACTORS THAT INHIBIT CHANGE
Empowerment	Disempowerment
Active interest in client as a person	Hostility, disinterest
Empathy	Confrontation
Making client feel need for change	Making client feel that she or he is not responsible for change
Advice on how to change	Ordering client to change
Involving client in the change process	Giving client a passive role
Environment supportive of recovery	Environment does not support recovery

does not mean protecting them from the natural consequences of their behavior! It is through these consequences that the client will come to see the need for change.

Confrontation and Other Techniques

In the latter half of the 20th century, clinical theory, supported by anecdotal evidence, made clinicians believe that heavy confrontation was necessary for the rehabilitation process to begin (W. R. Miller & White, 2007). This has proven to be a therapeutic myth that is enshrined in rehabilitation-training programs. Unfortunately, there is little evidence that such confrontation helps the client to begin or make behavioral change (W. R. Miller & White, 2007; W. R. Miller & Rollnick, 2002). Research has shown that as the level of confrontation increases, so does the level of client resistance. This makes sense, because one factor that predicts successful treatment is the client's satisfaction with the rehabilitation process (Hser, Evans, Huang, & Anglin, 2004). However, there is also a danger that the health care professional will become too passive, failing to focus on the problems that the client has encountered (or possibly will encounter) if they continue to abuse chemicals (Washton & Zweben, 2006).

In contrast to confrontation, *empathy* for the client's struggle has been found to be more appropriate. Where confrontation is necessary, it should be infused with caring and concern for the client with a focus on the problems encountered or anticipated rather than on the individual (Ramsay & Newman, 2000). The client should not be "shamed" into conformity, but should be allowed to develop the skills necessary to abstain from substance abuse by utilizing the resources at hand. This is a slow process, to be sure, but it also empowers clients to then learn that they have the resources necessary to change and how to apply these resources. The

therapist serves as a guide and confidant, helping the client explore behavioral alternatives while achieving a sense of self-efficacy. Such a therapeutic style places emphasis on the client's ability to achieve and responsibility for personal change, not heavy confrontation. The therapist advises, helps the client develop behavioral alternatives, and develop a sense of self-efficacy. In this manner, it is hoped that the therapist can guide the client to a substance free lifestyle.

The Minnesota Model of Substance Abuse Treatment

George Vaillant (2000) identified four factors that were common to all substance abuse rehabilitation programs: (a) compulsory supervision, (b) introduction of and use of competing behavior to replace the SUD, (c) new love relationships (in the sense of a commitment to recovery rather than substance use), and (d) increased spirituality and religiosity. The "Minnesota model" of substance abuse treatment met all four of these criteria, and dominated the therapeutic scene for the last half of the 20th century. It still remains a strong influence on both inpatient and outpatient rehabilitation programs (Foote, 2006; Ringwald, 2002).

The Minnesota model was developed in the 1950s by Dr. Daniel Anderson. In order to earn money to finish his college program of study, Dr. Anderson worked as an attendant at the now-defunct Willmar State Hospital, in Willmar, Minnesota. Following graduation, Dr. Anderson returned there to work as a recreational therapist. He was assigned to work with the alcoholics, which was considered the least desirable position at the time. Anderson was himself influenced by the work of Mr. Ralph Rossen, who was to later become the Minnesota State Commissioner of Health. At the same time, the growing influence of Alcoholics

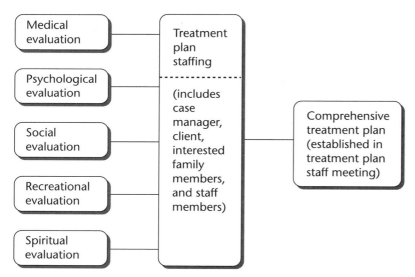

FIGURE 31-1 Flowchart of the Evolution of a Treatment Plan

Anonymous was used by Dr. Anderson and a staff psychologist at the state hospital by the name of Dr. Jean Rossi as a means of understanding and working with the alcohol-dependent person. They were supported in this new approach by the medical director of the hospital, Dr. Nelson Bradley (Larson, 1982).

These individuals joined together in an effort to better understand and treat the alcohol-dependent patients sent to the state hospital. Each person represented a different profession and thus contributed a different perspective about the client's needs, strengths, areas of weakness, and the issues that needed to be addressed in order to prepare the individual for a life without alcohol. A spiritual advisor by the name of Rev. John Keller was also assigned to the treatment team. With his arrival, the staff had "knowledge of medicine, psychology, AA, and theology together under one roof to develop a new and innovative treatment program" (Larson, 1982, p. 35).

This new treatment model, the Minnesota Model, was developed for work with alcohol-dependent people. It has since been applied to the treatment of all forms of substance abuse. The Minnesota model was centered around the *treatment team* approach, in which the skills of a substance abuse rehabilitation counselor, psychologist, physicians, nurses, recreational therapists, and clergy were brought together to work with the client. Each professional was allowed to make recommendations for the areas to focus on, and the document that emerges from this process was identified as the *treatment plan*. Other interested parties such as family members, probation/parole officers, and the client were also

invited to participate in the process of building a treatment plan. The treatment team meeting was chaired by the individual who was ultimately responsible for the execution of the treatment plan, and who is thus identified as the patient's case manager.

The treatment plan that emerged was multimodal, offering a wide variety of individualized goals and treatment recommendations. It identified specific problem areas that needed to be addressed and behavioral measurements by which each goal could be assessed. A target date for completion of that goal was also identified. The treatment plan itself will be discussed in more detail later in this chapter, but a flow chart of the treatment plan process might look like that in Figure 31-1.

One strength of the Minnesota model of rehabilitation was in its redundancy and the multiprofessional treatment team. The chemical dependency counselor did not need to be a "jack of all trades, master of none," but could make referrals to other members of the treatment team in response to the client's shifting needs. This feature helped to make the Minnesota Model one of the treatment program models for more than 50 years, although under managed care initiatives it has been modified or replaced by other treatment formats.

Reaction to the Minnesota Model

The Minnesota model has not met with universal approval or acceptance. One early challenge was based on the fact that although it was designed for working with alcohol-dependent people, it was rapidly applied for use with individuals with addictions to other compounds as well. There has been little research into whether the Minnesota model is equally effective with these other forms of drug addiction, but it is still often applied in this capacity in spite of the fact that researchers such as McPherson, Yudko, Afsarifad et al. (2009) have found that it has been ineffective in the treatment of CNS stimulant addiction.

The Minnesota model draws heavily on the principles of Alcoholics Anonymous (AA),[4] and participation in AA is required as part of the program. Yet AA is not in itself a form of treatment, and there is no clear evidence that AA is effective for individuals who were coerced into treatment. Surprisingly, even in cases where there is a wide discrepancy between the spiritual orientation of the rehabilitation program and the individual's own spiritual beliefs, there was no negative influence on the client's self-reported desire to drink (Sterling et al., 2006). Such discrepancies did not appear to increase premature termination from treatment, nor did it appear to slow progress in the rehabilitation process, according to Sterling et al. Thus the apparent contradiction in the Minnesota model in that participants are required to join an organization centered on spiritual growth does not appear to be a major issue at this time.

Another challenge to the Minnesota model was the arbitrary decision that treatment should last 28 days. There was little evidence to support the need for a 28-day treatment program, although it did become something of an industry standard for a number of years. Indeed, this 28-day treatment stay once served as a guide for insurance company reimbursement policies. This resulted in a cycle in which clients were admitted to a 28-day treatment program not based on their needs, but because the insurance companies would pay for a treatment stay of just 28 days!

In spite of the enthusiasm with which it was received, there has been little evidence to suggest that the Minnesota model of treatment is effective (R. K. Hester & Squires, 2004; McCrady, 2001). Fortunately, it has become almost extinct, except in a few private treatment centers where the client is able to "self-pay" for extended substance abuse treatment (Monti et al., 2002).

Other Treatment Formats for Substance Use Disorders

In the years since the Minnesota model was introduced, and especially since the managed care initiatives of the 1990s, health care professionals have explored a number of alternative treatment formats to allow them to work with individuals with SUDs that do not involve inpatient rehabilitation programs. In the following section we will briefly examine some of the more common treatment models that have emerged in the last four decades.

Detoxification

Technically, the term *detoxification* refers to the process of removing any toxin from the body. A second, related definition refers to the medical management of a person's withdrawal from alcohol or drugs (Haack, 1998). Research has shown that the majority of those individuals who go through a "detox" program for their SUD will relapse without further treatment (Craig, 2004). Thus "detox" is not considered a form of treatment itself, but a prelude to the rehabilitation process (Gerada, 2005; Leshner, 2001a, 2001b: McPherson Yudko, Afsarifadet al., 2009; Tinsley et al., 1998).

The goal of the detoxification process is to offer the individual a safe, humane withdrawal from alcohol or illicit drugs. The patient's safety is assured, to the degree that this is possible, by having a physician who is both trained and experienced in this process supervise the detoxification process. Under the physician's supervision the detoxification process will be carried out either on an outpatient basis if possible or on an inpatient basis if necessary.

Although detoxification from alcohol has traditionally been carried out in a hospital setting, in reality only 10–15% of alcohol-dependent people will require hospitalization for "detox" (Anton; 2005; Blondell, 2005). Patients who have a serious physical or psychiatric illness, have been unable to successfully complete an outpatient detoxification program in the past, have a history of alcohol withdrawal seizures, or are geographically isolated are among those who should be referred to an inpatient detoxification program (Anton, 2005). With careful screening, it is possible to identify those individuals who might qualify for an outpatient detoxification program, thus saving both the client and the insurance company significant amounts of money (Blondell, 2005).

Outpatient detoxification from alcohol is called "ambulatory detoxification" or "social detoxification" (Blondell, 2005). To see whether a given individual qualifies for such a program, the individual must be evaluated by a physician, nurse practitioner, or other trained professional. Then the patient is started on a detoxification program immediately. A nurse will stop by the patient's home once or twice a day to monitor

---

[4]Discussed in Chapter 35.

the patient's blood pressure, check to ensure that the patient has abstained from further alcohol use, and monitor the patient's health status as necessary. If the patient should relapse, a referral to an inpatient detoxification center or hospital would be necessary (Anton, 2005).

The individual's drug abuse history plays an important role in whether that person is referred to an inpatient or outpatient detoxification program. Some of the drugs of abuse, such as the barbiturates or benzodiazepines, can cause severe, life-threatening problems during detoxification. In some cases, patients can be monitored at home by another responsible adult, and placed on a gradual "taper"[5] regimen to allow them to safely reduce and eventually stop their abuse of these compounds. If the patient's environment does not allow for such an outpatient detoxification program, or if the patient's SUD should be of sufficient intensity, then a referral to an inpatient detoxification program is automatically made. Urine toxicology testing is automatically carried out both to ensure that the patient is taking recommended medications and to rule out the abuse of compounds that require inpatient detoxification (Blondell, 2005). In spite of strident cries from individuals who are opiate-dependent, withdrawal from these compounds is rarely life threatening,[6] but because of the tendency for such patients to relapse, inpatient "detox" is usually more successful than outpatient detoxification for this class of medications.

Many rehabilitation professionals believe that "detox" programs should function as a "funnel" for guiding patients into a treatment program. When detoxification is carried out in a freestanding clinic (as opposed to a hospital setting), many patients fail to go on to enter rehabilitation (W. R. Miller & Rollnick, 2002). It is possible that a proportion of these individuals do seek treatment either elsewhere or at a different time, but there has been no research into this possibility. To complicate matters, the charge has been made that detoxification centers housed in a hospital or rehabilitation center setting function as little more than recruitment centers for that treatment program. To avoid this problem, staff should inform patients of their treatment options, including the possible transfer to another rehabilitation program, and make sure that this is documented in the patient chart to avoid subsequent charges of conflict of interest.

The individual who is going through detoxification should be closely monitored by medical staff to detect signs of possible drug overdose, seizures, and medication compliance, and to ensure that the client does not continue to abuse chemicals while in "detox." Unfortunately, it is not uncommon for the client to decide to "help out" the withdrawal process by taking additional alcohol or drugs. This is often defended by the patient on the grounds that the medical staff has not provided sufficient pharmacological support during the patient's detoxification, a charge that might be well founded. In such situations, medical staff should review the patient's medication needs and, if sufficient, confront the patient about this illicit-chemical use.

Detoxification programs are subject to a number of abuses. Some individuals will "check in to detox" to find a place to hide from drug debts or to escape from the police. Opiate-addicted people have been known to enter a "detox" program to be cleansed of illicit drugs and allow their tolerance to opioids to drop, making it less expensive for them to return to opioid use upon discharge.[7] Thus although detoxification programs provide a valuable service, they are also vulnerable to abuses.

Videotape/Self-Confrontation

In the late 1980s and early 1990s, a technique was used in which videotapes were made of the individual shortly upon admission to a detoxification unit. This was viewed as a technique to show clients what they looked like under the influence of chemicals, in the hope that it would provide a degree of motivation for clients to discontinue the use of alcohol or drugs. There is little data to support this technique, and some data suggests that it might actually contribute to higher client dropout rates (R. K. Hester & Squires, 2004; W. R. Miller & White, 2007). A few programs still utilize this procedure, although for the most part it has been discontinued by treatment or rehabilitation programs.

Acupuncture

This is a form of "alternative medicine" that has on occasion been utilized in the treatment of SUDs. Anecdotal reports suggest that this procedure has a calming effect on the patient and reduces "craving" for alcohol or drugs. The theory behind this technique is beyond the scope of this text, but in practice small, sterile

---

[5]See Glossary.

[6]This is based on the belief that the patient is abusing *only* opioids.

[7]Unfortunately, it is not uncommon in this situation for patients to misjudge their drug dosage following detoxification, and overdose on opioids because of this (possibly with fatal results).

needles are inserted into specific spots on the body in an attempt to liberate or block the body's energy. There is limited evidence supporting the effectiveness of acupuncture in the rehabilitation of substance abusers, which appear to be about as effective as placebos when used to treat substance abusers (Ernst, 2002; R. K. Hester & Squires, 2004). This conclusion appears to be supported by the findings of Margolin et al. (2002), who found that acupuncture alone does not appear to be an effective treatment for cocaine addiction.

Family/Marital Therapies

Although viewed with a measure of disdain in the middle of the 20th century, family and marital therapies have proven to be valuable components to substance abuse rehabilitation programs and are now considered an integral part of treatment (Fals-Stewart, Lam, & Kelley, 2009). The goal of such ancillary therapy is to help the spouse and family members learn how to support the patient's efforts to achieve and maintain abstinence (Work Group on Substance Use Disorders, 2007). Another goal is to identify marital-conflict issues that might have contributed to the individual's SUD so that they might be addressed (Fals-Stewart et al., 2009).

The terms *marital therapy* and *family therapy* are generic terms applied to a number of different therapeutic approaches including the psychodynamic, family systems, structural, and behavioral family therapy approaches. Within the field of substance abuse rehabilitation, the best known and most common form of family therapy is the *family disease model*, which postulates that substance abuse in the family unit is an illness of the entire family and not just the substance abuser (Fals-Stewart et al., 2003, 2004). Proponents of this model believe that every member of the family plays a role, and the therapist(s) works to identify the role that the SUD plays within the family. For example, some people will use alcohol as a way to punish their partners, whereas others will use alcohol to make themselves "numb" to what they perceive as rejection by their partner.

In families where a member has an SUD, communications patterns tend to be confused or unhealthy, supporting the individual's SUD (Alter, 2001). Boundaries within the family are fluid or do not exist at all. Familial defenses often become *interlocking*, allowing the family to maintain a form of stability even in the face of rehabilitation efforts. Power roles within the family with a member with an SUD are often assumed by other family members, who then resist efforts for them to relinquish these roles so that the now-recovering family member might assume them again. All of these forces contribute to efforts to undermine or resist any effort to change by the addicted individual, including efforts at abstinence.

Given the impact that an individual's SUD has on the marriage and familial unit, marital or family therapy can be a valuable adjunct to treatment, and its importance has repeatedly been demonstrated in the clinical literature (Fals-Stewart et al., 2004). For example, the team of Neto, Labaz, Agular, and Chick (2008) found that social support provided by an adult who is close to the recovering alcoholic (usually the spouse) resulted in significantly longer periods of abstinence in the first 180 days following treatment, with the mean time for relapse being approximately 150 days. But family/marital counseling is a specialized area of expertise, which requires special training and supervision to be effective. It should not be attempted unless the therapist has the appropriate training and experience in family or marital therapy.

Individual Therapy Approaches[8]

There are a wide variety of individual therapy techniques that might be applied during substance abuse rehabilitation, including psychodynamic, motivational interviewing, cognitive-behavioral, Gestalt, and psychodrama, to cite some of the many different schools of individual psychotherapy currently in use both in the traditional mental health area as well as in substance abuse rehabilitation programs. Long viewed as being less effective than therapy groups, individual therapy offers the advantage of allowing clients to discuss issues that they find too personal to discuss in a group format (victimization issues, sexual orientation, guilt over past behavior(s), and so on) with an individual therapist with whom they have an established therapeutic relationship. Depending on the client's assessed level of care needs, individual counseling might be the appropriate form of treatment for a given individual.

A major disadvantage of the individual therapy session in substance abuse rehabilitation is that the client receives feedback from only the therapist. Further, the individual therapist is more vulnerable to manipulation than might occur in a group therapy format (discussed in the next section), as different group members might

---

[8]Substance abuse rehabilitation professionals who are in training and who are using this text to learn more about substance abuse are encouraged to explore these various individual therapy approaches in more detail, and to receive the appropriate training necessary to successfully apply each technique when working with an individual client.

more easily identify a manipulative effort by the client than an individual therapist is likely to see. Thus most rehabilitation and aftercare programs (discussed later in this chapter) utilize a mix of individual and group therapy formats, allowing that program to take advantage of the strengths of each form of treatment while avoiding many of the weaknesses inherent in either form of rehabilitation.

Group Therapy Approaches[9]

Group therapy is the most common modality through which psychosocial change is attempted (D. W. Brook, 2008). Unfortunately, the term *group therapy* is a generic term for a wide variety of therapeutic approaches carried out in a group setting, including cognitive-behavioral therapy, rational-emotive therapy, Gestalt therapy, psychodynamic group therapy, psychodrama, assertiveness training, and so on (Work Group on Substance Use Disorders, 2007). To complicate matters, it is not clear at this time which group format(s) are most effective for rehabilitation programs (Tomb, 2008).

Group therapy offers a number of advantages over individual therapy formats (Connors et al., 2001). One of the most important advantage is that the therapy group allows one staff person to work with a number of patients at the same time. Another advantage is that group members are able to offer each other feedback, rather than to rely passively on the professional's feedback. They can learn directly from other group members what has or has not worked for them, and help each other identify unhealthy behaviors. Through the group therapy process individuals' self-esteem might be enhanced, because they are offered the opportunity to form healthy, non-substance-centered relationships for perhaps the first time in their lives (D. W. Brook, 2008). Further, patients who are more advanced in recovery can become behavioral models for those just starting the rehabilitation process. Finally, by recreating the client's family of origin within the group setting, people are able to work on the interpersonal deficits from childhood (such as attachment disorders) that contributed to the development of their addiction (D. W. Brook, 2008).

Individual psychotherapy sessions are a useful adjunct to group therapy, allowing clients to discuss special problems that they might hesitate to discuss in a group setting. However, clients are usually encouraged to bring most of their concerns to the therapy group, which might meet one or more times daily. Cognitive-behavioral therapies help the client to identify self-defeating thoughts and the painful affective states that are caused by these thoughts, a process that is especially effective when working with personality-disordered patients. For example, the client who asserts "When I am hurting, I need alcohol (or drugs) to cope" might have another group member point out three different occasions where the client was able to cope without the use of chemicals and how this belief is thus flawed. In turn, this peer feedback might force clients to look at the black-and-white thinking that they use to assess the need for chemical abuse. A psychodynamic therapy group could allow clients to better understand the psychological forces that supported their addiction, whereas a psychodrama group format might allow clients to resolve conflicts that have blocked their recovery efforts to date through the appropriate simulations.

One very useful form of treatment group is the *coping skills* group. Many of those individuals with substance use problems began to abuse chemicals when they were children or adolescents, blocking the process of developing interpersonal coping skills necessary for adulthood (Monti et al., 2002). Social skills training might include *substance use refusal skills* training as well as helping the patient learn how to engage in non-substance-related pleasant activities (T. J. Morgan, 2003). Refusal skills training might take place within a group setting, where different group members take on different roles to help the individual learn how to refuse opportunities to use chemicals. Social skills training programs might help a client learn interpersonal skills to engage in non-substance centered recreational activities, as well as to learn how to feel more confident when interacting with others.

Although group therapy formats are very useful in the rehabilitation of substance abusers, it is necessary to carefully screen potential group members. Acutely suicidal or homicidal clients should be referred to individual therapists or hospitalized immediately, depending on the individual's needs (D. W. Brook, 2008). People who are unwilling or incapable to maintaining group confidentiality should not be admitted or retained in the group (D. W. Brook, 2008). Individuals who are in the acute stage of a psychotic episode should be excluded from therapy groups, as should

---

[9]Substance abuse rehabilitation students who are in training and who are using this text to learn more about substance abuse are encouraged to explore the various group therapy approaches in more detail, and to receive the appropriate training to allow them to understand when a given technique is most appropriate and how to successfully utilize a given form of group therapy.

group members who wish to utilize the group setting as a venue for selling drugs (D. W. Brook, 2008). These rules apply to community-based self-help groups as well as institutionally based therapy groups. However, when these rules are observed therapy groups might play a major role in the individual's rehabilitation from a substance use disorder.

Biofeedback Training

A number of studies have been carried out investigating the applicability of biofeedback programs to substance abuse rehabilitation. Biofeedback is a process where the individual is provided real-time information about internal body functions such as brain wave or skin resistance patterns. Depending on the modality selected (that is, muscle tension, skin temperature brain wave patterns, heart rate, and so forth) the individual might be taught to modify that body function at will, without the use of alcohol or illicit chemicals. This discovery in itself often helps a client understand that it is possible to change body states, such as how to relax, without the use of chemicals. It is possible for biofeedback programs to thus encourage the development of self-efficacy as patients develop skills to change body states once thought to only be alterable through the use of chemicals. There is preliminary evidence that supports the use of such techniques in rehabilitation programs, although there is no standardization as to the modalities used or the methods by which these modalities might be modified.

Harm Reduction[10] (HR) Model

In contrast to the Minnesota model is the harm reduction (HR) model. The HR model does not attempt to help the individual abstain from chemicals, at least not a first. It is based on the assumption that it is possible to change the behavior(s) of individuals who have SUDs over time, reducing the immediate consequences of their continued substance abuse. Eventually, it is hoped, individuals will accept abstinence as a goal, but even if they do not they are reducing the damage being done by their use of chemicals. Nicotine replacement therapy is one example of this process. Many individuals find it difficult to stop using the nicotine replacement therapy that they used in their smoking cessation program. However, their continued use of the nicotine in the spray or inhaler reflects the intake of just one chemical: nicotine. There are over 4500

known compounds in cigarette smoke, including many known to cause cancer, so continuous nicotine therapy avoids exposure to at least 4499 of the other compounds found in cigarette smoke.

Another good example of the HR model are methadone maintenance[11] programs. It is thought that by providing the opioid-dependent person medication in a controlled manner, the individual will be less likely to share needles, inject illicit drugs, engage in criminal behavior(s), and so on. Needle exchange programs might also be viewed as a form of harm reduction. Because many infectious diseases can be spread through the sharing of contaminated needles,[12] needle exchange programs help to limit the spread of infections that both destroy the health of the intravenous drug abuser and ultimately result in increased Medicare/Medicaid costs or higher insurance premiums. If a needle exchange program prevents just one or two new cases of an infection such as AIDS per year in a given community, the program will have paid for itself. Unfortunately, in spite of the obvious advantages of this process, there is strong resistance toward needle exchange programs in many regions of this country (Reuter, 2009).

Hypnosis

There has been little systematic research into the effectiveness of hypnosis in treating SUDs. The limited research that has been carried out usually involves the use of hypnosis to treat nicotine addiction, and there is little evidence to suggest that this treatment modality is viable in the long term (Work Group on Substance Use Disorders, 2007).

Yoga or Medication

As is true with hypnosis, there has been little systematic research into the possible application of yoga, or similar relaxation procedures, in the treatment of substance use disorders. There is, however, a rich body of research data supporting the use of yoga as a means to reduce stress, and it has been found to be a useful adjunct in the treatment of depression. Thus its use in the treatment of substance use disorders would seem to make clinical sense at this time, especially because by definition the SUDs reflect an imbalance in the individual's life.

Yoga and other stress management techniques have been in use for thousands of years. It would appear that

[10]Also known as *harm minimization*.

[11]Discussed in Chapter 33.

[12]Discussed in Chapter 36.

the utilization of such stress-reduction techniques as yoga would be of value as an adjunct to rehabilitation programs, especially with those individuals who engage in the abuse of substances for relief from stress. However, it is necessary for the patient to (a) learn the philosophy and (b) *practice* the techniques. Substance-abusing clients are famous for their inability to tolerate delay and their demands for immediate *relief* from real or perceived discomfort. These are characteristics that make it difficult to engage clients to learn to utilize yoga or similar procedures. However, for those who do learn how to use such procedures, it is frequently possible for substance-abusing patients to learn how to cope with stressors without the use of chemicals, and in the process discover self-efficacy.

The Treatment Plan

The substance abuse rehabilitation professional will have a wide range of techniques, many of which were briefly discussed earlier, to bring to bear on the problem of a substance-abusing client. The therapist and client should together develop a *treatment plan* to guide the client during the rehabilitation process. The treatment plan is based on the information obtained during the assessment process discussed in the last chapter. It "serves as the plan of action for pursuing the identified goals of treatment" (Connors et al., p. 82). Although different rehabilitation centers might utilize different formats, depending on the treatment format being utilized and the certification requirements for that specific health care facility, the treatment plan should be a written document. In some states it is a required part of rehabilitation and is viewed as a legal document.

All treatment plans share certain similarities. First, the treatment plan should provide a brief summary of the problem(s) that brought the client into treatment. An example of this might be that the "client is alcohol dependent." Some treatment plans include a brief summary of the client's physical and emotional health, whereas other formats include the client's own input into the rehabilitation process. In addition to the generalized statements of goals, specific objectives[13] are identified. Using the previous example, the objective might be "Client will successfully complete alcohol

detoxification process as measured by staff assessments of patient status, within 5 days."

Next there is a summary of the *discharge criteria*, listing the steps necessary for the client to accomplish in order for treatment to be successfully completed. Using the previous example, the client's progress in ingesting an adequate diet, which may counteract some of the dietary deficiencies associated with alcohol dependence could be stated as: "The client will consume 80% of meals provided 95% of the time for 3 days, as measured by staff report." Finally, there is a summary of those steps that are to be made a part of the client's aftercare program (discussed later in this chapter). Again, using the previous hypothetical example, this might be a statement such as "Client to identify a rehabilitation program that (she or he) wishes to enter by the time (she or he) is deemed medically ready for discharge, and make arrangements to enter that treatment program."

An example of a treatment plan goal for a hypothetical 24-year-old polydrug addict (cocaine, alcohol, marijuana, and occasionally benzodiazepines or opioids), who has a 3-year history of addiction to these compounds, might be as follows:

Problem: Client has been addicted to chemicals for the last 3 years, by self-report.

Long-term goal: Total abstinence from alcohol and drugs.

Methodology: (1) Successful completion of detoxification program, as measured by staff and patient report.

Methodology: (2) Successful completion of residential treatment program.

Methodology: (3) That patient take Naltrexone as prescribed 95% of the time.

Methodology: (4) That patient have "clean" urine test results 100% of the time, as measured by laboratory reports.

Methodology: (5) That patient identify community support group(s) and join same to develop substance-free support system.

Methodology: (6) That patient identify substance-free housing before discharge or within 30 days of admission to treatment.

Each of the target goals might be modified, or additional goals added as needed. For example, patients who indicate that they "just can't say 'no' to drug

---

[13]A *goal* is a generalized statement, such as "I want to lose weight." An objective is a measurable expression of that goal, such as "I want to lose 10 pounds."

dealers" might have the following additional objective added to the treatment plan:

> *Methodology: (7)* That patient demonstrate appropriate refusal skills in role-play simulations 100% of the time, as measured by staff report and patient report of comfort level using these techniques.

Aftercare Programs

Because substance use disorders are viewed as chronic, relapsing disorders, treatment does not end with the individual's discharge from an inpatient or outpatient rehabilitation program. Rather, participation in a *continuing-care* or *aftercare* program is recommended. Such programs have been found to significantly contribute to client abstinence rates (Ritsher et al., 2000; G. R. Smith et al., 2006). Aftercare programs work on the assumption that rehabilitation does not end with discharge from intensive treatment, but is the first step that the client takes on the road to long-term recovery.

These aftercare programs usually are carried out in a group format and focus on issues such as (a) maintenance of goals made in treatment and (b) helping the individual avoid relapsing back to active substance use (J. R. McKay et al., 1998). Individual therapy sessions with a professional rehabilitation counselor are utilized as an adjunct to the group therapy sessions. A major component of aftercare programs is helping the client identify mistaken beliefs that might contribute to relapse ("It is all right for me to drink beer, but I have to stay away from the hard stuff," or "Marijuana can't hurt you; it is natural, and natural things can't hurt you!"). Another goal of an aftercare program is to help clients learn self-monitoring skills to help them take responsibility for their recovery program. Such self-monitoring skills are a crucial part of an aftercare program because it has been found that "the benefits of abstinence in the first year operate in part through … building self-efficacy to abstain from alcohol use" (Maisto, Clifford, Stout, & Davis, 2008, p. 735). An important component in the development of such self-efficacy is the identification of high-risk situations in which the client is more likely to relapse[14] (being around those who are abusing alcohol or illicit drugs, as suggested in the hypothetical examples offered earlier in this paragraph) *and* the development of coping skills through which the client might deal with such high-risk situations.

In addition to participation in the aftercare program, clients are often expected to also attend self-help group meetings on a regular basis.[15] Aftercare groups might help clients learn to address medical issues such as chronic pain without relapsing, offer feedback, guidance, and support for clients addressing such needs as transitional housing and employment, guidance toward appropriate posttreatment family or marital counseling, and encouragement for the client to report "urges" or thoughts that might contribute to a relapse to the group. Should clients relapse, the group should offer encouragement as clients struggle to rebuild their recovery program, and help them examine their previous recovery system to identify problem areas that may have contributed to the relapse.

Chapter Summary

This chapter reviews some of the varieties of individual therapy applicable to the Minnesota model of treatment, which long dominated the inpatient rehabilitation programs. Individual therapy sessions were viewed as ancillary to the residential process for the most part, although in reality such therapy might be the most appropriate level of care for the client. The need for the therapist to develop a formal treatment plan was discussed, as were various treatment modalities such as detoxification from chemicals, biofeedback, marital and/or family therapies, group psychotherapy, and the role of blood and urine samples in the rehabilitation of the client were briefly explored.

---

[14]Relapse prevention is discussed in Chapter 32.

[15]Discussed in Chapter 35.

The Process of Treatment

Introduction

It is common for the average person on the street, and many people in the health care field, to speak of recovery from an SUD as if it were a single step. In reality, the SUDs are often *wrongly* viewed as acute conditions, like a broken leg or infection, that can be fixed by brief episodes of treatment.

In contrast to this perspective, substance abuse rehabilitation programs should be viewed as a form of *disease management* similar to the disease management programs developed for hypertension or diabetes (McLellan, 2008). As such, although the starting point is clearly defined, the end point remains elusive, just as the end point for disease management programs for diabetes or hypertension are not clearly defined. The concept of disease management of the SUDs is not unreasonable, for recovery from an SUD takes time, innumerable visits with rehabilitation professionals, and so on. This process parallels the process of disease management for other chronic medical conditions. In this chapter the process of recovery will be reviewed.

The Decision to Seek Treatment

Clients will decide to enter a rehabilitation program for a number of reasons, and vary in their motivation for a major life change such as abstinence from a desired substance (Cooney et al., 2005). The assessment process should identify whether the individual is a substance *abuser* or a person who is *addicted* to alcohol or drugs, as well as the severity of the consequences of that SUD for the individual (death from liver failure, a lengthy prison sentence, and so on) (Kessler et al., 2001). People who enter a formal rehabilitation program tend to be more impaired and to have more severe life problems than those who are able to abstain without entering a formal treatment program (R. H. Moos, 2003). People who seek professional assistance with an SUD usually have been addicted for 5–8 years or have engaged in heavy substance abuse for 10–19 years prior to seeking treatment (Kessler et al., 2005). People who are addicted to substances that result in a greater level of immediate impairment (cocaine, for example) will seek treatment earlier than those individuals who are addicted to alcohol, which requires time before its negative effects begin to manifest (Kessler et al., 2005). All of these issues must be considered during the treatment-planning process.

Methods of Treatment

There are different therapeutic methods utilized in the therapeutic process. In this section we will examine some of the more common methods in use.

Motivational Interviewing

The core elements of motivational interviewing (MI) involve expressing empathy for the client, helping clients see that there are discrepancies between their goals and values and their behavior, avoiding resistance to change by assisting clients to conclude that they need to change the target behavior, avoiding resistance to change, and supporting clients during the change process (Adamson & Sellman, 2008). In MI, "resistance" is viewed as a therapeutic mismatch between the client's stage of growth, therapeutic goals, and the treatment approach being utilized (W. R. Miller & Rollnick, 2002). An example of this might be found in cases where the client's goal is to find a way to drink "socially," whereas the therapist's goal is for total abstinence. The client's continued use of alcohol normally would be interpreted as a sign of resistance, not of a therapeutic mismatch between therapist and client goals.

Although the initial research studies were quite supportive of MI and its application to the treatment of alcohol use disorders, long-term (5-year) follow-up studies have failed to demonstrate increased efficacy of MI approaches to treatment as compared with non-directive therapy approaches or no counseling at all (Adamson & Sellman, 2008). There is a need for further research into the elements of MI that are effective and those that must be modified to enhance efficacy.

Cognitive-Behavioral Approaches

There are a number of closely related forms of cognitive-behavioral therapy. Their application to substance abuse rehabilitation is based on the assumption that individuals have developed a series of false or irrational assumptions on which their SUD rests. One such thought is that "I can't cope without using _____." Cognitive-behavioral approaches are usually carried out in a series of either 8–16 group or individual therapy sessions designed to help the individual identify these irrational thoughts and address them. In cases such as the preceding example, the therapist might work with clients to help them see where they have indeed coped with problems without resorting to substance use, and how black-and-white thinking contributes to the problem of relapse.

Voucher-Based Reinforcement

The process of voucher-based treatment involves the distribution of vouchers worth a certain number of "points," or even credit at a local store, for periods of abstinence confirmed through urine toxicology testing. Such a program might award voucher worth various point values that clients could use to buy a desired item (a stereo, for example), if they were to accumulate the desired number of points (in the stereo example, perhaps 500 points). After a period of weeks, the client might have accumulated a sufficient number of points to purchase the desired item, and the points are then traded in so that the client might "buy" it. Such approaches are used to reinforce the early stages of abstinence, when the client is most prone to relapse. Actual money is not used, as this would be a relapse trigger for the client, but points that could be traded in only at a specified store would lack the potential to serve as a relapse trigger, and this process has been found to enhance abstinence in the early stages of recovery.

The Stages of Recovery

For decades, clinicians have struggled to develop a system that would identify the stages of recovery from a substance use disorder, a process that is made even more difficult by the fact that there is virtually no research into the natural history of the SUDs! Clinical lore suggests that SUDs are chronic, progressive conditions, whereas clinical research suggests that a significant percentage of those people who meet the diagnostic criteria for an SUD in their late teens or early 20s will either have discontinued or at least greatly reduced their substance use by their late 20s (Heyman, 2009). Those people who are most likely to continue to have an active SUD as they progress through life are those who have a concurrent psychiatric or medical problem (Heyman, 2009).

Currently, a number of different stage recovery models have been proposed. The challenge, however, has been to establish a theoretical system that could then be tested and applied to clinical practice. To date, few of the proposed classification systems have received widespread acceptance by clinicians. For example, McLellan (2008) reviewed a tripartite model of treatment. The first step is detox/stabilization. During this phase the individual is stabilized medically, detoxification from alcohol or drugs is carried out, and the individual is prepared for the rehabilitation process. Depending on the substance(s) being abused and the patient's state of health, this process can be completed in just a few days, or might require weeks. Again, depending on the substance(s) being abused, the patient's health, and social resources, the detoxification might be carried out on either an outpatient or inpatient basis.

Step two is the actual process of rehabilitation, which will involve individual and group therapy as well as adjunctive programs (family/marital therapy, for example) as deemed necessary. Again, this process might be carried out on either an outpatient or an inpatient basis, depending on the patient's needs and available resources. After this stage is completed, the individual will enter the third stage: continuing care.[1] During this step, rehabilitation focuses on helping the individual abstain from chemical abuse by utilizing abstinence resources developed in the second stage, and finding ways around obstacles that were identified only after the individual attempted to abstain from alcohol or drugs.

In the latter part of the 20th century, a different, more detailed theoretical model of the change process was introduced by James Prochaska (J. O. Prochaska, 2002; J. O. Prochaska, DiClemente, & Norcross, 1992). This model postulated that individuals moved from one stage to the next on their road to recovery, and that people in different stages of change have different characteristics and needs than those in other stages of change (Connors et al., 2001; Sadock & Sadock, 2007). The first of these theoretical stages is that of *precontemplation* (A. W. Blume, 2005; Connors et al., 2001; J. O. Prochaska, 1998, 2002). Individuals in this stage are still actively abusing chemicals and have no thought of trying to abstain from alcohol or illicit drugs in the next 6 months. If they have thought about abstinence, their continued substance use is viewed as presenting more reasons to continue to engage in substance use than consequences.

The challenge for the substance abuse rehabilitation professional working with clients in this stage of the change process is to (a) teach them the negative effects of their substance use, (b) teach them the dangers of continued substance use, (c) address their ambivalence to change, (d) help clients envision an alternative lifestyle, (e) help clients identify barriers that might block this attempt at a lifestyle change, and (f) help enhance the clients' self-esteem so they will believe that a lifestyle change is possible (A. W. Blume, 2005; Ramsay & Newman, 2000; G. S. Rose, 2001). It is important for rehabilitation center staff to avoid focusing on behavioral change issues at this point, as clients still do not view their substance use disorder as being a major

problem (Connors et al., 2001). The main emphasis of treatment at this stage should be to help clients think about an alternative (drug-free) lifestyle. It is during this stage that defense mechanisms such as denial and rationalization are most prominent (Ramsay & Newman, 2000). If clients are in treatment under external pressure, they might also attempt to use compliance as a defense against actual lifestyle change (A. W. Blume, 2005). The stages in the process of recovery are shown in Figure 32-1.

It is only during the stage of *contemplation* that individuals begin to entertain vague thoughts of stopping alcohol or drug use "one of these days." About 40% of substance abusers are in this stage. There is no firm date set for quitting, although clients EW actively thinking about quitting at some point within the next 6 months. However, they remain ambivalent about change while simultaneously also experiencing a growing sense of dissatisfaction with their present lifestyle. A client might express a wish that "if you could arrange for me to continue to use, without the consequences" during this phase, and might remain in this stage for months or years. But clients are not working toward recovery during this phase, although they might begin to engage in preliminary action that moves them closer to actively attempting to change. For example, three-pack-a-day cigarette smokers might slowly reduce their cigarette consumption to a pack a day, in anticipation of eventually quitting.

For the therapist working with a client in the contemplative stage, the challenge is to (a) enhance motivation to change, (b) awaken within the client a desire for spiritual growth,[2] and, (c) help the client make a firm decision to change. It is not uncommon for clients during this stage to express amazement at how much their SUD has impacted the family, for example. An alcohol-dependent man might, after adding up the combined costs of medical treatment, court fines, lost employment, and the physical cost of the alcohol consumed, discover that his alcohol use disorder has resulted in a financial loss that totals well into six digits. "My God, I drank [the equivalent of the purchase price of] a house" clients might exclaim after adding up the accumulated costs induced by their alcohol use disorder, for example. Another technique that often works is to develop a worksheet on which the pros of continued substance use are compared with the negative consequences of continued substance use.

---

[1]This step is often mistakenly called *aftercare*, because the term *aftercare* implies that treatment has finished. However, because the term is deeply entrenched in the clinical literature, *aftercare* will be used in this text.

[2]See Chapter 27.

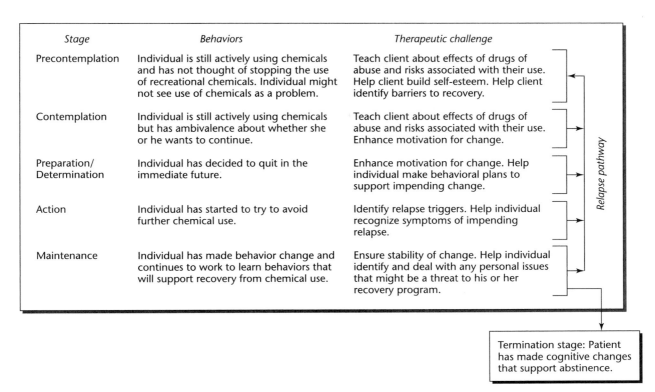

Stage	Behaviors	Therapeutic challenge
Precontemplation	Individual is still actively using chemicals and has not thought of stopping the use of recreational chemicals. Individual might not see use of chemicals as a problem.	Teach client about effects of drugs of abuse and risks associated with their use. Help client build self-esteem. Help client identify barriers to recovery.
Contemplation	Individual is still actively using chemicals but has ambivalence about whether she or he wants to continue.	Teach client about effects of drugs of abuse and risks associated with their use. Enhance motivation for change.
Preparation/ Determination	Individual has decided to quit in the immediate future.	Enhance motivation for change. Help individual make behavioral plans to support impending change.
Action	Individual has started to try to avoid further chemical use.	Identify relapse triggers. Help individual recognize symptoms of impending relapse.
Maintenance	Individual has made behavior change and continues to work to learn behaviors that will support recovery from chemical use.	Ensure stability of change. Help individual identify and deal with any personal issues that might be a threat to his or her recovery program.

Relapse pathway

Termination stage: Patient has made cognitive changes that support abstinence.

FIGURE 32-1 The Stages of Recovery
SOURCE: Based on Prochaska (1998) and Prochaska et al. (1992).

The next stage is the stage of *preparation.* Clients are now ready to change their attitude and behavior(s), usually within the next month, and might even have made the initial steps in the change process (Connors et al., 2001). Very few individuals reach this or the next stage(s). The therapeutic goal during this stage is for the therapist to assist the client in making realistic decisions and to set realistic goals. Another therapeutic goal is for the therapist to address maladaptive thoughts that support continued substance use ("I can keep a bottle in my house for friends, as long as I do not actually use it myself," for example). A danger is that the client's unrealistic goals or maladaptive thoughts during this effort will undermine further efforts to change.

During the *action* phase, clients make concrete steps to modify the identified problem behavior. They implement their behavior change plan, often encountering problems as they identify how the original change plan was flawed. The therapeutic goals during this phase center around (a) optimizing opportunities for individual growth, (b) being alert for signs that clients are experiencing problems, (c) encouraging clients to

begin the process of building a substance-free support system, (d) helping clients deal with the "emotional roller coaster" experienced during this period, and (e) helping clients be realistic about the pace of their recovery ("I can handle being in a relationship, now," a hypothetical client might say after only two months of abstinence).

If clients are able to abstain from alcohol or drugs for at least 6 months, they will enter the *maintenance* stage of recovery. During this phase, individuals develop behaviors supportive of recovery, addressing problem areas ignored during the period of active chemical abuse (employment or marital relationships, for example) and confronting personal issues that contributed to or exacerbated the SUD. Ultimately only 20% of clients with an SUD enter this phase (J. O. Prochaska, 2002). During this phase, individuals learn how to cope with "using" thoughts or "urges" to return to chemical use, increasing their self-efficacy and belief that they can succeed in the behavior change. Increased self-efficacy at the end of the first year of abstinence, including a lower number of days in which alcohol was consumed and lower amount of alcohol consumed per drinking day, appears to be a predictor of abstinence at the end of a 3-year period of time (Maisto et al., 2008). The therapeutic challenge during this stage is for the therapist to function as a parent-substitute, mentor, cheering section, and guide for clients, to ensure the stability of change and identify issues that might undermine their recovery program.

Relapse[3] is an ever-present danger. In years past this was viewed as a "treatment failure" by many health care professionals. This view has been challenged. The addictions are chronic, relapsing disorders similar to cancer, diabetes, or hypertension. Most certainly patients who fail to get their blood pressure under control after a trial of one hypertensive medication would not be classified as a "treatment failure," and there is no reason why a different criterion should be applied to the rehabilitation process. Some diabetic patients are "brittle" and require repeated hospitalizations for stabilization and treatment planning, and yet they are not called a "treatment failure."

Recovery from the SUDs is a dynamic process that will often move through the various stages of change in a cyclical rather than a linear manner (Connors et al., 2001; J. O. Prochaska, 1998, 2002). The comparison to how patients work through the stages of grief might not be inappropriate here. In both cases the client will be very vulnerable to internal and external cues that reawaken old thought patterns. Recovering smokers might, upon smelling cigarette smoke, start to think about how nice it was to sneak out of the office at about this time of the day to have a cigarette. Recently bereaved people might, upon hearing a song once shared with a loved one, find themselves mired in the pain and misery of mourning their substance of choice, again.

This is one of the more frustrating aspects of substance abuse rehabilitation. Clients might make a step forward, then fall back two steps. Over time, they might again reach the point where they take the step forward, and this time take yet another step forward. A comparison with recovery from nicotine addiction is not out of place here. Periods of smoking abstinence are intermixed with periods of active smoking, which hopefully will become less frequent and shorter in duration as the person learns to live without cigarettes. This is not to say that rehabilitation professionals should accept continued substance abuse as being unavoidable. Rather, this is to say that the process of recovery from an SUD differs from one individual to the next, and that

relapse is a constant danger against which both the client and the therapist must be on guard.

One motivational factor against relapse is the client's assessment of the alternatives to continued substance use (Heyman, 2009). Clients will reassess the benefits and consequences of abstinence differently at each stage of the recovery process (J. A. Cunningham, Sobell, Gavin, Sobell, & Breslin, 1997). If the client's assessment that the benefits of abstinence do not outweigh the perceived benefits of continued substance use, that person is unlikely to abstain from alcohol or illicit drugs. The treatment professional must thus continually reassess the client's perception of benefits and consequences of continued substance use throughout the rehabilitation process.

The model suggested by J. O. Prochaska et al. (1992) appears to apply both to those individuals who seek professional assistance in learning how to abstain from chemicals and to those who recover from an SUD without professional assistance. Upon reflection this makes sense, because "natural" recovery from substance use disorders is the norm rather than the exception (Heyman, 2009; Walters, Rogers, Saunders, Wilkinson, & Towers, 2003). Both "natural" and "assisted" recovery work toward the same goal: abstinence from substance abuse. It is only natural that they would follow the same process and similar steps to reach that common goal.

Nowinski (2003) suggested an alternative model of recovery to the model suggested by Prochaska. The first stage of the Nowinski model is that of *acceptance*. This might be achieved either by the individual reaching the decision that the consequences of further substance abuse outweigh the perceived benefits or through participation in a self-help group such as Alcoholics Anonymous.[4] If professional assistance is utilized to help individuals recover from their SUD, they have the option of utilizing either outpatient or inpatient rehabilitation programs. The goal of all of these programs during this stage is the same: to assist clients in accepting the reality of their SUD, and the pain and harm caused by this disorder. It is also imperative that clients understand that willpower alone will not guarantee abstinence from alcohol or drugs. Indeed, this belief may be utilized to avoid actual acceptance of the individual's SUD. "I can deal with it on my own" is a common refrain heard by health care professionals working with substance abusers; "I just need to apply myself to not use, again."

---

[3]Discussed in more detail in Chapter 34.

[4]Discussed further in Chapter 35.

It is not until clients have reached the second stage of recovery in the Nowinski (2003) model, that of *surrender*, that they become willing to begin to make the lifestyle changes necessary to support recovery. This is often a difficult step for alcohol or drug abusers to achieve. Because of their denial, they tend to believe that they have an inordinate amount of control not only over themselves, but also over their substance use disorder, and surrender does not come easily to one who is in charge of one's life, now does it? During this stage, the substance abuse rehabilitation professional works to help clients both recognize the impact of their SUD on themselves and others, and learn how to accept powerlessness as a step toward recovery. This is not always an easy process, even if the client is well motivated. It is much more difficult to accomplish when clients are unmotivated to recognize, accept, or change unhealthy behaviors in their lives.

Reactions Against Stage Models of Recovery

The stage models of recovery just outlined have not met with universal acceptance. This is to be expected, because few new theoretical constructs are accepted without criticism, review, modification, and possibly extensive revision. In the field of psychology, stage models tend to pass through several stages before final acceptance:

1. First, there is a phase of uncritical acceptance following the introduction of the new model.
2. After a short period of time, guarded criticism is offered about possible problems with the new theoretical model.
3. The criticism increases in volume and frequency until the theoretical model is awash in a sea of hostility.
4. The theoretical model is relegated to the archives or textbooks as an illustration of the process under consideration, because not every person progresses through each step in the same order as originally postulated.
5. Finally, the model is accepted as a general outline of a process within which there is individual variation.

To use an analogy, compare the reaction to Albert Einstein's original paper on the theory of relativity in 1905. His theory was scorned because he was only a patent clerk in Switzerland who had the audacity to think that he could solve this vexing problem, and only a few people in the field of theoretical physics actually tried to understand his theory. It is now accepted as the solution to the problem of how matter and energy are related to each other.

In the field of substance abuse rehabilitation, stage models such as those discussed in this text are often viewed as holy gospel. In reality such models are "at best descriptive rather than explanatory" (Davidson, 1998, p. 32). One person might remain in a given stage of recovery for months or even years. Another person might make rapid progress through that same stage in a matter of weeks. It is not that the model of change is incorrect, but rather that it is a reflection of the *average* individual's progression down the path to recovery. Each individual follows his or her own path.

Although the stages-of-change model suggested by Prochaska (J. O. Prochaska et al., 1992) has an elegant beauty, suggesting that it is accurate and true, it has actually received only limited support from research scientists. Gossop, Steward, and Marsden (2007) found, for example, that although patients had improved in the year following discharge from treatment, there was little correlation between their progress and the various measures of readiness to change. Indeed, it was found that those patients with the highest measured levels of readiness to change were also the same people who tended to be using the highest levels of heroin at the end of the 1-year follow-up period! This may reflect a greater measure of desperation on the part of heroin addicts who were unable to change, or it might indicate that the current stage models of change are not applicable to every form of SUD. There is obviously a need for further research in this area.

Then What Works in Predicting Recovery From SUDs?

One of the most frustrating tenets of substance abuse rehabilitation work is the expectation that those people in treatment for the abuse of a compound(s) are automatically the same as those people who are not in a rehabilitation program. This bias has distorted both clinical research and the development of rehabilitation models because it ignores the fact that many, perhaps a majority, of those people with a substance use disorder never seek professional assistance for their SUD (Heyman, 2009). Clinical research has demonstrated that almost 50% of those people who met the diagnostic criteria for substance dependence did not report even one sign of a current SUD in the past 12 months by the age of 24, and that by the age of 37 this figure had increased to 75%!

Which raises an interesting problem: We do not know what factors predict recovery from a substance use disorder, mainly because only a minority of those people with a substance use disorder actually are ever admitted to a treatment program. Those admitted to a rehabilitation program are possibly the *least likely* to be able to discontinue their substance use (Heyman, 2009). Generalizations from those people in a substance abuse rehabilitation program to *all* people with a substance use disorder might be ill advised. We simply do not know how to answer the question posed at the start of this section.

With that caveat in mind, it is possible to tentatively state that there are a multitude of factors that interact to support, or detract from the individual's recovery efforts. It has been found, for example, that "ongoing environmental factors can augment or nullify the short term influence of an intervention [program]" (R. H. Moos, 2003, p. 3). Many of these factors, such as a substance-abusing spouse for example, simply lie outside of the counselor's control. Unfortunately, many substance abuse rehabilitation professionals overestimate the impact that their treatment program might have on a given client. It has been found that "relatively stable factors in people's lives, such as informal help and ongoing social resources, tend to play a more enduring role" (R. H. Moos, 2003, p. 3) in assisting people's recovery efforts. Treatment might best be envisioned as the foundation for a recovery program, not that it will turn clients' lives around and save them from utter destruction.

The foundation on which a client's recovery might be established appear to involve issues such as:

- Interpersonal relationships: *Individuals who drink more have been found to have few interpersonal resources to draw upon for support.*
- Cognitive reappraisals: *Many former drinkers report that their realization that alcohol was causing physical and emotional damage to their lives was the point where they decided to stop drinking.*
- Demographic variables: *Individuals who drink more tend to come from lower socioeconomic groups, which may then provide fewer social supports necessary for recovery.*
- Severity of the SUD: *Physical problems, health issues, or legal problems may serve as warning signs that the individual has started to reach problematic levels of substance use.*

- Involvement in AA or religious groups: *This may help individuals better understand the damage that their SUD has caused, while providing social support for recovery.*
- Individual expectations and self-evaluation: *This will help to shape individuals' perception of recovery, their perception of barriers to recovery, and self-concept issues that might assist or undermine recovery efforts.*

A further factor that should be considered is the congruence between the individual's expectations and goals and those of the therapist. A client who wishes to attempt to be a "social drinker" might not participate in a rehabilitation program with a counselor who insists that abstinence is the only possible outcome for therapy.[5] Individuals who do not view themselves as being capable of abstaining from a chemical(s), or who utilized a drug(s) to make themselves numb to feelings of low self-esteem might have trouble in a recovery program until these issues are adequately addressed. There are so many variables that can influence a given individual's recovery program that only general statements about the "path to recovery" might be made.

Should Abstinence Be the Goal of Treatment?[6]

This question is fiercely debated. Clients often do not wish to abstain from substance abuse but just learn how to *control* it. Rehabilitation professionals often hold that abstinence is the more appropriate goal, thus establishing the grounds for a goal conflict from the outset of treatment. Yet there are reasons why abstinence should be the appropriate goal, in spite of the client's wishes or hopes. Abstinence from alcohol or illicit drugs reduces the possibility of interpersonal conflict, health care problems, and the financial strain inherent in purchasing a drug(s) of abuse.

Thus rehabilitation centers focus on total abstinence from alcohol and/or drugs as the goal of treatment. However, there are age differences in the willingness to accept abstinence as a treatment goal. There is evidence that drinkers under the age of 25 abstinence-based treatment does not appear to improve the success rate following treatment. For people under the age of 25,

---

[5]See Breakout Discussion #1 for Chapter 34 in Student Workbook.

[6]This topic is also reviewed in more detail in Breakout Discussion #1, in Student Workbook.

abstinence-based goals did not appear to improve the success rate for treatment, for reasons that could not be determined from their data. This is consistent with the observations of George E. Vaillant (1995, 1996; Vaillant & Hiller-Sturmhofel, 1996) who, in his work with alcohol-dependent individuals, found that rather than maintain abstinence, the subjects in his studies tended to alternate between periods of abstinence and more or less problematic drinking.

These findings raise interesting questions about the appropriate goal(s) of treatment. Most treatment centers advocate total abstinence as the only acceptable outcome of rehabilitation, a goal that is achieved and maintained by only a small percentage of those who enter substance abuse rehabilitation program. The method(s) by which a rehabilitation program achieves this goal is evaluated in terms of client abstinence rates from alcohol or drugs at the end of a given period (usually 3, 6, or 12 months). However, usually such assessments reflect more the ideology of the assessor more than the results of sound scientific research (Muir, 2008). Thus should total abstinence be a goal for a client who does not share this objective? If so, how should this goal be introduced to the client in a manner that does not immediately cause resistance? The approach suggested by McLellan (2008) of accepting rehabilitation as a form of disease management, similar to how physicians attempt to control diabetes or hypertension, is more appropriate.

Specific Points to Address in Substance Abuse Rehabilitation

During the rehabilitation process, there are a wide range of issues that must be resolved to successfully work with the client with an SUD. The first, as noted previously, is whether total abstinence should be the appropriate goal. Another issue is what form of substance abuse rehabilitation should be initiated. The answer to this question varies, depending on the substance(s) being abused.

Alcohol

Substance abuse rehabilitation professionals need to work with clients to (a) identify consequences of their AUD, (b) assess its impact on not only themselves but also on their families and significant others, (c) determine whether they thought that abstinence was a worthy goal in light of this understanding, and (d) determine what factors motivated their use of alcohol or might serve as a barrier to recovery. A client who says "I am only here to please my probation officer" has identified a significant barrier to recovery (no desire to do more than achieve a degree of impression management), for example. The therapist in this case must assist the client in internalizing a desire to change for personal reasons, not because of external pressure.

A significant problem that asserts itself not only with alcohol but with all of the substances of abuse is the *illusion of control*. Clients might go into a bar and drink only soda for the evening while on "pass," and then claim that they have achieved the ability to control their desire to drink and thus are ready to graduate from treatment. This problem is discussed in more detail in Chapter 34, but in brief this client is on the brink of a major relapse. Clients like these might next have one or two beers, without suffering any adverse consequences, and on these grounds dismiss everything that they learned while in treatment, setting the stage for an ultimate relapse.

Narcotic Analgesics

The goal of abstinence for people addicted to a narcotic analgesic is one that depends on the length of time that they have been addicted and their motivation for a drug-free lifestyle. A person who has only recently become addicted to a narcotic and who is highly motivated to abstain will present a different clinical picture from the person who has been addicted to narcotics for the past 10 years and is interested only in a methadone maintenance program.[7] Simple detoxification from narcotics is not the answer: 90% of those opioid-dependent people who completed a detox program return to the abuse of chemicals within 6 months (Schuckit, 2006a, 2006b).

A pair of research studies under the direction of Y. Hser supported the pessimistic outcome for opioid addiction (Hser, Hoffman, Grella, & Anglin, 2001; Hser, Anglin, & Powers, 1993). The authors of these studies followed a group of opioid-dependent individuals who had been arrested in California; and 24 years after their initial assessment, it was found that only 22% of the original sample of 581 individuals were opiate free (Hser et al., 1993). An additional 7% of the original research sample were on a methadone maintenance program, and 10% reported just occasional episodes of narcotics abuse. Unfortunately, almost 28% of the original sample had died in the 20-year period

---

[7]Discussed in Chapter 33.

between their initial arrest and the 24-year follow-up, with the causes of death being homicide, suicide, and accidents, in that order.

At the time of the 34-year follow-up, almost half of the original sample of 581 individuals were found to have died (Hser et al., 2001). This was almost equal to the number of original subjects who were opioid free, as confirmed by urine toxicology testing, and an additional 10% of the original subjects refused to submit to urine toxicology testing. Hser et al. concluded on the basis of their data that heroin abuse patterns were "remarkably stable" (p. 503) over the course of the study, with some subjects relapsing back to active opioid dependence after as much as 15 years of abstinence. The authors suggested that heroin addiction was a lifelong condition, with severe social and medical consequences.

However, it should also be noted that the Hser et al. (2001) study found that a significant percentage of their original research sample were opioid free, a finding consistent with other studies that have found that more than one-third of opioid-dependent people will eventually achieve a drug-free lifestyle. This opioid-free lifestyle is usually achieved around only 9 years after the individual first became addicted to opioids (Jaffe, 2000).

At this point in time there are opioid agonist replacement therapies[8] that, although not a perfect solution to the problem of narcotics addiction, at least offer the promise of helping individuals to control their craving for opioids while they address other life issues. Further, as research has demonstrated, approximately one-third of opioid-dependent people will eventually become free of narcotics after an extended struggle with their SUD. Thus the question of whether abstinence or opioid agonist therapies is the goal of treatment should be a joint decision between the therapist (or therapeutic team) and the client.

CNS Stimulants

Unfortunately, there is virtually no research into the factors that might contribute to or protect against the development of an addiction to CNS stimulants. There are no proven genetic markers to identify those individuals who are at high risk for the development of an addiction to this class of medications. Even if there were such genetic markers, would this deter people interested in abusing these medications from doing so if they were aware that they might be at high risk for addiction?

Traditionally, addiction to the CNS stimulants is not in itself grounds for admission to an inpatient detox facility. One exception to this is the possibility that individuals have one of a number of medical complications caused or exacerbated by their abuse of CNS stimulants, which may prove to be life-threatening unless they were to be monitored by health care professionals during the withdrawal process. Another exception is when patients are also addicted to compounds such as alcohol, where withdrawal can potentially be life threatening. Yet a third exception to this rule is when individuals have developed a suicidal depression as a result of CNS stimulant withdrawal. A qualified health care professional should assess each client, keeping in mind that the client's state of mind, past history of suicidal thinking or attempts, current medical status, support systems, and history of success or failure at past detoxification attempts, all help to determine the client's specific needs for a given level of care.

CNS stimulant withdrawal proceeds through both an acute and an extended withdrawal phase. Some of the emotional and physical problems experienced during both the acute and extended withdrawal phases may serve as relapse "triggers" for the client, and thus must be addressed by the attending health care staff. However, available evidence suggests that for those individuals who are able to remain abstinent from CNS stimulants such as cocaine for 12 weeks, up to 80% will remain drug-free for the first 6 months following treatment. But as will be discussed in Chapter 34, even people with extended periods of abstinence will find themselves suddenly experiencing periods of "craving" for CNS stimulants, usually in response to external stimuli associated with past substance abuse (songs, smells, physical appearance of a person seen in passing, and so on).

One very real problem in working with the CNS stimulant abuser is that the individual often has forgotten what a drug-free lifestyle is like. This underscores the need for *relapse prevention*[9] training as well as social support groups such as Alcoholics Anonymous, Narcotics Anonymous, Cocaine Anonymous, or one of the emerging faith-based support groups.

Marijuana Abuse

Although it has been estimated that only 10% of those who abuse marijuana eventually become addicted to it, marijuana addiction is still a very real phenomenon.

---

[8]Discussed in Chapter 33.

[9]Discussed in Chapter 34.

It is difficult to convince adolescents or young-adult abusers of this danger, and it is rare for a person with an SUD to abuse *only* marijuana. Further, it is rare for a person who is addicted to marijuana to present for treatment, unless there is some form of external coercion.

Total abstinence from all drugs of abuse is thought to be imperative when working with the marijuana abuser or addict (D. Smith, 2001). Compounds that cause any of the psychoactive effects of marijuana would reawaken memories of marijuana use and thus serve as a relapse "trigger." Further, because many individuals use marijuana as a way to cope with negative feelings, rehabilitation professionals must help the client learn non-drug-centered coping mechanisms for these negative feelings. A complete assessment of the client's motivation for marijuana use, and the development of alternative coping mechanisms for these problems, is imperative. Ancillary support services such as community-based support groups are also of value.

Smoking Cessation

This topic is reviewed in Chapter 16. However, in earlier editions of this text it was also discussed in this chapter. To minimize redundancy, this topic is discussed only in Chapter 16.

Anabolic Steroids

It is important to keep in mind that the individual's motivation to abuse anabolic steroids is rarely the same as that seen in other drug abusers. The individual's motivation for abusing these compounds will need to be identified. For example, anabolic steroid abusers who believes that these compounds will enhance their physical appearance will present with a different motivation than the steroid abusers who wish to build muscle strength.

Medical supervision of the steroid abuser is mandatory. The physician can order blood and urine tests that, although they do not directly indicate anabolic steroid abuse, do strongly hint that the patient has continued to abuse these compounds. The physician is also in the best position to confront the anabolic steroid abuser, who might otherwise dismiss a substance abuse rehabilitation professional's attempts at intervention with a wall of denial and medical jargon that the counselor is ill prepared to refute. The physician on the other hand can identify specific test results that warn of cardiac, liver, or other organ damage induced by the abuse of these compounds, and dismiss the client's semi-informed rationalizations of harmlessness with the facts.

A very real problem in working with anabolic steroid abusers is that many of the complications caused (or exacerbated) by these compounds do not appear until years after the individual started to abuse them. High school football players, for example, will often dismiss warnings that the anabolic steroids can exacerbate the buildup of atherosclerotic plaque. These problems are decades away, at least in their opinion, and winning is everything, is it not? As was discussed in the chapter on child and adolescent substance use disorders, adolescents (and young adults) do not process information about the dangers associated with substance abuse in the same manner that older adults do, as was discussed in Chapter 23, and the substance abuse rehabilitation professional needs to keep this in mind when working with a steroid abuser.

The client's motivation for abusing steroids should be identified, and coexisting disorders (such as body image problems) should be identified and addressed. Proper nutritional guidance will often prove to be a valuable adjunct to rehabilitation as clients learn that they can achieve many of the same desired effects without the use of steroids. Group therapy with other recovering anabolic steroid abusers may prove to be of value. Community-based support groups may also prove useful, but there are very few such support groups devoted only to individuals who have abused anabolic steroids.

Hallucinogen Abuse

Individuals who abuse hallucinogens rarely have the same motivation as those people who abuse alcohol or narcotics. Although many of these compounds may induce a sense of euphoria, abusers tend to point to their desire to induce sensory distortions. This often is done by people who believe that they are more creative when under the influence of these compounds, which is a source of motivation that is virtually never seen in narcotic analgesic abusers, for example. Although the potential danger(s) of hallucinogen abuse are limited,[10] the use of these compounds does impact psychosocial functioning and is illegal, and these are factors that the rehabilitation center staff might wish to emphasize in working with clients who abuse these compounds.

---

[10]MDMA's effects on memory being an exception to this rule.

Chapter Summary

In this chapter, two different stage models of the recovery process were identified and discussed. The most popular model was introduced by J. O. Prochaska et al. (1992). This model suggests that although progress is not linear, individuals who wish to make behavioral change(s) move from a precontemplation period, in which no behavioral change is being considered, into a phase where they are starting to consider the possibility of a behavioral change, known as contemplation. The individual may remain in this stage for a number of months, or even years, thinking about the possibility of attempting a major behavioral phase "one of these days," but without firm plans to do so starting on a specific date.

Individuals in the contemplation phase struggle with a vague sense of dissatisfaction with their present life circumstances. Fully 80% percent of people with an SUD are in the first two stages of this model, and only a small percentage of those with an SUD move to the action phase. It is during the action phase that the person attempts to make the behavioral change(s) being contemplated. After achieving a substance-free lifestyle for at least 6 months, the individual enters the maintenance phase, working to identify and develop behavior(s) that will assist in maintaining the behavioral change(s) achieved to date. The maintenance phase blends into the termination phase after about 5 years of abstinence. Only 20% of those who move beyond the contemplation phase ultimately reach this phase, underscoring the need for more research into the factors that motivate the person to move from one stage to the next.

Also discussed were some of the factors that might support the individual's attempt at abstinence, and factors specific to each class of drugs of abuse that rehabilitation professionals must consider in working with clients abusing those compounds.

CHAPTER 33

Pharmacological Interventions for Substance Use Disorders[1]

Introduction

Pharmacotherapy, or the utilization of select pharmaceuticals to treat a specific condition, often is used in the treatment of a wide range of medical disorders. Pharmaceutical companies, however, have not demonstrated any significant interest in developing agents for treating people with SUDs, in part because they view this market as being too limited (Ciraulo, 2004; Nutt, Robbins, & Stimson, 2005). This is unfortunate, as such treatments are often valuable adjuncts to the rehabilitation process (Lukas, 2006; Rounsaville, 2006). Most of the pharmaceutical agents currently in use to treat SUDs are compounds originally developed to treat other conditions and were by chance found to also be useful as adjuncts to treating SUDs (Ciraulo, 2004). In this chapter, we will examine some of the more common pharmacological interventions used to treat substance use disorders.

The Theory Behind Pharmacotherapy of SUDs

Lukas (2006) identified several subgroups of medications that might be utilized as adjunctive treatments for SUDs: (a) medications that control withdrawal symptoms, (b) medications that control the individual's "craving" for drugs, (c) aversive agents that cause dysphoria when certain compounds are used, (d) compounds used to treat concurrent psychiatric disorders, (e) agonist compounds used in certain "maintenance" programs, and (f) medications used to treat drug overdoses. Only minimal discussion of another category of compounds, psychopharmaceuticals used to treat mental illness, will be included in this text.[2] All of the medications discussed in this chapter fall into one or more of the categories suggested by Lukas (2006). A very real danger in using pharmaceuticals to treat substance use disorders is that such people are "enamored" (Washton & Zweben, 2006, p. 103) with pills. Their use might thus be, for at least some substance abusers, an extension of their "addictive thinking" rather than an adjunct to treatment.

---

[1]The information provided in this chapter, like the information provided in the rest of this text, is intended to illustrate the manner in which certain medications are used by physicians to treat illicit drug use. It is neither intended for nor should it be used as a guide for the treatment of any given individual(s).

[2]There are a number of psychiatric textbooks that provide excellent discussions of how these compounds are applied to the treatment of mental illness, and if interested in learning more about these compounds, the reader is advised to seek information through these sources.

Pharmacological Treatment of Alcohol Use Disorders

There are two subcategories of medications used in the treatment of AUDs: (a) those medications used to control the symptoms of the alcohol withdrawal syndrome and (b) aversive agents that cause dysphoria when the individual ingests alcohol. We will begin our discussion with the medications used to control the alcohol withdrawal syndrome.

Pharmaceutical Treatment of the Alcohol Withdrawal Syndrome (AWS)

In the first decade of the 20th century, the benzodiazepines are accepted as the treatment of choice for controlling the symptoms of the AWS (Bayard, McIntyre, Hill, & Woodside, 2004; Daeppen et al., 2002; Mariani & Levin, 2004; A. McKay et al., 2004). Physicians use these medications to first control the withdrawal symptoms and then to safely titer the dose down over a period of time so that the patient avoids most of the discomfort and risks associated with the AWS. The intermediate or long-acting benzodiazepines are the compounds of choice, as they avoid the danger of "rebound" withdrawal symptoms caused by between-dose variations in the blood benzodiazepine levels. Some physicians advocate the use of diazepam,[3] lorazepam, or chlordiazepoxide to control the AWS.

However, there is a minor controversy as to how these compounds should be employed. Some physicians advocate a fixed-dosing regimen, in which a specified amount of the selected benzodiazepine is administered on a schedule. Such a program might center around the administration of an oral dose of 50–100 mg of chlordiazepoxide every 6 hours, with an additional dose of 25–100 mg administered every hour until the withdrawal symptoms are controlled, and then over a period of days the dosage level is reduced until the patient is medication free. If diazepam is used, the dosage level is usually between 5 and 20 mg every 6 hours until the symptoms are controlled, although in an extreme case a daily accumulated dose of 2000 mg/day was necessary to control the AWS (Bayard et al., 2004).

Most physicians now advocate a symptom-driven approach to the pharmacological treatment of the AWS (A. McKay et al., 2004). Symptom-driven withdrawal programs allow for the dose to be adjusted depending on the patient's observed symptoms, resulting in significantly lower daily total benzodiazepine dosage

level (Bayard et al. 2004; Daeppen et al., 2002). If the patient should experience higher levels of agitation or hallucinations, a low dose of an antipsychotic medication such as haloperidol can be added to the patient's regimen to further augment the pharmacological support being offered to the patient (Bayard et al., 2004).

There is some research evidence suggesting that the anticonvulsant medication carbamazepine might be a safe alternative to use in mild to moderate intensity AWS. This medication has been used for this purpose in Europe with great success (Bayard et al., 2004). The initial dose utilized is 800 mg, and then this is reduced by 200 mg/day over the next 5 days (Bayard et al., 2004). An advantage of carbamazepine over the benzodiazepines is that it is not sedating, and like the benzodiazepines appears to reduce the individual's "craving" for alcohol during the withdrawal process.

The team of Addolorato et al. (2007) suggested that the compound *Baclofen*® might be useful during both the acute withdrawal phase as well as during the postwithdrawal phase because it appears to lower the individual's "craving" for alcohol during this period. There is ongoing research both to replicate the original findings and to determine the correct dosage level to offer the greatest benefit to the patient.

Pharmacological Treatment of the Alcohol Use Disorders

In spite of the terrible damage wrought by the AUDs, it is surprising to learn that there are just four medications specifically sanctioned for the treatment of the AUDs (Sherman, 2008): (a) disulfiram, (b) oral naltrexone, (c) injected extended release naltrexone, and (d) acamprosate. Other compounds have either "off-label"[4] applications of medications used for other purposes to treat the AUDs, or are being investigated as possible agents to use in treating AUDs. Although these compounds have met with limited success, and there is research under way to identify new compounds that might be of value in treating AUDs, it should be noted that to date there are no criteria to identify those people who would benefit most from pharmacological treatment(s) for AUDs (Aldhous, 2010).

Disulfiram

At the 1949 annual meeting of the American Psychiatric Association, the team of Barrera, Osinski, and Davidoff (1949/1994) presented a paper on using the

---

[3]The benzodiazepines are discussed in more detail in Chapter 7.

[4]See Glossary.

medication Antabuse® (disulfiram[5]) as an antidipsotrophic[6] compound. The compound would cause "unpleasant effects" when mixed with alcohol, and as such seemed to show promise in the treatment of alcohol use disorders. These "unpleasant effects" were discovered quite by accident by workers in rubber factories who were experimenting with disulfiram as a possible way to vulcanize rubber. Many of these workers would stop off for a drink or two after work, only to become violently ill from an unsuspected interaction between the alcohol and the disulfiram ingested through their skin (Bohn, 2001).

A few years later, researchers searching for a way to treat worm infestations in animals administered disulfiram to the animals, and then went to have a few drinks with coworkers before going home. Like their counterparts in the rubber industry, they also experienced an unpleasant effect between the alcohol and the disulfiram that they had inadvertently absorbed through the skin. A veterinarian observed the interaction and suggested that perhaps disulfiram might be useful in treating alcoholism (Bohn, 2001). It was developed as such a medication and is the oldest antidipsotrophic medication in use (Sherman, 2008).

Clinically, disulfiram interferes with the biotransformation of alcohol by destroying the enzyme aldehyde dehydrogenase. This enzyme normally breaks down acetaldehyde, an intermediate metabolite produced during the alcohol biotransformation process, which normally is broken down very rapidly in the drinker's body. Without this enzyme, acetaldehyde, which is about 30 times as toxic to the body as alcohol, builds up in the body, causing discomfort as the toxin levels increase (Moalem & Prince, 2007). As the acetaldehyde levels increase further and further into the toxic range, the drinker will experience facial flushing, heart palpitations, a rapid heart rate, difficulty in breathing, nausea, vomiting, and hypotension (Schuckit, 2006a, 2006b; Sofuoglu & Kosten, 2004). *The dislfiram/alcohol reaction can be fatal,* especially in cases where the individual has ingested large amounts of alcohol or is sensitive to the interaction effects of these compounds. Thus immediate medical treatment is necessary to help ensure the patient's survival.

Under normal conditions it takes 3–12 hours after disulfiram was first ingested before it can block the alcohol biotransformation process. Thus physicians usually prescribe a 3- to 5-day "loading dose" period in which the medication is administered daily, to establish a therapeutic blood level of disulfiram in the patient's blood. When patients whose disulfiram level has reached that therapeutic level ingest alcohol, they will usually experience the interaction within about 30 minutes of the time they first began to drink. Because of its long half-life, disulfiram is usually administered only two or three times a week after the loading dose period. On rare occasions it is administered daily. Disulfiram remains fully effective for 24–48 hours, and in most cases there is no alcohol-disulfiram interaction after 6–7 days; although there are reports of such reactions taking place 14 days after the patient's last use of disulfiram in rare cases.

The alcohol-disulfiram interaction continues for between 30 and 180 minutes, although there are isolated cases where this interaction has continued for longer than this. It must be stated again that the alcohol-disulfiram interaction effect can be fatal, and patients with this condition should be brought to a hospital emergency room for assessment and medical support, as needed. Factors that influence the strength of the alcohol-disulfiram interaction include (a) the length of time that the person has been taking disulfiram, (b) the amount of time since the last dose of disulfiram was ingested, (c) the amount of alcohol ingested, and (d) the individual's biochemistry. As with any other medication, the biochemistry of some people is such that their bodies biotransform disulfiram at a more rapid rate than the average person, which will weaken the alcohol-disulfiram effect if they should drink at a time when their blood disulfiram level was lowest.

When used properly, disulfiram was thought to provide an additional source of support for the drinker in early abstinence during a moment of weakness, because it takes a number of days for disulfiram to be eliminated from the body. This allows the drinker time for "second thoughts" and a possible recommitment toward the goal of abstinence. To help patients understand the consequences of mixing alcohol with disulfiram, some treatment centers advocate a learning process in which patients receive a "loading" dose of disulfiram over the course of several days and then is allowed to ingest a small amount of alcohol. This will induce the alcohol-disulfiram interaction effect under controlled conditions, in the hopes that drinkers will then be less likely to carry out this experiment on their own after discharge from treatment.

Disulfiram, like all pharmaceutical agents, has an extensive list of side effects. Before 1970, megadoses

---

[5]This is the generic name.

[6]Literally, *antidipsomania,* a term popular in the 19th and early 20th centuries for alcoholism. Both terms are obsolete.

of disulfiram[7] were used, causing such side effects as delirium, depression, anxiety, manic, and psychotic reactions. The recommended dose of disulfiram has been drastically reduced to only 250–500 mg per dose since then; however, it is still recommended that patients with diabetes, hypothyroidism, cerebral damage, epilepsy, nephritis, or women who are pregnant not use disulfiram (Gitlow, 2007). At the dosage levels currently in use, identified side effects include skin rash, fatigue, halitosis, a rare and potentially deadly form of hepatitis, peripheral neuropathies, hallucinations, and potential damage to the optic nerve (Schuckit, 2006a, 2006b; Tekin & Cummings, 2003). There are also indications that it may exacerbate the symptoms of schizophrenia and may interfere with male sexual performance. Further, disulfiram is not recommended for elderly patients because it may contribute to cardiovascular problems for these patients (Drew et al., 2010).

There are a number of potential disulfiram-medication interactions that need to be considered. It potentiates the effects of the anticonvulsant medication phenytoin.[8] and patients with a seizure disorder who take phenytoin should consult with a physician before taking disulfiram to avoid the danger of medication toxicity (*Monthly Prescribing Reference*, 2008). Disulfiram also potentiates the effects of oral anticoagulants, a matter of some concern for patients who are anticoagulant therapy, as well as the antibiotic isoniazid, used to treat tuberculosis. Its use is contraindicated in patients who are receiving (or have recently received) metronidazole, alcohol, or "hidden" alcohol, often found in elixirs, certain foods, or aftershave products.

There are many other problems associated with disulfiram use as an adjunct to treatment. Medication compliance is difficult, and only 20% of those prescribed disulfiram take it as prescribed (Myrick & Wright, 2008; Rounsaville, 2006). Researchers have attempted to develop disulfiram implants that would provide a long-term supply of medication that could be absorbed over extended periods of time, however research has failed to demonstrate that these preparations result in any significant increase in abstinence rates over the traditional oral forms (Bohn, 2001). Because of its limited effectiveness, and the danger of disulfiram-induced side effects, its use is becoming increasingly rare (Standridge & DeFranco, 2006). It has been found that disulfiram is no more effective than a placebo as a support to abstinence (Bohn, 2001; K. M.

Carroll, 2003; Mariani & Levin, 2004; Sofuoglu & Kosten, 2004). This lack of effectiveness may be due, in part, to the fact that disulfiram does not reduce the individual's "craving" for alcohol in the early stages of abstinence.

Naltrexone

It has been found that alcohol ingestion causes the release of endogenous opioids within the brain's "pleasure center," especially the mu opioid receptor. It is thus logical to assume that any compound that blocks the mu receptor will reduce the individual's incentive to drink. This has been found to be true when naltrexone, a mu opioid agonist, is administered (Mariani & Levin, 2004). Initial expectations for naltrexone® as the "magic bullet" that would control urges to relapse have failed to be supported by subsequent research. One study found that 50% of patients on naltrexone relapsed within the first 12 weeks (Kiefer et al., 2003). A number of studies have failed to find *any* benefit from naltrexone in preventing relapse back to active alcohol abuse (Mariani & Levin, 2004). Further, there is evidence of a dose-dependent toxic effect on the liver, limiting its use for patients with some form of liver damage.

But there is some evidence suggesting that naltrexone is of limited value in the treatment of a subform of alcohol dependence known as "reward" drinkers. Such individuals crave alcohol, and when they give in to these cravings and drink, they experience a profoundly rewarding experience. Naltrexone blocks the reward cascade, thus reducing the incentive for these individuals to consume alcohol (Myrick & Wright, 2008). This would explain why, although naltrexone does not prevent the initial "slip," it does appear to reduce the chance that the "slip" will become a full-blown "relapse" (Volpicelli, 2005). There is also evidence suggesting that individuals with a familial history of alcohol use disorders may be more likely to benefit from naltrexone than patients who do not have a familial history of an AUD, although the mechanism for this effect is not known at the present time (Gilman et al., 2007).

Medication compliance with naltrexone is a problem. Forty percent of patients prescribed this medication discontinue taking it within 30 days, and 60% within 90 days (K. M. Carroll, 2003). To address this issue, a time-released form of naltrexone has been developed and marketed under the brand name Vivitro® (Prescribing Information, 2006). This form of naltrexone is injected once a month, but although it helps to control the "craving" for alcohol in the early stages of recovery, its high cost prohibits its use by many patients (Garbutt et al., 2005).

---

[7]In case you wanted to know, these dosage levels were 1–2g per dose, which is to say 1000–2000 mg per dose.

[8]Often sold under the brand name of Dilantin.

Acamprosate[9]

Acamprosate (sold in the United States under the brand name Campral®) has been used by physicians as an aid to the treatment of alcohol use disorders since 1989 (Hunter & Ochoa, 2006). Acamprosate is derived from the amino acid taurine, which itself has effects similar to those of alcohol (Stahl, 2008). Like ethyl alcohol and taurine, acamprosate inhibits the glutamate receptors while enhancing GABA receptors. This compound appears to limit the release of glutamate both during and after the period of alcohol withdrawal. This appears to be accomplished through a drug-induced alteration of the calcium channels in neurons, slowing the responsiveness of those neurons to stimulation (K. M. Carroll, 2003; Hunter & Ochoa, 2006; Mariani & Levin, 2004; Overman, Teter, & Guthrie, 2003). This action both blocks some of the rewarding actions of alcohol and limits the "craving" for alcohol reported by many alcohol-dependent people in the early stages of recovery (Stahl, 2008).

Acamprosate has a limited side effect profile, and there is no evidence of a "rebound" effect when it is discontinued (Hunter & Ochoa, 2006). There has not been evidence of acamprosate abuse. Its safety profile even allows it to be used during acute alcohol withdrawal (Gual & Lehert, 2005). There are no reports of drug interactions between acamprosate and other pharmaceuticals, including disulfiram (Overman et al., 2003). Between 10 and 17% of patients started on this medication will experience transient diarrhea, which usually resolves within a few days (Hunter & Ochoa, 2006; Standridge & DeFranco, 2006). Other rare side effects include depression, nausea, drowsiness, dry mouth, and increased sexual desire (Hunter & Ochoa, 2006). It is excreted virtually unchanged by the kidneys (Overman et al., 2003; Sherman, 2000a). There is some evidence suggesting that it might improve sleep during the early stages of recovery (Stanner et al., 2006). This is an advantage, because sleep disturbance is a common complaint in patients in the early stages of recovery.

Unfortunately, medication compliance is a problem because this medication must be taken three times a day. Further, the clinical evidence supporting the use of acamprosate is limited, with some studies finding no difference in abstinence rates between those patients who use this pharmacological support and those who do not (Anton et al., 2009; Gitlow, 2007). Thus further research must be carried out to determine whether acamprosate has a role in the treatment of alcohol use disorders and, if so, how it might most effectively be utilized.

The compounds just discussed are those that are approved for the treatment of alcohol use disorders. In the section that follows, we will examine some of the compounds that are thought to be of value or that are being examined as a possible pharmaceutical aid to the recovery from alcohol use disorders.

Topiramate

This medication was originally introduced for the control of epilepsy. Topiramate enhances the effects of GABA in the brain, blocking the rewarding effects of alcohol and thus the individual's incentive to drink. Preliminary studies support the theory that it might prove useful as a tool to treat alcohol use disorders as well. The team of Baltieri, Daro, Ribeiro, and de Andrade (2008) found that 67% of their research sample had remained abstinent at the end of 4 weeks of treatment, 62% remained abstinent at the end of 8 weeks, and 46% were still abstinent at the end of 12 weeks of treatment. All three of these abstinence figures were significantly better than those achieved with naltrexone or a placebo, the authors reported.

This might be the mechanism by which topiramate reduces the frequency of alcohol use by chronic drinkers (B. A. Johnson et al., 2007; Mariani & Levin, 2004; Sofuoglu & Kosten, 2004). It has also been found that patients on topiramate had a significantly lower level of liver enzymes (suggesting abstinence) as compared with those people who did not receive this medication, and achieve a higher level of function (B. A. Johnson et al., 2008; Rubio, Martinez-Gras, & Manzanares, 2009). These studies would suggest that topiramate might be a valuable asset in the pharmacological treatment of alcohol use disorders in younger adult drinkers. However, because topiramate can induce cognitive impairment in older drinkers, its use in this population is not recommended (Drew et al., 2010).

Baclofen®

Experimental research suggests possible value in alcohol dependence, because it is not hepatotoxic (Addolorato et al., 2007). It appears to reduce alcohol withdrawal distress at least as well as diazepam (Addolorato et al., 2008). However, the long-term effectiveness of this compound in treating alcohol dependence is still being explored. At this time its use as a pharmacological support for the treatment of the alcohol use disorders is still experimental.

Aripipraole

Aripipraole, an agent used to treat both psychotic disorders as well as the bipolar disorders, has been

---

[9]The chemical name for this compound is *calcium acetylhomotaurinate*.

recommended as an aid to the treatment of the alcohol use disorders (Kranzler et al., 2008). Although this medication has been found to reduce alcohol's ability to induce euphoria through its ability to block dopamine receptors, it also increases alcohol-induced sedation in a small study (Kranzler et al., 2008). Although the original results were promising, there is a need for additional study into the utility of this compound to help treat alcohol use disorders, according to the authors.

Nalmefene

This is an opioid antagonist similar to naltrexone in terms of its chemical structure (Mason, Salvato, Williams, Ritvo, & Cutler, 1999). However, nalmefene has a longer half-life than does naltrexone, and it also binds more effectively at the mu, kappa, and receptor sites, which are the neurotransmitter receptor sites that are thought to be involved in alcohol-induced euphoria. This would suggest that this compound is at least as effective as naltrexone as a pharmacological support for the treatment of the alcohol use disorders, but there has been little interest in exploring the application of this compound in this manner.

Buspirone

Initial research suggested that buspirone might have value as a pharmacological support of the treatment of alcohol use disorders. However, subsequent research has found that buspirone is of value only for individuals who had a preexisting anxiety disorder who were abusing alcohol as a form of self-medication (Mariani & Levin, 2004).

Metronidazole

Metronidazole is an antibiotic compound that was considered as a possible adjunct to the treatment of the alcohol use disorders in the 1970s. This medication, when mixed with alcohol, will induce a disulfiram-like response. However, subsequent research has failed to suggest that metronidazole is effective as an antidipsotrophic[10] medication (R. K. Hester & Squires, 2004).

Lithium

In the last decades of the 20th century, there was a great deal of research into the possible use of lithium to treat the alcohol use disorders. Lithium is an element that has been found useful in the treatment of the bipolar affective disorders.[11] Early research was promising, but subsequent research failed to replicate the early

research evidence, and it is generally assumed that lithium is of value only for those individuals who have a concurrent alcohol use disorder and a bipolar disorder.

Ondansetron

This compound has been used to treat early-onset alcoholism in Europe with some success (B. A. Johnson et al., 2000). It is based on the theory that early-onset alcoholism might be the result of a serotonergic system dysfunction. Ondansetron is an experimental 5-HT_3 blocker. The 5-HT_3 receptor site is one of the serotonin subtypes, and has been found to be involved in the subjective experience of alcohol-induced pleasure. So by blocking this receptor subtype, it would be possible to reduce the individual's incentive to use alcohol because the drinker would derive no pleasure from the alcohol use. A disadvantage of this compound is its relatively short half-life. The individual must take it twice a day, with the result that the drinker could discontinue its use a day or so before drinking, with minimal to no drug-induced blockage of the 5-HT_3 receptor. At this point, ondansetron remains an experimental compound.

Selective Serotonin Reuptake Inhibitors (SSRIs)

Given the theory behind the use of ondansetron as a 5-HT_3 blocker, one would assume that the SSRIs would also be useful in the treatment of the AUDs. Unfortunately, these compounds have proven to be ineffective in the treatment of the alcohol use disorders, unless the patient should have a concurrent depressive disorder (Bohn, 2001; Mariani & Levin, 2004).

Varenicline

There is preliminary evidence based on research studies in which this compound (sold under the brand name of Chantix® for smoking cessation) was found to also be useful as an aid to alcohol use cessation. The team of McKee et al. (2009) found that heavy-drinking people who also smoked were less likely to smoke when given varenicline than were those who received a placebo. They also reported having fewer periods of "craving" for alcohol. The authors found that 80% of their research sample did not drink during the study period, as compared with only 30% of those who received a placebo, suggesting that there is need for further study into varenicline as a possible aid to alcohol use cessation.

Prazosin

There is some evidence supporting that prazosin, an alpha-1 adrenergic antagonist, might be useful in the treatment of alcohol dependence (T. L. Simpson et al., 2008). This compound is normally used to treat hypertension

---

[10]See Glossary.

[11]Formerly known as *manic depression*.

and is sold under a variety of brand names. A research study involving only 24 subjects did find that those who received this medication reported drinking fewer days of the week as opposed to the control group, although there was no difference between the two groups as to the amount of alcohol consumed per session.

Part Summary

Although the search for pharmacological agents that might assist the alcohol-dependent person abstain from future alcohol use is limited, there is evidence that some current, and experimental, compounds might assist the individual in this task. Major pharmaceutical companies, however, are not committed to the search for such compounds, and if such a medication were to be found, it probably will be as an incidental finding for a pharmaceutical introduced for another disease state. Further, there is a danger of "mission creep" (Aldhous, 2010, p. 43), which is to say that if a new medication were to be proven effective in the treatment of the AUDs, then physicians might be tempted to say to a patient, "You show signs of *possibly* having an AUD, so let's put you on this medication as a precaution." Another form of "mission creep" is when the diagnostic criteria become less strict, allowing the number of potential patients who could be legitimately be prescribed a new medication to increase.[12] Finally, there are no diagnostic criteria that can be used to identify those individuals who might best benefit from pharmacotherapy for an alcohol use disorder (Aldhous, 2010).

Pharmacological Treatment of Amphetamine Use Disorders

At this point, there are no known, reliable pharmacological treatments for the amphetamine use disorders (Haney, 2008; Jayaram-Lindstrom, Hammarberg, Beck, & Franck, 2008; McLellan, 2008). Scientists are exploring a number of lines of research in an attempt to identify such a compound(s) (Ling et al., 2006; Winslow et al., 2007). Although the amphetamines and cocaine are both classified as CNS stimulants, it

should be pointed out that medications under investigation for possible use in treating amphetamine addiction might not work for people addicted to cocaine, nor would the reverse automatically be true (Haney, 2008).

Buproprion

Initial clinical trials have indicated that this compound might help to block the "craving" that many amphetamine abusers, especially methamphetamine abusers, experience in the early stages of recovery. Further research to confirm these initial research studies is ongoing at this time (Rawson & Ling, 2008).

Modafinil

Modafinil, a compound sold to treat narcolepsy, appears to hold some promise in the treatment of methamphetamine abuse or addiction through its ability to activate some of the nerve pathways involved in attentiveness without initiating the reward cascade (Rawson & Ling, 2008; Vocci & Elkashef, 2009). Further research into the utility of this compound in the treatment of the amphetamine use disorders is needed (Vocci & Elkashef, 2009).

Naltrexone

There is preliminary evidence suggesting that naltrexone can reduce the incentive to abuse amphetamines (Jayaram-Lindstrom et al., 2008). The causal mechanism for this effect is not clear, however, because naltrexone blocks the endogenous opiate receptors involved in the pleasure cascade, which might block the ability of the amphetamines to induce euphoria and thus remove the incentive for their use. The authors found that 62% of their research sample who were placed on naltrexone remained compliant with taking the medication, and that at week 12 of the study these subjects reported less subjective "craving" for amphetamines than did those who were not on naltrexone. Research into the possibility utility of this compound in the pharmacological treatment of amphetamine addiction continues at this time (Vocci & Elkashef, 2009).

Topiramate

As an anticonvulsant, this compound helps to normalize neural activity, especially in seizure focal points in the brain. This action suggests that it might also help to normalize neural functioning during the period of acute withdrawal from an amphetamine compound such as methamphetamine. Research into this possibility is in progress at this time (Rawson & Ling, 2008; Vocci & Elkashef, 2009).

Gamma-Vinyl-GABA (Vigabatrin®)

This is an anticonvulsant medication approved for use in Europe but not in the United States. It functions as a

---

[12]An excellent example of this process might be seen in the marketing and prescribing tactics used by pharmaceutical companies that produce medications prescribed for "erectile dysfunction." Over the past 20 years or so, the suggested use of these medications went from men with pathological erectile dysfunction to all men who experience erectile dysfunction even if it is a normal part of aging. In receiving such a medication, those individuals with milder forms of this problem are also exposed to the dangers inherent in any medication use.

dopamine receptor antagonist in the nucleus accumbens, which is involved in the reward cascade. It is under investigation as a possible pharmacological treatment for the amphetamine use disorders at this time (Vocci & Elkashef, 2009).

Immunological Therapies

There are also a number of studies attempting to use the immune system to "attack" amphetamine (especially methamphetamine) molecules in the circulation. This would prevent the amphetamine molecule from binding at the receptor site, thus preventing it from inducing any sense of pleasure (Vocci & Elkashef, 2009).

Pharmacological Interventions for Cocaine Use Disorders

At least 19 compounds have been considered as a possible pharmaceutical intervention(s) for cocaine abuse or addiction, without a single compound being found to be effective in this role (Payer & London, 2009). It is also important to point out that although both the amphetamines and cocaine are classified as CNS stimulants, there is little reason to suspect that a compound found to be useful in treating the addiction to amphetamines would automatically be effective in treating cocaine addiction (Haney, 2008).

At one point researchers thought that the antidepressant medication might help control postcocaine "craving," but research did not support this expectation (Kosten & O'Connor, 2003). Surprisingly, there is an emerging body of evidence suggesting that disulfiram[13] might reduce cocaine postwithdrawal "craving" by increasing norepinephrine levels in the brain during the early stages of recovery (Sofuoglu & Kosten, 2004). This compound also functions as an indirect dopamine agonist by inhibiting the action of the enzyme dopamine beta hydroxylase. When patients on disulfiram abuse cocaine, they will experience an intense feeling of dysphoria (Kampman, 2005; Rounsaville, 2006). Although disulfiram does not eliminate the problem of cocaine abuse, it does appear to hold promise in the treatment of cocaine addiction.

There also is preliminary evidence that the β-blocker (or beta blocker) propranolol might also prove useful during acute cocaine withdrawal (Kampman, 2005). This is accomplished by a β-blocker-induced reduction in people's sensitivity to both adrenalin and noradrenalin, thus reducing their feelings of anxiety and agitation during this period (Kampman, 2005).

Another medication that is being examined as a possible pharmacological support for the treatment of the cocaine use disorders is *Baclofen*®, a muscle relaxant that is apparently able to reduce the individual's emotional responsiveness to conditioned cocaine use cues (Kampman, 2005). Finally, the anticonvulsant topiramate also appears to have a modest effect in helping to prevent a relapse back to active cocaine use following detoxification (Kampman, 2005).

Experimental Pharmacological Interventions for the Cocaine Use Disorders

In an interesting approach to the treatment of cocaine abuse or addiction, researchers have explored the use of the antipsychotic medication aripiprazole to block cocaine craving in rats and found that the experimental animals were less likely to resume self-administration of cocaine if they received aripiprazole (Feltstein, Altar, & See, 2007). This effect was dose-dependent, with those rats receiving the highest doses having the lowest rates of apparent cocaine-seeking behaviors. Because aripiprazole blocks the dopamine receptor sites in the brain, and cocaine affects these same receptor sites, the observed effects do make clinical sense. However, further research is needed to determine whether this medication would be effective in treating human subjects with the same results as those observed in the original experiment.

Buprenorphine

The initial research studies suggested that this compound might be useful in the treatment of cocaine abuse or dependence. However, subsequent research has failed to consistently replicate the original studies, suggesting that this medication probably is not effective in the treatment of cocaine use disorders (Kosten et al., 2008). Research into the possible utility of this medication in the pharmacological treatment for cocaine is ongoing.

Clonidine

Early experimental studies have suggested that this antihypertensive might be useful in curbing cocaine "craving" (Kosten et al., 2008).

Desipramine

There is mixed evidence that this antidepressant compound might reduce cocaine "craving," but it is useful in depressed cocaine abusers.

Gabitril®

There is also evidence that a medication used as an adjunct to control seizures known by the generic

---

[13]Discussed earlier in this chapter.

name tiagabine might be of use in treating cocaine craving during the early stages of recovery. This compound functions as a GABA reuptake blocker, thus enhancing the sedating effects of GABA[14] during the early stages of recovery (Heidbreder & Hagan, 2005).

Immunological Methods

Researchers are also attempting to teach the body's immune system to attack cocaine molecules (Sergio, 2008). This is done by attaching a foreign molecule, such as a biological toxin, known to trigger a strong immune system response to the cocaine molecules. When the immune system "learns" to attack the cocaine molecules, it will hopefully neutralize it before it reaches the brain, before it can induce any euphoria for the abuser (Sergio, 2008). This approach appears to have promise, although the initial vaccine was found to be only 38% effective in stimulating the addict's body into producing sufficient numbers of antibodies to suppress cocaine's effects, and that these effects lasted for only about 2 months, thus making revaccination necessary every 2 months (Martell et al., 2009).

Methadone

Animal research suggests the possibility that methadone (discussed later) might prove of value in the treatment of cocaine addiction (Leri et al., 2008). Leri et al. concluded that steady-state methadone elevated the mu opioid receptor mRNA expression in the nucleus accumbens and basolateral amygdala regions of the rat brain, reducing the reinforcing effects of cocaine for the experimental animals. However, the applicability of this research to humans remains unproven. Although these medications appear promising, to date no single medication, or combination of medications, has emerged to provide pharmacological support during the early stages of recovery from cocaine addiction.

Tiagabine

This compound is a GABA reuptake inhibitor and has been found to reduce the frequency of cocaine use and the amount of cocaine use in research subjects over a 10-week period of time (Kosten et al., 2008).

Topiramate

Originally introduced as an anticonvulsant, this compound appears to reduce the desire to abuse cocaine,

but the original studies must be replicated to ensure that it is indeed effective when used to treat cocaine use disorders (Kosten et al., 2008).

Pharmacological Treatment of Inhalant Use Disorders

There are no known pharmacological treatments specifically for the inhalant use disorders (Brust, 2004). Depending on the comorbid conditions, as well as inhalant-induced medical complications, a wide range of compounds might be employed to assist the individual in recovering from the abuse of these compounds.

Pharmacological Treatment of Marijuana Use Disorders

At this time, there are no medications that specifically treat marijuana use disorders (Sheff et al., 2007). An interesting study conducted by F. R. Levin et al. (2004) attempted to utilize the effects of the anticonvulsant medication divalproex sodium to treat marijuana abuse. The subjects in this study reported lower levels of marijuana "craving" while taking divalproex sodium, but there was little evidence of sustained abstinence from marijuana use in this research sample. The compounds buspirone and rimonabant have demonstrated some promise in controlling marijuana "craving," although it would appear that cognitive-behavioral psychotherapy and/or behavioral psychotherapy offers greater promise in marijuana dependence (Benyamina, Lecacheux, Blecha, Reynaud, & Lukasiewcz, 2008).

Pharmacological Treatment of Narcotic Use Disorders

There are three subcategories of medications used in the treatment of opioid use disorders (OUDs): (a) medications to treat opioid overdoses, (b) medications used to control the symptoms of the opioid withdrawal syndrome, and (b) opioid agonist agents to block opioid withdrawal symptoms. Each of these subgroups of compounds will be discussed in turn.

Medications to Treat Opioid Overdose

The mainstay treatment is Narcan (naloxone hydrochloride), with appropriate medical support (respiratory support and the like). This compound is a pure opioid antagonist and is available only in intravenous form (Thompson PDR, 2007). When injected, it

---

[14]Or counteracting the activating effects of NMDA, depending on how you want to look at it.

reverses the sedation, respiratory depression, and hypotension induced by an opioid overdose, with the effects usually beginning within 2 minutes. Unfortunately, it has a relatively short half-life (estimated at approximately 30–80 minutes) and so multiple doses might be necessary before the patient has completely recovered from the overdose. A second side effect of Narcan is that it will induce the opioid withdrawal syndrome at the same time that it is reversing the opioid overdose.

The pharmacokinetics of Narcan are quite well studied. It is metabolized in the liver, and 25–40% of the original dose is excreted in the urine within 6 hours (Thompson PDR, 2007). There is limited protein binding noted, and this compound will cross the placenta into the fetal circulation.[15] It is not known at the present time whether this compound will cross over into breast milk.

Compounds to Treat Opioid Withdrawal

The opioid withdrawal syndrome can cause some degree of physical distress to the patient being withdrawn from narcotic analgesics. This is true for the patient who has been receiving narcotic analgesics after an extended period of medical treatment, or for the person who is physically dependent on any of the legal or illegal opioids available for abuse. In this section, we will examine the medications most commonly utilized to help control the symptoms of the opioid withdrawal syndrome.

The opioid withdrawal syndrome does not automatically mean that the patient is an opioid abuser or addict. Patients who have suffered a severe injury that requires extended hospitalization, or repeated hospitalizations, and who are prescribed narcotic analgesics will often develop an Iatrogenic[16] addiction, although many physicians find it less threatening to patients to refer to their condition as a reflection of the process of a degree of neuroadaptation[17] to the prescribed medication(s). To minimize the patient's withdrawal distress, physicians will often set up a gradual "taper" program to allow the individual's body to gradually adapt to lower doses of narcotic analgesics, minimizing the physical distress, with the goal being that the patient will eventually be discontinue the use of narcotic analgesics.

Methadone

Methadone is often used by physicians for the "taper" process described in the last paragraph. It is also used for opioid withdrawal in cases of opioid dependence. The extended half-life of methadone makes it ideal for opioid withdrawal programs. Although some physicians and many members of the general public believe that methadone withdrawal for the opioid addict is a waste of time, in reality it does not appear possible at this time to determine who will remain abstinent from opioids even after just 4 weeks' time (Dijkstra, De Jong, Krabbe, & Van der Staak, 2008). This fact alone would appear to justify methadone as an aid to opioid withdrawal. Further, various forms of pharmacological support during the opioid withdrawal process increase the chance that the patient will remain in abstinence-centered rehabilitation programs for a longer period of time following the completion of the withdrawal process (Dijkstra et al., 2008).

Although it is possible to carry out a methadone "taper" on an outpatient basis, most programs do so on an inpatient basis. Successful completion rate for an outpatient opioid detoxification regimen is only 17%, as opposed to 80% of those who are detoxified on an inpatient unit (Polydorou & Kleber, 2008). Also, there is a danger that patients have also been abusing other compounds besides narcotic analgesics, a fact that they might have conveniently not mentioned at the time of their assessment for methadone-based opioid withdrawal but that might have life-threatening withdrawal syndromes of their own. In addition to the threat to the patient's life, polysubstance abuse or addiction reduces the patient's potential for successfully completing the withdrawal sequence, and of accepting a referral to a rehabilitation program. Inpatient detoxification programs also avoid the danger of medication diversion, because the patient receives the prescribed dose of methadone as administered by staff. Finally, inpatient detoxification allows for medical supervision of the patients in case of unreported concurrent medical problems.

Initially the patient is observed until the onset of withdrawal symptoms. Then oral doses of methadone are administered in increments of 10 mg/hour until the withdrawal symptoms are brought under control (E. D. Collins & Kleber, 2004; Polydorou & Kleber, 2008). This then becomes the starting dose for the withdrawal sequence on day 2, when the patient receives this same dose all at once. Perhaps, in a hypothetical case, a patient required eight 10 mg doses before his or her withdrawal symptoms were initially brought under control. On day 2 this patient would receive a single 80 mg

---

[15]This is a matter of some concern, because it means that the fetus will also immediately go into opioid withdrawal if the mother was an opioid addict, even if the fetus is in utero.

[16]See Glossary.

[17]See Glossary.

dose, usually in the morning. Then the patient's daily dose of methadone is reduced by 5–10 mg/day until she or he is completely withdrawn from all narcotics (E. D. Collins & Kleber, 2004). Sometimes the physician will order a slower taper when the daily dose reaches 10 mg/day, perhaps reducing the individual's daily methadone dose by only 2 mg/day, a process that remains unproven in terms of patient retention (E. D. Collins & Kleber, 2004).

Patients must be reminded that when their daily methadone reaches 30 mg (or in some cases less), they will experience some degree of withdrawal distress. There is no symptom-free withdrawal, and it is at this point that patient retention becomes a problem. Extended withdrawal regimens, some lasting up to 180 days, have been used in the hopes of improving patient retention. This approach does not appear to be more effective than the traditional 5- to 21-day methadone withdrawal cycle (P. G. O'Connor, 2000). An interesting approach is the slow reduction of the patient's daily methadone requirements until the individual reaches a 30 mg/day dosage level. At this point the patient is switched to buprenorphine (discussed in the next section) and then tapered from buprenorphine over the appropriate period of time (Polydorou & Kleber, 2008). There is a need for further research into the efficacy of this approach.

Buprenorphine

This compound, used in some opioid agonist programs, has also become a popular agent for control of the withdrawal symptoms from narcotics. When used in this capacity, patients are observed until they demonstrate moderate level withdrawal symptoms, a process that usually requires 8–12 hours. At that point 2–4 mg of buprenorphine are administered in a sublingual dose (Polydorou & Kleber, 2008). If the withdrawal symptoms continue for another hour, another 2–4 mg of buprenorphine are administered in a sublingual dose. Yet a third sublingual dose of 2–4 mg of buprenorphine might be necessary to control the individual's withdrawal symptoms in extreme cases. Once the withdrawal symptoms are controlled, the individual's daily dose of buprenorphine is slowly reduced (usually at a rate of 1–2 mg/day) until the "taper" is completed.

Clonidine

Clonidine was originally developed as an antihypertensive agent. It also has a mild analgesic effect, although it is rarely if ever used in this capacity (Polydorou &

Kleber, 2008). As was discussed in Chapter 11, narcotic analgesics suppress the action of the locus ceruleus region of the brain. This region of the brain becomes hyperreactive during narcotics withdrawal, contributing to the individual's distress. Clonidine, which is technically an alpha-2 adrenergic agonist, helps to suppress the activity of the locus ceruleus, reducing the individual's withdrawal discomfort and withdrawal distress. However, it has been found that clonidine-assisted withdrawal by itself results in significantly higher patient dropout rates than does a withdrawal regimen in which clonidine is used in combination with other compounds (R. D. Weiss et al., 2008). This would seem to reflect the fact that clonidine does not completely control the individual's "craving" for opioids.

Another disadvantage of clonidine-assisted withdrawal is that this compound is an antihypertensive and can cause abnormally low blood pressure levels (increasing the risk of patient falls) in many people. Also, many patients have learned to combine clonidine with methadone, alcohol, benzodiazepines, or other compounds to induce a feeling of euphoria. Thus health care professionals must closely monitor the patient to both ensure patient safety and minimize the danger of nonprescribed drug use during the withdrawal process.

Experimental Methods of Opiate Withdrawal

Ultra-Rapid Opiate Withdrawal

In the late 1990s the concept of ultra-rapid opiate withdrawal was introduced. Developed at the Center for Investigation and Treatment of Addiction (CITA) in Israel, the process of ultra-rapid detoxification from opiates is carried out when the patient is in a chemically induced coma to minimize or totally avoid opiate withdrawal–related discomfort (Whitten, 2006). After the coma is induced, the patient receives both clonidine and opiate antagonists, and the entire withdrawal process is completed within a single day. Although there was a great deal of media attention when this procedure was first introduced, follow-up studies have revealed that it is only about as effective as traditional methods of opioid detoxification (E. D. Collins, Kleber, Whittington, & Heitler, 2005; Polydorou & Kleber, 2008; Whitten, 2006). There is little evidence to suggest that patients who go through this process are more likely to abstain from further opioid abuse than those who are detoxified through traditional methods, raising questions as to the need for such a costly and dangerous process[18] (Brust, 2004; E. D. Collins & Kleber, 2004; Kosten & O'Connor, 2003; Whitten, 2006).

Opiate Agonist Agents

The use of opioid agonist agents is based on the theory that, by blocking some of the opioid receptor sites, it will be possible to control, if not avoid, the patient's withdrawal symptoms without inducing euphoria. In this part, we will look at the commonly used opioid agonist agents.

Methadone

Perhaps the best known of the opiate agonist agents currently in use to treat opiate addiction is methadone. Methadone is a synthetic narcotic analgesic developed by German chemists in World War II for use in treating battlefield injuries. It is well absorbed following oral intramuscular and intravenous injections (Toombs & Kral, 2005). Methadone is increasingly used to treat persistent pain, such as that encountered with certain ongoing medical disorders, as well as the control of opiate withdrawal symptoms, and in the context of methadone maintenance programs (MMPs).

The utilization of methadone to treat persistent pain often results in some confusion in patients who associate it only with the treatment of drug addicts. "I am not an addict!" is a refrain often heard from patients who find out that their doctor has prescribed methadone for them. In such cases it is necessary to explain that methadone was originally developed as a narcotic analgesic. It is necessary to explain to these patients that the extended half-life of methadone allows physicians to treat pain with fewer episodes of "breakthrough" pain that might add to the patients' discomfort. This does not imply that patients are addicted to opioids, it should be pointed out, but only that their physician has prescribed a long-acting narcotic analgesic to help control their pain.

When used properly as an adjunct to the rehabilitation of people addicted to opioids, methadone is relatively safe.[19] The mortality associated with methadone maintenance programs is 1500% lower than untreated opiate addiction, a fact that supports its use in the control of opioid withdrawal symptoms for those who are addicted to narcotics ("Methadone Overdose in MMT," 2007). The vast majority of deaths associated with methadone use are caused by overdoses of methadone obtained from illicit sources. However, the danger of drug–drug interactions between prescribed methadone and other prescription medications can also result in a fatal reaction ("Methadone Overdose in MMT," 2007). However, even therapeutic doses of methadone have the potential to cause cardiac arrhythmias, as discussed later in the section Complications of Prescribed Methadone Use.

There are approximately 1200 methadone maintenance clinics in the United States at this time ("OTPs: Past, Current, Future—Part III," 2008). Although this number would seem impressive, in reality only about 20% of the estimated 810,000 opioid-dependent people in the United States are thought to be in a methadone maintenance program at any one time (Lipman, 2008; O'Brien, 2008). Access to these programs is limited: The average waiting period between the time that an opiate-dependent person applies for admission to a methadone maintenance program and final admission is 10.6 weeks, and four states have no methadone maintenance programs at all in spite of the significantly higher death rate for untreated opioid addicts ("Methadone Overdose in MMT," 2007).

History

The use of methadone to control the "craving" for narcotics that so often disrupts efforts at rehabilitation was first explored by Drs. Dole and Nyswander in the mid-1960s (Dole, 1988; Dole & Nyswander, 1965). There was a wave of heroin addition in the United States at the time, and the standard treatment[20] had proven inadequate to meet the need for rehabilitation at the time. Dole and Nyswander (1965) suggested that long-term opioid abuse caused permanent changes in the brain's structure on a cellular level, and that these changes contributed to addicts' experience of "craving" for opioids if they could not obtain their drugs. This "craving" was hypothesized to continue for months, or even years, after the individual's last use of a narcotic, prompting the individual to start to abuse opioids to feel "normal" again (Dole & Nyswander, 1965). Dole and Nyswander (1965) hypothesized that if a compound could be found that would block the individual's craving for opioids, it would then be possible for the individual to participate in a psychosocial rehabilitation program.

---

[18]There is a risk every time that anesthesia or a drug-induced coma is utilized, even in a hospital setting.

[19]All medications carry a degree of risk, even when used as prescribed.

---

[20]There were just two treatment centers for narcotics addicts in the 1960s, both controlled by the federal government. These programs essentially provided just detoxification services for opioid addicts, who in most cases returned to narcotics use shortly after their discharge from the treatment center.

Dole and Nyswander found that subanalgesic doses of oral methadone would block the individual's craving for opioids for at least 24 hours (Kreek, 2000). However, in an excellent example of how one department of the federal government does not know what another department is doing, the Drug Enforcement Administration (DEA) threatened to arrest Dole and Nyswander (both federal employees working for another federal agency) for conducting this line of research ("After 40 Years the Basics of MMT Are Still Valid," 2005). Eventually, the DEA relented, and Dole and Nyswander were allowed to continue their research.

Pharmacokinetics and Clinical Application

It has been found that in order to prevent withdrawal symptoms from opioids, only 25–35% of the opioid receptor sites need to be occupied (Kreek, 2000; Schottenfeld, 2008). Further, the pharmacokinetics of methadone made it possible for once-daily administration for the control of opioid withdrawal symptoms. These factors made methadone "corrective but not curative" of opioid addiction (Dole, 1988, p. 3025). In spite of its potential in controlling withdrawal symptoms, methadone does not change the individual's personality, vocational skills, or support system (Gerada, 2005). Following stabilization on methadone, the individual will still require psychosocial counseling (Dole, 1988), and it might be a number of years before significant social or vocational progress is seen (Schottenfeld, 2008).

As noted in the last paragraph, to be effective the patient must receive a sufficient dose of methadone to block "craving" for narcotics, which research has found requires a minimal dosage level of 80 mg/day (Dole & Nyswander, 1965). Unfortunately, at least one-third of existing programs prescribe no more than 60 mg/day for the program participants (D'Aunno & Pollack, 2002).[21] This can cause the patient to experience subclinical withdrawal symptoms, contributing to the risk of relapse to active drug abuse.

When utilized appropriately, methadone maintenance programs have been found to be cost-effective, with each dollar invested in such programs ultimately providing a return of $38 to society through reduced health care costs, less criminal activity, and increased employment (Clausen, Anchersen, & Waal, 2008; Zarkin, Dunlap, Hicks, & Mamo, 2005). In spite of these apparent advantages, methadone maintenance is still extremely controversial (Khantzian, 2003a).

Complications of Prescribed Methadone Use

If patients on a MMP are injured and require analgesia, MMP participants require *more* of a narcotic analgesic to achieve the same degree of pain relief as opioid non-abusers (Schottenfeld, 2008; Toombs & Kral, 2005). Methadone occupies less than 35% of mu opioid receptors to block "craving" for narcotics, a level far too low to achieve significant levels of analgesia (Schottenfeld, 2008). Unfortunately, many physicians continue to dismiss the need for additional analgesic medications because patients "are on methadone and shouldn't need any additional medications" following surgery or injury, causing many patients in MMPs to suffer needless, often extreme pain following an accident or injury.

A second, overlapping concern is the potential for multiple health care providers to be working with the same individual (Walley, Farrar, Cheng, Alford, & Samet, 2009). Research has found that the primary health care provider was unaware of the patient's participation in a methadone maintenance program in 30% of the cases, and in part because of this fragmentation of care 69% of patients on a methadone maintenance program were receiving concurrent prescriptions for at least one medication that could interact with the methadone with potentially fatal results (Walley et al., 2009). Another important patient safety consideration is that methadone has the potential to induce or exacerbate potentially fatal cardiac arrhythmias, including *Torsade de Pointes* (Justo, Gal-Oz, Paran, & Seltser, 2006; Roden, 2004; Tatro, 2009).[22] Periodic reassessment of the patient's cardiac risk status, including serial electrocardiogram (EKG) studies, should be carried out by the prescribing physician (Schottenfeld, 2008).

Application of Methadone in Maintenance Programs

Following stabilization on methadone, the patient's medication is usually administered once a day, although some of the more progressive programs allow for "split dosing" to allow the patient to take part of the dose of methadone over a span of time. This medication is usually administered in liquid form to minimize the risk of drug diversion and is often mixed with fruit juice to make it easier to swallow. Patients who meet the federal and program guidelines may be permitted "take-home" dosing privileges, receiving a designated number of doses to be taken at home as per their medication schedule.

---

[21]Often this is because the state legislature prohibits the use of higher doses than this.

[22]Discussed in Chapter 11.

It is recommended that patients remain involved with the MMP for a minimum period of 1 year to allow them sufficient time to address problems in living. For some patients the commitment to methadone is a life-long one, again reflecting that their addiction can be arrested but not cured. Although psychosocial support services have been found to be useful adjuncts to the individual's rehabilitation, they are rarely offered. M. K. Kraft, Rothbard, Hadley, McLellan, and Asch (1997) concluded that three counseling sessions a week per client was the most cost-effective in helping clients abstain from heroin use. Such counseling is labor intensive, and unfortunately most programs have become little more than drug distribution centers, some providing subtherapeutic doses of methadone while making no effort to provide actual rehabilitation services (J. F. Kauffman, 2003a, 2003b).

Methadone and Chronic Pain

About 37% of patients on a methadone maintenance program will report severe, chronic or persistent pain, whereas 60% will report some level of pain even while on methadone maintenance (D. T. Barry et al., 2009). There is virtually no clinical literature on how to address these problems in the patient on methadone maintenance programs, although evidence would suggest that the treatment of coexisting psychiatric problems (depression and the like) will often reduce the patient's pain intensity (D. T. Barry et al., 2009). Nonopioid therapies to reduce pain (physical therapy and so on) are also of assistance. It should be noted that, in spite of strident claims to the contrary, chronic pain does not appear to be associated with an increase in the abuse of other compounds (D. T. Barry et al., 2009).

Criticism of Methadone Maintenance Programs

Dole developed the model of methadone maintenance on the theory that opioid agonist treatment was similar to the role that insulin played in the control of diabetes (Kleber, 2002). This analogy, although useful in understanding the role that methadone might play in the pharmacological treatment of opioid dependence, is not automatically true. It is just a conceptual model and does not make opioid dependence a true disease state just because the analogy is useful (Marlowe & DeMatteo, 2003, 2004).

Critics of the methadone maintenance program model also suggest that it is simply switching addiction from the drug(s) obtained from illicit sources to an addiction to a drug obtained from a legal source (Joseph, 2004; Kauffman, 2003a, 2003b; Kleber, 2002).

Many MMP patients also abuse alcohol or cocaine, both compounds that speed the biotransformation of the methadone. In many cases they then claim a need for a higher dose of methadone than was originally prescribed to avoid withdrawal symptoms (Karch, 2009; Mendelson & Mello, 2008). Other participants in MMPs use these compounds while on methadone because they find that they enjoy the mixture of these chemicals. Further, many patients on methadone maintenance programs attempt to obtain prescriptions (or illegal sources) for propoxyphene,[23] which enhances the effects of methadone and causes the user to experience a sense of euphoria. Other patients attempt to obtain benzodiazepines through either legal or illegal sources in an attempt to enhance the methadone-induced euphoria ("Dangers of Benzodiazepine Abuse During MMT," 2009). Both medications are ingested simultaneously for this reason, exposing the individual to the risk of benzodiazepine addiction and the potential for an overdose from the combined effects of these two medications.

At the very least these observations suggest that MMPs are not the ultimate answer to the problem of opioid dependence. Dole (1989) acknowledged as much when he observed that methadone is "highly specific for the treatment of opiate addiction" (p. 1880), doing little to block the euphoric effects of other forms of substance abuse. Further, it was acknowledged that medication diversion was a problem (Dole, 1995). There is anecdotal evidence that some opiate-dependent people will purchase illicit methadone to carry out a methadone "taper" at home, reducing their drug dosage requirements. Finally, there is a significant dropout rate for patients in MMPs. These observations support the observation that MMPs are not the ultimate answer to the problem of opioid dependence.

Buprenorphine

This compound is a chemical cousin to morphine and is sold under the brand name of Suboxone®. When administered intravenously it is thought to be 25–50 times as potent as morphine.[24] A standard conversion formula is that 0.3 mg of buprenorphine has the same analgesic potential as 10 mg of morphine (Fudala & O'Brien, 2005). It can be administered through intramuscular or intravenous injections, but is rapidly destroyed by gastric secretions and so oral dosing is

---

[23]The legal production of which, as noted in Chapter 11, has now been discontinued in the United States.

[24]The side effects of buprenorphine are reviewed in Chapter 11.

impossible. It can, however, be administered sublingually. It is extensively biotransformed by the liver after being administered in this method, limiting its effectiveness as an analgesic. However, this characteristic, in combination with the ability to bind to the mu opioid receptor site for periods of time far beyond the time that it activates these receptor sites, makes it of value as an oral opioid agonist that can be used in much the same manner as methadone. It also makes it virtually impossible to overdose on buprenorphine (G. B. Collins & Leak, 2008).

Unlike methadone, buprenorphine does not appear to cause any delay in psychomotor or cognitive performance (M. Weiss, 2007). It is highly lipid bound (96%), providing a reservoir of medication that can control opioid withdrawal symptoms for an extended time (M. Weiss, 2007). When administered sublingually, it is absorbed by the blood-rich tissues that line the mouth. The bioavailability of buprenorphine is only 30–50% of that achieved after an intravenous dose (Donaher & Welsh, 2006). The medication that is absorbed then blocks the opioid receptor sites, acting much as methadone does in blocking the opioid withdrawal symptoms without inducing a significant degree of euphoria. Sublingual doses of 2–8 mg/day of buprenorphine are about as effective as 65 mg of methadone (Donaher & Welsh, 2006). However, some patients require more than 8 mg/day of buprenorphine, and doses up to 32 mg/day in divided doses might be necessary in extreme cases (Donaher & Welsh, 2006; Sofuoglu & Kosten, 2004).

A major advantage of buprenorphine is that the withdrawal syndrome experienced when a patient discontinues this medication are not as long nor as intense as those seen during the methadone withdrawal syndrome (Glasper, de Wet, Bearn, & Gossop, 2007; P. G. O'Connor, 2000). Anecdotal evidence would suggest that it is better suited for patients who do not have long-standing opioid dependence problems, and *at best it is only as effective as methadone* in controlling opioid withdrawal symptoms (Donaher & Welsh, 2006). Further, there is a significant problem with drug diversion, as intravenously administered buprenorphine has some abuse potential (U.S. Department of Health and Human Services, 2004). For this reason buprenorphine is often mixed with naloxone, which will precipitate opiate withdrawal if the tablet is crushed and injected (Leinwand, 2000). Further, some centers advocate that buprenorphine be administered only in a supervised setting, so that the patient is not sent home with tablets that might later be diverted.

A major disadvantage of buprenorphine is that opioid-dependent patients must be *totally* abstinent from opioids for a matter of several days in order to avoid a drug-induced withdrawal cycle when they start buprenorphine (U.S. Department of Health and Human Services, 2004). It has also been found to interact with a wide range of other compounds, including (but not limited to) benzodiazepines, alcohol, or other CNS depressants that might cause a potentially fatal drug potentiation effect. Buprenorphine has also been found to interact with many antiviral agents used to treat HIV infection (Fiellin, Rosenheck, & Kosten, 2001; Tatro, 2009). Also, its use with children or adolescents has not been approved by the Food and Drug Administration, which is a problem given the growing problem of adolescent opioid addiction (Fiellin, 2008).

An interesting experimental modification of buprenorphine was reported by Bai-Fang et al. (2004). The authors utilized an experimental polymer microencapsulated long-acting form of buprenorphine to be injected into the user's body. This allowed for the gradual release of buprenorphine over a 4- to 6-week period of time, blocking narcotic-induced euphoria and allowing the patient to gradually discontinue the use of narcotics without significant distress, according to the authors. This method did demonstrate some promise, but has not been more fully developed as of this time.

Naltrexone

Originally this compound was developed for the treatment of the alcohol use disorders, and as discussed in this context earlier in this chapter, it also has been found to be of limited value in the treatment of opioid use disorders. Naltrexone is an opioid antagonist blocking the mu opioid receptor site. Oral doses of naltrexone are well absorbed, and peak blood levels are achieved in about an hour. The half-life of naltrexone has been estimated to be between 3.9 and 10.3 hours, and clinical research suggests that naltrexone blocks the euphoric effects of abused opiates for up to 72 hours after it was last ingested.

The theory behind the use of naltrexone is that by blocking the euphoric effects of the opioids, the individual would have little incentive to abuse this class of medications. It does, however, present the danger of inducing the opioid withdrawal syndrome if administered before the patient has completely detoxified from the opioids. Some opioid abusers have tried to "shoot through" naltrexone by using exceptionally large doses of opiates, in spite of the danger of a potentially fatal overdose, and thus patients on naltrexone should be warned not to attempt this. When used as an adjunct to the treatment of the opioid use disorders, 100 mg of the medication is usually administered every other day, with the patient receiving 150 mg on Friday to block opioid craving over the weekend.

Although it would seem to be useful in the treatment of opiate abuse and addiction, naltrexone is not a "magic bullet" for the opioid use disorders (Kraly, 2009). There is no extinction for the drug "craving" while the patient is on naltrexone, and the patient should be warned of this problem. Further, there is no *unequivocal* benefit from the use of this compound in the treatment of opiate use disorders (Kraly, 2009). It appears to be most effective for those patients who are motivated to follow treatment recommendations. Finally, the vast majority of patients started on naltrexone discontinue the use of this medication within 6 months.

In 2006 a time-release, injected form of naltrexone was introduced under the brand name of Vivitrol (Prescribing Information, 2006). The applicability of this preparation in the treatment of opioid dependence has not been determined. However, its high price would prohibit its widespread use in the treatment of opioid use disorders if it is found to be effective in the treatment of opioid use disorders. One study (Ngo, Tait, & Hulse, 2008) found that patients who had received naltrexone implants were more likely to require hospitalization for treatment of nonopioid overdoses in the first 6 months of the study, and after a 3-year follow-up period it was found that those patients in the naltrexone-implant sample were then more likely to require hospitalization for (or die from) nonopiate overdoses. The authors called for further research into their observed findings to attempt to replicate these results. Thus the applicability of naltrexone to the long-term treatment of opioid use disorders has not been proven.

LAAM

Initial research suggested that LAAM[25] was useful as an opiate agonist agent that would function much like methadone maintenance. The extended half-life of LAAM (>48 hours as compared with methadone's approximate 24-hour half-life) added the additional advantage that the patient would need to come in for dosing every only second or third day rather than daily as in methadone maintenance programs. Unfortunately, shortly after it was introduced it was discovered

that LAAM could induce potentially fatal cardiac arrhythmias at therapeutic doses, and the production of this product in the United States was discontinued in 2004 (Ivanov et al., 2006).

Experimental Compounds for Opiate Use Disorders

Ibogaine, an alkaloid obtained from the root bark of the shrub *Tabernathe iboga,* has been considered as a possible agent for the treatment of opioid use disorders. This shrub grows in certain regions of Africa and has some hallucinogenic properties (M. Abrams, 2003). Either because of or in spite of this characteristic, ibogaine is reputed to eliminate the individual's "craving" for opioids, especially in the earliest stages of recovery (Glick & Maisonneuve, 2000). Scientists are uncomfortable with the use of ibogaine itself, as evidence suggests that at high doses it can cause neural damage, and it can induce side effects that are intolerable for many users.

However, researchers have also discovered that the major metabolite of ibogaine, a compound called noribogaine, might prove useful (M. Abrams, 2003). This compound has a half-life of several weeks and a chemical structure that lends itself to manipulation by scientists who hope to find a way to retain its reputed benefits while avoiding the harsh side effects (Glick & Maisonneuve, 2000). An experimental compound known as 18-MC appears to accomplish this goal, but there are still many misconceptions and governmental bureaucratic hurdles that stand in the way of the clinical application of this compound, if it is found to be effective in human subjects.

Pharmacological Treatment of the Tobacco Use Disorders

Nicotine has been shown to be the most addictive of the vast number of compounds found in cigarette smoke, and thus has been the focus of a great deal of clinical research. The most common method by which nicotine is abused is by smoking cigarettes, which is a process through which nicotine is rapidly introduced into the circulation and from there to the brain. The addictive nature of nicotine is such that many pharmacological interventions for the tobacco use disorders center on nicotine replacement therapies. This both limits the individual's exposure to other chemicals, because nicotine is but one of the menagerie of compounds found in tobacco products, and allows for a gradual reduction in nicotine dosage levels over an extended period.

---

[25]Or, *L-alpha-acetylmethadol.*

Nicotine Replacement Systems

Nicotine Gum

Nicotine-containing gum was first introduced as a prescription-only compound in 1984, but later became available without a prescription (Anczak & Nogler, 2003). It was hypothesized that this would provide a safe, convenient nicotine replacement mechanism for the smoker who wished to quit. The initial research suggested that 27% of patients who utilized nicotine-containing gum were smoke-free 6 months after the start of their abstinence program. However, subsequent research has shown that the true abstinence rate for smokers who utilize nicotine-containing gum is no higher than that achieved by a placebo (Okuyemi, Nollen, & Ahluwalia, 2006).

Smokers who elect to use nicotine-containing gum either as the primary tool or as an adjunct to their smoking cessation program must learn a new way to chew the gum in order to gain maximum effect. The individual must learn to chew the gum once or twice and then "park" it between the gum and the cheek for a few moments, before repeating the procedure. When this procedure is followed, 90% of the nicotine in that piece of gum is released within the first 30 minutes. However, a 2 mg piece of nicotine-containing gum will allow the user to achieve a blood nicotine level that is only about one-third as that achieved by smoking a cigarette. Although the 4 mg preparation doubles this blood nicotine level, it still falls short of the amount of nicotine released into the blood by cigarette smoking. This may result in "craving" for additional nicotine on the part of the smoker, who then discontinues the attempt to quit.

Further, nicotine-containing gum has been found to have many side effects, such as sore gums, excessive salivation, nausea, anorexia, headache, and the formation of ulcers on the gums where the person "parked" the gum. Beverages with a high acid content, such as orange juice or coffee,[26] also block the absorption of the nicotine from the gum. So former-smokers-to-be must closely monitor the form of their beverage intake to avoid such compounds that might negate the benefits of the gum. A recently identified danger in such nicotine-containing gum is that the nicotine in the gum might up-regulate the Fox_{M1} gene in the tissues that come into contact with the gum, increasing the individual's risk for the development of oral cancer (Gemenetzidis et al., 2009).

Transdermal Nicotine Patches

Transdermal nicotine patches have been found to be moderately effective. They have been found to reduce the insomnia so often reported by smokers who attempt to quit on their own, which is an advantage. It is generally assumed that only 3% of those who attempt to quit smoking on their own will be able to do so. The 10-16% success rate of smoking cessation for the first 6 months is thus a significant improvement, but this still means that 85% of smokers who attempt to quit fail to do so on this attempt at smoking cessation. This may reflect the fact that, in contrast to the nearly instantaneous delivery of nicotine to the circulation achieved with cigarette smoking, transdermal nicotine patches require approximately an hour for blood nicotine levels to reach their peak. This time delay is hardly appropriate for a behavioral modification program designed to extinguish an undesired behavior. Finally, the blood nicotine levels achieved through the use of the transdermal nicotine patch often are lower than those achieved by the process of smoking, inducing a "craving" for additional nicotine.

However, there is a very real danger should the smoker attempt to supplement their nicotine levels by smoking. Individuals who smoke either while still wearing the nicotine patch or within an hour of removing the transdermal nicotine patch are vulnerable to a nicotine toxicity that may potentially be fatal. It is recommended that if individuals should feel the need for additional nicotine, they use nicotine-containing gum, or in extreme cases (as in a three-to-four-pack-a-day smoker) multiple skin patches might be used under the supervision of a physician.

The transdermal nicotine patch can cause skin irritation, and so different sites around the body should be utilized on different days. Nicotine transdermal patch use has been associated with abnormal or disturbing dreams, insomnia, diarrhea, and a burning sensation where the patch is attached to the skin. Also, although it might seem obvious that the user would remove the previous day's transdermal patch before attaching a new one, there have been cases where the patient has left the old skin patches in place.

The former smoker is vulnerable to smoking "cues" in the first weeks and months following smoking cessation, and some patients become either psychologically or physically dependent on the transdermal nicotine patch. From a harm-reduction viewpoint, this is an acceptable compromise because there are over 4500 known compounds in cigarette smoke, and only 1 in the nicotine transdermal patch (Gitlow, 2007).

---

[26]How many people smoke cigarettes but never drink coffee?

Nicotine Nasal Spray

A nicotine-based nasal spray has recently been introduced, which is available only by prescription (Sofuoglu & Kosten, 2004). The user will administer one "puff" of the spray to each nostril where the nicotine will be absorbed by the blood-rich tissues of the sinuses. The spray can be used up to 40 times a day. Within 10 minutes of administration, the blood nicotine level will reach two-thirds of the level seen when a smoker smokes one cigarette (Anczak & Nogler, 2003). Initially, it was suggested that patients use this product for less than 6 months, in part because of a concern that they might become addicted to the nicotine spray. However, there has been little evidence that such addictions have developed (Anczak & Nogler, 2003). A degree of sinus irritation is possible from this spray, but there has been little research into whether this degree of sinus irritation is the same as that seen when an individual smokes a cigarette. Smokers who used the nasal spray were less likely to gain weight during their cessation attempt, and tended to gain less weight than those who did not use the spray. Just under one-third of those who attempt to quit using this method remained smoke free 6 months after quitting, as opposed to just 14% of those who received a placebo (Okuyemi et al., 2006).

In the late part of the 1990s, McNeil Pharmaceuticals introduced a nicotine "inhaler" for use by those smokers who were attempting to quit. The inhaler was housed in a device similar to that of a cigarette or cigar filter. This device was to be used in place of cigarettes, although it was held in the hand in a manner similar to the way that cigarettes are held. It will deliver 4 mg of nicotine out of the 10 mg that is in the cartridge to the user and is designed for short-term use. Twenty-three percent of those who used the inhaler remained cigarette free for 6 months, as compared to just 11% of those who received a placebo (Okuyemi et al., 2006).

Combination Therapies

An interesting approach was utilized by Piper et al. (2009), who found that although the transdermal nicotine patch was somewhat effective in helping smokers quit, the combination of oral nicotine lozenges and transdermal nicotine patches produced significantly higher abstinence rates than monotherapies such as transdermal patches or bupropion alone. The study did not utilize nicotine lozenges plus varenicline, which was a shortcoming of the study, but did suggest that the combination of transdermal nicotine patches and oral nicotine lozenges offered greater effectiveness to smokers *if* they

complied with medication-dosing schedules. The authors found that medication compliance was an issue, with a positive correlation between compliance with dosing and smoking cessation.

Non-nicotine Replacement Pharmaceuticals for Smoking Cessation

Although it might be argued that nicotine replacement therapies reflect a form of "pharmaceutical" intervention for smoking cessation, in this section we will discuss nonreplacement methods of smoking cessation intervention.

Bupropion

In addition to its primary effects on the serotonin and dopamine neurotransmission systems, this is an antidepressant compound, sold under the brain name of Wellbutrin®, that has a mild acetylcholine reuptake blocking effect. This side effect of bupropion was found to control the craving for cigarettes in former smokers who were taking this antidepressant for the treatment of a depressive disorder. Further research demonstrated that 21–30% of those patients taking this medication as an aid to smoking cessation were able to remain smoke free for 6 months, as opposed to only 10–19% of those receiving a placebo (Okuyemi et al., 2006). Bupropion was then marketed as an aid to smoking cessation under the brand name of Zyban®. However, questions have been raised concerning possible increased risk for aggression during the process of smoking cessation.

Chantix® (Varenicline)[27]

Varenicline was introduced as an aid to smoking cessation in 2006 (Alfonso, 2008). In the time since it was introduced, varenicline has been found to be the most effective pharmacological intervention for smoking cessation currently available, although it is not perfect, and there is a need for research into other pharmacological agents that might assist smoking cessation (Ebbert, 2009). Varenicline functions as a partial agonist at selected nicotinic acetylcholine receptor sites,[28] partially stimulating these receptor sites without activating the dopamine cascade necessary to cause pleasure-blocking nicotine from these receptor sites when the individual smokes (Chantix Prescribing Information, 2006). Maximum blood levels are achieved 3–4 hours after a single dose, and steady-state blood levels are achieved about 3–4 days of regular use at prescribed doses (Chantix

---

[27]The generic name for this compound.

[28]Technically the $\partial 4\beta 2$ receptor site.

Prescribing Information, 2006). Less than 20% of varenicline is protein bound, and the elimination half-life of this compound is about 24 hours with 92% of this drug being excreted in its original form (Chantix Prescribing Information, 2006).

The side effect profile for varenicline includes (but is not limited to) nausea, abdominal pain, flatulence, visual problems, depression, suicidal thoughts or attempts, mood swings, vivid (sometimes frightening) dreams,[29] and rare reports of angina pectoris, myocardial infarction, dry eyes, blurred vision, and gingivitis (Chantix Prescribing Information, 2006; D. Rogers & Pies, 2008). The original product safety and efficacy studies excluded people with psychiatric histories. The Food and Drug Administration requires a special warning for prescribers to the effect that varenicline use is associated with increased aggression and possible suicidal thinking (Price, 2009), although there is reason to suspect that claims that varenicline induces or contributes to suicidal thinking might be unfounded (McClure et al., 2009).[30] It should be noted that people with a preexisting history of depression who were placed on this medication tended to report feelings of tension or agitation during the first 3 weeks of treatment, as well as irritability, anger, continued depression, confusion, and problems with concentration (McClure et al., 2009). However, because patients with a preexisting psychiatric history were excluded from the original product safety and efficacy trials, the relationship between varenicline use and psychiatric symptoms remains unclear according to McClure et al.

Still, in 2008 the Federal Aviation Administration mandated that pilots and air traffic controllers could not use this compound in part because of its side effect profile. It is acknowledged that varenicline "is not a panacea for smoking cessation" (Klesges, Johnson, & Somes, 2006, p. 95). The benefits appear to last only about 12 weeks, possibly because of the process of neuroadaptation to the drug's effects (A. Smith, 2008).

Experimental Compounds for Smoking Cessation

Buspirone

It was once thought that buspirone might counteract the anxiety and agitation often experienced by smokers in the early stages of smoking cessation. However, subsequent research failed to support this theory, and it is not utilized as an aid to smoking cessation unless the smoker experiences high levels of anxiety during the smoking cessation process (Covey et al., 2000).

Clonidine

A number of clinicians have attempted to utilize the antihypertensive drug clonidine to control the craving for nicotine often reported in the early stages of smoking cessation. Although the initial studies were promising, subsequent research suggested that the side effects were so severe for the average user that it was not useful as an initial approach to smoking cessation (Anczak & Nogler, 2003). However, it might prove useful in the subpopulation of smokers who experience high levels of agitation when they attempt to quit smoking (Covey et al., 2000).

Inversine (Mecamylamine)

This is an antihypertensive compound that is an acetylcholine receptor antagonist, blocking the receptor sites in the brain. This compound would then block the individual's craving for cigarettes and has been moderately successful in smoking cessation programs, although it has not found widespread use in this application.

iSmoke®

This is an experimental method of smoking cessation, sometimes referred to as "e-cigarettes," that is available over the Internet from the United Kingdom (Thomson, 2009). The "cigarette" is based on microprocessor technology in which a computer "chip" causes the end of the "cigarette" to glow red and releases a measured amount of vaporized nicotine for the smoker to inhale. This product is available in a number of different strengths offering different nicotine levels to different users. This feature makes iSmoke® useful in smoking cessation programs, according to the manufacturer, because users can slowly reduce the amount of nicotine being administered until they are cigarette free.

There are mixed claims about the effectiveness of this device, and its use is quite controversial. Advocates point out that it does not produce the "sidestream" smoke that results in environmental tobacco smoke. They also point to the fact that it does not expose the user to the wide variety of other compounds in tobacco smoke besides nicotine, thus making it safer to use than traditional cigarettes. Detractors point out that it is heavier than a traditional cigarette and does not produce the aroma found when a cigarette is smoked (Thomson, 2009). It also produces limited amounts of the nitrosamines, which are carcinogenic compounds found in abundance

[29]Sometimes called "Chantix dreams."

[30]This is not unusual during drug efficacy and safety trials on the grounds that the psychiatric disorder is a variable that might confound the results of the study.

in cigarette smoke, as well as acetaldehyde produced by the small amounts of ethyl alcohol used in the iSmoke® cartridge (Thomson, 2009). The amount of acetaldehyde produced by the iSmoke® cartridge is quite small, however, and is rapidly biotransformed into metabolites that are then eliminated from the body.

Its safety or effectiveness as a smoking cessation aid have not been demonstrated, and the World Health Organization does not support the use of this product. This product is not commercially available in the United States at this time, and might be classified as a prescription-only product for those who wish to attempt to quit smoking (Thomson, 2009). Until proven effective, this product must be considered experimental, at best.

Nortriptyline

This antidepressant is viewed as a second-line smoking cessation agent, in part because of its toxicity and potential for a fatal overdose if taken in excess. However, it might be useful in working with depressed cigarette smokers, and there is a need for further research into the potential use of this compound in smoking cessation (T. P. George & Weinberger, 2008).

Silver Acetate

This is a compound used in Europe for many years as an aid to smoking cessation. It is available in a form of chewing gum and as a lozenge. When a person who has used silver acetate–containing chewing gum or lozenge smokes, they will experience a noxious, metallic taste, providing an immediate punishment that will help the smoker extinguish the desire to smoke. This compound is also quite dangerous. Massive doses can result in a *permanent* discoloration of the skin and body organs. Still, it is being examined as a possible aid to smoking cessation.

Clozapine

Clozapine is an "atypical" antipsychotic medication that has been shown in a small number of studies to reduce the symptoms not only of psychosis but also of substance abuse in dual-diagnosis patients (Lybrand & Caroff, 2009). The use of other "atypical" antipsychotic medications as an aid to the treatment of SUDs, especially in those patients with a comorbid psychotic disorder, has yielded mixed results, but do suggest that there is a need to determine whether these compounds offer any promise of assisting the substance abuser (with or without a psychotic condition) to abstain from alcohol or the other drugs of abuse.

Chapter Summary

The pharmacological treatment of the substance use disorders, like the treatment of all other disease states, involves the application of selected medications to either control the manifestations of that disease or cure it. Pharmaceutical companies often invest significant amounts of money to develop a compound(s) for these purposes, but dismiss the need to search for compounds to treat the substance use disorders because the market is too limited to provide a reasonable financial return on their investment. Thus most of the pharmacological compounds in use for the treatment of SUDs are actually medications used to treat other conditions, which have been found to also be useful as a pharmacological adjunct to the treatment of substance use disorders.

Several subgroups of medications utilized as adjunctive treatments for SUDs were reviewed: (a) medications that control withdrawal symptoms, (b) medications that control the individual's "craving" for drugs, (c) aversive agents that cause dysphoria when certain compounds are used, (d) compounds used to treat concurrent psychiatric disorders, (e) agonist compounds used in certain "maintenance" programs, and (f) medications used to treat drug overdoses. Also, experimental methods through which the body's immune system might be trained to attack specific drug molecules for cocaine and possibly the amphetamines were reviewed.

CHAPTER 34

Relapse and Other Problems Frequently Encountered in Substance Abuse Rehabilitation

Introduction

Research has repeatedly demonstrated that treatment is more effective than criminal justice sanctions as a way of dealing with substance use disorders (SUDs). But it also is not a panacea, either. There are numerous problems that might arise for the client in both inpatient and outpatient rehabilitation programs. In this chapter, we will look at some of the more common, and more serious, problems encountered by rehabilitation professionals working with the substance abuser.

Limit Testing by Clients

Clients in therapeutic relationships, including those with SUDs, will often "test" therapeutic limits. This is done either consciously or unconsciously by the client, in order to determine whether the therapist can be trusted or, in some cases, if it is possible to find a way to control the therapist. Limit testing takes many different forms: The client might repeatedly miss appointments, or call to cancel a previously scheduled appointment at the last moment. Other clients might abuse alcohol or drugs while in a rehabilitation program. Such situations present the therapist with opportunities to demonstrate that "dependability" and "consistency" are part of the foundation to rehabilitation. For example, treatment programs that warn clients that a certain number of "dirty" urine toxicology test results[1] will result in discharge from that program

tend to have greater success than programs that fail to set such limits.

The Counselor and Treatment "Secrets"

One common method of manipulation often attempted by clients is they request an individual conference with a staff member and then confess to a rules infraction. Sometimes such confessions are made to a student or intern at the rehabilitation facility. The client then begs the staff member to keep this a secret, for fear of being discharged from the program, put into jail by a probation officer who learns of this chemical use, divorce by an angry spouse, and so on. The substance abuse rehabilitation professional who honors this request then enters into a state of collusion with the client. This becomes a relationship in which the staff person, who is attempting to help the client outgrow addictive thinking, becomes an enabler of that client. Further, the

---

[1]Discussed later in this chapter.

client can then use this silence on the part of the staff member as leverage for blackmail ("If you don't do [*fill in the blank*], I will tell them how you didn't report my relapse!").

The proper response to this problem is for staff people to immediately properly document the material discussed, in writing and through proper channels. This might be a memo or an entry into the client's progress notes. Staffers should also discuss the revelation with their immediate supervisor. This is all done without malice, in order both to ensure uniform enforcement of the rules and to protect the staff person's reputation.

Treatment Noncompliance

In no other sphere of medicine is the social stigma associated with the SUDs so apparent as it is when it is argued that because such programs suffer from high dropout rates, they are not effective. These arguments are not made in other areas of medicine, where patient noncompliance is also a problem. They are reserved for those who work in the field of addiction medicine.

To illustrate the double standard applied to the field of addictions rehabilitation, consider the contrast between oncology treatment programs and substance abuse treatment programs. Cancer programs do not insist that the patient be in remission before being admitted for treatment, yet it is not uncommon for both inpatient and outpatient drug rehabilitation programs to require this before admitting a person for treatment (Blume, 2005). A patient with diabetes who is repeatedly admitted to the hospital for stabilization of their medical disorder is called a "brittle" diabetic. The alcohol- or drug-dependent person who relapses is called a "treatment failure." Although proponents of the public health model point out that both conditions are chronic, relapsing medical disorders, only in the field of addiction medicine is rehospitalization referred to as a treatment "failure."

Treatment noncompliance is an ongoing problem in all fields of medicine. It has been found that patients with a chronic illness who have received a prescription for a medication to treat that disorder take their medication as prescribed only 50–60% of the time (Shea, 2006). Older people who are prescribed a medication called digoxin for their heart condition were found to have their prescriptions filled so rarely that it was estimated that they were taking their medication only 111 days of the year (Shea, 2006).

TABLE 34-1 MEDICATION NONCOMPLIANCE	
CONDITION	NONCOMPLIANCE RATE
Epilepsy medication	30–50%
High blood pressure	30–60%
Lipid-lowering agents	25–30%
Antidepressant medication	30–40%
Immunosuppressive agents	18%
Antidiabetic medication	30–50%
Anticoagulant medication	30%
Antiasthma medication	20–60%

Table 34-1 provides a summary of different medical conditions and the rate of medication noncompliance for each disorder.

The problem of treatment noncompliance reflects, in part, people's denial and defensiveness surrounding their medical condition (R. Rogers, 2008). This issue would seem to be of obvious importance in the treatment of various medical disorders, and yet treatment noncompliance[2] has not been emphasized in the training of most physicians (Shea, 2006). Medication noncompliance is not limited to substance abusers, although the two problems do overlap. Moderate-level drinkers are less likely to have prescriptions filled than are nondrinkers (Bryson et al., 2008). The authors found that only 58% of moderate and heavy alcohol users had their prescriptions for antihypertensive and lipid control agents filled, as opposed to 64% of nondrinkers.[3] Of those advised to enter a rehabilitation program by medical professionals, less than one-third follow through with this recommendation.

However, the issue of treatment noncompliance in the field of substance abuse rehabilitation is a significant problem. Clients who request detoxification often fail to complete the detoxification cycle because of concurrent medical problems, unwillingness to experience the withdrawal process, "urges" to abuse drugs, encouragement from others to restart drug use, and so on (Franken & Hendriks, 1999). Myrick and Wright (2008) reported that 90% of chronic drinkers could be detoxified through "social" or outpatient detoxification programs, but that only 70% complete the process. Of this number, half go on to substance abuse rehabilitation (35% of those who enter outpatient

---

[2]Also called *nonadherence.*

[3]Which still means that just over one-third of nondrinkers also failed to have their prescriptions for antihypertensive medications filled.

detoxification). Although rehabilitation program professionals have attempted to identify personality traits that might help in the early identification of those people at risk for premature termination of patient treatment, to date this search has been unsuccessful (W. R. Miller, 2003). To complicate matters, clients' willingness to enter a rehabilitation program might not reflect their level of motivation to make a major lifestyle change such as achieving abstinence (Connors et al., 2001).

Substance abuse rehabilitation programs suffer from significant levels of patient attrition. Factors such as previous social isolation, solitary drinking, not being married, having no children, and being unemployed are all associated with a higher probability of premature termination from treatment for male clients. There has been little research into the factors that might predict premature termination from treatment for women. However, as is true in virtually every other area of medicine, treatment noncompliance is a major problem in the field of substance abuse rehabilitation.

Lapse and Relapse

At first the title for this section might confuse the reader who is unfamiliar with the field of substance abuse rehabilitation. However, both phenomena are frequently encountered, and often present a point of confusion even for rehabilitation professionals because there is no firm boundary between a *lapse* and a *relapse*. For the sake of this text, a lapse will be defined as when individuals *initially* abuses a compound after a period of abstinence, such as the first puff of a marijuana cigarette or the first swallow of alcohol. This brings them to a decision point: Do they reaffirm their commitment to abstinence and not proceed further, or do they continue to abuse the chemical(s)? In the latter case, they will have relapsed.

The term *relapse* is drawn from the medical model of the addictions and reflects a state where the patient falls back into an active disease state after a period of remission (Marlatt & Witkiewitz, 2005). An example would be a patient who had developed cancer of the liver, had that region of the liver excised surgically, and was free from any sign of liver cancer for 3 years following the surgery. Then, in this hypothetical example another malignant growth was discovered at the 3-year postsurgical evaluation. That patient would be said to have relapsed. In the field of addictions rehabilitation, however, a lapse does not automatically lead to a relapse. The guiding philosophy of many programs is that the two are the same. This treatment philosophy is at odds with the fact that whereas 99% of treatment programs aspire to the goal of total abstinence, only a minority of those who graduate from substance abuse rehabilitation treatment will completely abstain from further alcohol or drug use (Leavitt, 2003). This is clearly seen in the observation that 50–90% of those treated for an SUD relapse at least once during the first 90 days following completion of a treatment program, and that, in the case of alcohol, 45–50% will have returned to their pretreatment level of alcohol consumption within a year of their discharge from treatment (Polivy & Herman, 2002).

Although these statistics would suggest a rather pessimistic view of the efficiency of treatment for SUDs, eventually 40% of patients with an SUD achieve abstinence either alone or with professional assistance (Gitlow, 2007). To put this figure into perspective, this rate of recovery is almost three times that seen with lung cancer. An additional 20% of those treated for an SUD return to periods of problematic use, whereas the remaining 40% go on to develop a progressive SUD that might ultimately prove fatal (Gitlow, 2007). Again, to put this figure into perspective, up to 85% of lung cancer patients die within 5 years of the initial diagnosis. To again use the analogy of lung cancer, the addictions can be *arrested,* but can never be *cured* (Gitlow, 2007). Relapse prevention is defined as a self-management program designed to assist individuals in arresting their addiction to the best degree possible (Marlatt & Donovan, 2005). Within this context, individuals' relapse is not a sign that treatment failed, any more than would diabetic patients' rehospitalization for stabilization be a sign that their treatment regimen failed.

The team of Witkiewitz and Masyn (2008) concluded after their analysis of 563 individuals who had relapsed to active alcohol use that there were three different paths following the initial lapse. Following the initial relapse, the first group engaged in infrequent, moderate alcohol use, according to the authors. A second group were those individuals who initially engaged in heavy alcohol use, but whose frequency of alcohol use gradually became less and less frequent over time. The final group were those people who returned to a pattern of heavy alcohol use. Surprisingly, the majority of their sample reported returning either to total abstinence or to infrequent and moderate alcohol use following their lapse back to drinking (Witkiewitz & Masyn, 2008). The authors also found that coping skills at the time of the individual's first lapse were positively related to less frequent and less intense alcohol use at the time of relapse.

It has been suggested that relapse is triggered by one or more of the following mechanisms: (a) drug exposure (to either the same or another compound), (b) stress exposure, or (c) cue reexposure (environmental cues previously associated with substance use) (Boles, 2007; Clay et al., 2008). It must also be recognized that there are different neural circuits involved in the initiation of substance use and those that contribute to a relapse (Leamon et al., 2008). Thus situations that contributed to the initiation of use (and thus activated certain neural networks) are not the same as those neural networks that might contribute to relapse.

These mechanisms interact, providing an almost endless number of individual pathways toward the person's relapse. Drug exposure may be unintentional (such as when a recovering smoker rounds a corner outside of work and encounters a cloud of cigarette smoke from coworkers who smoke). It also might be the result of a prescription from a physician (for example, a former alcohol-dependent person who receives a prescription for a benzodiazepine, then relapses as a result of the similarity of effects between these two compounds). Drug exposure holds the potential to reactivate the reward pathways once stimulated by the compound(s) of abuse, initiating a neurochemical cascade that can cause urges and thoughts about the chemical use, again.

Stress exposure is a frequent relapse trigger (Haney, 2008). It has been discovered that when exposed to significant levels of stress, men and women will activate regions of the brain that control habit-based behaviors, not those regions of the brain involved in cognitive assessment and control (Elton & Kilts, 2009). Thus when faced with stress, the person's first response might be to fall back on the habit of using chemicals as a means to deal with the stress, not to adequately assess the situation and then select the most appropriate behavioral response. However, stress as a relapse trigger often takes unexpected forms. It is not the experience of stress that triggers a relapse but the individual's loss of hope, demoralization, and depression in the face of stress that appears to activate the habit-based substance use response (Elton & Kilts, 2009; W. R. Miller & Harris, 2000). If individuals believe that they are able to cope with the demands being placed on them by life, they are less likely to break down under that stressor and relapse.

It is important to keep in mind that stressors take many different forms. Social isolation[4] can cause urges to use chemicals and thus function as a relapse trigger. Another form of stress exposure is the end of a marriage, or loss of custody of children through divorce or other mechanisms[5] (Boles, 2007). Physical illness is a significant stressor and often can induce thoughts of new chemical abuse. For example, the physical sensations experienced when a person has a bad cold or influenza often are similar to those sensations of unmedicated opiate withdrawal. Unfortunately, for individuals who have suffered a traumatic event, and especially those people who have developed posttraumatic stress disorder (PTSD), memories can serve as relapse triggers (Work Group on Substance Use Disorders, 2007).

Finally, through the process of associative learning, a large number of external cues are associated with substance use. One rarely recognized factor in relapse is the individual's sense of *smell* (A. Levin, 2008). Clinically, this makes sense because human evolution has resulted in a process through which the process of smelling something also activates memory centers. In ages past, being able to recognize the smell of a predator and then rapidly recognizing the smell as a source of danger would be advantageous. A side effect of this evolutionary adaptation is that smell might also trigger memories associated with substance use. For the alcohol-dependent person, for example, the smell of cigarette smoke might be associated with the experience of being in a bar, where cigarette smoking is pervasive. Surprisingly, few treatment centers even mention the possibility that smells can act as relapse triggers.

Marlatt and Wikiewitz (2005) identified a number of factors that might contribute to a relapse back to active chemical abuse or protect against such a problem:

- Self-efficacy: *Individuals' confidence in their ability to cope with high-risk situations, thoughts, urges, and so on.*
- Outcome expectancies: *Individual expectations about the outcome of substance use should the person relapse. Euphoric recall[6] often is activated by outcome expectancies.*

---

[4]Which in part explains the need for participation in a substance-free support group.

[5]Such as when the state asserts that the parent is unfit to retain custody, for example.

[6]See Glossary.

- Craving: *Although "craving" in itself is a poor predictor of relapse, it might be triggered by substance use cues (sights, smells, sounds), which in turn trigger memories of past substance use. For example, a former smoker might see a cigarette that has been stubbed out in the bottom of an ashtray, initiating "craving" for a cigarette.*
- Motivation: *People's motivation for change, or commitment to change, plays an important role in whether they relapse or remain abstinent.*
- Coping style: *This poorly understood determinant of relapse reflects the individual's ability to call upon learned coping skills to deal with substance use cues.*
- Emotional states: *There is a strong association between substance use and relapse. Negative emotions are more often seen in cases of a full relapse, whereas positive states appear to be more often associated with behavioral lapses.*
- Interpersonal support: *The individual's access to a strong, substance-free support system during times of craving contributes to continued abstinence* if the individual calls upon this resource.

For each of these forces, one must also consider the proximal[7] or distal[8] relationship of that factor to the individual's relapse (D. M. Donovan, 2005). People's genetic heritage is often overlooked as a distal factor for relapse in that their biological heritage may make them more likely to be susceptible to substance use cues (D. M. Donovan, 2005; Westphal, Wasserman, Masson, & Sorenson, 2005). A more proximal relapse trigger might be the need to have blood drawn for medical testing, where the feel of a needle entering the skin reawakens memories of past injected drug abuse for IV drug abusers.

Factor analysis has yielded three categories of proximal warning signs for potential relapse (D. M. Donovan, 2005): (a) *cognitive factors,* (b) *emotional states,* and (c) *behavioral characteristics* of the client. These factors interact within individuals, moving them either closer to or further from a potential relapse. Cognitive factors have also been called *maladaptive thoughts*[9] by

various authors (Beck, 2004; Daley & Marlatt, 2005; D. S. Keller, 2003). Examples of such maladaptive thoughts include: "I can control it, now" or "I have learned enough to avoid relapsing" or the ever-popular "I will stay out of trouble if I only bring $20 with me to the bar. I only leave when I have spent it all." Maladaptive thoughts might allow the individual to (a) convert normal sources of stress into excessive stress and justification for continued substance use (example: "I cannot *stand* to feel this way!"),[10] (b) transform distress into craving (example: "In order to cope with this, I need to use NOW!"), or (c) rationalize a potential relapse as being acceptable (example: "Surely I can handle *just one.*") (Beck, 2004).

Another category of maladaptive thoughts reflects the individual's *desire for indulgence* (Blume, 2005). Many people view substance use as a reward for past behavior(s), thus believing "I *deserve* a drink after all that I've done!" Other people may view substance use as a way to escape life's pressures, if only for a while. Planned or unplanned meetings with substance-abusing "friends" offer the individual a sympathetic ear (while they indulge in substance use) and thus represent a high-risk situation for a potential relapse (Blume, 2005; Westphal et al., 2005). Such maladaptive thoughts must be identified and then the appropriate countermeasure(s) taken, to ensure that the individual can remain abstinent. The last example, for instance, offers an illustration as to why a substance-free support group is so important.

A frequently encountered situation is the situation where clients find that abstinence either does not bring the immediate rewards felt with substance use or they are faced with life's adversities without their usual substance-based coping mechanisms. A hypothetical client who has been abstinent for 6 months only to be informed that he has a serious, potentially life-threatening medical problem would be hard pressed not to at least think of returning to chemical use as a way of "coping" or of at least making themselves "numb" to external reality. A second hypothetical client

---

[7]Proximal forces are those in close temporal proximity to the event in question. For example, hitting a major pothole in the road might cause a driver to lose control of the motor vehicle and thus is the proximal cause of the resulting accident.

[8]Distal forces are those that are more distant from the event in question. To use the example cited previously, the winter's freeze-thaw cycles might have weakened the pavement, allowing the pothole to form, eventually causing the accident discussed in the last footnote.

[9]Often referred to in 12-step groups as "stinking thinking."

[10]A technique that the author of this text often calls upon when dealing with this maladaptive thought is to paint a graphic picture of $1 million in $20 bills. Then the client is asked whether she or he could deal with that feeling for 24 hours, at the end of which they would receive the $1 million dollars. If the client says "yes," it is then pointed out to the client that they have just demonstrated that they *can* deal with the stressor, and how they are responding to the stressor with addictive thinking ("I can only cope with this problem by using!"). The next step is to develop a coping mechanism to cope with that form of urge to use chemicals.

who, after 6 months of hard-won recovery, returns home to be informed that her spouse has filed for a divorce might very well wonder where the rewards of abstinence are to be found if she is hit in the face with such realities.

Although clinical evidence has identified negative emotional states such as anger, fear, or confusion as possible relapse triggers, it is surprising to learn that *positive* emotional states might also serve as a relapse trigger as well. This surprising discovery reflects a process through which the individual seeks a way to ensure that the positive feelings experienced thus far will continue. Clients thus need to learn to experience life as it unfolds and not try to control or negate it by chemical abuse. Negative life events happen to us all, not just to those in the early stages of recovery, although the person in the earliest stages of recovery might not understand this fact yet.

Another common cognitive error is when the client takes a *short-term view of recovery*. It has been discovered that if clients remain abstinent for 6 years, they are unlikely to relapse. Treatment staff must thus work with clients to help them understand that they must remain on their guard until recovery becomes a lifestyle, which will take a number of years to accomplish. Like many postsurgical patients, clients in the early stages of recovery must learn not to attempt tasks that they are not ready to deal with yet.

Social pressure was found to play a significant role in the individual's return to alcohol or drug abuse by Zywiak et al. (2006). The authors based this conclusion on their analysis of data from 592 people enrolled in a larger research study called "Project 'MATCH'" and found three classes of relapse: (a) negative affect or family influences, (b) craving cued relapses, and (c) social pressure. The third category accounted for more than 58% of the identified relapse events according to the authors. The authors of this study also found that motivational interviewing procedures seemed to provide greater protection against social pressure–induced relapse events than other forms of intervention utilized in the Project MATCH study.

Spiritual issues have been found to both lead back to and away from continued substance abuse (Gitlow, 2007). Such issues might include the client's ongoing feelings of shame, worthlessness, or lack of feeling "grounded," especially in the early stages of recovery. These spiritual issues often overlap with psychological stressors that can trigger a relapse. A frequently overlooked factor is that substance use often fills a need in the client's life. The bar, for example, might offer social

contacts for an otherwise socially isolated person who is hesitant to initiate social contact out of a fear of rejection. Thus the individual's core personality is a distal relapse trigger that may predispose some people to relapse (D. M. Donovan, 2005; Chiauzzi, 1990, 1991). Individuals who tend to have a compulsive component to their personality makeup are especially vulnerable to relapse because of psychological pressures. Such people do not react well to even minor changes in their daily routine. Dependent personalities,[11] for example, often utilize alcohol or illicit drugs as a way to cope with their anxiety in social situations. Dependent people also may have difficulty refusing alcohol or drugs when confronted with people who offer chemicals to them.

People with passive-aggressive traits, for example, tend to be unwilling to accept personal responsibility for their behavior and blame others for mistakes. "He offered it to me" is a common cry after a relapse. "I did not want to be rude and not accept it!" In this manner, the responsibility is placed on the person who offered the compound in question, not on the person who relapsed. In contrast to this is the narcissistic personality. Narcissistic personalities tend to view themselves as being above the rules that govern everyday society. They are quite self-centered and have trouble admitting to weakness of any kind. These characteristics make it hard for them to ask for help if tempted to use alcohol or drugs. Finally, a number of personality subtypes struggle with impulsiveness, distrust of others, and rebellion. Many people view the traditional path to recovery as a form of control being imposed on them, for example. These (and other) personality types must be viewed as distal relapse triggers that must be addressed if clients are to achieve long-term recovery.

Clients with substance use disorder often, when moving toward abstinence, turn to *substitute addictions* as a way to trigger the reward pathways once engaged by the chemical(s) of abuse. Examples of such substitute addicts include the use of other chemicals. Alcohol-dependent people might turn to beer rather than hard liquor, rationalizing this as being "safe" because of the comparatively low alcohol content of beer and the fact that they had trouble only after consuming hard liquor. OxyContin[12]-addicted people might discontinue the use of opioids but later admit that they have started to

---

[11]The issue of personality type is reviewed in the *DSM-IV-TR* (American Psychiatric Association, 2000), in Sadock and Sadock (2007), as well as in many books on psychopathology.

[12]Discussed in Chapter 11.

engage in heavy marijuana abuse. There are endless ways that people in the early stages of recovery might attempt to substitute one behavior for their SUD. The recovering alcoholic, for example, might turn to gambling, and about a quarter of recovering alcohol-dependent people eventually develop a compulsive-gambling problem. Drug rehabilitation professionals must learn to inquire about such substitute addictions. Urine toxicology testing[13] is often of value in detecting unauthorized compounds in the individual's body, which would suggest the possibility of a relapse, if not the development of a substitute addiction.

A relapse does not suddenly happen. It is preceded by a series of subtle, often irrelevant warning signs that might, if clients are sensitive to them, alert them to the impending danger. But few clients are sensitive to these warning signs, at least in the earlier stages of recovery (Daley & Marlatt, 2005). The relapse itself is the last step in a chain of decisions, many of which are apparently innocent and often made unconsciously, that ultimately result in the relapse (D. S. Keller, 2003). A client's decision not to have a prescription for Antabuse[14] refilled is a decision that appears to be innocent by itself, however, in combination with other decisions (such as participation in company-sponsored softball games where beer is available) might ultimately lead to the individual's relapse back to active drinking.

Relapse is a *process* and not a single event. Each individual decision is referred to as a "mini-decision." In the hypothetical example cited earlier, the person's decision not to have a prescription for Antabuse refilled on the grounds that it is too expensive is but one step on the road to the ultimate relapse. Placing themselves in danger by their participation in company-sponsored softball games where beer is freely available is yet another mini-decision that contributed to their relapse. It is possible to reconstruct the relapse step-by-step.

A very real danger is for clients to place themselves in *high-risk* situations, which expose them to both relapse cues and opportunities to use again. The client might, for example, go to a bar "to hear my brother's band play." The desire to hear a brother's band play is innocent enough. The setting where the band is working is the high-risk situation. One does not have to walk very far to obtain alcohol if that person is in a bar, and soon the soda that one is drinking pales as the person begins to remember past drinking experiences

in that environment. Other high-risk situations involve interpersonal conflict (Daley & Marlatt, 2005; D. S. Keller, 2003). People who have just had a disagreement with a spouse, for example, may be in a high-risk situation if they were accustomed to using alcohol or drugs to cope with their angry feelings in the past. For some clients, the simple act of receiving a paycheck places them in a high-risk situation, as they now have money with which to buy alcohol or drugs.

Substance abuse rehabilitation professionals must help the client identify high-risk situations and develop the appropriate coping skill(s) to deal with that problem. This increases the client's self-efficacy and self-confidence. However, clients should also be warned that even if they do develop that coping skill, it does not mean that they are ready to place themselves in the high-risk situation again. A client who has been coached in alcohol-refusal skills still is not ready to go to a bar to hear a brother's band play, for example. Temptation is just around the corner, and those refusal skills might not be up to the task even if the client should call upon them.

One time of special vulnerability is the Christmas holiday season. For some people the stress of being around family members, their potential alcohol use (even if on a social basis), and family squabbles are all potential relapse triggers (Aldhous, 2009). For others, the pain of being alone over the holiday season is a potential relapse trigger. Thus one must help clients develop coping mechanisms for dealing with the holidays without drinking by developing alternative coping plans and coping skills (such as leaving the room when others are drinking, or asking that they not consume alcohol when the individual is in the room, or going to support group meetings, for example) to help the client avoid relapsing back to active alcohol use during this time of stress.

To help the client develop skills necessary for long-term recovery from alcohol, instruments such as the Inventory of Drinking Situations (IDS-100)[15] may help identify high-risk situations for the alcohol-dependent person. Staff then can help the client learn how to cope with such problem areas. A recovering friend might be asked to go with the client to a sister's wedding, to ensure that the client does not ingest alcohol at the wedding reception. Other techniques might include having the client carry a reminder card(s) with step-by-step instructions on how to deal with the

---

[13]Discussed later in this chapter.

[14]Discussed in Chapter 33.

[15]A 100-item questionnaire that will shed light on situations where the person is most likely to drink.

TABLE 34-2 MOST COMMON CAUSES OF RELAPSE

CATEGORY	DESCRIPTION OF SITUATION	PERCENTAGE OF CASES
Negative emotional states	Patient is experiencing feelings of frustration, anger, anxiety, depression, boredom, and so on.	35%
Peer pressure	Pressure comes from either a single person or a group of people (coworkers, for example) to resume the use of a chemical(s) (tobacco, for example).	20%
Interpersonal conflict	There is conflict between the client and a close friend, spouse, child, employer, employee, and so on.	16%
"Craving" for drugs or alcohol	Person becomes preoccupied with use of alcohol or drugs, especially in early abstinence.	9%
Testing personal control	Patients expose themselves to a high-risk situation to see whether they can resist the urge to use alcohol or other chemicals.	5%
Negative physical states	Person is experiencing illness, postsurgical distress, or acute injury, for example.	3%

NOTE: Based on Daley and Marlatt (2005) and Dimneff and Marlatt (1995).

potential relapse situation, limiting the chance of a relapse. Although it is not possible to identify every high-risk situation, Table 34-2 identifies many of the more common antecedents to relapse.

It is possible to anticipate many such problem areas and help the client develop the appropriate behavioral coping skills for many of these problem areas, although as noted it is impossible to anticipate every possible relapse risk situation (Daley & Marlatt, 2005; Witkiewitz & Marlatt, 2004). Further, the research evidence supporting the concept of relapse prevention training has been mixed (R. K. Hester & Squires, 2004; Irvin, Bowers, Dunn, & Wang, 1999). Relapse prevention programs do seem to be of value in helping the individual cope with the sense of demoralization, anger, and depression that identify those people most prone to relapse (W. R. Miller & Harris, 2000). Further, continued involvement in "relapse prevention" programs involving both individual and/or group therapy sessions does seem to increase the individual's chances of achieving long-term abstinence (J. R. McKay, 2006). It is even possible to integrate relapse prevention work with community-based support group work[16] to provide ongoing individual and group support for the individual during times of crisis. However, these steps are not a guarantee, and even people involved in the most comprehensive of relapse prevention programs will slip back into substance abuse, or active addiction.

Acute Injury

Patients with substance use disorders are often at higher risk for acute injury than nonabusers. However, the substance-abusing patient who presents with a traumatic injury presents the health care professional with many therapeutic dilemmas (P. J. Woods & Bartley, 2008). For example, if an opioid addict should present at a hospital emergency room with a broken arm, and even after the administration of a medication that would normally provide adequate analgesia the patient requests additional pain medication, is this patient drug seeking or has the patient's pain been undertreated?[17]

All too often, pain is inadequately treated even in patients with no history of a substance use disorder. Health care accreditation agencies have recognized that pain is too frequently undertreated and have made this a priority for their attention. Thus *all* patient reports of pain should be accepted and assessed, and appropriate attempts made to address the pain (P. J. Woods & Bartley, 2008). It would be immoral for the health care professional to dismiss patients' claims that they are still in pain simply because "they are only an addict," or, in cases where patients are on an opioid agonist program, to dismiss their request

---

[16]Alcoholics Anonymous, Narcotics Anonymous, or any of the other emerging secular or faith-based support groups.

[17]To complicate matters, as if this author would ever do such a thing, patients on an opioid agonist treatment program (methadone or suboxone) often require *more* medication to achieve a given degree of analgesia because some of the opioid receptor sites are blocked by the agonist used to control withdrawal symptoms.

for additional analgesic medications as irrelevant because "they are already on methadone." This dismissal could prove rather embarrassing for the health care professional if the ever-so-casually dismissed pain was proven to be an indicator of a potentially treatable condition.

The client's substance abuse history will be one of the factors that will influence the patient's perception of pain following an injury. Opioid-dependent patients who present with a fractured arm, for example, might require *more* pain medication for adequate analgesia simply because of their acquired high tolerance to narcotic analgesics, a fact that is often forgotten or misunderstood by health care professionals attending to the patient's needs (P. J. Woods & Bartley, 2008).

Another danger is that the use of analgesics, even if appropriate under normal conditions, may predispose individuals to a relapse if they were to be recovering from an SUD, especially an opiate use disorder. Thus issues surrounding relapse prevention must be addressed immediately after the patient's stabilization. Recovering alcohol-dependent people, for example, might find themselves reexperiencing some of the same sensations achieved by their abuse of alcohol if placed on a sedating agent such as a barbiturate or benzodiazepine, even if the use of this compound is medically warranted. The similarity of effects would then trigger strong urges to use alcohol again, potentially causing a major relapse on the part of the client.

Although this discussion is not exhaustive, it does illustrate how even substance-abusing patients might present with legitimate complaints of pain in the acute-care setting. Unfortunately, such patients have also been known to abuse health care facilities to obtain desired medications. Health care professionals are thus forced to engage in a very thorough investigation to determine whether the patient's complaints are real or unfounded, often in a setting where they have limited time to address the matter. Tests such as the Opioid Risk Tool or the Screener and Opioid Assessment for Patients-Revised will help with this process (Jackman, Purvis, & Mallett, 2008). Even without the use of these instruments, substance abuse rehabilitation professionals must address the issue of how patients' use of a prescribed substance for what was deemed to be a medically appropriate reason might impact their SUD or recovery program. This is a complicated matter, which varies from patient to patient and within the same patient over time.

Chronic Pain[18]

It has been estimated that more than 20% of the general population in the United States, or 50 million people, live with a chronic (or persistent) pain disorder (CPD) (Porreca & Price, 2009; M. B. Smith, 2008). In about half of these cases, the CPD will resolve within a year. Some of these individuals will have a concurrent substance use disorder, which complicates the treatment of each disorder. Research has shown that 37% of methadone maintenance program patients present with severe CPD issues and that 60% will report having persistent pain of some kind (D. T. Barry et al., 2009; Schottenfeld, 2008). In some cases the pain is persistent, whereas in other cases it is intermittent. Unfortunately, there has been little research into the phenomenon of CPD, which is unfortunate because it is logical to assume that this problem will become more common as a result of the aging population and the sedentary lifestyles so commonly seen in today's world (Pohl, 2007).

The symptoms of persistent pain differ from those of acute pain. It is not uncommon for patients with acute pain to describe the experience differently than patients with CPD. Patients suffering from acute pain will often use words such as *sharp* or *cutting* to describe their pain, where individuals with chronic pain will describe their pain as "dull" or "aching," more diffuse, and with an ill-defined focal point (Jackman et al., 2008; M. B. Smith, 2008). In chronic-pain patients, the neural network associated with pain perception becomes very sensitive to stimulation of the affected area[19] (M. B. Smith, 2008).

Persistent pain can be quite refractory to medical treatment, leaving the patient to suffer significant distress. This can contribute to feelings of hopelessness, depression, and possible suicidal thinking by patients, who desire a way of escaping from what they view as a hopeless situation. Such patients also might adopt a pain-entered coping style, limiting their exposure to situations that might cause or exacerbate their pain. Although patients view these adaptations as useful, they often cause long-term disruption to their life and hold the potential to exacerbate their pain over time (M. B. Smith, 2008).

Persistent pain disorders are a challenge to medical professionals, many of whom have little or no training

---

[18]The problem of chronic pain in methadone-maintained patients is discussed in Chapter 33.

[19]Technically, a state of *hyperalgesia* is said to exist.

in working with these patients. If the patient should also have a history of an SUD, the health care professionals working with that patient become even more cautious out of a fear of medication misuse or diversion, and the possibility that prescribed treatment might exacerbate the patient's substance use disorder[20] (P. Compton & Athanasos, 2003). Many physicians simply refuse to treat patients with these coexisting disorders. The dilemma is this: People with substance use disorders are not immune from CPDs. Substance-abusing patients are not immune to accidental injuries with long-term sequelae, degenerative joint disorders, or back problems. However, because the narcotic analgesics[21] normally play a major role in the treatment of acute and possibly chronic pain, the health care professional is forced to determine which substance-abusing patient requires pharmacological treatment as opposed to other treatment options[22] to achieve the optimal outcome. This is not always an easy task, especially because patients with an SUD who also have a persistent pain disorder are a very difficult subpopulation to work with even under the best of conditions.

Some substance-abusing patients use complaints of continued pain to obtain additional medications, which can be sold or traded for other, more desired compounds. Such cases confirm the fears of physicians who seek to avoid this danger. Other patients will seek additional narcotic analgesics to self-medicate nonpain issues such as insomnia, depression, loneliness, and anxiety (P. Comptom & Athanasos, 2003). As a group, patients with coexisting CPD and SUDs are less likely to respond to a pain management program that does not provide large doses of narcotic analgesics, more likely to be noncompliant with program rules, and less likely to consider non-narcotic or non-drug-related pain management techniques (biofeedback, physical therapy, and so forth).

Even patients who do not have an SUD may, through the process of neuroadaptation, find that their pain is no longer controlled at what was once an effective dosage level of a narcotic analgesic. Their demand for more medication does not, as many health care professionals fear, reflect an SUD. Rather, this process reflects the phenomenon of *pseudo-addiction*. Once the patients' pain has been adequately addressed, they usually do not make demands for additional pain medication(s). Their vocal demands for additional pain medications, however, are very similar to that of a substance-abusing patient who desires more narcotic analgesics for personal gain. The physician must discriminate between the legitimate needs of the former group of patients, while avoiding the administration of unnecessary drugs to the latter group.

Even compliant patients with an SUD may be less tolerant of pain because of acquired partial tolerance to the pain medication(s) being administered (G. Chang, Chen, & Mao, 2007; P. Compton & Athanasos, 2003). This can be seen in the observation that extended treatment with methadone (as in methadone maintenance programs) alters the individual's pain sensitivity (G. Chang et al., 2007). Some physicians believe that it is useful to withhold narcotic analgesics from patients with concurrent SUDs, although there is little evidence to support this therapeutic myth. The essential question is whether a hypothetical patient who did not have an SUD would require the requested medications to provide an acceptable level of analgesia.

Patients with an SUD should not be forced to endure unnecessary pain because of their SUD. To assist the attending physician in making the determination as to the appropriate medication decisions, a treatment team that works together closely, is in constant contact, uses consultations with appropriate treatment professionals when needed, and uses a *treatment contract* are of value. The treatment contract will specify that the patient must (a) use only one specified pharmacy and (b) use only one doctor (except in emergency situations). In the latter case, the patient–physician contact must be reported to the patient care coordinator within 72 hours so that the treatment team can determine whether there was a legitimate need for the patient to see another doctor or not. The treatment contract should also specify that patients will be required to submit to urine toxicology testing on a random basis and that they will be called back for "pill counts" to make sure that they are taking prescribed medications per instructions.[23]

The treatment contract should state that the patient understands that nonopioid treatments such as physical therapy, or nonopioid pharmaceuticals (gabapetin or

---

[20]Technically, the term for this fear is *opiophobia*.

[21]Discussed in Chapter 15.

[22]Physical therapy, alternative medicine, chiropractic medicine, and so on.

---

[23]Patients who should have 18 pills of a specified medication left when called back for a "pill count," but who only have 12 pills in the bottle should raise suspicion that either they are taking more than was prescribed or are diverting medication.

valproate, for example), as well as psychosocial support and lifestyle changes (dieting, exercising, and the like) will be utilized as indicated (Cheatle & Gallagher, 2006; Jackman et al., 2008). Unfortunately, rural health care professionals rarely have access to treatment teams such as the one just outlined and must face the problem of chronic-pain patients within their home communities. Still, the patient should be expected to sign a treatment contract such as the one just outlined, with it clearly specifying that failure to adhere to the provisions of this contract are grounds for termination of treatment.

A fear among physicians treating chronic-pain patients with narcotic analgesics is that the continued use of these medications will induce an addiction. It has been suggested that younger, male patients, and those who have access to a larger supply of medication that they can take without medical supervision, are at highest risk for developing an opioid use disorder or of medication misuse (Edlund et al., 2007). To combat these problems, having the medication dispensed in smaller lots (such as every second day), or by having a trusted family member dispense the medication, or in smaller communities by having the patient report to the physician's office to have the medication(s) dispensed by the office nurse, are all options.

It is imperative for health care professionals working with substance-abusing chronic-pain patients to understand that the lifestyle of addicted people often makes them intolerant of incomplete solutions or of lengthy treatments. "I want what I want, and I want it *now!*" is the mantra of a large percentage of these individuals, forcing the medical staff to establish boundaries almost immediately and to rigidly enforce them. A violation of the pain contract by a patient who "only wanted some more pain relief" by taking nonprescribed medications should be considered grounds for termination of treatment. Once the word is spread that a given pain management program *expects* cooperation, there will be fewer such cases to deal with.

Unfortunately, the mainstay of treatment of acute pain, the narcotic analgesics, are effective for the short-term control of pain (<16 weeks), but the long-term effectiveness of such compounds for longer periods of time (>16 weeks) has been less than clear (Blondell & Ashrafioun, 2008). Although there are promises of nonopioid medications that will treat chronic pain on the distant horizon, the narcotic analgesics (often in combination with other techniques) will remain the treatment of choice at least for the immediate future.

Early Recovery and Sexual Activity

It is important for health care professionals to recognize that people with an SUD might have learned to associate the use of certain compounds (such as cocaine, for example) with sexual activity. Through associational learning, they might have come to believe that "normal" sex involves the use of these chemicals and now find that intimacy is not as rewarding without the use of these chemicals (Gitlow, 2007). Other people might find interpersonal intimacy rather uncomfortable without using a chemical(s), possibly because of feelings of inadequacy or social anxiety. Still a third group of substance abusers have been the victims of sexual assault at some point in their lives, and they have learned to use the anxiolytic[24] effect of alcohol, marijuana, or other compounds to make themselves "numb" to the feelings reawakened by sexual contact.

For all three subgroups of people, interpersonal intimacy without the use of alcohol or illicit chemicals might prove to be frightening. Indeed, some people will have abused alcohol or illicit drugs for so long that they have no memories to guide them in a relationship without a chemical in their system. For example, a hypothetical 50-year-old father of three children might report that he has not been intimate with his wife for the last 15 years of their marriage without having some alcohol in his system and that he is afraid of possibly being rejected by her.

For all three subgroups of substance abusers, interpersonal intimacy might serve as a relapse "trigger." It is not unusual for clients to also keep these fears to themselves, in large part out of shame, or be unwilling to discuss them to an opposite-sex therapist. A referral to a therapist of the same sex who will then assess the role that alcohol or drugs have played in that person's sexual activity would be appropriate, and appropriate referrals to a licensed, experienced sex therapist, individual psychologist, social worker experienced in marital therapy, or other professional should be made.

"Cravings" and "Urges"

It is interesting to note that in spite of the importance attached to the concepts of drug use "craving" or "urges" by substance abuse rehabilitation professionals, there is no standard definition of either term; nor is there an objective way to measure either construct

---

[24]See Glossary.

(Anton, 1999; Ciraulo et al., 2003; R. D. Weiss et al., 2003). Different researchers use the same terms in different ways, contributing to confusion not only between professionals but also in the popular media about the experience of a drug use thought and a relapse.

A drug use thought is just that: a thought. A client who, at the end of a hard day's work, might think that "a cold one [beer] would be nice, now" has just experienced a drug use thought. The experience is transitory, as are all thoughts. Clients should be taught that such drug use thoughts are normal, especially in the early stages of recovery. These thoughts are the result of associational learning. In the hypothetical example just cited, the client might very well have learned to associate a beer(s) with the end of the workday. In such a case, having such a thought is normal. *Acting* on that thought is inappropriate. We all have thoughts, and if the truth be told we all occasionally think about doing some inappropriate things (for example, "I wonder what it would be like to rob a bank?"). Most of us do not act on those thoughts.

Drug *craving* is an intense, subjective emotional and physical experience for the individual, which varies in intensity between individuals. People might find that they are responding as they normally would if they were about to use a chemical(s), such as having sweaty palms, feeling anxious, increased heartbeat, and possibly increased salivation, or the other physical sensations that they came to associate with substance use. They focus almost compulsively on drug use cues and may view themselves as being overwhelmed by these feelings. Neurologically, this experience appears to parallel the reduction in glutamate receptor sites in the nucleus accumbens region of the brain in the early stages of recovery, as well as blood flow changes in the brain's reward system (Tapert et al., 2003; F. Weiss, 2005).

Thus drug cravings are the subjective experience experienced while the brain adapts to the absence of the drug(s) of abuse during the early stages of recovery. The craving might be triggered by an internal stimulus (a thought or physical sensation, for example) or an external drug use cue (seeing a used hypodermic needle in the gutter, for example). These drug use cues trigger a subjective experience of craving for the individual. Unfortunately, because of the process of neuroplasticity, urges become stronger if the individual gives in to them even once because neural pathways (and associated receptor sites) increase when used (J. M. Schwartz & Beyette, 1996). The reverse process, extinction, will require that the brain rewire itself, a process that takes time. During this process, the individual will experience craving and urges to return to the use of chemicals.

Surprisingly, because craving for a chemical is a subjective experience, the same symptoms of craving might be interpreted as intense by one person, as moderate by a second, and as quite weak by a third person (R. D. Weiss et al., 2003). The experience of craving waxes and wanes in intensity during the first 12 weeks of abstinence, and clients should be warned that their craving will be most intense during this period (G. Carol, Smelson, Losoczy, & Ziedonis, 2001). However, clinical experience suggests that after the first 90 days, the individual's experience of craving will become less intense and less frequent, information that might offer the client some hope to cling to during the early days of recovery.

It is important to keep in mind that there is a vast difference between a *hard choice* to abstain from chemicals and *no choice* but to abuse those chemicals (Gendel, 2006). Urges and cravings are not the same as obligations to use alcohol or drugs (Heyman, 2009). Such cognitive experiences are just part of the early recovery phase. Clients should both be warned to expect them and trained in how to respond to them.

The "Using" Dream

A phenomenon that is both frequently encountered and has not been well researched, is the "using" dream. These dream experiences may be quite frightening to the person in the early stages of recovery. Clients will report having awakened after having a dream in which they just used drugs or alcohol that was so intense and seemed so real that they had trouble separating reality from the dream experience for the first few seconds after awakening. Such dreams may be a "relapse" trigger or may make clients wonder about their commitment to recovery. It is thus important to warn clients that these dreams are common and usually not a sign of impending relapse.

There are two types of dreams: (a) the rapid eye movement (REM) dream, which accounts for about 85% of dream experiences, and (b) the non-REM dream, which accounts for about 15% of dreams. Dreams that take place during REM sleep are noted for bizarre, intense imagery that often makes no logical sense: A long-dead relative walks through the wall in the dream, and the dreamer simply asks, "Would you like some tea?" (Doweiko, 2002). Non-REM dreams tend to be rather dull and involve the dreamer carrying out routine tasks.

During both REM and non-REM dreams, there is a neuromuscular blockade that prevents the body from acting on motor movement commands generated by the sensory motor region of the cortex during sleep. The brain's production of acetylcholine[25] drops significantly during dream sleep, which appears to be part of the psychomotor blockade that develops during REM sleep. If awakened, the dreamer will recall vague sensations of not being able to move normally, intense emotions, and confusing, often irrational thoughts.

Another process that seems to take place during the REM dream is that the brain practices the fight-or-flight response. Dreaming is a safe time to do this, because the body is unlikely to act out on the motor movement commands involved in the fight-or-flight response. During REM dreams the amygdala[26] is exceptionally active, a fact that supports this theory. These fight-or-flight response emotional memories are intense sensations of fear and anxiety, feelings that might carry over into the dream's waking state for a few seconds.[27] In the normal waking brain, it is the duty of the cortex to make sense of internal and external sensations, and if the dreamer is feeling fear, then there must be something in the dream experience that initiated that fear. Memories of substance abuse would certainly cause dreamers to feel anxious if they were committed to abstinence.

The outcome of these two processes is that (a) dreamers have vague memories of not being able to move naturally in the dream, memories that closely simulate their experience(s) while under the influence of chemicals, and (b) dreamers recall feeling anxious, if not very frightened, during the dream state as the brain's neurochemical balance shifts from the dreaming state to the waking state. A relapse would be a situation that could trigger such intense emotions. Fortunately, anticipatory guidance[28] will help clients deal with such dreams. Further, as the associational memories between substance use and various substance use cues weaken over time, these "using" dreams will become less intense and less frequent over time. It seems rare for clients to report such dreams after the first 3 months of recovery, although on rare occasions clients will report such dreams and as having awakened with the thought on their minds, "Why would I ever want to do *that*?"

Toxicology Testing
Urine[29]

The issue of urine toxicology testing is one of the more controversial issues in the field of substance abuse rehabilitation. It is one of the most common and most cost-effective methods by which substance abuse might be detected (Bolnick & Rayburn, 2003; Cowan, Osselton, & Robinson, 2005; Nordgren & Beck, 2004). There are also legal standards and laws involved in the collection and interpretation of urine toxicology tests, which vary from state to state, that define the manner in which urine samples can be collected, the chain-of-evidence standards that must be met, the methods by which the urine sample can be tested, and who can legally interpret the test results (Standbridge, Adams, & Zotos, 2010).[30]

The assessor must understand, however, that a positive urine toxicology test is not, in itself, sufficient to diagnosis an addiction and should not be substituted for a clinical interview and medical evaluation (U.S. Department of Health and Human Services, 2004). Urine toxicology testing is an adjunct to assessment and treatment; it is not a form of treatment in its own right. Although a powerful tool in the treatment of the addictions, like all medical tests an improperly conducted urine toxicology test or a laboratory error can invalidate the results of that test. If the collection process is not properly carried out, the urine sample might suggest traces of substance abuse where the client had not engaged in such acts,[31] or fail to detect evidence of substance abuse where the client had engaged in such activities[32] (Levy, Harris, Sherritt, Angulo, & Knight, 2006). Thus urine toxicology testing is not a perfect process, and to minimize this problem rigid adherence to the proper collection procedures is imperative.

---

[25]See Glossary.

[26]See Glossary.

[27]A process called *dream carryover*. Through this process, the dreamer continues to experience emotions generated during the dream during the first few seconds of consciousness.

[28]A fancy term for helping clients anticipate that certain experiences might happen to them, so that they might mentally prepare for them.

[29]The information provided in this section is designed to illustrate the known strengths and weaknesses of urine toxicology tests. It is not intended for, and should not be used as, a guide for prosecution or employment sanctions.

[30]Generally the Certified Medical Review Officer (see Glossary) carries out these duties.

[31]Technically a false-positive test result.

[32]Technically a false-negative test result.

The urine collection process is invasive, especially in cases where close supervision is necessary. It is necessary to obtain the client's *written* consent at the time of collecting the urine sample for toxicology testing. Some programs include this as part of the treatment contract or as a condition of continued employment at a particular business under certain conditions. This document will then identify the fact that clients were informed that they might be asked to submit to urine toxicology testing at any time.

A positive urine toxicology test does not indicate the degree of *impairment* should a prohibited compound be detected (L. A. R. Stein & Rogers, 2008). Insurance companies and employers argue that even the smallest trace of a drug in a person's urine after an accident is evidence of impairment in spite of the lack of scientific research in this area ("Predicting Drug-Related Impairment," 2004). Unfortunately, a positive urine toxicology test suggests only that the individual might have used the compound(s) in question during the detection window for that compound(s). Other than proving that the compound or drug metabolites in question were possibly present, the urine test results cannot be used to judge level of impairment (Jemionek, Copley, Smith, & Past, 2008). There has been virtually no research to correlate the measured level of a compound(s) in a person's system with degree of impairment other than alcohol (L. A. R. Stein & Rogers, 2008). One advantage of urine toxicology testing is that it supplements clients' self-reports about their recent substance use (N. Katz & Fanciullo, 2002). Within the limits of such testing technology, urine toxicology test results can (a) help confirm client medication compliance and (b) help determine whether the client is abstaining from illicit alcohol or drug use, especially in the previous 1–3 days (Dolan, Rouen, & Kimber, 2004; Standbridge et al., 2010).

The process of urine toxicology testing is not a single, uniform process. It is a generic term for a number of different toxicology test procedures after the urine sample is collected. *Thin layer chromatography* (TLC) is the most commonly utilized procedure, especially when large numbers of urine samples must be screened for illicit-drug use (Craig, 2004). The results are often available in less than 2 hours, but are reported only as either positive or negative (Craig, 2004). This test is best suited for the initial testing of urine samples (Craig, 2004). *Gas liquid chromatography* (GC) is a more expensive and labor-intensive procedure that is often used to confirm "positive" TLC test results (Craig, 2004). The test equipment is quite expensive,

and the technician(s) who carries out the test(s) must receive special training in this procedure. However, GC provides a lower number of false-positive results than TLC and provides quantitative levels of the chemical(s) detected in the individual's urine (Craig, 2004).

Another form of urine toxicology tests are the *immunoassay* family of tests. J. A. Collins (2009) identified five different immunoassay procedures currently in use: (a) radioimmunoassay (rarely used now), (b) enzyme immunoassay, (c) fluoroimmunoassay, (d) kinetic microparticle immunoassay, and (e) lateral flow immunoassay.[33] Immunoassay procedures utilize antibodies to detect certain substances (Standbridge et al., 2010). Such tests offer the advantage of being rapid and can be used to test large numbers of urine samples for the initial screening (Craig, 2004). However, structural similarities between certain compounds may result in false-positive test results, a process known as *cross-reactivity* (J. A. Collins, 2009; Craig, 2004). Through this process the reagent used to detect one class of illicit chemicals reacts to another, possibly unrelated compound. An excellent example of this is when people with an allergy have ingested a therapeutic dose of certain nasal decongestants, only to have a urine toxicology test the next day suggest that they had abused an amphetamine compound. On some tests the use of dextromethorphan at therapeutic doses may indicate that the individual had abused phencyclidine (Mozayani, 2009; Traub, 2009).

"It is important to keep in mind," J. A. Collins (2009) observed, "that cross-reactivities and interferences may change with reagent lot changes, new formulations and variable antibody specificity" (p. 31). Thus the process of cross-reactivity is not static but is affected by a number of variables. The person or lab conducting the test must constantly remain informed as to the variables that might affect the test outcome with each of the reagents utilized on an ongoing basis. Further, physical disease states such as proteinuria,[34] nitrites, ketones, or blood in the urine, as well as bacterial and fungal infections can cause nonspecific cross-reactivity between these compounds and the immunoassay procedure being used (J. A. Collins, 2009).

It is because of such false-positive test results that confirmatory testing must *always* be carried out. Procedures such as the *gas chromatography/mass*

---

[33]The specific methodology for each procedure is rather complicated to discuss, and readers are referred to J. A. Collins's (2009) text for more information if they are interested in this information.

[34]See Glossary.

spectrometry (GC/MS) test, although very labor intensive, expensive, and limited to testing only a small number of urine samples at a time, will provide confirmation through a different methodology if the initial immunoassay test suggested illicit drug use. In many states, GC/MS results may be introduced as legal evidence of illicit-drug use. However, some of the compounds advertised as being able to break down metabolites of illicit-drug use are able to do so, although this process might take hours or days. Thus if too much time between the immunoassay test and the GC/MS test should pass, the initial test could suggest drug use, whereas the GC/MS test indicates no evidence of illicit drug use (Jones, 2009). Test manufacturers are constantly exploring new ways to identify such adulterated urine samples, whereas companies that manufacture such products are constantly seeking ways to foil the latest detection methods (G. R. Jones, 2009).

Although urine toxicology testing is a valuable therapeutic tool, it is not perfect. Some compounds will not be detected by standard urine toxicology tests, such as some of the congeners[35] of phencyclidine (PCP), which have the same psychoactive effects but that are not detected by standard urine toxicology tests for phencyclidine (Traub, 2009). Further, each drug offers a "detection window," after which time it is unlikely that urine tests will detect rare or occasional abuse of that compound. An additional consideration is that most commercial drug-screening kits do *not* test for every possible drug of abuse (Verebey, Buchan, & Turner, 1997). Many commercial urine toxicology test kits do not test for compounds such as LSD, fentanyl, Dilaudid, MDMA, Rohypnol, some of the synthetic and semisynthetic narcotic analgesics, and many of the "designer" drugs. The detection of these compounds may require special, very expensive tests (Vereby, Buchan, & Turner, 1997). Further, urine toxicology procedures will not detect signs of illicit-drug use until at least 6 hours after the individual's use of a compound, as the body needs time to begin the biotransformation and elimination processes before urine toxicology testing can detect evidence of substance use (Juhnke, 2002).

False-positive test results are a significant problem with the relatively unsophisticated on-site test kits used by many employers, parents, and law enforcement officials. Some of these tests have a false-positive rate of 30–35% (Schuckit, 2006a, 2006b; "Why Confirmatory Testing Is Always a Necessity," 1997). Because of the problem of false-positive test results, health care professionals should *always* confirm the initial results by independent toxicology testing at a certified laboratory. Further, because there are so many different urine toxicology tests available on the market, health care professionals should request a written summary from the manufacturer or laboratory as to the (a) methods used by the laboratory to test the urine sample the accuracy of the test procedures utilized, (b) the specific chemicals that can be detected by that method, (c) the detection windows for various compounds, and (d) what other compounds can yield false-positive test results. This summary should be updated on a regular basis to ensure that treatment staff are familiar with the strengths and weaknesses of the test methodology being utilized at that center on an ongoing basis.

Clients' Attempts at Deception

It is not uncommon for substance-abusing clients to attempt to manipulate the urine toxicology test to avoid having their recent illicit-drug use detected. A very obvious maneuver is to simply not keep a scheduled appointment if the client has reason to anticipate being asked to submit to urine toxicology testing ("I have to work, honest!" or the ever-popular "My car won't start!") (Gitlow, 2007). There are also a number of products that have properties to remove "toxins" from the body or correct electrolyte imbalances induced by the clients' attempts to "flush" their body with large amounts of fluids (Coleman & Baselt, 1997; Gwinnell & Adamec, 2006). It is possible that some of these compounds will work, and health care professionals might wish to consult with toxicology laboratories to determine which compounds might work and how their use might be detected.

Clients have been known to ingest large amounts of fluid in the hope of either (a) flushing the drug metabolites from their bodies or (b) at least dilute them so much that they will not be detected by the drug test. If possible, the specific gravity, acidity level, and creatinine levels of the urine sample submitted should be assessed to determine whether a given urine sample is appropriate for testing or altered through such methods (Coleman & Baselt, 1997).

Another method by which illicit-drug abusers might attempt to manipulate the urine toxicology test results is by *urine substitution*. The client will use a "clean" (that is, drug-free) urine sample, possibly hidden in a balloon or small bottle, that can be substituted for their own urine sample if nobody is watching them closely. This is easily done is most cases, because the majority

---

[35]A compound with a very similar chemical structure to another identified chemical, in this case phencyclidine (PCP).

of urine toxicology test samples are not collected under supervision (Sutheimer & Cody, 2009). Even if urine samples for toxicology testing are collected under supervision, there are companies that also will sell a rather realistic-looking artificial penis, so that the male client might submit a substituted urine sample while being observed. The urine is held in a storage container that is squeezed, forcing it through a tube and into the collection bottle, just as would occur if the man were to normally submit to urine toxicology testing. If done properly, the results are very realistic. An extreme method of deception is a urine substitution method through which clients will void their bladder, then insert a catheter and fill their bladder with another person's urine to provide a urine sample for testing if asked[36] (L. A. R. Stein & Rogers, 2008).

Clients who have been asked to submit to urine toxicology testing have been known to claim to be unable to urinate when somebody is watching them in an attempt to avoid supervised urine collection, or to "accidentally" dip the urine sample collection bottle into the toilet water. The specific gravity and level of acidity of the "urine sample" will reveal this attempt at deception, because toilet bowl water has a different specific gravity and acidity level than does human urine. Some treatment centers add a coloring agent to the toilet water, to foil these attempts at substitution. Further, toilet water is usually rather cool when compared with the human body, and *urine is always within 1–2 degrees of the core body temperature* if the temperature of the urine sample were to be tested within 4 minutes of the time that it was collected (N. Katz & Fanciullo, 2002). This fact is embarrassing to those clients who attempt to simulate a normal body temperature for the urine sample to be substituted by putting the sample into a microwave oven prior to reporting for toxicology testing. Temperature testing at the time of collection will thus help to identify urine samples that are unusually warm/cool, alerting staff to possible attempts at deception.

Yet another method that clients use to try to foil urine toxicology testing is to substitute other compounds as "urine." A partial list of compounds submitted as "urine" by various clients includes apple juice, citrus-flavored sodas, diluted tea, ginger ale, lemonade, salt water, plain tap water, and white grape juice. Again, testing the sample's specific gravity and acidity

TABLE 34-3 SAMPLE LIST OF AGENTS USED IN ATTEMPTS TO HIDE DRUG ABUSE
Ammonia
Bleach
Blood
Drano*
Ethanol
Gasoline
Kerosene
Lemon juice
Liquid soap
Peroxide
Vinegar
Table salt
Sodium bicarbonate
Vitamin C

level (as well as the amount of sugar in the sample!) will detect these attempts at substitution. Other drug abusers believe that it is possible to "hide" evidence of illicit-drug use by adding a foreign chemical(s) to the urine sample. Table 34-3 contains a partial list of adulterants used at one time or another to disguise urine samples tainted with illicit drug metabolites.

On rare occasions, the addition of such compounds to a urine sample will actually hide evidence of recent illicit-drug use, although they also alter the chemical characteristics of the "urine" sample submitted (Schuckit, 2006a, 2006b). Some compounds will make the urine sample more alkaline than possible for human urine, for example (S. C. Jenkins, Tinsley, & Van Loon, 2001). Small amounts of the compound alum will hide metabolites of methamphetamine in a urine sample, but at the cost of changing the acidity of the sample, which can be detected by treatment or laboratory staff when they check the sample's acidity level.

Urine toxicology testing should be carried out on a random basis (Juhnke, 2002). Some court-associated outpatient programs assign a "color" to each client, who must then call a central telephone number to see whether clients with that color will be called in for urine testing that morning. In residential programs, clients might be selected at random and told that they are to report for urine toxicology testing; then they are escorted to the collection site so that they do not sneak into their room and pick up a chemical or urine

---

[36]This process, however, exposes the individual to all of the risks inherent in using a catheter, and to potential infectious organisms in the urine of the person who supplied the urine sample to be substituted.

substitution sample. The information reviewed next provides an overview of the detection windows for various compounds commonly abused.[37]

Alcohol

Under normal conditions, clients will show traces of alcohol in their urine for only about the same time as it can be detected in their breath. Thus breath analysis is the preferred method of detecting alcohol in a person's body, although later confirmatory testing in a certified laboratory might be carried out by law enforcement officials. Recently a urine toxicology test for alcohol was introduced to detect a metabolite of ethyl alcohol known as *ethyl glucuronide*. This compound is specific to alcohol use and remains in the individual's blood for up to 5 days after the person's last drink. Unfortunately, there is a growing body of evidence that suggests that exposure to alcohol through such things as hand sanitizer[38] might also cause a positive test result (Kirn, 2006). Given the popularity of such products, the results of the ethyl glucuronide test must be interpreted with caution.

Amphetamine Compounds

In the casual user, amphetamine compounds might be detected for 24–48 hours (Bolnick & Rayburn, 2003; Greydanus & Patel, 2005; Schuckit, 2006a, 2006b). However, high doses of ephedrine or pseudoephedrine might cause a false-positive test result. For this reason, federal guidelines require that amphetamine molecules be identified through specific testing procedures such as the gas liquid chromatography (GC) test (discussed earlier) in order to rule a urine sample positive for amphetamine compounds such as methamphetamine. In the case of methamphetamine, it is important to keep in mind that once ingested, the body breaks methamphetamine down into amphetamine, but ephedrine or pseudoephedrine are not biotransformed into this compound. This allows the presence or absence of amphetamine or methamphetamine to be confirmed by the appropriate test procedures after the initial test results suggest amphetamine use.

Benzodiazepines

Depending on the specific benzodiazepine being used, urine toxicology tests might reveal evidence of benzodiazepine use for 1–4 weeks after their last use (Craig, 2004). Schuckit (2006a, 2006b) suggested a shorter

detection window of only 3 or more days. This discrepancy appears to reflect whether one is testing a rare abuser of a benzodiazepine or a chronic user. The benzodiazepine Rohypnol (flunitrazepam) is technically a member of the benzodiazepine family of compounds, but is not legally available in the United States. Routine toxicology tests will not detect it, although special tests can detect it in a urine sample if the test is carried out within 60 hours of the time that it was ingested. These tests are usually available only to law enforcement agencies investigating date rape claims.

Cocaine

Depending on the route of administration, the frequency with which the individual abuses cocaine, and the amount of cocaine abused, it is possible to detect metabolites of cocaine in urine for 72–96 hours (C. Jenkins et al., 2005; Schuckit, 2006a, 2006b). Heavy abusers might continue to test positive for cocaine metabolites for up to 10 days after their last use of this compound (Traub, 2009). Greydanus and Patel (2005) suggested that chronic cocaine abusers could test positive on urine toxicology screens for up to 2 weeks after their last use of this compound, whereas Schuckit (2006a, 2006b) simply stated that chronic abusers would test positive for "several days" (p. 30) after their last cocaine use.

One of the exceptions to this rule is when the patient is using a prescribed product with traces of cocaine in it, such as certain skin lotions. If the patient were to be using one of these compounds, this would produce a false-positive test result. Fortunately these skin lotions are available only by prescription and thus it is rare for this situation to arise (Ahrendt & Miller, 2005). Passive absorption of cocaine is possible for a physician or dentist, if their practice brings them into frequent contact with this compound, in which case they will have metabolites of cocaine in their urine for 72–96 hours (Gitlow, 2007). Fortunately, it would be relatively easy to determine whether that health care professional's job duties did indeed bring them into frequent contact with cocaine.

LSD

LSD might be detected in a person's urine for up to 8 hours after it was last used, but the laboratory must use special testing procedures to detect this substance (Craig, 2004).

Marijuana

Although the cannabinoids have been the most commonly detected illicit substance in urine toxicology tests for more than 20 years, the detection of marijuana through urine toxicology testing remains rather

---

[37]This information is provided for illustrative purposes only. It is not intended for and should not be used as the basis for employment screening, legal, or other purposes.

[38]Many brands of hand sanitizer contain ethyl alcohol.

complicated (Huestis, 2009). The excretion of marijuana metabolites from the body is variable, but correlates well with the amount of marijuana used by the individual (Goodwin et al., 2008). The rare social user will have traces of THC in their urine for 3–5 days after they last used marijuana (Greydanus & Patel, 2005; Goodwin et al., 2008; Schuckit, 2006a, 2006b). There is a persistent myth on the streets that a person who smokes marijuana will have traces of THC in their urine for 30 days after their last use of marijuana, and casual abusers will often repeat this myth as if it were gospel to try and avoid sanctions for illicit substance abuse.

The unusually heavy, chronic marijuana smoker[39] *will* build up significant THC reserves in their bodies, which will leak back into the blood through osmosis for between 20 and 45 days depending on the frequency with which they used marijuana and the potency of the marijuana smoked (Greydanus & Patel, 2005; C. Jenkins et al., 2001). Exceptionally heavy marijuana smokers have been known to have measurable amounts of THC in their urine for up to 2 months after their last use ("Weight Loss and the Release of THC from fat," 2009).[40] N. Katz and Fanciullo (2002) suggested that a habitual marijuana smoker might test positive for THC for up to 80 days, although this figure has not been supported by other researchers.

The reason why habitual marijuana abusers tend to test positive for marijuana for such extended periods of time is that after smoking, THC enters the body's adipose tissues and is slowly released back into the circulation after the abuser stops marijuana use. To avoid controversy, it has been suggested that clients submit to daily urine toxicology testing until their urine sample fails to show evidence of marijuana abuse for 3 straight days. The program staff must make sure that the patient does not have a prescription for the compound Marinol, which is a form of synthetic THC used to treat chemotherapy-induced nausea, as this will register as marijuana on urine toxicology tests.[41]

Occasionally, clients will attempt to claim that they have THC in their system as a result of passive inhalation. Passive inhalation of marijuana smoke to allow the individual to absorb sufficient marijuana smoke to test positive on urine toxicology testing has been called "extraordinarily unlikely" (Ahrendt & Miller, 2005, p. 962). However, it *is* possible to passively inhale enough marijuana smoke to test positive for it on a urine toxicology test. To do so it is necessary to sit in an airtight chamber so filled with marijuana smoke that people would need swimmer's goggles to protect their eyes from the irritating effects of the smoke ("Oral Fluid Drug Testing," 2005). Most motor vehicles or houses are not airtight, and so the claim of passive inhalation is not supported by the evidence.

MDMA

Ecstasy can be detected for 24–48 hours after it was used, but special urine toxicology testing must be carried out to detect it (Craig, 2004).

PCP

In the casual abuser, phencyclidine can be detected for 48–72 hours after it was last used (C. Jenkins et al., 2001). Craig (2004) offered a detection window of 2–8 days for the casual abuser and up to 21 days for the chronic abuser. Depending on the testing methodology utilized, some over-the-counter medications can cause false-positive reactions, and thus confirmatory testing should be carried out to confirm the initial test results (Ahrendt & Miller, 2005).

Hair Sample Testing

Whenever a person ingests a chemical, molecules of that substance are circulated throughout the body. In many cases molecules of that compound are then incorporated into the body's cells, including the hair cell follicles and ultimately the hair. Scientists have developed the technology to detect drug metabolites of many illicit drugs in the hair of the abuser. It has been suggested that because this is true, the collection of hair samples would be less intrusive than collecting urine samples, and much more difficult to falsify. Hair samples also offer a detection window of 7–100 days (Gwinnel & Adamec, 2006; L. A. R. Stein & Rogers, 2008; Sutheimer & Cody, 2009). This extended detection window foils the attempt of drug abusers to avoid detection by abstaining from drug use for a few days before a urine toxicology test (Craig, 2004). Although some drug abusers think that they can foil this process if they shave their heads, *any* body hair can be used for such tests.

---

[39]Which is to say somebody who smokes marijuana daily or more often, and not a reference to body size.

[40]It should be pointed out that "measurable amounts" is not the same as THC levels above the detection threshold utilized by the Department of Transportation to identify active marijuana abusers.

[41]One favorite trick of drug addicts is to obtain a blank prescription sheet and have a friend fill out the form as if it were a standing order for Marinol. If their marijuana use is then detected by a toxicology test, they can show the prescription sheet and claim that it was the prescription drug that was detected, not illicit marijuana. Thus such prescriptions should be verified with the physician who supposedly prescribed the Marinol if THC is detected in a urine toxicology test.

Advocates of hair follicle testing point out that this procedure is far less intrusive than urine toxicology testing. However, there have been several challenges to the use of hair tests for toxicology testing. The Food and Drug Administration (FDA) has warned that several of the test kits sold might result in false-positive test results on occasion ("FDA Revised Guidelines, Label Warnings," 2004). Further, initial positive results should be confirmed by a second test that utilizes a different methodology (Sutheimer & Cody, 2009). One study found that in 60 out of 100 individuals tested, the preliminary positive results for opiate abuse were not supported by confirmatory testing ("FDA Revised Guidelines, Label Warnings," 2004). Further, fully 50% of the preliminary positive results for amphetamine abuse, 10% of the preliminary "positive" results for marijuana abuse, and 2% of the preliminary "positive" results for cocaine abuse were found to be false-positive results upon confirmatory testing.

Marijuana abusers will often claim passive exposure to marijuana smoke as an explanation for the positive test results. M. Uhl and Sacks (2004) suggested that the test try to detect metabolites *other* than THC, such as 11-nor-delta-9-tetra-hydrocannabinol-9-carboxylic acid (THCA), to differentiate between actual marijuana use and passive exposure to marijuana. This metabolite is produced *only* when the person has abused marijuana, not through passive exposure, and for this reason hair samples from people exposed to marijuana smoke failed to reveal evidence of THCA when tested (M. Uhl & Sacks, 2004). This discovery will allow actual marijuana abusers to be identified and foil their claim of passive exposure to marijuana smoke.

Detractors to the process of hair testing point out that a number of hair strands must be removed. Craig (2004) suggested that as many as 40–60 hair strands be removed. Further, it is hard, if not impossible, to detect *when* the individual indulged in illicit-drug use. In theory, hair grows at the rate of 1 centimeter per month, which if true would allow the tester to estimate the time since the user last used that compound. Questions have also been raised whether this estimate of the hair growth rate is the same for all ethnic groups (Gitlow, 2007; Sutheimer & Cody, 2009). Further, 15% of hair follicles are either in a resting phase or ready to fall out at any given time, factors that can potentially influence the accuracy of hair toxicology testing. Hair toxicology tests cannot detect substance use in the 7 days prior to the collection of the hair samples and does not detect alcohol use (Gwinnell & Adamec, 2006; Juhnke, 2002). Research has found that different laboratories often provide different results for the same hair sample (Sutheimer & Cody, 2009), and there are no standardization in hair collection and preparation procedures between laboratories. These observations raise questions as to the validity of hair sample toxicology testing (L. A. R. Stein & Rogers, 2008; Sutheimer & Cody, 2009). For these and other reasons, the federal government has discontinued the practice of testing hair samples to detect illicit-drug use ("How Long Does Cocaine Remain in the Hair of Former Users?", 2009) for job sites where such testing is mandated.

Even if there is evidence of illicit-drug use detected in hair strand testing, this does not provide information on the level of *impairment* caused by the individual's drug abuse (Juhnke, 2002; L. A. R. Stein & Rogers, 2008). The fact that hair toxicology testing requires the removal of hair from the body, as opposed to the collection of urine, a waste product expelled from the body, makes it of limited value in serial toxicology tests (Craig, 2004). Thus there are strong objections to the use of hair toxicology testing, making its applicability uncertain at this time.

Saliva

Another emerging technology is the use of saliva to test for traces of alcohol or drug use. New techniques make this procedure attractive for workplace drug-testing programs. There are a number of variables that must be resolved before the accuracy of saliva drug testing can be established because "saliva flow can … be decreased due to menopausal hormone changes, stress, smoking, anti-cholinergic drugs that inhibit [the] parasympathetic nerve impulses, anticonvulsants, and tranquilizers" (C. M. Moore, 2009, p. 206).

Saliva toxicology testing is also hampered by a smaller detection window than is possible with urine toxicology testing (C. M. Moore, 2009). The test results are available in approximately 20 minutes and, depending on the substance, might offer a detection window of 1–36 hours (Dolan et al., 2004; L. A. R. Stein & Rogers, 2008). As with any screening procedure, confirmatory testing is necessary to rule out false-positive results.

Sweat

A number of companies offer skin patches impregnated with compounds designed to react to and reveal evidence of illicit-drug use. Such detection devices are useful for continuous monitoring of the individual over a 1- to 14-day period (Kadehjian & Crouch, 2009; L. A. R. Stein & Rogers, 2008). The sweat drug detection patch is designed to allow passage of water molecules through, while stopping the larger drug molecules that had diffused into the sweat from the circulation (Kadehjian & Crouch, 2009). However, illicit-drug use will not be detected for several hours after the individual abused the compound because it requires time for the drug molecules to diffuse into the sweat glands.

To avoid detection, some abusers will remove the skin patch the day that it was applied and then reapply it 6 or 7 days later, when they report to their probation officer, employer, and so forth to have it removed. Such tampering is evident to the skilled patch user because the patch is designed to separate internal membranes from the outer shell if it is removed before being examined (Kadehjian & Crouch, 2009). Although some clients might claim that their skin naturally produces an oil(s) that will cause the patch to fall off or that it just fell off while they were taking a shower, these claims are dubious because it is extremely unlikely that the patch will just fall off on its own. Further, although clients might claim that the patch tested positive for one or more substances because of environmental contamination, research has shown that this is virtually impossible except under specialized laboratory conditions (Kadehjian & Crouch, 2009).

Insurance Company Reimbursement Policies

Although Congress has passed a law that requires parity in insurance coverage for mental health and substance abuse problems, it has yet to be determined the degree to which this law will alter insurance company reimbursement policies for substance abuse treatment. This is a matter of significant concern because decisions about treatment are often shaped by funding availability (Leamon et al., 2008). Striking a fair balance between the need for medical treatment and funding availability has proven difficult, and one approach to this problem is known as *managed care* (MC). MC has essentially been called medical rationing by accountants, and it can be argued that the needs of the individual are subservient to the company's desire to save money. This clearly seen in the manner in which many managed care companies refuse to pay for services by a PhD-level psychologist with thousands of hours of training and experience, but will reimburse a master's degree clinician with a markedly lower level of training as a "mental health counselor." Rapid, cheap symptom reduction (not resolution of the problem) is the goal in many cases.

In the time since the MC programs were introduced, it has become clear that this is a system that rations health care access in all but name (Sanchez & Turner, 2003). MC has also been found to cut the cost charged to the insurance provider, while doing little to change long-term health care risks for the clients (Ceren, 2003; J. O. Prochaska, 2002). Many health care providers have started to refer to "managed care" as "managed profits" because of the way that the system limits the amount of money distributed by insurance companies for designated services.

In the time since the MC initiatives in the 1990s, it has become clear that such programs, by refusing to recognize (and pay for) the medical necessity of inpatient treatment for most cases of drug and alcohol dependence, [have] largely dismantled the '28 day' inpatient alcohol and drug [rehabilitation] programs (Jaffe & Anthony, 2005, p. 1151, parentheses in original deleted).

Since the introduction of MC, only approximately 10% of all substance abusers are initially referred to residential treatment programs (McLellan, 2008). Further, in spite of research findings that indicate that the longer that individuals are involved in treatment programs the more likely they will abstain from alcohol or drugs, authorization for treatment stays of 14 days or less have become the norm (Ceren, 2003; Daley & Marlatt, 2006; Olmstead, White, & Sindelar, 2004; D. D. Simpson, 2004). MC programs frequently require "prior authorization," in which an insurance company representative whose credentials are often "questionable and whose role is to cut costs" (Ceren, 2003, p. 77) must be consulted prior to the initiation of any but emergency care. Further, MC programs aggressively push for pharmaceutical treatment(s) of identified conditions rather than for behavioral treatments (Breggin, 2008).

The money that the insurance company must spend paying for health care for identified forms of "disease" is considered a financial loss[42] for that company. The insurance company thus attempts to maximize inflow of money, while limiting payments distributed. One way to do this is to exclude as many people as possible from participation in the program because they had a "preexisting condition." Another way to limit losses is to avoid identification of patients with a disorder(s). To this end, only 34% of insurance companies *required* that the physician screen for substance use or mental health disorders when doing a physical examination (Horgan, Garnick, Merrick & Hoyt, 2007). If the insurance company will not reimburse for a specific

---

[42]Or, an operating expense.

procedure, the physician is less likely to carry it out, increasing the chance that the client's mental health or substance use disorder will not be detected. Thus even if the insurance company does offer parity for treatment provided to a client, if that disorder is never detected, then it is unlikely that the insurance company will have to pay for that treatment.

A third way for insurance companies to limit financial loss is to adopt a very conservative definitive of "disease." *Symptom reduction* is often identified as the goal of "treatment," and to accomplish this the insurance company adopts a very liberal interpretation of what is considered "recovery." Is the patient still having delirium tremens? Then, if not, should not the patient be ready for discharge in the next 24 hours, for example. Although research has demonstrated that older drinkers might require up to 30 days to completely detoxify from the effects of their chronic drinking, insurance company benefits often are limited to 5–7 days for "detoxification" *and* treatment. Although such policies might be considered cost effective, a sad consequence of this process is that many clients are referred to aftercare before they have finished detoxification.

Finally, managed care companies place great emphasis on "evidence-based practice." This is a term that refers to treatment procedures that follow rigid treatment protocols, often established by companies with financial interests in the development of these protocols, based on research studies that exclude significant numbers of research subjects because of confounding variables that might make interpretation of the data difficult, to provide data that in many cases is nothing more than "a radical misconception about scientific knowledge that may serve ideological prejudices (and managed care business practices) but clearly does not serve the pursuit of truth" (Frattaroli, 2001, p. 163). Many of the research studies that emerge from this process are so restrictive, and so many potential research subjects are excluded, that the results are meaningless for practice in the real world. Further, 31% of research articles present outcomes that were different than the stated purpose of the original study design (Ewart, Lausen, & Millian, 2009), which is to say that after analysis of the data the purpose of the study was changed to reflect the obtained data.

Medication efficacy studies often are of limited duration (4–8 weeks for the most part), whereas clinicians work with patients for months, if not years. The long-term effectiveness of medications whose "effectiveness" was proven in a study that followed carefully screened research subjects for 8–12 weeks is of limited value to the clinician who advocates that an unscreened patient follow a specific treatment protocol for months or years. Yet it is on the basis of such "research" that "evidence-based practice" is often defined.

Finally, although clinicians placed great hopes on the Mental Health Parity Act, the final version of this law did not define mental health or substance abuse treatment benefits with any degree of clarity, and such benefits are not even mandated unless mental health benefits are already included in the individual's insurance plan (Sussman, 2009)! About all that this law did was mandate that if mental health benefits were included in the company insurance plan, such benefits were to be provided on a level consistent with coverage for other forms of disease covered by the insurance company's policy. However, the employer simply needed to select a benefits package that did not include provisions for mental health benefits, and then there would be no need for "parity" with other benefits (Sussman, 2009). In this manner Congress helped address the problems of underfunded treatment programs.

It will be interesting to see how much insurance premiums increase on the basis of the new "parity" law. Full parity for the treatment of mental health and substance use disorders was estimated to increase insurance premiums just pennies each month (Goldman et al., 2006; Greenfield, 2005). Whether insurance companies increase the monthly premiums by just this amount remains to be seen.

Psycho-Educational Intervention Programs

The Drug Abuse Resistance Education (D.A.R.E.) and similar programs are quite popular. Such programs are based on the theory that teaching children about the harmful effects of alcohol or drugs while helping them build self-esteem would somehow inoculate them against the desire to abuse chemicals in later life. The DARE program is usually led by a local police officer and is carried out in the classroom setting. Other programs utilize the services of various mental health or school guidance professionals. Although there is a great deal of anecdotal support for such programs, there is only limited clinical research data suggesting that they are effective, and most certainly it can be argued that such programs have not reached their full potential for curbing childhood or adolescent substance use disorders (Spoth et al., 2009).

Critics of psycho-educational programs such as DARE are growingly increasingly vocal, challenging the need for such programs for a number of reasons. It has been pointed out that psycho-educational programs are a form of primary intervention for possible substance use disorders. If a specific child or adolescent requires a more intensive level of treatment, the school system usually responds that this is not an educational systems issue (Zunz, Ferguson, & Senter, 2005). Thus school districts that utilize programs such as psycho-educational programs fail to offer the full continuum of care, leaving those students most in need without assistance. Other critics point out that these programs usually provide negative propaganda about the effects of alcohol or drugs, an approach that has never been demonstrated to work (Leavitt, 2003; Walton, 2002). At best, the critics of psycho-educational programs note that the "evidence suggests that, although knowledge can be increased and expressed attitudes may be changed, affecting drinking behavior through school programs is a very difficult task" (B. Room et al., 2005, p. 525).

There is no reason to suspect that changing other forms of substance use behavior would be different. The vast amounts of information provided to the participants will, at best, provide a temporary modification of the individual's behavior (Reyna & Farley, 2006/2007). Indeed, there is evidence that programs such as DARE are counterproductive, increasing the student's curiosity about the drugs of abuse (McPherson Yudko, Murray-Bridges et al., 2009). When children or adolescents experiments\ with a recreational substance (or know of a friend who has done so) and they find that the dreaded consequences did not happen to them, the credibility of the information provided is lost.

Critics of psycho-educational programs suggest that such programs continue because they give the *illusion* of doing something about the growing problem of childhood and adolescent substance use disorders (Leavitt, 2003). This possibility is supported by the observation made earlier that students are not provided with the full continuum of care and that those students most in need are not served by psycho-educational programs. Fortunately, many school districts are starting to fight back against such programs, citing their lack of proven success and the loss of classroom instruction time as reasons for rejecting such programs.

Chapter Summary

Even after a given client has been identified as being in need of either outpatient or inpatient substance abuse rehabilitation, the obstacles facing that client are often daunting. Some clients will challenge the accuracy of the diagnosis or the accuracy of urine toxicology test results. Some may come to treatment sessions under the influence of chemicals. Even if clients consent to treatment, their health care insurance provider must be contacted, "prior authorization" must be obtained for the treatment program, and continual justifications for treatment beyond the limited number of days that the insurance company authorizes provided for extensions of the initial treatment period must be authorized.

Treatment noncompliance is an ongoing problem in a wide range of medical conditions, but if a substance-abusing patient is noncompliant, the medical profession often just labels the patient as being a hopeless alcohol or drug addict and turns away. Even if the client successfully completing treatment, there are the obstacles facing the client: relapse cues and triggers, and prejudice by health care providers toward patients with an SUD. Although treatment staff may recommend extended aftercare programs for the client, many resist such recommendations or fail to actively participate in such programs. There are other obstacles facing the client, which are discussed in this chapter.

CHAPTER 35

Support Groups to Promote and Sustain Recovery

Introduction[1]

For many years, Alcoholics Anonymous (AA)[2] has had a "near exclusive dominance" (W. White & Nicolaus, 2005, p. 59) as a community-based support group for those who had an alcohol use disorder. It has been estimated that 95% of substance abuse rehabilitation programs utilize some kind of 12-step group model similar to that offered by AA and that recovering center staff are quite disinterested in treatment approaches that do not utilize such an approach (Brigham, 2003). Professional support is quite strong for 12-step-based approaches, as evidenced by the observation by McPherson, Yudko, Afsarifard et al. (2009), who suggested that participation in 12-step groups is an essential element in recovery.

However, in the past two decades there have been a growing number of secular support groups that reject many of the core elements of the AA program, offering alternatives for those who feel uncomfortable with the spiritual emphasis in the traditional 12-step group movement, for example. In this chapter we will briefly examine the role that self-help groups play in the recovery from a substance use disorder.[3]

---

[1]In earlier editions of this text, the 12 steps of the Alcoholics Anonymous program were reviewed as part of the chapter introduction. Permission to do so was kindly granted by the Alcoholics Anonymous World Services, Inc. For this edition, the 12 steps have been moved to Appendix 5.

[2]Over the years, the membership of Alcoholics Anonymous has evolved from one in which the members exclusively abused alcohol to one where members usually have a substance use disorder involving multiple substances. However, because the AA program was originally designed for people with an alcohol use disorder, this focus will be retained when discussing Alcoholics Anonymous.

[3]A health care provider might assume a degree of liability when referring a specific individual to a self-help group. Salzer and Kundera's (2010) paper provides an excellent overview of this issue. Health care providers should consult an attorney for the state(s) in which they practice to become aware of the specific liabilities that they assume when making a referral to a self-help group.

The History of Alcoholics Anonymous

There were many diverse forces that were to blend over time to form the organization that was to become known as Alcoholics Anonymous. First, there was the social atmosphere in the United States, which has traditionally placed great emphasis on public confession, contrition, and salvation through spirituality. These were elements of a nondenominational religious movement known as the Oxford Group, which also came to influence the evolving self-help group. Finally, there was the attempted psychoanalysis of an American alcoholic by Carl Jung. The former was especially influential, providing to the AA movement a strong belief in free will and personal responsibility (Committee on Addictions of the Group for the Advancement of Psychiatry, 2002).

Historically, AA is thought to have been founded on June 10, 1935, the day that an alcoholic physician had his last drink (Nace, 2005a). Shortly before this the physician, Dr. Robert Holbrook Smith ("Dr. Bob"), had a meeting with a stock broker, William G. Wilson. William "Bill" Wilson was struggling to protect his newly established sobriety while on a business trip to a new city. After making several telephone calls to various people who he hoped might help him, somebody suggested that he talk to Dr. Smith, who was actively drinking. He did so, but rather than ask for support in his own struggle to abstain from alcohol he began to talk about why he wanted to abstain from alcohol. At the end of the meeting, he concluded that he now understood why he made the original decision to quit drinking and thanked Dr. Bob for listening. The self-help philosophy of AA was born from this moment.

At first AA struggled to find itself, as evidenced by the fact that within the first 3 years there were only three AA groups and only a scattering of success stories. But the fledgling movement continued to grow slowly, and by the fourth year of its existence there were about 100 members in isolated AA groups (Nace, 2005a). To guide the newcomers, those early members who had achieved abstinence decided to write of their struggle to abstain and to share their discoveries with others. These reports were then compiled into the first edition of the book *Alcoholics Anonymous,* published in 1939, now called the "Big Book" of AA. The organization continued to grow during the last half of the 20th century, until it reached an estimated 97,000 AA "clubs" located in 150 different countries, involving a total estimated membership of over 2 million active members (Nace, 2005a). Perhaps 5 million people in the United States attend a self-help group because of alcohol or drug use disorders at least once each year ("New Nationwide Report Reveals That 5 Million People Participate in Self-Help Groups Each Year," 2008).[4]

Elements of AA

There are several elements that contribute to the effectiveness of a self-help group such as AA, not the least of which is that it is freely available to all (Ries, Galanter, & Tonigan, 2008). Further, such programs are widely available (the city of Seattle, Washington, alone has at least 1,200 meetings a week) (Ries et al., 2008). Further, all people involved have *shared the same problem.* By definition a self-help group is just that: a *self*-help group, and as such should be self-governing. A self-help group also does not attempt to provide psychotherapy, but rather *through example and feedback offers an educational experience* for the participant. Self-help groups place great emphasis on *individual responsibility* for a one's problems in a person who has made a personal commitment to change (Committee on Addictions of the Group for the Advancement of Psychiatry, 2002). To this end, the individual *chooses to participate* in the group process. Self-help groups place great emphasis on anonymity, a factor that separate them from social groups. Finally, there is only a *single purpose* to the group, which again differentiates it from social groups. The early members of AA freely borrowed from the fields of religion and medicine to mold a program that worked for them, the famous "12 steps," which form the core of this self-help movement.

A Breakdown of the Twelve Steps

At the core of AA are the 12 steps.[5] These steps are not required for members but are *suggested* as a way that a person *might* achieve lasting recovery (Beazley, 1998). A central tenet of both the 12 steps and AA as a whole is that individuals' resources alone are inadequate to help them abstain from alcohol. It is only through a commitment to a support group that people are able to draw upon the strength of the entire group in their battle to abstain from alcohol (Davison, Pennebaker, & Dickerson, 2000; "How Alcoholics Anonymous Works," 2007). In this

---

[4]Although these statistics appear to be in conflict with each other, the former statistic discusses *active* members in AA, whereas the latter statistic addresses how many people attend a self-help group in a given year. Attending a meeting once a year does not make one an "active" member of that group.

[5]In Appendix 5.

sense, AA might be viewed as functioning as a form of folk psychotherapy that aids personal growth through a series of successive approximations toward a better life. The 12 steps might be viewed as these successive approximations.

New members are not encouraged to seek the "cause" of their alcohol use disorder (AUD). An analogy that might be appropriate here is the difference between understanding *why* a ship is sinking (the "cause") and what people do with this knowledge (their response to the problem). The individual's AUD is accepted as a given fact. "It is not so much *how* you came to AA, as what you are going to do now that you are here," one hypothetical member might say to a newcomer. New members are not admonished for relapsing. Members in AA know that this is an ever-present danger. However, it is the goal of the group to offer individuals a new lifestyle that they hopefully will adopt in place of their alcohol-centered former lives. The 12 steps are one guide to this transition.

In the process of following the 12-step program, individuals encounter the first of many paradoxes in the AA program: The first step is the only one that actually mentions alcohol by name. This step asks individuals to make a conscious choice to admit that they are powerless over alcohol on the deepest level of their being. This process requires a conscious choice, for it requires great humility and an admission of defeat in the sense that people admit that they have been unable to deal with their AUD on their own. In so doing, people also must make a conscious decision to view their best "friend" (alcohol) as part of the problem. The 12 steps guide individuals through this process.

The 12 steps fall into three groups, the first of which includes Steps 1–3. These steps focus on helping individuals make a profound choice: that of surrender and turning their life over to a "Higher Power" of their choice. The only requirement for a Higher Power is that this indeed be something greater than themselves. Programs that suggest that a doorknob, for example, could be a Higher Power serve only to belittle the 12 steps. But by turning one's life over to a Higher Power, one moves alcohol from the center of one's mental arena and begins to relate not to a chemical, but to the Higher Power. The first goal of new members in this phase is simply to abstain and to establish a relationship with the Higher Power of their choice.

Steps 4–9 are a series of change-oriented procedures designed to help individuals (a) identify, (b) confront, and (c) ultimately overcome the personal character shortcomings that are thought to support their addiction. These steps allow individuals a mechanism through which they might work through the guilt that arises from past misdeeds and recognize the limits of personal responsibility. Individuals are encouraged to develop a recovery-centered support system, something that is often alien to them in the early stages of recovery and also to their family. People learn the disease concept of alcoholism as viewed by AA, the mechanism by which to find help (sponsor, recovering friends, and so forth) and the means to access help when needed (calling one's sponsor, a friend who is also in recovery, and so on). Guilt felt by individuals for alcohol-centered behavior(s) is replaced by a sense of gratitude for assistance offered and the learning of new ways of living. It is during this phase that individuals must identify and then face resentments for past harm that they have suffered, and learn to "let go" of these resentments and forgive the person who caused this harm.

Finally, Steps 10–12 challenges the individual to continue to build on the foundation established in earlier steps. Part of this process includes a continued search to identify additional personal shortcomings, which are then addressed by that person. The person has also hopefully learned to suspend judgment about others and to beware of the false pride that could lead back to a relapse. Spiritual growth continues to be encouraged, and finally, in Step 12 the individual is encouraged to carry this message of hope to others.

Although the AA program is one designed to aid spiritual growth, this process is not rapid. Indeed, the foundation of spiritual defects on which alcoholism is said to rest is resistant to change, and the process of rebuilding the "self" can take many years. Beazley (1998) suggested that individuals must remain actively involved in AA for at least 5 years to allow the process of spiritual growth to proceed. But once this process is started, individuals begin to wonder how they could possibly have lived otherwise. This is the promise held forth by proponents of Alcoholics Anonymous. The 12 steps are not forced on any member. Rather, they are offered as a guide to assist the person in a program of spiritual growth, and there are those who insist that the 12 steps were instrumental in saving their lives.

The Relationship Between Alcoholics Anonymous and Religion

One complaint often heard by those people who are resistant to participating in AA is that they do not like the "religious" aspect of the program. For some people, this complaint is a convenient excuse not to participate in an AA group. For others, this hesitancy reflects individual confusion over the manner in which the words *faith, religion* and *spirituality* are used interchangeably within this culture. There are very real differences between these words. Religion is an *organized set of beliefs* that are encoded in certain texts considered sacred by believers and are viewed as providing answers to life's questions by those who belong to that faith community (Ameling & Povilonis, 2001). Faith is viewed as the expression of belief in the face of ever-present doubt.

Although the following quote is quite old, it does illustrate that within the AA program, alcoholism is viewed as a "spiritual illness, and drinking as a symptom of that illness. The central spiritual 'defect' of alcoholics [is] described as an excessive preoccupation with self . . . Treatment of the preoccupation with self is the core of AA's approach" (McCrady & Irvine, 1989, p. 153). Within this framework, compulsive alcohol use is viewed as the opposite of true spiritual growth, and it has been found that there is a strong relationship between spirituality and abstinence from alcohol (Nace, 2005a; E. A. R. Robinson, Cranford, Webb, & Brower, 2007). In contrast to the focus on alcohol as the person's answer to life's problems, true spirituality is a reflection of the individual's search for meaning in life. Many people find that this search involves establishing a relationship with a Higher Power as they perceive this to be. This relationship might be expressed through participation in a formal religion, but this is not required. It is, however, a source of endless confusion by those who view AA from the outside and those who are just starting the journey to recovery.

The difference between spirituality and religion was perhaps best summarized by McDargh (2000), who observed that "religion is for those who are afraid of going to hell . . . spirituality is for those who have already been here [as a result of their SUD]." Within this context, it is possible to view the person with an alcohol use disorder as having found a "higher power" in alcohol (or, by extension, the other drugs of abuse) (Ringwald, 2002). Twelve-step programs seek to help the individual switch from the higher power of alcohol to a more benign one (Wallace, 2003). It is through this process that AA presents itself as a program for *spiritual* growth but not as a religious movement (Vaillant, 2000; Wallace, 2003). To better understand this point, it is helpful to view religion as the *form,* whereas spirituality is the *content* of belief. The spiritual aspect of

the AA program helps the new member to "let go," a concept that many newcomers find confusing. However, "having faith is not a question of clinging to a particular set of beliefs, a particular set of . . . practices or psychotherapeutic techniques. Having faith . . . requires that we let go of what we are clinging to" (Rosenbaum, 1999, p. xii). In the case of alcohol-dependent people, it is often found that they are clinging to old resentments and the belief that the chemical is the *only* way to cope, have fun, and so on.

The AA program is not forced upon the individual, but the 12 steps are suggested as a road to recovery. Participation in AA requires that the individual at least be *receptive* to the possibility that there is another way and have a true desire to quit drinking. In the early stages, it is sufficient that the person just be receptive to the possibility that there is another way, one that requires a conscious decision to take this alternative path. The first step on this alternative path is the decision to turn personal will over to God, as the individual should understand this Higher Power to be. The emphasis on spiritual growth in the AA program rests on the dual assumptions that (a) each person desires a relationship with a Higher Power, and (b) that it is people's distorted perception of "self" as being the center of the universe that makes them vulnerable to alcoholism (McDargh, 2000; Ringwald, 2002). Those who turn to alcohol often have only a vague sense of a Higher Power (if even that), and thus they need to make a consciousness decision to begin an ongoing dialogue with their Higher Power. This in turn will assist them in learning how to correct their distorted perception(s), deal with conflict, and how to have fun without the use of alcohol.

As part of this ongoing dialogue with the Higher Power, individuals are encouraged to carry out a daily self-examination similar to that of the *Examen* or *Conscious Examen* proposed by Ignatius as one of the foundations of the Jesuit order of the Catholic Church. In the Examen, people enter into an ongoing dialogue with their Higher Power, while they examine their thoughts, desires, and resentments. It is up to individuals to select their Higher Power and then make a conscious choice to enter into a relationship with that Higher Power. The conscious choice then makes individuals active participants in the recovery process, as opposed to being "patients" who lie passively for treatment to be performed on them (Nowinski, 2003). In this manner AA offers a program of spiritual growth, without a religious dogma, which might offend some members.

One "A" Is for Anonymous

Anonymity is central to the AA program ("Understanding Anonymity," 1981), and when honored, it is a major advantage of 12-step groups (Ries et al., 2008). This is a major reason why most AA meetings are "closed." There are three types of closed meetings, all of which are restricted to members:

1. The first type is a "discussion" meeting. The group leader has identified a topic applicable to the recovery program of all members (getting along with others, for example), which is discussed at the meeting.
2. The second type is a general meeting, in which members are encouraged to discuss their recovery programs, problems that they might have encountered, what is working for them, and so on.
3. The third type is a "step" meeting, in which one of the 12 steps is identified, and the whole focus of the meeting is on that step and how it applies to every member, their understanding of that step, and so on. Some AA groups rotate through the 12 steps every 3 months, whereas other groups devote an entire month to each of the steps. There is no established protocol as to how to carry out "step" meetings.

The only requirement to join an AA group is that the individual have an honest desire to learn how to abstain from alcohol. Then there are the "open" meetings. In the "open" meeting, any interested person can attend. One or two volunteers will speak about how the program helped them abstain from alcohol, and visitors are encouraged to ask questions about AA and how it works. For some people with an SUD, attending an open meeting is less threatening as a first step into recovery than going to a closed meeting. After attending one or two open meetings, individuals are then encouraged to begin to attend closed meetings for personal growth.

Anonymity is a cornerstone of the AA meeting. Who attends AA meetings, what is said at a meeting, and who said it is supposed to remain at the meeting. This presents a dilemma for AA groups that allow people who are court mandated or employer mandated to attend. To obtain confirmation that they did indeed attend the meeting, people must ask another AA member to sign some form of attendance verification, thus violating the anonymity of AA meetings. In this manner, the requirements of the court system and that of AA conflict. However, the attendee is still expected to have somebody sign an attendance confirmation form or else face the judge's wrath.

Another aspect of anonymity is that no single person can assume the role of speaking for the entire AA group ("Understanding Anonymity," 1981). This allows each member of the group to strive for humility, which is a cornerstone of the AA group. Each member is equal to the others, and there is no "board of directors" for the local AA group. Rather, special *service boards* or committees are set up by the group as the need arises. These boards remain answerable to the group as a whole. The members of the service board or committee are "but trusted servants; they do not govern" (*Twelve Steps and Twelve Traditions*, 1981, p. 10).[6] Further, because of the equality of members, interpersonal conflict is hopefully avoided or at least minimized.

Alcoholics Anonymous and Outside Organizations

Each Alcoholics Anonymous group is both not-for-profit and self-supporting. The group is autonomous financially, supporting itself only through donations made by members. Further, each member is prohibited from contributing more than $1,000 per year, and outside donations are discouraged, lest conflict develop within the group as to how the financial windfall should be utilized. As stated in *Twelve Steps and Twelve Traditions* (1981), AA groups will not "endorse, finance, or lend the AA name to any related facility or outside enterprise, lest problems of money, property and prestige divert us from our primary purpose" (p. 11). Thus many AA groups meet in churches, which donate the use of the room(s) for the meeting. Some AA groups, however, do purchase independent buildings in which to hold meetings. These structures are not called *Alcoholics Anonymous* buildings, as this would violate the sanction outlined earlier. In many cases the structures are called *Alono* buildings or something similar, but the name Alcoholics Anonymous is not used in the building's name.

The Primary Purpose of Alcoholics Anonymous

The AA group movement seeks to first provide a program for living to guide the newcomer during the transition stage between active alcohol use. This is

---

[6]*Twelve Steps and Twelve Traditions* of Alcoholics Anonymous will not be reviewed in this book. Interested readers are invited to review the text, which can be purchased from the Alcoholics Anonymous World Services, Inc. Web site.

accomplished not by preaching at the member, but by presenting a simple, realistic picture of the disease of alcoholism in the form of other members who have experienced the same (or similar) problems as a result of their own alcohol use disorder. Confrontation, when used, takes a different form than the word normally suggests: In AA, members share their own life stories, making a public confession of sorts in which they give examples of the lies, deceptions, and rationalizations that they used to support their own alcohol use disorder. In so doing, speakers present a picture of themselves when they were at a stage similar to that of new members, hoping that the new members will see themselves and the need to join AA now rather than suffer all of the consequences that the speakers outlined in their history.

Service to others is also a central theme in AA, since:

> *Even the newest of newcomers finds undreamed rewards as he tries to help his brother alcoholic, the one who is even blinder than he . . . And then he discovers that by divine paradox of this kind of giving that he has found his own reward, whether his brother has yet received anything or not.* (Twelve Steps and Twelve Traditions, *1981, p. 109*)

In this statement one finds one of the paradoxical components of AA: By helping you, I find part of my own recovery from alcohol. If people were speakers at a meeting, they would first of all seek to help themselves by an admission that they were powerless over their alcohol use. This is not an admission of *helplessness* but only that they were powerless (Wallace, 2003). By joining AA and with the admission of powerlessness, members seek the strength of the group as a whole. By admitting the reality of their own alcohol use disorder, speakers are reminded of "what *my* life was like, and by having shared it with you, I am reminded again of the reason why I will not return to drinking, again."

This is the method by which Bill Wilson, in his first meeting with Dr. Robert Smith,[7] was able to recommit himself to his own recovery. He did not preach but simply spoke about his own history, and then thanked Dr. Smith for listening to his story. In a sense, the speaker asserts that "I am a mirror of yourself, and just as you can not look into a mirror without seeing your own reflection, so you can not look at me without seeing a part of yourself." In so doing, the speaker benefits from sharing this message as well as the recipient (Zemore, Kaskutas, & Ammon, 2004).

---

[7]Often referred to as "Dr. Bob" in the AA group movement.

Three factors have been found to determine the success of AA: First is the frequency with which individuals attend meetings. People who attend a meeting a month will receive less benefit from the group process than those who attend two meeting a week, for example. Second is individuals' level of participation in the meeting. Clients who sit quietly in the back of the hall and then slip away at the end of the meeting will derive less benefit than those who actively participate in meetings, ask questions, meet with members after the meeting to discuss points that they are confused about, and so on.

Active AA involvement appears to reflect some of the forces that predict successful efforts to change (Brigham, 2003; Moos & Moos, 2006; Nace, 2003). Finally, there is the emphasis not on long-term recovery, but on simply keeping the focus on "one day at a time." Individual members are encouraged not to worry about distant problems, but to keep the focus on the problems that might undermine their recovery program today. They will have time to worry about tomorrow's problems when tomorrow arrives, or so it is believed.

Active participation in AA allows individuals to begin to develop a substance-free support system that they can call on when experiencing a weak moment, and that offers an alternative source of interpersonal contact beyond what was once achieved only through alcohol.

Outcome Studies: The Effectiveness of Alcoholics Anonymous

It is important to keep in mind that in the time since its inception, virtually every element of AA has been challenged and defended. Many substance abuse and health care workers view AA as being *the* single most important element of an individual's recovery program. In spite of this clinical lore, there has been relatively little research into (a) whether people referred to Alcoholics Anonymous actually attend group meetings, (b) the degree of their involvement or participation in these meetings, and (c) the effectiveness of the 12-step group (Ferri, Amato, & Davoli, 2006).

One study that did attempt to address some of these issues was conducted by the team of Kaskutas et al. (2005). This study shed light on the posttreatment AA participation of 349 people who had entered a formal treatment program for an AUD. The authors found that the posttreatment AA involvement of their research subjects fell into four subgroups:

- Low AA involvement: *These people attended AA just during the first year following treatment.*
- Medium AA involvement: *Individuals in this subgroup attended about 60 AA meetings in the first year following discharge from treatment, but had slightly increased their level of AA involvement by the fifth year following discharge.*
- High initial AA involvement: *Individuals in this subgroup attended 200 meetings in the first year following the discharge from treatment, with a slight decrease in their level of AA involvement by the end of their fifth year following discharge.*
- Declining AA involvement: *Individuals in this subgroup initially attended 200+ AA meetings in the first year following discharge from treatment, but by the end of the fifth year following discharge this had fallen to about 6 meetings/year.*

Further, the team of Kaskutas et al. (2005) found that there was a correlation between level of AA group involvement, with 79% of those people in Group 1 abstinent[8] from alcohol and 73% of those people whose level of AA group involvement placed them in the Group 2 still abstinent from alcohol at the end of the 5th year. Sixty-one percent of those individuals who fell into Group 3 were still abstinent from alcohol at the end of the 5th year, whereas 43% of those in Group 4 were still abstinent at the time of the follow-up study. Brust (2007a) suggested that AA had a success rate of 34%, but did not elaborate as to the criteria utilized to reach this conclusion. Lemonick and Park (2007) suggested that AA was effective "about 20% of the time" (p. 42).

There is a growing body of evidence that suggests that 12-step-oriented treatment programs have higher success rates and lower costs than programs without such a focus (Humphreys & Moos, 2007; Ries et al., 2008). Humphreys and Moos (2007) found that treatment programs that included 12-step group involvement were both 30% less expensive than cognitive-behavioral programs and that 30% more clients from the 12-step involvement group were alcohol-free at the end of 2 years. These findings suggest that 12-step programs can serve an important adjunctive role in substance abuse rehabilitation programs.

Data obtained from national surveys[9] have found that the average AA member has 84 months of sobriety, that 18% have been alcohol-free for more than 60 months, and that 30% have less than 12 months of recovery to their credit (Nace, 2003). These statistics compare very well against the 8-year abstinence rate for those people who were in formal treatment programs[10] (Timko, Moos, Finney, & Lesar, 2000).

Participation in AA group meetings appears to be a more realistic measure of the effectiveness of these self-help groups than simple attendance. Those individuals who have been found to be less active in group meetings appear to be those who are most likely to relapse (Chappel & DuPont, 1999; Gitlow, 2007). Unfortunately, although people might claim to have attended several 12-step group meetings recently, they sat in the back of the room, arrived late, left early, never spoke with anyone, and didn't have a sponsor (Gitlow, 2007, pp. 226–227). The need for individuals to be actively involved in a 12-step group makes sense, because programs such as Alcoholics Anonymous offers such things as (a) external supervision, (b) substitute dependency, (c) new abstinence-centered supportive relationships in place of alcohol-centered relationships, and (d) increased spirituality (Vaillant, 2000, 2005). For any of these factors to work, individuals must be actively involved in the self-help group process.[11] Further, involvement in the process of helping newcomers to AA appears to also assist the helpers in their struggle to maintain abstinence, an observation that reinforces the need for active participation in the AA program to assist individuals in their recovery (Pagano, Friend, Tonigan, & Stout, 2004).

Thus although many 12-step-based rehabilitation programs require 12-step group involvement while the person is in treatment, AA group involvement *after* discharge from treatment is positively correlated with sobriety (Brigham, 2003; Moos & Moos, 2006b; Nace, 2003). Moos and Moos (2006b) found, for example, that individuals who remained active in AA following discharge from treatment had better outcomes than did

---

[8]Which the authors of this study defined as no alcohol use in the past 30 days.

[9]One problem with surveys is that those people who choose to participate in the study are, by definition, different from those who decline to do so.

[10]A complicating factor in such studies is that the preponderance of formal treatment programs either are 12-step centered or require participation in 12-Step groups while the person is in treatment.

[11]Some clients have been known to drive to the meeting site, sit in their car in the parking lot, then leave when they see people start to come out of the building, and then tell their probation officer, counselor, and the like that they did "attend a meeting."

those who did not, and that people who participated in AA by attending at least 27 meetings in the first year following discharge were more likely to be abstinent in both the second year following discharge and again 16 years later. Thus involvement in AA appears to mirror individuals' efforts to make meaningful changes in other areas of their life, such as developing nonchemical means to cope with stress.

The benefits of participation in a 12-step group remain unproven, although there is a tendency for individuals who remain abstinent to be involved in a 12-step group (Zemore et al., 2004). Unfortunately, although proponents of 12-Step groups such as AA advocate continued involvement as being critical to the individual's recovery program, the majority of people either fail to join or fail to consistently participate in such groups (Zemore et al., 2004). These observations do raise questions about the effectiveness of self-help groups such as Alcoholics Anonymous.

Unfortunately, the very nature of AA or similar self-help groups virtually makes it impossible to design a study that would isolate those elements that might help make AA effective and the patient characteristics of those who are most likely to benefit from a 12-step group such as Alcoholics Anonymous (Gernstein, 2003). By definition, people who join AA are *not* representative of those who have an AUD, if only because of their decision to join Alcoholics Anonymous.[12] Those people who drop out of AA are, by the very fact that they dropped out of this self-help group movement, different from those who remain active in it. Given the fact that at the end of 3 months at least half of the new members who joined will have dropped out, and that at the end of 1 year 95% of new members will have stopped attending meetings (Nace, 2003), it must be asked how representative those who remain in this self-help group program are of alcohol-dependent individuals.

Although these studies are suggestive, there is still insufficient evidence at this time to answer the question whether AA is effective in the treatment of alcohol use disorders at this time.[13] One point of continuous confusion is the AA program's emphasis on spirituality as opposed to religion. The available evidence does not suggest that individual members' beliefs about religion change while they participate in Alcoholics Anonymous, although they do grow spiritually (E. A. R. Robinson et al., 2007). This spiritual growth is then associated with a higher abstinence rate, according to the authors. It is assumed that spirituality-based recovery programs might be most effective for those people who had strong beliefs prior to the onset of their alcohol use disorder (Cooney et al., 2005).

Narcotics Anonymous[14]

In 1953, a new self-help group that followed the Alcoholics Model was founded that called itself *Narcotics Anonymous* (NA). Although this group honors its debt to Alcoholics Anonymous, the members believed that:

> *We follow the same path with only a single exception. Our identification as addicts is all inclusive in respect to any mood-changing, mind-altering substance. "Alcoholism" is too limited a term for us; our problem is not a specific substance, it is a disease called "addiction."* (Narcotics Anonymous, *1982, p. x*)

To the members of NA, the problem was the common disease of addiction. This self-help group emerged for those whose only "common denominator is that we failed to come to terms with our addiction" (Narcotics Anonymous, 1982, p. x). But many outsiders view the major difference between AA and NA as being one of emphasis. Alcoholics Anonymous addresses only alcohol use disorders, whereas Narcotics Anonymous addresses addiction to chemicals including alcohol.

The growth of NA has been exceptional. Currently there are more than 25,000 chapters of NA, with more than a quarter of a million active members (Ringwald, 2002). Each self-help group offers a similar 12-step program, offering the person with an addiction a day-by-day program for recovery. This is not surprising, because NA members based their program on AA. One major difference appears to be that AA speaks only about *alcoholism* whereas NA addresses *addiction* to other compounds. Some people are quite comfortable going to AA and believe that it offers them all that they need to address their SUD. Other people believe that NA is a better group for them, because it addresses substance use disorders other than just alcoholism. There appears to be no inherent advantage of one program over the other. It is more important to determine which group works best for which individual.

---

[12]Yet it was on a sample drawn from members of AA that Jellinek (1960) based his research on alcoholism, raising questions about the validity of his research.

[13]See Breakout Discussion # 2 for Chapter 35, on the Internet.

[14]Alcoholics Anonymous and Narcotics Anonymous are not affiliated with each other, however there is an element of cooperation between the two organizations (M. Jordan, personal communication, February, 27, 1989).

Al-Anon and Alateen

The book *Al-Anon's Twelve Steps and Twelve Traditions* provides a short history of this movement. In brief, while substance abusers were attending one of the early AA meetings, their partners would meet to talk about different topics, including their significant other. At some point the decision was made to adapt the same 12 steps that their partner found so helpful in their own recovery program, and the Al-Anon movement was born. At the start of the 21st century, there are an estimated 30,000 Al-Anon groups in the United States with an estimated 390,000 members (Gwinnell & Adamec, 2006; W. L. White, 2005).

Although at first each group modified the 12 steps as they felt necessary, by 1948 the wife of one of the co-founders of AA became involved in the growing organization, and over time a uniform support group for members of AA members emerged. This was a self-help group movement that was in response to the fact that 86% of family members in which there was an alcohol-dependent person felt that their mental health had suffered because of the AUD of the other person (Gwinnell & Adamec, 2006). The program that evolved from this phenomenon was known as the Al-Anon Family Support Group, which made minor modification to the *Twelve Steps and Twelve Traditions* of AA to make them applicable to the needs of family members.

Surprisingly, family members find it useful to attend Al-Anon meetings even if the substance-abusing member continues to abuse chemicals. This not only allows family members to learn how to deal with the stress of a substance-abusing member, but in approximately 20% of the cases the substance-abusing individual eventually agrees to enter a treatment program (O'Farrell & Fals-Stewart, 2008).

Alateen

By 1957, it was recognized that teenagers presented special needs and concerns, and the Al-Anon program was modified to provide a group for these individuals, which came to be called *Alateen*. Currently, it is thought that there are 2300 Alateen groups in the United States (Capretto, 2007; Gwinnell & Adamec, 2006). Alateen programs follow the same 12-step program outlined in the Al-anon program, but provide an opportunity for teenagers to come together to share their experiences and problems and provide encouragement to each other. The group also provides information about the disease of alcoholism, how these teens did not "cause" the alcoholism in their families, how to detach from the alcoholism in their families, and how they can build a rewarding life in spite of the continued AUD in their family.

Support Groups Other Than 12-Step Groups

There has been a great deal of criticism aimed at 12-step groups such as AA or NA because of their emphasis on spirituality or their failure to empower women, for example. In response to this criticism, several new support groups have emerged, many of which will be discussed next.

Rational Recovery[15]

The Rational Recovery (RR) movement attempted to apply the tenets of cognitive-behavioral psychology to the problem of substance use disorders. This movement discontinued group meetings in January 2000. This step was necessary because it was believed that group meetings impeded the individual's progress toward recovery (A. T. Horvath, 2005). In the place of group meetings, RR utilizes services available through books, videos, and Internet-based material designed to help individuals recognize and then change "addictive thoughts" that contribute to their continued abuse of chemicals. This program uses different methodology than does Alcoholics Anonymous, and suggests that the one-day-at-a-time philosophy of AA is counterproductive rather than supportive of a recovery program (Rational Recovery Systems, Inc., 2008).

Self Management and Recovery Training (SMART)[16]

This program was started in 1985 and maintains a Web page on the Internet. SMART was originally part of the Rational Recovery movement but broke away from it in 1994 (A. T. Horvath, 2000, 2005). The SMART program draws heavily on cognitive-behavioral schools of therapy and has four central goals for adults with SUDs: (a) to enhance and maintain the individual's attempt to abstain from alcohol or drugs, (b) to help the individual learn how to cope with thoughts or cravings about chemicals, (c) to help the individual resolve old conflicts and problem behaviors, and (d) to help the individual develop a lifestyle balance (Gernstein, 2003; A. T. Horvath, 2000). The SMART program maintains that individuals' abuse of alcohol or other

---

[15]www.rational.org

[16]www.smartrecovery.org

chemicals is the result of self-defeating thoughts such as "I have a *right* to use _____!" or that their abuse of chemicals is not really the cause of all of their problems. Yet another category of dysfunctional thoughts are those that allow individuals to rationalize their relapse back to active substance use ("You made me so angry that I went out and drank!").

SMART groups believe that virtually any approach to recovery will be of some value to individuals and thus encourage participation in traditional 12-step groups (A. T. Horvath, 2000). About 10% of SMART group members also participate in AA groups (Gernstein, 2003). Participants are taught how to view abstinence as a form of self-affirmation and how not to rely on substance use for good feelings about themselves. This program has been found to be moderately effective for clients with an internal locus of control.

Secular Organizations for Sobriety (SOS)[17]

This self-help group was founded in 1986, and by the year 2000 it was estimated that there were more than 2000 SOS groups in existence, although the program has been viewed as struggling by some (Gernstein, 2003). SOS groups are a response to what is perceived as a heavy emphasis on spirituality in traditional 12-step groups (Ringwald, 2002). The guiding philosophy is heavily influenced by the cognitive-behavioral psychotherapy principles, and stresses personal responsibility, the role of critical thinking in recovery, and the identification of each individual's "cycle of addiction" (A. T. Horvath, 2005).

The SOS model postulates that the addictions rest on three elements: (a) the physiological need for the chemical brought about by tolerance, (b) the learned habit of using a chemical(s) as a way to cope, and (c) the denial of (a) and (b) (A. T. Horvath, 2005). In contrast to traditional 12-step groups, which suggest that individuals must rely on a Higher Power to abstain, SOS holds that individuals have the potential to learn how to live without chemicals within themselves (Ringwald, 2002). The program takes a neutral stance toward participation in traditional 12-step groups, and a significant portion of members are either currently attending a 12-step group or have done so in the past.

Women for Sobriety (WFS)[18]

This self-help group movement was started in 1976 by Jean Kirkpatrick, who passed away in June of 2000 at

the age of 77 years (A. T. Horvath, 2000). This organization is specifically for women, in response to the belief that traditional 12-step groups have failed to address how recovery from the addictions requires different forms of support for men and women. There are 13 core statements or beliefs in WFS, which are designed to assist the member in building self-esteem and a new perspective of the "self" that is not based on the use of chemicals. Unlike more traditional 12-step groups, WFS members are encouraged to leave the group when they feel that they are ready to graduate from the program and assume responsibility for their own recovery program (Ringwald, 2002). Thus the small number of active members actually does an injustice to the program, because only a fraction of the members are actively involved in the program at any time.

Moderation Management (MM)[19]

Moderation Management was founded in 1993 and has been quite controversial since its inception. The founder, Shirley Kishline, was frustrated with traditional 12-step group programs. She had been referred to 12-step-based treatment programs, but her own addiction to alcohol was never firmly established in her mind and she believed that she was only a "problem drinker" (Kishline, 1996, p. 53). Ms. Kishline defined a problem drinker as a person who consumed only 35 drinks per week and who had experienced only mild to moderate alcohol-related problems. The Alcohol-dependent people, in contrast, were those who would experience severe withdrawal symptoms if they should discontinue the use of alcohol.

Moderation Management recommended that *moderation* is a more appropriate goal than abstinence for many people. They also point out that 9 out of 10 "problem drinkers" avoid more traditional 12-step groups and that they shun the traditional label of "alcoholic" ("What Is Moderation Management?", 2008). Members of MM were encouraged to work on the goal of consuming no more than four standard drinks in any given 24-hour period (A. T. Horvath, 2005).

Initially, the MM concept gained support, and MM groups were established in approximately 25 states. Then Ms. Kishline was involved in a motor vehicle accident while under the influence of alcohol in which her vehicle struck another, killing a man and his son. Her measured blood alcohol level was 0.260, or

---

[17]www.secularsobriety.org

[18]www.womenforsobriety.org

[19]www.moderation.org

more than three times the level defined as legally intoxication in that state (Noxon, 2002). She was charged with vehicle manslaughter and convicted. This dealt a strong blow to the MM movement. The teachings of MM are not totally contrary to those of more traditional 12-step groups. Further, research did suggest that most members drawn to MM were those who had low-severity alcohol use problems and were disinterested in traditional 12-step groups (A. T. Horvath, 2005; Humphreys, 2003). However, research has found that at best only about 18% of people once dependent on alcohol can learn to drink in moderation again (Lilienfeld, Lunn, Ruscio, & Beyerstein, 2010). It is not clear how the arrest of the founder of Moderation Management or its low measured success rate[20] will affect the MM program movement.

LifeRing[21]

This program is another alternative to traditional 12-step groups. It is based in Oakland, California, and still is a relatively small movement. LifeRing rejects more traditional 12-step groups in part because of what it views as the inflexible nature of such groups. LifeRing maintains grounds that there are multiple paths to recovery, as opposed to the single path suggested by traditional 12-step groups. Further, LifeRing maintains that the individual's spirituality is a private matter. However, members are not discouraged from attending more traditional 12-step groups either.

Individuals are encouraged to develop a recovery program that will fit their needs, guided by the central philosophy of "whatever works" for them. Currently there are meetings in about 20 states and four foreign countries. Members tend to be white, middle-aged, college-educated individuals, with slightly more male members (58%) than female members (42%) (W. White & Nicolaus, 2005).

Faith-Based Recovery Initiatives

There is a growing trend for recovery programs to be established to function within the religious doctrine(s) of different churches. Such programs range from well-established to fledgling programs, and there are too many to discuss here. Collectively there is limited evidence that secular treatment approaches are more effective than more traditional 12-step programs (Leamon et al., 2008).

Challenges to the Traditional 12-Step Movement

Although the 12-step movement has established an almost irreproachable status in the addictions recovery community, it is not without a small, vocal group of critics. In this section we will review some of the criticism of the Alcoholics Anonymous program, which as the earliest program to be established has drawn the greatest level of criticism. However, each point addressed could also be applied to the other 12-step group movements discussed earlier.

It is often pointed out in traditional 12-step group meetings that, whereas people might be *recovering* from an SUD, they have never *recovered or been cured* (Fletcher, 2003; Gilliam, 1998). Indeed, the very concept of *psychosocial health* is not addressed in the 12-step model (Gilliam, 1998). Rather, individuals are told that they must continue to attend AA in order to keep their alcohol dependence at bay. Yet the AA "Big Book" repeatedly speaks of people having "recovered" from alcohol dependency and as no longer needing to attend meetings to maintain sobriety (Fletcher, 2003). This fact, critics of the movement point out, is quietly ignored by proponents of the disease model as advocated by the 12-step programs.

Another criticism of traditional 12-Step groups is that they are based on a fundamentalist tradition of the 1840s known as the Washington Revival (W. White & Nicolaus, 2005). This was essentially a white, conservative Protestant movement that replaced the physicians and ministers who were providing temperance lectures with lay people who were "reformed" or "reforming" (W. White & Nicolaus, 2005, p. 58). The influence of this movement on the early Alcoholics Anonymous movement might be seen in the emphasis on public confession of one's addiction to alcohol (W. White & Nicolaus, 2005). The leaders of the Washington Revival were later charged with "the sin of humanism" (W. White & Nicolaus, 2005, p. 59), which is to say placing their own will above that of God, and were subsequently discredited by the religious authorities of the time. The lessons of attempting to establish a secular recovery group were remembered, however, and eventually these lessons helped to form the foundation of the Oxford Group, which immediately preceded the formation of Alcoholics Anonymous.

---

[20]In response to those critics who will scream that 18% is a significant success rate, would you want to undergo a surgical procedure that had an 82% failure rate (possibly leaving the patient with no benefit, possible significant medical sequelae, or even death)?

[21]www.unhooked.com

These lessons were heeded by the founders of Alcoholics Anonymous, who attempted to strike a middle ground between secularity of the Washington Revival and the religious orientation of the Oxford group. However, state courts have ruled that Alcoholics Anonymous is essentially a religious movement. This ruling is based in part on the program's heavy emphasis on an external, possibly supernatural Higher Power that individuals must "surrender" to as part of their recovery program (Gernstein, 2003; Wallace, 2003). The courts have repeatedly ruled in various states that forcing a given individual to attend such a group violates the law (Peele, 2004b). This does not prevent local courts from offering the person with an AUD, the option to attend AA as an alternative to incarceration.[22] When the program is forced upon the individual, the potential exists that it can be more harmful than helpful (Szalavitz, 2006). This may be one reason why only 33% (Lilienfeld et al., 2010) to 50% (Nace, 2005a) of new members remain active in AA 3 months after their initial meeting. To further complicate matters, there is research evidence suggesting that those people who are court mandated to attend AA following an arrest for driving a motor vehicle while intoxicated have a *higher* recidivism rate and worse subsequent driving records (as evidenced by motor vehicle accidents, for example) than those sentenced to incarceration by the courts (Bufe, 1998).

Another challenge to the 12-step group movement is based on the fact that there were only a limited number of people (100) who had achieved abstinence when the 12 steps were formulated. The worldview of these early members was formed during the Great Depression of the 1930s and was designed to deflate the individual's ego on the assumption that grandiosity was a common characteristic of alcohol-dependent people. This core assumption has since been viewed as disempowering to individuals who join a 12-step group, and the applicability of these assumptions to the person living in the second decade of the 21st century, almost 80 years later, has been questioned.

Further, the AA program is a one-size-fits-all program, which demands conformity to a single approach to recovery (Gilliam, 1998). It has even been charged that 12-step groups follow a process of "indoctrination" (Bufe, 1998, p. 6) and fear. Individuals are repeatedly warned that the disease of alcoholism will automatically progress and that they must rely on the strength of the group to overcome individual weakness and avoid a relapse. These assertions are not supported by the clinical research,[23] which suggests that alcohol-dependent people rarely follow the downward spiral thought to be inescapable by AA but alternate between periods of more and less abusive drinking (Vaillant, 2000). Further, the 12-step program does not attempt to address the issue that alcohol use disorders can take many forms and that there is no single road to alcoholism. Rather, individuals are offered a single program as a road to recovery. Indeed, Szalavitz (2006) took this criticism even further, noting that the 12-step program has been adopted virtually unchanged to address a wide range of maladaptive behaviors such as overeating, heroin addiction, compulsive shopping, and so on. Not only is it a one-size-fits-all program, but it is a "one treatment model fits all problems" approach as well!

It is a common belief that a "spiritual awakening" by one of the original founders of Alcoholics Anonymous, "Bill" Wilson, was a critical step in the evolution of this self-help group movement. A little known fact however is that this "spiritual awakening" was possibly based on his having received a belladonna injection administered by his physician to help him overcome the acute effects of alcohol withdrawal[24] (Bufe, 1998). Thus one of the foundation stones on which Alcoholics Anonymous was founded may have at the very least been a medication side effect, if not the result of the combined effects of the alcohol withdrawal process and the belladonna.

Another criticism of 12-step programs is their emphasis on waiting until the individual "hits bottom" and reaches a state of spiritual desperation. In any other field of psychological or psychiatric treatment, waiting for the individual to experience to "hit bottom" would be branded abusive by the mental health community (Fletcher, 2003). Although this belief is growing less and less common in Alcoholics Anonymous, there are still those who espouse that it is necessary for the alcoholic to reach this step before attempting to intervene.

Still another criticism of the 12-step group movement is that it is based not on a foundation of scientific research, but on testimonials by individuals who assert that it was indeed essential to their recovery. Anecdotal stories, though perhaps very moving, do not constitute

---

[22]Thus technically, the individual "chooses" to attend the 12-step group meetings.

[23]This clinical research, however, is ignored on the grounds that researchers just do not understand the disease of addiction, as will be discussed later in this chapter.

[24]This was an acceptable treatment method for alcohol withdrawal symptoms at the time.

scientific research data supporting claims that AA (or similar groups) is effective. However, just as individuals who were "recovered" or "recovering" replaced physicians or ministers as speakers at temperance meetings, in many 12-step meetings one person is a designated speaker who affirms how the group saved his or her life. Feedback from mental health professionals is often dismissed because they "do not understand" the disease of addiction, or because they have "not been there."[25] In contrast to this program, participants are elevated to the role of "experts" because they were once actively addicted to chemicals (Szalavitz, 2006).

Finally, research has demonstrated that only about 20% of those who join AA will abstain from alcohol for the rest of their lives (Lilienfeld et al., 2010). As these various points of criticism suggest, although the 12-step group movement may have played a major role in the recovery, there are many points of contention suggesting that these programs are not a panacea for individuals with alcohol (or, by extension, other drug) use disorders.

Chapter Summary

Alcoholics Anonymous was one of the first self-help groups and has grown into the predominant, almost exclusive self-help group model for individuals with an alcohol use disorder. The program emerged as the first 100 members of the fledgling AA group movement who achieved long-term abstinence met to discuss the common elements that contributed to their recovery. This consensus resulted in the famous 12 steps of the AA program.

The AA program is designed to place emphasis on spiritual growth, without addressing religious issues. It is confrontative, without using confrontation, relies on external support for advertising or financial resources, and is not required of members but simply offered as a road that members might find useful in their quest for recovery from alcoholism. There is no "board of directors," and members who serve in various capacities do so as being an equal among equals. The growth of AA was slow initially, but has become a worldwide movement, with chapters in virtually every nation around the world, and has a total membership in the millions.

Questions have been raised as to whether AA is an effective adjunct to treatment for people with an alcohol use disorder. By extension, these same questions apply to self-help groups modeled after the AA program. There is preliminary evidence suggesting that AA is a useful adjunct to the treatment of some, but not all, people with an alcohol use disorder. Variations of this program have been applied to other problems, such as being the spouse of a person with an AUD (Al-Anon) and being the child of a person with an AUD (Alateen).

The Alcoholics Anonymous model was also modified and applied to other drugs of abuse, resulting in programs such as Narcotics Anonymous, which was reviewed in this chapter. It has also been applied to a variety of non-drug-related compulsive behaviors such as compulsive eating, compulsive shopping, and so on. Further, there are a number of emergent self-help programs that reject one or more of the tenets of the Alcoholics Anonymous program but that still attempt to help individuals find abstinence from alcohol and other drugs of abuse.

---

[25]So, when you are having a heart attack, will you demand that you be cared for *only* by a physician who has "been there" by having a prior heart attack?

CHAPTER 36

Substance Use Disorders and Infectious Disease[1]

Introduction

As a group, alcohol and illicit-drug users are approximately twice as likely as nonusers to use the services of a hospital emergency room and seven times as likely to require hospitalization (Laine et al., 2001). Following hospitalization, individuals with an SUD tend to require longer hospital stays before being ready for discharge as well (Laine et al., 2001). A major reason for this fact is the increased risk for infectious disease found in people with an SUD.

SUDs contribute to infectious disease(s) through a variety of mechanisms. Chronic alcohol use depletes the body of essential nutrients, reducing the effectiveness of the immune system, whereas aspiration of material regurgitated can contribute to pneumonia. Intravenous drug use, rarely carried out under antiseptic conditions, pushes bacteria normally found on the skin into the circulation, bypassing the body's normal defenses against such invasion. Shared compounds for smoking (such as marijuana) allows infectious microorganisms in the lungs to be passed from one person to the next. The general environment in which illicit-drug abusers live also predisposes them to infections. Some of the infectious diseases more commonly encountered in illicit-drug abusers include peripheral cellulitis, skin abscesses, pneumonias, lung abscesses, brain abscesses, various viral diseases, and tetanus. In this chapter, we will discuss some of the more common infections associated with the SUDs.

---

[1]The author would like to express his appreciation to John P. Doweiko, MD, for his review of this chapter for technical accuracy.

Why Is Infectious Disease Such a Common Complication for People with an SUD?

There are many answers to this question. The general state of malnutrition so often found in people with an SUD can compromise the effectiveness of the body's immune system. Methamphetamine addicts might subsist on a "diet" of soda and candy bars, for example. Alcohol-dependent people might, if asked, assert that they did indeed have dinner last night. When the matter is pursued however, drinkers might admit that they had two bags of peanuts, some pretzels from the bowl on the bar, and half a hamburger, along with almost a dozen bottles of beer, a diet that is hardly going to support a healthy immune system. Further, there is evidence that alcohol use by itself can impair the immune system.

Sterile Technique

The conditions under which illicit-drug abusers inject their drug(s) of choice make some form of infection almost certain. This is because the injected drug abuser rarely uses the "sterile technique" used by health care professionals. If a compound must be injected into the body, health care professionals will use a new, sterile needle, and prepare the injection site with either alcohol or an antiseptic solution before injecting a sterile compound into the patient's body. The needle is then discarded. In contrast to this process, intravenous drug addicts usually just find a vein and insert the needle without even attempting to wash the injection site with soap and water. In the process the addicted person will also push microorganisms found on the surface of the skin into the body, effectively bypassing the body's normal defenses.

Contamination

Illicit drugs are often contaminated with various microscopic pathogens, which are then injected directly into the body if the drug is administered via intravenous injection. Surprisingly, although pharmaceutical preparations are highly prized among illicit-drug abusers because of their purity and known potency, they also might become contaminated as the abuser prepares the capsule or tablet for injection. The tablet or contents of the capsule are crushed into a fine powder so that it can be prepared for injection. The flat surface that is selected for this process, however, might be contaminated, transferring microorganisms to the compound about to be injected. If they are forced to share the same needle, some IV drug abusers do not even attempt to sterilize it. At best they might lick the needle to clear off residual blood, and in the process transfer bacteria such as *Nesseria sica* and *Streptococcus viridans* to the needle surface. These are bacteria normally found in the human mouth where the body has developed defenses against them, but by injecting them directly into the body, these defenses are avoided.

Some intravenous drug abusers do attempt to rinse the rig[2] in tap water. This process contaminates the needle with various microorganisms normally found in tap water (which when swallowed are destroyed by the body's defenses). These microorganisms are then injected directly into protein-rich muscle tissue or the general circulation, depending on the method by which the compound is abused, again side-stepping the body's natural defenses against such microscopic invaders. The stage is now set for either a localized or systemic infection.

The list of infectious diseases that might be transferred from one IV drug abuser to the next through contaminated needles includes (but is not limited to) the various viral forms of hepatitis (discussed later in this chapter), HIV-1 (the virus that causes AIDS),[3] syphilis, and even malaria. Some of the more commonly encountered infections seen in substance abusers are discussed next.

Assorted Bacterial Infections Seen in Intravenous Drug Abusers

Endocarditis

This is a bacterial infection of the valves of the heart. Normally, only 1 in every 20,000 people develop this condition, which can be the result of such things as community-acquired pneumonia (discussed later). But intravenous drug abusers are considered a high-risk population, with 1 in every 500 developing this disorder (D. J. Robinson, Lazo, Davis, & Kufera, 2000). One reason for this is the chronic exposure to the irritating chemicals often used as adulterants.[4] But another cause is the failure of intravenous drug abusers to follow sterile technique: Many of the strains of bacteria that are

---

[2]See Glossary.

[3]Also discussed later in this chapter.

[4]Discussed in Chapter 37.

introduced into the body colonize the tissues of the heart valves upon reaching them, establishing ongoing endocarditis. Finally, shared needles may transfer bacteria from one person with endocarditis to another abuser, who then goes on to become addicted in turn.

Necrotizing Fasciitis

This is a bacterial infection in which subcutaneous tissues are attacked by strains of bacteria normally found only on the surface of the skin (S. B. Karch, 2009). Cocaine abusers might be especially vulnerable to this condition, possibly because of the vasoconstrictive effects of this compound. However, any IV drug abuser who fails to utilize proper sterile technique will push any bacteria at the injection site through the skin into the subcutaneous tissues, where they might establish an active infection. As the bacteria destroy the tissues under the skin, they might also be carried by the circulation to other organs of the body. The surface of the skin can appear to be normal until late in the disease cycle, making diagnosis difficult. Necrotizing fasciitis is a life-threatening and frequently fatal infection.

Skin Abscesses

The intravenous, or subcutaneous, drug abuser is vulnerable to bacterial infections at the injection site. Some of the adulterants mixed with heroin or cocaine will cause or at least exacerbate skin abscesses. These adulterants are usually not water soluble, irritating surrounding tissues, and because the injection site is rarely washed with an antiseptic solution, bacteria normally found on the skin are pushed into the blood-rich tissues under the skin when a compound is injected. These abscesses may become life threatening, require prolonged treatment, and leave the abuser with scars at the infection site for the rest of their lives . . . if they survive. Such infections are often lethal for the intravenous drug abuser.

The Pneumonias

Technically, the term *pneumonia* refers to an acute infection of the lungs, usually caused by bacteria or fungi.[5] It is usually diagnosed by radiological examination[6] of the lungs. Although pneumonia can develop in nonabusers, conditions such as the alcohol use disorders, immune systems disorders, cigarette smoking,

extreme age, vitamin malabsorption syndromes, and malnutrition all can contribute to the development of a pneumonia in a patient. People with an AUD, for example, are twice as likely to develop bacterial pneumonia than are nondrinkers.

Fungal Pneumonia

The development of a fungal pneumonia is a common complication of HIV infection (discussed later in this chapter) and of heroin use/abuse (S. B. Karch, 2009). Heroin abuse interferes with the normal function of the immune system, reducing the body's ability to defend itself against these pathogens. But many samples of illicit heroin are also contaminated with fungi, which when injected into the body are transported by the circulation to the lungs where they can establish an infection site. Fungal pneumonia frequently requires surgical removal of the infected tissues and the use of antibiotic compounds for an extended period of time.

Aspirative Pneumonia

There is a strong relationship between the alcohol use disorders and aspirative pneumonia, although many of the other drugs of abuse also can cause this condition. The chronic use of alcohol places the drinker at risk for various forms of lung infection (Kershaw & Guidot, 2008). If individuals should aspirate while regurgitating, they would be vulnerable to two different potentially life-threatening dangers. First, the material being regurgitated might be aspirated into the lungs, blocking the air passages. If the drinker is unable to clear the airway in time, hypoxia and possible death may be the result (J. L. Johnson & Hirsch, 2003). A second problem is that even if this threat is avoided, some of the material aspirated could possibly start to decompose in the lungs, establishing a growth medium for bacteria.

To further complicate matters, chronic alcohol use alters the normal pattern of bacterial growth in the mouth and throat, again allowing these pathogens access to the lungs if they are aspirated. Even in persons whose immune system has not been weakened by malnutrition and vitamin malabsorption syndromes, the respiratory system has few defenses against these microorganisms because they are normally found in other regions of the body (S. B. Karch, 2009; Marik, 2001). The true incidence of aspiration pneumonia in the community is not known, because many cases are misdiagnosed as either *community-acquired* or *nosocomial* forms of pneumonia (J. L. Johnson & Hirsch, 2003).

---

[5]Plural of the word *fungus*.

[6]A fancy term for X-rays.

It is known that this is a common problem among people with an SUD, is potentially fatal, and is always a medical emergency that should be assessed and treated by trained medical professionals.

Community-Acquired Pneumonia (CAP)

Intravenous drug abusers, cigarette smokers, and people with alcohol use disorders are all at increased risk for a condition known as community-acquired pneumonia (CAP) (S. B. Karch, 2009). Each year in the United States between 2 and 3 million people contract community-acquired pneumonia. Infected individuals will pass the offending bacteria, usually *Streptoccus pneumoniae,* to others through aspiration or inhalation of droplets that form when the person coughs (Musher, 2008). People living in close, crowded quarters (such as shelters for the homeless, day-care centers, and so on) are more likely to spread *S. pneumoniae* to those around them (Musher, 2008). People whose immune system was compromised by malnutrition, vitamin malabsorption syndromes, or conditions that reduce the effectiveness of the immune system such as HIV infection have a reduced resistance to the offending bacteria, making it more likely to contract CAP. Cigarette smokers are especially vulnerable to a form of CAP caused by the bacteria *Haemophilus influenzae.*

Mild cases of CAP might be treated on an outpatient basis, but eventually 20% of individuals with this condition will require hospitalization, and 45,000 people die each year from CAP in spite of medical care. Individuals with comorbid conditions, such as people with an SUD, are more likely to require hospitalization either for the infection itself or for infection-related complications such as meningitis or endocarditis. Fortunately, a vaccine was introduced in the early 1980s that will provide a degree of protection against *S. pneumoniae*–induced CAP (Musher, 2008).

Acquired Immune Deficiency Syndrome (AIDS)
A Short History of AIDS

In 1981 scientists had collected data suggesting that a previously unknown disease was spreading through the United States. In affected people, the immune system would fail, leaving them vulnerable to a range of rare "opportunistic infections" rarely seen except in those people whose immune system had been seriously compromised. Initially this disorder was found mainly in homosexual males, then it began to appear in intravenous drug abusers and people who had received a blood transfusion.

Researchers named this disorder the *acquired immune deficiency syndrome,* or AIDS, and concluded that it was the result of a viral infection from a previously unknown agent. Scientists now believe that the HIV-1 virus "jumped" from chimpanzees to humans in Africa approximately between the years 1884 and 1924, although it is possible that isolated cases of HIV-1 infection did occur in humans prior to this time ("Scientists Trace AIDS Virus Origin to 100 Years Ago," 2008). However, with the rise of an urban culture in Africa, and the development of rapid, efficient road transport systems, the virus was able to move into large population areas, enabling it to develop a pool of infected individuals who then would pass the infection on to others. Before this, travel in Africa was so difficult that even if people were to become infected, it was unlikely that they would survive long enough to leave the local geographic area and then, lacking further victims, it would die out.

Within a short period of time researchers identified the causal agent: a virus that they named the *human immunodeficiency virus* (HIV). It was originally thought that this was a single virus, but other members of the same general family of viruses were identified and assigned a number. The virus that causes AIDS in humans is usually referred to as "the AIDS virus" or "HIV," although some centers utilize the more correct term *HIV-1.*

What Is AIDS?

Technically, AIDS is not a disease in its own right. Rather, it is a *constellation* of symptoms, a syndrome, the most important of which is the breakdown of the individual's immune system over time (Welsby, 1997). As the HIV infection progresses, the untreated patient develops and dies from an infection, neoplasm, or other condition once easily controlled by the body's immune system.

Where Did HIV Come From?

Current research evidence suggests that both the HIV-1 and the HIV-2 viral infections are caused by a virus that jumped from one species to another. When this happens, the "new" virus causes a far more serious disease than it did in the original host species, which has had time to adapt to the virus (David Baltmore, quoted in Svitil, 2003). Some examples of other diseases that have jumped from one species into humans includes the West

Nile virus, hantavirus, and Ebola (David Baltimore, quoted in Svitil, 2003).[7] This is known as a "transspecies jump," and in such a jump, the virus changes during the course of a jump, adapting to its new host. The transspecies jump is the virus's most important means of long-term survival. Species go extinct; viruses move on (R. Preston, 1999, p. 54).

One of the remarkable facts of HIV-1 is that it apparently made the jump from its original host to humans in the past 100 years. We are thus able to watch a biological process take place in the span of our lifetime. There is little, if any, credible evidence that the virus was intentionally released into the population to target homosexual males or other minority-group members, or that it is divine retribution for past sins (Vaughn, 2006).

The Scope of HIV Infection

In the time since its discovery, an estimated 60 million people around the world have contracted the HIV virus, about two-thirds of whom are still alive (Silvestri, 2009; C. Wilson, 2008). Every day, an additional 7000 people contract HIV around the world, which means that there are 2.4 million new cases of HIV infection on this planet each year (Harmon, 2010; C. Wilson, 2008). It has been estimated that another 66,000 people become infected with HIV in the United States each year (Harmon, 2010). In the span of half a century, AIDS has been transformed from an obscure virus to the fourth most common cause of death around the world (Markel, 2004, p. 176; see also Lashley, 2006).

Most of those who have died from HIV infection or who are currently infected with this virus are in the Third World, especially the sub-Sahara region of Africa (Rhame, 2009). Although only 11% of the world's population lives in this part of the world, 67% of the world's HIV infections, 70% of new infections each year, and 75% of HIV-related deaths each year are found here (Rhame, 2009). In the United States, 1 to 1.18 million people have been infected with HIV, with perhaps as many as 25% not knowing that they have been infected (Centers for Disease Control and Prevention, 2008). Globally, an estimated 33 million people are thought to have died from AIDS, including

545,000 people in the United States (Centers for Disease Control and Prevention, 2008). These figures are estimates. Unfortunately, HIV infection in the United States is most often a disease of youth, with approximately half of those who contract the infection being under the age of 25 when they are infected (Khalsa, 2006).

How Does AIDS Kill?

Every species of bacteria, virus, or fungus has a characteristic pattern of protein molecules in the walls of its cells. The immune system learns to recognize the specific molecular pattern in these disease-causing microorganisms, and to attack them. The first time that the body is exposed to a new pathogen, it must rely on generalized disease-fighting cells known as *lymphocytes*. These generalists roam through the body, seeking out and attacking microorganisms with a foreign protein pattern in their cell walls. During this time, the body "learns" to produce disease-specific antibodies, a process that may take hours, days, weeks, or in some cases years. After they are formed, however, these antibodies drift through the body, searching for the specific invading pathogens for which they were tailor made, and the person is said to be "immune" to that disease.

But the AIDS virus differs from many of the traditional viral invaders with which the body has to cope. HIV infects the very cells sent out by the body to destroy it: the CD4 cells of the immune system (H. Bell, 2009). It accomplishes this by taking advantage of a protein complex in the wall of the CD4 cells to use as a binding site. The CD4 cells, also known as the T-helper cells, are lymphocytes, the generalists that roam the body looking for foreign invaders (Covington, 2005; Markel, 2004). It has been estimated that between 93 and 99% of the total number of HIV viral particles in the infected person's body can be found in the CD4 cells. Small concentrations of the virus particles are found in the cells of the retina, the brain, the testes, and other regions of the body (Pomerantz, 1998, 2003). These sites provide a reservoir of viral particles that might re-infect the person whose body had otherwise been cleansed of the virus (Pomerantz, 1998, 2003).

In the early 1980s, clinicians believed that the virus entered a "latency" phase during the first weeks or months following infection. It is now known that the virus begins to replicate almost immediately after it gains admission to the human body, and that the apparent "latency" period was actually an illusion caused by the fact that the first blood tests for the virus searched not for the virus itself, but for the lymphocytes specific to the AIDS virus. Because it might take the body up to

---

[7] R. J. Glasser (2004) stated that there are more than 1400 microorganisms that can infect humans, of which approximately half were originally caused infections in an animal species and jumped to the human population. It has been estimated that scientists have identified 1% of the bacterial species and 4% of the viral species found on this planet (R. J. Glasser, 2004).

9 months to start to produce these HIV-specific "antibodies," scientists were left with the illusion that the virus went through a latency phase.

The viral infectious process often is confusing to the person who is not a health care professional. Essentially, once a virus particle enters the target cell, it "reprograms" the cell's genetic material so that the cell now starts to produce thousands of copies of that virus. Eventually, billions of cells are involved in the process of producing new viral particles, and each time the host cell is full to the point of bursting, it does just that: The cell ruptures, spewing thousands of new viral particles into the body. However, during the replication process HIV becomes "sneaky." First, the HIV-1 virus has been found to have three proteins in the viral coat that render it invisible to the body's immune system after it infects a cell (Schaefer, Wonderlich, Roeth, Leonard, & Collins, 2008). One of these proteins then marks the infected cell so that it will not be attacked by the virus a second time, according to Schaefer et al.

Then, each time that the AIDS virus replicates in the victim's body, it produces slightly different copies of itself. The specific mechanism for this is quite technical and well beyond the scope of this text. However, in brief HIV tends to be "sloppy" during the process of replication, allowing subtle mistakes to slip into the genetic code of each new generation of virus particles. These new "daughter" virus particles are also called "mutations" or "variants" (Forstein, 2002). These variants are released back into the general circulation, but because they do not have the exact molecular pattern of the original viral particle, the body must learn to produce antibodies against these "new" invaders as well. At the end of the person's life, the body might literally contain billions of slightly different viral particles, overwhelming the immune system. As the immune system weakens, various opportunistic infections once easily controlled by the immune system develop. Indeed, in about 20% of cases, the development of opportunistic infections is the first sign that the person is infected with HIV (Silvestri, 2009). The overwhelmed immune system, faced with billions of different HIV virus forms, breaks down and an opportunistic infection develops that takes the patient's life.

The Chain of HIV Infection

In spite of its reputation, HIV is a rather fragile virus and is not easily transmitted from one person to another. There are three methods of transmission: (a) sexual contact (homosexual or heterosexual) with an infected partner, (b) transmission of the virus from an infected mother to an infant either during birth or through breast-feeding, and (c) exposure to HIV-infected blood by direct inoculation (sharing intravenous needles, blood transfusion from an infected donor, organ transplant from an infected donor, and so on) (Lashley, 2006). Sax (2003) estimated that the odds of contracting HIV after sharing a needle with an infected person one time are 1:150. The odds of contracting HIV after a single episode of unprotected vaginal sex was estimated at between 1:300 and 1:1000 (Sax, 2003). The risk for a health care worker who suffers an accidental "needle stick" has been estimated as between 0.3% and 0.9% (Fauci & Lane, 2008; D. L. Longo & Fauci, 2008). This method of possible HIV transmission will not be discussed further in this text.

Sexual contact (heterosexual or homosexual) is the most common method of HIV transmission in this country ("HIV Infection Among Injection Drug Users—34 States, 2004–2007," 2010). High-risk heterosexual contact, defined as being where one partner or the other is infected with HIV, is the second most common method of transmission, whereas the sharing of intravenous needles by drug abusers or addicts is the third most common method of disease transmission in the United States at this time ("HIV Infection Among Injection Drug Users—34 States, 2004–2007," 2010). HIV infection among intravenous drug abusers has been reported in 120 countries around the world (Arasteh & des Jarlais, 2008). In the United States, there has been an 80% drop in the number of people who contract HIV through shared intravenous needles (Centers for Disease Control and Prevention, 2009a). Although blood transfusions were a potential route of HIV transmission in the 1980s, the development of appropriate blood-screening tests has virtually eliminated blood transfusions as a source of new HIV infections (Rhame, 2009).

The means of HIV infection varies between men and women in the United States. For men who become infected, approximately 70% of new cases of HIV each year in the United States involved homosexual contact between males, whereas 25% were the result of sharing of contaminated intravenous needles and 15% involve having sex with an infected woman (Fiellin, 2008; Vaughn, 2006; Work Group on HIV/AIDS, 2000). In contrast to the pattern of disease transmission in men, 75% of women contract the infection as a result of unprotected sexual activity with an infected partner. The other 25% contract the infection through the shared use of intravenous needles (Work Group on HIV/AIDS, 2000). It has been estimated that up to 25% of

HIV-infected individuals of either sex are unaware of that they are infected. These people thus unknowingly pass the infection on to their sexual partner(s) or those with whom they share needle(s). Another, admittedly rare, method of HIV transmission is known as "vertical transmission." During this process an infected woman passes the virus on to her baby, usually during childbirth. The odds of vertical transmission are markedly reduced if the mother is fully compliant with an aggressive antiviral medication regimen (Havens, 2009), and if the mother is compliant, the risk of vertical transmission is <1% (Rhame, 2009). It is also possible for the mother to infect the infant through breast-feeding (Fauci & Lane, 2008).

Research into HIV-1 has shown that there are subtypes of the HIV virus, each of which has a different distribution pattern around the world. The "B" strain is the most common form of HIV in the United States, Europe, South America, and Australia, whereas the "E" subtype is found mainly in Asia and Africa. This latter form is more easily transmitted between an infected and uninfected partner during sexual activity, which reflects the most common mode of transmission for this subtype of HIV in those regions of the world.

Stages of HIV Infection

Sax (2003) identified six stages of the typical HIV infection:

1. Viral transmission: This is point where a previously uninfected person first contracts HIV.
2. Acute HIV infection: Within 1–4 weeks of Stage 1, 50–90% of newly infected people develop a mild, flulike syndrome. This may be dismissed by the individual, and because the symptoms are vague and nonspecific might be misdiagnosed by the physician, if consulted. *If* physicians are suspicious, they might order an HIV *viral load* test, but it might take 2–6 weeks between Stage 1 and the time that the viral load test will detect the first virus particles in the patient's blood (Sax, 2003; Yu & Daar, 2000).[8] It should be noted that during this time, although the body has not started to produce an HIV-specific immune response, the

individual remains capable of passing the infection on to others.

3. Seroconversion: This occurs within 6 months of the date of infection and marks the point where the individual's body has started to mount an HIV-specific immune response. It is at this point that HIV-specific antibodies are first found in the individual's blood. The individual is now said to be *seropositive,* or *HIV positive.* Those people who do not show signs of an HIV-specific immune response are said to be *seronegative.* There are two possible reasons why a person might be seronegative: (a) They have never been exposed to HIV, or (b) it is still too soon for blood tests to detect an HIV-specific immune response. It is recommended that the individual be retested 3 months later to rule out this possibility. Obviously, if individuals engages in a high-risk behavior, they will have to wait 6 more months before having a blood test to detect a HIV-specific immune response and then 3 more months for confirmatory testing. If the individual has a positive test, follow-up testing should be performed to rule out a false-positive result on the initial test. Once the HIV-specific immune system response is detected, physicians will usually order a viral load test, which provides a measure of the patient's status (Mylonakis et al., 2001).

4. Asymptomatic infection: At this point the HIV infection be detected only through blood tests, although the virus is replicating in the patient's body and can be passed on to others.

5. Symptomatic HIV infection: At this point the individual's immune system has started to break down, allowing opportunistic infections to begin to develop. Such infections include "thrush," cervical dysplasia or cancer, constant low-grade fever, unexplained weight loss, and development of peripheral neuropathies (Sax, 2003).

6. Acquired immune deficiency syndrome (AIDS): The body produces special cells to fight off microorganisms, known as the CD4+ T (sometimes called the *T-helper* cells). Normally there are between 1000 and 1200 CD4+ T cells per cubic milliliter of blood. When the number of CD4+ T cells falls below 200 per cubic milliliter of blood, the individual becomes vulnerable to various opportunistic infections that are the hallmark of AIDS. One common bacterial infection frequently encountered at this stage is tuberculosis (TB), which is 100 times more common in those people infected

---

[8]The current HIV viral load tests can detect as few as 20 virus particles per cubic milliliter of blood (Mylonakis, Pailou, & Rich, 2001; Work Group on HIV/AIDS, 2000). As long as the viral load in the patient's blood is less than the level of detection, the infection can slip under the "radar" of modern medicine.

with HIV than in the general population (Bartlett, 1999). In many cases TB is the first sign that a person has AIDS, and the infection seems to progress more rapidly in HIV-infected people (Raviglione & O'Brien, 2008).

Life Expectancy for People With HIV-1 Infection

Prior to the development of antiviral medications for HIV-infected people, the mean survival time after the person contracted the infection was 10 years (D. A. Cooper, 2008). About 10% percent of those people who were infected were "rapid progressers" who developed AIDS within 5 years of infection, whereas about 10% percent of those infected were "slow progressers" who took an exceptionally long time to progress to the AIDS stage.[9] Although great strides have been made in developing medications that will slow the replication of the virus, even with the best antiviral treatments available the average HIV-infected person is thought to lose 10 potential years of life (D. A. Cooper, 2008).[10] Infected people who are also active intravenous drug addicts are thought to lose approximately 20 years of potential life span to the combined effects of HIV infection and their SUD (D. A. Cooper, 2008).

The Treatment of HIV Infection

One of the most important factors in the treatment of HIV infection is early detection so that antiviral therapies can immediately be initiated. Unfortunately, it is not uncommon for the infection to be detected only about 1–3 years before the onset of AIDS (Carr & Lynfield, 2009; Shouse et al., 2009). This reflects, in part, the complacency that has developed in the general public, who have mistakenly come to believe that HIV/AIDS no longer presents a threat.

Once infected, a very important component of HIV treatment is the patient's nutritional status (Hendricks & Gorbach, 2009). Intravenous drug abusers typically lack access to adequate food sources, and even when appropriate food is ingested illicit drugs can interfere

with the absorption of many vitamins and minerals needed for adequate health (Hendricks & Gorbach, 2009). Thus treatment professionals must pay close attention to patients' dietary habits to ensure adequate intake of appropriate foods, including various micronutrients that might influence immune system function (Hendricks & Gorbach, 2009). One such micronutrient is *selenium*. Individuals who took a selenium supplement as prescribed were found to have no increase in viral load levels and an increase in the CD4 T cell count (Hurwitz et al., 2007). Hurwitz et al. concluded that the daily supplementation of the diet with selenium was an inexpensive way to both suppress the virus replication process and increase the CD4 T cell count. Further research into the impact of dietary malabsorption syndromes on the health status of HIV-infected patients is necessary.

In addition to dietary adherence, pharmaceutical companies have developed an ever-growing number of antiviral agents to assist in the fight against AIDS. These antiviral agents have changed the clinical picture of HIV infection in the United States from an automatic death sentence to that of a chronic disease such as diabetes or heart disease (Kuhl, 2002). Unfortunately, (a) these compounds slow but do not eliminate the replication of the AIDS virus, and (b) the high cost of obtaining these medications prohibits some people from being treated (Craig, 2004). Currently, there are four classes of antiviral agents used against HIV: (a) *nucleoside/nucleotide analogs,* (b) *fusion inhibitors,* (c) *protease inhibitors,* and (d) *nonnucleoside reverse transcriptase inhibitors* (Clavel & Hance, 2004; Godwin, 2004). The method by which each drug interferes with viral replication is very complex, but a brief summary of the different classes of antiviral agents and their mechanism of action is in Appendix 3.

To combat the problem of viral resistance to the antiviral medication(s) being administered, the physician will prescribe medications from different classes of antiviral agents (W. K. Henry, Alozie, & Bonham, 2009). Once termed HAART, or "highly active antiretroviral therapy," this process has also been called CART ("combination antiretroviral therapy"). The antiviral medications have proven quite effective in controlling HIV, turning what was once a fatal disease into a chronic, manageable illness, *if* the patient is compliant in taking the medications as prescribed. It has been estimated that the patient must take a minimum of 80–90% of the prescribed medication doses at the proper time to achieve maximum effect and limit the

---

[9]The introduction of effective antiviral treatments made it impossible to determine the median survival time for slow progressers.

[10]This figure assumes that the person has been infected with HIV just once. There is strong evidence that suggests that subsequent infection with HIV from other sources (infected sexual partner or intravenous drug use involving a shared IV needle with an infected person) might accelerate the progression of HIV to the stage of AIDS (D. M. Smith et al., 2004).

development of strains of HIV that are resistant to the medications (J. C. Scott & Marcotte, 2010). Unfortunately, up to 40% of patients on HAART medication programs are not compliant with taking their medications as prescribed. Patients who have an ongoing SUD, who are depressed, or who have unrealistic expectations for the treatment process often are noncompliant with medication dosing. To further complicate matters, the side effects of the current generation of antiviral agents might be quite debilitating for the patient, making the problem of medication compliance difficult.

Although antiviral medications might slow the replication of HIV in the human body, they do not eliminate the virus from the body. To date, the complete eradication of HIV from the body remains a goal that has not been achieved. To accomplish this, it would be necessary to eliminate every one of the estimated *1 trillion* (100,000,000,000) of the virus particles found in the body, including those within infected cells to achieve a total cure (J. Doweiko, personal communication, 2010). Thus a total cure for HIV infection remains an elusive goal at this time.

AIDS and Suicide

There is a great deal of controversy about the relationship between HIV infection and suicide. It is currently thought that individuals infected with the AIDS virus are 7–36 times as likely to commit suicide as an uninfected person the same age (Roy, 2003; Treisman, Angelino, & Hutton, 2001). The period of greatest risk appears to be the period immediately after individuals learn that they have been infected with the virus. It is thus recommended that a suicide risk assessment be carried out with each patient with HIV, and periodically after treatment has started.

AIDS and Kaposi's Sarcoma

When AIDS was first identified in the early 1980s, physicians thought that a rare form of cancer known as Kaposi's sarcoma was a manifestation of this disease. This misunderstanding was result of the fact that 40% of individuals infected with HIV also developed Kaposi's sarcoma (Antman & Chang, 2000). However, since then it has been discovered that Kaposi's sarcoma is caused by a virus from the herpes virus family (Antman & Chang, 2000) and thus is a separate disorder from HIV. It should also be noted that because both the hepatitis C virus (discussed later) can also be transmitted through contaminated intravenous needles, at least 33% of HIV-positive patients are also infected with the hepatitis C virus.

AIDS and Neurocognitive Dysfunction

Shortly after the individual is infected with the HIV virus, the virus enters the brain where it is able to cause inflammation and the accumulation of neurotoxic compounds such as the cytokines. This in turn will activate the brain's defensive immune response system, resulting in the destruction of both neurons and glial cells (J. C. Scott & Marcotte, 2010). This appears to be the mechanism for neurocognitive problems that are found in at least 50% of those people infected with HIV (J. C. Scott & Marcotte, 2010). The degrees of neurocognitive deficit can range from very mild to severe and were classified by J. C. Scott and Marcotte (2010) as follows:

Asymptomatic: Neuropsychological test performance at least two standard deviations below expectations in two of five areas assessed, but patient retains ability to carry out activities of daily living (ADLs).[11]

Minor neurocognitive deficits: In addition to aforementioned criteria, individuals have a mild impairment in their ability to carry out ADLs but do not meet the criteria for dementia.

HIV-associated dementia: Neuropsychological test scores are at least two standard deviations below norm on two of the five areas assessed, and individuals show a marked impairment in their ability to carry out ADLs.

Strict medication adherence has been found to reduce the probability that individuals will develop HIV-related neurocognitive problems or at least the severity of such deficits if they develop (J. C. Scott & Marcotte, 2010).

HIV Infection and Employment

It has been estimated that HIV infection results in a $22,000 per year reduction in earning potential for the individual (J. C. Scott & Marcotte, 2010). Because many insurance companies are unwilling to pay for the high cost of programs such as HAART, many individuals who are infected with HIV seek disability status through such programs as Social Security, so that their medications will be paid for by other agencies.

Part Summary

The acquired immune deficiency syndrome (AIDS) has been identified as the end stage of a viral infection

---

[11]See Glossary.

caused by the human immunodeficiency virus (HIV), a blood-borne virus that is a member of a family of viruses that share certain common characteristics. Over time, different members of the HIV family of viruses have been identified, which are now identified by numbers (HIV-1, HIV-2, and so on). AIDS is now known to be the end stage of an infection by either HIV-1 or, more rarely, HIV-2 (Lashley, 2006). Initially, infection with either virus was a virtual death sentence, and prior to the introduction of effective antiviral medications, the average survival period between initial infection and death from an opportunistic infection(s) was approximately 10 years. The new antiviral medications have transformed HIV infection from a virtual death sentence to that of a chronic disease that can be controlled, such as diabetes or heart disease, and there is a glimmer of hope that it might be possible to actually cure an infected person of this disease, although this remains a very distant goal.

Tuberculosis

Tuberculosis (TB) is one of the oldest diseases known to plague *Homo sapiens* and was perhaps the most feared infectious disease throughout history (J. Roth, 2009). TB has plagued humankind for at least the last 500,000 years (C. E. Barry & Cheung, 2009; Raviglione & O'Brien, 2008). In that time, it has been estimated that TB has killed approximately *1 billion* people, a number that far surpasses the estimated 40 million deaths around the world caused by the influenza epidemic of 1918–1920, or the total estimated number of deaths caused by the bubonic plague (J. Roth, 2009). Between the years 1600 and 1900, one in every five deaths in Europe is thought to have been caused by TB (MacKenzie, 2007). Nor has the infection become less lethal: At the start of the 21st century TB is the second most common cause of death from an infectious disease on the planet, surpassed only by HIV infection (J. Roth, 2009).

Globally, tuberculosis is widespread: Almost one-third of the world's population is thought to be infected with TB, with an additional 9 million more people[12] contracting the infection each year (Schurr, 2007). Infectious disease specialists have suggested that infections that result in the rapid death of the host tend to be self-defeating, because the host will die before passing the disease on to a large number of other people. TB has solved this problem by slowly killing the host, as evidenced by the fact that in spite of the large number of infected people around the world, only 1.6 million people die from TB each year. This allows each infected person to pass the infection to 10–15 other people, maintaining the chain of infection from one generation to the next (C. E. Barry & Cheung, 2009).

In the United States at the start of the 20th century, approximately 50–65% of infected individuals would die within 5 years of the initial infection. The introduction of effective antitubercular medications in the mid-20th century in the industrial world made death from tuberculosis in the United States very rare (C. E. Barry & Cheung, 2009). Thus 98% of TB-related deaths occur in the Third World countries, where such treatments are difficult or even impossible to obtain (C. E. Barry & Cheung, 2009; Raviglione & O'Brien, 2008).

Several factors contributed to the decline of TB infections in the United States. First, the development of appropriate diet guidelines in the early part of the 20th century helped infected individuals to minimize the damage wrought by the infection, extending lives that would otherwise have been cut short by this disease. Second, the introduction of effective antibiotic treatments in the mid-20th century also contributed to the decline of TB in this country (Simon, 2007). Finally, J. Roth (2009) also suggested that more-susceptible individuals might have succumbed to the infection over the generations, whereas more-resistant people either did not become infected or at least were able to resist the infection longer, thus shaping the development of the human genome over time.

What Is Tuberculosis?

TB is an infection caused by the bacterium *Mycobacterium tuberculosis* (Hauck, Neese, Panchal, & El-Amin, 2009; Raviglione & O'Brien, 2008). This strain of bacteria replicates very slowly and has a protein molecule pattern in the cell wall that leaves it virtually unaffected by many antibiotics used to treat other bacterial infections. *M. tuberculosis* seems to prefer oxygen-rich organs in the body such as the lungs, although cases have been found involving virtually every other organ system in the body (Markel, 2004; Raviglione & O'Brien, 2008). There is even evidence that *M. tuberculosis* can live without oxygen (C. E. Barry & Cheung, 2009).

There are a number of actors that help to determine whether a given individual might develop TB. Environmental factors such as intensity of exposure and malnutrition, combined with the individual's genetic

---

[12]This number is estimated to reflect only 60% of the actual total, because many countries do not track and report TB-related deaths (Raviglione & O'Brien, 2008).

predisposition and poor health all interact to influence the possibility of a person developing TB (Raviglione & O'Brien, 2008; Schurr, 2007). The higher the number of risk factors that people have, the greater the danger of their contracting TB.[13] There is also preliminary evidence suggesting that dietary or metabolic factors that influence individuals' ability to absorb vitamin D also influence their odds of contracting TB (Wilkinson et al., 2000). Given that individuals with an alcohol or other substance use disorder often have a poor diet, the vitamin D hypothesis might help to explain why this subgroup tends to be at high risk for TB infection. Paradoxically, obesity seems to offer some degree of protection against tuberculosis (J. Roth, 2009).

How Is Tuberculosis Transmitted, and How Does It Kill?

The usual mode of transmission is on microscopic droplets of liquid expelled whenever the host sings, talks, coughs, or sneezes. These droplets might remain suspended in midair for extended periods of time, allowing other people to breathe them into their own lungs (Markel, 2004). In the healthy individual. the pulmonary defenses destroy more than 90% of the inhaled *M. tuberculosis* bacteria (Raviglione & O'Brien, 2008). However, in cases where the person's pulmonary defenses are compromised by poor health, malnutrition, or concurrent infection, it becomes more difficult for the body to effectively eject *M. tuberculosis* before it establishes itself in the lungs. In these cases the immune system attempts to mount a counterattack. The initial wave of the immune system response is when the body's *macrophages* engulf the invading bacteria, surround them, and wall them inside little pockets known as granulomas. In response, *M. tuberculosis* enters a dormant state in the granulomas where it might remain for years if not decades.

If the individual's immune system becomes compromised by another infection or malnutrition, the body loses its ability to isolate *M. tuberculosis* in the granulomas. It then becomes possible for the bacteria to burst out and invade the surrounding tissue. This is known as *reactivation TB,* which accounts for a large percentage of all cases of TB in the United States at this time (Markel, 2004). It is at this point that the body attempts to use a different strategy to attack the

invading bacteria: The lymphocytes are called upon to destroy the bacteria. Unfortunately, during this process the lymphocytes also release a toxin that destroys the surrounding tissue. In the case of a TB infection in the lungs, less and less of the lung is able to properly function, and eventually the patient dies of pulmonary failure.

The Treatment of TB

Unfortunately, physicians and public health officials became complacent about TB, and in many cases treatment programs were rapidly scaled back or eliminated entirely. Then around 1984, health care professionals were stunned to find a growing number of cases of TB in this country. These infections did not represent new cases of TB for the most part, but were "reactivation" cases of TB in patients whose infection was formerly latent (Markel, 2004). Researchers soon discovered that between 10 and 15 million people in the United States had a latent TB infection, providing a "pool" of infected people, each of whom had the potential to infect others (Hauck et al., 2009).

The bacteria that causes tuberculosis is also evolving in ways that makes it resistant to the antibiotics used to treat it (Migliori, De Laco, Besozzi, & Cirillo, 2009). Currently, it is estimated that 5% of new cases of TB around the globe are resistant to at least one of the drugs normally used to treat this infection (World Health Organization, 2008). More alarmingly, strains of tuberculosis have been identified that are resistant to *every* known medication used to treat the disorder (C. E. Barry & Cheung, 2009; Migliori et al., 2009).

There are many reasons for the development of drug-resistant strains of tuberculosis. Patient noncompliance with prescribed medications was a major factor in the development of treatment-resistant tuberculosis (C. E. Barry & Cheung, 2009; Markel, 2004; Simon, 2007). When the patient initially starts antibiotic therapy for tuberculosis, those strains most susceptible to the chemical will die off first, leaving more-resistant bacteria behind. These bacteria then reproduce to fill the void, and when passed on to other people infect them with a strain of tuberculosis that is slightly more resistant to the antibiotic(s) used to treat this infection. This process is an example of biological evolution by the organism to meet environmental conditions, because the antibiotic is essentially just another environmental challenge for the organism to surmount in order to survive.

Other factors that contribute to the development of treatment-resistant TB is limited access to medical care or failure to follow through with recommended

---

[13]For example, if people who have a genetic predisposition making them more susceptible to TB infection are also malnourished but were never exposed to the bacteria that cause TB, they would never develop the infection.

treatment(s). In the Third World countries, access to appropriate treatments is limited at best and often impossible to obtain except by the very wealthy segment of the population that can afford the proper treatments. This is most clearly seen in the fact that globally the greatest proportion of treatment-resistant TB cases is found in countries where medical care is difficult or impossible to obtain (World Health Organization, 2008). Although access to health care and effective treatment for tuberculosis is available in the United States, the lifestyle of typical alcohol- or drug-dependent people makes treatment compliance a low priority for those who are both infected with TB and have an SUD. This contributes to the problem of new treatment-resistant strains of TB in this country.

Although there has been a great deal of attention paid to the problem of treatment-resistant TB by the mass media, physicians still have a number of medications that they can call upon to treat the person who has tuberculosis. These second-line medications are not as effective as first-line antitubercular drugs, and the treatment regiments might require that the patient take medications three to four times a day for up to 24 months (J. Cohen, 2004; Markel, 2004). There are new drugs under development that will cut the treatment regimen to just a single week-long course of antibiotics, but these medications will require years before they are available for clinical use (J. Cohen, 2004). Further, it should be noted that the eradication of an active TB infection does *not* confer any degree of protection against possible reinfection should the person again be exposed to *M. tuberculosis*.

One complication to the treatment of tuberculosis is substance abuse among patients with TB. Oeltmann, Kammerer, Pevzner, and Moonan (2009) found that 18.7% of the 28,650 patients examined also had an SUD, with alcohol being the most commonly abused substance. Given alcohol's ability to damage the liver, and the fact that many of the medications used to treat TB are metabolized in the liver, this finding has clinical significance for patients currently being treated for this disorder. It might be necessary for the physician to extend the period of active treatment in such patients, according to Oeltmann et al. Patients with a concurrent SUD were also found to be less likely to adhere to the medication program, and medication adherence must often be monitored by a health care professional to ensure that the patient completes the entire course of treatment. Thus the SUDs are a significant complicating factor for the treatment of tuberculosis and threaten to reawaken a plague that once killed millions of people around the world each year in pandemics that have shaped the course of history.[14]

Viral Hepatitis

The term *hepa* refers to the liver, whereas *titis* denotes an inflammation of the specified organ system. Thus the term *hepatitis* is a general term that means inflammation of the liver, which then must be qualified by the causal agent such as, for example, "alcohol-induced hepatitis" or "toxin-induced hepatitis." Viral hepatitis refers to an inflammation of the liver, induced by any of a number of different viral agents (Orr, 2008). In this section, we will briefly discuss some of the forms of viral hepatitis commonly encountered in the treatment of people with an SUD. Scientists have labeled each of the viral agents that can induce hepatitis by a letter to better classify them.

A Brief History of Viral Hepatitis

Physicians have long known that if people are exposed to water or food contaminated by fecal matter they might become ill with any of a wide variety of diseases.[15] But it was only in the 20th century that physicians began to understand that there were viral pathogens that might attack the liver. The first such virus to be identified was initially called just "viral hepatitis." But physicians also were aware that some patients developed hepatitis after receiving a blood transfusion, a condition that they called "serum hepatitis." In 1966 a virus that was classified as *hepatitis Type B* (HVB) was isolated. Unfortunately, it was soon discovered that HVA and HVB could not explain every case of what appeared to be viral hepatitis. It was hypothesized that yet another, undiscovered virus could also cause viral hepatitis in humans, and patients with hepatitis who did not appear to have either type A or type B hepatitis were said to have "non-A/non-B" hepatitis. Then in 1988,[16] an additional five viruses that could infect the human liver were identified, which are now classified as hepatitis type C (HVC), hepatitis type D (HVD), hepatitis type E (HVE), hepatitis type F (HVF), and hepatitis type G. Surprisingly, there is

---

[14]This topic lies outside of the scope of this book, although it is discussed in far more detail in infectious-disease textbooks.

[15]Cholera is another example of a disease that might be contracted through contracted through contact with water contaminated with fecal material, for example.

[16]Pearlman (2004) suggested that the hepatitis C virus was isolated in 1989, not 1988.

evidence to suggest that the virus that causes HVG is a distant genetic cousin to the virus that causes HVA.

Hepatitis A Virus

Method of Transmission

Viral hepatitis caused by the A virus (HVA) is most commonly transmitted by oral-fecal transmission[17] (Orr, 2008), although 5% of cases are thought to involve the sharing of a contaminated IV drug needle. People might be exposed to the virus by changing a diaper that is contaminated by fecal matter, or changing contaminated bed linens from a bed where an infected person was resting, and then failing to wash their hands. Other methods of transmission include swimming in contaminated water or having food products served that have not been properly cooked to ensure the death of pathogens, for example. Proper hand washing, appropriate food preparation, and not sharing IV needles are all ways to avoid exposure to HVA.

Syndrome Induced by HVA

After exposure to HVA, the individual will usually experience a flulike syndrome for about 4 weeks, although in 1% of cases the individual develops acute liver failure (Fontana, 2008). This is usually seen in older adults who contract HVA, but can occur in younger patients as well (Dienstag, 2008). Individuals remain contagious throughout the period in which they demonstrate symptoms of HVA infection, after which time they will have lifelong immunity to the virus (Orr, 2008).

Consequences of HVA Infection

HVA tends to be a time-limited disorder, although in very rare cases HVA infection can result in liver failure and the patient's death. In rare cases, the patient will develop *relapsing hepatitis* in the weeks to months after apparent recovery. This is rare, but if it does develop the patient will reexperience many of the symptoms of the original infection (Dienstag, 2008). This second episode is a manifestation that the original infection has not fully resolved. The individual remains infectious during this period, and hepatitis A viral particles have been found in fecal matter of people experiencing relapsing HVA, suggesting that they remain infectious during this time. Once patients recover from the HVA infection, they will have lifelong immunity to this virus.

Hepatitis B Virus

Method of Transmission

The virus that causes hepatitis type B (HVB) has six known subtypes, all of which are quite contagious. It has been estimated that this virus is 100 times as contagious as the virus that causes HIV infection.[18] Further, although the virus that causes AIDS will die within minutes after exposure to air, scientists believe that HVB can continue to live on contaminated surfaces such as countertops for *up to 7 days* after being deposited there by an infected person if the surface is not properly cleaned and can infect others.[19]

The hepatitis B virus is a blood-borne disease, which requires exposure to the body fluids of an infected person. Known methods of hepatitis B viral transmission include sharing a toothbrush or a razor, sexual contact with an infected partner, or even simply kissing an infected person. The virus can be transmitted through blood transfusions, although blood donations are now screened for donors, and the rate of infection is less than 1 case for every 250,000 units of blood administered. Because it can be contracted as a result of sexual intercourse, HVB is often classified as a sexually transmitted disease (STD) as well as a blood-borne pathogen.[20] Indeed, the transmission from an infected person to a noninfected partner during sexual intercourse is considered the most common method of HVB transmission in the United States at this time (Russo, 2004). Vertical transmission from an infected mother to the fetus during childbirth is possible, resulting in a low-grade lifelong infection for the baby following birth. This is the result of the "immunologic tolerance" that the baby's body develops for the virus (Dienstag, 2008, p. 1938). In spite of this immunologic tolerance, HVB infection may culminate in liver failure decades later in life (Dienstag, 2008).

Another common method of HVB transmission is the sharing of intravenous needles between drug abusers. IV drug abusers in a prison setting often try to avoid this by making the "yellow guy"[21] use the needle last, ignoring the fact that virus particles still will remain in the needle when it is next used hours or days later, thus passing the infection on to the next abuser. Research has shown that 45–90% of intravenous drug

---

[17]Which is one reason why washing your hands after using the toilet is so important.

[18]Discussed elsewhere in this chapter.

[19]Such as toys in day-care centers, countertops in restaurants or homes, and the like.

[20]Which is to say that the virus is found in all body fluids.

[21]Which is to say the guy who has jaundice.

abusers will have been exposed to HVB within a year of the time that they start to share intravenous drugs.

Syndrome Induced by HVB Infection

Individuals who have been infected by HVB might not demonstrate outward symptoms of an infection for 1–5 months after exposure, although blood tests will demonstrate an immune response to HVB within 1–12 weeks of the initial infection. The physical symptoms that eventually develop are similar to those seen with HVA infection, and will include such symptoms as anorexia, nausea, vomiting, fatigue, malaise, headache, photophobia, pharyngitis, and cough, followed 1–2 weeks later by symptoms of jaundice as the virus attacks the liver (Dienstag, 2008). These symptoms usually continue for 4–6 weeks, but on rare occasions can continue for as long as 4–12 months following infection. Once individuals have recovered from HVB infection, they are immune to the virus, and blood tests will reveal HVB-specific antibodies for the rest of their life (Orr, 2008).

Consequences of HVB Infection

The prognosis for the healthy person who contracts HVB is quite favorable, and 90–95% of previously healthy adults eventually recover completely (Dienstag, 2008). This has been disputed by Pungpapong, Kim, and Poterucha (2007), who utilized DNA-testing procedures and reported that they found traces of HVB in people who were thought to be virus free up to a decade after the acute infection resolved. Thus the question of whether healthy people infected with HVB fully recover or not has not been resolved.

One of the more dangerous consequences of HVB infection is acute liver failure. This complication has been estimated to develop in less than 1% of cases that occur in healthy adults (Fontana, 2008). However, the rate of fulminant liver failure for HVB patients is markedly increased if they also have contracted the hepatitis D virus (Dienstag, 2008).

The issue of whether the typical patient completely recovers from the acute HVB infection is unresolved, and physicians argue whether the virus is ever completely eliminated from the body of an infected individual. It is known that in 5–10% of cases the individual develops a chronic HVB infection. One of the manifestations of this chronic infection is the slow destruction of the patient's liver (Ganem & Prince, 2004; Pungpapong et al., 2007; Russo, 2004). Indeed, about 20% of patients with a long-term HVB infection will develop cirrhosis of the liver (Ganem & Prince, 2004). HVB-related cirrhosis causes the death of approximately 5000 people each year in the United States.

It was once thought that the virus directly caused the death of liver cells, but recent evidence has suggested that it is the body's immune response to the HVB infection that causes the liver damage rather than the virus itself (Dienstag, 2008; Ganem & Prince, 2004). Long-term HVB infection also is an indirect cause of death, as evidenced by the fact that people who have contracted HVB are 10 to 390 times more likely to develop liver cancer than a noninfected person, for example (Ganem & Prince, 2004; S. C. Gordon, 2000; Orr, 2008). Liver cancer is difficult to detect and treat and is usually fatal. It has been estimated that HVB-related cancer causes approximately 1200 deaths annually in the United States alone.

As if that were not enough, there is evidence that suggests that even if individuals recover from HVB infection, they are two to four times more likely than normal to develop cancer of the pancreas (Hassan et al., 2008). The causal mechanism for this is not known. People who are diabetic and who had past exposure to HVB were found to be seven times as likely to develop cancer of the pancreas than people without either disorder, according to Hassan et al.

Treatment of HVB Infection

Currently, the most effective treatment for HVB infection is prevention. Vaccines to prime the immune system against HVB infection have been developed and are recommended for people who might be exposed to this virus such as health care workers, the spouse of an infected person, children, and adolescents. Some school districts require proof of vaccination before allowing students to enter school for the academic year. Blood barrier precautions (gloves when handling blood products or other body fluids) are also helpful in preventing HVB transmission. A number of pharmaceuticals are being investigated as possible treatments for those who are already infected with HVB.

Hepatitis C Virus

Mode of Transmission

The virus that causes hepatitis type C (HVC) has six known subtypes. It is thought to be about 10 times as infectious as the HIV virus[22] and is classified as a blood-borne pathogen. HVC infection is a common complication of intravenous drug use, and it has been estimated that 66–93% of IV drug abusers in major cities will contract HVC during their drug use careers, and that 77% percent will do so in the 1st year of active

---

[22]Discussed elsewhere in this chapter.

intravenous drug abuse (Fiellin, 2008; Schottenfeld, 2008). Unfortunately, many experimental drug abusers who shared an intravenous needle only once or twice in their late teens or early 20s, even if they have long since forgotten this episode, are now discovering that this experiment had unanticipated long-term health consequences.

Surprisingly, many of those who discover that they are infected swear that they have never abused intravenously administered drugs. This may, in part, reflect the fact that HVC can be transmitted through sexual contact with an infected partner or through used tattoo needles (Davies, 2005). Approximately 15% percent of people who are infected with HVC contracted the infection through unprotected sex with an infected partner (Davies, 2005). Other sources of HVC infection include tattoos where unclean needles were used, organ transplants from infected donors, or occupational exposure to blood products, such as hemodialysis workers who might contract the infection as a result of their exposure to blood products at work (Dienstag, 2008). However, 60% of those infected with HVC contracted the infection through shared intravenous needles at some point in their lives, whereas 10% percent of HVC victims contracted the virus before the advent of effective blood-screening methods for blood donations. Currently, the risk of contracting HVC through a blood transfusion has been estimated at 1:2,300,000 (Dienstag, 2008). The HVC virus can also remain on surfaces and still be infectious for up to 4 days unless the contaminated surface is disinfected.[23] There is some controversy over whether HVC can be transmitted through the use of straws used by multiple people to inhale cocaine, but this is another possible source of HIV infection for those who never used intravenous drugs.

In the United States, an estimated 4 million people are thought to have been exposed to HVC, and 2.7 million people have a chronic HVC infection (Pearlman, 2004; Sylvestre, 2008; Willenbring, 2004). The latter statistic is important because, of those who develop a chronic HVC infection, about 1–5% will develop liver cancer each year. The causal mechanism for this association remains unknown (Orr, 2008). Approximately 20% of HVC-infected people will be able to fight off the infection, usually in the first 6 months after exposure to the virus (Davies, 2005; S. C. Hines, 2002; A. R. Woods & Herrera, 2002). Only a blood test

will reveal whether people have ever been exposed to HVC and whether they have a chronic infection.

Treatment is long and arduous, and the possibility of a cure varies from one genotype to another. If the HVC infection is cured through antiviral treatment, reinfection is possible should the person engage in high-risk behaviors such as continued intravenous drug use (Orr, 2008).

Consequences of HVC Infection

The acute period of illness following infection with HVC is less severe than that seen with HVA or HVB (Dienstag, 2008). In approximately 20% of the cases where people are infected with HCV, their body is able to overcome the infection, usually within the first 6 months (Davies, 2005; S. C. Hines, 2002; A. R. Woods & Herrera, 2002). It was once thought that in 20–25% of those people who were infected, the immune system was able to fight the infection to a "standstill." It is now thought that the virus just progresses more slowly in these people (Parini, 2003). In the remaining cases, HVC establishes a smoldering infection that will slowly destroy the individual's liver over a period of 20–30 years. Research has shown that up to 70% of patients who develop acute liver failure during the initial stage of HVC infection will fail to survive, as the liver is destroyed during the chronic phase (Fontana, 2008).

Even in cases where individuals have no outward sign of infection, they experience a slow, smoldering infection in which the liver is slowly attacked and destroyed over a period of years or decades. Twenty or 30 years after the victim was first infected, the cumulative level of liver damage might result in acute liver failure and the need for an emergency liver transplant to save the patient's life (Davies, 2005). Every day in the United States three people die as a result of HVC infection, and HVC-induced liver damage is the most common reason for liver transplantation in the United States at this time (Orr, 2008). Individuals with an alcohol use disorder or who abuse marijuana who also have an HVC infection seem to progress through the different stages of the disease more quickly than do nonabusers of alcohol or marijuana (Karsan et al., 2004; Sylvestre, 2008).

Treatment of HVC Infection

The most effective treatment for HVC infection is barrier precautions to prevent direct exposure to blood products and not sharing intravenous needles with others. Once the person becomes infected, the current

---

[23]A fact that makes you want to think twice about using public toilets, does it not?

treatment regimen is a combination of Interferon and ribavirin.[24,25] This combination has been found to be effective in 50–60% of cases, but results in side effects such as fever, chills, headache, anxiety, and concentration problems, so patient adherence to the treatment program is difficult to maintain. An unexpected complication of the current treatments for HVC infection is that even after apparent cures, low levels of the HVC virus might remain in people's T-cells[26] for extended periods of time, with the result being that they might remain capable of passing the virus on to others in spite of blood tests failing to find evidence of HVC infection (MacParland, Pham, Guy, & Michalak, 2009).

There are a number of medications in various stages of development that offer the promise of either controlling the virus or possibly eliminating it from the body. One such medication is being developed by Vertex Pharmaceuticals under the brand name of Telaprevir. This medication is a protease inhibitor, and early studies suggest that the addition of this compound to existing treatments for HVC might improve the cure rate by 50% over standard treatments and will require a treatment protocol that is only half as long as normal (Kapadia, 2008; T. B. Newman, Clay, Davis, McHutchison, & Liang, 2009). If this medication lives up to its initial promise and is approved for use, it will be a significant advancement against HVC infection.

Hepatitis D and E

These viral infections are only rarely found in the United States. Of the estimated 15 million people with hepatitis D (HVD) around the world, 70,000 are thought to live in the United States. There are an estimated 5000 new cases of HVD each year in this country (Karsan et al., 2004). It is interesting to note that HVD is an "incomplete" virus, which requires a concurrent infection by the hepatitis B virus to be able to infect the host. Because the largest proportion of people infected with HVB contracted that infection through contaminated IV needles, it should not be surprising to learn that many drug abusers with HVB have also been exposed to HVD at some point in their lives. Proper vaccination against HVB appears to have the added benefit of blocking HVD infection as well.

Although the HVE virus can be transmitted through direct contact with body fluids, the most common method of transmission of HVE appears to be exposure to water contaminated by a person infected with HVE. If infected, the only treatment for the person is supportive medical care. However, a vaccine has been developed for HVE that is both effective and safe to administer prior to possible exposure to this virus (Fontana, 2008).

Chapter Summary

Substance abusers are at high risk for a wide range of infectious diseases both as a direct result of their substance use and as an indirect consequence of their SUD. Individuals who share intravenous needles will spread pathogens from one person to the next. But the failure to follow "sterile technique" often results in the IV drug abuser "punching in" pathogens normally found only on the surface of the skin, where these bacteria and fungi then infect the abuser. This is an example of an indirect infectious-disease consequence of injected drug abuse, for example. Malnutrition, which is a side effect of drug use disorders, also is an indirect cause of infectious diseases in injection drug abusers.

People with alcohol use disorders share the dangers of malnutrition as a possible risk factor for infections. However, they are also at risk for aspiration of material being regurgitated, setting the stage for aspirative pneumonia. Injected drug use using contaminated needles also puts the person at risk for viral, fungal, and bacterial infections not normally found in the normal person. Some of these disorders include HIV infection and the various forms of infectious hepatitis. All of these disorders have the potential to kill the patient without (and sometimes even with) the best of medical care.

---

[24]This compound is a nucleoside analog compound that is taken orally.

[25]It should be noted that there are a number of compounds being investigated by the pharmaceutical industry that show promise in treating HVC and that might be introduced in the next decade.

[26]Component of the immune system.

CHAPTER 37

The Relationship Between Drugs and Crime

Introduction

Social scientists have been aware of the strong correlation between the substance use disorders (SUDs) and criminal activity. However, as statistics instructors repeat to their classes, correlation does *not* imply causality. It is possible that the substance misuse might predate criminal activity, or might develop after the individual has started to engage in criminal activity, or both might reflect the influence of a third unidentified factor shared by those who abuse chemicals and engage in criminal activity. The debate over which of these theories is the most accurate one has raged for decades (McCollister & French, 2002; Newcomb, Galif, & Carmona, 2001). However, adherents to all three theories agree that there is a strong correlational relationship between SUDs and criminal activity. In this chapter we will review this relationship and discuss some of the controversies that rage over these issues.

Criminal Activity and Drug Abuse: Partners in a Dance?

The relationship between substance misuse and criminal behavior is hardly an insignificant one. Globally 200 million people are thought to use an illegal drug(-s) at least once each year, and 4 million farmers are thought to be economically dependent on the cultivation of illegal crops ("Losing Tolerance With Zero Tolerance," 2005). In the United States, the cultivation and sale of domestically produced marijuana makes it *the biggest* cash crop raised in the United States at this time in spite of its legal status ("Grass Is Greener," 2007). These statistics suggest that the illicit-drug trade is an established aspect of modern society, not only in the United States but around the world.

The response to this worldwide epidemic of substance abuse has been to attempt to interdict supplies of illicit drugs before they reach the level of being sold on the street to individual abusers. The effectiveness of these efforts might be seen in the fact that in the last decade of the 20th century, the supply and scope of drug abuse around the world *increased* rather than dropped ("Losing Tolerance With Zero Tolerance," 2005). Depending on which facts one chooses to embrace and which facts are ignored, it is possible to argue that the substance use disorders are or are not causal agents in criminal activity. Delinquency usually *precedes* the development of the substance use disorders, and although individuals might outgrow delinquent behavior(s) with maturation, it is more difficult to outgrow SUDs (Husak, 2004). This little detail makes it difficult to argue that SUDs *caused* an individual's criminal behavior(s).

Elliott (1992) offered a different perspective on the relationship between SUDs and criminal behavior. The author suggested that both chemical abuse and criminal behavior are a reflection of the "decline in the power of cultural restraints" (p. 599) that periodically takes place in this culture. He supports his argument with the observation that Europe has suffered "tidal waves of crime" (p. 599) every few decades since the 14th century. A similar pattern has emerged in the United States over the past 200 years, and in each cycle there is "an erosion of personal integrity, widespread dehumanization, a contempt for life, material greed, corruption in high places, sexual promiscuity, *and an increased recourse to drugs and alcohol*" (Elliott, 1992, p. 599, italics added for emphasis).

There are multiple pathways between the SUDs and criminal activity, with new substance abuse both arising from and predicting criminal behavior (Newcomb et al., 2001). Early substance abuse was found to predict later criminal activity in a community sample, according to Newcomb et al. Substance abuse was found to impair impulse control, contributing to the tendency for the abuser to engage in socially inappropriate behavior(s). The authors found evidence of a "proneness toward criminality" (p. 190) was associated with SUDs. As was discussed in Chapter 20, early substance abuse is a common complication of such childhood behavior problems as the conduct disorders, and the findings of this study are consistent with conduct-disordered children's involvement with substances.

Alcohol, which is the most popular drug of abuse in this country, is also the substance most commonly involved in criminal activity (Husak, 2004). Twenty-one to 26% of people incarcerated for violent crimes report that they were under the influence of alcohol at the time of the offense, 3% reported having abused cocaine immediately prior to committing the offense, and just 1% were under the influence of heroin at the time of the criminal behavior (Husak, 2004; Nace, 2005b). Thus the compound most commonly associated with criminal behavior is the one that is legally obtained, which casts doubt on the theory that illicit substance use causes criminal activity in the majority of cases.

Criminal Activity and Personal Responsibility

The relationship between the SUDs and criminal behavior is complicated. One example of this is the fact that over 50% of opiate-dependent people have been arrested for a criminal act(s) before their first use of narcotics (Jaffe & Strain, 2005). Between 51 and 76% of adult males and 39–85% of adult females arrested for criminal activity have evidence of at least one illicit chemical in their bodies at the time of arrest (Farabee, Prendedrgast, & Carier, 2002; Makki, 2003). This raises a question: Is their criminal activity a reflection of their substance abuse or an extension of a pattern of antisocial behaviors that existed prior to their arrest?

If people are under the influence of a chemical(s) at the time of the offense, what is their level of responsibility? Is it the same as it would be had they not been under the influence of chemicals? The issue of personal responsibility is often side-stepped by the legal system through the assumption that drugs somehow interfered with the individual's ability to think coherently.[1] This position rests on the unproven assumption that substance use obliterates free will (Husak, 2004). In effect, it is an extension of the "demon rum" claim often made in the 19th and early 20th centuries (Walton, 2002). This position holds that "if intoxication is wrong, it is in large part these days because it is perceived to be guilty of inciting criminality and other antisocial activities in too many of those who regularly take intoxicants" (Walton, 2002, p. 75). Note that it is the *substance* that is blamed for the criminal behavior and not the individual. Proponents of this position believe that once individuals ingest alcohol or a drug, their ability to make rational choices is overwhelmed, thus inciting the criminal behavior. In some states, a "diminished capacity" defense might be used to mitigate against the full weight of the charges offense(s) committed under the influence of chemicals (Gendel, 2006; Husak, 2004). However, the legal system holds that the individual is still responsible for the decision to take the initial dose of alcohol or a drug.

The decision to bring the full weight of the legal system to bear on substance abusers demands that clear

---

[1]So, if people tend to engage in antisocial behaviors in general, but are unable to think clearly at the time of the current arrest because they are under the influence of alcohol or drugs, does this exonerate them of responsibility for the current criminal act?

decisions be made about what is acceptable behavior for individuals in society:

> [The] person to be blamed must have done something wrongful; no one can merit blame for conduct that is permissible. But whether and to what extent someone should be blamed is not simply a function of the wrongfulness of his conduct. We must also decide whether the wrongful act is fairly attributed to him, that is, whether he is responsible for it. (Husak, 2004, p. 405)

If people with an SUD act in a manner entirely consistent with that of a person with a substance use disorder, should they be punished? This is a legal conundrum. To punish people with an SUD simply because they have a substance use disorder violates the Eighth Amendment to the Constitution of the United States (Gendel, 2006). However, the courts have interpreted the law to the effect that individuals should not be punished for addictive *behavior* but they are still held accountable for behavior(s) that are clearly part of the addiction (Gendel, 2006). However, even this line of reasoning is not followed to the letter by those who prosecute drug offenders. Those people most likely to experiment with new drugs of abuse are white, middle-class, suburban males (Boyer, 2005). These individuals tend not to believe that they can be harmed by a drug(s) of abuse, and they have significant amounts of discretionary money at their command (Boyer, 2005). By the time that a new compound of abuse has reached the inner cities, it is already a well-established drug of abuse in other social circles (Boyer, 2005). However, the focus of antidrug criminal prosecutions tends to be on social groups other than white, middle-class, suburban males.

Manufactured Criminals

The national prohibition against the use of certain compound(s) has resulted in a situation where these compounds are available to those who abuse or are addicted to them only through illicit channels.[2] Because access to these chemicals is under the control of suppliers willing to break the law in return for a rather large profit, the usual laws of a free-market economy do not apply in the illicit-drug world (Reuter, 2009).

However, drug suppliers demand money for their product. To obtain this money individuals must engage in both legal and illegal activities. Some people exhaust personal finances, borrow money from family members, engage in theft, sell drugs to others for profit, or engage in prostitution (heterosexual or homosexual). People who engage in theft will get only a fraction of that item's actual worth, forcing them to steal even more to obtain the desired funds. It has been estimated that typical heroin addicts must steal $200,000 worth of material each year to support their addiction (M. J. Kreek, 1997). It can thus be argued that the national prohibition against the use of heroin (or other compounds deemed illegal, since a similar process exists for them) has contributed to the wave of crime that swept across the country in the latter half of the 20th century.

Drug Use and Violence: The Unseen Connection

Brust (2004) suggested that there were three categories of substance-related violence: (a) *pharmacological violence,* or drug-induced violent behavior; (b) *economic compulsive violence,* or violent crimes committed by a person to obtain money necessary to purchase illicit compound(s); and (c) *systemic violence,* or the violence that is associated with the illicit-drug distribution/sales network. All three forms of violent behavior(s) have been demonstrated by illicit-drug abusers.

The most commonly abused chemical, alcohol, provides an example of pharmacological violence. Approximately 50% of all sexual assaults, for example, are committed by men who have ingested alcohol (Abbey, Zawacki, Buck, Clinton, & McAuslan, 2001). Although one might argue that the disinhibition effects of alcohol might entice individuals to carry out a sexual assault that they might otherwise have not carried out, the date rape compounds such as GHB[3] and flunitrazepam[4] are intentionally used to facilitate sexual assault. As noted earlier, 21–26% of violent offenders are under the influence of alcohol at the time of their criminal assault (Nace, 2005b).

The effects of the amphetamines and cocaine provide excellent examples of pharmacological violence, because both compounds predispose the user toward violence both against others and against the self. Gold and Jacobs (2005) noted that cocaine abusers were more likely to die from homicide or suicide than were age-matched control subjects. There are many reasons for this: First, the lifestyle forced on those people who

---

[2]An exception to this rule are those individuals who have prescriptions for controlled substances, such as patients who receive prescriptions for narcotic analgesics to control pain.

[3]Discussed later in this chapter.

[4]Discussed in Chapter 7.

abuse these compounds bring them into frequent contact with people who are more likely to respond with violence either because of their premorbid personality or because of pharmacologically enhanced violent tendencies. Also, the behavior of a person under the influence of cocaine or the amphetamines might induce others to respond with violence, resulting in a "victim-precipitated homicide."

Earlier in this chapter, it was noted that the disinhibition effect of alcohol contributes to many sexual assaults each year in this country. It is not unreasonable to assume that the same mechanism might be involved in many homicides that take place each year in the United States. This is not to say that the alcohol use *caused* the individual to commit the homicide in every case. Rather, a significant percentage of homicides were planned in advance, and then the perpetrator(s) consumed alcohol to bolster their courage before committing the act. In other cases, the homicide is an unplanned act brought on during the heat of passion, in which individuals' self-control was reduced through their use of alcohol.

A common cause of substance-related death is criminal attack either by drug dealers, other addicted persons, or individuals looking for vulnerable people to prey upon. Drug dealers have been known to attack customers, safe in the knowledge that the victim is unlikely to go to the police to report a criminal attack when the victim has also been involved in criminal activity (drug use itself or the various activities that addicts must engage in to support their addiction). Drug dealers have also been known to kill clients for unpaid drug debts as a warning to others who might also owe the dealer money. They also have been known to kill bothersome clients by selling them a bag of exceptionally potent drugs so that the client will die of an overdose. On occasion, drug dealers have been known to sell cocaine addicts the powered residue of car battery acid that accumulates on the battery terminals, which then will kill the cocaine abuser when used.

Drug addicts have also been known to kill drug dealers, although it is not known at this time the frequency with which such assaults are premeditated. Rival drug dealers have been known to engage in gun battles over "turf,"[5] and it is not uncommon for a drug dealer to be dumped in front of a hospital emergency room by a rival, who speeds off before the police arrive. Sometimes the victims will live, but it is unlikely that they will provide the police with any useful information so as to avoid self-incrimination.[6]

Adulterants

It is rare for drugs of abuse to be sold to the individual drug abuser in their pure form ("Deadly Drug Adulterants," 2008). More commonly, the compound sold to the individual drug abuser has been highly adulterated. For example, upper-level drug dealers might buy a kilogram of cocaine, combine it with mannitol, and sell the 2 kilograms of resulting powder to lower-level drug dealers, doubling their profits ("Deadly Drug Adulterants," 2008). If the drug must pass through four or five levels of distributors, each of whom also adulterates the compound to increase profits, the final product might be one that is quite diluted.

Most commonly, adulterants are added by upper- and middle-level drug distributors to increase profits, a process known as "cutting" the drug. As a result of this process, the kilogram of coca paste that brought the farmer $1,000 in South America will be adulterated time and time again, until it averages about 45% purity when sold to the individual abuser. The ultimate cost of this single kilogram of cocaine will be approximately $70,000 when sold to the individual drug abuser because of various adulterants added to the mixture at different steps in the distribution process (Gold & Jacobs, 2005; Villalon, 2004).

The impact of adding an adulterant to an illicit drug is clearly demonstrated by the fact that "it costs approximately $300 to purchase enough coca leaves to produce a kilogram of cocaine, which retails for about $100,000 in the United States when sold in one-gram, two-thirds pure units [of cocaine]" (Reuter, 2009, p. 50). The other one-third of the cocaine are adulterants added to the cocaine at various stages in the production or distribution process to increase profits. A commonly encountered adulterant in cocaine is levamisole, a compound once used by physicians in the United States to treat roundworm infection and still used in veterinary medicine (Zhu, LeGatt, & Turner, 2009). Approximately one-third of the cocaine samples tested were found to contain levamisole, which is capable of inducing the blood disorder known as agranulocytosis[7] in rare cases.

---

[5]Usually a street corner on which to sell drugs, although on occasion the right to sell drugs in a certain part of the community.

[6]"Well Officer, I was just standing on the street corner, minding my own business and selling the occasional bag of heroin, when this guy pulls up in a car and shoots me so that he can sell heroin from that street corner!"

[7]The nature of this disorder lies outside of the scope of this text, and interested readers can learn more about this disorder by consulting the appropriate medical textbook.

Another example of this process is found in the illicit-narcotics production and distribution process: The opium farmer might be paid $90 for a kilogram of raw opium, which is then adulterated at each step of the distribution process, increasing profits by as much as 1600 times when the drug reaches the level of the individual abuser (Schuckit, 2006b). Street samples of illicit heroin in the United States have been found to range from 18 to 71% pure heroin ("How They Smack Up," 2005), which means that adulterants make up 31–82% of each sample sold on the streets.

As the examples provided in the last two paragraphs suggest, product reliability and safety are hardly priorities for those who traffic in illegal substances. Deception is also common. Abusers rarely have the time or resources to determine whether the product that they purchased was the product and potency claimed by the dealer, illustrating how in the world of illicit drugs "let the buyer beware!" Compounds are often misrepresented ("Oh yes, it's pure!") or in some cases do not even contain the compound that it is reputed to be. For example, less than 50% of the MDMA tablets sold actually contained that compound, with compounds such as caffeine, aspirin, cocaine, PCP, LSD, narcotics, GHB, Ketamine, dextromethorphan, and paramethoxyamphetamine (PMA) being sold under as MDMA (Grob & Poland, 2005).

One rarely considered aspect of drug adulteration is that these compounds have a potential to do damage to the abuser's body and the abuser's emotional state independent of the drug(s) of abuse. People who unknowingly smoke low-grade marijuana that has been intermixed with PCP to make it seem more powerful might suffer significant psychiatric harm if they have little or no experience with the effects of phencyclidine, for example. If the illicit drug is abused intravenously, the adulterants are injected directly into the abuser's body, bypassing the defensive acids and enzymes of the digestive tract (Leavitt, 2003). Popular belief suggests that drug dealers will mix deadly compounds in with the drug(s) being sold, although this is rarely done because it would (a) kill off the dealer's customer base, (b) be bad for business, and (c) give that drug dealer a bad reputation in a market where word-of-mouth advertising is the only form of advertising that exists ("Deadly Drug Adulterants," 2008). This is not to deny that toxic compounds are not intermixed with illicit drugs but that highly lethal compounds are rarely used to adulterate an illicit drug except on rare occasions. Still, either by accident or design, deadly adulterants are sometimes included in the mixture.

Identified categories of adulterants fall into one of five categories: (a) various forms of sugar, (b) stimulants, (c) local anesthetics, (d) toxins, and (e) any of a wide range of inert compounds that can be added to give the product bulk. Some of the compounds found in samples of illicit "drugs" include mannitol, lactose, glucose, caffeine, lidocaine, amphetamine compounds, quinine, and even on occasion heroin (Gold & Jacobs, 2005).[8] Marijuana is frequently adulterated, and it is not uncommon for up to half of the "marijuana" purchased to be seeds and woody stems that must be removed before it can be smoked. Low-potency marijuana has been known to be laced with other compounds such as Raid® insect spray, PCP, cocaine paste, dry cow manure,[9] alfalfa, apple leaves, catnip, cigarette tobacco, hay, licorice, mescaline, opium, wax, and wood shavings.

Samples of marijuana sold have been found to have been sprayed with a herbicide such as paraquat. Two compounds found in samples of marijuana recently purchased in Europe are homosildenafi (HS) and thiohomosildenafil (THS), compounds whose effects are very similar to that of the sildenafil family of compounds, which is sold in the United States as a treatment for "erectile dysfunction" ("Cannabis Booster," 2008). Authorities are not sure whether these compounds have been added to the marijuana to enhance the absorption of the psychoactive compounds in the smoke or to enhance the reputed aphrodisiac effect of marijuana. Unfortunately, scientists do not know how these compounds will affect the human body if smoked, because this is not the usual method of administration for the sildenafil compounds ("Cannabis Booster," 2008).

A partial list of the compounds found to be mixed with illicit cocaine samples can be found in Table 37-1. This is only a partial list, and new adulterants are being identified almost daily. As the list illustrates however, when it comes to the world of illicit drugs, let the buyer beware!

Because of the problem of adulterants, drug abusers prize pharmaceutical agents. These compounds are of known potency and are unlikely to be contaminated. However, they are mixed with "fillers" that help to give the tablet or capsule shape and form. When a drug abuser takes a compound orally, the digestive juices help to break down the inert compounds intermixed with pharmaceuticals to give them bulk and form. For example, methylphenidate tablets are mixed with talc, which helps to give the tablet form.

---

[8]Which can be a problem if you did not know that the product that you had purchased contained heroin, because this could lead to a potentially fatal overdose.

[9]Which may expose the user to salmonella bacteria.

TABLE 37-1 KNOWN ADULTERANTS IN ILLICIT DRUGS

ILLICIT COCAINE: KNOWN ADULTERANTS	ILLICIT PCP: KNOWN ADULTERANTS	ILLICIT HEROIN: KNOWN ADULTERANTS
Dextrose	Benzocain	Thepaine
Lactose	Procaine	Acetylcodeine
Mannitol	Caffeine	Quinine
Sucrose	Ketamine™	Phenobarbital
Caffeine	Magnesium Sulfate	Methqualone
Ephedrine	Ammonium chloride	Lidocaine
Phenylpropanolamine	Toluene	Caffeine
Phenertine		Diazepam
Methaqualone		Acetaminophen
Benzene		Fentanyl
Benzocaine		Arsenic
Heroin		Strychnine
Lidocaine		Vitamin C
Procaine		Toluene
Tetracaine		Ethanol
Inositol		Acetone
Corn starch		
Ascorbic acid		
Acetaminophen		
Aminopyrine		
Aspirin		
Boric acid		
Diphenhydramine		
Fentanyl		
Niacinamide		
Phenacetin		
Quinine		

NOTE: Based on Karch (2009) and B. A. Roth, Benowitz, and Olson (2007).

When crushed and injected, the talc in the methylphenidate tablet is injected into the body as well, forming micro-emboli in the circulation, which might potentially damage organs such as the heart, eyes, lungs, and brain (Greenhill, 2006). The same phenomenon is found when an illicit drug is abused: The adulterants may be introduced into the body, with unknown consequences. In many cases the adulterants cause local irritation to the tissue(s) into which it was injected, which then establishes the potential for an infection as the body's defenses break down at the site of injection.

The subject of adulterants is worthy of a book in its own right, for the various adulterants can damage virtually every organ in the body.

"Designer" Drugs

When a pharmaceutical company develops a new drug, it applies for a patent on that compound. This process requires, in part, that the chemists for that company identify the exact chemical structure of that drug molecule. After review by the Food and Drug Administration, the pharmaceutical company might be granted a patent for that specific drug molecule. In effect it becomes a molecule protected by copyright.

In the world of illicit drugs, much the same process is carried out, although the goal for the illicit-drug distribution system is not to "copyright" a compound but to find a chemical molecule that is not yet illegal. That chemical might then be sold without fear of criminal prosecution, at least until law enforcement agencies are able to have that drug molecule banned. Further, to create demand for products that they will then supply (for a rather large price), drug distributors often alter the chemical structure of existing drugs of abuse to find a "new" compound to sell. Because drug molecules are complex structures involving hundreds of atoms, it might be possible to develop dozens or even hundreds of variations on the "parent" drug. Many of these compounds are then sold, in the hope that one will become the latest craze and thus make the drug distributor rich. These compounds are called "designer" drugs, many of which are less potent than the original "parent" drug. Some designer drugs are as potent as the parent drug, whereas some are even more potent. All that it takes is for a chemist to alter the chemical structure parent drug molecule, possibly by as little as one atom.

To illustrate this process, assume that the illustration in Figure 37-1 is that of an illicit-drug "molecule" of a hallucinogenic compound. Admittedly, the "molecule" used to illustrate the process of making designer drugs has only four atoms as opposed to the thousands of molecules found in actual drug molecules, but it does serve to illustrate the process.

To create more demand, and possibly avoid criminal prosecution if the new variant has not yet been deemed illegal, the chemical structure of the original parent compound might be altered, possibly by adding just a single atom. Technically, this addition makes this a "different" drug, because the molecular structure is not exactly the same as that of the parent compound (see Figure 37-2).

The new compound is called an *analog* of the parent compound. It might be as potent as the original compound, but because of the altered chemical structure it might not have been deemed illegal, yet. The Food and Drug Administration does have the power to declare drug analogs illegal until a formal law can be passed, but to do so it is necessary for their chemists to identify the exact chemical structure of the analog. When this happens, it would be a simple matter to alter the chemical structure of the analog to build a new designer drug, starting the process over again. For example, see Figure 37-3.

The change might be very subtle, and either to escape criminal prosecution or to increase profits by creating a new product that illicit-drug distributors are willing to provide for a very high price, the chemical structure of the compound might be altered yet again, as in Figure 37-4.

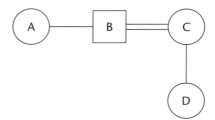

FIGURE 37-1 Parent Molecule

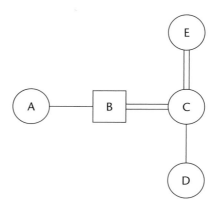

FIGURE 37-2 First Analog

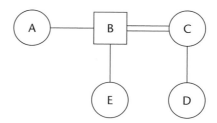

FIGURE 37-3 Second Analog

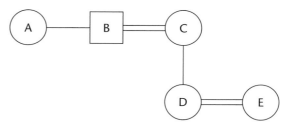

FIGURE 37-4 Third Analog

Although the "drug" molecule used to illustrate this process is a very simple one, it does serve to illustrate how it is possible to produce analogs of an original compound. In the case of real drug molecules, there might be dozens or even hundreds of possible analogs. We will examine some of those that have been identified by law enforcement agencies over the years.

Some Existing Drug Analogs
Analogs of the Amphetamines

The amphetamine molecule lends itself to experimentation, and several analogs of the parent amphetamine molecule have been identified to date. One is 2,5-dimethoxy-4-methylamphetamine, or the hallucinogen DOM, which is rarely used by illicit-drug abusers. The compound MDMA ("Ecstasy") is considered an analog of the amphetamines by some pharmacologists, and there are 184 known analogs of the MDMA molecule, some of which are known to have a psychoactive effect on the user. For example, the compound 3,4-methylenedioxyamphetamine, or MDEA, has a chemical structure that is very similar to that of MDMA and has very similar effects on the user. This substance is often sold under the name of "Eve." There have been isolated reports of deaths associated with MDEA abuse, and the long-term effects of this compound on the user are not known at this time.

Another designer drug is known as "Ya ba" ("Crazy medicine"). It is most commonly used in Southeast Asia, especially in Thailand where up to 5% of the populations admits to having used it at least once (Hilditch, 2000; Kurutz, 2003). Isolated cases of its use on the West Coast of the United States have also been reported. This compound, a blend of ephedrine, caffeine, methamphetamine, lithium (obtained from batteries), and some other chemicals obtained from household cleaning agents, provides an 8- to 12-hour "high." It can be inhaled, smoked, or used through a transdermal patch, but the preferred method of abuse is oral. Long-term use appears to contribute to suicidal or homicidal thoughts,[10] and most abusers follow a pattern of using the compound for 2–3 days followed by a day or two of deep sleep. Very little is known about the toxicology of Ya ba, which has not been subjected to clinical research studies by pharmacologists.

Analogs of Phencyclidine (PCP)

PCP is a popular drug molecule for illicit chemists to experiment with, and there have been at least 30 drug analogs of PCP identified to date. Some of these compounds are more potent than PCP, such as the compound N-ethyl-1-1phenylcyclohexylamine (also known as PCE) or the compound (1-(1-1-thienylcyclohexyl) piperidine) (or TCP). Other drug analogs of PCP are (1-(-phenylcyclohexyl)-pyrrolidine) (PHP) and (1-piperidinocyclohexanecarbonitrile) (PCC). These complex chemical names provide some idea of how the PCP parent molecule might be manipulated by chemists to develop other compounds.

Ketamine[11]

This compound is used as an anesthetic agent that does not cause the respiratory or cardiac depression caused by other anesthetics, making it of value in surgery in trauma cases (McDowell, 2005; Schultz, 2002). Ketamine has been classified as a Schedule III compound.[12] It has a fairly wide therapeutic window and thus is relatively safe when used as directed in a medical setting. It does have a shorter duration of action than PCP, with peak blood levels being seen approximately 20 minutes after it is ingested by mouth. When injected into a vein, such as when it is used as an anesthetic, its effects are seen with seconds (Sadock & Sadock, 2007). The analgesia induced by a single injection of Ketamine lasts about 40 minutes, but a dissociative state that lasts for hours after use is not uncommon (Sadock & Sadock, 2007). During this dissociative state the individual will have trouble forming memories, which makes this medication of value during the acute recovery stage following surgery. A common complication when it is used as a surgical anesthetic is a lack of concern for the environment or personal safety (Sadock & Sadock, 2007).

It is possible to manufacture Ketamine in illicit laboratories, but it is rather difficult to do this, so most commonly the Ketamine found on the streets is diverted, usually from veterinary supply companies because it is also used for surgery with animals (McDowell, 2005; Sadock & Sadock, 2007). It is a colorless and odorless compound that can be abused intranasally, orally, by inhalation,[13] or on rare occasions by intravenous injection (Sadock & Sadock, 2007). In a powdered form it might be intermixed with tobacco or marijuana and then smoked (Gahlinger, 2004). The fact that it is odorless and colorless makes it an ideal date rape drug because it can be slipped into the victim's drink without arousing suspicion, and its ability to induce anterograde[14] amnesia will reduce the chance that the rapist will be identified by the victim.

---

[10]Thus this compound's name.

[11]Or (2-o-chorophenyl)-2-methylamine chclohexanone), if you really must know.

[12]See Appendix 4.

[13]This is referred to as a "bump" by abusers who use this method.

[14]See Glossary.

When used orally, the effects are dose-dependent (Freese, Miotto, & Reback, 2002; Gahlinger, 2004). Dosage levels typically used by the Ketamine abuser are about one-half of that necessary to induce anesthesia, or about one-sixtieth of the LD50 for this compound, which reflects its large therapeutic window (McDowell, 2004, 2005). These dosage levels induce a sense of euphoria, visual hallucinations, a dissociative state, as well as vivid dreams (Freese et al., 2002; Gahlinger, 2004). Long-term abuse can induce memory problems (Gahlinger, 2004; C. J. A. Morgan, Muetzelfeldt, & Curran, 2009). Higher doses administered in a single setting will induce anesthesia, which again makes it useful for date rape situations. In exceptionally high doses, Ketamine can induce a "near death" experience, anxiety, hallucinations, a distorted sense of time, and a possible drug-induced psychosis (Brust, 2004).

In the brain, Ketamine binds at the NMDA receptor site, forcing a calcium ion channel to close (McDowell, 2004, 2005). This alters the rate at which that neuron can "fire." The elimination half-life of ketamine is 3–4 hours, and it is extensively biotransformed by the liver before elimination. Only about 3% of a single dose is excreted unchanged in the urine. Standard toxicology tests will not detect Ketamine, and so if a date rape situation is suspected a special toxicology test must be ordered to detect the drug or its metabolites. Some of the psychological effects of Ketamine when it is abused include hallucinations, hypertension, tachycardia, respiratory depression, paranoia, apnea, and "flashback" experiences in the days or weeks after the last weeks of this compound (Gahlinger, 2004; McDowell, 2004, 2005; Walton, 2002; Sadock & Sadock, 2007). Frequently, abusers experience deficits in the areas of spatial memory and pattern recognition on psychological tests, as well as delusional thought patterns, which appear to resolve with abstinence (C. J. A. Morgan et al., 2009).

Aminorex[15]

This compound was introduced in Europe as an aid to weight loss and sold under the brand name of Menocil® (S. B. Karch, 2009; Rasmussen, 2008). It was rapidly withdrawn from the pharmaceuticals market after it became apparent that this compound could induce fatal pulmonary hypertension, sometimes after just 4 weeks of use, and there is no legitimate application for this medication (S. B. Karch, 2009; Rasmussen, 2008).

It is still encountered by physicians on a sporadic basis, usually after it was sold to illicit-drug abusers under the guise of methamphetamine (S. B. Karch, 2009). It is easily synthesized, thus making it an attractive compound to manufacture in illicit-drug "labs," but was classified as a Schedule I[16] compound in April of 1989 and since then its use in the United States has virtually ended (S. B. Karch, 2009). The effects are not well documented but do appear to be similar to those of the amphetamines (S. B. Karch, 2009). Available evidence, based on research studies conducted before it was withdrawn from the market, suggest that Aminorex is rapidly absorbed after an oral dose, with peak blood levels being seen approximately 2 hours after the drug was ingested. The reported half-life is approximately 7.7 hours (S. B. Karch, 2009), and it is excreted virtually unchanged by the kidneys. Because of its legal status and potential for harm to the user, all clinical research into the effects of this compound was discontinued when it was withdrawn from the market. Its potential to cause other medical complications beyond pulmonary hypertension remains unknown at this time (S. B. Karch, 2009).

Gamma Hydroxybutyric Acid (GHB)

This compound was first identified in 1960 when scientists were doing research on the neurotransmitter GABA. Research has demonstrated that it is metabolized from GABA, the main inhibitory neurotransmitter in the brain. Initially there was some interest in this compound as a presurgical agent because its effects were thought to be similar to those of GABA. However, the usefulness of this compound as a pre-surgical agent was very limited, because (a) many patients experienced vomiting and seizures when recovering from its effects, (b) it has a rather narrow therapeutic window,[17] and (c) when used in a surgical setting other analgesics must still be administered to the patient (Tomb, 2008). These factors combined to make its use by physicians rather rare, although it is sold under the brand name of Xyrem® in the United States for the treatment of narcolepsy.[18]

Small amounts of GHB are normally found in the human kidneys, heart, muscle tissues, and brain, and it

---

[15]Technically, 2-amino-4-methyl-5-phenyl-2-oxazoline

[16]See Appendix 4.

[17]The LD$_{50}$ is only five times the therapeutic dose, thus making it easy for the abuser to overdose on this compound. The therapeutic window is made even smaller if the abuser is ingesting a CNS depressant such as alcohol simultaneously (Commission on Adolescent Substance and Alcohol Abuse, 2005; McDowell, 2005).

[18]See Glossary.

TABLE 37-2 GHB'S EFFECTS ON USER

DOSAGE LEVEL	EFFECT
0.1–1.5 mg/kg	sleep state with enhanced delta and REM sleep
10 mg/kg	euphoria, lowered inhibitions, amnesia (some reports of nausea, headache, itching, and vomiting reported at this dosage level)
20–30 mg/kg	In addition to aforementioned effects, light sleep and/or drowsiness
40–50 mg/kg	deep sleep state
60–70 mg/kg	deep coma, possible seizures
>70 mg/kg	Cardiopulmonary depression, seizures, respiratory depression, possible death

NOTE: Based on Commission on Adolescent Substance and Alcohol Abuse (2005), Koesters, Rogers, and Rajasingham (2002), and Rosenthal and Solhkhah (2005).

is thought to function as a neurotransmitter in that organ (McDowell, 2005; Drummer & Odell, 2001). As a neurotransmitter, GHB helps to mediate the sleep cycle, body temperature, and cerebral glucose metabolism, plays a role in the formation of memories, and possibly stimulates the release of the human growth hormone (Gahlinger, 2004; S. B. Karch, 2009; Weaver & Schnoll, 2008).

This latter effect was what made GHB use so attractive to muscle builders after the anabolic steroids were banned. Because of its widespread abuse, GHB was classified as a Schedule II compound[19] by the Drug Enforcement Administration in 2000, a move that might have contributed to the decrease of GHB use observed in the United States (Van Noorden, Van Dongen, Zitman, & Vergouwen, 2009). In response to this, body builders simply switched to any of a number of legal compounds that would be biotransformed into GHB after ingestion or to illicit sources of this chemical. Instructions how to make it are available over the Internet, but there are different formulas used, and the potency and purity of the obtained product is often open to question. However, the majority of users report taking this compound for recreational purposes and not for body-building purposes (S. B. Karch, 2009).

Clinically, it is well absorbed from the gastrointestinal tract following oral ingestion but on occasion is also injected intravenously by abusers. When ingested orally, GHB's effects begin within 10–30 minutes. Peak blood plasma levels are seen in between 20 and 40 minutes following a single oral dose, and it has a half-life of approximately 20 minutes (S. B. Karch, 2009). During the process of biotransformation, most of a single dose of GHB is excreted from the body as carbon dioxide, and only 2–5% is excreted from the

body unchanged. GHB's short half-life, combined with its ability to induce amnesia and escape detection by standard urine toxicology tests, are all characteristics that made it attractive as a date rape drug. However, a urine test has been developed to detect GHB in the first 12 hours after it was administered, thus limiting its attractiveness as a date rape compound because law enforcement authorities now have the technique to identify its use in date rape situations (Gwinnell & Adamec, 2006; S. B. Karch, 2009).

Subjectively, the effects of GHB are similar to those of alcohol, producing effects such as drowsiness, a sense of euphoria, and disinhibition (Van Noorden et al., 2009). When used concurrently with alcohol at high doses, it is possible that high doses of GHB will inhibit the biotransformation of the alcohol. This increases the risk of a possible alcohol overdose, which may prove fatal (Karch, 2009). GHB may cause seizures if used simultaneously with methamphetamine (Smith, 2001). Patients with HIV infection who are protease inhibitors should not ingest GHB, as the antiviral agents alter the user's body to biotransform many compounds, including GHB (Drummer & Odell, 2001).

Table 37-2 outlines some of GHB's effects on the user. In addition to those listed in the table, reported side effects of GHB include nausea, vomiting, tunnel vision, ataxia, confusion, agitation, dizziness, hypersalivation, hypotonia, and amnesia (Commission on Adolescent Substance and Alcohol Abuse, 2005; Gahlinger, 2004). Conservative, supportive medical care is the best treatment for a GHB overdose, although intubation and restraints might be necessary in extreme cases (Miro, Nogue, Espinoza, To-Figueras, & Sanchez, 2002).

Long-term abusers can become physically dependent on GHB, and there is a characteristic withdrawal syndrome that includes symptoms such as anxiety, tremor, insomnia, nausea, tachycardia, tremor, hypertension,

---

[19]See Appendix 4.

and a delirium tremens–like syndrome in heavy abusers who suddenly discontinue the use of GHB (Freese et al., 2002; Klein & Kramer, 2004; Rosenthal & Solhkhah, 2005; Van Noorden et al., 2009). These symptoms usually begin within 12 hours of the person's last use of GHB and can continue for up to 12–15 days. This withdrawal syndrome is potentially life threatening (Van Noorden et al., 2009). As the preceding information suggests, GHB is significantly more dangerous than was thought 20 or more years ago, and in spite of assurances from those who sell it should not be abused.

Phenethylamines[20]

There are more than 250 members of this family of compounds, including the natural compound mescaline, which is found in the peyote cactus of the American Southwest, the compound MDA, and the synthetic hallucinogen MDMA (Haroz & Greenberg, 2005; Strassman, 2005). Other compounds in this family include MMDA, DOET, DOB, 2C-I, and DOM, among others (Brust, 2007b; Shulgin & Shulgin, 2007).

Nexus[21]

Nexus is perhaps the best-known synthetic member of the phenylethylamines.[22] This compound is usually ingested orally, and a single dose of 10–20 mg will cause the user to experience intoxication, euphoria, and visual distortions or outright hallucinations for 6–8 hours. Doses above 50 mg result in extremely vivid, frightening hallucinations and morbid delusions (S. B. Karch, 2009). Side effects include nausea, abdominal cramps, pulmonary problems, and cough. In the brain the compound shows an affinity for the serotonin 5-HT receptor subtype. Clinical research into the pharmacokinetics of this compound is very limited because it was never intended for human use. Detection of this compound through urine toxicology tests is difficult, because it does not react with many reagents used to identify various drugs of abuse (S. B. Karch, 2009).

"Blue Mystic"

Another member of the phenethylamine family of compounds is 2C-T-7,[23] known as "Blue Mystic" (Boyer, 2005). It is thought that this compound is about 12 times as potent a hallucinogen as mescaline. This compound is often abused for its ability to induce visual hallucinations (S. B. Karch, 2009). Side effects can include nausea, cramps, seizures, and possible death from aspiration of material being regurgitated (Boyer, 2005). Beyond the fact that it has a narrow therapeutic window, and the difference between an effective dose and a toxic dose is only a matter of micrograms, very little is known about the pharmacokinetics of this compound.

DOB

The compound DOB[24] has effects similar to those of MDMA but they last longer. Its use is largely confined to Australia, although on occasion it is found as a contaminant or adulterant to MDMA or LSD (S. B. Karch, 2009). It is known that the effects begin 3–4 hours after the compound was ingested, and some of the symptoms might last for up to 24 hours (S. B. Karch, 2004; Shulgin & Shulgin, 2007). DOB use has been associated with blood vessel spasms and with seizures, both of which have the potential to be fatal (S. B. Karch, 2009). It is significantly more toxic than LSD, but specific pharmacokinetic studies are lacking at this time.

Paramethoxyamphetamine (PMA)

This is a potent hallucinogen, and its hallucinogenic potential appears to be approximately the same as LSD (S. B. Karch, 2009). It is very toxic, and a number of deaths have been attributed to its use (S. B. Karch, 2009). Some of the adverse effects from the use of this compound include tachycardia, hyperthermia, coma, seizures, arrhythmias, abnormal heart rhythm, and in isolated cases dangerously low blood sugar levels (S. B. Karch, 2009).

Tryptamines[25]

There are at least 200 compounds in this family of chemical agents, all of which have a chemical structure similar to that of the neurotransmitter serotonin (D. J. Brown, 2007). Some of the compounds in this family of chemicals include the hallucinogen psilocybin, DMT, DET, psilocin, and bufotenine. These compounds enjoyed various degrees of popularity in the 1960s and 1970s, but were classified as Schedule I[26] compounds by the Drug Enforcement Administration (Brust, 2007b; Haroz & Greenberg, 2005). Little is known about the pharmacokinetics of these compounds, although it is

---

[20]Shulgin and Shulgin (2007) provide an excellent overview of this family of compounds for those readers interested in learning more.

[21]Or 2,5 dimethoxyphenethylamine.

[22]In some communities it is sold under the names of Venus, Bromo, Erox, and XTC (S. B. Karch, 2009).

[23]Or 2,5-dimethoxy-4-(n)propylthiophenethylamine.

[24]Or 4-bromo-2,5-dimethoxyamphyetramine.

[25]Sometimes called the *indolealkylamines*.

[26]See Appendix 4.

known that many of these compounds are extensively biotransformed by the first-pass metabolism process and must be "snorted" or smoked to be effective (Haroz & Greenberg, 2005; A. A. Mueller, 2005.)

One member of this family of compounds is known by a variety of names, including *Foxy* or *Foxy Methoxy*[27] (Boyer, 2005; Meatherall & Sharma, 2005; A. A. Mueller, 2005). This compound appeared in the 1990s and was quickly classified as a Schedule I compound (A. A. Mueller, 2005). Unlike the other tryptamines, Foxy is not significantly affected by the first-pass metabolism effect and can be ingested orally. Although this compound has a different chemical structure than MDMA, the effects are very similar for the abuser, and it has the same potential for neurological damage as does Ecstasy. Little is known about the pharmacokinetics of this compound. It is known that when ingested orally the effects begin in about 20–30 minutes (A. A. Mueller, 2005). It can cause sexual stimulation and mild hallucinations, which are the desired effects. Side effects include (but are not limited to) anxiety, restlessness, anxiety, insomnia, and possible seizures (Meatherall & Sharma, 2005; A. A. Mueller, 2005). The tryptamines are able to induce a condition known as the "serotonin syndrome,"[28] and there is little reason to suspect that Foxy is exempt from this side effect (Boyer, 2005). There is evidence suggesting a synergistic effect between Foxy and compounds such as PCP, Ketamine, and marijuana, but little is known about the pharmacokinetics of this compound either in isolation or in combination with these compounds.

Psilocybin

Psilocybin is a naturally occurring tryptamine compound found in the mushroom *Psilocybe mexicana*, which is found in the northern part of Mexico and the American Southwest. The Aztecs called psilocybin the "flesh of the gods," suggesting that they were quite familiar with this compound and its ability to induce a mystical state of mind in the user (Griffiths, Richards, McCann, & Jesse, 2006). Research into the pharmacokinetics of psilocybin ended in the 1960s for the most part, and there is little known about the pharmacokinetics of this compound. It is known that high doses can induce seizures and confusional states, but fatalities that occur after the ingestion of psilocybin are most often the result of accidents or suicide rather than the direct effects of this compound (Filley, 2004).

Fentanyl

As was discussed in Chapter 11, fentanyl is a synthetic opioid. The basic fentanyl molecule is one that can be manufactured from a few ordinary industrial chemicals, although this process is rather difficult and lends itself to errors in the production process (S. B. Karch, 2009). Still, on occasion illicit-drug chemists will attempt to manufacture fentanyl for sale. The high potency of fentanyl can result in unintentional drug overdoses, some of which might be rapidly fatal. For example, when smoked (a popular method of fentanyl abuse), it is possible for one inhalation to prove fatal to the abuser ("Take Time to Smell the Fentanyl," 2004).

By making just a minor change in the basic fentanyl molecule, it is possible to produce fentanyl analogs[29] with various psychoactive effects. At least 12 such compounds have been identified to date. One analog has been found to extend fentanyl's effects from the normal 30–90 minutes to 4–5 hours. Another fentanyl analog extends the effects to 4–5 *days*. The compound 3-Methylfentanyl (or 3MF) is thought to be about 6000 times as potent as morphine, a characteristic that makes it a popular drug for snorting. Although these fentanyl analogs can be produced using easily available industrial chemicals, a simple mistake in the production process can produce compounds that are toxic and possibly fatal to the user.

Fry

There have been isolated reports of this compound in the United States. Fry is essentially marijuana soaked in formaldehyde and then laced with PCP (Klein & Kramer, 2004). Although euphoria is the desired effect of this mixture, it can produce a toxic psychosis, hallucinations, delusional thinking, panic, paranoia, reduced attention span, and loss of consciousness, in addition to brain and lung damage (Klein & Kramer, 2004).

Dextromethorphan (DXM)

This is a synthetic compound that is a chemical cousin to codeine. It is not a controlled compound as of this time (S. B. Karch, 2009). Dextromethorphan was originally marketed in the 1960s as an antitussive compound for treatment of mild- to moderate-intensity coughs (Haroz & Greenberg, 2005). In this context the user will ingest around 30 mg of dextromethorphan every 4–6 hours. It is a relatively effective cough suppressant, and more than 140 over-the-counter compounds are sold in the United States alone that contain dextromethorphan either as the primary or one of the primary ingredients (Bobo, Miller, & Martin, 2005).

---

[27]Or 5-meth-oxy-N,N, diisopropyltryptamine.

[28]See Glossary.

[29]See Glossary.

Dextromethorphan tends to concentrate in the brain, and the concentration of DXM in the brain is significantly higher than that found in the blood plasma (S. B. Karch, 2009). This is the site of its cough suppressant effects. DXM is biotransformed in the liver, and the primary metabolite of dexromethorphan is the compound *dextrorphan*. Thus dextromethorphan is actually a prodrug with the active metabolite actually causing its cough suppressant effects (S. B. Karch, 2009). This compound is extensively deactivated by the first-pass metabolism effect (S. B. Karch, 2009). However, about 10% of the general population lack the ability to produce an enzyme[30] necessary to biotransform dextromethorphan and are classified as "slow metabolizers" of this compound (S. B. Karch, 2009, p. 605). Whereas the effects of a typical dose of DXM last 4–6 hours in the average person, a single therapeutic dose will last 17–22 hours in a person deficient in this enzyme. The implications of this are especially important when one considers the dosage levels utilized by DXM abusers (discussed later).

DXM is also a compound that is frequently abused by adolescents. A powdered form of DXM is available over the Internet, and there are Web sites that will give step-by-step instructions on how to abuse DXM and what effects to look for at different dosage levels ("Escalating DXM Abuse Among Teenagers," 2007). The peak age of DXM abuse is about 15–16 years of age (Bryner et al., 2006). However, in contrast to the dosage levels utilized when a person wishes to control a cough, DXM abusers routinely ingest doses of between 150 and 2000 mg at one time (Brust, 2004).

In the brain, DXM functions as an NMDA[31] channel blocker and a serotonin reuptake blocker (Brust, 2004). At the doses typically utilized by DXM abusers, the compound can induce visual, tactile, and auditory hallucinations, a sense of euphoria, and an altered sense of time (Bobo et al., 2005; Haroz & Greenberg, 2005). At dosage levels of between 300 and 1000 mg/kg of body weight, the effects of DXM are similar to that of PCP (Bobo et al., 2005). The effects begin within 15–30 minutes and last for 2–6 hours (Haroz & Greenberg, 2005). Adverse consequences of DXM when abused include disorientation, paranoia, slurred speech, ataxia, tremor, nausea, vomiting, and nystagmus (Bobo et al., 2005). A DXM overdose[32]

might produce such symptoms as lethargy, slurred speech, hyperexcitability, ataxia, tremor, rigidity, tachycardia, hypertension, nystagmus, respiratory depression, acute psychosis, coma, and possible death from cardiovascular collapse. On rare occasions, DXM can also induce the serotonin syndrome.[33] As with any medication, all cases of possible dextromethorphan overdose should be assessed by a physician immediately.

Chapter Summary

The relationship between criminal activity and the substance use disorders is quite complex, and worthy of a book in its own right. The debate over whether those people most prone to criminal activity are drawn to the SUDs as well, or if criminal activity is a consequence of the lifestyle forced on those who wish to engage in substance abuse, continues to rage. Currently, it appears that both are applicable, depending on the individuals and their path toward addiction to a chemical.

At least some of the harm associated with the SUDs is a direct result of society's efforts at supply reduction through the "war" on drugs. By making chemical abuse illegal, society has both generated a new class of criminals (the abusers) and helped the growth of a class of criminals associated with the sale and distribution of drugs. Because it is a closed, illegal market, upper- and middle-level drug dealers often add various adulterants to the product that ultimately is sold to the illicit-drug abuser. These adulterants contribute to or cause various health consequences for the abuser, who then seeks medical assistance. This, in turn, places an additional burden on the health care system. There have been significant unanticipated consequences to making drugs of abuse illegal.

Further, to avoid criminal prosecution, those involved in the drug sales/distribution industry have been searching for new designer drugs, which are yet to be banned. When these compounds are identified by law enforcement officials and then outlawed, the search for other designer compounds that have not been banned begins anew. This search is spurred on by the criminal sanctions in place against the distribution and sale of illegal compounds. However, enforcement of these sanctions have resulted in a further demand on the overburdened court system, which will be discussed in the next chapter. Some of the more commonly encountered illicit drugs and their effects were reviewed.

---

[30]CYP2D6, which is part of the metabolic P-450 pathway of the liver.

[31]See Glossary.

[32]If the DXM was in a preparation that also included acetaminophen, which is common for many over-the-counter cough and cold medications, the abuser will be at risk for unknowingly ingesting an acetaminophen overdose (discussed in Chapter 15).

---

[33]See Glossary.

CHAPTER 38

The Debate Over Legalization[1]

When the United States is not invading some sovereign nation—or setting it on fire from the air, which is more fun for our simple-minded pilots—we're usually busy "declaring war" on something here at home. Anything we don't like about ourselves, we declare war on it. We don't do anything about it, we just declare war. "Declaring war" is our only public metaphor for problem solving. We have a war on crime, a war on poverty, a war on litter, a war on cancer, a war on violence, and [President] Ronald Reagan's ultimate joke, the war on drugs. More accurately, the war on the Constitution.

—*George Carlin (2001, p. 109)*

Introduction

The comedian George Carlin was, in the opinion of many, at his best when he was poking fun at current social and political trends. However, in a very real sense the quote at the start of this chapter is less of a joke than the general public realizes: It is the truth. The substance use disorders are the only medical (or psychiatric) condition in which the manifestations of that illness (in this case alcohol misuse or illicit-drug use) are addressed through the legal system (Heyman, 2009). A person with diabetes, a seizure disorder, or cancer does not need to fear arrest for being diabetic, having a seizure disorder, or having cancer. The person with a substance use disorder, however, is in danger of legal sanctions for engaging in the very behaviors that are used to define the disease!

Rational perspective about the problem of illicit drugs is "generally lacking" when the problem of illicit drugs is considered ("Drugs Drive Politicians Out of Their Minds," 2009, p. 5). Rather than following the recommendations of scientists or clinicians, governments choose to listen to the loud, moralistic special-interest groups that warn that to change existing policies on illicit drugs is to be "soft on crime" ("Drugs Drive Politicians Out of Their Minds," 2009). As J. T. Woods (2005) pointed out in another context,[2] "Law can rarely reform a people who have already succumbed to the allures of immediate gratification" (p. 212). In their attempt to achieve this goal in the arena of the substance use disorders, which most certainly provide immediate gratification for the user, the authorities have applied the weapons and tactics of World War I

---

[1]It is not the purpose of this chapter to advocate the legalization of compounds currently deemed illegal by law. Rather, it is the purpose of this chapter to stir debate within the class as to the question of legalization.

[2]The immorality of Roman society under Caesar Augustus.

(Walton, 2002).[3] The logic behind this approach has repeatedly been criticized, but still the same weapons and tactics are utilized to correct this social problem.

Further, as will be discussed in this chapter, the problem of illicit-drug use has been used as an excuse to negate many of the provisions of the U.S. Constitution. In a sense this country has been turned into a police state, a social change that is justified on the grounds that it will help to end illicit-substance use. To this end ever greater numbers of nonviolent offenders are sentenced to jail or prison on the pretense that this action will protect the public from illicit-drug abusers.[4] To make room in prison for these nonviolent drug abusers, individuals with violent criminal histories are released from prison before completion of their sentences. The success of this process might be seen in the fact that at the beginning of the 21st century the United States is the largest illicit-drug consumer in the world, using two-thirds of the world's illicit drugs (Dobbs, 2007). The illicit-drug market has been estimated to be a $400 billion industry (United Nations, 2008), and if the aforementioned estimate is correct, then our share of this illicit-drug trade is $264 billion each year. The United States is also spending at least an additional $200 billion per year to fight the "war on drugs."

There are also indirect costs of the "war on drugs" that will be discussed in this chapter. Statistics such as those just reviewed hardly reflect a resounding success. Yet just like the generals of World War I, politicians continue to reaffirm their commitment to following the same course of action year after year and point to each fractional reduction in drug use as proof that the "war on drugs" is working. In this chapter we will examine the issue of legalization of the drugs of abuse.

The "War" On Drugs: An Ongoing National Disaster

Future historians will view the "war" on drugs with disbelief. This "war" has raged for the better part of a century. It continues not because of the destructive potential of the drugs of abuse, but because of the irrational beliefs of those in command. An example of this was the social movement to legalize marijuana in the United States in the early 1970's. Then President Richard M. Nixon refused to consider this possibility because of a personal belief that people who consume alcohol do not use it for its intoxicating effects but for fun, whereas people who used marijuana were mainly those who were protesting against the then-current Vietnam war and whose substance use was part of the reason why they were protesting (Zeese, 2002).[5] There were also subtle racial undertones to the antidrug efforts of the Nixon administration, which were not discovered until the early years of the 21st century (Zeese, 2002). For example, possession of powdered cocaine (most prevalent in middle-class America) resulted in a much more lenient sentence than possession of an equal amount of "crack" cocaine (most prevalent in the inner cities).

---

[3]For those who have not studied history, generals in World War I would send wave after wave of infantry against an entrenched enemy whose machine guns and artillery literally mowed the attacking troops down like stands of wheat. This tactic was proven to be ineffective, cost thousands of soldiers their lives, but was never challenged or abandoned during World War I.

[4]Heyman (2009) argued that the majority of those who are incarcerated are in prison for the crime of drug sales and not possession of a controlled substance. Although it is tempting to argue that this will reduce drug availability, evidence suggests that it is at most a temporary solution, because other drug dealers quickly move in to fill the void.

---

[5]Would it come as a surprise to learn that President Richard M. Nixon was known to drink liquor on many occasions? Go figure...

The War on Drugs: The Fantasy

The "war" on drugs is based on four legs: (a) elimination of illicit compounds through destruction of raw materials, (b) the interdiction of drugs being shipped to this country, (c) legal sanctions against those who engage in the use of the substances deemed illegal by the government, and (d) treatment of those addicted to these compounds. We will examine each of these legs supporting the "war on drugs" in turn.

1. Elimination of Raw Materials

As a tactic, the elimination of the raw materials used to produce illicit drugs makes sense. If you eliminate the raw materials, then the compound cannot be produced and the problem is solved. The reality is far different. For example, during the administration of President George W. Bush,[6] a 5-year, multibillion-dollar program to try and eradicate cocaine cultivation in Colombia by spraying the fields where the coca plant is cultivated with an herbicide proved to be a failure. The farmers just moved over to the next valley and started to cultivate the coca plant there. The judicious use of bribes to prevent officials from targeting certain areas for attack also contributed to the failure of this program. Finally, much of the coca production was moved from Colombia to the neighboring countries of Bolivia and Peru, where it could also be cultivated. It is doubtful that this program had any major effect on the production of cocaine. Indeed, having caused a glut of cocaine on the illicit-drug market in the United States in the past decade, drug cartels targeted Europe as an untouched market, and now approximately 140 metric tons per year of cocaine (or a quarter of the world's annual production of illicit cocaine) are consumed there (Parenti, 2009).

Another example of the failure of precursor elimination might be seen in the ongoing battle over whether ephedrine should be outlawed or not. Ephedrine can be used in the production of methamphetamine. Although originally declared illegal, subsequent legal battles resulted in this decision being reversed, and producers of illicit methamphetamine either moved the production center to other countries where ephedrine is easily available or changed the process of producing methamphetamine to use pseudo-ephedrine, an over-the-counter cold remedy.

These (and a multitude of other) examples all suggest that the elimination of those products used in the production of illicit drugs has failed. However, this effort is necessary "because some of the plants that grow in the southern hemisphere are just plain evil. We know that because they're not stamped with labels like Bristol-Meyers, Squib, Eli Lilly or Pfizer. And it's vital that we understand that these southern hemisphere plants and their cultivators are to blame because the alternative is to believe that our national appetite for drugs is *our own problem*. And that's plain crazy talk" (Maher, 2002, p. 49, italics added for emphasis). As should be readily apparent by now, efforts at elimination of the raw materials used to produce the world's illicit drugs has been a failure.

2. Interdiction

The pages of history provide stunning evidence that the interdiction of illicit compounds is doomed to failure. The clearest example of this failure was the "Great Experiment" of Prohibition.

The Lessons of History: Prohibition The "Great Experiment" of Prohibition began in 1920 and ended in 1933.[7] Based on the theory that many of society's ills were caused by alcohol (the "demon rum"), the nonmedical use of alcohol was outlawed. Even when prescribed by physicians a patient could receive only 1 pint of liquor every 10 days (Pain, 2008). Because of this law, more than one physician concluded that his medical school education was negated by "a few farmers, lawyers, politicians and the like … who have the audacity to say to the medical profession of this country that they can't prescribe this or that…." (unknown physician, quoted in Pain, 2008, p. 45).[8]

Although Prohibition began in 1920, the per capita consumption of beer in the United States had reached its low point between 1911 and 1914 (Schweikart, 2008). The number of deaths from cirrhosis of the liver reached their lowest level in 1921, just a year after the start of Prohibition.[9] Further, by the end of Prohibition medical journal articles on alcohol had all but disappeared (Schweikart, 2008). One could argue that

---

[6]2000–2008.

[7]To his credit, Prohibition was passed over the veto of then President Woodrow Wilson. His successor, President Warren G. Harding, however, and the U.S. Senate, openly flouted the law by maintaining bars well stocked from the best of the liquor captured by federal agents, who interdicted alcohol shipments into the United States. However, Congress often exempts itself from laws passed to benefit the lowly citizens who voted for them.

[8]This is a charge that has been repeated when physicians encounter the federal ban against prescription marijuana.

[9]As was discussed in Chapter 5, it takes a number of years of chronic alcohol use for liver cirrhosis to develop. The fact that cases of cirrhosis reached their lower point in 1921 is indirect evidence that alcohol use had been falling before the start of Prohibition in 1920.

Congress willingly "closed the bar door after the horse was out," because Prohibition was passed after the problem began to resolve itself. Admittedly, the level of alcohol consumption continued to fall during the Prohibition years but it was never eliminated in this country (Schweikart, 2008).

However, Prohibition also ran headlong into what has been called the "law of unintended consequences."[10] Following the start of Prohibition, the homicide rate in the United States increased fourfold, whereas other forms of crime increased in frequency by 24% (McPherson, Yudko, Murray-Bridges et al., 2009). It has been argued that Prohibition did little more than contribute to a staggering increase in corruption by elected officials and law enforcement officers, a decline in civil rights, and profits for what might loosely be called "organized crime" (Lessig, 2009). Before the start of Prohibition, the activities of organized crime had mainly been limited to prostitution and illegal gambling. The emerging "organized-crime" organizations, sensing huge profits in providing alcohol to those who wished to drink in spite of Prohibition, quickly took control of the emerging illicit distribution system (M. Gray, 1998). So great was the demand for alcohol that at its height during Prohibition the distribution of illegal alcohol comprised 5% of the nation's gross national product (Schlosser, 2003). Viewed as a problem, Prohibition was passed to eliminate the negative effects of alcohol (the "demon rum" according to members of the Temperance movement). But the "cure" had bred an even more terrible disease: Organized-crime organizations soon started to fight among themselves to gain control of territories in which to distribute illegal alcohol. On occasion, these territorial negotiations were aided by the judicious use of explosives or by automatic-weapons fire from vehicles driving past a competitor's place of business.[11]

Another totally unanticipated consequence of Prohibition was that it forced those people who wanted to consume alcohol to switch from beer to hard liquor (M. Gray, 1998; McPherson, Yudko, Murray-Bridges et al., 2009). This is consistent with the theory that successful interdiction efforts might cause dealers to *increase* the potency of their product to encourage customer loyalty because of the difficulty of finding new customers during the time of increased police surveillance (Giles, 2009b). For alcohol, liquor presented the appeal of having less bulk, having a higher alcohol content, and not

spoiling as rapidly as beer. Before the start of Prohibition, typical drinkers would "sip" their drink(s) over an extended period, without evidence of widespread intoxication (A. Barr, 1999; M. Gray, 1998). With the start of Prohibition, drinkers shifted to a pattern of "binge" drinking, with the goal of rapidly achieving a state of intoxication (A. Barr, 1999; M. Gray, 1998). At the same time, individuals who did drink switched from beer to liquor, which allowed them to achieve the highest level of intoxication in the least amount of time (M. Gray, 1998). When Prohibition ended, drinkers retained this pattern of alcohol consumption. In this manner, the "Great Experiment" helped to shape the drinking habits of people for generations to come.

During the middle of the 20th century a similar process evolved, although the parallels with the Prohibition era were not recognized until much later. Researchers believe that the interdiction efforts of law enforcement authorities encouraged drug smugglers to switch from bulky, low-profit marijuana to cocaine. Pound for pound cocaine is less bulky, less smelly (and thus less likely to be detected by scent), more compact, and more lucrative to smuggle into the United States. Further, the interdiction efforts against cocaine dealers appear to have contributed to the development of drug gangs and a wave of violence that swept across the country in the 1980's and 1990's. By arresting the older, established drug dealers, the way was opened for inner-city, violence-prone, younger drug dealers to move into the business of selling cocaine and to fight over "turf" (Brust, 2004).

Another example of the law of unintended consequences might be seen in the efforts of law enforcement officials to interdict methamphetamine production in the United States. In the 1990s much of the methamphetamine was produced in small "mom and pop" laboratories that produced small amounts of methamphetamine for local consumption. By making these facilities a focus for law enforcement, the manufacture of methamphetamine was switched to "superlabs" outside of the United States that are capable of producing large amounts of relatively pure methamphetamine to be smuggled into this country (McPherson, Afsarifard et al., 2009; M. Smith, 2006).

Only a small percentage of the drugs that are produced and sent to be smuggled into this country are interdicted, and this results only in short-term, local reductions in drug availability. Given the level of profits involved, if one drug supplier is arrested, another will step into the void to sell drugs to those who desire them.

---

[10]See Glossary.

[11]Which sounds vaguely like the current situation between gangs selling drugs on the street corners and "crack" houses, does it not?

The policy toward interdiction ignores the fact that:

The more "effective" police activity is, the more [drug] prices rise, increasing the profits of smuggling, and the more likely it will be that drug purity and concentration will also increase, to make importation more cost-effective and detection more difficult. (Manderson, 1998, p. 589)

This was a lesson that law enforcement officials and those who make policy could have learned from Prohibition had they but stopped to read the history books: Interdiction just does not work (Reuter, 2009). In return for taking the risk of criminal prosecution, high-level suppliers arrange for drugs to be manufactured or smuggled into this country (usually by surrogates), where they are delivered to major cities and then funneled to outlying regions by middle-level distributors (Furst, Herrmann, Leung, Galea, & Hunt, 2004). The distributor at each level charges a high price for this service, which ultimately is passed on to the consumer. The product "markup" is rather high, for it is not part of the free-market economy, and is justified by the dealer's risk of arrest and prosecution. If one distributor is arrested, another person interested in such profits will simply step into the void.

3. Legal Sanctions

Manufactured Criminals   Because the abuse of illicit drugs is by definition illegal, those who abuse an illicit drug are classified as a "criminal" even if they do not engage in the sale, manufacture, or distribution of illicit drugs. Individuals with an SUD are then forced to use their drug(s) of choice under conditions that contribute to health care problems. These health care problems become another indirect cost of the "war on drugs," because by definition the illicit drugs are illegal. Abusers must often resort to criminal activity to support their SUD. Paradoxically, these consequences of the criminalization of certain compounds are then used to justify keeping them illegal.

Further, the methods used by law enforcement authorities involved in the "war on drug" are not respectful of those who are addicted to these compounds. It has been suggested that the drug enforcement agencies in the United States, especially the Drug Enforcement Administration (DEA), have become "as cruel as the rapacious drug dealers who just try to make money and don't about the people doing the drugs" (Doblin, quoted in Frood, 2008, p. 43). In other words, to "win" the "war on drugs," we have become just as violent and indifferent as the "enemy." To save a village (or nation), you must be prepared to destroy it.

Mandatory Sentencing   To stem the tide of a growing problem of narcotics abuse immediately following the end of World War II, Congress authorized the execution of heroin dealers (Walton, 2002). Some heroin dealers were executed. In spite of this drastic sanction, the number of narcotics abusers or addicts in the United States continued to increase (Walton, 2002), suggesting that the execution of drug dealers was not an effective deterrent. So, in the 1950's naturally Congress passed a new series of mandatory sentencing laws that dictated minimum sentences to be imposed on narcotics dealers. These laws met with almost universal acceptance and were loosely called the "Boggs Act." These laws were passed on the dubious assumption that it is possible to punish undesirable behaviors out of existence (Husak, 2004; Lundeen, 2002). One dissenting voice to the "Boggs Act" was that of James V. Bennett, the director of the U.S. Bureau of Prisons. He expressed strong reservations about the possible effectiveness of the Boggs Act, although he had not broken any laws in doing so. He was subsequently followed by agents of the Federal Bureau of Narcotics, who submitted regular reports to their superiors on the content of speeches that he made. In spite of the enthusiasm with which the Boggs Act was received and the reports filed by federal Bureau of Narcotics agents on the content of Mr. Bennett's views, it had become clear that Mr. Bennett was right: Mandatory minimum sentencing did little if anything to reduce the scope of narcotics abuse in the United States.

Congress then replaced the Boggs Act with a set of sentencing guidelines that allowed the presiding judge to assign appropriate sentences based on the merits of each case. However, in one of the great reversals of all time, just 14 years later Congress again embraced mandatory prison sentences as part of then President Ronald Reagan's renewed "war on drugs."[12] The mandatory sentences were encoded in the Sentencing Reform Act of 1984, which denied even first-time drug offenders the promise of early parole.[13] As a result of this new law, the prison system was soon overwhelmed with nonviolent first-time offenders who

---

[12]One has to wonder how many members of Congress voted in favor of these changes not because they thought that they might work, but because they were afraid of being accused of being "soft on crime" by their political rivals.

[13]Parole from prison was once a privilege offered to only a few offenders who demonstrated exceptional efforts toward rehabilitation. Now it is expected and is often viewed as a "right" of those being sentenced to prison. One will often hear freshly convicted inmates state that although they were sentenced to prison for 10 years, for example, their parole date is only 3 years away.

were serving lengthy mandatory sentences for drug-related convictions.

At this point in history, the largest category of incarcerated people are those convicted of drug-related offenses, usually the personal use of illicit compounds. Eighty-five percent of those arrested for marijuana-related offenses, for example, were not engaged in the sale or distribution of marijuana but had it only for personal use (Brust, 2004). The total number of people arrested for marijuana-related crimes (for example, possession) in 2001 exceeded the *combined* total number of people arrested that year for murder, manslaughter, forcible rape, robbery, and aggravated assault ("Marijuana Arrests," 2003).

An often overlooked aspect of the criminal prosecution and incarceration of those convicted of drug-related offenses is that it is expensive to put a person in prison. Estimates of the cost of incarceration range from between $45,000 and $93,000 per inmate per year[14] (L. B. Erlich, 2001). If there are between 400,000 and 800,000 people in prison for drug-related offenses, then approximately $74 billion a year is being spent just to keep those already convicted of a substance-related offense incarcerated. This is in addition to the cost of the "war on drugs" itself. Nor does the cost stop upon inmates' release from the penitentiary: Individuals who have been incarcerated earn 40% less than those who have never been incarcerated, thus reducing the amount of state and federal income taxes that they pay and increasing their subsequent dependence on state and federal supplementary funds for food stamps and the like. Individuals convicted of drug-related offenses are barred from state and federal tuition assistance programs for college or vocational-technical school costs, making it virtually impossible for the individual to train for a better job (McPherson, Yudko, Murray-Bridges et al., 2009). This after-punishment contributes to the high recidivism rate for drug offenders who are released from prison. In many cases they are pushed back into a life of crime because they can do little else to earn enough money to support themselves or their families.

In retrospect, the Boggs Act and the Sentencing Reform Act of 1984 were both failures. Consider, for example, that in spite of the widespread knowledge of the legal sanctions against illicit-drug use, "millions of people every year join the legions who have experimented with illegal substances" (Phillips & Lawton, 2004, p. 33). For virtually every action there is an unexpected consequence, a truism that has become enshrined as the "law of unintended consequences." If you wish to "get tough on crime" by throwing first-time drug offenders into jail or prison, it will become necessary to release violent offenders from prison to make room for newly convicted drug offenders. As a result of this unintended consequence, the average sentence served by a person convicted of homicide is approximately 9 years, whereas a person convicted of growing 100 marijuana plants could be sent to prison for up to 40 years[15] (Brust, 2004).

The Forfeiture Fiasco During his administration, President Ronald Reagan pressured Congress to become "tough on crime" by enacting a series of "zero tolerance" statutes. The possession of *any* amount of an illegal substance was grounds for criminal prosecution under these "zero tolerance" statutes. People were prosecuted for offenses as innocuous as having money in their wallet tainted by traces of cocaine, as if this was proof of their cocaine abuse. People found to have marijuana seeds in their car or boat were also vulnerable to prosecution. Only later was it proven that a significant percentage of the dollar bills in circulation were tainted by traces of cocaine simply by being rubbed up against another dollar bill that had traces of cocaine on it. It was also discovered that marijuana seeds blow in the wind. By then, however, the damage had been done and numerous people had been prosecuted under the guise of "zero tolerance."

Congress also passed a law allowing law enforcement authorities to confiscate property on the simple *suspicion* that it had been purchased with money made from the illicit-drug trade. The constitutional provisions against unlawful search and seizure were thus set aside. Law enforcement agencies no longer had to *prove* that the property had been purchased with money made from the sale of illegal drugs. They had only to state their belief that this was the case. Not surprisingly, in the time since this law was passed the forfeiture laws have been widely abused. Some police departments now *depend* on money and property seized under forfeiture laws for at least part of their operating budget. The level of abuse inherent in these laws might be seen in the fact that up to *80%* of the

---

[14]A figure that includes the cost of salaries for the staff who work in the prison, the physical plant itself, construction costs, food, medical care, and so on.

[15]Which, if you consider that the offender was 25 at the time of conviction, is essentially a life sentence.

money seized by federal authorities comes from people who are *never* indicted for criminal activity, much less tried in a court of law and convicted (Leavitt, 2003). Police in at least two states (Florida and Louisiana) have been identified as using minor traffic offenses as justification to seize money from motorists who have committed no illegal act other than that traffic law violation because it *might* be drug money (Leavitt, 2003).

The "forfeiture" laws *do* provide a provision that allows the citizen whose property was seized to seek the return of the property. This process requires individuals to file a lawsuit against the agency that seized the property, then provide proof in Court that they did not obtain the money or property from the illegal-drug trade. This process is expensive and time consuming, and the final cost of the process might be several times that of the property seized by authorities. Further, the agency that seized the property is not required to pay any form of interest on the material(s) seized. Few people are willing or have the financial resources to pay $4,000 in court costs to prove that the $1,000 that they had in their wallet for a vacation trip when stopped by the police was rightfully theirs, for example.

As should be obvious by now, the social experiment of trying to eliminate the illicit-drug trade through interdiction, incarceration, and punishment has been a failure. However, this does not stop law enforcement officials from trumpeting the minimal success of the past year and from hinting that for just a few billion dollars more it might be possible to "win" the war on drugs. Unfortunately, law enforcement and incarceration of offenders, often touted as "a panacea for the problem of illicit drug use" (Fulde & Wodak, 2007, p. 334), has yet to prove effective. Indeed, the mandatory sentencing laws were intended to discourage upper- and middle-level dealers from engaging in drug distribution activities. However, these individuals are able to trade their knowledge for lighter prison sentences or even just probation! As a result of this process, only a minority of those incarcerated in the federal prison system were midlevel drug distributors, and more than half of those incarcerated were either drug abusers or low-level dealers who sold drugs on the street corners.

4. Treatment[16]

The treatment of people who are not involved in the distribution or sale of illegal substances but who have a substance use disorder is a distant fourth when the funds for the "war on drugs" are distributed. The total expenditure for drug rehabilitation is estimated to be $15 billion from state and federal governments and $5 billion from insurance companies[17] (Carey, 2008). Arguments that rehabilitation is not effective break down in the face of studies that have found that incarceration has been estimated to cost 2 (Brust, 2004) to 10 times (S. L. Johnson, 2003) times as much as rehabilitation. Other research has suggested that for every dollar invested in treatment, the community saves from $4 to $12 (Breithaupt, 2001; Dobbs, 2007; Mee-Lee, 2002) to possibly as much as $50 (Garrett, 2000).[18] These figures do not mean that treatment is appropriate for every offender convicted of a drug-related crime. In spite of the claims of advocates, "the addiction treatment field [has] not met either public expectations for reduction of addiction ... or its own expectations to produce lasting abstinence" (McLellan, 2008, p. 94). However, neither is incarceration the answer for every offender convicted of a substance-related crime. There should be an attempt to balance the application of legal sanctions against those of treatment, to find the appropriate response to the crime committed by each individual.

The War on Drugs: The Reality

The "war on drugs" has been called a "march of folly" (Brust, 2004, p. ix), which few outside of Washington, DC, dare question (Reuter, 2009). To illustrate the "march of folly" inherent in the "war on drugs," in 1998 the United Nations pledged to win the war on drugs by the year 2008 (R. Room, 2009). The parade celebrating this victory was one that went down in the annals of history. Surely you remember where you were the moment that you heard about this victory!

The reality is that the drugs (or at least those who market and abuse them) have won. In its efforts to "win" this war, the United States has gone so far as to attempt to interfere with the internal affairs of other countries. One of many examples of this unwarranted, possibly illegal interference was seen in 2003, when the then "drug czar" of the United States accused Canada of trying to poison American youth by relaxing its internal

---

[16]Discussed in more detail in Chapter 32.

[17]An amount that might increase now that the federal government has passed a "parity" law that now requires that insurance companies reimburse for drug rehabilitation on a level equal to other health problems.

[18]These various estimates reflect, in part, different variables included from study to study. For example, one study might include long-term reductions in health care costs that another study does not include in its estimates of the savings that result from treatment.

marijuana possession laws (Reuter, 2009). This intrusion into the internal affairs of another country does provide, however, a fine example of how the weapons and tactics used in this "war" fail to work. For example, following the invasion of Afghanistan by U.S. armed forces an estimated $800 million per year was spent to eliminate the problem of illegal opium poppy cultivation in that country, without any apparent benefit (U.S. Special Envoy for Afghanistan and Pakistan, Richard Holbrooke, quoted in R. Room, 2009).

In spite of the moralistic stance by those who argue against illicit drugs, the antidrug media campaigns launched with great fanfare, as well as attempts at interdiction by law enforcement agencies, the problem of illicit-drug use has continued for over a century. In the name of protecting all citizens from the drugs of abuse, constitutional rights have been ignored or circumvented. We have reached the point where the property of a citizen might now be seized with the justification that it *might* have been purchased with money obtained from illegal-drug sales. Citizens are criminally prosecuted to save themselves from the scourge of illicit-drug use, which according to the American Medical Association is a disease. Many of these prosecutions are based on weak or nonexistent evidence (English, 2009).

The effectiveness of the "war on drugs" might be seen in the fact that in the early 1950's, when the population of the United States was approximately half of its current level, only 60,000 people were estimated to be addicted to narcotics (Ropper & Brown, 2005). In the time since then the United States has spent $2.5 *trillion*[19] (D. W. Fleming & Grey, 2008). Currently the population of the United States is a little more than double what it was in the early 1950's, and there are not the 120,000 people addicted to narcotics that one would expect if one simply doubled the 1950's population figure, but 1 *million* opioid-dependent people in the United States (Hasemyer, 2006; Tinsley, 2005). In spite of the massive expenditure of time, energy, and personnel on the "war on drugs," substance abusers spend more money for illicit drugs now than they do for cigarettes in the United States each year (Debusmann, 2006; Dobbs, 2007, Schlosser, 2003). These statistics hardly reflect a resounding success.

The failure of the "war on drugs" should not come as a surprise: We are fighting the war on both fronts. Collectively, we create the demand for illicit compounds, then spend billions of dollars to interdict the

compounds produced to meet this demand, and spend even more money to prosecute those who abuse these compounds and are arrested. We do so in spite of the awareness that past legislative and legal efforts to control illicit-substance use have all failed (McPherson, Yudko, Murray-Bridges et al., 2009). Rather than change a failed social policy, however, politicians blindly follow the same path, hoping for a different outcome.[20] This reflects, in part, the tendency for politicians to ignore scientific evidence in favor of "pander[ing] to public prejudice" (Nutt, 2009, p. 5).

A recent survey by the Hazelden Foundation revealed that 79% of those people sampled believe that the "war on drugs" has *not* been effective ("Americans Want Insurance to Cover Addiction; Unsure If It Does," 2009). Interdiction efforts have been so successful that there are 66% *more* hard-core drug addicts at the start of the 21st century than there were at the start of the last decade of the 20th century (Falco, 2005). Incarceration has also proven to be a magnificent success: In 1972 it was estimated that there were 200,000 jail and prison cells[21] in the United States, and a quarter of a century later there are *2 million* jail and prison cells in this country (Pepper, 2004). In spite of this fact, ever-growing numbers of people start to abuse drugs each year, politicians continue to maintain that it is possible for society to arrest its way out of the drug abuse problem, and the methodology used in this "war" does not seem to work. Yet the current policy continues.

The Drug War as Political Nonsense:

The analogy that can be made between the fairy tale "The Emperors' New Clothes" and the war on drugs is striking. The program has been shown to be a dismal failure, but nobody wants to say this publicly. Perhaps this is because the war on drugs is designed to give the *illusion* that politicians are doing *something* about this social problem, without having to face reality: It is our *demand* for drugs that is the foundation for the illicit-drug trade. As Delingpole (2009) noted, "In politics, unfortunately, fashion counts for rather more than integrity or ideology" (p. 9).

If politicians truly wanted to protect society from the dangers of substance abuse, then they would

---

[19]A trillion is a thousand billion, and a billion is a thousand million.

[20]One definition of insanity is doing the same thing over and over, hoping for a different outcome—which says something about the current "war on drugs," does it not?

[21]Jails are usually incarceration facilities at the county level. Prisons are incarceration facilities at either the state or federal level.

address the most destructive compounds being used today: cigarettes and alcohol. However, the focus of the war on drugs is on those mind-altering agents that do not make a profit for the large corporations who can hire lobbyists (Rasmussen, 2008). Collectively, alcohol and tobacco products cause or contribute to the deaths of almost 1 million people a year in the United States alone. Is it a coincidence that these industries also make lavish contributions to both major political parties on a regular basis? Cocaine, marijuana, heroin, and methamphetamine dealers do not make contributions to political parties, and their products are, by coincidence, classified as illegal.[22]

It is not the purpose of the preceding paragraph to argue that political contributions by what might loosely be called the "alcohol" or the "tobacco" industries are wrong. This is the political system in which we live. However, it *is* the purpose of the preceding paragraph (and the rest of this chapter) to make the reader question *why* the policies that are in place remain in place. A welcome voice of reason was offered by the U.S. Conference of Mayors, who publicly announced that the war on drugs was a failure (Curley, 2007).

Politicians do not listen to the voice of reason. Rather, they use the "it will happen to everybody" approach to generate the hysteria necessary to allow them to justify the war on drugs (Delingpole, 2009; Reuter, 2009). Dissenting voices must be suppressed, just as they were when Adolf Hitler first came to power in Germany in the 1930s. For example, the original draft of the federal Omnibus Crime Bill called for people who criticized the federal government's antidrug policies to be charged with *treason* and to be criminally prosecuted for that offense (Leavitt, 2003). The chairperson of the United Kingdom's Advisory Council on the Misuse of Drugs was dismissed in 2009 after voicing opinions that went counter to those of the government ("Drug Disarray," 2009).

Part Summary

To date, each of the corner posts of the war on drugs has achieved some degree of success and a significant degree of failure. It has been found that the more successful interdiction efforts prove to be, the higher the profit margin for smugglers and the greater the incentive for others to enter the drug distribution or sales business. It has proven impossible for society to arrest its way out of the drug abuse problem, and although treatment holds some degree of promise, it is also not the ultimate answer to the problem of drug use disorders sweeping across this country. Further, society does not address the issue that it is the demand for illicit drugs that fuels the "crisis" in illicit-drug use. Thus the war on drugs does not really address the basic problems in society that help to cause the problem, and those who openly call the war on drugs a failure are ignored, or their views are called unrealistic by those already committed to the same policies that have proven to be such a dismal failure.

The War on Drugs as a Drain on National Resources

Remember that incarceration is one of the centerpieces of the war on drugs. Having caught the drug distributors or users, prosecuted them, and convicted them, the question becomes one of what to do next? Incarceration is the answer, and it has been used with a vengeance: The expense of "treating" individuals with substance use disorders through the criminal justice system costs more than the SUD does to the individual or society (R. S. King, 2006). Currently many states are spending more on the construction of new jail or prison cells than they are on building college classrooms (Brust, 2004; M. L. Taylor, 2004).

An unintended consequence of the war on drugs is that the various states and communities become dependent on the salaries paid to those who staff the prisons built to house the influx of drug offenders. The same is true for construction companies that are contracted to build the new prisons. These agencies and states then have an impetus to maintain the current war on drugs. This is clearly seen in the repeated efforts by the DEA to keep marijuana classified as a controlled substance: If it were legalized, the number of illicit-drug users would be reduced from approximately 13 million people[23] to 3 million, making it hard for the DEA to justify its large budget to Congress (Walton, 2002). This is an example of how various agencies come to depend on the grants handed out by the federal and state governments for funding.

Other Consequences of the Prohibition Against Drug Abuse

Medical sociologists have observed that, because of existing prohibitions against the use of illicit drugs, abusers must use their limited supply of drugs under

---

[22]There is a lesson here, but I am not the one who suggested it!

[23]The number of illicit-drug abusers if marijuana abusers are included, as opposed to the number of illicit-drug abusers if marijuana abusers are no longer counted.

hazardous conditions. Some of the consequences include an increased risk of death for heroin abusers (6–20 times higher than for the general population) (Drummer & Odell, 2001). Some of the causes of death for intravenous drug abusers, for example, include drug overdose, infections (including AIDS), malnutrition, accidents, homicide, and suicide. The medical treatment of those who abuse illicit drugs and then develop associated illnesses is an indirect cost of the war on drugs, as is the social support(s) necessary for the families of those who are illicit-drug abusers.

An interesting social experiment involving the effort to address the illicit-drug problem was carried out in Portugal in 2001. The drug laws were revised so that they were less harsh and punishments proportional to the crime. Although the level of illicit-drug use remained approximately the same, the demand on the health care system for substance-related illness and deaths from illicit-drug use dropped (Nutt, 2009). This is not to say that illicit-drug use should be tolerated, but it does illustrate the consequences of the application of legal sanctions to address this social problem.

The Law and Morality: Where to Draw the Line?

In the modern war on drugs, federal and state authorities have applied legal sanctions against individuals who wish to use any of a long list of chemicals, or, in the case of alcohol, to use it beyond certain limits. If, as the American Medical Association argues, the substance use disorders are disease states, then these legal sanctions essentially turn these diseased people into criminals. However, the law is selective: Only certain substances or certain euphoric states are deemed worthy of criminal prosecution (Husak, 2004). Caffeine users, for example, achieve a drug-induced psychological state without fear of arrest or incarceration. Long-distance runners achieve the "runner's high" without fear of legal consequences (Husak, 2004). Drinkers, as long as they do not drive a motor vehicle while intoxicated or commit other crimes, can ingest alcohol to achieve a desired state of intoxication without fear of arrest.[24]

In the early 21st century, the line between legitimate medical purposes and recreational substance use has become rather uncertain. Some people will use a prescribed medication (let us use diazepam as an example)

to achieve a desired mood state, but if other people were to take the same medication without a prescription to achieve the same mood state, they could be charged with a crime (Husak, 2004). Should this be the case? It has been argued that personal, recreational drug use (as opposed to distribution of illicit chemicals to others) is a consensual crime. Are euphoric mood states grounds for legal sanctions? At what point does medical necessity blend into recreational drug use? If a man were to suffer from a clear case of erectile dysfunction, the prescribed use of a compound such as Viagra® would be appropriate. However, if another man were to ingest the same compound simply to enhance sexual performance, would this be grounds for criminal prosecution?[25] Both individuals may have obtained the same compound by prescription from a licensed physician, but where is the line between legitimate medical need and recreational use of that compound? As Rasmussen (2008) observed:

> The myth of a sharp divide between medical and nonmedical "recreational" drug use began to weaken. Some of the pharmaceuticals that people get from our modern medicine men suddenly began looking a lot like the illegal drugs that people take in alternative manners; perhaps some street "abusers" were actually self-medicating, and some legitimate patients were merely junkies hooked by the doctors and drug firms. (p. 175)

Imagine three hypothetical business executives. One will drink a martini(s) to relax after a hard day's work. The second will ingest a diazepam tablet for the same reason, whereas the last hypothetical person smokes marijuana at the end of the workday. The legal system tends to be exceptionally selective about where to draw the line, while failing to provide any rationale for this decision. If people use the wrong chemical to achieve a desired state of mind, they could be ruined by the legal consequences of that decision. Thus the war on drugs might be viewed as a war on those who attempt to alter their state of consciousness in socially unacceptable ways. The understanding of this reality may have helped the drug czar to reexamine the manner in which the United States attempts to deal with the U.S. drug abuse problem through referrals to treatment rather than incarceration (G. Fields, 2009).

---

[24]This assumes that the individual is not on bond, probation, or parole. In many cases, probation or parole agreements stipulate that the individual not ingest alcohol or illicit drugs as one of the conditions of the bond agreement, probation, or parole.

[25]Before you answer this question, there is evidence that sexual performance enhancement compounds are commonly abused by college students for recreational purposes. Should they be prosecuted for "criminal" activity?

The Debate Over Medicalization of Marijuana

Some of the compounds commonly abused today are accepted pharmaceutical agents. The benzodiazepines are one such group of compounds, and within certain limits so is cocaine. The amphetamine compounds are used to treat attention deficit-hyperactivity disorder (ADHD) in certain cases, as is methylphenidate. But if the subject of the medicalization of marijuana is raised, people immediately equate this with *legalization*, although the two are far different states. In reality, the medicalization of marijuana would simply place it on an equal footing with other accepted pharmaceuticals and allow researchers to identify components in marijuana that might be of value to health care professionals. As is true today for the other pharmaceuticals, the possession of any of these compounds without a prescription would be grounds for legal prosecution. The relationship between medicalization and legalization might best be viewed as shown in Figure 38-1.

Unfortunately, the federal government has maintained a stance that even doing basic research into possible medical applications of marijuana is illegal. They argue that (a) there are no *proven* uses for marijuana, and (b) you are forbidden to do research into possible medical applications of any compound found in the marijuana plant because of (a). Further, the issue has become even more complicated. The DEA recently threatened to suspend a physician's license to write prescriptions for supposedly writing prescriptions for certain illicit compounds, but the courts ruled that this was a violation of the physician's First Amendment rights under the Bill of Rights ("Medical Reprieve," 2003). This issue will be the subject of much debate for many years.

Legalization

Should marijuana be legalized? In the Netherlands, marijuana use is acceptable, and individuals are allowed to have small amounts of marijuana for personal use, if it was purchased in a government-approved coffee house. There is a tax placed on marijuana, providing a source of revenue. Illicit-drug distributors are still subject to arrest and prosecution, however. Thus the government-sanctioned use of marijuana is within strict limits, and the full power of the State is still applied to those who sell and distribute illicit marijuana.

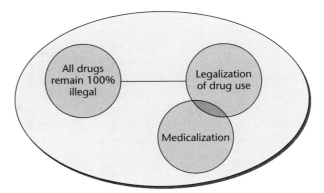

FIGURE 38-1 Medicalization and Legalization as Two Different Concepts

If you but breathe the word *legalization*, however, you are instantly engulfed by a multitude of political agendas, half truths, and illogical ideas, not the least of which is that you are "soft on crime." The war on drugs has deteriorated to the point where the *military* has been recruited to help law enforcement agencies stem the flow of drugs flowing into this country to meet the demand created by a minority of its citizens. Although the Obama administration's drug czar, Gil Kerlikowske, said that that "we're not at war with the people in this country" (quoted in G. Fields, 2009), the military is still involved in an attempt to stem the tide of illicit drugs to citizens who wish to alter their state of consciousness (Walton, 2002).

Proponents of the legalization of marijuana point out that such legalization, even with strict controls such as those put into place in the Netherlands, would remove a source of income from what is loosely called "organized crime." The appropriate taxes might serve as a source of an additional $33 billion per year in revenue for the government, which is hardly an insignificant amount[26] (Cafferty, 2009). Further, there is evidence that marijuana would soon lose its appeal to adolescents and young adults, many of whom use this compound as a form of rebellion (A. Barr, 1999). It has been argued that "if the appeal of drugs lies in their prohibited status, then we must expect that cannabis will soon be as fascinating as a new set of tax guidelines [if decriminalized]" (Walton, 2002, p. 137).

Walton did admit that there would possibly be a short-term increase in the number of marijuana

---

[26]Or, given the casual manner in which politicians in Washington toss around budgets of trillions of dollars (each $1 trillion is a thousand billion dollars), perhaps this figure is meaningless.

abusers, but as time passed the number of marijuana abusers would probably go down as marijuana would lose its appeal to many of those who are drawn to it now because it is illegal. As Greenwald (2009) noted, "The central myth which shields our failed drug laws from challenge and scrutiny is that decriminalization or legalization will cause an explosion of increased drug use. That is patently false" (p. 23). The author bases his conclusion on the recent decriminalization of drugs in Portugal, which did not result in a major increase in drug abuse. The legalization of at least marijuana has been tried in various countries in Europe, but those who set policy in this country have turned a blind eye to these alternative responses to the problem of illicit-drug abuse in this country.

Chapter Summary

Historically, the war on drugs is based on four legs: (a) elimination of illicit compounds through destruction of raw materials, (b) the interdiction of drugs being shipped to this country, (c) legal sanctions against those who engage in the use of the substances deemed illegal by the government, and apparently if all else fails (d) treatment of those addicted to these compounds. These policies have failed miserably in spite of an expenditure of $2.5 *trillion* since 1950 on the war on drugs.

Future historians may well conclude that the only groups to benefit from the war on drugs are (a) those involved in the illicit-drug trade, (b) street gangs involved in the daily distribution of the drugs and who profit from their sale, (c) the government employees whose job depends on the war on drugs, (d) politicians who talk about "getting tough" on crime by stamping down on the illicit-drug abuser, (e) construction company employees, whose jobs depend on building the prisons to house those convicted of drug-related offenses, (f) people hired to staff the aforementioned prisons, (g) various police departments, who have come to be dependent on the federal and state subsidies to fight the war on drugs, and (h) the terrorist groups who benefit from the sale of illegal drugs to fund their own activities.

The question of whether or not illegal drugs should be legalized and under what conditions is a social issue, not a medical one (Brust, 2004). There are many who argue that society should blindly "stay the course," even if that course is toward the shoals of financial ruin and social upheaval. It is clear that society cannot arrest its way out of the current situation, nor can it provide enough treatment beds (this assumes that the treatment would be effective the first time, and that the user not relapse, which further compounds the problem). There are no clear answers. It is not clear how to proceed or what new social policies might be required to address this social dilemma. However, as has been demonstrated in this chapter, there is a need for a long, *honest* examination of existing policies to find those that work and those that should be either modified or dismantled.

Sample Assessment:
Alcohol Abuse Situation

History and Identifying Information

Mr. John D_____[1] is a 35-year-old married white male from _____ County, Missouri. He is employed as an electrical engineer for the XXXXX Company, where he has worked for the last 3 years. Prior to this, Mr. D_____ was in the U.S. Navy, where he served for 4 years. He was discharged under honorable conditions and reported that he had only "a few" minor rules infractions. He was never brought before a court-martial, according to Mr. D_____.

Circumstances of Referral

Mr. D_____ was seen after having been arrested for driving while under the influence of alcohol. Mr. D_____ reported that he had been drinking with coworkers to celebrate a promotion at work. His measured blood alcohol level (BAL) was 0.150, well above the legal limit necessary for a charge of driving while under the influence. Mr. D_____ reported that he had "seven or eight" mixed drinks in approximately a 2-hour time span. By his report, he was arrested within a quarter hour of the time that he left the bar. After his initial court appearance, Mr. D_____ was referred to this evaluator by the court to determine whether Mr. D_____ has a chemical dependency problem.

Drug and Alcohol Use History

Mr. D_____ reports that he first began to drink at the age of 15, when he and a friend would steal beer from his father's supply in the basement. He would drink an occasional beer from time to time after that and first became intoxicated when he was 17, by Mr. D_____'s report.

When he was 18, Mr. D_____ enlisted in the U.S. Navy, and after basic training he was stationed in the San Diego area. Mr. D_____ reported that he was first exposed to chemicals while he was stationed in San Diego and that he tried both marijuana and cocaine while on weekend liberty. Mr. D_____ reported that he did not like the effects of cocaine and that he used this chemical only once or twice. He did like the effects of marijuana and reported that he would smoke one or two marijuana cigarettes obtained from friends perhaps once a month.

During this portion of his life, Mr. D_____ reports that he would drink about twice a weekend, when on liberty. The amount that he would drink ranged from "1 or 2 beers" to 12 or 18 beers. Mr. D_____ reported that he first had an alcohol-related blackout while he was in the Navy and that he "should" have been arrested for driving on base while under the influence of alcohol on several different occasions but was never stopped by the Shore Patrol.

Following his discharge from the Navy under honorable conditions at the age of 22, Mr. D_____ enrolled in college. His chemical use declined to the weekend use of alcohol, usually in moderation, but Mr. D_____ reported that he did drink to the point of an alcohol-related blackout "once or twice" in the 4 years that he was in college. There was no other

---

[1]This case is entirely fictitious. No similarity between any person, living or dead, is intended or should be inferred.

chemical use following his discharge from the Navy, and Mr. D_____ reports that he has not used other chemicals since the age of 20 or 21.

Upon graduation, at the age of 26, Mr. D_____ began to work for the XXXXX Company, where he is employed now. He met his wife shortly after he began work for the XXXXX Company, and they were married after a courtship of 1 year. Mr. D_____'s wife, Pat, does not use chemicals other than an "occasional" social drink. Exploration of this revealed that Mrs. D_____ will drink a glass of wine with a meal about twice a month. She denied other chemical use.

Mrs. D_____ reported that her husband does not usually drink more than one or two beers, and that he will drink only on weekends. She reported that the night he was arrested was "unusual" for him, in the sense that he is not a drinker. His employer was not contacted, but court records failed to reveal any other arrest records for Mr. D_____.

Mr. D_____ admitted to several alcohol-related blackouts, but none since he was in college. He denied seizures, DTs, or alcohol-related tremor. There was no evidence of ulcers, gastritis, or cardiac problems noted. His last physical was "normal" according to information provided by his personal physician. There were no abnormal blood chemistry findings, nor did his physician find any evidence suggesting alcoholism. Mr. D_____ denied having ever been hospitalized for an alcohol-related injury, and there was no evidence suggesting that he has been involved in fights.

On the Michigan Alcoholism Screening Test, Mr. D_____'s score of four (4) points would not suggest alcoholism. This information was reviewed in the presence of his wife, who did not suggest that there was any misrepresentation on his test scores. On this administration of the MMPI, there was no evidence of psychopathology noted. Mr. D_____'s MacAndrew Alcoholism Scale score fell in the normal range, failing to suggest an addictive disorder at this time.

Psychiatric History

Mr. D_____ denied psychiatric treatment of any kind. He did admit to having seen a marriage counselor "once" shortly after he married, but reported that overall he and his wife are happy together. Apparently, they had a question about a marital communications issue that was cleared up after one visit, which took place after 3 or 4 years of marriage.

Summary and Conclusions

At this time, there is little evidence to suggest an on-going alcohol problem. Mr. D_____ would seem to be a well-adjusted young man, who drank to the point of excess after having been offered a long-desired promotion at work. This would seem to be an unusual occurrence for Mr. D_____, who usually limits his drinking to one or two beers on the weekends. There was no evidence of alcohol-related injuries, accidents, or legal problems noted.

Recommendations

Recommend a light sentence, possibly a fine, limited probation, with no restrictions on license. It is also recommended that Mr. D_____ attend "DWI School" for 8 weeks to learn more about the effects of alcohol on driving.

The "Jellinek" Chart for Alcoholism

Following the publication of earlier editions of *Concepts of Chemical Dependency,* questions were raised concerning my decision not to mention the so-called Jellinek chart in this text. This chart, which is viewed as gospel within the alcohol/drug rehabilitation industry, purports to show the progression from social drinking to alcoholism, then on to recovery. Since the time of its introduction, the chart has been used to illustrate the "unalterable" progression of alcoholism to countless patients who were in the earlier stages of alcohol use problems, as well as to browbeat reluctant individuals into accepting the need for help with their supposed drinking problem. Variations of the chart have been developed for compulsive gambling, steroid abuse, compulsive spending, both heroin and cocaine addiction, and countless other disorders. An example of this chart is shown in Figure A2-1.

The problem is that Jellinek did *not* devise this chart! Even though it is often attributed to him, the chart is actually the work of Dr. Maxwell Glatt, a British physician who was so taken by Jellinek's work that he operationalized the *gamma* subtype of alcoholism in chart form. The chart, which addresses *only* the gamma subtype of alcoholism as suggested by Jellinek (1960), has mistakenly been accepted by countless alcohol/drug rehabilitation professionals as *the* chart that identifies the progression of *all* forms of alcoholism. As a result of this mistake many patients in rehabilitation programs, whose symptoms of alcohol use problems did not "fit" the progression of symptoms suggested in the chart, have been subjected to countless hours of confrontation because they were "in denial." Rather than perpetuate this misunderstanding, I decided not to make any reference to this chart in the text of *Concepts of Chemical Dependency.*

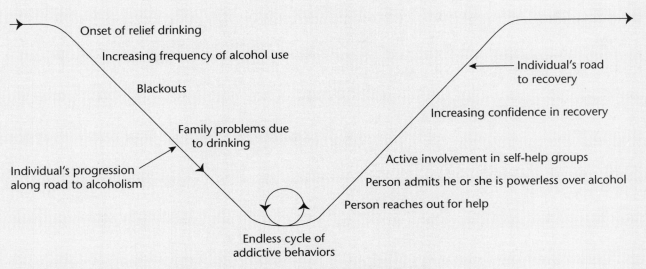

FIGURE A2-1 Alcohol Progression Chart Often Mistakenly Called the "Jellinek" Chart

Classes of Antiviral Drugs Currently in Use to Treat HIV Infection

Nucleoside/nucleotide analogs:	Compounds act as DNA chain termination agents, inhibiting the transcription of viral RNA into DNA in cells infected with the HIV-1 virus, thus inhibiting viral replication.
Non-nucleoside reverse transcriptase inhibitors:	Compounds that bind to and inhibit the action of the enzyme reverse transcriptase, which is essential for viral replication in infected cells.
Protease inhibitors:	Chemicals that block the action of a protein known as viral protease, which is necessary for viral replication.
Fusion inhibitors:	Compounds that block the protein complex on the host cell that the HIV-1 virus uses to bind to the cell wall.
Integrase inhibitors:	New class of antiviral agents designed to block the process by which the HIV-1 virus inserts DNA into host cell, forcing it to begin to manufacture copies of the HIV-1 virus to infect other cells.
Chemokine (C-Cmotif) inhibitors:	New class of antiviral agents that block effects of protein molecules in host cell wall (chemokine) that "pull" the molecular walls of the host cell and the virus together, allowing them to merge and thus fusion to occur.
Maturation inhibitors:	New class of antiviral agents under development. Maturation inhibitors interfere with the formation of a protein shell that normally surrounds the "daughter" virus particles, thus preventing full maturation and blocking the process by which new cells will be infected with the daughter virus particles once released.

Drug Classification Schedules

The Comprehensive Drug Abuse Prevention and Control Act of 1970 provided for the classification of all compounds into one of five categories, depending on their abuse potential and medical applications. It is one of the most confusing aspects of drug rehabilitation work for health care and drug rehabilitation professionals. It is also the system by which drugs are identified for legal prosecution. This classification system is based not on the pharmacological properties of a compound, but on its perceived abuse potential, and as noted all pharmaceuticals are classified as falling into one of five categories by the Drug Enforcement Administration (McPherson, Yudko, Murray-Bridges et al., 2009):

SCHEDULE	DEFINITION AND EXAMPLES
Schedule I compounds	Compounds with no recognized medical use. Examples: marijuana, LSD, MDMA, heroin
Schedule II compounds	Compounds with a recognized medical use, but with a very high abuse potential. Examples: morphine, amphetamine compounds
Schedule III compounds	Compounds with recognized medical use, but with a moderate abuse potential. Examples: ketamine, codeine
Schedule IV compounds	Compounds with recognized medical use, but with a mild abuse potential. Examples: phenobarbital, benzodiazepine compounds
Schedule V compounds	Compounds with recognized medical use, but with a low abuse potential. Example: buprenorphine

The Twelve Steps of Alcoholics Anonymous[1]

STEP ONE: We admitted that we were powerless over alcohol—that our lives had become unmanageable.

STEP TWO: Came to believe that a power greater than ourselves could restore us to sanity.

STEP THREE: Made a decision to turn our will and our lives over to the care of God as we understood Him.

STEP FOUR: Made a searching and fearless moral inventory of ourselves.

STEP FIVE: Admitted to God, to ourselves, and to another human being the exact nature of our wrongs.

STEP SIX: Were entirely ready to have God remove all these defects of character.

STEP SEVEN: Humbly asked Him to remove our shortcomings.

STEP EIGHT: Made a list of all persons we had harmed, and became willing to make amends to them all.

STEP NINE: Made direct amends to such people wherever possible, except where to do so would injure them or others.

STEP TEN: Continued to take personal inventory and when we were wrong, promptly admitted it.

STEP ELEVEN: Sought through prayer and meditation to improve our conscious contact with God as we understood Him, praying only for knowledge of His will for us, and the power to carry that out.

STEP TWELVE: Having had a spiritual awakening as a result of these steps, we tried to carry this message to alcoholics and to practice these principles in all our affairs.

---

[1]Reproduced with the kind permission of Alcoholics Anonymous World Services, Inc.

Glossary

Acetaldehyde Toxic compound, possibly carcinogenic, that is produced during the process of alcohol biotransformation and cigarette smoking. The biotransformation of acetaldehyde is blocked by disulfiram, making the individual who has consumed alcohol feel ill, which in theory should reduce the desire to drink.

Acetylcholine One of the major neurotransmitters. It is found mainly in the peripheral regions of the body, as acetylcholine carries out such functions as alerting the body to perceived danger, and the coordination of motor control functions. It also seems to be involved in the process of transmitting motor movement commands from the brain to the specific muscles involved in that action.

Adipose tissue Fat tissue.

ADLs Activities of daily living such as cooking, being able to dress one's self appropriately, handle financial decisions, and so on.

Agonist A chemical that activates a receptor site in a cell wall.

Albumin One of the primary protein molecules found in the general circulation.

Alcohol use disorder A term that is applied to individuals whose use of alcohol is far in excess of the norms for their social or cultural group. This term is slowly gaining popularity over the older terms *alcohol abuse* and *alcoholism*, in part because it is more inclusive, and it lacks the social stigma of these other terms.

Allele A variation of a gene.

Alveolar Pertaining to the little pockets in the lungs where the process of oxygen/carbon dioxide exchange is carried out.

Amnesia See: *Retrograde amnesia* or *anterograde amnesia.*

Amygdala A region in the brain that is shaped like an almond, located in each temporal lobe. This region is thought to be involved in the process of attaching emotional context to memory, and modulating emotional responses to external reality. This includes behaviors centered on the process of obtaining reward(s), and on the anxiety and panic responses.

Analog A chemical that is a variation of the chemical structure of another compound, producing a "new" drug. The original compound is known as the *parent* compound, whereas the variation is known as an *analog* of the parent compound.

Angina Pain in the heart caused by the muscle tissue of the heart suffering damage through a reduction in blood flow to that tissue.

Anhedonia Inability of people to take pleasure in activities that they once enjoyed. This condition is a feature of some personality disorders, major depression, and schizophrenia, and is seen in the drug withdrawal syndrome from various drugs of abuse.

Anorexia Loss of desire to eat for an extended period of time, thus resulting in weight loss.

Anorexic To cause a state of anorexia.

Anterograde amnesia Inability to remember events after a specific point in time. This condition usually results from any of a wide range of forms of neurological trauma or from a wide range of chemical compounds.

Alcohol-induced "blackouts" are a form of chemically induced state of anterograde amnesia. Other medications, such as Versed, a benzodiazepine often used in "conscious sedation" medical procedures, and Ketamine, also can induce this same effect.

Traumatic brain injury may also induce anterograde amnesia. It is not uncommon for patients who have been in a motor vehicle accident to assert that they could not remember events for the first few hours or days after the accident. It should be pointed out that anterograde and retrograde amnesia are not mutually exclusive and may coexist in the same patient.

Antidipsotrophic   An obsolete term used to identify compounds that would combat dipsomania, or chronic alcohol use.

Antipyretic   Against fever.

Antitussive   Agent used to control cough.

Anxiolytic   A compound that reduces the individual's subjective anxiety level.

Arteritis   Inflammation of an artery.

Aspirative pneumonia   A form of pneumonia that results when the individual aspirates stomach contents into the lungs during the process of vomiting. Bartlett (1999) identified two necessary components: (a) the aspiration of stomach contents into the lungs as a result of a breakdown of normal body defenses designed to prevent this, and (b) damage to lung tissue from gastric juices or bacterial infection.

Astrocytes   A form of glial cell in the brain that helps to provide physical support to the structure of the brain, as well as possibly play a role in the transfer of molecules from the blood to the neurons of the central nervous system (CNS)

Ataxia   Inability to properly coordinate muscle movements.

Attention deficit hyperactivity disorder (ADHD)
Behavioral disorder in which the individual lacks the ability to focus attention on the task at hand. There are two subtypes: the *inattentive* variety and the *hyperactive* variety. The latter is more often diagnosed, because children with this disorder are more likely to be recognized. It has been estimated that 3% of the children with ADHD will "mature out" of this condition each year, with the result being that for many individuals ADHD continues well into adulthood.

AUD   Abbreviation for *alcohol use disorder*.

Auto-amputation   A phenomenon in which the body essentially blocks the circulation to a limb so that the tissue dies. In the case of a limb, it will actually fall off. This is seen in cases of severe trauma, infection, or as a side effect of some chemicals.

Bacon, Roger   B. 1214 (?) - d. 1294. English friar, scientist, and philosopher.

Bibliotherapy   Use of assigned readings to help the client to better understand different concepts presented in individual or group therapy sessions.

Black market   System through which products are obtained outside of normal channels and then sold to those who are willing to pay for them for profit.

Blood–brain barrier   A structural component of blood vessels in the brain that blocks the passage of many toxins, bacteria, and other substances that might cause harm to the brain.

Body packers   Individuals who will ingest a compound, usually cocaine, wrapped in multiple condoms, in an attempt to smuggle the compound into a country such as the United States within their body. If one of the packages should rupture, the "packers" will be exposed to massive amounts of cocaine, probably with terminal results.

Cannabinoids   Compounds that are manufactured and used in the brain to regulate neurotransmission, especially the *dopaminergic* neurons.

Cardiomyopathy   Technically any disease of the myocardium, or the muscle tissue of the heart.

Catecholamines   A family of compounds, including epinephrine, a compound normally produced by the adrenal glands, and the neurotransmitters norepinephrine and dopamine. These compounds help to regulate various body functions. Norepinephrine, for example, functions as a neurotransmitter in the brain.

Cerebellar ataxia   Loss of motor coordination and balance caused by damage to the cerebrum.

Cerebellar atrophy   Shrinkage in the overall size of the cerebellum due to death of neurons in this region of the brain.

Cerebellum   In terms of the total number of neurons, the cerebellum is the largest part of the brain, in spite of its relatively small size. It is involved in the process of coordinating motor activities in the body.

Certified Medical Review Officer (CMRO)   Physician who has been trained in the interpretation of urine toxicology test results. The CMRO is also responsible for the integrity of the urine toxicology testing procedures utilized for interpretation of unexpected test results, and is charged with maintenance of patient confidentiality in testing process.

Cilia   Microscopic hairlike projections from the wall of various body organs, including the lungs, where they help to propel mucus to the top of the lungs, helping to expel foreign particles from the lungs.

Conduct disorders   A childhood condition marked by behavioral dyscontrol, acting-out behaviors, and sometimes poor academic achievement, in a child of normal intelligence.

Confabulation   A neurological disorder in which individuals are (a) unable to remember part of their past and (b) will make up a history. Without collateral information, individuals' rendition of their past might actually seem plausible in many cases, making the need for collateral information imperative to detect such cases.

Causes of confabulation include (but are not limited to) Korsakoff's syndrome. Thus it is imperative that the assessor rule out other possible causes of confabulation before assuming that it is alcohol related.

Contingency management   Process through which a person with a substance use disorder is trained to identify high-risk situations in advance, and then practices coping mechanisms to avoid relapsing.

Corticogenesis   Production and maturation of new neurons in the cortex region of the brain.

Cortisol   Enzyme normally found in the body, which is found at higher levels during times of stress. It is often referred to as a stress-fighting compound because of this.

C-reactive protein   Protein molecule involved in inflammatory response.

Creatinine   Waste product of muscle activity. This level is usually constant. Laboratories have established cut-off levels above or below which the urine is assessed as being suspicious because of abnormal creatinine levels.

Cross-tolerance   Process through which an individual's tolerance to one compound, say alprazolam, is transferred to other compounds in the same class, such as diazepam, as well as to similar compounds such as ethyl alcohol (all of which, in the example provided, are CNS depressants).

Cyclooxygenase   An enzyme involved in the process of prostaglandin production. One form of cyclooxygenase (COX-1) is involved in the regulation of kidney and stomach functions, where it carries out a protective function.

The second form of cyclooxygenase (COX-2) is produced by body tissues when damaged. About 60% of the chemical structure of COX-1 and COX-2 is the same. Unfortunately, the shared elements of the molecule is what is blocked by NSAIDs, which function as nonselective COX inhibitors. By blocking the action of both forms of cyclooxygenase, the NSAIDs interfere with the normal function of COX-1, when it is the effect of COX-2 that prompted the use of the NSAID. It is for this reason that patients with hypertension are advised not to use an NSAID unless directed to do so by a physician, or why patients taking aspirin for inflammation might suffer gastrointestinal damage, for example.

ΔFosB   A compound found in neurons that controls the process of manufacturing proteins within the neuron. ΔFosB is one of the *genetic transcription factors* that control when or if certain genes within the neuron become active, and is thought to be involved in the process of memory formation in some manner, possibly through the activation of certain genes in response to environmental experience(s).

Delta FosB   See: *ΔFosB*.

Diaphoresis   Perspiration, especially copious amounts.

Dimorphism   See: *Sexual dimorphism*.

Dissimulation   A situation where the client provides false information in response to a question or test item.

Doctor making   See: *Doctor shopping*.

Doctor shopping   Slang term for going to a number of different physicians until substance abusers find one who agrees that they might have a given condition and is willing to prescribe a desired substance for the treatment of a nonexistent or exaggerated condition.

Dopamine   Neurotransmitter utilized in the brain for such tasks as controlling behavior and mood, motivation and reward, learning, and some psychomotor functions, as well as being involved in the reward cascade.

Dopaminergic Nerve cells that use dopamine as their primary neurotransmitter.

Dysentery A painful infection of the lower intestinal tract, usually caused by the ingestion of contaminated water. The infected person will develop massive diarrhea, sometimes intermixed with blood and mucus. Unless the fluid loss caused by the diarrhea is rapidly controlled, dysentery can prove to be fatal after only a short period of time. Dysentery was common in the crowded, unsanitary military camps of the 1700s and 1800s, as well as in many cities throughout history, and major epidemics of dysentery were recorded throughout history before the cause of the disorder was identified.

Dysphoria Feelings of sadness, sorrow, depression, and so on. The opposite of *euphoria*.

Dysthymia The analogy to the former construct of "depressive neurosis" is not entirely inappropriate here. Technically, the term *dysthymia* means "ill humored." Patients with dysthymia demonstrate depressed mood that lasts most of the day and that is continuously present. Individuals will struggle with feelings of low self-esteem, guilt, inadequacy, irritability, and anger. They withdraw from others, lose interest in hobbies, and report that they have always felt depressed.

Unlike major depression, dysthymia begins early in life, often in childhood, and is most certainly present by young adulthood, although there is a subtype that does not manifest until middle age or even later in life. The symptoms must be present for at least 2 years prior to diagnosis, and the disorder has an intermittent course.

Edema Swelling of tissues immediately adjacent to injury.

Endocannabinoid One of a family of compounds bound within the brain or body where molecules of compounds found in marijuana bind. These natural, or endogenous, cannabis-like compounds carry out essential functions such as guiding the growth and neural cells in the cortex in utero and after birth, regulation of the immune system, and so on.

Enkephalins One of the family of endogenous opioids, involved in the process of regulating pain.

Epigenesis Process through which the environment impacts on how cells in the body produce protein molecules. Because this process is under the control of DNA, the environment has been found to alter the expression of cellular DNA. It has been suggested that these alterations in DNA might then be passed from one generation to the next.

Euphoric recall Tendency on the part of people to remember past experiences in a positive light, while overlooking negative experiences associated with that event(s). For example, heavy drinkers might drive by a bar, turn to their companion, and say, "Didn't we have a great time at the boss' birthday party?"—only to have the companion remind them that they both were also arrested for driving while under the influence of alcohol on the way home and both had to spend time in the county jail and pay a fine of over $1,000. These consequences are overlooked in favor of the positive memories of the night in question.

Executive functioning Essentially the ability of individuals to plan ahead, anticipate the consequences of their actions, and the like.

Externalizing disorder Cluster of psychiatric symptoms seen in the antisocial personality disorder in adults, conduct disorder in children, and/or attention deficit hyperactivity disorder (ADHD).

"Fast" metabolizer An individual whose body is, as a result of normal genetic variation(s), able to biotransform a compound more rapidly than average. This phenomenon is independent of those cases where the person is taking one compound that induces the biotransformation or metabolism of another through enzyme induction, for example.

Fillers When prepared for oral administration, pharmaceutical companies will mix the active agent with compounds designed to give the pill or capsule shape and form. These compounds are designed to be destroyed by gastric juices (thus releasing the active compound for absorption), or to break down in the gastrointestinal tract and release the active agent so that it might be absorbed.

Intravenous drug abusers who crush a pill or capsule bypass the defenses of the gastrointestinal tract, and run the risk that these "fillers" might cause a blockage in a vein or artery.

First-pass metabolism Over time, the body has developed a safety mechanism in which materials absorbed through the gastrointestinal tract are first carried to the liver, so that toxic compounds ingested might be subjected to detoxification before those compounds might injure the body. This is what is called the "first-pass metabolism" process.

Formication   The sensation of having unseen bugs crawling on or just under the skin. This sensation is often induced by large doses of some chemicals, such as the amphetamines or cocaine.

Free radicals   Molecules that, because of their ionic charge, are able to attach to and damage other molecules, thus disrupting the normal function of cells and possibly contributing to cellular death.

Free-radical molecules often contain an extra oxygen molecule, which will then "bind" to molecules found in cell walls, causing damage to them.

GABA   See: *Gamma-aminobutyric acid.*

Galactorrhea   Production of excess amounts of milk by the breast.

Gamma-amino-butyric acid   Also known as GABA. This neurotransmitter functions as the main inhibitory neurotransmitter in the brain. Approximately 20% of the receptor sites in the brain are thought to utilize GABA, including neurons in the *cortex, cerebellum, amygdala,* and *nucleus accumbens.*

It has been discovered that there are 20 subtypes of GABA receptors in the brain, and scientists are mapping the distribution pattern and function of these subtypes to better understand GABA's function in the brain.

Gastritis   Inflammation of the stomach lining.

Glial cells   There are a number of subtypes of glial cells in the brain, including Schwann cells, Muller cells, epithelial cells, oligodendrocytes, and astrocytes, to name a few. Collectively, the glial cells make up 90% of the cells in the brain. Yet for a long time they were dismissed as providing only structural and metabolic support for the neurons, which comprise 10% of the brain's mass.

Some glial cells have been found to "monitor" the neurotransmission process between neurons, and to modulate the process of neurotransmission at times. They have also been discovered to be capable of forms of intercellular communications that can utilize some of the same neurotransmitters as neurons, as well as distinctly separate forms of intercellular communications. Scientists are only now starting to understand that these cells are actively involved in the process of information processing, memory, and cellular repair following damage to the brain.

Glossitis   A very painful inflammation of the tongue.

Glucocorticoids   Class of steroids involved in the stress response process, metabolism of sugar in the body, suppression of the inflammatory response, and suppression of the immune system response.

Glutamate   A neurotransmitter that functions as an excitatory neurotransmitter within the brain. Excessive amounts of glutamate can prove to be neurotoxic, damaging or killing neurons in high doses.

Grave's disease   A dysfunction of the thyroid gland in which the thyroid produces too much thyroid hormone.

Gray matter   The neurons in the cortex of the brain appear gray during an autopsy, hence the name. In the living brain they have a vivid, reddish brown color under normal conditions, a sight that is rarely seen except by neurosurgeons.

The cortex is the region of the brain where the so-called "higher functions" such as thought and planning take place. Some regions of the cortex are also responsible for planning and initiation of psychomotor activities, speech, and hearing.

Hepatotoxicity   Toxic to the liver.

Hippocampus   A region of the brain that is thought to be involved in the processing of sensory information, as well as the formation and retrieval of memories.

HPA axis   The hypothalamus and pituitary regions of the brain along with the adrenal glands are involved in the body's response to real (or perceived) threats, ultimately increasing the release of stress-fighting hormones such as cortisol in the body.

Hyperthermia   Retention of body heat well above safe levels, which may prove fatal to the individual if not corrected before the brain is damaged by the abnormally high body temperature.

Hypokalemia   Abnormally low blood potassium levels.

Hypothalamus   Controls behaviors such as eating, fighting, sleep, and mating.

Hypothermia   Abnormally low body temperature, which if not corrected in a timely manner might result in the individual's death.

Hypnotic   A compound that can induce sleep or a sleeplike state.

Hypoxia   Reduced oxygen flow to the brain. This can result in organic brain damage if not corrected in a short period of time.

Iatrogenic   Literally, induced by a physician. This term is also often applied to conditions that are side effects of treatment of another disease, such as antibiotic-induced diarrhea where the antibiotic compound is used to treat a serious infection elsewhere in the body.

Isomer   One of two or more compounds with the same percentage of chemicals, but where the molecular structure of the chemical is slightly different.

Kindling   A process that has been called "reverse tolerance" by some scientists. Through the process of kindling, the brain becomes more and more sensitive to seizure triggers, which then initiates a seizure(s). Sometimes this process is called *sensitization.*

Law of unintended consequences   A rule that whenever a change is made, it alters the system in unforeseen ways, resulting in stressors and complications that were not expected when the original change was made.

An excellent example of this law is the application of high-cost, labor-intensive medical care to treat heart attack victims. This results in increased survival rates (the intended result), but also leaves a pool of heart attack survivors who require intensive medical monitoring afterward (unintended consequence).

Macrophage cells   Generalist cells from the immune system that help to clean up cellular debris and attack foreign cells. Macrophages are also involved in some aspect(s) of the immune response.

Meconium   A thick, green, tarlike substance that lines the intestinal tract of the fetus. This substance is usually excreted by the infant in the first few days after birth.

Occasionally, it is excreted before/during birth. If it is excreted prior to birth, physicians may try to dilute it by injecting sterile fluid into the uterus to dilute any meconium in that environment. If aspirated by the neonate during the birth process, it is called *meconium aspiration syndrome.* This is a medical emergency. Following birth it can prevent the infant's lungs from properly inflating and may cause pneumonia.

Medulla oblongata   Region of the brain, sometimes referred to as the brain stem, involved in the control of respiration and temperature regulation.

Melatonin   Hormone produced by the pineal gland in the brain, whose actions in the brain are still not well understood. It is thought that this compound plays a role in the regulation of human circadian rhythms.

Meningioma   A benign, slow-growing tumor of the central nervous system that is classified as a *space-occupying lesion* rather than an invasive tumor. Because

meningioma growth is so slow, the brain is often able to compensate for the tumor's presence. The meningioma is frequently found as an incidental discovery, such as when a patient has a C-T scan to rule out a fractured skull following a motor vehicle accident.

Meningiomas can grow over the years to an impressive size before producing symptoms that call attention to its presence. The symptoms produced by a meningioma depend on the specific location where it is located.

Microcephaly   A condition in which the baby's head is below the fifth percentile for infant head circumference for that age group.

Mnemonic   To assist memory, or make recall easier. A mnemonic device might be a series of letters that remind a person such as a health care professional to address certain issues. For example, the letters "A-B-C" remind the health care professional to immediately check the patient's *airway, breathing,* and *circulation.*

Monoamine oxidase   Enzyme produced by the brain to break down members of the neurotransmitter family known as *monoamines.*

Monoamine oxidase inhibitor   Any of a number of compounds that will block the actions of the enzyme monoamine oxidase.

Myocardial infarction   The blockage of blood to the tissue of the myocardium, which is to say the tissues of the heart. If this blood flow is not restored in a short period of time, the tissue will die. Often called a "heart attack" by the lay person.

Nalaxone   Naloxone is opioid antagonist which, because it is largely degraded by gastric acids is administered intravenously to counteract effects of a narcotic overdose.

Narcolepsy   Very rare neurological condition in which the patient will experience sudden attacks of sleep.

Necrosis   Death of body tissues.

Neuroadaptation   The process, once called "tolerance," by which the nervous system adapts to the constant presence of a foreign compound. This term is usually applied to the brain's adjustments to the constant presence of a prescribed chemical, whereas the term *tolerance* is applied to the same process when the person's body adapts to the presence of an illicit compound.

Neuroplasticity Ability of neurons to form new neural pathways in response to new experiences (what we call learning) and, to some degree, after neurological trauma.

Neurotoxin A chemical that is toxic to the neurons in the brain.

Neurotransmitter Any molecule that is released by one neuron to pass a chemical-electrical message on to the next neuron. This then causes the target neuron to respond to the chemical message passed on by the first neuron in a specific manner.

NMDA See: *N-Methyl-D-aspartate.*

N-Methyl-D-aspartate Protein that forms a receptor site in the neural wall for the excitatory neurotransmitter glutamate.

Norepinephrine One of the cat catecholamine family of neurotransmitters. In the central nervous system, norepinephrine serves a stimulatory function.

Nucleus accumbens Region of the brain thought to be responsible for reward and motivation. At one point, the nucleus accumbens was thought to be *the* reward center in the brain. It has now been discovered that environmental stimuli (both reinforcing and aversive) stimulate a release of dopamine from the nucleus accumbens, suggesting that it signals that there is a change in external environment that requires attention.

It is known that this region of the brain is involved with the process of integrating the individual's conscious activities with sensory stimuli. It is most active when the body encounters an *unexpected* event, either positive or negative. When a reward becomes anticipated, other regions of the brain seem to become involved in the reward cascade and the nucleus accumbens becomes less active.

Obstructive sleep apnea Condition in which the airway becomes blocked during sleep for longer than 10 seconds. The sleeping person must then struggle to reopen the airway, often through gasping, "snorting," or coughing. This is a medical problem that should be addressed by a physician if it is suspected to exist.

"Off-label" application The application of a pharmaceutical for a disease or condition that it is not normally licensed for. The Food and Drug Administration often will not approve an existing medication for a new use until it has conducted and/or supervised testing on the efficacy and safety of that compound in that application, a process that might take months or even years. During that time, physicians will often use the compound to treat a disease(s) or condition(s) based on research data from Europe or on anecdotal data.

Oppositional defiant disorder A behavioral disorder in which the child demonstrates temper outbursts, active refusal to comply with rules, and engage in annoying behaviors far in excess of what one would expect from the child on the basis of chronological age. There is an enduring pattern of negativistic, hostile, and defiant behaviors without the violations of social norms or rights of others.

Overpressure Above the ambient atmospheric pressure. In the case of surgical anesthetics, pure oxygen must also be supplied to the patient at overpressure, to avoid the danger of *hypoxia.*

Over-the-counter medication There are more than 100,000 compounds that can be purchased without a prescription, thus earning the title of an over-the-counter compound (Brody, 1994).

Peristalsis Rhythmic muscle contractions of the muscles that surround the intestines, pushing the ingested material through.

Pharmaceuticals (a) Compounds produced under supervision of various regulatory agencies, intended for the treatment of disease states in humans or (if veterinarian medications) animals. Such compounds are of a known potency, and purity. (b) Term applied to compounds intended for medical use that are diverted to the illicit-drug market. As such, they are often prized by drug abusers, because they are known to be pure and not adulterated as illicit drugs often are.

Pharmacokinetics The study of what happens to a compound and its effects after it is admitted into the human body. This includes the metabolites of that compound and their effect on the body as well.

Pituitary gland Structure in the brain that has been called the "master gland" in the body. It activates a number of other glands in the body through the release of hormones into the blood, thus controlling growth, to cite one example.

Polypharmacology Concurrent use of multiple agents. This may take place both in therapeutic settings and in the world of illicit-drug use. One danger of this practice is the *potentiation* or *synergistic* effect between compounds in the same class of chemicals.

Potentiation The pharmacological process through which the effects of one compound are reinforced by those of a second compound. This may prove to be fatal for the individual, if the combined effects of these chemicals overwhelms the body's normal maintenance mechanisms.

Prefrontal cortex Region of the brain that, among other things, is involved in complex cognitive and psychomotor processes including self-regulation of goal-directed behavior, working memory, problem solving, and response inhibition.

Presynaptic Involving the "upstream" neuron, which is to say the neuron that releases neurotransmitters into the synaptic junction to activate the next neuron in the neural network.

Priapism Extended, painful penile erection that may result in damage to the vasculature network of the penis, which might result in permanent erectile dysfunction.

Prime effect (of a drug) The desired effect of that compound. For example, people who have a fever might take an aspirin tablet with the goal of reducing their fever to a more tolerable level. Compare this with the *side effect* of a compound.

This is sometimes referred to as the *therapeutic effect* of that compound.

Prostaglandins Any of a family of compounds found in the body, some of which are involved in normal maintenance of body organs and some of which are involved in the inflammatory response following injury. These compounds are active in very low concentrations.

Proteinuria Presence of abnormal levels of protein in urine, which if found may indicate kidney damage or disease.

Pulmonary arteritis See: *Arteritis.*

REM "rebound" Increase in the duration and frequency of the REM sleep stage, often with intense, vivid imagery that might border on nightmares. This is thought to reflect the brain's attempt to "catch up" on lost REM sleep time from sleep deprivation or from drug-induced suppression of this stage of the sleep cycle.

Reperfusion Sudden restoration of blood flow to a region of the body that had been deprived of blood. The damage caused by the actual cessation of blood flow to that region of the body might be exacerbated by the sudden restoration of circulation to the affected cells.

Reticular activating system (RAS) A small region of the brain, possibly only 100 neurons in size, that is responsible for the individual's ability to focus attention on the task at hand.

Retrograde amnesia Inability of the individual to remember events prior to a specific time. This condition usually is the result of any of a number of forms of neurological trauma. It is not uncommon, for example, for patients to report that they were unable to remember having been in a motor vehicle accident, or that they have only incomplete memories of the accident and what happened in the moments before the accident.

Patients must be assessed individually to determine the degree to which their memory capacity has been affected. It should be pointed out that anterograde and retrograde amnesia are not mutually exclusive and may coexist in the same patient.

Reuptake pump Molecular structure located in the walls of a neuron that absorb molecules of a specific neurotransmitter after its release into the synapse, for recycling by the neuron.

Rhabdomyolysis Destruction of muscle tissue on a massive scale. When muscle tissues die, they release a compound known as myoglobin, which normally helps to store oxygen in the muscle cell.

During rhabdomyolysis, massive amounts of myoglobin are released in the circulation at once, which interferes with normal kidney function. In extreme cases this can cause kidney failure, cardiac arrhythmias, and even death.

Rig Slang term for device used for intravenous drug injection.

Sensitization effect Almost a form of "reverse" tolerance, in which the brain becomes hypersensitive to the effects of or presence of a compound (such as cocaine), causing effects such as seizures or even death from doses once easily tolerated without ill effect(s). The concept of an allergy might not be entirely inappropriate here.

Serotonergic Pertaining to or using serotonin.

Serotonin One of the major neurotransmitters found in the human brain. There are 19 known subtypes of serotonin, which are thought to control different functions in the brain.

Serotonin syndrome   A potentially life-threatening drug-induced neurological condition. In spite of the best of medical care, up to 11% of patients who develop this condition will fail to survive. Behavioral symptoms of the serotonin syndrome include irritability, confusion, increased anxiety, drowsiness, *hyperthermia, sinus tachycardia,* dilation of the pupils, nausea, muscle rigidity, and seizures.

The serotonin syndrome might develop up to 24 hours after patients start taking a medication that affects *serotonin.* In 50% of the cases, patients begin to develop the disorder within 2 hours of when they started to take the medication.

All suspected cases of serotonin syndrome should be assessed by a physician immediately as this condition can be potentially fatal. There is no specific treatment for serotonin syndrome, and the only treatment is supportive care (Boyer, 2005).

Sexual dimorphism   Subtle differences between male and female.

Side effect (of a drug)   The unintended effects of a chemical on the body. For example, if people take a dose of aspirin to reduce their fever, this is the primary effect. The ability of aspirin to also induce gastrointestinal bleeding is an undesired, or side effect of that compound.

Sleep apnea   A breathing disorder in which the individual's ability to breathe normally during sleep is disrupted. Complications of sleep apnea can include hypertension, heart rhythm disturbance, and possible death.

Sleep latency   The period of time between when people go to bed and when they finally fall asleep.

"Slow" metabolizer   As a result of normal genetic variation(s), there are individuals whose body is unable to biotransform/metabolize a compound more slowly than the average person. This phenomenon is independent of those cases where the person is taking one compound that blocks the biotransformation or metabolism of another.

Stroke   Interruption of blood flow to a region of the brain. In *ischemic* strokes, a blockage in a blood vessel forms, cutting the neurons that rely on that vessel off from the cerebral vasculature. Unless these neurons are able to draw on other blood vessels (collateral circulation), they will die. Statistically, 85% of strokes are ischemic strokes.

In a *hemorrhagic* stroke, a blood vessel in the cerebral vasculature ruptures. To prevent uncontrolled hemorrhage, the body then forms a blood clot in the damaged vessel, cutting off those neurons that depend on that vessel for access to the circulation off from oxygen and nutrients. In addition, free blood is very toxic to the neurons, so the blood that flows from the ruptured vessel causes additional damage to the brain. Statistically, about 15% of strokes are hemorrhagic strokes.

Synergistic response   A process through which two or more drugs of the same or similar mechanism of action reinforce the effects of the each other, causing a stronger-than-normal response to each compound. The synergistic effect can potentially be fatal. Often called *potentiation* between the two compounds.

Synesthesia   A phenomenon where information from one sensory modality slips over into another sensory interpretation system. People who possess this ability naturally will speak of how they are able to see colors in association with certain sounds, for example. This phenomenon, which can occur naturally in rare cases, can also be induced by some drugs of abuse.

Taper   A program in which gradually decreasing doses of a given compound are administered to patients so that they can safely be taken off that compound.

Tardive dyskinesia   Condition resulting in abnormal movements of muscles. Technically, the term *tardive* means "late," and *dyskinesia* refers to the abnormal muscle movements. This condition was often seen as a late complication of Parkinson's disease.

However, certain compounds have been found to exacerbate the development of this condition. The abnormal muscle movements previously seen only as a late complication of Parkinson's disease are now seen in younger people as either a side effect of medications or a side effect of some drugs of abuse.

Teratogen   A compound that permanently interferes with normal fetal growth and development.

Teratogenic   Harmful to the fetus.

Thiamine   One of the "B" family of vitamins. The B vitamins are thought to be involved in the maintenance of the nervous system. These vitamins are water soluble, allowing the body to absorb the amount that it needs and then excrete the rest in the urine.

Thrombosis A blood clot that has broken off from a larger clot and is blocking a blood vessel, thus starving the tissue that relies on that vessel for oxygen and nutrients.

Tinnitus Loss of hearing, and a persistent "ringing" in the ears, which can be induced by loud noises, illness, or certain medications. This will gradually clear if the offending medications are discontinued immediately, but may become permanent.

Torsade de pointes Cardiac arrhythmia that is potentially fatal.

Tourette's disease A movement disorder in which the person will engage in repetitive, stereotypical movements, and often engage in repetitive vocalizations.

Ventricular tachycardia Cardiac arrhythmia in which the normal pattern of electrical discharge/repolarization in the ventricles of the heart is interrupted, disrupting the normal heart rhythm. This condition is potentially fatal if not immediately corrected.

White matter A region of the brain comprised of nerve cells responsible for relay of information. The cortex is often referred to as "gray matter" after its appearance after death. In contrast to this, the other neurons in different regions of the brain assume a white color following death.

Abnormalities in the white matter of the brain will make it difficult for individuals to consider multiple viewpoints when making decisions, and in adolescents will result in the "one-track mind" so often seen during this phase of life.

References

Aanavi, M. P., Taube, D. O., Ja, D. Y., & Duran, E. F. (2000). The status of psychologists' training about and treatment of substance abusing clients. *Journal of Psychoactive Drugs, 31,* 441–444.

Abbey, A., Zawacki, T., Buck, P. O., Clinton, A. M., & McAuslan, P. (2001). Alcohol and sexual assault. *Alcohol Research and Health, 25*(1), 43–51.

ABC News. (2006). Light cigarettes just as addictive as full flavored. Retrieved from http://abcnews.go.com/health/story?it=2135345&page=1

Abrams, D. I., Hilton, J. F., Leiser, R. J., Shade, S. B., Elbeik, T. A., Aweeka, F. T., et al. (2003). Short-term effects of cannabinoids in patients with HIV-1 infections. *Annals of Internal Medicine, 139,* 258–288.

Abrams, M. (2003). The end of craving. *Discover, 24*(5), 24–25.

Abt Associates, Inc. (1995). *What America's users spend on illegal drugs, 1988–1993.* Washington, DC: Office of National Drug Control Policy.

Ackerman, J. P., Riggins, T., & Black, M. M. (2010). A review of the effects of prenatal cocaine exposure among school-aged children. *Pediatrics, 125*(3), 554–565.

Acosta, M. C., Haller, D. L., & Schnoll, S. H. (2005). Cocaine and stimulants. In R. J. Frances, S. I. Miller, & A. H. Mack (Eds.), *Clinical textbook of addictive disorders* (3rd ed.). New York: Guilford.

Adamson, S. J., & Sellman, J. D. (2008). Five-year outcomes of alcohol-dependent persons treated with motivational enhancement. *Journal of Studies on Alcohol and Drugs, 69,* 589–593.

Addiction and the problem of relapse. (2007). *Harvard Mental Health Letter, 23*(7), 4–7.

Addolorato, G., Leggio, L., Ferrulli, A., Cardone, S., Vonghia, L., Mirijello, A., et al. (2007). Effectiveness and safety of baclofen for maintenance of alcohol abstinence in alcohol-dependent patients with liver cirrhosis: A randomized, double-blind controlled study. *The Lancet, 370*(9603), 1915–1922.

Adler, D. S., & Underwood, A. (2002). Aspirin: The oldest new wonder drug. *Newsweek, CXXIX*(21), 60–62.

Adolescents with insomnia are at risk for future substance abuse and depression. (2008). *Neuropsychiatry Reviews, 9*(11), 22.

Adult use of prescription opioid pain medications—Utah, 2008. (2010). *Morbidity and Mortality Weekly Report, 59,* 153–157.

After 40 years, the basics of MMT are still valid. (2005). *Addiction Treatment Forum, 14*(4), 4–5.

Agency: More teens abusing inhalants. (2005). Retrieved from http://www.cnn.com.2005/HEALTH/03/22/drugs.inhalants.reut/index.html

Agrawal, A., Sartor, C. E., Lynskey, M. T., Grant, J. D., Perdagia, M. L., Grucza, R., et al. (2009). Evidence for interaction between age at first drink and genetic influences on *DSM-IV* alcohol dependence symptoms. *Alcoholism: Clinical and Experimental Research* (published online prior to print). doi: 10.1111/j.1530-0277.2009.01044x

Aharonovich, E., Liu, X., Samet, S., Nunes, D., Waxman, R., & Hasin, D. (2005). Post-discharge cannabis use and its relationship to cocaine, alcohol, and heroin use: A new prospective study. *American Journal of Psychiatry, 162,* 1507–1514.

Ahrendt, D. M., & Miller, M. A. (2005). Adolescent substance abuse: A simplified approach to drug testing. *Pediatric Annals, 34,* 956–963.

Alati, R., Al-Manum, A., Williams, G. M., O'Callaghan, M. O., Najman, J. M., & Bor, W. (2006). In utero alcohol exposure and prediction of alcohol disorders in early adulthood: A birth cohort study. *Archives of General Psychiatry, 63,* 1009–1016.

Alattar, M. A., & Scharf, S. M. (2008). Opioid-associated central sleep apnea: A case series. *Sleep Breath* (published online prior to print).

Albertson, T. E., Derlet, R. W., & van Hoozen, B. E. (1999). Methamphetamine and the expanding complications of amphetamines. *Western Journal of Medicine, 170,* 214–219.

Alcohol and minorities: An update. (2002). *Alcohol Alert, 43,* 1–2.

Alcohol and the liver. (1993). *Alcohol Alert, 29.* Washington, DC: National Institute on Alcohol Abuse and Alcoholism.

Alcohol and tobacco. (1998). *Alcohol Alert, 39.* Washington, DC: National Institute on Alcohol Abuse and Alcoholism.

Alcohol metabolism: An update. (2007). *Alcohol Alert, 72,* 1–5.

Aldhous, P. (2006). Breaking the cycle of drugs and crime. *New Scientist, 191*(2562), 6–7.

Aldhous, P. (2008). Beauty's in the eye of the beer holder. *New Scientist, 199*(2669), 12.

Aldhous, P. (2009). Shot keeps holiday drinkers on wagon. *New Scientist, 200*(2688), 12.

Aldhous, P. (2010). Prescription: Sobriety. *New Scientist, 205*(2072), 40–43.

Aldington, S., Williams, M., Nowitz, M., Weatherall, M., Pritchard, A., McNaughton, A., et al. (2007). Effects of cannabis on pulmonary structure, function and symptoms. *Thorax* (published online prior to print). doi: 101136/thx.2006.077081

Alfonso, R. (2008). FAA bans anti-smoking drug Chantix for pilots, air controllers. Retrieved from http://www.latimes.com/news/nationworld/washingtondc/lala-na-smokedrug22may,22,0,5923950.story

Alter, J. (2001, March). *Making marriage work: Communications in recovery.* Symposium presented to the Department of Psychiatry, Cambridge Hospital, Boston.

Alterman, A. I., McDermott, P. A., Cacciola, J. S., Rutherford, M. I., Boardman, C. R., & McKay, J. R. (1998). A typology of antisociality in methadone patients. *Journal of Abnormal Psychology, 107,* 412–422.

Ameling, A. I., & Povilonis, M. (2001). Spirituality, meaning, mental health, and nursing. *Journal of Psychosocial Nursing, 39*(4), 15–20.

American Academy of Pediatrics. (1998). Neonatal drug withdrawal. *Pediatrics, 101,* 1079–1089.

American Psychiatric Association. (2000). *Diagnostic and statistical manual of mental disorders* (4th ed., text revision). Washington, DC: American Psychiatric Publishing.

American Society of Addiction Medicine (ASAM). (2001). *ASAM Patient Placement Criteria for the Treatment of Substance-Related Disorders,* (2nd ed.—Revised). Chevy Chase, MD: Author.

American Society of Health System Pharmacists. (2008). *AHFS drug information.* Bethesda, MD: Author.

Americans want insurance to cover addiction; unsure if it does. (2009). Retrieved from http://www.hazelden.org/web/public/pr090209healthinsurance.page

America's most dangerous drug. (2005). *Newsweek, CXLIV*(6), 40–48.

Ames, G. M., Duke, M. R., Moore, R. S., & Cunradi, C. B. (2009). The impact of occupational culture on drinking behavior of young adults in the U.S. Navy. *Journal of Mixed Methods Research, 3* (published online prior to print). doi: 10.1177/1558689808328534

Aminoff, M. J., Greenberg, D. A., & Simon, R. P. (2005). *Clinical neurology.* New York: Lange Medical Books/McGraw-Hill.

Amtmann, D., Weydt, P., Johnson, K. L., Jensen, M. P., & Carter, G. T. (2004). Survey of cannabis use in patients with amyotrophic lateral sclerosis. *American Journal of Hospice & Palliative Care, 21*(2), 95–104.

Anand, U., Otto, W. R., Sanchez-Herrera, D., Facer, P., Yiangou, Y., Korchev, Y., et al. (2008). Cannabinoid receptor CB2 localisation and agonist-mediated inhibition of capsaicin response in human sensory neurons. *Pain, 138*(3), 667–680.

Anczak, J. D., & Nogler, R. A. (2003). Tobacco cessation in primary care: Maximizing interventional strategies. *Clinical Medicine & Research, 1*(3), 201–216.

Anda, R. F., Whitfield, C. L., Felitti, V. J., Chapman, D., Edwards, V. J., Dube, S. R., et al. (2002). Adverse childhood experiences, alcoholic parents, and later risk of alcoholism and depression. *Psychiatric Services, 53,* 1001–1009.

Anderson, C. E., & Loomis, G. A. (2003). Recognition and prevention of inhalant abuse. *American Family Physician, 68,* 869–874, 876.

Anderson, D. J. (1989). An alcoholic is never too old for treatment. *Minneapolis Star-Tribune, VII*(200), p. 7EX.

Andersson, J. (2008). HIV after 25 years: How to induce a vaccine? *Journal of Internal Medicine, 263,* 215–217.

Antman, K., & Chang, Y. (2000). Kaposi's sarcoma. *New England Journal of Medicine, 342,* 1027–1038.

Antoin, H., & Beasley, R. D. (2004). Opioids for chronic noncancer pain. *Postgraduate Medicine, 116*(3), 37–44.

Anton, R. F. (1999). What is craving? Models and implications for treatment. *Alcohol Research & Health, 23,* 165–173.

Anton, R. F. (2005). Alcohol use disorders. In R. E. Rankel & E. T. Pope (Eds.), *Conn's current therapy,* 2005. Philadelphia: Elsevier Saunders.

Anton, R. F., O'Malley, S. S., Ciraulo, D. A., Cisler, R. A., Coupe, D., Donovan, D. M., et al. (2006). Combined pharmacotherapies and behavioral interventions for alcohol dependence. *Journal of the American Medical Association, 295,* 2003–2017.

Antonio, R. (1997). The use and abuse of ephedrine. *Muscle & Fitness, 58*(10), 178–180.

Appleby, L., Dyson, V., Luchins, D. J., & Cohen, L. S. (1997). The impact of substance abuse screening on a public psychiatric inpatient population. *Psychiatric Services, 48,* 1311–1316.

Arasteh, K., & des Jarlais, D. C. (2008). Injection drug use, HIV, and what to do about it. *The Lancet* (published online). doi: 10.1016/SO140-6736(08)613124

Arehart-Treichel, J. (2004). Homelessness does not lead to increased substance abuse. *Psychiatric News, 39*(12), 9.

Arehart-Treichel, J. (2008). Psychiatric genetic counseling: Don't expect easy answers. *Psychiatric News, 43*(1), 20.

Armon, C. (2009). Smoking may be considered an established risk factor for sporadic ALS. *Neurology, 73,* 1693–1698.

Armstrong, M. A., Gonzales-Osejo, V., Lieberman, L., Carpenter, D. M., Pantoja, P. M., & Escobar, G. J. (2008). Perinatal substance abuse intervention in obstetric clinics decreases adverse neonatal outcomes. *Journal of Perinatology, 23,* 3–9.

Arria, A. M., & Wish, E. D. (2006). Nonmedical use of prescription stimulants among students. *Pediatric Annals, 35,* 555–571.

Asthma deaths blamed on cocaine use. (2007). *Forensic Drug Abuse Advisor, 9*(2), 14.

Athletes caught using a new steroid–THG. (2003). *Forensic Drug Abuse Advisor, 15,* 76–77.

A tree shrew's favorite tipple. (2008). *New Scientist, 199*(2667), 18.

August, G. J., Winters, K. C., Realmuto, G. M., Fahnhnorst, T., Botzet, A., & Lee, S. (2006). Prospective study of adolescent drug use among community samples of ADHD and non-ADHD participants. *Journal of the American Academy of Child and Adolescent Psychiatry, 45,* 824–832.

Autti-Ramo, I. (2000). Twelve-year follow-up of children exposed to alcohol in utero. *Developmental Medicine & Child Neurology, 42,* 406–411.

A very venerable vintage. (1996). *Minneapolis Star-Tribune, XV*(63), p. A16.

Ayd, F. J., Janicak, P. G., David, J. M., & Preskor, S. H. (1996). Advances in the pharmacotherapy of anxiety and sleep disorders. *Principles and Practice of Psychopharmacotherapy, 1*(4), 1–22.

Azar, B. (2008). Better studying through chemistry. *Monitor on Psychology, 39*(8), 32–34.

Baber, A. (1998). Addiction's poster child. *Playboy, 45*(5), 29.

Babor, T. F., Higgins-Briddle, J. C., Saunders, J. B., & Monterio, M. G. (2001). *The alcohol use disorders identification test: Guidelines for use in primary care* (2nd ed.). New York: World Health Organization.

Bach, A. K., Wincze, J. P., & Barlow, D. H. (2001). Sexual dysfunction. In D. H. Marlow (Ed.), *Clinical handbook of psychological disorders* (3rd ed.). New York: Guilford.

Bacher, I., Rabin, R., Woznica, A., Sacco, K. A., & George, T. P. (2010). Nicotinic receptor mechanisms in neuropsychiatric disorders: Therapeutic implications. *Primary Psychiatry, 17*(1), 35–41.

Back, S. E., & Payne, R. (2009). Gender and prescription opioid addiction. In K. T. Brady, S. E. Back, & S. F. Greenfield (Eds.), *Women & addiction.* New York: Guilford.

Badon, L. A., Hicks, A., Lord, K., Ogden, B. A., Meleg-Smith, S., & Varner, K. J. (2002). Changes in cardiovascular responsiveness and cardiotoxicity elicited during binge administration of Ecstasy. *Journal of Pharmacology and Experimental Therapeutics, 302,* 898–907.

Bagnardi, V., Blangiardo, M., La Vecchia, C., & Corrao, G. (2001). Alcohol consumption and the risk of cancer. *Alcohol Research & Health, 25,* 263–270.

Bai-Fang, X., Sobel, S. C., Sigmon, S. L., Walsh, R. E., Liebson, I. A., Nuwayser, E. S., et al. (2004). Open-label trial of an injection depot formulation of buprenorphine in opioid detoxification. *Drug & Alcohol Dependence, 73*(1), 11–22.

Bailey, C. P., & Connor, M. (2005). Opioids: Cellular mechanisms of tolerance and physical dependence. *Current Opinion in Pharmacology, 5*(1), 60–68.

Bailey, J. E., Campagna, E., Dart, R. C., & RADARS System Poison Center Investigators. (2008). The underrecognized toll of prescription opioid abuse on young children. *Annals of Emergency Medicine* (published online prior to print). doi: 10.1016/ j.annerergmed.2008.07.015

Baker, S. (2009). Building a better brain. *Discover, 30* (4), 54–59.

Balamuthsamy, S., & Desai, B. (2006). MRI changes in cocaine-induced toxic enceptalophy. *Psychiatry On-Line.* Retrieved June 21, 2006, from http://www .priory.com/psych/toxicencephelophy.pdf

Ballas, C. A., Evans, D. L., & Dinges, D. F. (2004). Psychostimulants in psychiatry: Amphetamine, methylphenidate and modfinil. In A. F. Schatzberg & C. B. Nemeroff (Eds.), *Textbook of psychophar-macology* (3rd ed.). Washington, DC: American Psychiatric Publishing.

Baltieri, D. A., Daro, F. R., Ribeiro, P. L., & de Andrade, A. G. (2008). *Addiction.* Retrieved from http://www.ncbi.him.hih.gov/pubmed/1855810? ordinlalpos=1itool=EntrezSystem2.Pentrez.pubm

Bambico, F. R., Katz, N., Debonnel, G., & Gobbi, G. (2007). Cannabinoids elicit antidepressant-like behavior and activate serotonergic neurons through the medial prefrontal cortex. *Journal of Neurosci-ence, 27*(43), 11700–11711.

Bambico, F. R., Nguyen, N. T., Katz, N., & Gobbi, G. (2009). Chronic exposure to cannabinoids during adolescence but not during adulthood impairs emotional behavior and monoaminergic neurotransmission. *Neurobiology of Disease* (published online prior to print). doi: 10.1016/j.nbd .2009.11.020

Bankole, A. J., & Ait-Daoud, N. (2005). Alcohol: Clinical aspects. In J. H. Lowinson, P. Ruiz, R. B. Millman, & J. G. Langrod (Eds.), *Substance abuse: A comprehensive textbook* (4th ed.). New York: Lippincott Williams & Wilkins.

Banta, J. E., & Montgomery, S. (2007). How often are substance use disorders diagnosed in outpatient settings? *American Journal of Drug and Alcohol Abuse, 33*(4), 583–593.

Banta-Greene, C. J., Field, J. A., Chiala, A. C., Sudakin, D. L., Power, L., & de Montigny, L. (2009). The spatial epidemiology of cocaine, methamphetamine and 3,4-methylenedioxymethamphetamine (MDMA) use: A demonstration using a population measure of community drug load derived from municipal wastewater. *Addiction* (published online prior to print). doi: 10.1111/j.1360-0433/2002 .20678.x

Barber, C. (2008). The medicated Americans. *Scientific American Mind, 19*(1), 44–51.

Barki, Z. H. K., Kravitz, H. M., & Berki, T. M. (1998). Psychotropic medications in pregnancy. *Psychiatric Annals, 28,* 486–500.

Barnett, J. E. (2009). The pernicious influence of the pharmaceutical industry: Who's minding the store? *The Independent Practitioner, 29*(1), 12–14.

Barnett, M. (2001). Alternative opioids to morphine in palliative care: A review of current practice and evidence. *Postgraduate Medical Journal, 77,* 372–378.

Baron, D., Garbely, J., & Boyd, R. L. (2009). Evaluation and management of substance abuse emergencies. *Primary Psychiatry, 16*(9), 41–47.

Baron, J. A., Cole, B. F., Sandler, R. S., Haile, R. W., Ahnen, D., Bresalier, R., et al. (2003). A randomized trial of aspirin to prevent colorectal adenomas. *New England Journal of Medicine, 348,* 891–899.

Barr, A. (1999). *Drink: A social history of America.* New York: Carroll & Graf.

Barr, C. S., Schwandt, M., Lindell, S. G., Chen, S. A., Goldman, D., Suomi, S., et al. (2007). Association of a functional polymorphism of the μ-opioid receptor gene with alcohol response and consumption in male rhesus macaques. *Archives of General Psychi-atry, 64*(3), 369–376.

Barr, R. G., Kurth, T., Stamfer, M. H., Buring, J. E., Hennekens, C. H., & Gaziano, J. M. (2007). Aspirin and decreased adult-onset asthma: Randomized comparisons from the Physician's Health Study. *American Journal of Respiratory and Critical Care Medicine, 175,* 120–125.

Barrera, S. E., Osinski, W. A., & Davidoff, E. (1994). The use of Antabuse (tetraethylthiuraddisulphide) in chronic alcoholics. *American Journal of Psychia-try, 151,* 263–267. (original work published 1949)

Barry, C. E., & Cheung, M. S. (2009). New tactics against tuberculosis. *Scientific American*, *300*(3), 6–69.

Barry, D. T., Beitel, M., Garnet, B., Joshi, D., Rosenblum, A., & Schottenfeld, R. S. (2009). Relations among psychopathy, substance use, and physical pain experiences in methadone-maintained patients. *Journal of Clinical Psychiatry*, *70*(9), 1213–1218.

Bartlett, J. G. (1999). *Management of respiratory tract infections* (2nd ed.). New York: Lippincott Williams & Wilkins.

Bartsch, A. J., Homola, G., Biller, A., Smith, S. M., Weijers, H.-G., Wiesbeck, G. A., et al. (2007). Manifestations of early brain recovery associated with abstinence from alcoholism. *Brain*, *130*, 36–47.

Baselt, R. C. (1996). Disposition of alcohol in men. In J. C. Garriott (Ed.), *Medicolegal aspects of alcohol* (3rd ed.). Tucson, AZ: Lawyers & Judges Publishing.

Batki, S. L. (2001, November 1). *Methamphetamine and MDMA*. Paper presented at the meeting of the American Society of Addiction Medicine, Washington, DC.

Batzer, W., Ditzer, T., & Brown, C. (1999). LSD use and flashbacks in alcoholic patients. *Journal of Addictive Diseases*, *18*(2), 57–63.

Bauld, L., Chesterman, J., Ferguson, J., & Judge, K. (2008). A comparison of the effectiveness of group based and pharmacy led smoking cessation treatment in Glasgow. *Addiction*, *104*, 308–318.

Bauman, M. H., & Rothman, R. B. (2007). Neurobiology of 3,4-methylenedioxymethamine (MDMA or Ecstasy). In S. B. Karch (Ed.), *Drug abuse handbook* (2nd ed.). New York: CRC Press.

Bayard, M., McIntyre, J., Hill, K. R., & Woodside, J. (2004). Alcohol withdrawal syndrome. *American Family Physician*, *56*, 1443–1450.

BBC News. (2006). US warns of "global meth threat." Retrieved from http://news.bbc.co.uk/2/hi/americas/4757179.stm

Beasley, R., Clayton, T., Crane, J., von Mutius, E., Lai, C. K. W., Montefort, S., et al. (2008). Association between paracetamol use in infancy and childhood, and the risk of asthma, rhinoconjunctivitis and eczema in children aged 6–7 years: Analysis from Phase Three of the ISAAC programme. *The Lancet*, *372*, 1039–1048.

Beattie, M. (1987). *Codependent no more*. New York: Harper & Row.

Beattie, M. (1989). *Beyond codependency*. New York: Harper & Row.

Beauvais, F. (1998). American Indians and alcohol. *Alcohol Health & Research World*, *22*, 253–259.

Beazley, H. (1998, March 3). *The integration of AA and clinical practice*. Paper presented at the Treating the Addictions seminar, Department of Psychiatry, Cambridge Hospital, Boston.

Bechara, A. (2006, August 12). *Decision making, impulse control, and loss of willpower to resist drugs: A neurocognitive perspective*. Symposium presented at the annual meeting of the American Psychological Association, New Orleans, LA.

Beck, A. T. (2004, March 5). *The cognitive-behavioral approach to addiction treatment*. Paper presented to the Department of Psychiatry, Cambridge Hospital, Boston.

Becklake, M. R., Ghezzo, H., & Ernst, P. (2005). Childhood predictors of smoking in adolescence: A follow-up study of Montreal school children. *Canadian Medical Association Journal*, *173*, 377–379.

Begley, S. (2007). *Train your mind, change your brain*. New York: Ballantine Books.

Behrendt, S., Wittchen, H., Fofler, M., Lieb, R., Lowe, N. C., Rehm, J., et al. (2008). Risk and speed of transitions to first alcohol dependence symptoms in adolescents: A 10-year longitudinal community study in Germany. *Addiction*, *103*(10), 1638–1647.

Belenko, S., Patapis, N., & French, M. T. (2005). Economic benefits of drug treatment: A critical review of evidence for policy makers. Retrieved from http//www.tresearch.org/resources/specials,2005Feb_economicbenefirts/pdf

Belhani, D., Fanton, L., Vaillant, F., Descotes, J., Manati, W., Tabib, A., et al. (2009). Cardiac lesions induced by testosterone: Protective effects of dexrazoxane and trimetazidine. *Cardiovascular Toxicology*, *9*(2), 64–69.

Bell, H. (2009). Outwitting HIV. *Minnesota Medicine*, *92*(10), 22–26.

Bell, R. A., Spangler, J. G., & Quandt, S. A. (2000). Smokeless tobacco use among adults in the southeast. *Southern Medical Journal*, *93*, 456–462.

Bell, T. (1996). Abuse or addiction? *Professional Counselor*, *11*(5), 12.

Bellack, A. S., Bennett, M., Gearon, J. S., Brown, C. H., & Yang, Y. (2006). A randomized clinical trial of a new behavioral treatment for drug abuse in people with severe and persistent mental illness. *Archives of General Psychiatry*, *63*, 426–432.

Bennett, P. N., & Brown, M. J. (2003). *Clinical pharmacology*. New York: Churchill Livingstone.

Benson, H. (2009, February 23–27). *Mind/body medicine: Components, research, techniques and application with the emphasis on the relaxation response*. Seminar presented by the Harvard Medical School Department of Continuing Education, Key Largo, FL.

Benson, R. T., & Sacco, R. L. (2000). Stroke prevention. *Neurologic Clinics of North America, 19*, 309–320.

Bentall, R. P. (2009). *Doctoring the mind*. New York: New York University Press.

Benton, S. A. (2009). *Understanding the high-functioning alcoholic*. Westport, CT: Praeger.

Benyamina, A., Lecacheux, M., Blecha, L., Reynud, M., & Lukasiewcz, M. (2008). Pharmacotherapy and psychotherapy in cannabis withdrawal and dependence. *Expert Review in Neurotherapy, 8*(3), 479–491.

Berent, S., & Alberts, J. W. (2005). *Neurobehavioral toxicology* (*Vol. 1*). New York: Taylor & Francis.

Berg, J. E. (2003). Mortality and return to work of drug abusers from therapeutic community treatment 3 years after entry. *The Primary Care Companion to the Journal of Clinical Psychiatry, 5*(4), 164–167.

Berger, J. S., Roncaglioni, M. C., Avanzini, F., Pangrazzi, I., Tognoni, G., & Brown, D. L. (2006). Aspirin for the primary prevention of cardiovascular events in women and men. *Journal of the American Medical Association, 295*, 306–313.

Berger, T. (2000). Nervous system. In G. Zernig, A. Saria, M. Kurz, & S. S. O'Malley (Eds.), *Handbook of Alcoholism*. New York: CRC Press.

Berghuis, P., Rajnicek, A. M., Morozuv, Y. M., Ross, R. A., Mulder, J., Urbán, G. M., et al. (2007). Hardwiring the brain: Endocannabinoids shape neuronal connectivity. *Science, 316*, 1212–1216.

Bermani, S. M., Kuczenski, R., McCracken, J. T., & London, E. D. (2009). Potential adverse effects of amphetamine treatment on brain and behavior: A review. *Molecular Psychiatry, 14*, 123–142.

Berry, J., & Mugford, G. (2007, April 28). *Addressing the epidemic of benzodiazepine overprescribing*. Seminar presented at the 38th Annual Medical-Scientific Conference of the American Society of Addiction Medicine, Miami, FL.

Bhattacharyya, S., Fusar-Poli, P., Borgwardt, S., Martin-Santos, R., Nosarti, C., O'Carroll, C., et al. (2009). Modulation of mediotemporal and ventrostriatal function in humans by Δ-9-tetrahydrocannabiinol. *Archives of General Psychiatry, 66*(4), 442–451.

Bhuvaneswar, C., & Chang, G. (2009). Substance use in pregnancy. In K. T. Brady, S. E. Back, & S. F. Greenfield (Eds.), *Women & addiction*. New York: Guilford.

Bialous, S. A., & Sarna, L. (2004). Sparing a few minutes for tobacco cessation. *American Journal of Nursing, 104*(12), 54–60.

Biederman, J., Monuteaus, M. C., Spencer, T., Wilens, T. E., Macpherson, H. A., & Faraone, S. V. (2008). Stimulant therapy and risk for subsequent substance use disorders in male adults with ADHD: A naturalistic controlled 10-year follow-up study (published online). doi: 10.1176/appi.ajp.2007.07091486

Big Tobacco's secret kiddie campaign. (1998). *Newsweek, CXXXI*(4), 29.

Bijttebier, P., Boethals, E., & Ansoms, S. (2006). Parental drinking as a risk factor for children's maladjustment: The mediating role of family environment. *Psychology of Addictive Behavior, 20*, 126–130.

Biller, A., Bartsch, A. J., Homola, L., & Bendszus, M. (2009). The effects of ethanol on human brain metabolites longitudinally characterized by proton MR spectroscopy. *Journal of Cerebral Blood Flow & Metabolism, 29*, 891–902.

Bisaga, A. (2008). Benzodiazepines and other sedatives and hypnotics. In M. Galanter & H. D. Kleber (Eds.), *The American Psychiatric Publishing textbook of substance abuse treatment*. Washington, DC: American Psychiatric Publishing.

Bjork, J. M., Grant, S. J., & Hommer, D. W. (2003). Cross-sectional volumetric analysis of brain atrophy in alcohol dependence: Effects of drinking history and comorbid substance use disorder. *American Journal of Psychiatry, 160*, 2038–2045.

Black, C. (1982). *It will never happen to me*. Denver, CO: MAC Printing and Publications.

Black, C. (2003, March 7). *The legacy of addictions: Looking at family patterns*. Symposium presented to the Department of Psychiatry, Cambridge Hospital, Boston.

Black, R. A., & Hill, D. A. (2003). Over-the-counter medications in pregnancy. *American Family Physician, 160*, 2038–2045.

Bloch, S., & Pargiter, R. (2002). A history of psychiatric ethics. *Psychiatric Clinics of North America, 25*, 509–524.

Blondell, R. D. (2005). Ambulatory detoxification of patients with alcohol dependence. *American Family Physician, 71*, 495–502.

Blondell, R. D., & Ashrafioun, L. (2008). Treatment opioid dependency and coexisting chronic nonmalignant pain. *American Family Physician, 78*(10), 1132–1133.

Blow, F. C., Serras, A. M., & Barry, K. L. (2007). Late-life depression and alcoholism. *Current Psychiatry Reports, 9,* 14–19.

Blum, A. (2008). Alchemy, the safer cigarette, and Phillip Morris. *The Lancet, 371,* 1644–1647.

Blum, D. (1998). Finding strength. *Psychology Today, 31*(3), 32–38, 66–67, 69, 72–73.

Blum, K. (1988). The disease process in alcoholism. *Alcoholism & Addiction, 8*(5), 5–8.

Blum, K. (2006). Quitting early. Retrieved from http//chicagotribune.com/business/bal_hs .smoke31mar31,1,880720.story?crack=1&cst=true

Blum, K., & Payne, J. E. (1991). *Alcohol and the addictive brain.* New York: Free Press.

Blume, A. W. (2005). *Treating drug problems.* New York: Wiley.

Blume, A. W., & de la Cruz, B. (2005). Relapse prevention among diverse populations. In G. A. Marlatt & D. M. Donovan (Eds.), *Relapse prevention— maintenance strategies in the treatment of addictive behaviors* (2nd ed.). New York: Guilford.

Blume, S. B., & Zilberman, M. L. (2004). Addiction in women. In M. Galanter & H. D. Kleber (Eds.), *The American Psychiatric Publishing textbook of substance abuse treatment* (3rd ed.). Washington, DC: American Psychiatric Publishing.

Blume, S. B., & Zilberman, M. L. (2005a). Addictive disorders in women. In R. J. Frances, S. I. Miller, & A. H. Mack (Eds.), *Clinical textbook of addictive disorders* (3rd ed.). New York: Guilford.

Blume, S. B., & Zilberman, M. L. (2005b). Alcohol and women. In J. H. Lowinson, R. B. Millman, & J. G. Langrod (Eds.), *Substance abuse: A comprehensive textbook* (4th ed.). New York: Lippincott Williams & Wilkins.

Boal, M. (2002). Designer drug death. *Rolling Stone, 888,* 44–49.

Bobo, W. C., Miller, S. C., & Martin, B. D. (2005). The abuse liability of dextromethorphan among adolescents: A review. *Journal of Child and Adolescent Substance Abuse, 14*(4), 55–75.

Bode, C., Maute, G., & Bode, J. C. (1996). Prostaglandin E2 and prostaglandin F2a biosynthesis in human gastric mucosa: Effect of chronic alcohol misuse. *Gut, 39,* 348–352.

Boese, A. (2007). Did they really do that? *The Scientist.* Retrieved from http://www.the_scientist./news/home/53568

Boffetta, P., Hecht, S., Gray, N., Gupta, P., & Straif, K. (2008). Smokeless tobacco and cancer. *The Lancet Oncology, 9*(9), 822.

Boffeta, P., & Straif, K. (2009). Use of smokeless tobacco and risk of myocardial infarction and stroke: Systematic review with meta-analysis. *British Medical Journal* (published online prior to print). doi: 10.1136/bmj.b3060

Bohn, M. (2001, June 1). *Alcoholism pharmacotherapy.* Paper presented at the Contemporary Issues in the Treatment of Alcohol and Drug Use Symposium, Milwaukee, WI.

Boles, S. C. (2007, April 26). *Neurochemistry review: Advances in anti-relapse pharmacotherapy of alcoholism.* Paper presented at the Ruth Fox Course for Physicians, 38th Medical-Scientific Conference of the American Society of Addiction Medicine, Miami, FL.

Bolla, K. I., & Cadet, J. L. (2007). Exogenous acquired metabolic disorders of the nervous system: Toxins and illicit drugs. In C. Goetz (Ed.), *Textbook of clinical neurology* (3rd ed.). Philadelphia: Saunders-Elsevier.

Bolnick, J. M., & Rayburn, W. F. (2003). Substance use disorders in women: Special considerations during pregnancy. *Obstetric and Gynecological Clinics of North America, 30,* 545–558.

Bonanno, G. A. (2004). Loss, trauma, and human resilience. *American Psychologist, 59,* 20–28.

Bondesson, J. D., & Saperston, A. R. (1996). Hepatitis. *Emergency Medical Clinics of North America, 14,* 695–718.

Bongar, B. (1997, August 12). *Suicide: What therapists need to know.* Seminar presented at the 1997 meeting of the American Psychological Association, Chicago.

Book, S. W., & Randall, C. L. (2002). Social anxiety disorder and alcohol use. *Alcohol Research & Health, 26,* 130–139.

Booth, M. (1996). *Opium: A history.* New York: St. Martin's-Griffin.

Borgwardt, S. J., Allen, P., Bhattacharyya, A., Fusar-Poli, P., Crippa, J. A., Seal, M. L., et al. (2008). Neural basis of Δ–9-tetrahydrocannabinol and cannabidol: Effects inhibition. *Biological Psychiatry, 64*(11), 966–973.

Borowsky, I. W., Ireland, M., & Resnick, M. D. (2009). Health status and behavioral outcomes for youth who anticipate a high likelihood of earth death. *Pediatrics, 124* (published online prior to print). doi: 10.1542.1542ped.2008-3425

Botre, F., & Pavan, A. (2008). Enhancement drugs and the athlete. *Neurological Clinics of North America*, *26*, 149–167.

Bottoroff, J. L., Johnson, J. L., Moffat, B. M., & Mulvogue, T. (2009). Relief oriented use of marijuana by teens. *Substance Abuse Treatment, Prevention and Policy*, *4*(7) (published online prior to print). doi: 10.1186/1747-597X-4-7

Bowen, M. (1985). *Family therapy in clinical practice*. Northvale, NJ: Jason Aronson.

Bowen, S. E., Batis, J. C., Mahammadi, M. H., & Hannigan, J. H. (2005). Abuse pattern of gestational toluene exposure and early postnatal development in rats. *Neurotoxicity & Teratology*, *27*, 105–116.

Boyd, C. J., McCabe, S. E., & Morales, M. (2005). College students' alcohol use: A critical review. In J. J. Fitzpatrick, J. S. Stevenson, & M. S. Sommers (Eds.), *Annual review of nursing research* (*Vol. 23*). New York: Springer.

Boyer, E. W. (2005, March 5). *Emerging drugs of abuse*. Paper presented at the Treating the Addictions seminar hosted by the Department of Psychiatry of Cambridge Hospital, Boston.

Bradley, K. A., Boyd-Wickizer, J., Powell, S., & Burman, M. L. (1998). Alcohol screening questionnaires in women. *Journal of the American Medical Association*, *280*, 166–171.

Bradley, K. A., Bush, K. R., Epler, A. J., Dobie, D. J., Davis, T. M., et al. (2003). Two brief alcohol screening tests from the Alcohol Use Disorders Identification Test (AUDIT): Validation in a female veterans affairs patient population. *Archives of Internal Medicine*, *163*, 821–829.

Brady, K. T., & Back, S. (2008). Women and addiction. In M. Galanter & H. D. Kleber (Eds.), *The American Psychiatric Publishing textbook of substance abuse treatment*. Washington, DC: American Psychiatric Publishing.

Brady, K. T., & Hartwell, K. (2009). Gender, anxiety and substance use disorders. In K. T. Brady, S. E. Back, & S. F. Greenfield (Eds.), *Women & addiction*. New York: Guilford.

Brady, K. T., Tolliver, B. K., & Verduin, M. L. (2007). Alcohol use and anxiety: Diagnostic and management issues. *American Journal of Psychiatry*, *164*, 217–221.

Brain Trauma Foundation. (2000). Use of barbiturates in the control of intracranial hypertension. *Journal of Neurotrauma*, *17*(6–7), 527–530.

Brambilla, C., & Colonna, M. (2008). Cannabis: The next villain on the lung cancer battlefield? *European Respiratory Journal*, *31*, 227–228.

Bravo, G. (2001). What does MDMA feel like? In J. Holland (Ed.), *Ecstasy: The complete guide*. Rochester, VT: Park Street Press.

Breggin, P. R. (1999). Letter to the editor. *Journal of the American Medical Association*, *281*, 1490–1491.

Breggin, P. R. (2008). *Brain-disabling treatments in psychiatry* (2nd ed.). New York: Springer.

Breiter, H. C. (1999, March 6). *The biology of addiction*. Symposium presented to the Department of Psychiatry of Cambridge General Hospital, Boston.

Breithaupt, D. (2001). Why health insurers should pay for addiction treatment. *Western Journal of Medicine*, *174*, 375–377.

Brekke, J. S., Prindle, C., Woo Bae, S., & Long, J. D. (2001). Risks for individuals with schizophrenia who are living in the community. *Psychiatric Services*, *52*, 1358–1366.

Brenhouse, H. C., & Anderson, S. L. (2008). Delayed extinction and stronger reinstatement of cocaine conditioned place preference in adolescent rats, compared to adults. *Behavioral Neuroscience*, *122*(2), 460–465.

Brigham, G. S. (2003). 12-step participation as a pathway to recovery: The Maryhaven experience and implications for treatment and research. *Science Practice & Perspectives*, *2*(1), 43–51.

Brink, S. (2004). The price of booze. *U.S. News & World Report*, *136*(4), 48–50.

Britt, J. P., & McGehee, D. S. (2008). Presynaptic opioid and nicotinic receptor modulation of dopamine overflow in the nucleus accumbens. *Journal of Neuroscience*, *28*, 1672–1681.

Britton, A., Marmot, M. G., & Shipley, M. (2008). Who benefits most from the cardio-protective protective properties of alcohol consumption—health freaks or couch potatoes? *Journal of Epidemiology and Community Health*, *62*(10), 905–908.

Brody, A. L., Mandelkern, M. A., London, E. D., Olmstead, R. E., Farahi, J., Scheibal, D., et al. (2006). Cigarette smoking saturates brain a4ß2 niotinic acetylcholine receptors. *Archives of General Psychiatry*, *63*, 907–915.

Brody, T. N. M. (1994). Clinical pharmacokinetics. In T. M. Brody, J. Larner, K. Minneman, & H. C. Neu (Eds.), *Human pharmacology: Molecular to clinical* (2nd ed.). St. Louis, MO: Mosby.

Bronisch, T., Hofler, M., & Lieb, F. (2008). Smoking predicts suicidally: Findings from a prospective community study. *Journal of Affective Disorders* (published online). doi: 10.10.16jad.2007.10.010

Brook, D. W. (2008). Group therapy. In M. Galanter & H. D. Kleber (Eds.), *The American Psychiatric Publishing textbook of substance abuse treatment.* Washington, DC: American Psychiatric Publishing.

Brook, J. S., Pahl, K., & Rubenstone, E. (2008). Epidemiology of addiction. In M. Galanter & H. D. Kleber (Eds.), *The American Psychiatric Publishing textbook of substance abuse treatment.* Washington, DC: American Psychiatric Publishing.

Brooks, J. T., Leung, G., & Shannon, M. (1996). Inhalants. In L. Friedman, N. F. Fleming, D. H. Roberts, & S. E. Hyman (Eds.), *Source book of substance abuse and addiction.* New York: Williams & Wilkins.

Brower, K. J., Aldrich, M. S., Robinson, E. A. R., Zucker, R. A., & Greden, J. F. (2001). Insomnia, self-medication and relapse to alcoholism. *American Journal of Psychiatry, 158,* 399–404.

Brown, A. (2007). Sensationalising our drug and alcohol problems is failing public health. *Nursing Times, 103*(10), 12.

Brown, D. (2006). Nicotine up sharply in many cigarettes. Retrieved from http://www.washington post.com./wp/dyn/content/article/s006/08/30/AR2006083001418.html

Brown, D. J. (2007). Psychedelic healing? *Scientific American Mind, 18*(6), 60–65.

Brown, E. S. (2005). Bipolar disorder and substance abuse. *Psychiatric Clinics of North America, 28,* 415–425.

Brown, R. (2006). Speaking of "poppycock" … a reply to the *Wall Street Journal. ASAM News, 21*(3), 5–6.

Brown, R. L., Leonard, T., Saunders, L. A., & Papasoulioutis, O. (1997). A two-item screening test for alcohol and other drug problems. *The Journal of Family Practice, 44,* 151–160.

Brown, S., & Lewis, V. (1995). The alcoholic family: A developmental model of recovery. In S. A. Brown (Ed.), *Treating alcoholism.* New York: Jossey-Bass.

Brown, S. A. (1985). *Treating the alcoholic: A developmental model of recovery.* New York: Wiley.

Brown, S. A., McGue, M., Maggs, J., Schulenberg, J., et al. (2009). Underaged alcohol use. *Alcohol Research & Health, 32*(1), 41–52.

Brown, T. M., & Stoudemire, A. (1998). *Psychiatric side effects of prescription and over-the-counter medications.* Washington, DC: American Psychiatric Publishing.

Bruckner, J. V., & Warren, D. A. (2003). Toxic effects of solvents and vapors. In C. D. Klassen & J. B. Watkins (Eds.), *Casarett and Doull's essentials of toxicology.* New York: McGraw-Hill.

Bruijnzeel, A. W., Repetto, M., & Gold, M. S. (2004). Neurobiological mechanisms in addictive and psychiatric disorders. *Psychiatric Clinics of North America, 27,* 661–674.

Brunton, L. L., Lazo, J. S., & Parker, K. L. (2006). *Goodman & Gilman's the pharmacological basis of therapeutics* (11th ed.). New York: McGraw-Hill.

Brunton, L., Parker, K., Blumenthal, D., & Buston, L. (2008). *Goodman & Gilman's manual of pharmacology and therapeutics.* New York: McGraw-Hill.

Brust, J. C. M. (1998). Acute neurologic complications of drug and alcohol abuse. *Neurological Clinics of North America, 16,* 503–519.

Brust, J. C. M. (2004). *Neurological aspects of substance abuse* (2nd ed.). New York: Elsevier Butterworth-Heinemann.

Brust, J. C. M. (2007a). Alcoholism. In J. C. M. Brust (Ed.), *Current diagnosis and treatment in neurology.* New York: Lange Medical Books/McGraw-Hill.

Brust, J. C. M. (2007b). Drug abuse. In J. C. M. Brust (Ed.), *Current diagnosis and treatment in neurology.* New York: Lange Medical Books/McGraw-Hill.

Bryner, J. K., Wang, U. K., Hul, J. W., Bedodo, M., MacDougall, C., & Anderson, I. B. (2006). Dextromethorphan abuse in adolescence. *Archives of Pediatrics and Adolescent Medicine, 160,* 1217–1222.

Bryson, C. L., Au, D. H., Sun, H., Williams, E. C., Kivlahan, D. R., & Bradley, K. A. (2008). Alcohol screening scores and medication nonadherence. *Annals of Internal Medicine, 149,* 795–803.

Buber, M. (1970). *I and thou.* New York: Scribner's.

Buckley, P. F. (2006). Prevalence and consequences of the dual diagnosis of substance abuse and severe mental illness. *Journal of Clinical Psychiatry* (Suppl. 7), 5–9.

Buckman, J. F., Yusko, D. A., White, H. R., & Pandina, R. J. (2009). Risk profile of male college athletes who use performance-enhancing drugs. *Journal of Studies on Alcohol & Drugs, 70,* 919–923.

Budney, A. J., Moore, B. A., Bandrey, R. G., & Hughes, J. R. (2003). The time course and significance of cannabis withdrawal. *Journal of Abnormal Psychology, 112,* 393–402.

Budney, A. J., Roffman, R., Stephens, R. S., & Walker, D. (2007). Marijuana dependence and its treatment. *Addiction Science & Clinical Practice, 4*(1), 4–16.

Budney, A. J., Sigmon, S. C., & Higgins, S. T. (2003). Contingency management in the substance abuse treatment clinic. In F. Rogers, J. Morgenstern, & S. T. Walters (Eds.), *Treating substance abuse: Theory and technique* (2nd ed.). New York: Guilford.

Bufe, C. (1998). *Alcoholics Anonymous: Cult or cure* (2nd ed.). Tuscon, AZ: See Sharp Press.

Buffenstein, A., Heaster, J., & Ko, P. (1999). Chronic psychotic illness from methamphetamine. *American Journal of Psychiatry, 156,* 662.

Buhrich, N., Weller, A., & Kevans, P. (2000). Misuse of anticholinergic drugs by people with serious mental illness. *Psychiatric Services, 51,* 928–929.

Buia, C., Fulton, G., Park, A., Shannon, E. M., & Thompson, D. (2000). The lure of Ecstasy. *Time, 155*(23), 62–68.

Buka, S. L., Shenassa, E. D., & Niaura, R. (2003). Elevated risk of tobacco dependence among offspring of mothers who smoked during pregnancy: A 30-year prospective study. *American Journal of Psychiatry, 160,* 1978–1984.

Bureau of Justice Statistics. (2008, June 6). Slower growth in the nation's prison and jail populations. Press release.

Buring, J., & Ferrari, N. (2006). Take an aspirin and.... *Newsweek, CXLVII*(17), 71.

Burns, D. M. (2008). Nicotine addiction. In A. S. Fauci, E. Braunwald, D. L. Kasper, S. L. Hauser, D. L. Longo, J. L. Jameson, & J. Loscalzo (Eds.), *Harrison's principles of internal medicine* (17th ed.). New York: McGraw-Hill.

Burns, E. (2007). *The smoke of the gods.* Philadelphia: Temple University Press.

Busch, A. B., Weiss, R. D., & Najavits, L. M. (2005). Co-occurring substance use disorders and other psychiatric disorders. In R. J. Frances, S. I. Miller, & A. H. Mack (Eds.), *Clinical textbook of addictive disorders* (3rd ed.). New York: Guilford.

Butz, A. M., Pulsifer, M .B., Belcher, H. M. E., Leppert, M., Lears, M. K., Donithan, M., et al. (2005). Infant head growth and cognitive status at 36 months in children with *in-utero* drug exposure. *Journal of Child & Adolescent Substance Abuse, 14*(4), 15–39.

Byington, D. B. (1997). Applying relational theory to addictions treatment. In S. L. A. Straussner & E. Zelvin (Eds.), *Gender and addictions*. Northvale, NJ: Jason Aronson.

Cabaj, R. P. (1997). Gays, lesbians and bisexuals. In J. H. Lowinson, P. Ruiz, R. B. Millman, & J. G. Langrod (Eds.), *Substance abuse: A comprehensive textbook* (3rd ed.). New York: Lippincott Williams & Wilkins.

Cabaj, R. P. (2005). Gays, lesbians and bisexuals. In J. H. Lowinson, P. Ruiz, R. B. Millman, & J. G. Langrod (Eds.), *Substance abuse: A comprehensive textbook* (4th ed.). New York: Lippincott Williams & Wilkins.

Caetano, R., Clark, C. L., & Tam, T. (1998). Alcohol consumption among racial/ethnic minorities: Theory and research. *Alcohol Health & Research World, 22,* 229–242.

Cafferty, J. (2009). *Commentary: War on drugs is insane.* Retrieved from http://www.cnn.com/2009/POLITICS/03/31/cafferty.legal.drugs/index.html

Cahill, T. (1998). *The gifts of the Jews.* New York: Doubleday.

Cahill, T. (2006). *How the Irish saved civilization.* New York: Doubleday.

Calfee, R., & Fadale, P. (2006). Popular ergogenic drugs and supplements in young athletes. *Pediatrics, 117,* e557–e559.

California judges get tougher on science. (1997). *Forensic Drug Abuse Advisor, 9*(8), 61.

Callaway, J. C., & McKenna, D. J. (1998). Neurochemistry of psychedelic drugs. In S. B. Karch (Eds.), *Drug abuse handbook.* New York: CRC Press.

Cannabis booster. (2008). *New Scientist, 200*(2968), 6.

Cannabis chemical clue to colon cancer. (2008). *New Scientist, 199,*(2668), 17.

Cape, G. S. (2003). Addiction, stigma and movies. *Acta Psychiatricia Scandinavica, 107,* 163–169.

Capretto, N. A. (2007, April 26). *Addiction: A family disease.* Paper presented at the Ruth Fox Course for Physicians, 38th Medical-Scientific Conference of the American Society of Addiction Medicine, Miami, FL.

Carey, B. (2008). Drug rehabilitation or revolving door? Retrieved from http:www.nytimes.com/2008/12/23/health/23reha.html?pagewanted=1&_r=2&hy?8dpc

Carlin, G. (2001). *Napalm and silly putty.* New York: Hyperion.

Carmona, R. H. (2004). *The health consequences of smoking: A report of the Surgeon General.* Washington, DC: Centers for Disease Control and Prevention.

Carol, G., Smelson, D. A., Losonczy, M. F., & Ziedonis, D. (2001). A preliminary investigation of cocaine craving among persons with and without schizophrenia. *Psychiatric Services, 52*, 1029–1031.

Carpenter, S. (2001). Research on teen smoking cessation gains momentum. *APA Monitor, 32*(6), 54–55.

Carr, P., & Lynfield, R. (2009). Why HIV still matters in Minnesota. *Minnesota Medicine, 92*(10), 36–37.

Carroll, C. M., & Ball, S. A. (2005). Assessment of cocaine abuse and dependence. In D. M. Donovan & G. A. Marlatt (Eds.), *Assessment of addictive behaviors* (2nd ed.). New York: Guilford.

Carroll, K. M. (2003). Integrating psychotherapy and pharmacotherapy in substance abuse treatment. In D. M. Donovan & G. A. Marlatt (Eds.), *Treating substance abuse: Theory and technique* (2nd ed.). New York: Guilford.

Carroll, K. M., Ball, S. A., Martino, S., Nich, C., Babuscio, T. A., Nuro, K. F., et al. (2008). Computer assisted delivery of cognitive-behavioral therapy for addiction: A randomized trial for CBT4CBT. *American Journal of Psychiatry* (published online). doi: 10.1176/appi.ajp.2008.071111835

Carroll, K. M., Smelson, D. A., Losonczy, M. F., & Ziedonis, D. (2001). A preliminary investigation of cocaine craving among persons with and without schizophrenia. *Psychiatric Services, 52*, 1029–1031.

Carvey, P. M. (1998). *Drug action in the central nervous system.* New York: Oxford University Press.

Casavant, M. J., Blake, K., Griffith, J., Yates, A., & Copley, L. M. (2007). Consequences of use of anabolic androgenic steroids. *Pediatric Clinics of North American, 54*, 677–690.

Caspers, K., Amdt, S., Yucuis, R., McKirgan, L., & Spinks, R. (2010). Effects of alcohol and cigarette use disorders on global and specific measures of cognition in middle age adults. *Journal of Studies on Alcohol and Drugs, 71*, 192–200.

Castro, F. G., Barrington, E. H., Walton, M. A., & Rawson, R. A. (2000). Cocaine and methamphetamine: Differential addiction rates. *Psychology of Addictive Behaviors, 14*, 390–396.

CDC: 1 million living with HIV in US. (2005). Retrieved from http://www.cnn.com/2005/HEALTH/conditions/06/13/hiv.cases.ap.index.html

Centers for Disease Control and Prevention. (2004). *The health consequences of smoking: What it means to you.* Washington, DC: U.S. Government Printing Office.

Centers for Disease Control and Prevention. (2007). Types of alcoholic beverages usually consumed by students in 9th–12th grades—four states, 2005.

Morbidity and Mortality Weekly Report, 56(29), 737–740.

Centers for Disease Control and Prevention. (2008). HIV/AIDS in the United States. *Centers for Disease Control and Prevention fact sheet* (August 2008 revision). Washington, DC: Author.

Centers for Disease Control and Prevention. (2009a). HIV-associated behaviors among injecting-drug users—23 cities, United States, May 2005–February 2006. *Morbidity and Mortality Weekly Report, 58*, 329–332.

Centers for Disease Control and Prevention. (2009b). Alcohol use among pregnant and nonpregnant women of childbearing age—United States, 1991–2005. *Morbidity and Mortality Weekly Report, 58*(19), 529–532.

Center for Substance Abuse Research. (2006). Alcohol, marijuana, Adderall, and Ritalin perceived to be most easily available drugs misused among undergraduates. *CESAR FAX, 15*(43), 1.

Center for Substance Abuse Research. (2008). Alcohol & marijuana have highest rates of continued use in the year after initiation: Heroin and crack cocaine have the highest rates of dependence. *Substance Use and Abuse, 17*(15), 1.

Cepeda, M. S., Alvarez, H., Morales, O., & Carr, D. B. (2004). Addition of ultralow dose naloxone to postoperative morphine PCA: Unchanged analgesia and opioid requirement but with decreased incident of opioid side effects. *Pain, 107*, 41–46.

Ceren, S. L. (2003) Warning: Managed care may be dangerous to your health. *The Independent Practitioner, 23*(2), 77.

Chaloupka, F. J. (2008). Smoking, food insecurity, and tobacco control. *Archives of Pediatric Medicine, 162*(11), 1096–1098.

Chambers, R. A., Sajdyk, T. J., Conrow, S. K., Lafuze, J. E., Fitz, S. D., & Shekhar, A. (2007). Neonatal amygdala lesions: Co-occurring impact on social/fear related behavior and cocaine sensitization in adult rats. *Behavioral Neuroscience, 121*, 1316–1327.

Chan, A. T., Manson, J., Feskanich, D., Stampfer, M. J., Colditz, G. A., & Fuchs, C. S. (2007). Long-term aspirin use and mortality in women. *Archives of Internal Medicine, 167*, 562–572.

Chan, A. T., Obino, S., & Fuchs, C. S. (2007). Aspirin and the risk of colorectal cancer in relationship to the expression of COX-2. *New England Journal of Medicine, 356*, 2131–2142.

Chang, G. (2001, March 2). *Gender and addictions.* Symposium presented to the Department of Psychiatry of Cambridge Hospital, Boston.

Chang, G. (2006, August 10). *Screening instruments and brief interventions for prenatal alcohol use.* Symposium presented at the annual meeting of the American Psychological Association, New Orleans, LA.

Chang, G., Chen, L., & Mao, J. (2007). Opioid tolerance and hyperalgesia. *Medical Clinics of North America, 91,* 199–211.

Chang, J. C., Dada, D., Frankel, R. M., Rodriguez, K. L., Zickmund, S., Ling, B. S., et al. (2008). When pregnant patients disclose substance use: Missed opportunities for behavioral change counseling. *Patient Education and Counseling, 72*(3), 394–401.

Chantix prescribing information. (2006). New York: Pfizer Pharmaceuticals.

Chapman, C. R., & Okifuji, A. (2004). Pain: Basic mechanisms and conscious experience. In R. H. Dworkin & W. S. Brietbart (Eds.), *Psychosocial aspects of pain: A handbook for health care providers.* Seattle: IASP Press.

Chapman, S., & MacKenzie, R. (2010). The global research neglect of unassisted smoking cessation: Causes and consequences. *PLoS Medicine* (published online). doi: 10.1371/journal.pmed.1000216

Chappel, J. N., & DuPont, R. L. (1999). Twelve-step and mutual help programs for addictive disorders. *Psychiatric Clinics of North America, 22,* 425–446.

Charney, D. S. (2004). Outpatient treatment of comorbid depression and alcohol use disorders. *Psychiatric Times, 21*(2), 31–33.

Charney, D. S., Mihic, S. J., & Harris, R. A. (2006). Hypnotics and sedatives. In L. L. Brunton, J. S. Lazo, & K. L. Parker (Eds.), *The pharmacological basis of therapeutics* (11th ed.). New York: McGraw-Hill.

Chassin, L., Flora, D. B., & King, K. M. (2004). Trajectories of alcohol and drug use and dependence from adolescence to adulthood: The effects of familial alcoholism and personality. *Journal of Abnormal Psychology, 113,* 483–498.

Chatlos, J. C. (1996). Recent developments and a developmental approach to substance use disorders: A biopsychosocial treatment approach. *Current Psychiatry Reports, 8*(5), 371–376.

Chau, D. L., Shull, J., & Mason, M. N. (2005). End-of-life pain: Pharmacological and psychosocial perspectives. *Psychiatric Times, 22*(11), 16–17.

Cheatle, M. D., & Gallagher, R. M. (2006). Chronic pain and comorbid mood and substance use

disorders: A biopsychosocial treatment approach. *Current Psychiatry Reports, 8*(5), 371–376.

Chen, C. K., Lin, S. K., Sham, P. C., Ball, D., Loh, E. W., Hsiao, C. C., et al. (2003). Pre-morbid characteristics and co-morbidity of methamphetamine users with and without psychosis. *Psychological Medicine, 33,* 1407–1414.

Chen, C. M., Smith, G. D., Harbord, R. M., & Lewis, S. J. (2008). Alcohol intake and blood pressure: A systematic review implementing a Mendelian randomized approach. *PLoS Med, 5,* e52. doi: 10.137/journal.pmed.0050052

Chen, C. M., Yoon, Y., Hi, H., & Lucas, D. L. (2007). Alcohol and hepatitis C mortality among males and females in the United States: A life table analysis. *Alcoholism: Clinical and Experimental Research, 31,* 285–292.

Cheng, A. T. A., Gau, S. F., Chen, T. H. H., Chang, J., & Chang, Y. (2004). A 4-year longitudinal study of risk factors for alcoholism. *Archives of General Psychiatry, 61,* 184–191.

Cherny, N. I., & Foley, K. M. (1996). Nonopioid and opioid analgesic pharmacology of cancer pain. *Hematology/Oncology Clinics of North America, 10,* 79–102.

Cherpitel, C. J., & Ye, Y. (2008). Trends in alcohol- and drug-related ED and primary care visits: Data from the US National Surveys (1995–2005). *American Journal of Drug and Alcohol Abuse, 34*(5), 576–583.

Chiauzzi, E. (1990). Breaking the patterns that lead to relapse. *Psychology Today, 23*(12), 18–19.

Chiauzzi, E. (1991). *Preventing relapse in the addictions.* New York: Pergamon.

China's healthcare woes. (2008). *New Scientist, 200*(2679), 11.

Chopra, D. (1997). *Overcoming addictions.* New York: Three Rivers Press.

Chou, R., Fanciullo, G. J., Fine, P. G., Adler, J. A., Ballantyne, J. C., Davies, P., et al. (2009). Clinical guidelines for the use of chronic opioid therapy in chronic noncancer pain. *The Journal of Pain, 10*(2), 113–130.

Chugh, T., Socoteanu, C., Reinier, K., Walts, J., Jui, J., & Gunson, K. (2008). A community-based evaluation of sudden death associated with therapeutic levels of methadone. *The American Journal of Medicine* (published online). doi: 10.1016/j.amjmed.2007.10.009

Chung, P. J., Garfield, C. F., Elliott, M. N., Ostroff, J., Ross, C., Jernigan, D. H., et al. (2009). Association between adolescent viewership and alcohol advertising on cable television. *American Journal of Public Health* (published online prior to print). doi: 10.2105/AJPH.2008.146423

Chung, T., Colby, S. M., Barnett, N. P., Rohsenow, D. J., Spirto, A., & Monti, P. M. (2000). Screening adolescents for problem drinking: Performance of brief screens against *DSM-IV* alcohol diagnoses. *Journal of Studies on Alcohol, 61*, 579–587.

Cigarette smoking among adults—United States. 2007. (2007). *Morbidity and Mortality Weekly Report, 57*(45), 1121–1126.

Ciraulo, D. A. (2004, March 5). *A pharmacological approach to treatment.* Paper presented at the Treating the Addictions conference sponsored by the Department of Psychiatry of Cambridge Hospital, Boston.

Ciraulo, D. A., Ciraulo, J. A., Sands, B. F., Knapp, C. M., & Sarid-Segal, O. (2005). Sedative-hypnotics. In H. R. Kranzler & D. A. Ciraulo (Eds.), *Clinical manual of addiction psychopharmacology.* Washington, DC: American Psychiatric Publishing.

Ciraulo, D. A., & Nace, E. P. (2000). Benzodiazepine treatment of anxiety or insomnia in substance a use patients. *American Journal on Addictions, 9*, 276–284.

Ciraulo, D. A., Piechniczek-Buczek, J., & Iscan, E. N. (2003). Outcome predictors in substance use disorders. *Psychiatric Clinics of North America, 26*, 381–409.

Ciraulo, D. A., & Sarid-Segal, O. (2005). Sedative-, hypnotic-, or anxiolytic-related disorders. In B. J. Sadock & V. A. Sadock (Eds.), *Kaplan & Sadock's comprehensive textbook of psychiatry* (8th ed.). New York: Lippincott Williams & Wilkins.

Ciraulo, D. A., Shader, R. I., Greenblatt, D. J., & Creelman, W. (2006). *Drug interactions in psychiatry* (3rd ed.). New York: Lippincott Williams & Wilkins.

Clark, D. B., Martin, C. S., & Cornelius, J. R. (2008). Adolescent-onset substance use disorders predict young mortality. *Journal of Adolescent Health, 42*(6), 637–639.

Clark, D. B., Vanyukrov, M., & Cornelius, J. (2002). Childhood antisocial behavior and adolescent alcohol use disorders. *Alcohol Research & Health, 26*, 109–115.

Clark, R. E., Xie, H., & Brunette, M. F. (2004). Benzodiazepine prescription practices and substance abuse in persons with severe mental illness. *Journal of Clinical Psychiatry, 65*(2), 151–155.

Clausen, T., Anchersen, K., & Waal, H. (2008). Mortality prior to, during and after opioid maintenance treatment (OMT): A national prospective cross-registry study. *Drug and Alcohol Dependence, 94*(1–3), 151–157.

Clavel, F., & Hence, A. J. (2004). HIV drug resistance. *New England Journal of Medicine, 350*, 1023–1035.

Clay, S. W., Allen, J., & Parran, T. (2008). A review of addiction. *Postgraduate Medicine, 120*(2), E01–7.

Cloak, C. C., Ernst, T., Fujii, L., Hedemark, B. A., & Chang, L. (2009). Lower diffusion in white matter of children with prenatal methamphetamine exposure. *Neurology* (published online prior to print). doi: 10.1212/01.wn1.0000346516.49126.20

Cloninger, C. R., Bohman, M., & Sigvardsson, S. (1981). Inheritance of alcohol abuse: Cross-fostering analysis of adopted men. *Archives of General Psychiatry, 38*, 861–868.

Cloninger, C. R., Sigvardsson, S., & Bohman, M. (1996). Type I and Type II alcoholism: An update. *Alcohol Health & Research World, 20*(1), 18–23.

Cloud, J. (2002). Is pot good for you? *Time, 160*(19), 62–66.

Cocaine and the brain. (2004). *Forensic Drug Abuse Advisor, 6*(9), 67.

Codependency. (1990). *The Wellness Letter, 7*(1), 7.

Coghlan, A. (2006a). Let's hear it again for red wine. *New Scientist, 190*(2551), 8.

Coghlan, A. (2006b). Trials for drug that gets to heart of HIV. *New Scientist, 190*(2555), 16–17.

Coghlan, A. (2008). Plans drawn up for a war on drink. *New Scientist, 198*(2652), 6–7.

Coghlan, A. (2009). Which way to turn on cannabis law? *New Scientist, 201*(2689), 6–7.

Cohen, J. (2004). New TB drug promises shorter, simpler, treatment. *Science, 306*, 1872.

Cohen, J., Collins, R., Darkes, J., & Gwartney, D. (2007). A league of their own: Demographics, motivations and patterns of abuse of 1,955 male adult non-medical anabolic steroid users in the United States. *Journal of the International Society of Sports Nutrition* (published online). doi: 10:1186/1550-2783-4-12

Cohen, L. R., & Gordon, S. M. (2009). Co-occurring eating and substance use disorders. In K. T. Brady, S. E. Back, & S. F. Greenfield (Eds.), *Women & addiction.* New York: Guilford.

Cohen, L. R., & Hien, D. A. (2006). Treatment outcomes for women with substance abuse and PTSD who have experienced complex trauma. *Psychiatric Services, 57*, 100–106.

Cohen, M. (2000). *Counseling addicted women*. Thousand Oaks, CA: Sage.

Coker, M. (1997). Overcoming sexism in A.A.: How women cope. In S. L. A. Straussner & E. Zelvin (Eds.), *Gender and addictions*. Northvale, NJ: Jason Aronson.

Cole, J. Q., & Yonkers, K. A. (1995). Nonbenzodiazepine anxiolytics. In A. F. Shatzberg & C. B. Nemeroff (Eds.), *Textbook of psychopharmacology*. Washington, DC: American Psychiatric Publishing.

Coleman, E. D., & Balelt, R. C. (1997). Efficacy of two commercial products for altering urine drug test results. *Journal of Toxicology: Clinical Toxicology, 35*(6), 637–642.

Collins, E. D., & Kleber, H. D. (2004). Opioids. In M. Galanter & H. D. Kleber (Eds.), *The American Psychiatric Publishing textbook of substance abuse treatment* (3rd ed.). Washington, DC: American Psychiatric Publishing.

Collins, E. D., Kleber, H. D., Whittington, R. A., & Heitler, N. E. (2005). Anesthesia-assisted vs buprenorphine- or clonidine-assisted heroin detoxification and naltrexone introduction: A randomized trial. *Journal of the American Medical Association, 294*, 903–913.

Collins, G. B., & Leak, B. C. (2008). Buprenorphine revolutionizes treatment for opiate dependence. *Cleveland Clinic Insights, 2008*, 2–3.

Collins, J. A. (2009). Screening: Immunoassays. In J. D. Robero-Miller & B. A. Goldberger (Eds.), *Handbook of workplace drug testing* (2nd ed.). Washington, DC: AACC Press.

Collins, R. L., & McNair, L .D. (2002). Minority women and alcohol use. *Alcohol Research & Health, 26*(4), 251–256.

Colliver, J. D., Compton, W. M., Gfroerer, J. C., & Condon, T. (2006). Projecting drug use among aging baby boomers in 2020. *Annals of Epidemiology, 16*(4), 257–265.

Comerci, G. D., Fuller, P., & Morrison, S. F. (1997). Cigarettes, drugs, alcohol & teens. *Patient Care, 31*(4), 57–83.

Commission on Adolescent Substance and Alcohol Abuse. (2005). In D. L. Evans, E. B. Foa, R. E. Gur, H. Hendin, C. P. O'Brien, M. E. P. Seligman, & B. T. Walsh (Eds.), *Treating and preventing adolescent mental health disorders*. New York: Guilford.

Committee on Addictions of the Group for the Advancement of Psychiatry. (2002). Responsibility and choice in addiction. *Psychiatric Services, 53*, 707–713.

Committee on Child Health Care Financing and Committee on Substance Abuse. (2001). Improving substance abuse prevention, assessment and treatment financing for children and adolescents. *Pediatrics, 108*, 1025–1029.

Committee on Secondhand Smoke Exposure and Acute Coronary Events. (2009). *Secondhand smoke exposure and cardiovascular effects: Making sense of the evidence*. Washington, DC: National Academy of Science.

Community Anti-Drug Coalitions of American (1997, June 19). *The meth challenge: Threatening communities coast to coast*. Interactive live national teleconference.

Compton, M. T., Kelly, K. E., Ramsay, C. E., Pringle, M., Goulding, S. M., Esterberg, M. L., et al. (2009). Association of pre-onset cannabis, alcohol and tobacco use with age of prodrome and age of onset of psychosis in first-episode patients. *American Journal of Psychiatry, 166*(11), 1251–1257.

Compton, M. T., & Ramsay, C. E. (2009). The impact of pre-onset cannabis use on age at onset of prodromal and psychotic symptoms. *Primary Psychiatry, 16*(4), 35–43.

Comptom, P., & Athanasos, P. (2003). Chronic pain, substance abuse and addiction. *Nursing Clinics of North America, 38*, 525–537.

Comptom, W. M., Cottler, L. B., Jacobs, J. L., Ben-Abdallah, A., & Spitznagel, E. L. (2003). The role of psychiatric disorders in predicting drug dependence treatment outcomes. *American Journal of Psychiatry, 160*, 890–895.

Comptom, W. M., Grant, B. F., Colliver, J. D., Glantz, M. D., & Stinson, F. S. (2004). Prevalence of marijuana use disorders in the United States 1991–1992 and 2001. *Journal of the American Medical Association, 291*, 2114–2121.

Comptom, W. M., Thomas, Y. F., Stinson, F. S., & Grant, B. F. (2007). Prevalence, correlates, disability, and comorbidity of *DSM-IV* drug abuse and dependence in the United States: Results from the national epidemiologic survey on alcohol and related conditions. *Archives of General Psychiatry, 64*, 566–576.

Comtois, K. A., Schiff, M. A., & Grossman, D. C. (2008). Psychiatric risk factors associated with postpartum suicide attempt in Washington State, 1992–2001. *American Journal of Obstetrics & Gynecology, 199*(2), 120.e1–120.e5.

Concar, D. (1997). Deadly combination. *New Scientist, 155*, 2090–2091.

Concern at new "legal high" drugs. (2008). BBC News. Retrieved from http://news:bbc/cp/uk_news/politics/7670752.stm

Conen, D., Tedrow, U. B., Cook, N. R., Mororthy, M. V., Buring, J. E., & Albert, C. M. (2008). Alcohol consumption and risk of incident atrial fibrillation. *Journal of the American Medical Association, 21,* 2489–2496.

Congeni, J., & Miller, S. (2002). Supplements and drugs used to enhance athletic performance. *The Pediatric Clinics of North America, 49,* 435–461.

Conner, L. C., Le Fauve, C. E., & Wallace, B. C. (2009). Ethnic and cultural correlates of addiction among diverse women. In K. T. Brady, S. E. Back, & S. F. Greenfield (Eds.), *Women & addiction.* New York: Guilford.

Connor, K. R., Hesselrock, M. V. M., Schuckit, M. A., Hirsch, J. K., Knox, H. L., Meldrum, S., et al. (2006). Precontemplated and impulsive suicide attempts among individuals with alcohol dependence. *Journal of Studies on Alcohol, 67,* 95–101.

Connor, K. R., Li, Y., Meldrum, S., Duberstein, P. R., & Conwell, Y. (2003). The role of drinking in suicidal ideation: Analysis of Project MATCH data. *Journal of Studies on Alcohol, 64,* 402–408.

Connors, G. J., Donovan, D. M., & DiClemente, C. C. (2001). *Substance abuse treatment and the stages of change.* New York: Guilford.

Conroy, D., Arnedt, J. T., & Brower, K. J. (2008). Insomnia in patients with addictions: A safer way to break the cycle. *Current Psychiatry, 7*(5), 97–109.

Cooney, N. L., Kadden, R. M., & Steinberg, H. R. (2005). Assessment of alcohol problems. In D. M. Donovan & G. A. Marlatt (Eds.), *Assessment of addictive behaviors* (2nd ed.). New York: Guilford.

Cooper, D. A. (2008). Life and death in the CART era. *The Lancet, 372,* 266–267.

Cooper, J. R., Bloom, F. E., & Roth, R. H. (2003). *The biochemical basis of neuropharmacology* (8th ed.). New York: Oxford University Press.

Cornwell, E. E., Blezberg, H., Belmahos, G., Chan, L. S., Demetriades, D., Stewart, B. M., et al. (1998). The prevalence and effect of alcohol and drug abuse on cohort-matched critically injured patients. *The American Surgeon, 64,* 461–465.

Correia, C. J. (2005). Behavioral theories of choice. In M. Earlywine (Ed.), *Mind-altering drugs: The science of subjective experience.* New York: Oxford University Press.

Corrigan, J. D., Bonger, J., Lamb-Hart, G., Heinmann, A. W., & Moore, D. (2005). Increased substance abuse treatment compliance for persons with traumatic brain injury. *Psychology of Addictive Behavior, 19*(2), 131–139.

Corrigan, P. W., Lurie, B. D., Goldman, H. D., Slopen, N., Medasani, K., & Phelan, S. (2005). How adolescents perceive the stigma of mental illness and alcohol abuse. *Psychiatric Services, 56,* 544–560.

Could brain abnormality predict drug addiction? (2008). *Science Daily.* Retrieved from http://www.sciencedaily.com/releases/2008/10/081022222911.htm

Covey, L. W., Sullivan, M. A., Johnston, A., Glassman, A. H., Robinson, M. D., & Adams, D. P. (2000). Advances in non-nicotine pharmacotherapy for smoking cessation. *Drugs, 59,* 17–31.

Covington, L. W. (2005). Update on antiviral agents for HIV and AIDS. *Nursing Clinics of North America, 40,* 149–165.

Cowan, D., Osselton, D., & Robinson, S. (2005). Drug testing. In D. Nutt, T. W. Robbins, G. V. Stimson, M. Ince, & A. Jackson (Eds.), *Drugs and the future.* New York: Academic Press.

Cox, S., Posner, S. F., Kourtis, A. P., & Jamieson, D. J. (2008). Hospitalizations with amphetamine abuse among pregnant women. *Obstetrics & Gynecology, 111*(2), 341–347.

Cozolino, L. (2002). *The neuroscience of psychotherapy.* New York: Norton.

Craig, R. J. (2004). *Counseling the alcohol and drug dependent client.* New York: Norton.

Crego, A., Holguin, S. R., Prada, M., Mota, N., et al. (2009). Binge drinking affects attentional and visual working memory process in young university students. *Alcoholism Clinical and Experimental Research, 33*(11), 1870–1879.

Crews, F. T. (2008). Alcohol-related neurodegeneration and recovery. *Alcohol Research & Health, 31,* 377–388.

Croft, H. A. (2006). Physical handling of prescription stimulants. *Pediatric Annals, 35*(8), 86–97.

Crosby, A. E., Espitia-Hardeman, V., Hill, H. A., Ortega, L., et al. (2009). Alcohol and suicide among racial/ethnic populations—17 states, 2005–2006. *Morbidity and Mortality Weekly Report, 58*(23), 637–641.

Cross, C. L., & Ashley, L. (2007). Trauma and addiction. *Journal of Psychosocial Nursing, 45*(1), 24–31.

Crowley, T. J. (2007). Adolescents and substance-related disorders. In J. B. Saunders, M. A. Schuckit, P. J. Sirovatka, & D. A. Reiger (Eds.), *Diagnostic issues in substance use disorders.* Washington, DC: American Psychiatric Publishing.

Crowley, T. J., & Sakai, J. (2004). Neurobiology of alcohol. In M. Galanter & H. D. Kleber (Eds.), *The American Psychiatric Publishing textbook of substance abuse treatment* (3rd ed.). Washington, DC: American Psychiatric Publishing.

Crowley, T. J., & Sakai, J. (2005). Inhalant-related disorders. In B. J. Sadock & V. A. Sadock (Eds.), *Kaplan & Sadock's comprehensive textbook of psychiatry* (8th ed.). New York: Lippincott Williams & Wilkins.

Cruz, M. T., Bajo, M., Schweitzer P., & Roberto, M. (2008). Shared mechanisms of alcohol and other drugs. *Alcohol Research & Health, 31*(2), 137–147.

Cumsille, P. E., Sayer, A. G., & Graham, J. W. (2000). Perceived exposure to peer and adult drinking as predictors of growth in positive alcohol expectancies during adolescence. *Journal of Consulting and Clinical Psychology, 68,* 531–536.

Cunniff, C. (2003, May 28). *Fetal alcohol syndrome: Diagnosis, treatment, and public health.* Paper presented at the Continuing Medical Education Symposium, Gundersen Lutheran Medical Center, La Crosse, WI.

Cunningham, J. A., Sobell, L. C., Gavin, D. R., Sobell, M. B., & Breslin, F. C. (1997). Assessing motivation for change: Preliminary development and evaluation of a scale measuring the benefits and costs of changing alcohol or drug use. *Psychology of Addictive Behaviors, 11,* 107–114.

Cunningham, J. K., Liu, L. M., & Callaghan, R. (2009). Impact of US and Canadian precursor regulation on methamphetamine purity in the United States. *Addiction, 104,* 441–453.

Cupp, M. J. (1999). Herbal remedies: Adverse effects and drug interactions. *American Family Physician, 59,* 1239–1244.

Curley, B. (2007). U.S. mayors declare drug war a failure. Retrieved from http:www.jointogether.org/news/features/2007/us-mayors-declare-drug-war.html

Curran, H. V., Collins, R., Fletcher, S., Kee, S. C. Y., Woods, B., & Iliffe, S. (2003). Older adults and withdrawal from benzodiazepine hypnotics in general practice: Effects on cognitive function, sleep, mood and quality of life. *Psychological Medicine, 33,* 1223–1237.

Cutler-Triggs, C., Fryer, G. E., Miyoshi, T. J., & Weitzman, M. (2008). Increased rates and severity of child and adult food insecurity in households with adult smokers. *Archives of Pediatric and Adolescent Medicine, 162*(11), 1056–1062.

Daeppen, J. B., Gache, P., Landry, U., Sekera, E., Schweizer, V., Gloor, S., et al. (2002). Symptom-triggered versus fixed doses of benzodiazepine for alcohol withdrawal. *Archives of Internal Medicine, 162,* 1117–1121.

Daghestani, A. N., Dinwiddie, S. H., & Hardy, D. W. (2001). Antisocial personality disorder in and out of correctional and forensic settings. *Psychiatric Annals, 31*(7), 441–446.

Dajer, T. (2005). Why is she so short of breath? *Discover, 26*(3), 21–22.

Dalen, J. T. (2007). Aspirin resistance: Is it real? Is it clinically significant? *The American Journal of Medicine, 120,* 1–4.

Daley, D. C., & Marlatt, G. A. (2005). Relapse prevention. In J. H. Lowinson, P. Ruiz, R. B. Millman, & J. G. Langrod (Eds.), *Substance abuse: A comprehensive textbook* (4th ed.). New York: Lippincott Williams & Wilkins.

Daley, D. C., & Marlatt, G. A. (2006). *Overcoming your alcohol or drug problem (therapist's guide).* New York: Oxford University Press.

Daling, J. R., Doody, D. R., Sun, X., Trabert, B. L., Weiss, N. S., Chen, C., et al. (2009). Association of marijuana use and incidence of testicular germ cell tumors. *Cancer* (published online). doi: 10.1002/cncr.24159

Dalley, J. W., Fryer, T. D., Brichard, L., Robinson, E. S., Theobald, D. E., Lääne, K., et al. (2007). Nucleus accumbens D2/D3 receptors predict trait impulsivity and cocaine reinforcement. *Science, 315,* 1267–1270.

Danaei, G., Ding, E. L., Mozaffarian, D., Taylor, B., Rehm, J., Murray, D. J., et al. (2009). The preventable causes of death in the United States: Comparative risk assessment of dietary, lifestyle and metabolic risk factors. *PLoS Medicine.* Retrieved from http:ww//www.plosmedicine.org/article/info%3Adoi%2F10.1317%Fjournal.pmed.1000058

Danaei, G., Vander Hoorn, S., Lopez, A. D., Murray, C. J., Ezzati, M., & Comparative Risk Assessment Collaborating Group (Cancers). (2006). Causes of cancer in the world: Comparative risk assessment of nine behavioural and environmental risk factors. *The Lancet, 19*(9449), 1784–1793.

Dangers of benzodiazepine abuse during MMT. (2009). *Addiction Treatment Forum, 19*(2), 6–7.

Daniels, A. (2009). Is there a "right" to health care? *The Wall Street Journal.* Retrieved from

http://online.wsj.com/article_email/sb100014240529
702035173045743061706770645070.html

Danjou, P., Paty, P., Fruncillo, R., Worthington, P., Unruh, M., Cevallos, W., et al. (1999). A comparison of the residual effects of zaleplon and zolpidem following administration 5 to 2 h before awakening. *Analytical Chemistry, 45*(3), 777–780.

D'Arcy, Y. (2005). Conquering pain. *Nursing 2005, 35*(3), 36–41.

Daubin, C., Quentin, C., Goulle, J., Guillotin, D., Lehoux, P., Lepage, O., et al. (2008). Refractory shock and asystole related to tramadol overdose. *Clinical Toxicology, 45*(8), 961–964.

D'Aunno T., & Pollack, N. A. (2002). Changes in Methadone treatment practices. *Journal of the American Medical Association, 288*, 850–856.

Davey, M. (2005). Grisly effects of one drug: Meth mouth. Retrieved from http:www.nytimes.com/2005/06/11/national/11meth.hmtl?ex-1120104000en=82c41a6f61399c01&emc-etal

Davidson, R. (1998). The transtheoretical model. In W. R. Miller & N. Heather (Eds.), *Treating addictive behaviors* (2nd ed.). New York: Plenum.

Davies, P. (2005). Long-dormant threat surfaces: Deaths from hepatitis C are expected to jump. *The Wall Street Journal, CCXLV*(105), D-1.

Davis, W. R., & Johnson, B. D. (2008). Prescription opioid use, misuse, and diversion among street drug users in New York City. *Drug & Alcohol Dependence, 92*(1–3), 267–276.

Davison, K. P., Pennebaker, J. W., & Dickerson, S. S. (2000). Who talks? *American Psychologist, 55*, 205–217.

Day, E., Bentham, P., Callaghan, R., Kuruvilla, T., & George, S. (2004). Thiamine for Wernicke-Korsakoff syndrome in people at risk from alcohol abuse. *The Cochrane Database of Systematic Reviews, 2*, CD004033.

Day-Cameron, J. M., Muse, L., Hauenstein, J., Simmons, L., & Correia, C. J. (2009). Alcohol use by undergraduate students on their 21st birthday: Predictors of actual consumption, anticipated consumption and normative beliefs. *Psychology of Addictive Behaviors, 23*, 695–701.

Dayton, T. (2005). Discovering life after blame: A new model of the addicted/traumatized family system. *Counselor, 6*(1), 12–17.

Deadly drug adulterants. (2008). *Forensic Drug Abuse Advisor, 20*(6), 47–48.

"Deadly in pink" report targets Big Tobacco. (2009). Retrieved from http://tobaccofreekids.org/reports/wo,en_new/report/deadlyinpink_02182009_FINAL.pdf

De Bellis, M. D., Clark, D. B., Beers, S. R., Soloff, P. H., Boring, A. M., Hall, J., et al. (2000) Hippocampal volume in adolescent-onset alcohol use disorders. *American Journal of Psychiatry, 157*, 737–744.

Debusmann, B. (2006). US war on drugs: Elusive victory, disputed statistics. Retrieved from http://www.alertnet.org/thenews/newsdesk/NO371862.htm

de la Torre, R., Farré, M., Roset, P. N., Pizarro, N., Abanades, S., Segura, M., et al. (2004). Human pharmacology of MDMA: Pharmacokinetics, metabolism, and disposition. *Therapeutic Drug Monitoring, 26*(2), 137–144.

DeLeon, G. (2008). Therapeutic communities. In M. Galanter & H. D. Kleber (Eds.), *The American Psychiatric Publishing textbook of substance abuse treatment*. Washington, DC: American Psychiatric Publishing.

Delingpole, J. (2009). *Welcome to Obamaland: I have seen the future and it doesn't work*. Washington, DC: Regnery.

Dembosky, A. (2009). Marijuana smoke is a carcinogen, California board rules. *Mercury News*. Retrieved from http://www.mercurynews.com/politics/ci_12644670?nclick_check=1

Dervaux, A., Baylé, F. J., Laqueille, X., Bourdel, M. C., & Le Borgne, M.-H., Olié, J.-P., et al. (2001). Is substance abuse in schizophrenia related to impulsivity, sensation seeking, or anhedonia? *American Journal of Psychiatry, 158*, 494–494.

Deteriorating home life puts kids at risk. (2009). *New Scientist, 201*(2701), 14.

DeVane, C. L. (2004). Principles of pharmacokinetics and pharmacodynamics. In A. F. Schatzberg & C. B. Nemeroff (Eds.), *Textbook of psychopharmacology* (3rd ed.). Washington, DC: American Psychiatric Publishing.

DeVane, C. L. (2009). Sex differences in pharmacokinetics and pharmacodynamics. In K. T. Brady, S. E. Back, & S. F. Greenfield (Eds.), *Women & addiction*. New York: Guilford.

DeVane, C. L., & Nemeroff, C. B. (2002). 2002 guide to psychotropic drug interactions. *Primary Psychiatry, 9*(3), 28–51.

DeVour, M. C. (1999). What is moderate drinking? *Alcohol Health & Research World, 23*(1), 5–14.

DeWilde, B., Dom, G., Hulstjn, W., & Wabbe, B. (2007). Motor functioning and alcohol dependence. *Alcoholism: Clinical and Experimental Research, 31*, 1820–1825.

Dickensheets, S. (2001). Roid rage. *Playboy*, *48*(7), 128–129, 156–162.

Dickinson, A. (2000). Smoke screen. *Time*, *155*(11), 92.

DiClemente, C. C., Bellino, L. E., & Neavins, T. M. (1999). Motivation for change and alcoholism treatment. *Alcohol Health and Research World*, *23*(2), 86–92.

DiClemente, C. C., & Prochaska, J. O. (1998). Toward a comprehensive, transtheoretical model of change. In W. R. Miller & N. Heather (Eds.), *Treating addictive behaviors* (2nd ed.). New York: Plenum.

Dienstag, J. J. (2006). Hepatitis C: A bitter harvest. *Annals of Internal Medicine*, *144*, 770–771.

Dienstag, J. J. (2008). Acute viral hepatitis. In A. S. Fauci, E. Braunwald, D. L. Kasper, S. L. Hauser, D. L. Longo, J. L. Jameson, & J. Loscalzo (Eds.), *Harrison's principles of internal medicine* (17th ed.). New York: McGraw-Hill Medical.

Diercks, D. B., Gonarow, G. C., Kirk, J. D., Jois-Bilowich, P., Hollander, J. E., Weber, J. E., et al. (2008). Illicit stimulant use in a United States heart failure population presenting to the emergency department (from the Acute Decompensated Heart Failure National Registry Emergency Module). *American Journal of Cardiology*, *102*(9), 1216–1219.

DiFranza, J. R., Savageau, J. A., Fletcher, K. O'Loughlin, J., Pbert, L., Ockene, J. K., et al. (2007). Symptoms of tobacco dependence after brief intermittent use: The development and assessment of nicotine dependent in youth study. *Archives of Pediatrics & Adolescent Medicine*, *171*, 704–710.

DiFranza, J. R., Savageau, J. A., Fletcher, K., Pbert, L., O'Loughlin, J., McNeill, A. D., et al. (2007). Susceptibility to nicotine dependence: The Development and Assessment of Nicotine in Youth 2 Study. *Pediatrics*, *120*(4), e-974–e983 (published online). doi: 10.1542/peds.2007-0027

Dijkstra, B. J. M., De Jong, C. A. J., Krabbe, P. F. M., & van der Staak, C. P. F. (2008). Prediction of abstinence in opioid-dependent patients. *Journal of Addiction Medicine*, *2*(4), 194–201.

Dill, P. L., & Wells-Parker, E. (2006). Court-managed treatment for convicted drinking drivers. *Alcohol Research & Health*, *29*(1), 41–48.

Diller, L. H. (1998). *Running on Ritalin*. New York: Bantam Books.

Dilts, S. L., & Dilts, S. L. (2005). Opioids. In R. J. Frances, S. I. Miller, & A. H. Mack (Eds.), *Clinical textbook of addictive disorders* (3rd ed.). New York: Guilford.

Dimneff, L. A., & Marlatt, G. A. (1995). Relapse prevention. In R. K. Hester & W. R. Miller (Eds.), *Handbook of alcoholism treatment approaches* (2nd ed.). New York: Allyn & Bacon.

Disney, E. R., Elkins, I. J., McGue, M., & Iacono, W. G. (1999). Effects of ADHD, conduct disorder, and gender on substance abuse in adolescence. *American Journal of Psychiatry*, *156*, 1515–1521.

Dixit, A. R., & Crum, R. M. (2000). Prospective study of depression and risk of heavy alcohol use in women. *American Journal of Psychiatry*, *157*, 751–758.

Dobbs, L. (2007). The war within, killing ourselves. Retrieved from http://www.cnn.com/2007/US/02/13/Dobbs.Feb14/index.html

Doble, A., Martin, I. L., & Nutt, D. (2004). *Calming the brain*. New York: Martin-Dunitz.

Doctors often skip health behavior conversations with teens. (2008, December 1). News release. Center for the Advancement of Health.

Doghramji, K. (2003). When patients can't sleep. *Current Psychiatry*, *2*(5), 40–50.

Doidge, N. (2007). *The brain that changes itself*. New York: Viking.

Dokoupil, T. (2009). Can booze cure men's fashion phobia? Upscale stores hope spirits boost sales. *Newsweek*. Retrieved from http://blog.newsweek .comblogs/thehumancondition/archive/2009/07/08/can-booze-cure-men's-fashion-phobia?

Dolan, K., Rouen, D., & Kimber, J. (2004). An overview of the use of urine, hair, sweat and saliva to detect drug use. *Drug & Alcohol Review*, *23*(2), 213–217.

Dole, V. P. (1988). Implications of methadone maintenance for theories of narcotic addiction. *Journal of the American Medical Association*, *260*, 3025–3029.

Dole, V. P. (1989). [Letter to the editor]. *Journal of the American Medical Association*, *261*(13), 1880.

Dole, V. P. (1995). On federal regulation of methadone treatment. *Journal of the American Medical Association*, *274*, 1307.

Dole, V. P., & Nyswander, M. A. (1965). Medical treatment for diacetylmorphine (heroin) addiction. *Journal of the American Medical Association*, *193*, 545–656.

Donaher, P. A., & Welsh, C. (2006). Managing opioid addiction with buprenorphine. *American Family Physician*, *73*, 1573–1578.

Donovan, D. M. (2005). Assessment of addictive behaviors for relapse prevention. In D. M. Donovan & G. A. Marlatt (Eds.), *Assessment of addictive behaviors* (2nd ed.). New York: Guilford.

Donovan, J. E., Molina, B. S. G., & Kelly, T. M. (2009). Alcohol outcome expectancies as socially shared and socialized beliefs. *Psychology of Addictive Behaviors, 23,* 248–259.

D'Onofrio, G., & Degutis, L. C. (2004). Screening and brief intervention in the emergency department. *Alcohol Research & Health, 28*(2), 63–72.

D'Onofrio, G., Rathlev, N. K., Ulrich, A. S., Rish, S. S., & Freedland, E. S. (1999). Lorazepam for the prevention of recurrent seizures related to alcohol. *New England Journal of Medicine, 340,* 915–919.

Don't buy it. (2006). *New Scientist, 190*(2547), 15.

Dooldeniya, M. D., Khafagy, R., Mashaly, H., Browning, A. J., Sundaram, S. K., & Biyani, C. S. (2007). Lower abdominal pain in women after binge drinking. *British Medical Journal, 335,* 992–993.

Doubeni, C. A., Li, W., Fouayzi, H., & DiFranza, J. R. (2008). Perceived accessibility as a predictor of youth smoking. *Annals of Family Medicine, 6,* 323–330.

Doweiko, H. (1999). Substance use disorders as a symptom of a spiritual disease. In O. J. Morgan & M. Jordan (Eds.), *Addiction and spirituality: A multidisciplinary approach.* St. Louis, MO: Chalice Press.

Doweiko, H. E. (2002). Dreams as an unappreciated therapeutic avenue for cognitive-behavioral therapists. *Journal of Cognitive Psychotherapy, 16*(1), 29–38.

Dowling, G. J., Weiss, S. R. B., & Condon, T. P. (2008). Drugs of abuse and the aging brain. *Neuropsychopharmacology, 33,* 209–218.

Drake, R. E. (2007). Management of substance use disorder in schizophrenia patients: Current guidelines. *CNS Spectrums, 12*(10), 27–32.

Drake, R. E., Essock, S. M., Shaner, A., Carey, A., Minkoff, K., Kola, L., et al. (2001). Implementing dual diagnosis services for clients with mental illness. *Psychiatric Services, 52,* 469–476.

Drake, R. E., & Mueser, K. T. (2002). Co-occurring alcohol use disorder and schizophrenia. *Alcohol Research & Health, 26,* 99–102.

Drake, R. E., Mueser, K. T., Brunette, M. F., & McHugo, G. J. (2004). A review of treatments for people with severe mental illnesses and co-occurring substance use disorders. *Psychiatric Rehabilitation Journal, 27*(4), 360–374.

Dreher, M. C., Nugent, K., & Hudgins, R. (1994). Prenatal marijuana exposure and neo-natal outcomes in Jamaica: An ethnographic study. *Pediatrics, 93,* 254–260.

Drew, S. M., Wilkins, K. M., & Trevisan, L. A. (2010). Managing medications and alcohol misuse by your older patients. *Current Psychiatry, 9*(2), 21–24, 27–28, 41.

Driessen, M., Meier, S., Hill, A., Wetterling, T., Lange, W., & Junghanns, K. (2001). The course of anxiety, depression and drinking behaviors after completed detoxification in alcoholics with and without comorbid anxiety and depressive disorders. *Alcohol & Alcoholism, 36,* 249–255.

Drinking and driving. (1996). *Alcohol Alert, 37.* Washington, DC: National Institute on Alcohol Abuse and Alcoholism.

Druesne-Peccolo, D., Tehard, B., Mallet, Y., Gerber, M., Norat, T., Hercberg, S., et al. (2009). Alcohol and genetic polymorphisms: Effect on risk of alcohol-related cancer. *The Lancet Oncology, 10,* 173–180.

Drug and Alcohol Services Information System. (2007). *Adolescent treatment admissions by gender: 2005.* Washington, DC: Substance Abuse and Mental Health Services.

Drug disarray. (2009). *New Scientist, 204*(2733), 6.

Drugs drive politicians out of their minds. (2009). *New Scientist, 201*(2695), 5.

Drugs in sports: New problems in doping detection. (2009). *Forensic Drug Abuse Advisor, 21*(9), 68–69.

Drug war is lost. (2005). *New Scientist, 185*(1490), 4.

Drug war success claims challenged. (2006). Retrieved from http//www.jointogether.org./news/head-lines/inthenews/2006/drug-war-success-claims.html

Drummer, O. H., & Odell, M. (2001). *The forensic pharmacology of drugs of abuse.* New York: Oxford University Press.

Dube, C., Rostom, A., Lewin, G., Tsertsvandez, A., Barrowman, N., Code, C., et al. (2007). The use of aspirin or primary prevention of colorectal cancer: a systematic review prepared for the U.S. Prevention Services Task Force. *Archives of General Medicine, 146,* 365–375.

Dube, S. R., Anda, R. F., Felitti, V. J., Chapman, D. P., Williamson, D. F., & Giles, W. H. (2001). Childhood abuse, household dysfunction, and the risk of attempted suicide throughout the life span. *Journal of the American Medical Association, 286,* 3089–3096.

Dube, S. R., Asman, K., Malarcher, A., Carabollo, R., & Office on Smoking and Health, National Center for Chronic Disease Prevention and Health Promotion, CDC. (2009). Cigarette smoking among adults and trends in smoking cessation—United States, 2008.

Morbidity and Mortality Weekly Report, 58, 1227–1232.

Dubovsky, S. (2005). Benzodiazepine receptor agonists and antagonists. In B. J. Sadock & V. A. Sadock (Eds.), *Kaplan & Sadock's comprehensive textbook of psychiatry* (8th ed.). New York: Lippincott Williams & Wilkins.

Dudley, R. (2004). Ethanol, fruit ripening, and the historical origins of human alcoholism in primate frugivory. *Integrative and Comparative Biology, 44*(94), 315–323.

Dumais, A., Lesage, M., Alda, M., Rouleau, G., Dumont, M., Chawky, N., et al. (2005). Risk factors for suicide in major depression: A case-controlled study of impulsive and aggressive behaviors in men. *American Journal of Psychiatry, 162,* 2116–2124.

Dunigan, R. (2009, March 6). *Addiction treatment with diverse populations.* Paper presented at the Treating the Addictions seminar hosted by the Harvard Medical School Department of Continuing Education, Boston.

Dunn, K. M., Sauders, K. W., Rutter, C. M., Banta-Green, S. C., Merrill, J. O., Sullivan, M. D., et al. (2010). Opioid prescriptions for chronic pain and overdose. *Archives of Internal Medicine, 152,* 85–92.

DuPont, R. L. (2002). Clinical approaches to drug offenders. In G. G. Leukefeld, F. Tims, & D. Farabee (Eds.), *Treatment of drug offenders.* New York: Springer.

DuPont, R. L., & DuPont, C. M. (1998). Sedative/hypnotics and benzodiazepines. In R. J. Frances & S. I. Miller (Eds.), *Clinical textbook of addictive disorders* (2nd ed.). New York: Guilford.

Dyehouse, J. M., & Sommers, M. S. (1998). Brief intervention after alcohol-related injuries. *Nursing Clinics of North America, 33,* 93–104.

Eagleman, D. (2007). 10 unsolved mysteries of the brain. *Discover, 28*(8), 54–59, 75.

Earlywine, M. (2005). Cannabis: Attending to subjective effects to improve drug safety. In M. Earlywine (Ed.), *Mind-altering drugs: The science of subjective experience.* New York: Oxford University Press.

Ebbert, J. O. (2009). Emerging drugs for the treatment of alcohol dependence. *Expert Opinion on Emerging Drugs, 14*(1), 23–32.

Echeburua, E. de Medina, R. B., & Aizpiri, J. (2005). Alcoholism and personality disorders: An exploratory study. *Alcohol & Alcoholism, 40*(4), 323–326.

Eckholm, E. (2008). Courts give addicts a chance to straighten out. Retrieved from http://www.nytimes.com/2008/10/15/us/15drugs.html?_r=1

Edenberg, H. J. (2007). The genetic of alcohol metabolism. *Alcohol Research & Health, 30,* 5–13.

Edlund, M. J., Booth, B. M., & Feldman, Z. L. (2009). Perceived need for treatment for alcohol use disorders: Results from two national surveys. *Psychiatric Services, 60,* 1618–1628.

Edlund, M. J., Steffick, D., Hudson, T., Harris, K. M., & Sullivan, M. (2007). Risk factors for clinically recognized opioid abuse and dependence among veterans using opioids for chronic, non-cancer pain. *Pain, 129*(3), 355–362.

Eggan, S. M., Hashimoto, T., & Lewis, D. A. (2008). Reduced cortical cannabinoid 1 receptor messenger RNA and protein expression in schizophrenia. *Archives of General Psychiatry, 65,* 772–784.

Eisenberg, E. R., & Galloway, G. P. (2005). Anabolic-androgenic steroids. In J. H. Lowinson, P. Ruiz, R. B. Millman, & J. G. Langrod (Eds.), *Substance abuse: A comprehensive textbook* (4th ed.). New York: Lippincott Williams & Wilkins.

el-Guebaly, N. (2008). Cross-cultural aspects of addiction. In M. Galanter & H. D. Kleber (Eds.), *The American Psychiatric Publishing textbook of substance abuse treatment.* Washington, DC: American Psychiatric Publishing.

el-Guebaly, N., Cathcart, J., Currie, S., Brown, D., & Gloster, S. (2002). Smoking cessation approaches for persons with mental illness or addictive disorders. *Psychiatric Services, 53,* 1166–1170.

Ellgren, M., Spano, S. M., & Hurd, Y. L. (2006). Adolescent cannabis exposure alters opium intake and opioid limbic neuronal populations in adult rats. *Neuropsychopharmacology* (advance publication online). doi: 10.1038/sjnpp.1301127

Ellickson, P. L., Martino, S. C., & Collins, R. L. (2004). Marijuana use from adolescence to young adulthood: Multiple developmental trajectories and their associated outcomes. *Health Psychology, 23*(3), 299–307.

Elliott, F. A. (1992). Violence. *Archives of Neurology, 49,* 595–603.

Ellis, A., McInerney, J. F., DiGiuseppe, R., & Yeager, R. J. (1988). *Rational emotive therapy with alcoholics and substance abusers.* New York: Pergamon.

Elton, A., & Kilts, C. D. (2009). The role of sex differences in the drug addiction process. In K. T. Brady, S. E. Back, & S. F. Greenfield (Eds.), *Women & addiction.* New York: Guilford.

Emanuele, M. A., Wezeman, F., & Emanuele, N. V. (2002). Effects of alcohol on female reproductive function. *Alcohol Research & Health, 26*(4), 274–281.

Encrenaz, G., Kovess-Masfethy, V., Jutand, M., Carmona, E., et al. (2009). Use of psychoactive substances and health care in response to anxiety and depressive disorders. *Psychiatric Services, 60*(3), 351–357.

Engels, R. C., & ter Bogt, T. (2004). Outcome expectancies and Ecstasy use in visitors of rave parties in the Netherlands. *European Addiction Research, 10*(10), 152–162.

English, T. J. (2009). Dope. *Playboy, 56*(11), 66–68, *69*, 150–156.

Erickson, C. K. (2007). *The science of addiction.* New York: Norton.

Erlich, L. B. (2001). *A textbook of forensic addiction medicine and psychiatry.* Springfield, IL: Thomas.

Erlich, P. F., Brown, J. K., & Drongowski, R. (2006). Characterization of the drug-positive adolescent trauma population: Should we, do we, and does it make a difference if we test? *Journal of Pediatric Surgery, 41*(5), 927–930.

Ernst, E. (2002). Complementary therapies for addictions: Not an alternative. *Addiction, 1*, 2–3.

Escalating DXM abuse among teenagers. (2007). *Forensic Drug Abuse Advisor, 19*(1) 2–3.

Espeland, K. E. (1997). Inhalants: The instant, but deadly high. *Pediatric Nursing, 23*(1), 82–86.

Estfan, B., Mahmoud, F., Shaheen, P., Davis, M. P., et al. (2007). Respiratory function during parenteral opioid titration for cancer pain. *Palliative Medicine, 21*(2), 81–86.

Eubanks, L. M., Rogers, C. J., Beuscher, I. V., Koob, G. F., Olson, A. J., Dickerson, T. J., et al. (2006). A molecular link between the active component of marijuana and Alzheimer's disease pathology. *Molecular Pharmaceutics,* 10.1021/mp060066mS15 43-8384(06)00066-9.

Europeans heaviest drinkers in the world. (2006). Retrieved from http://www.iol.co/za/index.php? set_id-31&art_id+vn20060604115400426c580480

Evans, K., & Sullivan, J. M. (2001). *Dual diagnosis* (2nd ed.). New York: Guilford.

Ewart, R., Lausen, H., & Millian, D. (2009). Undisclosed changes in outcomes in randomized controlled trials: An observational study. *Annals of Family Medicine, 7*, 542–546.

Ewing, J. A. (1984). Detecting alcoholism: The CAGE questionnaire. *Journal of the American Medical Association, 252*, 1905–1907.

Ezzati, M., Henley, S. J., Lopez, A. D. & Thun, M. J. (2005). Role of smoking in global and regional cancer epidemiology: Current patterns and data needs. *International Journal of Cancer, 116*(6), 963–971.

Fadem, B. (2009). *Behavioral science* (5th ed.). New York: Wolters Kluwer/Lippincott Williams & Wilkins.

Falco, M. (2005). US federal drug policy. In J. H. Lowinson, P. Ruiz, R. B. Millman, & J. G. Langrod (Eds.), *Substance abuse: A comprehensive textbook* (4th ed.). New York: Lippincott Williams & Wilkins.

Fallon, J. H., Keator, D. B., Mbogori, J., Taylor, D., & Potkin, S. G. (2005). Gender: A major determinant of brain response to nicotine. *International Journal of Neuropsychopharmacology, 8*(1), 17–26.

Fals-Stewart, W., Lam, W. K. K., & Kelley, M. L. (2009). Behavioral couple therapy. In K. T. Brady, S. E. Back, & S. F. Greenfield (Eds.), *Women & addiction.* New York: Guilford.

Fals-Stewart, W., O'Farrell, T. J., & Birchler, G. R. (2003). Family therapy techniques. In F. Rotgers, J. Morgenstern, & S. T. Walters (Eds.), *Treating substance abuse: Theory and technique* (2nd ed.). New York: Guilford.

Fals-Stewart, W., O'Farrell, T. J., & Birchler, G. R. (2004). Behavioral couple's therapy for substance abuse: Rationale, methods and findings. *Science & Practice Perspectives, 2*(2), 30–40.

Farabee, D., Prendergast, M., & Carier, J. (2002). Alcohol, the "un-drug." *Psychiatric Services, 53*, 1375–1376.

Farrell, A. D., & White, K. S. (1998). Peer influences and drug use among urban adolescents: Family structure and parent-adolescent relationship as protective factors. *Journal of Consulting and Clinical Psychology, 66*, 284–258.

Fauci, A. S., & Lane, H. C. (2008). Human immunodeficiency virus disease: AIDS and related disorders. In A. S. Fauci, E. Braunwald, D. L. Kasper, S. L. Hauser, D. L. Longo, J. L. Jameson, & J. Loscalzo (Eds.), *Harrison's principles of internal medicine* (17th ed.). New York: McGraw-Hill Medical.

Fazel, S., Långstrom, N., Hjern, A., Grann, M., & Lichtenstein, P. (2009). Schizophrenia, substance abuse, and violent crime. *Journal of the American Medical Association, 301*(19), 2016–2023.

FDA revised guidelines, label warnings. (2004). *Forensic Drug Abuse Advisor, 16*(4), 26–27.

Feilding, A., & Morrison, P. (2010). Safer skunk. *New Scientist, 205*(2774), 22–23.

Feltstein, M. W., Alter, C. A., & See, R. E. (2007). Aripipazole blocks reinstatement of cocaine seeking in an animal model of relapse. *Biological Psychiatry, 61*(5), 582–590.

Fergusson, D. M., Boden, J. M., & Horwood, J. (2009). Tests of causal links between alcohol abuse or dependence and major depression. *Archives of General Psychiatry, 66*(3), 260–266.

Fergusson, D. M., Horwood, J., Lunskey, M. T., & Madden, P. A. F. (2003). Early reactions to cannabis predict later dependence. *Archives of General Psychiatry, 60*, 1033–1039.

Fernandez, H. H., Eisenschenk, S., & Okun, M. S. (2010). *Ultimate review for the neurology boards* (2nd ed.). New York: Demosmedical.

Ferri, M., Amato, L., & Davoil, M. (2006). Alcoholics Anonymous and other 12-step programs for alcohol dependence. *The Cochrane Database of Systematic Reviews, 3.*

Fetro, J. V., Coyle, K. K., & Pham, P. (2001). High risk behaviors among middle school students in a large majority–minority school district. *Journal of School Health, 71*(1), 30–37.

Feuillet, L., Mallet, S., & Sparad, M. (2006). Two girls with neurocutaneous symptoms cause by mothball intoxication. *New England Journal of Medicine, 355*, 423–424.

Fields, G. (2009). White House Czar calls for end to "war on drugs." *Wall Street Journal.* Retrieved from http://online.wsj.com/article/SB1242258915276173 97.html

Fields, R. D. (2009). Marijuana hurts some, helps others. *Scientific American Mind, 20*(5), 17.

Fiellin, D. A. (2008). Treatment of adolescent opioid dependence. *Journal of the American Medical Association, 300*, 1057–2058.

Fiellin, D. A., Rosenheck, R. A., & Kosten, T. R. (2001). Office-based treatment for opioid dependence: Reaching new patient populations. *New England Journal of Medicine, 355*, 423–424.

Figueredo, V. M. (1997). The effects of alcohol on the heart. *Postgraduate Medicine, 101*, 165–176.

Filley, C. M. (2004). Encephalopathies. In M. Rizzo & P. J. Elsinger (Eds.), *Behavioral neurology and neuropsychology.* Philadelphia: Saunders.

Fineschi, V., Riezzo, I., Centini, F., Silingardi, E., Licata, M., Beduschi, G., et al. (2005). Anabolic steroid abuse and heart disease. *International Journal of Legal Medicine, 15*, 1–6.

Finger, W. W., Lund, M., & Slagel, M. A. (1997). Medications that may contribute to sexual disorders: A guide to assessment and treatment in family practice. *Journal of Family Practice, 44*, 33–44.

Finnegan, L. P., & Kandall, S. R. (2005). Maternal and neonatal effects of alcohol and drugs. In J. H. Lowinson, P. Ruiz, R. B. Millman, & J. G. Langrod (Eds.), *Substance abuse: A comprehensive textbook* (4th ed.). New York: Lippincott Williams & Wilkins.

Finnegan, L. P., & Kandall, S. R. (2008). Perinatal substance use. In M. Galanter & H. D. Kleber (Eds.), *The American Psychiatric Association textbook of substance abuse treatment* (4th ed.). Washington, DC: American Psychiatric Publishing.

Fiore, M. C. (2006, September 9). *Tobacco use and dependence: Current recommendations and new treatment options.* Paper presented at the Continuing Medical Education Symposium, Gundersen Lutheran Medical Center, La Crosse, WI.

Fiore, M. C., Hatsukam, D. K., & Baker, T. B. (2002). Effective tobacco dependence treatment. *Journal of the American Medical Association, 288*, 1768–1771.

Fiorillo, C. D., Tobler, P. N., & Schultz, W. (2003). Discrete coding of reward probability and uncertainty by dopamine neurons. *Science, 299*, 1898–1902.

First shots in the war on alcohol. (2009). *New Scientist, 204*(2730), 5.

Fisher, S. L., Bucholz, K. K., Reich, W., Fox, L., Kuperman, S., Kramer, J., et al. (2006). Teenagers are right—parents do not know much: An analysis of adolescent-parent agreement on reports of adolescent substance use, abuse and dependence. *Alcoholism: Clinical and Experimental Research, 30*(10), 1699–1710.

Flaum, M., & Schultz, S. K. (1996). When does amphetamine-induced psychosis become schizophrenia? *American Journal of Psychiatry, 153*, 812–815.

Fleming, C. B., Mason, W. A., Mazza, J. J., Abbott, R. D., & Catalano, R. F. (2008). Latent growth modeling of the relationship between depressive symptoms and substance use during adolescence. *Psychology of Addictive Behaviors, 22*(2), 186–197.

Fleming, D. W., & Grey, J. P. (2008). This is the U.S. on drugs. Retrieved from http://www.latimes.com/news/opinion/commentry/la-oe-fleming5-2008julo5%2co%2C3205714.story

Fleming, M. F. (1997). Strategies to increase alcohol screening in health care settings. *Alcohol Health & Research World, 21*, 340–347.

Fleming, M., Mihic, S. J., & Harris, R. A. (2006). Ethanol. In L. L. Brunton, S. J. Lazo, & K. L. Parker (Eds.), *The pharmacological basis of therapeutics* (11th ed.). New York: McGraw-Hill.

Fletcher, M. (2003, March 8). *Sober for good: Variety of solutions for drinking problems*. Paper presented at the Treating the Addictions seminar hosted by the Department of Psychiatry of Cambridge Hospital, Boston.

Flora, C. (2005). Tough love. *Psychology Today, 38*(6), 40–41.

Fogarty, M. (2003). Depending on cigarettes, counting on science. *The Scientist, 17*(6). Retrieved from http://www.the-scientist.com/yr2003/mar/feature_030324.html

Folks, D. G., & Burke, W. J. (1998). Sedative-hypnotics and sleep. *Clinics in Geriatric Medicine, 14*, 67–86.

Fonda, D. (2001). Why tobacco won't quit. *Time, 157*(26), 38–39.

Fontana, R. J. (2008). Acute liver failure including acetaminophen overdose. *Medical Clinics of North America, 92*, 761–794.

Foote, J. (2006, March 4). *Evidence-based treatments meet reality: Misunderstandings, compromises, and promises*. Symposium presented by the Department of Psychiatry, Cambridge Hospital, Boston.

Ford, W. E. (2000). Medical necessity and psychiatric managed care. *Psychiatric Clinics of North America, 23*, 309–317.

Fored, C. M., Ejerblad, E., Linblad, P., Fryzek, J. P., Dickman, P. W., Signorello, L. B., et al. (2001). Acetaminophen, aspirin and chronic renal failure. *New England Journal of Medicine, 345*, 1801–1808.

Forstein, M. (2002, February 2). *Sex, drugs and HIV: A clinician's nightmare*. Paper presented at the Treating the Addictions seminar presented by the Department of Psychiatry of Cambridge Hospital, Boston.

Forsyth, C. B., Tang, Y., Shaikh, M., Zhang, L., Keshavarzian, A. (2009). Alcohol stimulates activation of snail, epidermal growth factor receptor signaling, and biomarkers of epithelial-mesenchymal transition in colon and breast cancers. *Alcoholism: Clinical and Experimental Research* (published online prior to print). doi: 10.1111/j.1530-0277.2009. 01061.x

Fortgang, E. (1999). Is pot bad for you? *Rolling Stone, 87*, 53, 101.

Fox, H., & Shina, R. (2009). Stress, neuroendocrine response and addiction in women. In K. T. Brady, S. E. Back, & S. F. Greenfield (Eds.), *Women & addiction*. New York: Guilford.

Frank, D. A., Augustyn, M., Knight, W. G., Pell, T., & Zuckerman, B. (2001). Growth, development and behavior in early childhood following prenatal cocaine exposure. *Journal of the American Medical Association, 285*, 1613–1625.

Franken, I. A. H., & Hendriks, V. M. (1999). Predicting outcome of inpatient detoxification of substance abusers. *Psychiatric Services, 50*, 813–817.

Franklin, J., & Markarian, M. (2005). Substance abuse in minority populations. In R. J. Frances, S. I. Miller, & A. D. Mack (Eds.), *Clinical textbook of addictive disorders* (3rd ed.). New York: Guilford.

Franklin, J. E. (1989). Alcoholism among blacks. *Hospital & Community Psychiatry, 40*, 1120–1122, 1127.

Frattaroli, E. (2001). *Healing the soul in the age of the brain*. New York: Penguin-Putnam.

Freeborn, D. (1996). By the numbers. *Minneapolis Star-Tribune, 15*(94), D2.

Freedenthala, S., Vaughn, M. G., Jensona, J. M., & Howerd, M. O. (2007). Inhalant use and suicidality among incarcerated youth. *Drug and Alcohol Dependence, 90*(1), 81–88.

Freedman, R. (2008). Cannabis, inhibitory neurons, and the progressive course of schizophrenia. *American Journal of Psychiatry, 165*, 416–419.

Freese, T. E., Miotto, K., & Teback, C. J. (2002). The effects and consequences of selected club drugs. *Journal of Substance Abuse Treatment, 23*(2), 151–156.

Freiberg, M. S., & Samet, J. H. (2005). Alcohol and coronary heart disease: The answer awaits in a randomized controlled trial. *Circulation, 112*, 1379–1380.

Freimuth, M. (2005). *Hidden addictions*. New York: Jacob Aronson.

Fricchione, G. (2004). Generalized anxiety disorder. *New England Journal of Medicine, 251*, 675–682.

Frierson, R. L., Melikian, M., & Wadman, P. C. (2002). Principles of suicide risk assessment. *Postgraduate Medicine, 112*(3), 65–71.

Fromm, E. (1956) *The art of loving*. New York: Harper & Row.

Fromm, E. (1968). *The revolution of hope*. New York: Harper & Row.

Frood, A. (2008). The antagonism and the ecstasy. *New Scientist, 199*(2671), 42–43.

Fryer, S. L., Schweinburg, B. C., Bjorkquist, O. A., Frank, L. R., Mattson, S. N., Spadoni, A. D., et al. (2009). Characterization of white matter microstructure in fetal alcohol spectrum disorders. *Alcoholism: Clinical and Experimental Research, 33*(3), 1–8.

Fudala, P. J., & O'Brien, C. P. (2005). Buprenorphine for the treatment of opioid addiction. In J. H. Lowinson, P. Ruiz, R. B. Millman, & J. G. Langrod (Eds.), *Substance abuse: A comprehensive textbook* (4th ed.). New York: Lippincott Williams & Wilkins.

Fulde, G. W. O., & Wodak, A. (2007). Ice: Cool drug or real problem? *Medical Journal of Australia, 186,* 334–335.

Fuller, P. G., & Sajatovic, M. (1999). *Drug information handbook for psychiatry.* Cleveland, OH: Lexi-Comp.

Furst, R. T., Herrmannk, C., Leung, R., Galea, J., & Hunt, K. (2004). Heroin diffusion in the mid-Hudson region of New York State. *Addiction, 99*(4), 431–441.

Furstenberg, F. (2010). Passage to adulthood. *The Prevention Researcher, 17*(2), 3–7.

Fusar-Poli, P., Crippa, J. A., Bhattacharyya, S., Borgwardt, S. J., Allen, P., Martin-Santos, R., et al. (2009). Distinct effects of Δ–9-tetrahydrocannabinol and cannabidiol on neural activation during emotional processing. *Archives of General Psychiatry, 66*(1), 95–105.

Gahlinger, P. M. (2004). Club drugs: MDMA, gamma-hydroxybutyrate (GHB), Rohypnol, and Ketamine. *American Family Physician, 69,* 2919–2927.

Gallagher, L. (2005). Stone Age beer. *Discover, 26*(11), 54–59.

Galloway, G. P. (1997). Anabolic-androgenic steroids. In J. H. Lowinson, P. Ruiz, R. B. Millman, & J. G. Langrod (Eds.), *Substance abuse: A comprehensive textbook* (3rd ed.). New York: Lippincott Williams & Wilkins.

Ganem, D., & Prince, A. M. (2004). Hepatitis B virus infection—natural history and clinical consequences. *New England Journal of Medicine, 350,* 1118–1129.

Garbutt, J. C., Kranzler, H. R., O'Malley, S. S., Gastfriend, D. R., Pettinati, H. M., Silverman, B. L., et al. (2005). Efficacy and tolerability of long-acting injectable Naltrexone for alcohol dependence. *Journal of the American Medical Association, 293,* 1617–1625.

Garfinkel, D., Zisapel, N., Wainstein, J., & Laudon, M. (1999). Facilitation of benzodiazepine discontinuation by melatonin. *Archives of Internal Medicine, 159,* 2456–2460.

Garrett, L. (1994). *The coming plague.* New York: Farrar, Strauss Giroux.

Garrett, L. (2000). *Betrayal of trust.* New York: Hyperion.

Garriott, J. C. (1996). Pharmacology and toxicology of ethyl alcohol. In J. C. Garriott (Ed.), *Medioclegal aspects of alcohol* (3rd ed.). Tucson, AZ: Lawyers and Judges Publishing.

Garry, P. (1995). Oh, judge, can't you make them stop picking on me? *Minneapolis Star-Tribune, 14*(106), 10A.

Gastfriend, D. R. (2004a, March 5). *Patient treatment matching: What works for whom and why.* Paper presented to the Department of Psychiatry at Cambridge Hospital, Boston.

Gastfriend, D. R. (2004b). Patient placement criteria. In M. Galanter & H. D. Kleber (Eds.), *The American Psychiatric Publishing textbook of substance abuse treatment* (3rd ed.). Washington, DC: American Psychiatric Publishing.

Gastfriend, D. R., & McLellan, A. T. (1997). Treatment matching. *Medical Clinics of North America, 81,* 945–966.

Gazzaniga, M. S. (2008). *Human.* New York: HarperCollins.

Gehricke, J. G., Potkin, S. G., Leslie, F. M., Loughlin, S. E., Whalen, C. K., Jamner, L. D., et al. (2009). Nicotine-induced brain metabolism associated with anger provocation. *Behavioral and Brain Functions, (5)* 5–19.

Gelernter, J., & Kranzler, H. R., (2008). Genetics of addiction. In M. Galanter & H. D. Kleber (Eds.), *The American Psychiatric Publishing textbook of substance abuse treatment.* Washington, DC: American Psychiatric Publishing.

Gemenetzidis, E., Bose, A., Riaz, A. M., Chaplin, T., Young, B. D., Ali, M., et al. (2009). FOXM1 upregulation is an early event in human squamous cell carcinoma and is enhanced by nicotine during malignant transformation. *PLoS One.* Retrieved from http://www.plosone.org/article/info%%2F10.1371%2Fjournal.pone.0004849

Gendel, M. H. (2006). Substance misuse and substance-related disorders in forensic psychiatry. *Psychiatric Clinics of North America, 29,* 649–673.

Genetics of drug addiction: The memory connection. (2009). *Addiction Treatment Forum, 18*(1), 6.

Genkinger, J. M., Spiegelman, D., Anderson, K. E., Bergkvist, L., Bernstein, L., van den Brandt, P. A., et al. (2009). Alcohol intake and pancreatic cancer risk: A pooled analysis of fourteen cohort studies.

Cancer Epidemiology, Biomarkers & Prevention, 18, 765–776.

George, R., & Regnard, C. (2007). Lethal opioids or dangerous prescribers? Palliative Medicine, 21(2), 77–80.

George, T. P., & Weinberger, A. H. (2008). Nicotine and tobacco. In M. Galanter & H. D. Kleber (Eds.), The American Psychiatric Association textbook of substance abuse treatment. Washington, DC: American Psychiatric Publishing.

Geppert, C. M., & Minkoff, K. (2004). Issues in dual diagnosis: Diagnosis, treatment and new research. Psychiatric Times, 21(4), 103–107.

Geppert, C. M. A. (2008). Aristotle, Augustine, and addiction. Psychiatric Times, 24(7), 40–42.

Gerada, C. (2005). Drug misuse: A review of treatments. Clinical Medicine, 51, 69–73.

Gerber, Y., Rose, L. J., Goldbourt, U., Genyamini, Y., Drory, Y., & Israel Study Group on First Acute Myocardial Infarction. (2009). Smoking status and long-term survival after first acute myocardial infarction. Journal of the American College of Cardiology, 54, 2383–2387.

Gernstein, J. (2003, March 8). SMART recovery: A group CBT approach to addictions. Paper presented at the Treating the Addictions symposium hosted by the Department of Psychiatry of Cambridge Hospital, Boston.

Get over it. (2006). New Scientist, 190(2550), 5.

Getzfeld, A. R. (2006). Essentials of abnormal psychology. New York: Wiley.

Ghaffar, O., & Feinstein, A. (2008). Multiple sclerosis and cannabis: A cognitive and psychiatric study. Neurology (published online). doi: 10.1212/01wn10 000344046.23960.25

Ghoneim, M. M. (2004a). Drugs and human memory (part 1). Anesthesiology, 100, 987–1002.

Ghoneim, M. M. (2004b). Drugs and human memory (part 2). Anesthesiology, 100, 1277–1297.

Ghosh, D., Mishra, M. K., Das, S., Kaushik, D. K., & Basu, A. (2009). Tobacco carcinogen induces microglial activation and subsequent neuronal damage. Journal of Neurochemistry (published online prior to print). doi: 10.111/j.1471-4159 .06203.x

Giacchino, S., & Houdek, D. (1998). Ruptured varicies! RN, 61(5), 33–36.

Giancola, P. R., Levinson, C. A., Corman, M. D., Godlaski, A. J., Morris, D. H., Phillips, J. P., et al. (2009). Men and women, alcohol and aggression. Experimental and Clinical Psychopharmacology, 17(3), 154–164.

Giannini, A. J. (2000). An approach to drug abuse, intoxication and withdrawal. American Family Physician, 61, 2763–2774.

Gibson, A., Degenhardt, L., Mattick, R. P., Ali, R., White, J., & O'Brien, S. (2008). Exposure to opioid maintenance treatment reduces long-term mortality. Addiction, 103(3), 462–468.

Gilbertson, R., Ceballos, N. A., Prather, R., & Nixon, S. J. (2009). Effects of acute alcohol consumption in older and younger adults: Perceived impairment versus psych-motor performance. Journal of Studies on Alcohol and Drugs, 70(2), 242–252.

Giles, J. (2008). The immunity fix. New Scientist, 199(2667), 42–45.

Giles, J. (2009a). Doubts raised over brain scan findings. New Scientist, 201(2691), 11.

Giles, J. (2009b). Police crackdowns may encourage drug use. New Scientist, 203(2715), 9.

Gillham, O. (2005). What happened to ACA—adult children of alcoholics? Counselor, 6(1), 24.

Gilliam, M. (1998). How Alcoholics Anonymous failed me. New York: Morrow.

Gilman, J. M., Bjork, J. M., & Hommer, D. W. (2007). Parental alcohol use and brain volumes in early- and late-onset alcoholics. Biological Psychiatry, 62, 607–615.

Gilpin, N. W., & Kolb, G. F. (2008). Neurobiology of alcohol dependence. Alcohol Research & Health, 31(3), 185–195.

Girls are abusing steroids too. (2005). Retrieved fromhttp:www.cnn.com/2005/HEALTH/04/25/girls.steroids.ap/indexhtml

Gitlow, S. (2007). Substance use disorders (2nd ed.). New York: Lippincott Williams & Wilkins.

Glantz, S. A., Slade, J., Bero, L., Hanauer, P., & Barnes, D. E. (1996). The cigarette papers. Los Angeles: University of California Press.

Glasper, L. J., de Wet, C. J., Bearn, J., & Gossop, M. (2007). Comparison of buprenorphine and methadone in the treatment of opiate withdrawal: Possible advantages of buprenorphine for the treatment of opiate-benzodiazepine codependent patients? Journal of Clinical Psychopharmacology, 27, 188–192.

Glasser, J. (2002). Cycle of shame. U.S. News & World Report, 132(17), 26–33.

Glasser, R. J. (1998). The doctor is not in. Harper's Magazine, 296(1774), 35–41.

Glasser, R. J. (2004). We are not immune. Harper's Magazine, 309(1850), 35–42.

Glazer, D. G., & Wu, L. T. (2009). The epidemiology of at-risk and binge drinking among middle-aged and elderly community adults: National Survey on Drug Use and Health. *American Journal of Psychiatry* (published online prior to print). doi: 10.1176/1ppi .ajp.2009.09010016

Glennon, R. A. (2004). Neurobiology of hallucinogens. In M. Galanter & H. D. Kleber (Eds.), *The American Psychiatric Publishing textbook of substance abuse treatment* (3rd ed.). Washington, DC: American Psychiatric Publishing.

Glennon, R. A. (2008). Neurobiology of hallucinogens. In M. Galanter & H. D. Kleber (Eds.), *The American Psychiatric Publishing textbook of substance abuse treatment*. Washington, DC: American Psychiatric Publishing.

Glick, S. D., & Maisonneuve, I. M. (2000). Development of novel medications for drug addiction. In S. D. Glick & I. Maisonneuve (Eds.), *New medications for drug abuse*. New York: New York Academy of Sciences.

Godwin, C. (2004). What's new in the fight against AIDS. *RN, 67*(4), 46–52.

Going to pot. (2009). *Playboy, 56*(1), 22.

Gold, M. S. (2005). From the guest editor. *Psychiatric Annals, 35*(6), 458, 460.

Gold, M. S., & Dupont, R. L. (2008). Teens + marijuana: (Still) a dangerous mix. *Clinical Psychiatry News, 36*(7), 14.

Gold, M. S., Frost-Pineda, K., & Jacobs, W. S. (2004). Cannabis. In M. Galanter & H. D. Kleber (Eds.), *The American Psychiatric Association textbook of substance abuse treatment* (3rd ed.). Washington, DC: American Psychiatric Publishing.

Gold, M. S., & Jacobs, W. S. (2005). Cocaine and crack: Clinical aspects. In J. H. Lowinson, P. Ruiz, R. B. Millman, & J. D. Langrod (Eds.), *Substance abuse: A comprehensive textbook* (4th ed.). New York: Lippincott Williams & Wilkins.

Goldberg, I. J. (2003). To drink or not to drink? *New England Journal of Medicine, 348*, 163–164.

Goldkamp, J. S., White, M. D., & Robinson, J. B. (2002). *An honest chance: Perspectives on drug courts*. Washington, DC: U.S. Department of Justice.

Goldman, H., Frank, R. G., Burnam, A., Huskamp, H. A., Ridgely, M. S., Normand, S.-L. T., et al. (2006). Behavioral health insurance parity for federal employees. *New England Journal of Medicine, 354*, 1378–1386.

Goldschmidt, L., Richardson, G. A., Cornelius, M. D., & Day, N. L. (2004). Prenatal marijuana and alcohol exposure and academic achievement at age 10. *Neurotoxicology & Teratology, 26*(4), 52–532.

Goldsmith, R. J., & Garlapati, V. (2004). Behavioral interventions for dual diagnosis patients. *Psychiatric Clinics of North America, 27*, 709–725.

Goldstein, D. (2005). Blunt instrument. *New Scientist, 185*(2492), 23.

Goldstein, R. Z., & Volkow, N. D. (2002). Drug addiction and its underlying neurobiological basis: Neuroimaging evidence for the involvement of the frontal cortex. *The American Journal of Psychiatry, 150*, 1642–1652.

Goler, N. C., Armstrong, M. A., Taillac, C. J., & Osejo, V. M. (2008). Substance abuse treatment liked with prenatal visits improves perinatal outcomes: A new standard. *Journal of Perinatology* (published online). doi: 10.1038/jp2008.70

Gomberg, E. S. L. (2004). Ethnic minorities and the elderly. In M. Galanter & H. D. Kleber (Eds.), *The American Psychiatric Publishing textbook of substance abuse treatment* (3rd ed.). Washington, DC: American Psychiatric Publishing.

Gonzalez, R., Vasisileva, J., & Scott, J. C. (2009). Neuropsychological consequences of drug abuse. In I. Grant & K. M. Adams (Eds.), *Neuropsychological assessment of neuropsychiatric and neuromedical disorders* (3rd ed.). New York: Oxford University Press.

Goodnough, L. T., Brecher, M. E., Kanter, M. H., & AuBuchon, J. P. (1999). Transfusion medicine. *New England Journal of Medicine, 340*, 438–447.

Goodwin, R. S., Darwin, W. D., Chiang, C. N., Shih, M., Li, S.-H., & Huestis, M. A. (2008). Urinary elimination of 11-Nor-9-carbosy-Δ-9-tetrahydrocannabinol in cannabis users during continuously monitored abstinence. *Journal of Analytical Toxicology, 32*(8), 562–569.

Gordon, S. C. (2000). Antiviral therapy for chronic hepatitis B and C. *Postgraduate Medicine, 107*, 135–144.

Gordon, S. M. (2007). Women—barriers to substance abuse treatment. *Counselor, 8*(3), 22–28.

Gorman, D. (2003). The best of practices, the worst of practices: The making of science-based primary intervention programs. *Psychiatric Services, 54*, 1087–1089.

Gorter, R. W., Butorac, M., Cobland, E. P., & van der Sluis, W. (2005). Medical use of cannabis in the Netherlands. *Neurology, 64*, 917–919.

Gossop, M., Steward, D., & Marsden, J. (2007). Readiness for change and drug use outcomes after treatment. *Addiction, 102*, 301–308.

Gottleib, A. M. (1997). Crisis of consciousness. *Utne Reader, 79,* 45–48.

Gouzoulis-Mayfrank, E., Daumann, J., Tuchtenhagen, F., Pelz, S., Becker, S., Kunert, H.-J., et al. (2000). Impaired cognitive performance in drug-free users of recreational Ecstasy (MDMA). *Journal of Neurology, Neurosurgery and Psychiatry, 68,* 719–725.

Graber, M. A. (2007). Identifying and treating the methamphetamine abuser. *Emergency Medicine, 39,* 12–16, 47.

Graedon, J., & Graedon, T. (1996). *The people's pharmacy.* New York: St. Martin's Griffin.

Graham, J. R. (1990). *MMPI-2 assessing personality and psychopathology.* New York: Oxford University Press.

Graham, N. A., Polles, A., & Gold, M. S. (2007). Performance enhancing, non-prescription use of erectile dysfunction medications. *Journal of Addictive Diseases, 25*(Suppl. 1), 33–45.

Graham, S. (2009). A brief encounter. *The Independent Practitioner, 29*(1), 25.

Grahm, K., Massak, A., Demers, A., & Rehm, J. (2007). Does the association between alcohol consumption and depression depend on how they are measured? *Alcoholism: Clinical and Experimental Research, 31*(1), 78–88.

Grant, B. F., Dawson, D. A., Stonson, F. S., Dufour, M. C., Chou, S. P., & Pickering, R. P. (2006). The 12-month prevalence and trends in *DSM-IV* alcohol abuse and dependence: United States, 1991–1992 and 2001–2002. *Alcohol Research & Health, 29*(2), 79–93.

Grant, I., Heath, A. C., Bucholz, K. K., Madden, P. A. F., Agrawal, A., Statham, D. J., et al. (2007). Spousal concordance for alcohol dependence: Evidence for assortative mating or spousal interaction effect. *Alcoholism: Clinical and Experimental Research, 31*(5), 717–728.

Grant, J. E., Kushner, M. G., & Kim, S. W. (2002). Pathological gambling and alcohol use disorder. *Alcohol Research & Health, 26,* 143–150.

Grass is greener. (2007). *Playboy, 54*(4), 27.

Gray, J. D., Punsonim, M., Tabori, N. E., Melton, J. T., Fanslow, V., Ward, M. J., et al. (2007). Methylphenidate administration to juvenile rats alters brain areas involved in cognition, motivated behaviors, appetite and stress. *Journal of Neuroscience, 27,* 7196–7207.

Gray, M. (1998). *Drug crazy.* New York: Routledge.

Greely, H., Sahakian, B., Harris, J., Kessler, R. C., Gazzaniga, M., Campbell, P., et al. (2008). Towards responsible use of cognitive-enhancing drugs by the healthy. *Nature* (published online). doi: 10.1038/456702a

Green, C. A. (2006). Gender and use of substance abuse treatment services. *Alcohol Research & Health, 29*(1), 55–62.

Green, C. R., Munoz, D. P., Nikkel, S. M., & Reynolds, J. N. (2007). Deficits in eye movement control in children with fetal alcohol spectrum disorders. *Alcoholism: Clinical and Experimental Research, 31*(3), 500–511.

Green, J. (2002). *Cannabis.* New York: Thunder's Mouth Press.

Greenbaum, R. L., Stevens, S. A., Nash, K., Koren, G., & Rovet, J. (2009). Social cognitive and emotion processing abilities of children with fetal alcohol spectrum disorders: A comparison with attention deficit hyperactivity disorder. *Alcoholism Clinical and Experimental Research, 33*(10) (published online prior to print). doi: 10.1111/j.1530-0277 .2009.01003.x

Greenberg, B. H., & Bernard, D. D. (2005). *Contemporary diagnosis and management of heart failure.* Newtown, PA: Handbooks in Health Care.

Greenfield, S. F. (2003, March 7). *Gender differences in addiction: Findings and treatment implications.* Symposium presented to the Department of Psychiatry at Cambridge Hospital, Boston.

Greenfield, S. F. (2005). Is parity for the treatment of substance use disorders really sensible? *Psychiatric Services, 56,* 153–155.

Greenfield, S. F. (2007). *Alcohol use and abuse.* Cambridge, MA: Harvard Health Publications.

Greenfield, S. F., & Hennessy, G. (2008a). Assessment of the patient. In M. Galanter & H. D. Kleber (Eds.), *The American Psychiatric Publishing textbook of substance abuse treatment* (4th ed.). Washington, DC: American Psychiatric Publishing.

Greenhill, L. L. (2006). The science of stimulant abuse. *Pediatric Annals, 35,* 552–558.

Greenwald, G. (2009). Viewfinder. *New Scientist, 202*(2704), 23.

Grekin, E. R., Sher, K. J., & Wood, P. K. (2006). Personality and substance dependence symptoms: Modeling substance-specific traits. *Psychology of Addictive Behaviors, 20,* 415–424.

Grens, K. (2007). Scientists get hooked on a single transcription actor. *New Scientist.* Retrieved from http:///www.the_scientist.com/article/come/53236

Greydanus, D. E., & Patel, D. R. (2005). The adolescent and substance abuse: Current concepts. *Disease a Month, 51*, 391–431.

Griffin, K. W., Botvin, G. J., Scheier, L. M., Diaz, T., & Miller, N. L. (2000). Parenting practices as predictors of substance use, delinquency, and aggression among urban minority youth: Moderating effects of family structure and gender. *Psychology of Addictive Behaviors, 14*, 174–184.

Griffith, C. M., & Schenker, S. (2006). The role of nutritional therapy in alcoholic liver disease. *Alcohol Research & Health, 29*(4), 296–306.

Griffiths, R. R., Richards, W. A., McCann, U., & Jesse, R. (2006). Psilocybin can occasion mystical-type experiences having substantial and sustained personal meaning. *Psychopharmacology, 287*(3), 268–283.

Grinfeld, M. J. (2001). Decriminalizing addiction. *Psychiatric Times, 18*(3), 1, 5–6.

Grinspoon, L., Bakalar, J. B., & Russo, E. (2005). Marijuana: Clinical aspects. In J. H. Lowinson, P. Ruiz, R. B. Millman, & J. G. Langrod (Eds.), *Substance abuse: A comprehensive textbook*. New York: Lippincott Williams & Wilkins.

Griswold, K. S., Arnoff, H., Kernan, J. B., & Khan, L. S. (2008). Adolescent substance use and abuse: Recognition and management. *American Family Physician, 77*, 331–336.

Grob, C. S., & Poland, R. E. (2005). MDMA. In J. H. Lowinson, P. Ruiz, R. B. Millman, & J. G. Langrod (Eds.), *Substance abuse: A comprehensive textbook* (4th ed.). New York: Lippincott Williams & Wilkins.

Gross, J. (2008). New generation gap as older addicts seek help. Retrieved from http://www.nytimes.com/ 2008/03/06us/06abuse.html

Gruber, A. J., & Pope, H. G. (2002). Marijuana use among adolescents. *The Pediatric Clinics of North America, 49*, 389–413.

Gruber, A. J., Pope, H. G., Hudson, J. I., & Yurgelun-Todd, D. (2003). Attributes of long-term heavy cannabis abusers: A case-controlled study. *Psychological Medicine, 33*, 1415–1422.

Grucza, R. A., & Bierut, L. J. (2006). Cigarette smoking and the risk for alcohol use disorders among adolescent drinkers. *Alcoholism: Clinical and Experimental Research, 30*, 2046–2054.

Grucza, R. A., Bucholz, J. P., Rice, L. J., & Bierut, L. J. (2008). Secular trends in the lifetime prevalence of alcohol dependence in the United States: A re-evaluation. *Alcoholism: Clinical and Experimental Research, 32*(5), 763–770.

Grucza, R. A., Norberg, K., Bucholz, K. K., & Bierut, L. J. (2008). Correspondence between secular changes in alcohol dependence and age of drinking onset among women in the United States. *Alcoholism: Clinical and Experimental Research, 32*(8), 1493–1501.

Gual, A., & Lehert, P. (2005). Acamprosate during and after acute alcohol withdrawal: A double blind placebo-controlled study in Spain. *Alcohol and Alcoholism, 36*(5),413–418.

Guilbert, H., & Krawiec, M. (2003). Natural history of asthma. *Pediatric Clinics of North America, 50*, 523–538.

Gullu, H., Caliskin, M., Ciftci, O., Erdogan, D., Topcu, S., Yildirim, E., et al. (2007). Light cigarette smoking impairs coronary microvascular functions as severely as smoking regular cigarettes. *Heart* (published online). doi: 10.1136/hrt.2006.100255

Gunderson, E. W., & Stimmel, B. (2004). Treatment for pain in drug-addicted persons. In M. Galanter & H. D. Kleber (Eds.), *The American Psychiatric Publishing textbook of substance abuse treatment* (3rd ed.). Washington, DC: American Psychiatric Publishing.

Gunn, J. (2003). Psychopathy: An elusive concept with moral overtones. In T. Millon, E. Simonsen, M. Birket-Smith, & R. D. Davis (Eds.), *Psychopathy: Antisocial, criminal and violent behavior*. New York: Guilford.

Guo, J., Ibaragi, S., Zhu, T., Lou, L., Hu, G. F., Huppi, P. S., et al. (2008). Nicotine promotes mammary tumor migration via a signaling cascade involving protein kinase C and cdc42. *Cancer Research, 68*, 8473–8481.

Gupta, S. (2007). Keg parties and cardiacs. *Time, 169*(19), 76.

Gutstein, H. B., & Akil, H. (2006). Opioid analgesics. In L. L. Brunton, J. S. Lazo, & K. L. Parker (Eds.), *The pharmacological basis of therapeutics* (11th ed.). New York: McGraw-Hill.

Gwinnell, E., & Adamec, C. (2006). *The encyclopedia of addictions and addictive behaviors*. New York: Facts on File.

Haack, M. R. (1998). Treating acute withdrawal from alcohol and other drugs. *Nursing Clinics of North America, 33*, 75–92.

Haber, J. R. (2008). Alcohol and religion. *The Addictions Newsletter, 14*(3), 13–14.

Hahn, I. H., & Hoffman, R. S. (2001). Cocaine use and acute myocardial infarction. *Emergency Medical Clinics of North America, 19,* 493–510.

Hale, T. W. (2003). Medications in breast feeding mothers of preterm infants. *Pediatric Annals, 32,* 337–347.

Hall, A. J., Logan, J. E., Toblin, R. L., Kaplan, J. A., Kraner, J. C., Bixler, D. et al. (2008). Patterns of abuse among unintentional pharmaceutical overdose fatalities. *Journal of the American Medical Association, 300*(200), 2613–2620.

Hall, H., McPherson, S. B., Towe, L., & Yudko, E. (2009). Effects and diagnosis of methamphetamine use. In S. B. McPherson, H. V. Hall, & E. Yudko (Eds.), *Methamphetamine use—clinical and forensic aspects.* New York: CRC Press.

Hall, W., & Degenhardt, L. (2005). Cannabis-related disorders. In B. J. Sadock & V. A. Sadock (Eds.), *Kaplan & Sadock's comprehensive textbook of psychiatry* (8th ed.). New York: Lippincott Williams & Wilkins.

Hall, W., & Solowij, N. (1998). Adverse effects of cannabis. *The Lancet, 352,* 1611–1616.

Hallas, J., Bjerrum, L., Støvring, H., & Andersen, M. (2008). Use of a prescribed ephedrine/caffeine combination and the risk of serious cardiovascular events: A registry-based case-crossover study. *American Journal of Epidemiology, 168*(8), 966–973.

Halushka, M. K., & Halushka, P. V. (2002). Why are some individuals resistant to the cardioprotective effects of aspirin? *Circulation, 105,* 1620–1622.

Hampson, A. J., Grimaldi, M., Lolic, M., Wink, D., Rosenthal, R., & Axelrod, J. (2002). Neuroprotective antioxidants from marijuana. *Annals of the New York Academy of Sciences, 939,* 274–282.

Haney, M. (2008). Neurobiology of stimulants. In M. Galanter & H. D. Kleber (Eds.), *The American Psychiatric Publishing textbook of substance abuse treatment.* Washington, DC: American Psychiatric Publishing.

Hanley, M. (2004). Neurobiology of stimulants. In M. Galanter & H. D. Kleber (Eds.), *The American Psychiatric Publishing textbook of substance abuse treatment* (3rd ed.). Washington, DC: American Psychiatric Publishing.

Hansen, J., Winzeler, S., & Topolinski, S. (2010). When death makes you smoke: A terror management perspective on the effectiveness of cigarette on-pack warnings. *Journal of Experimental Social Psychology, 46*(1), 226–228.

Hanson, G. R., & Finkenstein, A. E. (2009). Basic neuropharmacological mechanisms of methamphetamine. In J. R. Roll, R. A. Rawson, W. Ling, & S. Shoptaw (Eds.), *Methamphetamine addiction—from basic science to treatment.* New York: Guilford.

Harkness, A., & Bratman, S. (2003). *Mosby's handbook of drug-herb and drug-supplement interactions.* Philadelphia: Mosby.

Harmon, K. (2010). Renewed hope. *Scientific American, 302*(1), 15–16.

Haroz, R., & Greenberg, M. I. (2005). Emerging drugs of abuse. *Medical Clinics of North America, 89,* 1259–1276.

Harper, C., & Matsumoto, I. (2005). Ethanol and brain damage. *Current Opinion in Pharmacology, 5,* 73–78.

Harrell, A., & Kleiman, M. (2002). Drug testing in criminal justice settings. In C. G. Leukefeld, F. Tims, & D. Farabee (Eds.), *Treatment of drug offenders.* New York: Springer.

Harrison, P. A., Fulkerson, J. A., & Beebe, T. J. (1998). *DSM-IV* substance use disorder criteria for adolescents: A critical examination based on a statewide school survey. *American Journal of Psychiatry, 155,* 486–492.

Hart, C. L., & Smith, G. D. (2009). Alcohol consumption and use of acute and mental health hospital services in the West of Scotland: Collaborative prospective cohort study. *Journal of Epidemiology and Community Health* (published online prior to print). doi: 10.1136/jech.2008.079764

Hart, K. E., & Fiissel, D. L. (2003). Do adult offspring of alcoholics suffer from poor mental health? A three-group comparison controlling for self-report bias. *Canadian Journal of Nursing, 35,* 52–72.

Hart, R. H. (1997). On the cannabinoid receptor: A study in molecular psychiatry. *Psychiatric Times, 14*(7), 59–60.

Hartwell, K. J., Tolliver, B. K., & Brady, K. T. (2009). Biologic commonalities between mental illness and addiction. *Primary Psychiatry, 16*(8), 33–39.

Hasemyer, D. (2006). Painkiller abuse a "huge problem," conference participants are told. Retrieved from http://www.signonsandiego.com/news/metro/20060411/news_.html

Hashimoto, J. G., & Wiren, K. M. (2007). Neurotoxic consequences of chronic alcohol withdrawal: Expressing profiling reveals importance of gender over withdrawal severity. *Neuropsychopharmacology* (published online). doi: 10.1038/sj.npp.1201494

Hasin, D. S., & Grant, B. F. (2002). Major depression in 6050 former drinkers. *Archives of General Psychiatry, 59,* 794–800.

Hasin, D. S., Stinson, F. S., Ogburn, E., & Grant, B. F. (2007). Prevalence, correlates, disability and comorbidity of *DSM-IV* alcohol abuse and dependence in the United States: Result from the National Epidemiologic Survey on Alcohol and Related Conditions. *Archives of General Psychiatry, 654,* 830–842.

Hassan, M. M., Donghui, L., el-Deeb, A. S., Wolff, R. A., Bondy, M. L., Davila, M., et al. (2008). Association between hepatitis B virus and pancreatic cancer. *Journal of Clinical Oncology, 26*(28), 4457–4562.

Hatsukami, D. K., & Fischman, M. W. (1996). Crack cocaine and cocaine hydrochloride. *Journal of the American Medical Association, 276,* 1580–1588.

Hatzipetros, T., Raudensky, J. G., Soghomonian, J. J., & Yamamoto, B. K. (2007). Haloperidol treatment after high dose methamphetamine administration is exictotoxic to GABA cells in substantia nigra para reticulata. *The Journal of Neuroscience, 27*(22), 5895–5902.

Hauck, F. R., Neese, B. H., Panchal, A. S., & El-Amin, W. (2009). Identification and management of latent tuberculosis infection. *American Family Physician, 79*(10), 879–886.

Haugh, R. (2006). Drunk denials. *Hospital & Health Networks, 80*(2), 1068–1069.

Havens, P. L. (2009, November). *HIV in pregnancy: Delivery options and virus load.* Wisconsin HIV providers teleconference.

He, J., Whelton, P. K., Vu, B., & Klag, M. J. (1998). Aspirin and risk of hemorrhagic stroke. *Journal of the American Medical Association, 280,* 1930–1935.

Healy, B. C., Ali, E. N., Guttmann, C. R. G., Chitnis, T., Glanz, B. I., Buckle, G., et al. (2009). Smoking and disease progression in multiple sclerosis. *Archives of Neurology, 66*(7), 858–864.

Heavy drinkers "lie to doctors." (2008). *BBC News.* Retrieved from http://newsvote.bbc.uk/mpapps/pagetools/print/news.bbc.co.uk/2/hi/health/7737367.stm?ad=1

Hecht, S., Carmella, S. G., Murphy, S. E., Riley, W. T., Le, C., Luo, X., et al. (2007). Similar exposure to a tobacco specific carcinogen in smokeless tobacco users and cigarette smokers. *Cancer Epidemiology Biomarkers & Prevention, 16,* 1657–1572.

Hecht, S., & Hatsukami, D. (2005). Reducing harm caused by tobacco. *Minnesota Medicine, 88,* 40–43.

Hefrich, Y. R., Yu, L., Ofori, A., Hamilton, T. A., Lambert, J., King, A., et al. (2007). Effects of smoking on aging of photoprotected skin. *Archives of Dermatology, 14*(3), 397–402.

Hegab, A. M., & Luketic, V. A. (2001). Bleeding esophageal varicies. *Postgraduate Medicine, 109*(2), 75–76, 81–86, 89.

Heidbreder, C. A., & Hagan, J. J. (2005). Novel pharmacotherapeutic approaches to the treatment of drug addiction and craving. *Current Opinion in Pharmacology, 5,* 107–118.

Heil, S. H., & Subramanian, M. G. (1998). Alcohol and the hormonal control of lactation. *Alcohol Health & Research World, 22*(3), 178–184.

Heinemann, A. W., & Rawal, P. H. (2005). Disability and rehabilitation issues. In J. H. Lowinson, P. Ruiz, R. B. Millman, & J. G. Langrod (Eds.), *Substance abuse: A comprehensive textbook* (4th ed.). New York: Lippincott Williams & Wilkins.

Heinz, A. (2006). Staying sober. *Scientific American Mind, 17*(2), 56–61.

Heinz, A., Ragan, P., Jones, D. W., Hommer, D., Williams, W., Knable, M. B., et al. (1998). Reduced central serotonin transporters in alcoholism. *American Journal of Psychiatry, 155,* 1544–1549.

Heller, A., Bubula, N., Lew, R., Heller, B., & Won, L. (2001). Gender-dependent enhanced adult neurotoxic response to methamphetamine following fetal exposure to the drug. *Journal of Pharmacology and Experimental Therapeutics, 298,* 1–11.

Henderson, G., Morton, J., & Little, H. (2005). Drug abuse: From gene through cell to behavior. *Current Opinions in Pharmacology, 5,* 1–3.

Henderson, L. A. (1994). Adverse reactions. In L. A. Henderson & W. A. Glass (Eds.), *LSD: Still with us after all these years.* New York: Lexington Books.

Hendricks, K., & Gorbach, S. (2009). Nutrition issues in chronic drug users living with HIV infection. *Addiction Science & Clinical Practice, 5*(1), 1623.

Henry, J., & Rella, J. (2001). Medical risks associated with MDMA use. In J. Holland (Ed.), *Ecstasy: The complete guide.* Rochester, VT: Park Street Press.

Henry, W. K., Alozie, O. K., & Bonham, S. (2009). Peering into the future. *Minnesota Medicine, 92*(10), 50–54.

Hernandez-Avila, C., & Pierucci-Lagha, A. (2005). Inhalants. In H. R. Kranzler & D. A. Ciraulo (Eds.), *Clinical manual of addiction psychopharmacology.* Washington, DC: American Psychiatric Publishing.

Herning, R. I., Better, W., & Cadet, J. L. (2001). Marijuana abusers are at increased risk for stroke: Preliminary evidence from cerebrovascular perfusion data. *Annals of the New York Academy of Sciences, 939*, 413–415.

Herning, R. I., Better, W., & Cadet, J. L. (2008). EEG of chronic marijuana users during abstinence: Relationship to years of marijuana use, cerebral blood flow, and thyroid function. *Clinical Neurophysiology, 119*, 321–331.

Herzog, W., Aversano, T., & Atlantic CPORT Investigators and Coordinators. (2007). Gender differences in the effect of traditional cardiac risk factors on age of presentation with STEMI. *Circulation, 116*(2), 317.

Hesselbrock, V. M., & Hesselbrock, M. N. (2007). Are there empirically supported and clinically useful subtypes of alcohol dependence? In J. B. Saunders, M. A. Schuckit, P. J. Sirovatka, & D. A. Regier (Eds.), *Diagnostic issues in substance disorders.* Washington, DC: American Psychiatric Publishing.

Hester, R. K., & Squires, D. D. (2004). Outcome research. In M. Galanter & H. D. Kleber (Eds.), *The American Psychiatric Publishing textbook of substance abuse treatment* (3rd ed.). Washington, DC: American Psychiatric Publishing.

Hester, T. (2008). Study: NJH loses money through nonviolent drug sentences. Retrieved from http://www.newsday.com/news/local/wire/newjersey/ny/-bc-nonviolentdrugoff0528may28,0,128334.story

Heyman, G. M. (2009). *Addiction: A disorder of choice.* Cambridge, MA: Harvard University Press.

Heymann, P. (2008, March 1). *Narcotics, youth and the Internet.* Paper presented at the Treating the Addictions seminar hosted by the Department of Psychiatry of Cambridge Hospital, Boston.

Higgins, E. S. (2009). Do ADHD drugs take a toll on the brain? *Scientific American Mind, 20*(4), 38–43.

Hildebrandt, E. (2008). *$70 billion a year for drug laws while predators remain free.* Retrieved from http://www.salem-news.com/articles/may242008/pot_culture_5-24-08.php

Hildebrandt, T., Langenbucher, J., Carr, S., Sanjuan, P., & Park, S. (2006). Predicting intentions for long-term anabolic-androgenic steroid use among men: A covariance structure model. *Psychology of Addictive Behaviors, 20*, 234–240.

Hilditch, T. (2000). Ya ba. *Gear, 2*(11), 86–88.

Hill, D. B., & Kugelmas, M. (1998). Alcoholic liver disease. *Postgraduate Medicine, 103*, 261–275.

Hill, K. G., Hawkins, J. D., Catalano, R. F., Abbott, R. D., & Guo, J. (2005). Family influences on the risk of daily smoking initiation. *Journal of Adolescent Health, 37*, 202–210.

Hill, P., Dwyer, K., Kay, T., & Murphy, B. (2002). Severe chronic renal failure in association with oxycodone addiction: A new form of fibillary glomerulopathy. *Human Pathology, 33*, 783–787.

Hiller, M. L., Knight, K., Rao, S. R., & Simpson, D. D. (2002). Assessing and evaluating mandated correctional substance abuse treatment. In C. G. Leukefeld, F. Tims, & D. Farabee (Eds.), *Treatment of drug offenders.* New York: Springer.

Hilts, P. J. (1994). Labeling on cigarettes a smoke screen. *St. Paul Pioneer Press, 146*(5), 1A, 6A.

Hilts, P. J. (1996). *Smoke screen.* New York: Addison-Wesley.

Hines, L. M., Stampfer, K. M. J., Ma, J., Gaziano, J. M., Ridker, P. M., Hankinson, S. E., et al. (2001). Genetic variation in alcohol dehydrogenase and the beneficial effect of moderate alcohol consumption on myocardial infarction. *New England Journal of Medicine, 344*, 549–555.

Hines, S. C. (2002). Progress against hepatitis C infection. *Patient Care, 36*(3), 11–20.

Hingson, R. (2003, March 7). *College-age drinking.* Symposium presented to the Department of Psychiatry at Cambridge Hospital, Boston.

Hingson, R. W., Heeren, T., & Winter, M. R. (2006). Age at drinking onset and alcohol dependence at age onset, duration and severity. *Archives of Pediatric and Adolescent Medicine, 160*, 739–746.

Hingson, R. W., Zha, W., & Weigzman, E. R. (2009). Magnitude of and trends in alcohol-related mortality and morbidity among US college students ages 18–24, 1998–2005. *Journal of Studies on Alcohol and Drugs,* (Suppl. 16), 12–20.

Hitsman, B., Moss, T. G., Montoya, I. D., & George, T. P. (2009). Treatment of tobacco dependence in mental health and addictive disorders. *Canadian Journal of Psychiatry, 54*(6), 368–378.

HIV infection among injection drug users—34 states, 2004–2007. (2010). *Weekly Morbidity and Mortality Report, 303*(2), 1291–1295.

Hoag, H. (2008). Sex on the brain. *New Scientist, 199*(2665), 28–31.

Hobson, J. A. (1999). *Dreaming as delirium.* Cambridge, MA: MIT Press.

Hobson, J. A. (2001). *The dream drugstore.* Cambridge, MA: MIT Press.

Hobson, J. A. (2005). *13 dreams Freud never had.* New York: Pi Press.

Hoffman, R. S., & Hollander, J. E. (1997). Evaluation of patients with chest pain after cocaine use. *Critical Care Clinics of North America, 13,* 809–828.

Hogan, M. J. (2000). Diagnosis and treatment of teen drug use. *Medical Clinics of North America, 84,* 927–966.

Holland, W. W., & Fitzsimons, B. (1991). Smoking in children. *Archives of Disease in Childhood, 66,* 1269–1270.

Holleran, R. S. (2002). The problem of pain in emergency care. *Nursing Clinics of North America, 37,* 67–78.

Holm, K. J., & Goa, K. L. (2000). Zolpidem. *Drugs, 59,* 865–889.

Holzel, K. L., Weiser, A. K., Berner, M. M., & Harter, M. (2008). Meta analysis: Are 3 questions enough to detect unhealthy alcohol use? *Annals of Internal Medicine, 149*(12), 878–888.

Hommer, D. W., Momenan, R., Kaiser, E., & Rawlings, R. R. (2001). Evidence of a gender-related effect of alcoholism on brain volumes. *American Journal of Psychiatry, 158,* 198–204.

Hopfer, C. M., Mikulich, S. K., & Crowley, T. J. (2000). Heroin use among adolescents in treatment for substance use disorders. *Journal of the American Academy of Child and Adolescent Psychiatry, 39,* 1316–1323.

Hopko, D. R., Lachar, D., Bailley, S. E., & Varner, R. V. (2001). Assessing predictive factors for extended hospitalization at acute psychiatric admission. *Psychiatric Services, 52,* 1367–1373.

Horgan, C. M., Garnick, D. W., Merrick, E. L., & Hoyt, A. (2007). Health care requirements for mental health and substance abuse screening in primary care. *Journal of General Internal Medicine, 22*(7), 930–936.

Horgan, J. (2005). The electric kool-aid clinical trial. *New Scientist, 185*(2488), 36–39.

Horney, K. (1964). *The neurotic personality of our time.* New York: Norton.

Horvath, A. T. (2000). SMART recovery. *The Addictions Newsletter, 7*(2), 11.

Horvath, A. T. (2005). Alternative support groups. In J. H. Lowinson, P. Ruiz, R. B. Millman, & J. G. Langrod (Eds.), *Substance abuse: A comprehensive textbook* (4th ed.). New York: Lippincott Williams & Wilkins.

Horvath, T. (2007). 9th circuit rules government officials personally liable for mandated 12-step attendance. *The Addictions Newsletter, 14*(3), 16.

How alcoholics anonymous works. (2007). *Harvard Mental Health Letter, 24*(1), 4–6.

How long does cocaine remain in the hair of former users? (2009). *Forensic Drug Abuse Advisor, 21*(7), 52–53.

How they smack up. (2005). *Playboy, 52*(4), 25.

Hser, Y., Anglin, M. D., & Powers, K. (1993). A 24-year follow-up of California narcotics addicts. *Archives of General Psychiatry, 50,* 577–584.

Hser, Y., Evans, E., Huang, D., & Anglin, D. M. (2004). Relationship between drug treatment services, retention and outcomes. *Psychiatric Services, 55,* 767–774.

Hser, Y., Hoffman, V., Grella, C. E., & Anglin, M. D. (2001). A 33-year follow-up of narcotics addicts. *Archives of General Psychiatry, 58,* 503–508.

Hubbard, J. B., Franco, S. E., & Onaivi, E. S. (1999). Marijuana: Medical implications. *American Family Physician, 60,* 2583–2593.

Huddleston, C. W., Freeman-Wilson, K., & Boone, D. L. (2004). *Painting the current picture: A national report card on drug courts and other problem-solving court programs in the United States.* Alexandria, VA: National Drug Court Institute.

Hudziak, J., & Waterman, G. S. (2005). Buspirone. In B. J. Sadock & V. A. Sadock (Eds.), *Kaplan & Sadock's comprehensive textbook of psychiatry* (8th ed.). New York: Lippincott Williams & Wilkins.

Huestis, M. A. (2009). Cannabinoids. In J. D. Robero-Miller & B. A. Goldberger (Eds.), *Handbook of workplace drug testing* (2nd ed.). Washington, DC: AACC Press.

Huffing can kill your child. (2004). *CBS Evening News.* Retrieved from http://www.cbsnews.com/stories/2004/06/01eveningnews/main610528.shtml

Hughes, J. R. (2005). Nicotine-related disorders. In B. J. Sadock & V. A. Sadock (Eds.), *Kaplan & Sadock's comprehensive textbook of psychiatry* (8th ed.). Baltimore: Lippincott Williams & Wilkins.

Hughes, T. L., Wilsnack, S. C., Szalacha, L. A., Johnson, T., Bostwick, W. B., Seymour, R., et al. (2006). Age and racial/ethnic differences in drinking and drinking-related problems in a community sample of lesbians. *Journal of Studies on Alcohol, 67,* 579–590.

Humphreys, K., (2003). A research based analysis of the moderation management controversy. *Psychiatric Services, 54,* 621–622.

Humphreys, K., & Moos, R. H. (2007). Encouraging posttreatment self-help involvement to reduce demand for continuing care services: Two-year clinical and utilization outcomes. *Alcoholism: Clinical and Experimental Research, 31*(4), 64–68.

Hung, J. (2003). Aspirin for cardiovascular disease prevention. *Medical Journal of Australia, 179,* 147–152.

Hunger leaves its mark on fetal DNA. (2008). *New Scientist, 200*(2680), 12.

Hunnault, C. C., Mensinga, T. T., de Vries, I., Hermien, H., Hoek, J., Kruidenier, M., et al. (2008). Delta-9-tetrahydrocannabinol (THC) serum concentrations and pharmacological effects in males after smoking a combination of tobacco and cannabis containing up to 69 mg THC. *Psychopharmacology, 202*(2), 161–170.

Hunter, K., & Ochoa, R. (2006). Acamprosate (Campral) for treatment of alcoholism. *American Family Physician, 74,* 645–646.

Hurcom, C., Copello, A., & Orford, J. (2000). The family and alcohol: Effects of excessive drinking and conceptualizations of spouses over recent decades. *Substance Use & Misuse, 35,* 473–502.

Hurt, R. D., & Robertson, C. R. (1998). Prying open the door to the tobacco industry's secrets about nicotine. *Journal of the American Medical Association, 280,* 1173–1181.

Hurwitz, B. E., Klaus, J. R., Llabre, M. M., Gonzalez, A., Lawrence, P. J., Maher, K. J., et al. (2007). Suppression of human immunodeficiency virus type 1 viral load with selenium supplementation: A randomized controlled trial. *Archives of Internal Medicine, 167,* 148–154.

Husak, D. N. (2004). The moral relevance of addiction. *Substance Use & Misuse, 39,* 399–436.

Hutchison, R. (2004). COX-2—selective NSAIDs. *American Journal of Nursing, 104*(3), 52–55.

Hyman, S. E. (2005, March 4). *Addictions and the brain: An update.* Seminar presented at the Cambridge Hospital Department of Psychiatry, Boston.

Hymowitz, N. (2005). Tobacco. In R. J. Frances, S. I. Miller, & A. H. Mack (Eds.), *Clinical textbook of addictive disorders* (3rd ed.). New York: Guilford.

Ikehara, S., Iso, H., Toyoshima, H., Date, C., Yamamoto, A., Kikuchi, S., et al. (2008). Alcohol consumption and mortality from stroke and coronary heart disease among Japanese men and women. *Stroke* (published online prior to print). doi: 10.1161/STROKE/AHA.108528288

Ilgen, M. A., Jain, A., Lucas, E., & Moos, R. H. (2007). Substance use disorder treatment and a decline in attempted suicide during and after treatment. *Journal of Studies of Alcohol & Drugs, 68,* 503–509.

Illicit drug use among older adults. (2009, December 29). *The NSDUH Report.* News Release: National Survey on Drug Use and Health.

Increase in fatal poisonings involving opioid analgesics in the United States, 1999–2006. (2009, September 22). Centers for Disease Control and Prevention, Press release.

Insomnia in later life. (2006). *Harvard Mental Health Letter, 23*(6), 1–5.

International Narcotics Control Board. (2008). *Report of the International Narcotics Control Board for 2008.* New York: United Nations.

Iqbal, M. M., Sobhan, T., & Ryals, T. (2002). Effects of commonly used benzodiazepineson the fetus, the neonate and the nursing infant. *Psychiatric Services, 53,* 39–49.

Ireland, T. (2001). The abuse connection. *Counselor, 2*(3), 14–20.

Irvin, J. E., Bowers, C. A., Dunn, M. E., & Wang, M. C. (1999). Efficacy of relapse prevention: A meta-analytic review. *Journal of Consulting and Clinical Psychology, 67,* 563–570.

Isaacson, J. H., & Schorling, J. B. (1999). Screening for alcohol problems in primary care. *Medical Clinics of North America, 83,* 1547–1563.

Isensee, B., Hans-Ulrich, W., Stein, M. B., Hofler, M., & Lieb, R. (2003). Smoking increases the risk of panic. *Archives of General Psychiatry, 60,* 692–700.

Ishida, J. H., Peters, M. G., Jin, C., Louie, D., Tan, V., Bacchetti, P., et al. (2008). Influence of cannabis use on severity of hepatitis C disease. *Clinical Gastroenterology and Hepatology, 6,* 69–75.

Is there a genetic basis for drug addiction? (2008). *Forensic Drug Abuse Advisor, 20*(6), 44–46.

Is there a genetic basis for methamphetamine resistance? (2008). *Forensic Drug Abuse Advisor, 20*(6), 46–47.

Ivanov, I. S., Schulz, K. P., Palmero, R. C., & Newcorn, J. H. (2006). Neurobiology and evidence-based biological treatments for substance abuse disorders. *CNS Spectrums, 11*(11), 864–877.

Iverson, L. (2005). Long-term effects of exposure to cannabis. *Current Opinion in Pharmacology, 5,* 69–72.

Jackman, R. P., Purvis, J. M., & Mallett, B. S. (2008). Chronic nonmalignant pain in primary care. *American Family Physician, 78*(10), 1155–1162.

Jackson, D., Jackson, L. M., & Hawkey, C. J. (2000). COX-2 selective nonsteroidal anti-inflammatory drugs. *Drugs, 59*(6), 1207–1216.

Jackson, V. A., Sesso, H. D., Buring, J. E., & Gasiano, M. (2003). Alcohol consumption and mortality in men with preexisting cerebrovascular disease. *Archives of Internal Medicine, 163,* 1189–1193.

Jacobs, E. J., Thun, M. J., Bain, E. B., Rodriguez, C., Henley, S. J., & Calle, E. E. (2007). A large cohort study of long-term daily use of adult-strength aspirin and cancer incidence. *Contemporary Nurse, 23*(2), 321–330.

Jacobus, J., McQueeny, T., Bava, S., Schweinsburg, B. C., Frank, L. R., Yang, T. T., et al. (2009). White matter integrity in adolescents with histories of marijuana use and binge drinking. *Neurotoxicity and Teratology* (published online prior to print). doi: 10.1016/j.ntt.2009.07.006

Jaffe, J. H. (2000). Opioid-related disorders. In H. I. Kaplan & B. J. Sadock (Eds.), *Comprehensive textbook of psychiatry* (7th ed.). Baltimore: Lippincott Williams & Wilkins.

Jaffe, J. H., & Anthony, J. C. (2005). Substance-related disorders: Introduction and overview. In B. J. Sadock & V. A. Sadock (Eds.), *Kaplan & Sadock's comprehensive textbook of psychiatry* (8th ed.). Baltimore: Lippincott Williams & Wilkins.

Jaffe, J. H., & Jaffe, A. B. (2004). Neurobiology of opioids. In M. Galanter & H. D. Kleber (Eds.), *The American Psychiatric Publishing textbook of substance abuse treatment* (3rd ed.). Washington, DC: American Psychiatric Publishing.

Jaffe, J. H., Ling, W. H., & Rawson, R. A. (2005). Amphetamine (or amphetamine-like) related disorders. In B. J. Sadock & V. A. Sadock (Eds.), *Kaplan & Sadock's comprehensive textbook of psychiatry* (8th ed.). New York: Lippincott Williams & Wilkins.

Jaffe, J. H., Rawson, R. A., & Ling, W. H. (2005). Cocaine-related disorders. In B. J. Sadock & V. A. Sadock (Eds.), *Kaplan & Sadock's comprehensive textbook of psychiatry* (8th ed.). New York: Lippincott Williams & Wilkins.

Jaffe, J. H., & Strain, E. C. (2005). Opioid-related disorders. In B. J. Sadock & V. A. Sadock (Eds.), *Kaplan & Sadock's comprehensive textbook of psychiatry* (8th ed.). New York: Lippincott Williams & Wilkins.

James, L. P., Farrar, H. C., Komoroski, E. M., Wood, W. R., Graham, C. J., Bornemeier, R. A., et al. (1998). Sympathomimetic drug use in adolescents presenting to a pediatric emergency department with chest pain. *Journal of Toxicology: Clinical Toxicology, 36,* 321–329.

Javitt, D., & Zukin, S. R. (2005). Phencyclidine (or phencyclidine-like) related disorders. In B. J. Sadock

& V. A. Sadock (Eds.), *Kaplan & Sadock's comprehensive textbook of psychiatry* (8th ed.). New York: Lippincott Williams & Wilkins.

Jayaram-Lindstrom, N., Hammarberg, A., Beck, O., & Franck, J. (2008). Naltrexone for the treatment of amphetamine dependence: A randomized, placebo-controlled trial. *American Journal of Psychiatry, 165,* 1442–1448.

Jeffreys, D. (2004). *Aspirin: The remarkable story of a wonder drug.* New York: Bloomsbury.

Jellinek, E. M. (1952). Phases of alcohol addiction. *Quarterly Journal of Studies on Alcohol, 13,* 673–674.

Jellinek, E. M. (1960). *The disease concept of alcoholism.* New Haven, CT: College and University Press.

Jemionek, J. F., Copley, C. L., Smith, M. L., & Past, M. R. (2008). Concentration distribution of the marijuana metabolite Δ-9-tetrahydrocannabinol-9-carboxylic acid and the cocaine metabolite benzoylecgonine in the Department of Defense urine drug-testing program. *Journal of Analytical Toxicology, 32*(6), 408–416.

Jenkins, A. J. (2007). Pharmacokinetics: Drug absorption, distribution and elimination. In S. B. Karch (Ed.), *Drug abuse handbook* (2nd ed.). New York: CRC Press.

Jenkins, A. J., & Cone, E. J. (1998). Pharmacokinetics: Drug absorption, distribution and elimination. In S. B. Karch (Ed.), *Drug abuse handbook.* New York: CRC Press.

Jenkins, S. C., Tinsley, J. A., & van Loon, J. A. (2001). *A pocket reference for psychiatrists* (3rd ed.). Washington, DC: American Psychiatric Publishing.

Jernigan, T. L., Gamst, A. C., Archibald, S. L., Fennema-Notestine, C., Mindt, M. R., Marcotte, T. L., et al. (2005). Effects of methamphetamine dependence and HIV infection on cerebral morphology. *American Journal of Psychiatry, 162,* 1461–1472.

Jerslid, D. (2001). *Happy hours.* New York: HarperCollins.

Johns, A. (2001). Psychiatric effects of cannabis. *British Journal of Psychiatry, 178,* 116–122.

Johnson, B. A. (2010). Medication treatment of different types of alcoholism. *American Journal of Psychiatry, 167,* 639–647.

Johnson, B. A., Ait-Daoud, M., Bodwen, C. L., DiClemente, Mao, L., Beyers, K., et al. (2003). Oral topiramate for treatment of alcohol dependence: A randomized control trial. *The Lancet, 361,* 167–185.

Johnson, B. A., Devous, M. D., Ruiz, P., & Ait-Daud, N. (2001). Treatment advances for cocaine-induced ischemic stroke: Focus on diphdropyridine-class calcium channel blockers. *American Journal of Psychiatry, 158,* 1191–1198.

Johnson, B. A., Roache, J. D., Javors, M. A., DiClemente, C. C., Cloninger, C. R., Prihoda, T. J., et al. (2000). Ondansetron for reduction of drinking among biologically predisposed alcohol patients. *Journal of the American Medical Association, 284,* 963–970.

Johnson, B. A., Rosenthal, N., Capece, J. A., Wiegand, F., Mao, L., Beyers, K. et al. (2008). Topiramate for treating alcohol dependence: A randomized controlled trial. *Journal of the American Medical Association, 298*(14), 1641–1651.

Johnson, B. A., Rosenthal, N., Capece, J. A., Wiegand, F., Mao, L., Beyers, K., et al. (2008). Improvement of physical health and quality of life of alcohol-dependent individuals with topiramate treatment: US multisite randomized control trial. *Archives of Internal Medicine, 168*(11), 1188–1199.

Johnson, C., Drgon, T., Liu, Q., Walther, D., Edenberg, H., Rice, J., et al. (2006). Pooled association genome scanning for alcohol dependence using 104,268 SNPs: Validation and use to identify alcoholism vulnerability loci in unrelated individuals from the collaborative study on the genetics of alcoholism. *American Journal of Medical Genetics, 141B*(8), 844–853.

Johnson, J. L., & Hirsch, S. (2003). Aspiration pneumonia. *Postgraduate Medicine, 113*(3), 99–112.

Johnson, S. (2006). *The ghost map.* New York: Riverhead Books.

Johnson, S. L. (2003). *Therapist's guide to substance abuse intervention.* New York: Academic Press.

Johnson, V. E. (1980). *I'll quit tomorrow.* San Francisco: Harper & Row.

Johnson, V. E. (1986). *Intervention.* Minneapolis, MN: Johnson Institute Books.

Johnston, L. D., O'Malley, P. M., Bachman, J. G., & Schulenberg, J. E. (2009). *National survey results on drug use from the Monitoring the Future Study, 1975–2007.* Bethesda, MD: National Institute on Drug Abuse.

Johnston, L. D., O'Malley, P. M., Bachman, J. G., & Schulenberg, J. E. (2008). *National survey results on drug use from the Monitoring the Future Study, 1975–2008.* Bethesda, MD: National Institute on Drug Abuse.

Johnston, L. D., O'Malley, P. M., Bachman, J. G., & Schulenberg, J. E. (2009). *Monitoring the future: National results on adolescent drug use.* Bethesda, MD: National Institute on Drug Abuse.

Johnston, S. C., & Elkins, J. S. (2008). Neurological complications of hypertension. In M. J. Aminoff (Ed.), *Neurology and general medicine* (4th ed.). New York: Churchill Livingstone.

Jones, A. W. (1996). Biochemistry and physiology of alcohol: Application to forensic sciences and toxicology. In J. C. Garriott (Ed.), *Medicolegal aspects of alcohol* (3rd ed.). Tuscon, AZ: Lawyers & Judges Publishing.

Jones, E. M., Knutson, D., & Haines, D. (2004). Common problems in patients recovering from chemical dependency. *American Family Physician, 68,* 1971–1978.

Jones, G. R. (2009). Introduction. In J. D. Robero-Miller & B. A. Goldberger (Eds.), *Handbook of workplace drug testing* (2nd ed.). Washington, DC: AACC Press.

Jones, J. H., & Weir, W. B. (2005). Cocaine-associated chest pain. *Medical Clinics of North America, 39,* 1323–1342.

Jones, R. T. (2005). Hallucinogen-related disorders. In B. J. Sadock & V. A. Sadock (Eds.), *Kaplan & Sadock's comprehensive textbook of psychiatry* (8th ed.). New York: Lippincott Williams & Wilkins.

Jones, R. T., & McMahon, J. (1998). Alcohol motivations as outcome expectancies. In A. G. Eashton & M. S. Gold (Eds.), *Treating addictive behaviors* (2nd ed.). New York: Guilford.

Jonnes, J. (2002). Hip to be high: Heroin and popular culture in the twentieth century. In D. F. Musto, P. Korsmeyer, & T. W. Malucci (Eds.), *One hundred years of heroin.* Westport, CT: Auburn House.

Jorgensen, E. D. (2001, March 3). *Dual diagnosis in treatment-resistant adolescents.* Paper presented at the Treating the Addictions seminar hosted by the Department of Psychiatry of Cambridge Hospital, Boston.

Jorgensen, E. D. (2008, March 1). *Adolescent addictions: What we can and cannot do to help.* Paper presented at the Treating the Addictions seminar hosted by the Department of Psychiatry of Cambridge Hospital, Boston.

Joseph, H. (2004). Feedback/feedforward. *Addiction Treatment Forum, 13*(2), 3–4.

Joseph, H., & Langrod, J. (2005). The homeless. In J. H. Lowinson, P. Ruiz, R. B. Millman, & J. G. Langrod (Eds.), *Substance abuse: A comprehensive textbook* (4th ed.). New York: Lippincott Williams & Wilkins.

Joyner, M. J. (2004). Designer doping. *Exercise and Sport Science Reviews*, *32*(3), 81–82.

Juhnke, G. A. (2002). *Substance abuse assessment and diagnosis*. New York: Brunner/Routledge.

Juliana, P., & Goodman, C. (2005). Children of substance-abusing parents. In J. H. Lowinson, P. Ruiz, R. B. Millman, & J. G. Langrod (Eds.), *Substance abuse: A comprehensive textbook* (4th ed.). New York: Lippincott Williams & Wilkins.

Julien, R. M. (2005). *A primer of drug action* (10th ed.). New York: Worth.

Justo, D., Gal-Oz, A., Paran, Y., & Seltser, D. (2006). Methadone-associated Torsades de pointes (polymorphic ventricular tachycardia) in opioid-dependent patients. *Addiction*, *101*(9), 1333–1338.

Kadehjian, L. J., & Crouch, D. J. (2009). Sweat testing. In J. D. Robero-Miller & B. A. Goldberger (Eds.), *Handbook of workplace drug testing* (2nd ed.). Washington, DC: AACC Press.

Kalantar-Zaden, K., Nguyen, M. K., Chang, R., & Kurtz, I. (2006). Fatal hyponatremia in a young woman after Ecstasy ingestion. *Nature Clinical Practice Nephrology*, *2*(5), 283–288.

Kalivas, P. W. (2003). Predisposition to addiction: Pharmacokinetics, pharmacodynamics and brain circuitry. *American Journal of Psychiatry*, *160*(3), 1–3.

Kallberg, H., Jacobsen, S., Bengtsson, C., Pedersen, M., Padyukov, L., Garred, P., et al. (2008). Alcohol consumption is associated with decreased risk of rheumatoid arthritis: Results from two Scandinavian case-control studies. *Annals of the Rheumatic Diseases*. doi: 10.1136/ard2007.086314

Kamienski, M., & Keogh, J. (2006). *Pharmacology demystified*. New York: McGraw-Hill.

Kaminer, W. (1992). *I'm dysfunctional—you're dysfunctional*. New York: Addison-Wesley.

Kaminer, Y. (1999). Addictive disorders in adolescents. *Psychiatric Clinics of North America*, *22*, 275–288.

Kaminer, Y. (2001). Adolescent substance abuse treatment: Where do we go from here? *Psychiatric Services*, *52*, 147–149.

Kaminer, Y. (2008). Adolescent substance abuse. In M. Galanter & H. D. Kleber (Eds.), *The American Psychiatric Publishing textbook of substance abuse treatment* (3rd ed.). Washington, DC: American Psychiatric Publishing.

Kaminer, Y., & Buckstein, O. G. (2005). Adolescent substance abuse. In R. J. Frances & S. I. Miller (Eds.), *Clinical textbook of addictive disorders* (3rd ed.). New York: Guilford.

Kaminer, Y., & Tarter, R. E. (2004). Adolescent substance abuse. In M. Galanter & H. D. Kleber (Eds.), *The American Psychiatric Association textbook of substance abuse treatment* (3rd ed.). Washington, DC: American Psychiatric Publishing.

Kampman, K. M. (2005). New medications for the treatment of cocaine dependence. *Psychiatry*, *2*(12), 44–48.

Kanayama, G., Barry, S., Hudson, J. I., & Harrison, G. P. (2006). Body image and attitudes towards male role models in anabolic-androgenic steroid users. *American Journal of Psychiatry*, *163*(4), 697–703.

Kanayma, G., Cohane, G. H., Weiss, R. D., & Pope, H. G. (2003). Post anabolic-androgenic steroid use among men admitted for substance abuse treatment: An under-recognized problem? *Journal of Clinical Psychiatry*, *64*, 156–160.

Kandall, S. R. (1999). Treatment strategies for drug-exposed neonates. *Clinics in Perinatology*, *26*, 231–243.

Kandel, D. B., & Chen, K. (2000). Types of marijuana users by longitudinal course. *Journal of Studies on Alcohol*, *61*, 367–378.

Kapadia, R. (2008). Get yourself some healthy profits. *Smart Money*, *17*(11), 84–89.

Karam-Hage, N. M. (2004). Treating insomnia in patients with substance use/abuse disorders. *Psychiatric Times*, *21*(2), 55–56.

Karan, L. D., Haller, D. L., & Schnoll, S. H. (1998). Cocaine and stimulants. In R. J. Frances & S. I. Miller (Eds.), *Clinical textbook of addictive disorders* (2nd ed.). New York: Guilford.

Karch, D., Cosby, A., & Simon, T. (2006). Toxicology testing and results for suicide victims—13 states, 2004. *Morbidity and Mortality Weekly Report*, *55*(46), 1245–1248.

Karch, S. B. (2009). *The pathology of drug abuse* (4th ed.). New York: CRC Press.

Karlamangla, A. S., Sarkisian, C. A., Mako, D. M., Dedes, H., Liao, D. H., Kim, S., et al. (2009). Light to moderate alcohol consumption and disability: Variable benefits by health status. *American Journal of Epidemiology*, *169*(1), 96–104.

Karsan, H. A., Rojter, S. E., & Saab, S. (2004). Primary prevention of cirrhosis. *Postgraduate Medicine*, *115*, 25–30.

Karst, M., Salim, K., Bunstein, S., Conrad, I., Hoy, L., & Schneider, U. (2003). Analgesic effect of the synthetic cannabinoid CT-3 on chronic neuropathic pain. *Journal of the American Medical Association*, *290*, 1757–1762.

Kaskutas, L. A., Ammon, L., Delucchi, K., Room, R., Bond, J., & Weisner, C. (2005). Alcoholics anonymous careers: Patterns of AA involvement five years after treatment entry. *Alcoholism: Clinical and Experimental Research, 29*(11), 1983–1990.

Katz, N., & Fanciullo, G. J. (2002). Role of urine toxicology testing in the management of chronic opioid therapy. *The Clinical Journal of Pain, 18,* 576–582.

Katz, W. A. (2000). *Pain management in rheumatologic disorders.* USA: Drugsmartz Publications.

Katzung, G. B. (1995). Introduction. In B. G. Katzung (Ed.), *Basic & clinical pharmacology* (6th ed.). Norwalk, CT: Appleton & Lang.

Kauffman, J. F. (2003a). Methadone treatment and recovery for opioid dependence. *Primary Psychiatry, 10*(9), 61–64.

Kauffman, J. F. (2003b, March 8). *Recovery and methadone treatment.* Paper presented at the Treating the Addictions seminar sponsored by the Department of Psychiatry of Cambridge Hospital, Boston.

Kauffman, S. A. (2008). *Reinventing the sacred.* New York: Basic Books.

Kaufman, M. (2006). Smoking in U.S. declines sharply. Retrieved from http://www.washingtonpost.comwp-dyn/content/article/2006/03/08AR2006030802368.html

Kaufman, M. J., Levin, J. M., Ross, M. H., Lang, N., Rose, S. L., Kukes, T. J., et al. (1998). Cocaine-induced vaso-constriction detected in humans with magnetic resonance angiography. *Journal of the American Medical Association, 279,* 376–380.

Kavanagh, D. J., McGrath, J., Saunders, J. B., Dore, G., & Clark, D. (2002). Substance misuse in patients with schizophrenia. *Drugs, 62*(5), 743–756.

Kaye, A. D., Gevirtz, C., Bosscher, H. A., Duke, J. B., Frost, E. A., Richards, T. A., et al. (2003). Ultrarapid opiate detoxification: A review. *Canadian Journal of Anesthesia, 50*(7), 633–671.

Keller, D. S. (2003). Exploration in the service of relapse prevention: A psychoanalytic contribution to substance abuse treatment. In F. Rotgers, J. Morgenstern, & S. T. Walters (Eds.), *Treating substance abuse: Theory and technique* (2nd ed.). New York: Guilford.

Keller, R. W., & Snyder-Keller, A. (2000). Prenatal cocaine exposure. In S. D. Glick & I. B. Maisonneuve (Eds.), *New medications for drug abuse.* New York: New York Academy of Sciences.

Kelly, J. F., Finney, J. W., & Moos, R. (2005). Substance use disorder patients who are mandated to treatment: Characteristics, treatment process, and 1- and 5-year outcomes. *Journal of Substance Abuse Treatment, 28*(3), 213–223.

Kelly, J. P., Cook, S. F., Kaufman, D. W., Anderson, T., Rosenberg, L., & Mitchell, A. A. (2008). Prevalence and characteristics of opioid use in the US adult population. *Pain, 138,* 507–513.

Kelly, V. A., & Saucier, J. (2004). Is your patient suffering from alcohol withdrawal? *RN, 67*(2), 27–31.

Kendler, K. S., & Prescott, C. A. (1998). Cocaine use, abuse and dependence in a population-based sample of female twins. *British Journal of Psychiatry, 173,* 345–350.

Kendler, K. S., Thornton, L. M., & Pederson, N. L. (2000). Tobacco consumption in Swedish twins reared apart and reared together. *Archives of General Psychiatry, 173,* 345–350.

Kenfield, S. A., Stampfer, M. J., Rosner, B. A., & Colditz, G. A. (2008). Smoking and smoking cessation in relation to mortality in women. *Journal of the American Medical Association, 299*(17), 2037–2047.

Kenny, P. J., Chen, S. A., Kitamura, O., Markou, A., & Koob, G. F. (2006). Conditioned withdrawal drives heroin consumption and decreases reward sensitivity. *Journal of Neuroscience, 26,* 5894–5900.

Kerrigan, M. (2008, October 29). *Mothers issues after delivery.* Seminar presented at the Wisconsin State Methadone Providers Meeting, Madison.

Kershaw, C. D., & Guidot, D. M. (2008). Alcoholic lung disease. *Alcohol Research & Health, 31*(1), 66–75.

Kessler, R. C., Aguilar-Gaxiola, S., Berglund, P. A., Caraveo-Anduaga, DeWit, D. J., Greenfield, S. F., et al. (2001). Patterns and predictors of treatment seeking after onset of a substance use disorder. *Archives of General Psychiatry, 58,* 1065–1071.

Keyes, M., Legrand, L. N., Iacono, W. G., & McGue, M. (2008). Parental smoking and adolescent problem behavior: An adoption study of general and specific effects. *American Journal of Psychiatry, 165,* 1338–1344.

Khalsa, A. M. (2006). Prevention, counseling, screening, and therapy for the patient with newly diagnosed HIV infection. *American Family Physician, 73,* 271–280.

Khan, R., Morrow, L. J., & McCarron, R. M. (2009). How to manage complications of the 5 most abused substances. *Current Psychiatry, 8*(11), 35–47.

Khantzian, E. J. (2003a, March 8). *Introductory comments by moderator.* Symposium presented to the Department of Psychiatry, Cambridge Hospital, Boston.

Khantzian, E. J. (2003b). The self-medication hypothesis revisited: The dually diagnosed patient. *Primary Psychiatry, 10*(9), 47–48, 53–54.

Khat calls. (2004). *Forensic Drug Abuse Advisor, 16*(3), 19–21.

Khurana, M., & Schubiner, H. (2007). ADHD in adults: Primary care management. *Patient Care—Neurology and Psychiatry, 1*(1), 11–15, 27.

Khushalani, N. I. (2008). Cancer of the esophagus and stomach. *Mayo Clinic Proceedings, 83*(6), 712–722.

Kiefer, F., Jahn, H., Tarnaske, T., Helwig, H., Briken, P., Holzbach, R., et al. (2003). Comparing and combining naltrexone and acamprosate in relapse prevention of alcoholism. *Archives of General Psychiatry, 60*, 92–99.

Kieser, R. J. (2005, July 13). *Methadone and pregnancy.* Seminar presented at the Wisconsin State Methadone Providers Meeting, Madison.

Kilbourne, J. (2002, February 2). *Deadly persuasion: Advertising and addiction.* Symposium presented to the Department of Psychiatry, Cambridge Hospital, Boston.

Kilmer, J. R., Palmer, R. S., & Cronce, J. M. (2005). Assessment of club drug, hallucinogen, inhalant and steroid use and misuse. In D. M. Donovan & G. A. Marlatt (Eds.), *Assessment of addictive behaviors* (2nd ed.). New York: Guilford.

Kilts, C. (2004). Neurobiology of substance use disorders. In A. F. Schatzberg & C. B. Numeroff (Eds.), *Textbook of psychopharmacology* (3rd ed.). Washington, DC: American Psychiatric Publishing.

Kim, Y., Teylan, M. A., Baron, M., Sands, A., Nairn, A. C., & Greengard, P. (2009). Methylphenidate-induced spine formation and Δ-FosB expression in nucleus accumbens. *Proceedings of the National Academy of Sciences* (published online prior to print). doi: 10.1073/pnas.0813170106

King, G. R., & Ellinwood, E. H. (2005). Amphetamine and other stimulants. In J. H. Lowinson, P. Ruiz, R. B. Millman, & J. G. Langrod (Eds.), *Substance abuse: A comprehensive textbook* (4th ed.). New York: Lippincott Williams & Wilkins.

King, M., McKeown, E., Warner, J., Ramsay, A., Johnson, K., Cort, C., et al. (2003). Mental health and quality of life of gay men and lesbians in England and Wales: Controlled, cross-sectional study. *The British Journal of Psychiatry, 183*, 552–558.

King, R. S. (2006). *The next big thing? Methamphetamine in the United States.* Washington, DC: The Sentencing Project.

Kinsella, L. J., & Riley, D. E. (2007). Nutritional deficiencies and syndromes associated with alcoholism. In C. Goetz (Ed.), *Textbook of clinical neurology* (3rd ed.). Philadelphia: Saunders-Elsevier.

Kirisci, L., Mezzich, A., & Tarter, R. (1995). Norms and sensitivity of the adolescent version of the Drug Use Screening Inventory. *Addictive Behaviors, 20*, 149–157.

Kirisci, L., Vanyukov, M., & Tarter, R. (2005). Detection of youth at high risk for substance use disorders: A longitudinal study. *Psychology of Addictive Behaviors, 19*, 243–252.

Kirn, T. F. (2006). New alcohol test appears fallible. *Clinical Psychiatry News, 34*(6), 48.

Kishline, A. (1996). A toast to moderation. *Psychology Today, 29*(1), 53–56.

Klatsky, A. L. (2002). Alcohol and wine in health and disease. In D. K. Das & F. Ursini (Eds.), *Annals of the New York Academy of Sciences* (Vol. 957). New York: New York Academy of Sciences.

Klatsky, A. L. (2003). Drink to your health? *Scientific American, 288*(2), 74–81.

Klatsky, A. L., Morton, C., Udaltsova, N., & Friedman, G. D. (2006). Coffee, cirrhosis and transaminase enzymes. *Archives of Internal Medicine, 166*(11), 1190–1195.

Kleber, H. D. (2002). Methadone: The drug, the treatment, the controversy. In D. F. Musto, P. L. Korsmeyer, & T. W. Malucci (Eds.), *One hundred years of heroin.* Westport, CT: Auburn House.

Klein, M., & Kramer, F. (2004). Rave drugs: Pharmacological considerations. *AANA Journal, 72*(1), 61–67.

Kleinig, J. (2004). Ethical issues in substance use and intervention. *Substance Use & Misuse, 39*(3), 369–398.

Klesges, R. C., Johnson, K. C., & Somes, G. (2006). Varenicline for smoking cessation. *Journal of the American Medical Association, 296*, 94–95.

Klotz, F., Garle, M., Granath, F., & Thiblin, I. (2006). Criminality among individuals testing positive for the presence of anabolic androgenic steroids. *Archives of General Psychiatry, 63*, 1274–1279.

Kluger, J. (2006). Balding, wrinkled, and stoned. *Time.* Retrieved from http://www.time.com/time/magazine/article/0,9171,1149389,00.html

Knapp, C. (1996). *Drinking: A love story.* New York: Dial Press.

Knapp, C. M., Ciraulo, D. A., & Jaffe, J. (2005). Opiates: Clinical aspects. In J. H. Lowinson, P. Ruiz,

R. B. Millman, & J. G. Langrod (Eds.), *Substance abuse: A comprehensive textbook* (4th ed.). New York: Lippincott Williams & Wilkins.

Knapp, C. M., Ciraulo, D. A., & Kranzler, H. R. (2008). Neurobiology of alcohol. In M. Galanter & H. D. Kleber (Eds.), *The American Psychiatric Publishing textbook of substance abuse treatment.* Washington, DC: American Psychiatric Publishing.

Knauer, S. (2002). *Recovering from sexual abuse, addictions, and compulsive behaviors.* New York: Haworth Social Work Practice Press.

Knight, J. R. (2000, February 1). *Adolescent substance use: New strategies for early identification and intervention.* Symposium presented to the Department of Psychiatry, Cambridge Hospital, Boston.

Knight, J. R. (2002, February 1). *Adolescent substance abuse: New strategies for early identification and intervention.* Paper presented at the "Treating the Addictions" symposium, Boston.

Knight, J. R. (2003). No dope. *Nature, 426*(2963), 114–115.

Knight, J. R. (2005, March 4). *Adolescent substance abuse: New strategies for early identification and intervention.* Symposium presented to the Department of Psychiatry, Cambridge Hospital, Boston.

Knight, J. R., Harris, S. K., Sherritt, L., Van Hook, S., Lawrence, N., Brooks, T., et al. (2007). Prevalence of positive substance abuse screen results among adolescent primary care patients. *Archives of Pediatric and Adolescent Medicine, 16*, 1035–1041.

Knudsen, H. K. (2009). Adolescent-only substance abuse treatment: Availability and adoption of components of quality. *Journal of Substance Abuse Treatment, 36*(2), 195–204.

Knudsen, H. K., Roman, P. M., & Ducharme, L. J. (2004). The availability of psychiatric programs in private substance abuse treatment centers, 1995–2004. *Psychiatric Services, 55*, 270–273.

Kobeissy, F. H., O'Donoghue, M. B., Golden, E. C., Larner, S. F., et al. (2007). Performance enhancement and adverse consequences of MDMA. *Journal of Addictive Diseases, 25*(Suppl. 1), 47–59.

Koenig, H. G. (2001). Religion, spirituality and medicine: How are they related, and what does it mean? *Mayo Clinic Proceedings, 76*, 1189–1191.

Koesters, S. C., Rogers, P. D., & Rajasingham, C. R. (2002). MDMA (Ecstasy) and other club drugs: The new epidemic. *Pediatric Clinics of North America, 49*, 415–433.

Kolb, G. F. (2008). Neurobiology of addiction. In M. Galanter & H. D. Kleber (Eds.), *The American*

Psychiatric Publishing textbook of substance abuse treatment.* Washington, DC: American Psychiatric Publishing.

Kondro, W. (2003). Athlete's "designer steroid" leads to widening scandal. *The Lancet, 362*, 1466.

Konstan, M. W., Schluchter, M. D., Xue, W., & Davis, P. B. (2007). Clinical use of ibuprofen is associated with slower FEV1 decline in children with cystic fibrosis. *American Journal of Respiratory and Critical Care Medicine, 176*, 1084–1089.

Koob, A. (2009). *The root of thought.* Upper Saddle River, NJ: FT Press.

Koob, G. F. (2008). Neurobiology of addiction. In M. Galanter & H. D. Kleber (Eds.), *The American Psychiatric Publishing textbook of substance abuse treatment.* Washington, DC: American Psychiatric Publishing.

Kosten, T. R., & George, T. P. (2002). The neurobiology of opioid dependence: Implications for treatment. *Science & Practice Perspectives, 1*(1), 13–20.

Kosten, T. R., & O'Connor, P. G. (2003). Management of drug and alcohol withdrawal. *New England Journal of Medicine, 348*, 1786–1795.

Kosten, T. R., & Sofuoglu, M. (2004). Stimulants. In J. H. Lowinson, P. Ruiz, R. B. Millman, & J. G. Langrod (Eds.), *Substance abuse: A comprehensive textbook* (3rd ed.). New York: Lippincott Williams & Wilkins.

Kosten, T. R., Sofuoglu, M., & Gardner, T. J. (2008). Clinical management: Cocaine. In M. Galanter & H. D. Kleber (Eds.), *The American Psychiatric Publishing textbook of substance abuse treatment.* Washington, DC: American Psychiatric Publishing.

Kovalesky, A. (2004). Women with substance abuse concerns. *Nursing Clinics of North America, 39*, 205–217.

Kraft, M. K., Rothbard, A. B., Hadley, T. R., McLellan, A. T., & Asch, D. A. (1997). Are supplementary services provided during methadone maintenance really cost effective? *American Journal of Psychiatry, 154*, 1214–1219.

Kraft, U. (2006). Natural high. *Scientific American Mind, 17*(4), 60–65.

Krain, A., Wisnivesky, J. P., Garland, E., & McGinn, T. (2004). Prevalence of human immunodeficiency virus testing in patients with hepatitis B and C infection. *Mayo Clinic Proceedings, 79*, 51–56.

Kraly, F. S. (2009). *The unwell brain.* New York: Norton.

Krambeer, L. L., von McKnelly, W., Gabrielli, W. F., & Penick, E. C. (2001). Methadone therapy for opioid dependence. *American Family Physician, 63,* 2404–2410.

Kranzler, H. R., & Ciraulo, D. A. (2005a). Alcohol. In H. R. Kranzler & D. A. Ciraulo (Eds.), *Clinical manual of addiction psychopharmacology.* Washington, DC: American Psychiatric Publishing.

Kranzler, H. R., & Ciraulo, D. A. (2005b). Sedative-hypnotics. In H. R. Kranzler & D. A. Ciraulo (Eds.), *Clinical manual of addiction psychopharmacology.* Washington, DC: American Psychiatric Publishing.

Kranzler, H. R., Covault, J., Pierucci-Lagha, A., Chan, G., Douglas, K., Arias, A. J., et al. (2008) Effects of aripiprazole on subjective and physiological responses to alcohol. *Alcoholism: Clinical and Experimental Research, 32*(4), 573–579.

Krasopoulos, G., Brister, S. J., Beattie, W. S., & Bushanan, M. R. (2008). Aspirin resistance and risk of cardiovascular morbidity: Systematic review and meta-analysis. *British Medical Journal* (published online). doi: 10.1136/bmj.29430.529549BE.

Kraus, J. F., & Chu, L. D. (2005). Epidemiology. In J. M. Siler, T. W. McAlister, & S. C. Yudofsky (Eds.), *Textbook of traumatic brain injury.* New York: CRC Press.

Kreeger, K. (2003). Inflammation's infamy. *The Scientist, 17*(4), 28.

Kreek, M. J. (1997, September 29). *History and effectiveness of methadone treatment.* Paper presented at the NIDA Heroin Use and Addiction Conference, Washington, DC.

Kreek, M. J. (2000). Methadone-related opioid agonist pharmacotherapy for heroin addiction. In S. D. Glick & I. B. Maisonneuve (Eds.), *New medications for drug abuse.* New York: New York Academy of Sciences.

Kreek, M. J. (2008). Neurobiology of opiates and opioids. In M. Galanter & H. D. Kleber (Eds.), *The American Psychiatric Publishing textbook of substance abuse treatment.* Washington, DC: American Psychiatric Publishing.

Kreslake, J. M., Wayne, G. F., Alkpert, H. R., Hoh, H. K., & Connolly, G. N. (2008). Tobacco industry control of menthol in cigarettes and targeting of adolescents and young adults. *American Journal of Public Health* (published online). doi: 10.2105/AJPH.2007.125542

Kriechbaum, N., & Zernig, G. (2000). Adolescent patients. In G. Zernig, A. Saria, M. Kurz, & S. S. O'Malley (Eds.), *Handbook of alcoholism.* New York: CRC Press.

Kruelwitch, C. J. (2005). Alcohol consumption during pregnancy. In J. J. Fitzpatrick, J. S. Stevenson, & M. S. Sommes (Eds.), *Annual review of nursing research (Vol. 23).* New York: Springer.

Kubo, A., Levin, T. R., Block, G., Rumore, G. J., Quesenberry, C. P., Buffler, P., et al. (2009). Alcohol types and sociodemographic characteristics as risk factors for Barrett's esophagus. *Gastroenterology, 136*(3), 806–815.

Kuhl, D. (2002). *What dying people want.* New York: Public Affairs.

Kuntsche, E., Simons-Morton, B., Fotiou, A., ter Bogt, T., Kokkevi, A., & Health Behavior in School-Aged Children Study. (2009). Decrease in adolescent cannabis use from 2002–2006 and links to evenings out with friends in 31 European and North American countries and regions. *Archives of Pediatrics and Adolescent Medicine, 163*(2), 119–125.

Kuper, H., Boffeta, P., & Adami, H. O. (2002). Tobacco use and cancer causation: Association by tumor time. *Journal of Internal Medicine, 252,* 206–224.

Kurutz, S., (2003). Kill 'em all. *Playboy, 50*(9), 49.

Kwok, M., Schooling, C. M., Ho, L., Leung, S., Mak, H. K., McGhee, S. M., et al. (2008). Early life second-hand smoke exposure and serious infectious morbidity during the first eight years: Evidence from Hong Kong's "Children of 1997" birth cohort. *Tobacco Control.* doi: 10.1136tc.2007.023887

Lack of funding for the war on drugs. (2008). *Forensic Drug Abuse Advisor, 20*(7), 55–56.

Lai, S., Lima, J. A. C., Lai, H., Vlahov, D., Celentano, D., Tong, W., et al. (2005). Human immunodeficiency virus 1 infection, cocaine, and coronary calcification. *Archives of Internal Medicine, 165,* 690–695.

Lakhan, S. E., & Rowland, M. (2009). Whole plant cannabis extracts in the treatment of spasticity in multiple sclerosis: A systematic review. *BMC Neurology, 9*(59) (published online prior to print). doi: 10.1186/1471-2377-9-59

Lambert, N. M., Fincham, F. D., Marks, L. D., & Stillman, T. F. (2010). Invocations and intoxication: Does prayer decrease alcohol consumption? *Psychology of Addictive Behaviors, 24,* 209–219.

Lamon, B., Gadegbeku, B., Martin, J. L., Beicheler, M. B., & the SAM Group. (2005). Cannabis intoxication and fatal road crashes in France: Population based case-control study. *British Medical Journal, 331,* 1371.

Landau, J., & Garrett, J. (2006). *Invitational intervention: A step by step guide for clinicians helping families engage resistant substance abusers in treatment.* New York: Haworth.

Larimer, M. E., & Kilmer, J. R. (2000). Natural history. In G. Zernig, A. Saria, M. Kurz, & S. S. O'Malley (Eds.), *Handbook of alcoholism.* New York: CRC Press.

Larson, K. K. (1982). Birthplace of the Minnesota Model. *Alcoholism, 3*(2), 34–35.

Lashley, F. R. (2006). Transmission and epidemiology of HIV/AIDS: A global view. *Nursing Clinics of North America, 41,* 339–354.

Latimer, W. W., Newcomb, M., Winters, K. C., & Stinchfield, R. D. (2000). Adolescent substance abuse treatment outcome: The role of substance abuse problem severity, psychosocial and treatment factors. *Journal of Consulting and Clinical Psychology, 68,* 684–696.

Laure, P., & Binsinger, C. (2007). Doping prevalence among preadolescent athletes: A 4-year follow-up. *British Journal of Sports Medicine* (published online). doi: 10.1136/bjsm.2007.035733

Laurence, D. R., & Bennett, P. N. (Eds.). (1992). *Clinical pharmacology* (7th ed.). New York: Churchill Livingstone.

Lawton, G. (2009). If you party now, will you pay later? *New Scientist, 201*(2695), 8–9.

Le, A.D., Li, Z., Funk, D., Shram, M., Li, T. K., & Shaham, Y. (2006). Increased vulnerability to nicotine self-administration and relapse in alcohol-naive offspring of rats selectively bred for high alcohol intake. *Journal of Neuroscience, 26,* 1872–1879.

Leamon, M. H., Wright, T. M., & Myrick, H. (2008). Substance-related disorders. In R. E. Hales, S. C. Yudofsky, & G. O. Gabbard (Eds.), *The American Psychiatric Publishing textbook of psychiatry* (5th ed.). Washington, DC: American Psychiatric Publishing.

Leavitt, F. (2003). *The real drug abusers.* New York: Rowman & Littlefield.

Lee, C. M., Geisner, I. M., Patrick, M. E., & Neighbors, C. (2010). The social norms of alcohol-related negative consequences. *Psychology of Addictive Behaviors, 24,* 342–348.

Lee, C. M., Lewis, M. A., & Neighbors, C. (2009). Preliminary examination of spring break alcohol use and related consequences. *Psychology of Addictive Behaviors, 23,* 689–694.

Lee, M. T., Garnick D. W., Miller, K., & Horgan, C. M. (2004). Adolescents with substance abuse: Are health plans missing them? *Psychiatric Services, 55,* 116.

Lee, W. K., & Rega, T. J. (2002). Alcoholic cardiomyopathy: Is it dose-dependent? *Congestive Heart Failure, 8*(6), 303–306.

Leeds, J., & Morgenstern, J. (2003). Psychoanalytic theories of substance abuse. In F. Rotgers, J. Morgenstern, & S. T. Walters (Eds.), *Treating substance abuse: Theory and technique* (2nd ed.). New York: Guilford.

Leeman, R. F., Toll, B. A., Taylor, L. A., & Volpicelli, J. R. (2009). Alcohol-induced disinhibition expectancies and impaired control as prospective predictors of problem drinking in undergraduates. *Psychology of Addictive Behaviors, 23,* 553–563.

Le Foll, B., & Goldberg, S. R. (2005). Cannabinoid CB1 receptor antagonists as promising new medications for drug dependence. *Journal of Pharmacology and Experimental Therapeutics, 312*(3), 875–883.

Lehrman, S. (2004). Sobering shift. *Scientific American, 290*(4), 22, 24.

Leinwand, D. (2000). New drugs, younger addicts fuel push to shift treatment from methadone clinics. *USA Today, 18*(179), 1–2.

Leistikow, B. N., Kabit, Z., Connolly, G. N., Clancy, L., & Alpert, H. (2008). Male tobacco smoke load and non-lung cancer mortality associations in Massachusetts. *BMC Cancer, 8*(341). Retrieved from http://www.biomedcentral.com/1471-2407/8/341

Lemonick, M. D., & Park, A. (2007). The science of addiction. *Time, 170*(3), 42–48.

Lender, M. E. (1981). The disease concept of alcoholism in the United States: Was Jellinek first? *Digest of Alcoholism Theory and Application, 1*(1), 25–31.

Leonard, K. E., & Mudar, P. (2003). Peer and partner drinking and the transition to marriage: A longitudinal examination of selection and influence processes. *Psychology of Addictive Behaviors, 17,* 115–125.

Leri, F., Zhou, Y., Goddard, B., Levy, A. M., Jacklin, D., & Kreek, M. J. (2008). Steady-state methadone blocks cocaine seeking and cocaine-induced gene expression alterations in the rat brain. *European Neuropsychopharmacology* (published online). doi: 10.1016/j.euroneuro.2008.09.004

Leshner, A. I. (2001a, March 2). *Addiction and the brain.* Paper presented to the Department of Psychiatry of Cambridge Hospital, Boston.

Leshner, A. I. (2001b, November 2). *Recent developments in drug addiction research.* Paper presented to the American Society of Addiction Medicine Symposium, Washington, DC.

Lessig, L. (2009). Our new prohibition. *Playboy*, *56*(4), 115–116.

Lester, B. M., El-Sohly, M., Wright, L., Smeriglio, V. L., Verter, J., Bauer, C. R., et al. (2001). The maternal lifestyle study: Drug use by meconium toxicology and maternal self-report. *Pediatrics*, *107*, 309–317.

Leung, C. C., Lam, T. H., Ho, K. S., Yew, W. W., et al. (2010). Passive smoking and tuberculosis. *Archives of Internal Medicine*, *170*(3), 287–292.

Levin, A. (2008). Might following your nose increase alcoholism risk? *Psychiatric News*, *43*(1), 21.

Levin, F. R., McDowell, D., Evans, S., Nunes, E., Akerele, E., Donovan, S., et al. (2004). Pharmacotherapy for marijuana dependence: A double-blind, placebo-controlled pilot study of divalproex sodium. *American Journal on Addictions*, *13*, 21–32.

Levin, J. D. (2002). *Treatment of alcoholism and other addictions*. Northvale, NJ: Jacob Aronson.

Levin, M. R. (2009). *Liberty and tyranny*. New York: Threshold Editions.

Levis, J. T., & Garmel, G. M. (2005). Cocaine-related chest pain. *Emergency Medical Clinics of North America*, *23*, 1083–1103.

Levisky, J. A., Karch, S. B., Bowerman, D. L., Jenkins, W. W., et al. (2003). False-positive RIA for methamphetamine following ingestion of an ephedra-derived herbal product. *Journal of Analytical Toxicology*, *27*(3), 123–124.

Levitz, J. S., Bradley, T. P., & Golden, A. L. (2004). Overview of smoking and all cancers. *Medical Clinics of North America*, *88*, 1655–1675.

Levy, T. M., & Orlans, M. (1998). *Attachment, trauma and healing*. Washington, DC: CWLA Press.

Levy, S., Harris, S. K., Sherritt, L., Angulo, M. & Knight, J. R. (2006). Drug testing of adolescents in ambulatory medicine. *Archives of Pediatric and Adolescent Medicine*, *160*, 146–150.

Lewis, B. A., Singer, L. T., Short, E. J., Minnes, S., et al. (2004). Four-year language outcomes of children exposed to cocaine in utero. *Neurotoxicology & Teratology*, *26*(5), 617–627.

Lewis, D. C. (1997). The role of the generalist in the care of the substance-abusing client. *Medical Clinics of North America*, *81*, 831–843.

Lewis, M. L. (1937). Alcohol and family casework. *Social Casework*, *35*, 8–14.

Lezak, M. D., Hannay, H. J., & Fischer, J. S. (2004). Toxic conditions. In M. D. Lezak, D. B. Howieson, & D. W. Loring (Eds.), *Neuropsychological assessment* (4th ed.) New York: Oxford University Press.

Li, G., Baker, S. P., Smialek, J. E., & Soderstrom, C. A. (2001). Use of alcohol as a risk factor for bicycling injury. *Journal of the American Medical Association*, *285*, 893–896.

Lieber, C. S. (1996). *Metabolic basic of alcoholic liver disease*. Paper presented at the 1996 annual Frank P. Furlano, MD memorial lecture, Gundersen Lutheran Medical Center, La Crosse, WI.

Lieber, C. S. (1998). Hepatic and other medical disorders of alcoholism: From pathogenesis to treatment. *Journal of Studies on Alcohol*, *59*(1), 9–25.

Lilienfeld, S. O., Lunn, S. J., Ruscio, J., & Beyerstein, B. L. (2010). *50 great myths of popular psychology: Shattering widespread misconceptions about human behavior*. New York: Wiley-Blackwell.

Lindman, R. E., Sjoholm, B. A., & Lang, A. R. (2000). Expectations of alcohol-induced positive affect: A cross-cultural comparison. *Journal of Studies on Alcohol*, *61*, 681–687.

Ling, W., Rawson, R., & Shoptaw, S. (2006). Management of methamphetamine abuse and dependence. *Current Psychiatry Reports*, *8*(5), 335–354.

Ling, W., Wesson, D. R., & Smith, D. E. (2005). Prescription drug abuse. In J. H. Lowinson, P. Ruiz, R. B. Millman, & J. G. Langrod (Eds.), *Substance abuse: A comprehensive textbook* (4th ed.). New York: Lippincott Williams & Wilkins.

Lipman, J. J. (2008). The methadone poisoning epidemic. *The Forensic Examiner*, *17*(2), 38–46.

Lipton, B. H. (2008). Revealing the wizard behind the curtain. In D. Goleman, G. Small, G. Braden & B. Lipton (Eds.), *Measuring the immeasurable: The scientific case for spirituality*. Boulder, CO: Sounds True Press.

Llewellyn, D. J., Lang, L. A., Langa, K. M., Naughton, F., & Matthews, F. E. (2009). Exposure to secondhand smoke and cognitive impairment in non-smokers: National cross sectional study with cotinine measurement. *British Medical Journal*, *338* (published online prior to print). doi: 10.1136/bmj.b462

LoCastro, J. S., Potter, J. S., Donovan, D. M., Couper, D., & Pope, K. W. (2008). Characteristics of first-time alcohol treatment seekers: The COMBINE study. *Journal of Studies on Alcohol & Drugs*, *69*, 885–895.

London, E. D., Simon, S. L., Berman, S. M., Mandelkern, M. A., Lichtman, A. M., Bramen, J., et al. (2004). Mood disturbances and regional cerebral metabolic abnormalities in recently abstinent methamphetamine abusers. *Archives of General Psychiatry*, *61*, 74–84.

Longo, D. L., & Fauci, A. S. (2008). The human retroviruses. In A. S. Fauci, E. Braunwald, D. L. Kasper, S. L. Hauser, D. L. Longo, J. L. Jameson, & J. Loscalzo (Eds.), *Harrison's principles of internal medicine* (17th ed.). New York: McGraw-Hill Medical.

Longo, L. P. (2005, April 4). *Identification and management of alcohol dependence.* Paper presented at symposium, Gundersen Lutheran Medical Center, La Crosse, WI.

Longo, L. P., & Johnson, B. (2000). Addiction: Part I. *American Family Physician, 61,* 2401–2408.

Longo, L. P., Parran, T., Johnson, B., & Kinsey, W. (2000). Addiction: Part II. *American Family Physician, 61,* 2401–2408.

Lopez, W., & Jeste, D. V. (1997). Movement disorders and substance abuse. *Psychiatric Services, 48,* 634–636.

Losing tolerance with zero tolerance. (2005). *The Lancet, 365,* 629–630.

Louie, A. K. (1990). Panic attacks—When cocaine is the cause. *Medical Aspects of Human Sexuality, 24*(12), 44–46.

Lovasi, G. S., Roux, A. V. D., Hoffman, E. A., Kawut, S. M., et al. (2010). Association of environmental tobacco smoke exposure in childhood with early emphysema in adulthood among nonsmokers. *American Journal of Epidemiology, 171*(1), 54–62.

Lovecchio, F., Pizon, A., Riley, B., Sami, A., et al. (2007). Onset of symptoms after methadone overdose. *American Journal of Emergency Medicine, 25*(1), 57–59.

Lovinger, D. M. (2008). Communication networks in the brain. *Alcohol Research & Health, 31,* 196–214.

Luggen, A. S. (2006). Alcohol and the older adult. *Advice for Nurse Practitioners, 14*(1), 47–52.

Lukas, S. E. (2006, March 3). *The neurobiological basis of drug and alcohol abuse: How it directs treatment initiatives.* Paper presented at the Treating the Addictions seminar sponsored by the Department of Psychiatry, Cambridge Hospital, Boston.

Lundström, E., Kaillberg, H., Alfredsson, L., Klareskog, L., & Padyukov, K. (2009). Gene-environmental interaction between the DRB1 shared epitope and smoking in the risk of anti-citrullinated protein antibody-positive arthritis: All alleles are important. *Arthritis & Rheumatism, 60*(6), 1597–1603.

Lybrand, J., & Caroff, S. (2009). Management of schizophrenia with substance use disorders. *Psychiatric Clinics of North America, 32,* 821–833.

Lynam, D. R., Milich, R., Zimmerman, R., Novak, S. P., Logan, T. K., Martin, C., et al. (1999). Project DARE: No effects at 10-year follow-up. *Journal of Consulting and Clinical Psychology, 67,* 590–593.

Lynch, G., & Granger, R. (2008). *Big brain—The origins and future of human intelligence.* New York: Palgrave Macmillan.

Lynch, W. J., Potenza, M. N., Cosgrove, K. P., & Mazure, C. M. (2009). Sex differences in vulnerability to stimulant abuse. In K. T. Brady, S. E. Back, & S. F. Greenfield (Eds.), *Women & addiction.* New York: Guilford.

Lynskey, M. T., & Hall, W. (2001). Attention deficit hyperactivity disorder and substance use disorders: Is there a causal link? *Addiction, 96,* 815–822.

Lynskey, M. T., & Lukas, S. E. (2005). Cannabis. In H. R. Kranzler & D. A. Ciraulo (Eds.), *Clinical manual of addiction psychopharmacology.* Washington, DC: American Psychiatric Publishing.

Lundeen, E. (2002). On the implications of drug legalization. *The Independent Practitioner, 22*(2), 175–176.

Lundqvist, T. (2005). Cognitive consequences of cannabis use: Comparison with abuse of stimulants and heroin with regard to attention, memory, and executive function. *Pharmacology, Biochemistry & Behavior, 81*(2), 319–330.

Lynskey, M., & Lukas, S. E. (2005). Cannabis. In H. R. Kranzler & D. A. Ciraulo (Eds.), *Clinical manual of addiction psychopharmacology.* Washington, DC: American Psychiatric Publishing.

MacCoun, R. J., & Reuter, P. (2001). Evaluating alternative cannabis regimes. *British Journal of Psychiatry, 178,* 123–128.

MacKenzie, K. (2007). The white plague. *New Scientist, 193*(2596), 44–47.

MacParland, S. A., Pham, T. N. Q., Guy, C. S., & Michalak, T. K. (2009). Hepatitis C virus persisting after clinically apparent sustained virological response to antiviral therapy retains infectivity in utero. *Hepatology, 49*(5), 1431–1441.

Maher, B. (2002). *When you ride ALONE you ride with bin Laden.* Beverly Hills, CA: New Millennium Press.

Mahoney, D. (2006). Teens and steroids: A dangerous mix. *Clinical Psychiatry News, 14*(6), 50–51.

Maisto, S. A., Clifford, P. R., Stout, R. L., & Davis, C. M. (2008). Factors mediating the association between drinking in the first year after alcohol treatment and drinking at three years. *Journal of Studies on Alcohol & Drugs, 69,* 728–737.

Makki, T. (2003). Substance use, psychological distress and crime. *Medical Journal of Australia, 179,* 399–400.

Malanga, C. J. (2009). Still no time for complacency. *Neurology, 72,* 2062–2063.

Malik, B., & Stillman, M. (2009). Pain syndromes. In S. I. Savitz & M. Ronthal (Eds.), *Neurology review for psychiatrists.* New York: Lippincott Williams & Wilkins.

Malinin, A. I., Callahan, K. P., & Serebruany, V. L. (2001). Paradoxical activation of major platelet receptors in the methadone-maintained patient after a single pill of aspirin. *Thrombosis Research, 104,* 297–299.

Mamer, M., Penn, A., Wildmer, K., Levin, R. I., & Maslansky, R. (2003). Coronary artery disease and opioid use. *American Journal of Cardiology, 93,* 1295–1297.

Mancall, E. (2008). Nutritional disorders of the nervous system. In J. J. Aminoff (Ed.), *Neurology and general medicine* (4th ed.) New York: Churchill Livingstone.

Manderson, D. R. A. (1998). Drug abuse and illicit drug trafficking. *Medical Journal of Australia, 12,* 588–589.

Mann, C. C., & Plummer, M. L. (1991). *The aspirin wars.* New York: Knopf.

Mann, J. (2000). *Murder, magic and medicine* (2nd ed.). New York: Oxford University Press.

Mansvelder, H. D., Keath, J. R., & McGehee, D. S. (2002). Synaptic mechanisms underlie nicotine-induced excitability of brain reward areas. *Neuron, 33,* 905–919.

Marcus, D. A. (2003). Tips for managing chronic pain. *Postgraduate Medicine, 113*(4), 49–50, 55–56, 59–60, 63–66, 98.

Marcus, G. (2008). *Kluge.* New York: Houghton Mifflin.

Maremmani, I., Pacini, M., Lamanna, F., Pani, P. P., et al. (2010). Mood stabilizers in the treatment of substance use disorders. *CNS Spectrums, 15*(2), 95–109.

Margolin, A., Kleber, H. D., Avants, S. K., Konefal, J., Gawin, F., Stark, E., et al. (2002). Acupuncture for the treatment of cocaine addiction. *Journal of the American Medical Association, 287,* 55–63.

Mariani, J. J., & Levin, F. R. (2004). Pharmacotherapy for alcohol-related disorders: What clinicians should know. *Harvard Review of Psychiatry, 12,* 351–366.

Marijuana arrests. (2003). *Forensic Drug Abuse Advisor, 15*(1) 7.

Marijuana-related deaths? (2002). *Forensic Drug Abuse Advisor, 14*(1), 1–2.

Marik, P. E. (2001). Aspiration pneumonitis and aspiration pneumonia. *New England Journal of Medicine, 344,* 665–671.

Markarian, M., & Franklin, J. (2005). Substance abuse in minority populations. In R. J. Frances & S. I. Miller (Eds.), *Clinical textbook of addictive disorders* (3rd ed.). New York: Guilford.

Markel, H. (2000). Easy answer might not be the right one. *New York Times, CL* (51551), D8.

Markel, H. (2004). *When germs travel.* New York: Pantheon Books.

Marlatt, G. A., Baer, J. S., Kivlahan, D. R., Dimeff, L. A., Larimer, M. E., Quigley, L. A., et al. (1998). Screening and brief intervention for high-risk college student drinkers: Results from a 2-year follow-up assessment. *Journal of Consulting and Clinical Psychology, 66,* 604–615.

Marlatt, G. A., & Donovan, D. M. (2005). Introduction. In G. A. Marlatt & D. M. Donovan (Eds.), *Relapse prevention: Maintenance strategies in the treatment of addictive disorders* (2nd ed.). New York: Guilford.

Marlatt, G. A., & Witkiewitz, K. (2005). Relapse prevention for alcohol and drug problems. In G. A. Marlatt & D. M. Donovan (Eds.), *Relapse prevention: Maintenance strategies in the treatment of addictive behaviors* (2nd ed.). New York: Guilford.

Marlowe, D. B., & DeMatteo, D. S. (2003). Drug policy by analogy: Well, it's like this … *Psychiatric Services, 54,* 1455–1456.

Marsa, L. (2005). A generation out of control? *Ladies Home Journal, CXXI*(4), 162–164, *168,* 173–174.

Marsch, L. A., Bickel, W. K., Badger, G. J., Stothart, M. E., Quesnel, K. J., Stanger, C., et al. (2005). Comparison of pharmacological treatments for opioid-dependent adolescents. *Archives of General Psychiatry, 62,* 1157–1164.

Marsicano, G., Wotjak, C. T., Azad, S. C., Bisogno, T., Rammes, G., Cascio, M. G., et al. (2002). The endogenous cannabinoid system controls extinction of aversive memories. *Nature, 418,* 530–535.

Martell, B.A., O'Connor, P.G., Kerns, R.D., Becker, W.C., Morales, K. H., Kosten, T. R., et al. (2007). Systematic review: Opioid treatment for chronic back pain: Prevalence, efficacy, and association with addiction. *Annals of Internal Medicine, 146,* 116–127.

Martell, B. A., Orson, F. M., Poling, J., Mitchell, E., Rossen, R. D., Gardner, T., et al. (2009). Cocaine vaccine for the treatment of cocaine dependence in methadone-maintained patients. *Archives of General Psychiatry, 66*(10), 1116–1123.

Martensen, R. L. (1996). From papal endorsement to southern vice. *Journal of the American Medical Association, 276,* 1615.

Martin, B. R. (2004). Neurobiology of marijuana. In M. Galanter & H. D. Kleber (Eds.), *The American Psychiatric Publishing textbook of substance abuse treatment* (3rd ed.). Washington, DC: American Psychiatric Publishing.

Martin, N. M., Abu Dayyeh, B. K., & Chung, R. T. (2008). Anabolic steroid abuse causing recurrent hepatic adenomas and hemorrhage. *World Journal of Gastroenterology, 14*(28), 4573–4575.

Mash, D.C., Ouyang, Q., Pablo, J., Basile, M., Izenwasser, S., Lieberman, A., et al. (2003). Cocaine abusers have an overexpression of synuclein in dopamine neurons. *Journal of Neuroscience, 23,* 2564–2571.

Mason, B. J., Salvato, F. R., Williams, L. D., Ritvo, E. C., & Cutler, R. B. (1999). A double-blind, placebo-controlled study of oral nalmefene for alcohol dependence. *Archives of General Psychiatry, 56,* 719–724.

Masten, A. S. (2001). Ordinary magic: Resilience processes in development. *American Psychologist, 56,* 227–238.

Masten, A. S., Fade, V. B., Zucker, R. A., & Spear, L. P. (2009). A developmental perspective on underaged alcohol use. *Alcohol Research & Health, 32*(1), 3–15.

Matochik, J. A., Eldreth, D. A., Cadet, J. L., & Bolla, K. I. (2005). Altered brain tissue composition in heavy marijuana abusers. *Drug and Alcohol Dependency, 77,* 23–30.

Mattingley, J. S., & Groon, L. C. (2008). Wernicke encephalophy: Is the Gundersen Lutheran Alcohol Detoxification Protocol sufficient? *The Gundersen Lutheran Medical Journal, 5*(1), 13–16.

Mayeda, S., & Sanders, M. (2007). Counseling difficult-to-reach adolescent male substance abusers. *Counselor, 8*(2), 12–18.

Maze, I., Covington, H. E., Dietz, D. E., LaPlant, Q., Renthal, W., Russo, S. J., et al. (2010). Essential role of histone methyltranserase G9a in cocaine-induced plasticity. *Science, 327*(5962), 213–216.

McAnalley, B. H. (1996). Chemistry of alcoholic beverages. In J. C. Garriott (Ed.), *Medicolegal aspects of alcohol* (3rd ed.). Tucson, AZ: Lawyers and Judges Publishing.

McCabe, S. E., Cranford, J .A., & Boyd, C.J. (2006). The relationship between past-year drinking behaviors and nonmedical use of prescription drugs: Prevalence of co-occurrence in a national sample. *Drug & Alcohol Dependence, 84*(3), 281–288.

McCabe, S. E., Cranford, J. A., Morales, M., & Young, A. (2006). Simultaneous and concurrent polydrug use of alcohol and prescription drugs: Prevalence, correlates and consequences. *Journal of Studies on Alcohol and Drugs, 67*(4), 529–537.

McCabe, S. E., West, B. Y., Morales, M., Cranford, J. A., & Boyd, C. J. (2009). Does early onset of nonmedical use of prescription drugs predict subsequent prescription drug abuse and dependence? Results from a national study. *Addiction, 102*(12), 1920–1930.

McCann, U. D., Sgambati, F. P., Schwartz, A. R., & Ricaurte, G. A. (2009). Sleep apnea in young abstinent recreational MDMA (Ecstasy) consumers. *Neurology, 73,* 2011–2017.

McClain, C. (2006). Smoking 1 cigarette stiffens heart. Retrieved from http:///www.azstarnet.commetro/129277

McClemon, F. J., Westman, E. C., Rose, J. D., & Lutz, A. M. (2007). The effects of food, beverages, and other factors on cigarette palatability. *Nicotine & Tobacco Research, 9*(4), 505–510.

McClosky, M. S., & Berman, M. E. (2003). Alcohol intoxication and self-aggressive behavior. *Journal of Abnormal Psychology, 112,* 306–311.

McClure, J. B., Swan, G. E., Jack, L., Catz, S. L., Zbikowski, S. M., McAfee, T. A., et al. (2009). Mood side-effects and smoking outcomes among persons with and without probable lifetime depression taking verenicline. *Journal General Internal Medicine.* Retrieved from http://www.springerlink.com/content/77207452k3822r3v/fulltext.html

McCollister, K. E., & French, M. T. (2002). The economic cost of substance-abuse treatment in criminal justice settings. In G. G. Leukefeld, F. Tims., & D. Farabee (Eds.), *Treatment of drug offenders.* New York: Springer.

McCord, J., Jneid, H., Hollander, J. E., de Lemos, J. A., Cercek, B., Hsue, P., et al. (2008). Management of cocaine-associated chest pain and myocardial infarction. A scientific statement from the American Heart Association Acute Cardiac Care Committee of the Council on Clinical Cardiology. *Circulation, 117,* 1897–1907.

McCrady, B. S. (2001). Alcohol use disorders. In D. H. Barlow (Ed.), *Clinical handbook of psychological disorders* (3rd ed.). New York: Guilford.

McCrady, B. S., & Irvine, S. (1989). Self-help groups. In R. K. Hester & W. R. Miller (Eds.), *Handbook of alcoholism treatment approaches.* New York: Pergamon Press.

McDargh, J. (2000, March 4). *The role of spirituality in the recovery process.* Paper presented at the Treating the Addictions seminar hosted by the Department of Psychiatry of Cambridge Hospital, Boston.

McDonagh, M., & Peterson, K. (2006). *Drug class review on pharmaceutical treatments for ADHD: Final report, 2006*. Portland: Evidence-Based Practice Center, Oregon Health and Science Center.

McDowell, D. M. (2004). MDMA, ketamine, GHB and the "club drug" scene. In M. Galanter & H. D. Kleber (Eds.), *The American Psychiatric Publishing textbook of substance abuse treatment* (3rd ed.). Washington, DC: American Psychiatric Publishing.

McDowell, D. M. (2005). Marijuana, hallucinogens and club drugs. In R. J. Frances, S. I. Miller, & A. H. Mack (Eds.), *Clinical textbook of addictive disorders* (3rd ed.). New York: Guilford.

McGillicuddy, N. B., Rychtarik, R. G., Morsheimer, E. T., & Burke-Storer, M. R. (2007). Agreement between parent and adolescent reports of adolescent substance use. *Journal of Child and Adolescent Substance Abuse, 16*(4), 59–78.

McGovern, P. E. (2009). *Uncorking the past*. Los Angeles: University of California Press.

McGowan, L. M. E., Dekker, G. A., Chan, E., Stewart, A., Chappell, L. C., Hunter, M., et al. (2009). Spontaneous preterm birth and small for gestational age infants in women who stop smoking early in pregnancy: Prospective cohort study. *British Medical Journal* (published online prior to print). BMJ 2009;338:b.1081

McGrath, J., Welham, J., Scott, J., Varghess, D., Degenhardt, L., Hayatbakhsh, M. R., et al. (2010). Association between cannabis use and psychosis related outcomes using sibling pair analysis in a cohort of young adults. *Archives of General Psychiatry, 67*(5) (published online prior to print). doi: 10.1001/archgenpsychiatry.2010.6

McGuinness, T. M. (2006). Nothing to sniff at: Inhalant abuse and youth. *Journal of Psychosocial Nursing, 44*(8), 15–18.

McGuinness, T. M., & Fogger, S. A. (2006). Hyperanxiety in early sobriety. *Journal of Psychosocial Nursing, 44*(1), 22–27.

McGuire, L. (1990). The power of non-narcotic pain relievers. *RN, 53*(4), 28–35.

McIlveen, J. W., Mullaney, D., Weiner, M. J., Diaz, N., & Horton, G. (2007). Dysthymia and substance abuse: A new perspective. *Counselor, 8*(2), 30–34.

McKay, A., Koranda, A., & Axen, D. (2004). Using a symptom-triggered approach to manage patients in acute alcohol withdrawal. *MEDSURG Nursing, 13*(1), 15–20, 31.

McKay, J. R. (2006). Continuing care in the treatment of addictive disorders. *Current Psychiatry Reports, 8*, 355–362.

McKee, S. A., Harrison, E. L. R., O'Malley, S. S., Krishnan-Sarin, S., Shi, J., Tetrault, J. M., et al. (2009). Varenicline reduces alcohol self-administration in heavy-drinking smokers. *Biological Psychiatry* (published online prior to print). doi: 10.10/j.biopsych.2009.09.029

McLellan, A. T. (2001, March 2). *Is addiction treatment effective: Compared to what?* Symposium presented to the Department of Psychiatry, Cambridge Hospital, Boston.

McLellan, A. T. (2008). Evolution in addiction treatment, concepts and methods. In M. Galanter & H. D. Kleber (Eds.), *The American Psychiatric Publishing textbook of substance abuse treatment*. Washington, DC: American Psychiatric Publishing.

McNichol, E., Horowicz-Mehler, N., Risk, R. A., Bennett, K., Gialeli-Goudas, M., Chew, P. W., et al. (2003). Management of opioid side effects in cancer-related and chronic noncancer pain: A systematic review. *The Journal of Pain, 4*(5), 231–256.

McPherson, S. B., Afsarifard, F., Hall, H. V., Yudko, E., & Rodriguez, P. (2009). Global perspective on methamphetamine. In S. B. McPherson, H. V. Hall, & E. Yudko (Eds.), *Methamphetamine use—clinical and forensic aspects*. New York: CRC Press.

McPherson, S. B., Yudko, E., Afsarifard, F., & Freitas, T. (2009). Treatment. In S. B. McPherson, H. V. Hall, & E. Yudko (Eds.), *Methamphetamine use—Clinical and forensic aspects*. New York: CRC Press.

McPherson, S. B., Yudko, E., Murray-Bridges, L., Rodriguez, P., & Lindo-Moulds, P. (2009). The history of drug control. In S. B. McPherson, H. V. Hall, & E. Yudko (Eds.), *Methamphetamine use—Clinical and forensic aspects*. New York: CRC Press.

McQueeny, T., Schweinsburg, G. B., Schweinsburg, A. D., Jacobus, J., Bava, S., Frank, L. R., et al. (2009). Altered white matter integrity in adolescent binge drinkers. *Alcoholism Clinical and Experimental Research, 21*. Retrieved from http://www3.interscience.wiley.com/journal/122343078

McRae-Clark, A., & Price, K. L. (2009). Women and marijuana dependence. In K. T. Brady, S. E. Back, & S. F. Greenfield (Eds.), *Women & addiction*. New York: Guilford.

McVoy, M., & Findling, R. (2009). Child and adolescent psychopharmacology update. *Psychiatric Clinics of North America, 32,* 111–133.

Meatherall, R., & Sharma, P. (2005). Foxy, a designer tryptamine hallucinogen. *Journal of Analytical Toxicology, 25*(4), 313–317.

Medical reprieve. (2003). *Playboy, 50*(3), 60.

Medication-assisted treatment (MAT) during pregnancy—Part 1. (2009). *Addiction Treatment Forum, 19*(3), 4–5.

Medina, K. L., Price, J., Harper, E., Logan, P., & Sheer, P. K. (2008, August 14). *Ecstasy consumption and executive functioning: Gender aspects.* Poster presentation at the meeting of the American Psychological Association, Boston.

Medina, K. L., Shear, P. K., & Schafer, J. (2006). Memory functioning in polysubstance-dependent women. *Drug and Alcohol Dependence, 84*(3), 248–265.

Mee-Lee, D. (2002, February 1). *Clinical implications of four generations of addiction treatment: We've come a long way baby—or have we?* Symposium presented to the Department of Psychiatry at Cambridge Hospital, Boston.

Mee-Lee, D., & Gastfriend, D.R. (2008). Patient placement criteria. In M. Galanter & H. D. Kleber (Eds.), *The American Psychiatric Publishing textbook of substance abuse treatment.* Washington, DC: American Psychiatric Publishing.

Meier, B. (2003). *Pain killer: A wonder drug's trail of addiction and death.* New York: Rodale Press.

Meldrum, M. L. (2003). A capsule history of pain management. *Journal of the American Medical Association, 290,* 2470–2475.

Melton, L. (2007). What's your poison? *New Scientist, 193*(2590), 30–33.

Mendelson, J. H., & Mello, N. K. (2008). Cocaine and other commonly abused drugs. In A. S. Fauci, E. Braunwald, D. L. Kasper, S. L. Hauser, D. L. Longo, J. L. Jameson, & J. Loscalzo (Eds.), *Harrison's principles of internal medicine* (17th ed.). New York: McGraw-Hill.

Mendelson, J. H., Mello, N. K., Schuckit, M. A., & Segal, D. S. (2006). Cocaine, opioids and other commonly abused drugs. In S. L. Hauser (Ed.), *Harrison's neurology in clinical medicine.* New York: McGraw-Hill.

Mendyk, S. L., & Fields, D .W. (2002). Acute psychotic reactions: Consider "dip dope" intoxication. *Journal of Emergency Nursing, 28,* 432–435.

Menegaux, F., Steffen, C., Bellec, S., Baruchel, A., Lescoeur, B., Leverger, G., et al. (2006). Maternal coffee and alcohol consumption during pregnancy, parental smoking, and risk of childhood acute leukemia. *Cancer Detection and Prevention, 29*(6), 487–493.

Merton, T. (1961). *New seeds of contemplation.* New York: New Directions Publishing.

Merton, T. (1978). *No man is an island.* New York: New Directions Publishing.

Messinis, L., Kyprianidou, A., Malefaki, S., & Papathanasoupoulos, P. (2006). Neuropsychological deficits in long-term frequent cannabis users. *Neurology, 66,* 737–739.

Methadone–cipro interactions. (2002). *Forensic Drug Abuse Advisor, 14*(1), 5–6.

Methadone overdose in MMT. (2007). *Addiction Treatment Forum, 16*(3), *1,* 3–6.

Metzner, R. (2002). The role of psychoactive plant medicines. In C. S. Grob (Ed.), *Hallucinogens.* New York: Penguin Putnam,.

Meyer, J. S., & Quenzer, L.F. (2005). *Psychopharmacology.* Sunderland, MA: Sinauer Associates.

Meyer, R. E. (1996). The disease called addiction: Emerging evidence in a 200-year debate. *The Lancet, 347,* 162–166.

Meyers, D. G., Neuberger, J. S., & He, J. (2009). Cardiovascular effect of bans on smoking in public places. *Journal of the American College of Cardiology, 54,* 1249–1255.

Migliori, G. B., De Laco, G., Besozzi, G., & Cirillo, C. R. (2009). First tuberculosis cases in Italy resistant to all tested drugs. *Eurosurveillance, 12*(20), 3194.

Miles, H. Johnson, S., Amponsah-Afuwape, S., Finch, E., Leese, M., & Thornicroft, G. (2003). Characteristics of subgroups of individuals with psychotic illness and a comorbid substance use disorder. *Psychiatric Services, 54,* 554–561.

Millar, H. (2009). The hidden epidemic of very young alcoholics. *San Francisco Chronicle.* Retrieved from http://www.sfgate.com/cgi-bin/article.cgl?f=/g/a/2009/07/16hearstmagfamily300674.DTL

Miller, G. M. (2008, February 29). *The neurobiology and genetic susceptibility of addiction.* Paper presented at the Treating the Addictions seminar hosted by the Department of Psychiatry of the Cambridge Health Alliance, Boston.

Miller, L., Davies, M., & Greenwald, S. (2000). Religiosity and substance use and abuse among adolescents in the National Comorbidity Survey. *Journal of the American Academy of Child and Adolescent Psychiatry, 39,* 1190–1197.

Miller, M. C. (2005). What are the dangers of methamphetamine? *Harvard Mental Health Letter, 22*(2), 8.

Miller, M. C. (2007). Drug diversion by adolescents. *Harvard Mental Health Letter, 24*(1), 8.

Miller, M. C. (2008). Songs, lyrics, stress, and substance abuse in adolescents. *Harvard Mental Health Letter, 24*(11), 8.

Miller, N. S. (1999). Mortality risks in alcoholism and effects of abstinence and addiction treatment. *Psychiatric Clinics of North America, 27*, 371–383.

Miller, N. S. (2004). Prescription opiate medications: Medical uses, consequences, laws and controls. *Psychiatric Clinics of North America, 27*, 689–708.

Miller, N. S., & Adams, J. (2006). Alcohol and drug disorders. In J. M. Silver, T. W. McAllister, & S. C. Yudofsky (Eds.), *Textbook of traumatic brain injury.* Washington, DC: American Psychiatric Publishing.

Miller, N. S., & Brady, K. T. (2004). Preface. *Psychiatric Clinics of North America, 27*, xi–xviii.

Miller, T. R., Levy, D. T., Spicer, R. S., & Taylor, D. M. (2006). Societal costs of underaged drinking. *Journal of Studies on Alcohol and Drugs, 67*, 519–528.

Miller, W. R. (2003, March 7). *What really motivates change? Reflections on 20 years of motivational interviewing.* Symposium presented to the Department of Psychiatry at Cambridge Hospital, Boston.

Miller, W. R., & Brown, S. A. (1997). Why psychologists should treat alcohol and drug problems. *American Psychologist, 52*, 1269–1279.

Miller, W. R., & Harris, R. J. (2000). A simple scale of Gorski's warning signs for relapse. *Journal of Studies on Alcohol, 61*, 759–765.

Miller, W. R., & Rollnick, S. (2002). *Motivational interviewing* (2nd ed.). New York: Guilford.

Miller, W. R., & White, W. (2007). Confrontation in addiction treatment. *Counselor, 8*(4), 12–30.

Milne, D. (2007). Perception of sleep quality linked to drinking relapse. *Psychiatric News, 42*(5), 29.

Milstein, J. M. (2008). Introducing spirituality in medical care. *Journal of the American Medical Association, 299*, 2440–2441.

Minkoff, K. (1997). Substance abuse versus substance dependence. *Psychiatric Services, 48*, 867.

Minkoff, K. (2008, October 20). *Changing the world: Welcoming, accessible recovery-oriented, culturally-fluent, comprehensive, continuous, integrated systems of care for individuals and families with psychiatric and substance use disorders.* Seminar presented at

Gundersen Lutheran Medical Center, La Crosse, WI.

Miro, O., Nogue, S., Espinoza, G., To-Figueras, J., & Sanchez, S. (2002). Trends in illicit drug emergencies: The emerging role of gamma hydroxybutyrate. *Clinical Toxicology, 40*, 129–135.

Mithoefer, M., Mithoefer, A., & Wagner, M. (2008). *Methylenedioxymethamphetamine(MDMA)-assisted psychotherapy in subjects with chronic posttraumatic stress disorder: A Phase II clinical trial completed 19 September 2008.* Poster presented at the 24th Annual Meeting of the International Society of Traumatic Stress Studies, Chicago.

Mittleman, M. A., Lewis, R. A., Maclure, M., Sherwood, J. B., & Muller, J. E. (2001). Triggering myocardial infarction by marijuana. *Circulation, 103*, 2805–2809.

Moalem, D., & Prince, J. (2007). *Survival of the sickest.* New York: HarperCollins.

Modesto-Lowe, V., & Fritz, E. M. (2005). The opio-dergic-alcohol link: Implications for treatment. *CNS Drugs, 19*(8), 693–707.

Modesto-Lowe, V., & Kranzler, H. R. (1999). Diagnosis and treatment of alcohol-dependent patients with comorbid psychiatric disorders. *Alcohol Research & Health, 23*(2), 144–149.

Moeller, F. G., & Dougherty, D. M. (2001). Antisocial personality disorder, alcohol, and aggression. *Alcohol Research & Health, 25*(1), 5–11.

Moffett, S. (2006). *The three-pound enigma.* Chapel Hill, NC: Algonquin Books.

Moir, D., Rickert, W. S., Levasseur, G., Larouse, Y., Maertens, R., White, P., et al. (2007). A comparison of mainstream and sidestream marijuana and tobacco cigarette smoke produced under two machine smoking conditions. *Chemical Research in Toxicology, 21*(2), 494–502.

Mokdad, A. H., Marks, J. S., Stroup, D. F., & Gerberding, J. L. (2004). Actual causes of death in the United States, 2000. *Journal of the American Medical Association, 291*, 1238–1245.

Montgomery, D. P., Plate, C. A., Jones, M., Jones, J., Rios, R., Lambert, D. K., et al. (2008). Using umbilical cord tissue to detect fetal exposure to illicit drugs: A new multicentered study in Utah and New Jersey. *Journal of Perinatology, 28*, 750–753.

Monthly Prescribing Reference. (2008). *12*(2), 54.

Monti, P. M., Kadden, R. M., Rohsenow, D. J., Cooney, N. L., & Abrams, D. B. (2002). *Treating alcohol dependence* (2nd ed.). New York: Guilford.

Moon, M. A. (2008a). Smoking associated with cognitive decline in middle age. *Clinical Psychiatry News, 36*(7), 37.

Moon, M. A. (2008b). Methylnaltrexone relieves opioid-induced constipation. *Clinical Psychiatry News, 36*(7), 44.

Mooney, L., Glasner-Edwards, S., Rawson, R. A., & Ling, W. (2009). Medical effects of methamphetamine use. In J. R. Roll, R. A. Rawson, W. Ling, & S. Shoptaw (Eds.), *Methamphetamine addiction—From basic science to treatment.* New York: Guilford.

Moore, C. M. (2009). Drugs of abuse in oral fluid. In J. D. Robero-Miller & B. A. Goldberger (Eds.), *Handbook of workplace drug testing* (2nd ed.). Washington, DC: AACC Press.

Moos, B. S. (2005). Paths of entry into Alcoholics Anonymous: Consequences for participation and readmission. *Alcoholism: Clinical and Experimental Research, 29*(10), 1858–1868.

Moos, R. H. (2003). Addictive disorders in context: Principles and puzzles of effective treatment and recovery. *Psychology of Addictive Behaviors, 17,* 3–12.

Moos, R. H., & Moos, B. S. (2005). Paths of entry into Alcoholics Anonymous: Consequences for participation and readmission. *Alcoholism: Clinical and Experimental Research, 29*(10), 1858–1868.

Moos, R. H. & Moos, B. S. (2006a). Participation in treatment and Alcoholics Anonymous: A 16-year follow-up of initially untreated individuals. *Journal of Clinical Psychology, 62*(6), 735–750.

Moos, R. H. & Moos, B. S. (2006b). Treated and untreated individuals with alcohol use disorders: Rates and predictors of remission and relapse. *International Journal of Clinical and Health Psychology, 6*(3), 513–526.

Moos, R. H., Moos, B. S., & Andrassy, J. M. (1999). Outcomes of four treatment approaches in community residential programs for patients with substance use disorders. *Psychiatric Services, 50,* 1577–1583.

Morgan, C. J. A., Muetzelfeldt, L., & Curran, H. V. (2009). Ketamine use, cognition and psychological wellbeing: A comparison of frequent, infrequent and ex-users and non-using controls. *Addiction, 104*(1), 77–87.

Morgan, P. T., Pace-Schott, E. F., Sahl, Z. H., Coric, V., et al. (2006). Sleep, sleep-dependent procedural learning and vigilance in chronic cocaine users: Evidence for occult insomnia. *Drug and Alcohol Dependence, 82*(3), 238–249.

Morgan, T. J. (2003). Behavioral treatment techniques for psychoactive substance use disorders. In F. Rotgers, J. Morgenstern, & S. T. Walker (Eds.), *Treating substance abuse: Theory and technique* (2nd ed.). New York: Guilford.

Morton, J. (2005). Ecstasy: Pharmacology and neurotoxicity. *Current Opinion in Pharmacology, 5,* 79–86.

Mosier, W. A. (1999). Alcohol addiction: Identifying the patient who drinks. *Journal of the American Academy of Physician's Assistants, 12*(5), 25–26, 28–29, 35–36, 38, 40.

Moss, H. B., Chen, C. M., & Yi, H. (2007). Subtypes of alcohol dependence in a nationally representative sample. *Journal of the American Academy of Physician's Assistants, 91*(2–3), 149–158.

Moss, J., & Rosow, C E. (2008). Development of opioid antagonists: New insights into opioid effects. *Mayo Clinic Proceedings, 83*(10), 1116–1130.

Motluk, A. (2004). Intemperate society. *New Scientist, 183*(2461), 28–33.

Motluk, A. (2006). To your good health. *New Scientist, 191*(2560), 31–34.

Motluk, A. (2008). Body's own drug damps down fear. *New Scientist, 198*(2657), 12.

Movig, K. L. L., Mathijssen, M. P. M., Nagel, P. H. A., van Egmond, J., de Gier, J. J., Leufkens, H. J., et al. (2004). Psychoactive motor use and the risk of motor vehicle accidents. *Accident Analysis and Prevention, 36,* 631–636.

Mozayani, A. (2009). Phencyclidine. In J. D. Robero-Miller & B. A. Goldberger (Eds.), *Handbook of workplace drug testing* (2nd ed.). Washington, DC: AACC Press.

Mueller, A. A. (2005). New drugs of abuse update: Foxy methoxy. *Journal of Emergency Nursing, 30*(5), 507–508.

Mueser, K. T., Noordsy, D. L., Drake, R. E., & Fox, L. (2003). *Integrated treatment for dual disorders.* New York: Guilford.

Muggli, M. E., Ebbert, J. O., Robertson, C., & Hurt, R. D. (2008). Waking a sleeping giant: The tobacco industry's response to the polonium 210 issue. *American Journal of Public Health, 98*(9), 1643–1650.

Muir, H. (2008). Science rules OK! *New Scientist, 198*(2657), 40–43.

Mukamal, K. J., Maclure, N., Mueller, J. E., & Mittleman, M. A. (2008). An exploratory prospective study of marijuana use and mortality following acute myocardial infarction. *American Heart Journal, 155*(3), 465–470.

Mulder, J., Aguado, T., Keimpema, E., Barabas, K., Ballester Rosado, C. J., Nguyen, L., et al. (2008). Endocannabinoid signaling controls pyramidal cell specification and long-range axon patterning. Retrieved from http://www.pnas.org/cgti/content/abstract/0803545105v1?

Mundle, G. (2000). Geriatric patients. In G. Zernig, A. Saria, M. Kurz, & S. S. O'Malley (Eds.), Handbook of alcoholism. New York: CRC Press.

Mundt, M. P., Zakletskala, L. I., & Flemming, M. F. (2209). Extreme college drinking and alcohol-related injury risk. Alcoholism: Clinical and Experimental Research, 33, 1532–1538.

Musher, M. M. (2008). Pneumococcal infections. In A. S. Fauci, E. Braunwald, D. L. Kasper, S. L. Hauser, D. L. Longo, J. L. Jameson, & J. Loscalzo (Eds.), Harrison's principles of internal medicine (17th ed.). New York: McGraw-Hill Medical.

Musto, D. F. (1991). Opium, cocaine and marijuana in American history. Scientific American, 265(1), 40–47.

Myers, B. J., Dawson, K. S., Britt, G. C., Lodder, D. E., et al. (2003). Prenatal cocaine exposure and infant performance on the Brazelton Neonatal Behavioral Assessment Scale. Substance Use & Misuse, 38(14), 2065–2096.

Mylonakis, E., Paliou, M., & Rich, J. D. (2001). Plasma viral load testing in the management of HIV infection. American Family Physician, 63, 483–490.

Myrick, H., & Wright, T. (2008). Clinical management of alcohol abuse and dependence. In M. Galanter & H. D. Kleber (Eds.), The American Psychiatric Publishing textbook of substance abuse treatment. Washington, DC: American Psychiatric Publishing.

Nace, E. P. (2003). The importance of Alcoholics Anonymous in changing destructive behavior. Primary Psychiatry, 10(9), 65–68, 71–72.

Nace, E. P. (2005a) Alcoholics Anonymous. In J. H. Lowinson, P. Ruiz, R. B. Millman, & J. G. Langrod (Eds.), Substance abuse: A comprehensive textbook (4th ed.). New York: Lippincott Williams & Wilkins.

Nace, E. P. (2005b). Alcohol. In R. J. Frances, S. I. Miller, & A. H. Mack (Eds.), Clinical textbook of addictive disorders (3rd ed.). New York: Guilford.

Naimi, T. S., Brewer, R. D., Mokdad, A., Denny, C., Serdula, M. K., & Marks, J. S. (2003). Binge drinking among US adults. Journal of the American Medical Association, 289, 70–75.

Narcotics Anonymous. (1982). Van Nuys, CA: Narcotics Anonymous World Service Office.

National Center on Addiction and Substance Abuse at Columbia University. (2000, May 10). CASA releases physician survey. Press release.

National Center on Addiction and Substance Abuse at Columbia University. (2009a). Shoveling up II: The impact of substance abuse on federal, state, and local budgets. New York: Author.

National Center on Addiction and Substance Abuse at Columbia University. (2009b). National survey of American attitudes on substance abuse XIV: Teens and parents. Press release. Retrieved from http//www.casacolumbia.org/absolutem/templates/Pressreleases.aspx?articleid=566&zoneid=66

National Survey on Drug Use and Health. (2006). The NSDUH Report 22, Office of Applied Studies. Washington, DC: SAMHSA.

National Survey on Drug Use and Health. (2008). Use of specific hallucinogens: 2006. The SUDUH Report, Office of Applied Studies. Washington, DC: SAMHSA.

Nazi meth on the rise. (2003). Forensic Drug Abuse Advisor, 15, 77–78.

Neergaard, L. (2004). Dieters, bodybuilders will lose ephedra: FDA ban takes effect April 12. Milwaukee Journal Sentinel, 122(84), 3A.

Neighbors, C., Pedersen, E. R., & Roberts, T. (2009). 21 bottles of beer in my bloodstream: Extreme drinking on 21st birthdays among college students. The Addictions Newsletter, 16(3), 14–15.

Nelson, E. C., Heath, A. C., Bucholz, K. K., Madden, P. A., Fu, Q., Knopik, V., et al. (2004). Genetic epidemiology of alcohol-induced blackouts. Archives of General Psychiatry, 61, 257–273.

Nelson, R. (2007). Younger onset of alcohol dependence correlates with less help seeking. CNS News, 9(1), 19, 25.

Nelson, T. (2000, March 29–31). Pharmacology of drugs of abuse. Seminar presented by the Division of Continuing Studies, University of Wisconsin, Madison.

Nelson, T. F., Xuan, Z., Lee, H., Weitzman, E. R., & Wechsler, H. (2009). Persistence of heavy drinking and ensuing consequences at heavy-drinking colleges. Journal of Studies on Alcohol and Drugs, 70(5), 726–734.

Nemeroff, C. B., & Putnam, J. S. (2005). Barbiturates and similarly acting substances. In B. J. Sadock & V. A. Sadock (Eds.), Kaplan & Sadock's comprehensive textbook of psychiatry (8th ed.). New York: Lippincott Williams and Wilkins.

Nestler, E.J. (2005). The neurobiology of cocaine addiction. *Science & Practice Perspectives*, *3*(1), 4–10.

Neto, D., Labaz, R., Agular, P., & Chick, J. (2008). Effectiveness of sequential combined treatment in comparison with treatment as usual in preventing relapse in alcohol dependence. Retrieved from http://www.ncbi.him.hig.gov/pubmed/1885241?ordinalpos=1itool=EntrezSystem2.PEntrez.com

Neubauer, D. N. (2005). *Insomnia*. Montvale, NJ: Thompson Healthcare.

Newberg, A., & Walkman, M. R. (2009). *How God changes your brain*. New York: Random House.

Newcomb, M. D., Galaif, E. R. & Carmona, J. V. (2001). The drug-crime nexus in a community sample of adults. *Psychology of Addictive Behaviors*, *15*, 185–193.

Newcorn, J. H., & Ivanov, I. (2007). Psychopharmacological treatment of attention-deficit/hyperactivity disorder and disruptive behavior disorders. *Pediatric Annals*, *36*, 564–574.

Newman, J. L., & Mello, J. K. (2009). Neuroactive gonadal steroid hormones and drug addiction in women. In K. T. Brady, S. E. Back (Eds.), *Women & addiction*. New York: Guilford.

Newman, T. B., Clay, C. M., Davis, G. L., McHutchison, J. G., & Liang, T. J. (2009). Combination therapy for hepatitis C infection. *New England Journal of Medicine*, *340*, 1207.

New nationwide report reveals that 5 million people participate in self-help groups each year. (2008). Substance Abuse & Mental Health Services Administration. Retrieved from http://oas.samhsa.gov.2kb/selfHelp/selfHelp.cmf

New York remains cocaine capital of the world. (2007). *Forensic Drug Abuse Advisor*, *19*(1), 7.

Ngo, H. T. T., Tait, R. J., & Hulse, G .K. (2008). Comparing drug-related hospital morbidity following heroin dependence treatment with methadone maintenance or naltrex-one implantation. *Archives of General Psychiatry*, *65*(4), 457–465.

Nichol, P. E., Krueger, R. F., & Iacono, W. G. (2007). Investigating gender differences in alcohol problems: A latent trait modeling approach. *Alcoholism: Clinical & Experimental Research*, *31*, 783–794.

Nicoll, R. A., & Alger, B. E. (2004). The brain's own marijuana. *Scientific American*, *291*(6), 68–75.

Nichols, D. E. (2006). Commentary. *Psychopharmacology*, *187*, 284–286.

NIDA info facts. (2007). Washington, DC: National Institute on Drug Abuse.

Nielson, D. A., Virkkunen, M., Lappalainen, J., Eggert, M., Brown, G. L., Long, J. C., et al. (1998). A tryptophan-hydroxylase gene marker for suicidality and alcoholism. *Archives of General Psychiatry*, *55*, 593–602.

Nisbet, P. A. (2000). Age and the lifespan. In R. W. Maris, A. L. Berman, & M. M. Silverman (Eds.), *Comprehensive textbook of suicidology*. New York: Guilford.

Nishno, S., Mishma, K., Mignot, E., & Dement, W.C. (2004). Sedative-hypnotics. In A. F. Schatzberg & C. B. Nemeroff (Eds.), *Textbook of psychopharmacology* (3rd ed.). Washington, DC: American Psychiatric Publishing.

Niv, N., Pham, R., & Hser, Y. (2009). Racial and ethnic differences in substance abuse service needs and outcomes in California. *Psychiatric Services*, *60*, 1350–1356.

No dope on dope. (2006). *New Scientist*, *190*(2549), 6.

Noe, A. (2009). *Out of our heads*. New York: Hill and Wang.

Nordgren, H. K., & Beck, O. (2004). Multicomponent screening for drugs of abuse: Direct analysis of urine by LC-MS-GS. *Therapeutic Drug Monitoring*, *26*(1), 90–97.

Norris, K. (1996). *The cloister walk*. New York: Riverhead Books.

Norton-Hawk, M. (2009, March 6). *Social class, drugs, and prostitution: Everything old is new again*. Paper presented at the Treating the Addictions seminar hosted by the Harvard Medical School Department of Continuing Education, Boston.

Nowak, R. (2004). How our brains fend off madness. *New Scientist*, *183*(2462), 13.

Nowak, R. (2008). Something for the pain. *New Scientist*, *199*(2672), 13.

Nowinski, J. (2003). Facilitating 12-step recovery from substance abuse and addiction. In F. Rotgers, J. Morgenstern, & S. T. Walters (Eds.), *Treating substance abuse: Theory and technique* (2nd ed.). New York: Guilford.

Noxon, C. (2002). The trouble with rehab. *Playboy*, *49*(3), 86–88, 152, 154, 156–157.

Nunes, E. V., & Levin, F. R. (2006). Treating depression in substance abusers. *Current Psychiatry Reports*, *8*(5), 363–370.

Nurnberger, J. I., & Bierut, L. J. (2007). Seeking the connections: Alcoholism and our genes. *Scientific American*, *296*(4), 46, 48–53.

Nutt, D. (2009). A dangerous attitude to drugs. *New Scientist*, *204*(2733), 5.

Nutt, D., Robbins, T., & Stimson, G., (2005). Drug futures 2025. In D. Nutt, T. W. Robbins, G. V. Stimson, M. Ince, & A. Jackson (Eds.), *Drugs and the future*. New York: Academic Press.

O'Brien, C. P. (2005). Benzodiazepine use, abuse and dependence. *Journal of Clinical Psychiatry*, 66(Suppl. 2), 28–33.

O'Brien, C. P. (2006). Drug addiction and drug abuse. In L. L. Brunton, J. S. Lazo, & K. L. Parker (Eds.), *Pharmacological basis of therapeutics* (11th ed.). New York: McGraw-Hill.

O'Brien, C. P. (2008). A 50-year-old woman addicted to heroin. *Journal of the American Medical Association*, 300(3), 314–321.

O'Connor, A. D., Rusyniak, D. E., & Bruno, A. (2005). Cerebrovascular and cardiovascular complications of alcohol and sympathomimetic drug abuse. *Medical Clinics of North America*, 89, 1343–1358.

O'Connor, P. G. (2000). Treating opioid dependence—New data and new opportunities. *New England Journal of Medicine*, 343, 1332–1333.

Oehmichen, M., Auer, R. N., & Konig, H. G. (2005). *Forensic neuropathology and associated neurology*. New York: Springer-Verlag.

Oeltmann, J. E., Kammerer, J. S., Pevzner, E. S., & Moonan, P. K. (2009). Tuberculosis and substance abuse in the United States, 1997–2006. *Archives of Internal Medicine*, 169, 189–197.

O'Farrell, T. J., & Fals-Stewart, W. (2008). Family therapy. In M. Galanter & H. D. Kleber (Eds.), *The American Psychiatric Publishing textbook of substance abuse treatment*. Washington, DC: American Psychiatric Publishing.

Office of National Drug Control Policy. (2006). *National drug control strategy*. Washington, DC: U.S. Government Printing Office.

Office of National Drug Control Policy. (2008, June 12). New report finds highest-ever levels of THC in U.S. marijuana. Press release.

Okuyemi, K. S., Nollen, N. L., & Akhluwalia, J. S. (2006). Interventions to facilitate smoking cessation *American Family Physician*, 74, 262–271.

Oliva-Marston, S. E., Yang, P., Mechanic, L. E., Bowman, E. D., Pine, S. R., Loffredo, C. A., et al. (2009). Childhood exposure to secondhand smoke and functional mannose binding lectin polymorphisms are associated with increased cancer risk. *Cancer Epidemiology Biomarkers & Prevention*, 18(12), 3375–3383.

Olmedo, R., & Hoffman, R. S. (2000). Withdrawal syndromes. *Emergency Medical Clinics of North America*, 18, 273–288.

Olmstead, D. H., White, W. D., & Sindelar, J. (2004). The impact of managed care on substance abuse treatment services. *Health Services Research*, 39(2), 319–343.

Olson, J. (2006) *Clinical pharmacology made ridiculously simple* (3rd ed.). Miami, FL: MedMaster.

O'Meara, A. (2009). *Chasing medical miracles*. New York: Walker & Co.

Oncken, C. A., & George, T. P. (2005). Tobacco. In H. R. Kranzler & D. A. Ciraulo (Eds.), *Clinical manual of addiction psychopharmacology*. Washington, DC: American Psychiatric Publishing.

Oral fluid drug testing. (2005). *Forensic Drug Abuse Advisor*, 17, 27–28.

Ordorica, P. I., & Nace, P. E. (1998). Alcohol. In R. J. Frances & S. I. Miller (Eds.), *Clinical textbook of addictive disorders* (2nd ed.). New York: Guilford.

Orr, D. A. (2008, October 31). *Protecting high-risk adults against vaccine preventable hepatitis (VPH)*. Seminar presented to the Wisconsin State Methadone Providers Meeting, Madison.

O'Shea, E., Escobedo, I., Orio, L., Sanchez, V., Navarro, M., Green, A. R., et al. (2005). Elevation of ambient room temperature has differential effects on MDMA-induced 5-HT and dopamine release in striatum and nucleus accumbens of rats. *Neuropsychopharmacology*, 30(7), 1312–1323.

Osher, F. C., & Drake, R. E. (1996). Reversing a history of unmet needs: Approaches to care for persons with co-occurring addictive and mental disorders. *American Journal of Orthopsychiatry*, 66, 4–11.

Ostacher, M. J., & Sachs, G. S. (2006). Update on bipolar disorder and substance abuse: Recent findings and treatment strategies. *Journal of Clinical Psychiatry*, 67(9), e10.

OTPs: Past, current, future—part III. (2008). *Addiction Treatment Forum*, 17(3), 1, 4–5.

Otsuka, R., Watanabe, H., Hirata, K., Tokai, K., Muro, T., Yoshiyama, M., et al. (2001). Acute effects of passive smoking on the coronary circulation in healthy young adults. *Journal of the American Medical Association*, 286, 436–441.

Otto, R. K., Lang, A. R., Megargee, E. I., & Rosenblatt, A. I. (1989). Ability of alcoholics to escape detection by the MMPI. *Critical Items*, 4(2), 7–8.

Outslay, M. G. (2006). Understanding ecstasy. *Journal of the American Association of Physician Assistants*, 19(7), 42–47.

Overman, G. P., Teter, C. J., & Guthrie, S. K. (2003). Acamprosate for the adjunctive treatment of alcohol dependence. *The Annals of Pharmacotherapy*, 37, 1090–1099.

Owen, F. (2007). The dark side of the summer of love. *Playboy*, *54*(7), 56–60, 122–128.

Owen, F. (2008). The Adderall effect. *Playboy*, *55*(10), 50–52, 128.

Pagano, J., Graham, N. A., Frost-Pineda, K., & Gold, M. S. (2005). The physician's role in recognition and treatment of alcohol dependence and comorbid conditions. *Psychiatric Annals*, *35*(6), 473–481.

Pagano, M. E., Friend, K. B., Tonigan, S., & Stout, R. L. (2004). Helping other alcoholics in Alcoholics Anonymous and drinking outcomes: Findings from Project MATCH. *Journal of Studies on Alcohol*, *65*, 766–773.

Page, J. (2001). Take two aspirin and call me in the morning. *Smithsonian*, *32*(5), 96–105.

Pain, S. (2008). Two pints, twice a day. *New Scientist*, *200*(2680), 44–45.

Palmer, N. D., & Edmunds, C.N. (2003). Victims of sexual abuse and assault: Adults and children. In T. L. Underwood, & C. Edmunds (Eds.), *Victim assistance*. New York: Springer.

Palmstierna, T. (2001). A model for predicting alcohol withdrawal delirium. *Psychiatric Services*, *52*, 820–823.

Pankiewicz, J. (2008, November 19). *Optimizing clinical outcomes throughout the course of schizophrenia*. Eli Lilly & Co.-sponsored presentation in La Crosse, WI.

Papastefanou, C. (2007). Radiation dose from cigarette tobacco. *Radiation Protection Dosimetry*, *123*(1), 68–73.

Papathanasopoulous, P., Messinis, L., Epameinondas, L., Kastellakis, A., & Panagis, G. (2008). Multiple sclerosis, cannabinoids and cognition. *The Journal of Neuropsychiatry and Clinical Neurosciences*, *20*(1), 36–51.

Paradowski, J. (2008). *Methadone, pregnancy and infant care*. Seminar presented at the Wisconsin State Methadone Providers Meeting, Madison.

Parekh, R. (2006, March 3). *Adolescent substance use and abuse*. Paper presented at the Treating the Addictions workshop sponsored by the Department of Psychiatry of Cambridge Hospital, Boston.

Parent, J. M., & Aminoff, M. J. (2008). Seizures and general medical disorders. In M. J. Aminoff (Ed.), *Neurology and general medicine* (4th ed.). New York: Churchill Livingstone.

Parenti, C. (2009). The drug coast. *Playboy*, *56*(2), 38–40, 98, 100–105.

Pargament, K. I. (2007). *Spirituality integrated psychotherapy*. New York: Guilford.

Parini, S. (2003). Hepatitis C. *Nursing*, *33*(4), 57–63.

Park, A., Sher, K. J., & Krull, J. L. (2009). Selection and socialization of risky drinking during the college transition: The importance of microenvironments associated with specific living units. *Psychology of Addictive Behaviors*, *23*, 404–414.

Parkinson-like symptoms linked to illicit Kat use. (2008). *Forensic Drug Abuse Advisor*, *20*(4), 27–28.

Parrott, A., Morinan, A., Moss, M., & Scholey, A. (2004). *Understanding drugs and behavior*. New York: Wiley.

Parrott, D. J., & Giancola, P. R. (2006). The effect of past-year heavy drinking on alcohol-related aggression. *Journal of Studies on Alcohol*, *67*, 122–130.

Passie, T., Hartmann, U., Schnieder, U., Emrich, H. M., & Kruger T. H. (2005). Ecstasy (MDMA) mimics the post-orgasmic state: Impairment of sexual drive and function during acute MDMA—effects may be due to increased prolactin secretion. *Medical Hypotheses*, *64*(5), 899–903.

Patel, M., Belson, M.G., Wright, D., Lu, H., et al. (2005). Methylendioxy-N-methamphetamine (Ecstasy)-related myocardial hypertrophy: An autopsy study. *Resuscitation*, *66*(2), 197–202.

Patkar, A. A., Vergare, M. J., Batka, V., Weinstein, S. P., & Leone, T. (2003). Tobacco smoking: Current concepts in etiology and treatment. *Psychiatry*, *66*(3), 183–199.

Patock-Peckham, J. A., & Morgan-Lopez, A. A. (2006). College drinking behaviors: Mediational links between parenting styles, impulse control, and alcohol-related outcomes. *Psychology of Addictive Behaviors*, *20*(2), 117–125.

Paton, A. (1996). The detection of alcohol misuse in accident and emergency departments grasping the opportunity. *Journal of Accident & Emergency Medicine*, *13*, 306–308.

Patrick, D. D. (2003). Dual diagnosis' substance-related and psychiatric disorders. *Nursing Clinics of North America*, *38*, 67–73.

Patrizi, R., Pasceri, V., Sciahbase, A., Summara, F., Rosano, G. M. C., & Lioy, E. (2006). Evidence of cocaine-related coronary artery atherosclerosis in young patients with myocardial infarction. *Journal of the American College of Cardiology*, *10*, 2120–2122.

Patterns and trends in inhalant use by adolescent males and females: 2002–2005. (2007). National Survey on Drug Use and Health. Washington, DC: U.S. Department of Health and Human Services.

Paula, C. A., Au, R., Fredman, L., Massaro, J. M., Seshadri, S., Decarli, C., et al. (2008). Association of alcohol consumption with brain volume in the Framingham study. *Archives of Neurology* 65(10), 1363–1367.

Payer, D., & London, E. D. (2009). Methamphetamine and the brain. In J. R. Roll, R. A. Rawson, W. Ling, & S. Shoptaw (Eds.), *Methamphetamine addiction—from basic science to treatment*. New York: Guilford.

Payne, R. A., Back, S. E., Wright, T., Hartwell, K., & Brady, K. T. (2009). Alcohol dependence in women: Comorbidities can complicate treatment. *Current Psychiatry, 8*(6), 52–59.

Pearlman, B. L. (2004). Hepatitis C infection: A clinical review. *Southern Medical Journal, 97*, 365–373.

Pearson, A. (2009). *Addressing the challenges of substance abuse and brain injury*. Paper presented at the 10th Annual Managing Challenging Situations in Brain Injury Care, Brooklyn Park, MN.

Peart, J., & Gross, G. (2004). Morphine-tolerant mice exhibit a profound and persistent cardioprotective phenotype. *Circulation, 109*, 1219–1222.

Pechnick, R. N., & Ungerleider, J. T. (2004). Hallucinogens. In M. Galanter & H. D. Kleber (Eds.), *The American Psychiatric Publishing textbook of substance abuse treatment* (3rd ed.). Washington, DC: American Psychiatric Publishing.

Peck, M. S. (1997a). *The road less traveled & beyond.* New York: Simon & Schuster.

Peele, S. (2004a). The surprising truth about addiction. *Psychology Today, 37*(3), 43–46.

Peele, S. (2004b). Is AA's loss psychology's gain? *Monitor on Psychology, 35*(7), 86.

Peles, E., Hetzroni, T., Bar-Hamburger, R., Adelson, M., & Shreiber, S. (2007). Melatonin for perceived sleep disturbances associated with benzodiazepine withdrawal among patients in methadone maintenance treatment: A double-blind randomized clinical trial. *Addiction, 12*, 1947–1953.

Pell, J. P., Haw, S., Cobbe, S., Newby, D. E., Pell, A. C. H., Fischbacher, C., et al. (2008). Smoke-free legislation and hospitalizations for acute coronary syndrome. *New England Journal of Medicine, 359*, 482–491.

Pendlebury, J. D., Wilsin, R. J. A., Bano, S., Lumb, K. J., Schneider, J. M., & Hasan, S. U. (2008). Respiratory control in neonatal rats exposed to prenatal cigarette smoke. *American Journal of Respiratory and Critical Care Medicine, 177*, 1255–1261.

Pennock, P. E. (2007). *Advertising sin and sickness.* DeKalb, IL: NIU Press.

Pepper, B. (2004). Responding to co-occurring disorders. *Psychiatric Services, 55*, 343.

Perkonigg, A., Goodwin, R. D., Fiedler, A., Behrendt, S., Beesdo, K., Lieb, R., et al. (2008). The natural course of cannabis use, abuse and dependence during the first decades of life. *Addiction, 103*(9), 439–449.

Perry, P. J., Alexander, B., Liskow, B. I., & DeVane, C. L. (2007). *Psychotropic drug handbook* (8th ed.). New York: Lippincott Williams & Wilkins.

Peters, B. B. (2007, April 26). *Fetal alcohol spectrum disorders: Its impact on the fetus to adults*. Paper presented at the Ruth Fox Course for Physicians, 38th Medical-Scientific Conference of the American Society of Addiction Medicine, Miami, FL.

Peterson, A. M. (1997). Analgesics. *RN, 60*(4), 45–50.

Petrakis, I. L., Gonzalez, G., Rosenheck, R., & Krystal, J. H. (2002). Comorbidity of alcoholism and psychiatric disorders. *Alcohol Research & Health, 26*(2), 81–89.

Pettit, J. L. (2000). Melatonin. *Clinical Reviews, 10*(6), 87–88, 91.

Pfefferbaum, A., Rosenbloom, M. J., Serventi, K., & Sullivan, E. V. (2004). Brain volume, RBC status and hepatic function in alcoholics after 1 and 4 weeks of sobriety: Predictors of outcome. *American Journal of Psychiatry, 158*, 188–197.

Pharmacokinetics of MDMA (Ecstasy) studied. (2008). *Forensic Drug Abuse Advisor, 20*(5), 35–36.

Phelps, D. (1996). Records suggest nicotine enhances. *Minneapolis Star-Tribune, 15*(5), 1A, 22A.

Phillips, H., & Lawton, G. (2004). The intoxication instinct. *New Scientist, 184*(2473), 32–39.

Pies, R. W. (2003, March 7). *Antidepressants and alcohol: How do they mix?* Symposium presented to the Department of Psychiatry, Cambridge Hospital, Boston.

Pies, R. W. (2005). The top 10 adverse drug reactions in psychiatry. *Psychiatric Times, 22*(11), 22–23.

Piette, J. D., Heisler, M., & Wagner, T. H. (2004). Cost-related medication underuse. *Archives of Internal Medicine, 164*, 1749–1755.

Pigott, T. A., Walker, M. H., Tietelbaum, S. A., & Lu, C. (2009). Sex differences and neurotransmitter systems in addiction. In K. T. Brady, S. E. Back, & S. F. Greenfield (Eds.), *Women & addiction*. New York: Guilford.

Pihl, R. O. (1999). Substance abuse: Etiological considerations. In T. Millon, P. H. Blaney, & R. D. David (Eds.), *Oxford textbook of psychopathology*. New York: Oxford University Press.

Pinel, J. P. J. (2003). *Biopsychology* (5th ed.). New York: Allyn & Bacon.

Pinker, S. (2002). *The blank slate: The modern denial of human nature.* New York: Oxford University Press.

Pinsky, D. (2008). Playboy interview. *Playboy 55*(7), 45–48, 120–122.

Piper, M. E., Smith, S. S., Schlam, T. R., Fiore, M. C., Jorenby, D. E., Fraser, D., et al. (2009). A randomized placebo-controlled clinical trial of 5 smoking cessation pharmacotherapies. *Archives of General Psychiatry, 66*(11), 1253–1262.

Pletcher, M. J., Kiefe, C., Sidney, C., Carr, J. J., Lewis, C. E., & Hulley, S. B. (2005). Cocaine and coronary calcification in young adults: The Coronary Artery Risk Development in Young Adults (CARDIA) study. *American Heart Journal, 150,* 921–926.

Pliszka, S. R. (1998). The use of psychostimulants in the pediatric patient. *Pediatric Clinics of North America, 45,* 1085–1098.

Pohl, M. (2007). Chronic pain, opioids and addiction. *Counselor, 8*(4), 34–41.

Polivy, J., & Herman, C. P. (2002). If at first you don't succeed. *American Psychologist, 57,* 596–601.

Polydorou, S., & Kleber, H. D. (2008). Detoxification of opioids. In M. Galanter & H. D. Kleber (Eds.), *The American Psychiatric Publishing textbook of substance abuse treatment.* Washington, DC: American Psychiatric Publishing.

Pomerantz, R. J. (1998). How HIV resists eradication. *Hospital Practice, 33*(9), 87–90.

Pomerantz, R. J. (2003). Cross-talk and viral reservoirs. *Nature, 424,* 136–137.

Ponnappa, B. C., & Rubin, E. (2000). Modeling alcohol's effects on organs in animal models. *Alcohol Research & Health, 24*(2), 93–104.

Pope, C. A., Burnett, R. T., Krewski, D., Jerrett, M., Shi, Y., Calle, E. E., et al. (2009). Cardiovascular mortality and exposure to airborne fine particulate matter and cigarette smoke: Shape of exposure–response relationship. *Circulation* (published online prior to print). doi: 10.1161/CIRCULATIONHA.109857888

Pope, H. G., & Brower, K. J. (2004). Anabolic androgenic steroids. In M. Galanter & H. D. Kleber (Eds.), *The American Psychiatric Publishing textbook of substance abuse treatment* (3rd ed.). Washington, DC: American Psychiatric Publishing.

Pope, H. G., & Brower, K. J. (2005). Anabolic-androgenic steroid abuse. In B. J. Sadock & V. A. Sadock (Eds.), *Kaplan & Sadock's comprehensive textbook of psychiatry* (8th ed.). New York: Lippincott Williams & Wilkins.

Pope, H. G., & Brower, K. J. (2008). Treatment of anabolic-androgenic steroid-related disorders. In M. Galanter & H. D. Kleber (Eds.), *The American Psychiatric Publishing textbook of substance abuse treatment.* Washington, DC: American Psychiatric Publishing.

Pope, H. G., Gruber, A. J., Hudson, J. I., Huestis, M. A., & Yugelin-Todd, D. (2001). Neuropsychological performance in long-term cannabis abusers. *Archives of General Psychiatry, 58,* 909–915.

Pope, H. G., Kouri, E. M., & Hudson, J. I. (2000). Effects of supraphysiologic doses of testosterone on mood and aggression. *Archives of General Psychiatry, 57,* 133–147.

Pope, H. G., Phillips, K. A., & Olivardia, R. (2000). *The Adonis complex: The secret crisis of male body obsession.* New York: Free Press.

Porcerelli, J. H., & Sandler, B. A. (1998). Anabolic-androgenic steroid abuse and psychopathology. *The Psychiatric Clinics of North America, 21,* 829–833.

Porreca, F., & Price, T. (2009). When pain lingers. *Scientific American Mind, 20*(5), 34–41.

Potent pot. (2008). *New Scientist, 198*(2661), 7.

Potenza, M. N., Fiellin, D. A., Heninger, G. R., Rounsaville, B. J., & Mazure, C. M. (2002). Gambling: An addictive behavior with health and primary care implications. *Journal of General Internal Medicine, 17*(9), 721–732.

Potenza, M. N., Kosten, T. R., & Rounsaville, B. J. (2001). Pathological gambling. *Journal of the American Medical Association, 286,* 141–144.

Predicting drug-related impairment. (2004). *Forensic Drug Abuse Advisor, 16*(3), 21–22.

Prem, S., & Uzoma, M. (2004). Marijuana-induced transient global amnesia. *Southern Medical Journal, 97*(8), 782–784.

Prenatal cocaine exposure not linked to bad behavior in kids. (2006). *Science Daily.* Retrieved from http://www.sciencedaily.com/releases/2006/05/06050222048.html

Prescribing information. (2006). Frazer, PA: Caphalon.

Preston, R. (1999). The demon in the freezer. *The New Yorker, LXXV*(18), 44–61.

Preuss, U. W., Schickit, M. A., Smith, T. L., Danko, G. P., Bucholz, K. K., Hesselbrock, M. N., et al. (2003). Predictors and correlates of suicide attempts over 5 years in 1,237 alcohol-dependent men and women. *American Journal of Psychiatry, 160,* 56–63.

Preuss, U. W., & Wong, W. M. (2000). Comorbidity. In G. Zernig, A. Saria, M. Kurz, & S. S. O'Malley (Eds.), *Handbook of alcoholism.* New York: CRC Press.

Price, L. H. (2009). Modafinil: A different kind of stimulus package. *The Brown University Psychopharmacology Update, 20*(9), 9.

Primack, B. A., Dalton, M. A., Carroll, M. V., Agerwal, A. A., & Fine, M. J. (2008). Content analysis of tobacco, alcohol and other drugs in popular music. *Archives of Pediatrics & Adolescent Medicine, 162* (2), 169–175.

Primack, J. R., & Abrams, N. E. (2006). *The view from the center of the universe.* New York: Riverhead Books.

Prochaska, J. O. (1998, September 17). *Stage model of change.* Paper presented at symposium, Gundersen Lutheran Medical Center, La Crosse, WI.

Prochaska, J. O. (2002, February 1). *Stages of change: 25 years of addiction treatment.* Symposium presented to the Department of Psychiatry, Cambridge Hospital, Boston.

Prochaska, J. O., DiClemente, C. C., & Norcross, J. C. (1992). In search of how people change. *American Psychologist, 47,* 1102–1114.

Prochaska, J. J., Gill, P., Hall, S. E., & Hall, S. M. (2005). Identification and treatment of substance misuse on an inpatient psychiatry unit. *Psychiatric Services, 56,* 347–349.

Propoxyphene pharmacokinetics. (2009). *Forensic Drug Abuse Advisor, 21*(5), 37–38.

Przekop, P., & Lee, T. (2009). Persistent psychosis associated with *Salvia divinorum* use. *American Journal of Psychiatry, 166,* 832.

Pumariega, A. D., & Kilgus, M. D. (2005). Adolescents. In J. H. Lowinson, P. Ruiz, R. B. Millman, & J. G. Langrod (Eds.), *Substance abuse: A comprehensive textbook* (4th ed.). New York: Lippincott Williams & Wilkins.

Pungpapong, S., Kim, W. R., & Poterucha, J. J. (2007). Natural history of hepatitis B infection: An update for clinicians. *Mayo Clinic Proceedings, 82,* 967–975.

Putnam, F. W. (1989). *Diagnosis and treatment of multiple personality disorder.* New York: Guilford.

Quednow, B. B., Jessen, F., Kuhn, K. U., Maier, W., Daum, I., & Wagner, M. (2006). Memory deficits in abstinent MDMA (Ecstasy) users: Neuropsychological evidence of frontal dysfunction. *Journal of Psychopharmacology, 20*(3), 373–384.

Qureshi, A., & Lee-Chiong, T. (2004). Medications and their effects on sleep. *Medical Clinics of North America, 88,* 751–766.

Raby, W. N. (2009). Comorbid cannabis misuse in psychotic disorders: Treatment strategies. *Primary Psychiatry, 16*(4), 29–34.

RachBeisel, J., Scott, J., & Dixon, L. (1998). Co-occurring severe mental illness and substance use disorders: A review of recent research. *Psychiatric Services, 50,* 1427–1434.

Raghaven, A. V., Decker, W. W., & Meloy, T. D. (2005). Management of atrial fibrillation in the emergency department. *Emergency Clinics of North America, 23,* 1127–1139.

Raj, A., & Sheehan, D. (2004). Benzodiazepines. In A. F. Schatzberg & C. B. Nemeroff (Eds.), *Textbook of psychopharmacology* (3rd ed.). Washington, DC: American Psychiatric Publishing.

Ramadan, M .I., Werder, S. F., & Preskorn, S. H. (2006). Protect against drug–drug interactions with anxiolytics. *Current Psychiatry, 5*(5), 16–28.

Ramcharan, S., Meenhorst, P. L., Otten, J. M. M. B., Koks, C. H. W., de Boer, D., Maes, R. A., et al. (1998). Survival after massive Ecstasy overdose. *Journal of Toxicology: Clinical Toxicology, 36,* 727.

Ramsay, J. R., & Newman, C. F. (2000). Substance abuse. In F. M. Dattilo & A. Freeman (Eds.), *Cognitive-behavioral strategies in crisis intervention* (2nd ed.). New York: Guilford.

Randle, K. D., Estes, R., & Cone, W. P. (1999). *The abduction enigma.* New York: Forge.

Rao, U., Hammen, C. L., & Poland, R. E. (2009). Mechanisms underlying the comorbidity between depressive and addictive disorders in adolescents: Interactions between stress and HPA activity. *American Journal of Psychiatry, 166*(3), 361–369.

Rasmussen, N. (2008). *On speed: The many lives of amphetamine.* New York: New York University Press.

Rational Recovery Systems, Inc. (2008). Organization Web site. https://rational.org/index.php?id=1

Raviglione, M. C., & O'Brien, R. J. (2008). Tuberculosis. In A. S. Fauci, E. Braunwald, D. L. Kasper, D. L. Longo, J. L. Jameson, & J. Loscalzo (Eds.), *Harrison's principles of internal medicine* (17th ed.). New York: McGraw-Hill Medical.

Raw data. (2008). *Playboy, 55*(9), 29.

Raw data. (2009a). *Playboy, 56*(4), 22.

Raw data. (2009b). *Playboy, 56*(6), 24.

Raw data. (2010). *Playboy, 57*(2), 23.

Rawson, R. A., & Ling, W. (2008). Clinical management: Methamphetamine. In M. Galanter & H. D. Kleber (Eds.), *The American Psychiatric Publishing textbook of substance abuse treatment.* Washington, DC: American Psychiatric Association.

Rawson, R. A., Sodano, R., & Hillhouse, M. (2005). Assessment of amphetamine use disorders. In

D. M. Donovan & G. A. Marlatt (Eds.), *Assessment of addictive behaviors* (2nd ed.). New York: Guilford.

Reading, E. (2007, April 26). *Conscious contact: Religious experience in search of the spiritual.* Paper presented at the Ruth Fox Course for Physicians, 38th Medical-Scientific Conference of the American Society of Addiction Medicine, Miami, FL.

Reduced hospitalizations for acute myocardial infarction after implementation of a smoke-free ordinance—city of Pueblo, Colorado, 2002–2006. (2008). *Morbidity and Mortality Weekly Report, 57*(51), 1373–1377.

Redmond, E. M., Morrow, D., Kunkiml, S., Miller-Graziano, C. L., & Cullen, J. P. (2008). Acetalhyde stimulates monocyte adhesion in a P-selectin- and THF-dependent manner. *Circulation* (published online prior to print). doi: 10.1016/jatherosclerosis.2008.10.008

Reed, S. C., & Evans, S. M. (2009). Research design and methodology in studies of women and addiction. In K. T. Brady, S. E. Back, & S. F. Greenfield (Eds.), *Women & addiction.* New York: Guilford.

Rehm, J., Mathers, C., Popova, S., Thavorncharoensap, M., Teerawattananon, Y., & Patra, J. (2009). Global burden of disease and injury and economic cost attributable to alcohol use and alcohol-use disorders. *The Lancet, 373*(9682), 2223–2233.

Rehm, J., Patra, J., & Popova, S. (2007). Alcohol drinking cessation and its effects on esophageal and head and neck cancers: A pooled analysis. *International Journal of Cancer, 121*(5), 1132–1137.

Reich, R. R., & Goldman, M. S. (2005). Exploring the alcohol expectancy memory network: The utility of free associates. *Psychology of Addictive Behavior, 19,* 317–325.

Reichert, V. C., Folan, P., Bartscherer, D., Jacobsen, D., Fardellone, C., Metz, C., et al. (2007). A comparison of older smokers versus younger smokers being treated for tobacco dependence. *Chest Meeting Abstracts 2007, 132,* 409b.

Reichert, V. C., Seltzer, V., Efferen, L. S., & Kohn, N. (2005). Women and tobacco dependence. *Medical Clinics of North America, 889,* 1467–1481.

Reiman, E. M. (1997). Anxiety. In A. J. Gelenberg & E. L. Bassuk (Eds.), *The practitioner's guide to psychoactive drugs* (4th ed.). New York: Plenum.

Rempel, M. (2005). *Recidivism 101: Evaluating the impact of your drug court.* New York: Center for Court Innovation.

Renner, J. A. (2004a). Alcoholism and alcohol abuse. In T. A. Stern & J. B. Herman (Eds.), *Massachusetts General Hospital psychiatry update and board preparation* (2nd ed.). New York: McGraw-Hill.

Renner, J. A. (2004b). How to train residents to identify and treat dual diagnosis patients. *Biological Psychiatry, 56,* 810–816.

Repetto, M., & Gold, M. S. (2005). Cocaine and crack: neurobiology. In J. H. Lowinson, P. Ruiz, R. B. Millman, & J. G. Langrod (Eds.), *Substance abuse: A comprehensive textbook* (4th ed.). New York: Lippincott Williams & Wilkins.

Resilience. (2006). *Harvard Mental Health Letter, 23*(6), 5–6.

Reuter, P. (2009). Do no harm. *The American Interest, 4*(4), 46–52.

Reuter, P., & Pollack, H. (2006). How much can treatment reduce national drug problems? *Addiction, 101*(3), 341–347.

Rexrode, K. M., Buring, J. E., Glynn, R. J., Stampfer, M. J., Youngman, L. D., & Gaziano, J. M. (2001). Analgesic use and renal function in men. *Journal of the American Medical Association, 286,* 315–321.

Reyna, V. F., & Farley, F. (2006/2007). Is the teen brain too rational? *Scientific American Mind, 17*(6), 58–65.

Reynolds, E. W., & Bada, H. S. (2003). Pharmacology of drugs of abuse. *Obstetrics and Gynecology Clinics of North America, 30,* 501–522.

Rhame, F. (2009). Let's not forget the third world. *Minnesota Medicine, 92*(10), 38–39.

Rhee, S. H., Hewitt, J. K., Young, S. E., Corley, R. P., Crowley, T. J., & Stallings, M. C. (2003). Genetic and environmental influences on substance initiation, use and problems use in adolescents. *Archives of General Psychiatry, 60,* 1256–1264.

Ricaurte, G. A., Langston J. W., & McCann, N. (2008). Neuropsychiatric complications of substance abuse. In M. J. Aminoff (Ed.), *Neurology and general medicine* (4th ed.). New York: Churchill Livingstone.

Ricaurte, G. A., Yuan, J., Hatzidimitriou, G., Branden, C., & McCann, U. D. (2002). Severe dopaminergic neurotoxicity in primates after a common recreational dose regimen of MDMA (Ecstasy). *Science, 297,* 2260–2263.

Richards, J. R. (2000). Rhabdomyolsis and drugs of abuse. *Journal of Emergency Medicine, 19,* 51–56.

Ries, R. K., Galanter, M., & Tonigan, J. B. (2008). Twelve-step facilitation. In M. Galanter & H. D. Kleber (Eds.), *The American Psychiatric*

Publishing textbook of substance abuse treatment. Washington, DC: American Psychiatric Publishing.

Riggs, P. D. (2003). Treating adolescents for substance abuse and comorbid psychiatric disorders. *Science & Practice Perspectives, 2*(1), 18–28.

Rigler, S. K. (2000). Alcoholism in the elderly. *American Family Physician, 61,* 1710–1716.

Rimsza, M. E., & Moses, K. S. (2005). Substance abuse on college campus. *Pediatric Medical Journal, 310,* 555–559.

Ringwald, C. D. (2002). *The soul of recovery.* New York: Oxford University Press.

Rist, P. M., Berger, K., Buring, J. E., Kase, C. S., Gaziano, J. M., & Kurth, T. (2010). Alcohol consumption and functional outcome after stroke in men. *Stroke, 41,* 141–146.

Ritsher, J. B., Moos, R. H., & Finney, J. W. (2000). Relationship of treatment orientation and continuing care to remission among substance abuse patients. *Psychiatric Services, 53,* 595–601.

Roane, B. M., & Taylor, D. J. (2008). Adolescent insomnia as a risk factor for early adult depression and substance abuse. *Sleep, 31*(10), 1351–1356.

Roane, K. R. (2000). A scourge of drugs strikes a pious place. *US News & World Report, 128*(9), 26–28.

Robbe, D., Montgomery, S. M., Thome, A., Rueda-Orozco, P. E., McNaughton, B. L., & (2006). Cannabinoids reveal importance of spike timing coordination in hippocampal function. *Nature Neuroscience, 9,* 1526–1533.

Roberts, R. Q., Jacobson, D. J., Girman, C. J., Rhodes, T., Lieber, M. M., & Jacobsen, S. J. (2002). A population-based study of daily nonsteroidal anti-inflammatory drug use and prostate cancer. *Mayo Clinic Proceedings, 77,* 219–225.

Roberts, S. (2004). Dual diagnosis. *Schizophrenia Digest, 2*(1), 30–34.

Robinson, D. J., Lazo, M. C., Davis, T., & Kufera, J. A. (2000). Infective endocarditis in intravenous drug users: Does HIV status alter the presenting temperature and white cell count? *Journal of Emergency Medicine, 19,* 5–11.

Robinson, E. A. R., Cranford, J. A., Webb, J. R. & Brower, K. J. (2007). Six-month changes in spirituality, religiousness, and heavy drinking in a treatment-seeking sample. *Journal of Studies on Alcohol and Drugs, 68*(2), 282–290.

Robson, D., (2009). Fuming. *New Scientist, 202*(2702), 34–37.

Robson, P. (2001). Therapeutic aspects of cannabis and cannabinoids. *British Journal of Psychiatry, 178,* 107–115.

Rochester, J. A., & Kirchner, J. T. (1999). Ecstasy (3,4-Methylenedioxymethamphetamine): History, neurochemistry and toxicity. *Journal of the American Board of Family Practice, 12,* 137–142.

Roden, D. M. (2004). Drug-induced prolongation of the QT interval. *New England Journal of Medicine, 350,* 1013–1022.

Rodriguez, J., Jiang, R., Johnson, W. C., MacKenzie, B. A., Smith, L. J., & Barr, R. G. (2010). The association of pipe and cigar use with cotinine levels, lung function, and airflow obstruction. *Annals of Internal Medicine, 152,* 1–28.

Rodriguez, S. C., Olguin, A. M., Miralles, C. P., & Valdrich, P. F. (2006). Characteristics of meningitis caused by ibuprofen. *Medicine, 85,* 214–220.

Rogers, D., & Pies, R. (2008). General medical drugs associated with depression. *Psychiatry, 5*(12), 28–41.

Rogers, R. (2008). Detection strategies for malingering and defensiveness. In R. Rogers (Ed.), *Clinical assessment of malingering and deception* (3rd ed.). New York: Guilford.

Rohde, P., Lewinsohn, P. M., Kahle, C. W., Seeley, J. R., & Brown, R. A. (2001). Natural course of alcohol use disorders from adolescence to young adulthood. *Journal of the American Academy of Child and Adolescent Psychiatry, 40,* 83–90.

Rohde, P., Lewinsohn, P. M., Seeley, J. R., Klein, D. N., Andrews, J. A., & Small, J. W. (2007). Psychosocial functioning of adults who experienced substance use disorders as adolescents. *Psychology of Addictive Behaviors, 21,* 155–164.

Rosenthal, R. N., & Solhkhah, R. (2005). Club drugs. In H. R. Kranzler & D. A. Ciraulo (Eds.), *Clinical manual of addiction psychopharmacology.* Washington, DC: American Psychiatric Publishing.

Roshsenow, D. J., Howland, J., Arnedt, J. T., Almeida A. B., Greece, J., Minsky, S., et al. (2009). Intoxication with bourbon versus vodka: Effects on hangover, sleep, and next-day neurocognitive performance in young adults. *Alcoholism: Clinical and Experimental Research* (published online prior to print). doi: 10.1111/j.1050-0277.2009.01116.x

Roiser, J. P., Cook, L. J., Cooper, J. D., Rubinsztein, D. C., & Sahakian, B. J. (2005). Association of a functional polymorphism in the serotonin transporter gene with anormal emotional processing in Ecstasy users. *American Journal of Psychiatry, 162,* 609–612.

Roldan, C. J., & Patel, M. M. (2008). Intracranial complications of cocaine abuse. *Emergency Medicine, 40*(10), 37–40.

Rollo, K. L., Sane, A., & Ewen, B. (2007). Meth: The crystal that kills. *Nursing 2007 Critical Care, 2*(1), 54–56.

Romach, M. K., Glue, P., Kampman, K., Kaplan, H. L., Somer, G. R., Poole, S., et al. (1999). Attenuation of the euphoric effects of cocaine by the dopamine D1/D5 antagonist Ecopipam (SCH 39166). *Archives of General Psychiatry, 56*, 1101–1106.

Room, B., Babor, T., & Rehm, J. (2005). Alcohol and public health. *The Lancet, 365*, 519–530.

Room, R. (2009). Get real, drug czars. *New Scientist, 202*(2709), 22–23.

Ropper, A. H., & Brown, R. H. (2005). *Adams and Victor's principles of neurology* (8th ed.). New York: McGraw-Hill.

Ropper, A. H., & Samuels, M. A. (2009). *Adams and Victor's principles of neurology* (9th ed.). New York: McGraw-Hill.

Rose, G. S. (2001, March 2). *Motivational interviewing.* Symposium presented to the Department of Psychiatry of Cambridge Hospital, Boston.

Rose, I. M. (1988). *The body in time.* New York: Wiley.

Rose, J. E., Behm, F. M., Westman, E. C., Mathew, R. J., London, E. D., Hawk, T. C., et al. (2003). PET studies of the influences of nicotine on neural systems in cigarette smokers. *American Journal of Psychiatry, 160*, 323–333.

Rosen, I. M., & Maurer, D. M. (2008). Reducing tobacco use in adolescents. *American Family Physician, 77*, 483–490.

Rosenbaum, R. (1999). *Zen and the heart of psychotherapy.* New York: Brunner/Mazel.

Rosenbloom, D. L. (2000, March 3). *The community perspective on addictions: Joining together.* Symposium presented by the Department of Psychiatry, Cambridge Hospital, Boston.

Rosenbloom, D. L. (2005, March 4). *Cultural aspects of adolescent use and misuse of alcohol.* Symposium presented by the Department of Psychiatry, Cambridge Hospital, Boston.

Rosenbloom, M. J., & Pfefferbaum, A. (2008). Magnetic resonance imaging of the living brain. *Alcohol Research & Health, 31*, 362–376.

Rosenthal, R. N., & Solhkhah, R. (2005). Club drugs. In H. R. Kranzler & D. A. Ciraulo (Eds.), *Clinical manual of addiction psychopharmacology.* Washington, DC: American Psychiatric Publishing.

Ross, G. R. (2002, June 6). *Child and adolescent alcohol and drug use.* Seminar presented by the Cross Country University, Milwaukee, WI.

Ross, S. (2008). The mentally ill substance abuser. In M. Galanter & H. D. Kleber (Eds.), *The American Psychiatric Publishing textbook of substance abuse treatment.* Washington, DC: American Psychiatric Publishing.

Rostain, A. (2008). Attention-deficit/hyperactivity disorder in adults: Evidence-based recommendations for management. *Postgraduate Medicine, 20*(3), 27–38.

Roth, B. A., Benowitz, N. L., & Olson, K. R. (2007). Emergency management of drug abuse. In S. B. Karch (Ed.), *Drug abuse handbook* (2nd ed.). New York: CRC Press.

Roth, J. (2009). Evolutionary speculation about tuberculosis and the metabolic and inflammatory processes of obesity. *Journal of the American Medical Association, 301*(24), 2586–2588.

Rothman, R. B., Vu, N., Partilla, J. S., Roth, B. L., Hufeisen, S. J., Compton-Toth, B. A., et al. (2003). In vitro characterization of ephedrine-related stereoisomers at biogenic amine transporters and the receptorome reveals selective actions as norepinephrine transporters substrates. *Journal of Pharmacology and Experimental Therapeutics, 307*, 138–145.

Rothenbergher, A., & Banaschewski, T. (2004). Informing the ADHD debate. *Scientific American Mind, 14*(5), 50–55.

Rounsaville, B. J. (2004). Treatment of cocaine dependence and depression. *Biological Psychiatry, 56*, 803–809.

Rounsaville, B. J. (2006, March 3). *Biopsychosocial interventions for addiction treatment.* Paper presented at the Treating the Addictions workshop sponsored by the Department of Psychiatry, Cambridge Hospital, Boston.

Rourke, S. B., & Grant, I. (2009). The neurobehavioral correlates of alcoholism. In I. Grant & K. M. Adams (Eds.), *Neuropsychological assessment of neuropsychiatric and neuromedical disorders* (3rd ed.). New York: Oxford University Press.

Rouse, S. V., Butcher, J. N., & Miller, K. B. (1999). Assessment of substance abuse in psychotherapy clients: The effectiveness of the MMPI-s substance abuse scales. *Psychological Assessment, 11*(1), 101–107.

Roy, A. (2001). Characteristics of cocaine-dependent patients who attempt suicide. *American Journal of Psychiatry, 158*, 1215–1219.

Roy, A. (2003). Characteristics of HIV patients who attempt suicide. *Acta Psychiatrica Scandinavica, 107*, 41–44.

Ruben, D. H. (2001). *Treating adult children of alcoholics.* New York: Academic Press.

Rubio, G., Martinez-Gras, I., & Manzanares, J. (2009). Modulation of impulsivity by topiramate: Implications for the treatment of alcohol dependence. *Journal of Clinical Psychopharmacology, 29*(6), 584–589.

Russo, M. (2004). Hepatitis B. *Emergency Medicine, 36*(3), 18–19.

Russo, M. W. (2006). Acetaminophen overdose and acute liver failure. *Emergency Medicine, 38*(8) 15–17.

Rutkowski, B. A. & Maxwell, J. C. (2009). Epidemiology of methamphetamine use. In J. R. Roll, R. A. Rawson, W. Ling, & S. Shoptaw (Eds.), *Methamphetamine addiction—From basic science to treatment.* New York: Guilford.

Ryan, A. M., Malboeuf, C. M., Bernard, M., Rose, R. C., & Phipps, R. P. (2006). Cycloxy-genase-2 inhibition attenuates antibody responses against human papilloma-viruslike particles. *Journal of Immunology, 177,* 7811–7819.

Rychtarik, R. G., Connors, G. J., Whitney, R. B., McGillicuddy, N. B., et al. (2000). Treatment settings for persons with alcoholism: Evidence for matching patients to in-patient versus outpatient care. *Journal of Consulting and Clinical Psychology, 68,* 277–289.

Rylkova, D., Bruijnzeel, A. W., & Gold, M. S. (2007). Anabolic steroid abuse: Neurobiological substrates and psychiatric comorbidity. *Journal of Addictive Diseases, 25*(Suppl. 1), 33–45.

Sacks, O. (1970). *The man who mistook his wife for a hat.* New York: Harper & Row.

Sacks, O. (2008). *Musicophilia: Tales of music and the brain.* New York: Vintage.

Sadeghejad, A., Ohar, J. A., Zheng, S. L., Sterling, D. A., Hawkins, G. A., Meyers, D. A., et al. (2009). ADAM33 polymorphisms are associated with COPD and lung function in long term tobacco smokers. *Respiratory Research* (published online prior to print). doi: 10.1186/1465-9921-10-21

Sadock, B. J., & Sadock, V. A. (2007). *Kaplan and Sadock's synopsis of psychiatry* (10th ed.). New York: Lippincott Williams & Wilkins.

Saitz, R. (1998). Introduction to alcohol withdrawal. *Alcohol Health & Research World, 22*(1), 5–12.

Salazar, M., Carracedo, A.,, Salanueva, I. J., Hernandez-Tiedra, S., Lorente, M., Egia, A., et al. (2009). Cannabinoid action induces autophagy-mediated cell death through stimulation of ER stress in human glioma cells. *Journal of Clinical Investigation* (published online prior to print). doi: 10.1172/JCI37948

Salerno, S. (2005). *Sham: How the self-help movement made America helpless.* New York: Random House.

Salo, R., Nordahl, T. E., Galloway, G. P., Moore, C. D., et al. (2009). Drug abstinence and cognitive control in methamphetamine-dependent individuals. *Journal of Substance Abuse Treatment.* Retrieved from http://www.journalofsubstanceabusetreatment.com/article/S0740-5472(09)00032-4

Salzer, M. S., & Kundra, L. B. (2010). Liability issues associated with referrals to self-help groups. *Psychiatric Services, 61*(1), 6–8.

Salzman, S. (2008, February 25–29). *Essential psychopharmacology: A master's class.* Seminar offered by the Harvard Medical School, Ocean Reef Club, Key Largo, FL.

Samenuk, D., Link, M. S., Homoud, M. K., Contreras, R., et al. (2002). Adverse cardiovascular events temporally associated with Ma Huang, an herbal source of ephedrine. *Mayo Clinic Proceedings, 77,* 12–16.

Samet, S., Waxman, R., Hazenbuehler, M., & Hasin, D. S. (2007). Assessing addiction: concepts and instruments. *Addiction Science & Clinical Practice, 4*(1), 19–30.

Sampson, H. W. (2002). Alcohol and other risk factors affecting osteoporosis risk in women. *Alcohol Research & Health, 26*(4), 294–298.

San, L., Arranz, B., & Martinez-Rega, J. (2007). Antipsychotic drug treatment of schizophrenic patients with substance use disorders. *European Addiction Research, 13,* 230–243.

Sanchez, L. M., & Turner, S. M. (2003). Practicing psychology in the era of managed care. *American Psychologist, 58,* 116–129.

Sanna, P. P., & Koob, G. F. (2004). Cocaine's long run. *Nature Medicine, 10*(4), 340–341.

Santora, P. B., & Hutton, H. E. (2008). Longitudinal trends in hospital admissions with co-occurring alcohol/drug diagnoses, 1994–2002. *Journal of Substance Abuse Treatment, 35*(1), 1–12.

Satel, S. L. (2000, March 3). *The limits of drug treatment and the case for coercion.* Symposium presented to the Department of Psychiatry, Cambridge Hospital, Boston.

Satel, S. L., & Farabee, D. J. (2005). The role of coercion in drug treatment. In J. H. Lowinson, P. Ruiz, R. B. Millman, & J. G. Langrod (Eds.), *Substance abuse: A comprehensive textbook* (4th ed.). New York: Lippincott Williams & Wilkins.

Satre, D. D., Mertens, J. R., Arean, P. A., & Weisner, C. (2004). Five-year alcohol and drug treatment outcomes in older adults versus middle-aged and young adults in managed care program. *Addiction, 99,* 1286–1297.

Sattar, S. P., & Bhatia, S. (2003). Benzodiazepine for substance abusers: Yes or no? *Current Psychiatry, 2*(5), 25–34.

Saum, C. A., & Inciardi, J. A. (1997). Rohypnol misuse in the United States. *Substance Use and Misuse, 32,* 723–731.

Sauret, J. M., Marinides, G., & Wang, G. K. (2002). Rhabdomyolysis. *American Family Physician, 65,* 907–912.

Savage, S. R., Kirsh, K. L., & Passik, S. D. (2008). Challenges in using opioids to treat pain in persons with substance use disorders. *Addiction Science & Clinical Practice, 4*(2), 4–25.

Sax, P. E. (2003). HIV infection. In B. A. Cunha (Ed.), *Antibiotic essentials.* Royal Oak, MI: Physician's Press.

SBIRT Research Collaborative Group. (2007). The impact of screening, brief intervention, and referral for treatment on emergency department patients with alcohol use. *Annals of Emergency Medicine, 50,* 699–710.

Schaefer, M. R., Wonderlich, E. R., Roeth, J. F., Leonard, J. A., & Collins, K. L. (2008). HIV-1 nef targets MHC-I and CD4 for degradation via a common ß-COP dependent pathway in T cells. *PLoS Pathogens* (published online). doi: 10.137/journal.ppat.1000131

Schaler, J. A. (2000). *Addiction is a choice.* Chicago: Open Court.

Schanzer, B. M., First, M. B., Dominguez, B., Hasin, D. S., & Canton, C. L. M. (2006). Diagnosing psychotic disorders in the emergency department in the context of substance abuse. *Psychiatric Services, 57,* 1468–1473.

Schirmer, M., Wiedermann, C. & Konwalinka, G. (2000). Immune system. In G. Zernig, A. Saria, M. Kurz, & S. S. O'Malley (Eds.), *Handbook of alcoholism.* New York: CRC Press.

Schlaepfer, T. E., Strain, E. C., Greenberg, B. D., Preston, K. L., Lancaster, E., Bigelow, G. E., et al. (1998). Site of opioid action in the human brain: Mu and kappa agonists subjective and cerebral blood flow effects. *American Journal of Psychiatry, 155,* 470–473.

Schlit, T., de Win, M. L., Koeter, M., Jaker, D. J., Korf, D. J., van den Brink, W., et al. (2007). Cognition in novice Ecstasy users with minimal exposure to other drugs. *Archives of General Psychiatry, 64,* 728–736.

Schlosser, E. (2003). *Reefer madness.* New York: Houghton Mifflin.

Schmid, H., Bogt, T. T., Godeau, E., Hublet, A., Dias, S. F., & Fotiou, A. (2003). Drunkenness among young people: A cross-national comparison. *Journal of Studies on Alcohol, 29*(1), 49–52.

Schmidt, L., Greenfield, T., & Mulia, N. (2006). Unequal treatment: Racial and ethnic disparities in alcoholism treatment services. *Alcohol Research & Health, 29*(1), 49–54.

Schmitz, J. M., & Delaune, K. A. (2005). Nicotine In J. H. Lowinson, P. Ruiz, R. B. Millman, & J. G. Langrod (Eds.), *Substance abuse: A comprehensive textbook* (4th ed.). New York: Lippincott Williams & Wilkins.

Schnoll, S. H., & Weaver, M. F. (2004). Phencyclidine and ketamine. In M. Galanter & H. D. Kleber (Eds.), *The American Psychiatric Publishing textbook of substance abuse treatment* (3rd ed.). Washington, DC: American Psychiatric Publishing.

Schomerus, G., Matschinger, H., & Angermeyer, M.C. (2006). Alcoholism: Illness beliefs and resource allocation preference of the public. *Drug & Alcohol Dependence, 82*(3), 204–210.

Schorling, J. B., & Buchsbaum, D. G. (1997). Screening for alcohol and drug abuse. *Medical Clinics of North America, 81,* 845–865.

Schottenfeld, R. S. (2008). Opioid maintenance treatment. In M. Galanter & H. D. Kleber (Eds.), *The American Psychiatric Publishing textbook of substance abuse treatment.* Washington, DC: American Psychiatric Publishing.

Schuckit, M. A. (1994). Low level of response to alcohol as a predictor of future alcoholism. *American Journal of Psychiatry, 151,* 184–189.

Schuckit, M. A. (2005). Alcohol-related disorders. In H. I. Kaplan & B. J. Sadock (Eds.), *Comprehensive textbook of psychiatry* (8th ed.). Baltimore: Williams & Wilkins.

Schuckit, M. A. (2006a). *Drug and alcohol abuse: A clinical guide to diagnosis and treatment* (6th ed.). New York: Springer.

Schuckit, M. A. (2006b). Alcohol and alcoholism. In S. L. Hauser (Ed.), *Harrison's neurology in clinical medicine* (5th ed.). New York: McGraw-Hill.

Schuckit, M. A. (2008a). Alcohol and alcoholism. In A. S. Fauci, E. Braunwald, D. L. Kasper, S. L. Hauser, D. L. Longo, J. L. Jameson, & J. Loscalzo (Eds.), *Harrison's principles of internal medicine* (17th ed.). New York: McGraw-Hill.

Schuckit, M. A (2008b). Opioid drug abuse and dependence. In A. S. Fauci, E. Braunwald, D. L. Kasper, S. L. Hauser, D. L. Longo, J. L. Jameson, & J. Loscalzo (Eds.), *Harrison's principles of internal medicine* (17th ed.). New York: McGraw-Hill.

Schuckit, M. A. (2009). Alcohol-related disorders. In B. J. Sadock, V. A. Sadock, & P. Ruiz (Eds.), *Kaplan & Sadock's comprehensive textbook of psychiatry* (9th ed.). New York: Lippincott Williams & Wilkins.

Schuckit, M. A. (2010). Opioid drug abuse and dependence. In S. L. Hauser & S. A. Josephson (Eds.), *Harrison's neurology in clinical medicine* (2nd ed.). New York: McGraw-Hill.

Schuckit, M. A., & Tapert, S. (2004). Alcohol. In M. Galanter & H. D. Kleber (Eds.), *The American Psychiatric Publishing textbook of substance abuse treatment* (3rd ed.). Washington, DC: American Psychiatric Publishing.

Schultz, C. H. (2002). Earthquakes. In D. E. Hogan & J. L. Burnstein (Eds.), *Disaster medicine*. New York: Lippincott Williams & Wilkins.

Schurr, E. (2007). Is susceptibility to tuberculosis acquired or inherited? *Journal of Internal Medicine, 261*(2), 106–110.

Schwartz, J. M., & Beyette, B. (1996). *Brain lock: Free yourself from obsessive-compulsive behavior.* New York: HarperCollins.

Schwartz, R. H., & Wirth, P. W. (1990). Potential substance abuse detection among adolescent patients: Using the Drug and Alcohol Problem (DAP) Quick Screen, a 30-item questionnaire. *Clinical Pediatrics, 29,* 38–43.

Schweikart, L. (2008). *48 liberal lies about American history (that you probably learned in school)*. New York: Sentinel Books.

Scientists call for stronger warnings for acetaminophen. (2002). *La Crosse Tribune, 99*(153), A1, A8.

Scientists trace AIDS virus origin to 100 years ago. CNN. Retrieved from http://www.cnn.com/2008/TECH/science/10/01/aids.virus.origin.ap/index.html

Scott, C. G. (2000). Ethical issues in addiction counseling. *Rehabilitation Counseling Bulletin, 43*(4), 209–214.

Scott, I. (1998). A hundred-year habit. *History Today, 48*(6), 6–8.

Scott, J. C., & Marcotte, T. D. (2010). Everyday impact of HIV-associated neurocognitive disorders. In T. D. Marcotte & I. Grant (Eds.), *Neuropsychology of everyday functioning*. New York: Guilford.

Segerstrom, S. C. (2008). *Doing optimism.* In D. Goleman, G. Small, G. Braden & G. Lipton (Eds.), *Measuring the immeasurable: The scientific case for spirituality.* Boulder, CO: Sounds True Press.

Sekine, Y., Iyo, M., Ouchi, Y., Matsunaga, T., Tsukada, H., Okada, H., et al. (2001). Methamphetamine-related psychiatric symptoms and reduced brain dopamine transporters studied with PET. *American Journal of Psychiatry, 158,* 1206–1214.

Sekine, Y., Ouchi, Y., Takei, N., Yoshikawa, E., Nakamura, K., Futatsubashi, M., et al. (2006). Brain serotonin transporter density and aggression in abstinent methamphetamine abusers. *Archives of General Psychiatry, 63,* 90–100.

Selzer, M. (1971). The Michigan Alcoholism Screening Test: The quest for a new diagnostic instrument. *American Journal of Psychiatry, 127,* 1653–1658.

Seppala, M. D. (2004). Dilemmas in diagnosing and treating co-occurring disorders: An addiction professional's perspective. *Behavioral Healthcare Tomorrow, 13*(4), 42–47.

Sergio, P. (2008). New weapons against cocaine addiction. *Scientific American Mind, 19*(2), 54–57.

Sessa, B. (2005). Can psychedelics have a role to play in psychiatry once again? *British Journal of Psychiatry, 186,* 457–458.

Setlik, J., Gond, G. R., & Ho, M. (2009). Adolescent prescription ADHD medication abuse is rising along with prescriptions for these medications. *Pediatrics, 124,* 875–880.

Setola, V., Hufeisen, S. J., Grande-Allen, J., Vesely, I., et al. (2003). 3,4-Methylene-dioxymethamphetamine (MDMA, Ecstasy) induces fenfluramine-like proliferation actions in human cardiac valvular intertial cells in vitro. *Molecular Pharmacology, 63,* 1223–1229.

Shaffer, H. J. (2001, March 2). *What is addiction and does it matter?* Symposium presented to the Department of Psychiatry, Cambridge Hospital, Boston.

Shalev, A. Y. (2009). Posttraumatic stress disorder and stress-related disorders. *Psychiatric Clinics of North America, 32,* 687–704.

Sharma, P. (2003, March 5). *Tylenol, the wonder drug.* Paper presented at the Continuing Medical Education Symposium, Gundersen Lutheran Medical Center, La Crosse, WI.

Sharp, C. W., & Rosenberg, N .L. (2005). Inhalants. In J. H. Lowinson, P. Ruiz, R. B. Millman, & J. G. Langrod (Eds.), *Substance abuse: A comprehensive textbook*. New York: Lippincott Williams & Wilkins.

Sharp, M. J., & Getz J. G. (1998). Self-process in comorbid mental illness and drug abuse. *American Journal of Orthopsychiatry, 68,* 639–644.

Shea, C. W. (2006). Alcohol dependence treatment. *Advances in Addiction Treatment, 1*(1), 12–14.

Shea, S. C. (2002). *The practical art of suicide assessment.* New York: Wiley.

Shea, S. C. (2006). *Improving medication adherence.* New York: Lippincott Williams & Wilkins.

Shear, M. K. (2003). Optimal treatment of anxiety disorders. *Patient Care, 37*(5), 18–32.

Sheff, D., Warren, L., Ketcham, K. & Eban, K. (2007). In J. Hoffman & S. Foremke (Eds.), *Addiction: Why can't they just stop?*. New York: Rodale Press.

Shekelle, P. G., Hardy, M. L., Morton, S. C., Maglione, M., Mojica, W. A., Suttorp, M. J., et al. (2003). Efficacy and safety of ephedra and ephedrine for weight loss and athletic performance. *Journal of the American Medical Association, 289,* 1537–1545.

Shem, S. (1978). *The house of God.* New York: Dell.

Shenk, J. W. (1999). America's altered states. *Harper's Magazine, 298*(1788), 38–52.

Shenouda, S. K., Lord, K. C., McIlwain, E., Lucchesi, P. A., & Varner, K. J. (2008). Ecstasy produces left ventricular dysfunction and oxidative stress in rats. *Cardiovascular Research, 79,* 662–670.

Shepard, D. S., Larson, M. J., & Hoffmann, N. G. (1999). Cost-effectiveness of substance abuse services. *Psychiatric Clinics of North America, 22,* 385–400.

Shepard, J. P., Sutherland, I., & Newcombe, R. G. (2006). Relation between alcohol, violence, and victimization in adolescence. *Journal of Adolescence, 29*(4), 239–253.

Sher, K. J. (1991). *Children of alcoholics.* Chicago: University of Chicago Press.

Sher, K. J., & Wood, M. D. (2005). Subjective effects of alcohol: II. In M. Earlywine (Ed.), *Mind-altering drugs: The science of subjective experience.* New York: Oxford University Press.

Sher, K. J., Wood, M. D., Richardson, A. E., & Jackson, K. M. (2005). Subjective effects of alcohol: I. In M. Earlywine (Ed.), *Mind-altering drugs: The science of subjective experience.* New York: Oxford University Press.

Sherer, R. A. (2006). Drug abuse hitting middle-aged more than Gen-Xers. *Psychiatric Times.* Retrieved from http://www.psychiatrictimes.com/showarticle.jtml?articleid=185303195

Sherman, C. (2008). Drug therapy for alcohol dependence. *Clinical Psychiatry News 36*(7), 37.

Shermer, M. (2008). Why you should be skeptical of brain scans. *Scientific American Mind, 19*(5), 66–71.

Sherwood, B. (2009). *The survivors club.* New York: Grand Central Publishing.

Shipley, R., & Rose, J. (2003). *Quit smart.* Durham, NC: QuitSmart Smoking Resources, Inc.

Shivani, R., Goldsmith, R. J., & Anthenelli, R. M. (2002). Alcoholism and psychiatric disorders. *Alcohol Research & Health, 26,* 90–98.

Shouse, R. L., Kajese, T., Hall, H. I., Valleroy, L. A., et al. (2009). Late HIV testing—34 states, 1996–2005. *Morbidity and Mortality Weekly Report.* Retrieved from http://www.cdc.gov/mmwr/preview/mmwrhtml/mm5824a2htm

Shulgin, A., & Shulgin, A. (2007). *Pihkal: A chemical love story.* Berkeley, CA: Transform Press.

Siegel, D. (2008). Reflections on the mindful brain. In D. Goleman, G. Small, G. Braden & G. Lipton (Eds.), *Measuring the immeasurable: The scientific case for spirituality.* Bolder, CO: Sounds True Press.

Silvestri, N. J. (2009). Central nervous system infections. In S. I. Savitz & M. Ronthal (Eds.), *Neurology review for psychiatrists.* New York: Lippincott Williams & Wilkins.

Simkin, D. R. (2002). Adolescent substance use disorders and comorbidity. *Pediatric Clinics of North America, 49,* 463–477.

Simon, H. B. (2007). Old bugs learn new tricks. *Newsweek, CXLVIII*(24), 74, 77.

Simpson, D. D. (2004). A conceptual framework for drug treatment process and outcomes. *Journal of Substance Abuse Treatment, 27,* 99–121.

Simpson, T. L., Saxon, A. J., Meredith, C. W., Malte, C. A., McBride, B., Ferguson, L. C., et al. (2008). A pilot trial of the alpha-adrenergic antagonist prazosin for alcohol dependence. *Alcohol Clinical and Experimental Research* (published online prior to print).

Singer, E. A., Palapattu, G. S., & van Wjingarrden, E. (2008). Prostate-specific antigen levels in relation to consumption of nonsteroidal anti-inflammatory drugs and acetaminophen. *Cancer 113* (published online). doi: 10.1002/cncr.23806

Sinha, R. (2000). Women. In G. Zernig, A. Saria, M. Kurz, & S. S. O'Malley (Eds.), *Handbook of alcoholism.* New York: CRC Press.

Sirotin, Y. B., & Das, A. (2009). Anticipatory haemodynamic signals in sensory cortex not predicted by local neuronal activity. *Nature, 457,* 475–479.

Sklair-Tavron, L., Ski, W. X., Lane, S. B., Harris, H. W., Bunney, B. S., & Nestler, E. J. (1996). Chronic morphine induces visible changes in the morphology of mesolimbic dopamine neurons. *Proceedings of the National Academy of Sciences, 93,* 11202–11207.

Slade, J., Breo, L. A., Hanauer, P., Barnes, D. E., & Glantz, S. A. (1995). Nicotine and addiction. *Journal of the American Medical Association, 274,* 225–233.

Slutske, W. S., Heath, A. C., Madden, P. A. F., Bucholz, K. K., et. al., (2002). Personality and the genetic risk for alcohol dependence. *Journal of Abnormal Psychology, 111,* 124–133.

Slutske, W. S., Hunt-Carter, E. E., Nabors, R. E., Sher, K. J., Bucholz, K. K., Madden, P. A., et al. (2004). Do college students drink more than non-college attending peers? Evidence from a population-based female twin study. *Journal of Abnormal Psychology, 113,* 530–540.

Small, M. F. (2002). What you can learn from drunk monkeys. *Discover, 23*(7), 40–47.

Smith, A. (2008). Antismoking drugs go up in smoke. Retrieved from http://money.cnn.com.2008/03/11/news/companies/antismoking

Smith, B. H., Molina, B. S., & Pelham, W. E. (2002). The clinically meaningful link between alcohol use and attention deficit hyperactivity disorder. *Alcohol Research & Health, 26,* 122–129.

Smith, D. (1997, May). *Prescription drug abuse.* Paper presented at the Wis-SAM symposium Still Getting High: A 30-Year Perspective on Drug Abuse, Gundersen Lutheran Medical Center, La Crosse, WI.

Smith, D. (2001, June 1). *All the rave—what's pop in substance abuse.* Paper presented at the Contemporary Issues in the Treatment of Alcohol and Drug Abuse Symposium, Milwaukee, WI.

Smith, D. M. (2007). Managing acute acetaminophen toxicity. *Nursing 2007, 37*(1), 58–63.

Smith, D. M., Wong, J. K., Hightower, G. K., Kolesch, K., Ignacio, C. C., Daar, E., et al. (2004). Incidence of HIV superinfection following primary infection. *Journal of the American Medical Association, 292,* 1177–1178.

Smith, G. E., & Wesson, D. R. (2004). Benzodiazepines and other sedative-hypnotics. In M. Galanter & H. D. Kleber (Eds.), *The American Psychiatric Publishing textbook of substance abuse treatment* (3rd ed.). Washington, DC: American Psychiatric Publishing.

Smith, G. R., Burnam, M. A., Mosley, C. L., Hollenberg, J. A., Mancino, M., & Grimes, W. (2000). Reliability and validity of the substance abuse outcomes module. *Psychiatric Services, 57,* 1452–1460.

Smith, G. S., Keyl, P. M., Hadley, J. A., Barlety, C. L., Foss, R., Tolbert, W., et al. (2001). Drinking and recreational boating fatalities. *Journal of the American Medical Association, 286,* 2974–2980.

Smith, J. E., Meyers, R. J., & Delaney, H. D. (1998). The community reinforcement approach with homeless alcohol-dependent individuals. *Journal of Consulting and Clinical Psychology, 66,* 541–548.

Smith, L. M., Chang, L., Yonekura, M. L., Gilbride, K., Kuo, J., Poland, R. E., et al. (2001). Brain proton magnetic resonance spectroscopy and imaging in children exposed to cocaine in utero. *Pediatrics, 107,* 227–231.

Smith, L. M., Chang, L., Yonekura, M. L., Grob, C., Osborn, D., & Ernst, T. (2001). Brain proton magnetic resonance spectroscopy in children exposed to methamphetamine in utero. *Neurology, 57*(2), 255–260.

Smith, M. (2006). APA: Pure "ice" fueling methamphetamine epidemic. Retrieved from http://www.metpagetoday.com/2005meetingcoverage/2005APAMeeting/tb/3391

Smith, M. B. (2008). Chronic pain and psychotherapy: One psychiatrist's view. *Primary Psychiatry, 14*(9), 55–68.

Smothers, B. A., Yahr, H. T., & Ruhl, C. (2004). Detection of alcohol use disorders in general hospital admissions in the United States. *Archives of Internal Medicine, 164,* 749–756.

Smucker, W. D., & Hedayat, M. (2001). Evaluation and treatment of ADHD. *American Family Physician, 64,* 817–829.

Smyth, B., Hoffman, V. I., Fan, J., & Hser, Y. (2007). Years of potential life lost among heroin addicts 33 years after treatment. *Preventative Medicine, 44*(4), 369–374.

Sneider, J. T., Pope, H., Silveri, M. M., Simpson, N. S., Gruber, S. A., & Yurgelun-Todd, D. A. (2006). Altered regional blood volume in chronic cannabis smokers. *Experimental and Clinical Psychopharmacology, 14,* 422–428.

Sobell, M. B., & Sobell, L. C. (2007). Substance use, health and mental health. *Clinical Psychology, 14*(1), 1–3.

Sofuoglu, M., & Kosten, T. R. (2004). Pharmacologic management of relapse prevention in addictive disorders. *Psychiatric Clinics of North America, 27,* 622–648.

Sofuoglu, M., & Mooney, M. (2009). Subjective responses to intravenous nicotine: Greater sensitivity in women than in men. *Experimental and Clinical Psychopharmacology, 17*(2), 63–69.

Sokol, R. J., Delaney-Black, V., & Nordstrom, B. (2003). Fetal alcohol spectrum disorder. *Journal of the American Medical Association, 290,* 2966–2999.

Solomon, D. H., Glynn, R. J., Levin, R., & Avorn, J. (2002). Nonsteroidal anti-inflammatory drug use and acute my6ocardial infarction. *Archives of Internal Medicine, 162,* 1099–1104.

Solomon, J., Rogers, A., Kate., P. & Lach, J. (1997). Turning a new leaf. *Newsweek, CXXIX*(13), 50.

Solotaroff, P. (2002). Killer bods. *Rolling Stone, 889,* 54–56, 58–59, 72, 74.

Solowij, N., Stephens, R. S., Roffman, R. A., Babor, T., Kadden, R., Miller, M., et al. (2002). Cognitive functioning of long-term heavy cannabis users seeking treatment. *Journal of the American Medical Association, 287,* 1123–1131.

Sommer, W. (2005, November 11). *Alcoholism and other addictions: Basic science and clinical applications.* Seminar presented at the Psychopharmacology & Neuroscience Course: Update 2005, Bethesda, MD.

Sommers, C. H., & Satel, S. (2005). *One nation under therapy.* New York: St. Martin's Press.

Sonne, S. C., & Brady, K. T. (2002). Bipolar disorder and alcoholism. *Alcohol Research & Health, 26,* 103–108.

Sorter, M. T. (2010). Adolescents in crisis: When to admit for self-harm or aggressive behavior. *Current Psychiatry, 9*(1), 35–39, 45–46.

South American drug production increases. (1997). *Forensic Drug Abuse Advisor, 9*(3), 18.

Soyka, M. (2000). Alcohol-induced psychotic disorders. In G. Zernig, A. Saria, M. Kurz, & S. S. O'Malley (Eds.), *Handbook of alcoholism.* New York: CRC Press.

Spear, L. P. (2002). The adolescent brain and the college drinker: Biological basis of propensity to use and misuse alcohol. *Journal of Studies on Alcohol, 63*(2) (Suppl. 14), 71–81.

Spear, L. P. (2010). *The behavioral neuroscience of adolescence.* New York: Norton.

Spencer, T. J. (2008). Adult ADHD: Diversion and misuse of medications. *CNS Spectrums, 13*(10) (Suppl. 15), 9–15.

Spencer, T., Biederman, J., Wilens, T., Faraone, T., Prince, J., Gerard, K., et al. (2001). Efficacy of a mixed amphetamine salts compound in adults with attention deficit/hyperactivity disorder. *Archives of General Psychiatry, 58,* 775–782.

Spiller, H. A., & Krenzelok, E. P. (1997). Epidemiology of inhalant abuse reported to two regional poison centers. *Journal of Toxicology: Clinical Toxicology, 35,* 167–174.

Spoth, R., Greenberg, M., & Turrisi, R. (2009). Overview of preventive interventions addressing underaged drinking. *Alcohol Research & Health, 32*(1), 53–66.

Squeglia, L. M., Spandoni, A. D., Infante, A., Myers, M. G., & Tapert, S. F. (2009). Initiating moderate to heavy alcohol use predicts changes in neuropsychological functioning for adolescent girls and boys. *Psychology of Addictive Behaviors, 23,* 715–722.

Srisurapanont, M., Marsden, J., Sunga, A., Wada, K., & Monterio, M. (2003). Psychotic symptoms in methamphetamine psychotic inpatients. *International Journal of Neuropsychopharmacology, 6*(4), 347–352.

Stahl, S. M. (2008). *Essential psychopharmacology* (3rd ed.). New York: Cambridge University Press.

Stahler, G. J., Mennis, J., Cotlar, R., & Baron, D. A. (2009). The influence of neighborhood environment on treatment continuity and rehospitalization in dually diagnosed patients discharged from acute inpatient care. *American Journal of Psychiatry, 166,* 1258–1268.

Stamp out drugs. (2003). *Playboy, 50*(7), 52.

Standbridge, J. B., Adams, S. M., & Zotos, A. P. (2010). Urine drug screening: A valuable office procedure. *American Family Physician, 81,* 635–640.

Standbridge, J. B., & DeFranco, G. M. (2006). The clinical realities of using drugs to fight alcoholism. *Patient Care, 40*(3), 13–20.

Stanner, L., Boeijinga, P., Thierry, G. I., Gendre, I., Muzet, M., Landron, F., et al. (2006). Effects of acamprosate on sleep during alcohol withdrawal: A double-blind, placebo-controlled polysomnographic study in alcohol-dependent subjects. *Alcoholism: Clinical & Experimental Research, 30,* 1492–1499.

Stanwood, G. D., & Levitt, P. (2007). Prenatal exposure to cocaine products produced unique developmental and long-term changes in dopamine D1 receptor activity and subcellular distribution. *The Journal of Neuroscience, 27*(1), 152–157.

Stark, M. J., Rhode, K., Maher, J. E., Pizacano, B. A., Dent, C. W., Bard, R., et al. (2007). The impact of clean indoor air exemptions and preemptive policies on the prevalence of a tobacco-specific lung carcinogen among nonsmoking bar and restaurant workers. *American Journal of Public Health* (published online). doi: 10.2015/AJPH.2006.094086

Stauber, R. E., Trauner, M., & Fickert, P. (2000). Gastrointestinal system and pancreas. In G. Zernig, A. Saria, M. Kurz, & S. O'Malley (Eds.), *Handbook of alcoholism*. New York: CRC Press.

Steele, T. E., & Morton, W. A. (1986). Salicylate-induced delirium. *Psychosomatics, 27*(6), 455–456.

Stein, B., Orlando, M., & Sturm, R. (2000). The effect of copayments on drug and alcohol treatment following inpatient detoxification under managed care. *Psychiatric Services, 51*, 195–198.

Stein, L. A. R., & Rogers, R. (2008). Denial and misreporting of substance abuse. In R. Rogers (Ed.), *Clinical assessment of malingering and deception*. New York: Guilford.

Stein, S. M., & Friedmann, P. D. (2001). Generalist physicians and addiction care. *Journal of the American Medical Association, 286*, 1764–1765.

Steinbrook, R. (2008). The AIDS epidemic—A progress report from Mexico City. *New England Journal of Medicine, 359*, 885–887.

Steinhubl, S. R., Bhatt, D. L., Brennan D. M., Montalescot, G., Hankey, G. J., Ekelboom, J. W., et al. (2009). Aspirin to prevent cardiovascular disease: The association of aspirin dose and clopidogrel with thrombosis and bleeding. *Archives of Internal Medicine, 150*, 379–386.

Stephens, A., Logina, I., Liguts, V., Aldins, P., Eksteina, I., Platkajis, A., et al. (2008). A Parkinsonian syndrome in methcathinone users and the role of manganese. *New England Journal of Medicine, 358*, 1000–1017.

Stephens, M. (2008). Supplements and sports: Honest advice. *American Family Physician, 78*, 1025.

Stephens, R. S., & Roffman, R. A. (2005). Assessment of cannabis use disorders. In D. M. Donovan & G. A. Marlatt (Eds.), *Assessment of addictive disorders* (2nd ed.). New York: Guilford.

Sterling, R. C., Weinstein, S., Hill, O., Gottheil, E., Gordon, S. M., & Shorie, K. (2006). Levels of spirituality and treatment outcome: A preliminary examination. *Journal of Studies on Alcohol, 67*, 600–606.

Sternbach, H. (2003). Serotonin syndrome. *Current Psychiatry, 2*(5), 14–24.

Steroids and growth hormones make users "really ripped." (2003). *Forensic Drug Abuse Advisor, 15*, 74–76.

Stetter, F. (2000). Psychotherapy. In G. Zernig, A. Saria, M. Kurz, & S. S. O'Malley (Eds.), *Handbook of alcoholism*. New York: CRC Press.

Stevens, J. C., & Pollack, M.H. (2005). Benzodiazepines in clinical practice: Consideration of their long-term use and alternative agents. *Journal of Consulting and Clinical Psychology, 66*(Suppl. 2), 21–27.

Stevenson, J. S. (2005). Alcohol use, misuse, abuse and dependence in later adulthood. In J. J. Fitzpatrick, J. S. Stevenson, & M. S. Somers (Eds.), *Annual review of nursing research* (*Vol. 23*). New York: Springer.

Stevenson, J. S., & Somers, M. S. (2005). The case for alcohol research as a focus of study by nurse researchers. In J. J. Fitzpatrick, J. S. Stevenson, & M. S. Somers (Eds.), *Annual review of nursing research* (*Vol. 23*). New York: Springer.

Stewart, S. A. (2005). The effects of benzodiazepines on cognition. *Journal of Medical Psychiatry, 66*(Suppl. 2), 9–13.

Sticherling, C., Schaer, B. A., Ammann, P., Maeder, M., & Osswald, S. (2005). Methadone-induced Torsade de pointes tachycardias. *Swiss Medical Weekly, 135*(19–20), 282–285.

Stillman, M. J., & Stillman, M. T. (2007). Choosing nonselective NSAIDS and selective COX-2 inhibitors in the elderly. *Geriatrics, 62*(22), 26–34.

Stimmel, B. (1997a). *Pain and its relief without addiction*. New York: Haworth Medical Press.

Stimmel, B. (1997b). *Drug abuse and social policy in America: The war that must be won*. Paper presented at the 1997 annual Frank P. Furlano, MD, memorial lecture, Gundersen Lutheran Medical Center, La Crosse, WI.

Stitzer, M. (2003). *Nicotine addiction and tobacco dependence*. Seminar presented at the 2003 meeting of the American Psychological Association, Toronto, Canada.

Stix, G. (2009). Turbocharging the brain. *Scientific American, 301*(4), 46–55.

Stone, P., & Edwards, P. (1970). *1776*. New York: Penguin Books.

Stoschitzky, K. (2000). Cardiovascular system. In G. Zernig, M. Kurz, & S. S. O'Malley (Eds.), *Handbook of alcoholism*. New York: CRC Press.

Stout, P. R. (2009). Opioids. In J. D. Robero-Miller & B. A. Goldberger (Eds.), *Handbook of workplace drug testing* (2nd ed.). Washington, DC: AACC Press.

Strandberg, A. Y., Strandberg, T. E., Pitkala, K., Salomaa, V., Tilvis, R. S., & Mittinen, T. A. (2008). The effect of smoking in midlife on health-related quality of life in old age. *Archives of Internal Medicine, 168*(18), 1968–1974.

Strassman, R. (2005). Hallucinogens. In M. Earlywine (Ed.), *Mind-altering drugs: The science of subjective experience*. New York: Doubleday.

Strauch, B. (2003). *The primal teen*. New York: Doubleday.

Sturmi, J. E., & Diorio, D. J. (1998). Anabolic agents. *Clinics in Sports Medicine, 17*, 261–282.

Substance abuse adds millions to Medicaid's total health care costs. (2008, December 30). Substance Abuse Policy Research Program, press release.

Substance abuse and dependence among women. (2005, August 5). *National Survey on Drug Use and Health*.

Substance Abuse and Mental Health Services Administration. (2005). *Results from the 2004 National Survey on Drug Use and Health: National Findings*. Rockville, MD: Author.

Substance Abuse and Mental Health Services Administration. (2009). *Results from the 2008 National Survey on Drug Use and Health: National Findings*. Rockville, MD: Author.

Sull, J. W., Sang-Wook, Y., Nam, C. M., & Ohrr, H. (2009). Binge drinking and mortality from all causes and cerebrovascular disease in Korean men and women. *Stroke* (published online prior to print). doi: 10.1161/STROKEAHA.109.556027

Sullivan, M. G. (2007). Heavy alcohol use hastens death by up to 25 years: Neuro-psychiatric patients at great risk. *Clinical Psychiatry News, 35*(8), 1.

Sundaram, R., Shulman, L., & Fein, A. M. (2004). Trends in tobacco use. *Medical Clinics of North America, 88*, 1391–1397.

Suppes, T., & Keck, P. E. (2005). *Bipolar disorder: Treatment and management*. Kansas City, MO: Compact Clinicals Medical Publishers.

Suris, J. C., Akre, C., Berchtold, A., Jeannin, A., & Michaud, P. (2007). Characteristics of cannabis users who have never smoked tobacco. *Archives of Pediatrics & Adolescent Medicine, 161*(11), 1042–1047.

Sussman, N. (2009). Mental health parity act becomes the law on October 3, 2009. *Primary Psychiatry, 16*(10), 10–11.

Sussman, N., & Westreich, L. (2003). Chronic marijuana use and the treatment of mentally ill patients. *Primary Psychiatry, 19*(9), 73–76.

Sutheimer, C. A. & Cody, J. T. (2009). Subversion of regulated workplace drug testing—Specimen adulteration and substitution. In J. D. Robero-Miller & B. A. Goldberger (Eds.), *Handbook of workplace drug testing* (2nd ed.). Washington, DC: AACC Press.

Svitil, K. A. (2003). What, me worry about SARS? *Discover, 24*(8), 19–20.

Swann, A. C. (2009). Behavioral neurochemistry and pharmacology. In S. I. Savitz & M. Ronthal (Eds.), *Neurology review for psychiatrists*. New York: Lippincott Williams & Wilkins.

Swartz, M. S., Wagner, H. R., Swanson, J. W., Stroup, T. S., McEvoy, J. P., McGee, M., et al. (2006). Substance use and psychosocial functioning in schizophrenia among new enrollees in the NIMH CATIC study. *Psychiatric Services, 57*, 1110–1116.

Swegle, J. M., & Logemann, C. (2006). Management of common opioid-induced adverse effects. *American Family Physician, 74*, 1347–1354.

Swift, R., & Davidson, D. (1998). Alcohol hangover. *Alcohol Health & Research World, 22*, 54–60.

Swift, R. M. (2005, January 22). *The etiology of alcohol abuse and dependence: What happens in the brain?* Seminar presented at the Four Seasons Hotel, Chicago.

Sylvestre, D. (2008). Hepatitis C for addiction professionals. *Addiction Science & Clinical Practice, 4*(1), 34–42.

Szalavitz, M. (2005). Give us the drugs. *New Scientist, 185*(2484), 19.

Szalavitz, M. (2006). *Help at any cost*. New York: Riverhead Books.

Szasz, T. S. (1997). Save money, cut crime, get real. *Playboy, 44*(1), 121, 190.

Tabakoff, B., & Hoffman, P. L. (2004). Neurobiology of alcohol. In M. Galanter & H. D. Kleber (Eds.), *The American Psychiatric Publishing textbook of substance abuse treatment* (3rd ed.). Washington, DC: American Psychiatric Publishing.

Tacke, U., & Ebert, M. H. (2005). Hallucinogens and phencyclidine. In H. R. Kranzler & D. A. Ciraulo (Eds.), *Clinical manual of addiction psychopharmacology*. Washington, DC: American Psychiatric Publishing.

Take time to smell the fentanyl. (1994). *Forensic Drug Abuse Advisor, 6*(5), 34–35.

Talty, S. (2003). The straight dope. *Playboy, 50*(11), 89–92.

Taming drug interactions. (2003). *Addiction Treatment Forum, 12*(4), 1, 6.

Tan, J. S. L., Mitchel, P., Kifley, A., Flood, V., Smith, W., & Wang, J. J. (2008). Smoking and long-term incidence of age-related macular degeneration: The

Blue Mountains study. *Archives of Ophthalmology,* *125*, 1089–1095.

Tan, W. C., Lo, C., Jong, A., Xing, L., Vollmer, W. M., Buist, S. A., et al. (2009). Marijuana and chronic obstructive lung disease: A population-based study. *Canadian Medical Association Journal, 180*(8) (published online prior to print). doi: 10.1503/cmaj.081040

Tannu, N., Mash, D. C., & Hemby, S. E. (2006). Cytosolic proteomic alterations in the nucleus accumbens of cocaine overdose victims. *Molecular Psychiatry* (published online). doi: 10.1038/sj.mp.4001914

Tapert, S. F., Caldwell, L., & Burke, C. (2004/2005). Alcohol use and the adolescent brain: Human studies. *Alcohol Research & Health, 28*(4), 205–212.

Tapert, S. F., Cheung, E. H., Brown, G. S., Frank, L. R., Paulus, M. P., Schweinsburg, A. D., et al. (2003). Neural response to alcohol stimuli in adolescents with alcohol use disorder. *Archives of General Psychiatry, 60,* 727–735.

Tarter, R. E., Vanyukov, M., Kirisci, L., Reynolds, M., & Clark, D. B. (2006). Predictors of marijuana use in adolescents before and after illicit drug use: Examination of the gateway hypothesis. *American Journal of Psychiatry, 163,* 2134–2140.

Tashkin, D. B. (2005). Smoked marijuana as a cause of lung injury. *Archives for Chest Disease, 63*(2), 93–100.

Tatro, D. S. (2009). *Drug interaction facts.* St. Louis, MO: Wolters Kluwer.

Tavris, C. (1990). One more guilt trip for women. *Minneapolis Star-Tribune, 8*(341), A21.

Tavris, C. (1992). *The mismeasure of women.* New York: Simon & Schuster.

Taylor, M. L. (2004). Drug courts for teenagers can be effective. *La Crosse Tribune, 101*(61), 16.

Taylor, S., McCracken, C. F. M., Wilson, K. C. M., & Copeland, J. R. M. (1998). Extended and appropriateness of benzodiazepine use. *British Journal of Psychiatry, 173,* 433–438.

Teicher, M. H. (2002). Scars that won't heal: The neurobiology of child abuse. *Scientific American, 286*(3), 68–75.

Tekin, S., & Cummings, J. L. (2003). Hallucinations and related conditions. In K. M. Heilmann & E. Valenstein (Eds.), *Clinical neuropsychology* (4th ed.). New York: Oxford University Press.

Terplan, M., Smith, E., Kozloski, M., & Pollack, H. A. (2009). Methamphetamine use among pregnant women. *Obstetrics & Gynecology, 113*(6), 1285–1291.

Terry, M. B., Gammon M. D., Zhang, F. F., Tawfik, H., Teitelbaum, S. L., Britton, J. A., et al. (2004). Association of frequency and duration of aspirin use and hormone receptor status with breast cancer risk. *Journal of the American Medical Association, 291,* 2433–2440.

Tetrault, J. M., Crothers, K., Moore, B. A., Mehra, R., Concato, J., & Fiellin, D. A. (2007). Effects of marijuana smoking on pulmonary function and respiratory complications: A systematic review. *Archives of Internal Medicine, 167*(3), 229–235.

Thatcher, D. L., & Clark, D. B. (2008). Adolescents at risk for substance use disorders. *Alcohol Research & Health, 31*(2), 168–176.

The drug index. (1995). *Playboy, 42*(9), 47.

Thevis, M., Thomas, A., Kihler, M., Beuck, S., & Schanzer, W. (2009). Emerging drugs: Mechanism of action, mass spectrometry and doping control analysis. *Journal of Mass Spectrometry, 44*(4), 442–460.

Thombs, D. L., O'Mara, R. J., Tsukamoto, M., Rossheim, M. E., Weiler, R. M., Merves, M. L., et al. (2010). Event-level analysis of energy drink consumption and alcohol intoxication in bar patrons. *Addictive Behaviors, 35*(4), 325–330.

Thompson, J. P. (2004). Acute effects of drugs of abuse. *Clinical Medicine, 3*(2), 123–126.

Thompson PDR. (2007). *2007 physician's desk reference* (61st ed.). Montvale, NJ: Author.

Thomson, H. (2009). iSmoke. *New Scientist, 201*(2695), 32–35.

Thomson, W. M., Poulton, R., Broadbent, J. M., Moffit, T.E., Caspi, A., Beck, J. D., et al. (2008). Cannabis smoking and periodontal disease among young adults. *Journal of the American Medical Association, 299*(5), 525–531.

Tildesley, E. A., & Andrews, J. A. (2008). The development of children's intentions to use alcohol: Direct and indirect effects of parent alcohol use and parenting behaviors. *Psychology of Addictive Behaviors, 22,* 326–339.

Tillich, P. (1957). *The dynamics of faith.* New York: Harper & Row.

Timko, C., Moos, R. H., Finney, J. W., & Lesar, M. D. (2000). Long-term consequences of alcohol use disorders: Comparing untreated individuals with those in Alcoholics Anonymous and formal treatment. *Journal of Studies on Alcohol, 61,* 529–540.

Tinsley, J. A. (2005). Drug abuse. In R. E. Rakel & E. T. Pope (Eds.), *Conn's current therapy, 2005*. Philadelphia: Elsevier Sanders.

Tinsley, J. A., Finlayson, R. E., & Morse, R. M. (1998). Developments in the treatment of alcoholism. *Mayo Clinic Proceedings, 73*, 857–863.

Tobacco. (2009). *A to Z health guide—How to live longer and better*. New York: Time.

Tomb, D. A. (2008). *House officer series: Psychiatry* (7th ed.). New York: Lippincott Williams & Wilkins.

Tominaga, G. T., Carcia, G., Dzierba, A., & Wong, J. (2004). Toll of methamphetamine on the trauma system. *Archives of Surgery, 139*, 844–847.

Toneatto, T., Sobell, L. C., Sobell, M. B., & Rubel, E. (1999). Natural recovery from cocaine dependence. *Psychology of Addictive Behaviors, 13*, 259–268.

Tong, E. K., & Glantz, S. A. (2007). Tobacco industry efforts undermining evidence linking secondhand smoke with cardiovascular disease. *Circulation, 116*(16), 1845–1854.

Toombs, J. D., & Kral, L. A. (2005). Methadone treatment for pain states. *American Family Physician, 71*, 1353–1358.

Torregrossa, M. M., & Kalivas, P. W. (2009). Addictive processes. In G. G. Berntson & J. T. Cacioppo (Eds.), *Handbook of neuroscience for the behavioral sciences*. New York: Wiley.

Trachtenberg, M. C., & Blum, K. (1987). Alcohol and opioid peptides: Neuropharmacological rationale for physical craving of alcohol. *American Journal of Drug and Alcohol Abuse, 13*(3), 365–372.

Trafton, J. A., & Gifford, E. V. (2008). Behavioral reactivity and addiction: The adaption of behavioral response to reward opportunities. *Journal of Neuropsychiatry and Clinical Neurosciences, 20*(1), 23–35.

Trandon, K. (2007). Yoga: An excellent therapeutic adjunct for outpatient therapy. *Counselor, 8*(5), 12–17.

Traub, S. J. (2009). Substance abuse and neurotoxicity. In S. I. Savitz & M. Ronthal (Eds.), *Neurology review for psychiatrists*. New York: Lippincott Williams & Wilkins.

Tresch, D. D., & Aronow, W. S. (1996). Smoking and coronary artery disease. *Clinics in Geriatrics Medicine, 12*, 23–32.

Treweek, J., Wee, S., Kopob, G. F., Dickerson, T. J., & Janda, K. D. (2007). Self-vaccination by methamphetamine glycation products chemically links chronic drug abuse and cardiovascular disease. *Proceeds of the National Academy of Sciences* (published online June 25, 2007). doi: 10.1073/pnas.0701328104

Triesman, G. J., Angelino, A. F. & Hutton, H. E. (2001). Psychiatric issues in the management of patients with HIV infection. *Journal of the American Medical Association, 286*, 2857–2864.

Trocki, K. F., Drabble, L. A., & Midanik, L. T. (2009). Tobacco, marijuana, and sensation seeking: Comparisons across gay, lesbian, bisexual and heterosexual groups. *Psychology of Addictive Behaviors, 23*, 620–631.

Tsai, V. W., Anderson, C. L., & Vaca, F. E. (2010). Alcohol involvement among young female drivers in US fatal crashes: Unfavorable trends. *Injury Prevention, 16*, 17–20.

Tse, W., & Koller, W. C. (2004). Neurologic complications of alcoholism. In W. J. Weiner & C. G. Goetz (Eds.), *Neurology for the non-neurologist* (5th ed.). New York: Lippincott Williams & Wilkins.

Tuncel, M., Wang, Z., Arbique, D., Fadel, P. J., Victor, R. J., Vongpatanasin, W., et al. (2002). Mechanism of the blood-pressure raising effects of cocaine in humans. *Circulation, 105*, 1054–1059.

Twelve steps and twelve traditions of Alcoholics Anonymous. (1981). New York: Alcoholics Anonymous World Services.

Uhl, G. R., Liu, Q., Drgon, T., Johnson, C., Walther, D., Rose, J. E., et al. (2008). Molecular genetics of successful smoking cessation. *Archives of General Psychiatry, 65*(6), 683–693.

Uhl, M., & Sachs, H. (2004). Cannabinoids in hair: Strategy to prove marijuana hashish consumption. *Forensic Science International, 145*, 143–147.

Underaged alcohol use: Findings from the 2002–2006 National Surveys on Drug Use and Health. (2008). Washington, DC: Substance Abuse and Mental Health Services Administration.

Understanding anonymity. (1981). New York: Alcoholics Anonymous World Services.

Ungvarski, P. J., & Grossman, A. H. (1999). Health problems of gay and bisexual men. *Nursing Clinics of North America, 34*, 313–326.

United Nations. (2008). *2008 world drug report*. New York: United Nations Publications.

Unwin, B. K., Davis, M. K., & De Leeuw, J. B. (2000). Pathological gambling. *American Family Physician, 61*, 741–749.

Upadhyaya, H. P., & Gray, K. M. (2009). Adolescent substance use and the role of gender. In K. T. Brady, S. E. Back, & S. F. Greenfield (Eds.), *Women & addiction*. New York: Guilford.

U.S. Department of Health and Human Services. (2004). *Clinical guidelines for the use of burprenorphine in the treatment of opioid addiction: A treatment improvement protocol.* Washington, DC: U.S. Government Printing Office.

U.S. face of drug abuse grows older. (2006). Retrieved from http:www.msnbc.msn.com/id/128396/01/html

Utah judge strikes down FDA ban on ephedra. (2005). Retrieved from http://www.cnn.com/2005/LAW04/04/14/ephedra.suit.ap/index.html

Vadez, C., Salto, M., Gyetfal, B. M., Oros, M., Szakall, I., Kovacs, K. M., et al. (2007). Glutamate receptor metabotropic 7 is *cis*-regulated in the mouse brain and modulates alcohol drinking. *Genomics, 90*(6), 670–702.

Vaglum, P. (2003). Antisocial personality disorder and narcotic addiction. In T. Millon, E. Simonsen, E. Birket-Smith, & R. D. Davis (Eds.), *Psychopathy: Antisocial, criminal and violent behavior.* New York: Guilford.

Vaillant, G. E. (1990). We should retain the disease concept of alcoholism. *The Harvard Medical School Mental Health Letter, 9*(6), 4–6.

Vaillant, G. E. (1995). *The natural history of alcoholism revisited.* Cambridge, MA: Harvard University Press.

Vaillant, G. E. (1996). A long-term follow-up of male alcohol abuse. *Archives of General Psychiatry, 53,* 243–249.

Vaillant, G. E. (2000, March 4). *Alcoholics Anonymous: Cult or magic bullet?* Symposium presented to the Department of Psychiatry, Cambridge Hospital, Boston.

Vaillant, G. E. (2005). Alcoholics Anonymous: Cult or cure? *Australian and New Zealand Journal of Psychiatry, 39,* 431–436.

Vaillant, G. E., & Hiller-Sturmhofel, S. (1996). The natural history of alcoholism. *Alcohol Health & Research World, 20,* 152–161.

Vanable, P. A., King, A. C., & deWit, H. (2000). Psychometric screening instruments. In G. Zernig, A. Saria, M. Kurz, & S. S. O'Malley (Eds.), *Handbook of alcoholism.* New York: CRC Press.

van den Bree, M., & Pickworth, W. B. (2005). Risk factors predicting changes in marijuana involvement in teenagers. *Archives of General Psychiatry, 62,* 311–319.

Vanderah, T. W. (2006). Pathophysiology of pain. *Medical Clinics of North America, 91,* 1–12.

Vandry, R. G., Budney, A. J., & Ligouori, A. (2008). A within-subject comparison of withdrawal symptoms during abstinence from cannabis, tobacco and both substances. *Drug and Alcohol Dependence, 92,* 48–54.

van Hook, S., Harris, S. K., Brooks, T., Careym, P., Kossack, R., Kulig, J., et al. (2007). The "Six T's": Barriers to screening teens for substance abuse in primary care. *Journal of Adolescent Health, 40*(5), 456–461.

van Noorden, M. S., van Dongen, L. C., Zitman, F. G., & Vergouwen, T. A. (2009). Gamma-hydroxybutyrate withdrawal syndrome: Dangerous but not well known. *General Hospital Psychiatry, 4,* 394–396.

Varlinskaya, E. I., & Spear, L. P. (2006). Ontogeny of acute tolerance to ethanol induced social inhibition in Sprague-Dawley rats. *Alcoholism: Clinical and Experimental Research, 30,* 1833–1844.

Vaughan, E .L., Corbin W. R., & Fromme, K. (2009). Academic and social motives and drinking behavior. *Psychology of Addictive Behaviors, 23,* 564–576.

Vaughn, A. (2006). Substance abuse, medications, HIV and the community. *Nursing Clinics of North America, 41,* 355–369.

Vedantam, S. (2006). Millions have misused ADHD stimulant drugs, study says. Retrieved from http://www.washingtonpost.com.wp-dyn/content/article/2006/02/24ar2006022401733?htmareferrer=email article

Vega, C., Kwoon, J. V., & Oavine, S. D. (2002). Intracranial aneurysms: Current evidence and clinical practice. *American Family Physician, 66*(4), 601–608.

Veld, B. A., Ruitenberg, A., Hofman, A., Launer, L. J., van Duijn, C. M., Stijnen, T., et al. (2001) Nonsteroidal anti-inflammatory drugs and the risk of Alzheimer's disease. *New England Journal of Medicine, 345,* 1515–1521.

Venkatakrishnan, K., Shader, R. I., & Greenblatt, D. J. (2006). Concepts and mechanisms of drug disposition and drug interactions. In D. A. Ciraulo, R. I. Shader, D. J. Greenblatt, & W. Creelman (Eds.), *Drug interactions in psychiatry* (3rd ed.). New York: Lippincott Williams & Wilkins.

Vereby, K., Buchan, B. J., & Turner, C. E. (1998). Laboratory testing. In R. J. Frances & S. I. Miller (Eds.), *Clinical textbook of addictive disorders* (2nd ed.). New York: Guilford.

Vernooij, M. W., Haag, M. D. M., van der Lugt, A., Hofman, A., Krestin, G. P., Stricker, B. H., et al. (2009). Use of antithrombotic drugs and the presence of cerebral microbleeds. *Archives of Neurology,*

66(6) (published online prior to print). doi: 1001/archneurol.2002.42

Vetter, V. L., Elia, J., Erickson, C., Berger, S., et al. (2008). Cardiovascular monitoring of children and adolescents with heart disease receiving medications for attention deficit/hyperactivity disorder. *Circulation* (published online). doi: 10.1161/CIRCULATIONAHA.107.189473

Viamontes, G. I., & Beitman, B. D. (2006). Neural substrates of psychotherapeutic change. *Psychiatric Annals, 36*, 238–246.

Vik, P., Cellucci, T., Jarchow, A., & Hedt, J. (2004). Cognitive impairment in substance use. *Psychiatric Clinics of North America, 27*, 97–109.

Villalon, C. (2004). Cocaine country. *National Geographic, 206*(1), 34–55.

Vitacco, M. J. (2008). Syndromes associated with deception. In R. Rogers (Ed.), *Clinical assessment of malingering and deception* (3rd ed.). New York: Guilford.

Vital signs. (2007). *Clinical Psychiatry News, 35*(7), 1.

Vlad, S. C., Miller, D. R., Kowall, N. W., & Felson, D. T. (2008). Protective effects of NSAIDs on the development of Alzheimer's disease. *Neurology, 70*, 1672–1677.

Vocci, F., & Elkashef, A. (2009). Pharmacological treatment of methamphetamine addiction. In J. R. Roll, R. A. Rawson, W. Ling, & S. Shoptaw (Eds.), *Methamphetamine addiction—From* basic science to treatment. New York: Guilford.

Volkow, N. D. (2006a, August 12). *Addiction: The neurobiology of free will gone awry*. Symposium presented at the annual meeting of the American Psychological Association, New Orleans, LA.

Volkow, N. D. (2006b). Steroid abuse is a high-risk route to the finish line. *NIDA Notes, 21*(1), 2.

Volkow, N. D., Fowler, J. S., Logan, J., ALexoff, D., Zhu, W., Telang, F., et al. (2009). Effects of modafinil on dopamine and dopamine transporters in the male human brain. *Journal of the American Medical Association, 301*(11), 1148–1154.

Volkow, N. D., & Swanson, J. M. (2003). Variables that affect the clinical use and abuse of methylphenidate in the treatment of ADHD. *American Journal of Psychiatry, 160*(11), 1909–1918.

Volkow, N. D., Wang, G. J., Fowler, J. S., Logan, J., Gatley, S. J., Gifford, A., et al. (1998). Prediction of reinforcing responses to psychostimulants in humans by brain dopamine D2 receptor levels. *American Journal of Psychiatry, 156*, 1440–1443.

Vollmer, G. (2006). Crossing the barrier. *Scientific American Mind, 17*(3), 34–39.

Volpicelli, J. R. (2005). New options for the treatment of alcohol dependence. *Psychiatric Annals, 35*(6), 484–491.

Vonlaufen, A., Wilson, J. S., Pirola, R. C., & Apte, M. V. (2007). Role of alcohol metabolism in chronic pancreatitis. *Alcohol Research & Health, 30*, 48–54.

Vornik, L. A., & Brown, E. S. (2006). Management of comorbid bipolar disorder and substance abuse. *Journal of Clinical Psychiatry, 67* (Suppl. 7), 24–30.

Vourakis, C. (1998). Substance abuse concerns in the treatment of pain. *Nursing Clinics of North America, 27*, 675–687.

Vuchinich, R. E. (2002). The president's column. *Addictions Newsletter, 10*(1), 1, 5.

Vul, E., Harris, C., Winkielman, P., & Pashler, H. (2009). Puzzlingly high correlations in fMRI studies of emotion, personality and social cognition. Retrieved from http://www.pashlet.com/Articles/Vul-etal-2008inpress.pdf

Wade, N. (2009). *The faith instinct*. New York: Penguin Press.

Wadland, W. C., & Ferenchick, G. S. (2004). Medical comorbidity in addictive disorders. *Psychiatric Clinics of North America, 27*, 675–687.

Wagner, E. F. (2009). Improving treatment through research: Directing attention to the role of development in adolescent treatment success. *Alcohol Research & Health, 32*(1), 67–75.

Wakefulness drug: New safety concerns. (2009). *A to Z health guide—how to live longer and better.* New York: Time.

Walker, D. D., Venner, K., Hill, D. E., Myers, R. J., & Miller, W. R. (2004). A comparison of alcohol and drug disorders: Is there evidence for a developmental sequence of drug abuse? *Addictive Behaviors, 29*(4), 817–823.

Wallace, J. (2003). Theory of 12-step oriented treatment. In F. Rotgers, J. Morgenstern, & S. T. Walters (Eds.), *Treating substance abuse: Theory and technique* (2nd ed.). New York: Guilford.

Walley, A. Y., Farrar, D., Cheng, D. M., Alford, D. P., & Samet, J. H. (2009). Are opioid-dependence and methadone maintenance treatment (MMT) documented in the medical record? A patient safety issue. *Journal of General Internal Medicine, 24*(9), 1007–1011.

Walsh, J. K., Pollak, C. P., Scharf, M. B., Schweitzer, P. K., & Vogel, G. W. (2000). Lack of residual sedation following middle of the night zaleplon administration in sleep maintenance insomnia. *Clinical Neuropharmacology, 23*(1), 17–21.

Walsh, K., & Alexander, G. (2000). Alcoholic liver disease. *Postgraduate Medicine, 76*, 280–286.

Walters, S. T., Rotgers, F., Saunders, B., Wilkinson, C., & Towers, T. (2003). Theoretical perspectives on motivation and addictive behaviors. In F. Rotgers, J. Morgenstern, & S. T. Walters (Eds.), *Treating substance abuse: Theory and technique* (2nd ed.). New York: Guilford.

Walton, S. (2002). *Out of it: A cultural history of intoxication.* New York: Harmony Books.

Wannamethee, S. G, Camargo, C. A., Manson, J. A. E., Wllett, W. C., & Rimm, E. B. (2003). Alcohol drinking patterns and risk of type 2 diabetes mellitus among younger women. *Archives of Internal Medicine, 163*, 1329–1336.

Washton, A. M., & Zweben, J. E. (2006). *Treating alcohol and drug problems in psychotherapy practice.* New York: Guilford.

Watkins, K. E., Burnam, A., Kung, F. Y., & Paddock, S. (2001). A national survey of care for persons with co-occurring mental and substance use disorders. *Psychiatric Services, 52*, 1062–1068.

Watson, S. J., Benson, J. A., & Joy, J. E. (2000). Marijuana and medicine: Assessing the science base. *Archives of General Psychiatry, 57*, 547–552.

Wattendorf, D. J., & Muenke, M. (2005). Fetal alcohol spectrum disorders. *American Family Physician, 72*, 279–282, 285.

Wayne, G. F., & Connolly, G. (2009). Regulatory assessment of brand changes in the commercial tobacco market. *Tobacco Control* (published online prior to print). doi: 1136/fc2009.030502

Watters, E. (2006). DNA is not destiny. *Discover, 27*(11), 23–37, 75.

Weafer, J., Fillmore, M. T., & Milich, R. (2009). Increased sensitivity to the disinhibiting effects of alcohol in adults with ADHD. *Experimental and Clinical Psychopharmacology, 17*(2), 113–121.

Weathermon, R., & Crabb, D. W. (1999). Alcohol and medication interactions. *Alcohol Research & Health, 23*(1), 40–54.

Weaver, M. F., Jarvis, M. A., & Schnoll, S. H. (1999). Role of the primary care physician in problems of substance abuse. *Archives of Internal Medicine, 159*, 913–924.

Weaver, M. F., & Schnoll, S. H. (2008). Hallucinogens and club drugs In M. Galanter & H. D. Kleber (Eds.), *The American Psychiatric Publishing textbook of substance abuse treatment.* Washington, DC: American Psychiatric Publishing.

Wegscheider-Cruse, S. (1985). *Choice-making.* Pompano Beach, FL: Health Communications.

Wegscheider-Cruse, S., & Cruse, J. R. (1990). *Understanding co-dependency.* Pompano Beach, FL: Health Communications.

Weight loss and the release of THC from fat. (2009). *Forensic Drug Abuse Advisor, 21*(8), 58–59.

Weiner, D. A., Abraham, M. E., & Lyons, J. (2001). Clinical characteristics of youths with substance use problems and implications for residential treatment. *Psychiatric Services, 52*, 793–799.

Weiss, C. J., & Millman, R. B. (1998). Hallucinogens, phencyclidine, marijuana and inhalants. In R. J. Frances & S. I. Miller (Eds.), *Clinical textbook of addictive disorders* (2nd ed.). New York: Guilford.

Weiss, F. (2005). Neurobiology of craving, conditioned reward and relapse. *Current Opinion in Pharmacology, 5*, 9–19.

Weiss, M. (2007). Drugs of abuse. In K. Z. Bezchlibnyk-Butler, J. J. Jeffries, & A. S. Virani (Eds.), *Clinical handbook of psychotropic drugs* (17th ed.). Ashland, OH: Hogrefe & Huber.

Weiss, R. D., Griffin, M. L., Mazurick, C., Berkan, B., Gastfriend, D. R., Frank, A., et al. (2003). The relationship between cocaine craving, psychosocial treatment, and subsequent cocaine use. *American Journal of Psychiatry, 160*, 1320–1325.

Weiss, R. D., Potter, J. S., & Iannucci, R. A. (2008). Inpatient treatment. In M. Galanter & H. D. Kleber (Eds.), *The American Psychiatric Publishing textbook of substance abuse treatment.* Washington, DC: American Psychiatric Publishing.

Welch, S. P. (2005). The neurobiology of marijuana. In J. H. Lowinson, P. Ruiz, R. B. Millman, & J. G. Langrod (Eds.), *Substance abuse: A comprehensive textbook* (4th ed.). New York: Lippincott Williams & Wilkins.

Wells, J. E., Horwood, L. J., & Fergusson, D .M. (2006). Stability and instability in alcohol diagnosis from ages 18 to 21 and ages 21 to 25 years. *Alcohol & Drug Dependence, 81*(2), 157–165.

Wells, K. E., Paddock, S. M., Zhang, L., & Wells, K. B. (2006). Improving care for depression in patients with comorbid substance misuse. *American Journal of Psychiatry, 163*, 125–132.

Wells, S. K., Graham, K., & Purcell, J. (2009). Policy implications of the widespread practice of "pre-drinking" or "pre-gaming" before going to public drinking establishments—are current prevention strategies backfiring? *Addiction, 104*(1), 4–9.

Welsby, P. D. (1997). An HIV view of the human condition. *Postgraduate Medicine, 73*, 609–610.

Wesson, D. R., & Smith, D. E. (2005). Sedative-hypnotics. In J. H. Lowinson, P. Ruiz, R. B. Millman, & J. G. Langrod (Eds.), *Substance abuse: A comprehensive textbook* (4th ed.). New York: Lippincott Williams & Wilkins.

Westermeyer, J. (1995). Cultural aspects of substance abuse and alcoholism. *The Psychiatric Clinics of North America, 18*, 589–620.

Westermeyer, J., Eames, S. L., & Nugent, S. (1998). Comorbid dysthymia and substance disorder: Treatment history and cost. *American Journal of Psychiatry, 155*, 1556–1560.

Westfall, T. C., & Westfall, D. P. (2006). Adrenergic agonists and antagonists. In L. L. Brunton, J. S. Lazo, & K. L. Parker (Eds.), *The pharmacological basis of therapeutics* (11th ed.). New York: McGraw-Hill.

Westover, A. N., Nakonezny, P. A., & Haley, R. W. (2008). Acute myocardial infarction in young adults who abuse amphetamines. *Drug and Alcohol Dependence, 96*, 49–56.

Westphal, J., Wasserman, D. A., Masson, C. L., & Sorenson, J. L. (2005). Assessment of opioid. In D. M. Donovan & G. A. Marlatt (Eds.), *Assessment of addictive behaviors* (2nd ed.). New York: Guilford.

What is moderation management? (2008). Retrieved from http://www.moderation.org/whatismm.shtml

Wheeler, K., & Malmquist, J. (1987). Treatment approaches in adolescent chemical dependency. *The Pediatric Clinics of North America, 158*, 86–95.

White, A. M. (2003). What happened? Alcohol, memory blackouts and the brain. *Alcohol Research & Health, 27*(2), 186–196.

White, H. R., & Jackson, K. (2004/2005). Social and psychological influences on emerging adult drinking behavior. *Alcohol Research & Health, 28*, 182–190.

White, M. P. (2009). Medication dosing in anxiety disorders: What the evidence shows. *Primary Psychiatry, 16*(10), 21–28.

White, P. T. (1989). Coca. *National Geographic, 175*(1), 3–47.

White, W., & Nicolaus, M. (2005). Styles of secular recovery. *Counselor, the Magazine for Addiction Professionals, 6*(4), 58–61.

White, W. L. (2005). Fire in the family: Historical perspectives on the intergenerational effects of addiction. *Counselor, 6*(1), 20–23, 25.

Whitten, L. (2006). Study finds withdrawal no easier with ultrarapid opiate detox. *NIDA Notes, 21*(1), 4.

Whitten, L. (2008a). Gene experiment confirms a suspected cocaine action. *NIDA Notes, 24*(1), 8–10.

Whitten, L. (2008b). Basic sciences discoveries yield novel approaches to analgesia. *NIDA Notes, 22*(1), 1, 12–15.

Why confirmatory testing is always a necessity. (1997). *Forensic Drug Abuse Advisor, 9*(4), 25.

Why do the mentally ill die younger? *Time Health & Science*. Retrieved from http://www.time.com/time/article/0,8599,1863220,00.html

Wild, T. C., Cunningham, J., & Hobdon, K. (1998). When do people believe that alcohol treatment is effective? The importance of perceived client and therapist motivation. *Psychology of Addictive Behaviors, 12*, 93–100.

Wilens, T. E. (2006). Attention deficit hyperactivity disorder and substance use disorders. *American Journal of Psychiatry, 163*, 2059–2063.

Wilkinson, R. J., Llewelyn, M., Tossi, A., Patel, P., et al. (2000). Influence of vitamin D deficiency and vitamin D receptor polymorphisms on tuberculosis among Gujarati Asians in West London: A case-control study. *The Lancet, 355*, 618–621.

Willenbring, M. L. (2004). Treating co-occurring substance use disorders and hepatitis C. *Psychiatric Times, 21*(2), 53–54.

Willi, C., Bodenmann, P., Ghali, W. A., Faris, P. D., & Cornuz, J. (2007). Active smoking and the risk of type 2 diabetes. *Journal of the American Medical Association, 298*, 2654–2664.

Williams, B. R., & Baer, C. L. (1994). *Essentials of clinical pharmacology in nursing* (2nd ed.). Springhouse, PA: Springhouse.

Williams, D. A. (2004). Evaluating acute pain. In R. H. Dworkin & W. S. Breitbart (Eds.), *Psychosocial aspects of pain: A handbook for health care providers*. Seattle: IASP Press.

Williams, H., Dratcu, L., Taylor, R., Roberts, M., & Oyefeso, A. (1998). Saturday night fever: Ecstasy related problems in a London accident and emergency department. *Journal of Accident and Emergency Medicine, 15*, 322–326.

Williams, T. (2000). High on hemp: Ditchweed digs in. *Utne Reader, 98*, 72–77.

Wills, T. A., Sandy, J. M., Yaeger, A. M., Cleary, S. D., & Shinar, Q. (2001). Coping dimensions, life stress and adolescent substance use: A latent growth analysis. *Journal of Abnormal Psychology, 110*, 309–323.

Wilson, B. A., Shannon, M. T., Shields, K. M. & Stang, C. L. (2007). *Prentice-Hall's Nurse's Drug Guide, 2007.* Upper Saddle River, NJ: Prentice-Hall.

Wilson, C. (2005). Miracle weed. *New Scientist, 185*(2485), 38–41.

Wilson, C. (2008). Safer sex in a pill. *New Scientist, 200*(2683), 40–43.

Windle, M., Spear, L. P., Fuligni, A. J., Angold, A., Brown, J. D., Pine, D., et al. (2009). Transitions into underaged and problem drinking. *Alcohol Research & Health, 32*(1), 3040.

Winegarden, T. (2001, September 7). *Antipsychotic use in special populations.* Teleconference sponsored by Astra-Zeneca Pharmaceuticals, La Crosse, WI.

Winkelman, J. W. (2006). Diagnosis and treatment of insomnia. *Monthly prescribing reference.* New York: Prescribing Reference.

Winning the war on drugs? (2007). *Forensic Drug Abuse Advisor, 19*(7), 56.

Winslow, B. T., Voorhees, K. I., & Pehl, K. L. (2007). Methamphetamine abuse. *American Family Physician, 76*(8), 1169–1174.

Winters, K. C., & Kaminer, Y. (2008). Screening and assessing adolescent substance use disorders in clinical populations. *Journal of the American Academy of Child and Adolescent Psychiatry, 47*(7), 740–744.

Wiseman, B. (1997). Confronting the breakdown of law and order. *USA Today, 125*(2620), 32–34.

Witkiewitz, K., & Marlatt, G. A. (2004). Relapse prevention for alcohol and drug problems. That was Zen, this is Tao. *American Psychologist, 59*(4), 224–235.

Witkiewitz, K., & Masyn, K. E. (2008). Drinking trajectories following an initial lapse. *Psychology of Addictive Behaviors, 22*(2), 157–167.

Woititz, J. G. (1983). *Adult children of alcoholics.* Pompano Beach, FL: Health Communications.

Wolf, M. E. (2006). Addiction. In G. J. Siegel, R. W. Albers, S. T. Brady, & D. L. Price (Eds.), *Basic neurochemistry* (7th ed.). New York: Elsevier Academic Press.

Wolfe, H. C. (2009), March 7. *Here's why you need to be aware of inhalant abuse: The hidden addiction.* Paper presented at the Treating the Addictions seminar hosted by the Harvard Medical School Department of Continuing Education, Boston.

Wolin, S. J., & Wolin, S. (1993). *The resilient self.* New York: Villard Books.

Wolin, S. J., & Wolin, S. (1995). Resilience among youth growing up in substance-abusing families. *Pediatric Clinics of North America, 42,* 415–429.

Woloshin, S., Schwartz, L. M., & Welch, H. G. (2008). The risk of death by age, sex, and smoking status in the United States: Putting health risks in context. *Journal of the National Cancer Institute, 100*(12), 845–853.

Wood, R. I. (2004). Reinforcing aspects of androgens. *Psychology & Behavior, 83*(2), 279–289.

Woods, A. R., & Herrera, J. L. (2002). Hepatitis C: Latest treatment guidelines. *Consultant, 42,* 1233–1243.

Woods, J. H., & Winger, G. (1997). Abuse liability of flunitrazepam. *Journal of Psychopharmacology, 17* (Suppl. 3), 1s–57s.

Woods, J. R. (1998). Maternal and transplacental effects of cocaine. *Annals of the New York Academy of Sciences, 846,* 1–11.

Woods, J. T. (2005). *How the Catholic Church built Western civilization.* Washington, DC: Regnery Publishing.

Woods, P. J., & Bartley, M. K. (2008). Improve pain management in patients with substance abuse. *Nursing 2008 Critical Care, 3*(1), 19–27.

Woody, G. E., Poole, S. A., Subramaniam, G., Dugosh, K., Bogenscchultz, M., Abbott, P., et al. (2008). Extended versus short-term buprenorphine-nalaxone for treatment of opiate-addicted youth: A randomized trial. *Journal of the American Medical Association, 300*(17), 2003–2011.

Worchester, S. (2006). Survey: Teens use inhalants more, worry about risks less. *Clinical Psychiatry News, 34*(6), 28.

Work Group on HIV/AIDS. (2000). Practice guidelines for the treatment of patients with HIV/AIDS. *American Journal of Psychiatry, 157*(11), Supplement.

Work Group on Substance Use Disorders. (2007). Treatment of patients with substance use disorders (2nd ed). *American Journal of Psychiatry, 164* (Supplement).

World Health Organization. (2006). Tobacco-free initiative. Retrieved from http://www.who.int/tobacco/research/cancer/en/

World Health Organization. (2008). *Anti-tuberculosis drug resistance in the world* (Report No. 3). New York: Author.

Wright, R. (2009). *The evolution of God.* New York: Little, Brown.

Wu, L. T., & Ringwalt, C. L. (2005). Alcohol dependence and use of treatment services among women in the community. *American Journal of Psychiatry, 161,* 1790–1797.

Wu, L. T., & Ringwalt, C. L. (2006). Use of alcohol treatment and mental health services among adolescents with alcohol use disorders. *Psychiatric Services, 57,* 84–92.

Wuethrich, B. (2001). Getting stupid. *Discover, 22*(3), 56–63.

Wunsch, J. (2007, April 26). *Trends in adolescent drug use.* Paper presented at the Ruth Fox Course for Physicians, 38th Medical-Scientific Conference of the American Society of Addiction Medicine, Miami, FL.

Wyman, P. A., Moynihan, H., Eberly, S., Cox, C., Cross, W., Jin, X., et al. (2007). Association of family stress with natural killer cell activity and frequency of illness in children. *Archives of Pediatrics & Adolescent Medicine, 161,* 228–234.

Wynn, G. H., Oesterheld, J. R., Cozza, K. L., & Armstrong, S. C. (2009). *Clinical manual of drug interaction principles for medical practice.* Washington, DC: American Psychiatric Publishing.

Yeh, H. C., Duncan, B. B., Schmidt, M. I., Wang, N., & Brancati, F.L. (2010). Smoking, smoking cessation, and risk for type 2 diabetes mellitus: A cohort study. *Archives of Internal Medicine, 152*(1), 10–17.

Yeo, K., Wijetunga, M., Ito, H., Efird, J. T., Tay, K., Seto, T. B., et al. (2007). The association of methamphetamine use and cardiomyopathy in young patients. *The American Journal of Medicine, 120,* 165–171.

Young, E. (2008). Strange inheritance. *New Scientist, 199*(2664), 28–33.

Young adult drinking. (2006). *Alcohol Alert, 68,* 1–2.

Yu, K., & Daar, E. S. (2000). Primary HIV detection. *Postgraduate Medicine, 107,* 114–122.

Yucel, M., Solowij, N., Respondek, C., Whittie, S., Fornito, A., Pantelis, C., et al. (2008). Regional brain abnormalities associated with long-term heavy cannabis use. *Archives of General Psychiatry, 65*(6), 694–701.

Yudko, E., Hall, H. V., & McPherson, S. B. (2009). Mechanisms of methamphetamine action. In S. B. McPherson, H. V. Hall, & E. Yudko (Eds.), *Methamphetamine use—Clinical and forensic aspects.* New York: CRC Press.

Yudko, E., & McPherson, S. B. (2009). MDMA. In S. B. McPherson, H. V. Hall, & E. Yudko (Eds.), *Methamphetamine use—Clinical and forensic aspects.* New York: CRC Press.

Zahr, N. M., & Sullivan, E. V. (2008). Translational studies of alcoholism. *Alcohol Research & Health, 31*(3), 215–230.

Zajicek, J., Fox, P., Sanders, H., Wright, D., Vickery, J., Nunn, A., et al. (2003). Cannabinoids for treatment of spasticity and other symptoms related to multiple sclerosis (CAMS study): Multicentre randomised placebo-controlled trial. *The Lancet, 362*(8), 1517–1526.

Zakhari, S. (2006). Overview: How is alcohol metabolized by the body? *Alcohol Research & Health, 29*(4), 245–254.

Zarkin, G. A., Dunlap, L. J., Hicks, K. A., & Mamo, D. (2005). Benefits and costs of methadone treatment: Results from a lifetime simulation model. *Health Economics, 14,* 1133–1150.

Zax, D. (2008). Washington's boyhood home. *Smithsonian, 39*(6), 24–28.

Zealberg, J. J., & Brady, K. T. (1999). Substance abuse and emergency psychiatry. *Psychiatric Clinics of North America, 22,* 803–817.

Zeese, K. B. (2002). From Nixon to now. *Playboy, 49*(9), 49.

Zelvin, E. (1997). Codependency issues of substance-abusing women. In S. L. A. Straussner & E. Zelvin (Eds.), *Gender and addictions.* Northvale, NJ: Jason Aronson.

Zemore, S. E., Kaskutas, L. A., & Ammon, L. N. (2004). In 12-step groups, helping helps the helper. *Addiction, 99*(8), 1015–1023.

Zerekh, J., & Michaels, B. (1989). Co-dependency. *Nursing Clinics of North America, 24*(1), 109–120.

Zernig, G., & Battista, H. J. (2000). Drug interactions. In G. Zernig, A. Saria, M. Kurz, & S. S. O'Malley (Eds.), *Handbook of alcoholism.* New York: CRC Press.

Zevin, S., & Benowitz, N. L. (1998). Drug-related syndromes. In S. B. Karch (Ed.), *Drug abuse handbook.* New York: CRC Press.

Zevin, S., & Benowitz, N. L. (2007). Medical aspects of drug abuse. In S. B. Karch (Ed.), *Drug abuse handbook* (2nd ed.). New York: CRC Press.

Zhang, Y., Picetti, R., Butelman, E. R., Schussman, S. D., Ho, A., & Kreek, M. J. (2008). Behavioral and neurochemical changes induced by oxycodone differ between adolescent and adult mice. Neuropsychopharmacology (published online). doi: 10.1038/npp.2008.134

Zhang, Y., Woods, R., Chaisson, C. E., Neogi, T., et. al., (2006). Alcohol consumption as a trigger of recurrent gout attacks. *American Journal of Medicine, 119,* e13–e88.

Zhao, Z. Q., Gao, Y. J., Sun, Y. G., Zhao, C. S., Gereau, R. W., IV, Chen, Z.-F. (2007). Central serotonergic neurons are differentially required for opioid analgesia, but not for morphine tolerance or morphine reward. *Proceedings of the National Academy of Sciences* (published online). doi: 10.103/pnas.0705740104

Zhu, N. Y., LeGatt, D. F., & Turner, A. R. (2009). Agranulocytosis after consumption of cocaine adulterated with Levamisole. *Annals of Internal Medicine, 150*(4), 287–289.

Ziedonis, D., & Brady, K. (1997). Dual diagnosis in primary care. *Medical Clinics of North America, 81,* 1017–1036.

Zilberman, M. L. (2009). Substance abuse across the lifespan in women. In K. T. Brady, S. E. Back, & S. F. Greenfield (Eds.), *Women and addiction.* New York: Guilford.

Zimberg, S. (1995). The elderly. In A. M. Washton (Ed.), *Psychotherapy and substance abuse.* New York: Guilford.

Zimberg, S. (1996). Treating alcoholism: An age-specific intervention that works for older patients. *Geriatrics, 51*(10), 45–49.

Zimberg, S. (2005). Alcoholism and substance abuse in older adults. In R. J. Frances, S. I. Miller, & A. H. Mack (Eds.), *Clinical textbook of addictive disorders* (3rd ed.). New York: Guilford.

Zimmer, C. (2008). *Microcosm.* New York: Pantheon Books.

Zisserman, R. N., & Oslin, D. W. (2004). Alcoholism and at-risk drinking in the older population. *Psychiatric Times, 21*(2), 50–53.

Zucker, R. A., Donovan, J. E., Masten, A. S., Mattson, M. E., & Moss, H. B. (2009). Developmental processes and mechanisms: Ages 0–10. *Alcohol Research & Health, 32*(1), 16–29.

Zuckerman, B., Frank, D. A., & Mayes, L. (2002). Cocaine-exposed infants and developmental outcomes. *Journal of the American Medical Association, 287,* 1990–1991.

Zukin, S. R., Sloboda, Z., & Javitt, D.C. (2005). Phencyclidine. In J. H. Lowinson, P. Ruiz, R. B. Millman, & J. G. Langrod (Eds.), *Substance abuse: A comprehensive textbook* (4th ed.). New York: Lippincott Williams & Wilkins.

Zunz, S. J., Ferguson, N. L., & Senter, M. (2005). Post-identification support for substance dependent students in school-based programs: The weakest link. *Journal of Child and Adolescent Substance Abuse, 14*(4), 77–92.

Zur, O. (2005). The psychology of victimhood. In R. H. Wright & N. A. Cummings (Eds.), *Destructive trends in mental health.* New York: Routledge.

Zweig, C., & Wolf, S. (1997). *Romancing the shadow.* New York: Ballantine Books.

Zylka, M. J., Sowa, N. A., Taylor-Blake, B., Twomey, M. A., Voikar, V., & Vihko, P. (2008). Prostatis acid phosphatase is an ectonucleotidase and suppresses pain by generating adenosine. *Neuron, 60,* 111–122.

Zywiak, W. H., Stout, R. L., Longabaugh, R., Dyck, I., Connors, G. J., & Dyck, I. (2006). Relapse-onset factors in Project MATCH: The relapse questionnaire. *Journal of Substance Abuse Treatment, 31*(4), 341–354.

Index

referral, circumstance of, 371
REM rebound
  alcohol and, 57
  barbiturates and, 69
  benzodiazepines and, 81
residential treatment programs, 391–394
  detox, 391
  hospital-based, 391–392
  therapeutic communities, 392–394
respiratory depression, 150–151
  alcohol and, 40 (table), 60
  analgesics and, 150
  benzodiazepine-induced, 79, 80
  GHB and, 499
  inhalants and, 185 (table)
  methadone, 145
  naproxen and, 208
  narcotic analgesic related, 150–151
  opiate overdose and, 141, 142 (table), 161
  PCP and, 172 (table)
  See also sleep apnea
reticular activating system (RAS) and bar-
    biturates, 90
retrograde transmitter molecule, 126
reuptake pumps, 29
reward process, 335
Reye's syndrome, 205
Ritalin. *See* methylphenidate
Rhabdomyolysis, 62
Rohypnol. *See* flunitrazepam
"roid rage," 195
room deodorizer, as inhalant, 187
Rossen, Ralph, 399
Rossi, Jean, 400
Rozerem (ramelteon), 85
rules of codependency, 300–301
"rum fits", 62 (footnote)
"rush"
  cocaine-induced, 110, 113, 114
  dosage levels and, 156
  women and, 251
Rush, Dr. Benjamin, 345

salvia divinorum, 179–180, 236
saliva, testing, 457
schizophrenia and dual diagnosis patients,
    322–323
Screener and Opioid Assessment for
    Patients-Revised, 447
secondary neurotransmitter molecules, 28
"secrets," treatment, 439–440
Secular Organizations for Sobriety (SOS), 470
sedative-hypnotic withdrawal syndrome, 77
seizures
  aspirin, 208
  benzodiazepines withdrawal, 77 (table),
    81, 86
  cocaine-induced, 118
  ephedrine and, 89
  GHB and, 498, 499
  hallucinogens and, 167

ibuprofen overdose and, 208
inhalant-induced, 185 (table), 185
LSD-induced, 170
MDMA-induced, 176 (table), 177, 178
methylphenidate, 90, 91
methamphetamine, 101
narcotics use and, 151, 160
opiate abuse and, 144, 239
PCP-induced, 172 (table), 173
zaleplon and, 116
selective serotonin reuptake inhibitors
    (SSRIs), 424
Self-Management and Recovery Training.
    See SMART
serotonin
  alcohol and, 29, 38
  buspirone and, 82, 83, 436
  cocaine, 111
  LSD and, 167, 170
  marijuana and, 286
  MDMA and, 175, 176, 178, 347
  steroids and, 195
serotonin syndrome
  buspirone, as cause of, 83, 436
  cocaine-induced, 111
  DXM and, 502
  MDMA-induced, 101, 178
  tryptamines and, 501
side effects of chemicals, 18–19
SIDS. *See* sudden infant death
sigma receptor, 142 (table)
syndrome (SIDS), 233, 235, 238 (table)
silver acetate, 438
single photon emission computed tomogra-
    phy (SPECT) scan, 141
site of action, of chemical agent, 21, 27–28
skin abscesses, 476
"skin popping," 20
SLE (systemic lupus erythematosus), 206
sleep apnea
  alcohol use and, 41, 60
  benzodiazepines and, 79
  MDMA, 176
  tobacco use and, 218
  zolpidem and, 84
slow metabolizers, 24
SMART (Self Management and Recovery
    Training), 469–470
Smith, Robert, 466
smoking machines, 131
sn-2 arachidonyglycerol (2-AG), 126, 127
sniffing death syndrome, 186
"snorting," 112–113, 184
social detoxification, 401
social learning and drug use, 12
social use, defined, 15
society, response to drug abuse, 7–8
Sonata, 84
SOS (Secular Organizations for Sobriety),
    470
"speed run," 100

spiritual disorder theory of addiction,
    353–362
  circle of addiction, 358
  defense mechanisms, 362
  false pride, 361–362
  games of addiction, 358–360
  growth of, 358
  illusion of a purpose, 356
  lifestyles and, 359
  loss of the soul, 354–356
  mind-body, 357
  overview of, 353
  pain of life, 357
  philosophy of, 356–357
  recovery, 360–361
spiritus, 356
SSRIs (selective serotonin reuptake inhibi-
    tors), 42, 73, 129, 170, 195, 323, 424
"stacking" steroids, 193
stage models, 413
standardized tests, 370
steady state, of compounds, 25
steroids, 189–197
  abuse of and addiction to, 190–191
  addictive potential of, 196
  adolescent growth pattern and,
    190, 191, 196, 197
  anabolic recovery, 417
  anabolic-androgenic, 190
  central nervous system (CNS), effects
    on, 195
  complications of abuse, 193–196
  death caused by abuse of, 194
  defined, 190
  depression caused by, 195
  digestive system, effects on, 194
  disorders, 195–196
  drug interactions, 196
  as gateway drug, 196
  heart disease, effects on, 194–195
  kidneys, effects on, 194
  legal status of, 191–192
  liver, effects on, 194
  medical uses of, 190
  methods of use, 192–193
  overview, 196–197
  pharmacology of, 192
  preadolescents and, 191, 192
  pyramid doses, 192
  psychosis, drug-induced, 195
  recovery from abuse, 191
  reproductive system, effects on, 194
  "roid rage," 195
  scope of the problem, 191
  side effects, 193, 195–196
  sources of, 192–193
  violence, caused by abuse of, 195
  withdrawal syndrome, 195, 196
STP. *See* DOM
Strattera® (Atomoxetine Hydrochloride),
    95–96